HELP YOUR KIDS WITH
Language Arts

- Grammar
- Punctuation
- Spelling
- Communication skills

HELP YOUR KIDS WITH
Language Arts

A STEP-BY-STEP VISUAL GUIDE TO GRAMMAR, PUNCTUATION, AND WRITING

Senior Project Editor Victoria Pyke
Project Editors Carron Brown, Camilla Gersh, Matilda Gollon, Ashwin Khurana
US Editor John Searcy

Managing Editor Linda Esposito
Managing Art Editor Diane Peyton Jones
Publishers Laura Buller, Andrew Macintyre

Preproduction Controller Adam Stoneham
Senior Producer Gemma Sharpe

Senior Designer Jim Green
Project Designers Paul Drislane, Hoa Luc, Mary Sandberg

Publishing Director Jonathan Metcalf
Associate Publishing Director Liz Wheeler
Art Director Phil Ormerod

Jacket Editor Manisha Majithia
Jacket Designer Laura Brim

First American Edition, 2013
Published in the United States by
DK Publishing
345 Hudson Street
New York, New York 10014

Copyright © 2013, 2019 Dorling Kindersley Limited
DK, a Division of Penguin Random House, LLC
15 16 17 10 9 8 7 6 5 4 3 2 1
001—313518—Jan/2019

All rights reserved.
Without limiting the rights under the copyright reserved above, no part of this publication may be reproduced, stored in or introduced into a retrieval system, or transmitted, in any form, or by any means (electronic, mechanical, photocopying, recording, or otherwise), without the prior written permission of the copyright owner.
Published in Great Britain by Dorling Kindersley Limited.

A catalog record for this book is available from
the Library of Congress.

ISBN 978-1-4654-0849-5

DK books are available at special discounts when purchased in bulk for sales promotions, premiums, fund-raising, or educational use. For details, contact: DK Publishing Special Markets, 375 Hudson Street, New York, New York 10014 or SpecialSales@dk.com.

Printed in China

A WORLD OF IDEAS:
SEE ALL THERE IS TO KNOW

www.dk.com

LINDA B. GAMBRELL is Distinguished Professor of Education at Clemson University. She is past president of the International Reading Association (IRA), Literacy Research Association, and the Association of Literacy Educators and Researchers. In 2004, she was inducted into the Reading Hall of Fame. She is a former classroom teacher and reading specialist. Linda has written books on reading instruction and published articles in major literacy journals, including *Reading Research Quarterly*, the *Reading Teacher*, and the *Journal of Educational Research*.

SUSAN ROWAN is a former Head of English and Leading English and Literacy Adviser for a London borough. She has a Certificate in Education (Bishop Otter College of Education), a BA in English and History (Macquarie University, Australia), and an MBA—Education (University of Nottingham). With more than twenty-five years of teaching experience, Susan now works as an independent English and Literacy consultant supporting schools in London and southeast England.

DR. STEWART SAVARD is an eLibrarian in the Comox Valley of British Columbia. He has written a number of papers on the development of school libraries, the use of online and paper resources, and strategies for working with students to prevent plagiarism. Stewart also has extensive experience as a classroom and Learning Assistance teacher. He has worked on almost twenty books.

Foreword

The ability to speak and write well is essential for good communication in everyday life and in school. Our messages—whether spoken or written—need to be clear and easy for others to understand. While the importance of proper speaking and writing skills is often lost in our world of texting, e-mailing, and instant messaging, these skills are very important. Good speaking and writing skills help get a message across clearly and accurately, and give it credibility. Writing that is riddled with errors of grammar, punctuation, and spelling will reflect poorly on the writer, even if he or she is very knowledgeable about a topic. A good command of the English language and basic communication skills can lead to better grades in school and give a student a clear advantage over someone who is less skilled in language usage.

The rules of grammar, punctuation, and spelling, and the skills needed to communicate effectively can be bewildering. That's why *Help Your Kids with Language Arts* is an essential resource. This book presents examples that help to make the rules of grammar, punctuation, spelling, and communication clear and accessible. Wondering whether to say "you and me" or "you and I"? This book will provide an easy-to-understand explanation.

This book sets out to explain in simple terms the rules of clear and effective speaking and writing. It is divided into four chapters that focus on the key English language arts topics: grammar, punctuation, spelling, and communication skills. The information within each chapter is designed to make these English language arts interesting and enjoyable to learn. Engaging examples supported by step-by-step, simple-to-follow explanations will make even the most confusing concepts easy to grasp. This book will equip parents with the information they need to help students develop the skills required to communicate effectively in both speaking and writing.

As a former teacher, I am very aware of the importance of good communication skills. Success in school and in life is enhanced by these skills. *Help Your Kids with Language Arts* is an essential resource because throughout life we refine our use of the English language—always striving for clear and accurate communication with others.

LINDA B. GAMBRELL

abbreviations, accents, **acronyms**, adjectives, **adverbs**, alliteration, **apostrophes**, Arabic numerals, **articles**, asterisks, **auxiliary verbs**, brackets, **bullet points**, capital letters, **clauses**, collective nouns, **colloquialisms**, colons, **commands**, commas, **common nouns**, compound sentences, **compound words**, conditional sentences, **conjunctions**, consonants, **dangling participles**, dashes, **dialects**, direct speech, **ellipses**, exclamations, **exaggeration**, figures of speech, **first person**, fragments, **gender**, homographs, **homonyms**, homophones, **hyperbole**, hyphens, **idioms**, indefinite pronouns, **indicative mood**, indirect questions, **infinitives**, interjections, **irregular verbs**, italics, **jargon**, linking verbs, **main clauses**, misplaced modifiers, **moods**, morphemes, **negatives**, noun phrases, **nouns**, numbers, **objects**, ordinal numbers, **parentheses**, participles, **personal pronouns**, phonetics, **phrasal verbs**, phrases, **pitch**, plural nouns, **possessive determiners**, prefixes, **prepositional phrases**, present participles, **pronouns**, proper nouns, **puns**, punctuation, **question marks**, questions, **quotations**, relative pronouns, **reported speech**, rhetorical questions, **Roman numerals**, roots, **sentences**, silent letters, **singular**, slang, **subject**, subordinate clauses, **suffixes**, syllables, **tautology**, tenses, **third person**, tone, **verbs**, voices, **vowels**

CONTENTS

FOREWORD	6
WHY LEARN THE RULES?	10
SPOKEN AND WRITTEN LANGUAGE	12
ENGLISH AROUND THE WORLD	14

1 GRAMMAR

The purpose of grammar	18
Parts of speech	20
Nouns	22
Plurals	24
Adjectives	26
Comparatives and superlatives	28
Articles	30
Determiners	32
Pronouns	34
Number and gender	36
Verbs	38
Adverbs	40
Simple tenses	42
Perfect and continuous tenses	44
Participles	46
Auxiliary verbs	48
Irregular verbs	50
Verb agreement	52
Voices and moods	54
Phrasal verbs	56
Conjunctions	58
Prepositions	60
Interjections	62
Phrases	64
Clauses	66
Sentences	68
Compound sentences	70
Complex sentences	72
Using clauses correctly	74
Managing modifiers	76
Commonly misused words	78
Negatives	80
Relative clauses	82
Idioms, analogies, and figures of speech	84
Colloquialisms and slang	86
Direct and indirect speech	88

2 PUNCTUATION

What is punctuation?	92
Periods and ellipses	94
Commas	96
Other uses of commas	98
Semicolons	100
Colons	102
Apostrophes	104
Hyphens	106
Quotation marks	108
Question marks	110
Exclamation points	112
Parentheses and dashes	114
Bullet points	116
Numbers, dates, and time	118
Other punctuation	120
Italics	122

3 SPELLING

Why learn to spell?	126
Alphabetical order	128
Vowel sounds	130
Consonant sounds	132
Syllables	134
Morphemes	136
Understanding English irregularities	138
Roots	140

Prefixes and suffixes	142
Hard and soft letter sounds	144
Words ending in -e or -y	146
Words ending in -tion, -sion, or -ssion	148
Words ending in -able or -ible	150
Words ending in -le, -el, -al, or -ol	152
Single and double consonant words	154
The "*i* before *e* except after *c*" rule	156
Capital letters	158
Silent letters	160
Compound words	162
Irregular word spellings	164
Homonyms, homophones, and homographs	166
Confusing words	168
Other confusing words	170
Abbreviations	172
British and American spellings	174
More British and American spellings	176

4 COMMUNICATION SKILLS

Effective communication	180
Picking the right words	182
Making sentences interesting	184
Planning and research	186
Paragraphing	188
Genre, purpose, and audience	190
Reading and commenting on texts	192
Layout and presentational features	194
Writing to inform	196
Newspaper articles	198
Letters and e-mails	200
Writing to influence	202
Writing to explain or advise	204
Writing to analyze or review	206
Writing to describe	208
Writing from personal experience	210
Writing a narrative	212
Writing for the Web	214
Writing a script	216
Re-creations	218
Checking and editing	220
The spoken word	222
Debates and role plays	224
Writing a speech	226
Presentation skills	228

5 REFERENCE

Reference—Grammar	232
Reference—Punctuation	236
Reference—Spelling	238
Reference—Communication skills	244
Glossary	248
Index	252
Acknowledgments	256

Why learn the rules?

THERE ARE MANY BENEFITS TO LEARNING AND MASTERING THE RULES OF THE ENGLISH LANGUAGE.

The rules of English are indispensable and will help English speakers of all ages in a variety of situations, from sending a simple e-mail and giving travel directions to writing the next best-selling novel.

English is the primary language of **news** and **information** in the world.

Ways with words

The rules or skills of English can be divided into four major areas. These areas show how words should be organized in a sentence, how they should be spelled and punctuated, and how they should be used in specific situations.

Grammar
Grammar rules show how different types of words—such as nouns and adjectives—should be put together in a sentence to create fluent and clear writing.

Punctuation
Punctuation refers to the use of symbols—such as periods, question marks, commas, and apostrophes—to tell the reader how to read a piece of writing.

Spelling
Spelling rules help English speakers understand and remember the ways in which letters and groups of letters combine to form words.

Communication skills
Communication skills help English speakers interact with others effectively: for instance, when writing a letter, passing on instructions, or delivering a speech.

Access all areas

A solid grasp of English will help students succeed in all subject areas, not just in English lessons. Whether writing a science report, instructing a basketball team as captain, or auditioning for a play, English language skills help students fulfill their potential.

English language skills can help students succeed in all subject areas.

Report Card

Student: Paul Drislane

Course	Percentage	Grade
English	97%	A
Math	94%	A
Science	90%	A
History	92%	A
Geography	97%	A
Drama	93%	A
Phys. Ed.	95%	A

WHY LEARN THE RULES? | 11

Dream job

When applying for jobs, good English language skills can make all the difference. Knowing the rules will help a candidate write a perfect application, and speak clearly and confidently in an interview. All employers, regardless of the industry, look for candidates who can express themselves correctly and assertively because these skills are valuable in most jobs every day.

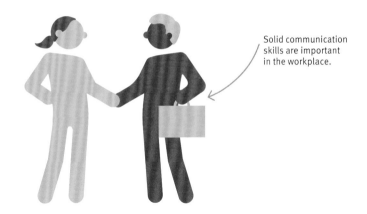

Solid communication skills are important in the workplace.

Time out

Language is used creatively in a variety of social situations, from a rowdy sports game to a sophisticated stage show. At a big game, fans sing rhyming and repetitive chants filled with playful jokes or insults directed at the opposing team. In the theater, actors perform dramatic, evocative lines to express feelings of love, passion, sadness, or anger. Whether watching a funny movie, reading a newspaper, or listening to a pop song, a person who has a good working knowledge of English will get the most out of these experiences.

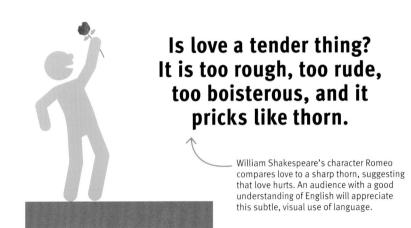

Is love a tender thing? It is too rough, too rude, too boisterous, and it pricks like thorn.

William Shakespeare's character Romeo compares love to a sharp thorn, suggesting that love hurts. An audience with a good understanding of English will appreciate this subtle, visual use of language.

Travel the world

English is one of the most popular languages spoken across the globe, and it's the main language used in the business world. Fluency in the language makes it easier to travel to English-speaking places for work or vacations. What's more, a knowledge of grammatical terms makes learning other languages easier.

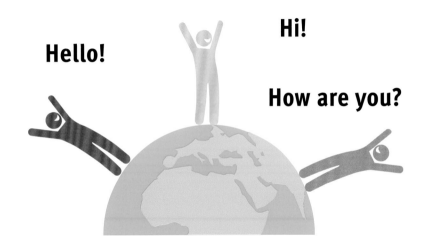

Spoken and written language

BOTH WRITTEN AND SPOKEN ENGLISH HAVE UNIQUE FEATURES.

It's important to understand the differences between written and spoken language—as well as the different uses within each—to improve these two types of communication.

The **earliest known written language** was **Sumerian**, which developed in **Mesopotamia** (modern-day Iraq) in about 2600 BCE.

Written language
Pieces of writing such as novels, letters, and newspaper articles are carefully constructed because writers usually have time to think about the words and sentences they use. This means that written English is organized into complete sentences and uses formal vocabulary and correct grammar.

Dear Jane,

I am having a wonderful time in Thailand. It's a beautiful country with a fascinating culture. The sun shines every day, so we spend most of our time at the stunning beaches, sunbathing and snorkeling. I would love to come back another year.

Love from Nick x

Jane Palmer
28 Maple Street
Springfield, IL 62704
USA

Written English should be in complete sentences.

Spoken language
In general, spoken language is more spontaneous than written language, so it contains features such as repetition, pauses, and sounds like *er* or *um*. Words are often left out or shortened to speed up a conversation, and the vocabulary and pronunciation varies according to the background of the speaker.

The words *I had an* have been left out.

The words *yeah* and *awesome* are informal words used in speech.

Hey, Jane! Yeah, awesome trip, thanks. Good weather, good beaches...um... we went snorkeling, too. Can't wait to go back another time.

People often repeat words when they are speaking.

It is more common to shorten or abbreviate words in spoken language. Here, *cannot* has been shortened to *can't* and *I* has been omitted.

People pause and fill silences with sounds when they speak.

Writing spoken language

Some pieces of writing intentionally mimic the features of spoken English. For instance, the dialogue in novels or dramatic scripts is often written to sound spontaneous, and uses words and spellings that suggest the background of the characters, to make them more authentic.

Yarra Creek

Episode 14: The Big Invitation

Scene: It's a sunny day. Mario and Darren meet while collecting their mail on the driveway.

Mario: G'day Darren. D'ya wanna drop by for a barbie this arvo?

Darren: Yeah, no plans, mate. Catch ya later.

- *G'day* is a word used in Australian speech for "hello."
- The informal phrase *catch ya later* is used instead of *see you later*. *You* is written as *ya* to show how the word should be pronounced.
- The words *Do you want to* have been written as they should be pronounced by the actor.
- The word *barbie* means "barbeque" and *arvo* means "afternoon."

Formal or informal

In general, spoken English can be less formal than written English; however, there are important exceptions. For instance, a text message to a friend may be informal, but a work presentation should be delivered in formal language. The level of formality depends on the situation and the audience.

Written:
- a postcard to a family member
- an e-mail to a potential employer
- a text message to a friend
- a letter to a politician
- a serious newspaper article
- a play script about teenagers

Spoken:
- a chat to a friend on the telephone
- a response in a job interview
- a joke
- a work presentation
- an interview on a talk show
- a news broadcast on television

△ Informal
▲ Formal

△ **Formal or informal**
Some types of written English need to use formal language, while others can be informal. The same is true for spoken English. It depends on the particular situation.

English around the world

ENGLISH IS USED THROUGHOUT THE WORLD, BUT NOT ALWAYS IN THE SAME WAY.

Many countries throughout the world use the English language, but the way it's used—especially spoken—can differ hugely between regions, even within the same country.

Spread the word

The English language can be traced back to a combination of Anglo-Saxon dialects more than 1,500 years old. It started to spread around the world from the 1600s onward, when the British began to explore and colonize, taking their language with them. Today, the English language continues to grow in popularity, especially in Southeast and eastern Asia, where English is seen as the preferred language for business and trade with Western countries.

1. In the Caribbean and Canada, historical links with the UK compete with geographical, cultural, and economic ties with the United States, so their language reflects both British and American forms of English.

2. Most of South America speaks Spanish or Portuguese because Spain and Portugal once had empires there. However, in a few countries in Central and South America—such as Guyana, which achieved independence from Great Britain in 1966—the official language is English.

Spot the differences

After the English language was taken to North America, the spelling of certain words started to change. Published in 1828, *An American Dictionary of the English Language* established spellings such as *center* and *color* (instead of the British spellings *centre* and *colour*), creating a broader acceptance of American and British English as two distinct entities. These variations in spelling still exist today.

▷ **Spelling and punctuation**
British and American English use different spellings and punctuation. For example, verbs such as *criticise* are spelled with an *s* in British English but a *z* in American English. American English often uses longer dashes and more commas in a list than British English.

The new musical *Hello Darling* has been (cancelled) after just nine performances (—) the shortest run in the (theatre's) history. The show has been severely (criticised) after many jokes caused (offence). One critic described the (humour) as "crude, dated and unimaginative".

British version ⟶

⟵ American version

The new musical *Hello Darling* has been (canceled) after just nine performances (—) the shortest run in the (theater's) history. The show has been severely (criticized) after many jokes caused (offense). One critic described the (humor) as "crude, dated, and unimaginative."

ENGLISH AROUND THE WORLD   **15**

3. North America was the first English-speaking colony, but it developed a distinct form of English with different spellings.

4. English became the dominant language in Great Britain during the Middle Ages (5th to 15th centuries).

5. A 2010 survey found that around two-thirds of Europeans can speak some English.

6. Today, English is an international language of business, and is taught in schools in many Asian countries, including Japan and China.

7. In India and parts of Africa, English was imposed as the administrative language through centuries of colonial rule, but—in most cases—it was spoken only as a second language by the local populations.

8. The expansion of the British Empire during the 1700s in Australia and New Zealand saw European populations quickly outnumber indigenous populations, and English became the dominant language.

What's that?

English speakers around the world use different words and pronunciation, according to their background, age, and sense of identity. An accent is the way in which the words are pronounced, while a dialect refers to the use of certain vocabulary and grammatical constructions. In the UK alone, there are many distinctive dialects, such as Geordie (Newcastle), Brummie (Birmingham), and Doric (northeast Scotland). Similarly, around the world, English is spoken and written in many different ways, so that some common objects are called by different names in Britain, America, Canada, and Australia.

fizzy drink soda pop

flip-flops thongs

knapsack backpack rucksack

A path at the side of the road for pedestrians is called a *pavement* in Britain, a *sidewalk* in North America, and a *footpath* in Australia.

pavement sidewalk footpath

jumper sweater

The British call a knitted garment with long sleeves a *jumper*. In North America, this is called a *sweater*.

sweet pepper bell pepper capsicum

trousers pants

trainers runners sneakers

Grammar

The purpose of grammar

THE STRUCTURE OF A LANGUAGE IS KNOWN AS ITS GRAMMAR.

Words are the building blocks of language. Grammar is a set of rules that determines how these building blocks can be put together in different combinations to create well-formed phrases, clauses, and sentences, which enable and enrich conversation.

> The **first** published **book** about English **grammar**, *Pamphlet for Grammar*, was written by **William Bullokar** in 1586.

Evolving languages

All languages change over time. As a language evolves, its grammar adapts to incorporate new words and ways of organizing them. Different languages have different sets of rules, so sentences are formed in different ways, even if they mean the same thing. Thus, it's often difficult to translate sentences exactly from another language into English.

▷ **English word order**
This is a grammatically correct sentence in English. The verb *read* follows the subject, *I*, and the adjective *good* follows the linking verb *was*.

I read my sister's book, which was good.

▷ **Old English word order**
This sentence has been translated into Old English, and then translated directly back into modern English. The first part of the sentence still makes grammatical sense in modern English, but in the second part of the sentence, the verb is now at the end.

I read the book of my sister, which good was.

▷ **German word order**
This sentence has been translated into German, and then translated directly back into English. The word order is the same as that of the Old English sentence, because Old English is a Germanic language.

I read the book of my sister, which good was.

Learning grammar

When a child learns a language, he or she absorbs information about how that language is structured. This knowledge is refined as the child learns to read and write. Although much of this learning is subconscious, some grammatical rules simply have to be learned.

I'm coming with you, aren't I?

Wrong! What you meant to say was, "I'm coming with you, am I not?"

THE PURPOSE OF GRAMMAR

Parts of speech

Words are grouped together according to the functions they perform in a sentence. There are ten parts of speech in English. Nouns (or pronouns) and verbs are essential to the structure of a sentence, but it's the other parts of speech, including adjectives, adverbs, conjunctions, and prepositions, that make a sentence interesting.

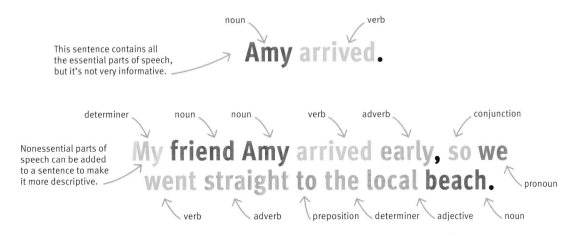

Structuring sentences

Without the rules of grammar, words would be placed in a random order, and no one would be able to understand what anyone else was saying. An ability to communicate effectively comes from following these rules. A sentence must also be correctly punctuated for it to make sense. Grammar explains which order to put words in, while punctuation marks such as periods and commas indicate how the sentence should be read.

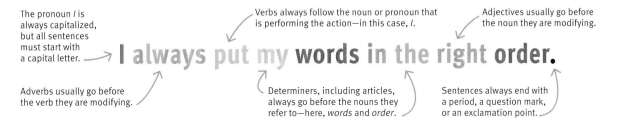

Everyday grammar

A good grasp of grammar enables people to speak and write clearly and concisely, and to understand all kinds of reading material. These skills are invaluable when it comes to job applications, as employers will always show a preference for candidates who have submitted grammatically correct applications. Similarly, candidates who can express themselves clearly will be more successful in interviews. Good grammar improves creative writing, too, and even the best-known writers—past and present—have followed a few simple rules.

"My suffering left me sad and gloomy."

The opening line from Yann Martel's *Life of Pi* follows the rules because it starts with a noun, followed by a verb, and includes adjectives that make the sentence memorable.

Parts of speech

WORDS ARE THE BUILDING BLOCKS OF LANGUAGE, BUT THEY MUST BE ARRANGED IN A RECOGNIZABLE ORDER.

SEE ALSO	
Nouns	22–23 ⟩
Verbs	38–39 ⟩
Voices and moods	54–55 ⟩
Phrases	64–65 ⟩
Clauses	66–67 ⟩
Sentences	68–69 ⟩

Parts of speech refer to the way in which particular words are used. Some words can be classified as more than one word type, and they change type according to the sentence they belong to.

Word types
The main parts of speech are nouns, verbs, adjectives, pronouns, adverbs, prepositions, and conjunctions. Interjections are also important, since they are used so often in everyday speech. Nouns (or pronouns) and verbs are the only essential components of a sentence.

▽ **Different roles**
Each type of word performs a different function. Some depend on others for sense; some exist solely to modify others.

Noun
A word used to name a person, animal, place, or thing.

EXAMPLES
William, mouse, supermarket, ladder, desk, station, ball, boy

ball

Adjective
A word used to describe a noun or pronoun.

EXAMPLES
shiny, dangerous, new, bouncy, noisy, colorful, wooden

colorful ball

Verb
A word that expresses an action or a state of being.

EXAMPLES
run, be, kick, go, think, do, play, stumble, touch

kick the ball

Adverb
A word that describes and adds information to a verb or a verb phrase.

EXAMPLES
quickly, soon, very, rather, too, almost, only, quietly

quickly kick the ball

Pronoun
A word that takes the place of a noun.

EXAMPLES
he, she, them, him, we, you, us, mine, yours, theirs

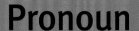
kick the ball to **him**

Preposition
A word that indicates the relationship between two people or things, usually in terms of where they are.

EXAMPLES
with, under, on, behind, into, over, across

kick the ball **behind** you

PARTS OF SPEECH   21

Putting words together

For speech to make sense, words must be linked to other words in the right way to form sentences. Imagine a sports team—each player representing one word. A lone player cannot achieve very much, but, teamed with other players and following strict rules, he can achieve a lot. These rules of play are like grammar—they determine both direction and purpose.

When we are joined together, we make a great team.

Conjunction
A word used to link words and clauses.

EXAMPLES
and, but, so, yet, or, neither, nor, because

bat **and** ball

Interjection
A word that usually occurs alone and expresses emotion.

EXAMPLES
oh, hello, ah, ouch, phew, yuck, hooray, help, er, um, oops

ouch!

Article
A word used with a noun to refer to a specific person or thing, or someone or something in general.

EXAMPLES
a, an, the

the ball

Determiner
A word used in front of a noun to denote something specific or something of a particular type. Articles are also determiners.

EXAMPLES
those, many, my, his, few, several, much, many

my ball

Summary sentence

article — noun — adverb — verb — determiner — adjective — noun — preposition — interjection

The **boy** quickly kicked his bouncy **ball** past a **defender,** but in his **haste** he stumbled. *oops!*

article — noun — conjunction — preposition — determiner — noun — pronoun — verb

Nouns

NOUNS ARE USED TO NAME PEOPLE, ANIMALS, PLACES, OR THINGS.

Nouns are often known as "naming" words. Every sentence must include at least one noun or pronoun. Most nouns can be either singular or plural, and can be divided into two main groups: common and proper nouns.

SEE ALSO	
Plurals	24–25 ⟩
Articles	30–31 ⟩
Determiners	32–33 ⟩
Pronouns	34–35 ⟩
Verbs	38–39 ⟩
Verb agreement	52–53 ⟩

Common nouns (concrete)

Common nouns are used all the time to describe everyday objects, animals, places, people, and ideas. They do not have a capital letter unless they appear at the start of a sentence. Every sentence must contain a noun, and this noun is usually a common noun. Common nouns that describe things that can be seen and touched are known as concrete nouns.

book   bread   girl
goat   birds   piece

Common nouns (abstract)

A type of common noun, abstract nouns are more difficult to define. Unlike concrete nouns, which refer to physical things, abstract nouns refer to ideas, feelings, occasions, or time—things that can't be seen or touched.

love   happiness   trust
bravery
afternoon   health

The goat's afternoon was ruined down and snatched the piece of

- With the exception of some abstract nouns, if the word **the** can be put **in front of a word** and the resulting combination **makes sense**, then that word is a **noun**.
- Nouns can often be recognized by their **endings**. Typical endings include **-er, -or, -ist, -tion, -ment**, and **-ism**: writ**er**, visit**or**, dent**ist**, competi**tion**, argu**ment**, critic**ism**.

GLOSSARY

Abstract noun The name given to something that cannot be touched, such as a concept or a sensation.

Collective noun The name given to a collection of individuals—people or things.

Concrete noun The name given to an ordinary thing, such as an animal or object.

Noun phrase Several words that, when grouped together, perform the same function as a noun.

Proper noun The name given to a particular person, place, or thing, which always starts with a capital letter.

Prepositional phrase A preposition such as *in* or *on* followed by a noun or pronoun that together act as an adjective (describing a noun) or an adverb (describing a verb) in a sentence.

NOUNS 23

The word *time* is the most **commonly used noun** in the **English** language.

Common nouns (collective)
Another type of common noun, collective nouns refer to a group of things or people. They are usually singular words that represent a number of things. Different collective nouns refer to different concrete nouns, and the collective nouns used to describe groups of animals are especially varied.

a **crowd** of people
a **swarm** of bees
a **flight** of stairs
a **bunch** of grapes
a **flock** of birds

Identifying noun phrases
A noun phrase is made up of a noun and any words that are modifying that noun. These modifying words are usually articles such as *the* or *a*, determiners such as *my*, *this*, or *most*, adjectives such as *happy* or *hungry*, or prepositional phrases such as *in the field*. Noun phrases perform exactly the same role as common nouns in a sentence.

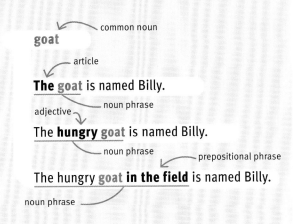

when a **flock of birds** swooped bread from **Emily's** hand.

Proper nouns
A proper noun is the name given to a particular person or place, or to a religious or historical concept or period. Proper nouns always start with a capital letter. This helps to distinguish them from common nouns. The most common proper nouns are the names of people or places, but titles, institutions, days of the week, and events and festivals are also proper nouns.

Type of proper noun	Examples
Names of people	John, Sally Smith, Queen Elizabeth II
Titles	Mr., Miss, Sir, Dr., Professor, Reverend
Places, buildings, and institutions	Africa, Asia, Canada, New York, Red Cross, Sydney Opera House, United Nations
Religious names	Bible, Koran, Christianity, Hinduism, Islam
Historical names	World War I, Ming Dynasty, Roman Empire
Events and festivals	Olympic Games, New Year's Eve
Days of the week, months	Saturday, December

Plurals

A NOUN'S PLURAL FORM IS USED WHEN THERE IS MORE THAN ONE OF SOMETHING.

> **SEE ALSO**
> ‹ 22–23 Nouns
> Comparatives and superlatives 28–29 ›
> Verb agreement 52–53 ›
> Prefixes and suffixes 142–143 ›

The word *plural* refers to the form a noun takes when more than one thing is being mentioned. Most nouns have distinctive singular and plural forms.

Regular plural nouns

The most common way to make a noun plural is to add *s* or *es* to the end of the singular form. Most nouns take the ending -s, except for those ending in -s, -z, -x, -sh, -ch, or -ss, which take the suffix (ending) -es.

One dragon
Two dragons

One wish
Two wishes

Follow the rules

Some nouns are given different plural endings to make them easier to pronounce. In most cases, it's possible to follow a few simple rules. If a word ends in -y, for example, and it has a vowel before the final -y, the plural is formed in the usual way: An *s* is added. If the final -y is preceded by a consonant, however, the *y* must be changed to *i*, followed by the ending -es.

If a word, such as *cactus*, has been borrowed from **Latin**, the Latin **plural** form (here, *cacti*) is often used.

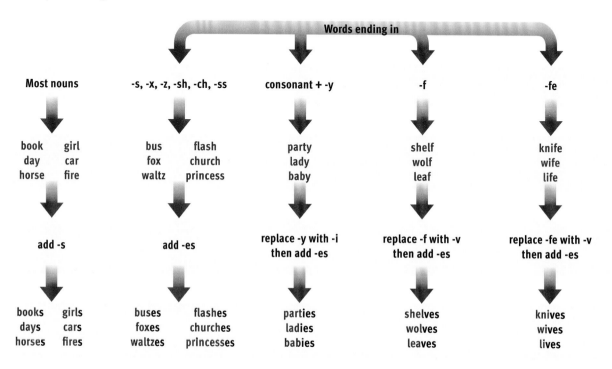

PLURALS

Irregular plural nouns

Some words just don't follow the rules. Although many nouns that end in -o are made plural by adding an s, others take the ending -es. Some nouns change their spelling completely when they become plural, while others do not change at all. Words that originate from Latin and Greek often have irregular plural endings. These exceptions have to be learned.

- If the plural form of a **noun** is used in a sentence, the **verb** that follows it must also be **plural**.
- Do not confuse **plural** words with the **possessive**. For example, "There are **two Jasons** [plural] in my class, and this is **Jason's car** [possessive]."

Singular	Plural
belief	beliefs
chief	chiefs
cliff	cliffs
roof	roofs

Words ending in -f usually change their endings to -ves.

Singular	Plural
quiz	quizzes

Words ending in -z usually take the regular -es ending.

Words ending in -o usually take the -s ending.

Singular	Plural
echo	echoes
hero	heroes
potato	potatoes
tomato	tomatoes

Singular	Plural
analysis	analyses
appendix	appendices
crisis	crises

Words of Latin or Greek origin often have irregular plural forms.

Some words change their spelling completely.

Singular	Plural
child	children
woman	women
person	people
man	men
foot	feet
tooth	teeth
goose	geese
mouse	mice
ox	oxen

Singular	Plural
sheep	sheep
deer	deer
moose	moose
series	series
scissors	scissors

Some words don't change at all.

Some nouns have two plural forms.

Singular	Plural
hoof	hooves or hoofs
dwarf	dwarves or dwarfs
mango	mangoes or mangos
buffalo	buffaloes or buffalo
index	indexes or indices
focus	focuses or foci

Staying singular

Collective nouns such as *flock* or *crowd* have plural forms, but usually appear in the singular. Some nouns do not have a plural form at all, even though they usually represent multiple things. Furniture, for example, is a singular word, but it may encompass a table, a chair, a sofa, and a cabinet.

furniture   education   information   homework   livestock   evidence   weather   knowledge

GLOSSARY

Collective noun The name given to a collection of individuals—people or things.

Plural noun When more than one person or thing is being described.

Suffix An ending made up of one or more letters that is added to a word to change its form—for example, from singular to plural.

Adjectives

ADJECTIVES ARE WORDS OR PHRASES THAT MODIFY OR DESCRIBE NOUNS OR PRONOUNS.

A noun by itself does not offer much information. If a man wanted to buy a shirt in a store, he would need to narrow down what he was looking for by using descriptive words like *thin* or *silky*. These words are known as adjectives.

SEE ALSO	
‹ 22–23 Nouns	
Comparatives and superlatives	28–29 ›
Articles	30–31 ›
Pronouns	34–35 ›
Verbs	38–39 ›
Adverbs	40–41 ›
Commas	96–99 ›
Writing to describe	208–209 ›

- If you are unsure whether a word is an adjective or something else, see if it answers questions such as: **What kind? Which one? How much? How many?**
- Adjectives should be used **sparingly**, for effect. Too many adjectives can make a sentence difficult to follow.

Describing words

Most adjectives describe attributes (characteristics) of nouns or pronouns and answer the question *What is it like?* They are used to compare one person or thing to other people or things. Adjectives are usually placed directly in front of the noun—a position known as the attributive position.

the weary painter
(adjective in attributive position — noun)

The weary painter took off his and ate a day-old Chinese

GLOSSARY

Attributive position When an adjective is placed directly in front of the noun or pronoun that it is modifying.
Clause A group of words that contains a subject and a verb.
Linking verb A verb that joins the subject of a sentence to a word or phrase—often an adjective—that describes the subject.
Predicate position When an adjective follows a linking verb at the end of a sentence.
Proper noun The name given to a particular person, place, or era, which always starts with a capital letter.

Compound adjectives

Compound adjectives are made up of more than one word. When two or more words are used together as an adjective in front of a noun, they are usually hyphenated. This shows that the two words are acting together as a single adjective.

This two-word adjective means "not fresh today."

day-old meal

"Proper" adjectives

Some nouns can be modified and used before other nouns as adjectives. These include proper nouns, such as the names of places. Adjectives formed from proper nouns should always start with a capital letter. They often end in -an, -ian, and -ish.

Chinese
Australian   **English**
Roman

ADJECTIVES

Identifying adjectives

Adverbs such as *very* or *extremely* can be used to exaggerate the state of a subject. These adverbs are sometimes confused with adjectives. A simple way of checking whether a word is an adjective or an adverb is to break down a sentence, pairing each descriptive word in turn with the noun to see if the resulting phrase makes sense.

A **hungry**, **decidedly** **weary** painter

A **hungry** painter ✓ — This is an adjective, because the phrase makes sense.

A **decidedly** painter — This is not an adjective, because the phrase doesn't make sense. It is an adverb.

A **weary** painter ✓ — This is also an adjective, because the phrase makes sense.

Listing adjectives

If one word is not enough to describe something, use several adjectives. Each adjective should be separated from the next by a comma. If there is a list of adjectives at the end of the clause, the last adjective must be preceded by *and*.

blue, green, and white overalls

- Place a comma between adjectives in a list.
- The last adjective should follow the word *and*.

• Avoid using two adjectives together that mean the same thing: for example, "the hungry, starving, ravenous tennis player." This **unnecessary repetition** of the same idea using different words is known as **tautology**.

blue, green, and white overalls

meal because he felt ravenous.

Predicate adjectives

Many adjectives can also be placed at the end of a sentence, following a verb. This is known as the predicate position. A verb used in this way is called a linking verb, because it connects a subject with a descriptive word. Common linking verbs include *seem*, *look*, *feel*, *become*, *stay,* and *turn*.

he felt ravenous

- linking verb
- adjective in predicate position

Adjective endings

Many adjectives can be recognized by their endings. Knowing these endings can help to distinguish adjectives from adverbs and verbs.

Ending	Examples
-able/-ible	comfort**able**, remark**able**, horr**ible**, ed**ible**
-al	fiction**al**, education**al**, logic**al**, nation**al**
-ful	bash**ful**, peace**ful**, help**ful**, beauti**ful**
-ic	energet**ic**, man**ic**, dramat**ic**, fantast**ic**
-ive	attract**ive**, sensit**ive**, impuls**ive**, persuas**ive**
-less	home**less**, care**less**, end**less**, use**less**
-ous	raven**ous**, mischiev**ous**, fam**ous**, nerv**ous**

Comparatives and superlatives

ADJECTIVES CAN BE USED TO COMPARE NOUNS OR PRONOUNS.

SEE ALSO	
‹ 22–23 Nouns	
‹ 26–27 Adjectives	
Prepositions	60–61 ›
Syllables	134–135 ›

Comparatives and superlatives are special types of adjectives that are used to compare two or more things. Most comparatives are formed using the ending -er, and most superlatives are formed using the ending -est.

- **Never use double** comparatives or double superlatives—"more prettier" and "most prettiest" are wrong.
- Not every adjective has a comparative or superlative form. *Unique*, *square*, *round*, *excellent*, and *perfect* are all words that can't be graded.

Comparatives

A comparative adjective is used to compare two people or things. It is formed by adding the ending -er to all one-syllable adjectives and some two-syllable adjectives. When two nouns are being compared in a sentence, they are usually linked using the preposition *than*.

The Ferris wheel is bigger than the carousel.

This word is used to link the two nouns being compared: the Ferris wheel and the carousel.

The Ferris wheel is bigger than the the biggest ride of all. The ghost

Superlatives

Superlative adjectives can be used to compare two or more people or things. They are formed by adding the ending -est to one-syllable adjectives, and using the word *the* in front of them: "the biggest ride."

big
bigger
biggest

small
smaller
smallest

thin
thinner
thinnest

REAL WORLD
Biggest and best

Multiple superlatives are often used in advertisements to sell things, whether they're books, vacations, or circus attractions. Words like *greatest*, *best,* and *cheapest* enable a seller to exaggerate the quality or value of the product being sold, making it more appealing to potential customers. Superlatives should be used in moderation in formal text, however.

COMPARATIVES AND SUPERLATIVES

Identifying irregular adjective spellings

Some adjectives do not follow the rules when it comes to forming their comparatives or superlatives. If an adjective already ends in -e (*rude*), only -r needs to be added to make it comparative (*ruder*), and -st, to make it superlative (*rudest*). Words ending in -y or a vowel and a single consonant have to change their endings.

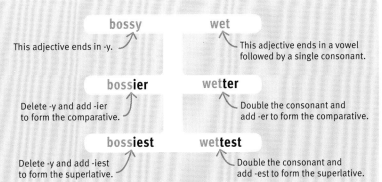

bossy — This adjective ends in -y.
bossier — Delete -y and add -ier to form the comparative.
bossiest — Delete -y and add -iest to form the superlative.

wet — This adjective ends in a vowel followed by a single consonant.
wetter — Double the consonant and add -er to form the comparative.
wettest — Double the consonant and add -est to form the superlative.

Exceptions

Some two-syllable adjectives, such as *lovely*, can take either form of the comparative or superlative (see "Awkward adjectives"). Other adjectives change completely when they are used to compare things. These comparative and superlative forms have to be learned.

Adjective	Comparative	Superlative
good	better	best
bad	worse	worst
much	more	most
many	more	most
little	less	least
quiet	quieter or more quiet	quietest or most quiet
simple	simpler or more simple	simplest or most simple
clever	cleverer or more clever	cleverest or most clever
lovely	lovelier or more lovely	loveliest or most lovely

carousel, but the roller coaster is train is the most frightening.

Awkward adjectives

If adding the ending -er or -est results in an odd-sounding adjective, the comparative and superlative are formed using the words *more* or *most* before the adjective. This applies to most two-syllable adjectives and all adjectives with three or more syllables.

The ghost train is the most frightening.

The superlative *frighteningest* is hard to say, so—because *frightening* has three syllables—the superlative is formed using *most*.

Articles

THERE ARE TWO TYPES OF ARTICLES: DEFINITE AND INDEFINITE.

Articles are a type of adjective and a type of determiner. They are always used with a noun. Similarly, many singular forms of nouns must be used with an article.

SEE ALSO	
‹ 22–23 Nouns	
‹ 24–25 Plurals	
‹ 26–27 Adjectives	
Determiners	32–33 ›

The definite article

The definite article is *the*. It always precedes a noun, and refers to a specific person or thing. This person or thing may have been mentioned before, or there may be only one to talk about. Alternatively, it may be clear from the context which noun is being referred to.

the rhinoceros

There is only one rhinoceros on the bus, so the definite article is used.

In **many languages**, including French, German, and Spanish, **the article** tells the reader whether a word is **feminine**, **masculine**, or **neutral**. In **English**, very **few words** have a **gender**.

The rhinoceros and his best a bus to visit the struggling

The indefinite article

The indefinite article, *a* or *an*, is used to refer to any one person or thing. Words that begin with consonants (*bus*) use *a*, while words that start with a vowel (*a, e, i, o,* or *u*) or a silent *h*, such as *hour*, use *an* to make pronunciation easier. The indefinite article also indicates that someone or something belongs to a specific group. For example, "The animal is a giraffe" explains that this particular animal is one of many members of a group of animals known as giraffes.

The indefinite article indicates that this could be one of a number of buses, whereas the definite article *the* would refer to one particular bus.

a bus

The form *an* is used before a vowel to make it easier to say.

an elephant

Articles and adjectives

If a noun is preceded by one or more descriptive adjectives, the article goes before the adjective. The resulting phrase (article + adjective + noun) is known as a noun phrase. If the indefinite article is used in front of an adjective that begins with a vowel, the form *an* is used.

The article precedes the adjective *struggling*, which goes before the noun *ostrich*.

the struggling ostrich

The adjective *anxious* begins with a vowel, so *an* is used.

an anxious rhinoceros

ARTICLES

Identifying when to use an article

If a singular noun can be counted, this noun will require an article—definite or indefinite. For example, "I saw elephant today" doesn't make sense. Some nouns, such as *happiness*, *information*, and *bread*, do not have a plural form, and therefore cannot be counted. These nouns can be used without an article (zero article) or with the definite article. They never take the indefinite article.

elephant
This noun can be counted, so the definite or indefinite article can be used.

one elephant
two elephants

the elephant

an elephant

bread
This noun cannot be counted.

one bread
two breads

The definite article can be used for a specific piece of bread.

the bread

The zero article is used for the concept of bread in general.

bread

---

friend, **an** elephant, took ostrich at flying school.

The zero article

Some words, such as *school*, *life,* and *home*, take the definite article when a particular one is being referred to, and the indefinite article when one of several is being described. When these words are used to describe a general concept, such as being at school, the article is removed. This absence of an article is known as the zero article.

at flying school
This describes school as a concept—a place where a person goes to learn something—so the zero article (no article) is used.

at the flying school next to the zoo
This describes a particular school—the one next to the zoo—so *the* is required.

- Many **geographical areas** and features, including **rivers**, **deserts**, and **oceans**, use the **definite article**: for example, the North Pole, the Pacific Ocean, or the Rocky Mountains.

- If an **article** is at the beginning of the **title** of a work, such as *The Secret Garden*, it should start with a **capital letter**.

- **Unique things**, such as **the sun**, always take *the*.

- Watch out for words that begin with a **vowel** that **sounds like a consonant**, such as *university*. These take the indefinite article *a*, rather than *an*.

Determiners

DETERMINERS ARE ALWAYS PLACED BEFORE A NOUN, AND HELP TO DEFINE IT.

SEE ALSO	
‹ 20–21 Parts of speech	
‹ 22–23 Nouns	
‹ 26–27 Adjectives	
‹ 30–31 Articles	
Pronouns	34–35 ›
Verb agreement	52–53 ›

Articles are determiners, and other determiners work in much the same way: They are used in front of nouns to indicate whether something specific or something of a particular type is being referred to.

Determiners and adjectives

Determiners are often considered to be a subclass of adjectives and, like adjectives, they belong to nouns and modify nouns. Unlike adjectives, there is rarely more than one determiner for each noun, nor can determiners be compared or graded. They precede the noun and include words like *several*, *those*, *many*, *my,* and *your*, as well as articles (*the*, *a,* and *an*) and numbers.

The determiner always precedes any adjectives, which, in turn, precede the noun.

several (determiner) **furious** (adjective) **members** (plural noun)

- **Many sentences do not make sense without determiners.** Adjectives, by contrast, are optional; they color the words rather than glue them together.
- Most **noun phrases** only use **one determiner**, but there are exceptions: for example, "all the bats" and "both my cats."

Several furious members of the broomsticks. "That witch has nine

definite article — *the*

GLOSSARY

Cardinal number A counting number such as *one*, *two*, or *twenty-one*.

Linking verb A verb such as *be* that joins the subject of a sentence to a word or phrase—often an adjective—that describes the subject.

Ordinal number The form of a number that includes *first*, *second*, and *twenty-first*.

Demonstrative determiners

Demonstrative determiners give an idea of distance between the speaker and the person or thing that he or she is referring to. *This* (singular) and *these* (plural) are used to describe things that are nearby. *That* (singular) and *those* (plural) are used for things that are farther away.

This indicates a witch who is not present at the meeting. → **that witch**

The witches are discussing a noise they can hear—that of shrieking bats—so *this* is used. → **this noise**

DETERMINERS   33

Identifying determiners

Sometimes determiners look very similar to adjectives. One way of figuring out whether a word that precedes a noun is a determiner or an adjective is to try placing the word at the end of a sentence, following a linking verb such as *be*. If the sentence makes sense, that word is an adjective; if it does not make sense, it is a determiner.

Several furious members

This is an adjective, because the sentence makes sense.

The members **are furious**.

↑ linking verb

This is a determiner, because the sentence does not make sense.

The members **are** several.

• Some words, such as *each* or *all*, are used both as **determiners and pronouns**. The rule to remember is that a **determiner is always followed by a noun**, whereas a pronoun replaces a noun.

Possessive determiners

The possessive determiners *my*, *your*, *his*, *her*, *its*, *our*, and *their* are used before nouns to show ownership. They should not be confused with possessive pronouns—for example, *mine*, *yours*, *ours*, and *theirs*—which replace, rather than precede, the noun.

their broomsticks

The broomsticks (plural noun) belong to the witches.

"...coven held a meeting on their ... shrieking bats!" they grumbled.

indefinite article

Numbers and quantifiers

Cardinal and ordinal numbers and other words that express quantity are considered to be determiners when they appear before a noun. These include *much*, *most*, *little*, *least*, *any*, *enough*, *half*, and *whole*. Beware of determiners such as *much* (singular) and *many* (plural) that can only modify singular or plural nouns.

nine shrieking bats

This cardinal number is being used before a noun phrase (*shrieking bats*) as a determiner.

much noise

This determiner can only be used with a singular noun.

many bats

This determiner can only be used with a plural noun.

Interrogative determiners

Interrogative determiners include *which* and *what* and are used before a noun to ask a question.

Which witch?

What noise?

Pronouns

PRONOUN MEANS "FOR A NOUN," AND A PRONOUN IS A WORD THAT TAKES THE PLACE OF A NOUN.

SEE ALSO	
‹ 22–23 Nouns	
‹ 30–31 Articles	
‹ 32–33 Determiners	
Number and gender	36–37 ›
Prepositions	60–61 ›
Commonly misused words	78–79 ›
Relative clauses	82–83 ›

Without pronouns, spoken and written English would be very repetitive. Once a noun has been referred to by its actual name once, another word—a pronoun—can be used to stand for this name.

Using pronouns
If the full name of a noun were used each time it had to be referred to, sentences would be long and confusing. Pronouns are useful because they make sentences shorter and therefore clearer. The noun is still required when someone or something is referred to for the first time.

Rita loves playing the **guitar**.
She finds **it** relaxing.

- This personal pronoun represents *Rita*, the subject.
- This personal pronoun represents *playing the guitar*, the object.

Types of pronouns
There are seven types of pronouns, which are used for different purposes. Do not confuse these with determiners or adjectives, which modify rather than replace nouns.

• *I* is the only pronoun that is spelled with a **capital** letter.

Personal pronouns
These **represent people, places, or things**. They vary according to whether the noun being replaced is the subject of a sentence (performing the action) or the object (receiving the action).

I, you, he, she, it, we, you, they (subject)
me, you, him, her, it, us, you, them (object)

She gave **them** a guitar lesson.
- This pronoun represents the singular subject.
- This pronoun represents the plural object.

Possessive pronouns
These **show ownership and replace possessive** noun phrases. Don't get these confused with possessive determiners such as *my* and *your*, which precede but do not replace the noun.

mine, yours, his, hers, its, ours, yours, theirs

The guitar is **hers**.
- This pronoun replaces the possessive noun phrase *Rita's guitar*.

Relative pronouns
These **link one part of a sentence to another** by introducing a relative clause that describes an earlier noun or pronoun.

who, whom, whose, which, that, what

Rita is the person **who** plays the guitar.
- This pronoun is describing *Rita*, the subject.

Reflexive pronouns
These **refer back to an earlier noun or pronoun** in a sentence, so the performing and receiving of an action apply to the same person or thing. They cannot be used without the noun or pronoun that they relate to.

myself, yourself, himself, herself, ourselves, themselves

She taught **herself**.
- This pronoun refers back to the earlier pronoun *she*.

Demonstrative pronouns

These **function as subjects or objects** in a sentence, replacing nouns. Don't confuse these with demonstrative determiners, which precede but do not replace the noun.

this, that, these, those

This pronoun is acting as the subject of the sentence.

This is my instrument.

Interrogative pronouns

These are **used to ask questions** and represent an unknown subject or object.

who, whom, what, which, whose

This pronoun represents the subject, an unknown musician.

Who is playing?

Indefinite pronouns

These **do not refer to any specific person or thing**, but take the place of nouns in a sentence.

somebody, someone, something, anybody, anyone, anything, nobody, no one, nothing, all, another, both, each, many, most, other, some, few, none, such

I haven't seen anyone.

This represents an unknown person, the object of the sentence.

- As a rule, **a pronoun cannot be modified** by an **adjective** or **adverb** in the way that a noun can be: For example, "the sad I" does not make sense. Some exceptions include **"what** else" and **"somebody** nice."
- *Somebody* and *someone* **mean the same thing**, as do *anybody* and *anyone*, *everybody* and *everyone*, and *nobody* and *no one*.

Talking about myself

Many people wrongly opt for the reflexive form *myself* because they are unsure whether to use *I* or *me*. Reflexive pronouns should only be used to refer back to a specific noun or pronoun that has already been mentioned in the sentence. This noun or pronoun is usually (but not always) the subject.

I imagined myself on the stage.

This reflexive pronoun correctly refers back to the subject, *I*.

Rita performed for Ben and myself.

This wrongly used reflexive pronoun has no noun to refer back to—there is no *I* in the sentence.

Identifying when to use *I* or *me*

People often make mistakes when deciding whether to use the personal pronouns *I* or *me*. To figure out which to use, split the sentence into two short sentences. It should then become clear which one is right. Remember to put others first in a sentence.

Me and Ben enjoyed the concert. ✗

This doesn't make sense, so *me* is wrong. → Me enjoyed the concert. ✗

Ben enjoyed the concert. ✓

This makes sense, so *I* is the correct pronoun. → I enjoyed the concert. ✓

Always place others first. → Ben and I enjoyed the concert. ✓

If the pronoun follows a preposition, the object personal pronoun *me* should be used.

This is a preposition, so the subject pronoun *I* is wrong.

It was a late night **for** Ben and I. ✗

It was a late night **for** Ben and me. ✓

The object pronoun *me* now correctly follows the preposition *for*.

Number and gender

PRONOUNS AND DETERMINERS MUST AGREE WITH THE NOUNS TO WHICH THEY RELATE.

In English, there are no personal pronouns or possessive determiners that can be used to refer to someone without identifying whether that person is male or female. This often results in mismatched combinations of singular nouns and plural pronouns or determiners.

SEE ALSO	
‹ 24–25 Plurals	
‹ 32–33 Determiners	
‹ 34–35 Pronouns	
Verbs	38–39 ›
Verb agreement	52–53 ›

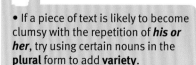

- If a piece of text is likely to become clumsy with the repetition of **his or her**, try using certain nouns in the **plural** form to add **variety**.

GLOSSARY

Indefinite pronoun A pronoun such as *everyone* that refers to nobody or nothing specific.

Number The term used to identify a noun or pronoun as singular or plural.

Personal pronoun A pronoun that takes the place of a noun and represents people, places, or things.

Possessive determiner A word that is used before a noun to show ownership.

Matching numbers

Pronouns must agree in number (singular or plural) with the nouns they represent. Plural nouns or pronouns must be followed by plural pronouns or determiners, and singular nouns or pronouns must be followed by singular pronouns or determiners.

Pronoun	Determiner
I	my
you	your
he	his
she	her
it	its
we	our
you	your
they	their

They were preparing for their
told his students that everyone

- When using the word **each**, think about **"each one,"** as it makes it easier to remember that **each** is always followed by a **singular pronoun** or **determiner**.

- Some words, such as **each** and **all**, are used both as **determiners** and as **pronouns**. Remember that a determiner is always used in front of a noun, whereas a pronoun replaces a noun.

Indefinite pronouns

Indefinite pronouns such as *everyone* and *anything* often cause problems. Although they appear to refer to more than one person or thing, these pronouns are, in fact, singular words. One way of establishing whether a pronoun is singular or plural is to put the verb form *are* right after it. If the resulting combination sounds wrong, then that pronoun is singular.

Singular	Plural
everyone is	both are
somebody is	all are
something is	many are
each is	most are
nothing is	others are
another is	few are

NUMBER AND GENDER

Identifying who's who

If there is more than one person or thing in a sentence, it must be clear which pronoun refers to which person or thing. If it is not clear, the sentence needs to be reworded. Alternatively, the name of the relevant person can be repeated to make it clear who is doing what.

In this case it was Anna's first climb, not Emily's, so the name *Anna* has been repeated to make this clear.

Emily wanted **Anna** to come, although it was **her** first climb. ✗
It is unclear whether it was Emily's first climb or Anna's.

Although it was **her** first climb, **Emily** wanted **Anna** to come. ✓
This sentence has been reordered so that the pronoun is next to the subject it relates to—it was Emily's first climb, not Anna's.

Emily wanted **Anna** to come, although it was **Anna's** first climb. ✓

Misusing *their*

The plural form *they* doesn't have a gender, and people often use this form when speaking or writing to avoid having to distinguish between males and females. In many cases, this results in a singular noun or pronoun being paired with a plural determiner. The only way to avoid this problem is to use *his or her* instead of *their* for the singular, or to make the noun plural and use *their*.

Everyone had to bring his or her own rope.
The indefinite pronoun *everyone* is singular, so the determiners *his* and *her* are used to refer to a group made up of males and females.

The students had to bring their own ropes.
The sentence has been reworded to include a plural subject (*students*), so the plural determiner *their* can be used. The object (*ropes*) has been made plural as well.

climbing expedition. The instructor had to bring his or her own rope.

Male or female?

Sometimes it's hard to know whether to use *he*, *she*, or *they* when referring to both men and women. Historically, writers used the masculine pronouns and determiners *he*, *his*, *him*, and *himself* to represent both sexes, but this approach is now considered outdated. Assumptions about male and female roles should also be avoided.

The instructor told his students to bring ropes.
This sentence refers to a specific instructor, who is known to be male, so the determiner *his* is correct.

An instructor must carry spare ropes for his or her students.
This sentence refers to an unknown instructor, who could be male or female, so the determiners *his* and *her* are required.

Instructors must carry spare ropes for their students.
Sometimes it's clearer to use both the noun and the determiner in the plural form.

Verbs

MOST VERBS ARE ACTION WORDS.

A verb is the most important word in a sentence; without it, the sentence would not make sense. Verbs describe what a person or thing is doing or being.

SEE ALSO	
‹ 22–23 Nouns	
‹ 26–27 Adjectives	
‹ 34–35 Pronouns	
Adverbs	40–41 ›
Simple tenses	42–43 ›
Perfect and continuous tenses	44–45 ›
Irregular verbs	50–51 ›

Verbs, subjects, and objects

All sentences require both a verb and a subject. The subject (a noun or pronoun) is the person or thing doing the action (a verb). Many sentences also have an object. The direct object (also a noun or pronoun) is the person or thing that is receiving the action.

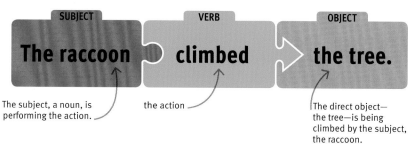

The subject, a noun, is performing the action.

the action

The direct object—the tree—is being climbed by the subject, the raccoon.

▷ **The indirect object**
The indirect object is the person or thing indirectly affected by the action of the verb. It always goes before the direct object, and typically right after the verb. Indirect objects never occur without a direct object.

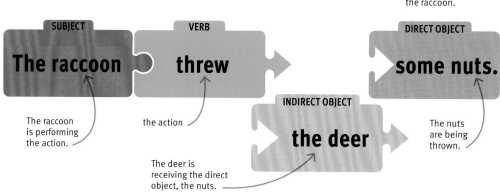

The raccoon is performing the action.

the action

The nuts are being thrown.

The deer is receiving the direct object, the nuts.

Transitive verbs

Action verbs can be divided into two types—transitive and intransitive. A transitive verb always occurs with an object. It carries an action across from the subject to the direct object. If you can ask and answer the question *who?* or *what?* using the verb, then it is transitive.

This object answers the question "What did the fire destroy?"

A fire destroyed **the forest.**

SUBJECT | TRANSITIVE VERB | OBJECT

Intransitive verbs

Intransitive verbs do not need an object—they make sense on their own. Common intransitive verbs include *arrive*, *sleep*, and *die*. Some verbs, such as *escape*, can be both transitive and intransitive.

Here, *escaped* is used as an intransitive verb—it makes sense without an object.

The animals escaped.

SUBJECT | INTRANSITIVE VERB

Linking verbs

A linking verb links the subject of a sentence to a word or phrase that describes the subject. Linking verbs either relate to the senses (*feel*, *taste*, *smell*, *look*, *hear*) or to a state of existence (*be*, *become*, *appear*, *remain*). The most common linking verb is *be*.

subject — This linking verb is a past form of the verb *be*. — This adjective describes the state of mind of the rabbits.

The rabbits were **frightened**.

Identifying a linking verb

The simplest way to identify a linking verb is to substitute a form of *be* for the verb. If the resulting sentence makes sense, that verb is a linking verb. If it doesn't make sense, the verb is an action verb.

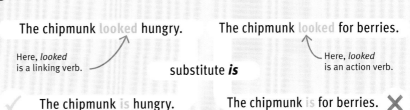

The chipmunk looked hungry.   The chipmunk looked for berries.

Here, *looked* is a linking verb.   Here, *looked* is an action verb.

substitute *is*

✓ The chipmunk is hungry.   The chipmunk is for berries. ✗

The infinitive

The infinitive is the simplest form of a verb—the form that is used in dictionaries. It can be used on its own, but is almost always preceded by *to*. Unlike verbs, infinitives never change in form. They can be used as nouns, adjectives, or adverbs in a sentence.

The chipmunk needed **to eat**.

subject — This infinitive is acting like a noun, such as *food*, would act because it is the object of the sentence.

He found a grasshopper **to eat**.

subject — This infinitive is acting like an adjective, because it is modifying the object of the sentence; it adds the information that the grasshopper is edible.

A well-known exception to the **subject–verb–object** rule comes from the Christian marriage service: "With this ring, **I thee wed**."

REAL WORLD
To boldly go or to go boldly?

Split infinitives occur when an adverb, such as *boldly*, is placed between the infinitive and the preceding *to*. It's preferable to keep the *to* next to the verb, but avoiding a split infinitive can make a sentence awkward. Split infinitives can be used sparingly for emphasis, to avoid confusion, or for a more natural reading order. A famous example is from the opening lines of the 1960s *Star Trek* television series: "To boldly go where no man has gone before."

GLOSSARY

Intransitive verb A verb that does not require an object.
Linking verb A verb, such as *be*, that connects the subject of a sentence to a word or phrase—often an adjective—that describes the subject.
Object The noun or pronoun that is receiving the action of the verb.
Subject The noun or pronoun that is performing the action of the verb.
Transitive verb A verb that must be used with an object.

Adverbs

AN ADVERB MODIFIES A VERB, AN ADJECTIVE, OR ANOTHER ADVERB.

The word *adverb* essentially means "to add to a verb," and this is what adverbs mostly do. They provide information about how, when, where, or how often something is happening, and to what degree.

SEE ALSO	
‹ 26–27 Adjectives	
‹ 28–29 Comparatives and superlatives	
‹ 38–39 Verbs	
Conjunctions	58–59 ›
Phrases	64–65 ›
Clauses	66–67 ›
Managing modifiers	76–77 ›

When and how often?

Adverbs of time indicate when something is happening, while adverbs of frequency indicate how often it is happening. These adverbs modify verbs, and can occupy different positions in a sentence—usually at the beginning or end of a clause.

yesterday   soon
today   now
then   later

adverbs of time

always   rarely
usually   again
sometimes never

adverbs of frequency

Where?

Adverbs of place work in the same way as adverbs of time and frequency. They modify verbs and tell the reader more about where something is happening.

away   nowhere   there
everywhere   upstairs
        abroad
here   out

Yesterday we went out. We left an extremely large dog saw us.

Forming common adverbs

Most adverbs in English are formed by adding the ending -ly to an adjective, but there are some exceptions. Some adjectives, such as *lovely* or *holy*, also end in -ly, so it's important not to confuse these with adverbs.

Adjective ending	Rule	Adverb
-l (beautiful, wonderful)	Add -ly	beautiful**ly**, wonderful**ly**
-y (pretty, busy, hungry)	Change -y to -i, then add -ly	prett**ily**, bus**ily**, hungr**ily**
-le (comfortable, reputable)	Change -e to -y	comfortab**ly**, reputab**ly**
-ic (enthusiastic, ecstatic)	Add -ally	enthusiastic**ally**, ecstatic**ally**
-ly (friendly, daily)	Use an adverbial phrase	in a friendly way, every day

ADVERBS

How?

Adverbs that describe how actions are performed are known as adverbs of manner. They are formed from adjectives and modify verbs. These adverbs can be placed before or after the verb, or at the beginning or end of a clause. Like adjectives, most adverbs of manner and frequency can be graded by adverbs of degree, such as *very*, *quite*, or *almost*. These are always placed directly before the adjective or adverb they describe.

This adverb of degree is modifying the adverb of manner quietly—*it indicates how quietly they left.*

We left very quietly

This adverb of manner is at the end of a clause, and is modifying the verb left—*it is describing how they left.*

an extremely **large dog**

This adverb of degree is modifying the adjective large—*it is explaining how large the dog was.*

- Some **adverbs of degree**, such as ***just***, ***only***, ***almost***, and ***even***, must be placed immediately in front of the word they are modifying: for example, "I have **just** arrived."

Sentence adverbs

Sentence adverbs are unusual because they do not just modify a verb—they modify the whole sentence or clause containing that verb. They usually express the likelihood or desirability of something happening, and include words like *unfortunately*, *probably*, and *certainly*. They can also be used to influence the reader.

This adverb is modifying a whole clause, meaning "it is unfortunate that an extremely large dog saw us."

unfortunately **an** extremely **large dog saw us**

very quietly, **but** unfortunately **We'll run more** quickly **next time.**

Comparing adverbs

Like adjectives, adverbs of manner can be compared. To form the comparative, *more* is usually added before the adverb. In the same way, *most* is added before the adverb to form the superlative.

more quickly
most quickly

The three **most common adverbs** in English are *not*, *very*, and *too*.

GLOSSARY

Adverbial phrase A group of words such as "in July of last year" that perform the same role as an adverb and answer questions such as: How? When? Where? How often?

- ***Then*** is an **adverb of time**, and should **not** be used as a **conjunction**. When joining two clauses together, use a conjunction such as *and* before *then*.
- **Don't overuse adverbs.** In the phrase "absolutely fabulous," the adverb ***absolutely*** adds nothing to the adjective ***fabulous***, which already implies high levels of enthusiasm for something.

Simple tenses

THE TENSE OF A VERB INDICATES WHEN AN ACTION TAKES PLACE.

Unlike most parts of speech, verbs change their form. These different forms, known as tenses, indicate the timing of an action, which is performed by the first, second, or third person.

SEE ALSO	
❰ 34–35 Pronouns	
❰ 38–39 Verbs	
❰ 40–41 Adverbs	
Perfect and continuous tenses	44–45 ❱
Auxiliary verbs	48–49 ❱
Irregular verbs	50–51 ❱

Picking the right person
Each verb must express a person (first, second, or third), a number (singular or plural), and a tense (past, present, or future). There are three persons in English. These identify who is taking part in a conversation.

The word **tense** comes from the **Latin** word *tempus*, which means **"time."**

▷ **The first person**
The first person represents the speaker, and uses the personal pronouns *I* or *me* if the speaker is alone, and *we* or *us* if the speaker is accompanied.

singular
I sing

plural
We sing

▷ **The second person**
The second person addresses the reader or listener, and uses *you* for both singular and plural.

singular
You sing

plural
You sing

▷ **The third person**
The third person represents everyone and everything else, and uses the singular pronouns *he* and *him*, *she* and *her*, and *it*, and the plural pronouns *they* and *them*.

singular
She sings

plural
They sing

SIMPLE TENSES

The present simple tense

The present simple tense is used to express a constant or repeated action that is happening right now. It can also represent a widespread truth: For example, "I smile all the time." Regular verbs in the present tense use the infinitive, except for the third person singular, which uses the infinitive plus the ending -s.

I smile **We** smile
You smile **You** smile
She smiles **They** smile

The third person singular is formed by adding an *s*.

The past simple tense

The past simple tense expresses an action that began and ended in the past. Regular past tense verbs are formed using the infinitive, followed by the ending -ed.

The first, second, and third person take the same form of the verb in the past tense—for both singular and plural.

I laughed **We** laughed
You laughed **You** laughed
She laughed **They** laughed

The future simple tense

The future simple tense is used to express actions that will occur in the future. Regular verbs in the future tense are formed using the auxiliary verb *will*, followed by the infinitive.

I will cry **We** will cry
You will cry **You** will cry
She will cry **They** will cry

The auxiliary verb *will* is used to create the future simple tense.

- Another way of forming the **future simple tense** is to place *am*, *is*, or *are* before *going to*, followed by the infinitive. This form is useful when the action being described is definitely going to happen. For example, **"It is going to explode."**
- The three basic tenses are the present, the past, and the future. Each of these tenses has a **simple** form, a **continuous** form, a **perfect** form, and a **perfect continuous** form.

GLOSSARY

Auxiliary verb A "helping" verb like *be* or *have* that joins the main verb in a sentence to the subject.

Infinitive The simplest form of a verb: the form that is used in dictionaries.

Perfect and continuous tenses

THESE TENSES GIVE MORE INFORMATION ABOUT WHEN AN ACTION IS HAPPENING, AND HOW LONG IT GOES ON FOR.

SEE ALSO	
‹ 38-39 Verbs	
‹ 42-43 Simple tenses	
Participles	46-47 ›
Auxiliary verbs	48-49 ›
Irregular verbs	50-51 ›

GLOSSARY

Auxiliary verb A "helping" verb like *be* or *have* that links the main verb in a sentence to the subject.
Past participle The form of a verb that usually ends in -ed or -en.
Present participle The form of a verb that ends in -ing.

The perfect tenses refer to actions that are completed over a period of time. The continuous tenses are used to emphasize that an action is ongoing at a particular point in time.

The present perfect tense

The perfect tenses describe actions that span a period of time but have a known end. The present perfect tense refers either to an action that happened at an unspecified time in the past, or to an action that began in the past and continues in the present. It is formed using the past participle, preceded by the auxiliary verb form *have* or—for the third person singular—*has*.

This refers to an action that happened at some point in the past.

I have disappeared
You have disappeared
She has disappeared

We have disappeared
You have disappeared
They have disappeared

This refers to an action that began in the past and continues in the present.

She has lived here for ten years.

The third person singular is formed using has *instead of* have.

The past perfect tense

The past perfect tense describes an action that happened in the past before something else happened. It is formed in the same way as the present perfect tense, but using the auxiliary verb form *had* before the past participle.

I had escaped
You had escaped
It had escaped

We had escaped
You had escaped
They had escaped

By the time **the guard** noticed, **I** had escaped.

This action finished before the second action (the guard noticing) started.

The future perfect tense

The future perfect tense describes an action that will occur at some point in the future before another action. For example, "He will have offended again before we catch him."

I will have offended
You will have offended
He will have offended

We will have offended
You will have offended
They will have offended

This tense is formed using the past participle, preceded by will have.

PERFECT AND CONTINUOUS TENSES

The present continuous tense

Continuous or progressive tenses are used to describe actions or situations that are ongoing. The present continuous tense expresses an action that is continuing at the same time that something else is happening. This tense is formed using the present participle, preceded by *am, are,* or *is*.

I am hiding
You are hiding
She is hiding

We are hiding
You are hiding
They are hiding

I am hiding in a tree until **it** gets dark.

The action *hiding* is continuing at the same time that it starts to get dark.

The past continuous tense

The past continuous tense describes a past action that was happening at the same time that another action occurred. For example, "They were falling asleep when they heard a loud crash."

I was falling
You were falling
He was falling

We were falling
You were falling
They were falling

This tense is formed in the same way as the present continuous tense, but using *was* or *were* instead of *am, is,* or *are*.

The future continuous tense

The future continuous tense describes an ongoing action that is going to happen in the future. Like the other continuous forms, the present participle is used, but it is preceded by *will be*.

I will be watching
You will be watching
She will be watching

We will be watching
You will be watching
They will be watching

Perfect continuous tenses

Like simple continuous tenses, perfect continuous tenses describe ongoing actions. Like perfect tenses, these actions end at some point in the present, past, or future. Perfect continuous tenses are also formed using the present participle.

Tense	Form	Example
Present perfect continuous	have/has been + present participle	I have been hiding since dawn.
Past perfect continuous	had been + present participle	The guard had been searching all day.
Future perfect continuous	will have been + present participle	They will have been following my trail.

REAL WORLD
Verbal dynamism

Some verbs sound strange when they are used in the continuous tenses. For something to be ongoing, it needs to be something active, such as running or eating. Verbs that do not imply an action, but instead refer to a state of affairs—for example, *know, own, love,* or *feel*—cannot be used in the continuous tenses. Although it has become a familiar expression, the slogan "I'm lovin' it" is grammatically wrong. Maybe that's why everyone remembers it.

Participles

PARTICIPLES ARE FORMED FROM VERBS.

There are two participles: the past and the present. They are used with auxiliary verbs like *have* and *be* to form tenses, and on their own as adjectives. The present participle can also be used as a noun.

SEE ALSO	
‹ 26–27 Adjectives	
‹ 38–39 Verbs	
‹ 42–43 Simple tenses	
‹ 44–45 Perfect and continuous tenses	
Auxiliary verbs	48–49 ›
Voices and moods	54–55 ›
Managing modifiers	76–77 ›
Silent letters	160–161 ›

Past participles as verbs

Combined with the auxiliary verb *have*, past participles are used to form the perfect tense of a verb. Regular past participles are formed in the same way as the simple past tense, using the infinitive, plus the ending -ed. Common irregular past participle endings include -en, -t, or -n. The past participle of a few verbs is the same as the infinitive, and some, such as *tell*, change their spelling completely.

INFINITIVE	+ -ED	REGULAR PAST PARTICIPLE
look	+ -ed	looked

irregular past participles

taken   built   grown   cut   told
frozen   kept   seen   become   begun
broken   lost   worn   come   written

Josh had looked everywhere for been hoping to do some ice-

• Don't use the **wrong participle** as an **adjective**. An "interested cat" is not the same as an "interesting cat."

GLOSSARY

Auxiliary verb A "helping" verb like *be* or *have* that joins the main verb in a sentence to the subject.

Gerund The name given to the present participle when it is used as a noun.

Linking verb A verb that joins the subject of a sentence to a word or phrase that describes the subject.

Present participles as verbs

Present participles are used with the auxiliary verb *be* to form verbs in the continuous tense. They are formed using the infinitive and the ending -ing. Unlike past participles, all present participles have the same ending. If the infinitive ends in a silent -e (for example, *hope*), the -e is dropped before the -ing ending is added.

INFINITIVE	+ -ING	PRESENT PARTICIPLE
want	+ -ing	wanting
hope	+ -ing	hoping

PARTICIPLES 47

Past participles as adjectives

Past participles can be used on their own as adjectives to modify nouns. They are placed either before the noun or pronoun they describe, or after it, following a linking verb.

This past participle is being used as an adjective before the noun it describes (skates).

his broken skates

His skates were broken.

Here, the past participle is being used as an adjective after the noun it describes (skates), following the linking verb were.

Identifying a gerund phrase

Participle phrases act as adjectives, whereas gerund phrases act as nouns, which can be described by adjectives. Since gerund phrases are always singular, it is possible to check whether a phrase is a gerund phrase by substituting the pronoun *it*.

Emptying his cupboard, Josh found them.

The pronoun it has been substituted for the phrase, and the resulting sentence doesn't make sense, so the phrase is a participle phrase.

It, Josh found them. ✗

Emptying his cupboard, Josh found them. ✓

This participle phrase is acting as an adjective, describing Josh.

Repairing the skates was a priority.

The pronoun it has been substituted for the phrase, and the resulting sentence makes sense, so the phrase is a gerund phrase.

It was a priority.

Repairing the skates was a priority. ✓

---

his broken skates. He had
skating, but they were missing.

Present participles as nouns

When the present participle of a verb is used as a noun, it is called a gerund. Like nouns, a gerund (one word) or a gerund phrase (multiple words) can be used as the subject or object of a sentence.

subject

He wanted to do some ice-skating.

The gerund phrase ice-skating is acting as the object of this sentence.

Present participles as adjectives

Like past participles, present participles can be used as adjectives. They can be placed before or after the noun or pronoun that they modify.

This present participle is being used as an adjective after the pronoun it describes (they), following the linking verb were.

They were missing.

the missing skates

This present participle is formed from the verb miss, and is describing the noun skates.

Auxiliary verbs

SOME VERBS HELP TO FORM OTHER VERBS.

Often called "helping verbs," auxiliary verbs can be used in front of other verbs to form tenses, negative sentences, and the passive voice, or to express different moods.

SEE ALSO
- ‹ 34–35 Pronouns
- ‹ 38–39 Verbs
- ‹ 42–43 Simple tenses
- ‹ 44–45 Perfect and continuous tenses
- ‹ 46–47 Participles
- Voices and moods 54–55 ›
- Negatives 80–81 ›
- Question marks 110–111 ›

Helpful properties
Auxiliary verbs are known as helping verbs because they perform several different roles. Their main job is to help form different tenses, but they are also used to create negative sentences, turn statements into questions, and add emphasis to speech.

Must is the **only verb** in English to have a **present** but **no past** form.

▷ **Forming tenses**
Auxiliary verbs are used to link the main verb to the subject, helping to form different tenses. The future, perfect, and continuous tenses all rely on auxiliary verbs.

The present participle is used to form the present continuous tense.

▷ **Forming negatives**
Auxiliary verbs are the only verbs that can be made negative. A negative sentence is formed by placing the word *not* between the auxiliary verb and the main verb.

▷ **Forming questions**
In a statement, the subject always comes before the verb. Auxiliary verbs can switch places with their subjects in order to form questions.

▷ **Adding emphasis**
Auxiliary verbs can also be used for emphasis, particularly when the speaker wants to contradict a previous statement.

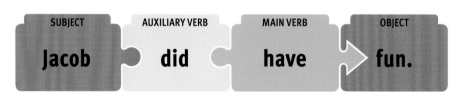

Primary auxiliary verbs

The verbs *be*, *have*, and *do* are known as the primary auxiliary verbs. Primary auxiliary verbs can be used as the main verb in a sentence, or they can be used with participles to form tenses. These verbs also have participles of their own. Auxiliary verbs are irregular verbs, and are irregular even in the present tense.

Verb form	be	have	do
Infinitive	be	have	do
First person (present)	am, are	have	do
Second person (present)	are	have	do
Third person (present)	is, are	has, have	does, do
Past participle	been	had	done
Present participle	being	having	doing

- Only the **primary auxiliaries**—***be***, ***have***, and ***do***—can **change** their form. **Modal auxiliaries** always take the **same form**.
- ***Might*** is the past tense of ***may***, so *might* is always used when talking about something that might have happened previously.
- Sometimes modal auxiliaries are used to add **emphasis** to a decision or a command. Using ***will*** instead of ***am going to*** for the **first person** future tense makes a statement sound more determined: for example, "I **will** go to the party."

Modal auxiliary verbs

Common auxiliary verbs that cannot be used on their own are known as modal auxiliary verbs. These include *can*, *will*, *should*, *may*, and *must*, and they are used with action verbs to express a command, an obligation, or a possibility. Modal auxiliaries are unusual because they do not have an infinitive form or participles, nor—unlike primary auxiliaries and regular verbs—do they take the ending -s for the third person singular.

He can go.

The third person singular modal auxiliary does not take an -s; "he cans" doesn't make sense.

Modal auxiliary	Use	Example
can	Used to express a person's ability to do something.	I can run fast.
could	Used to show possibility; also the past form of *can*.	I could run faster.
may	Used to ask permission to do something, or to express a possibility.	May I come?
might	Used to express a small possibility; also the past form of *may*.	I might run away.
must	Used to indicate a strong obligation.	I must come.
ought	Used to express a sense of obligation.	I ought to stay.
shall	Used to form the future simple tense, and to show determination.	I shall run faster.
should	Used to express obligation.	I should come.
will	Used to form the future simple tense, and to show determination or issue a command.	You will come!
would	Used to express a polite question or a wish, or to indicate the consequence of a conditional sentence; also the past form of *will*.	Would you like to come? I would love to come. If I were to come, I would have fun.

# Irregular verbs

SOME VERBS HAVE ONE OR MORE IRREGULAR FORMS.

The past tense and past participles of all regular verbs are formed in the same way. By contrast, irregular verbs are unpredictable, and take a variety of verb endings. Some change their spelling completely. It is essential to learn these.

SEE ALSO	
‹ 38–39	Verbs
‹ 42–43	Simple tenses
‹ 44–45	Perfect and continuous tenses
‹ 46–47	Participles
‹ 48–49	Auxiliary verbs

Forming irregular verbs

The simple past tense and past participle of regular verbs are formed using the ending -ed (or -d, if the infinitive form already ends in -e). Irregular verbs do not follow this pattern. They take different endings, and the vowel of a verb often changes to form the past tense.

regular simple past tense of discover, *with the ending -ed*

Grace discovered her shoes a week after her sister had swiped them.

regular past participle of swipe, *with the ending -d*

irregular simple past tense of find

Grace found her shoes a week after her sister had stolen them.

irregular past participle of steal

- **Auxiliary verbs** are **irregular,** and—unlike other irregular verbs—the verbs *be, have,* and *do* are irregular **even in the present tense.**

Some of the **most common verbs** in the **English** language are **irregular** verbs.

GLOSSARY

Auxiliary verb A "helping" verb like *be* or *have* that joins the main verb in a sentence to the subject.

Infinitive The simplest form of a verb: the form that is used in dictionaries.

Past participle The form of a verb that usually ends in -ed or -en. It is used with the auxiliary verbs *have* and *will* to form the perfect tenses.

Identifying when to use *lie* and *lay*

The irregular verbs *lie* and *lay* are often mixed up in everyday speech. The past tense of the verb *lie* (meaning "to be in a resting position") is the same as the infinitive form of the verb *lay* (meaning "to place something" or "to enforce"). The mistake most speakers make is to use the past tense form of *lie*—"lay"—when the present tense or infinitive form is required.

I need to lay down. ✗

It is clear from the context of the sentence that the infinitive *lie* is required, rather than the infinitive *lay*.

I need to lie down. ✓

Here, the irregular past tense form of the verb *lie* has been used correctly.

I lay down. ✓

I lay down the law. ✗

I laid down the law. ✓

Here, the irregular past tense form of the verb *lay* has been used correctly.

Common irregular verbs

Many well-known verbs do not take the standard ending -ed when they are used in the past tense or as past participles. The past tense forms and past participles of some irregular verbs look very different from the infinitive form. All of these verb forms have to be learned.

Infinitive form	Simple past tense	Past participle
be	was/were	been
become	became	become
begin	began	begun
blow	blew	blown
break	broke	broken
bring	brought	brought
build	built	built
buy	bought	bought
catch	caught	caught
choose	chose	chosen
come	came	come
cost	cost	cost
creep	crept	crept
cut	cut	cut
do	did	done
draw	drew	drawn
drink	drank	drunk
drive	drove	driven
eat	ate	eaten
fall	fell	fallen
feel	felt	felt
find	found	found
fly	flew	flown
freeze	froze	frozen
get	got	got or gotten
give	gave	given
go	went	gone
grow	grew	grown
hang	hung	hung
have	had	had
hear	heard	heard
hold	held	held
keep	kept	kept
know	knew	known
lay	laid	laid

Infinitive form	Simple past tense	Past participle
lead	led	led
leave	left	left
let	let	let
lie	lay	lain
lose	lost	lost
make	made	made
mean	meant	meant
meet	met	met
mistake	mistook	mistaken
pay	paid	paid
put	put	put
ride	rode	ridden
rise	rose	risen
run	ran	run
say	said	said
see	saw	seen
sell	sold	sold
send	sent	sent
set	set	set
shake	shook	shaken
sit	sat	sat
sleep	slept	slept
speak	spoke	spoken
spend	spent	spent
spin	spun	spun
stand	stood	stood
steal	stole	stolen
stick	stuck	stuck
swear	swore	sworn
swim	swam	swum
take	took	taken
teach	taught	taught
tear	tore	torn
tell	told	told
think	thought	thought
throw	threw	thrown
understand	understood	understood
wear	wore	worn
weep	wept	wept
win	won	won
write	wrote	written

Verb agreement

THE NUMBER OF THE SUBJECT DICTATES THE NUMBER OF THE VERB.

Like nouns and pronouns, a verb can be singular or plural in number, but it must match the subject to which it relates. Sometimes it's hard to know whether a noun is singular or plural, leading to errors in verb agreement.

SEE ALSO	
‹ 22–23 Nouns	
‹ 24–25 Plurals	
‹ 34–35 Pronouns	
‹ 36–37 Number and gender	
‹ 38–39 Verbs	
‹ 42–43 Simple tenses	
Prepositions	60–61 ›

Singular or plural?

The key to correct verb agreement is to follow this simple rule: If the subject is singular, the verb must be singular; if the subject is plural, the verb must also be plural.

The **competitors have** arrived, and the **Mighty Musclemen contest is** about to start.

— subject
— The subject is plural so the verb must be plural.
— subject
— The subject is singular so the verb must be singular.

• Some nouns sound plural but are actually treated as **singular**. These include **mathematics** and **politics**, as well as **proper nouns** such as *United States* or *Philippines*.

🔍 Identifying the subject

One problem occurs when the wrong word is identified as the subject. This often happens when the subject and verb are separated by a prepositional phrase. When the prepositional phrase is removed from the sentence, it becomes clear which noun or pronoun is the true subject.

The **box of extra weights are** ready. ✗
— This is a prepositional phrase, made up of the preposition *of*, the adjective *extra*, and the noun *weights*.

The **box are** ready. ✗
— The prepositional phrase has been removed from the sentence, so it is now clear that the subject (*box*) is singular.

The **box is** ready. ✓
— The subject is singular, so the singular verb form *is* is used.

The **box of extra weights is** ready. ✓
— The prepositional phrase has been put back into the sentence, and the verb now agrees with the subject.

Collective nouns

Most collective nouns (for example, *class* or *crowd*) are singular words, because they can be made plural (*classes*, *crowds*). However, some collective nouns, including *team*, *staff*, and *couple*, can be singular or plural. A good general rule to follow is to consider whether the noun is acting as a unit or whether the noun is made up of individuals acting in different ways.

My **team has** won.

— Here, the team represents a unit, so the singular form of the verb is used.

The **team are** divided in their feelings.

— Here, the individual members of the team are acting in different ways, so the plural form of the verb is used.

Multiple subjects

If a sentence contains more than one noun, and these nouns are joined by *and*, they almost always take a plural verb. These are known as compound subjects. Phrases such as *along with* and *as well as* separate the subjects, however. In these cases, the verb should agree with the first subject, regardless of whether the second subject is singular or plural. By contrast, if a singular subject is joined to a plural subject and separated by *or* or *nor*, the verb agrees with the nearest subject.

- When the phrase **the number of** precedes the subject of a sentence, the subject is considered to be singular: "The number of weights used **is** variable." By contrast, the phrase *a number of* makes a subject plural: "A number of different weights **are** used."
- Expressions of **quantity**, such as **time, money, weight,** or **fractions**, are treated in the same way as **collective nouns**. For example, "**Half** of Tyler's allowance **is** spent on exercise equipment."

Tyler and his brother **Matt** are competing.

◁ **Compound subjects**
The subjects *Tyler* and *Matt* are acting together, and are joined by *and*, so they take the plural form.

Matt's **size as well as** his **strength** is awesome.

◁ **Separate subjects**
The subjects *size* and *strength* are acting separately, so the verb is singular to match the first subject, *size*.

Neither Tyler's **neck nor** his **arms** are small.

◁ **Mixed subjects**
The plural subject *arms* is closer to the verb than the singular subject *neck*, so the verb is plural. With mixed subjects, always put the plural subject closest to the verb.

Indefinite pronouns

Most indefinite pronouns can be easily identified as singular or plural. *Both*, *several*, *few*, and *many*, for example, are always plural. Some, however, are singular words that refer to plural things. These include *each*, *everyone*, and *everything*.

▽ **Agreeing with prepositional phrases**
Five indefinite pronouns can be singular or plural, depending on the context. These are *all*, *any*, *most*, *none*, and *some*. Only when these pronouns occur do prepositional phrases determine whether a verb should be singular or plural.

Most of the contest is over.

- indefinite pronoun
- This prepositional phrase is singular because the noun *contest* is singular, so the verb also has to be singular.

Most of the competitors have left.

- indefinite pronoun
- This prepositional phrase is plural, because the noun *competitors* is plural.
- The verb is plural to match the prepositional phrase.

Number	Indefinite pronoun
singular	everybody, everyone, everything, somebody, someone, something, anybody, anyone, anything, nobody, no one, nothing, neither, another, each, either, one, other, much
plural	both, several, few, many, others
singular or plural	all, any, most, none, some

Voices and moods

SENTENCES IN ENGLISH CAN BE EXPRESSED IN DIFFERENT VOICES AND DIFFERENT MOODS.

SEE ALSO	
‹ 38–39 Verbs	
‹ 42–43 Simple tenses	
‹ 46–47 Participles	
‹ 48–49 Auxiliary verbs	
‹ 50–51 Irregular verbs	
Sentences	68–69 ›
Newspaper articles	198–199 ›

There are two voices in English. These determine whether the subject of a sentence is performing or receiving an action. Mood is the form of the verb that conveys the attitude in which a thought is expressed.

The active voice

Verbs can be used in two different ways. These are known as voices. The active voice is simpler than the passive voice. In an active sentence, the subject is performing the action of the verb, and the object is receiving it.

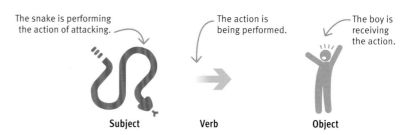

The snake is performing the action of attacking.
The action is being performed.
The boy is receiving the action.

Subject — Verb — Object

The snake attacked the boy.

The passive voice

In a passive sentence, the word order is reversed so that the subject is receiving the action and the object is performing it. The passive voice is formed using the auxiliary verb *be* followed by a past participle. The performer of the action is either identified using the preposition *by* or not included at all.

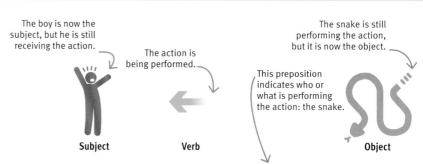

The boy is now the subject, but he is still receiving the action.
The action is being performed.
The snake is still performing the action, but it is now the object.
This preposition indicates who or what is performing the action: the snake.

Subject — Verb — Object

The boy was attacked by the snake.

REAL WORLD
Passive persuasion

The passive voice is often used on official signs, because it is perceived as less confrontational than the active voice. In these situations, it is also often unnecessary to state who is performing the action.

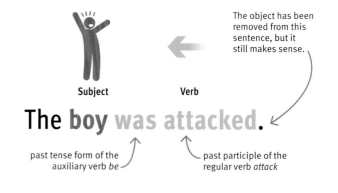

Subject — Verb

The boy was attacked.

past tense form of the auxiliary verb *be*
past participle of the regular verb *attack*

The object has been removed from this sentence, but it still makes sense.

VOICES AND MOODS

The indicative mood
There are three main moods in English. Most verbs are used in the indicative mood, which indicates an actual condition, as opposed to an intended, expected, or believed condition. This mood is used to state facts.

This sentence states a fact—something that was the case at some point in the past—so it is in the indicative mood.

The boy was terrified.

The imperative mood
The imperative mood is used to give commands or make requests. Exclamations are often in the imperative mood; these always end with an exclamation point.

This command is also an exclamation.

This is a request.

Go away! Please leave me alone.

The subjunctive mood
The subjunctive mood is rarely used in English, and it can only be identified in the third person form or with the verb *be*. It is used after verbs and phrases that express an obligation or a desire, such as *demand*, *require*, *suggest*, or *it is essential that*, and it indicates that the obligation or desire may not be fulfilled.

GLOSSARY
Auxiliary verb A "helping" verb like *be* or *have* that links the main verb in a sentence to the subject.
Exclamation A sentence that expresses a strong emotion, such as surprise, or a raised voice, and ends with an exclamation point.
Modal auxiliary verb An auxiliary verb that is used with an action verb to express a command, an obligation, or a possibility.
Past participle The form of a verb that ends in -ed or -en. It is used with the auxiliary verb *be* to form the passive voice.

▷ **Third person**
To form most subjunctive verbs, the final *s* is removed from the third person form.

He demanded that the zookeeper remove the snake.

The present subjunctive follows the verb phrase *demanded that*. It is used because the zookeeper might not remove the snake.

▷ **Exception**
The main exception is the verb *be*, which takes the form *be* for the present tense and *were* for the past tense.

The zookeeper requested that the boy be quiet.

The present subjunctive follows the verb phrase *requested that*. The zookeeper wants the boy to be quiet, but the boy might not be quiet.

Identifying the subjunctive in conditional sentences

Conditional sentences are used to indicate that the action of a main clause ("going to the beach") can only happen if a certain condition, contained in a subordinate clause, is fulfilled ("if the weather is hot"). Most conditional sentences start with *if* or *unless*. If the action being described is almost certain to happen, the indicative mood is used. If the action being described is hypothetical (impossible to predict), the past tense form of the subjunctive mood should be used.

Many conditional sentences start with *if*.

If the weather...

They will almost certainly go to the beach if the weather is hot, so the indicative mood is used.

If the weather is hot, we will go to the beach. ✓

If the weather were hot, we would be happier. ✓

The weather is not hot, so the belief that they would be happier is a hypothetical situation, which requires the subjunctive verb form *were*.

The modal auxiliary verb *would* usually appears in conditional sentences with the subjunctive.

Phrasal verbs

NEW VERBS ARE FORMED BY ADDING AN ADVERB OR A PREPOSITION TO AN EXISTING VERB.

SEE ALSO	
‹ 38–39 Verbs	
‹ 40–41 Adverbs	
Prepositions	60–61 ›
Hyphens	106–107 ›

A phrasal verb is a compound of a verb and an adverb, a verb and a preposition, or a verb, an adverb, and a preposition. Phrasal verbs work like regular verbs, but they are mostly used in informal speech.

Adverb phrasal verbs

Composed of an existing verb followed by an adverb, an adverb phrasal verb works in the same way as a regular verb—as a single unit. The adverb is essential to the phrasal verb's meaning, either intensifying the sense of the preceding verb or changing its meaning entirely. Adverbs like *up*, *down*, *out*, or *off* are often used to form phrasal verbs.

The adverb *up* changes the meaning of the verb *get*, resulting in a phrasal verb that means "to rise, usually after sleeping," rather than "to receive or obtain."

I got up early.

adverb phrasal verb

Most **new verbs** in the **English** language are **phrasal verbs**.

- The small words used to form phrasal verbs—**adverbs** and **prepositions**—are often known as **particles**.
- Phrasal verbs are **never hyphenated**.

I got up early because Daniel
We ran into Paulo, who was

Prepositional phrasal verbs

Prepositional phrasal verbs consist of a verb followed by a preposition, such as *by*, *after*, *in*, *on*, or *for*. The preposition links the verb to the noun or pronoun that follows—the direct object. Prepositional phrasal verbs are always transitive, but unlike adverb phrasal verbs, prepositional phrasal verbs cannot usually be separated by the direct object (see "Word order").

talk about
stand by
listen to
call on
take after
wait for
run into

Versatile verbs

Only a handful of adverbs and prepositions are needed to create a range of phrasal verbs with different meanings. Using a different phrasal verb can completely change the meaning of a sentence. For example, "Paulo is looking after the game" means that he is in charge of the game.

PHRASAL VERBS

GLOSSARY

Direct object The noun or pronoun that is receiving the action of the verb.
Intransitive verb A verb that does not require an object.
Transitive verb A verb that must be used with an object.

Word order

Like regular verbs, phrasal verbs can be transitive or intransitive. Transitive phrasal verbs require a direct object to receive the action, while intransitive phrasal verbs, such as *get up* or *eat out*, make sense without an object. The verb and adverb in a transitive adverb phrasal verb can usually be separated by the direct object.

Daniel was taking me out for lunch.

direct object

This adverb phrasal verb is transitive, so it can be separated by the direct object.

Identifying when a phrasal verb can be separated

Some transitive phrasal verbs can be separated by a direct object; others cannot be separated. A simple way to test whether a phrasal verb is separable or inseparable is to place the pronoun *it* (representing the direct object) between the verb and the adverb or preposition. If the resulting phrase makes sense, that phrasal verb can be separated.

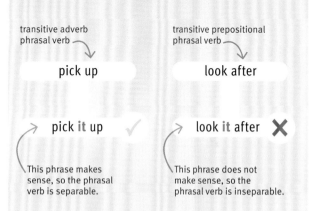

transitive adverb phrasal verb: **pick up**
transitive prepositional phrasal verb: **look after**

pick it up ✓
This phrase makes sense, so the phrasal verb is separable.

look it after ✗
This phrase does not make sense, so the phrasal verb is inseparable.

was taking me out for lunch.
looking forward to the game.

look forward to
look over
look out
look through
look at
look after

Adverb-prepositional phrasal verbs

Some phrasal verbs are made up of a verb, followed by an adverb and a preposition. Like prepositional phrasal verbs, these must have a direct object, and the parts of the phrasal verb cannot be separated by this object.

Paulo was looking forward to the game.

verb
adverb
preposition
direct object

Conjunctions

A CONJUNCTION CONNECTS WORDS, PHRASES, AND CLAUSES.

Also known as connectives, conjunctions are used to link two or more parts of a sentence. These parts can be of equal importance, or a main clause can be linked to a subordinate clause using a subordinator.

SEE ALSO	
Phrases	64–65 ⟩
Clauses	66–67 ⟩
Compound sentences	70–71 ⟩
Complex sentences	72–73 ⟩
Using clauses correctly	74–75 ⟩
Commas	96–99 ⟩

- Relative pronouns such as **who**, **whom**, **which**, and **that** are used in the same way as subordinators.
- It's a good idea to avoid starting a sentence with conjunctions like **because** or **and** because this practice often results in **incomplete sentences**.

Coordinating conjunctions

Without conjunctions, writing would be made up of numerous short sentences. Conjunctions are used to create longer sentences, preventing text from becoming stilted. Coordinating conjunctions are used to link words, phrases, or clauses of equal importance. They include the words *and*, *but*, *or*, *nor*, *yet*, *for,* and *so*.

roses and sunflowers

This coordinating conjunction is being used to link two types of flowers.

Flora tried to water her roses and
She cut both the hedge and the

- Never use a comma to link two main clauses. **Main clauses** should only be linked using a **conjunction**, a **semicolon**, or a **colon**.

GLOSSARY

Main clause A group of words that contains a subject and a verb and makes complete sense on its own.

Subordinate clause A group of words that contains a subject and a verb but depends on a main clause for its meaning.

Pairs of conjunctions

Conjunctions can be single words or phrases, and they often appear in pairs. Pairs such as *both–and*, *either–or*, and *not only–but also* are sometimes known as "correlative conjunctions" because the conjunctions work together. The two parts must be placed directly before the words they are joining.

pair of conjunctions

She cut both the hedge and the tree.

nouns being joined by the pair

Identifying when to use a semicolon

Adverbs such as *however*, *accordingly*, *besides*, and *therefore* can also be used as conjunctions to join two main clauses. Unlike coordinating conjunctions and subordinators, these adverbs must be preceded by a semicolon and followed by a comma.

She was confident. She hadn't cut the hedge before.
— two main clauses

She was confident, but she hadn't cut the hedge before.
— coordinating conjunction separating two main clauses

She was confident; however, she hadn't cut the hedge before.
— This adverb is being used as a conjunction, so it must be preceded by a semicolon and followed by a comma.

Coordinating multiple subjects

When a coordinating conjunction is used to link two main clauses with different subjects, a comma should be placed before the conjunction. This helps to show where one main clause ends and another begins.

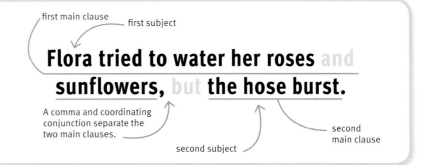

Flora tried to water her roses and sunflowers, but the hose burst.

- first main clause
- first subject
- A comma and coordinating conjunction separate the two main clauses.
- second subject
- second main clause

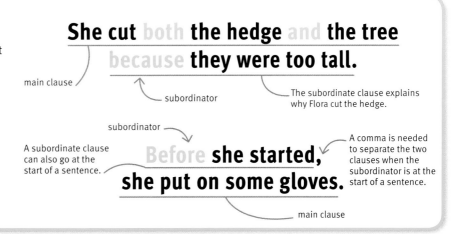

Subordinators

Subordinators or subordinating conjunctions are used to connect words, phrases, and clauses of unequal importance. A subordinate clause adds information to a main clause, explaining why, where, or when something is happening. Subordinate clauses start with subordinators like *before*, *if*, *because*, *although*, and *while*, and can be placed at the beginning or end of a sentence.

She cut both the hedge and the tree because they were too tall.

- main clause
- subordinator
- The subordinate clause explains why Flora cut the hedge.

Before she started, she put on some gloves.

- subordinator
- A subordinate clause can also go at the start of a sentence.
- A comma is needed to separate the two clauses when the subordinator is at the start of a sentence.
- main clause

Prepositions

PREPOSITIONS CONNECT NOUNS AND PRONOUNS TO OTHER WORDS IN A SENTENCE.

SEE ALSO	
‹ 20–21 Parts of speech	
‹ 22–23 Nouns	
‹ 30–31 Articles	
‹ 34–35 Pronouns	
‹ 56–57 Phrasal verbs	
Phrases	64–65 ›
Commas	96–99 ›

Prepositions never appear alone. They are short words that convey the relationship of a noun or pronoun to another part of a sentence—often the physical position of one thing in relation to another.

Simple prepositions

Prepositions are common in written and spoken English. They usually appear as part of a prepositional phrase, and include words like *for*, *about*, *with*, *of*, and *on*. A prepositional phrase is made up of a preposition followed by its object, which is a noun, pronoun, or noun phrase.

for — preposition
a — article
long — adjective
bicycle ride — noun phrase and object of the preposition

- In **formal writing**, **sentences** should **not end** with **prepositions**, but this practice is common in spoken English. "What are you talking about?" is a good example.
- **Prepositional phrases** only ever contain the **object** of a clause. They never contain the subject. In the sentence "They sped **down a hill**," *hill* is the object, and *they* is the subject.

Daisy went for a long bicycle ride down a hill and through a stream.

Winston Churchill, objecting to strict rules about **prepositional word order**, famously said, "That is nonsense **up with which** I shall not put."

Parallel prepositions

Writers can improve their sentences by using consistent language. If different prepositions are required for different nouns, they must all be included in the sentence. If one preposition is being used to introduce a series of nouns, it only needs to be used before the first noun. The same preposition can be used before each noun, but this is repetitive.

The noun objects *hill* and *stream* require different prepositions, so both must be included in the sentence.

They raced down a hill and through a stream.

This preposition applies to both nouns, so it only needs to appear before the first item in this list.

They sped through a stream and a forest.

Identifying prepositional phrasal verbs

A prepositional phrasal verb is made up of a verb followed by a preposition. This type of verb must have an object, but the preposition cannot be separated from its verb by this object. If the preposition part of a prepositional phrasal verb is removed, the sentence will not make sense.

Daisy was **annoyed** and **afraid of** Ed's poor cycling skills. ✗

If the phrase and afraid is removed, the sentence does not make sense.

Daisy was **annoyed of** Ed's poor cycling skills. ✗

This phrasal verb does make sense on its own.

Daisy was **afraid of** Ed's poor cycling skills. ✓

The correct preposition has been added into the sentence. — *object, a noun phrase*

Daisy was **annoyed by** and **afraid of** Ed's poor cycling skills. ✓

Using prepositional phrases

Prepositional phrases can be used like adjectives and adverbs to modify nouns or verbs. They can offer more detail about an object so that the reader knows what or whom is being referred to, or they can point to where something is, or when or why something happened.

This prepositional phrase is working as an adjective because it is describing a noun, eagle.

Daisy saw an eagle in a tree.

This prepositional phrase is working as an adverb, because it is describing where they raced.

They raced down a hill.

ride **with** Ed. They raced **down** and stopped **next to** a bridge.

Complex prepositions

Sometimes simple prepositions are used with one or two other words to form complex prepositions, which act as a single unit. Like one-word prepositions, these come before nouns or pronouns in prepositional phrases and can act as adjectives or adverbs.

except for
next to
out of
as for
in front of
in spite of
along with

GLOSSARY

Adjective prepositional phrase A prepositional phrase that describes a noun.

Adverb prepositional phrase A prepositional phrase that describes a verb.

Noun phrase A phrase made up of a noun and any words that are modifying that noun, such as articles or adjectives.

Object The noun or pronoun that is receiving the action of the verb.

Prepositional phrasal verb A verb followed by a preposition, which together act as a single unit.

Prepositional phrase A preposition followed by a noun, pronoun, or noun phrase that together act as an adjective (describing a noun) or an adverb (describing a verb) in a sentence.

Interjections

INTERJECTIONS ARE WORDS OR PHRASES THAT OCCUR ALONE AND EXPRESS EMOTION.

Interjections are considered a part of speech, but they play no grammatical role in a sentence. They are single words or phrases that are used to exclaim, protest, or command, and rarely appear in formal writing.

SEE ALSO	
❰ 20–21 Parts of speech	
Sentences	68–69 ❱
Colloquialisms and slang	86–87 ❱
Commas	96–99 ❱
Exclamation points	112–113 ❱

Emotional words

Interjections occur frequently in spoken English. They are useful in informal writing—particularly in narratives or scripts—since they help convey the emotions of a character, but they are only used in formal writing as part of a direct quotation. New interjections to describe different emotions are invented all the time, and they vary from region to region.

Emotion	Interjection
pain	ouch, ow, oh
disgust	yuck, ugh, ew
surprise	eek, yikes, ooh, wow, eh, well, really
elation	hooray, yippee, ha, woo-hoo, whoopee
pleasure	mmm, yeah
relief	phew, whew, whoa
boredom	blah, ho-hum
embarrassment	ahem, er
disappointment	aw, meh, pfft
dismay	oh no, oh, oops
panic	help, ah, uh oh
irritation	hmph, huh, hey, oy
disapproval	tsk-tsk, tut-tut
realization	aha, ah
pity	dear, alas, ahh
doubt	hmm, er, um

- **Use interjections in moderation**, or not at all. They rarely improve a piece of writing.

Using interjections

Interjections that express strong emotions such as dismay or surprise usually function as exclamations, appearing alone as single words or phrases followed by an exclamation point. Milder emotions tend to be expressed using an interjection followed by a comma.

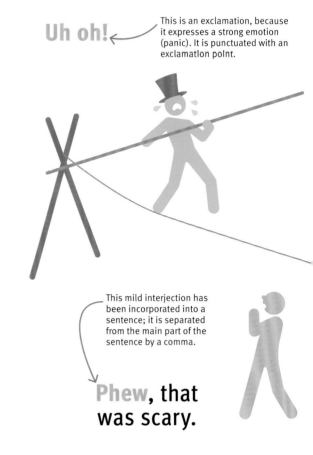

Uh oh! — This is an exclamation, because it expresses a strong emotion (panic). It is punctuated with an exclamation point.

This mild interjection has been incorporated into a sentence; it is separated from the main part of the sentence by a comma.

Phew, that was scary.

INTERJECTIONS

REAL WORLD
Eureka!

Albert Einstein is reputed to have uttered the interjection *Eureka!* on coming up with his special theory of relativity. *Eureka* is a Greek word, meaning "I have found it." Similar moments of revelation may be marked by interjections like *aha!* or *hooray!*—the benefit being that a single-word interjection conveys much more emotion than a simple sentence.

Interruptions and introductions

Many English speakers use the interjections *er* or *um* to fill pauses in their speech, such as when they are unsure of what to say. These are sometimes called hesitation devices. *Yes*, *no*, and variations of the two are also interjections, as are other introductory expressions such as *indeed* and *well*. These can be used alone in response to a question or statement.

I, er, have no idea what has happened to, um, the snake charmer.

Commas are used on either side of a mild interjection such as a hesitation device if it appears in the middle of a sentence.

Yes, he's been gone for ages. Where is he?

The interjections *yes* and *no* are used at the start of a sentence, followed by a comma, or on their own.

Greetings

Everyday greetings like *hello*, *hi*, *goodbye,* and even *yoo-hoo* are interjections, functioning on their own or as part of a sentence. Like other interjections, if a greeting is removed from a sentence, the meaning of that sentence is not affected.

Hello, what are you doing?

Asides

Interjections are often used in parentheses to indicate an aside or an action. This is particularly useful in a play script, because it indicates the tone of a sentence and gives directions to the actors.

The snake charmer is (cough!) temporarily unavailable.

This aside tells the speaker to pause and cough—in this case, indicating that the speaker doesn't necessarily believe what he or she is saying.

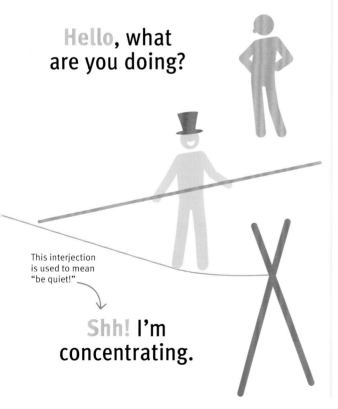

This interjection is used to mean "be quiet!"

Shh! I'm concentrating.

Phrases

A PHRASE IS A GROUP OF WORDS THAT MAKE UP PART OF A SENTENCE.

Phrases add information to a sentence, but they only make complete sense as part of a sentence. A phrase does not contain a verb, and it can perform the function of an adjective, an adverb, or a noun.

SEE ALSO	
‹ 22–23 Nouns	
‹ 26–27 Adjectives	
‹ 40–41 Adverbs	
‹ 46–47 Participles	
‹ 60–61 Prepositions	
Managing modifiers	76–77 ›

Adjective phrases

Like adjectives, adjective phrases describe nouns or pronouns. An adjective phrase usually starts with an adverb or a preposition. It can be placed before or after the noun or pronoun it describes.

very red-faced
↑ adverb

This adjective phrase is made up of an adverb followed by an adjective, and it can be used after the noun it describes.

the very red-faced drummer

This adjective phrase can also be placed before the noun it describes.

of the band
preposition ↗

This is an adjective phrase because it is giving more information about the members, a noun.

The drummer, very red-faced,
The shocked members of the band

- **Phrases** can be used **instead of one-word adjectives** or **adverbs** to make a piece of writing more **interesting**.

Most **dictionary definitions** are **adjective phrases**.

Noun phrases

A noun phrase is made up of a noun and any words that are modifying that noun, including articles, determiners, and adjectives or adjective phrases. Noun phrases work in exactly the same way as nouns in a sentence.

This is a noun phrase because it is performing the action of the verb—hiding. This noun phrase is the subject of the sentence.

the shocked members of the band

This adjective phrase forms part of the noun phrase.

the drummer
↗ article

This is a simple noun phrase consisting of an article and a noun.

PHRASES

Adverbial phrases
Like adverbs, adverbial phrases describe verbs, adjectives, and other adverbs. They answer questions such as: How? When? Why? Where? How often?

angrily across the stage

This is an adverbial phrase because it is describing how ("angrily") and where ("across the stage") the drummer strode.

behind their instruments

This is an adverbial phrase because it is describing where the members of the band hid.

GLOSSARY
Adjective phrase A group of words that describe a noun or pronoun.

Adverbial phrase A group of words such as "in July of last year" that perform the same role as an adverb and answer questions such as: How? When? Why? Where? How often?

Noun phrase Several words that, grouped together, perform the same function as a noun.

Prepositional phrase A preposition such as *in* or *on* followed by a noun or pronoun that together act as an adjective (describing a noun) or an adverb (describing a verb) in a sentence.

strode angrily across the stage.
hid behind their instruments.

Prepositional phrases
Prepositional phrases are the most common type of phrase, but they always act as either adjectives or adverbs in a sentence, modifying nouns or verbs. They are therefore contained within—or make up—adjective or adverbial phrases. A prepositional phrase is made up of a preposition, along with the noun or noun phrase that follows it.

behind their instruments
preposition

This prepositional phrase is acting as an adverb, because it is modifying the verb *hid*.

across the stage
preposition

This prepositional phrase is also acting as an adverb, because it is modifying the verb *strode*.

of the band
preposition

This prepositional phrase is acting as an adjective, because it is describing the noun *members*.

Clauses

A CLAUSE IS THE KEY ELEMENT OF A SENTENCE.

A clause is a group of words that contains a subject and a verb. It can form part of a sentence, or a complete simple sentence. Clauses can be main or subordinate, and they can behave like adjectives or adverbs.

SEE ALSO	
❬ 22–23 Nouns	
❬ 26–27 Adjectives	
❬ 40–41 Adverbs	
❬ 58–59 Conjunctions	
Sentences	68–69 ❭
Compound sentences	70–71 ❭
Complex sentences	72–73 ❭
Using clauses correctly	74–75 ❭
Relative clauses	82–83 ❭

Main clauses

Also known as an independent clause, a main clause includes a subject and a verb and expresses a complete thought. Main clauses are the same as simple sentences, because they have to make sense on their own.

Subordinate clauses

A subordinate clause (also called a dependent clause) contains a subject and a verb, but it does not make sense on its own. It depends on a main clause for its meaning. Subordinate clauses often explain or add more information about where or when things happen, or how they are done. Relative and adverbial clauses are types of subordinate clause.

🔍 Identifying main and subordinate clauses

Both main and subordinate clauses have a subject and a verb, but only main clauses make sense on their own. The easiest way to identify a subordinate clause is to look for relative pronouns, such as *which* or *that*, or subordinators, such as *because* or *although*.

The cat went outside, although it was raining.
— This sentence is made up of two clauses.

The cat went outside.
— This is a main clause, because it contains a subject and a verb, and makes complete sense on its own.

although it was raining
— This is a subordinate clause, because it contains a subject (here, a pronoun), a verb, and a subordinator, and it does not make sense on its own.

Relative clauses

Relative clauses are also known as adjective clauses, and they are a type of subordinate clause. Like adjectives and adjective phrases, relative clauses describe nouns and pronouns. Unlike adjectives, they can only be placed after the noun or pronoun they are modifying. Relative clauses always start with one of the relative pronouns *who*, *whom*, *whose*, *which,* or *that*, which acts as the subject or the object of the clause.

▽ **Subject**
The relative pronoun *which* is the subject of this relative clause, which describes a noun.

▷ **Object**
Here, the relative pronoun *which* is the object of the clause—it is receiving the action of the verb *did*.

Adverbial clauses

An adverbial clause is a type of subordinate clause that behaves like an adverb. It gives additional information about how, when, where, and why something is happening. Adverbial clauses start with subordinators such as *because*, *although*, *after*, *while*, since, *as,* and *until*.

▷ **Why?**
This adverbial clause explains why the cat did something, but it does not make sense without a main clause.

▷ **When?**
This adverbial clause explains when the cat did something, but it does not make sense without a main clause.

GLOSSARY

Adverbial phrase A group of words that behave in the same way as an adverb and answer questions such as: How? When? Why? Where? How often?

Object The person or thing that is receiving the verb's action.

Relative pronoun A pronoun that links one part of a sentence to another by introducing a relative clause, which describes an earlier noun or pronoun.

Subject The person or thing that is performing the action.

Subordinator A conjunction used to connect words, phrases, and clauses of unequal importance.

- A **main clause** can be turned into a **subordinate clause** by adding a **subordinator**—for example, "**because** the cat slept."

Sentences

THERE ARE MANY DIFFERENT TYPES OF SENTENCES, VARYING IN COMPLEXITY.

SEE ALSO	
❮ 38–39 Verbs	
❮ 54–55 Voices and moods	
❮ 64–65 Phrases	
❮ 66–67 Clauses	
Compound sentences	70–71 ❯
Complex sentences	72–73 ❯
Periods and ellipses	94–95 ❯
Question marks	110–111 ❯
Exclamation points	112–113 ❯

A sentence is a unit of written language that contains a subject and a verb and makes complete sense on its own. It must begin with a capital letter and end with a period, exclamation point, or question mark.

Simple sentences

A simple sentence is the same as a main clause. It must have a subject and one main verb, and it must express a single idea. The subject is the person or thing that does the action (the verb), but one subject can be made up of more than one person or thing. Most simple sentences also include an object, which is the person or thing receiving the action.

The chef cooked.
- capital letter
- subject: The chef
- verb: cooked
- A period ends the sentence.

The chef and his friends ate the delicious meal.
- The subject can represent more than one person or thing.
- object: the delicious meal
- Descriptive words and phrases can be added to give more information, but if there is still only one verb, it remains a simple sentence.

Statements

A statement is a sentence that conveys a fact or piece of information. The subject always comes before the verb. Most simple sentences are statements, and statements end with a period.

The pie had exploded.
This is a statement because it states a fact and ends with a period.

Questions

A question is a sentence that asks for information and ends with a question mark. Unlike a statement, the subject is placed after the verb. Only auxiliary verbs can change places with their subjects, so a question must include an auxiliary verb like *be*, *do*, or *can*. Many questions also start with question words such as *why*, *when*, *where*, and *how*.

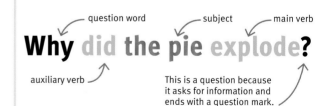

Why did the pie explode?
- question word: Why
- auxiliary verb: did
- subject: the pie
- main verb: explode
- This is a question because it asks for information and ends with a question mark.

- **Shorter sentences** tend to be **more effective** at getting a message across.
- It's important to **vary the sentence construction** in a piece of writing, so that it does not become monotonous.
- **Simple sentences** can be used to **create tension** in a story.

SENTENCES **69**

Identifying a sentence

A main clause becomes a sentence once it starts with a capital letter and ends with a period, question mark, or exclamation point. All sentences must have a subject and a verb, and make sense without any additional information.

✗ the chef loves cooking

↳ This is not a sentence because it does not begin with a capital letter and end with a period.

✓ The chef loves cooking.

✗ What is.

This is not a sentence because it doesn't have a subject, nor does it make sense, and because the question word *what* at the beginning indicates that a question is being asked.

✓ What is he cooking?

✗ something is burning!

↳ This is not a sentence because it does not start with a capital letter.

✓ Something is burning!

Commands

A command is a sentence that gives an order or an instruction. Instructions are most effective when they are written in simple sentences. The subject in a command is implied, rather than present—it is the person who is receiving the command. Orders usually end with an exclamation point, while instructions tend to end with a period.

Do not open **the oven!**

↲ This sentence gives an order, so it ends with an exclamation point.

↳ The implied subject is the person who is being told not to open the oven.

Please do not touch **the pie.**

↳ The implied subject is the person who is being asked not to touch the pie.

↳ This sentence gives a polite instruction, so it ends with a period.

Exclamations

An exclamation works in the same way as a statement, but it expresses a strong emotion, such as surprise or horror. Exclamations always end with an exclamation point.

The pie had exploded!

↲ The use of an exclamation point instead of a period adds emotion to a statement, making it seem more dramatic.

The **shortest complete sentence** in the **English** language is "I am."

REAL WORLD
"Careful you must be..."

When the simple rules of sentence construction are not followed, sentences become very hard to understand. The *Star Wars* character Yoda's speech is a good example. Instead of speaking in sentences that follow the subject–verb–object pattern, Yoda muddles his sentences so that the object comes first, followed by the subject, and then the verb. The result is confusing.

GLOSSARY

Auxiliary verb A "helping" verb like *be* or *have* that joins the main verb in a sentence to the subject.

Main clause A group of words that contains a subject and a verb and makes complete sense on its own.

Object The person or thing that is receiving the action of the verb.

Subject The person or thing that is performing the action of the verb.

Compound sentences

A COMPOUND SENTENCE IS A SENTENCE THAT HAS MORE THAN ONE MAIN CLAUSE.

SEE ALSO	
‹ 58–59 Conjunctions	
‹ 66–67 Clauses	
‹ 68–69 Sentences	
Complex sentences	72–73 ›
Semicolons	100–101 ›
Colons	102–103 ›

Compound sentences are made up of two or more main clauses, but no subordinate clauses. The main clauses are linked using conjunctions, and the resulting sentence conveys different ideas of equal importance.

Joining main clauses

Compound sentences are a useful way of connecting two or more ideas of equal importance. They help improve the flow of a piece of writing, as many successive simple sentences can be uncomfortable to read. To form most compound sentences, two main clauses—each containing a subject and a verb—are joined together using a coordinating conjunction like *and*, *but*, or *so*. A comma is used before the coordinating conjunction to separate the two clauses.

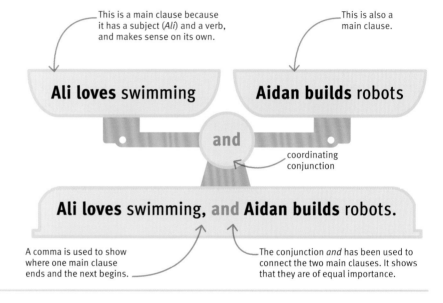

Using conjunctions

There are seven main coordinating conjunctions, and these are used in different ways. The conjunction *and* is used to join two things that are alike, or to show that one thing follows the other. *But* is used to contrast one idea with another, while *so* indicates that the second thing occurs as a result of the first. *Yet* is used to mean "nevertheless," *or* and *nor* are used to link alternatives, and *for* is used in compound sentences to mean "because."

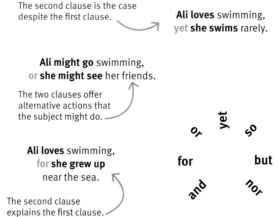

COMPOUND SENTENCES   71

Joining multiple main clauses
Sometimes three (or more) main clauses are joined together. If the resulting sentence is a list of main clauses containing similar ideas, a comma is used to separate the first two main clauses, and a conjunction is used before the third clause.

A comma is used to separate the first two main clauses in a list of three clauses.

Ali loves swimming, **Aidan builds** robots, and **Sophie enjoys** reading.

A coordinating conjunction is used to join the third main clause to the second main clause.

Using semicolons
Another way to form a compound sentence is to link two main clauses using a semicolon. A semicolon performs the same role as a conjunction, and can therefore be replaced by a conjunction. It shows that two clauses are closely related and equally important.

The two main clauses are giving two different, but closely related, pieces of information about Aidan, so they can be linked using a semicolon.

Aidan builds robots; **he** also **repairs** motorcycles.

The same two clauses can also be linked using a conjunction.

Aidan builds robots, and **he** also **repairs** motorcycles.

Using colons
A colon can also be used to form a compound sentence. Rather than connecting two similar ideas, a colon is used to show that the second main clause is an explanation of the first main clause. Unlike a semicolon, a colon cannot be replaced by a conjunction.

Aidan has an unusual hobby: **He builds** robots.

These two main clauses are linked using a colon, because the second clause is an explanation of the first clause.

GLOSSARY
Coordinating conjunction A word that connects words, phrases, and clauses of equal importance.

Main clause A group of words that contains a subject and a verb and makes complete sense on its own.

Subject The person or thing that is performing the action of the verb.

Subordinate clause A group of words that contains a subject and a verb but depends on a main clause for its meaning.

- **Never use a comma to join two main clauses.** Main clauses can only be connected using a conjunction, a semicolon, or a colon.
- If the two **main clauses** use the **same subject** and are linked using a **conjunction**, the subject can be left out of the second clause. If the sentence is short, no comma is required before the conjunction. For example, "Ali loves swimming **but** hates running."

Complex sentences

A COMPLEX SENTENCE CONTAINS AT LEAST ONE SUBORDINATE CLAUSE.

SEE ALSO	
‹ 58–59 Conjunctions	
‹ 66–67 Clauses	
‹ 70–71 Compound sentences	
Managing modifiers	76–77 ›
Semicolons	100–101 ›
Colons	102–103 ›
Making sentences interesting	184–185 ›

Unlike a compound sentence, which contains only main clauses, a complex sentence is made up of a main clause and one or more subordinate clauses. The subordinate clause depends on the main clause for its meaning.

Ranking ideas

Complex sentences are useful because they can be used to indicate that one idea is more important than another. The secondary idea is contained in a subordinate clause, which has a subject and a verb, but does not make sense without the main clause to which it is attached. Subordinate clauses add information to main clauses.

Zoe put on her coat ← main clause
because it was cold.

— This is a subordinate clause because it explains why Zoe put on her coat, but does not make sense on its own.

Linking subordinate clauses

Subordinate clauses usually start with a relative pronoun such as *which* or *that*, a participle such as *dancing* or *shouting*, or a subordinator such as *because* or *although*. Many subordinators, including *where*, *when*, and *while*, give a clear indication of the type of information they are offering.

MAIN CLAUSE
Zoe had fun at the dance class

SUBORDINATE CLAUSES

where she met a new friend.

which finished late.

while the music played.

although she was tired.

until it was time to go home.

dancing with her friends.

Identifying dangling participles

Subordinate clauses often start with a participle, which describes the action being performed by the subject of the main clause. If a subordinate clause that starts with a participle is put in the wrong place in a sentence, it is described as "dangling," because it has no subject to hold on to. The clause should always be placed next to the subject it describes.

Talking to a friend, the music deafened Zoe.
— This is a dangling participle because it is modifying the wrong noun—*music*.

The music was **talking to a friend**.
— Check which noun the subordinate clause is modifying by moving the noun so that it relates to the clause.

Zoe was **talking to a friend**.
— The correct noun is now being modified.

Talking to a friend, Zoe was deafened by the music.
— Rewrite the sentence so that the correct noun is next to the subordinate clause.

Clause order

Subordinate clauses that start with relative pronouns always follow the noun or pronoun they are describing. If a subordinate clause starts with a subordinator or a participle, however, it can occupy different positions in a sentence.

▷ **Ending a sentence**
When a subordinate clause is placed at the end of a sentence, no comma is required to separate the clauses unless the sentence is long and would otherwise be confusing.

The subordinate clause is separated from the main clause by a subordinator, so no comma is required.

Rob hid in a corner **because he hated dancing.**

▷ **Starting a sentence**
If the subordinate clause is placed at the start of a sentence, however, it must be separated from the main clause that follows by a comma.

This subordinate clause is at the beginning of the sentence, so a comma is required to separate the two clauses.

Until the class was over, Rob hid in a corner.

▷ **Sitting in the middle**
Similarly, if a subordinate clause breaks up a main clause, a comma is required at the start and end of the clause to separate it from the main clause.

This subordinate clause has split the main clause into two parts, so commas are required to show which parts belong to which clauses.

Rob**, feeling bored,** hid in a corner.

Multiple subordinate clauses

As long as a complex sentence contains at least one main clause, more than one subordinate clause can be used. The easiest way to construct a complex sentence is to start with a main clause and then add the subordinate clauses, one at a time.

> **GLOSSARY**
>
> **Main clause** A group of words that contains a subject and a verb and makes complete sense on its own.
>
> **Relative pronoun** A pronoun that links one part of a sentence to another by introducing a relative clause, which describes an earlier noun or pronoun.
>
> **Subject** The person or thing that is performing the action of the verb.
>
> **Subordinate clause** A group of words that contains a subject and a verb but depends on a main clause for its meaning.
>
> **Subordinator** A conjunction used to connect words, phrases, and clauses of unequal importance.

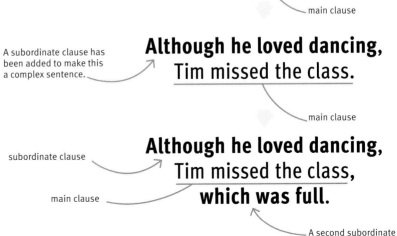

Tim missed the class.

main clause

A subordinate clause has been added to make this a complex sentence.

Although he loved dancing, Tim missed the class.

main clause

subordinate clause

main clause

Although he loved dancing, Tim missed the class, which was full.

A second subordinate clause has been added.

Using clauses correctly

CLAUSES MUST BE PUT IN A CERTAIN ORDER FOR A SENTENCE CONTAINING SEVERAL CLAUSES TO MAKE SENSE.

SEE ALSO	
‹ 64–65	Phrases
‹ 66–67	Clauses
‹ 68–69	Sentences
‹ 70–71	Compound sentences
‹ 72–73	Complex sentences

A main clause must make complete sense on its own, while a subordinate clause only makes sense when it is connected to a main clause. When clauses are put in the wrong place in a sentence, the meaning of that sentence changes.

Breaking sentences down

Certain rules must be followed for a complex sentence to make sense. If a sentence is broken down into its component parts, it has to be clear which clause refers to which subject. Each clause must have its own subject and verb, and a main clause must express a complete thought.

This is a main clause because it makes sense on its own.

This subordinate clause explains why Lauren (the subject of the sentence) was upset.

Lauren was upset because she had lost her swimsuit, which was new.

This subordinate clause is placed at the end of the sentence because it describes the swimsuit, not Lauren.

🔍 Identifying a misplaced clause

If a clause describes someone or something, it needs to be placed as close as possible to the person or thing it describes. Sometimes a phrase or another clause gets in the way, and the whole meaning of a sentence changes as a result. When this happens, the sentence should be reworded so that the potentially confusing clause is placed next to the person or thing that it describes.

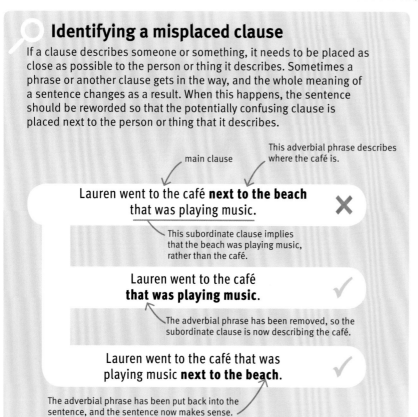

main clause

This adverbial phrase describes where the café is.

Lauren went to the café **next to the beach** that was playing music. ✗

This subordinate clause implies that the beach was playing music, rather than the café.

Lauren went to the café **that was playing music**. ✓

The adverbial phrase has been removed, so the subordinate clause is now describing the café.

Lauren went to the café that was playing music **next to the beach**. ✓

The adverbial phrase has been put back into the sentence, and the sentence now makes sense.

GLOSSARY

Adverbial phrase A group of words such as "in July of last year" that perform the same role as an adverb and answer questions such as: How? When? Why? Where? How often?

Main clause A group of words that contains a subject and a verb and makes complete sense on its own.

Subject The person or thing that is performing the action of the verb.

Subordinate clause A group of words that contains a subject and a verb but depends on a main clause for its meaning.

Split subject and verb

Some subordinate clauses can be placed in the middle of a sentence, separating the different parts of a main clause. If the subject of a sentence is too far away from its verb, the meaning of that sentence will be difficult to follow, so long subordinate clauses are best placed at the beginning or end of a sentence.

▷ **Separated**
This sentence is hard to follow, because the verb, *felt*, is separated from its subject, *Lauren*, by a long subordinate clause.

Lauren, after walking to the café, buying two scoops of ice cream, and eating them hungrily, **felt ill.**

▷ **Reunited**
The sentence has been reorganized so that the subject of the main clause, *Lauren*, is now next to its verb.

After walking to the café, buying two scoops of ice cream, and eating them hungrily, **Lauren felt ill.**

Avoiding sentence fragments

Sentence fragments are parts of sentences that do not contain all the pieces needed to make a complete sentence. In the context of a conversation, sentence fragments can be meaningful. Once the context has been removed, however, sentence fragments make no sense at all, so they are rarely used in writing.

▽ **Recognizing fragments**
Many sentence fragments do not contain a subject or a verb, and they only make sense in context: for example, as the answer to a question.

What would you like?

Vanilla-and-fudge ice cream.

sentence fragment

REAL WORLD
Fragmented advertising

Sentence fragments are often used in advertising, since the product being advertised provides the context. An advertiser's main concern is that the brand is prominent, so the name of this brand normally appears at the start or in the middle of the sentence fragment. Sometimes advertisements are more memorable simply because they sound wrong.

▽ **Making sentences**
If a sentence fragment has been removed from its context, the subject and verb need to be reinstated. A written sentence should never have to rely on the sentences around it for its sense.

subject
I would like vanilla-and-fudge ice cream.
verb

Managing modifiers

A MODIFIER IS A WORD, PHRASE, OR CLAUSE THAT DESCRIBES ANOTHER WORD, PHRASE, OR CLAUSE.

Used correctly, modifiers make sentences more descriptive and therefore more interesting. If a modifier is put in the wrong place in a sentence, however, it can alter the whole meaning of that sentence.

SEE ALSO
‹ 26–27 Adjectives
‹ 40–41 Adverbs
‹ 46–47 Participles
‹ 64–65 Phrases
‹ 66–67 Clauses
‹ 74–75 Using clauses correctly

Misplaced adverbs

Common one-word modifiers include the adverbs *only*, *almost*, *just,* and *nearly*. These adverb modifiers are usually placed right before the word they modify. If a modifier is in the wrong place, the intended meaning may not be clear, and the modifier may end up modifying the wrong person or thing.

— This means that I spoke to Maria very recently, and asked her to lunch.

I **just** asked Maria to lunch.

I asked **just** Maria to lunch.

— This means that I asked Maria to lunch, and no one else.

— This means that I was tempted to eat a whole pie, but I didn't eat any of it.

I **almost** ate a whole pie.

— This means that I ate the pie, and ate most of it.

I ate **almost** a whole pie.

The comedian Groucho Marx **humorously** used a **misplaced modifier**: "One morning I shot an elephant **in my pajamas**. How he got into my pajamas I'll never know."

Misplaced adjectives

Like adverb modifiers, adjective modifiers should be placed as close as possible to the person or thing they describe. Misplaced adjectives tend to occur when a noun is described by several words.

This adjective is describing a silver woman, not a silver bracelet.

Jim found a **silver** woman's bracelet.

Jim found a woman's **silver** bracelet.

— The adjective is now describing a silver bracelet that belongs to a woman.

GLOSSARY

Dangling participle When a modifying phrase or clause that starts with a participle is put in the wrong place in a sentence, it is described as "dangling," because it has no subject to hold on to.

Main clause A group of words that contains a subject and a verb and makes complete sense on its own.

Misplaced modifier A modifier that has been placed so far from the person or thing it is intended to modify that it appears to modify a different person or thing.

Participle The form of a verb that ends in -ing (present participle) or -ed or -en (past participle).

Subject The person or thing that is performing the action of the verb.

Subordinate clause A group of words that contains a subject and a verb but depends on a main clause for its meaning.

Managing Modifiers

Misplaced prepositional phrases

Prepositional phrases often end up in the wrong place. If a modifier is a phrase, it should still be placed next to the person or thing it is modifying. If a prepositional phrase is placed elsewhere in a sentence, it may not convey the intended message.

Laura went for a walk with the dog *in her new boots*.

This prepositional phrase is modifying the dog, so the dog is wearing the new boots.

Laura went for a walk *in her new boots* with the dog.

This prepositional phrase is now modifying the main clause, "Laura went for a walk," so it is Laura who is wearing the boots.

- When writing, always **reread** a finished piece of text before showing it to anyone. As the writer, it's **easy to overlook** potentially **amusing** or **misleading word order**.
- A good way to check for **misplaced modifiers** in a sentence is to **single out** any **modifying words** or phrases by **underlining** or **highlighting** them. It is then easier to see which modifiers relate to which nouns, and **move** any that are in the **wrong place**.

Identifying squinting modifiers

If a modifier is placed between two phrases or clauses, it can be difficult to figure out which phrase or clause it relates to. This type of modifier is often referred to as a squinting modifier, because it looks in two different directions at the same time. The only way to resolve this ambiguity is to move the modifier so that there can be no confusion.

This adverb could be modifying the verb *swim*, in which case the sentence is saying that the people who often swim are the ones who will get stronger.

People who swim **often** will get stronger.

Alternatively, *often* could be modifying the phrase "will get stronger," in which case the sentence is saying that people in general will often get stronger if they swim.

People who **often** swim will get stronger. ✓

The modifying adverb has been moved so that there is no ambiguity, and the people who often swim are the ones who will get stronger.

People who swim will **often** get stronger. ✓

The modifying adverb has been moved to avoid confusion, and the sentence is saying that people in general will often get stronger if they swim.

Dangling participles

Subordinate clauses that start with a participle often cause confusion. This type of clause must be next to its subject, which should also be the subject of the sentence. If the clause is put in the wrong place, it will modify the wrong thing; similarly, if the intended subject is left out of a sentence, that sentence will not make sense. When these errors occur, they are known as dangling participles.

Driving past, the camel was asleep.

In this sentence, the sleeping camel is doing the driving. The intended subject (the person who was driving) has been left out of the sentence.

Driving past, he saw a sleeping camel.

The sentence has been reworded so that the participle *driving* now modifies a subject, *he*, which is also the subject of the sentence.

Commonly misused words

SOME GRAMMATICAL ERRORS OCCUR FREQUENTLY.

SEE ALSO	
‹ 26–27 Adjectives	
‹ 34–35 Pronouns	
‹ 40–41 Adverbs	
‹ 48–49 Auxiliary verbs	
Relative clauses	82–83 ›
Idioms, analogies, and figures of speech	84–85 ›
Apostrophes	104–105 ›
Confusing words	168–171 ›

It's common to make grammatical mistakes when speaking, but when these mistakes are transferred to writing, the meaning of a sentence is often affected. Most of these problems result from confusion between two words.

That or which?
Use *that* for restrictive relative clauses, which introduce essential information, and *which* for nonrestrictive relative clauses, which introduce additional, nonessential information.

The cats **that are black** are sleeping.

The cats, **which are black**, are sleeping.

May or might?
The auxiliary verb *may* implies a possibility that something will happen, while *might* indicates a real uncertainty. If something is unlikely to happen, use *might*.

I **may** go for a swim later.

You **might** encounter a shark.

Can or may?
Can refers to a person's ability to do something, whereas *may* is used to ask permission. These auxiliary verbs are not interchangeable.

Can you cook?

May I come?

I or me?
The simplest way to know which pronoun to use is to remove the other person from the sentence. It should then become obvious. Always remember to put the other person or people first.

Isabella, Rosie, and **I** went to a café.
— "I went to a café" makes sense, so this is correct.

Rosie bought coffee for Isabella and **me**.
— "Rosie bought coffee for me" makes sense, so this is correct.

Who or whom?
Think of *who* as representing *he* or *she*, and *whom* as representing *him* or *her*. If in doubt, rephrase the sentence and substitute *he/she* or *him/her*.

Finn, **who** loved snow, went outside.
— The substituted clause would be "he loved snow."

Finn found Greg, **whom** Finn had telephoned earlier.
— The substituted clause would be "Finn had telephoned him."

Whether or if?

Whether does not mean the same thing as *if*. *Whether* is used in sentences where there are two or more alternatives, while *if* can only be used when there are no alternatives.

She couldn't decide **whether** to run **or** hide.

She doesn't know **if** anything will happen.

Its or it's?

Use the possessive determiner *its* when describing a thing that belongs to something, and the contraction *it's* to represent *it is*.

It's back!

its back

Could have or could of?

In speech, the contracted form of *could have*, *could've*, is often mistakenly interpreted as *could of*. *Could of* is wrong and should never be used.

You **could have** told me!

Literally

Literally means "actually" or "in a real sense." It should only be used to describe things exactly as they happened. Anything else is figurative, not literal.

Fewer or less?

Fewer is used for things that can be counted, while *less* is used for hypothetical quantities—things that cannot be counted.

I got **fewer** than ten birthday presents this year.

I have **less** work to do than he has.

Bring or take?

If an object is being moved toward the subject, the verb *bring* should be used. If it is being moved away, the verb *take* should be used.

Should I **bring** a book to read?

You can **take** one of my books.

Good or well?

Good is an adjective, so it is used to describe nouns. *Well* is mostly used as an adverb to describe verbs, adjectives, or other adverbs. However, it can also be used as an adjective to mean "healthy." *Good* does not mean "healthy," so it shouldn't be used in that sense.

A **good** chef eats **well**, so stays **well**.

This adjective is describing the noun *chef*. — This adverb is describing the verb *eats*. — This adjective means "healthy."

I **literally** erupted with laughter!

Negatives

A NEGATIVE TURNS A POSITIVE STATEMENT INTO A NEGATIVE ONE.

In order to show that something is incorrect or untrue in English, a positive statement has to be turned into a negative one—usually by adding the word *not* after an auxiliary verb. Double negatives should be avoided.

SEE ALSO	
‹ 34–35	Pronouns
‹ 40–41	Adverbs
‹ 42–43	Simple tenses
‹ 44–45	Perfect and continuous tenses
‹ 48–49	Auxiliary verbs
‹ 52–53	Verb agreement
Apostrophes	104–105 ›

REAL WORLD
Satisfied?
When British rock band the Rolling Stones sang "I can't get no satisfaction" in 1965, they canceled the negative *can't* out with the negative *no*. But despite the double negative, the meaning was clear, and listeners worldwide understood the band to be thoroughly dissatisfied.

Forming negative sentences
Auxiliary verbs are the only verbs that can be made negative. If a sentence does not contain an auxiliary verb, one must be added. The negative word *not* is then placed directly after the auxiliary verb. The resulting combination is known as a negative auxiliary.

AUXILIARY VERB	NEGATIVE WORD	MAIN VERB
had is will	not	been going go

Frank had not been to a German
believe he wouldn't try a curried

Contractions
In negative sentences, the auxiliary verb and the negative word *not* can be combined and shortened to form contractions, with an apostrophe to represent the missing letter or letters. Common negative contractions include *haven't* (have not) and *can't* (cannot).

Auxiliary verb	Negative word	Contraction
would	not	wouldn't
do	not	don't
should	not	shouldn't
could	not	couldn't
will	not	won't

Most negative contractions are formed by joining the two words and removing the *o* from *not*.

There are some exceptions: Here, the *i* from *will* has also been changed to *o*.

NEGATIVES

Identifying a double negative

A double negative is when two negative words appear in a single clause. Although the two negative words are usually intended to convey a single negative thought—and this usage is understood in colloquial English—in reality, one negative plus another negative equals a positive. If a clause includes two negative words, one of them should be removed.

There are two negatives in this sentence, so the resulting meaning is that Frank did want more food.

Frank **didn't** want **no** more food. ✗

There is now only one negative in the sentence, so it conveys its intended meaning.

✓ Frank **didn't** want more food.

Frank **wanted no** more food. ✓

The past tense auxiliary verb form *did* has been removed, so the verb *want* has to be put in the past tense.

There is now only one negative in the sentence, so it conveys its intended meaning.

GLOSSARY

Auxiliary verb A "helping" verb like *be* or *have* that connects the main verb in a sentence to the subject. These are the only verbs that can be made negative.

Clause A grammatical unit that contains a subject and a verb. Sentences are made up of one or more clauses.

• ***Not*** is the most common negative word, but other words can be used in the same way. These range from ***never*** and ***no***, the most forceful, to ***seldom***, ***barely***, and ***hardly***, which reflect smaller degrees of negativity.

Negative pronouns

Some indefinite pronouns are already in a negative form, and therefore don't need to be made negative using *not*. These include *nobody*, *no one*, *nothing*, and *none*.

There is no need to add the word *not* after this auxiliary verb, because *nobody* is a negative word.

Nobody could believe he wouldn't try a curried sausage.

Nobody is a singular pronoun, so the verb must be singular.

restaurant before. **Nobody** could sausage. He **disliked** spicy food.

Positive thinking

Most statements use fewer words and are more convincing if they are written in a positive way. Even negative words can be used in a positive sentence structure.

This negative word means "did not like," but it can be used in a positive sentence.

He disliked spicy food.

Negative structure	Positive structure
did not like	disliked
was not honest	was dishonest
did not pay attention	ignored
could not remember	forgot
did not start on time	started late
is not attractive	is unattractive

Relative clauses

ALSO KNOWN AS ADJECTIVE CLAUSES, RELATIVE CLAUSES MODIFY NOUNS.

Relative clauses add information to a sentence using the relative pronouns *who*, *whom*, *whose*, *that*, and *which*. Restrictive relative clauses add essential details, while nonrestrictive clauses add nonessential details.

SEE ALSO	
‹ 34–35	Pronouns
‹ 64–65	Phrases
‹ 66–67	Clauses
‹ 72–73	Complex sentences
‹ 74–75	Using clauses correctly
‹ 76–77	Managing modifiers
Commas	96–99 ›

• Make sure that the **relative clause** is **next** to the **noun** or **pronoun** that it is **modifying**. Otherwise, it may end up modifying the wrong person or thing.

• Sometimes a relative clause can be used to **modify** the **rest of the sentence**, rather than a single noun or pronoun. In the following sentence, the relative clause is describing the whole first part of the sentence: "Joe did not look sorry, **which was normal.**"

Nonrestrictive relative clauses

There are two types of relative clauses: nonrestrictive and restrictive. Also known as "nondefining" or "nonessential" clauses, nonrestrictive relative clauses offer additional information about a noun. They are separated from the rest of a sentence by commas, because the information they provide is supplementary, rather than essential.

Nonrestrictive clauses require commas.

The principal, who hated chaos, felt calm.

This nonrestrictive relative clause gives more detail about the principal, but it can be removed without affecting the meaning of the sentence.

The principal, who hated chaos, felt
Joe, whom he had summoned. Joe

Relative pronouns

Relative clauses always follow the noun or pronoun that they modify. They start with one of five relative pronouns, which act as either the subject or the object of the relative clause. *Who* always acts as the subject, while *whom* always acts as the object. The relative pronouns *who*, *whom*, and *whose* are used to refer to people, while *which* and *that* are used to refer to things.

This is the object of the relative clause—the person who was summoned.

whom he had summoned

This is the subject of the relative clause.

This is the subject of the relative clause—the person who hated chaos.

who hated chaos

This is the object of the relative clause.

RELATIVE CLAUSES

Identifying when a pronoun can be omitted

Sometimes a relative pronoun can be omitted from a relative clause without affecting the sense of a sentence. This only works if the pronoun is the object of the clause—the person or thing receiving the action.

restrictive relative clause

Joe had to clean up the mess that the toad had made. ✓

that the toad had made
— *subject*

This is the object of the relative clause, so it can be omitted without changing the meaning of the sentence.

Joe had to clean up the mess the toad had made. ✓

The sentence makes sense without the relative pronoun and object *that*.

• Although **whom** is grammatically correct, **who** is almost always used instead in **everyday** English.

GLOSSARY

Clause A grammatical unit that contains a subject and a verb. Sentences are made up of one or more clauses.

Object The person or thing that is receiving the action of the verb.

Relative pronoun A pronoun that links one part of a sentence to another by introducing a relative clause, which describes an earlier noun or pronoun.

Subject The person or thing that is performing the action of the verb.

Which or *that*?

Historically *which* and *that* were interchangeable, and could be used for either type of relative clause. It is now usual practice to use *that* for restrictive clauses (see below) and *which* for nonrestrictive clauses. This helps to differentiate one type of information from the other.

The principal felt calm, which was unusual.

This is a nonrestrictive relative clause, because it gives extra—but not essential—information about the principal.

Joe held the toad that had escaped.

This is a restrictive relative clause, because it helps to identify which toad is being described.

calm, which was unusual. He eyed
held the toad that had escaped.

Restrictive relative clauses

Restrictive relative clauses are sometimes called "defining" or "essential" clauses, because they identify who or what is being referred to and are therefore vital to the meaning of a sentence. Restrictive clauses are not separated from the rest of a sentence by commas.

Joe held the toad that had escaped.

This relative pronoun is acting as the subject of the relative clause—the thing that did the escaping.

This is a restrictive relative clause—it identifies which toad had escaped.

Idioms, analogies, and figures of speech

CERTAIN DEVICES ARE USED TO MAKE SPEECH AND WRITING MORE INTERESTING AND PERSUASIVE.

SEE ALSO	
Writing to describe	208–209 ⟩
Writing from personal experience	210–211 ⟩
Writing a narrative	212–213 ⟩

Figures of speech are used to create different effects, usually to emphasize a point or help an audience visualize something. Idioms would be meaningless if they were not familiar expressions, while analogies are a useful tool for explaining things.

The word *metaphor* comes from the **Greek** word *metapherin*, which means **"transfer."**

Idioms

An idiom is a word or phrase that means something completely different from the word or words it is made up of. The meanings of idioms have little or no relation to the literal meanings of their component parts, but they make sense because they are familiar expressions. Different regions have different idioms.

This idiom is used to refer to someone who watches a lot of television.

couch potato

This idiom means "to get into bed."

hit the sack

down in the dumps

This idiom is used to refer to someone who is feeling miserable.

Analogies

Analogies are used to explain what something is by likening that thing to another thing and identifying similarities. An analogy is not a figure of speech, but it works like an extended metaphor or simile: It compares an unfamiliar thing to a familiar thing, and then lists the shared characteristics. Baking a cake, for instance, can be used as an analogy for writing. Both require careful planning and specific ingredients, and are designed to suit a particular audience.

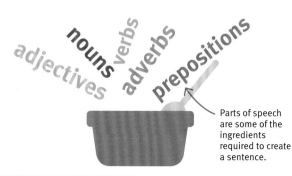

Parts of speech are some of the ingredients required to create a sentence.

REAL WORLD
Avoiding clichés

Clichés are expressions or ideas that have been overused to the point where they have almost lost their original meanings and serve only to annoy the reader. Clichés such as "best-kept secret," "expect the unexpected," and "the best just got better" are common in slogans and advertisements, but it is always more effective to write something original.

IDIOMS, ANALOGIES, AND FIGURES OF SPEECH

Figures of speech

Figures of speech are useful language tools that allow a writer or speaker to persuade, emphasize, impress, or create a mental image. Words and phrases are used out of their literal contexts to create different, heightened effects. When a person claims to be "starving," for example, that person is unlikely to be dying of hunger; rather, he or she is simply very hungry.

- Try to **invent new, interesting metaphors** when writing rather than copying existing ones.

Alliteration
The same letter or sound is used at the start of multiple words for effect.

Catherine **c**arefully **c**ombined **c**old **c**offee **c**ake and **k**iwi fruit.

Simile
The words *like* or *as* are used to compare two things.

She is **as** plump **as** a peach, but she moves **like** a ballerina.

Metaphor
One thing is described as being a different thing, resulting in a comparison between the two.

Her cheeks **are** sun-blushed apples.

Euphemism
A mild word or phrase is substituted for a word or phrase that might cause offense.

She has **ample** proportions (she is overweight).

Pun
Also known as word play, the multiple meanings of a word are used to create humor.

She gave me her measurements as **a round figure**.

Hyperbole
A statement is grossly exaggerated.

She said she could **eat a rhinoceros**.

Personification
An object or animal is given human qualities.

The food **called** to her.

Oxymoron
Two terms are used together that contradict each other.

The pie looked **terribly tasty**.

Onomatopoeia
A word is used that mimics the sound of what it stands for.

She **burped** noisily.

Anaphora
A word or phrase is repeated at the start of successive clauses for emphasis.

She ate the pie; **she ate** the cake; **she ate** the kiwi fruit.

Irony
One thing is said but the opposite thing is meant, usually for humor or emphasis.

I admired her **charming** table manners (her manners were poor).

Understatement
Something is made out to be smaller or less important than it really is.

She said she had enjoyed her **light lunch**.

Colloquialisms and slang

COLLOQUIALISMS AND SLANG ARE FORMS OF INFORMAL SPOKEN LANGUAGE.

Colloquialisms are words or phrases that are used in ordinary, informal speech. Slang is even less formal, and is often only recognized by the members of a particular group. Slang includes words or phrases that may be considered taboo.

SEE ALSO	
‹ 12–13 Spoken and written language	
‹ 14–15 English around the world	
‹ 84–85 Idioms, analogies, and figures of speech	
Genre, purpose, and audience	190–191 ›
Newspaper articles	198–199 ›
The spoken word	222–223 ›
Writing a speech	226–227 ›

Colloquialisms

English speakers use a variety of informal words and phrases that differ from region to region but are recognized by most native speakers. These words and phrases are called colloquialisms, which stems from the Latin word for "conversation."

Colloquialisms are an important part of relaxed conversation (known as colloquial speech), but they should not be used in formal speech or writing. Most colloquialisms are labeled in dictionaries as "informal" or with the abbreviation "colloq."

Some slang terms are used so often that they become **universal**—the slang word *cool*, meaning **"fashionable"** or **"great,"** is one example.

fella
dude   fellow
chap guy
geezer
     gent
buddy

man

scratch
loot   dough
greenbacks
bread
moola   bones

money

REAL WORLD
Rhyming slang

Rhyming slang, also known as Cockney rhyming slang, originated in the East End of London in the nineteenth century. It is formed by replacing a common word with a phrase that rhymes with it. Often, the rhyming part of this phrase is then removed, so the resulting slang term bears little or no resemblance to the original common word. The word *phone*, for example, is translated into rhyming slang as the phrase "dog and bone," which is then shortened to "dog."

Shortened forms

Some words have both a formal meaning and a colloquial meaning. The word *kid*, for example, can refer to a baby goat or, informally, to a child. Colloquialisms are often shorter and easier to say than the word or words they represent. Common colloquialisms therefore include shortened forms of longer words and words that have been combined. They also include abbreviations, such as *ROFL* ("rolling on the floor laughing"), which are used in text messages and e-mail chats in place of longer expressions.

Shortened form	Formal term
'cos	because
ain't	is not
gonna	going to
wanna	want to
BRB	be right back
BTW	by the way
DND	do not disturb
LOL	laugh out loud
TTYL	talk to you later

Slang

Slang is only used in informal speech or, sometimes, in works of fiction. It is used in place of conventional words for things that are familiar, but possibly uncomfortable, to the speaker, and includes words that are considered taboo in most contexts. Slang words are labeled as "slang" in dictionaries. Different slang words are adopted by different groups of speakers—especially teenagers. They vary across small geographic areas and change frequently over time.

Slang term	Meaning
awesome	incredible, very good
bummed	depressed
chick	girl, woman
chillin'	being calm and relaxed
epic fail	a failure of huge proportions
wack	inferior
gross	repulsive
hardcore	intense
hater	an angry or jealous person
hissy fit	tantrum
hot	attractive
lame	unfashionable, of poor quality
my bad	it was my mistake
noob	someone unfashionable, a newcomer
sick	very good
sweet	excellent, very good
tool	someone stupid

Sick! That was hardcore.

   ?

Changing meanings

New slang words are invented all the time, and existing slang words often change their meanings from one generation to the next. For example, the slang term *busted* used to refer to something that was broken. The term then evolved to describe what happened when someone was caught doing something wrong. In modern slang, *busted* is sometimes used to refer to an unattractive person. Existing slang words are also often combined to form new ones.

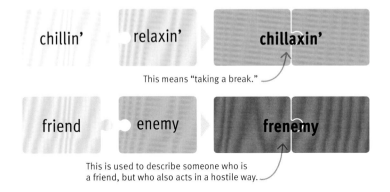

chillin' + relaxin' → **chillaxin'**
This means "taking a break."

friend + enemy → **frenemy**
This is used to describe someone who is a friend, but who also acts in a hostile way.

Jargon

Jargon is a type of slang. It is the name for the technical vocabulary that is used by a particular profession. Jargon is usually unintelligible to those outside the profession, but enables those within it to refer to things concisely and without explanation.

assistance from other officers — suspect vehicle

Call for **backup**! We have an **S/V** and the **perp** is **on the run**.

perpetrator (the person who has committed a crime) — trying to avoid being captured

Direct and indirect speech

THERE ARE TWO WAYS OF REPRESENTING SPEECH IN WRITING.

When a person's exact words are reproduced in writing within quotation marks, this is known as direct speech. When a person's speech is reported, using neither the exact words nor quotation marks, it is called indirect or reported speech.

SEE ALSO	
‹ 22–23 Nouns	
‹ 34–35 Pronouns	
‹ 36–37 Number and gender	
‹ 38–39 Verbs	
‹ 40–41 Adverbs	
‹ 42–43 Simple tenses	
Quotation marks	108–109 ›
Writing a narrative	212–213 ›

Direct speech

Direct speech is always contained within quotation marks, indicating words that are spoken aloud by someone. Direct speech is usually written in the present tense (as it is spoken), and is accompanied by a simple clause in the past tense that tells the reader who is speaking.

What are your symptoms?

"What are your symptoms?" the doctor asked.

- This direct speech gives the exact words of the doctor, so it is contained within quotation marks.
- A comma is usually used to separate direct speech from its accompanying clause, but a question mark or exclamation point can be used instead.
- This simple clause explains who is speaking.

Indirect speech

Indirect speech is also known as reported speech, because it is an account—or report—of what someone has said. Indirect speech does not require quotation marks. It is usually written in the past tense, because it is describing what someone has said. The present tense is occasionally used when reporting something that has always been—and remains—the case.

- **Be careful** when **converting speech** from direct to indirect. It must be clear from the **context** of the sentence or the **word order** which **pronoun** refers to which **person**.
- When writing **dialogue**, a **new line** should be started for **each new speaker**.

▷ **Reporting back**
These are not Peter's exact words, but they recount what he said, so this is an example of indirect speech.

Peter explained that **his** thumb kept twitching.

- The third person is used because Peter is not the narrator.

▷ **Stating facts**
This indirect speech is reporting an unchanging fact, so the present tense is used.

He told the doctor that **he spends** all his time playing video games.

- This means that he always has, does, and will spend his time playing video games.

Identifying characters

Alternating between different forms of speech makes a narrative more interesting to read. When converting direct speech (first person) to indirect speech (third person), it's important to take into account who is speaking, and to whom, and to change the relevant nouns and pronouns to match.

The doctor said, "I fear that you have gamer's thumb."

- In direct speech, the speaker is usually identified.
- The doctor is talking to his patient, whom the context has identified as Peter.

The doctor said he fears that he has gamer's thumb.

- In most cases, it is possible to find out whether a character is male or female by looking at the surrounding text.
- The direct speech has been converted to indirect speech, but it now sounds as though the doctor is the sufferer.
- This is still in the present tense; indirect speech is usually written in the past tense.

The doctor said he feared that Peter had gamer's thumb.

- It is now clear who is speaking to whom, and the indirect speech is in the past tense.

Time and space

If direct speech is being recounted (turned into indirect speech) in a different place and at a different time from where and when it happened, the adverbs and adverb phrases used must match the new situation. For example, the direct speech "Go to the hospital today!" would be recounted a week later in the following way: He was told to go to the hospital that day.

Direct speech	Indirect speech
now	then
here	there
this (morning)	that (morning)
next (week)	the following (week)
today	that day
tomorrow	the next day/the following day
yesterday	the previous day/the day before

Varying verbs

The most common verbs used to report speech are *said*, *told*, and *asked*. Indirect speech can be made more interesting if the writer uses a variety of reporting verbs. The verbs used in the simple clauses that indicate who said what in direct speech can be varied in the same way.

- **Indirect speech** often uses the words **said**, **asked**, or **told**, but don't **confuse** it with **direct speech**, which is always in **quotation marks**.

▷ **Descriptive direct speech**
The verb *sobbed* encourages the reader to sympathize with Peter. *Said* would not have this effect.

"I feel like a freak!" sobbed Peter.

▷ **Interesting indirect speech**
Use unusual verbs such as *promised* and *begged* to add emotion to indirect speech.

The doctor promised that Peter's symptoms were curable. Peter begged him to help.

Punctuation

What is punctuation?

PUNCTUATION REFERS TO THE MARKS USED IN WRITING THAT HELP READERS UNDERSTAND WHAT THEY ARE READING.

Sometimes words alone are not enough to convey a writer's message clearly. They need a little help from punctuation marks to illustrate relationships between words, pauses, or even emotions.

Several of the main **punctuation marks** also have **uses** in **mathematical** notation.

Punctuation marks

There are twelve commonly used punctuation marks. Using punctuation marks correctly and carefully makes it possible for a writer to convey his or her message clearly. Punctuation can also enable the writer to control whether text is read quickly or slowly.

Period
This marks the end of a sentence.

EXAMPLE
The dog slept.

Ellipsis
This represents an unfinished sentence or omitted text.

EXAMPLE
Everything seemed calm, but then...

Comma
This joins or separates elements in a sentence.

EXAMPLE
Hearing a cat, he jumped up.

Semicolon
This joins two main clauses or separates items in a list.

EXAMPLE
He ran after the cat; it ran up a tree.

Colon
This introduces text in a sentence.

EXAMPLE
He was interested in one thing: chasing the cat.

Apostrophe
This marks the possessive or omitted text.

EXAMPLE
The dog's owner couldn't see the cat.

WHAT IS PUNCTUATION?

Why we need punctuation
Some people might argue that writing would be simpler without punctuation. However, writers have something to say and want readers to understand exactly what they mean. Punctuation makes this possible.

	What punctuation does to writing
yes	This word has no punctuation marks. It is just a sequence of letters that together form a word. The reader can read this word in any way.
Yes.	This is a statement. It has a period (.), which marks the end of the sentence. This tells the reader to read the word calmly, as it states a fact.
Yes?	This is a question. It has a question mark (?) at the end of the sentence. It tells the reader to read the word as a question, with a slightly raised voice.
Yes!	This is an exclamation. It has an exclamation point (!) at the end of the sentence, which tells the reader to read it with emotion.
y-e-s	The letters of the word *yes* are separated here by hyphens (-). These tell the reader to read the individual letters slowly and carefully.

Hyphen
This joins or separates words or parts of words.

EXAMPLE
The single-minded dog barked at the cat.

Quotation marks
These enclose direct speech or quotations.

EXAMPLE
"Come on, Fido," his owner called.

Question mark
This marks the end of a direct question.

EXAMPLE
What are you doing?

Exclamation point
This marks the end of an exclamation.

EXAMPLE
Come here, now!

Parentheses
These surround additional information in a sentence.

EXAMPLE
The dog (tail between his legs) followed his owner.

Dash
This signals extra information in a sentence.

EXAMPLE
The cat—pleased with itself—leaped out of the tree.

Periods and ellipses

SEE ALSO	
‹ 54–55 Voices and moods	
‹ 68–69 Sentences	
Exclamation points	112–113 ›
Capital letters	158–159 ›
Abbreviations	172–173 ›

A PERIOD ENDS A SENTENCE, WHEREAS AN ELLIPSIS INDICATES THAT A SENTENCE IS UNFINISHED.

A period marks the end of a complete statement. It can also be used to show that a word has been abbreviated. An ellipsis represents text omitted from a sentence.

- If an **abbreviation** with a period comes at the end of a sentence, no additional period is needed. For example, "The undersea experiment commenced at 4:00 p.m."

Ending a statement
A period is used at the end of a statement. There is no space before a period, but a space is left after one. It is followed by a capital letter at the start of the next sentence.

The undersea experiment ended.
This period marks the end of the sentence.

The undersea experiment ended. said, "Swim to the surface

REAL WORLD
Web and e-mail addresses
The period is used today in website and e-mail addresses. In these situations, it is known as a "dot" and functions as a separator between the parts of the address. Unlike in normal writing, the dot is stated when the address is read aloud, so the example here would read "w-w-w-dot-d-k-dot-com."

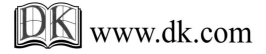

Commands
Some commands, including orders and polite requests, end with a period. For commands that express greater emotion, such as anger or surprise, an exclamation point should be used.

Swim to the surface.
This period marks the end of this request.

Get out of the water!
This exclamation point expresses urgency.

PERIODS AND ELLIPSES

- When using **abbreviations**, be consistent and either always use periods, or never use them.
- Most **acronyms**, such as **NASA** or **NATO**, should be written without periods.

In **telegrams**, the word *STOP* was used to mark the **end of a sentence** instead of a period, because it **cost less** than punctuation.

Abbreviations

A period can be used at the ends of certain abbreviations, representing letters that have been omitted. For example, *Dr.* stands for "Doctor." Some abbreviations, such as those for metric measurements and US states, are never spelled with a period.

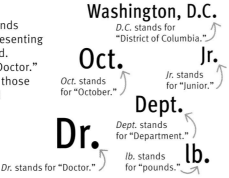

Washington, D.C.
D.C. stands for "District of Columbia."

Oct.
Oct. stands for "October."

Jr.
Jr. stands for "Junior."

Dept.
Dept. stands for "Department."

Dr.
Dr. stands for "Doctor."

lb.
lb. stands for "pounds."

GLOSSARY

Abbreviation A shortened form of a word, often with one or more periods to represent missing letters.

Acronym An abbreviation made up of the initial letters of a series of words and in which the letters are pronounced as they are spelled, rather than as separate letters.

Command A sentence that gives an instruction.

Statement A sentence that conveys a fact or piece of information.

Leading scientist Dr. Fisher
Wait, I forgot to tell you…"

Ellipses

Three periods in a row are called an ellipsis. An ellipsis indicates that a sentence has been left unfinished, as when a speaker drifts into silence or is cut off abruptly. Ellipses can also represent omitted text within quotations.

I thought…
This ellipsis means that the speaker suddenly stopped speaking. No period is needed.

Could I…?
A question mark or exclamation point is kept after an ellipsis.

This ellipsis stands for the missing words from the start of the sentence in the quotation. The missing words could be "Today we heard that."

The report said that "…Dr. Fisher…is correct.…The island is near…"

This ellipsis indicates missing text. Some style guides suggest placing spaces before and after the ellipsis.

If text is omitted after a complete sentence, the ellipsis is placed after the final punctuation mark.

Commas

COMMAS ARE USED TO SEPARATE ELEMENTS IN A SENTENCE.

Commas clarify information by separating words, phrases, or clauses. They are used to organize information into groups, sorting it so a sentence is understood correctly.

SEE ALSO	
‹ 62–63 Interjections	
‹ 64–65 Phrases	
‹ 66–67 Clauses	
‹ 82–83 Relative clauses	
Other uses of commas	98–99 ›
Parentheses and dashes	114–115 ›

Introductions

Sometimes, a sentence begins with a clause, phrase, or word that sets the scene and leads the way to where the main action begins in the second half of the sentence. A comma is placed after the introduction to make the reader pause and anticipate the main information. An introduction to a sentence could be a word such as *However*, a phrase such as *Three years ago* or a clause such as *If this happens*.

This is an introductory phrase.

Once upon a time, there was a garden.

A comma is placed after the introductory phrase, before the main information is revealed.

The main information follows the comma.

This is an introductory clause.

When Lisa visited the garden, she saw a flower.

The main information comes after the comma.

A comma is placed after the introductory clause.

Working in pairs

If a sentence is interrupted by an additional phrase that is not essential to the understanding of the sentence, a comma is placed on either side of the phrase, like two parentheses. Without the commas, the information is treated as essential.

Sometimes, the interruption is placed at the beginning or end of a sentence. In these cases, only one comma is used, since a comma is never placed at the start or end of a sentence.

A flower, like a sock, can be striped.

The interruption is placed within a pair of commas to separate nonessential information.

A flower can be striped, like a sock.

A comma is placed before an interruption at the end of a sentence.

A flower like a sock can be striped.

Without the commas, the information becomes part of the main sentence and changes its meaning.

A comma is placed after an interruption at the start of a sentence.

Like a sock, a flower can be striped.

- Often, **quotations** are used without introductions, so no comma is needed. For example: **The guide says that this is "the best garden in France."**
- Don't use a comma if the first part of the quotation ends with an **exclamation point** or a **question mark**. For example: "Stop!" Tom cried. "The bridge is dangerous."

GLOSSARY

Adverb A word that describes the way something happens.
Clause A grammatical unit that contains a subject and a verb.
Conjunction A word used to connect phrases and sentences.
Direct speech Text that represents spoken words.
Interjection A word or phrase that occurs alone and expresses emotion.
Phrase A group of words that does not contain a verb.

Direct speech

In direct speech, a comma should be used between the introduction to the speech and the direct speech itself. The introduction can be at the start, end, or middle of the sentence. When in the middle, use a comma on either side of the introduction, between the first and second parts of the sentence.

A comma is placed before the quotation mark, after the introduction.

Grandma asked, "Can we find more of these flowers?"

A comma is placed before the quotation mark, before an introduction.

A comma is placed before the quotation mark after the introduction.

"The flowers," Lisa said, "are always in bloom in May."

Direct address

Commas are always used when someone is spoken to directly, by name. The placement of the comma depends on where the name appears in a sentence. The commas work in the same way as around an interruption: commas to either side of the name when it appears in the middle of a sentence, a comma after the name when it starts a sentence, and a comma before the name when it comes at the end of a sentence.

- If an **interruption** is taken out of a sentence, the sentence should still make sense.
- Commas with **interjections** such as *stop* or *help* work in the same way as those for direct address.

Let's eat Grandma.

In this example, the comma is missing, so Grandma is about to be eaten.

Let's eat, Grandma.

A comma is placed before the name when it appears at the end of a sentence.

Other uses of commas

COMMAS CAN BE USED TO JOIN MULTIPLE MAIN CLAUSES, REPRESENT OMITTED WORDS, AND SEPARATE ITEMS IN LISTS.

SEE ALSO	
‹ 26–27 Adjectives	
‹ 58–59 Conjunctions	
‹ 70–71 Compound sentences	
‹ 72–73 Complex sentences	
‹ 96–97 Commas	
Semicolons	100–101 ›
Numbers, dates, and time	118–119 ›

Sentences can be joined using a comma with a conjunction to create the right pace and variety in writing. A comma is also used to avoid repetition and to separate words or phrases in lists.

Commas to join clauses

Commas are used with conjunctions to join two or more main clauses to make a sentence. The comma before the last main clause is followed by one of these conjunctions: *and*, *or*, *but*, *nor*, *for*, *yet*, or *so*. If two clauses are short and closely linked, the comma can be omitted.

REAL WORLD

Comma butterfly

A comma is also a type of butterfly with a small, white marking on the underside of each of its wings that resembles the punctuation mark.

Walkers turn left, joggers turn right, but cyclists go straight.

- start of first main clause
- A comma separates the first two main clauses in a set of three.
- start of second main clause
- start of third main clause
- A comma is placed before the conjunction *but*.

Sit here and enjoy the view.

- start of first main clause
- start of second main clause
- No comma is needed before the conjunction because it joins two short, closely related main clauses.

Commas and omitted words

When avoiding repetition that would make a sentence long and possibly boring, a comma can be used to represent the omitted words.

In the first month of the year, the flower was orange; in the second, red; and in the third, yellow.

- A comma is placed after the introductory phrase.
- Each of these commas represents the omitted word *month*.

- Use a **semicolon** to join two related sentences together without a conjunction.
- A **comma** can be used only with the **conjunctions** *and*, *or*, *but*, *for*, *nor*, *yet*, or *so* to **join clauses**.
- **Avoid** using **too many commas**. When a sentence contains a lot of pauses, it is difficult to read.

Commas in lists

Commas are used to separate words or phrases in a list. A good way to test if the comma is in the correct position is to replace it with one of the conjunctions *and* or *or*. If the sentence doesn't make sense with *and* or *or*, don't add a comma.

The **comma** is one of the **most misused** punctuation marks.

Each interest is separated by a comma from another interest in the list.

The last word in the list is joined by a comma followed by the word *and*.

My interests are walking, flowers, birds, and gardening.
My interests are walking flowers, birds, and gardening.

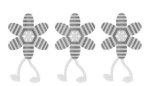

Since there is no comma separating *walking* and *flowers*, the interest is *walking flowers*.

The comma before the conjunction is known as a "serial comma" and is useful for preventing ambiguity.

Commas with adjectives

A list of adjectives in front of a noun can be treated in two different ways. If each adjective modifies the noun, add a comma to separate them. However, if an adjective describes a combination of words that come after, no comma is needed. There are two ways to check if a comma should be used.

First, if *and* can be added between the adjectives, a comma should be placed between them. Second, swap the adjectives. If the meaning hasn't changed, it's correct to use a comma to separate the adjectives.

I saw a yellow, flying saucer.

When the comma is placed here, each adjective describes the noun separately: The saucer is flying and yellow.

I saw a blue flying saucer.

With no comma, the adjective *blue* describes the *flying saucer*.

GLOSSARY

Adjective A word that describes a noun.
Conjunction A word used to connect phrases and clauses.
Main clause A group of words that contains a subject and a verb and makes complete sense on its own.
Noun A word that refers to a person, place, or thing.
Verb A word that describes an action.

- The **serial comma**, set after the second-to-last item of the list, is especially useful when there are two instances of **and** in a sentence. For example, "The blue, pink, and black-and-white flowers have grown."

Semicolons

SEMICOLONS CONNECT SECTIONS OF TEXT THAT ARE CLOSELY RELATED.

SEE ALSO	
‹ 58–59 Conjunctions	
‹ 66–67 Clauses	
‹ 94–95 Periods and ellipses	
‹ 96–99 Commas	
Colons	102–103 ›

Semicolons can be used to indicate a close relationship between main clauses or to separate complex items in a list. They also precede certain adverbs when they are used as conjunctions.

- **Never use** a semicolon to **connect a main clause to a subordinate clause**. A comma and a conjunction should be used. For example, "Sam had two red T-shirts, **which** were new."
- **Use** a semicolon to **connect two main clauses** that are not joined by a conjunction.

Connecting

A semicolon is used to join two main clauses and show that they are of equal importance and closely related. These clauses can stand alone as separate sentences, or they can be connected by a comma and a conjunction.

May was warm; it was pleasant.

This clause is closely related to the previous main clause because it provides information as to why May was pleasant.

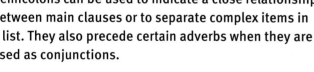

Identifying when to use a semicolon

Many people have trouble deciding when to use a colon or a semicolon. Both are used to connect two main clauses that are closely related, but the colon indicates specifically that the second sentence is a direct explanation or a result of the first.

The weather was dreadful.   It rained every day.

The weather was dreadful: It rained every day. ✓

The second clause explains why the weather was dreadful, so a colon is used to connect the two sentences.

It was freezing.   He was grateful for his coat.

The second clause does not explain why it was freezing, nor is it a direct result of it being freezing, so a semicolon is used to connect the two sentences.

It was freezing; he was grateful for his coat. ✓

SEMICOLONS

Many **writers**, such as James **Joyce**, George **Orwell**, and Kurt **Vonnegut** have **refused** to use semicolons, deeming them pointless.

GLOSSARY

Clause A grammatical unit that contains a subject and a verb. Sentences are made up of one or more clauses.

Main clause A clause that makes complete sense on its own.

Subordinate clause A clause that provides additional information but depends on the main clause for it to make sense.

REAL WORLD

Ben Jonson's *English Grammar*

English dramatist Ben Jonson (1572–1637) is widely credited as the first person to set down rules on how to use semicolons in English. His book *English Grammar*, first published in 1640, systematically examined the period, comma, semicolon, and colon. Before this, there were no accepted standards on how to use these marks.

Before adverbs

A semicolon precedes certain adverbs, such as *however*, *therefore*, *consequently*, and *nevertheless*, when they are used as conjunctions to connect clauses.

However is used as a conjunction here, so it is preceded by a semicolon.

June was hot; however, some cities were rainy.

June was hot; however, some Texas; and Boston, England.

Lists

When a sentence includes a list in which some or all of the items already contain commas, semicolons are used to separate the list items. This makes the sentence easier to follow.

Without the semicolons, the reader might mistake *Texas* and *England* for cities.

Some cities were rainy: London; Paris, Texas; and Boston, England.

Commas separate cities from regions.

A region is needed to clarify which *Paris* the text is referring to.

A region is needed to clarify which *Boston* the text is referring to.

Colons

THE COLON SEPARATES PARTS OF A SENTENCE, WHILE ALSO INDICATING A CLOSE RELATIONSHIP BETWEEN THEM.

A colon connects a main clause with another clause, a phrase, or a word. It can be used to provide an explanation or for emphasis, or to introduce a list or quoted material.

> **SEE ALSO**
> ‹ 70–71 Compound sentences
> ‹ 96–99 Commas
> ‹ 100–101 Semicolons
> Quotation marks 108–109 ›
> Bullet points 116–117 ›

Explanations
A colon shows that what follows a main clause is an explanation of it. The section following the colon can be a main clause, or just a word.

This main clause provides an explanation of what her secret is.

They know her secret: She is obsessed with socks.

Emphasis
A colon can be used to emphasize a point in a text, by causing the reader to pause before reading that point.

The single word emphasizes that she's interested in only one thing.

She thinks about one thing: socks.

Lists
A colon is also used to introduce a list. The section preceding the colon should be a complete statement, but the section following the colon can be just a simple list of things.

Her socks have the following patterns: striped, spotted, and paisley.

This is the introduction to the list.

The items in the list follow the colon.

The colon is also used in math for **ratios** or **scales**. For example, **3:1** means a ratio of **three to one**.

> **GLOSSARY**
> **Clause** A grammatical unit that contains a subject and a verb. Sentences are made up of one or more clauses.
> **Main clause** A clause that makes complete sense on its own.
> **Subordinate clause** A clause that provides additional information but depends on the main clause for it to make sense.

REAL WORLD
Emoticons

In the digital world, punctuation marks, especially the colon, are used to create informal graphic representations of emotions known as "emoticons." The most frequently used marks are the colon, semicolon, and parenthesis, but almost any punctuation mark can be used.

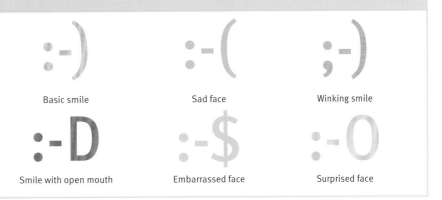

Quotes

A colon is often used to introduce quoted text, especially literary quotations, where the author's exact words are repeated.

Quoted text follows the colon.

She was quoted in the newspaper: "I love socks!"

Titles

A colon is sometimes found in the titles of works of literature, film, art, and music. If the title is followed by a subtitle, a colon separates the two.

main title — The subtitle follows the colon.

Socks: The Sure-footed Life of a Collector

Bible references

When giving a Bible reference, the chapter and verse are separated by a colon.

book of the Bible

A colon separates the chapter and verse.

1 Corinthians 13:12 — verse

chapter

- A colon never follows a **verb**.
- A **dash** can be used instead of a colon, but a **colon creates a greater pause** and a sense of anticipation for what follows it. Use a dash for emphasis and drama.
- A colon should be followed by **one space**.
- The **first word** following a colon should be **lowercase**, unless it begins a main clause.

Apostrophes

APOSTROPHES SHOW POSSESSION OR OMISSION.

The apostrophe is used to create the possessive form of nouns and represents letters that have been omitted in contractions. It can also be used to create a few unusual plural nouns.

SEE ALSO	
‹ 32–33 Determiners	
‹ 48–49 Auxiliary verbs	
‹ 80–81 Negatives	
Other confusing words	170–171 ›

Missing letters

An apostrophe represents missing letters in a contraction, which is when a word or words are shortened by omitting letters. There are about 100 common contractions. Only auxiliary verbs such as *be* and *have* can be used in this way.

Original form	Contracted form	Original form	Contracted form
it is	it's	he had; he would	he'd
she is	she's	I will	I'll
who is	who's	you will	you'll
I am	I'm	who will	who'll
you are	you're	is not	isn't
we are	we're	has not	hasn't
they are	they're	cannot	can't
I have	I've	could not	couldn't
we have	we've	will not	won't
would have	would've	did not	didn't

Rafael **wasn't** happy that the his name with two **f's** on

REAL WORLD
Apostrophe catastrophe

The use of apostrophes in plurals in commercial signs is widespread. This type of mistake is sometimes called a "greengrocer's apostrophe."

Plural forms

Occasionally, apostrophes are used to create plural forms where adding an *s* on its own would cause confusion, as when an abbreviation or a single letter is made plural. There are very few words that are pluralized in this way. Most plurals of regular nouns are formed by adding only an *s*.

with two **f's**

Without the apostrophe, it would be unclear that the phrase is talking about the letter *f*.

APOSTROPHES

- Place an apostrophe where letters have been **omitted**. This is not always where the words have joined.
- Another way to form the **possessive of a noun** is to swap the position of the owner and the item it owns and connect them with the word *of*. For example, instead of writing "the Netherlands**'s** tulips," write "the tulips **of** the Netherlands."

Apostrophes frequently appear in non-English **surnames**, such as **O'Neill**, **N'Dor**, and **D'Agostino**.

Forming the possessive

An apostrophe marks a noun's possession (ownership) of something. There are two forms of possessive apostrophes. The first, an apostrophe followed by an *s* (-'s), shows possession of a singular noun. The second, an apostrophe after the *s* (-s'), shows possession of a plural noun ending in *s*.

play's new director

To form the possessive of a singular noun, add an apostrophe, followed by the letter s.

The new director belongs to the play, which is singular.

grapes' seeds

When forming the possessive of a plural that ends in s, only an apostrophe is added.

The seeds belong to grapes, which is plural.

women's story
people's faces

If a plural word ends in any letter other than s, such as e, i or n, an apostrophe is added, followed by the letter s.

play's new director had spelled Socrates's revised script.

Words ending in s

In the past, some grammar styles have recommended that the possessive of a proper noun ending in *s* be written with only an apostrophe, and no additional *s*. Today, an *s* is generally added in all cases.

The possessive of Socrates is Socrates's rather than Socrates'.

Socrates's revised script

The possessive of Jess is Jess's rather than Jess'.

Jess's disbelief

GLOSSARY

Auxiliary verb A "helping" verb that is used with other words to form contractions.

Contraction A shortened form of a word or words, in which letters are omitted from the middle and replaced with an apostrophe.

Hyphens

HYPHENS ARE USED TO EITHER JOIN OR SEPARATE WORDS OR PARTS OF WORDS.

Sometimes two terms need to be shown to be connected, so that they are treated as one. Alternatively, a separation between terms may need to be emphasized. A hyphen can be used for both of these purposes.

SEE ALSO	
‹ 26–27 Adjectives	
‹ 56–57 Phrasal verbs	
Numbers, dates, and time	118–119 ›
Alphabetical order	128–129 ›
Syllables	134–135 ›
Roots	140–141 ›
Prefixes and suffixes	142–143 ›

Clarity

A hyphen is essential when the meaning of a phrase might be confused. When a hyphen is used between two or more words, it is a compound modifier indicating that the words work together to modify another word.

big-hair society

This hyphen indicates that the society is interested in big hair.

big hair society

Without the hyphen, the hair society is big.

The celebrated big-hair society for a get-together about their

Verbs into nouns

When a phrasal verb is made into a noun, it is hyphenated. Phrasal verbs themselves are never hyphenated. For example, the phrasal verb *get together* in "Let's get together and talk about it" isn't hyphenated, but a hyphen is used when it becomes a noun: "for a get-together."

a break-in   **a get-together**

   a hang-up   **an eye-opener**

a write-up   **a put-down**

- **Compound modifiers** that contain adverbs **ending in -ly**, such as "extraordinarily hairy experience," are **never hyphenated**.
- Names of **centuries** used as modifiers should be **hyphenated** before the noun, as in "twentieth-century issues."
- A hyphen is used to **break a long word** in two **between two syllables** at the **end of a line**.

HYPHENS

Prefixes

Hyphens are sometimes needed in words with prefixes. Many need to be hyphenated to avoid confusion with words spelled in a similar way. A hyphen is also often added when a prefix ending in a vowel is joined to a root word beginning with a vowel, in order to avoid having two vowels side-by-side. The prefix self- is always followed by a hyphen. Finally, a hyphen is needed when adding a prefix to a capitalized word or to a date.

re-formed ← The hyphen indicates that the society formed again. Without a hyphen, the word *reformed* means "changed for the better."

co-owner ← This hyphen is needed to divide the two *o*'s because *coowner* is hard to read.

self-service ← The prefix self- always has a hyphen following it.

pre-Roman ← A hyphen follows a prefix before a capital letter.

post-1500 ← A hyphen follows a prefix before a date.

GLOSSARY

Compound modifier A term used to describe a noun that combines two or more words.

Phrasal verb A verb composed of a verb followed by an adverb or a preposition that act together as a single unit.

Prefix A group of letters attached to the start of a word that can change the original word's meaning.

Root word A word to which prefixes and suffixes can be added.

Suffix A group of letters attached to the end of a word that can change the original word's meaning.

Writing numbers

Hyphens are needed when writing out fractions, or numbers from twenty-one (21) to ninety-nine (99).

twenty-four   three-quarters

re-formed after twenty-four years
beard- and hair-loss issues.

Suspended hyphens

Occasionally, a hyphen is found alone at the end of a word. This is called a suspended hyphen, and it occurs when two or more compound modifiers describing one noun and connected by *or*, *and*, or *to* use the same word. To avoid repetition, the first instance of the word is omitted and replaced with a hyphen.

beard- and hair-loss issues

This suspended hyphen followed by *and* indicates that there were both beard-loss and hair-loss issues.

Compound modifiers

When two or more words are used together to modify another word, a hyphen is often needed to show that these modifying words are acting as a single unit. These compound modifiers are almost always hyphenated when they precede the noun, but not when they follow the noun, unless a hyphen is needed for clarity.

hair-loss issues ← noun

A compound modifier before the noun is hyphenated.

A compound modifier after the noun is not hyphenated.

issues of hair loss

Quotation marks

QUOTATION MARKS INDICATE DIRECT SPEECH OR QUOTED MATERIAL.

SEE ALSO	
‹ 88–89 Direct and indirect speech	
‹ 96–99 Commas	
‹ 102–103 Colons	
Italics	122–123 ›
Reading and commenting on texts	192–193 ›
Writing to inform	196–197 ›
Writing to analyze or review	206–207 ›
Writing a narrative	212–213 ›

Quotation marks, sometimes simply called quotes, are always used in pairs. In addition to indicating speech or a quotation, they can also signal unusual words.

GLOSSARY

Direct speech Text that represents spoken words.
Italics A style of type in which the letters are printed at an angle to resemble handwriting.
Quotation Text that reproduces another author's exact words.

Direct speech

Quotation marks surround direct speech (text that represents spoken words). The material within quotation marks can be split into two sections at either end of the sentence, with text in the middle to explain who is speaking. Quoted material can also be placed at the beginning, in the middle, or at the end of a sentence.

This direct speech is at the beginning of the sentence.

The punctuation that is part of the direct speech is placed within the quotation marks.

This text explains who has just spoken.

DIRECT SPEECH **SPEAKER**

"Do pandas eat meat?" one visitor asked.

This text explains who is about to speak.

A comma is placed before the direct speech.

This direct speech is at the end of the sentence.

SPEAKER **DIRECT SPEECH**

One visitor asked, "Do pandas eat meat?"

Do pandas eat meat?

Unusual words

Quotation marks can be used to separate particular words or phrases within text. These can indicate that another author's words are being used, that the words are unusual, or that the author does not take the expression seriously.

The zookeeper said that the panda show was "thrilling," but three pandas were asleep.

The writer has placed quotation marks around this word to suggest that he or she did not find the show as thrilling as expected, based on how it had been described.

QUOTATION MARKS

Identifying where to place punctuation

In direct speech, a comma is used to separate the text that explains who is speaking from the spoken words. Periods and commas should always go within the quotation marks, while question marks and exclamation points should be left outside unless they are part of the quoted speech. If the end of the direct speech falls at the end of the sentence, only one punctuation mark is needed. When reproducing a quotation, the punctuation and capitalization of the text should be written exactly as it appears in the original text.

The zookeeper continued "Pandas are very agile." ✗

Quotation marks are placed around direct speech.

The zookeeper continued, "Pandas are very agile." ✓

This introduces the speech. / A comma is placed before the direct speech. / Periods are always placed before the closing quotation mark.

Can you believe the panda cub "can fit on your hand?" ✗

Quoted material is placed within quotation marks.

Can you believe the panda cub "can fit on your hand"? ✓

The question mark goes outside the quotation marks because it is not part of the quoted material.

Single quotation marks

Single quotation marks are used for quotations within quotations. Any double quotation marks within direct speech or a quotation are changed to single quotation marks to distinguish the words they surround from the rest of the speech or quotation.

- Quotation marks are used to **surround quotations** in the **same way** as they surround **direct speech**.
- In British English, **single quotation marks** are sometimes used in place of double quotation marks for **quoted speech**. Some **US newspapers** also use this style for headlines.

SPEAKER: The zookeeper said,

DIRECT SPEECH: "I wouldn't call pandas 'cuddly.'"

The direct speech is marked by double quotation marks.

The zookeeper is quoting someone else's description of pandas, so the quoted word is within single quotation marks.

REAL WORLD
Air quotes

Air quotes are quotation mark shapes created with a person's hands when speaking. They serve to highlight unusual words, as quotation marks can in writing, and add a hint of sarcasm to the person's speech.

Titles of short works

Quotation marks are used for the titles of short works, such as short stories, articles, and song titles. The titles of longer works, such as books and movies, are italicized.

The name of the article is in quotation marks.

The article "Panda Facts" was an eye-opener.

Question marks

A QUESTION MARK SIGNALS THE END OF A SENTENCE THAT ASKS A QUESTION.

SEE ALSO	
‹ 34–35 Pronouns	
‹ 68–69 Sentences	
‹ 88–89 Direct and indirect speech	
‹ 108–109 Quotation marks	
Exclamation marks	112–113 ›
Italics	122–123 ›

Usually, a period is used to indicate the end of a sentence. However, if the sentence is a question rather than a statement, it should end with a question mark.

Direct questions

A sentence that asks a question and expects an answer in response is a direct question, and requires a question mark. In direct questions, the subject (a noun or pronoun) follows the verb. This is in contrast to the word order of a statement, in which the verb follows the subject. Many direct questions start with question words, such as *when*, *who*, *where*, *why*, or *how*.

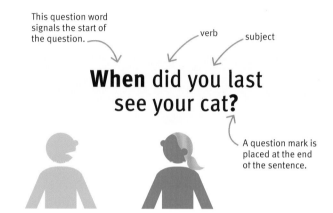

This question word signals the start of the question.

verb

subject

When did you last see your cat?

A question mark is placed at the end of the sentence.

Embedded questions

An embedded question is one that appears within a longer sentence, following an introductory phrase. The word order for an embedded question follows that of a statement, with the subject preceding the verb. This makes the question sound more polite. If the full sentence asks a question, it requires a question mark.

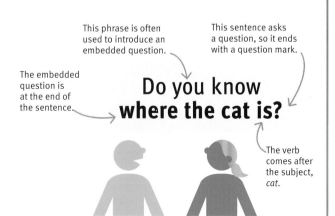

The embedded question is at the end of the sentence.

This phrase is often used to introduce an embedded question.

This sentence asks a question, so it ends with a question mark.

Do you know where the cat is?

The verb comes after the subject, *cat*.

Indirect questions

An indirect question always ends in a period. This type of question states what has been asked, rather than directly asking a question. It does not repeat the speaker's exact words, and usually does not require an answer. Indirect questions never end in a question mark.

He asked me if I knew where the cat was.

This is an indirect question because it does not require an answer, and it ends in a period.

QUESTION MARKS

- A question can be **just a word**, such as *Who?*, *What?*, *Where?*, *When?*, *Why?*, or *How?*
- A question mark **should not** normally **be used with another punctuation mark**. One **exception** is when a **period** is used with an abbreviation at the end of a sentence. For example, "Should we meet at 3:00 p.m.?"
- When a question mark appears within a title that is **italicized**, the question mark should also be italicized.

In **Spanish**, an **inverted question mark** (¿) is used to indicate the **beginning** of a question, in addition to the question mark at the end.

Tag questions

A tag question is one that can be added to the end of a statement. The speaker prompts the listener to respond in a certain way, and then adds the question to the end for confirmation. Tag questions follow a comma at the end of a statement.

This is a statement that makes sense on its own.

You don't think I'm responsible, **do you?**

This is the question, but it cannot appear on its own because it doesn't make sense without the rest of the sentence.

Rhetorical questions

A rhetorical question is a question that is asked only to stress a point. It often contains a note of emotion or sometimes exaggeration. No response is expected, since the answer to the question is either obvious or cannot be known. Rhetorical questions are punctuated with a question mark.

Do I look like a cat thief?

No response is expected, because the speaker does not think she looks like a cat thief.

REAL WORLD

Can we help you?

Occasionally, question marks are used to indicate tourist information points on signs. Signs like this exist in many places, but are particularly useful for tourists in countries where the spoken language is written in a different alphabet, such as in Japan.

GLOSSARY

Abbreviation A shortened form of a word, often with one or more periods to represent missing letters.

Italics A style of type in which the letters are printed at an angle to resemble handwriting.

Phrase A group of words that does not contain a verb.

Question A sentence that asks for information.

Statement A sentence that conveys a fact or piece of information.

Subject The person or thing that is performing the action of the verb.

Exclamation points

EXCLAMATION POINTS ARE USED AT THE END OF EXCLAMATIONS.

SEE ALSO	
⟨ 54–55 Voices and moods	
⟨ 62–63 Interjections	
⟨ 68–69 Sentences	
⟨ 110–111 Question marks	
Parentheses and dashes	114–115 ⟩

An exclamation point indicates the end of an exclamation, which is a sentence that expresses a writer's strong emotions. It can also be used for emphasis.

Emotions
The exclamation point is used at the end of an exclamation to express a strong emotion, such as surprise, excitement, or anger, or a raised voice.

This is so unexpected!

Surprise!

I love cheese!

Fear!

I'm allergic to cheese!

Stop nibbling on the cheese!

Excitement!

Anger!

- Use exclamation points **sparingly** in **formal writing**. They rarely improve a piece of writing.
- If it is unclear whether or not an exclamation point is needed, remember that it is **usually preferable to end a statement with a period.**

GLOSSARY

Exclamation A sentence expressing a strong emotion, such as surprise, or a raised voice.

Interjection A word or phrase that occurs alone and expresses emotion.

Question A sentence that asks for information.

REAL WORLD
Comics
Exclamation points are a feature of comic books. Some comics use them in almost every sentence. An exclamation point can also be part of an illustration, used on its own next to a character's head to indicate surprise, or with interjections representing sounds, such as *Pow!* or *Zap!* In the 1950s, the exclamation point was called a "bang." This may be because the exclamation point often appeared on its own in a speech bubble next to the barrel of a gun to show that it had just been fired.

Exclamations

Almost any type of sentence can be made into an exclamation. The most common types of exclamations are emotional statements, commands, and interjections.

Exclamation points are **rarely** used in **names**, but the name of the Canadian town of **Saint-Louis-du-Ha! Ha!** officially has two.

Statements
A statement, which normally ends in a period, can be made into an exclamation if it conveys an emotion. An emotional statement ends with an exclamation point instead of a period.

There's a mouse in the kitchen!

Commands
Exclamation points are often used in commands, especially when they are direct orders rather than polite requests.

Be quiet and don't move suddenly!

Interjections
Interjections—words usually exclaimed in urgency or surprise—are some of the most common types of exclamations. Interjections are often single words rather than sentences.

Help!

Emphasis
Exclamation points are often placed next to interruptions within parentheses or dashes to add emphasis to an interruption. Never use an exclamation point alongside a question mark.

The interruption uses an exclamation point to emphasize how grateful the speaker was.

Our hero (thankfully!) arrived just in time.

- **One exclamation point** has a greater impact than several, so using **more than one** exclamation point **should be avoided**.

Identifying exclamations

Sentences beginning with *what* and *how* can either ask or state something, so the only way to know which punctuation mark to use is to understand what the sentence is saying and how it is being said.

What a nightmare this is?

What a nightmare this is! ✓

This sentence is stating something, not asking something. It is an exclamation, so it requires an exclamation point rather than a question mark.

What is a nightmare!

What is a nightmare? ✓

This sentence is asking something, not exclaiming something. It is a question, so it requires a question mark rather than an exclamation point.

Parentheses and dashes

PARENTHESES AND DASHES INDICATE A STRONG INTERRUPTION WITHIN A SENTENCE.

SEE ALSO	
‹ 88–89 Direct and indirect speech	
‹ 96–99 Commas	
‹ 106–107 Hyphens	
Numbers, dates, and time	118–119 ›
Abbreviations	172–173 ›

Parentheses and dashes allow writers to interrupt the normal run of a sentence and insert additional information. Parentheses are always used in pairs around the extra text, while dashes can be used alone or in pairs.

• **Parentheses** can be used around an *s* to show that there may be **one or more** of something: for example, "boy(s)."

Parentheses for interruptions
Parentheses surround extra information that is added to a sentence. The extra text disrupts the normal run of the sentence but can easily be removed without changing the meaning. Parentheses can also be used to enclose an entire sentence, which is punctuated in the same way as any other sentence.

(which was late)
⮜ This gives extra information, which could be removed without affecting the overall meaning of the sentence.

The driver bought a new watch. (His old one had stopped working.)
This sentence gives more information, but can be removed without spoiling the story.
The period is contained within the parentheses.

The freight train (which was late [with] lychees (exotic fruit)." Afte

Brackets
Brackets clarify text within a quotation or provide additional information. The information in brackets is not part of the original quotation.

"laden [with] lychees"
This is part of a quotation.
Brackets show that a word has been changed from or added to the original quote.

Parentheses for clarification
Parentheses are used around information providing clarification, such as an alternative name or spelling, a translation, or a definition.

lychees (exotic fruit)
The information inside these parentheses defines what lychees are.

PARENTHESES AND DASHES   115

- **Brackets** are used within a quotation with the italicized Latin word *sic*, which is used to show that words within a **quotation** have been **reproduced exactly** as they were written. For example, "I heard that the farmer, Mr. Cwpat [*sic*], is alive."
- If using a keyboard that doesn't have a dash, typing **two hyphens (--)** is an acceptable substitute. **Never use a dash** in place of a hyphen, though.

A dash is **longer than a hyphen**. On old-fashioned **typewriters**, **two hyphens** typed one after the other were used instead of a **dash**.

Dashes for interruptions

Dashes perform the same function as parentheses, surrounding additional information in a sentence. While parentheses must always be used in pairs, only one dash is required if the interruption comes at the beginning or end of a sentence.

—by all accounts—

The sentence would still make sense without the part within the dashes, so this part could be removed.

It was a long wait—the longest I'd ever had.

No spaces should be left between the dash and the surrounding words.

This part of the sentence gives additional information about how long the wait was.

was—by all accounts—"laden 5–6 hours, it finally arrived.

Dashes for ranges

A dash can be used to express ranges of numbers, as in the case of dates or page references. In these situations, only the first and last numbers are written. Technically, ranges require the use of a shorter dash called an "en dash," as opposed to the longer "em dash." A dash also expresses ranges of months or days of the week, and it can be used to indicate the direction of travel.

5–6 hours

This means "5 to 6 hours." If the word *from* is written before the number, use *to*, not a dash.

Monday–Friday

This includes Tuesday, Wednesday, and Thursday.

the Trys–Qysto route

This means that the route goes from Trys to Qysto.

Punctuation

Bullet points

BULLET POINTS DRAW THE READER'S ATTENTION TO THE KEY POINTS IN A DOCUMENT.

Bullet points are used to create lists. Bulleted items appear in technical documents, websites, or presentations as a way of condensing important information into brief phrases or sentences.

SEE ALSO	
‹ 98–99 Other uses of commas	
‹ 100–101 Semicolons	
‹ 102–103 Colons	
Layout and presentational features	194–195 ›
Writing to inform	196–197 ›
Writing to explain and advise	204–205 ›
Presentation skills	228–229 ›

Key points

Bulleted items are used to emphasize important points in a document by separating them from the main text and presenting them as a list. This enables the reader to process essential information right away. The bulleted text can be written as complete sentences, phrases, or single words.

> We'll need to be fully prepared for the mission briefing. We'll have to make sure the jet pack is tuned up. We should also get the sewing kit out to finish off the penguin costumes we started last week. Finally, we'll need to dismantle the kite and pack it up as kit.

This running text provides a lot of detail.

SLIDE 1

Before the mission briefing, we'll need to complete several tasks:
- tune up the jet pack
- finish the penguin costumes
- pack up the kite kit

Only the most important information from the text is given here.

Writing bulleted items

Bulleted information has a greater impact if the items are of similar lengths and written in the same way. If the first item starts with a verb, for example, the remaining items should do the same. This creates a balanced list that is easy to follow and gives the items equal importance.

SLIDE 2

On the mission, we'll have to do the following activities:
- go undercover
- impersonate penguins
- follow people
- jump out of helicopters

The bulleted items are all of a similar length.

All of the bulleted items begin with verbs.

BULLET POINTS

- **Use bullet points sparingly:** A few bulleted sections have a greater impact than many.
- **Numbered lists** are an alternative to bulleted lists. These are usually indented and punctuated in the same way as bulleted lists.

Although the most common style of **bullet point** is •, there are many other options, such as º, –, or ◊.

REAL WORLD
Presentations

Speakers often use bulleted lists as visual aids when giving presentations. When addressing a large audience within a short time frame, it's important to get the message across clearly and effectively. Bulleted lists are ideal for this purpose.

Punctuating bulleted text

Bulleted information should be indented from the main text. The text introducing the bullet points should be followed by a colon. Different rules apply depending on whether or not the bulleted items are full sentences.

SLIDE 4

Remember to bring these items:
- a water pistol
- a unicycle
- a pogo stick
- roller skates

The bulleted information is indented from the main text.

A colon is placed after the introductory sentence.

These points are phrases, so they begin with lowercase letters.

Lowercase points require no punctuation.

◁ **Lowercase bullets**
If the bulleted items are not full sentences, they can begin with a lowercase letter. In general, no punctuation is required at the end of lowercase bullet points.

◁ **Complete sentences**
If the bulleted items are complete sentences, each one needs to begin with a capital letter and end with a period, question mark, or exclamation point.

SLIDE 5

The director asked these questions:
- Do I need winter clothes?
- Will there be pirates?
- Can I bring my pig?
- Will we receive any gadgets?

Each of these points is a complete sentence, beginning with a capital letter and ending with a question mark.

Numbers, dates, and time

NUMBERS ARE REPRESENTED IN WRITING AS BOTH NUMERALS AND WORDS.

SEE ALSO	
‹ 94–95	Periods and ellipses
‹ 96–99	Commas
‹ 102–103	Colons
‹ 106–107	Hyphens
‹ 114–115	Parentheses and dashes
Abbreviations	172–173 ›

In addition to mathematical calculations, numerals are sometimes used in writing. They are especially useful for writing dates and time, and decimals and numbers over one hundred.

The **Arabic numbering system** is more accurate than the **Roman system** because it includes the **number zero**.

- When writing a **range of numerals**, as in page references, write the first and last page of the reference and **separate the numerals** with a dash: for example, 14–17 (which includes pages 15 and 16).
- When writing informally, **years can be abbreviated** using an apostrophe followed by the last two numerals, as in "the summer of '97."

Writing out numbers
Fractions and numbers up to one hundred should be written out as words, unless the text uses numbers frequently, as in scientific or mathematical works.

eight spaceships

The numeral 8 is written out.

GLOSSARY

Arabic numerals Everyday numerals such as 1, 2, and 3.
Roman numerals Numbers represented by certain letters of the alphabet, such as *i*, *v*, and *x*.

Flying on board **eight** spaceships, discovered **325** comets on **April 10**

Arabic numerals
Everyday numerals are called Arabic numerals because Arabs introduced them to Europe from India. The ten characters are 0, 1, 2, 3, 4, 5, 6, 7, 8, and 9. These are combined to represent every possible number.

325 comets

Use Arabic numerals for numbers over one hundred.

Dates
Numerals are always used for the day and year of a date. When writing years of more than four digits, as in 10,000 BCE, a comma is used. If the month comes first, a comma is needed between the date and year, and after the year when the date appears in the middle of the sentence.

Date format	Example
day-month-year	The discovery on 10 April 2099 was exciting.
month-day-year	The discovery on April 10, 2099, was exciting.
year-month-day	The discovery on 2099 April 10 was exciting.

NUMBERS, DATES, AND TIME

Identifying when to use words or numerals

If a sentence begins with a number—even a very high number—the number should be written out in words, or the sentence should be rewritten to avoid starting with a number.

325 comets were discovered. ✗
Sentences should never start with numerals.

Three hundred twenty-five comets were discovered. ✓
This number has been written out because it is at the start of the sentence. This option is not ideal with longer numbers.

The aliens discovered **325** comets. ✓
This sentence has been reworded and is the more successful version.

Roman numerals

Roman numerals use the letters *i* (one), *v* (five), *x* (10), *l* (50), *c* (100), *d* (500), and *m* (1,000) from the alphabet to represent numbers. Numbers over ten are a combination of these letters. Both upper- and lowercase Roman numerals are used to refer to acts and scenes in plays—for example, "Act IV, scene i." Uppercase Roman numerals are sometimes used in names of royalty, such as "King Henry VIII." Lowercase Roman numerals can be used for page references—for example, "xiv–xvii."

If a lower Roman numeral is placed before a larger one, subtract it from the larger number, so ix is 10 (x) minus 1 (i) = 9.

Roman	Number	Roman	Number
I, i	1	XX, xx	20
II, ii	2	L, l	50
III, iii	3	C, c	100
IV, iv	4	CD, cd	400
V, v	5	CDX, cdx	410
VI, vi	6	D, d	500
VII, vii	7	CM, cm	900
VIII, viii	8	M, m	1,000
IX, ix	9	MCMXC	1,990
X, x	10	MMXIII	2,013

the aliens from planet Squark IV
2099, between 1:30 and 11:00 p.m.

Time

Numerals are usually used to write the time of day, with a colon separating the hour from the minutes. If expressing time in quarters or halves, or when using the phrase *o'clock*, the time should be written in words.

Between **1:30** and **11:00 p.m.**
time in numerals — *time in words*
This abbreviation stands for "post meridiem" and refers to the afternoon.

Between **half past one** and **eleven o'clock.**

- In numbers over a thousand, a **comma** is placed before every group of **three digits, except within addresses** – for example, **20,000** and **300,000**.
- When writing the time of day using the phrase *o'clock*, **spell out** the number—for example, "eleven o'clock."

Other punctuation

SLASHES, AT SIGNS, AMPERSANDS, AND ASTERISKS ARE A FEW OF THE LESS COMMONLY USED PUNCTUATION MARKS.

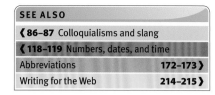

SEE ALSO
- ‹ 86–87 Colloquialisms and slang
- ‹ 118–119 Numbers, dates, and time
- Abbreviations 172–173 ›
- Writing for the Web 214–215 ›

Slashes are used in web addresses, to show alternatives, to represent a period of time, and in units of measurement. "At" signs (@), ampersands (&), asterisks (*), and pound signs (#) usually represent omitted words or letters.

The **at sign** was originally used to represent a **Spanish unit of weight** called an *arroba*.

Slashes in Internet addresses
Slashes are used to write Internet addresses. In this situation, they are called "forward slashes" and link the address of a minor page to that of a main site.

— Style Skunks' main website   — linked "news" page

www.styleskunks.com/news

Slashes for alternatives
Slashes are used to show alternatives such as *and/or* and *he/she*. These are found in technical documents, such as forms, or where space is limited, as in newspaper articles. It is usually better to write the alternatives out.

— This means that she looked for shoes or hats, or both.

She looked for shoes and/or hats.

At signs
The at sign is used to write e-mail addresses. It separates the unique user name from the name of the host domain.

— host domain

user name ↘

questions@styleskunks.com

Ampersands
The ampersand represents the word *and*. It is found in the names of businesses and organizations, and is used in academic references.

— This could also be written "Squirrels and Swirls."

She loved the fashion label Squirrels **&** Swirls.

OTHER PUNCTUATION

Asterisks

Asterisks are used to show that there is extra information at the bottom of the page. The extra information is known as a footnote. They are also used in newspaper articles when a direct quotation includes a word that is too offensive to be written in full. An asterisk represents each letter that has been omitted from the work. This reduces the word's impact, but it remains recognizable to readers who are familiar with it.

The asterisk leads the reader to a footnote explaining that the socks are low quality.

Free socks* will be included with all shoe orders.

- To mark the **omission of** one or more **words** from a passage, never use an asterisk; an **ellipsis (…)** should be used instead.

- If there is a need for **more than one footnote** on a page, use one **asterisk (*)** for the first footnote reference, and **two asterisks (**)** for the second, but do not use more than three in a sequence. In this case, numbering the footnotes would be a better option.

- When writing a **long Internet address** that breaks at the end of a line, break it after a slash—after ".com/" for example.

Pound signs

Found on every telephone keypad, the pound sign, also known as the number sign or hash, represents the word *number* in informal writing. It is usually preferable to write the word *number* instead.

It was the #1 fashion website in the world.

This means "number one."

REAL WORLD
Twitter

The social networking service Twitter has adopted some of the less commonly used punctuation marks and given them a new significance. The at sign, for example, is used before someone's user name to mention or reply to that user, while the pound sign is used to add "tags" to words, making them searchable by other users.

- **Slashes** are found in certain abbreviations. For example, *c/o* appears in addresses and means "care of," while *miles/hour* means "miles per hour."

- The **ampersand (&)** should never be used in place of the word *and* in formal writing, nor should the **at sign** be used in place of the word *at*.

Italics

ITALICS ARE LETTERS THAT ARE PRINTED AT AN ANGLE TO RESEMBLE HANDWRITING.

Words or phrases are styled in italic letters to distinguish them from the surrounding text. Italics may indicate a title, a foreign word or phrase, or emphasis.

SEE ALSO	
‹ 108–109	Quotation marks
‹ 112–113	Exclamation points
‹ 114–115	Parentheses and dashes
‹ 120–121	Other punctuation
Capital letters	158–159 ›
Abbreviations	172–173 ›

Foreign words

Foreign words or phrases that have not been adopted into the English language should be written in italics. These are sometimes followed by a translation, either in parentheses or quotation marks. Genus and species names of living things are Latin words and should always be italicized. The genus starts with a capital letter, while the species is written in lowercase letters.

The foreign word is italicized. The translation is placed in parentheses.

oma (grandma)

The genus is capitalized. The species is written with lowercase letters.

Bombus terrestris (bumblebee)

The scientific name is italicized. The common name is placed in parentheses.

My *oma* (grandma) loves the
I think *Big Beach Splash!*, a film

- If it is unclear whether a **foreign word** should be italicized or not, look it up in a **dictionary**. If the word is not in an English dictionary, it should be italicized.
- **Proper names** are **not italicized** even if they are in a different language—for example, Londres (French for London).

Punctuation

Do not italicize punctuation following words in italics unless it is part of the title or phrase being italicized.

The exclamation point is in italics because it is part of the movie title.

Big Beach Splash!,

The comma is not italicized because it is not part of the movie title.

ITALICS 123

Titles

Italic type is used to write the titles of long works, such as books, journals, movies, or musical compositions. Shorter works, such as poems or short stories, are written in quotation marks. The names of ships should also be italicized.

Big Beach Splash! — movie title

Surfing is Simple — book title

Italicize	Do not italicize
• titles of printed matter such as books, newspapers, journals, magazines, very long poems, and plays	• the name of a holy book such as the Bible or the Koran • chapters within a book, articles in a newspaper or magazine, titles of short stories or poems—put these in quotation marks
• titles of movies, and radio and television programs	• individual episodes of a radio or television program—put these in quotation marks
• names of specific ships, submarines, aircraft, spacecraft, and artificial satellites	• the abbreviations before a ship's name: RMS *Titanic*, USS *Arizona* • a brand of vehicle: Rolls-Royce, Boeing 747 • names of trains
• long musical compositions such as albums and operas	• titles of songs and short compositions—put these in quotation marks
• works of art, such as paintings and sculptures	• buildings and monuments: the Empire State Building, the Statue of Liberty

book *Surfing is Simple*, but about surfing, is *much* better.

Emphasis

Italics can be used when a writer wants to emphasize certain words or draw attention to a contrast between two terms. They may also indicate that the word or phrase should be given greater emphasis when spoken.

The movie is *much* better.

This word has been italicized to emphasize how much better the speaker thinks the movie about surfing is, compared to the book.

This style is called **italic** because it was first used in **Italy** in **1501**.

• When **writing by hand** or typing with a device that does not have italics, underline the word or phrase instead.

Spelling

Why learn to spell?

SPELLING IS IMPORTANT FOR BOTH READING AND WRITING.

Rules can help with spelling; however, there are many exceptions to these rules, which can sometimes make spelling difficult. Learning to spell well is worth the effort, since it helps a writer convey meaning clearly.

Letters

There are twenty-six letters in the English alphabet, which can be written as lowercase or capital letters. These letters also make specific sounds, with some making more than one sound. In special cases, two letters—such as *c* and *h*—combine to produce one unique sound different from any individual letter sound, such as *ch* in *change*. Understanding when to use lowercase and capital letters helps improve spelling, and better spelling increases the overall quality of writing.

The word *alphabet* comes from the **first two letters** of the **Greek** alphabet: *alpha* and *beta.*

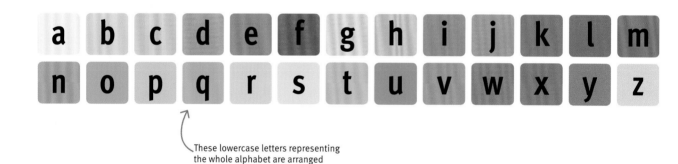

These lowercase letters representing the whole alphabet are arranged in alphabetical order.

The QWERTY keyboard—named after the first six letters and arranged in capital letters—was put in this order so that the most common letters were not close together, thereby avoiding mistakes that caused jams in early typewriters.

Meanings

Many English words come from Latin or Greek, and learning to recognize these roots and understand what they mean can help with spelling. For example, *mar* is the Latin word for "sea," and it is used in the English words *marine* and *maritime*. A common Greek example is *dec*, which means "ten," and this is used in the English words *decade* and *decathlon*. Some root words, such as *build*, which comes from the Old English word *byldan*, are instantly recognizable and form the basis for other related words, including *building*, *builder*, and *rebuild*.

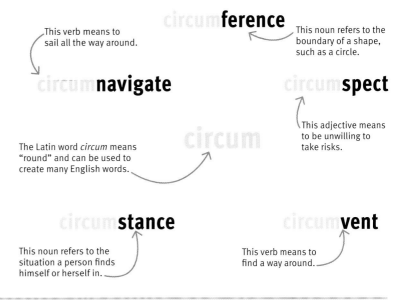

Word beginnings and endings

Some words can have an extra part added to them, which results in a new word. This addition is called a prefix (word beginning) or a suffix (word ending) and can change the meaning of the word. For example, *social* acquires the opposite meaning when the prefix anti- is added, resulting in *antisocial*. However, when the suffix -ite is added to the same root word, the result is *socialite*, which refers to a person who enjoys social activities.

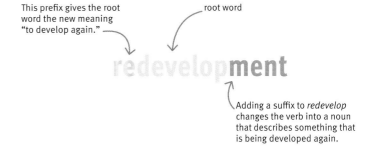

Choose the right words

In some cases, spelling errors can produce a different meaning from the one expected. This is especially true when words that are spelled differently but pronounced the same (homophones) create unintentional, but sometimes amusing, results.

Replace with *mousse* for a type of dessert.

Replace with *yew* for a species of tree.

Replace with *current* for a body of moving water.

Mike ate a lemon **moose** under the **ewe** tree, then went for a swim. The **currant** caught him, and he let out a **whale**. Suddenly it was a scary **plaice**. If he didn't **dye**, he'd have an epic **tail**.

Replace with *wail* for a high-pitched cry.

Replace with *place* for a specific point or location.

Replace with *die* to describe the end of living.

Replace with *tale* for a type of story.

Alphabetical order

ALPHABETICAL ORDER IS A SIMPLE WAY OF ORGANIZING GROUPS OF WORDS.

SEE ALSO	
‹ 126–127 Why learn to spell?	
Capital letters	158–159 ›
Abbreviations	172–173 ›
Planning and research	186–187 ›

From a short list of students in a classroom to a long index in a book, alphabetical order makes information easy to store and find.

Sorting a list

Alphabetical order is the arranging of words based on where their initial letters are in the alphabet. Using this system, words are sorted by their first letters, then by their second letters, and so on. For example, the words *buy* and *biscuit* both begin with the letter *b*, but the second letter in each word is different: The letter *i* in *biscuit* comes before the letter *u* in *buy*, so *biscuit* would come before *buy* in an alphabetical list.

- If a long word has the same letters as a short word, but then goes further—such as *cave* and *caveman*—the **short word (e.g. *cave*) will always come first** in a dictionary.
- The alphabet is **useful for locating a seat** in a theater or a book in a library, as rows are usually labeled in alphabetical order.

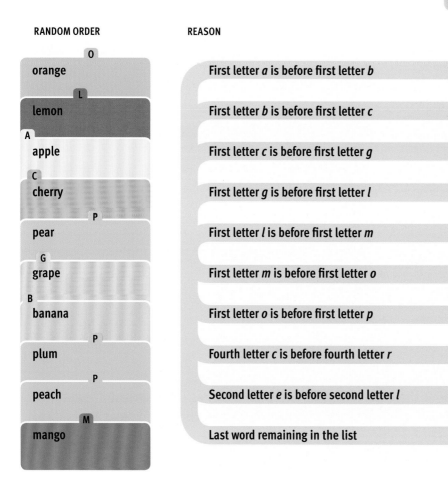

RANDOM ORDER

orange
lemon
apple
cherry
pear
grape
banana
plum
peach
mango

REASON

First letter *a* is before first letter *b*
First letter *b* is before first letter *c*
First letter *c* is before first letter *g*
First letter *g* is before first letter *l*
First letter *l* is before first letter *m*
First letter *m* is before first letter *o*
First letter *o* is before first letter *p*
Fourth letter *c* is before fourth letter *r*
Second letter *e* is before second letter *l*
Last word remaining in the list

ALPHABETICAL ORDER

apple
banana
cherry
grape
lemon
mango
orange
peach
pear
plum

ALPHABETICAL ORDER

Special cases

Organizing words according to their initial letters does not always work. For example, abbreviations, capital letters, and numerals need to be treated in special ways. In all cases, however, it is important to be consistent.

The English **alphabet** is based on the **Latin** alphabet of the **Romans**.

king cobra
kingfisher
king penguin

If terms consist of more than one word, treat them as if they were written without the space. In this example, the list is arranged by looking at the fifth letter.

Treat capitalized words in exactly the same way as lowercase words.

Hague, The
Hamburg
High Wycombe

blueberry
Coconut Island
date

If a phrase contains an article, such as *the*, ignore it and sort by the second word.

Sacramento
St. (Saint) Helier
Salzburg

Arrange any abbreviated terms as if they were spelled out.

Names of people are arranged by surnames, so the first name comes after the comma.

Dahl, Roald
Meyer, Stephenie
Twain, Mark

Π (Pi)
101 Dalmations
Toy Story

Collect terms with symbols or numerals at the beginning.

The dictionary

A dictionary is a collection of words and their definitions in alphabetical order. The words are arranged this way to make it easier for somebody to find a word and check its spelling or definition.

handwriting
writing done by hand, not typed or printed

The first three letters begin with the letters *han*, but the fourth letter *d* in *handwriting* comes before the letter *g* in *hang*.

hang
to support something from above

This word appears after the four-letter word *hang* because it has a fifth letter, *a*.

hanga**r
a very large building where aircraft are stored

Ignore the hyphen (-) and arrange the word by the fifth letter, *g*.

hang-g**lider
a huge kite that a person can hang from

The third letter *p* comes after the third letter *n* in *hang-glider*.

happ**en
to take place

happy
pleased and content

The fifth letter *y* comes after the fifth letter *e* in *happen*, so this is the last word.

REAL WORLD

Indexes

An index is a list of important topics in a reference book that is arranged in alphabetical order. Next to each key topic, a page number (or several page numbers) refers to the location of that key topic in the book. This makes it quicker and easier for the reader to find specific information.

Vowel sounds

THE ENGLISH ALPHABET CONTAINS FIVE VOWELS: *A*, *E*, *I*, *O*, AND *U*.

Each vowel has a short or long phoneme, or sound. Each sound made by a vowel can be written down as a grapheme—one or more letters that represent a sound.

SEE ALSO	
‹ 120–121 Other punctuation	
‹ 126–127 Why learn to spell?	
‹ 128–129 Alphabetical order	
Consonant sounds	132–133 ›
Syllables	134–135 ›
Silent letters	160–161 ›
Irregular word spellings	164–165 ›

Short vowel sounds

A vowel can sound short, or abrupt. For example, the word *rat* has a short "a" sound and the grapheme that represents this sound is *a*. A more complex word, such as *tread*, has a short "e" sound and the grapheme is *ea*. The letter *y* sometimes takes the place of a vowel. For example, the word *gym* has a short "i" sound but the grapheme is *y*.

The **Taa language**, spoken mainly in Botswana, has **112 different sounds**.

▷ **Short "a"**
This sound is represented only by the grapheme *a*.

c**a**t

▷ **Short "e"**
This sound is represented by the graphemes *a*, *ai*, *e*, *ea*, *eo*, and *ie*.

m**a**ny   s**ai**d   r**e**ptile
h**ea**d   l**eo**pard   fr**ie**nd

▷ **Short "i"**
This sound is represented by the graphemes *e*, *i*, *o*, *u*, and *y*.

pr**e**tty   **i**nsect   w**o**men
b**u**sy   rh**y**thm

▷ **Short "o"**
This sound is represented by the graphemes *a* and *o*.

s**a**lt   **o**ctopus

▷ **Short "u"**
This sound is represented by the graphemes *o*, *ou*, and *u*.

d**o**ve   y**ou**ng   b**u**ffalo

Long vowel sounds

A vowel can sound long, or stretched. For example, the word *alien* has a long "a" sound at the beginning of the word and the grapheme that represents this sound is *a*. A more complex word, such as *monkey*, has a long "e" sound in its second syllable and the grapheme is *ey*.

- **The letter y is a consonant when it is the first letter of a syllable that has more than one letter,** such as *yellow*. If *y* is anywhere else in the syllable, it acts like a vowel: In the word *trendy*, it sounds like an "e."

a
▷ **Long "a"**
This sound is represented by the graphemes *a, ai, aigh, ay, a–e, ei, eigh,* and *ey*.

apron   snail   straight   ray
snake   reindeer   sleigh   they

▷ **Long "e"**
This sound is represented by the graphemes *e, ea, ee, ei, ey, e–e, ie,* and *y*.

he   beaver   cheetah   ceiling
donkey   these   thief   smelly

▷ **Long "i"**
This sound is represented by the graphemes *i, eigh, I, ie, igh, i–e, y, ye,* and *y–e*.

bison   height   I   pie   night
pike   fly   eye   type

▷ **Long "o"**
This sound is represented by the graphemes *o, oa, oe, ol, ou, ough, ow,* and *o–e*.

cobra   goat   toe   folk
soul   dough   crow   antelope

▷ **Long "u"**
This sound is represented by the graphemes *u, ew, ue,* and *u–e*.

unicorn   chew
barbecue   use

Complex vowel sounds

In addition to short and long vowel sounds, there are also complex vowel sounds in English. For example, the grapheme *oo* makes two different sounds depending on the word: a short vowel sound, as in the word *hook*, or a long vowel sound, as in the word *loot*.

Complex vowel sound	Examples
aw	**aw**ful, **au**thor
oi	t**oi**l, ann**oy**
ow	h**ou**se, c**ow**
oo (short)	l**oo**k, p**u**t
oo (long)	m**oo**t, s**ui**t

Consonant sounds

THERE ARE 21 CONSONANTS IN THE ENGLISH LANGUAGE: THE WHOLE ALPHABET MINUS THE FIVE VOWELS.

SEE ALSO	
‹ 120–121 Other punctuation	
‹ 126–127 Why learn to spell?	
‹ 128–129 Alphabetical order	
‹ 130–131 Vowel sounds	
Syllables	134–135 ›
Silent letters	160–161 ›

Most consonants have one phoneme, or sound, but some have multiple sounds. Like vowels, consonants are written down as graphemes—letters that represent sounds.

Single consonant sounds

Single consonant sounds are sounds that are represented by consonants. For example, the single consonant sound "f" is heard in the word *fan*, and this is represented by the grapheme *f*. However, the single consonant sound "f" can also be heard in the word *phase*; here, it is represented by the grapheme *ph*. The letters *c*, *q*, and *x* do not have single consonant sounds, but are often paired with other letters to form digraphs or blends.

b ▽ The "b" sound
This consonant is represented by the graphemes *b* and *bb*.

bat   rabbit

d ▽ The "d" sound
This consonant is represented by the graphemes *d*, *dd*, and *ed*.

dog   puddle   rained

▽ The "f" sound
This consonant is represented by the graphemes *f*, *ff*, *gh*, and *ph*.

flamingo   puff
laugh   dolphin

▽ The "g" sound
This consonant is represented by the graphemes *g*, *gh*, *gg*, and *gu*.

girl   ghost
haggle   guinea

h ▽ The "h" sound
This consonant is represented by the graphemes *h* and *wh*.

hen   who

j ▽ The "j" sound
This consonant is represented by the graphemes *ge*, *gg*, *gi*, *gy*, *j*, and *dge*.

gerbil   suggest   giraffe
gymnast   jaguar   badger

▽ The "k" sound
This consonant is represented by the graphemes *c*, *cc*, *ch*, *ck*, *k*, and *que*.

cat   raccoon   chameleon
duck   kitten   mosque

▽ The "l" sound
This consonant is represented by the graphemes *l* and *ll*.

lion   bull

m ▽ The "m" sound
This consonant is represented by the graphemes *m*, *mb*, *mm*, and *mn*.

mouse   lamb
hummingbird   column

n ▽ The "n" sound
This consonant is represented by the graphemes *gn*, *kn*, *n*, and *nn*.

gnome   knot   newt   sunny

p ▽ The "p" sound
This consonant is represented by the graphemes *p* and *pp*.

pig   puppy

r ▽ The "r" sound
This consonant is represented by the graphemes *r*, *rh*, *rr*, and *wr*.

rat   rhinoceros
parrot   wren

s ▽ The "s" sound
This consonant is represented by the graphemes *c*, *s*, *sc*, *ss*, and *st*.

cell   salamander
science   hiss   whistle

CONSONANT SOUNDS

▽ **The "t" sound**
This consonant is represented by the graphemes *bt*, *t*, *th*, *tt*, and *ed*.

dou**bt** **t**iger **th**yme ca**tt**le jump**ed**

▷ **The "v" sound**
This consonant is represented by the graphemes *f* and *v*.

o**f** do**v**e

▷ **The "w" sound**
This consonant is represented by the graphemes *w*, *wh*, and *u*.

walrus **wh**ale peng**u**in

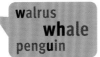

▷ **The "y" sound**
This consonant is represented by the graphemes *i* and *y*.

on**i**on **y**ak

▽ **The "z" sound**
This consonant is represented by the graphemes *s*, *ss*, *x*, *z*, and *zz*.

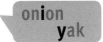
plea**s**e sci**ss**ors **x**ylophone **z**ebra bu**zz**

Digraphs

A digraph is a single sound that is made by combining two letters. For example, the word *shining* begins with the digraph "sh" and is represented by the grapheme *sh*. This digraph can appear in other words, such as *action*, but in this case it is written as *ti*.

Digraph	Grapheme	Examples
ch	ch, t, tch	**ch**icken, na**t**ure, ha**tch**
ng	n (before k), ng	mo**n**key, hatchli**ng**
sh	ce, ch, ci, sh, ss, ti	o**ce**an, **ch**ef, spe**ci**al, **sh**eep, mi**ss**ion, mo**ti**on
th (voiceless)	th	slo**th**
th (voiced)	th	fea**th**er
zh	ge, s	bei**ge**, vi**s**ion

REAL WORLD
NATO phonetic alphabet

The NATO phonetic alphabet is used to avoid confusion when spelling words verbally. Each word is spoken in place of the name of the letter. Radio broadcasters in the military and aviation industries use this alphabet.

A	Alpha	N	November
B	Bravo	O	Oscar
C	Charlie	P	Papa
D	Delta	Q	Quebec
E	Echo	R	Romeo
F	Foxtrot	S	Sierra
G	Golf	T	Tango
H	Hotel	U	Uniform
I	India	V	Victor
J	Juliet	W	Whiskey
K	Kilo	X	X-ray
L	Lima	Y	Yankee
M	Mike	Z	Zulu

Blends

Consonant blends are two or more consonants that join together. They can appear at the beginning or end of a word. Like digraphs, they are never separated, but the individual sound that is represented by each letter is heard. For example, the word *bright* begins with the blend *br*, and the individual letters—*b* and *r*—are clearly heard.

Blend	Examples	Blend	Examples
bl	**bl**ock	pl	**pl**um
br	**br**ead	pr	**pr**etzel
cl	**cl**am	pt	ada**pt**
cr	**cr**acker	sc	**sc**allop
ct	perfe**ct**	sch	**sch**ool
dr	**dr**ink	scr	**scr**ape
fl	**fl**oor	sk	**sk**eleton
fr	**fr**uit	sk	whi**sk**
ft	si**ft**	sl	**sl**ither
gl	**gl**aze	sm	**sm**oke
gr	**gr**apefruit	sn	**sn**ack
lb	bu**lb**	sp	**sp**aghetti
ld	mi**ld**	sp	cri**sp**
lf	se**lf**	sph	**sph**ere
lk	mi**lk**	spl	**spl**atter
lm	e**lm**	spr	**spr**inkle
ln	ki**ln**	squ	**squ**id
lp	pu**lp**	st	**st**eak
lt	ma**lt**	st	toa**st**
mp	cho**mp**	str	**str**awberry
nd	gri**nd**	sw	**sw**eet
nk	dri**nk**	tr	**tr**out
nt	mi**nt**	tw	**tw**in

Syllables

BREAKING UP WORDS INTO SYLLABLES CAN HELP WITH PRONUNCIATION AND SPELLING.

SEE ALSO	
‹ 120–121 Other punctuation	
‹ 130–131 Vowel sounds	
‹ 132–133 Consonant sounds	
Roots	140–141 ›
Prefixes and suffixes	142–143 ›

Every English word consists of one or more syllables. Separating words into syllables helps split complex words into simple, easy-to-remember parts.

Sounding out syllables

One way to determine the correct pronunciation of a word is to break it up into syllables and say each part aloud. For example, the word *melody* can be broken up into three syllables: *me*, *lo*, and *dy*. Single syllable words, such as *cook* and *shop*, are never divided. There are certain rules about how to break up a word.

▷ **Long vowel sounds and consonants**
If the first part of the word makes a long vowel sound and a consonant comes between two vowels, the word is usually divided before the consonant.

Sa makes a long vowel sound.

sa-ving

The consonant *v* is between two vowels, *a* and *i*.

▷ **Single-letter syllables and special sounds**
Never separate two or more letters that together make a single sound. A long vowel sounded alone forms a syllable by itself.

Ph sounds like an *f*.

O makes a long vowel sound.

phys-i-o-ther-a-py

Th makes a unique sound.

▷ **Short vowel sounds and consonants**
If the first part of the word makes a short vowel sound and a consonant comes between two vowels, the word is usually divided after the consonant.

▷ **Prefixes and suffixes**
A prefix is divided from the root word. If the word ends in the suffix -le and this is preceded by a consonant, the word is divided before the consonant.

▷ **Identical consonants and different vowel sounds**
Two identical consonants next to each other are separated. The word is also divided where two different vowel sounds meet. Most suffixes are separated from the root word.

Mod makes a short vowel sound.

mod-est

The consonant *d* is between two vowels, *o* and *e*.

The prefix *re-* is separated from *handle*.

re-han-dle

The suffix *-le* is preceded by the consonant *d*.

Identical consonants are separated.

Here, *di* and *ate* make different vowel sounds.

im-me-di-ate-ly

The suffix *-ly* is separated from *immediate*.

REAL WORLD
Haiku poetry

Haiku is a traditional Japanese form of poetry that usually consists of 17 syllables. Although Japanese haiku is printed in a vertical line (pictured), in English it is often written over three lines, with five syllables in the first and third lines, and seven syllables in the middle line.

A Haiku by Bashō
Written in Kanazawa in 1689

GLOSSARY

Consonant A letter of the alphabet that is not a vowel.

Prefix A group of letters attached to the start of a word that can change the original word's meaning.

Suffix A group of letters attached to the end of a word that can change the original word's meaning.

Vowel One of the five letters *a*, *e*, *i*, *o*, and *u*.

Word stress

When a word has more than one syllable, one of the syllables is always louder than the others in spoken English—this is the syllable that is stressed.

Rule 1
In many English words, the stress is on the first syllable.

dam-age

Rule 2
A word with a prefix or suffix usually has the stress on the root word.

in-ter-**rup**-tion

Rule 3
In words beginning with de-, re-, in-, po-, pro-, or a- the first syllable is usually not stressed.

pro-**gres**-sive

Rule 4
Two vowels together in the last syllable often indicate a stressed last syllable.

sus-**tain**

Rule 5
A word with a double consonant in the middle puts stress on the syllable before the consonant.

mid-dle

Rule 6
The stress is usually on the syllable preceding the suffixes -tion, -ity, -ic, -ical, -ian, -ial, and -ious.

im-i-**ta**-tion

Rule 7
The stress is usually on the second syllable before the suffix -ate.

o-**rig**-i-nate

Rule 8
If none of 1–7 apply, in words with three or more syllables, one of the first two syllables is usually stressed.

sym-pho-ny

Iambic pentameter

Syllables are often used in literature to give sentences a lilting rhythm and to emphasize certain parts of a word. A poetic form called iambic pentameter consists of ten syllables in each line. The ten syllables are divided into five pairs of alternating unstressed and stressed syllables. The rhythm in each line resembles the "da-DUM" sound of a heartbeat.

The only English letter whose name has more than one syllable is **w**, which is pronounced **"duh-bull-you."**

▷ **Shakespearean syllables**
Many people have used this technique, including the English playwright William Shakespeare (1564–1616). This famous line is taken from his tragedy *Macbeth*.

Is **this** - a **dag** - ger **I** - see **be** - fore **me**

The first syllable in a pair is unstressed and represents the quieter "da" in the heartbeat rhythm.

The second syllable in the pair is stressed and represents the louder "DUM" in the heartbeat rhythm.

Morphemes

A MORPHEME IS THE SMALLEST MEANINGFUL PART OF A WORD.

All words are made up of at least one morpheme. An understanding of morphemes can help with spelling, since a morpheme in one word can apply to other similar words.

SEE ALSO	
‹ 20–21 Parts of speech	
‹ 22–23 Nouns	
‹ 24–25 Plurals	
‹ 26–27 Adjectives	
‹ 38–39 Verbs	
‹ 40–41 Adverbs	
‹ 104–105 Apostrophes	
Roots	140–141 ›
Prefixes and suffixes	142–143 ›

Free and bound morphemes

There are two types of morphemes: free and bound. Free morphemes are separate words, and can form the root of a longer word. Bound morphemes are parts of words—usually prefixes or suffixes—that attach to a free morpheme. For example, the word *cats* has two morphemes: The noun *cat* is the free morpheme and the suffix *-s* is the bound morpheme.

fortunate
This free morpheme is an adjective that refers to good luck or success.

fortunately
This suffix is a bound morpheme and changes the free morpheme into an adverb.

unfortunately
This prefix is another bound morpheme and gives the adverb the opposite meaning.

Adding information

A bound morpheme can add information to a free morpheme without changing the basic meaning of the word. For example, adding the bound morpheme *-est* to the end of the free morpheme *fast* results in the word *fastest*. The meaning has become more specific.

Rule 1
Adding the bound morpheme *-s* to the end of a free morpheme results in a plural word.

cup / cup**s**

The cup**s** are very large.

Rule 2
To show possession, add the bound morpheme *-s* and an apostrophe to the end of a free morpheme.

swimmer / swimmer**'s**

The swimmer**'s** goggles were too small.

GLOSSARY

Adjective A word that describes a noun.
Adverb A word that modifies the meaning of a verb, adjective, or other adverb.
Noun A word that refers to a person, place, or thing.
Prefix A group of letters attached to the start of a word that can change the original word's meaning.
Suffix A group of letters attached to the end of a word that can change the original word's meaning.
Verb A word that describes an action.

Rule 3
The comparative form occurs when the bound morpheme *-ier* is added to the end of a free morpheme.

hungry / hungr**ier**

He was hungr**ier** than his friends.

Rule 4
The superlative form occurs when the bound morpheme *-est* is added to the end of a free morpheme.

long / long**est**

It was the long**est** day ever.

Acting in a different way

Some words add more than just detail. For example, the free morpheme and adjective *kind* can combine with the bound morpheme ending -ness, which forms the noun *kindness*. The meaning of a word can also change. For example, the word *helpful* can acquire the opposite meaning when the bound morpheme un- is added, which results in the word *unhelpful*.

- Understanding morphemes can help with unfamiliar words. Take **demagnetize**: the morpheme is the noun **magnet**, but the **suffix -ize** changes it to a verb. However, the newly created word **magnetize** acquires the opposite meaning when the **prefix de-** is added, and refers to the act of making something **less magnetic**.

Rule 1
The bound morpheme ending -ness changes an adjective into a noun.

bright / bright**ness**

It is very bright in this room.

This room's bright**ness** is overwhelming.

Rule 2
The bound morpheme ending -ion changes a verb into a noun.

act / act**ion**

She wanted to act in the play.

The play contained many act**ion** scenes.

Rule 3
The bound morpheme -ful attaches to the end of a noun and changes it into an adjective.

spite / spite**ful**

The annoyed boy ignored his sister out of spite.

The spite**ful** boy became very annoyed.

Rule 4
The bound morpheme un- attaches to the start of a word to give it the opposite meaning.

helpful / **un**helpful

The helpful boy carried the bags.

The **un**helpful boy did not carry the bags.

In the field of linguistics, **morphology** is the identification, analysis, and description of words that **form a language**, including root words and parts of speech.

Understanding English irregularities

THE ENGLISH LANGUAGE HAS BEEN SHAPED BY MANY LANGUAGES.

SEE ALSO	
⟨ 86–87 Colloquialisms and slang	
Roots	140–141 ⟩
Hard and soft letter sounds	144–145 ⟩
Irregular word spellings	164–165 ⟩

English has its foundations in Latin and Greek and continues to evolve as foreign words are adopted. With so many influences, it is understandable that English has so many spelling irregularities.

Latin influences

Latin is more than 2,000 years old and originated in the Roman Empire. English has adopted Latin at different times in history. In the years of the Roman Empire (27 BCE–476 CE), contact with Rome introduced new vocabulary. During the Middle Ages (fifth–fifteenth centuries CE), Latin was the language of the Church, which exerted an enormous influence on language—in fact, the first printed books were religious texts. In subsequent centuries, people invented words for new things by combining existing Latin words.

cominitiāre — This Latin word means "to begin" and is the origin of the English word *commence*.

superbus — This Latin word means "superior" and is the origin of the English word *superb*.

verbatim — This Latin word means "word for word" and is still used today.

Greek influences

Ancient Greek literature and myths have greatly influenced the English language. Most Greek terms in English were created by combining Greek roots to describe things named in modern times, such as *dinosaur*. For this reason, Greek words are usually technical words used in medicine and science.

skeleton — This Greek word means "dried up" and is the same as the English word *skeleton*.

pharmakon — This Greek word refers to a place that dispenses medicine and is the origin of the English word *pharmacy*.

deinos and *saurus* — In Greek, the word *deinos* means "terrible" and *saurus* means "lizard." When combined, they form the origin of the English word *dinosaur*.

REAL WORLD
The Domesday Book

The Domesday Book was written in Latin and compiled in 1085–1086 CE. It is Britain's earliest public record, and was drawn up on the orders of King William I to describe the resources of late eleventh-century England. Latin was the language used for government documents and by the Church, and continued to be used for important documents up to Victorian times.

Old English influences

A more familiar-sounding form of English began when the Anglo-Saxons came from continental Europe to England in about the fifth century CE. English from this time is now referred to as Old English and it was related to German. Modern English words that derive from Old English usually have one or two syllables, and refer to everyday things, such as food, animals, parts of the body and family relationships. Old English words are usually spelled differently from the modern equivalent, but they are often pronounced in a similar way.

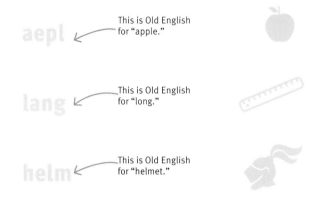

aepl — This is Old English for "apple."

lang — This is Old English for "long."

helm — This is Old English for "helmet."

French influences

One of the languages that has influenced English the most is French—a Latin-based language. This is because for about 300 years after the Norman Conquest in 1066, the most powerful people in England spoke a form of French called Norman. For this reason, many English words relating to government, law, money, and warfare come from the French language.

parler — This French word means "to speak" and is the origin of the English word parliament.

recrue — This French word refers to untrained soldiers and is the origin of the English word recruit.

saudier — This French word refers to a person who is paid for military service and is the origin of the English word soldier.

Other influences

There are many other languages that have influenced English over time. For example, the English words *bangle* and *shampoo* derive from Hindi words, and *alligator* and *canoe* derive from Spanish words.

Language of origin	Examples
French	ballet, cuisine
German	hamburger, kindergarten
Italian	fresco, graffiti
Spanish	anchovy, bonanza
Dutch	cookie, tulip
Arabic	algebra, giraffe
Sanskrit	guru, karma
Hindi	bandanna, cheetah
Persian	balcony, lilac
Russian	gulag, mammoth
Czech	pistol, robot
Norwegian	fjord, ski
Dravidian (Indian subcontinent)	mango, peacock
African languages	jumbo, zombie
American Indian languages	chocolate, igloo
Chinese	ketchup, tea
Japanese	origami, tsunami

The most famous remnant of **Old English** is ***Beowulf***. This epic poem survives in a **single manuscript** dating to sometime between the **eighth and eleventh centuries CE**. The author's identity remains a mystery.

140 SPELLING

Roots

THE ROOT IS THE PART OF A WORD THAT CONTAINS MEANING, EVEN WITHOUT A PREFIX OR SUFFIX.

SEE ALSO	
‹ 136–137 Morphemes	
‹ 138–139 Understanding English irregularities	
Prefixes and suffixes	142–143 ›

A root can be an existing English word or part of a word, and it usually originates from Latin or Greek. Learning to identify roots can help with spelling and building vocabulary.

Whole root words

English includes many whole root words, which often stem from Greek or Latin. These words cannot be separated into smaller words, since they are already in their simplest form. However, a whole root word can be made longer by adding a prefix or suffix. For example, the word *build* can become *building*, *builder* and *rebuild*. Each new word has a different meaning, but they are all related to the whole root word.

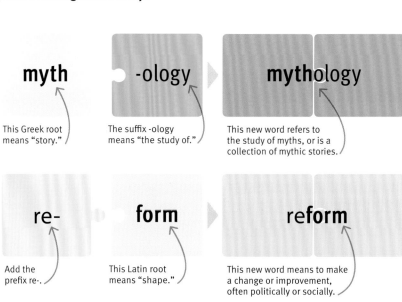

Partial root words

The root is not always a complete English word. Adding a suffix, or a prefix and a suffix, however, can extend a Latin or Greek root to create a recognizable English word. For example, the Latin word *aud*, meaning "hear," forms the root of many familiar English words, including *audio*, *audience*, *audition,* and *auditorium*. Although these words mean different things, they are all related to the original root word.

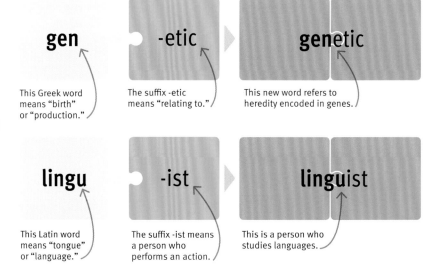

Latin root words

There are nearly 1,000 Latin root words used in English. Many of these words were introduced through French, which stems from Latin, after the Norman conquest of England in 1066.

Latin root	Meaning	Examples
aqua, aque	water	**aqua**rium, **aqua**tic, **aque**duct
bi	two	**bi**annual, **bi**cycle, **bi**nary
cent	one hundred	**cent**ipede, **cent**ury, per**cent**
circum	round	**circum**ference, **circum**navigate, **circum**stance
form	shape	con**form**, **form**ation, trans**form**
jud	judgment	ad**jud**icate, **jud**ge, **jud**icial
liber, liver	free	**liber**ation, **liber**ty, de**liver**
liter	letter (alphabet)	**liter**al, **liter**ate, **liter**ature
mater, matr	mother	**mater**nity, **matr**iarch, **matr**only
min	small	**min**iature, **min**imum, **min**ority
pater, patr	father	**pater**nal, **patr**iotic, **patr**on
quad	four	**quad**rant, **quad**ratic, **quad**rilateral
terr	earth	extra**terr**estrial, **terr**ain, **terr**itorial
tri	three	**tri**angle, **tri**cycle, **tri**nity
uni	one	**uni**corn, **uni**form, **uni**versal

When words **share** the same root—such as *employ* in the words *employee*, *employer*, and *employment*—they are known as a **word family**.

Greek root words

There are hundreds of Greek roots used in English, especially relating to science. For example, *scope* in Greek means "to examine," and is seen in many English words, such as *microscope* and *telescope*.

Greek roots	Meanings	Examples
aero	air	**aero**bics, **aero**sol, **aero**space
bibl, biblio	book	**Bibl**e, **biblio**graphy, **biblio**phile
bio	life	anti**bio**tic, **bio**graphy, **bio**logy
cycl, cyclo	circle	bi**cycl**e, **cycl**ical, **cyclo**ne
dec	ten	**dec**ade, **dec**agon, **dec**athlon
dem, demo	people	epi**dem**ic, **demo**cracy, **demo**graphy
mega	great	**mega**lomania, **mega**phone, **mega**ton
pan	all	**pan**demic, **pan**orama, **pan**theism
path	feeling	**path**ology, sym**path**y, tele**path**y
phobia	fearing	agora**phobia**, arachno**phobia**, claustro**phobia**
phos, photo	light	**phos**phorus, **photo**graph, **photo**synthesis
poly	many	**poly**gon, **poly**math, **poly**technic
psych	spirit	**psych**iatry, **psych**ic, **psych**ology
tele	far off	**tele**kinetic, **tele**phone, **tele**vision
therm	heat	exo**therm**ic, **therm**al, **therm**ometer

- There's **no easy way** to **recognize** whether a root is **Latin** or **Greek**. The best way to find out is to look the word up in a **dictionary**. The origin of the root will be mentioned in the entry.

GLOSSARY

Prefix A group of letters attached to the start of a word that can change the original word's meaning.

Suffix A group of letters attached to the end of a word that can change the original word's meaning.

Prefixes and suffixes

PREFIXES AND SUFFIXES ARE COLLECTIVELY CALLED AFFIXES.

Prefixes are added to the start of a word and suffixes are added to the end of a word. They can change a word's meaning or its part of speech, or—combined with a partial root word—create a new word.

SEE ALSO	
‹ 106–107 Hyphens	
‹ 136–137 Morphemes	
‹ 140–141 Roots	
Words ending in -e or -y	146–147 ›
Words ending in -tion, -sion, or -ssion	148–149 ›
Words ending in -able or -ible	150–151 ›
Words ending in -le, -el, -al, or -ol	152–153 ›
Single and double consonant words	154–155 ›

Prefixes

A prefix is added to the start of a root to change the meaning of that root or create a new word. For example, the root word *do* acquires the opposite meaning when the prefix un- (meaning "not") is added, resulting in the word *undo*. When the prefix demo- (meaning "common people" in Greek) is added to the partial root *crat* (meaning "rule" in Greek), it results in the whole English word *democrat*. Other prefixes can be added to the root *crat* to form the English words *aristocrat*, *autocrat*, and *bureaucrat*.

• Most **prefixes** are not separated from the root by a **hyphen**. However, **ex-** (as in "former") and **self-** are **always** followed by a **hyphen**.

Prefixes	Meaning	Examples	Prefixes	Meaning	Examples
a-, an-	not	**a**typical, **an**onymous	intro-	in	**intro**duction
ab-	away from	**ab**normal	mid-	middle	**mid**way
ad-	toward	**ad**vance	mis-	wrongly	**mis**conception
al-	all	**al**most	non-	not	**non**sense
all-	all	**all**-knowing	out-	more than others	**out**standing
ante-	before	**ante**room	out-	separate	**out**house
anti-	against	**anti**social	over-	too much	**over**do
be-	make	**be**friend	para-	beyond, beside	**para**normal
co-, col-,	together	**co**operate, **col**laborate,	per-	through	**per**form
com-, con-		**com**munity, **con**fidence	post-	after	**post**war
de-	opposite	**de**tach	pre-	before	**pre**mature
de-	down	**de**cline	pro-	for	**pro**active
dis-	not	**dis**embark	re-	again	**re**apply
em-, en-	cause to	**em**battle, **en**amor	retro-	back	**retro**spective
ex-	out of, from	**ex**port	se-	away from	**se**gregate
ex-	former	**ex**-husband	self-	oneself	**self**-confidence
extra-	beyond	**extra**ordinary	sub-	under	**sub**marine
fore-	before	**fore**arm	super-, sur-	over, above	**super**natural, **sur**vive
im-, in-	in	**im**port, **in**come	sus-	under	**sus**pect
im-, in-,	not	**im**mature, **in**credible,	trans-	across	**trans**mit
ir-		**ir**rational	ultra-	beyond	**ultra**sound
inter-	among	**inter**national	un-	not	**un**cover
intra-	within	**intra**mural	under-	beneath, below	**under**mine

Suffixes

A suffix is added to the end of a root—which is either a whole word or part of a word—and changes its meaning or its part of speech. For example, adding the suffix -ant (meaning a person who performs an action) to the end of the word *account* results in a new word with a new meaning: *accountant*. On the other hand, the verb *exist* becomes the noun *existence* when the suffix -ence ("state of") is added.

REAL WORLD
Techno-prefixes

New affixes appear in English all the time, largely due to rapidly changing technology. For example, the prefix e- (meaning "electronic") was created to form words such as *e-mail* and *e-commerce*. Similarly, the prefix cyber-, which refers to information technology, is used in the words *cyberspace* and *cybercafé*.

Suffixes	Meaning	Examples
-able, -ible	able to	sustain**able**, sens**ible**
-acy	state or quality	conspir**acy**
-age	action of	advant**age**
-age	collection	assembl**age**
-al	act of	deni**al**
-al, -ial	having characteristics of	season**al**, controvers**ial**
-ance, -ence	state of	defi**ance**, compet**ence**
-ant, -ent	person who performs an action	account**ant**, stud**ent**
-ate	become	infl**ate**
-cian	profession of	techni**cian**
-cy	state of being	accura**cy**
-dom	place or state of being	free**dom**
-ed	past tense	stopp**ed**
-en	made of	gold**en**
-en	become	bright**en**
-ent	state of being	differ**ent**
-er, -or	person who performs an action	drumm**er**, investigat**or**
-er	more	short**er**
-ery	action of	robb**ery**
-ery	place of	bak**ery**
-esque	reminiscent of	pictur**esque**
-est	the most	short**est**
-ette	small	mason**ette**
-ful	full of	cheer**ful**
-hood	state of	child**hood**
-ia, -y	state of	amne**sia**, monarch**y**

Suffixes	Meaning	Examples
-ic, -tic, -ical	having characteristics of	histor**ic**, poet**ic**, radi**cal**
-ice	state or quality	just**ice**
-ify	make	magn**ify**
-ing	present participle	hopp**ing**
-ish	having the quality of	child**ish**
-ism	the belief in	modern**ism**
-ist	one who	art**ist**
-ite	one connected with	social**ite**
-ity, -ty	quality of	real**ity**, socie**ty**
-ive, -ative, -itive	tending to	pass**ive**, superl**ative**, sens**itive**
-less	without	use**less**
-like	resembling	child**like**
-ling	small	half**ling**
-ly	how something is	friend**ly**
-ment	condition of, act of	entertain**ment**
-ness	state of	happi**ness**
-ous, -eous, -ious	having qualities of	ridicul**ous**, nause**ous**, cur**ious**
-s, -es	more than one	otter**s**, fox**es**
-ship	state of	friend**ship**
-sion, -ssion, -tion	state of being	intru**sion**, permi**ssion**, classifica**tion**
-some	tending to	cumber**some**
-ward	in a direction	back**ward**
-y	characterized by	storm**y**

Hard and soft letter sounds

THE LETTERS *C* AND *G* CAN MAKE HARD AND SOFT SOUNDS.

SEE ALSO	
‹ 130–131 Vowel sounds	
‹ 132–133 Consonant sounds	
Silent letters	160–161 ›
Irregular word spellings	164–165 ›

The letter that follows *c* or *g* determines if a word has a hard or soft sound. This sound can occur in any part of the word, not just at the beginning.

- Sometimes, **a word** has a **hard "c" sound** that is followed by the letter *e* or *i*. In these cases, the letter *h* is added to make the *c* hard. Some example words include **chemist** (the letter *e*) and **chiropractic** (the letter *i*).

The hard and soft *c*

The letter *c* makes a hard sound when it appears before any letter other than *e*, *i*, or *y*. A soft *c* sounds like an *s*—as in *silly*—and can be heard in words where *c* occurs before the letters *e*, *i*, or *y*.

▷ **Hard "c" sounds**
There are many words in English with a hard "c" sound. A word like *cartoon* has a hard "c" sound because *c* precedes the letter *a*.

cartoon   **cow**   **crack**
recall   **uncle**   **porcupine**

▷ **Soft "c" sounds**
These words all have a soft "c" sound. The word *cereal* has a soft "c" sound because *c* precedes the letter *e*.

cereal   **circus**   **cyan**
decent   **pencil**   **fancy**

Words with both "c" sounds

Sometimes, one word includes a hard and a soft "c" sound. These are unusual in English; however, they do follow the same rules.

circulate   **bicycle**
soft "c" sound / hard "c" sound   soft "c" sound / hard "c" sound

Most words with a **soft c** or **g** come from **Latin**.

clearance   **vacancy**
hard "c" sound / soft "c" sound   hard "c" sound / soft "c" sound

HARD AND SOFT LETTER SOUNDS

The hard and soft g

The letter g makes a hard sound when it appears before any letter other than e, i, or y. The soft g sounds like a j—as in jelly—and usually comes before the letters e, i, or y.

- Some words have a **hard "g" sound** that is followed by an "e" or "i" sound. In such cases, the **letter** u is added to make a hard "g" sound, as seen in **guess** (the letter e) and **guide** (the letter i).

▷ **Hard "g" sounds**
The hard "g" sound is common in English. The word *glue* has a hard "g" sound because g precedes the letter *l*.

galaxy   green   gullible
igloo   lagoon   fragrant

▷ **Soft "g" sounds**
These words have a soft "g" sound. The word *gene* has a soft "g" sound because g precedes the letter *e*.

gene   ginger   gymnast
angel   legible   allergy

Words with both "g" sounds

There are some words that include a hard and a soft "g" sound. There are not many words in English that have both sounds.

geography
soft "g" sound / hard "g" sound

gorgeous
hard "g" sound / soft "g" sound

garage
hard "g" sound / soft "g" sound

gigantic
soft "g" sound / hard "g" sound

Hard g exceptions

Some words make a hard sound even if g precedes the letters e, i, or y. These exceptions to the rule just have to be learned, so, if uncertain, check the correct spelling in a dictionary.

geese   baggy
giggle   gear   girl
craggy   get
       geyser
gill   giddy
       gift

These are some common exceptions to the hard g rule.

Words ending in -e or -y

WORDS ENDING IN -E OR -Y OFTEN CHANGE THEIR SPELLINGS WHEN A SUFFIX IS ADDED.

SEE ALSO
‹ 130–131 Vowel sounds
‹ 132–133 Consonant sounds
‹ 140–141 Roots
‹ 142–143 Prefixes and suffixes
Silent letters 160–161 ›

The final -e in words is usually silent. If a suffix is added, the -e is sometimes dropped. A final -y sometimes changes to an *i* when a suffix is added.

Root word	Suffix	New word
argue	-ment	argument
awe	-ful	awful
due	-ly	duly
nine	-th	ninth
true	-ly	truly
whole	-ly	wholly
wise	-dom	wisdom

△ **Exceptions**
There are many exceptions to the rules, some of which are listed in this table.

Words ending in -e

The silent -e serves an important function by changing the vowel sound of the previous syllable. For example, the words *plan* and *plane* are distinguished in spelling only by the silent -e, and this difference is reflected in the way they are pronounced. When adding a suffix, the spelling of words ending in a silent -e follows certain rules.

▷ **Rule 1**
If a word ends in a silent -e, the silent -e is dropped when a suffix beginning with a vowel is added.

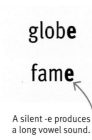

A silent -e produces a long vowel sound.

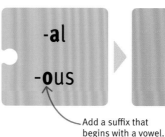

Add a suffix that begins with a vowel.

The silent -e is replaced by a suffix that begins with a vowel.

▷ **Rule 2**
If a word ends in a silent -e, the silent -e is kept when a suffix beginning with a consonant is added.

A silent -e produces a long vowel sound.

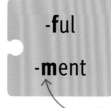

Add a suffix that begins with a consonant.

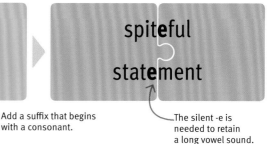

The silent -e is needed to retain a long vowel sound.

▷ **Rule 3**
If a word ends in -ce or -ge, the silent -e must be retained with the suffixes -able and -ous.

A silent -e can follow the letter *c* or *g*.

Add the relevant suffix.

The silent -e is needed to retain a soft "c" or "g" sound.

WORDS ENDING IN -E OR -Y

> **GLOSSARY**
>
> **Prefix** A group of letters attached to the start of a word that can change the root word's meaning.
>
> **Root** The smallest part of a word without a prefix or suffix attached.
>
> **Suffix** A group of letters attached to the end of a word that can change the root word's meaning.
>
> **Syllable** A unit of pronunciation that has one vowel sound.

- The **suffix -y acts as a vowel**, so, if adding it to words ending in a silent -e, drop the silent -e. For example, *ice* becomes *icy* and *spice* becomes *spicy*.

Words ending in -y

Words that end in -y can also change spelling when a suffix is added. The main factor that determines this spelling change is whether the final -y is preceded by a consonant or a vowel.

▷ **Exceptions**
Like words ending in -e, there are exceptions to the rules for words ending in -y.

Root word	Suffix	New word
day	-ly	daily
dry	-ness	dryness
shy	-ly	shyly
shy	-ness	shyness
sly	-ly	slyly
sly	-ness	slyness

▷ **Rule 1**
If a word ends in a consonant and -y, the -y is replaced by *i* when any suffix except for -ing is added.

beauty — **-ful** ▷ **beautiful**
apply — **-ance** ▷ **appliance**

Here, a consonant is followed by a -y ending.
Any suffix can be added, except -ing.
The -y is replaced by the letter *i*.

▷ **Rule 2**
If a word ends in a -y preceded by a vowel, the -y is kept when a suffix is added.

annoy — **-ed** ▷ **annoyed**
play — **-er** ▷ **player**

Here, a vowel is followed by a -y ending.
Add a suffix that begins with any letter.
Keep the -y ending rather than changing it to *i* to avoid having three vowels in a row.

▷ **Rule 3**
If a word ends in a -y, the -y is kept when the suffix -ing is added.

fly — **-ing** ▷ **flying**
copy — **-ing** ▷ **copying**

This word ends in -y.
Add the suffix -ing.
The -y ending is needed to avoid a double *i*.

Words ending in -tion, -sion, or -ssion

THREE DIFFERENT SUFFIXES CAN REPRESENT THE "SHUN" SOUND AT THE END OF A WORD.

The suffixes -tion, -sion, and -ssion make a "shun" sound. Certain rules are helpful when choosing the correct ending to put at the end of a word.

SEE ALSO	
‹ 22–23	Nouns
‹ 38–39	Verbs
‹ 130–131	Vowel sounds
‹ 132–133	Consonant sounds
‹ 136–137	Morphemes
‹ 140–141	Roots
‹ 142–143	Prefixes and suffixes

GLOSSARY

Consonant A letter of the alphabet that is not a vowel.
Noun A word that refers to a person, place, or thing.
Suffix A group of letters attached to the end of a word that can change the original word's meaning.
Verb A word that describes an action.
Vowel One of the five letters *a, e, i, o,* and *u*.

Words ending in -tion

The suffix -tion means "the act of." For instance, *digestion* means "the act of digesting." Most verbs that take the -tion ending already end in -t, so only -ion needs to be added. This suffix is the most common ending.

▷ **Rule 1**
If a verb ends in -t, then add -ion to avoid a double *t* before the suffix.

This verb ends with -t.

This suffix borrows the *t* from the verb.

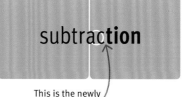

This is the newly formed noun.

▷ **Rule 2**
If a verb ends in -te, then remove the *e* and add -ion.

This verb ends with -te.

This suffix borrows the *t* from the verb.

The final *e* is dropped before the suffix is added, resulting in this noun.

▷ **Rule 3**
Some verbs drop the last letter and add an extra vowel before the suffix. To find out which vowel to add, always check a dictionary.

This verb ends with an -e.

In this case, add the letter *a*.

The full suffix is needed here.

The final *e* is dropped before the vowel and suffix are added, resulting in this noun.

WORDS ENDING IN -TION, -SION, OR -SSION

Words ending in -sion

The suffix -sion means "the state of." For example, *conclusion* means "the state of concluding." There are about 50 words in common use that end in -sion. Most verbs change their endings in order to add the suffix.

▷ **Rule 1**
If the verb ends in -se, then remove the e and add -ion because s is already present.

This verb ends with -se.

This suffix borrows the s from the verb.

The final e is dropped before the suffix is added, resulting in this noun.

precise → -ion → precision

▷ **Rule 2**
This suffix is used when the verb ends in -d, -l, -r, -s, or -t. Usually, the last letter of the verb is dropped in order to add -sion and turn the verb into a noun.

extend → -sion → extension

This verb ends with -d.

The full suffix is needed here.

The final d is dropped before the suffix is added, resulting in this noun.

Words ending in -ssion

This suffix -ssion means "the result of." For example, *impression* means "the result of impressing." Usually, a verb needs to change its ending before the suffix is added.

▷ **Rule 1**
If a verb ends in -ss, then just add -ion.

This verb ends with -ss.

This suffix borrows the ss from the verb.

This is the newly formed noun.

discuss → -ion → discussion

▷ **Rule 2**
If the verb ends with a -t, then remove it and add -ssion.

omit → -ssion → omission

This verb ends with -t.

The full suffix is needed here.

The final t is dropped before the suffix is added, resulting in this noun.

Unusual spellings

Some words that end with a "shun" sound do not follow the rules and just need to be learned. If unsure about the correct spelling, always check a dictionary.

Ending	Examples
-sian	A**sian**, Rus**sian**
-xion	comple**xion**, crucifi**xion**
-cion	coer**cion**, suspi**cion**
-cean	crusta**cean**, o**cean**

The only words in which the **"sh" sound** at the start of the last syllable is spelled with the letters *sh* are **cushion** and **fashion**.

Words ending in -able or -ible

SPELLING WORDS WITH SIMILAR-SOUNDING SUFFIXES CAN BE CONFUSING.

> **SEE ALSO**
> ‹ 26–27 Adjectives
> ‹ 136–137 Morphemes
> ‹ 140–141 Roots
> ‹ 142–143 Prefixes and suffixes
> ‹ 144–145 Hard and soft letter sounds
> Single and double consonant words 154–155 ›

The suffixes -able and -ible both mean "able to." For example, *adaptable* means "able to adapt." However, it can be difficult to decide which suffix to use, as they are not interchangeable.

> **GLOSSARY**
> **Adjective** A word that describes a noun.
> **Suffix** A group of letters attached to the end of a word that can change the original word's meaning.
> **Syllable** A unit of pronunciation that has one vowel sound.
> **Verb** A word that describes an action.
> **Vowel** One of the five letters *a*, *e*, *i*, *o*, and *u*.

Words ending in -able

The suffix -able is usually added to complete words to turn them into adjectives. Learning a few simple rules makes it easier to decide which suffix to use. More words end in -able than -ible, so, if in doubt, choose -able. Best of all, check the correct spelling in a dictionary.

▷ **Rule 1**
Words ending in -able are usually formed from two separate words that make sense individually.

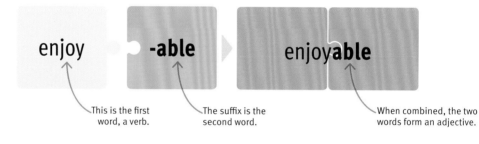

This is the first word, a verb.
The suffix is the second word.
When combined, the two words form an adjective.

▷ **Rule 2**
When -able is added to a word that ends in -e, the *e* is usually removed.

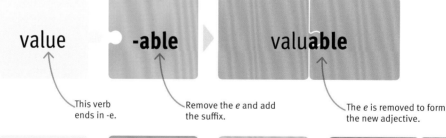

This verb ends in -e.
Remove the *e* and add the suffix.
The *e* is removed to form the new adjective.

▷ **Rule 3**
Often, if a word ends in -y, the *y* is replaced with an *i* before the suffix -able is added.

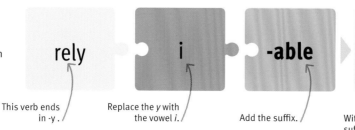

This verb ends in -y.
Replace the *y* with the vowel *i*.
Add the suffix.
With the addition of the suffix, the verb *rely* has been changed into an adjective.

Words ending in -ible

The suffix -ible is usually added to partial root words, many of which have Latin or Greek origins, but it can also be added to complete words. Several rules help to distinguish words that end in -ible from those that end in -able.

▷ **Rule 1**
Most words ending in -ible cannot be divided into two English words that make sense on their own. The suffix is needed in order to make a whole word.

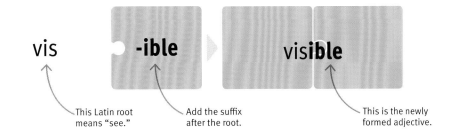

This Latin root means "see."
Add the suffix after the root.
This is the newly formed adjective.

▷ **Rule 2**
Words with *s* or *ss* before the ending usually take -ible. If they end in a vowel, the vowel is dropped.

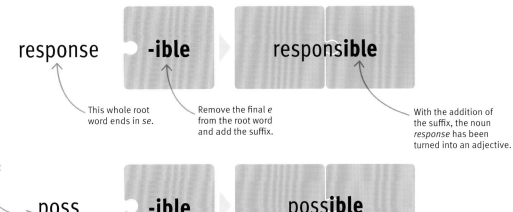

This whole root word ends in *se*.
Remove the final *e* from the root word and add the suffix.
With the addition of the suffix, the noun *response* has been turned into an adjective.

This partial root word ends in a double *s*.

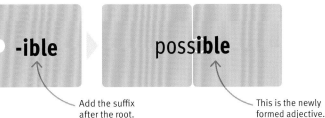

Add the suffix after the root.
This is the newly formed adjective.

Soft and hard "c" and "g" sounds

Words that end in -able usually have a hard "c" or "g" sound. In contrast, words that end in -ible usually have a soft "c" or "g" sound.

Hard "c" or "g" sounds	Soft "c" or "g" sounds
ami**cable**	for**cible**
communi**cable**	invin**cible**
despi**cable**	redu**cible**
indefati**gable**	le**gible**
navi**gable**	tan**gible**

The word *uncopyrightable* is the **longest** English **word** in normal use that contains no letter more than **once**.

• Many words that **begin with** *a* use the **suffix** that also begins with *a*: -able. Some common examples include *adorable*, *advisable*, and *available*.

Words ending in -le, -el, -al, or -ol

THESE WORD ENDINGS ARE NOT USUALLY SUFFIXES.

> **SEE ALSO**
> ‹ 22–23 Nouns
> ‹ 26–27 Adjectives
> ‹ 38–39 Verbs
> ‹ 136–137 Morphemes
> ‹ 140–141 Roots
> ‹ 142–143 Prefixes and suffixes

Similar-sounding word endings like -le, -el, -al, and -ol can cause spelling difficulties. However, there are some guidelines that can help with using them. As with all tricky spellings, a dictionary is a valuable checking tool.

Words ending in -le

The most common of these word endings is -le. This word ending is not a suffix because it does not change the meaning or part of speech of a root word. The -le word ending is usually found in nouns (such as *table*), verbs (such as *tickle*), and adjectives (such as *vile*).

edi*b*le
The letter *b* has a stick and comes before -le.

sam*p*le
The letter *p* has a tail and comes before -le.

wrin*k*le
The letter *k* has a stick and comes before -le.

dan*g*le
The letter *g* has a tail and comes before -le.

△ **The rule**
Words ending in -le are often preceded by a letter with a stick or tail—part of the letter reaching high, as in *b*, or low, as in *p*.

Some other **common words** that end with **-ol** use **oo** to create a long vowel sound, as in the words *cool*, *pool*, *school*, and *tool*.

> article
> missile   regale   role
> textile   bicycle   bale
> chronicle   axle   capsule
> docile   hostile   debacle
> revile
> aisle

Of course, a number of words that end with -le do not follow this rule. Some commonly used ones are listed here.

> **GLOSSARY**
>
> **Adjective** A word that describes a noun.
> **Noun** A word that refers to a person, place, or thing.
> **Root** The smallest part of a word without a prefix or suffix attached.
> **Suffix** A group of letters attached to the end of a word that can change the word's meaning.
> **Verb** A word that describes an action.
> **Vowel** One of the five letters *a*, *e*, *i*, *o*, and *u*.

WORDS ENDING IN -LE, -EL, -AL, OR -OL

Words ending in -el and -al

As is the case with -le, the word endings -el and -al generally do not act as suffixes because they are not changing a root word's meaning or part of speech.

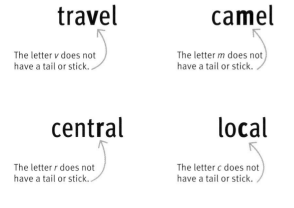

△ **The rule**
Words ending in -el and -al are often preceded by a letter without a stick or tail (part of the letter reaching high or low).

-el exceptions	-al exceptions
angel	acquittal
bagel	betrayal
chapel	capital
compel	coastal
decibel	frugal
gel	fundamental
gospel	homicidal
hostel	hospital
hotel	judgmental
model	mental
nickel	municipal
parallel	orbital
propel	petal
scalpel	portal
snorkel	verbal

△ **Exceptions to the rule**
As with words ending in -le, there are a number of exceptions, which end in -el or -al but do not follow this rule.

The -al ending as a suffix

The word ending -al can also be used as a suffix because it can sometimes change the meaning of a root word. Words that end with this suffix are usually nouns or adjectives.

▽ **The rule**
The -al ending can act as a suffix that attaches to a root word, which can be a whole word or part of a word.

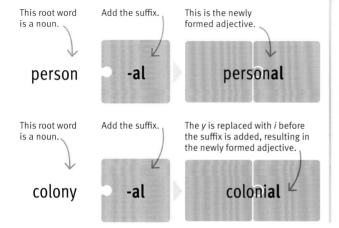

Words ending in -ol

On rare occasions, -ol is also used as a word ending. This ending is usually found in nouns and verbs. If in doubt, always check the spelling in a dictionary before using it.

Here are ten nouns and verbs that end with -ol.

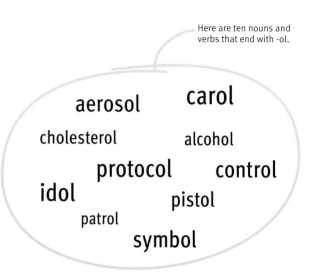

Single and double consonant words

SINGLE AND DOUBLE CONSONANTS USUALLY SOUND THE SAME.

SEE ALSO	
‹ 130–131	Vowel sounds
‹ 132–133	Consonant sounds
‹ 134–135	Syllables
‹ 136–137	Morphemes
‹ 140–141	Roots
‹ 142–143	Prefixes and suffixes
‹ 144–145	Hard and soft letter sounds
‹ 152–153	Words ending in -le, -el, -al, or -ol
Silent letters	160–161 ›
Compound words	162–163 ›

It is not always obvious if a word contains a single or a double consonant—some spellings just have to be learned. However, there are a few rules that can help.

Consonants and short vowel sounds

In words with more than one syllable, if the first syllable is stressed and has a short vowel sound, then the following consonant is doubled. For example, the word *letter* has a double *t* because the first syllable, *let*, is stressed and has a short vowel sound. Compare this to *retire*, which does not have a double *t*. This is because the stress is on the second syllable, *tire*, which has a long vowel sound.

• The letters *h*, *w*, *x*, and *y* are **never** doubled, even when a suffix beginning with a **vowel** is added. For example, the consonant is not doubled in the words **washed**, **drawer**, **fixable**, and **flying**.

de**p**art
The letter *p* is not doubled because the stress is on the second syllable, *part*.

ha**mm**er
The letter *m* is doubled because the stress is on the first syllable, *ham*.

pre**p**are
The letter *p* is not doubled because the stress is on the second syllable, *pare*.

va**ll**ey
The letter *l* is doubled because the stress is on the first syllable, *val*.

Exceptions to the rule

Many words do not follow the rule above. In most cases, these are root words and are therefore not attached to a prefix or suffix. Some of these words, such as *melon*, have a single consonant after a short vowel sound. Double consonants can also occur after unstressed syllables, as in *correct*. These exceptions can make spelling difficult, so check a dictionary if uncertain.

Single consonant	Double consonant
comet	accept
domino	accumulate
epic	correct
galaxy	effect
lizard	necessary
melon	occur
palace	recommend
radish	sufficient
valid	terrific

Double consonants and suffixes

Consonants that come at the end of a word are often doubled when a suffix is added. This mostly applies to verbs. For example, the final consonant of the verb *sit* is doubled after adding the suffix -ing, which results in the word *sitting*.

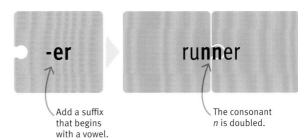

• Consonants are **doubled** when adding a **prefix** or **another word** that ends with the same letter as the first letter of the root. For example, the prefix **mis-** and root **spell** combine to make **misspell**.

▷ **Rule 1**
When adding a suffix that begins with a vowel, such as -er, to a verb that has one syllable and ends with a short vowel sound and a consonant, the final consonant is often doubled.

The syllable *run* has a short vowel sound and ends with a consonant.

Add a suffix that begins with a vowel.

The consonant *n* is doubled.

▷ **Rule 2**
When adding a suffix that begins with a vowel, such as -ing, to a verb with more than one syllable, which ends with a short vowel sound and a consonant, the final consonant is usually doubled.

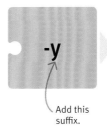
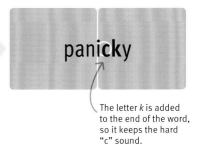

The second syllable, *gin*, ends with a short vowel sound and a consonant.

Add a suffix that begins with a vowel.

The consonant *n* is doubled.

▷ **Rule 3**
When adding a suffix that begins with *e*, *i*, or *y* to a verb that ends in *c*, the final consonant is not doubled. Instead, the letter *k* is added after *c* in order to keep the hard "c" sound.

panic → -y → panicky

The word ends with the letter *c*.

Add this suffix.

The letter *k* is added to the end of the word, so it keeps the hard "c" sound.

GLOSSARY

Consonant A letter of the alphabet that is not a vowel.
Prefix A group of letters attached to the start of a word that can change the original word's meaning.
Suffix A group of letters attached to the end of a word that can change the original word's meaning.
Syllable A unit of pronunciation that has one vowel sound.
Vowel One of the five letters *a*, *e*, *i*, *o*, and *u*.

In English, ***bookkeeper*** and ***bookkeeping*** are the only words with **three** consecutive **double letters**.

The "*i* before *e* except after *c*" rule

THE "*I* BEFORE *E* EXCEPT AFTER *C*" RULE IS USED TO REMEMBER SPELLINGS CONTAINING *IE* OR *EI*.

This rule has been used for more than 150 years, and it works in the majority of cases. There are, however, many exceptions to the rule, and it's best to learn these and to be aware of them.

SEE ALSO	
‹ 130–131 Vowel sounds	
‹ 138–139 Understanding English irregularities	
Irregular word spellings	164–165 ›

• There are **no *cein*** words in the English language. If a *c* is followed by an *ie/ei* combination then an *n*, the spelling should **always be *ie***, as in ***science***.

The rhyme

A useful rhyme was created to help people remember the "*i* before *e*" rule. Originally, it consisted of only two lines, but it has been expanded over the years to include some exceptions to the rule.

The start of the rhyme means that *i* usually comes before *e* in words that contain an "ee" sound, such as *thief*.

I before e,
Except after c
When the sound is "ee"
Or when sounded as "ay,"
As in neighbor and weigh,
But leisure and seize
Do as they please.

However, when the "ee" sound comes after the letter *c*, the *e* goes before the *i*, as in *receive*.

The *e* also goes first when the sound in the word is "ay," as in *eight*.

The end of the rhyme notes that there are some words that don't follow any particular rule.

REAL WORLD
Loan words

A word that has been borrowed from another language is called a loan word. Many loan words use an *e* before *i* spelling. These words include *geisha* from Japanese, *sheikh* from Arabic, and *rottweiler* from German. Many names borrowed from foreign languages are also spelled with the *e* first, such as *Keith*, *Heidi*, *Neil*, and *Sheila*.

• If in **doubt**, always use a **dictionary** to confirm whether a word uses *ie* or *ei*.

THE "*I* BEFORE *E* EXCEPT AFTER *C*" RULE

Single syllable sounds

As mentioned in the rhyme, the sound of the *ie* or *ei* can be used to figure out which letter combination is right. There are four main rules to remember if the *ie/ei* is pronounced as one syllable. However, most of the rules have exceptions, which have to be learned.

Rule 1
If the sound is "ee," the *i* goes before the *e*.

niece, belief, achieve, field

There are numerous exceptions to this rule that have to be learned.

protein, seize, either, leisure, caffeine

Rule 2
If the "ee" sound follows the letter *c*, the *e* goes first.

receive, receipt, deceit, ceiling

One exception to this rule is when the *ci* sounds like "sh."

ancient, conscience, species

The rule also doesn't apply to words ending in *y* that have been modified.

fancied, policies, bouncier

Rule 3
The *e* goes before the *i* if the sound is "ay" or "eye."

eight, height, feisty

Sometimes, the "eye" sound can also be heard when the *i* goes before *e*.

die, pie, lie, cried

Rule 4
The *e* goes before the *i* if the sound is "eh," as in *met*.

heifer, their, heir

exceptions to this rule

friend, unfriendly

Double syllable sounds

If the *i* and *e* are pronounced as two different sounds, it's easy to figure out which letter comes first. If the "i" sound is pronounced first, then the *i* comes first in the spelling, and vice versa.

di-et, a-li-en, sci-ence, so-ci-e-ty

Pronounced *i* then *e*
In these words, the *i* syllable is said first, so the *i* comes first in the spelling.

de-i-ty, see-ing, be-ing, re-ig-nite, here-in

Pronounced *e* then *i*
In these words, the *e* syllable is said first, so the *e* comes first in the spelling.

Capital letters

THE MOST COMMON USE OF A CAPITAL LETTER IS AT THE BEGINNING OF A SENTENCE.

In addition to starting sentences, capital letters are used for the names of people and places, and expressions of time, such as days of the week.

SEE ALSO	
⟨ 22–23 Nouns	
⟨ 34–35 Pronouns	
⟨ 68–69 Sentences	
⟨ 92–93 What is punctuation?	
⟨ 94–95 Periods and ellipses	
Abbreviations	172–173 ⟩
Making sentences interesting	184–185 ⟩
Checking and editing	220–221 ⟩

Starting a sentence
The first word of a sentence begins with a capital letter. This draws the reader's attention and emphasizes the beginning of the new sentence. A capital letter follows a period, an exclamation point, or a question mark at the end of the previous sentence.

On that
— The first word in a sentence begins with a capital letter.

Expressions of time
Days of the week, months of the year, and national and religious holidays, such as Christmas, are all written with capital letters. However, the names of the seasons, such as winter, are never capitalized. Historical periods and events, such as the Industrial Revolution and the Olympic Games, are always capitalized.

Saturday
— The days of the week are always capitalized.

Bronze **A**ge
— Both letters are capitalized for this historical period.

Halloween
— Celebrations are always capitalized.

On that **S**aturday afternoon in **O**livia as she hurried to meet her

• Remember to begin every **quotation** with a capital letter.

A, H, I, M, O, T, U, V, W, X, and **Y** are all **symmetrical** capital letters.

REAL WORLD
Capital letters and titles

The titles of books, plays, songs, newspapers, movies, and poems require capital letters. Smaller words within a title, such as the articles *a* and *the*, or the prepositions *of* and *in*, are not usually capitalized unless they are at the start of a title. For example, *The New York Times* spells *The* with a capital *T* because it is the first word of the newspaper's title.

CAPITAL LETTERS

- Unlike other pronouns, such as *you*, *he*, *she*, *it*, and *them*, *I* is **always spelled** with a **capital letter**.

The English alphabet **originally only had capital letters**. Lowercase letters were introduced in the **eighth century CE**.

Identifying when to use capital letters

It's important to use capital letters correctly so it's clear where one sentence ends and another begins. Proper nouns must also be capitalized, so that the names of people or places, or expressions of time, can be easily distinguished from other common things.

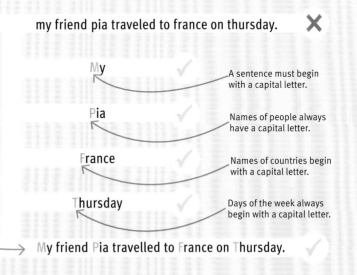

my friend pia traveled to france on thursday. ✗

My ✓ — A sentence must begin with a capital letter.

Pia ✓ — Names of people always have a capital letter.

France ✓ — Names of countries begin with a capital letter.

Thursday ✓ — Days of the week always begin with a capital letter.

All the capital letters are used correctly here. → **M**y friend **P**ia travelled to **F**rance on **T**hursday. ✓

San **F**rancisco, the rain drenched friends at the **K**atwalk **C**afé.

People and places

Proper nouns, such as the names of people or places, always begin with a capital letter. A capital letter is also required when describing a specific place, such as "the South," which may refer to the southern region of a country. However, capital letters are not required when indicating a general direction, as in "north of the shopping center."

San **F**rancisco — A city requires a capital letter. For cities with two parts, both words are capitalized.

Olivia — The name of a person must be capitalized.

River **N**ile — Both parts of this specific river name are capitalized.

Katwalk **C**afé — Both parts are capitalized as they form the name of a place of business.

Disneyland — This is the name of a place, so it is capitalized.

Africa — Names of continents are capitalized.

Silent letters

A SILENT LETTER IS WRITTEN BUT NOT PRONOUNCED.

English includes many words with silent letters. This can sometimes make spelling difficult; however, learning to recognize certain patterns can help with spelling these words.

> **SEE ALSO**
> ‹ 130–131 Vowel sounds
> ‹ 132–133 Consonant sounds
> ‹ 134–135 Syllables
> ‹ 136–137 Morphemes
> ‹ 156–157 The "*i* before *e* except after *c*" rule
> Irregular word spellings 164–165 ›

Silent letters

Letters that do not affect the sound of a word are called silent letters. In many cases, these letters were once clearly heard, but over time the pronunciation of the words has changed, even though the spelling has stayed the same.

If the silent *n* is removed, it does not change the sound of this word—but it would be misspelled.

Letter	When it can be silent	Examples
a	before or after another vowel	**a**isle, coco**a**, he**a**d
b	after *m*	crum**b**, lim**b**, thum**b**
	before *t*	de**b**t, dou**b**t, su**b**tle
c	after *s*	mus**c**le, s**c**ent, s**c**issors
d	before or after *n*	We**d**nesday, han**d**some, lan**d**scape
e	at the end of a word	giraff**e**, humbl**e**, lov**e**
g	before *h*	dau**g**hter, thou**g**h, wei**g**h
	before *n*	campai**g**n, forei**g**n, **g**nome
h	at the beginning of a word	**h**eir, **h**onest, **h**our
	after *ex*	ex**h**austing, ex**h**ibition, ex**h**ilarate
	after *g*	g**h**astly, g**h**ost, g**h**oul
	after *r*	r**h**apsody, r**h**inoceros, r**h**yme
	after *w*	w**h**ale, w**h**eel, w**h**irlpool
k	before *n*	**k**nee, **k**night, **k**now
l	before *d*	cou**l**d, shou**l**d, wou**l**d
	before *f*	beha**l**f, ca**l**f, ha**l**f
	before *m*	a**l**mond, ca**l**m, pa**l**m
n	after *m*	autum**n**, hym**n**, solem**n**
p	before *n*	**p**neumatic, **p**neumonia, **p**neumonic
	before *s*	**p**salm, **p**sychiatry, **p**sychic
	before *t*	**p**teranodon, **p**terodactyl, recei**p**t
t	before *ch*	ca**t**ch, stre**t**ch, wi**t**ch
	after *s*	cas**t**le, Chris**t**mas, lis**t**en
u	with other vowels	b**u**ilding, co**u**rt, g**u**ess
w	before *r*	**w**reck, **w**rite, **w**rong
	with *s* or *t*	ans**w**er, s**w**ord, t**w**o

SILENT LETTERS

Auxiliary letters

An auxiliary letter is a type of silent letter that can change the pronunciation of a word. For example, if the letter *a* in *coat* is removed, this would spell another word, *cot*, which sounds different and has a different meaning from *coat*.

Here, the silent *e* is an auxiliary letter because, if it is removed, the sound changes. It would also be confused with the existing word *kit*.

Letter	When it can be silent	Examples
a	after *o*	bo**a**t, co**a**t, go**a**t
b	after *m*	clim**b**, com**b**, tom**b**
c	before *t*	indi**c**t
d	before *g*	ba**d**ge, do**d**ge, ju**d**ge
e	at the end of a word	hop**e**, kit**e**, sit**e**
g	after *i* and before *n*	beni**g**n, desi**g**n, si**g**n
	after *i* and before *m*	paradi**g**m
h	after *c*	ac**h**e
i	only in one word	bus**i**ness
l	before *k*	fo**l**k, ta**l**k, wa**l**k
	before *m*	ca**l**m, pa**l**m
s	after *i*	ai**s**le, i**s**land
w	before *h*	**w**ho, **w**hom, **w**hose

Regional variations

One aspect that varies from one accent to the next is the silencing and sounding of particular letters. The English language includes a range of regional accents, each with its own peculiarities. Even so, two people raised in the same region might pronounce the same word differently.

Some speakers don't pronounce the final *r* in this word.

Letter	When it can be either silent or heard	Examples
h	before *e*	**h**erb
	after *w*	w**h**ich, w**h**ip, w**h**iskey
r	after a vowel	bo**r**n, ca**r**, sta**r**
t	before or after another consonant	of**t**en, fas**t**en, **t**sunami

About **60 percent** of English words contain a **silent letter**.

- Some words that contain silent letters stem from **other languages**. The words *knife*, *knock* and *know*, which all have a **silent k**, are **Old Norse** words. The words *bright*, *daughter* and *night*, which all contain the **silent gh**, are **Anglo-Saxon** words.

Compound words

A NEW WORD FORMED FROM THE UNION OF TWO WORDS IS CALLED A COMPOUND WORD.

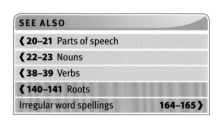

SEE ALSO	
‹ 20–21 Parts of speech	
‹ 22–23 Nouns	
‹ 38–39 Verbs	
‹ 140–141 Roots	
Irregular word spellings	164–165 ›

A compound word is made up of two smaller words that have been joined together. There are many compound words in the English language.

Adding detail

Some words are joined to other words to add detail, making the resulting compound word more specific. For example, the word *house* can modify the word *boat* to create the new compound word *houseboat*. The word *boat* can be modified again with other words, such as *motor* and *steam*, to create new compound words that describe other types of boats: For example, *motorboat* and *steamboat*.

The word *house* modifies the word *boat* to specify a type of boat: a *houseboat*.

 house  boat **houseboat**

The word *cheese* modifies the word *cake* to specify a type of cake: *cheesecake*.

 cheese cake **cheesecake**

- Most compound words are nouns. Verbs formed from two words tend to stay as two words: For example, the verb *turn around* **can be distinguished from the compound word** *turnaround*—a noun that usually refers to the act of processing or completing something.

GLOSSARY

Noun A part of speech that refers to a person, place, or thing.
Verb A part of speech that describes an action.

Word 1	Word 2	Compound word
air	craft	aircraft
baby	sitter	babysitter
book	keeper	bookkeeper
card	board	cardboard
dish	washer	dishwasher
fire	place	fireplace
ginger	bread	gingerbread
horse	shoe	horseshoe
key	hole	keyhole
news	paper	newspaper
river	side	riverside
snow	flake	snowflake
sun	rise	sunrise
tax	payer	taxpayer
wall	paper	wallpaper

New meaning

This type of compound word is formed when two smaller words are combined to form a new word that is unrelated to the original words. For example, *hogwash* is made up of two words, *hog* (a type of swine) and *wash* (to cleanse). When combined, these words form the compound word *hogwash*—a noun that describes something as nonsense.

The word *glove* combines with the word *fox*, resulting in a type of plant: *foxglove*.

fox   glove   **foxglove**

The word *tail* combines with the word *pony*, resulting in a type of hairstyle: a *ponytail*.

pony   tail   **ponytail**

Word 1	Word 2	Compound word
block	buster	blockbuster
cart	wheel	cartwheel
heart	beat	heartbeat
honey	moon	honeymoon
in	come	income
life	style	lifestyle
lime	light	limelight
master	piece	masterpiece
off	shoot	offshoot
over	come	overcome
scare	crow	scarecrow
show	case	showcase
sleep	walk	sleepwalk
type	writer	typewriter
wind	shield	windshield

Some languages, such as German and Finnish, **can combine three words**. For example, *Farbfernsehgerät* means "color television set" in German.

- Two words can be joined together to form a compound word if the combination creates **one idea or item**, such as *afterlife* or *backbone*. If two words do not create one idea or item, they should stay separate.

REAL WORLD
Evolving compound words

Some words go together so often that they might at first seem to be compound words, such as *post office*, *half moon*, and *ice cream*. Many words begin as two separate words (*wild life*), then become hyphenated (*wild-life*), and then, eventually, become a compound word (*wildlife*).

Irregular word spellings

SOME SPELLINGS DON'T FOLLOW ANY RULES.

The only way to remember irregular spellings is to learn them. However, there are ways to do this that are more fun than just staring at the words.

> SEE ALSO
> ⟨ 134–135 Syllables
> ⟨ 138–139 Understanding English irregularities
> ⟨ 156–157 The "*i* before *e* except after *c*" rule

Weird words

Some words are difficult to spell because they are not spelled like they sound. For example, *said* rhymes with *led* and *fed* but is spelled very differently. Other irregular spellings are tricky because they go against common rules. For example, the word *foreign* does not follow the "*i* before *e* except after *c*" rule.

- One way to learn a spelling is to put up **reminders** everywhere. Write the **troublesome word** in **large letters**, and then put it on the **wall** or anywhere around the house where it will be seen **throughout the day**.

A
accidentally
again
archaeology
asthma

E
Egypt
embarrassed
enough
especially

L
lawyer
leopard
liaison

S
school
soldier
straight
surprise

B
beautiful
because
beginning
beige

F
fluorescent
foreign
forty

M
mischievous

N
nuisance

T
Tuesday
tomorrow
tongue
twelfth

C
circuit
conscience
cough
country

G
geography
graffiti
guarantee

O
ocean

P
particularly
people
pharaoh
psychology

V
vicious

H
height

W
weird

D
definitely
disappear
disguise
does

J
jeopardy
jewel

R
raspberry
restaurant
rhythm
rough

Y
yacht
young

K
knee

IRREGULAR WORD SPELLINGS

Write it out
One technique to learn a spelling is to look at the word, cover it up, write it out from memory, then check it. Do this as many times as necessary until the word is right.

LOOK

COVER

WRITE

CHECK

What's the problem?
Another way to learn an irregular spelling is to investigate what makes it so difficult. Look at the word and underline the part that is strange or hard to remember. Highlighting the problem will make it easier to recall.

le*o*pard — The *o* is silent.

rest*au*rant — The *au* sounds like it should be spelled *er*.

twel*fth* — It's strange that this word uses an *f* and *th* to make the final sound.

Speak differently
If a word isn't written how it sounds, say it out loud, pronouncing it so that it does match the spelling.

defin*I*Tely — Try stressing *it* to remember that it isn't spelled *at*.

WED NES DAY — Say this word in its separate parts to make it easier to spell.

particul*ARLY* — Start to stress the *arly* to remember that it isn't spelled *erly*.

Words within words
Another trick is to look for smaller words in longer ones. This will associate the longer word with the smaller word. Visualizing these small words with pictures will make spelling the longer word much easier.

Draw images like this to visualize the words within words.

There is a **rat** in sep**a**rate

Silly sayings
Making up ridiculous phrases can help people to remember spellings. These are called mnemonic devices. One method is to think of a phrase whose words begin with each letter in the tricky word. Other sayings can remind people of the number of particular letters in a word.

RHYTHM — **R**hythm **H**elps **Y**our **T**wo **H**ips **M**ove

Each word in the saying starts with a letter from the spelling.

BECAUSE — **B**ig **E**lephants **C**an't **A**lways **U**se **S**mall **E**xits

NECESSARY — One **c**offee with two **s**ugars

This saying reminds people that the word has one *c* and two *s*'s.

Homonyms, homophones, and homographs

SOME WORDS HAVE THE SAME PRONUNCIATION OR SPELLING BUT MEAN DIFFERENT THINGS.

SEE ALSO	
‹ 78–79 Commonly misused words	
‹ 140–141 Roots	
‹ 142–143 Prefixes and suffixes	
‹ 160–161 Silent letters	
‹ 164–165 Irregular word spellings	
Writing to describe	208–209 ›

Variations in pronunciation or spelling are what distinguish homonyms, homophones, and homographs. Using the correct word is important for both spoken and written English.

Homonyms
Words with the same spelling and pronunciation, but different meanings, are called homonyms. For example, the word *fair* can refer to an event with games and rides or to the idea of treating somebody in a reasonable way.

The word **homonym** come from the Greek **homos**, which means "**same**," and **onyma**, which means "**name**."

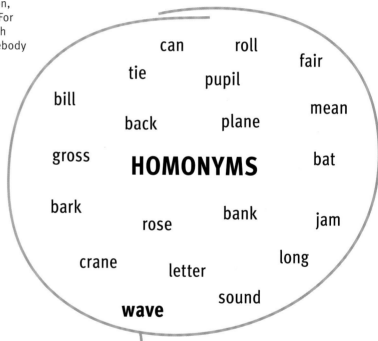

HOMONYMS: can, roll, fair, tie, pupil, bill, back, plane, mean, gross, bat, bark, rose, bank, jam, crane, letter, long, sound, wave

Homonyms have the same pronunciation and spelling.

REAL WORLD
Crossword puzzles
Crossword puzzles can be difficult without a good understanding of homonyms, homophones, and homographs. The clues in cryptic crosswords take advantage of the confusion caused by these words in order to mislead the reader.

▷ **Wave**
The homonym *wave* has several meanings. These include the kind of wave caused by ocean currents, as well as the movement of a hand as a greeting gesture or signal.

Homophones

Words with identical pronunciation but different spellings and meanings are called homophones, which means "same sound" in Greek. Most homophones come in pairs, such as *reed* and *read*; however, there are also some groups of three words, as in *to*, *too*, and *two*.

Homophones have the same pronunciation but different spellings.

HOMOPHONES

- which/witch
- read/reed
- to/too/two
- week/weak
- dear/deer
- pair/pear
- buy/by/bye
- stair/stare
- knight/night
- cite/site/sight
- I/eye
- sent/cent/scent
- for/four
- bare/bear
- die/dye

△ **Pear and pair**
The words *pear* and *pair* are homophones. The first word refers to an edible fruit, and the second word means two of something.

Homographs

Words that are spelled the same but pronounced differently, with different meanings, are called homographs, which means "same writing" in Greek. For example, the word *tear* can refer to a watery discharge from the eye or a rip in something.

Homographs have different pronunciations but the same spelling.

HOMOGRAPHS

- reject
- putting
- minute
- bow
- tear
- content
- live
- lead
- object
- wind
- bass
- contract
- refuse
- produce
- wound
- row
- project
- close
- does
- sow

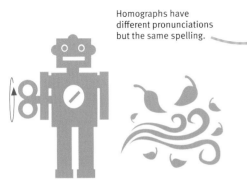

△ **Wind**
The homograph *wind* has two meanings. One relates to a turning or twisting action, and the other refers to a strong breeze.

Confusing words

SIMILAR-SOUNDING WORDS CAN BE DIFFICULT TO SPELL.

SEE ALSO	
‹ 136–137 Morphemes	
‹ 142–143 Prefixes and suffixes	
‹ 162–163 Compound words	
‹ 166–167 Homonyms, homophones, and homographs	
Other confusing words	170–171 ›

English includes many words that look and sound the same, or nearly the same. Recognizing small differences in pronunciation can help with spelling.

Noun and verb confusion

Some nouns and verbs are often confused because of their similar or identical pronunciation. In some cases, a small change in the sound of a word can indicate a different part of speech, as in the noun *advice* and verb *advise*. More often, however, words have the same pronunciation but a different spelling and meaning, as in *effect* and *affect*.

advice or **advise**
This noun refers to guidance. / This verb means to offer suggestions.

Their **advice** was helpful. / I asked her to **advise** me.

altar or **alter**
This noun refers to a table in a church. / This verb means to change something.

The priest stood at the **altar**. / He tried to **alter** the results.

breath or **breathe**
This noun refers to air taken in or out of the lungs. / This verb means to take air in and out of the lungs.

She took a deep **breath**. / He had to **breathe** hard while jogging.

ceiling or **sealing**
This noun refers to the upper surface of a room. / This verb means to close securely.

The new light hung from the **ceiling**. / The plumber is **sealing** the gap.

device or **devise**
This noun refers to a piece of equipment. / This verb means to plan or invent.

I bought a new phone **device**. / The team will **devise** a website.

effect or **affect**
This noun refers to the result of an action. / This verb means to have an impact on.

The protest had a positive **effect**. / The fight **affect**ed him badly.

lesson
This noun refers to a period of teaching.

 or

lessen
This verb means to reduce.

She enjoyed her piano **lesson**.

I must **lessen** my grip on the rope.

weight
This noun refers to mass contained by an object.

 or

wait
This verb means to stay or delay an action.

The bag's **weight** is immense.

I must **wait** for my brother.

Commonly misspelled words

There are many other words that sound the same or similar to each other, but have different spellings and meanings. In all cases, it's important to use the correct word in order to be understood, particularly in written form. If uncertain which is the correct word to use, check a dictionary.

Word	Example sentence
are	Those boys **are** always getting into trouble.
hear	I could **hear** the plane flying overhead.
know	The taxi driver didn't **know** the way to my house.
lose	There was no way she could **lose** in the finals.
passed	He **passed** the present to his friend.
weather	The **weather** report predicted snowfall.

Word	Example sentence
our	**Our** team was invited to the national championships.
here	**Here** is the latest photo of my family.
now	There is **now** a café where my house used to be.
loose	My friend's **loose** change fell out of his pocket.
past	She drove **past** the park on the way home.
whether	I am not sure **whether** to wear my coat today or not.

One or two words?

Some phrases have different meanings according to whether they are spelled as one word or two. For example, the single word *everyday* means routine or commonplace, whereas *every day* means each day.

Word	Example sentence
anyone	**Anyone** caught smoking will be punished.
already	Our passports have **already** been inspected.
altogether	The song was **altogether** inappropriate.
everyday	I was wearing **everyday** clothes around the house.
maybe	**Maybe** one day they will uncover the truth.

Phrase	Example sentence
any one	**Any one** of those people could be to blame.
all ready	We are **all ready** to board the plane.
all together	The paintings were exhibited **all together** for the first time.
every day	I need to use a hairdryer **every day** after my shower.
may be	There **may be** more than one culprit.

• Learning the meanings of commonly used **roots**, **prefixes**, and **suffixes** can help with confusing words.

Other confusing words

MISSPELLED WORDS OFTEN ARISE FROM CONFUSED MEANINGS.

Some words are misunderstood and therefore spelled incorrectly. Choosing the wrong word can alter the meaning of a sentence, which may confuse the reader.

SEE ALSO
‹ 104–105 Apostrophes
‹ 166–167 Homonyms, homophones, and homographs
‹ 168–169 Confusing words

Confused meanings

Some words are incorrectly spelled because their meanings are not properly understood. In some cases, two words may sound similar, which only adds to the confusion.

With such words, the difference in meaning and spelling has to be learned; there is no trick or rule to remember. Consult a dictionary if in doubt about which word to use.

adapt **adopt**
This refers to making something suitable. | This can mean to follow an idea or method.

A fish can **adapt** to a new habitat. | They will **adopt** the new policy.

conscience **conscious**
This refers to a sense of right or wrong. | This means to be aware or awake.

Her **conscience** told her to confess. | He was **conscious** of his faults.

disinterested **uninterested**
This refers to an impartial person. | This means having no interest.

The **disinterested** reporter is talking. | He is **uninterested** in the show.

distinct or **distinctive**
This refers to something that is different. | This means a feature of a person or thing.

There are two **distinct** cell types. | She had a **distinctive** voice.

historic **historical**
This refers to something famous in history. | This means something linked to the past.

The moon landing is a **historic** event. | The museum held **historical** relics.

regretful **regrettable**
This refers to the feeling of regret. | This means to give rise to regret.

She was **regretful** for her actions. | The loss of jobs was **regrettable**.

OTHER CONFUSING WORDS

Triple trouble

Sometimes, three words sound very similar but mean different things. In such cases, be extra careful to understand the differences between the three words and learn the spellings.

though
This means the same as the word *however*.

 or

through
This means into one end and out of the other.

 or

thorough
This refers to something that is well done or complete.

He still wanted to go shopping, **though**.

He walked **through** the crowd.

He conducted a **thorough** investigation.

quit
This means to leave, usually permanently.

 or

quiet
This refers to making little or no noise.

 or

quite
This usually refers to the greatest extent or degree.

The journalist **quit** her job at the newspaper.

It seemed eerily **quiet** along the street.

The story made **quite** an impression on her.

More confused meanings

There are many examples of words that are widely and repeatedly misspelled because their meanings are not clearly understood. Always reread the sentence to make sure the correct word is used.

Word	Example
accident	The bicycle **accident** left her with a large bruise.
angel	The religious text mentioned an **angel**.
desert	It was very hot in the middle of the **desert**.
elicit	The father tried to **elicit** a response from his son.
envelop	The fog was about to **envelop** the town.
lightening	The hairdresser was **lightening** my hair.
rational	There was no **rational** reason for her behavior.

Word	Example
incident	There was an **incident** of bullying on the team.
angle	Every **angle** in a square is the same size.
dessert	My favorite **dessert** is key lime pie.
illicit	The airport confiscated **illicit** food from the man.
envelope	He put the letter in an **envelope**.
lightning	The **lightning** storm caused havoc.
rationale	She explained the **rationale** for her decision.

REAL WORLD
Funny puns

Tabloid newspapers are renowned for their use of puns in headlines. Puns take advantage of the potential confusion between words that sound the same to create jokes or wry commentary.

Abbreviations

A WORD OR PHRASE THAT IS WRITTEN IN A SHORTENED FORM IS CALLED AN ABBREVIATION.

SEE ALSO	
‹ 94–95 Periods and ellipses	
‹ 158–159 Capital letters	
‹ 164–165 Irregular word spellings	
Picking the right words	182–183 ›

The English language contains many abbreviations, which are used to represent longer words or phrases in speech, or where space is limited. In some cases, the abbreviation is better known than the full name.

The symbol @ is an abbreviation for "at" and is used in **e-mail addresses** and **text messsages**.

Common abbreviations

The way an abbreviation is written usually depends on the category to which it belongs. Often, a period is used to represent missing text. For abbreviated Latin phrases, periods are used after each letter. Abbreviations that are formed from the initial letters of a group of words usually don't use periods.

REAL WORLD
NASA

One of the world's most recognized abbreviations is the name of the American government agency NASA, which stands for the National Aeronautics and Space Administration. The first letter from each word forms this acronym—an abbreviation that is pronounced as a word, not as separate letters. The NASA logo shown here is on the side of a space shuttle.

Abbreviation	Words in full
3-D	three-dimensional
a.m.	*ante meridiem* (Latin); before noon (English)
b.	born (indicating birth date)
BCE	before the Common Era
Brit.	British
C	Centigrade or Celsius
CE	Common Era
dept.	department
DIY	do-it-yourself
ed.	edition or editor
e.g.	*exempli gratia* (Latin); for example (English)
est.	established or estimated
EST	Eastern Standard Time
etc.	*et cetera* (Latin); and the rest (English)
EU	European Union
F	Fahrenheit
FAQ	frequently asked questions
GMT	Greenwich Mean Time
HTML	HyperText Markup Language

Abbreviation	Words in full
i.e.	*id est* (Latin); that is (English)
IOU	I owe you
LED	light-emitting diode
long.	longitude
MD	medical doctor
Mr.	Mister
Mrs.	Mistress (referring to wife)
PDF	Portable Document Format
percent	*per centum* (Latin); in each hundred (English)
p.m.	*post meridiem* (Latin); after noon (English)
PM	Prime Minister
Pres.	President
P.S.	*post scriptum* (Latin); written after (English)
PTO	please turn over
SMS	Short Message Service
UK	United Kingdom
US	United States
USB	Universal Serial Bus
www	World Wide Web

ABBREVIATIONS

Shortenings

A shortening is a representation of a single word, typically in lowercase letters. Usually, the beginning or the end of a word is dropped; in rare cases, both the beginning and end of a word are omitted. The use of a period depends on whether the abbreviation is formal or informal. Occasionally, shortening results in spelling changes, as when *bicycle* is changed to *bike*.

advertisement ▶ **ad**
The first two letters produce this informal word.

in**flu**enza ▶ **flu**
The three middle letters make this informal word.

latitude ▶ **lat.**
The first three letters create this formal abbreviation, which requires a period.

we**blog** ▶ **blog**
The last four letters create this informal word.

Contracted abbreviations

A contracted abbreviation occurs when letters from the middle of a word are removed. These words are usually related to a position or qualification. This type of abbreviation usually begins with a capital letter. A period is normally used at the end of a contracted abbreviation.

Docto**r** ▶ **Dr.**
Take out the middle four letters to get this abbreviation.

Junio**r** ▶ **Jr.**
Remove the middle four letters to form this abbreviation.

Limit**e**d ▶ **Ltd.**
Remove the letters *imi* and *e* to make this abbreviation.

Ser**g**ean**t** ▶ **Sgt.**
Remove the letters *er* and *ean* to create this abbreviation.

Initialisms

An initialism is created from the first letter of each word. Each letter is pronounced separately and written in capital letters. Initialisms generally don't require periods between the letters.

United **S**tates of **A**merica ▶ **USA**

British **B**roadcasting **C**orporation ▶ **BBC**

Digital **V**ideo **D**isc ▶ **DVD**

Acronyms

An acronym is a word formed from the initial letters of a group of words. It is different from an initialism because it is pronounced as it is spelled, not as separate letters. Acronyms are written in capital letters and without periods.

Acquired **I**mmuno**D**eficiency **S**yndrome ▶ **AIDS**

North **A**tlantic **T**reaty **O**rganization ▶ **NATO**

Personal **I**dentification **N**umber ▶ **PIN**

British and American spellings

BRITISH AND AMERICAN WORDS ARE OFTEN SPELLED USING DIFFERENT ENDINGS.

In British English, the *l* is often doubled before a suffix, but not in American English. Words that end in -ise, -yse, -ce, -re, and -our in British English may also be spelled differently in American English.

> **SEE ALSO**
> ⟨ 142–143 Prefixes and suffixes
> ⟨ 154–155 Single and double consonant words

English-language spelling was first **standardized** by the English writer **Samuel Johnson** in 1755.

Doubling the letter *l*

Words that are written with a double *l* in British English are often written with only a single *l* in American English. This usually occurs when a suffix, such as -or, -ed, -er, or -ing, is added to a word ending in a single *l*.

British English	American English
cancelled	canceled
counsellor	counselor
fuelled	fueled
jeweller	jeweler
marvelled	marveled
modelling	modeling
quarrelled	quarreled
traveller	traveler

Words ending in -ise or -ize and -yse or -yze

Most words that end with -ise or -yse in British English end with -ize or -yze in American English. However, the -ize and -yze spellings are also widely used in Britain.

British English	American English
analyse	analyze
criticise	criticize
hypnotise	hypnotize
mobilise	mobilize
modernise	modernize
organise	organize
recognise	recognize
visualise	visualize

Words ending in -ce or -se

Certain words that end with -ce in British English end with -se in American English. Depending on the part of speech, some words, such as *practice* and *licence*, are spelled in two different ways in British English, whereas this distinction is ignored in American English.

British English	American English
defence	defense
licence (noun); license (verb)	license (noun and verb)
offence	offense
pretence	pretense
practice (noun); practise (verb)	practice (noun and verb)

BRITISH AND AMERICAN SPELLINGS

Words ending in -re or -er

Many British words that end with -re are spelled with -er in American English. This difference is commonly seen in the spelling of metric measurements, such as *metre* and *litre* in British English, compared to *meter* and *liter* in American English.

British English	American English
calibre	caliber
centre	center
fibre	fiber
lustre	luster
meagre	meager
sombre	somber
spectre	specter
theatre	theater

Words ending in -our or -or

Words that end with -our in British English often end with -or in American English. However, in British English, when one of the endings -ous, -ious, -ary, -ation, -ific, -ize, or -ise is added to a noun that ends in -our, the -our is usually changed to -or. For example, *humour* becomes *humorous*, and *glamour* becomes *glamorise*.

British English	American English
behaviour	behavior
colour	color
flavour	flavor
humour	humor
labour	labor
neighbour	neighbor
rumour	rumor
vigour	vigor

Same spelling

Many British and American words are spelled the same, regardless of the rules. In most cases, there is no reason for this and the words just have to be learned. If uncertain, check how words are spelled in a dictionary.

rebelled **endurance** **feather**

mediocre

advertise **exercise**

fooling **actor**

REAL WORLD
Webster's Dictionary

Noah Webster (1758–1843) is frequently credited with introducing American spelling. Webster wanted to emphasize a unique American cultural identity by showing that Americans spoke a different language from the British. He also advocated spelling words phonetically. In 1828, he published *An American Dictionary of the English Language*, which forms the basis of American spelling to this day.

- American and British spellings are both **correct**, as long as one or the other is used **consistently**.
- Occasionally, American English uses the British spelling for **names**, as in the case of the space shuttle ***Endeavour*** or **Ford's Theatre** in Washington, D.C.

More British and American spellings

SPELLING DIFFERENCES BETWEEN BRITISH AND AMERICAN ENGLISH CAN SOMETIMES AFFECT A WORD'S PRONUNCIATION.

SEE ALSO
‹ 142–143 Prefixes and suffixes
‹ 146–147 Words ending in -e or -y
‹ 154–155 Single and double consonant words
‹ 160–161 Silent letters
‹ 162–163 Compound words

Small differences between British and American spellings do not usually change the meaning of a word. However, British English may use two words to indicate two meanings, whereas American English uses the same word for both meanings.

Different sounds or words

A minor change in the spelling of a word can affect its sound, even if the meaning is the same. Occasionally, British and American English use different words to mean the same thing.

British English	American English
aeroplane	airplane
aluminium	aluminum
disorientated	disoriented
pavement	sidewalk
sledge	sleigh or sled

Different meanings

Sometimes, British English uses two words that sound the same but with different spellings to indicate different meanings. American English uses the same word for both meanings.

The **Oxford English Dictionary** is widely thought to be the **authority** on the English language and includes both **British** and **American** spellings.

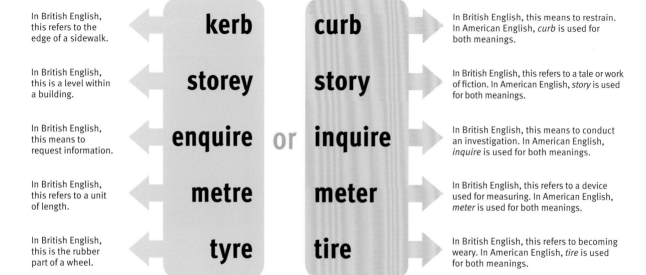

In British English, this refers to the edge of a sidewalk. — **kerb** / **curb** — In British English, this means to restrain. In American English, *curb* is used for both meanings.

In British English, this is a level within a building. — **storey** / **story** — In British English, this refers to a tale or work of fiction. In American English, *story* is used for both meanings.

In British English, this means to request information. — **enquire** or **inquire** — In British English, this means to conduct an investigation. In American English, *inquire* is used for both meanings.

In British English, this refers to a unit of length. — **metre** / **meter** — In British English, this refers to a device used for measuring. In American English, *meter* is used for both meanings.

In British English, this is the rubber part of a wheel. — **tyre** / **tire** — In British English, this refers to becoming weary. In American English, *tire* is used for both meanings.

Silent vowels

In British English, some words have two vowels in a row, one of which is silent. In American English, this silent vowel is usually dropped.

British English	American English
anaemia	anemia
foetus	fetus
manoeuvre	maneuver
paediatric	pediatric
palaeontology	paleontology

Past tenses ending in -ed or -t

When verbs are written in the past tense, their spellings can differ between British and American English. This is mainly the case with verbs in which the last letter is *l*, *m*, or *n*. American English uses the regular ending -ed, whereas British English often uses the irregular ending -t.

British English	American English
burnt or burned	burned
dreamt or dreamed	dreamed
learnt or learned	learned
smelt or smelled	smelled
spelt or spelled	spelled

Retaining or dropping the silent -e

Certain words in American English do not have a silent -e ending, while British spelling usually retains the silent -e. This pattern occurs most commonly when a suffix, such as -ment, has been added to a word that ends in a silent -e.

British English	American English
acknowledgement	acknowledgment
ageing or aging	aging
axe	ax
judgement	judgment
useable or usable	usable

- Some words that are **hyphenated** in British English are **compound words** in American English. For example, British English uses *ear-splitting* and *kind-hearted*, while American English uses *earsplitting* and *kindhearted*.

REAL WORLD
Mid-Atlantic English

In the early part of the twentieth century, many American actors, such as Katharine Hepburn, tried to cultivate an accent that was neither obviously American nor British. This was sometimes called "mid-Atlantic English." The fashion for this accent has disappeared, and today the term is used to refer to written English that avoids obvious "Britishisms" or "Americanisms."

Communication skills

COMMUNICATION SKILLS

Effective communication

GOOD COMMUNICATION SENDS THE RIGHT MESSAGE.

To communicate means to exchange ideas and information with others. Communicating effectively means exchanging ideas and information with others in such a way that they understand precisely what is meant.

Everyday communication

Communicating effectively isn't just about writing an A-grade essay. People need to pass on information in many different scenarios every day. Most communication has a desired effect: for example, to give the recipient information or to persuade them to do something.

Sending an invitation
Giving a friend advice
Making a complaint
Giving travel directions
Selling an item on the Internet
Auditioning for a play

Good communication skills can help in many different situations.

Getting the message

Bad communication will not have the desired effect. For example, an unclear recipe will produce an inedible cake, a lackluster political speech will lose votes, and an incomplete party invitation will confuse the intended guests, who may fail to show up.

This version gives precise details about the time and location.

Please join me to celebrate my birthday on

Saturday, July 14, at 7:00 p.m.

My address is
44 Culver Street, Eureka, CA 95501.

The dress code is formal.

This invitation does not specify what time or where the party is taking place.

> I'm having a party next Saturday. It would be great to see you there. Remember to dress up.

The term *dress up* is vague and could refer to costumes or formal attire.

The exact dress code is specified.

EFFECTIVE COMMUNICATION

Sending the right message
In order to send clear and effective messages, it's important to consider various factors.

LET'S PARTY!
Don't miss the celebration of the year on

Saturday, July 14, at 7:00 p.m.

There will be **food, dancing, fireworks, magic,** and **much, much more**.

My address is
44 Culver Street, Eureka, CA 95501.

HOW TO GET HERE

Tone
Picking the right tone is important. Tone refers to the mood or feeling of a text. For example, a party invitation should be enthusiastic, an advice column should be sympathetic, and a business letter should be formal and serious.

Language
Effective communication should be written using appropriate language. The choice of vocabulary and sentence structures will help to communicate the right message.

Layout
The font size and color, the arrangement of text on the page, and the use of images can simplify a message or draw attention to pieces information. The layout of some forms of communication, such as newspaper articles and letters, follows specific conventions.

Method
It's important to pick the right method of communication, such as an e-mail, newspaper article, or leaflet. People also communicate verbally in a debate or by giving a speech. Nonverbal methods of communication, such as body language and eye contact, should also be considered.

Audience
A message needs to be tailored to its audience. For example, a piece of writing for young children may use simple and fun language, while an adult audience will understand more complicated vocabulary.

This sounds fun...

Purpose
All communication has a purpose. This is the effect that the message should have on the audience. For example, it may be to encourage them to go to a party, to give them advice, or to pass on news.

Picking the right words

EFFECTIVE COMMUNICATION USES VARIED AND APPROPRIATE VOCABULARY.

> **SEE ALSO**
> ‹ 26–27 Adjectives
> ‹ 84–85 Idioms, analogies, and figures of speech
> ‹ 86–87 Colloquialisms and slang
> Genre, purpose, and audience 190–191 ›
> Writing to inform 196–197 ›
> Newspaper articles 198–199 ›
> Writing to describe 208–209 ›
> Writing for the Web 214–215 ›

It's important to pick words that are clear and suit the purpose and audience of the text. Using the same words all the time can be boring, so try to use a varied range of vocabulary.

Avoid overused words

Using a wide range of vocabulary makes a piece of writing more entertaining and original. Here are some overused words to avoid, such as *got* and *great*, and some alternatives, known as synonyms.

very

pleasant   agreeable
charming
incredibly   truly   delightful
unusually
extremely

countless
nice
many   numerous
myriad   acquired
obtained   thrilling
received   entertaining
amusing
enjoyable

lots of   finally   next
wonderful   later
fabulous   incredible   got
fantastic   great   then   fun

Less is more

It's important not to use several words when one will do. Overly long phrases might seem impressive, but they are often unclear. Most long phrases can be replaced with shorter versions.

👍 **Look up** any **new** words and find out what they mean. Then, write them down and try to use them in the **future**.

REAL WORLD
Military jargon

Members of the armed forces use jargon to communicate with one another for speed and secrecy. Many of these terms are abbreviations of longer phrases. For example, *DPV* is an abbreviation for "Desert Patrol Vehicle."

Unclear version	Concise version
she is of the opinion that	she thinks that
concerning the matter of	about
in the event that	if
regardless of the fact that	although
due to the fact that	because
in all cases	always
he is a man who	he
a small number of	a few

PICKING THE RIGHT WORDS

How formal
The words people use depend on the situation they're in and the person they're talking to. In informal situations, people tend to use colloquial words, but when writing to someone they don't know, or someone in authority, they use formal vocabulary.

> Hey, man. This homework sucks. I just don't get it.

A text message to a friend can include slang, such as "Hey, man" and "sucks."

> Dear Mrs. Jones,
>
> Jake experienced some difficulties in completing last night's homework. Although he tried very hard, he could not understand the exercise. He may need some extra help so that he can finish the work.
>
> Yours truly,
> Sheila Jessop

A letter to a teacher should be written in formal language.

Word play
Writers also choose words to entertain readers. By using particular combinations of words, they can create humor and sound patterns. There are three main types of word play: puns, alliteration, and assonance.

Puns
A pun is a play on words. It exploits the multiple meanings of a word, or similar sounding words, to create humor.

Once **a pun** a time...

Alliteration
Alliteration is the effect created when words next to or close to each other begin with the same letter or sound. It is often used in newspaper headlines.

Thomas **T**urner **t**ripped over the **t**able.

Assonance
Assonance is the effect created by the repetition of vowel sounds. It is often used in poetry.

Is it **true you** like **blue**?

Getting technical
Jargon is the term for words or phrases that are only used and understood by members of a particular group or profession. For example, doctors, lawyers, and sports professionals use certain terms to communicate quickly and effectively. However, it's best to avoid using jargon outside of these circles, since it can be meaningless to other people.

Get me his **vitals**.

Doctors use this term to refer to patients' vital statistics, such as their pulse, body temperature, and breathing rate.

Making sentences interesting

THE BEST PIECES OF WRITING USE SENTENCES THAT ARE CLEAR BUT ALSO INTERESTING TO READ.

SEE ALSO	
‹ 26–27 Adjectives	
‹ 40–41 Adverbs	
‹ 58–59 Conjunctions	
‹ 60–61 Prepositions	
‹ 68–69 Sentences	
‹ 70–71 Compound sentences	
‹ 72–73 Complex sentences	
Writing a narrative	212–213 ›

A text containing very similar sentences will be boring to read. Using a variety of sentence types with plenty of detail will make a piece of writing more engaging.

Pick and mix
Good writers vary the types of sentences that they use in their work. Lots of short sentences can make a piece of writing monotonous and disjointed. Using some longer sentences instead helps the writing flow and links ideas together. There are three main types of sentences to choose from.

A monster was on the loose. It came out at night and its howls filled the air. People said that the monster had green fur and red eyes, although no one had ever seen it.

- This simple sentence contains the subject *monster* and the main verb *was*.
- This compound sentence has two main clauses linked by the conjunction *and*.
- This complex sentence contains a main clause and a subordinate clause.

Change of pace
Rather than using a random mixture of sentences, it's possible to select a particular type of sentence for effect—for example, to change the pace or add tension or excitement.

She began to run. The monster followed. Her heart was racing. The monster wasn't far behind. She had to make a decision. She jumped into the lake.

A string of short sentences in a story can create excitement.

Pulling herself out of the water, she could see light from the cottage in the distance. She scrambled up the riverbank, and ran through the mud, under the oak trees, around the bend in the road, and up the path. She was home.

Using a short sentence after a very long one can relieve tension.

"If we don't all gather together and track down the bloodthirsty monster, our children will not be safe on the streets and we will not be able to sleep soundly in our beds. We need to act now."

A long sentence in a speech can reinforce the seriousness of a problem.

Following the long sentence with a short sentence can make a powerful final point.

MAKING SENTENCES INTERESTING

A fresh start

Good writers avoid starting all the sentences in a paragraph in the same way because it sounds monotonous. Sentences can easily be rewritten to stop this from happening.

All these sentences start with the same word, there.

There was a chill in the air as Jessica walked through the woods. **There** was nobody around. **There** was a sudden growl in the distance.

This passage gives exactly the same information, but in a more interesting way.

There was a chill in the air as Jessica walked through the woods. Nobody was around. Suddenly, she heard a growl in the distance.

Add detail

Adding extra detail using adjectives and adverbs will make a sentence more informative and interesting. The position of an adverb can also be changed to vary the sentence structure.

This sentence isn't very interesting.

Jessica backed away from the monster.

Adding an adverb tells the reader about the way the girl is moving. The adjective describes the mood of the monster.

Jessica **nervously** backed away from the **angry** monster.

Moving the adverb changes the structure of the sentence.

Nervously, Jessica backed away from the angry monster.

GLOSSARY

Main clause A group of words that contains a subject and a verb and makes complete sense on its own.

Subordinate clause A group of words that contains a subject and a verb but depends on a main clause for its meaning.

- Add more detail to a sentence by using **prepositions**, which tell the reader **where** something is or **when** something is happening. Prepositions include *about, across, after, at,* and *under*.

- Use a variety of **conjunctions** to link clauses and make sentences **flow** from one to another. These are **connecting words**, such as *so, because, until, whereas,* and *but*.

REAL WORLD
Exciting commentary

Sports commentators often describe the events of a game or race with very short sentences. This makes the commentary as fast-paced and exciting as the event itself. It's particularly effective for radio commentaries when listeners can't see the action, but are relying on the commentary to create the mood.

Planning and research

IT IS ESSENTIAL TO PLAN A PIECE OF WRITING.

Good writers always plan their work—on paper rather than in their heads. Planning helps a writer generate ideas, organize them into a clear structure, and avoid leaving anything out.

SEE ALSO	
Paragraphing	188–189 ⟩
Writing to inform	196–197 ⟩
Newspaper articles	198–199 ⟩
Letters and e-mails	200–201 ⟩
Writing to influence	202–203 ⟩
Writing to explain and advise	204–205 ⟩
Writing to analyze or review	206–207 ⟩
Writing to describe	208–209 ⟩
Writing from personal experience	210–211 ⟩

First scribbles

The best way to start planning a project is to jot down any relevant ideas, words, and phrases. One method is to use a mind map. At this stage in the planning process, it is useful to think of as many relevant ideas as possible—they can be cut down later.

▷ **Map out ideas**
A mind map is a visual method of writing down notes. The free structure of a mind map can make it a very effective way to generate ideas. However, a simple list is also fine.

- Use **official** or well-known publications or websites for research to ensure that the information is **accurate**.
- Try to **cross-reference** any facts or statistics with another source for accuracy.
- Keep a file called "Bibliography" open whenever working on a project and **regularly update** it.

The idea for the piece of writing goes in the middle.

Ideas are written around the edge.

Research

It's important to research a piece of writing in order to gain a good overall understanding of a topic, and to gather specific examples, quotations, or statistics. Sources for research include books, websites, and newspapers. To avoid plagiarism (copying someone else's work), always rephrase the sentences.

Write down the source for each statistic, quotation, and fact.

At a later stage, color code each note to show which paragraph it will be used in.

Put quotation marks around quotations now to avoid plagiarism later.

Worldwide obesity has more than doubled since 1980. (World Health Organization Report, 2012)

"Physical inactivity is an independent risk factor for coronary heart disease—in other words, if you don't exercise, you dramatically increase your risk of dying from a heart attack when you're older." Dr. John Hobbs

▷ **Neat notes**
Notes should be neat, organized, and as detailed as possible. Disorganized or incomplete notes will hinder the writing process, and the information may have to be found again.

PLANNING AND RESEARCH

Bibliography

When doing research, it's essential to keep a running list of sources to create a document called a bibliography. This should include all books, magazines, websites, and television programs used for the project. Each source should go on a single line, with periods or commas between details, and a period at the end.

- Put the author's last name first.
- The book title should be in italics or underlined.
- Find the publisher and the publication date on one of the first few pages of the book.

Roberts, Alice. *The Complete Human Body Book.* New York: DK Publishing, 2010.

John Hobbs, Doctor, interviewed on 3/3/2013.

http://www.who.int/dietphysicalactivity/childhood/en/

- Include the full addresses of any websites.
- Include the details of any people who were interviewed.

The plan

The next stage is to organize the ideas and research into a clear structure using paragraphs. A piece of writing needs to start with an introduction that states what the work is about. Each new idea forms a new paragraph. Finally, a conclusion sums everything up. Paragraphs need to follow a clear progression: for example, in order of importance or chronology (date order).

A plan should include the main points that will be made in each paragraph.

It isn't necessary to use full sentences in a plan, but always use complete sentences when writing the final piece.

It's useful to give each paragraph a color and go back to the notes and color each note according to which paragraph it relates to. This will make it easier to find the right notes during writing.

▷ **Going according to plan**
Using a plan will keep a piece of writing focused. However, it's common to add, take out, or move ideas around during writing.

Introduction
Background information. How young people today get less exercise than ever. This is linked to bad health and delinquency. Include shocking statistics.

1. It's easy to change
Exercise like running, starting a soccer team, and walking is cheap and doesn't require equipment. It doesn't take up much time—give figures.

2. Health benefits
Exercise makes you happier, helps you lose weight, improves fitness levels. Include some statistics.

3. Social benefits
Team sports are sociable—young people will mix with others and make more friends. Keeps young people out of trouble. Encourages healthy competitive and team spirit.

4. Long-term benefits
A generation with fewer health problems. More success in professional sports.

Conclusion
How the worrying situation discussed in the introduction could change. Vision for the future. Quote from Olympic champion.

Paragraphing

PARAGRAPHS ARE USED TO ORGANIZE A PIECE OF WRITING.

It's important to structure a long piece of writing, such as an essay, article, or letter, into paragraphs. This will break the text up into separate points, which will make it easier to read.

SEE ALSO	
‹ 58–59 Conjunctions	
‹ 184–185 Making sentences interesting	
‹ 186–187 Planning and research	
Reading and commenting on texts	192–193 ›

Starting an introduction with a question will catch the reader's attention.

> What's your excuse? Perhaps you don't like getting sweaty, you have no time, or you're just plain lazy. Whatever the reason, you're not alone; fewer and fewer young people are getting enough exercise. However, sports offer numerous health and social benefits, so it's time to stop complaining and get moving.

One way of starting a new paragraph is to indent the first line.

This paragraph is about the health benefits of exercise.

> ...Thus, regular exercise will not only improve your long-term health, but also make you feel happier and less stressed out.
>
>   In addition to the health benefits, playing sports can improve your social life. It is an opportunity to see your friends on a regular basis and to meet new people by joining a team.

The next sentences are about social benefits, so they start a new paragraph.

A good start

The opening paragraph should state what a piece of writing is about. It also needs to grab the reader's attention so that he or she wants to read on. The first line should be something strong and original, such as a quotation, a rhetorical question, or a statistic.

The great American basketball player Michael Jordan once said, "I can accept failure, but I can't accept not trying."

Start an introduction with a famous or memorable quotation.

Are you putting yourself at risk? People who don't get enough exercise dramatically increase their risk of developing heart disease.

Use a shocking fact to make an impact.

New idea, new paragraph

All the sentences in a paragraph should be related to one another. A new point of discussion requires a new paragraph. Start the new paragraph by indenting the first few words of the text or by skipping a line.

Another way to start a new paragraph is to skip a line.

> ...Thus, regular exercise will not only improve your long-term health, but also make you feel happier and less stressed out.
>
> In addition to the health benefits, playing sports can improve your social life. It is an opportunity to see your friends on a regular basis and to meet new people by joining a team.

PARAGRAPHING

REAL WORLD
Once upon a time...

Fiction writers need to write good opening lines to draw readers into the story. For example, the author J.K. Rowling starts the first chapter of *Harry Potter and the Deathly Hallows* with these lines: "The two men appeared out of nowhere, a few yards apart in the narrow, moonlit lane."

Topic sentences

It can be effective to start a paragraph with a topic sentence. This is a statement that introduces the main idea in the paragraph. The rest of the paragraph needs to expand on the topic sentence or give evidence to back it up. This method can help keep a piece of writing focused.

The health benefits of regular exercise cannot be ignored.

> This bold statement is a topic sentence. The rest of the paragraph will discuss the health benefits that it refers to.

Overall, there is no excuse. Getting regular exercise will reduce your chances of developing heart disease and other serious illnesses. In the short term, it will make you healthier, happier, and more energetic. Finally, it's an excellent way to meet new people, have fun, and perhaps discover a new talent.

> A conclusion should make a decisive final statement.

> Link a conclusion back to points in the introduction to give the piece cohesion.

- Referring **back** to points made in previous paragraphs makes a piece of writing more **connected** because it shows that the piece has been considered as a whole.
- Do not make **completely new** points in a conclusion.

A lasting impression

A conclusion should summarize the main points made in a piece of writing and make a decisive judgment about the topic. It should refer back to the original question and, ideally, any points made in the introduction. A sophisticated conclusion can end by referring to the wider implications of the question, and leave the reader with something to think about.

If you start now, perhaps you could be climbing the Olympic podium one day.

> A conclusion should repeat the main points.

> A final, memorable statement in a piece of writing is sometimes called a "clincher."

Seamless links

A good piece of writing should be cohesive. This means that the sentences, paragraphs, and ideas are all linked together in a flowing way. Sentences and paragraphs can be connected using linking words or phrases. However, use these sparingly.

on the other hand **by contrast** **however** **nevertheless** *to contrast one idea with another*	**therefore** **thus** **as a result of** **accordingly** *to give logical reasons*
first **next** **first of all** **finally** *to order ideas in a sequence*	**also** **moreover** **furthermore** **in addition** *to develop an idea*

Genre, purpose, and audience

ALL NONFICTION TEXTS HAVE A CLEAR GENRE, PURPOSE, AND AUDIENCE.

> **SEE ALSO**
> ‹ 86–87 Colloquialisms and slang
> ‹ 180–181 Effective communication
> ‹ 182–183 Picking the right words
> ‹ 186–187 Planning and research
> Reading and commenting on texts 192–193 ›

Writers need to consider what type of text they are writing, as well as for whom they are writing and why. These factors influence the presentation style and language used.

Genre

A nonfiction text is one based on facts, rather than a story. The different types, or genres, of nonfiction text all have their own features and conventions. For example, a newspaper or magazine article will have a headline at the top and text written in columns, whereas a letter includes the sender's address at the top.

- **Newspaper article** — Newspaper stories are written in columns with a headline at the top.
- **Leaflet** — Leaflets are sheets of paper folded into three, with information on each segment.
- **Letter** — Letters can be formal or informal, but both types are laid out with the sender's address at the top.

GENRE: Advertisement, Website, Newspaper article, Blog, Leaflet, Script, Speech, Letter

The genre, purpose and audience of a text need to be considered together. All three factors influence the features of a piece of writing.

Purpose

The purpose of a text is the reason that it was written. For example, an encyclopedia entry about Paris is supposed to inform the reader, whereas an advertisement for a vacation in Paris is intended to persuade the reader to visit. Even though they are about the same subject, these two texts would have very different features.

- **To inform** — Texts written to inform contain lots of facts and need to be very clear.
- **To advise** — Pieces of advice will have a sympathetic tone.
- **To influence** — Persuasive texts contain opinions.

PURPOSE: To inform, To advise, To influence, To analyze, To describe

> • Sometimes a text can be written for **more than one purpose**. An advertisement for pimple cream might give customers **advice** about their skin, but will also try to **persuade** them to buy the product.

GENRE, PURPOSE, AND AUDIENCE

GLOSSARY

Adjective A describing word that tells the reader more about a noun.

Colloquialism A word or phrase used in informal speech.

Fact A statement that can be proved.

Jargon Specialized terms that are understood and used by a select, often professional, group of people.

Slang Words and phrases that are used in informal speech and often only understood by a select group of people.

REAL WORLD
Television audiences

Television advertising executives design advertisements to appeal to their target audience. For example, they might use actors who remind viewers of themselves. They will also aim to show the advertisements during television programs that are related to their product. Thus, advertisements for new food products might be shown during the break in a cooking show, because people who watch cooking shows are more likely to buy food products.

AUDIENCE

- Teachers — A text written for a particular group of professionals can use terms that only they will understand.
- Adults
- Environmentalists — A piece written for a group of people who believe in something strongly can reinforce and flatter their opinions.
- General public — Something written for a general audience should be simple enough to be understood by everyone. However, it should not be patronizing, because it needs to appeal to adults as well as children.
- Teenagers
- Young children

In some languages, such as French, speakers use **different words** depending on **who** they are talking to. For example, the French word for "you" is *tu* in an **informal** situation, but it is *vous* in a **formal** situation.

Audience

A nonfiction text always has a target audience. For example, it might be for adults, teenagers, or children. It could be for people with a particular interest or specialized knowledge, or it may be designed to appeal to a general audience. The key aspects of the text need to be tailored to attract this target audience.

Audience	Some common features
Adults	Sophisticated vocabulary, longer sentences, detailed subject matter, smaller font size, longer pieces of writing, formal tone and language
Young children	Simple vocabulary, short sentences, larger font size, simple subject matter, pictures and color to keep them interested
Teenagers	Slang, colloquial language, informal tone, humor, subject matter that seems relevant to them
Professionals	Jargon or specialized terms that are understood by them

Reading and commenting on texts

IT'S USEFUL TO BE ABLE TO INTERPRET AND WRITE ABOUT DIFFERENT PIECES OF WRITING.

SEE ALSO	
‹ 88–89 Direct and indirect speech	
‹ 102–103 Colons	
‹ 108–109 Quotation marks	
‹ 190–191 Genre, purpose and audience	
Layout and graphical elements	194–195 ›
Writing to influence	202–203 ›

When answering a question about a text, a writer needs to understand the question, find the right information in the text and use it to write a focused answer.

Understand the question

The first step is to read the question and understand what it is asking. Even a well-crafted answer will get no marks if it does not answer the question. Underlining the key words in the question will make it easier to focus on what is being asked.

What do you learn from the <u>opening paragraph</u> about…

This question only asks about the opening paragraph, so don't make comments about the rest of the text.

What are the <u>four main reasons</u> that the writer gives…

How does the writer use <u>language</u> to <u>persuade the reader</u> that…

This question is asking specifically about language, so there is no need to write about presentation.

The right information

The next stage is to read the text and look for the relevant information or features. It is useful to underline the words, sentences or passages that will help answer the question. Sometimes a question will refer to two texts.

TEXT 1

<u>Are your parents always nagging you to eat breakfast?</u> Well, this time they're right. In the morning, your body needs <u>fuel</u>, just like a <u>car</u>. Once you've <u>filled up</u>, you'll be ready <u>to hit the road</u>.

compares the body to a car

Underline sections that will be useful when writing an answer.

Write observations and notes around the text.

This extract has the same subject matter as Text 1, but is written in complex, scientific language.

TEXT 2

Recent studies outline the many health benefits of eating a <u>nutritious</u> breakfast. In the morning, the body's <u>glycogen</u> stores start to <u>deplete</u>. Without breakfast, a person soon begins to feel <u>fatigued</u>.

- **Read** the whole text first. It is important to get an **overall idea** of what the text is about before analyzing the details.
- Refer to the text frequently, but be **selective**—**don't copy** out whole chunks of text.
- Become more **familiar** with different types of texts and the techniques they use by **reading** texts from **everyday life**, such as newspapers and even brochures.

Provide evidence

When writing about a text, every point made must be backed up with evidence. This can be made up of a quotation (the exact words from the text), or a reference (a description of the pictures, structure, or layout). If using a quotation, it must be surrounded by quotation marks to separate it from the answer.

> The first extract was written to persuade young children to eat a healthy breakfast. It starts by asking the reader a question: "Are your parents always nagging you to eat breakfast?" The writer has also used phrases such as "fuel," "filled up," and "hit the road" to compare the process of eating breakfast to the process of filling a car up with fuel.

Long quotations need to be preceded by a colon. If it's longer than four lines, skip a line before the quotation.

Short quotations can be embedded in the text.

Explain why

After giving an example, it is essential to explain what it shows about the text. This will make the point clear.

This answer gives an example.

> The writer has used words such as "fuel," "filled up," and "hit the road" to compare eating breakfast to filling a car up with fuel. This simple comparison makes the process easier for young children to understand. It also makes the text more fun, so it will hold a young audience's attention.

It then explains why this feature of the text is effective.

Fact or opinion?

Facts are pieces of information that can be proved. Opinions are what people believe or think. It is important to see the difference between fact and opinion when figuring out the purpose of a text. In general, informative texts use facts, whereas persuasive texts use personal opinions. Sometimes a text will use both.

This statement is presented as a fact, but it is actually an opinion, because not everyone would agree with it.

This sentence states a fact.

Superflake cereal is made from wheat and oats.

Superflake cereal is delicious.

Comparing texts

When comparing two texts, do not write about one text and then the other. Comparisons must be drawn between the two, which means picking out the similarities and differences. Some useful terms for making comparisons include *both texts*, *similarly*, *by contrast*, *on the other hand*, *whereas*, and *in comparison*.

These words help to compare and contrast the two texts.

> **Both** texts are about the importance of a nutritious breakfast and both try to persuade the reader to eat more healthily. However, they use very **different** language techniques. **Whereas** the first text, for young children, uses simple language and basic explanations, the second text, for adults, goes into much **more** detail and uses scientific terms such as "glycogen stores"...

Layout and presentational features

THE WAY THAT A TEXT IS PRESENTED ADDS TO ITS OVERALL IMPACT.

> **SEE ALSO**
> ‹ 116–117 Bullet points
> ‹ 122–123 Italics
> ‹ 192–193 Reading and commenting on texts
> Writing to inform 196–197 ›
> Newspaper articles 198–199 ›
> Writing for the Web 214–215 ›
> Re-creations 218–219 ›

Layout refers to the way that a text is organized on a page. Presentational features are the individual elements, such as pictures, headlines, fonts, and color.

Headline
Headlines sit at the top of newspaper and magazine articles, leaflets, and sometimes advertisements. Headlines are usually in bold text and capital letters so that they stand out and attract the reader's attention.

Font
The font refers to the size, shape, and color of the text. Large fonts are often used for children, because they are easier to read. Colorful text and fun shapes are also used for a young audience, while serious pieces of writing are printed in a small standard font. Bold and italic fonts are used to draw attention to headings or certain words and phrases.

MYSTERIOUS INTRUDERS

This subheading could be printed in a fun font if the article were for children.

Bullet points
Bullet points are used to break up a dense block of text into a clear list of individual points. This makes the information easier to read and absorb.

SUPERNATURAL

Recently revealed statistics show a record number of supernatural sightings in the local area. The police have recorded 31 ghost sightings in the past five years, along with 25 reports of UFOs, 15 zombies, 10 vampires, and 8 witches.

MYSTERIOUS INTRUDERS

Often the calls appear to be serious incidents, such as intruders at a property, but then turn out to be something more mysterious. The police claim that the time spent answering the calls costs the force thousands of dollars every year.

More strange sights
- There have been 14 sightings of big cats in the past five years, as well as eight reported injuries blamed on big cats.
- Six people have claimed that they have seen a sea monster. Apparently, it resembles a huge alligator with purple scales.
- A ghost ship has been seen on four occasions on the harbor rocks. In 1876, a ship was wrecked on this exact spot.

LAYOUT AND PRESENTATIONAL FEATURES

REAL WORLD
Effective images

Charity advertisements often show images of the people or animals that they want to help. These are effective because they make the issue more real for the audience, and let them imagine the positive effect that their money would have for the cause.

- When analyzing the layout of a piece, **don't just identify** the features—**explain why** they are **effective**.

Photographs and graphics
Images can be used for effect or to give more information. For example, an advertisement for a hair product might show a picture of a model with extremely glossy hair to persuade the audience to buy a new shampoo. A newspaper report about a terrible flood might show a photograph of the affected area to demonstrate exactly what has happened. Graphs and diagrams are used to make complicated topics or statistics clear.

SIGHTINGS SURGE

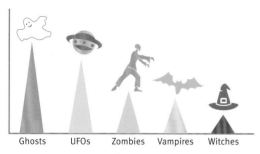

The most common supernatural sightings are of ghosts.

Caption
Photographs and diagrams are usually accompanied by a short sentence that explains what the image is about. This is called a caption.

ZOMBIE WAS MOVIE EXTRA

Most of the sightings are easily and quickly explained. In 2011, a reported zombie sighting turned out to be a movie extra taking his lunch break. Another caller raised the alarm after seeing something suspicious floating in the air on a Saturday night: "I saw a big, orange, glowing sphere rising from the ground." The sighting turned out to be a Chinese lantern.

Subheading
Subheadings are used to break up a long text into shorter chunks, so that it's easier to read. They also summarize the content of the next paragraph, which helps the reader find the section they're interested in reading.

"I saw a big, orange, glowing sphere rising from the ground."

Pull quote
Newspaper and magazine articles often include quotes from eyewitnesses or experts. To draw attention to particularly interesting quotes, the words can be lifted out from the article and repeated elsewhere on the page, usually in bolder or larger type.

Writing to inform

THE MAIN PURPOSE OF SOME PIECES OF WRITING IS TO GIVE THE READER INFORMATION.

SEE ALSO	
‹ 54–55 Voices and moods	
‹ 116–117 Bullet points	
‹ 194–195 Layout and presentational features	
Newspaper articles	198–199 ›
Letters and e-mails	200–201 ›

Informative texts, such as leaflets, encyclopedias, newspaper reports, and letters, give the reader information about a topic. Some texts also tell the reader how to do something, by giving instructions.

Simple but detailed

Informative writing should give readers the details they need to know, clearly. It should include lots of facts, presented in short paragraphs and using simple vocabulary.

Sierra Nevada of California

3.7 million visitors

A headline at the top of a leaflet tells the reader what it is about.

YOSEMITE NATIONAL PARK

Yosemite National Park covers nearly 761,268 acres (3,081 sq km) of mountainous terrain in the Sierra Nevada of California. The park attracts more than 3.7 million visitors each year.

There are countless ways to explore and have fun in Yosemite National Park.

Pictures of the place show the reader what it looks like and make the leaflet look attractive.

REAL WORLD
DIY dilemma

Sometimes people buy furniture in separate parts that need to be put together at home. The buyer needs to follow a set of instructions in order to assemble the item. Often, the instructions are not very clear, which can lead to a great deal of frustration.

WRITING TO INFORM

Bite-sized chunks

It's effective to break down detailed text into short sections, so that the information is easy to find and absorb. Subheadings are useful for guiding readers through the text and leading them to important details. Bullet points divide up the information even further.

Bullet points divide up the information.

- Avoid using unnecessarily **complicated** language that may **obscure** the information.
- Use **adverbs**, such as *carefully* or *quickly*, in **instructions** to give the reader more information on **how** to do something.

Here are some of the activities we have to offer:

Biking
More than 12 miles (19 km) of paved cycle paths are available in the park.

Birdwatching
Try to spot some of the 262 species of birds recorded in Yosemite.

Hiking
Get your hiking boots on and explore the park by foot.

Fishing
Following the regulations, see what you can catch in the lakes and rivers.

Horse riding
Saddle up and enjoy the park's majestic views on horseback.

Please remember:
- Stay on the trails.
- Drink plenty of water.
- Do not litter.

Not just a pretty picture

Adding images and color makes an informative text look more fun, but can also make the details clearer. Diagrams and maps show the reader something, rather than just telling them.

HOW TO GET HERE

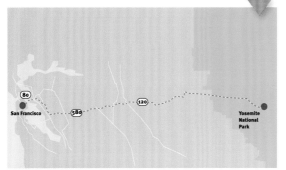

Driving instructions
From San Francisco

1. Take the Bay Bridge (Interstate 80) east.
2. Take Interstate 580 east, following signs for Tracy/Stockton to Interstate 205.
3. Follow Interstate 205 to Highway 120.
4. Take Highway 120 into Yosemite National Park.

Numbered steps create an easy-to-follow sequence.

Easy instructions

Instructions are a type of informative text. They include travel directions, recipes, and product manuals. They are usually written in a numbered, step-by-step format. Commands are also used to give firm and clear instructions.

Commands tell the reader what to do.

Take Highway 120 into Yosemite National Park.

Newspaper articles

NEWSPAPERS INFORM AND ENTERTAIN THE READER.

Journalists use certain techniques to inform and engage their readers. The specific content and language used in an article depend on the type of publication and the intended audience.

SEE ALSO
❮ 54–55 Voices and moods
❮ 190–191 Genre, purpose, and audience
❮ 192–193 Reading and commenting on texts
❮ 194–195 Layout and presentational features
❮ 196–197 Writing to inform

Which paper?
Some newspapers focus on serious, in-depth articles, while other papers run more sensational stories, such as political scandals or celebrity gossip. The scope of a paper also affects its content. National newspapers report on national or global events, but regional newspapers focus on local community finances, politics, and events, which are more relevant to local people.

MARKETS FALL AS ECONOMIC CRISIS CONTINUES

◁ Some newspapers choose to run serious stories.

HOLLYWOOD COUPLE SPLITS

◁ Other newspapers focus on celebrity stories.

SCHOOL TO CLOSE

◁ Local newspapers report local news.

A local grandmother was rescued from her burning home on Saturday by her pet dog. Shirley Williams, 65, was in bed with the flu when the blaze broke out at approximately 2:00 p.m., following an electrical fault.

Her golden retriever, Star, was in the backyard, but risked his life by bounding

Details, details, details
News articles need to explain what happened, where, why, and who was involved. All good journalists include as many details as possible in their stories, such as names, ages, and times.

Shirley Williams, 65, was in bed with the flu when the blaze broke out at approximately 2:00 p.m., following an electrical fault.

Drama
Newspapers often use exaggerated or dramatic language to catch the reader's attention and make an article more exciting to read.

blaze

◁ The word *blaze* sounds more dramatic than *fire*.

NEWSPAPER ARTICLES

> **GLOSSARY**
>
> **Alliteration** The repetition of certain letters or sounds for effect.
>
> **Headline** The statement at the top of an article that tells the reader what it is about.
>
> **Pun** The use of a word or phrase that has two meanings for comic effect.
>
> **Quote** To repeat the words of a person. Quotations need to be surrounded by quotation marks.

Sales of **printed newspapers** have **declined** in recent years because many people read the news **online**.

HERALD

RDOG
AVES SICK
GRANNY

...o the fire. He led her to safety through ...smoke and flames. Local firefighter Joe ...t, who later arrived at the scene, said, ...e would have gotten there too late. That ...g saved her life." ...hirley is recovering in the hospital. The ...yor has commended Star for his bravery.

Headlines
Headlines tell the reader what a story is about. They are short and dramatic and often use techniques such as alliteration or puns to grab attention and sell copies.

SUPERDOG SAVES SICK GRANNY

Using three words in a row beginning with the letter s creates a snappy headline.

Stay active
The news is usually written in the active rather than the passive voice. This is because sentences in the active voice are shorter, easier to read, and convey a sense of immediacy, which makes the news sound more exciting.

he led her — The active voice makes the story sound immediate.

she was led — The passive voice would make the story less engaging.

In their words
Journalists quote experts to give a news story authority. They also interview and quote the people who were involved. This makes the story seem more real for the reader.

"That dog saved her life."

Short and snappy
People often read newspapers in a rush, so journalists need to get the information across quickly and simply. Sentences and paragraphs should be short and clear.

Shirley is recovering in the hospital.

Letters and e-mails

LETTERS AND E-MAILS ARE FORMS OF CORRESPONDENCE ADDRESSED TO A SPECIFIC PERSON OR GROUP.

Different types of correspondence are used in certain situations, for different purposes. It is important to set out each type correctly.

SEE ALSO	
‹ 118–119 Numbers, dates, and time	
‹ 188–189 Paragraphing	
‹ 196–197 Writing to inform	
Writing to influence	202–203 ›
Writing to explain or advise	204–205 ›
Writing from personal experience	210–211 ›

Formal letters
Formal letters are written to someone the writer doesn't know, or to someone in authority, such as a teacher or a politician. Examples of formal letters include job application letters and complaint letters. People send complaint letters about faulty products or bad service in a hotel or restaurant.

The **first e-mail** was sent in **1971**. Today, more than **294 billion** e-mails are sent every day.

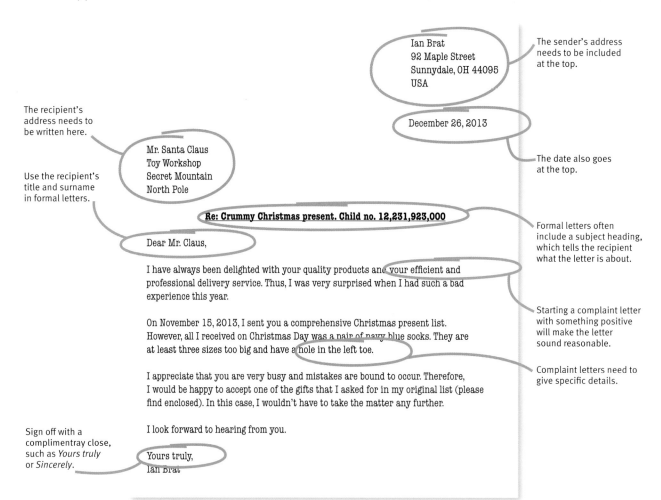

Ian Brat
92 Maple Street
Sunnydale, OH 44095
USA

— The sender's address needs to be included at the top.

December 26, 2013

— The date also goes at the top.

The recipient's address needs to be written here.

Mr. Santa Claus
Toy Workshop
Secret Mountain
North Pole

Use the recipient's title and surname in formal letters.

Re: Crummy Christmas present. Child no. 12,231,923,000

Dear Mr. Claus,

I have always been delighted with your quality products and your efficient and professional delivery service. Thus, I was very surprised when I had such a bad experience this year.

On November 15, 2013, I sent you a comprehensive Christmas present list. However, all I received on Christmas Day was a pair of navy blue socks. They are at least three sizes too big and have a hole in the left toe.

I appreciate that you are very busy and mistakes are bound to occur. Therefore, I would be happy to accept one of the gifts that I asked for in my original list (please find enclosed). In this case, I wouldn't have to take the matter any further.

I look forward to hearing from you.

Sign off with a complimentray close, such as *Yours truly* or *Sincerely*.

Yours truly,
Ian Brat

Formal letters often include a subject heading, which tells the recipient what the letter is about.

Starting a complaint letter with something positive will make the letter sound reasonable.

Complaint letters need to give specific details.

LETTERS AND E-MAILS

Informal letters include the sender's address at the top, but they do not need the recipient's address.

The date needs to be included at the top.

Informal letters can be addressed to the recipient's first name.

Informal letters can have a chattier tone and include some small talk.

This phrase is friendlier than *Yours truly* or *Sincerely*.

Santa Claus
Toy Workshop
Secret Mountain
North Pole

January 5, 2014

Dear Rudolf,

I hope you are sticking to your New Year's resolutions! How is the diet going?

Mrs. Claus and I wanted to thank you for hosting a fantastic New Year's Eve party. It was great fun for us all to celebrate together after a busy few weeks.

I hope that we can see you for dinner soon.

Best wishes
Santa

Informal letters

Informal letters are used for someone the sender knows, such as a friend, a family member, or a person of the same age or younger. They might describe a place or experience, pass on news, or thank the recipient for something. Informal letters have a chattier tone, but still follow a set layout.

- A **job application** letter gives an employer the **first impression** of a candidate, so it needs to be perfect.
- A complaint letter should be **firm but polite**. A **rude** letter will only **annoy** the recipient and reduce the chance of an apology or compensation.

E-mails

E-mails to friends or family don't have to follow any particular rules. However, e-mails to people the sender doesn't know should use appropriate language and have a clear structure. More and more correspondence is now sent via e-mail, so writing an e-mail isn't an excuse to be sloppy.

E-mails need to have an appropriate and descriptive subject heading.

An e-mail should have a focused structure and use clear paragraphs.

Professional e-mails should end with a complimentary close, just like letters.

Send **Save** **Discard**

To: Joe@toycollege.com

Subject: Junior Toymaker Vacancy

Attach a file

Dear Joe,

Thank you very much for your recent application for the Junior Toymaker position.

I have read your résumé and would be delighted to meet with you for an interview. Would 2:00 p.m. next Thursday be convenient?

Please let me know.

Kind regards,
Santa Claus

Writing to influence

SOME TEXTS SEEK TO CHANGE AN AUDIENCE'S VIEWS OR BEHAVIOR.

SEE ALSO	
‹ 186–187 Planning and research	
‹ 188–189 Paragraphing	
‹ 190–191 Genre, purpose, and audience	
Writing to describe	208–209 ›
Writing a speech	226–227 ›

Pieces of writing that argue or persuade seek to influence the audience. However, there are subtle differences between arguing and persuading.

A strong argument

An argument tends to acknowledge the opposite opinion while providing well-reasoned arguments against it. For example, if someone were to argue that cats were better than dogs, that person would not simply list all the good things about cats. He or she would acknowledge why some people prefer dogs, then argue against those points.

Reasons why people prefer dogs to cats
- Dogs are more intelligent than cats. Cats are smart enough to hunt, wash, and fend for themselves.
- Cats are unkind because they bring dead mice into the house. This is their way of showing affection.
- Cats are unsociable. They are friendly but don't demand constant attention—an annoying characteristic of dogs.

To plan an argument, list the reasons why people take the opposite point of view.

Try to disprove each point with a counterargument.

Powers of persuasion

A persuasive piece is more one-sided and emotional than an argument. It often coaxes the audience to act: for example, to buy a product, join an organization, or donate money to charity.

- Persuasive writing should be firm but **not aggressive**.
- **Real-life stories** add emotion to a piece of writing.
- Use **confident language**, such as *you will* and *definitely*, rather than *you might* and *possibly*.

Persuasive writing does not accept the opposite opinion.

This type of writing coaxes the reader to act now.

GLOSSARY

Exaggeration Representing something as larger or better than it actually is.

Hyperbole An extreme form of exaggeration that is not necessarily taken seriously, but grabs the reader's attention.

Rhetorical question A question that does not need an answer but is used for effect.

Superlative The form of an adjective or adverb that suggests the greatest or least of something.

Writing to Influence

Get your own way
Writers use particular methods to influence their audiences' opinions. These are called rhetorical devices. Writing that persuades uses more of these techniques than writing that argues.

Repetition rules
Sometimes a word, phrase, or structure is repeated to make an idea stick in the audience's mind, and convince them that it's true. Lists of three are a particularly common technique.

Dogs are loyal. Dogs are friendly. Dogs are the best!

Ask the experts
Writers use facts, statistics, and quotations from reliable and authoritative sources to back up their points and make them sound more convincing.

According to one recent study at Queen's University, Belfast, dog owners suffer from fewer medical problems than cat owners.

The **Ancient Greeks** called the art of using language to persuade "the art of rhetoric."

Tearjerkers
Some words and phrases make the reader feel an emotion, such as pain, sadness, guilt, or anger. Once the reader is feeling this way, they are often more susceptible to persuasion.

Cats bring comfort and friendship to the old, frail, and lonely.

Rhetorical questions
A rhetorical question is a question that does not require or expect an answer. However, it makes the reader reflect on points that he or she may not have considered.

Is a cat fun? Can you play fetch with a cat?

Getting personal
Addressing the audience directly with *you* will make them feel more involved. Using *we* can form a relationship between the writer and audience, and encourage the audience to trust and believe the writer.

We all know that you don't have to take cats for constant walks.

Simply the best
Exaggeration is used to emphasize a point and to grab an audience's attention. Exaggeration often includes superlatives, such as *the best*, *the worst*, and *the cheapest*. Extreme exaggeration is called hyperbole.

I couldn't live without my cat. My cat is my whole world.

REAL WORLD
I'm talking to you
This poster from 1914 was used to persuade men to join the British army in World War I. It shows Lord Kitchener, the British Secretary of State for War, telling the audience that their country needs them. By looking directly at the audience and addressing them with the word *YOU*, Lord Kitchener made a very effective appeal.

Writing to explain or advise

EXPLANATIONS AND PIECES OF ADVICE GIVE THE READER MORE THAN THE BASIC FACTS.

SEE ALSO	
‹ 186–187	Planning and research
‹ 188–189	Paragraphing
‹ 190–191	Genre, purpose, and audience
‹ 192–193	Reading and commenting on texts
‹ 196–197	Writing to inform
‹ 202–203	Writing to influence

Writing to explain and writing to advise can be confused with writing to inform. However, explanations and pieces of advice include reasons, feelings, and suggestions, as well as information.

Extra explanation
An explanation gives reasons. For example, it can explain why or how an event has happened, or why someone feels a certain way.

Explaining experiences
People are sometimes asked to explain their views on a topic, or the reason an experience was important or difficult. These types of explanations should not only describe the topic or event, but also the feelings involved.

> **I've lost all my confidence**

How and why
Explanations tell the reader how or why something happened, not just what happened. They use linking words and phrases to show cause and effect.

> **this is because**
> **as a result of this**
> **therefore**

STOP THE STENCH!

Dear Annie,
I have a serious problem with smelly feet. It sounds silly, but it has an impact on my entire life. Not only does the smell irritate me, but other people have started to notice and make jokes. I've lost all my confidence and I can't even go to my friends' houses anymore because I'm too frightened to take off my shoes. What can I do?

Anonymous, 14

Dear Anonymous,

Don't worry—you're not alone! Stinky feet are a common problem. This is because there are more sweat glands in the feet than anywhere else in the body. When your feet release sweat, bacteria on the skin break it down. This process releases that cheesy smell.

WRITING TO EXPLAIN OR ADVISE

Good advice
A piece of advice tells someone the best, easiest, or quickest way to do something, or suggests how to solve a problem.

Sympathy
Advice needs to be authoritative but friendly. Using a sympathetic and positive tone will encourage the reader.

> **the good news is**   **don't worry**

The good news is that there are lots of simple ways to stop the stench. First of all, you should wash your feet and change your socks every day. You could also try special foot deodorants, but I find that spraying normal deodorant on your feet works just as well. A guaranteed way to get rid of the smell is to wash your feet with an antibacterial soap. If you do this twice a day, you should banish smelly feet within a week.

Here are some other useful tips:
- Wear socks and shoes made from natural fibers because they let your feet breathe, unlike synthetic materials.
- Wear open-toed sandals in the summer and go barefoot at home in the evenings.
- See a doctor if these simple measures don't help.

Good luck.

Yours truly,

Annie

• A good explanation must be **well structured** in order to deliver the information in a **clear** and **logical** way.

Personal pronouns
A writer can address the reader directly by using *you*, or refer to his or her personal opinion with *I*. This helps to build a relationship with the reader, who should then be more receptive to the advice.

> **you could**   **I find**

Suggestions
Strong suggestions such as *you should* are effective because they encourage the reader to act. However, it's best to include a few gentler suggestions, such as *you could* or *you might*, to maintain a friendly tone.

> **you should wash your feet**

Strong suggestions tell the reader what to do.

Guaranteed results
The text needs to show how the advice will help. It should emphasize what will happen if the advice is or is not followed.

> **If you do this twice a day, you should banish smelly feet within a week.**

Bullet points
Advice leaflets or columns often break down the information into bullet points, so that the reader can read and follow the pieces of advice easily.

Writing to analyze or review

THESE TWO TYPES OF WRITING BREAK DOWN A TOPIC AND DISCUSS ITS KEY PARTS.

SEE ALSO
‹ 42–43 Simple tenses
‹ 186–187 Planning and research
‹ 188–189 Paragraphing
‹ 190–191 Genre, purpose, and audience

Both an analysis and a review discuss a subject in depth. However, while an analysis gives a balanced judgement, a review is usually opinionated and personal.

GLOSSARY
First person narrative When an author writes a piece from his or her point of view, using *I* and *my*.
Objective When a piece of writing is not influenced by personal opinions.
Subjective When a piece of writing is influenced by personal opinions.
Third person narrative When an author writes from a detached or outside point of view.

Balanced judgment

An analysis is an investigation of a topic. Unlike a persuasive piece of writing or a review, an analysis remains objective, which means that it is not influenced by personal feelings. It will look at the good and bad points of a subject, and come to a fair conclusion. A useful way to plan a balanced analysis is to use a table, listing arguments for and against.

Against reality television	For reality televison
Television producers make shows vulgar and offensive in order to boost ratings.	Reality television is popular and producers should give viewers what they want.
It encourages people to pursue celebrity status, rather than success through education and hard work.	If someone doesn't want to watch a show, they can change the channel or turn off the television.
The contestants are humiliated and treated poorly, which sets a bad example for viewers.	Some shows tackle important problems in society, such as unhealthy eating.
All the shows follow the same formula, and no creativity is involved in the making of a program.	Reality television tells us more about human nature, and how people behave in certain situations.

Distant and detached

To maintain the objectivity of an analysis, it's best to write in the third person and use an impersonal tone. For example, starting a sentence with the words *It is often argued* does not reveal the writer's personal opinion.

It is often argued…

It seems likely…

There is evidence to suggest…

Many people believe…

It is sometimes stated…

Writing to Analyze or Review

Rave reviews

A review is a piece of writing that provides a focused description and evaluation of an event or a publication, such as a book or a movie. It is much more subjective than an analysis, and is therefore written in the first person, with many personal opinions.

The travel website **TripAdvisor** contains more than **75 million** consumer **reviews** and opinions.

Sneak preview

The first part of a review should give a short summary of the movie, book, show, or other event without giving everything away. It should give the reader a general idea of what it is about.

Movie preview

TAKE TO THE FLOOR 2

The rooftop tango scene is stunning and very moving.

Take to the Floor 2 is the latest in a series of teen dance dramas to spin into theaters. As usual, the story focuses on two young dancers from the opposite sides of town. When street kid Chad wins a scholarship to a prestigious dance school, he finds it hard to fit in. Then, one day, he catches the eye of ballet dancer Ellie, who is wowed by his moves.

Many of the dance scenes are spectacular, from a rooftop tango in the pouring rain to a shopping mall salsa extravaganza. The cast members are all highly trained movers; however, their acting skills were left at the stage door. Ellie and Chad fail to bring their sizzling dance-floor chemistry into the dialogue, which is disappointing.

Take to the Floor 2 is nothing new; the plot certainly doesn't offer any surprises. However, the film is saved by its show-stopping dance scenes and pumping soundtrack. Overall, it's incredibly fun to watch, even if you end up feeling like you've seen it all before.

The good and the bad

The middle part of a review should go into more detail about the strengths and weaknesses of the subject. It might discuss the acting in a play, the quality of writing in a book, or the use of special effects in a movie. It is important to back up any comments with examples.

The verdict

The final paragraph in a review should be a summarizing statement about the subject, and an overall recommendation—a final judgment on whether the subject is worth watching, seeing, or reading.

- An analysis should be **structured** clearly, using **paragraphs**. Discuss one point of view first, followed by the other. Finally, come to a **balanced conclusion**.
- When writing a review, think about the **audience** and what they will **want to know** about the subject being reviewed.

Writing to describe

DESCRIPTIVE WRITING TELLS THE READER WHAT SOMETHING OR SOMEONE IS LIKE.

SEE ALSO	
‹ 26–27	Adjectives
‹ 40–41	Adverbs
‹ 84–85	Idioms, analogies, and figures of speech
‹ 182–183	Picking the right words
‹ 184–185	Making sentences interesting
Writing a narrative	212–213 ›

Many types of writing use description, from stories to advertisements. Descriptive writing uses particular words to paint a vivid image of something in the reader's head.

The senses

When writing to describe, it's important to appeal to the reader's senses. By describing what something looks, sounds, and feels like, a writer will allow the reader to imagine something in detail. Not all of the senses may be relevant, but try to think about as many as possible.

• One way to structure a description is to describe it **location by location**, as if moving around a scene with a video camera.

> Barbara walked into the kitchen and was confronted by a **rush of warm air** and the **smell of something sweet**. On the counter was a **triple-layer chocolate cake** with **fudge icing oozing** down the sides. She **eagerly cut** a slice and **stuffed** it into her mouth. The chocolate sponge was **rich** and **bitter** with a slight **nutty** flavor. The **sugar sprinkles crackled** in her mouth and got **stuck in her teeth**. Suddenly, the **doorbell rang**. Barbara jumped, and her **cake splattered** across the floor.

Describe what something looks, feels, smells, tastes, and sounds like.

REAL WORLD
Too good to miss

Advertising executives use description to create tempting pictures in an audience's mind to persuade them to buy something. For example, they might describe hair as *smooth*, *glossy*, and *rich* to sell a new shampoo or hair dye. Alternatively, an advertisement for a beach resort could include descriptions such as *azure blue*, *gently lapping waves*, and *golden sands*.

Descriptive details

Readers won't be able to imagine something unless they are given details. By selecting particular words, writers can add extra information and make a sentence more descriptive.

> She reached for a slice of cake and put it in her mouth.

△ **Lacking detail**
This sentence doesn't tell the reader very much about the scene.

> She reached **quickly** for a **big** slice of **sticky, delicious** cake and **eagerly** put it in her mouth.

(adverb, adjective)

△ **Adjectives and adverbs**
The addition of adjectives and adverbs instantly makes the sentence more evocative.

Using this word is a more precise way to describe the big slice.

> She **grabbed** a **wedge** of **sticky, delicious chocolate** cake and **stuffed** it in her mouth.

△ **Precise vocabulary**
Sometimes it's better to use precise vocabulary that includes description within the words themselves.

> She **tentatively** reached for a **sliver** of **fattening** cake and **sneakily popped** it in her mouth.

△ **Different choices**
By using different descriptive words, a writer can give a sentence a totally different feel.

Figurative language

Figurative language is an exaggerated style of writing that draws comparisons between things to create a more vivid description.

Simile
A simile compares one thing to another by using the words *as* or *like*.

Her cheeks were pink **like** strawberries.

Metaphor
A metaphor is a word or phrase that describes something as if it were something else.

A **wave** of terror washed over him.

Personification
Personification is when human actions or feelings are given to objects or ideas.

The wind **screamed** and **howled**.

Onomatopoeia
Onomatopoeia is when a writer uses words that mimic the sound they stand for.

The leaves **crunched** underfoot.

Writing from personal experience

WHEN SOMEONE WRITES ABOUT THEIR LIFE OR PERSONAL EXPERIENCES, IT'S CALLED AUTOBIOGRAPHICAL WRITING.

SEE ALSO	
‹ 34–35 Pronouns	
‹ 184–185 Making sentences interesting	
‹ 188–189 Paragraphing	
‹ 204–205 Writing to explain or advise	
‹ 208–209 Writing to describe	
Writing a narrative	212–213 ›
Writing for the Web	214–215 ›
Writing a speech	226–227 ›

Autobiography is a genre in itself, but it can also be used in other types of writing, such as a speech or an advice leaflet, to give a more personal touch.

A life less ordinary

Everyday life may not seem very interesting, but readers find other people's lives fascinating. Earliest memories, embarrassing incidents, or particularly happy, sad, scary, or proud moments all make good topics. Readers also enjoy finding out about experiences that are very different from their own, such as celebrating certain festivals or living in different places.

This is my life

When writing a complete autobiography (from birth to the present day), it's important to work out the right order of events. One way to do this is to create a life map. This is a visual way of plotting events, and can be accompanied by pictures to suggest memories. Rather than listing every single memory, writers often give an autobiography a theme. For example, it might focus on a struggle from rags to riches or a love of sports.

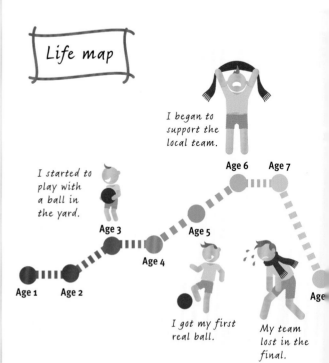

- Don't make up a whole experience, but it is acceptable to **embellish** a story slightly if it is going to make the story more **dramatic** or **entertaining**.

REAL WORLD
Travel writing

Travel writing is very different from the text found in travel guidebooks, which usually lists information. Pieces of travel writing recount the author's own travel experiences, including his or her feelings, opinions, and amusing anecdotes.

Edited highlights

Autobiographical writing is informative but also needs to be entertaining, so it shouldn't list boring details. For example, there's no need to give a minute-by-minute account of a game. It's much more interesting to tell the reader about feelings and reactions, such as fear, pride, or disappointment.

I felt sick and panicky all morning before the big game. We needed to win and I'd finally made the team. I had everything to prove.

Make it real

An autobiography tells stories, and the best stories include plenty of description. Describing sights, sounds, emotions, and tastes will allow the reader to picture the experience as vividly as the writer can remember it.

It was a hot night in the stadium. The noise of the supporters was deafening, and their chants boomed across the field like a roll of thunder in a storm.

Add character

Autobiographical writing needs to showcase the writer's unique personality. Therefore, it often includes his or her personal opinions, likes and dislikes, strange habits, and favorite vocabulary. Funny details add humor and give the piece character.

I was wearing my lucky socks. I had eaten my usual peanut butter sandwich and pet the cat three times. I was ready to play the game of my life!

You and me

An autobiography will naturally include the words *I* and *my*, but it can also be effective to address the reader using *you*. This is called direct address and helps to create a relationship with readers, making them feel more involved in the story.

I'm sure you've been on the losing side before, or watched your team miss that crucial shot. So you know what it feels like to be emotionally crushed by a loss.

Writing a narrative

A NARRATIVE IS A PIECE OF WRITING THAT TELLS A STORY.

A story is an account of events linked by cause and effect. All stories need a narrator, a plot, characters, and a setting. Some stories also include dialogue to show conversations between characters.

> SEE ALSO
> ‹ 34–35 Pronouns
> ‹ 108–109 Quotation marks
> ‹ 182–183 Picking the right words
> ‹ 184–185 Making sentences interesting
> ‹ 208–209 Writing to describe

Whose view?
The narrator is the person telling the story. If the narrator is a character in the story recounting the events from his or her point of view, the narrative is in the first person. If the narrator is uninvolved in the story and always refers to characters as *he*, *she*, or *they*, then the story is written in the third person.

First person (main character)
Stories in the first person are often narrated by the main character, or protagonist, of the story.

The scoundrels had deceived me, so I made them walk the plank!

The word *his* shows that this story is in the third person.

The ruthless captain made his crew walk the plank.

The word *my* shows that this story is in the first person.

My master is the most fearsome pirate sailing the seven seas.

First person (minor character)
Not all stories in the first person are told by the main character. Using a minor character as a narrator gives a different angle.

Third person
A narrative written in the third person tells the story from the author's or an outsider's point of view.

Don't lose the plot
The plot is what turns a list of events into a story. All the events happen for a reason and are caused by the actions and decisions of the characters. A good plot needs to have a clear beginning, middle (usually the main part of the action), and end.

△ **Beginning**
The beginning introduces the main characters and the situation that they are in. One classic plotline starts with the main character facing a problem.

△ **Middle**
The middle of the plot often shows the character trying to overcome the problem. The main event or turning point in the plot usually happens in the middle of the story.

△ **End**
The end brings the story to a resolution. The main character may have solved his or her problem. Alternatively, a plot "twist" may introduce an unexpected ending.

Heroes and villains

A good story needs to have interesting characters that the reader cares about. Usually, there is a main character, or hero. There are also villains, who stop the hero from reaching his or her goals, and allies, who help the hero. Each character should be distinctive, with unique physical or personality traits.

cunning, arrogant, moody, selfish, nasty, quick-tempered, stubborn, rude

adjectives to describe bad characters

adjectives to describe good characters

honest, enthusiastic, kind, caring, humorous, patient, helpful, modest

The perfect setting

The setting is the time, place, and situation where the action happens. The right setting will give the story mood and atmosphere. For example, a pirate story could be set on a deserted tropical island in the seventeenth century. Describing a setting in detail will enable the reader to imagine what it is like.

Dramatic dialogue

Using dialogue in a story can reveal more about the characters and advance the plot. It should be concise and dramatic—overly long or pointless pieces of dialogue should be avoided. Choosing phrases such as *he grumbled*, *he screamed,* or *he gasped* instead of *he said* also adds more drama.

The island was **deserted**, except for the **multicolored** birds **circling** overhead. The **golden** sandy beach was **fringed** with **coconut** trees and **tropical** plants. A **ghostly** shipwreck in the distance was being **pounded** against the **craggy** rocks by **crashing** waves.

Words that contain description, such as sounds, paint a vivid picture of the scene.

Pieces of dialogue need to go in quotation marks.

"Is that you, Captain?" **shouted** the first mate.
"Of course it is. Now, hurry up and lower a boat to fetch me," **bellowed** the captain.

A new speaker's dialogue needs to go on a new line.

Use more interesting words as an alternative to *said*.

- Use a mixture of **long** and **short** sentences to build up **tension** and **suspense**.
- **Figurative language** such as the simile *as fast as a cheetah* can enrich the description in a narrative. However, use it **sparingly**—too much description can **distract** the reader from the action.

Writing for the Web

WRITING FOR THE WEB IS VERY DIFFERENT FROM WRITING FOR PRINT.

Online readers are usually trying to find specific information and will move on if the website isn't clear or doesn't tell them what they need to know. Web writers use specific techniques to keep readers interested.

SEE ALSO
‹ 86–87 Colloquialisms and slang
‹ 182–183 Picking the right words
‹ 184–185 Making sentences interesting
‹ 194–195 Layout and presentational features
‹ 196–197 Writing to inform
210–211 › Writing from personal experience

Easy on the eye
Reading words on a screen is harder than reading them on a printed page, so if online readers find something too difficult to read, they will click away. Therefore, online text should always be written in short and clear sentences and paragraphs.

Key words
The Web is huge and full of websites on the same topics. Web writers have to make their content easy to find by including the "key words" that users search for on search engines. This is called Search Engine Optimization (SEO). It means that headlines and subheadings should be obvious rather than obscure.

Go to kangaroo country
> This title is fun but would not always be found in searches for "Australia."

Go to Australia
> The word *Australia* will be picked up by search engines.

Go Travel

> Business websites sometimes include company logos.

FLIGHTS | HOTELS | TOURS | INSURANCE | AROUND THE WORLD | BUS/TRAIN/

Australasia travel guides
If you really want to get away from it all, you can't get much farther away than Australasia. Ride the waves on Australia's Gold Coast, hike through the mountains in New Zealand, or just relax on the beach in Fiji. Start planning your trip of a lifetime here.

Go to Australia
Australia has it all, from hip cities to idyllic islands to the remote outback. Scuba dive at the Great Barrier Reef, party in Sydney, or check out some fascinating wildlife.
Find out more...

Go to New Zealand
New Zealand is a thrill-seeker's paradise. Get your adrenaline rush from skydiving, white-water rafting, or bungee jumping. Or just take in the beautiful scenery.
Find out more...

Go to Fiji
If you want to relax on a stunning beach, Fiji won't disappoint. It has more than three hundred islands with crystal clear waters and beautiful coral reefs.
Find out more...

> Attractive images make the website and the places look appealing.

WRITING FOR THE WEB

Blogs

Blogs are a type of online journal written for an audience. They are usually written in an informal and personal style and should be entertaining to read. Bloggers often write in the style of casual speech (although the text should still be grammatically correct), so it's helpful to read a blog out loud to make sure that it has the right tone.

Tabs along the top of the page take the user to different sections of the site.

People read **online text** about **25 percent slower** than they can read printed material.

> **GLOSSARY**
>
> **Blog** An online journal containing the author's comments and reflections. It is updated regularly.
>
> **Hyperlink** A word, phrase, or icon on the World Wide Web, which, if clicked, takes the user to a new document or website.
>
> **SEO** Standing for "Search Engine Optimization," this is the process that increases the online visibility of a website so more Web users will visit it.

| ESSENTIALS | PLANNING | DESTINATIONS | VOLUNTEER | WORK

The Go Travel blog

Surfing at Bondi

I've finally made it Down Under!

It's early in the morning here, but I'm not on Aussie time yet so I thought I would update you all on my trip. Yesterday, I decided to cure my jet lag by throwing myself into the pounding surf at Bondi Beach!

Read more....

Blogs can include some slang. This is short for "Australian."

Give it some space

A clear layout also makes online text easier to read. It is often broken up into small paragraphs and bullet points and surrounded by plenty of white space. People often skim text when they are reading online, so clear and descriptive subheadings can help them find the information that they need.

Click on our interactive destination map

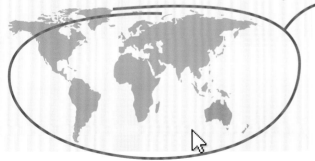

Interactive graphics present information in a more entertaining way and keep readers interested.

Act now

All writing has a purpose, whether to give readers information, or to make them buy something. The Web, more than any other medium, can allow readers to act on what they have read right away. It is therefore important to include active hyperlinks that take readers to extra information or to the checkout page.

 Get a quote by e-mail
Ask one of our team

Add to basket

Ask one of our team

Websites use links like this to encourage users to buy something.

Writing a script

VOICE-OVERS AND DRAMATIC SCRIPTS HAVE TO BE EFFECTIVE WHEN READ ALOUD.

SEE ALSO	
⟨ 88–89 Direct and indirect speech	
⟨ 114–115 Parentheses and dashes	
⟨ 196–197 Writing to inform	
⟨ 212–213 Writing a narrative	
The spoken word	222–223 ⟩
Writing a speech	226–227 ⟩

The words in a script are spoken to an audience, so they have to be easy to understand. Scripts also need to be laid out in specific ways, and include instructions for the people involved.

Voice-overs

A voice-over is the audio commentary that accompanies a short video, such as a documentary, an advertisement, or a nonprofit campaign film. A useful way to lay out a voice-over script is to use a table with columns.

Easy listening
A voice-over needs to be written in simple language so that listeners will understand what is said immediately. They can't go back and read sections again. Using simple sentences and words will also make a script easy for narrators to read, so they won't stumble over their words.

This column describes the images that will be shown on screen.

Each column shows different elements of a voice-over, plotted against time, in minutes.

Time	Images	Words	Sound effects
0:00	Beautiful and colorful images of rainforest plants and wildlife	The Amazon rainforest has the largest collection of plant and animal species in the world. Millions of weird and wonderful living things call this their home.	Peaceful jungle sounds
0:15	Shocking scene of deforestation	But for how long will this rainforest survive?	Silence
0:20	Zoom over deforestation	Silence	Silence

Words and pictures
In a voice-over script, the words need to relate to the images on screen, giving extra information about them. However, it is often effective to include occasional silences, so the audience can focus on and absorb what they see.

- The best way to test a voice-over is to read it **out loud**. If the narrator **runs out of breath**, or gets **confused**, the script needs to be **rewritten**.

On average, a narrator can read **180 words** out loud **per minute**.

Dramatic scripts

A dramatic script tells a story. However, unlike a written narrative, a script will be performed. Dramatic scripts can be for the theater, television, radio, or film. Each type has slightly different conventions, but they have some common features.

Directions

A script should include directions that tell everyone involved what to do. Directions indicate when actors should enter and exit, and in what tone they should perform a line. Other directions relate to lighting, sound effects, or camera shots, such as close-ups.

PROTEST

The title of the piece goes at the top.

Scene A park that is going to be demolished to make way for a shopping center. There are protest chants.

The setting and the characters involved in the scene are listed at the top.

Characters
MEADOW An environmental activist
DETECTIVE STUBBS A police officer

Directions show when characters enter and exit the scene. They should be in parentheses.

(MEADOW starts to climb a tree.)
(Enter DETECTIVE STUBBS.)

DETECTIVE STUBBS: What do you think you're doing?
MEADOW: (angrily) Saving our trees!
DETECTIVE STUBBS: Get down immediately!

Directions also include adverbs that tell actors how to perform their lines.

(MEADOW laughs and scrambles to the top of the tree.)
DETECTIVE STUBBS: Hey you, come back!

Dialogue

The dialogue refers to the conversation between characters. In a play, the plot is controlled by the dialogue and action, so the words need to tell the audience what is happening. The speech also needs to be convincing, so it should reflect the age, nationality, personality, and mood of each character.

Re-creations

THE REWRITING OF A TEXT IN A DIFFERENT FORM IS CALLED A RE-CREATION.

> **SEE ALSO**
> ‹ 42–43 Simple tenses
> ‹ 190–191 Genre, purpose, and audience
> ‹ 194–195 Layout and presentational features
> ‹ 198–199 Newspaper articles
> › 212–213 Writing a narrative

A piece of writing can be restyled in a variety of ways. For instance, a text such as a story could be rewritten as an autobiography or a newspaper article.

Transforming texts

A re-creation is turning one type of text into another. This can be done by simply changing the narrative viewpoint. For example, a third-person narrative could be turned into a first-person narrative. Similarly, a story could be retold in a different tense. A piece of writing can also be rewritten in a completely different form—a poem could inspire a story, or a play could become a newspaper article.

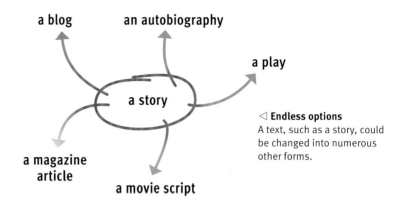

◁ **Endless options**
A text, such as a story, could be changed into numerous other forms.

REAL WORLD
Revised and updated

Sometimes writers rework classic stories to appeal to modern audiences. The action and characters are often moved into a modern setting. For example, the musical *West Side Story* is loosely based on William Shakespeare's *Romeo and Juliet*, but it is set in 1950s New York City.

The original

The best way to start a re-creation is to read and understand the original text. The rewritten form must include key details from the original version, such as events in the plot and the main characters. However, also think about minor details, such as the mood and atmosphere of the piece.

Highlight the important plot details in the original text.

extract from *Cinderella*

> The **king's son**, who was told that a great princess, who nobody knew, had arrived, ran out to receive her. He gave her his hand as she alighted from the coach, and **led her into the hall**, among all the company. There was immediately a **profound silence**. Everyone **stopped dancing**, and **the violins ceased to play**, so entranced was everyone with the **singular beauties** of the **unknown newcomer**.

Also look out for smaller details.

The makeover

The next stage is to think of an original way to transform the text into something else. It is best to choose a form that will suit the main events and characters in the original text. The revised version should use the correct features and layout for the new form.

- Be **creative** but stick to the important details. The new version should show an **understanding of the original text**.

◁ **Cinderella's story**
The story *Cinderella* could be rewritten as her autobiography. In this case, it should be narrated in the first person and include her thoughts and feelings.

Adding extra descriptive detail shows creativity.

> That night changed my life forever. I felt dizzy with excitement as I entered the ballroom. Women in multicolored dresses sashayed across the floor under sparkling chandeliers. The room was filled with the sound of guests chattering and violins playing. Then everything went silent. Everyone was looking at me.

Include details from the original text.

▷ **Royal scoop**
Cinderella could also inspire a scandalous newspaper article. In this case, the new text should be laid out with a headline and in columns, and the language should be short and snappy.

 THE CASTLE

WHO IS SHE?

The secret stunner left the ball in a hurry just before midnight.

PARTY PRINCE SPOTTED WITH MYSTERY WOMAN

It was a sight that broke hundreds of hearts. Prince Charming, 24, was seen dancing the night away with a new woman on Saturday evening.

The prince, who has publicly announced his intention to wed this year, was apparently bewitched by the beautiful blonde. Dressed in a floor-length metallic gown and glitzy glass slippers, she was the center of attention at the prince's annual ball.

One attendee said, "Everyone went silent when she entered the room. We were all entranced by her beauty."

Front-page stories usually have an eye-catching headline.

Newspaper articles often include alliteration (the use of words beginning with the same letter or sound).

These details come from the original text.

There have been more than **400** feature-length film and television **adaptations** of **William Shakespeare's** plays.

COMMUNICATION SKILLS

Checking and editing

CHECKING AND EDITING WILL IMPROVE A PIECE OF WRITING.

All writers make mistakes or have better ideas. It's important to leave enough time after finishing a piece of work to check for errors and improve the quality of the writing.

SEE ALSO	
‹ 52–53	Verb agreement
‹ 70–71	Compound sentences
‹ 72–73	Complex sentences
‹ 168–171	Confusing words
‹ 186–187	Planning and research
‹ 188–189	Paragraphing
‹ 190–191	Genre, purpose, and audience

The right answer
Even a perfect piece of writing will be poorly received if it answers the wrong question. When reviewing a piece of work, look at the question again, and make sure that the answer fulfills the brief.

— The answer should discuss language and presentational features.

Discuss how the website uses language and presentational features to persuade readers to visit the theme park.

— The answer should focus on how these features persuade the reader.

Discuss how the website uses language and presentational features to persuade readers to visit the theme park.

This website is designed to lure people to the Wild Waves Water Park. It is (particulery) aimed at young people who are on summer vacation. The range of images are persuasive. The selection shows groups of people who are obviously

Tricky words
One of the most important things to do is to check for spelling mistakes. To correct a spelling in handwritten work, put the mistake in parentheses, draw a line through it, and write the correct version above. Do not rely on spell-checkers—it's better to identify mistakes and learn the correct versions.

particularly
It is (particulery) aimed

Good grammar
Some grammatical mistakes to look out for include incomplete sentences, incorrect word order, and errors of verb agreement.

is
The range of images (are) persuasive.

— The subject *range* is singular, so the verb needs to be singular too.

Strict structure

Structuring a piece of text using paragraphs is very important. A new point of discussion requires a new paragraph. If a paragraph break is missing in a piece of handwritten work, mark it with a paragraph symbol (¶).

reader's attention. ¶ The language used

Use this symbol to show that there should be a new paragraph.

Perfect punctuation

Punctuation marks may look small, but they need to be used correctly. It's easy to make mistakes when writing quickly, so look out for errors such as misused commas and apostrophes.

The colorful text is really eye-catching, and it immediately grabs the reader's attention.

The two clauses need to be joined with a conjunction or a semicolon, not just a comma.

enjoying themselves and the reader will want to join the fun. The colorful text is really eye-catching, it immediately grabs the reader's attention. The language used on the website is really persuasive. For example, the text is full of verbs suggest movement. The writer has challenged the reader with rhetorical questions, such as "Do you dare to ride the rapids?"

Varied vocabulary

A polished piece of writing should contain a good range of vocabulary. Repeatedly used words should be replaced with synonyms or similar appropriate words to add variety. Adverbs, such as *very* and *really*, should not be overused.

The language used on the website is convincing.

The word *persuasive* can be replaced with a synonym. The adverb *really* can be cut out.

Something missing?

If a word has been left out in handwritten work, insert a caret symbol (∧) where the words should go and write them neatly above. To insert a longer passage, put an asterisk (*) where the new text should start, put another asterisk at the bottom or side of the work, and write the extra text next to it.

The text is full of verbs ∧ suggest movement*.
            that

Use the asterisk for longer passages.

Use this mark to add single words.

*, such as "splash," "zoom," "race," and "spin."

REAL WORLD
George W. Bush

The former US president George W. Bush didn't always check his work. He is famous for making grammatical errors, such as "Rarely is the question asked: Is our children learning?" He also once said, "The goals of this country is to enhance prosperity and peace."

The spoken word

THE SPOKEN WORD IS DIFFERENT FROM WRITTEN LANGUAGE IN MANY KEY RESPECTS.

A person's speech is influenced by various factors, such as where he or she is from and to whom he or she is talking. It's important to consider these factors when writing or analyzing spoken language.

SEE ALSO	
‹ 62–63 Interjections	
‹ 86–87 Colloquialisms and slang	
‹ 88–89 Direct and indirect speech	
‹ 94–95 Periods and ellipses	
Debates and role plays	224–225 ›
Writing a speech	226–227 ›
Presentation skills	228–229 ›

Standard English

Standard English is often considered the "correct" form of English, because it is grammatically correct and does not use any slang. It is usually spoken in a neutral accent without any regional pronunciation; this is called General American in North America, Received Pronunciation in the UK, and General Australian in Australia. Standard English is used in formal situations, by public officials, and traditionally by the media.

Good evening. Welcome to the nine o'clock news.

Standard English uses formal, unabbreviated vocabulary and correct grammar.

Dialect and accent

Varieties of spoken English have developed in different English-speaking countries across the world, and in the regions and communities within them. Each variety has its own colloquial vocabulary and grammatical constructions. These varieties are known as dialects. An accent is the way in which language is pronounced. People use dialectal words and constructions in informal situations.

Hello, my friend. How are you?

This person is talking in Standard English, but it sounds odd in an informal situation.

G'day, mate. How ya goin'?

This is Australian slang for *hello*. It is a contraction of the greeting *good day*.

This is slang for *friend*.

The words *you* and *going* are spelled like this to show how they are pronounced in Australia.

Hey, dude. What's up?

This is another slang word for *friend*, more commonly used in North America.

REAL WORLD
Soap operas

The actors in television soap operas set in a particular location will use the accents from that place. For example, the actors in the show *Dallas* have Texas accents. This makes the dialogue seem more authentic. If the actors don't speak like this themselves, they have to learn the accent.

Tone and pitch

Speakers adjust the tone and pitch of their voice according to what they are saying. For example, someone might sound sad and low-pitched if delivering bad news, but delighted and high-pitched if discussing good news.

Bao Bao, the world's oldest panda, has died at age 34.

In other news, the weather is going to be fantastic this weekend.

This sentence would probably be delivered in an upbeat tone.

Pauses and fillers

When people are thinking about what to say next, or lose their train of thought, they pause. Sometimes people fill the silence with a hesitation device, such as *er* or *huh*, or with a sigh.

Structure

People often leave out words and use incomplete sentences when they are having spoken conversations. Contractions such as *haven't* and *couldn't* are used more frequently in speech than in written text, because the words are easier to say and help make a conversation flow.

So...why did your team play so badly tonight?

An ellipsis stands for a pause when spoken language is written down.

Er...we...have no excuse.

Did you see the game last night?

Awesome, wasn't it?

This isn't a full sentence. The speaker is relying on what was said before for his or her words to make sense.

Yeah.

Reckon we're going to the playoffs now.

The word I has been left out, and we're has been used instead of we are. The informal verb reckon is often used in colloquial speech.

GLOSSARY

Accent The way in which a language is pronounced.
Colloquial A word used to describe the language that is used in informal, everyday speech.
Contraction A word that has been shortened by removing letters.
Dialect The informal vocabulary and grammar used by a particular social or geographic group of people.
Pitch The height of a sound.
Tone The feeling or mood projected by a voice—for example, happy, sad, angry, or excited.

Debates and role plays

DEBATES AND ROLE PLAYS ARE TYPES OF CONVERSATIONS THAT ARE PREPARED FOR IN ADVANCE.

A prepared conversation is very different from an informal chat with friends. Participants need to think about what they are going to say in advance, and consider how they should react to others.

SEE ALSO	
‹ 202–203	Writing to influence
‹ 206–297	Writing to analyze or review
‹ 216–217	Writing a script
‹ 222–223	The spoken word
Presentation skills	228–229 ›

• A **formal discussion** requires **formal language** so try to use Standard English.

The big debate
A debate is a formal discussion or argument about a topic. Participants need to express their own opinions confidently, and listen and respond to others.

I think Powerman is the best superhero because he has the most superhuman powers. He is **incredibly strong** and can **fly at supersonic speeds**.

Always back up an opinion with evidence.

Acknowledge the opposite point of view before disagreeing with it.

I understand your point. However, I think Birdman's lack of superpowers makes him more inspirational, **because** he has had to overcome challenges and learn his skills.

▷ **Prepare**
Participants need to convey their ideas and opinions. The best way to do this is to research the topic in detail, and consider the different points of view related to it. The most effective discussions will cover as many viewpoints as possible.

◁ **Listen and respond**
Listening is just as important as talking. Participants should show that they are listening to others by responding appropriately and asking relevant questions. They should either agree with someone and add to the point, or disagree and say why.

So, Melvin, **what do you think?** Maybe you prefer someone else, such as Tigerwoman?

Coax other participants to join in by asking questions.

Avoid hostile body language.

▷ **Involve others**
It's important to involve all the participants in a discussion and to act as a group. Everyone should be allowed to speak, without someone else talking over them. Quieter members of the group may need encouragement to join in.

◁ **Body language**
Body language helps participants interact with one another. Nodding in agreement is a simple way to do this. Making eye contact with everyone in the group, especially the speaker, is also effective. If someone folds their arms, it looks as if they don't want to be there.

Role plays

A role play is a made-up scenario in which participants each play a character. There isn't a script, so everyone needs to act spontaneously. The best way to prepare is to think about the character's personality, and how they would behave in the specific situation.

The first **American presidential debate** was between the candidates **John F. Kennedy** and **Richard Nixon** in 1960. It was one of the **most-watched** broadcasts in US television history.

Get inside their head

A good way to start is to imagine what the character would be thinking. Reflect on the person's story so far, and what they would think about the current situation. Consider their relationships with the other characters, and how they will behave around them.

Talk the talk

To make characters convincing, it's important to talk like them. An angry person might shout, a shy character might mutter his or her words, and an excited person might talk quickly. Use an appropriate accent if the person is from a particular country or region, and use the right vocabulary for the character's age group.

Walk the walk

The character's personality or mood should be reflected with appropriate body language. For example, a confident character would hold her head up high and her shoulders back and might walk with a swagger. A timid or uncomfortable character would look down at the ground, shuffle, slouch, and avoid eye contact.

Not you again!

REAL WORLD
In court

A criminal trial is a type of debate, because the lawyers argue about whether a defendant is guilty or not guilty. The prosecution and defense lawyers take turns making their points and giving evidence. A judge, and sometimes a jury, will give a verdict. A lawyer's ability to persuade can make all the difference in a trial's outcome.

- Introduce some **controversial points of view** in a discussion. Even if no one agrees with them, unusual ideas can get a debate going.
- Do not **shout**. Even if there is a disagreement, it's important to remain **polite**.

Writing a speech

A SPEECH IS A TALK ON A SUBJECT GIVEN TO AN AUDIENCE.

People make speeches for many different reasons, but they are often for work or social occasions. The techniques used for writing a speech are similar to those used in written work, but a speech must be effective when read aloud.

SEE ALSO	
⟨ 34–35 Pronouns	
⟨ 182–183 Picking the right words	
⟨ 188–189 Paragraphing	
⟨ 202–203 Writing to influence	
⟨ 222–223 The spoken word	
Presentation skills	228–229 ⟩

Talking point

Every speech needs to have a clear and passionate message for its audience. For example, a politician makes speeches to persuade people to vote for him or her, or to support his or her policies. Activists speak to raise awareness about an issue, such as animal rights.

- Informal speeches can include some **slang**, but it's best to use **Standard English** so that the audience will **understand** what is **being said**.

GLOSSARY

Alliteration The repetition of certain letters or sounds for effect.
Pronoun A word that takes the place of a noun, such as *I*, *me*, or *she*.
Rhetorical question A question that does not require an answer but is used for effect.
Slogan A short but memorable statement that sums up a message.
Standard English The form of English that uses formal vocabulary and grammar.

Ideas for my speech:
- *Save the Brussels sprout!*
- *When I met my favorite sports hero.*
- *Mullet hairstyles are a fashion disaster.*
- *Why I should be the next James Bond.*
- *Cell phones should not be banned in school.*

Structure

Like any piece of writing, a speech needs to have a focused structure, with a clear beginning, middle, and end.

I have a shocking secret. I like Brussels sprouts!

Brussels sprouts are incredibly good for you. There is more vitamin C in a sprout than an orange.

So, next time you eat dinner, give the little green things a chance.

△ **Beginning**
The opening lines should capture the audience's attention, with a joke, a surprising statistic, or an inspirational quote.

△ **Middle**
The middle part of the speech should deliver the main points, one by one. Each point should be backed up with evidence.

△ **End**
The last section needs to sum up the message of the speech and ideally end with something memorable.

WRITING A SPEECH

Smooth talker

Speechwriters use particular techniques to create interesting speeches that will engage an audience. Most importantly, they consider what the words will sound like when they are spoken out loud.

Rhetorical questions

Sometimes, a speaker will ask the audience a question, often without expecting an answer. Posing questions makes listeners feel involved and encourages them to think about something in depth.

You say that you hate Brussels sprouts, but have you ever given them a chance?

Repetition and lists

Repeating words and phrases gives a speech a good rhythm and emphasizes important words and ideas. Patterns of three are particularly common in speech writing. Listing subjects, places, or names can reinforce how many there are of something.

Sprouts are bursting with goodness. They are packed with **vitamin C, vitamin A, potassium, calcium, iron, and protein**.

Emotive and sensational language

A speech isn't just a list of events or a logical argument. It needs to appeal to the audience. Speechwriters use emotive language to evoke a response in the audience, such as sympathy, guilt, or excitement.

Every year, thousands and thousands of untouched Brussels sprouts are **thoughtlessly dumped** in the trash.

Pronouns

Using the pronouns *I*, *you*, or *we* in a speech can make it more personal. Speakers also use friendly terms of address, such as *friends* or *comrades*, to relate to the audience.

I changed my mind about Brussels sprouts. **You** can, too. **Together we** can make this vegetable popular again.

Slogans

Speeches often contain memorable statements called slogans, which sum up an argument. They are usually short and powerful, and sound good when spoken out loud, often because they use alliteration.

Bring **b**ack the **B**russels!

REAL WORLD

I would also like to thank...

Actors often give speeches when they win prizes at awards ceremonies. The Academy Awards have become famous for having overly long and emotional speeches. The record for the longest speech is still held by Greer Garson, who rambled on for seven minutes in 1942. Since then, ceremony organizers have imposed a 45-second rule, so speeches longer than 45 seconds are cut off by the orchestra.

The best speeches are often **short**. **Abraham Lincoln's Gettysburg Address**, one of the most famous speeches in history, lasted for less than **three minutes**.

Presentation skills

THE BEST PUBLIC SPEAKERS ARE CLEAR AND ENGAGING.

Even a well-written speech will be dull if it is badly presented. It's important to speak clearly and to engage an audience with the right tone of voice, body language, and even props.

SEE ALSO
‹ 116–117 Bullet points
‹ 202–203 Writing to influence
‹ 222–223 The spoken word
‹ 224–225 Debates and role plays
‹ 226–227 Writing a speech

Flash cards

It's tempting to read out a speech word by word, but a spontaneous delivery is more entertaining for an audience. It's best to learn as much of a speech as possible, and prepare small cards with the important points, quotations, and statistics to use as prompts.

Write the important points on a flash card. These can be written in note form.

Why I love Brussels sprouts
- I have a secret. I love Brussels sprouts!
- The day I changed my mind.
- They have a bad reputation but don't deserve it.
- Largest producer is the Netherlands, with 82,000 tons a year.

Include statistics because they are easy to forget.

Speak up

A speaker should never shout, but should project his or her voice so that it can be heard around the room. It's also important not to speak too quickly, as the audience may find it difficult to keep up. In fact, pausing occasionally can be very effective because it gives an audience time to think about what is being said. Finally, there is no need to hide an accent, but the pronunciation should be clear.

Some nutritional facts about Brussels sprouts
- Brussels sprouts contain more vitamin C than oranges. (pause)
- There is almost no fat in Brussels sprouts. (pause)
- Unlike most vegetables, Brussels sprouts are high in protein. (pause)

Include pauses on a flash card to show when to break for a few seconds.

Intonation

When people talk, their voices go up and down and get louder and quieter. This natural variation is called intonation. If a person's voice stays the same, it will sound robotic and put the audience to sleep. Stressing important words or phrases helps to create a good rhythm, and will emphasize those points.

Underline or highlight important words or phrases that need to be stressed.

History of Brussels sprouts
- Forerunners to the Brussels sprout were cultivated in Ancient Rome.
- American Founding Father Thomas Jefferson grew Brussels sprouts.
- Today, production is huge. Approximately 32,000 tons are produced in the United States every year.

Gestures and movement

Gestures can make a presenter seem more enthusiastic and engaging. Speakers often wave their hands around to emphasize certain points and catch an audience's attention. Walking around a room makes a delivery more personal because the speaker moves closer to certain individuals. Making eye contact with individuals in an audience is also important.

- A speaker must sound **enthusiastic**. If he or she sounds bored, the audience will be, too.
- It can be useful to **practice** a speech in front of a **mirror**.

Maintain eye contact to engage the audience.

△ **Enthusiasm**
Enthusiastic gestures, such as punching the air or waving, can make a speaker seem more passionate.

△ **Big ideas**
Some actions—for example, spreading out the arms—can emphasize the size of an issue.

△ **Distraction**
It's important not to move around too much. Awkward movements can distract an audience from what the speaker is saying.

Visual aids

Sometimes speakers use visual aids to engage their audiences. These include images, graphs, and diagrams that explain complicated information or make it more interesting. Summarizing key points on a projector slide or handout will also emphasize the most important details, and help the audience to remember them.

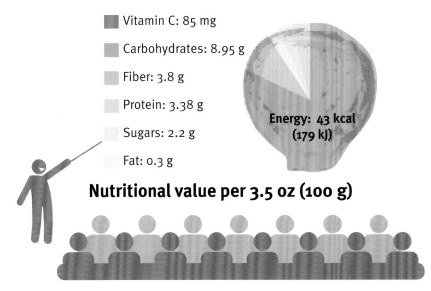

Vitamin C: 85 mg
Carbohydrates: 8.95 g
Fiber: 3.8 g
Protein: 3.38 g
Sugars: 2.2 g
Fat: 0.3 g
Energy: 43 kcal (179 kJ)

Nutritional value per 3.5 oz (100 g)

REAL WORLD
Dressing down

Public speakers even think about the way they dress when speaking to an audience. Some politicians or business professionals decide not to wear a suit and tie when making a speech to the public. By wearing more casual clothes, they hope that they will look more relaxed and approachable, so the audience will relate to them.

Reference

Grammar reference

Parts of speech

The different types of words that make up sentences are called parts of speech. Only nouns and verbs are essential elements of a sentence, but other parts of speech—such as adjectives and adverbs—can make a sentence more descriptive.

Part of speech	Meaning	Examples
noun	A name	cat, Evie, girl, house, water
adjective	Describes a noun or pronoun	big, funny, light, red, young
verb	Shows action or a state of being	be, go, read, speak, swim, walk
adverb	Describes verbs, adjectives and other adverbs, giving information on where, when and how much	briskly, easily, happily, here, loudly, quite, rather, soon, together, very
pronoun	Takes the place of a noun	he, she, you, we, them, it
preposition	Relates a noun or pronoun to another word in the sentence	about, above, from, in
conjunction	A joining word, used to link words and phrases	and, because, but, while, yet
interjection	An exclamation or remark	ah, hey, hi, hmm, wow, yes
article	Used with a noun to specify whether the noun is a particular person or thing, or something general	a, an, the
determiner	Precedes a noun and puts the noun in context	all, her, my, their, your

Negative and positive words and phrases

Some words have negative meanings—for example, *no*, *none*, *not*, *insult*, and *deny*. Other words can be made negative by adding a negative prefix, such as anti-, dis-, or un-, or suffix, such as -less. These words can then be used to make a sentence structure positive, which helps to simplify the sentence and make it easier to understand.

Negative structure	Positive structure
was not typical	was atypical
is not social	is antisocial
have no defenses	is defenseless
was not hydrated	was dehydrated
does not approve	disapproves
was not legal	was illegal
is not balanced	is imbalanced
was not direct	was indirect
was not spelled correctly	was misspelled
does not exist	is nonexistent
was not happy	was unhappy

Irregular verbs

Not all verbs follow the rules: Regular verbs follow a specific spelling pattern when they are converted into the past tense, but irregular verbs do not. Here are some of the irregular verbs and their past-tense and past-participle spellings.

Infinitive form	Simple past tense	Past participle
awake	awoke	awoken
bear	bore	born
beat	beat	beaten
bend	bent	bent
bind	bound	bound
bite	bit	bitten
burn	burned/burnt	burned/burnt
deal	dealt	dealt
dig	dug	dug
dream	dreamed/dreamt	dreamed/dreamt
feed	fed	fed
fight	fought	fought
forbid	forbade	forbidden
forget	forgot	forgotten
forgive	forgave	forgiven
forsake	forsook	forsaken
grind	ground	ground
hide	hid	hidden
hit	hit	hit
hurt	hurt	hurt
kneel	knelt	knelt
leap	leaped/leapt	leaped/leapt
light	lit	lit
overdo	overdid	overdone
prove	proved	proved/proven
read	read	read
ring	rang	rung
seek	sought	sought
shine	shone	shone
slay	slew	slain
stink	stank	stunk
tread	trod	trodden
wake	woke	woken
weave	wove	woven

Pronouns

Pronouns are used to represent nouns, so that sentences do not become repetitive. Singular nouns should be replaced by singular pronouns, and plural nouns should be replaced by plural pronouns. Some pronouns can be singular or plural.

Type	Singular	Plural
personal pronouns	I you he she it me him her	we you they us them
possessive pronouns	mine yours his hers its	ours yours theirs
relative pronouns	that what which who whom whose	that what which whose
reflexive pronouns	myself yourself himself herself	ourselves themselves
demonstrative pronouns	this that	these those
interrogative pronouns	who whom what which whose	what which
indefinite pronouns	all another any anyone anything each more most neither nobody none no one nothing other some somebody	all any both few many most none others several some

Common grammatical errors

Dangling participles
The introductory phrases in the first two sentences below set the sentence up for a noun that doesn't follow. This is called a "dangling participle" because the first part of the sentence is left dangling, with nothing to support or explain it. The noun that starts the second part of the sentence must be the noun that relates to the first part.

✗ **Smiling** from ear to ear, **the school** confirmed Jo's position on the debate team.

✗ **Smiling** from ear to ear, **Jo's position** on the school debate team was confirmed.

✓ **Smiling** from ear to ear, **Jo** learned that her position on the school debate team was confirmed.

Double negatives
Two negatives make a positive in math, and the same is true in language—two negative words in a sentence cancel each other out to upset the intended meaning.

✗ Charlie **couldn't** have **none** of the sweets.

✓ Charlie **could** have **none** of the sweets.

✓ Charlie **couldn't** have **any** of the sweets.

Incomplete sentences
A complete sentence must make sense, and to do this it must contain a subject and a verb. Even though the second sentence below is made up of only two words, it is complete because it has a subject and a verb. The first sentence is incomplete because it doesn't have a subject.

✗ Where is.

✓ I slept.

Misuse of *me*, *myself*, and *I*
If the following sentence is split into smaller parts, the sentence "Me traveled by train" is wrong.

✗ Luke and **me** traveled by train.

✓ Luke and **I** traveled by train.

Likewise, if this sentence is split into smaller parts, the sentence "It was a long journey for I" is wrong.

✗ It was a long journey for Luke and **I**.

✓ It was a long journey for Luke and **me**.

Myself always needs to have a subject to refer back to. There is no *I* or *me* in the first of the following sentences, so the use of *myself* in this instance is wrong.

✗ Luke wondered about **myself** in the same situation.

✓ I wondered about **myself** in the same situation.

Misplaced modifiers
A modifier needs to be close to the word that it is modifying; otherwise, confusion can occur. In the following sentence, the modifier *hot* should refer to the warmth of the porridge that Becky eats every morning, and not the heat of the bowl.

✗ Becky ate a **hot** bowl of porridge every morning.

✓ Becky ate a bowl of **hot** porridge every morning.

Misusing gender-neutral pronouns
Some pronouns, such as *they*, don't specify a gender. *They* is a plural pronoun and is sometimes misused in sentences where a singular pronoun is needed. In the following sentence, *they* is wrong because it is plural while the subject *someone* is singular. *They* should be replaced with *he or she,* or the sentence should be rewritten.

✗ If **someone** did that, then **they were** wrong.

✓ If **someone** did that, then **he or she was** wrong.

Split infinitives
An infinitive is the simplest form of a verb, such as *to run* or *to have*. It is preferable to keep the word *to* with the infinitive verb in a sentence. In the first sentence below, the adverb *secretly* has separated *to* from the verb *like*. This is a split infinitive and should be avoided.

✗ She used **to** secretly **like** football.

✓ She secretly used **to like** football.

Subject-verb disagreement
In the example below, the subject has been misidentified as *presents*—a plural noun—so the plural form of the verb (*were*) has been used. The subject of the sentence is actually the singular noun *sack*, so the singular form of the verb (*was*) should be used instead.

✗ The **sack** of presents **were** delivered late.

✓ The **sack** of presents **was** delivered late.

Non sequiturs
Literally translated, *non sequitur* means "it does not follow" and is an instance where one statement or conclusion doesn't logically follow from what was previously said or argued. Here are some examples:

You have a big nose. Therefore, your face looks young.

I will win the game. I have a hat.

Commonly misused words and expressions

Using *bored of* instead of *bored by* or *bored with*
✗ She was bored **of** studying.
✗ He was bored **of** the classes.
✓ She was bored **with** studying.
✓ He was bored **by** the classes.

Confusing *compared to* and *compared with*
Compared to should be used when asserting that two things are alike. In this sentence, Jess was like the best in the class.
✓ The teacher compared Jess **to** the best in the class.

Compared with should be used when comparing the similarities and differences between two things. In the sentence below, the teacher was considering how similar Jess was to the best in the class.
✓ The teacher compared Jess **with** the best in the class.

Using *different than* instead of *different from*
✗ The left side is different **than** the right side.
✓ The left side is different **from** the right side.

Using *like* as a conjunction instead of *as if* or *as though*
Like is correctly used as a preposition in the final example sentence; it should not be used as a conjunction.
✗ He acted **like** he didn't care.
✓ He acted **as though** he didn't care.
✓ It looks **like** a turtle.

Using *or* with *neither*
Either and *or* go together, and *neither* and *nor* go together.
✗ Use **neither** the left one **or** the right one.
✓ Use **either** the left one **or** the right one.
✓ Use **neither** the left one **nor** the right one.

Using *should of*, *would of*, and *could of* instead of *should have*, *would have*, and *should have*
Of is often wrongly used to mean *have* in spoken English.
✗ Steve **should of** stood up for himself.
✓ Steve **should have** stood up for himself.
✓ Steve **should've** stood up for himself.

Using *try and* and *go and* instead of *try to* and *go to*
The conjunction *and* is often wrongly used instead of the preposition *to* with the verbs *try* and *go*.
✗ We should **try and** change our flights.
✓ We should **try to** change our flights.
✗ I'll **go and** see the show.
✓ I'll **go to** see the show.

Using nouns as verbs
In spoken English, especially jargon, it is common for nouns to be used as verbs. This practice is best avoided.
✗ The fire will **impact** the environment.
✓ The fire will have **an impact** on the environment.

Rules for forming sentences

• A sentence must always contain a subject and a verb, start with a capital letter, and end with a period, question mark, or exclamation point. A sentence may also contain an object.

• The basic structure for a sentence to follow is subject–verb–object.

• Never join two main clauses using only a comma. Either separate the clauses into two separate sentences by using a period or a semicolon, or add a joining word such as *and* or *but* after the comma.

• Ensure that a sentence makes sense. If it doesn't make sense, one of the essential ingredients is probably missing, so the sentence is incomplete. For example, a subordinate clause does not make a complete sentence on its own; the main clause is also needed.

• Make sure that the subject and verb match. If the subject is singular, then the verb should be singular; if the subject is plural, then the verb should be plural.

• Use the active voice instead of the passive voice. The active voice is simpler, so the meaning is conveyed more clearly.

• Use positive sentence structure instead of negative sentence structure whenever possible in order to simplify sentences and make them easier to understand.

• Sentences should have a parallel structure. This means that the same patterns of words should be used to show that different parts of the sentence have equal importance.
✗ Darcy likes swimming, running, and to ride her bike.
✓ Darcy likes to swim, run, and ride her bike.

Punctuation reference

Punctuation mark	Name	How to use
.	period	• marks the end of a complete statement • marks the end of an abbreviated word
…	ellipsis	• marks where text has been omitted or an unfinished sentence
,	comma	• follows an introductory word, phrase, or clause • can be used as parentheses, to separate a nonessential part of a sentence • can be used with a conjunction to join two main clauses • separates words or phrases in a list • represents omitted words to avoid repetition in a sentence • can be used between an introduction to speech and the direct speech
;	semicolon	• separates two main clauses that are closely related • precedes adverbs such as *however*, *therefore*, *consequently*, and *nevertheless* to connect clauses • separates items in a complex list
:	colon	• connects a main clause to a clause, phrase, or word that is an explanation of the main clause or that emphasizes a point in the main clause • introduces a list after a complete statement • introduces quoted text
'	apostrophe	• marks a missing letter • indicates possession • creates plural forms if just adding an *s* is confusing
-	hyphen	• links two words in compound modifiers • can be used in fractions and in numbers from twenty-one to ninety-nine • joins certain prefixes to other words
" "	quotation marks	• can be used before and after direct speech and quoted text • separates a word or phrase in a sentence • can be used around titles of short works
?	question mark	• marks the end of a sentence that is a question
!	exclamation point	• marks the end of a sentence that expresses strong emotion • can be used at the end of an interruption to add emphasis
( )	parentheses	• can be used around nonessential information in a sentence • can be used around information that provides clarification
—	dash	• can be used in pairs around interruptions • marks a range of numbers (5–6 hours) • indicates direction of travel (Trys–Qysto route)
•	bullet point	• indicates a key point in a list
/	slash	• can be used to show an alternative instead of using the word *and* or *or*

Contractions

	be	will	would	have	had
I	I am / I'm	I will / I'll	I would / I'd	I have / I've	I had / I'd
you	you are / you're	you will / you'll	you would / you'd	you have / you've	you had / you'd
he	he is / he's	he will / he'll	he would / he'd	he has / he's	he had / he'd
she	she is / she's	she will / she'll	she would / she'd	she has / she's	she had / she'd
it	it is / it's	it will / it'll	it would / it'd	it has / it's	it had / it'd
we	we are / we're	we will / we'll	we would / we'd	we have / we've	we had / we'd
they	they are / they're	they will / they'll	they would / they'd	they have / they've	they had / they'd
that	that is / that's	that will / that'll	that would / that'd	that has / that's	that had / that'd
who	who is / who's	who will / who'll	who would / who'd	who has / who's	who had / who'd

Verbs and *not*	Contraction
is not	isn't
are not	aren't
was not	wasn't
were not	weren't
have not	haven't
has not	hasn't
had not	hadn't
will not	won't
would not	wouldn't
do not	don't
does not	doesn't
did not	didn't
cannot	can't
could not	couldn't
should not	shouldn't
might not	mightn't
must not	mustn't

Auxiliary verbs and *have*	would have	should have	could have	might have	must have
Contraction	would've	should've	could've	might've	must've

Common punctuation errors

Comma splice
A comma between two clauses creates a "comma splice" if it is used without a conjunction. The comma needs to be replaced with either a semicolon or a period, or the text can be rewritten to use a comma and a conjunction.

✗ You cook**,** I'll do the dishes.
✓ You cook**, and** I'll do the dishes.

Greengrocer's apostrophe
An unnecessary apostrophe incorrectly placed before the plural *s* is called a "greengrocer's apostrophe."

✗ carrot**'**s ✗ apple**'**s
✓ carrots ✓ apples

Hyphen in a compound modifier
Using a hyphen in a compound modifier that includes an adverb ending in -ly is incorrect. These compound modifiers are never hyphenated.

✗ cleverly-planned meeting
✓ cleverly planned meeting

Misuse of *your* and *you're*
Confusion between *your* and *you're* can be avoided by remembering that *you're* is a contraction made up of two separate words: *you* and *are*.

✗ It's in **you're** bag. ✗ **Your** mistaken.
✓ It's in **your** bag. ✓ **You're** mistaken.

Spelling reference

Commonly misspelled words

There are many difficult words in the English language that people struggle to spell correctly. Here are some of the most commonly misspelled words, with handy tips on how to spell them correctly.

Correct spelling	Spelling tips	Common misspelling
accommodation	there are two *c*'s and two *m*'s	accomodation
apparently	*ent* in the middle, not *ant*	apparantly
appearance	ends with **-ance**, not **-ence**	appearence
basically	ends with **-cally**, not **-cly**	basicly
beginning	double *n* in the middle	begining
believe	remember the "*i* before *e* except after *c*" rule	beleive or belive
business	starts with **busi-**	buisness
calendar	ends with **-ar**, not **-er**	calender
cemetery	ends with **-ery**, not **-ary**	cemetary
coming	there is only one *m*	comming
committee	double *m*, double *t*, and double *e*	commitee
completely	remember the last *e*; ends with **-tely**, not **-tly**	completly
conscious	remember the *s* before the *c* in the middle	concious
definitely	*ite* in the middle, not *ate*	definately
disappoint	there is one *s* and two *p*'s	dissapoint
embarrass	there are two *r*'s and two *s*'s	embarass
environment	remember the *n* before the *m*	enviroment
existence	ends with **-ence**, not **-ance**	existance
familiar	ends with **-iar**	familar
finally	there are two *l*'s	finaly
friend	remember the "*i* before *e* except after *c*" rule	freind
government	remember the *n* before the *m*	goverment
interrupt	there are two *r*'s in the middle	interupt
knowledge	remember the *d* before the *g*	knowlege
necessary	one *c* and two *s*'s	neccessary
separate	*par* in the middle, not *per*	seperate
successful	two *c*'s and two *s*'s	succesful
truly	there is no *e*	truely
unfortunately	ends with **-tely**, not **-tly**	unfortunatly
which	begins with **wh**	wich

SPELLING REFERENCE

Two words or one?
Some words in the English language are often used together, so it's easy to mistake them for a single word. Here are some phrases that many people fall into the trap of writing as one word instead of two.

a lot
bath time
blood sugar
cash flow
first aid

full time
hard copy
high chair
hip bone
home page

ice cream
life cycle
never mind
post office
race car

real time
seat belt
side effect
time frame
time sheet

Commonly confused words
The English language is full of similar-sounding words that have different meanings. It is essential, therefore, to spell the words correctly to achieve the correct meaning in a sentence. Here are some of the most commonly confused words that sound alike, with examples of their correct usage.

accept and except
I **accept** your apology.
Everyone was on the list **except** for me.

adverse and averse
She was feeling unwell due to the **adverse** effects of her medication.
He was lazy and **averse** to playing sports.

aisle and isle
The bride walked down the **aisle**.
They visited an **isle** near the coast of Scotland.

aloud and allowed
She read the book **aloud**.
He was **allowed** to choose which book to read.

amoral and immoral
Her **amoral** attitude meant that she didn't care if her actions were wrong.
He was fired from the company for **immoral** conduct.

appraise and apprise
The manager needed to **appraise** the employee's skills.
The lawyer arrived to **apprise** the defendant of his rights.

assent and ascent
He nodded his **assent**.
They watched the **ascent** of the balloon.

aural and oral
The **aural** test required her to listen.
The dentist performed an **oral** examination.

bare and bear
She went outside with **bare** feet.
The large **bear** roamed the woods.

break and brake
The chocolate was easy to **break** apart.
The car didn't **brake** fast enough.

broach and brooch
He decided to **broach** the subject for discussion.
She wore a pretty **brooch**.

capital and capitol
Richmond is the **capital** of Virginia.
The state **capitol** is an impressive building.

cereal and serial
He ate a bowl of **cereal** for breakfast.
She found the **serial** number on her computer.

complement and compliment
The colors **complement** each other well.
He paid her a **compliment** by telling her she was pretty.

cue and queue
The actor waited for his **cue** before walking on stage.
There are three jobs left in the printer **queue**.

desert and dessert
The **desert** is extremely hot and dry.
She decided to have cake for **dessert**.

pore and pour
He had a blocked **pore** on his nose.
She helped **pour** the drinks at the party.

principle and principal
The man was guided by strong **principles**.
He was given the role of the **principal** character.

stationary and stationery
The aircraft landed and remained **stationary**.
She looked in the **stationery** cabinet for a pen.

Tricky capitalized words

Certain words sometimes begin with a capital letter and other times they don't. It's important to know when to use a capital letter, so that written sentences make sense.

In some cases, capital letters are the only distinguishing factor between two words that are spelled the same way, but mean very different things.

Confused words	Lowercase meaning	Capitalized meaning
alpine and Alpine	relating to mountainous areas	relating to the Alps
august and August	majestic	the eighth month of the year
cancer and Cancer	a disease	a constellation and astrological sign
china and China	porcelain	a country in eastern Asia
earth and Earth	soil, dry land	the planet we live on
jack and Jack	a device for lifting heavy items	a male name
italic and Italic	a sloping typeface	relating to Italy
lent and Lent	the past tense of the verb *lend*	in Christianity, the period preceding Easter
march and March	to walk briskly and rhythmically	the third month of the year
marine and Marine	relating to the ocean	a member of the Marine Corps
mercury and Mercury	a chemical element	the closest planet to the Sun
nice and Nice	pleasant	a city in the south of France
pole and Pole	a long cylindrical object	a person from Poland
turkey and Turkey	a bird	a country in the Middle East

Common Latin and Greek roots

Latin root	Meaning	Examples
act	do	action, enact
ang	bend	angle, triangle
cap	head	capital, decapitate
dic	speak	dictate, predict
imag	likeness	image, imagination
just	law	justice, justify
ques	ask, seek	question, request
sci	know	conscience, science

Greek root	Meaning	Examples
arch	chief	archbishop, monarch
auto	self	autobiography, automatic
cosm	universe	cosmopolitan, cosmos
gen	birth, race	generation, genocide
log	word	apology, dialogue
lys	break down	analysis, catalyst
morph	shape	metamorphosis, morphology
phon	sound	symphony, telephone

Prefixes and suffixes

Prefixes	Meanings	Examples
aero-	air	**aero**dynamic, **aero**sol
agri-	of earth (relating to soil)	**agri**business, **agri**culturalist
ambi-	both	**ambi**guous, **ambi**valent
astro-	star	**astro**logy, **astro**naut
bio-	life, living things	**bio**diversity, **bio**fuel
contra-	against, opposite	**contra**band, **contra**dict
deca-	ten	**deca**de, **deca**hedron
di-, du-, duo-	two	**di**oxide, **du**et, **duo**tone
electro-	relating to electricity	**electro**lysis, **electro**magnet
geo-	relating to Earth	**geo**graphy, **geo**logy
hydro-	relating to water	**hydro**electricity, **hydro**power
infra-	below, beneath	**infra**red, **infra**stucture
kilo-	one thousand	**kilo**gram, **kilo**meter
mal-	bad	**mal**aise, **mal**nourished
maxi-	large	**maxi**mize, **maxi**mum
multi-	many	**multi**cultural, **multi**ply
nano-	one-billionth, extremely small	**nano**second, **nano**technology
ped-	foot	**ped**estrian, **ped**ometer
proto-	first	**proto**col, **proto**type
sy-, syl-, sym-, syn-	together, with	**sy**stem, **syl**lable, **sym**bol, **syn**thesis
tele-	distant	**tele**phone, **tele**scope

Suffixes	Meaning	Examples
-ade	action	block**ade**, masquer**ade**
-an	person, belonging to	guardi**an**, histori**an**
-ancy, -ency	state	vac**ancy**, ag**ency**
-ar, -ary	resembling	line**ar**, exempl**ary**
-ard, -art	characterize	wiz**ard**, bragg**art**
-ence, -ency	state	depend**ence**, emerg**ency**
-ess	female	lion**ess**, waitr**ess**
-fy	to make into	beauti**fy**, simpli**fy**
-iatry	healing, medical care	pod**iatry**, psych**iatry**
-ile	having the qualities of	project**ile**, sen**ile**
-or, -our	condition	hum**or**, glam**our**
-ory	having the function of	compuls**ory**, contribut**ory**
-phobia	fear of	agora**phobia**, arachno**phobia**
-ure	action	expos**ure**, meas**ure**
-wise	in the manner of	clock**wise**, like**wise**

Homonyms

Homonyms are words that have the same spelling and pronunciation, but different meanings.

Homonym	Meaning 1	Meaning 2	Meaning 3	Meaning 4
back	a person's back, from shoulders to hips	the back part of an object, opposite to the front	to go backward	in return
board	a thin, flat piece of wood	a decision-making body	regular meals	to get on to a ship or train
bore	to make a hole	a hollow part of a tube	a dull person or activity	to make someone weary
cast	to throw forcefully in a specific direction	to cause light or shadow to appear on a surface	to register a vote	actors in a drama
clear	easy to interpret or understand	having or feeling no doubt or confusion	transparent	free of obstacles
course	a route or direction	a dish forming one of the parts of a meal	the way in which something develops	a series of lessons on a particular subject
dock	an enclosed area of water in a port	the place in a court where defendants stand	to deduct, usually money	to cut short, for example, an animal's tail
fair	treating people equally or appropriately	light hair color or complexion	fine and dry weather	an event with exhibitions and amusements
tie	fabric worn around neck	to fasten with string or cord	the same score in a game	a bond that unites people

Homophones

Homophones are words with identical pronunciations, but different spellings and meanings.

Spelling 1	Meaning 1	Spelling 2	Meaning 2	Spelling 3	Meaning 3
aisle	a passage	isle	a small island	I'll	Contracted form of *I will*
buy	to purchase	by	through the agency of	bye	short for *goodbye*
cent	a monetary unit	scent	an odor	sent	past tense of the verb *send*
cite	to mention	sight	vision	site	a place
for	in support of	fore	situated in front	four	the number (4)
meat	animal flesh as food	meet	to get together	mete	to dispense a punishment
rain	precipitation from the sky	rein	a strip attached to a horse for guidance	reign	the period of rule by a monarch
raise	to lift something	rays	beams of light	raze	to completely destroy or demolish
vain	conceited	vane	a device for showing wind direction	vein	a blood vessel

Useful spelling rules

- The "ee" sound at the end of a word is almost always spelled with a **y**, as in **emergency** and **dependency**. There are exceptions to this rule, such as **fee** and **coffee**.

- When **all** and **well** are followed by another syllable, they only have one **l**, as in **already** and **welcome**.

- When **full** and **till** are joined to a root syllable, the final **l** should be dropped, as in **useful** and **until**.

- When **two vowels** go walking, **the first one** does the talking. This means that when there are two vowels next to each other in a word, the first one represents the sound made when spoken, while the second vowel is silent, as in **approach** and **leather**. There are some exceptions to this rule, including **great** and **build**.

- When words end in a **silent -e**, drop the **silent -e** when adding endings that begin with a vowel: for example, when adding **-ing** to **give** to form **giving**. Keep the **silent -e** when adding endings that begin with a consonant: for example, when adding **-s** to **give** to form **gives**.

- If a word ends with an "ick" sound, spell it using *ick* if it has one syllable, as in **click** and **brick**. If the word has two or more syllables, spell it using *ic*, as in **electronic** and **catastrophic**. Some exceptions to this rule include **homesick** and **limerick**.

- The letter **q** is usually followed by a **u**, as in **quiet** and **sequence**.

Mnemonics and fun spelling tips

affect and effect
Affect is the **a**ction; **e**ffect is the **re**sult.

dilemma
Emma faced a dil**emma**.

ocean
Only **c**ats' **e**yes **a**re **n**arrow.

misspells
Miss Pells never misspells.

desert and dessert
What's the difference between deserts and desserts? Desserts are sweeter with **two s's** for sugars.

soldier
Sol**die**rs sometimes **die** in battle.

difficulty
Mrs. **D**, Mrs. **I**, Mrs. **FFI**, Mrs. **C**, Mrs. **U**, Mrs. **LTY**.

height and weight
There is an **eight** in h**eight** and w**eight**.

secretary
A **secret**ary must keep a **secret**.

island
An island **is land** that is surrounded by water.

measurement
You should be **sure** of your mea**sure**ments before you start work.

piece
You have to have a **pie** before you can have a **pie**ce.

hear
H**ear** with your **ear**.

Communication skills reference

Synonyms

Good writers use a wide range of vocabulary. Rather than using the same word repeatedly, try to use different words that mean the same thing. These are known as synonyms. Some alternatives may give more information than the original choice: For example, *she whispered* tells the reader much more than *she said*.

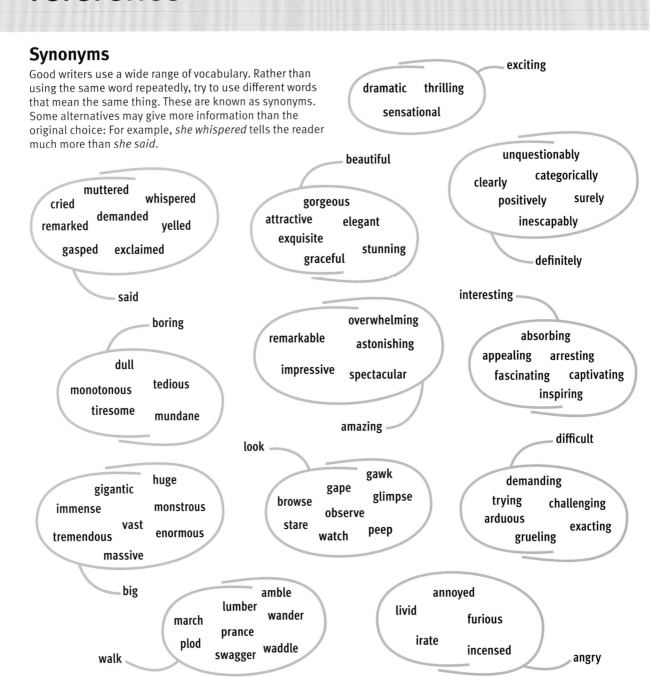

Adjectives to describe characters

The best stories include unique characters. Use unusual adjectives to describe a character's mood and personality.

absentminded	flamboyant	materialistic
argumentative	generous	morose
bossy	glamorous	optimistic
charismatic	gregarious	responsible
considerate	intelligent	ruthless
eccentric	intuitive	witty

Tautologies

Some phrases say the same thing twice. These are called tautologies and should be avoided because they are unnecessary.

Tautology	Reason to avoid
tiny little baby	*Tiny* and *little* mean the same thing.
a round circle	Circles are always round.
an old antique	An antique has to be old.
an unexpected surprise	All surprises are unexpected.
yellow in color	Something can't be yellow in anything other than color.
month of May	May is always a month.
new innovation	An innovation has to be new.

Clichés

A cliché is a colloquial expression that has been overused. Clichés should be avoided because they make a piece of writing unoriginal, and because they are informal and often ambiguous.

face the music
up in the air
as light as a feather
at the end of the day
at all costs
in a nutshell
on a roll
cost an arm and a leg

Emotive language

Writers use emotive language to have a greater emotional impact on their audience. This technique is useful when trying to persuade or entertain an audience. It's important to be aware of the effect this language can have in order to analyze and write emotive texts.

Normal version	Dramatic version
she cried	she wailed
a good result	a staggering result
disturbance in town square	riot in town square
school fire	school blaze
brave person	heroic citizen
unhappy workers	furious workers
animals killed	animals slaughtered
house prices fall	house prices plummet
problems in schools	chaos in schools

Less wordy

Using more words than necessary can obscure the meaning of a phrase. Concise writing is both clearer and more stylish.

Wordy version	Concise version
a considerable number of	many
are of the same opinion	agree
as a means of	to
at the present time	currently, now, today
at this point in time	now
give an indication of	show
has a requirement for	requires, needs
has the ability to	can
in close proximity to	near
in the absence of	without
in the course of	during
in the majority of instances	usually
in the very near future	soon
is aware of the fact	knows

REFERENCE

Cover letters

A cover letter is a formal letter written to accompany a résumé for a job application. It should be laid out like any formal letter, and include certain details that will promote the application. A good cover letter should be concise and no more than one page long.

The applicant's details go at the top right.

Joe Elf
Hollow Tree
Snowy Forest
North Pole

September 15, 2013

The date needs to be included under the applicant's address.

The employer's details go at the top left.

Mr. Santa Claus
Toy Workshop
Secret Mountain
North Pole

The first paragraph should state which role the applicant is applying for, and where he or she saw the vacancy.

Dear Mr. Claus,

I would like to apply for the position of Junior Toymaker advertised in the *North Pole Chronicle*. As requested, I have enclosed my résumé and two references.

The role would be an excellent opportunity for me to start my career in toy manufacturing. I believe that my internship experience and degree from the Toy College would make me an asset to the company.

I can be contacted at the address and phone number on my résumé. I am available for interview next week.

The middle of the letter needs to explain why the applicant wants the job, and what skills and experience he or she has.

Ending with a positive phrase will show enthusiasm.

I look forward to discussing this role with you soon.

Yours truly,

Joe Elf

Joe Elf

Citations

In academic work, writers have to cite their sources. This is to prove that they have not copied another scholar's writing, taken credit for someone else's ideas, or made up information. A citation needs to be added if another writer's direct words have been quoted, or his or her original ideas or findings are described. Statistics also need to be cited. There are several citation systems to choose from; however, the same system must be used throughout a piece of writing.

▷ **Numbering system**
In a numbering system, a small number is placed after each fact or quotation that needs to be cited. This corresponds to a numbered source placed at the bottom of the page, called a footnote. The details are repeated in the bibliography at the end of the work.

Pizza purists argue that pizzas should only be topped with tomatoes, herbs, and sometimes mozzarella. According to a prominent Italian food writer, "There are only two types of pizza—Marinara and Margherita. That is all I serve."[1]

1. Gennaro Rossi, *The Perfect Pizza* (London: Pizza Press, 2010), 9.

- The title of the book is written in italics.
- The location and name of the publisher appear in parentheses, separated by a colon. A publisher's name is followed by a comma and the publication date.
- The specific page reference(s) should also be included. There is no need to include abbreviations such as *p.* or *pp.*

▷ **Parenthetical system**
In a parenthetical system, citations appear in parentheses within the text. In North America, the two most common parenthetical systems are MLA style (shown here) and APA style, named after the Modern Language Association and the American Psychological Association, respectively.

Pizza purists argue that pizzas should only be topped with tomatoes, herbs, and sometimes mozzarella. According to a prominent Italian food writer, "There are only two types of pizza—Marinara and Margherita. That is all I serve" (Rossi 9).

- The last name of the author is included because it is not mentioned in the surrounding text. If the author's name is mentioned in the text, there is no need to include it in the citation.
- The exact page reference is always included.
- The period is placed outside the quotation marks, after the parentheses.

▷ **"Works Cited" list**
When using a parenthetical system, the rest of the information about the sources needs to be included in a "Works Cited" list at the end of the assignment. Unlike a bibliography, this list only includes the sources that have been quoted or paraphrased; it does not list books used for background research.

Romano, Silvio. *The History of Italian Cooking*. New York: Food Books, 1982. Print.

Rossi, Gennaro. *The Perfect Pizza*. London: Pizza Press, 2010. Print.

- The sources should be listed alphabetically by the author's last name.
- The title is italicized.
- The publisher's details are separated by a colon.
- End each entry with the medium of publication.

Glossary

abbreviation
A shortened form of a word, often with one or more periods to represent missing letters.

abstract noun
The name given to something that cannot be touched, such as a concept or a sensation.

accent
The way in which a language is pronounced, which varies across geographic areas.

acronym
An abbreviation made up of the initial letters of the main words in a phrase. These letters are pronounced as a word (rather than as separate letters), which represents the meaning of the original phrase.

active voice
When the subject of a sentence is performing the action of the verb, and the object is receiving it.

adjective
A word that describes a noun.

adjective phrase
A group of words that describe a noun or pronoun.

adjective prepositional phrase
A prepositional phrase that describes a noun.

adverb
A word that modifies the meaning of an adjective, verb, or other adverb.

adverb prepositional phrase
A prepositional phrase that describes a verb.

adverbial phrase
A group of words that behave in the same way as an adverb and answer questions such as: How? When? Why? Where? How often?

alliteration
The repetition of certain letters or sounds for effect.

Arabic numerals
Everyday numerals such as 1, 2, and 3.

attributive position
When an adjective is placed directly in front of the noun or pronoun that it is modifying.

auxiliary verb
A "helping" verb such as *be* or *have* that joins the main verb in a sentence to the subject. Auxiliary verbs are also used with other words to form contractions and negative sentences.

bibliography
A list of all the sources used in a piece of academic work.

blog
An online journal that contains the writer's comments and reflections. It is updated regularly.

cardinal number
A counting number such as *one*, *two*, *ten*, or *twenty-one*.

clause
A grammatical unit that contains a subject and a verb. Sentences are made up of one or more clauses.

collective noun
The name given to a collection of individuals—people or things.

colloquial language
The language that is used in everyday speech.

colloquialism
A word or phrase used only in informal speech.

command
A sentence that gives an instruction.

common noun
The name given to everyday objects, places, people, and ideas.

concrete noun
The name given to an ordinary, physical thing, such as an object or animal.

conjunction
A word or phrase used to connect words, phrases, and clauses.

consonant
A letter of the alphabet that is not a vowel.

contraction
A shortened form of a word or words, in which letters are omitted from the middle and replaced with an apostrophe.

coordinating conjunction
A word that connects words, phrases, and clauses of equal importance.

dangling participle
When a modifying phrase or clause that starts with a participle is put in the wrong place in a sentence, and has no subject to hold on to.

dialect
The informal vocabulary and grammar used by a particular social or geographic group.

direct object
The person or thing directly affected by the action of the verb.

direct speech
Text that represents spoken words and is written in quotation marks.

exaggeration
When something is represented as larger or better than it actually is.

exclamation
A sentence that expresses a strong emotion, such as surprise, or a raised voice, and ends in an exclamation point.

fact
A statement that can be proved.

first person narrative
When an author writes a piece from his or her point of view, using *I* and *my*.

gerund
The name given to the present participle when it is used as a noun.

headline
The statement at the top of an article that tells the reader what the article is about.

hyperbole
An extreme form of exaggeration that may not be taken seriously, but grabs the reader's attention.

hyperlink
A word, phrase, or icon on the World Wide Web, which, if clicked, takes the user to a new document or website.

indefinite pronoun
A pronoun such as *everyone* that refers to nobody or nothing specific.

indirect object
The person or thing indirectly affected by the action of the verb.

indirect question
A sentence that reports a question that has been asked, without expecting an answer, and ends in a period.

infinitive
The simplest form of a verb: the form that is used in dictionaries.

interjection
A word or phrase that occurs alone and expresses emotion.

intonation
The variation of pitch and loudness in a person's voice.

intransitive verb
A verb that does not require an object.

italics
A style of type in which the letters are printed at an angle to resemble handwriting.

jargon
A type of slang that includes specialized terms that are used and understood by a select, often professional, group of people.

linking verb
A verb, such as *be*, that joins the subject of a sentence to a word or phrase—often an adjective—that describes the subject.

main clause
A group of words that contains a subject and a verb and makes complete sense on its own.

metaphor
A word or phrase that is used to describe something as if it were something else.

misplaced modifier
A modifier that has been placed so far from the person or thing it is intended to modify that it appears to modify a different person or thing.

modal auxiliary verb
An auxiliary verb such as *could* that is used with an action verb to express a command, an obligation, or a possibility.

morpheme
The smallest meaningful part of a word.

noun
A part of speech that refers to a person, place, or thing.

noun phrase
Several words that, when grouped together, perform the same function as a noun.

number
The term used to identify a noun or pronoun as singular or plural.

object
The person or thing (a noun or pronoun) that is receiving the action of the verb.

objective
When a piece of writing is not influenced by the writer's personal opinions.

onomatopoeia
The use of words that mimic the sounds they represent.

opinion
A statement based on someone's personal view.

ordinal number
The form of a number that includes *first*, *second*, *tenth*, and *twenty-first*.

participle
The form of a verb that ends in -ing (present participle) or -ed or -en (past participle).

passive voice
When the subject in a sentence is receiving the action of the verb, and the object is performing it. It is formed using the auxiliary verb *be* and the past participle.

past participle
The form of a verb that usually ends in -ed or -en. It is used with the auxiliary verbs *have* and *will* to form the perfect tenses, and with the auxiliary verb *be* to form the passive voice.

personal pronoun
A pronoun such as *she* that takes the place of a noun and represents people, places or things.

personification
When human actions or feelings are given to objects or ideas.

pitch
The height of a sound.

plural noun
When more than one person or thing is being described.

possessive determiner
A word that is used before a noun to show ownership.

predicate position
When an adjective follows a linking verb at the end of a sentence.

prefix
A group of letters attached to the start of a word that can change the original word's meaning.

prepositional phrasal verb
A verb followed by a preposition, which together act as a single unit to describe an action.

prepositional phrase
A preposition followed by a noun, pronoun, or noun phrase that together act as an adjective (describing a noun) or an adverb (describing a verb) in a sentence.

present participle
The form of a verb that ends in -ing. It is used with the auxiliary verb *be* to form the continuous tenses.

pronoun
A word, such as *I*, *some*, or *who* that takes the place of a noun.

proper noun
The name given to a particular person, place, or thing, which always starts with a capital letter.

pun
The use of a word or phrase that has two or more meanings for comic effect.

question
A sentence that asks for information.

quotation
Text that reproduces another author's exact words, and is written in quotation marks.

quote
To repeat the words of a person.

relative pronoun
A pronoun such as *which* that links one part of a sentence to another by introducing a relative clause, which describes an earlier noun or pronoun.

rhetorical question
A question that does not require an answer but is used for effect.

Roman numerals
Numbers represented by certain letters of the alphabet, such as *i* (one), *v* (five), and *x* (ten).

root
A whole word or part of a word that can attach to a suffix or prefix.

SEO
Standing for "Search Engine Optimization," this is the process that increases the online visibility of a website, so more Web users will visit it.

simile
A phrase that compares one thing to another using *as* or *like*.

slang
Words and phrases that occur in informal speech and are often only used by a select group of people.

slogan
A short but memorable statement that sums up a message.

Standard English
The form of English that uses formal vocabulary and grammar.

statement
A sentence that conveys a fact or piece of information.

subject
The person or thing that is performing the action of the verb.

subjective
When a piece of text is influenced by the writer's personal opinions.

subordinate clause
A group of words that contains a subject and a verb but depends on a main clause for its meaning.

subordinator
A conjunction used to connect words, phrases, and clauses of unequal importance.

suffix
An ending made up of one or more letters that is added to a word to change its form or its meaning.

superlative
The form of an adjective or adverb that suggests the greatest or least of something.

syllable
A unit of pronunciation that has one vowel sound.

synonyms
Words that have the same or similar meanings.

tautology
Saying the same thing more than once using different words.

tense
The form of a verb that indicates the timing of an action.

third person narrative
When an author writes from a detached or outside point of view, using *he/his* or *she/her*.

tone
The feeling or mood projected by a voice: for example, happy, sad, angry, or excited.

transitive verb
A verb that must be used with an object.

verb
A part of speech that describes the action of a noun or pronoun, or a state of being.

vowel
One of the five letters *a*, *e*, *i*, *o*, or *u*.

Index

A

abbreviations 172–173
  alphabetical order 129
  colloquialisms 86
  italicization 123
  punctuation 94, 95, 111, 172, 173
  slashes 121
  spoken language 12
  US states 95
accents 15, 161, 177, 222, 225, 228
acronyms 95, 172, 173, 182
addresses 119, 121, 200, 201
adjective phrases 64
adjective clauses
  see relative clauses
adjectives 20, 26–27, 245
  attributive position 26
  using commas with 99
  comparatives 28
  compound adjectives 26
  descriptive language 209
  endings 27
  infinitives 39
  lists 27
  misplaced 76
  and nouns 23
  participles 47
  predicate position 27
  "proper" adjectives 26
  superlatives 28
  in writing, to add detail 185
adverbial clauses 67
adverbial phrases 64, 89
adverbs 20, 40–41, 89
  confusion with adjectives 27
  as conjunctions 59
  descriptive language 209
  in dramatic scripts 217
  in instructions 197
  misplaced 76, 77
  in phrasal verbs 56, 57
  in phrases 64
  split infinitives 39
  to add detail 185
  to vary sentences 185
advertising 75, 84, 191, 194
  images 195
  language 28, 208
advice, giving 205
affixes 142, 143
air quotes 109
alliteration 85, 183, 199, 219
alphabets 126, 159
  alphabetical order 128–129
  NATO phonetic alphabet 133

American spellings 14, 15, 174–177
ampersands (&) 120, 121
analogies 84
analysis 206, 207, 222
anaphora 85
apostrophes 104–105
  contractions 80, 104, 237
  greengrocer's apostrophe 104
arguments 202, 224
articles 21, 30–31
  and adjectives 30
  definite article 30, 31
  indefinite article 30, 31
  and nouns 23, 30
  zero article 31
articles (written works) 188, 190, 192, 198–199
  headlines 194, 196, 199
  images 195
  pull quotes 195
assonance 183
asterisks (*) 121, 221
at sign (@) 120, 121
atmosphere 212, 218
audience 181, 182, 191, 207
  formal or informal? 13
  influencing 202–203
  vocabulary 182, 191, 196, 198
autobiographical writing 211, 219

B

Bible references 103
bibliographies 186, 187, 243
blends 133
blogs 215
body language 181, 224, 225, 229
bold text 194, 195
brackets 114, 115
bring or *take*? 79
British spellings 14, 174–177
bullet points 116–117, 194, 197, 205, 215, 228
Bush, George W. 221

C

can or *may*? 78
capital letters 158–159, 240
  abbreviations 173
  alphabet 129, 159
  articles 31, 158
  bulleted text 117

headlines 194
  Latin words 122
  proper nouns 23, 26, 159
  sentences 68
  time, periods of 158
  titles of works 31, 158
captions 195
characters
  in a dramatic script 217
  in a narrative 212, 213, 245
children, communicating to 191, 194
clause order 73, 74
clauses 66–67
  adverbial clauses 67
  main 66, 72
    linking 58, 70–71, 98
  nonrestrictive clauses 82, 83
  relative clauses 67, 82–83
  restrictive clauses 83
  subordinate clauses 59, 66, 72
    placement of 73, 74, 75, 77
clichés 84, 245
clincher statements 189
collective nouns 23
  plurals 25
colloquialisms 86, 183, 191
colons 102–103
  introducing a list 102
  joining clauses 71, 102
  quotations 193
  ratio 102
  time 119
color 191, 194
comic books 112
commands 49, 55, 69, 94, 113
  advice 205
  instructions 197
commas 96–99
  in bibliographies 187, 247
  with conjunctions 59, 71, 98
  with direct address 97
  with direct speech 97, 108
  interjections 62, 63
  after introductions 96, 97
  in lists 99
  nonrestrictive clauses 82, 83, 96
  numbers 119
  for omitted words 98
serial comma 99
  subordinate clauses 73
  tag questions 111
commentary, sports 185
commenting on texts 192–193
communication

audience 181, 182, 191, 202–203, 207
  layout 181, 194–195, 201, 215
  planning 186–187, 202
  purpose 181, 190, 193, 215
  research 186–187
  spoken 12, 13, 185, 222–229
  tone 181, 184, 185, 201, 222
  vocabulary 181, 182–183, 191, 196, 198
  Web 214–215
  see also writing
comparing texts 193
comparatives 28
  bound morphemes 136
  irregular spellings 29
  with *more* or *most* 29
complaint letters 200, 201
compound adjectives 26, 106, 107
compound words 162–163
  American spelling 177
conclusions 187, 189
  analysis 206, 207
conjunctions 21, 58–59, 70
  correlative 58
  subordinators 59
connectives *see* conjunctions
consonants 132–133
  blends 133
  digraphs 133
  double consonants 154, 155
    British spelling 174
  graphemes 132–133
  sounds 132–133
  y 131, 147
contractions 79, 80, 104, 173, 222, 223, 237
creative writing 184
cross-references 186
crosswords 166

D

dangling participles 72, 77
dashes 14, 103, 115
  with interruptions 115
  ranges 115, 118
dates 118
  adding a prefix 107
  letters 200, 201
  ranges 115
debates 224, 225
dependent clauses
  see subordinate clauses
determiners 21, 32–33
  and adjectives 32

INDEX **253**

demonstrative determiners 32
interrogative determiners 33
and nouns 23, 32, 33
possessive determiners 33, 36, 37
and pronouns 36, 37
singular or plural 36, 37
see also articles
diagrams 195, 197, 229
dialects 14, 15, 222
dialogue 13, 88, 213, 217
dictionaries 64, 129
　abbreviations 86
　Oxford English Dictionary 176
　Webster's Dictionary 14, 175
digraphs 133
direct address 97, 203, 205, 211
direct speech 88, 89
　punctuation in 88, 97, 108–109
direction of travel 115
Domesday Book 138

E

editing 220–221
ellipses 95, 223
e-mails 94, 120, 200, 201
　language 86, 201
emoticons 103
emotion, expressing 62, 69
　exclamation points 112
　language 202–203, 245
　real-life stories 202
　rhetorical questions 111, 203
　in speech 89
emphasis
　colons 102
　commands 49, 55
　to contradict 48
　determination 49
　exaggeration 203
　exclamation points 113
　figures of speech 85
　intonation 228
　italicization 123, 194
　rhetorical questions 111, 203
　in sentences 184
errors, checking for 220–221
essays 109, 188
euphemism 85
exaggeration 203
exclamation points 112–113
　commands 55, 69, 94
　after an ellipsis 95

imperative mood 55
　and interjections 62
exclamations 69, 113
eye contact 181, 224, 229

F

facts 55, 68, 88, 190, 193, 196, 203
fewer or less? 79
fiction 189
figurative language 209, 213
figures of speech 85
flash cards 228
fonts 191, 194, 195
footnotes 121, 243
foreign words 122
formal writing 191
　exclamation marks 112
　letters 183, 200, 246
　and prepositions 60
　superlatives 28
fractions 107, 118
French words 139, 141

G

gender of words 30, 36, 37
genres 190
gerunds 47
good or well? 79
graphemes
　consonants 132–133
　vowels 130–131
graphs 195, 229
Greek root words 127, 138, 140, 141, 240
greetings 63, 222

H

haiku poetry 134
hashes see pound signs
headings, letters 200
headlines 194, 196, 199, 214
hesitation devices 63
holy books 123
homographs 167
homonyms 166, 242
homophones 127, 167, 242
humor, creating 183
hyperbole 85
hyperlinks 215
hyphens 106–107
　compound adjectives 26, 106, 107
　compound words 163, 177

in numbers 107
prefixes 107, 142
suspended 107

I

"i before e" rule 156–157
I or me? 78
iambic pentameter 135
idea generation 186, 187
idioms 84
images see pictures
indentation 188
independent clauses
　see main clauses
indexes 129
indirect speech 88, 89
informal language 86–87, 183, 191
　blogs 215
　letters 201
　spoken language 12, 13, 226
　see also colloquialisms, slang
initialisms 173
instructions 196, 197
interjections 21, 62–63, 97, 113
　asides 63
　emotion, expressing 62
　greetings 63
Internet see Web
interruptions 63
　using commas 97,
　using dashes 115
　adding emphasis 113
　using parentheses 114
introductions 187, 188
irony 85
italics 122–123, 194
its or it's? 79

J

jargon 87, 182, 183, 191
job seeking 11, 19, 200, 201, 240
Jonson, Ben 101

K

key words 192, 214

L

language 11, 191, 227
　descriptive 208, 209

e-mails 86, 201
English around the world 14–15
　figurative 209, 213
　persuasive 202–203, 245
layouts 194–195
　blogs 215
　letters 190, 200, 201
Latin words 122, 138
　abbreviations 172
　root words 127, 140, 141, 240
leaflets 190, 194, 196, 205
letters of the alphabet 126
letters, writing 188–189, 196
　complaint 200
　formal 183, 200
　informal 201
　layout 190, 200, 201
linking words and phrases 204
　see also conjunctions
lists 99, 101
　bullet points 116
　numbered 117
literally, use of 79
logos 214

M

magazine articles 190
　advice columns 205
　headlines 194, 196
　pull quotes 195
main clauses 66, 72
　linking 58, 70–71, 98
maps 197, 210
may or might? 78
measurements
　metric 95, 175
metaphor 84, 85, 209
mid-Atlantic English 177
mind maps 186
mnemonics 156, 165, 243
modifiers 76–77
　adverbs 41, 76
　compound words 162–163
　hyphens (compound modifiers) 106
　squinting 77
moods 54, 55
　imperative 55, 197
　indicative 55
　in narratives 213
　re-creations 218
　role play 225
　in scripts 217
　subjunctive 55
morphemes 136–137
morphology 137

N

names
  alphabetical order 129
  American spelling 175
  buildings and monuments 123
  in letter writing 200, 201
  proper nouns 23, 122, 159, 175
  vehicles 123
narratives 212–213
  changing viewpoints 218
narrators 212, 216
NATO phonetic alphabet 133
negatives 232
  contractions 80, 237
double negatives 80, 81
  sentences 48, 80
newspapers 190, 192, 198–199, 219
  advice columns 205
  headlines 194, 196, 199
  images 195
  pull quotes 195
nonfiction 190–191
  advice 205
  analysis 206, 207
  autobiographies 210–211
  reviews 207
  travel 211
nonrestrictive clauses 82, 83
note-taking 186, 187, 192
noun phrases 23, 30, 32, 60, 64, 65
nouns 22–23
  and adjectives 26
  abstract nouns 22
  collective nouns 22, 52
  common nouns 22
  compound words 162–163
  and determiners 32
  infinitives 39
  in phrases 23, 30, 60, 64, 65
  participles 47
  phrases 60, 64
  plurals 24–25
  possessives 105
  proper nouns 23, 122, 159
    used as adjectives 26
    American spelling 175
  as subjects 38
numbers 118–119
  alphabetical order 129
  Arabic numerals 118
  cardinal numbers 33
  dates 118
  as determiners 33
  instructions 197
  ordinal numbers 33
  ranges 115
  Roman numerals 119
  writing out 107, 118, 119

O

objects 38, 68
offensive words 121
Old English words 127, 139
omitted words
  asterisks 121
  contractions 80, 104, 237
  ellipses 95
  spoken language 12, 223
  see also abbreviations
onomatopoeia 85, 209
opinions 190, 193
  in arguments 202
  autobiographical writing 211
  reviews 207
  writing without 206
overused words 182, 221
oxymoron 85

P

page references 115, 119
paragraphs 187, 188–189, 221
  blogs 215
  e-mails 201
  indentation 188
  informative writing 196
  length 199
  opening paragraphs 188
  Web 214
parentheses 114, 247
  directions in scripts 217
  and interjections 63
  and interruptions 113, 114
  marking mistakes 220
participles 46–47
  dangling participles 72, 77
  past participles 44, 46, 51, 243
    as adjectives 47
    passive voice 54
  present participles 45, 46
    as adjectives 47
    as nouns 47
particles 56
parts of speech 20–21, 232
periods 94–95
  abbreviations 94, 172, 173
  bibliographies 187
  bulleted text 117
  ellipses 95
  indirect questions 110
  quotation marks 95
  sentences 68, 69
  time 119
  Web and e-mail 94
personality 211, 225
personification 85, 209
persuasive writing 202–203
phonemes 130, 132
phrasal verbs 56–57, 61, 106
phrases 64–65, 232, 239
  adjective 64
  adverbial 64
  long to short 182
  noun phrases 23, 30, 32, 60, 64, 65
  prepositional 23, 52, 53, 60, 65, 77
pictures 191, 195, 196, 197,
  life maps 210
  presentations 229
  scripts 216
plagiarism 186
plays *see* scripts
plots 212, 218
plurals
  using apostrophes 104
  bound morphemes 136
  collective nouns 25
  determiners 36, 37
  nouns 24–25
  using parentheses 114
  possessives 105
  pronouns 36
  verbs 25, 52–53
poetry
  assonance 183
  haiku 134
possession
  apostrophes 104–105
  bound morphemes 136
  determiners 33
  nouns 105
  pronouns 34
posters 203
pound signs 121
prefixes 107, 127, 134, 140, 142, 155, 241
  morphemes 136
prepositional phrases 52, 53, 60, 65
  misplaced 77
  and nouns 23
prepositions 20, 60–61
  and nouns 28
  passive voice 54
  in phrasal verbs 56, 57
  in phrases 52, 60, 61, 64, 65
  in writing 185
presentations 228–229
bulleted text 116–117
pronouns 20, 33, 34–35, 58, 243
  and adjectives 26
  demonstrative 35
  gender agreement 36–37
  indefinite 35, 36, 37, 53, 81
  interrogative 35
  negatives 81
  personal 34, 36, 37, 42, 203, 205, 211, 227
  I or *me*? 78
  possessive 34
  reflexive 34, 35
  relative 34, 67, 82, 83
  as subjects 38
  tenses 42
pronunciation
  accents 15, 161, 225, 228
  acronyms 173
  auxiliary letters 161
  dialects 14, 15
  hard and soft letter sounds 144–145, 151
  homonyms 166
  noun or verb? 168
  public speaking 228
  silent letters 160–161
  syllables 134–135
  word stress 135
public speaking
  see spoken language
punctuation 90–123, 236–237
punctuation marks 92–93, 236
puns 85, 183, 199

Q

quantity, expressing 33, 53
question marks 110–111
  after an ellipsis 95
  and quotation marks 88, 109
questions 68, 110–111, 224
  embedded 110
  indirect 110
  interrogative determiners 33
  interrogative pronouns 35
  rhetorical 111, 188, 203, 227
  tag 111
quotation marks 108–109
  dialogue 213
  direct speech 88, 108–109,
  double or single quotation marks 109
  quotations 109, 186, 193

INDEX

quotations 109, 193
　added or changed text in brackets 114, 115
　to begin a text or a speech 188, 226
　capital letters 158
　ellipses 95
　introducing quotations 97, 103, 193
　newspaper articles 199
　pull quotes 195
　sources 186, 193, 203, 247
QWERTY keyboard 126

R

reading, commenting and comparing 192–193
real-life stories 202, 210–211
re-creations 218–219
references
　Bible references 103
　cross-references 186
　as evidence 193, 207, 226
　page references 115, 119
relative clauses 67, 82–83
repetition 12, 199, 203, 227
research 186, 187
restrictive clauses 83
reviewing text 220–221
reviews 207
rhetorical devices 203
root words 127, 138, 140–141, 142, 151, 240

S

scientific names 122
scripts
　asides 63
　dramatic 217
　Roman numerals 119
　writing 216–217
semicolons 100–101
　before adverbs 101
　joining main clauses 59, 71, 100
　lists 101
sentence fragments 75
sentences 38, 68–69, 184–185
　active 54
　beginning of 185
　complex 72–73, 74
　compound 70–71
　conditional
　　subjunctive mood 55
　consistent language 60
　length 184, 191, 199

negative sentences 48, 80
pace, change of 184
positive sentences 81, 200
rules for forming 235
topic sentences 189
word groups 19
word order 18, 19, 38
　see also main clauses
settings 213, 217
sic 115
signs 54, 111
simile 85, 209
slang 86, 87, 183, 191, 215, 222
slashes 120, 121
slogans 227
sounding out letters 165
　accents, regional 161
　consonants 132–133
　　double 154, 155
　hard and soft sounds 144–145, 151
　homographs 167
　homonyms 166
　homophones 167
　silent letters 160–161
　vowels 130–131, 134, 243
　　i before *e* 157
　　short vowels 154
sources 186, 203, 247
speech
　direct 88, 89, 97, 108–109, 213
　indirect or reported 88, 89
　informal 86–87
speeches 226–227
spell-checkers 220
spelling 124–177, 238–243
　American spellings 14, 15, 174–177
　British spellings 14, 174–177
　confused meanings 170, 171
　consonants 154, 155
　homographs 167
　homonyms 166, 242
　homophones 167, 242
　"*i* before *e*" rule 156–157
　irregular words 164–165
　mnemonics 156, 165, 243
　morphemes 136–137
　noun or verb? 168
　one or two words? 169, 239
　past tense 177
　roots 140–141, 240
　silent letters 160–161, 177
　similar sounding words 167, 169, 171, 239
　sounding out 130–135, 144–145, 154, 165, 168

suffix rules 148–151, 153, 155
techniques for spelling 165
word endings (not suffixes) 152–153
split infinitives 39
spoken language 12, 13, 222–229
　debates 224, 225
　presentations 116–117, 228–229
　role plays 225
　speeches 226–227
　sports commentary 185
　see also speech
squinting modifiers 77
statements 68, 81, 94, 189
　exclamations 113
statistics 186, 188, 203, 226, 243
　graphs and diagrams 195
subheadings 194, 195, 197
　Web 214, 215
subject matter
　audience 191, 207
　newspaper articles 198
subjects 38, 52
　in clauses 66, 68, 69
　compound subjects 53
　omitting 71
　and voices 54
subordinate clauses 59, 66, 72
　placement of 73, 74, 75, 77
subordinators 59, 66, 67, 73
suffixes 127, 134, 140, 143, 241
　double consonants 155
　morphemes 136
　suffix rules with word endings
　　-able 150
　　-al 153
　　-e 146
　　-ible 151
　　-sion 149
　　-ssion 149
　　-tion 148
　　-y 147, 155
　unusual spellings 149
　vowels 155
superlatives 28, 29
　bound morphemes 136
　exaggeration 203
　irregular spellings 29
　with more or most 29
syllables 134–135
　iambic pentameter 135
　sounding out 134, 157
　word stress 135
synonyms 182, 221, 244

T

tables 206
tautology 27, 245
telegrams 95
television 191
tenses 42–45
　continuous tenses 45
　first person 42, 43
　　narratives 212, 218
　future
　　continuous tense 45, 46
　　perfect tense 44
　　simple tense 43, 233
　past 88, 177
　　continuous tense 45
　　perfect tense 44
　　simple tense 43, 51
　perfect tenses 44, 46
　present 88
　　continuous tense 45
　　perfect tense 44
　　simple tense 43
　second person 42, 43
　third person 42, 43, 44
　　analysis 206
　　indirect speech 88
　　narratives 212, 218
　　subjunctive mood 55
text messages 183
that or *which*? 78, 83
themes 210
time 119
　adverbs 40, 41
　capitalization 159
　in speech 89
　words or numbers? 119
titles of works 103
　capital letters 31, 158
　in quotation marks 109
　italicization 111, 123
Twitter 121

U

underlining 123, 192, 228
understatement 85

V

verb agreement 52–53
verbs 20, 38–39
　auxiliary 43, 44, 46, 48–49
　　can or *may*? 78
　contractions 104, 237
　may or *might*? 78
　modal 49
　negatives 80

passive voice 54
  primary 49
  in clauses 66
infinitive 39, 43
intransitive 57
irregular 49, 50–51, 233
linking verbs 27, 39
and moods 55
past participle 44, 46, 51, 233
phrasal 56–57, 61, 106
and plural nouns 25
present participle 45
in speech 89
tenses 42–43
transitive 38, 57
and voices 54
viewpoints 218, 224
vocabulary 181, 182–183, 191
  autobiographical writing 211
  descriptive language 209
  informative writing 196
  newspaper articles 198
  role play 225
voice-overs 216, 217
voices
  active 54, 199
  passive 54
vowels
  sounds 130–131, 134, 146 243

W

Web 94
  addresses 120, 121
  using for research 186, 187
  writing for 214–215
whether or if? 79
who or whom? 78, 82
word endings
  -able 27, 143, 146, 150, 151
  -al 27, 143, 146, 153
  -e 29, 46, 50, 146, 147, 150, 177
  -el 153
  -ible 27, 143, 151
  -le 40, 134, 152
  -ol 152, 153
  -sion 148, 149
  -ssion 143, 148, 149
  -tion 22, 148
  -y 24, 29, 40, 143, 147, 150, 155
  unusual spellings 149
word families 141
word order 18, 19
  adjectives 26, 27
  adverbs 41
  articles 30
  attributive position 26
  determiners 32
  negatives 48
  objects 38
  phrasal verbs 57
  predicate position 27
  questions 33, 48, 68, 110–111
  sentences 68
  statements 68
  voices 54
word origins 14, 127, 138–139, 161
  Greek 127, 138, 140, 141
  Latin 122, 127, 138, 140, 141
  loan words 156
  Old English 127, 139
word stress 135
writing 12
  answers 192–193, 220
  audience 13, 181, 182, 191, 202–203, 207
  blogs 215
  checking and editing 220–221
  cohesion 70, 184, 189
  comparing texts 193
  conclusions 187, 189, 207
  descriptive 208–209
  experiences 204, 210–211
  idea generation 186, 187
  to influence 202–203
  informative 196–197
  introductions 187, 188
  layouts 194–195, 201, 215
  letters 188, 190, 196, 201
    formal 183, 200
  narratives 212–213
  nonfiction 190
    advice 205
    autobiographies 210–211
    analysis 206, 207
    reviews 207
    travel 211
  paragraphs 187, 188–189, 196, 214, 215
  persuasive 202–203
  planning 187, 202
  plots 212, 218
  re-creations 218
  research 186, 187
  reviews 207
  scripts 216–217
  settings 213, 217
  sources 186, 203, 245
  stories
    to create excitement 184
    to create tension 184
  themes 210
  viewpoints 218
  Web 214–215

Acknowledgments

DORLING KINDERSLEY would like to thank David Ball and Mik Gates for design assistance, Mike Foster and Steve Capsey at Maltings Partnership for the illustrations, Helen Abramson for editorial assistance, Jenny Sich for proofreading, and Carron Brown for the index.

The publisher would like to thank the following for their kind permission to reproduce their photographs:

(Key: a-above; b-below/bottom; c-center; f-far; l-left; r-right; t-top)

29 Alamy Images: Niday Picture Library. **39** Alamy Images: Moviestore Collection Ltd. **45** Alamy Images: Kumar Sriskandan. Alamy Images: Kumar Sriskandan. **45** Alamy Images: Kumar Sriskandan. Alamy Images: Kumar Sriskandan. **54** Fotolia: (c) Stephen Finn. **63** Corbis: Bettmann. **69** Corbis: Susana Vera / Reuters. **75** Alamy Images: Vicki Beaver. **80** Corbis: Michael Ochs Archives. **84** Alamy Images: Stephen Finn. **86** Alamy Images: Jon Challicom. **98** Alamy Images: Papilio. **101** Corbis: Ken Welsh / * / Design Pics. **104** Alamy Images: Jamie Carstairs. **109** Getty Images: NBC. **111** Alamy Images: Eddie Gerald. **112** Alamy Images: flab. **121** Alamy Images: incamarastock. **134** Alamy Images: Phillip Augustavo. **138** Corbis: National Archives / Handout / Reuters. **143** Alamy Images: David Page. **156** Corbis: Franck Guiziou / Hemis. **158** Alamy Images: Martin Shields. **163** Dreamstime.com: Urosr. **166** Corbis: Darren Greenwood / Design Pics. **172** Corbis: Richard T Nowitz. **175** Getty Images. **177** Corbis: Bettmann. **182** Alamy Images: Paul David Drabble. **185** Dreamstime.com: Shariffc. **191** Corbis: JGI / Jamie Grill / Blend Images. **195** Used with kind permission of Dogs Trust, the UK's largest dog welfare charity with 18 rehoming centres nationwide and they never put down a healthy dog. **196** Alamy Images: Alistair Scott. **203** Alamy Images: Mary Evans Picture Library. **208** Corbis: Frank Lukasseck. **211** Alamy Images: Nancy G Photography / Nancy Greifenhagen. **214** Getty Images: Darryl Leniuk (b); Nicholas Pitt (t); Jochen Schlenker (c). **218** Corbis: John Springer Collection. **221** Alamy Images: Kristoffer Tripplaar. **222** The Kobal Collection: Warner Horizon TV. **225** Corbis: Heide Benser. **227** Corbis: GARY HERSHORN / X00129 / Reuters. **229** Corbis: Joshua Bickel

All other images © Dorling Kindersley
For further information see: www.dkimages.com

HELP YOUR KIDS WITH SCiEnCe

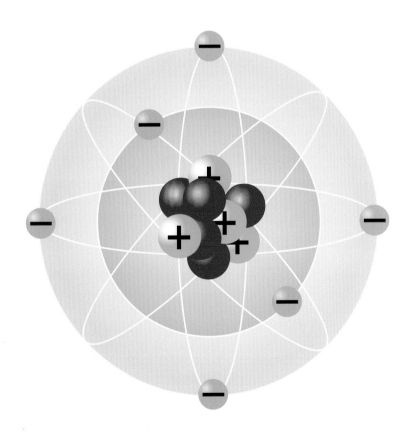

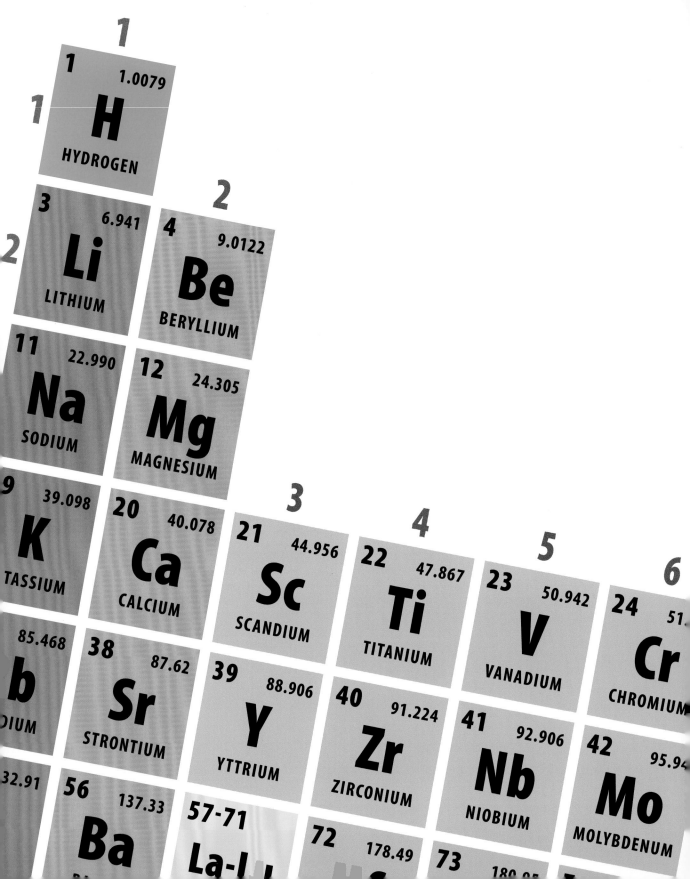

HELP YOUR KIDS WITH SCIENCE

A UNIQUE STEP-BY-STEP VISUAL GUIDE

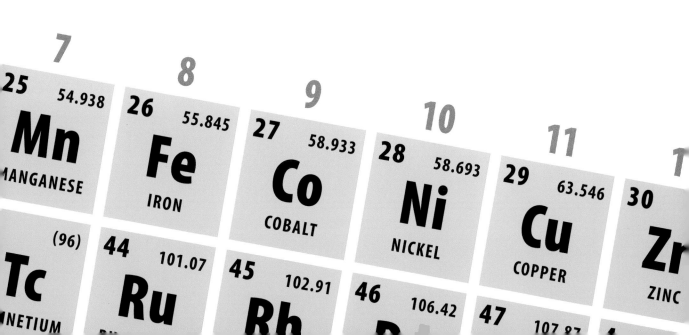

DORLING KINDERSLEY
Senior Editor Carron Brown
Project Editors Steven Carton, Matilda Gollon, Ashwin Khurana
US Editors Jill Hamilton, Rebecca Warren

Senior Designer Jim Green
Project Art Editor Katie Knutton
Art Editor Mary Sandberg
Designer Mik Gates
Packagers Angela Ball, David Ball

Managing Editor Linda Esposito
Managing Art Editor Diane Peyton Jones

Category Publisher Laura Buller

Senior Production Controller Erika Pepe
Production Editor Adam Stoneham

Jacket Editor Manisha Majithia
Jacket Designer Laura Brim

Publishing Director Jonathan Metcalf
Associate Publishing Director Liz Wheeler
Art Director Phil Ormerod

DORLING KINDERSLEY INDIA
Illustrations:
Managing Art Editor Arunesh Talapatra
Deputy Managing Art Editor Priyabrata Roy Chowdhury
Senior Art Editor Chhaya Sajwan
Art Editors Shruti Soharia Singh, Anjana Nair, Priyanka Singh, Shipra Jain
Assistant Art Editors Payal Rosalind Malik, Nidhi Mehra, Niyati Gosain, Neha Sharma, Jomin Johny, Vidit Vashisht

Editorial Assistance:
Deputy Managing Editor Pakshalika Jayaprakash
Senior Editor Monica Saigal
Project Editor Roma Malik

First American Edition, 2012
Published in the United States by
DK Publishing
345 Hudson Street
New York, New York 10014

Copyright © 2012, 2019 Dorling Kindersley Limited
DK, a Division of Penguin Random House, LLC
12 13 14 10 9 8 7 6 5 4 3 2 1
001—313518—Jan/2019

All rights reserved.
Without limiting the rights under the copyright reserved above, no part of this publication may be reproduced, stored in or introduced into a retrieval system, or transmitted, in any form, or by any means (electronic, mechanical, photocopying, recording, or otherwise), without the prior written permission of the copyright owner.
Published in Great Britain by Dorling Kindersley Limited.

A catalog record for this book is available from the Library of Congress.
ISBN 978-0-7566-9268-1

DK books are available at special discounts when purchased in bulk for sales promotions, premiums, fund-raising, or educational use. For details, contact:
DK Publishing Special Markets, 375 Hudson Street,
New York, New York, 10014 or SpecialSales@dk.com

Printed in China

A WORLD OF IDEAS:
SEE ALL THERE IS TO KNOW
www.dk.com

TOM JACKSON has written nearly 100 books and contributed to many more about science, technology, and natural history. Before becoming a writer, Tom spent time as a zookeeper, worked in safari parks in Zimbabwe, and was a member of the first British research expedition to the rain forests of Vietnam since the 1960s. Tom's work as a travel writer has taken him to the Sahara Desert, the Amazon jungle, the African savanna, and the Galápagos Islands—following in the footsteps of Charles Darwin.

DR. MIKE GOLDSMITH has a Ph.D. in astrophysics from Keele University, awarded for research into variable supergiant stars and cosmic dust formation. From 1987 until 2007 he worked in the Acoustics Group at the UK's National Physical Laboratory and was Head of the group for many years. His work there included research into automatic speech recognition, human speech patterns, environmental noise and novel microphones. He still works with NPL on a freelance basis and has recently completed a project to develop a new type of environmental noise mapping system. He has published more than forty scientific papers and technical reports, primarily on astrophysics and acoustics. Since 1999, Mike has written more than thirty science books for readers from babies to adults. Two of his books have been short-listed for the Aventis prize (now the Royal Society prize) for children's science books.

DR. STEWART SAVARD is the Science Head Teacher and district eLibrarian/eResource teacher in British Columbia's Comox Valley, Canada. Stewart has published papers on the role of Science Fiction and Science collections in libraries and helped edit 18 Elementary Science books. He is actively developing a range of school robotics programs.

ALLISON ELIA graduated from Brunel University in 1989, with a BSc (Hons) in Applied Physics. After graduating, she worked in Public Sector finance for several years, before realizing that her true vocation lay in education. In 1992 she undertook a PGCE in Secondary Science at Canterbury Christ Church College. For the past 18 years, Allison has taught Science in a number of schools across Essex and Kent and is currently the Head of Science at Fort Pitt Grammar School in Kent, UK.

Introduction

Science is vital to understanding everything in the Universe, from what makes the world go around to the workings of the human body. It explains why rainbows appear, how rockets work, and what happens when we flick a light switch. These may seem difficult subjects to get to grips with, but science needn't be complex or baffling. In fact, much of science depends on simple laws and principles. Learn these, and how they can be applied, and even the most complicated concepts become more straightforward and understandable.

This book sets out to explain the essentials of three key sciences—biology, chemistry, and physics. In particular, it focuses on the curricula for these subjects taught in schools worldwide for students between the ages of 9 and 16. This is often a crucial time for developing an understanding of science. Many children become confused by the terminology, equations, and sheer scale of some of the topics. Inevitably, parents—who themselves often have a limited understanding of science—are asked to help with homework. That is where this book can really come to the rescue.

Help Your Kids with Science **is designed to make all aspects of science easy and interesting. Beginning with a clear overview of what science is, each of the three sections is broken down into single-spread topics covering a key area of that science. The text is presented in short, easy-to-read chunks and is accompanied by clear, fully annotated diagrams and helpful equations. Explanations have been kept as simple as possible so that anyone—parent or child—can understand them.**

Another problem children often have with science is relating scientific concepts to real life. To help them make a connection, "Real World" panels have been introduced throughout the book. These give the reader a look at the practical applications of the science they've been reading about, and the exciting ways it can be used. Cross-references are used to link related topics and help reinforce the idea that many branches of science share the same basic principles. A useful reference section at the back provides quick and easy facts and explanations of terms used in the text.

As a former research scientist, I am only too aware of how science can seem bewildering. Even scientists can get stuck if they stray into an unfamiliar discipline or are the first to investigate a new line of study. The trick is to get a firm grasp on the basics, and that is exactly what this book sets out to provide. From there you can go on to investigate how the world around you works and explore the endless possibilities that science has to offer mankind.

DR. MIKE GOLDSMITH

Contents

INTRODUCTION by Dr. Mike Goldsmith	6
WHAT IS SCIENCE?	10
THE SCIENTIFIC METHOD	12
FIELDS OF SCIENCE	14

1 BIOLOGY

What is biology?	18
Variety of life	20
Cell structure	22
Cells at work	24
Fungi and single-celled life	26
Respiration	28
Photosynthesis	30
Feeding	32
Waste materials	34
Transport systems	36
Movement	38
Sensitivity	40
Reproduction I	42
Reproduction II	44
Life cycles	46
Hormones	48
Disease and immunity	50
Animal relationships	52
Plants	54
Invertebrates	56
Fish, amphibians, and reptiles	58
Mammals and birds	60
Body systems	62
Human senses	64
Human digestion	66
Brain and heart	68
Human health	70
Human reproduction	72
Ecosystems	74
Food chains	76
Cycles in nature	78
Evolution	80
Adaptations	82
Genetics I	84
Genetics II	86
Pollution	88
Human impact	90

2 CHEMISTRY

What is chemistry?	94
Properties of materials	96
States of matter	98
Changing states	100
Gas laws	102
Mixtures	104
Separating mixtures	106
Elements and atoms	108
Compounds and molecules	110
Ionic bonding	112
Covalent bonding	114
Periodic table	116
Understanding the periodic table	118
Alkali metals and alkali earth metals	120
The halogens and noble gases	122
Transition metals	124
Radioactivity	126
Chemical reactions	128
Combustion	130
Redox reactions	132
Energy and reactions	134
Rates of reaction	136
Catalysts	138
Reversible reactions	140
Water	142
Acids and bases	144
Acid reactions	146
Electrochemistry	148

Lab equipment and techniques	150
Refining metals	152
Chemical industry	154
Carbon and fossil fuels	156
Hydrocarbons	158
Functional groups	160
Polymers and plastics	162

3 PHYSICS

What is physics?	166
Inside atoms	168
Energy	170
Forces and mass	172
Stretching and deforming	174
Velocity and acceleration	176
Gravity	178
Newton's laws of motion	180
Understanding motion	182
Pressure	184
Machines	186
Heat transfer	188
Using heat	190
Waves	192
Electromagnetic waves	194
Light	196
Optics	198
Sound	200
Electricity	202
Current, voltage, and resistance	204
Circuits	206
Electronics	208
Magnets	210
Electric motors	212
Electricity generators	214
Transformers	216
Power generation	218
Electricity supplies	220
Energy efficiency	222
Renewable energy	224
The Earth	226
Weather	228
Astronomy	230
The Sun	232
The Solar System I	234
The Solar System II	236
Stars and galaxies	238
Origins of the Universe	240
Reference—Biology	242
Reference—Chemistry	244
Reference—Physics	246
Glossary	248
Index	252
Acknowledgments	256

What is science?

A SYSTEM INVOLVING OBSERVATIONS AND TESTS USED TO FIGURE OUT THE MYSTERIES OF THE UNIVERSE AND EXPLAIN HOW NATURE WORKS

The word "science" means "knowledge" in Latin, and a scientist is someone who finds out new things. Scientific knowledge is the best way of describing the Universe—how it works and where it came from.

Science is...

...a collection of knowledge that is used to explain natural phenomena. The knowledge is arranged so that any fact can be confirmed by referring to other previously known facts.

...a way of uncovering new pieces of knowledge. This is achieved using a process of observation and testing that is designed to confirm whether a proposed explanation of something is true or false.

Answering questions

Science is an effective method of explaining natural phenomena. The way of doing this is known as the scientific method, which involves forming a theory about an unexplained phenomenon and doing an experiment to test it. Strictly speaking, the scientific method can only show whether a theory is false or not false. Once tested, a false theory is obviously no good and is discarded. However, a "not false" theory is the best explanation of a phenomenon we have—until, that is, another theory shows it to be false and replaces it.

ice cream changes states from a solid to a liquid with heat

◁ **Solving problems**
Much of science is driven by practical problems that need answers, such as "Why does ice cream melt?" However, scientific breakthroughs also come about from pure curiosity about the Universe.

Measurements

Scientists need to make measurements as they gather evidence of how things behave. Saying a snake "was as long as an arm" is less useful than giving a precise length. Scientists use a system of measurements called the SI (Système International) units (see p.200), which include meters for length, kilograms for mass, seconds for time, and moles for measuring the quantity of a substance. All other units of measurement (eg, for force, pressure, or speed) are derived from the SI units. For this reason, metric units are given first throughout the book, with imperial equivalents in parentheses.

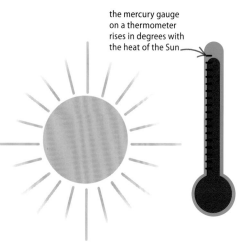

the mercury gauge on a thermometer rises in degrees with the heat of the Sun

◁ **Setting a scale**
The degrees marked on a thermometer show the temperature rising and falling. However, like all units, the difference between one degree and the next is not something that is set by nature. The sizes of the units are generally set because they are practical to use in scientific calculations.

WHAT IS SCIENCE? 11

Backing up knowledge

The reason science is such a reliable way of describing nature is because every new piece of knowledge added is only accepted as true if it is based on older pieces of knowledge that everyone already agrees upon. Few scientific breakthroughs are the work of a single mind. When outlining a discovery, scientists always refer to the work of others that they have based their ideas on. In so doing, the development of knowledge can be traced back hundreds, if not thousands, of years.

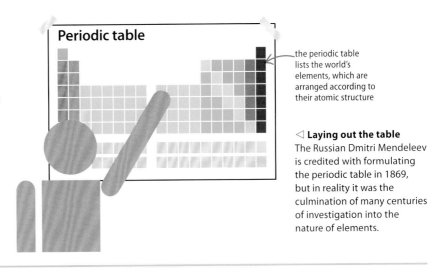

the periodic table lists the world's elements, which are arranged according to their atomic structure

◁ **Laying out the table**
The Russian Dmitri Mendeleev is credited with formulating the periodic table in 1869, but in reality it was the culmination of many centuries of investigation into the nature of elements.

Specialists

Modern science has been practiced for around 250 years, and in that time great minds have revealed a staggering amount about the nature of life, our planet, and the Universe. Early scientists investigated a wide range of subjects. However, no one alive today can have an expert understanding of all areas of scientific knowledge. There is just too much to know. Instead, scientists specialize in a certain field that interests them, devoting their working lives to unlocking the secrets of that subject.

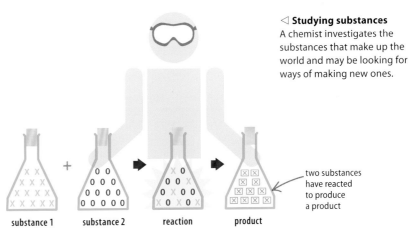

◁ **Studying substances**
A chemist investigates the substances that make up the world and may be looking for ways of making new ones.

two substances have reacted to produce a product

substance 1   substance 2   reaction   product

Applying science

Some scientists find explanations for natural phenomena because they are curious—they just like knowing. However, other scientists figure out how the latest understanding of nature might be put to practical use. Applied science and engineering is perhaps the best example of why science is such a powerful tool. If the knowledge discovered by scientists was not correct, none of our high-tech machines would work properly.

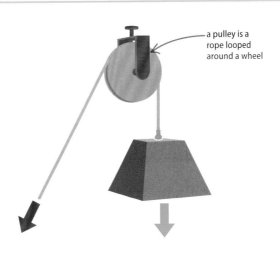

a pulley is a rope looped around a wheel

◁ **Using force**
Understanding forces and energy explains how it is easier to lift weights with a set of pulleys. For example, lifting a weight with two pulleys requires only half the force needed when using just one.

The scientific method

THE PROCESS BY WHICH IDEAS ABOUT NATURAL PHENOMENA ARE PROVEN TO BE LIKELY OR INCORRECT

All scientific investigations follow a process called the scientific method. They all begin with a flash of inspiration, where a scientist has a new idea about how the Universe might work.

Ask a question
All science begins with a person wondering why a natural phenomenon occurs in the way that it does. This may be in response to a previous discovery that gives rise to new areas of investigation.

Do background research
The next step is to observe the phenomenon, recording its characteristics. Learning more about it will help the scientist form a possible explanation that fits the acquired evidence.

Construct hypothesis
At this stage, the scientist sets out a theory for the phenomenon. This is known as a hypothesis. As yet, there is no proof for the hypothesis.

Test the hypothesis
The scientist now designs an experiment to test the hypothesis, and uses the hypothesis to predict the result. The experiment is repeated several times to ensure that the results are generally the same.

Try again
No experiment is ever a failure. When results disprove a hypothesis, the scientist can use that knowledge to reconsider the question, and provide a new hypothesis that supports the evidence.

Draw a conclusion
If the results of the experiment are not what is predicted by the hypothesis, then the theory about it is disproven. If the results match the prediction, then the hypothesis has been proven (for now).

PROVEN   **DISPROVEN**

Hypothesis is proven
The results of the experiment show that the hypothesis is a good way of describing what is happening during the natural phenomenon. It can therefore be used as an answer to the original question.

Hypothesis is disproven
The experiment shows that the natural phenomenon being investigated behaves in a different way from the one predicted by the hypothesis. Therefore this explanation cannot be not correct and the original question remains unanswered.

Report results
It is important for positive results to be announced publicly so other scientists can repeat the experiment and check that it was performed correctly. The results are reviewed by experts before the findings are accepted. This new knowledge then becomes a foundation on which to investigate even more ideas.

THE SCIENTIFIC METHOD

Question
Does adding salt to water have any effect on how fast it evaporates (turns from liquid into vapor)?

Background research
Saltwater's freezing point is lower than 0°C (the normal freezing point of pure water) because the dissolved salt gets in the way of the water molecules, making it harder for them to form into solid ice crystals.

Hypothesis
Salt makes it harder for water to form ice, lowering the freezing point. Therefore, does salt also lower the boiling point of water, making it easier to form water vapor? If so, saltwater will evaporate faster than freshwater.

Test the hypothesis
Divide some freshwater into two cups. Add some salt to one cup to make a salt solution. Weigh out 5 ml (0.17 fl oz) of each liquid and pour each amount into two identical shallow dishes. The water should be about 1 mm (0.04 in) deep. Leave the dishes in direct sunlight. Monitor them over a few hours to see which dish dries out first. The hypothesis predicts that the saltwater will evaporate first.

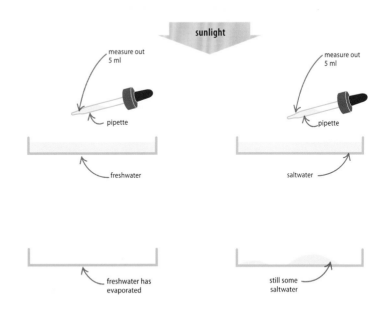

Results
The freshwater dish dries out first. What is the conclusion? Is the hypothesis false or not false?

Conclusion
The hypothesis is false.
Salt in the water does not make it evaporate faster.

Fields of science

SCIENCE IS DIVIDED INTO A NUMBER OF DISCIPLINES THAT EACH FOCUS ON INVESTIGATING SPECIFIC AREAS OF THE SUBJECT.

Modern scientists are all specialists who belong to one of dozens of disciplines. Some fields fall under the main subjects of biology, chemistry, and physics, while others combine knowledge of all three to uncover facts.

Biochemistry
Studying the chemical reactions that take place inside cells and which keep organisms alive.

Genetics
Understanding the way chemicals can carry coded instructions for making new cells and whole bodies.

Forensic science
Using scientific evidence to link criminals with crime scenes to help prove their guilt.

BIOLOGY
Any science that is concerned with living things is described as biology. Biologists investigate every aspect of life, from the working of a cell to how animals behave in large groups.

CHEMISTRY
This science investigates the properties of atoms and the many different substances atoms produce when combined in different ways. Chemistry forms a link between physics and biology.

Zoology
The area of biology that investigates everything there is to know about animals.

Botany
The area of biology that is concerned wholly with the study of plants.

Organic chemistry
Investigating carbon-based compounds, mostly derived from organic (once-living) sources.

Microbiology
The field of biology concerned with cell anatomy, using microscopes to see the structure of cells.

Ecology
Looking at communities of organisms and how they survive together in a habitat.

Electrochemistry
A field of chemistry that uses the energy in chemical reactions to produce electric currents.

Medicine
Applying knowledge of biochemistry, microbiology, and anatomy to diagnose and treat illnesses.

Paleontology
Studying fossilized remains of extinct animals and relating them to modern species.

Inorganic chemistry
Investigating the properties of all nonorganic (nonliving) substances.

FIELDS OF SCIENCE

Until the 17th century, scientists were known as **"natural philosophers."** Today's philosophers contend with subjects such as ethics, which cannot be tested by the scientific method.

Social sciences

These sciences are not linked directly with the "natural sciences" (eg, biology, chemistry, or physics). Instead, they apply scientific methods to investigate humanity. Examples include:

Anthropology
Studying the human species, especially how societies and cultures from around the world differ from one another.

Archaeology
Studying ancient civilizations from the remains of their homes and cities.

Economics
Developing theories as to how people and companies spend their money.

Geography
Researching the natural landscape and how humans use the land, such as where they build cities.

Psychology
Investigating the way the human mind works using scientific methods.

Geology
Investigating the processes that form rocks and shape our planet's landscape.

Nuclear chemistry
Studying the behavior of unstable atoms that break apart and release powerful radiation.

PHYSICS
With its name meaning "nature" in Greek, physics is the basis of all other sciences. It provides explanations of energy, mass, force, and light without which other sciences would not make sense.

Particle physics
Studying the particles that make up atoms and carry energy and mass throughout the Universe.

Thermodynamics
Studying the way energy flows through the Universe according to a series of unbreakable laws.

Mechanics
Understanding the motion of objects in terms of mass and how energy is transferred between them by forces.

Optics
Studying the behavior of beams of light as they reflect off or shine through different substances.

Wave theory
Explaining sound and other natural phenomena using an understanding of the behavior of waves.

Electromagnetism
Investigating electric currents and magnetic fields, and their uses in electronic devices.

Astronomy
Studying objects, such as planets, stars, and galaxies, in space.

Meteorology
Understanding the conditions that produce weather.

Applied science

This area of work takes pure scientific knowledge and uses it for practical purposes. Some applied sciences can be described as types of engineering. Examples include:

Biotechnology
Using the knowledge of genetics and biochemistry to make artificial organisms and biological machines.

Computer science
Building microchip processors and writing software instructions to build faster and smarter computers.

Materials science
Developing new materials with properties suited to a particular application.

Telecommunications
Making use of electromagnetism, radiation, and optics to send signals and information over long distances.

Biology

What is biology?

THE SCIENCE THAT INVESTIGATES EVERY FORM OF LIFE—HOW IT SURVIVES AND WHERE IT ORIGINATED.

Biology, or life science, is a vast subject that studies life at all scales, from the inner workings of a microscopic cell to the way whole forests behave.

What is life?

All life shares seven basic characteristics. These are not exclusive to life, but only living things have all seven. For example, a car can move, it "feeds" on fuel, excretes exhaust, and may even sense its surroundings, but these four characteristics do not make the car alive.

▷ **The seven characteristics**
Living things, or organisms, are incredibly varied. Even so, they all share the same seven characteristics that set them apart from nonliving things.

THE SEVEN REQUIREMENTS FOR LIFE	
Requirement	Description
movement	altering parts of its body in response to the environment
reproduction	being able to make copies of itself
sensitivity	able to sense changes in the surroundings
growth	increasing in size for at least a period of its life
respiration	converting fuels (eg, food) into useful energy
excretion	removing waste materials from its body
nutrition	acquiring fuel to power and grow its body

Taxonomy

The field of biology that organizes, or classifies, organisms is called taxonomy. Modern taxonomy groups organisms according to how they are related to each other (rather than just how they look). It involves placing all organisms in groups, or taxons, arranged in this hierarchy: domain, kingdom, phylum (or division in the plant kingdom), class, order, family, genus, and species. Animals and plants are part of the largest domain, Eukaryota.

◁ **Classification**
Taxonomy (see pages 20–21) shows us that some of these organisms are more closely related than others. For example, animals belong to the animal kingdom, whereas plants belong to the plant kingdom.

Microbiology

A cell is the smallest unit of life and that is what microbiologists study. They use microscopes to see inside cells and investigate how their minute inner machinery, often called organelles, functions to keep the cells alive. Microbiology has shown that not all cells are the same, which helps explain how bodies work and gives clues to how life started and has since evolved.

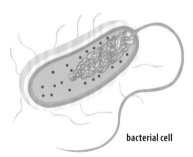

◁ **Seeing in detail**
This cutaway artwork shows the inner structure of a bacterial cell. Microbiologists (see page 23) view the tiniest details using powerful electron microscopes, which use a beam of electrons instead of light to magnify cells.

Physiology

Biologists are interested in the anatomy of living things—how bodies are made from tissues and organs. Physiology is the study of how an organism's anatomical features relate to a particular function. Physiologists may even study the fossils of extinct animals, such as dinosaurs, to make discoveries about their lives and deaths.

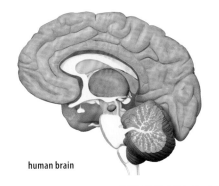

human brain

◁ **Nerve center**
The brain is a complex organ (a body part that has a specific function and is made of two or more kinds of tissue). The mass of nerve tissue is the main control center for the body (see page 68).

Ecology

The field of biology that investigates how communities of organisms live together is called ecology. Ecologists group wildlife into ecosystems, which occupy a specific living space or habitat. Scientists try to figure out the complex relationships between the members of an ecosystem. They may use their findings to help protect the habitat and its inhabitants from harmful human activities.

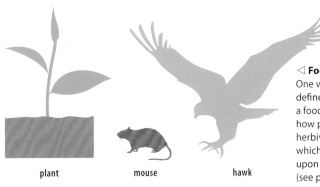

plant   mouse   hawk

◁ **Food chains**
One way that ecologists define an ecosystem is by a food chain, which tracks how plants are eaten by herbivorous animals, which in turn are preyed upon by predators (see pages 76–77).

Evolution

Biologists have discovered that living things can change, or evolve, to adapt to new habitats. The process is very slow, but it explains why the fossils of extinct organisms share features with today's wildlife. Evolution also explains how similar animals such as these finches have become slightly different from each other in order to suit how they live.

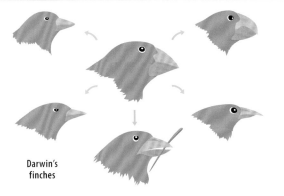

Darwin's finches

◁ **Bill shapes**
These species of Darwin's finch each target specific types of food, such as seeds or insects. As a result, their bills have all evolved into different shapes (see page 82).

Conservation

The more biologists reveal about the natural world, the more they find that many species are under threat of extinction. While extinction is a normal part of evolution, it appears that human activities, such as farming and industry, are making species die out much faster than normal. Conservationists use their knowledge of biology to protect endangered species and prevent unique habitats from being destroyed.

giant panda

◁ **Saving species**
Without conservation, the giant panda, a bamboo-eating bear from China, may have become extinct. It was threatened by hunting and loss of its mountain habitat.

Variety of life

LIFE ON EARTH IS ORGANIZED INTO RELATED GROUPS.

Scientists have attempted to make sense of Earth's biodiversity—its enormous variety of life—by classifying living things into different groups, according to how they look and how they are related.

SEE ALSO	
Fungi and single-celled life	26–27 ⟩
Plants	54–55 ⟩
Invertebrates	56–57 ⟩
Fish, amphibians, and reptiles	58–59 ⟩
Mammals and birds	60–61 ⟩

Three domains of life

Biologists estimate that there are about eight million species of living things on Earth today. The field of biology that organizes all these species into an understandable system is called taxonomy. Taxonomy arranges organisms in a hierarchy of groups. The largest groups are called domains. Most biologists divide life into three domains: Bacteria, Eukaryota, and the Archaea.

Bacteria
These simple-celled organisms live in all parts of Earth, from deep inside rocks to the guts of most eukaryotes. A few bacteria infect eukaryotes, causing diseases.

Eukaryota
This domain includes plants, animals, fungi, and some single-celled organisms. The Eukaryota is the only domain to contain multicellular organisms, where body cells work together to do different jobs.

Archaea come in many different shapes, from strands like these, to cubes, and even spherical varieties

Archaea
These are the oldest living things on Earth. They evolved more than 3.8 billion years ago out of the extreme conditions on Earth back then, and can still be found today in conditions too harsh for other life.

The word **"dolphin"** means "womb fish"—early biologists thought dolphins were related to fish, and not land mammals.

▷ **KINGDOM**
Eukaryota is the largest domain and it is the only one that is subdivided into kingdoms.

Classification

Taxonomists group organisms according to how they are related to each other. Group members have all evolved from a common ancestor at some point in the past. The further you go down the groups, the closer the similarities are between species.

Animal kingdom
Every animal belongs to this group. They all have multicellular bodies, must feed on other organisms to survive, and are usually able to respond rapidly to threats and problems.

Fungi kingdom
Until the middle of the 20th century, these organisms were considered a branch of the plant kingdom. Fungi are molds and mushrooms that live in damp habitats, and grow on their food, which they break down and absorb outside themselves.

Protist kingdom
The protists are a diverse group of eukaryotes that do not develop into specialized multicellular bodies. Instead they survive as single, solitary cells. However, a few species develop into clusters or colonies of individual cells.

Plant kingdom
Plants are multicellular organisms that make their own food by photosynthesis. Most plants are terrestrial or live in freshwater, and live in one place during their lifetime, although they can move in response to their environment.

Angiosperms
This division contains plants that produce seeds with a tough, protective coat. Angiosperms are the only plants to reproduce using flowers.

Eudicots
A class of angiosperms, eudicots have seeds with two cotyledons. A cotyledon is an embryonic leaf, which supplies food for the sprouting plant.

Rosales
The Rosales order of eudicots includes many popular flowering plants, as well as nettles, elms, mulberries, and hemp.

Rosaceae
This family contains many familiar fruits, such as apples, pears, plums, and peaches. Its other members include shrubs, such as rowans.

Rosa
Members of the *Rosa* genus are covered in prickles—sharp spikes that grow from the surface of the stem—and produce flowers known as roses.

Rosa centifolia
This species is the main one known as the garden rose. It has been bred into thousands of varieties with desirable colors, scents, and ways of growing, such as climbing.

Chordata
This phylum of animals contains the vertebrates (backboned animals), which includes birds, fish, reptiles, amphibians, and mammals.

Mammalia
This class of chordates is made up of animals that grow hair and feed their young on milk. Humans are mammals.

Carnivora
Carnivores are mammals that are specialized in hunting for food. The largest are bears, and the smallest are weasels.

Felidae
This is the cat family of mammal carnivores. The family is divided in two: the big cats (Pantherinae) can roar; the small cats (Felinae) cannot.

Panthera
The genus of big cats includes lions, tigers, jaguars, and leopards. Mostly these cats hunt alone, killing prey with crushing bites.

Panthera leo
The lion is the only social member of the cat family, living in groups called prides. Lions are found throughout Africa and in India.

▷ **PHYLUM and DIVISION**
Kingdoms are divided into phyla (animals) or divisions (plants).

▷ **CLASS**
Phyla are divided into classes.

▷ **ORDER**
Classes are divided into orders, which may be subdivided into suborders.

▷ **FAMILY**
Orders and suborders are organized into families.

▷ **GENUS**
A genus is a group of closely related species; some genera contain just one species.

▷ **SPECIES**
A species is a group of organisms that look similar and can reproduce with each other.

Cell structure

CELLS ARE THE BUILDING BLOCKS OF LIFE.

The cell is the basic unit of living things, with many millions working together to form an individual organism. Each cell is an enclosed sac containing everything it needs to survive and do its job.

SEE ALSO	
Cells at work	24–25 ❯
Fungi and single-celled life	26–27 ❯
Respiration	28–29 ❯
Photosynthesis	30–31 ❯
Disease and immunity	50–51 ❯
Genetics II	86–87 ❯

Animal cell

The average animal cell grows to about 10 µm across (a 100th of a millimeter) although single cells inside eggs, bones, or muscles can reach several centimeters across. Animal bodies contain a large number of cell types, each specialized to do different jobs. Some kinds of single-celled protists, such as amoebas and protozoans, have a cell body very similar in structure to the cells of animals.

Centrosome
This produces long and thin strands used for hauling objects around the cell.

Cytoplasm
A watery filling of the cell with minerals dissolved in it.

Mitochondrion
The power plant of the cell—it releases energy from sugars.

Rough endoplasmic reticulum (ER)
Networks of ribosome-studded tubes, where proteins are manufactured.

Smooth endoplasmic reticulum
Tubes manufacturing fats and oils, and processing minerals.

Nucleus
This contains the cell's genetic material, DNA—the instructions to build and maintain the cell.

Nucleolus
A dense region of the nucleus, which helps make ribosomes.

Ribosome
Genetic information in DNA is decoded here to make the proteins that build the cell.

Cell membrane
The selectively permeable outer layer through which certain substances pass in and out of the cell.

Golgi apparatus
Where newly made substances are packaged into membrane sacs, or vesicles, for transport around and out of the cell.

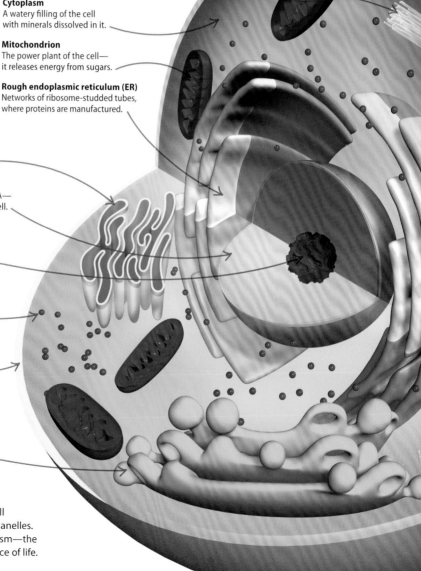

▷ **Animal cell construction**
The outer layer of most animal cells is a flexible membrane, which can take on any shape. The cell contains many types of tiny structures called organelles. Each one has a specific role in the cell's metabolism—the chemical processes necessary for the maintenance of life.

CELL STRUCTURE

Plant cell

The major difference between the cells of plants and animals is that plant cells are surrounded by a cell wall made of a lattice of cellulose strands. The space between the walls of neighboring cells is called the middle lamella. It contains a cement made of pectin, a sugary gel that joins the cells together.

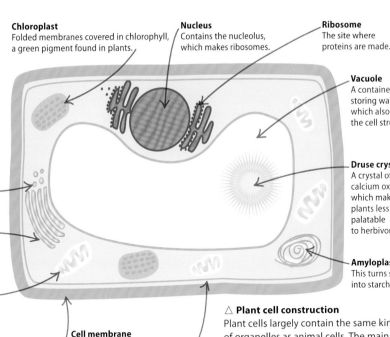

Chloroplast
Folded membranes covered in chlorophyll, a green pigment found in plants.

Nucleus
Contains the nucleolus, which makes ribosomes.

Ribosome
The site where proteins are made.

Vacuole
A container for storing water, which also gives the cell structure.

Druse crystal
A crystal of calcium oxalate, which makes plants less palatable to herbivores.

Amyloplast
This turns sugars into starches.

Vesicles
A membrane sac that can store or transport substances.

Golgi apparatus
This bags up substances into vesicles.

Mitochondrion
This creates the cell's power supply.

Cell wall
A lattice of cellulose, a tough polymer made from chains of glucose.

Cell membrane
The membrane is not attached to the wall, and moves as the cell shrinks and swells.

△ **Plant cell construction**
Plant cells largely contain the same kinds of organelles as animal cells. The main additions are the chloroplasts in the cells of green sections of the plant body. This is where photosynthesis occurs, the process that produces the plant's sugar fuel.

▽ **Membrane structure**
The cell's outer layer, or membrane, is selectively permeable—it allows only some things to enter and leave the cell. The membrane is made from double layers of fat chemicals called lipids. The "head" of a lipid is hydrophilic, meaning it mixes with water and substances on each side of the cell. The "tail" is hydrophobic—it is repelled by water, and forms a barrier that helps keep the cell's contents inside.

Lysosome
A bag of destructive enzymes that break down unwanted materials in the cell.

Hydrophilic head
The heads floats in the cytoplasm and extracellular liquids.

Hydrophobic tail
The two lipid layers connect by their tails to form a thin, water-repellent film on either side of the membrane.

REAL WORLD
Microscopic cells

Most cells are not visible to the naked eye, so microbiologists study them through microscopes. The first person to see cells in this way was 17th-century English scientist Robert Hooke. He named them cells after the small rooms used by monks. Today, microbiologists use dyes and lighting techniques to show a cell's internal structure, such as these human body cells (below).

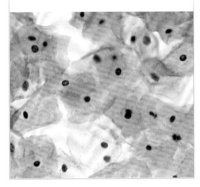

Cells at work

EACH CELL IS LIKE A MICROSCOPIC FACTORY.

SEE ALSO	
❮ 22–23 Cell structure	
Muscle contraction	39 ❯
Human senses	64–65 ❯

All the processes needed for life, such as releasing energy from food, removing waste materials, and growth, take place inside cells.

Cell transport

Cells process a wide range of chemicals. Inside the cell, large molecules such as proteins and even entire organelles are hoisted around by microtubules, which are also used in cell division. Some chemicals must be moved between organelles inside the cell, and others travel in and out through the cell membrane. Here are the main ways substances enter cells.

Bacteria cells can divide every 20 minutes, and one germ can grow to four billion trillion in 24 hours.

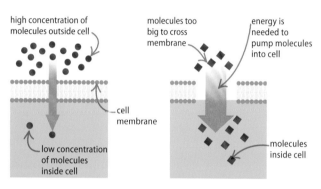

△ **Diffusion**
Diffusion happens when a substance spreads out, moving from areas of high concentrations to low.

△ **Active transport**
If a molecule is too big or is unable to dissolve in the cell membrane, it is moved across in a process that uses energy.

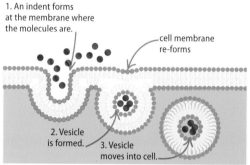

△ **Endocytosis**
If molecules are too big to be pumped into a cell by active transport, a cell uses energy to put them in a sac, called a vesicle. This vesicle is formed from the cell membrane, and breaks open to release its contents once inside. When a cell moves a vesicle of material out, it is called exocytosis.

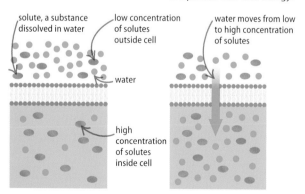

△ **Osmosis**
Osmosis is a type of liquid diffusion that takes place when solutions are separated by a membrane. Large dissolved molecules are blocked from diffusing into the cell. Instead, the water balances both sides, by moving from the low concentration side to the high.

REAL WORLD
Wilted flowers

Osmosis creates a force that moves water in and out of cells. When cut flowers are placed in freshwater, water floods into the plant cells by osmosis, making them full and rigid. When the water has gone, osmosis pulls the water out of the cells. The water evaporates, and the flowers wilt.

CELLS AT WORK **25**

Multicellular structures

A living body is made of billions of cells working together. To do that most effectively, the cells are specialized to do certain jobs. A collection of cells that performs a single function—such as producing the mucus in the nose—is called a tissue. Very often, tissues group together to perform a complex set of tasks. They are then described as an organ, such as the nose.

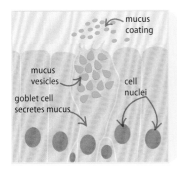

△ **Goblet cell**
This type of cell produces mucus (a mixture of water and a gooey protein called mucin) and other dissolved chemicals.

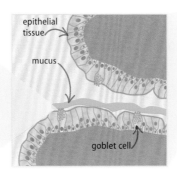

△ **Epithelial tissue**
Goblet cells form much of the epithelia, the tissue that lines the nose, windpipe, and gut. The mucus they produce protects the cells from chemical attack and dirt.

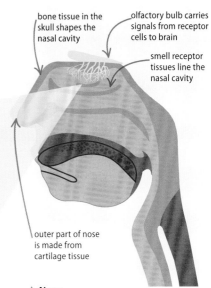

△ **Nose**
The nose is an organ that carries air in and out of the body. Muscle, cartilage, and bone tissues combine with epithelial tissue to help it do its job.

Cell division

A body grows because the number of its cells increases. This increase in number is achieved by cells dividing in half, to make two identical but fully independent cells. This type of cell division is called mitosis. It involves several stages, in which the cell's contents are split into two groups. That includes doubling the number of chromosomes (which carry the cell's genes).

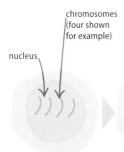

△ **1. Interphase**
Cell has usual number of 46 chromosomes inside it.

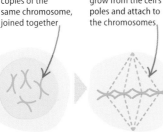

△ **2. Prophase**
Each chromosome is doubled, forming two chromatids.

△ **3. Metaphase**
The chromosomes line up in the middle of the cell.

△ **4. Anaphase**
The chromatids are pulled apart, to become separate chromosomes.

△ **5. Telophase**
The microtubules disappear, and the cells begin to divide.

△ **6. Cytokinesis**
Two daughter cells are formed, each with 46 chromosomes.

Fungi and single-celled life

LIFE ON EARTH INCLUDES ORGANISMS THAT ARE NEITHER ANIMAL NOR PLANT.

SEE ALSO	
‹ 20–21 Variety of life	
‹ 22–23 Cell structure	
Disease and immunity	50–51 ›

The life forms within the Bacteria and Archaea domains, and most of the protist kingdom, are single-celled and can be viewed only through a microscope. By contrast, members of the fungi kingdom can grow into the largest organisms in the natural world.

Bacteria

The cells of Bacteria are hundreds of times smaller than those of plants or animals. They do not have a nucleus. Instead, their DNA is stored as a tangled loop called a plasmid. There are no other large organelles bound by a membrane, and all the metabolic reactions occur in the cytoplasm. Many bacteria move by flapping a whiplike flagellum. The hairlike pili are used to attach the bacteria to surfaces.

Archaea

For many years, these microorganisms were considered to be types of Bacteria, and the two groups were classified together. However, recent DNA analysis suggests that Archaea are a totally separate group. Many archaea are extremophiles—they survive in extreme conditions, such as incredibly hot or cold places. It is likely that their ancestors evolved in the extreme habitats of the young Earth about 3.5 billion years ago.

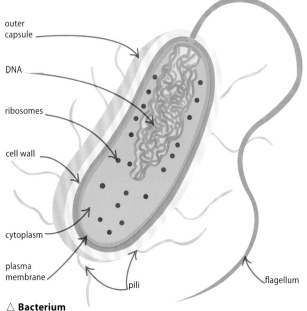

△ **Bacterium**
Most bacteria are surrounded by three layers. The plasma membrane is similar to the one in other types of cell. The cell wall is made of proteins and sugars. The starchy outer capsule, which stops the cell from drying out, is missing in some species.

▷ **Haloquadratum**
This archaea lives in brine pools, where the salt content kills most other life forms. It has a square cell (its name means "salt square") filled with gas bubbles that help it float. No one knows how the cell survives.

▽ **Pyrococcus**
Discovered in the super-hot water that gushes from hydrothermal vents on the deep ocean floor, this archaea's name means "fire sphere." Sunlight never reaches its habitat, and the archaea is sustained by chemicals in the hot water.

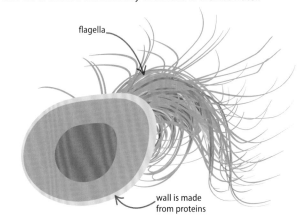

A **honey fungus** in Oregon, USA, is nearly 9 sq km (3.5 sq miles) in area, making it the **largest** single organism on Earth.

FUNGI AND SINGLE-CELLED LIFE

Fungi

The fungal kingdom includes mushrooms, molds, and yeasts. They are saprophytic organisms, which means they grow over a food source and secrete enzymes that digest it externally. Their cells are eukaryotic, with a nucleus and organelles like those of plants and animals. The cells are held inside a rigid cell wall made largely of chitin, the same material that crab shells and beetle wings are made of.

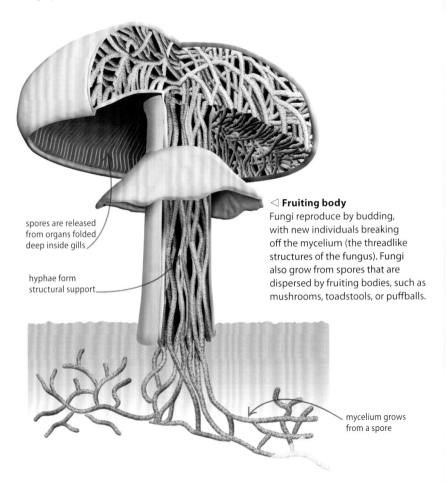

◁ **Fruiting body**
Fungi reproduce by budding, with new individuals breaking off the mycelium (the threadlike structures of the fungus). Fungi also grow from spores that are dispersed by fruiting bodies, such as mushrooms, toadstools, or puffballs.

- spores are released from organs folded deep inside gills
- hyphae form structural support
- mycelium grows from a spore

▷ **Hypha**
The main part of a fungus is called the mycelium. This is made up of many strands called hyphae, which are long tubes of cells that extend over food sources. Yeast are single-celled fungi and do not develop hyphae.

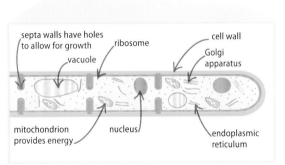

- septa walls have holes to allow for growth
- ribosome
- vacuole
- cell wall
- Golgi apparatus
- mitochondrion provides energy
- nucleus
- endoplasmic reticulum

Protists

This kingdom includes a wide variety of single-celled organisms. There are at least 30 different phyla and it is likely that at least some of them evolved separately from each other. The protist cell is very diverse, and can resemble that of an animal, plant, or fungus. Some species, such as Euglena, photosynthesize with chloroplasts, but also feed like animals.

▽ **Diatom**
These single-celled algae live in sunlit waters. They have an ornate cell wall made from silica. In the right conditions, diatoms produce thick blooms in the water. The silica skeletons of dead diatoms are one of the ingredients in clay.

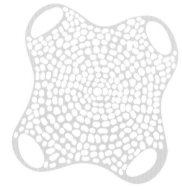

▽ **Ciliate**
Not every protist is motile (able to move). An amoeba alters the shape of its cell so its contents flow in one direction. Flagellates are powered by tail-like flagella, while ciliates (below) waft hairlike extensions called cilia (singular: cilium) to push themselves along.

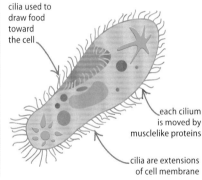

- cilia used to draw food toward the cell
- each cilium is moved by musclelike proteins
- cilia are extensions of cell membrane

Respiration

THE PROCESS OF RESPIRATION SUPPLIES ENERGY FOR LIFE.

All living things are powered by the energy released by a respiration reaction that takes place inside cells. This reaction needs a supply of oxygen taken from the surrounding air or water.

SEE ALSO	
Photosynthesis	30–31 ⟩
Combustion	130–131 ⟩
Redox reactions	132–133 ⟩
Energy	170–171 ⟩

Cellular respiration

Every cell produces its own energy by respiration. The process takes place in tiny power plants called mitochondria. A cell that uses a lot of energy, such as a muscle cell, has a large number of these organelles. Respiration is a chemical reaction in which glucose (a sugar and important source of energy) is oxidized (chemically combined with oxygen). As well as energy, the reaction produces carbon dioxide and water.

chemical equation for cellular respiration

glucose · oxygen · energy · water · carbon dioxide

$$C_6H_{12}O_6 + 6O_2 \longrightarrow 6H_2O + 6CO_2$$

▽ **Storing and releasing energy**
The energy released from respiration is stored by a chemical called adenosine triphosphate (ATP). The energy is used to add a phosphate (P) to adenosine diphosphate (ADP), to store energy. When needed elsewhere in the cell, the phosphate breaks off and releases the energy.

$$ADP + P = ATP \quad \text{energy gained}$$

$$ATP - P = ADP \quad \text{energy released}$$

▽ **Anerobic respiration**
If the cell cannot get enough oxygen to power respiration, it does it anaerobically, meaning "without air." This process produces lactic acid as a result, which is what makes hard-working muscles burn with fatigue. Anaerobic respiration releases only part of the energy in glucose, but the rest is released when oxygen is available again.

glucose · lactic acid

$$C_6H_{12}O_6 = 2C_3H_6O_3$$

Mitochondrion

A mitochondrion is surrounded by an outer membrane, similar to the one around a cell. There is another membrane inside that is folded in on itself. The folded areas are called cristae. The main enzymes that control the production of ATP are bonded to the inner membrane. This is where respiration happens. The cristae increase the surface area of the inner membrane, maximizing the space for the enzymes.

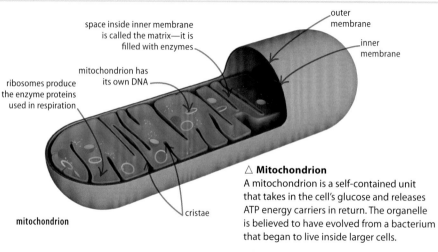

△ **Mitochondrion**
A mitochondrion is a self-contained unit that takes in the cell's glucose and releases ATP energy carriers in return. The organelle is believed to have evolved from a bacterium that began to live inside larger cells.

RESPIRATION

Gas exchange

Respiration requires a supply of oxygen, and the body also needs to remove the waste carbon dioxide it produces. The area through which these gases enter and leave the body is called the gas exchange surface. Lungs, gills, and the trachea tubes of insects are lined with these surfaces. A gas exchange surface is thin, moist, and well supplied with blood to take away the oxygen and deliver the waste carbon dioxide. The gases move in and out of the area by diffusion (see page 24).

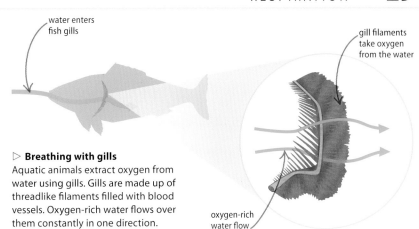

▷ **Breathing with gills**
Aquatic animals extract oxygen from water using gills. Gills are made up of threadlike filaments filled with blood vessels. Oxygen-rich water flows over them constantly in one direction.

Breathing with lungs

Most land vertebrates breathe using lungs. The process is called reciprocal breathing: oxygen-rich air is inhaled, gases are exchanged, and then the oxygen-depleted air is exhaled. The lungs of primitive vertebrates, such as salamanders, are simple sacs. The lungs of larger animals are effectively sponges of tissue, with a huge gas exchange surface.

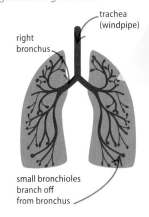

◁ **Alveoli**
At the end of each bronchiole are sacs called alveoli (singular: alveolus) where the gases are exchanged.

▷ **Lungs**
When you inhale, air is sucked into your lungs via your trachea, which branches into left and right bronchi, which in turn branch off into bronchioles.

▽ **Gas mixture**
The air we breathe is a mixture of gases. Only about a fifth of it is oxygen, which diffuses into the blood. There is about 100 times more carbon dioxide in exhaled air than in inhaled air.

Gas	Inhaled air %	Exhaled air %
nitrogen	78	78
oxygen	21	17
inert gas	1	1
carbon dioxide	0.04	4
water vapor	little	saturated

▷ **Reciprocal breathing**
To breathe in, the diaphragm moves down, enlarging the space in the chest. This lowers the pressure in the lungs, forcing in air from outside. To breathe out, the diaphragm goes up, reducing the space in the chest and pushing out the oxygen-depleted air.

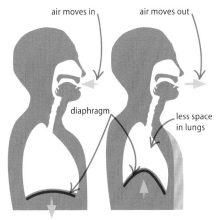

Photosynthesis

PLANTS MAKE THEIR OWN FOOD FROM SIMPLE INGREDIENTS AND SUNLIGHT.

SEE ALSO	
⟨ 24 Cell transport	
⟨ 28–29 Respiration	
Plants	54–55 ⟩
Food chains	76–77 ⟩
Energy	170–171 ⟩
Light	196–197 ⟩

Plants need sunlight to survive. They harness the energy in light to make food from carbon dioxide and water in a process called photosynthesis.

Light reaction

Photosynthesis is a chemical reaction that combines carbon dioxide gas and water to make a molecule of glucose. The glucose is the plant's food, and is sent around the plant to provide the energy it needs. The waste product of the process is oxygen. Photosynthesis itself is powered by sunlight. A chemical called chlorophyll in the leaves absorbs some of the light's energy and uses it to start the reaction.

carbon dioxide   water   glucose   oxygen

the Sun's energy is crucial for photosynthesis.

$$6CO_2 + 6H_2O \xrightarrow{sunlight} C_6H_{12}O_6 + 6O_2$$

chlorophyll in guard cells causes them to respond to light and open the stomata on the leaf

carbon dioxide from the air travels into the leaf through the stomata by diffusion (see page 24)

△ **Atmospheric carbon**
During photosynthesis, carbon atoms are taken from the atmosphere. These atoms are the building blocks of all organic (carbon-containing) compounds—in both plants and the animals that eat them.

Leaf

A leaf is a plant's solar panel. It is flattened to create a larger surface area to catch as much sunlight as possible. The light shines through the surface of the leaf, and photosynthesis occurs in the cells inside. Water arrives from the plant along a vessel that runs down the center of the leaf. Carbon dioxide comes into the plant from the surrounding air through pores called stomata on the underside of the leaf.

Upper epidermis
A layer of cells that forms the leaf's upper surface. These cells have a waxy coating to reduce the amount of water lost through evaporation.

Spongy mesophyll
Cells with large spaces between them where the gases circulate.

Water loss
Leaves lose water through evaporation and need a constant supply so they do not dry out.

Guard cells
A stoma is made of two guard cells, which move away from each other to open the pore when the Sun is shining, and move together to close it when it's dark.

Chloroplast
A green structure inside the cell where the chlorophyll is located.

Palisade cells
These column-shaped cells under the upper surface are where most of the photosynthesis takes place.

Vascular bundle
Xylem (blue) brings water and dissolved minerals to the leaf. Phloem (orange) takes away sucrose (see page 37).

Lower epidermis
The underside of the leaf is filled with pores called stomata (singular: stoma) that let gases in and out of the plant.

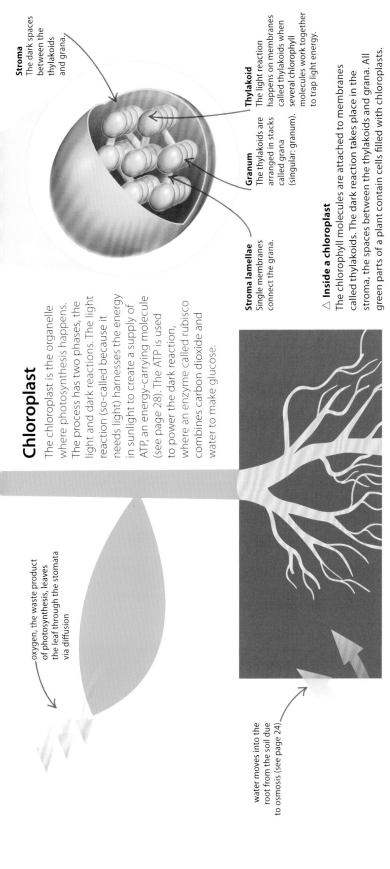

Chloroplast

The chloroplast is the organelle where photosynthesis happens. The process has two phases, the light and dark reactions. The light reaction (so-called because it needs light) harnesses the energy in sunlight to create a supply of ATP, an energy-carrying molecule (see page 28). The ATP is used to power the dark reaction, where an enzyme called rubisco combines carbon dioxide and water to make glucose.

Stroma
The dark spaces between the thylakoids and grana.

Thylakoid
The light reaction happens on membranes called thylakoids when several chlorophyll molecules work together to trap light energy.

Granum
The thylakoids are arranged in stacks called grana (singular: granum).

Stroma lamellae
Single membranes connect the grana.

△ **Inside a chloroplast**
The chlorophyll molecules are attached to membranes called thylakoids. The dark reaction takes place in the stroma, the spaces between the thylakoids and grana. All green parts of a plant contain cells filled with chloroplasts.

oxygen, the waste product of photosynthesis, leaves the leaf through the stomata via diffusion

water moves into the root from the soil due to osmosis (see page 24)

Chlorophyll

The chemical pigment chlorophyll is what makes most plants look green. Each chlorophyll molecule absorbs the red and blue light in sunlight, using its energy to power photosynthesis, and reflects the rest back. So what we see is the green light that is not used by photosynthesis reflected back.

△ **Absorption spectrum**
This graph shows the wavelengths, or colors, of light, that are absorbed by chlorophyll. The dip in the middle shows that yellows and greens are absorbed less than reds and blues.

(y-axis: amount of light absorbed; x-axis: wavelength of light (nanometers), 400–700)

REAL WORLD
Fall colors

Deciduous trees drop their leaves in winter, when it is too dark to photosynthesize efficiently. Before they are shed, the leaves change color—turning from green to brown. This change is due to the chlorophyll being absorbed by the plant for use in the next year. The fall colors are formed by pigments called carotenes that are left behind.

Feeding

THE PROCESS OF COLLECTING AND CONVERTING RAW MATERIALS INTO ENERGY.

SEE ALSO	
Waste materials	34–35 ⟩
Human digestion	66–67 ⟩
Human health	70–71 ⟩
Food chains	76–77 ⟩
Cycles in nature	78–79 ⟩

Not all living things feed—plants and other photosynthetic organisms make their own food. However animals, fungi, and many single-celled organisms survive by consuming other living things.

What is feeding?

An organism that feeds is called a heterotroph, a name that means "other eater." As the name suggests, heterotrophs collect the nutrients and energy they need by consuming other organisms. Plants are called autotrophs—"self-eaters"—because they generate everything they need to survive themselves. There are several modes of feeding and every organism specializes in getting its food in a specific way.

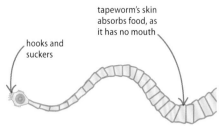

△ **Absorption**
The simplest feeding method is to absorb food through the surface of the body. A tapeworm hooks itself to the surface of a human's small intestine, then absorb nutrients through its skin.

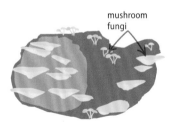

△ **External digestion**
A fungus is a saprophyte, meaning it grows over its food source, secreting enzymes that digest the food externally. Nutrients are then absorbed directly into its body.

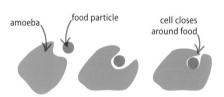

△ **Phagocytosis**
Single-celled organisms such as amoebas engulf their food, moving their cell membrane around it to form a sac in which the food is digested.

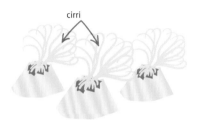

△ **Filter feeding**
Barnacles do not search for food, but sieve it from the water using their long, feathery legs, called cirri. Many shellfish, such as clams, are also filter feeders.

△ **Biting**
Only vertebrates, such as crocodiles, have jaws that open and close in a biting motion. The jaws are lined with teeth, which cut the food into manageable chunks before swallowing.

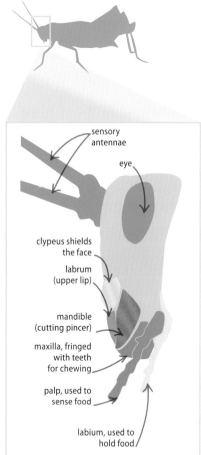

△ **Mouthparts**
Insects and other arthropods have complex mouthparts. A grasshopper's mouthparts are suited to cutting and chewing, but other insects have mouthparts that can be used for sucking, biting, or soaking up liquids.

Teeth

Digestion, the breaking up of food into simpler substances that can be used by the body, follows feeding. The first phase of this is often mechanical digestion, where hard, sharp teeth bite food into small chunks or chew it to a pulp. Some toothless animals, such as birds, grind their food internally in gizzards—muscular stomachs that use stones swallowed by the animals to help break up the food.

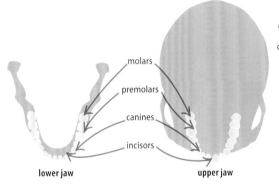

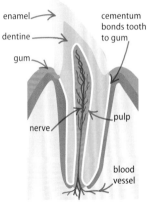

▷ **Human teeth**
Humans have four types of teeth. Incisors are used to slice and bite, and canines grip and rip. Molars and premolars are flat and are used for grinding food.

△ **Tooth anatomy**
A hard enamel cover is supported by softer dentine beneath. The pulp contains blood and nerve connections.

Types of consumer

Not all animals eat the same foods, and that difference is reflected in their teeth and jaws. Carnivores eat meat, so their teeth are often structured to help catch prey and rip it to shreds. Plant food is very tough, so herbivores (plant-eaters) use wide, grinding teeth to make it more digestible. Omnivores have teeth suited to a mixed diet of both meat and plants.

▽ **Hunter or hunted?**
Scientists can tell a lot about the way an animal lived by the shape, position, and condition of its teeth.

dolphins have many hooked teeth for gripping slippery fish, so they do not escape

lions have long fangs for gripping prey, while large premolars at the back of the jaw slice meat with a scissor action

the gap in a cow's teeth allows the animal to grab a new mouthful of grass while still chewing the last one

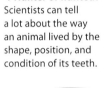

human teeth are adapted to a varied diet of fruits, hard seeds, and flesh

▷ **Rumination**
Chewing food once is not enough for large herbivores, such as cattle or antelopes. They regurgitate food, called cud, from the stomach to chew it a few more times during digestion. Ruminants rely on bacteria living in their complex stomachs to break down the tough cellulose (the main part of plant cell walls) in their food.

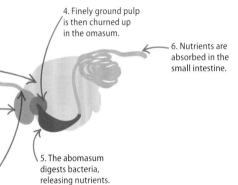

1. Swallowed food goes to the rumen, where it is mixed with digestive bacteria.

2. The second stomach chamber, the reticulum, receives cud, a mixture of food and stomach juices, from the rumen.

3. The reticulum pushes cud back up to the mouth for extra chewing.

4. Finely ground pulp is then churned up in the omasum.

5. The abomasum digests bacteria, releasing nutrients.

6. Nutrients are absorbed in the small intestine.

Waste materials

ANIMALS AND PLANTS USE A VARIETY OF METHODS TO GET RID OF THEIR WASTE MATERIALS.

SEE ALSO	
⟨ 32–33 Feeding	
Hormones	48–49 ⟩
Body systems	62–63 ⟩
Human digestion	66–67 ⟩

Excretion is the process of removing the waste produced by living bodies. This process is different to defecation, which is the release of the unused portion of food from the digestive tract.

Waste removal

A waste product is anything that the body cannot use. If they are allowed to build up in the body, they may become toxic. Nitrogen compounds from unneeded proteins form poisons that must be flushed away, and even carbon dioxide from respiration would make the blood dangerously acidic if it were not removed.

▽ **Getting rid of waste**
Organisms tackle their waste in different ways. The methods used to dispose of it safely depend on the nature of the waste and what resources are available. For example, fish flush waste out in water, but this method would dehydrate many animals, so other techniques are used.

REAL WORLD
Wandering albatross digestion
Soaring over the ocean, an albatross swoops down to catch its prey, such as a small fish or an octopus. While some food settles and is digested in the lower gut, a layer of nourishing oil floats to the top of the bird's stomach. This oil can then be regurgitated to feed its young.

Waste product	Organism	Excretory process	Explanation
ammonia	fish	break-down of proteins	ammonia is very poisonous, so it is excreted in very dilute urine by fish and other animals that have plenty of water available around them
urea	mammals	break-down of proteins	to save water, animals chemically convert ammonia into urea, which is soluble and can be excreted in liquid urine
uric acid	birds, reptiles	break-down of proteins	uric acid is a solid form of nitrogen-containing waste excreted as a white paste, which saves water but requires a lot of energy to process
carbon dioxide	all life	respiration of sugars	carbon dioxide, produced as a byproduct of respiration, is released from the body during gas exchange, for example, in the lungs or gills
oxygen	plants and algae	photosynthesis	although oxygen is useful, too much can upset some of the plant's processes, so unwanted oxygen is released through its leaves
feces	most animals	undigested food	unneeded food material, combined with other waste materials (including brown pigments from dead blood cells), is eliminated via the anus
salt	all organisms	balancing concentrations of body fluids	salts help with many body processes, but too much can cause cramps and dehydration, so it is excreted in sweat, urine, or through skin glands

WASTE MATERIALS 35

Kidneys and bladder

In humans—and other vertebrates—most waste products are filtered from the blood supply by the kidneys. The liquid produced—known as urine—trickles from each kidney through a long tube called a ureter. Both ureters empty into the bladder, a flexible bag in the pelvic region. When this is about half full, the weight of the liquid creates the urge to urinate. Urine is expelled from the bladder via a channel running through the genital region called the urethra.

▽ **Inside the kidneys**
A renal artery brings waste-filled blood to the kidney. The blood is dispersed to the outer regions, called the cortex, where the filtering happens in thousands of tiny units called nephrons. From there, the clean blood is returned to the body via a renal vein. Drops of the filtered waste are collected by the calyx, a multiheaded funnel that connects to the ureter.

Even **water** can be toxic, because too much in the body causes the brain to swell and can kill.

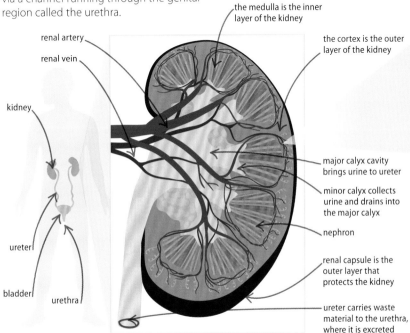

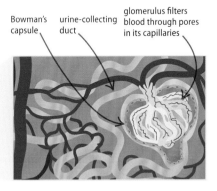

△ **Nephron**
Tiny blood vessels form into a netlike structure called a glomerulus. The liquid portion of the blood squirts out through the thin walls of the glomerulus into a bell-shaped Bowman's capsule. The solid blood cells cannot escape, but the waste material travels with the liquid through a series of tubules (tiny tubes) to a collecting duct that leads back through the medulla to the ureter.

Osmoregulation

The kidneys also carry out osmoregulation, controlling the amount of water in the body. When there is a lack of water, the nephron tubules reabsorb some of it from urine so it is not expelled unnecessarily. Osmoregulation is governed by a hormone called antidiuretic hormone, or ADH, which is produced by the pituitary gland.

▷ **Rising and falling**
The levels of ADH in the blood are constantly adjusting to maintain the right amount of water in the blood in a cycle, shown here.

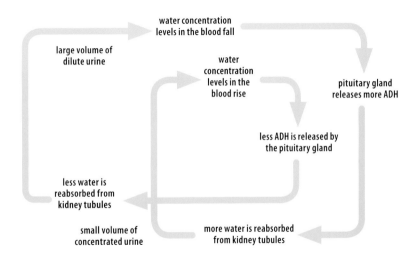

Transport systems

SUBSTANCES ARE MOVED AROUND INSIDE LIVING THINGS IN A VARIETY OF WAYS.

SEE ALSO	
‹ 24–25 Cells at work	
Disease and immunity	50–51 ›
Body systems	62–63 ›
Circulatory system	69 ›

The cells in a multicellular organism are specialized into certain roles and cannot survive on their own. The body's transport system brings them what they need to stay alive, and takes away their waste materials.

Circulation

Animals transport substances around their bodies in a liquid. In vertebrates, this liquid is blood, pumped along by a heart (or hearts) through a series of pipes, or vessels. Blood vessels reach all parts of the body, narrowing to thin-walled capillaries that deliver materials to cells by diffusion.

▷ **Arteries and veins**
The vessels that carry blood away from the heart are called arteries. They pulsate to push blood along, which can be felt through the skin in some places. Veins bring blood back to the heart.

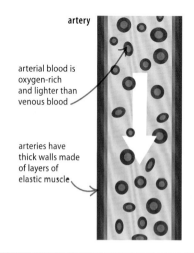

artery

arterial blood is oxygen-rich and lighter than venous blood

arteries have thick walls made of layers of elastic muscle

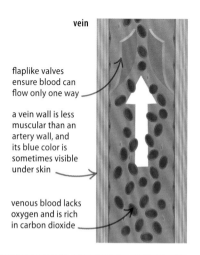

vein

flaplike valves ensure blood can flow only one way

a vein wall is less muscular than an artery wall, and its blue color is sometimes visible under skin

venous blood lacks oxygen and is rich in carbon dioxide

Composition of blood

Blood contains hundreds of compounds. About 55 percent of blood is a watery mixture known as plasma. This contains dissolved ions, hormones, and several proteins, such as the ones that form blood clots and scabs to seal breaks in vessels. The rest of the blood is made up of red and white blood cells and platelets.

Blood color ▷
Blood looks red because most of its cells contain an iron-rich pigment called hemoglobin. This substance bonds with oxygen arriving via the lungs and delivers it to body cells. A few invertebrates use copper-rich hemocyanin to do this, which makes their blood blue.

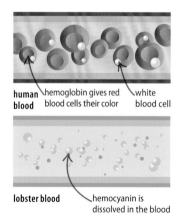

human blood — hemoglobin gives red blood cells their color — white blood cell

lobster blood — hemocyanin is dissolved in the blood

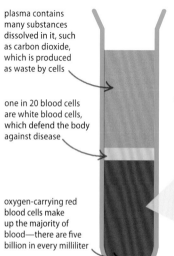

plasma contains many substances dissolved in it, such as carbon dioxide, which is produced as waste by cells

one in 20 blood cells are white blood cells, which defend the body against disease

oxygen-carrying red blood cells make up the majority of blood—there are five billion in every milliliter

▽ **Red blood cells**
Hemoglobin, the body's oxygen carrier, is held in red blood cells. These have a curved doughnut shape to maximize their surface area for collecting oxygen.

TRANSPORT SYSTEMS

Plant vascular system

The transport system of a plant is made up of two sets of vessels—xylem and phloem. Xylem carries water around the plant. Its stiff tubes run from the roots, up the stem, to the leaves. Phloem carries the sugar made in the leaves to the rest of the plant in the form of dissolved sucrose. Both types of vessel are made from columns of cells with openings at either end that form continuous pipes along which liquids can flow.

More than **100 million tons** of sugar are extracted from the sap stored in the phloem tubes of sugar cane **every year**.

REAL WORLD
Giant redwood

The largest trees in the world, such as these giant redwoods of California, USA, grow to around 361 ft (110 m) tall. Scientists estimate that this is about the maximum height for a tree, since the pressure needed to pump a continuous column of water any higher would cause the water to pull itself apart inside the tree, and never reach the top.

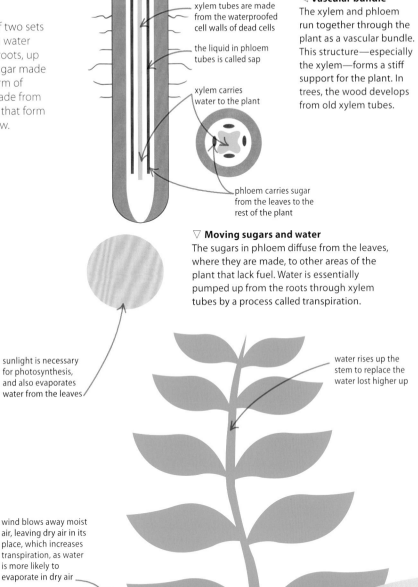

◁ **Vascular bundle**
The xylem and phloem run together through the plant as a vascular bundle. This structure—especially the xylem—forms a stiff support for the plant. In trees, the wood develops from old xylem tubes.

- xylem tubes are made from the waterproofed cell walls of dead cells
- the liquid in phloem tubes is called sap
- xylem carries water to the plant
- phloem carries sugar from the leaves to the rest of the plant

▽ **Moving sugars and water**
The sugars in phloem diffuse from the leaves, where they are made, to other areas of the plant that lack fuel. Water is essentially pumped up from the roots through xylem tubes by a process called transpiration.

- sunlight is necessary for photosynthesis, and also evaporates water from the leaves
- water rises up the stem to replace the water lost higher up
- wind blows away moist air, leaving dry air in its place, which increases transpiration, as water is more likely to evaporate in dry air
- water is drawn into roots—and up the xylem—by osmosis (see page 24)
- root hairs increase the surface area able to suck up water

Movement

ORGANISMS HAVE DEVELOPED DIFFERENT WAYS OF MOVING.

SEE ALSO	
Fish, amphibians, and reptiles	58–59 ⟩
Mammals and birds	60–61 ⟩
Body systems	62–63 ⟩

Organisms move by changing the shape of their body to propel themselves forward. In complex animals these body changes are controlled by muscles, bundles of protein that exert pulling forces on body parts.

Modes of locomotion

Animals move in order to find food, escape a threat, or locate mates. The precise mode of locomotion (movement) used depends heavily on their habitat. Plants and fungi cannot move in the same way—their stiff cell walls make their bodies too rigid. However, many single-celled organisms, such as most protists and algae, can move by using extensions called flagella or cilia in the search for food or better conditions.

△ **Flying**
Wings are modified limbs that create lift and thrust forces to carry birds, bats, and some insects through the air.

△ **Swinging**
Tree-dwellers require a large decision-making brain and nimble limbs to control climbing and jumping.

△ **Walking**
Most land animals walk on four legs (quadrupedal), although humans and flightless birds walk on two (bipedal).

△ **Burrowing**
Burrowers have powerful limbs for digging or are slender enough to be able to wriggle through soft soils.

△ **Floating**
The Portuguese man-of-war cannot move itself, but it is moved by tides, currents, and winds on the water's surface.

△ **Drifting**
Some microscopic plankton can swim, but most float freely in the water and are carried along by ocean currents.

△ **Swimming**
Aquatic animals that can swim strongly enough to control where they move in the water are called nektons.

△ **Staying still**
Some organisms spend their lives anchored in one spot, usually under water, and just move their limbs to catch food.

Snake locomotion

Snakes evolved from four-legged reptiles, with their ancestors losing their limbs over time. Their most common—and fastest—mode of movement is serpentine locomotion, using sideways curves.

muscle contracts on the outside of the curve to pull the body straight

the rear curve is now where the first one was

snake curves around bumps on the ground

the outer edge of curve does the pushing

the straightened front section moves forward

△ **1. Bunching up**
The body is pulled into wide curves so the rear end moves toward the head.

△ **2. Stretching out**
As the body straightens, the curved sections push against the rough ground.

△ **3. Gaining ground**
The head gains ground by moving forward, and then the sequence starts again.

MOVEMENT

Anchor points

Muscles exert a force by contracting, or pulling, and need a solid anchor point to pull against. This is the main function of a skeleton, with the bones connecting at joints, to allow it to move when muscles pull. Muscles cannot push, so they work in pairs, with each muscle pulling in the opposite direction to the other.

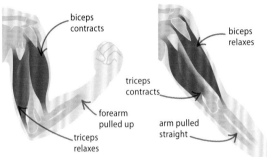

△ **Flex**
The biceps muscle contracts, pulling up on the forearm and causing the whole arm to bend at the elbow.

△ **Extend**
The triceps contracts, and the biceps relaxes, pulling the forearm down and straightening the arm.

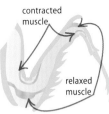

△ **Raised**
Arthropod exoskeletons contain pairs of muscles attached to their jointed inside surfaces.

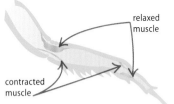

△ **Extended**
The exoskeleton does not bend when pulled by a muscle. Instead, the force is transferred to the joint, making the whole joint move.

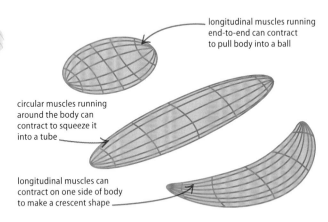

△ **Hydrostatic skeleton**
Worms and other soft-bodied animals have a hydrostatic skeleton—made of sacs of liquid surrounded by muscles. These have a fixed volume, but can be changed into different shapes using sets of circular and longitudinal muscles.

Muscle contraction

A muscle cell takes the form of a long fiber—up to 30 cm (12 in) long in a man's thigh. The cell contains many hundreds of nuclei and several bundles of myofibrils, which are made up of two protein filaments known as myosin and actin. Muscles contract when the two filaments move closer together in the cells. Millions of these tiny movements accumulate into a powerful contraction.

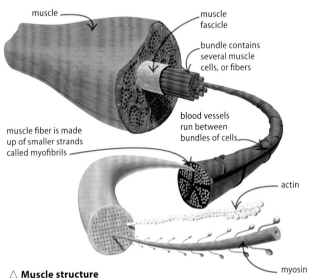

△ **Muscle structure**
Muscles are formed from a hierarchy of bundles. Even the smallest muscle contains several fascicles, which are bundles of muscle cells. In turn, the cells contain bundles of myofibrils that are filled with myosin and actin.

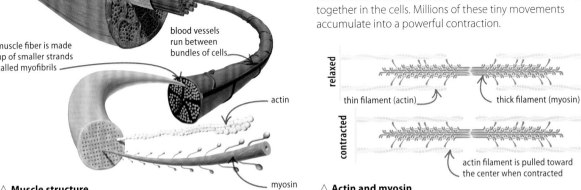

△ **Actin and myosin**
When a muscle receives an electric pulse from a nerve, the signal causes the thick myosin protein to haul itself along two actin strands, pulling them toward the center. When relaxed, the proteins spread apart again, and the muscle lengthens.

Sensitivity

LIVING ORGANISMS SENSE THEIR
ENVIRONMENT IN DIFFERENT WAYS.

SEE ALSO	
Human senses	64–65 ⟩
Functional groups	160–161 ⟩
Electromagnetic waves	194–195 ⟩
Light	196–197 ⟩
Sound	200–201 ⟩

All living things are sensitive to their surroundings, such as changes in light, sound, or chemistry. This sensitivity allows organisms to respond, for example to a threat, increasing their chances of survival.

Tropism

Plants can sense the factors in the environment that help them maximize their growth. This is called tropism. A seed is sensitive to gravity (gravitropism), so its roots grow down into the soil. The roots also turn toward water in the soil (hydrotropism), while the stem grows toward sunlight (phototropism). Phototropism causes a growing point (the meristem) to face the Sun by growing cells on one side of the stem longer than those of the other.

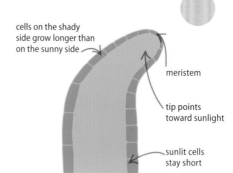

cells on the shady side grow longer than on the sunny side
meristem
tip points toward sunlight
sunlit cells stay short

◁ **Phototropism**
Sunlight inhibits the production of growth hormones or auxins. The cells on the shady side of the stem release auxins. That makes the cells in shade grow longer, while the cells on the sunny side stay short.

▷ **Compound eye**
Many arthropods have compound eyes, which have thousands of individual lenses. Each lens forms a small dot of an image, which overlaps with other dots to form a larger image.

lenses made from cone-shaped crystal can pick up slightest movements
pigment cells stop light leaking to other lenses
rhabdom channels light toward retina cell
each retina cell detects light
signal passes to nerve cell

Animal senses

The human senses of touch, smell, sight, hearing, and taste are all used by animals, but not in the same way. For example, a grasshopper hears with pressure-sensitive knees, a housefly tastes its food by standing on it (its taste buds are on its feet), while a moth detects smells with its feathery antennae. Some animals have senses that do not compare to human ones.

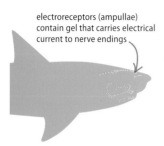

electroreceptors (ampullae) contain gel that carries electrical current to nerve endings

△ **Ampullae of Lorenzini**
Sharks have electroreceptors that pick up the electric fields produced by the muscles of other animals. This allows them to find prey in the dark water.

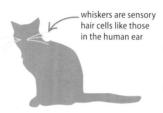

whiskers are sensory hair cells like those in the human ear

△ **Whiskers**
Whiskers are ultra-sensitive hairs used by mammals to feel their way in the dark. They are wider than the head, so the animal knows if it is heading into a tight spot.

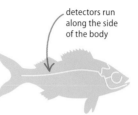

detectors run along the side of the body

△ **Lateral line**
Fish use a motion sensor, called the lateral line, running along the side of the body. It picks up the swirling water currents created by other animals moving nearby.

pits are on the snout

△ **Heat pits**
Pythons and vipers have hollow pits on their snouts that detect the body heat of warm-blooded prey. The pits also warn the snake if it should avoid the other creature.

SENSITIVITY

Nerve cell

Sensory organs send out signals to the rest of the body as electric pulses that run along nerves. Nerves are made up of bundles of long cells called neurons. The long, wirelike section of the cell is called the axon, and it carries the signal to the next cell in line. Charged ions flood in and out of the axon to create the electric pulse.

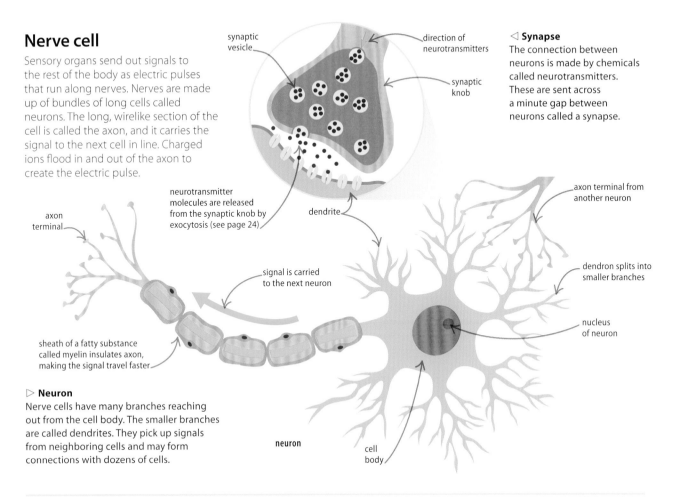

▷ **Synapse**
The connection between neurons is made by chemicals called neurotransmitters. These are sent across a minute gap between neurons called a synapse.

▷ **Neuron**
Nerve cells have many branches reaching out from the cell body. The smaller branches are called dendrites. They pick up signals from neighboring cells and may form connections with dozens of cells.

Reflex action

Information from the senses travels toward the brain through sensory neurons. In vertebrates, such as humans, these connect to the spinal cord, and the signal travels up to the brain through the cord. Any immediate response to the stimulus (such as a sharp pin) is sent out to the muscles by motor neurons right away. This means that reflex actions, such as withdrawing the hand from the source of pain, do not involve the brain, but are controlled by the spinal cord alone.

▷ **Reflex arc**
The nerve pathway controlling a reflex is called the reflex arc. The sensory nerve sends a signal to the spinal cord, where it connects directly to the motor neuron that signals to the muscles, causing them to move.

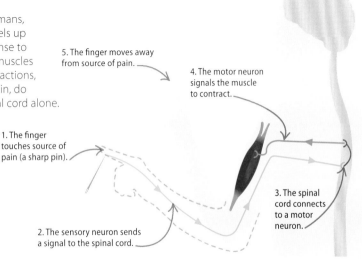

Reproduction I

SPECIES MUST REPRODUCE TO SURVIVE.

Reproduction is the main purpose of the natural world. Living things grow, feed, and survive in order to reproduce and makes copies of themselves.

SEE ALSO	
‹ 22–23 Cell structure	
‹ 25 Cell division	
Human reproduction	72–73 ›
Evolution	80–81 ›
Genetics I	84–85 ›

Asexual reproduction

When a single organism makes an exact copy of itself, the process is called asexual reproduction. The copy is genetically identical, a clone of the parent. Asexual reproduction can be useful for populating new habitats very quickly. However, because all the offspring are identical, a disease or other problem that affects one of them is likely to affect all the others, too.

New Mexico whiptail lizards are all asexual, but all females must "mock mate" with each other before laying eggs.

▽ Budding
The most basic form of reproduction is budding, in which a section of the parent breaks off, forming an independent individual. Many single-celled organisms reproduce by budding.

▽ Vegetative reproduction
Some plants send out side roots (called runners) or stems (stolons), that sprout daughter plants nearby. When the daughter plant is established, the connection with the parent breaks.

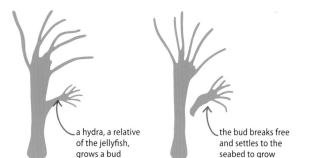
a hydra, a relative of the jellyfish, grows a bud on its side

the bud breaks free and settles to the seabed to grow independently

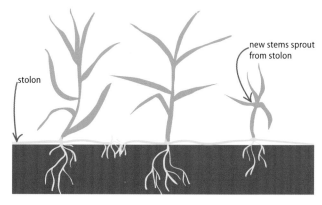
stolon

new stems sprout from stolon

▷ Sporogenesis
Fungi, primitive plants (such as ferns and moss), and even some parasitic worms reproduce by releasing hardy spores. These are tiny balls of cells, which can grow into new individuals.

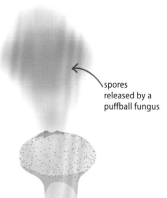
spores released by a puffball fungus

▷ Parthenogenesis
Parthenogenesis is a form of reproduction in which animals produce young without mating. Some female aphids give birth to daughters that are identical to themselves in every way except size.

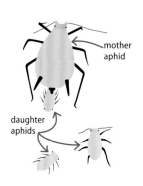
mother aphid

daughter aphids

Sexual reproduction

Sexual reproduction happens when two parents mix up their genes in order to produce offspring with their own unique genetic make-ups. Sexual reproduction requires each parent to produce gametes, or sex cells. While ordinary cells contain two full sets of genes—one from each parent—gametes have just a single set. In a process called fertilization, two gametes—one from each parent—fuse to form a zygote, the first cell of a new individual.

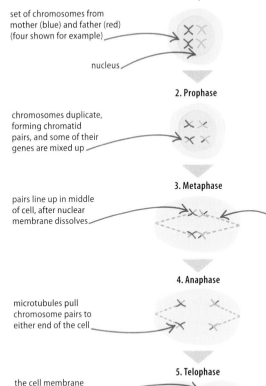

1. Interphase — set of chromosomes from mother (blue) and father (red) (four shown for example), nucleus

2. Prophase — chromosomes duplicate, forming chromatid pairs, and some of their genes are mixed up

3. Metaphase — pairs line up in middle of cell, after nuclear membrane dissolves; microtubules form at the cell's poles and attach to the pairs

4. Anaphase — microtubules pull chromosome pairs to either end of the cell

5. Telophase — the cell membrane forms across the cell

each daughter cell has a unique genetic make-up, different to each other and their parents' cells

◁ **Meiosis**
Gametes are produced using a special type of cell division—actually two divisions occurring together. In the first division, the number of chromosomes is halved. In the second division, the mechanisms are almost identical to the ones in mitosis.

▽ **Second division**
In the second division, each of the two cells pulls the chromosomes apart again. Once this is done, the cell membranes and nuclei form again, leaving four unique cells, with half the number of chromosomes of the original parent cells.

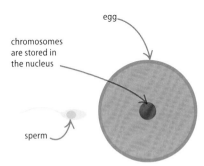

egg, chromosomes are stored in the nucleus, sperm

△ **Sperm and egg**
Male gametes are called sperm, and female ones are called eggs or ova (singular: ovum). Both contain half the usual number of chromosomes. A sperm's purpose is to deliver genes to the egg and it contains nothing else. By contrast, an egg cell needs to be huge to contain the nutrients required to grow a new individual after fertilization.

Animal development

After fertilization, the new individual (embryo) needs to develop and grow until it is ready to feed and live independently. The ways that animals produce their young depends on their habitat and biology.

▷ **Development strategies**
Small creatures, which are under constant threat of predators, produce lots of young quickly. Larger and better protected animals invest in protecting fewer young instead.

Method	Explanation	Example
ovuliparity	eggs are fertilized after being released by the female	fish, toads
oviparity	eggs are fertilized before release and often protected in a nest	birds
ovoviviparity	fertilized eggs retained in body until after hatching	seahorses
aplacental viviparity	young grow inside mother, feeding on eggs or siblings	some sharks
placental viviparity	young sustained by mother through placenta until birth	mammals

Reproduction II

ANIMALS AND PLANTS EMPLOY A RANGE OF STRATEGIES TO REPRODUCE.

SEE ALSO	
‹ 22–23 Cell structure	
Life cycles	46–47 ›
Plants	54–55 ›

Plants and animals employ a number of reproduction strategies to maximize their breeding potential. This may involve changing from one sex to another, or relying on other animals to aid in reproduction and dispersal of offspring.

Hermaphrodites

Sex cells are produced by organs known as gonads. The female gonad is the ovary; the male one is the testis. Animals that have both types of gonads at some point in their lives are known as hermaphrodites. Earthworms and land snails are simultaneous hermaphrodites, meaning they have both gonads at the same time. Nevertheless, they still need to find mates to breed.

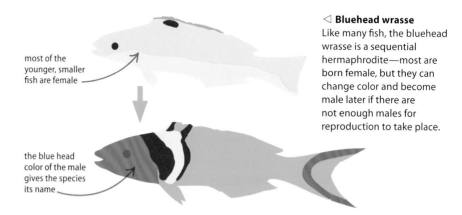

◁ **Bluehead wrasse**
Like many fish, the bluehead wrasse is a sequential hermaphrodite—most are born female, but they can change color and become male later if there are not enough males for reproduction to take place.

Marsupials

Most female mammals sustain a developing fetus inside the uterus or womb using a placenta. The placenta transfers oxygen and nutrients into the fetus's blood supply. The baby is born once it has developed enough to survive independently. The young of marsupials are born at an earlier stage of development than those of other mammals. Instead of being fed from a placenta in the uterus, they continue their growth in their mother's pouch, or marsupium.

▷ **Kangaroo**
Baby kangaroos, or joeys, are born after just 31 days of development inside the mother. They then make a dangerous journey from the birth canal, over the mother's fur to the safety of the mother's pouch.

Joeys are only about 2 cm (0.8 in) long when they are born and weigh less than 1 g (0.4 oz).

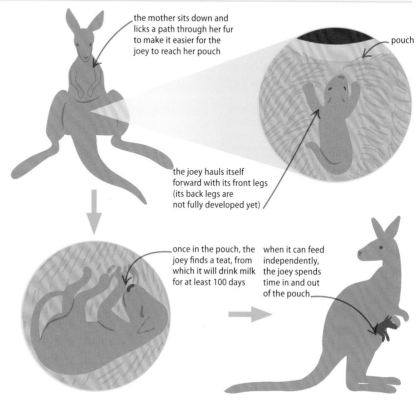

Flowering plants

The flower is the reproductive organ of a plant. It has male and female parts. The anthers produce pollen, which contain the male sex cells, while the ovary at the heart of the flower contains the ova (singular: ovum), or eggs. The other structures in the flower are there to aid the pollen from one flower getting to the stigma of another flower, from where the sex cells in the pollen travel to the ovary.

Fruit and seeds

When a plant ovum is fertilized, the ovary develops into a seed. The seed is an embryonic form of the adult plant, with a root, stem, and food store. A fruit is the coating around the seed, developed from the wall of the ovary. Fruits have evolved to have many functions.

▷ **Animal-pollinated flower**
This flower's bright petals and sweet smell attract insects that come to drink nectar, a sweet liquid produced at the center of the flower. The visiting insects pick up sticky pollen from the anther. When they visit another flower, the pollen transfers to that flower's stigma.

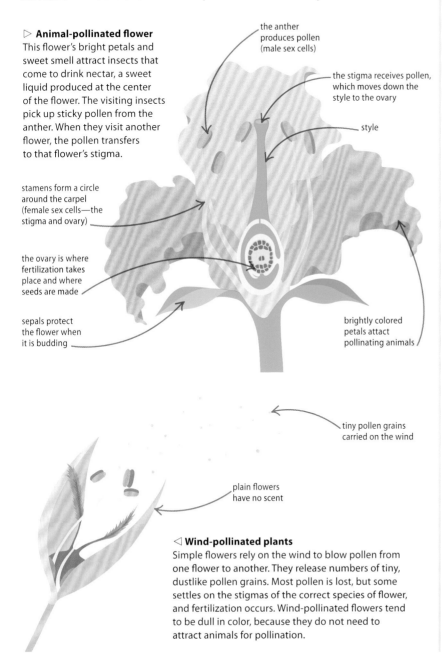

- the anther produces pollen (male sex cells)
- the stigma receives pollen, which moves down the style to the ovary
- style
- stamens form a circle around the carpel (female sex cells—the stigma and ovary)
- the ovary is where fertilization takes place and where seeds are made
- sepals protect the flower when it is budding
- brightly colored petals attract pollinating animals
- tiny pollen grains carried on the wind
- plain flowers have no scent

◁ **Wind-pollinated plants**
Simple flowers rely on the wind to blow pollen from one flower to another. They release numbers of tiny, dustlike pollen grains. Most pollen is lost, but some settles on the stigmas of the correct species of flower, and fertilization occurs. Wind-pollinated flowers tend to be dull in color, because they do not need to attract animals for pollination.

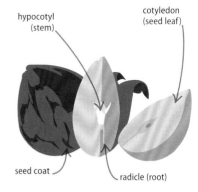

- hypocotyl (stem)
- cotyledon (seed leaf)
- seed coat
- radicle (root)

△ **Seeds**
The embryonic root and stem are ready to sprout from the seed during germination. They get their energy from a cotyledon—some seeds have two—which is an embryonic leaf structure packed with starch fuel.

- berry
- maple key
- coconut

△ **Different fruits**
The main job of a fruit is to protect the seed and help it move far away from the parent tree. Sweet fruits, such as berries, are eaten by animals and the seed is deposited later. A maple key is a wind-borne fruit, while the coconut is able to float vast distances across the ocean.

Life cycles

DIFFERENT PLANTS AND ANIMALS GROW TO MATURITY IN DIFFERENT WAYS.

SEE ALSO	
‹ 45 Fruits and seeds	
Plants	54–55 ›
Ecosystems	74–75 ›

The early, or juvenile, phase of a multicellular organism's life is devoted to growth. Organisms use a range of systems to reach an adult size, only then developing sexual organs and reproducing.

Germination

A seed is a plant embryo. It already has a root (radicle) and a tiny stem (plumule) inside. The embryonic leaf, called a cotyledon, is a food store that powers the first stage of growth, known as germination. Germination is stimulated by environmental conditions. Longer days—indicating the approach of spring—are a common cue. Some seeds require other cues, such as temperature changes, being soaked in water for a long period, or even heat from fire.

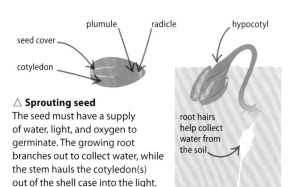

△ **Sprouting seed**
The seed must have a supply of water, light, and oxygen to germinate. The growing root branches out to collect water, while the stem hauls the cotyledon(s) out of the shell case into the light.

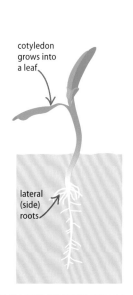

Plant life cycles

All flowering plants produce seeds but they do it according to one of three life cycles. Annual plants, such as grasses, sprout, seed, and then die all within one year. Biennials spend the first year growing a storage root, such as a carrot, which then resprouts and flowers in the second year. Perennials live for more than two years and produce repeated batches of seeds.

▽ **Annual (grass)**
The grass seed stays in the soil during winter, grows rapidly, and flowers within a few months. The plant drops new seeds onto the fresh soil before it dies.

▽ **Biennial (carrot)**
In the first year, leaves above ground fuel the creation of a carrot root, which remains even when the leaves and shoots die off over winter. The next spring, the carrot root's stored sugar fuels new shoots, rapid flowering, and seed production.

▽ **Perennial (oak tree)**
The oak tree grows for several years before flowering for the first time. Its seeds are dispersed by animals. During winters, the plant becomes dormant, before growing more and flowering again the following year.

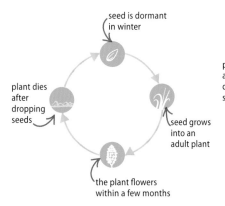

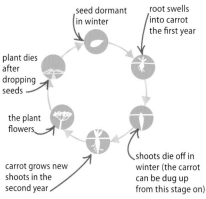

LIFE CYCLES

Metamorphosis

Animals that produce large numbers of young can find they are in direct competition for food with their own offspring. Many insects avoid this problem by having larval stages, which look and live in very different ways to the adults. A larva must undergo a complete metamorphosis, where its body rebuilds itself in the adult, sexually mature form. Other young insects are nymphs, which, unlike larvae, resemble their adult form.

REAL WORLD
Woolly bear caterpillar

The larvae of tiger moths are called woolly bears, and the species that live in the Arctic take years to reach adulthood. The woolly bears freeze solid during the long winters, and can only manage one molt during the short Arctic summer. After 14 molts and 14 years, the caterpillars finally pupate into tiger moths.

▷ **Incomplete metamorphosis**
The cicada nymph looks like its adult parent, but lacks wings. After several molts, the nymph reaches its largest size, called the final instar. During the next molt, it develops wings and sex organs and emerges as an adult, ready to reproduce.

▷ **Complete metamorphosis**
After hatching, the caterpillar (larva) is an eating machine and undergoes several molts as it outgrows its inflexible exoskeleton. Then it becomes a pupa, a dormant phase inside a protective case, where metamorphosis takes place. The insect emerges as an adult butterfly.

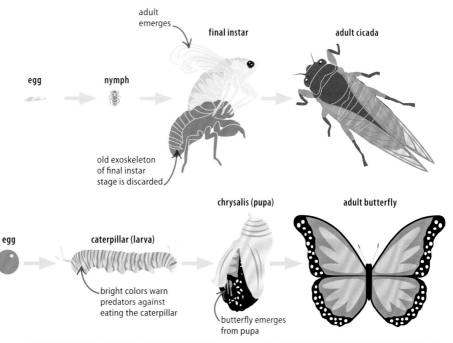

Reproductive strategies

Animals employ different strategies to ensure their offspring survive until they can reproduce. There are two main options: producing huge numbers of young, but leaving their survival to chance, or protecting just a few young, and giving them parental care and protection.

▷ **Pros and cons**
All reproductive strategies have advantages and disadvantages. An animal's place in the food chain and its habitat are the two factors that influence its reproductive strategy.

Animal	Type of care	Benefits	Costs
salmon	many thousands of eggs are laid each year	young can populate a new habitat quickly, and at least a few will always survive	effort kills the parents, and most young die before they reproduce
lion	one or two young are produced every few years; mother looks after them until adulthood	young are more likely to survive until adulthood, and help raise and protect younger siblings	investing energy into just a few young over many years is risky

Hormones

CHEMICAL MESSAGES CALLED HORMONES CONTROL DAY-TO-DAY BODY PROCESSES.

SEE ALSO
⟨ 24–25 Cells at work
⟨ 34–35 Waste materials
⟨ 36–37 Transport systems
⟨ 38–39 Movement
Radiating heat 189 ⟩

Complex life forms use hormones to control growth, metabolic rate, and to prepare the body for activity or sleep. Hormones are produced in special organs called glands throughout the body.

Glands

Any body part that secretes a substance is called a gland. Exocrine glands send chemicals out of the body. They include sweat, salivary, and the seminal gland, which releases semen. Hormones are produced by endocrine glands, which release substances into the blood and internal body fluids. From there, hormones are carried to the parts of the body that they influence.

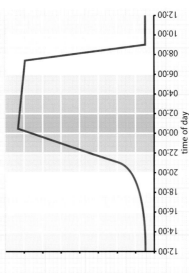

△ **Human hormones**
The glands shown here secrete hormones used in a variety of processes in the human body.

- pineal gland produces chemicals that make us sleepy
- pituitary gland produces hormones that influence urine and breast milk production, and other processes
- thyroid gland produces thyroxine, which controls the rate of metabolism of the body
- adrenal glands produce epinephrine to combat stress
- pancreas produces insulin to process sugar in food

△ **Melatonin**
This hormone is released by the pineal gland underneath the brain. Its production is linked to the time of the day. In humans, it is released in the evening to prepare the body for night time, making us sleepy. In nocturnal animals, it is activated to wake them up.

△ **Epinephrine**
This powerful hormone is released by the adrenal glands. It triggers the body's response to stress (the "fight-or-flight" response). When released, epinephrine (also known as adrenaline) gives an immediate energy boost to prepare the body to act. Some of the common signs of this are listed here.

Effect	Explanation	Purpose
skin goes pale	blood vessels in the skin contract	blood directed to muscles for movement
heart rate goes up	heart pumps more blood	oxygen reaches muscles faster
heavy breathing	lungs take bigger breaths	boost to oxygen supply

Thermoregulation

The human body maintains a constant body temperature so its metabolism runs at a constant rate. As a result, the body must conserve its heat in cold conditions and shed excess heat in warm ones. Its processes for keeping its body temperature steady are called thermoregulation.

▽ Hot and cold

Thermoregulation makes use of the basic principles of heat transfer. Heat is lost via skin flooded with warm blood, and also by the evaporation of sweat secreted on the skin. When cold, the body curls up to decrease its surface area and so reduce heat loss.

Hot conditions	Cold conditions
Vasodilation The blood vessels in the skin widen to allow warm blood to radiate heat into the air.	**Vasocontraction** The blood vessels contract, so less blood reaches the skin, reducing heat transfer.
Sweating As sweat evaporates, it takes some of the body's heat with it.	**Shivering** The rapid movement of muscles when shivering generates heat.
Pilorelaxation Body hair lies flat, allowing cool breezes to get close to the skin.	**Piloerection (goosebumps)** Body hair stands up, to keep a layer of warm air next to the body.
Stretching out Moving around allows heat to be lost from a larger surface area.	**Curling up** Curling tight reduces the surface area losing heat.

In **very cold water**, a human's heart rate slows and blood is sent only to the brain and vital organs to conserve oxygen—so the person can survive for several minutes without **breathing**.

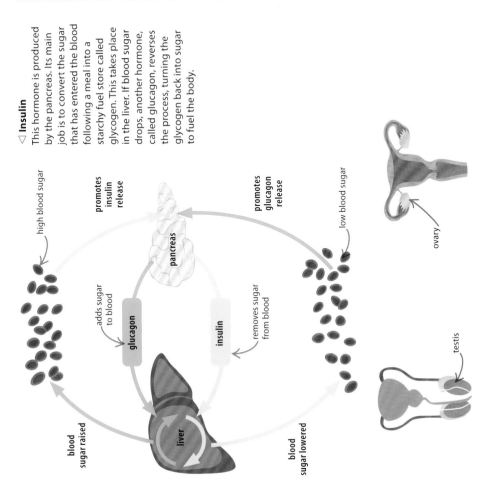

▽ Insulin

This hormone is produced by the pancreas. Its main job is to convert the sugar that has entered the blood following a meal into a starchy fuel store called glycogen. This takes place in the liver. If blood sugar drops, another hormone, called glucagon, reverses the process, turning the glycogen back into sugar to fuel the body.

△ Testosterone

The male hormone is produced by the testes (singular: testis), the male reproductive organs. As well as controlling the production of sperm, testosterone makes the body develop male characteristics, such as increased body hair and larger muscles. Testosterone also increases the willingness to fight (although it does not make you any better at it).

△ Estrogen

This is a female hormone produced by the ovaries. It is involved in the production of eggs, making them ready for reproduction on a monthly cycle. Estrogen is also responsible for making the body develop secondary sexual features, such as mammary glands and pubic hair during puberty.

Disease and immunity

WHEN THE BODY IS ATTACKED BY DISEASE-CAUSING ORGANISMS, IT HAS A RANGE OF RESPONSES.

SEE ALSO	
‹ 24–25 Cells at work	
‹ 26–27 Fungi and single-celled life	
Body systems	62–63 ›

The immune system is a highly complex defense system that looks for, and then destroys, foreign bodies that get inside the body. These foreign bodies use the body as a place to live and reproduce, which can cause illness.

Pathogens

The agents that cause disease are called pathogens. Most are living organisms, such as bacteria (often called germs), but illnesses are also caused by viruses, which are not generally considered to be living. The pathogens infect body tissues, and cause symptoms by killing cells, or by releasing poisons as they grow and spread.

Infection name	Type of pathogen	What it does	Symptom
streptococcus	bacterium	lives on skin and throat	sore throat
plasmodium	protist	kills body cells	malaria
threadworm	nematode worm	lives in intestines	itchy anus
H1N1	virus	invades body cells	fever and joint pain

△ **Pathogen table**
When pathogens invade the body, it is called an infection. Contagious diseases are those that pass from person to person, such as influenza. Other diseases are caught in other ways and do not spread so easily.

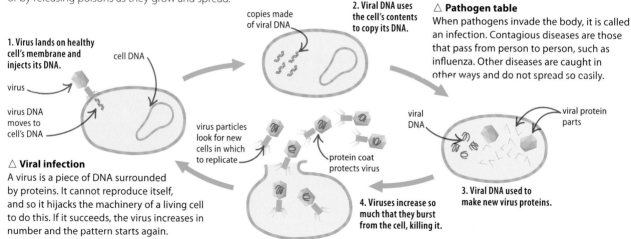

△ **Viral infection**
A virus is a piece of DNA surrounded by proteins. It cannot reproduce itself, and so it hijacks the machinery of a living cell to do this. If it succeeds, the virus increases in number and the pattern starts again.

White blood cells

White blood cells are the detectives of the body, patrolling the bloodstream looking for invaders. When they find one, the white blood cells copy the invading pathogen's antigen—the chemical marker on its surface. Then, the blood cells generate a protein, called an antibody, that flags the attacker for removal from the body. Amazingly, the immune system remembers the antibodies for all past attacks, and so can only be infected once by the same pathogen.

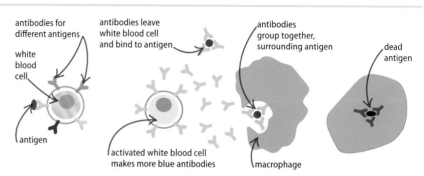

△ **1. Seeking**
The white blood cell recognizes the antigen on an object in the body as being foreign.

△ **2. Attacking**
Antibodies are released, and large white blood cells called macrophages engulf the antigen.

△ **3. Destroying**
Destructive enzymes called lysosomes finally kill the antigen inside the macrophage.

DISEASE AND IMMUNITY

Vaccination

The immune system is exploited by doctors to protect people from disease using vaccines. A vaccine introduces the antigens of a pathogen to the body—either in a chemical form, or a weakened strain that does not cause debilitating symptoms. The body responds to these antigens, and, if the actual pathogen enters the body at a later date, the immune system recognizes it and immediately kills it.

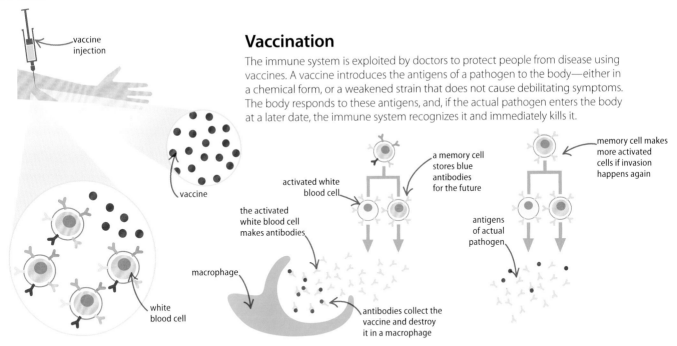

△ **1. Vaccination**
The vaccine is injected into the body, where it is detected by the white blood cells just like any other foreign antigen entering the body.

△ **2. Antibodies**
The white blood cells develop antibodies for the vaccine, which kill the vaccine antigens. The antibody is then stored in a memory cell.

△ **3. Fighting infection**
The real pathogen has the same antigen as the vaccine. If it enters the body, the immune system deploys the stored antibodies and the disease does not develop.

Healing skin

The body's first line of defense against attack is the skin. When the skin is broken by a cut or scrape, bacteria and other germs can get into the body. Therefore, blood rushes to the area, making it swell and helping seal the gap. The liquid blood quickly coagulates (thickens) into a solid scab that forms a temporary seal while the skin grows back.

Sufferers of **hemophilia** have a reduced ability to form blood clots, which can result in a small scrape causing them to bleed to death.

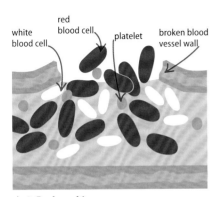

△ **1. Broken skin**
The blood floods into the gap in the skin. Tiny cells called platelets react to the skin proteins. They trigger swelling, which brings white blood cells to mop up any invaders.

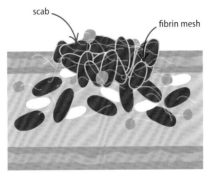

△ **2. Coagulation**
The platelets release the enzyme thrombin, which converts a soluble protein called fibrinogen into an insoluble one, fibrin. The fibrin forms a solid mesh across the gap.

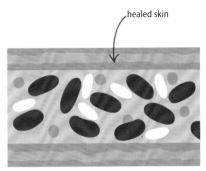

△ **3. Healing**
The temporary seal, or scab, lasts until the skin has grown back. When this happens, the inflammation reduces, and the fibrin dissolves back into the blood.

Animal relationships

ANIMALS LIVE TOGETHER IN DIFFERENT WAYS.

Competition for resources is central to animal life. Many species go it alone, but others team up to make life easier. This teaming-up may be between members of the same species, or involve completely different animals working together.

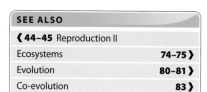

SEE ALSO	
‹ 44–45 Reproduction II	
Ecosystems	74–75 ›
Evolution	80–81 ›
Co-evolution	83 ›

Social groups

The strongest competition for survival is between members of the same species. Solitary animals avoid each other, so that competition is at a minimum. The animals that live in groups must strike a balance between the benefits of sticking together, and the increased competition for food and mates. Social groups range from simple ones that provide safety in numbers, to complex societies, where members hunt together and protect each other's young.

△ **Lion pride**
Prides feature one top male, who protects the rest and fathers all the cubs.

△ **Wolf pack**
Wolves work together to hunt animals much larger than themselves.

△ **Fish school**
Within a school, an individual has less chance of being picked off by a predator.

△ **Sheep flock**
Together, a flock is more likely to spot a threat before it gets too close.

A single **super colony** of Argentine ants runs 6,000 km (3,700 miles) along the southern European coast.

△ **Baboon troop**
Baboons work together to defend their young and secure food supplies.

△ **Okapi**
Living alone is best in a dense forest habitat where food is widely available.

Eusocial colony

The most highly social animals are ants, wasps, and bees. They are eusocial, which means there is division of labour, with different members of the colony performing specific jobs for the good of the whole. The colony works for their mother, the queen, to raise huge numbers of yet more sisters. All work is done by females. Only a few males are produced every year to mate with the next generation of queens.

woodcutter ants feed on fungus grown on a compost of cut leaf fragments

△ **Forager**
Foragers collect food from the surroundings and bring it back to the nest for the colony to eat.

eggs develop into more workers to help out in the colony

△ **Worker**
Small workers feed and clean the eggs, larvae, and pupae, and help build the nest.

queen is considerably larger than other ants

△ **Queen**
A large female controls the colony, and uses chemicals to stop other females from laying eggs.

wings used to fly to find a mate

△ **Male**
Male ants are produced at the end of summer. They die after they have mated with a queen.

ANIMAL RELATIONSHIPS

Symbiosis

When animals of two species cooperate with each other, the relationship is known as symbiosis. There are two types. In mutualistic relationships, both partners benefit from the actions of the other. Commensal relationships are rarer. They involve one animal benefiting from the association, while the other receives no benefit, but is not harmed either.

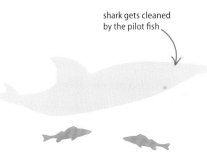

△ **Pilot fish and shark**
The small fish follow a large predator and snap up the leftovers from its meals, keeping the predator clean in the process.

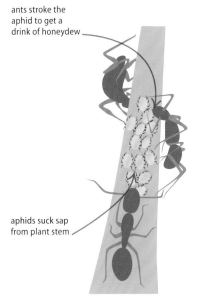

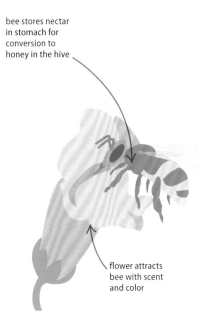

△ **Ants and aphids**
Aphids produce a sweet urine called honeydew. Ants protect a herd of aphids from predators, in order to feed on the aphids' honeydew.

△ **Honeybee and flower**
Flowers rely on honeybees to transfer their pollen to another plant. In return, the bees feed on nectar supplied by the plant.

△ **Oxpecker and impala**
An oxpecker bird lives on the back of a large herbivore, such as an impala. The bird feeds on ticks and insects living on the larger animal's hair and skin.

Parasites

A parasite is an organism that lives on or inside another, known as the host. The parasite either eats the body of the host or consumes some of its food. The host is disadvantaged by the relationship, but is not killed—if it was, the parasite would soon die as well in many cases. A parasitoid is an animal that does kill its host, generally as a larva eating it alive. Once the host is dead, the parasitoid takes on an independent mode of life (see page 91).

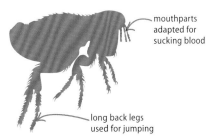

△ **Flea**
This insect is an ectoparasite, meaning it lives on the outside of the host. Fleas suck the blood of their hosts, moving to new ones in great leaps.

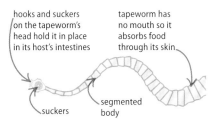

△ **Tapeworm**
This flatworm is an endoparasite, meaning it lives inside its host. Egg-carrying segments break off the worm and end up in the host's droppings, where they hatch and spread.

Plants

THE ORGANISMS THAT MAKE UP THE PLANT KINGDOM RANGE FROM SIMPLE MOSSES TO COMPLEX FLOWERING PLANTS.

The study of plants is called botany. Plants reach such huge sizes and are so widespread that botanists estimate there are 1,000 tonnes of living plant material for every tonne of animal.

SEE ALSO	
⟨ 20-21	Variety of life
⟨ 30-31	Photosynthesis
⟨ 37	Plant vascular system
⟨ 40	Tropism
⟨ 42-43	Reproduction I
⟨ 44-45	Reproduction II
⟨ 46	Plant life cycles
Carbon and fossil fuels	156-157 ⟩

The plant kingdom

There are thought to be around 300,000 species of plants, far fewer than animals. Unlike animals, plants are restricted to sunlit habitats to power photosynthesis, so they cannot grow in deep water or underground. They fall into three main groups: seaweeds (including algae), nonvascular land plants, and vascular plants (plants with xylem and phloem vessels). This last group makes up 90 percent of plant species.

▽ Seaweeds
anchored to rocks by structures called holdfasts, seaweeds are hardy plants that use leaflike structures called laminae to catch light for photosynthesis

▽ Mosses and liverworts
The most simple land plants are the mosses and liverworts. They do not have true leaves or roots. Without xylem or phloem to transport material, they are restricted in size and require a damp habitat. Mosses and liverworts reproduce using eggs and sperm that swim between plants.

moss — simple stems are flattened to catch light; the plant is held in place by extensions called rhizoids

▽ Ferns
Ferns are primitive vascular plants that do not produce seeds. They have roots and stems with bundles of xylem and phloem. These not only transport water and sugars, but also provide enough support for the plants to reach large sizes. Ferns include the first "trees", about 350 million years ago.

fern — structures on the fronds called sporangia disperse spores—which form new ferns; a young bud unfurls into a frond

▽ Gymnosperms
The first plants to reproduce using seeds were the gymnosperms, which include today's conifer trees, such as pines, cycads, and firs. Their scientific name means "naked seed," which refers to the way the seeds are not enclosed in a coat or fruit, as in the flowering plants (angiosperms) that evolved later.

pine cone — opening in top of female cone receives pollen from smaller male cones; pollen develops into a seed inside the cone, before the cone lets the seed fall to the ground

plant kingdom
- water
  - seaweeds
- land
  - non-vascular
    - mosses
  - vascular
    - ferns
    - gymnosperms
    - angiosperms (see below)

Angiosperms

Plants that reproduce using flowers are called angiosperms. Their seeds develop with a protective coat. They evolved from gymnosperms about 200 million years ago, and are the most common plant group, at least on land. Unlike the seeds of more primitive plants, angiosperm seeds include a starchy endosperm as a source of nutrition for the growing plant. Wheat, rice, and corn all come from endosperm seeds, and form much of the staple diet of humans.

The **largest flower** belongs to the corpse flower of Southeast Asia—it is 1 m (3 ¼ ft) wide and smells of rotting meat.

△ Fruit
Only angiosperms produce fruits. These fruits develop from the outer layers of the ovary after seeds have formed inside. The seeds are often spread by animals, who eat the fruit but cannot digest the seeds.

△ Wood
Tall trees are supported by dead xylem tubes that have been strengthened with a waterproof compound called lignin. The xylem grows out from the center. What remains of the original stem forms the bark.

△ Flower
The flower is the reproductive organ of a flowering plant. Most produce both pollen (male sex cells) and ova, or eggs (female sex cells). The flower is structured to disperse and collect pollen.

△ Leaf
Most angiosperms are broad-leaved. However, plants that live in extreme conditions—such as cacti—have spiked leaves to save water loss. Pine needles have the same function.

Dropping leaves

Botanists call the way plants drop their leaves abscission. Deciduous plants drop their leaves all in one go, generally in fall, because there will not be enough sunlight in winter to photosynthesize, and the leaves will be damaged by frost. New leaves grow in spring. An evergreen plant also drops its leaves, but evergreen abscission occurs continually throughout the year, along with new growth.

Climate	Conditions	Which?	Why?
tropical	wet and hot	evergreen	growth possible all year around
monsoon	rainy season	deciduous	avoid water loss through leaves
temperate	cold winter	deciduous	avoid frost damage to leaves
polar	short summer	evergreen	no time to grow new leaves for summer

▽ Evergreen or deciduous?
Evergreen plants live in places that are warm or cold all year, while deciduous species are adapted to habitats with changing seasons.

▽ Abscission
Leaf loss is triggered by changing conditions, such as shortening day lengths. The area at the base of the petiole has thin cell walls. These are broken when spongy bark expands underneath, breaking the water supply to the leaf, so the leaf falls away.

Many conifer seeds need to be frozen **over winter** before they will sprout.

Invertebrates

AN INVERTEBRATE IS AN ANIMAL WITHOUT A BACKBONE.

SEE ALSO
‹ 20–21 Variety of life
‹ 32 What is feeding?
‹ 39 Anchor points
‹ 42 Asexual reproduction
‹ 47 Metamorphosis
‹ 52–53 Animal relationships

The invertebrates are made up of dozens of phyla, many as distantly related to each other as they are to vertebrate animals. They range from microscopic to some of the largest creatures on Earth.

Arthropods

By far the largest group of invertebrates, the Arthropoda phylum includes insects (which make up 90 percent of the group), arachnids, and crustaceans. They all have a stiff exoskeleton made from chitin, a protein-based substance. All arthropods have legs made from several jointed sections; the phylum's name means "jointed foot." Insects are the only invertebrates that are able to fly.

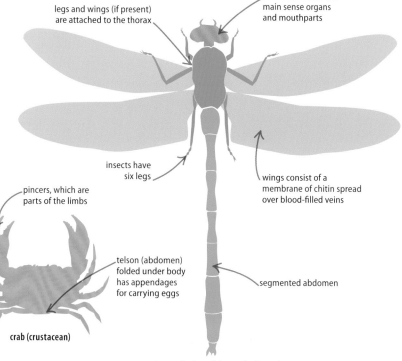

- cephalothorax, front body section
- abdomen
- arachnids have eight legs

spider (arachnid)

- pincers, which are parts of the limbs
- telson (abdomen) folded under body has appendages for carrying eggs

crab (crustacean)

- legs and wings (if present) are attached to the thorax
- the head houses the main sense organs and mouthparts
- insects have six legs
- wings consist of a membrane of chitin spread over blood-filled veins
- segmented abdomen

underneath view of dragonfly (insect)

Radiata

Most animals are bilaterally symmetrical, which means they can be divided into two halves that mirror each other. Radiata is a subkingdom (a group of phyla) made up of simple animals with round bodies. Radiata have both radial (symmetry around a fixed point, called the center) and bilateral symmetry. They do not have a mouth as such, but one body opening through which both food and waste pass. The main phylum is the Cnidaria, which includes corals, jellyfish, and anemones. Cnidarians have two types of body form, the polyp and the medusa.

▽ **Polyp**
The polyp is the upright form used by corals or sea anemones. They sit on the seabed with feeding tentacles facing upward, sifting food from the water.

- this opening is both the mouth and the anus
- feeding tentacle
- body stalk

▽ **Medusa**
Adult jellyfish are medusae, the bell-shaped form of cnidarians. Medusae are free swimming, and have stinging tentacles that hang down.

- a central stomach pouch distributes nutrients via canals that run through the body
- this opening is both the mouth and the anus
- stinging tentacle

INVERTEBRATES

Mollusks

The second-largest phylum of invertebrates is the mollusks. Mollusks range from filter-feeding bivalves and grazing gastropods to highly intelligent cephalopods. All mollusks share a common body plan. The main muscle is the "foot," which is used for locomotion in snails. In cephalopods, the foot is divided into tentacles, while bivalves use it to move and dig.

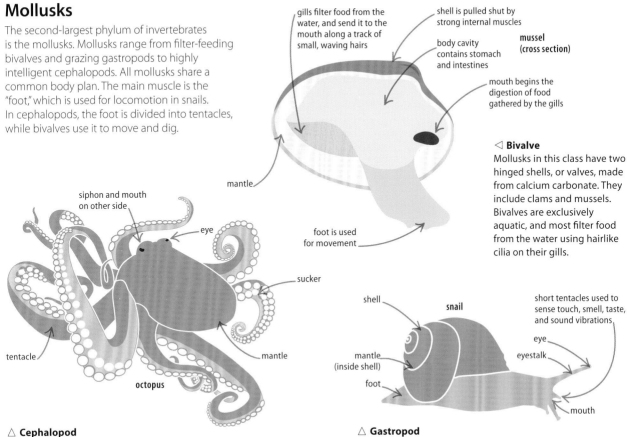

◁ **Bivalve**
Mollusks in this class have two hinged shells, or valves, made from calcium carbonate. They include clams and mussels. Bivalves are exclusively aquatic, and most filter food from the water using hairlike cilia on their gills.

△ **Cephalopod**
This class includes octopuses, squid, and the nautilus. All but the latter have evolved out of their shells. They catch food with suckered—and in many cases clawed—tentacles that surround a beaklike mouth. They squirt a jet of water from a funnel near their mouth, called the siphon, to move.

△ **Gastropod**
This class of mollusks includes snails, slugs, winkles, and limpets. They have one shell—although this can be either reduced in size or absent completely in slugs. Snails and slugs are the only mollusks to live on land, although they require damp habitats. Snails breathe using a lunglike cavity in the mantle.

Worms

Worms are simple animals. They all lack legs, but can live in a wide range of habitats from the deep sea to inside the bodies of other animals. About half of the nematodes, also known as roundworms, are intestinal parasites, while the rest live in soil. The platyhelminthes, or flatworms, are parasitic or aquatic. They do not have intestines, and absorb food through their skin.

▷ **Annelid**
Also known as segmented worms, the Annelid phylum includes ragworms living in the ocean, oligochaetes such as earthworms on land, and leeches, which can live in freshwater or on land. Small, hairlike structures called setae help earthworms to burrow and sense their environment, while a series of pseudohearts pumps blood around their bodies.

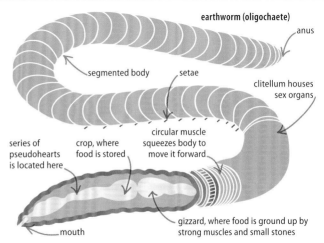

Fish, amphibians, and reptiles

THESE GROUPS ARE THE MOST PRIMITIVE VERTEBRATES (ANIMALS WITH BACKBONES).

SEE ALSO	
‹ 20–21 Variety of life	
‹ 34 Waste removal	
‹ 38 Snake locomotion	
‹ 40 Animal senses	
‹ 44 Hermaphrodites	
Mammals and birds	60–61 ›
Niches and factors	74 ›
Heat transfer	188–189 ›

Fish, amphibians, and reptiles are three classes of vertebrates, the group to which birds and mammals—including humans—belong.

What is a vertebrate?

Vertebrates make up most of the phylum Chordata. "Chordata" refers to a flexible supporting rod, called the notochord, that is present at some point in the life of all chordates. In most cases, it develops into a vertebral column—a chain of interlinked bones that form the spine, or backbone. This protects a spinal cord, a thick nerve bundle that connects the brain to the rest of the body.

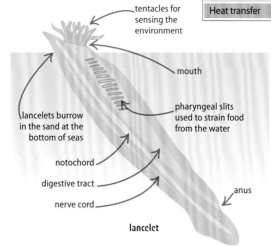

◁ **No skull**
The first vertebrates are thought to have looked like today's lancelets, simple aquatic animals that live on the seabed. Lancelets have no skull, unlike true vertebrates, but they share other features, including a notochord and pharyngeal slits (which form gills in fish).

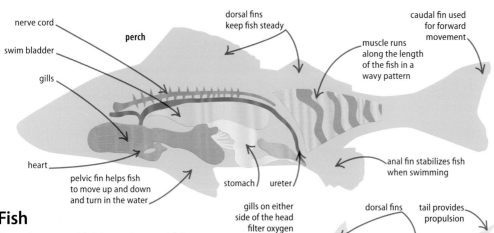

Fish

Several groups of fish have risen and fallen since the first fish evolved 500 million years ago (mya). There are two main groups of fish living in the world's marine and freshwater habitats today. The first have skeletons of bone and number about 20,000 species. The other group of 800 species includes the sharks and rays, which have skeletons made from cartilage—the same flexible tissue found in the outer part of the human ear.

◁ **Bony fish**
Bony fish, unlike cartilaginous fish, can control their buoyancy by altering the levels of gas in an internal float called the swim bladder.

◁ **Cartilaginous fish**
A shark's cartilaginous skeleton (in dark blue) and streamlined body shape help it move quickly through water. Flexible rods of cartilage stiffen the flat fins and tail lobes. The dorsal fins keep the shark from rolling over as swishes of its long tail power it through the water.

FISH, AMPHIBIANS, AND REPTILES

Reptiles

Reptiles were the first vertebrates to make the break from living in water completely. They became the ancestors of birds and mammals as a result. They are a varied group with several distinct branches, but all share two common features. They all have waterproofed keratin scales covering their skin, and their eggs all have waterproof shells to keep in their moisture, so they won't shrivel up out of water.

The **Johnstone river turtle** breathes underwater by absorbing oxygen through its anus.

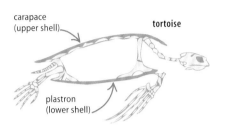
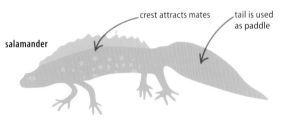

△ **Turtles and tortoises**
Turtles and tortoises evolved separately from dinosaurs and other reptiles. They have a defensive bony shell covered in giant horny scales (called scutes) attached to the ribs.

△ **Squamates**
Most of today's reptiles belong to this order, which includes lizards and snakes. Many snakes and a few lizards have venom glands, which are modified salivary glands, used for attacking prey.

△ **Crocodilians**
The crocodilians are archosaurs, a group of large reptiles that also included the dinosaurs. They are predatory hunters, waiting for prey to come close before snapping with powerful jaws.

Amphibians

Amphibians were the first creatures to live part of their life on land, evolving about 400 mya. They must return to water or moist habitats to lay eggs. After hatching, most amphibians spend their early growth phase in water, breathing with gills. They then transform—in a process called metamorphosis—into an air-breathing adult form that feeds on land.

△ **Newts and salamanders**
These amphibians were the first vertebrates to evolve a neck. Their neck lets them move their head from side to side, which is different from frogs and toads, who must move their whole body to look left or right.

REAL WORLD
Ectothermy

Fish, amphibians, and reptiles are ectothermic (cold-blooded), meaning their bodies are the same temperature as their surroundings. Ectotherms become more active in warm weather. Reptiles and amphibians influence their temperature by basking in the sun to heat up, or diving into water to cool down.

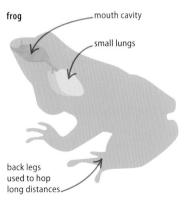

◁ **Frogs and toads**
Frogs are hunters that ambush prey using a sticky tongue and huge mouth. They have small lungs, and absorb much of their oxygen through their skin. Toads tend to have warty skin and legs designed for walking, while frogs have smoother skin and legs suited to hopping.

Mammals and birds

THESE GROUPS ARE WARM-BLOODED VERTEBRATES.

The vertebrate classes Aves (birds) and Mammalia (mammals) are among the most widespread groups of animal. They live on all continents and in almost all aquatic habitats.

SEE ALSO	
❮ 20–21 Variety of life	
❮ 32–33 Feeding	
❮ 38–39 Movement	
❮ 40 Animal senses	
❮ 42–43 Reproduction I	
❮ 58–59 Fish, amphibians, and reptiles	
Adaptations	82–83 ❯
Heat transfer	188–189 ❯

Endothermy

Birds and mammals are endothermic (warm-blooded) animals, meaning they maintain a constant body temperature. This requires energy to warm or cool the body, but it ensures that the animal's metabolism runs at a constant rate. As a result, its body systems function fully—even in colder habitats where ectothermic (cold-blooded) animals cannot survive. Endotherms have anatomical features to help them manage their body heat.

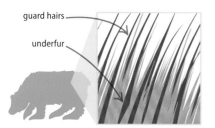

△ **Fur layers**
The hairs of many mammals are in two layers. The short underfur traps an insulating blanket of air. The longer, oily guard hairs keep out water, which would reduce the effectiveness of the underfur.

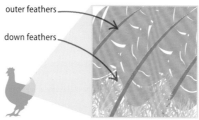

△ **Down insulation**
Birds prevent heat loss using fluffy down feathers that grow close to the body, under their outer feathers. Down traps air in pockets, insulating the body, and preventing valuable body heat from escaping.

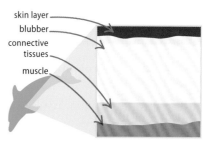

△ **Blubber**
In water, wet fur is a hindrance, so marine mammals have a thick insulating layer of blubber. This is a layer of soft fat, which has blood vessels running through it to help keep the animal warm.

Mammals

The largest vertebrates around today are mammals. The group gets its name from their mammary glands—modified sweat glands that produce milk. They are used by female mammals to suckle their young after birth. All mammals have at least a few hairs on their skin—although they are lost soon after birth in whales and dolphins. The hairs are made from keratin, the same waxy protein that builds reptile scales and bird feathers.

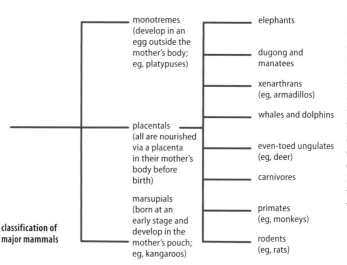

classification of major mammals

◁ **Mammal variety**
Mammals appeared around 200 million years ago (mya) as small insect-eaters similar to today's shrews. The great variety of species we see today evolved from these primitive ancestors after the dinosaurs became extinct 65 mya. By 30 mya, mammals were the dominant vertebrate group.

MAMMALS AND BIRDS

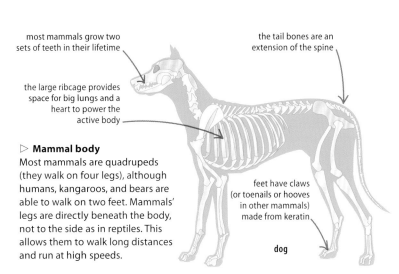

dog

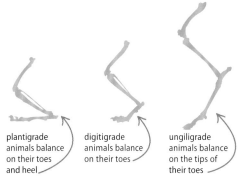

- most mammals grow two sets of teeth in their lifetime
- the large ribcage provides space for big lungs and a heart to power the active body
- the tail bones are an extension of the spine
- feet have claws (or toenails or hooves in other mammals) made from keratin
- plantigrade animals balance on their toes and heel
- digitigrade animals balance on their toes
- ungiligrade animals balance on the tips of their toes

▷ **Mammal body**
Most mammals are quadrupeds (they walk on four legs), although humans, kangaroos, and bears are able to walk on two feet. Mammals' legs are directly beneath the body, not to the side as in reptiles. This allows them to walk long distances and run at high speeds.

△ **Stances**
Mammals stand in three ways. Animals that walk long distances, such as humans and bears, are plantigrade. Digitigrade feet are used by agile animals that run and jump, such as dogs. Ungiligrade animals, such as horses, are suited to high-speed running.

Birds

The first birds evolved from forest-living dinosaurs about 150 mya. With about 10,000 species known, birds are the dominant flying vertebrates. Their wings are formed from long feathers attached to the bones of the forelimb. Feathers are stiff but lightweight, making them ideal for forming a rigid flight surface.

▽ **Bird skeleton**
Birds evolved from bipedal (upright-walking) dinosaurs. The wing is formed from the forelimb with thickened finger bones extending from the end to increase the length.

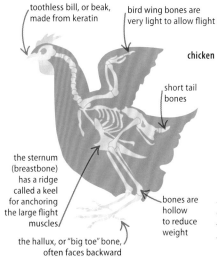

chicken

- toothless bill, or beak, made from keratin
- bird wing bones are very light to allow flight
- short tail bones
- the sternum (breastbone) has a ridge called a keel for anchoring the large flight muscles
- the hallux, or "big toe" bone, often faces backward
- bones are hollow to reduce weight

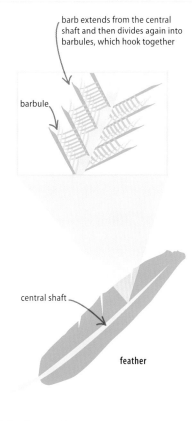

- barb extends from the central shaft and then divides again into barbules, which hook together
- barbule
- central shaft

feather

△ **Feather anatomy**
A feather is made of a branching network of hooked keratin filaments. Birds must frequently preen, applying oils that keep the filaments clean and hooked together into a flat surface.

- long, narrow wings create large lift force, enabling the bird to hang in the air — **gliding** (eg, albatross)
- long and wide wings catch updrafts — **soaring** (eg, eagle)
- rounded wings push bird upward — **rapid takeoff** (eg, pheasant)
- pointed wings allow rapid turns in flight — **high speed** (eg, swift)
- triangular-shaped wings allow rapid wingbeats — **hovering** (eg, hummingbird)

△ **Wing shape**
The shape of a bird's wing is a good indicator of how it flies. Scavenging birds need long, curved wings to glide, while ground birds need short wings to take off and get away from predators quickly.

Body systems

THE HUMAN BODY SYSTEMS THAT PERFORM SPECIFIC JOBS.

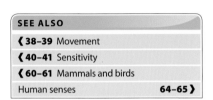

SEE ALSO
⟨ **38–39** Movement
⟨ **40–41** Sensitivity
⟨ **60–61** Mammals and birds
Human senses **64–65** ⟩

The human body takes between 18 and 23 years to develop to full size. Medical science divides the body into several body systems—each featuring a set of organs that work together to perform certain jobs.

Skeletal and muscular systems

Bones give strength and support to the body, and are the main tissue in the skeleton. An adult human skeleton is made up of about 200 bones. These are covered by about 640 skeletal muscles, each one connected by a stiff, cordlike tendon to a specific joint. As the muscle contracts (tightens), it pulls on that joint, creating movement in a variety of ways. Bones are joined to each other by bands of cartilage, called ligaments.

▽ **Muscular system**
There are two main sets of muscles in the human body. The skeletal muscles work in pairs to move the body, while smooth muscles produce rippling pulses in the digestive system and arteries, to push material along tubes.

▷ **Synovial joints**
Most joints are synovial joints—the bone ends have a covering of smooth cartilage and the space between them contains lubricating synovial fluid. Different kinds of joints allow different types of movement.

Pivot
The head rotates from side to side using a pivot joint in the neck.

Ball-and-socket
The shoulder can move in all directions thanks to a circular bone connected to a round socket.

Hinge
Like the hinge on a door, the elbow can move only in one plane—it cannot twist like other joints.

Saddle
Made of two curved bones, a saddle joint allows the thumb to move in two planes.

Ellipsoidal
The wrist has an oval bone sitting in a socket, allowing it to move in two planes—up-and-down, and side-to-side.

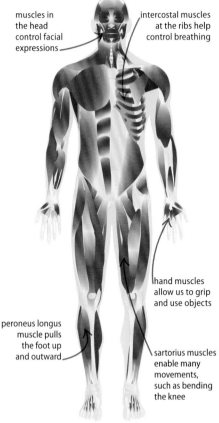

muscles in the head control facial expressions

intercostal muscles at the ribs help control breathing

hand muscles allow us to grip and use objects

peroneus longus muscle pulls the foot up and outward

sartorius muscles enable many movements, such as bending the knee

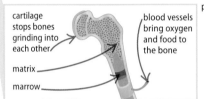

cartilage stops bones grinding into each other
matrix
marrow
blood vessels bring oxygen and food to the bone

△ **Bone structure**
Bones are made of living cells that secrete a matrix of flexible calcium phosphate. In the core, or marrow, of a bone red blood cells are manufactured.

Gliding
Gliding joints occur in many places in the skeleton, and are usually very small. They feature bones that are almost flat that can glide over each other.

BODY SYSTEMS

Other systems

The human body can be divided into a total of ten internal body systems (the skin and other outer body coverings can be counted as an external system). The organs and tissues in each system work closely together to perform the vital tasks that keep the body alive. If any one system fails, the other body systems cannot replace its function and are unable to work properly themselves.

△ **Respiratory system**
Centered on the lungs, this system takes oxygen, needed by the body, from the air and puts it into the blood.

△ **Endocrine system**
The glands that make up this system produce hormones and other secretions that control other body systems.

△ **Digestive system**
This system processes food to extract its nutrients, which are taken into the bloodstream.

△ **Urinary system**
The kidneys filter waste materials from the blood, which are then flushed away in urine.

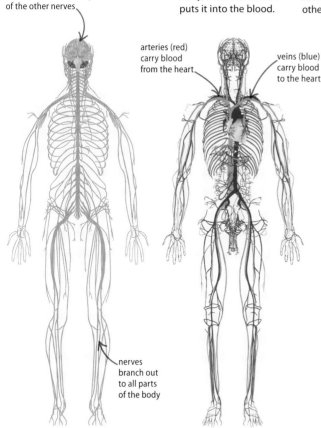

the brain and spinal cord control the activity of the other nerves

arteries (red) carry blood from the heart

veins (blue) carry blood to the heart

nerves branch out to all parts of the body

> When compressed, human bone is **four times** stronger than concrete.

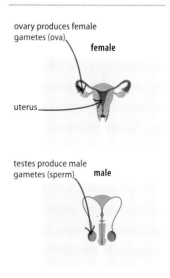

ovary produces female gametes (ova)

female

uterus

testes produce male gametes (sperm)

male

△ **Nervous system**
A network of nerves carries signals around the body as electric pulses. The brain and spinal cord form the central nervous system.

△ **Circulatory system**
This system takes blood pumped by the heart around the body. The blood delivers oxygen and other materials to body tissues.

△ **Lymphatic system**
Body cells leak slightly, so this system collects waste liquids that build up in tissues, and empties them into the circulatory system.

△ **Reproductive system**
The reproductive systems of males and females produce gametes, or sex cells. When these fuse, they form the first cell of a new person, which develops in the uterus.

Human senses

THE WAY WE GATHER INFORMATION ABOUT OUR SURROUNDINGS.

Our senses of hearing, vision, smell, taste, and touch constantly relay information to our brain about the world around us. The brain can then respond if necessary—such as moving us away from danger.

SEE ALSO	
‹ 40–41 Sensitivity	
‹ 62–63 Body systems	
Brain	68 ›
Optics	198–199 ›
Sound	200–201 ›

Hearing

The ear is a hypersensitive touch organ that picks up pressure waves moving through air, which make the eardrum vibrate. This vibration travels along three tiny bones, called the auditory ossicles, to the fluid-filled labyrinth, made up of the cochlea and semicircular canals. The sound waves become ripples in this labyrinth fluid, wafting hairlike sensory nerve endings that send signals on to the brain along the auditory nerve.

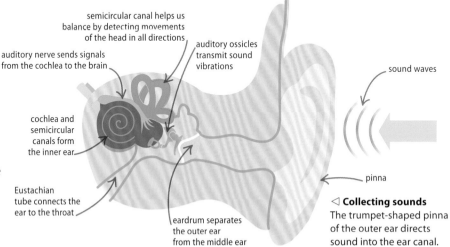

◁ **Collecting sounds**
The trumpet-shaped pinna of the outer ear directs sound into the ear canal.

Vision

The eye is like a camera. It lets in light through the pupil, a hole at the front that can adjust its size by contracting and relaxing the iris. The cornea and lens work together to focus the light onto the retina, a lining of light-sensitive cells at the back of the eye. The cells pick up the pattern of light falling across them, which is transmitted to the brain by the optic nerve and made into an image.

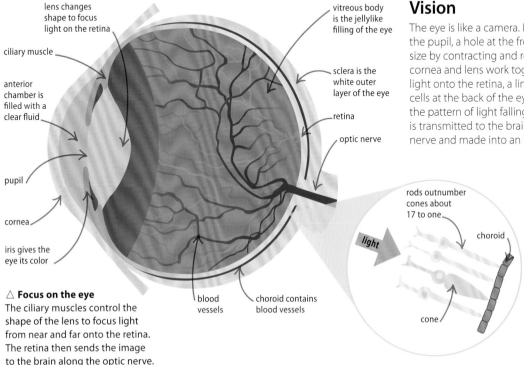

△ **Focus on the eye**
The ciliary muscles control the shape of the lens to focus light from near and far onto the retina. The retina then sends the image to the brain along the optic nerve.

◁ **Rods and cones**
The cells in the retina have light-sensitive pigments that produce electric nerve pulses when light hits them. Rod cells are used in night vision and cannot detect color. There are three types of cone cells, each sensitive to light within a different range of colors, and are used to produce color images by day.

HUMAN SENSES 65

Smell and taste

Our senses of smell and taste both involve collecting chemicals and analysing them. The nose collects chemicals carried in the air. Inside the nose, scent chemicals dissolve in the mucus lining of the nasal cavity (which also helps clean the air). The chemicals are detected by hairlike nerve endings that send signals to the brain. The tongue detects similar chemicals in food.

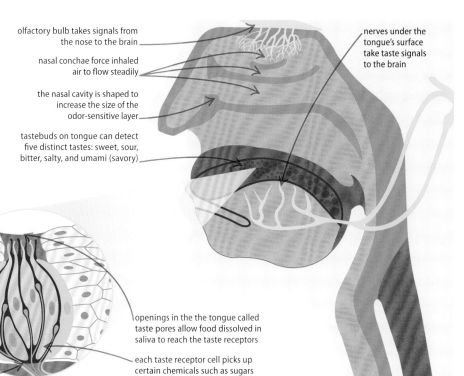

olfactory bulb takes signals from the nose to the brain

nasal conchae force inhaled air to flow steadily

the nasal cavity is shaped to increase the size of the odor-sensitive layer

tastebuds on tongue can detect five distinct tastes: sweet, sour, bitter, salty, and umami (savory)

nerves under the tongue's surface take taste signals to the brain

▷ Taste bud
Taste buds are located on the tongue, gums, and throat. They have nerve endings covered in proteins that can detect specific chemicals associated with certain foods, such as sweet sugar or sour acids.

the nerve endings send signals from the taste receptor cells to the brain

openings in the the tongue called taste pores allow food dissolved in saliva to reach the taste receptors

each taste receptor cell picks up certain chemicals such as sugars (sweet) and acids (sour)

▷ Skin
Mechanoreceptors pick up pressure, touch, stretching, vibration, and sharp pains. Heat and cold are picked up by thermoreceptors.

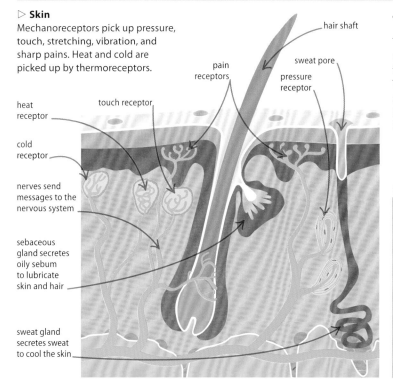

heat receptor
cold receptor
nerves send messages to the nervous system
sebaceous gland secretes oily sebum to lubricate skin and hair
sweat gland secretes sweat to cool the skin

touch receptor
pain receptors
hair shaft
sweat pore
pressure receptor

Touch

The sense of touch relies on several types of receptors, mainly located in the skin, but also found in muscles, joints, and internal organs. There are about 50 touch receptors for every square inch of skin, although more sensitive body parts, such as the fingertips and tongue, have more, while the back has fewer.

REAL WORLD
Braille

Fingertips (touch), and not eyes (vision), are used to read Braille. Letters are represented by patterns of between one and five small bumps, or dots, arranged in a grid. Skilled Braille readers can read about 200 words per minute.

Human digestion

THE DIGESTIVE SYSTEM PROCESSES THE FOOD WE EAT.

SEE ALSO	
‹ 62–63 Body systems	
Human health	70–71 ›
Catalysts	138–139 ›

Digestion is a complex process that breaks down food into simple substances. These fats, sugars, proteins, and other nutrients are then absorbed, leaving unwanted waste to be expelled.

The digestive tract

Food is digested in the digestive tract—the passage food takes from the mouth to the anus. Nutrients are absorbed in the intestines (also known as the gut). The material that cannot be digested is mixed with other waste products from the body, such as the brown pigments from old blood cells, and pushed out of the body through the anus.

▷ **Peristalsis**
In the mouth, saliva is mixed with the food and it is chewed to form a bolus (ball). Muscles along the walls of the esophagus (throat) contract in waves to push the bolus down to the stomach.

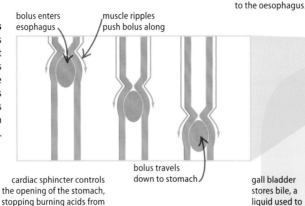

- bolus enters esophagus
- muscle ripples push bolus along
- cardiac sphincter controls the opening of the stomach, stopping burning acids from leaking into the esophagus
- bolus travels down to stomach

▷ **Stomach**
The stomach is an elastic, muscular sac that can stretch to hold up to 4 liters (8 pints). The stomach churns up the food and mixes it with powerful acids and enzymes, turning it into a liquid. It is then sent to the small intestine, and from there to the large intestine.

food in the stomach passes through the pyloric sphincter to the small intestine after it has been thoroughly mixed with enzymes

stomach wall is lined with mucus to protect it from the powerful digestive chemicals

- senses from the nose and tastebuds on tongue give flavor to food
- the tongue pushes food from the mouth to the pharynx
- pharynx connects the nose and mouth to the oesophagus
- salivary glands prod saliva, which begins dige
- esophagus
- liver takes the products of digestion and processes them into substances useful for the body
- gall bladder stores bile, a liquid used to break down fats
- stomach
- duodenum
- pancreas makes enzymes
- small intestine absorbs most of the chemicals from food
- rectum stores waste until it can be ejected from the anus
- large intestine absorbs water from food
- anus

HUMAN DIGESTION

▽ **Absorbtion of nutrients**
Most nutrients are absorbed in the part of the small intestine called the jejunum, which is lined with hairlike villi that increase the surface area of the gut wall.

▽ **Villi**
The intestines provide a surface area about the size of a tennis court to absorb nutrients. This is thanks to the villi, tiny hairlike projections that are supplied with blood and covered in epithelial cells, which are themselves lined with even smaller microvilli.

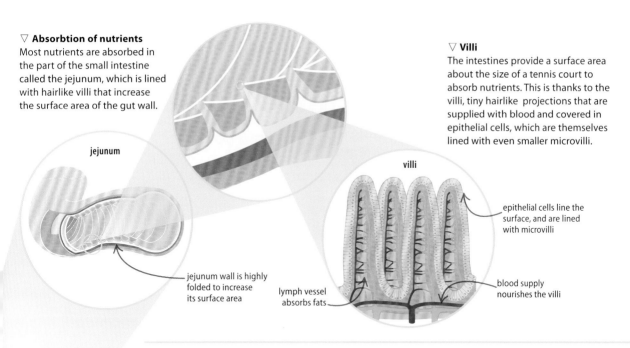

jejunum

villi

epithelial cells line the surface, and are lined with microvilli

jejunum wall is highly folded to increase its surface area

lymph vessel absorbs fats

blood supply nourishes the villi

Digestive chemicals

Digestion is both a physical and a chemical process. It starts in the mouth, when the teeth mechanically grind up the food. This pulp is mixed with saliva, which contains enzymes that work on the food. Enzymes target specific foods, dividing complex foods, such as starches and proteins, into smaller, simpler ingredients—sugar and amino acids respectively—that can absorbed more easily.

▽ **Chemical chart**
A range of digestive chemicals work on the food at each stage of its journey through the gut. The chemicals each have a specific role to play in breaking down the food, and are produced by glands and organs along the alimentary canal.

	Enzyme or other chemical	Function	Produced by
Mouth	lipase (enzyme)	digests fats	salivary gland
	amylase (enzyme)	digests starch	salivary gland
	mucin	lubricates food	salivary gland and gut lining
	bicarbonate (enzyme)	kills bacteria, neutralizes acids	salivary gland
Stomach	pepsin (enzyme)	digests proteins	stomach cells
	hydrochloric acid	kills bacteria	stomach cells
	rennin (enzyme)	digests milk	stomach cells
Small intestine	bile	aids digestion of fats	liver, via gall bladder
	trypsin (enzyme)	digest proteins	pancreas
	nuclease (enzyme)	digest nucleic acids	pancreas
	phospholipase (enzyme)	digests fats	pancreas
	amylase (enzyme)	digests starches	pancreas
	sucrase (enzyme)	digests sucrose	duodenum
	lactase (enzyme)	digests lactose (sugar found in milk)	duodenum
	maltase (enzyme)	digests maltose (sugar found in starch)	duodenum

Brain and heart

THE BODY'S MOST VITAL ORGANS
ARE THE BRAIN AND THE HEART.

The brain and the heart are the most important parts of the body. While the heart is the engine that keeps the body supplied with nutrients, the brain is the control center.

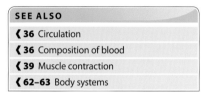

SEE ALSO
‹ 36 Circulation
‹ 36 Composition of blood
‹ 39 Muscle contraction
‹ 62–63 Body systems

Brain

The brain forms the main part of the central nervous system (CNS), which receives signals from every part of the body, and sends out responses if necessary. The brain is split into two halves, or hemispheres, made of masses of nerve cells that have thousands of high-speed connections with their neighbors. The outer layer of the brain is called the cerebral cortex, or gray matter, and the inner layer is called white matter.

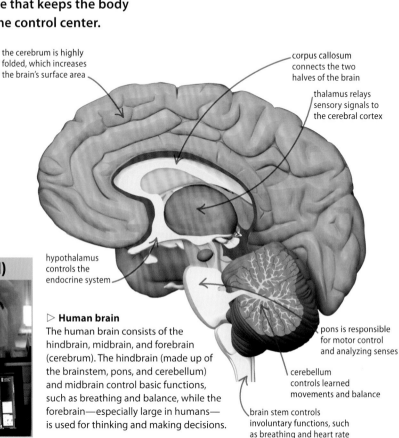

- the cerebrum is highly folded, which increases the brain's surface area
- corpus callosum connects the two halves of the brain
- thalamus relays sensory signals to the cerebral cortex
- hypothalamus controls the endocrine system
- pons is responsible for motor control and analyzing senses
- cerebellum controls learned movements and balance
- brain stem controls involuntary functions, such as breathing and heart rate

▷ **Human brain**
The human brain consists of the hindbrain, midbrain, and forebrain (cerebrum). The hindbrain (made up of the brainstem, pons, and cerebellum) and midbrain control basic functions, such as breathing and balance, while the forebrain—especially large in humans—is used for thinking and making decisions.

REAL WORLD
Magnetic resonance imaging (MRI)

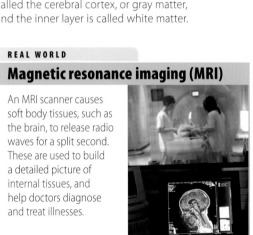

An MRI scanner causes soft body tissues, such as the brain, to release radio waves for a split second. These are used to build a detailed picture of internal tissues, and help doctors diagnose and treat illnesses.

Brain functions

Neuroscience, the study of the brain, has found that different areas of the cerebrum are devoted to specific functions. If one of the areas—often known as a cortex—is damaged, that function, such as speech or sight, ceases while the others continue unaffected. Neuroscientists have learned a lot about the human brain in recent years. For example, we now know that each cortex has more connections between its cells than there are stars in the Milky Way Galaxy.

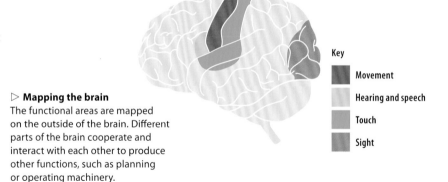

▷ **Mapping the brain**
The functional areas are mapped on the outside of the brain. Different parts of the brain cooperate and interact with each other to produce other functions, such as planning or operating machinery.

Key
- Movement
- Hearing and speech
- Touch
- Sight

Circulatory system

The human circulatory system is a double loop of vessels. The pulmonary loop carries deoxygenated blood to the lungs, where it picks up oxygen and releases carbon dioxide. The reoxygenated blood then goes back to the heart, where it enters the second loop, the systemic loop, which takes it around the body.

▷ **Vessel types**
The arteries (in red) take oxygenated blood to the tissues. The system of veins (in blue) then brings back the used, deoxygenated blood—which is then returned to the lungs. Capillary vessels run between the arteries and veins, carrying blood through the tissues.

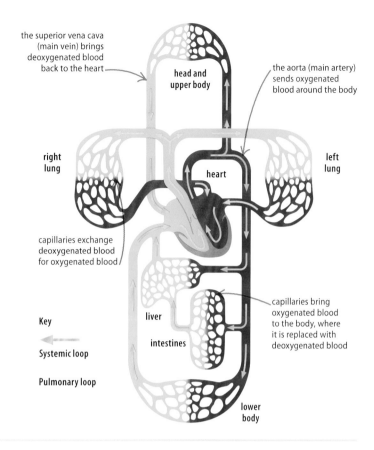

The **total length** of your circulatory system stretches an amazing 96,600 km (60,000 miles)—more than **twice** the distance around Earth.

In a heartbeat

The human heart is a powerful pump made from a type of muscle (cardiac) that never needs to rest—so a heart can keep working throughout a person's life. The heart has two sides, each one divided into an upper chamber called the atrium, and a lower chamber (the ventricles). The right side receives deoxygenated blood from the body. Reoxygenated blood is pumped out again from the left side.

The heart beats around **three billion times** in the average person's life.

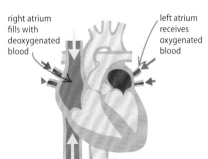

△ **Heart relaxed**
When the cardiac muscles are relaxed, deoxygenated blood flows into the right atrium from the vena cava, the main vein. Oxygenated blood flows into the left atrium.

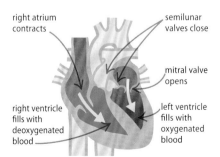

△ **Atria contract**
The contraction of the heart starts at the top, squeezing the atria, so the blood moves down into the ventricles. One-way valves prevent the blood from moving back into the atria.

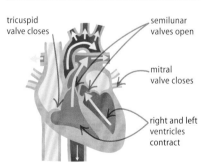

△ **Ventricles contract**
The lower part of the heart contracts, squeezing the ventricle. The right ventricle pumps the blood toward the lungs. The left ventricle pushes blood into the aorta (main artery).

Human health

DIET, EXERCISE, AND AVOIDING DANGEROUS SUBSTANCES HELP TO MAINTAIN A HEALTHY BODY.

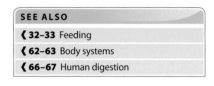

SEE ALSO
‹ 32–33 Feeding
‹ 62–63 Body systems
‹ 66–67 Human digestion

Medical science and improved living conditions have resulted in human life expectancies being twice, if not three times, those of prehistoric people. However, some aspects of a modern lifestyle are at odds with maintaining a healthy body.

Healthy eating

Food is made up of four groups of substances: carbohydrates, fats, proteins, and fiber. All four are essential for a nutritious diet. Carbohydrates are found in simple form in sugary food and in complex form in starchy food. Fiber is an indigestible form of carbohydrate that keeps the digestive tract healthy. Fats and oils are concentrated energy stores, and too much of them can lead to weight problems. Finally, protein, needed for muscles and digestion, is mainly found in animal-based foods, such as meat and dairy products, but is also found in beans, chickpeas, and lentils.

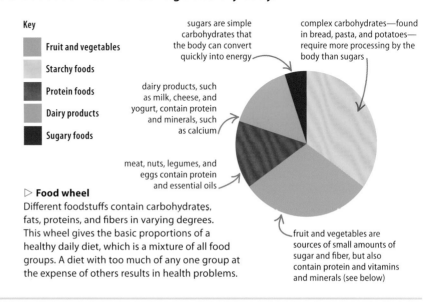

▷ **Food wheel**
Different foodstuffs contain carbohydrates, fats, proteins, and fibers in varying degrees. This wheel gives the basic proportions of a healthy daily diet, which is a mixture of all food groups. A diet with too much of any one group at the expense of others results in health problems.

Vitamins and minerals

A healthy diet contains a series of nutrients called vitamins. These are chemicals the body cannot make itself, which are essential for important metabolic processes. The health problems that vitamin deficiencies produce can usually be reversed by eating a balanced diet. The body also requires a supply of minerals, which are metals that are important for maintenance.

▷ **Required nutrients**
Humans require the following vitamins and minerals in small amounts in their diets.

Name	Beneficial for	Sources	Deficiency results in
vitamin A	good eyesight	liver, carrots, green vegetables	night blindness
vitamin B1	healthy nerves and muscles	eggs, red meat, and cereal	loss of appetite
vitamin B2	healthy skin and nails	milk, cheese, and fish	itchy eyes
vitamin B6	healthy skin and digestion	fish, bananas, and beans	inflamed skin
vitamin B12	healthy blood and nerves	shellfish, poultry, and milk	fatigue
vitamin C	healthy immune system	citrus fruits, kiwi, and fruits	scurvy
vitamin D	strong bones and teeth	sunlight and oily fish	rickets
vitamin E	removing toxins	nuts, green vegetables	weakness
folic acid	red blood cell formation	carrots, yeast	anemia
calcium	strong bones and healthy muscles	dairy products	bad teeth
iron	healthy blood and body cells	red meat and cereals	anemia
magnesium	healthy bones	nuts and green vegetables	insomnia
zinc	normal growth and immune system	meat and fish	growth retardation

HUMAN HEALTH

Body weight

The human body is primed to survive long periods of starvation. When food is available, the body lays down stores of fat to fuel the body during the lean times. In developed countries, food is always available, so people may become overweight, taking in more food than their body uses each day. This can lead to a variety of illnesses.

Key
- Obese
- Overweight
- Normal
- Underweight

▷ **Body mass index**
This chart is used to work out the healthiness of a person's weight-to-height ratio. Being overweight causes problems for the body, especially the circulatory system. People who are underweight may have a weaker immune system.

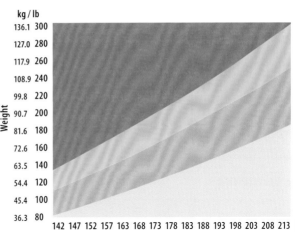

Exercise

The human body is built for walking long distances and having short bursts of activity. Modern working practices require people to sit still for long periods, so it is necessary these days to do regular exercise to keep the body in good condition. Exercise helps to burn the energy in food (measured in kilocalories, or calories for short), reducing weight gain due to overeating.

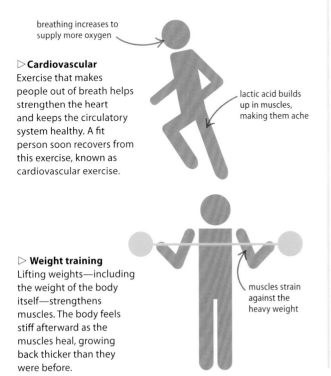

▷ **Cardiovascular**
Exercise that makes people out of breath helps strengthen the heart and keeps the circulatory system healthy. A fit person soon recovers from this exercise, known as cardiovascular exercise.

▷ **Weight training**
Lifting weights—including the weight of the body itself—strengthens muscles. The body feels stiff afterward as the muscles heal, growing back thicker than they were before.

Dangerous substances

Alcohol and tobacco products are sold legally to adults because they have a long history of use across the world, but they cause serious illness. Other substances—often just called drugs—are illegal, and cause many health and social problems.

▽ **Threats**
Misuse of alcohol, over-the-counter drugs, and smoking can lead to many health issues, both physical and mental. The main reason for this is addiction and dependency, which means the addict continues with the harmful behaviour and finds it hard to break away.

Activity	Associated health problems
tobacco smoking	cancer of lungs, mouth, esophagus, and pancreas; heart disease; lung problems, specifically emphysema, bronchitis, and scarring of lung tissue; addiction
alcohol use	physical damage to liver (cirrhosis); mental instability; poor judgment; dangerous behavior; increased risk of heart attack; inflammation of digestive tract and pancreas; addiction
drug use	mental and physical problems, depending on drug; severe addiction and dependency; risk of various cancers; addict may resort to crime to pay for drugs

BIOLOGY

Human reproduction

EVERY HUMAN BEING STARTS LIFE AS A TINY FERTILIZED EGG.

SEE ALSO	
‹ 43 Sexual reproduction	
‹ 62–63 Body systems	
Genetics I	84–85 ›
Genetics II	86–87 ›

Human reproduction begins with a sperm from a man combining with an egg inside a woman's uterus to produce an embryo. The baby develops for nine months inside the mother, sustained by a temporary organ called the placenta.

Sex organs

Gametes, or sex cells, are produced in sex organs or gonads. They carry a half set of chromosomes. The man produces sperm cells in organs called testes, while a woman produces egg cells (ova) in two ovaries. The ovaries release about 400 eggs in a woman's lifetime, at a rate of one every 28 days or so, while the testes produce many millions of sperm each day. Sperm cells are delivered to the cervix during sexual intercourse, and from there they swim into the oviduct (fallopian tube) to reach the single egg.

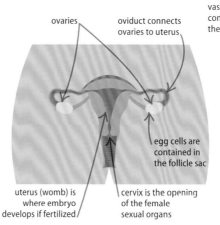

△ **Female sex organs**
The main function of the female sex organs is to provide a place where an embryo can grow. Once it has developed enough to survive independently, the baby is born.

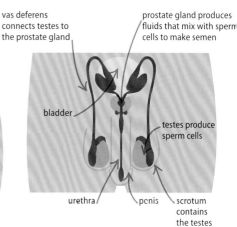

△ **Male sex organs**
The function of the male sex organs is to deliver sperm to the woman's uterus in a liquid called semen. The sperm cells make up about five percent of this mixture.

> The record for the **most children** with the same mother is 69, born in Russia in the 18th century.

Ovulation

The process of producing and releasing an egg cell, known as ovulation, is controlled by hormones. The amount of oestrogen rises, causing one follicle in one ovary to prepare an egg cell. The ripe egg bursts from the ovary and travels into the oviduct ready to meet a sperm. The rest of the follicle then releases another hormone, progesterone, which causes the lining of the uterus to thicken, ready to receive an embryo.

▽ **Hormones and ovulation**
The egg follicle produces oestrogen, which peaks on day 13 or 14. A few days later, the hormone progesterone causes the lining of the uterus to thicken, so it is ready to receive a fertilized egg cell. If fertilization does not happen, the progesterone level drops, and the thickened lining of the uterus is shed as menstrual blood. The process then repeats.

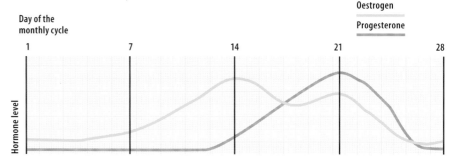

HUMAN REPRODUCTION

Fertilization

After ovulation, the egg travels toward the uterus along the oviduct. It lives for about 18 hours, during which time it is ready for a sperm to fertilize it. During fertilization, the half sets of DNA from both sex cells combine to make a full set. At this point the cell becomes a zygote, the first cell of a genetically unique individual. The zygote divides into a ball of cells, called a blastocyst.

▷ **Fusing cells**
A single sperm burrows into the much larger egg cell. It drops its tail-like flagella, and any sperm arriving afterward are blocked from getting in.

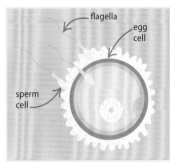

▷ **Implantation**
The blastocyst can survive only for a few days on its own. It must implant in the uterus wall within about ten days in order to receive oxygen and nutrients. Once it does this, it continues to divide into new cells, and is then called an embryo.

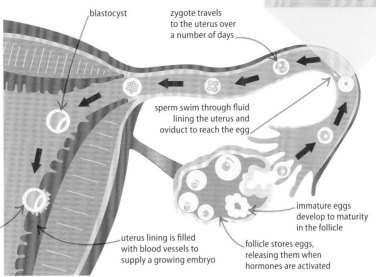

Gestation

From fertilization, the human embryo takes between 38 and 42 weeks to develop to the point where it can survive outside the uterus. The embryo is nourished by the placenta. Both develop from the same single blastocyst. Birth is triggered by a hormone released by the growing baby. This makes the cervix and vagina soften, and contractions of the uterus push the baby out.

▷ **Early development**
Every baby grows from a single cell called a zygote. This divides rapidly into a growing ball of cells. The cells differentiate into those that form the placenta, the membranes around the embryo, and the embryo itself. The cells that form the baby are identifiable after eight days of growth.

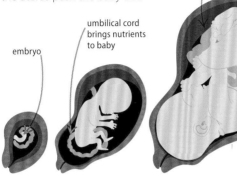

two months   five months   nine months

REAL WORLD
Fetal development

After about eight weeks of growth, the baby has all of its primary organs and recognizable human features. From this point it is known as a fetus. The development of a fetus can be monitored by scanning the womb with ultrasound to produce an image (below).

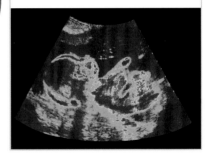

Ecosystems

THE SCIENCE OF ECOLOGY STUDIES HOW ORGANISMS FORM COMMUNITIES CALLED ECOSYSTEMS.

SEE ALSO	
‹ 52–53 Animal relationships	
Food chains	76–77 ›
Cycles in nature	78–79 ›
Adaptations	82–83 ›
Human impact	90–91 ›

An ecosystem is a complex set of relationships between the plants, animals, and other life forms that live in a habitat. These living things are also affected by other factors, such as weather and climate.

Niches and factors

Each species in an ecosystem occupies a niche—which means both the place and roles it carries out in the habitat. The mode of survival in any niche depends on the activity of other species in the ecosystem, such as predators looking for prey, or fast-growing algae using up the available resources. In a stable ecosystem, these influences, or factors, are in balance. If one factor changes, the rest of the ecosystem rebalances.

▽ **Wildlife community**
This freshwater ecosystem, like all ecosystems, is affected by physical factors, such as sunlight, climate, and fire, while its living members depend on each other for food.

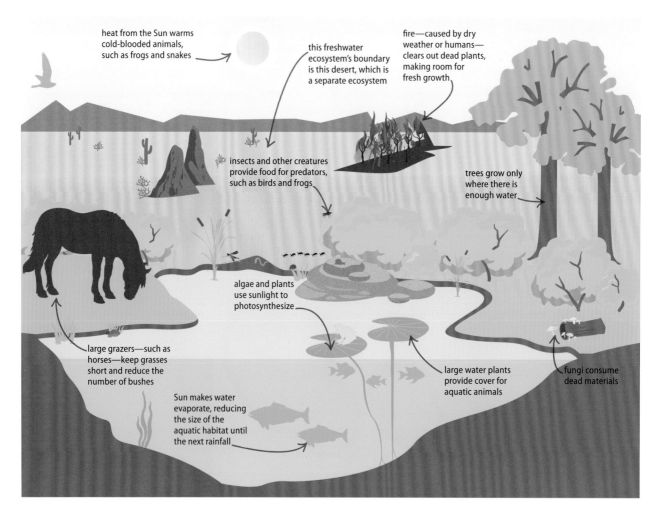

heat from the Sun warms cold-blooded animals, such as frogs and snakes

this freshwater ecosystem's boundary is this desert, which is a separate ecosystem

fire—caused by dry weather or humans—clears out dead plants, making room for fresh growth

insects and other creatures provide food for predators, such as birds and frogs

trees grow only where there is enough water

algae and plants use sunlight to photosynthesize

large grazers—such as horses—keep grasses short and reduce the number of bushes

large water plants provide cover for aquatic animals

fungi consume dead materials

Sun makes water evaporate, reducing the size of the aquatic habitat until the next rainfall

Predators and prey

Within an ecosystem, hunters and the hunted are closely linked. Their populations rise and fall in a repeating pattern. When there are a lot of prey animals, predators also increase in number, as there is more food to sustain them. However, more predators soon results in fewer prey, and the number of predators drops as there is less food available. Without many predators, the prey population rises again, and the cycle repeats.

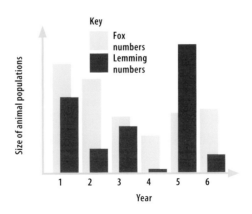

◁ **Foxes and lemmings**
This graph shows that, in years with high numbers of lemmings, Arctic foxes do well and have large numbers of pups. The next year, the lemming population falls as a result of this and the population of foxes decreases, too.

Biomes

The land habitats on Earth are grouped into ten climate zones, also known as biomes. Each biome is home to a particular set of animals and plants, which are adapted to the challenges of surviving in the different conditions. Desert animals must conserve water, while polar ones contend with long periods of extreme cold. Aquatic habitats are divided into marine and freshwater biomes.

Temperate forest
Trees grow in summer, before dropping their leaves and becoming dormant in winter.

Taiga
Conifer forests dominate the far north, where the cold and short summers are the main factors.

Polar
The temperature around the poles is below freezing for most of the year.

Temperate grassland
When there is too little rainfall for trees to grow, huge expanses of grass cover the land.

Savannah
In these warm, grass-covered regions, there is low rainfall and few trees.

Tropical forest
High rainfall and warm conditions all year result in thick jungles around the tropics.

Mountains
At high altitude, the air is thin (lacking oxygen) and temperatures are low.

Tundra
All but the upper layer of soil is permanently frozen, making it hard for plants to grow.

Chaparral
Also known as the Mediterranean biome, this region is filled with dry woodlands.

Desert
The driest parts of Earth have hardly any rainfall and very little vegetation.

Food chains

ENERGY PASSES ALONG FOOD CHAINS FROM PLANTS TO TOP CARNIVORES.

SEE ALSO	
‹ 32–33 Feeding	
‹ 74–75 Ecosystems	
Cycles in nature	78–79 ›
Adaptations	82–83 ›
Energy	170–171 ›

Living things require a supply of energy and nutrients to power, maintain, and grow their bodies. Scientists track how energy and nutrients move from one organism to another using food chains.

Producers and consumers

Food chains always begin with plants and other photosynthetic organisms, which are known as the producers. Animals and other heterotrophs (organisms that eat others to survive) are known as the consumers. The nutrients and energy gathered by the producers passes up the food chain via a series of consumers.

△ **Producer**
Green plants harness the energy of sunlight to power themselves, and are called producers.

△ **Primary consumer**
Herbivores, such as cows, eat only producers, and form the second step in the food chain.

△ **Secondary consumer**
Omnivores, such as raccoons, eat both producers and small primary consumers.

△ **Top predator**
The food chain ends with a powerful predator, such as an eagle or shark.

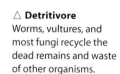

△ **Detritivore**
Worms, vultures, and most fungi recycle the dead remains and waste of other organisms.

Energy pyramid

Most of the energy consumed by organisms is given off as heat, becoming unavailable to the rest of the food chain, so less energy is passed onto the next level. As a result, the total quantity of organisms—the biomass—also decreases. This gives the food chain a pyramid structure—with many producers at the base, and fewer and fewer consumers at each stage above.

▷ **Trophic levels**
Scientists call each level of a food chain a trophic level—from the Greek word for food. As a rough estimate, only about 10 percent of the energy in one trophic level passes to the one above.

Top predator
Only a few large predators can survive in the top trophic level.

Secondary consumers
Many secondary consumers enjoy a very wide, omnivorous diet.

Primary consumers
Herbivores have easy access to plant food, but can fully digest only a small fraction.

Producers
Plants outweigh the animals in a food chain many times over.

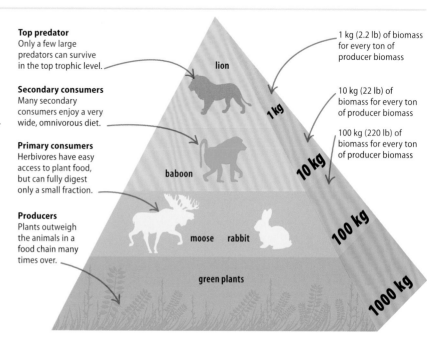

1 kg (2.2 lb) of biomass for every ton of producer biomass

10 kg (22 lb) of biomass for every ton of producer biomass

100 kg (220 lb) of biomass for every ton of producer biomass

FOOD CHAINS 77

Food webs

No food chain exists on its own. In real wildlife communities, the chains interlink to make a food web—a representation of an ecosystem. Food webs vary a great deal between habitats. They may contain a keystone species, through which a lot of the nutrients pass, or on which many other species in the web rely for food.

▽ **Arctic Ocean**
Despite being one of the coldest places on Earth, the Arctic has a rich food web. Minute algae called phytoplankton are the producers. Arctic cod is a keystone species, since many of the predators would die out without it.

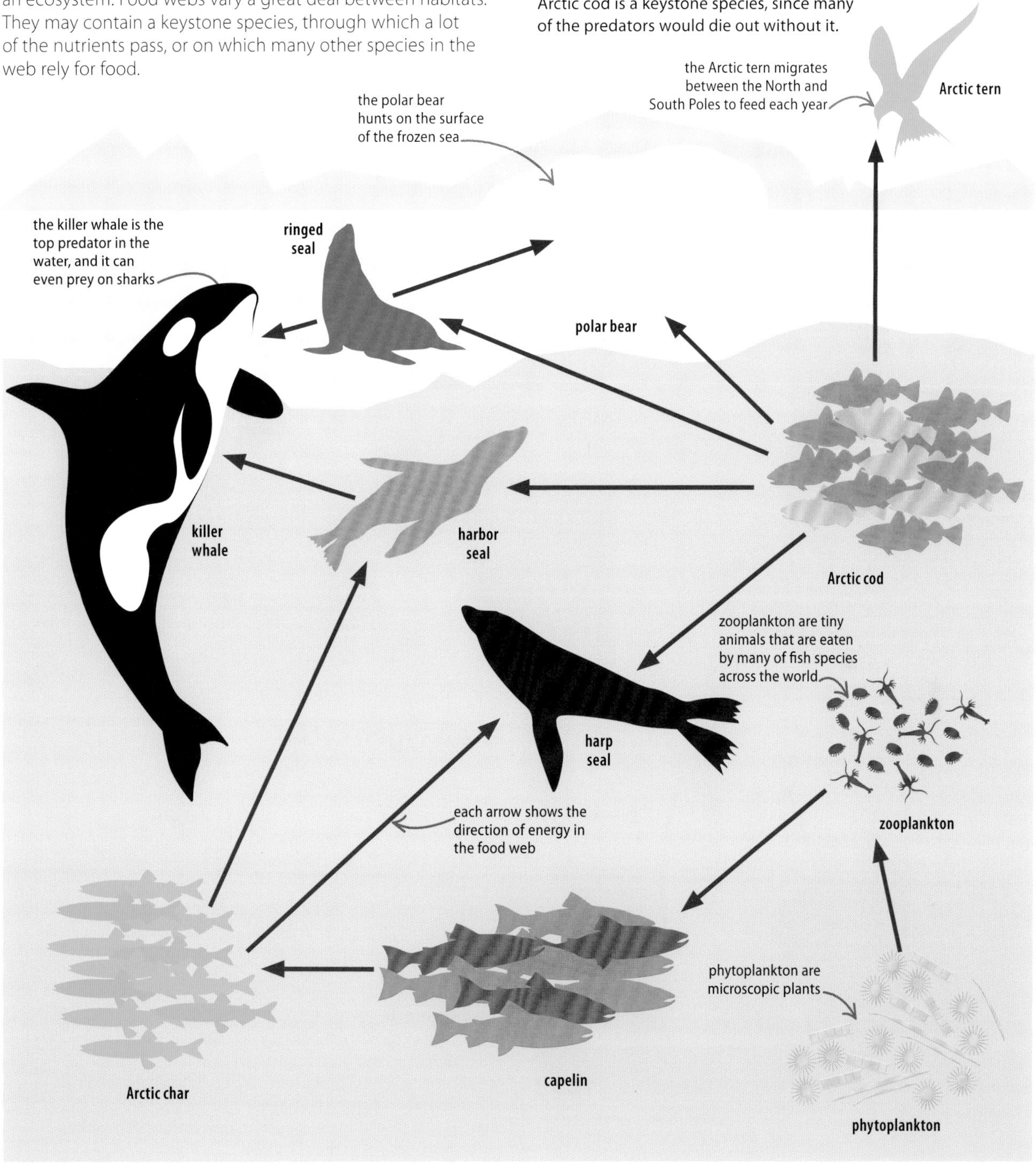

the Arctic tern migrates between the North and South Poles to feed each year

Arctic tern

the polar bear hunts on the surface of the frozen sea

the killer whale is the top predator in the water, and it can even prey on sharks

ringed seal

polar bear

killer whale

harbor seal

Arctic cod

zooplankton are tiny animals that are eaten by many of fish species across the world

harp seal

zooplankton

each arrow shows the direction of energy in the food web

phytoplankton are microscopic plants

Arctic char

capelin

phytoplankton

Cycles in nature

NUTRIENTS AND OTHER SUBSTANCES ARE RECYCLED IN THE ENVIRONMENT.

SEE ALSO	
‹ 28–29 Respiration	
‹ 30–31 Photosynthesis	
‹ 34–35 Waste materials	
Chemical industry	154–155 ›
Carbon and fossil fuels	156–157 ›

Living things require many nutrients—substances used to build their bodies. There is a finite supply of these in the environment, so they are recycled through the environment by biological, chemical, and physical processes—and also by human activities.

The carbon cycle

Carbon is essential to life. It is one of the most abundant elements in a living body and its atoms are in just about every chemical in cells. During photosynthesis, plants fix (collect) carbon dioxide from the atmosphere and turn it into sugars and other nutrients. These then pass to animals and other organisms that eat the plants. Eventually, the carbon in them is returned to the atmosphere as a waste product of respiration.

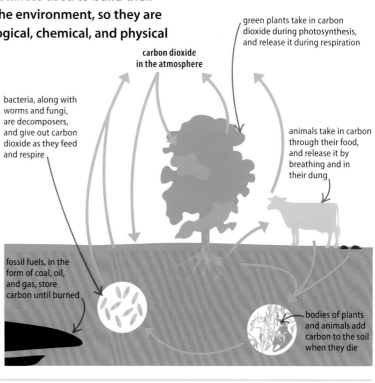

▷ Nonbiological factors
Carbon is not only cycled between the atmosphere and organisms. Carbonates, a combination of carbon and oxygen found in rocks and fossil fuels, are locked away underground for millions of years. Burning fossil fuels releases this carbon dioxide back into the atmosphere.

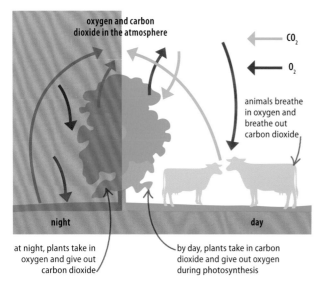

The oxygen cycle

Almost all organisms require a supply of oxygen, which is used in respiration to release energy from sugar. Organisms take in the oxygen and give out carbon dioxide (a waste product of respiration). However, oxygen does not run out, because it is constantly being replaced by the photosynthesis of plants. In this process carbon dioxide is taken in as a raw ingredient of glucose, and oxygen is given out as a waste material.

◁ Night and day
Plants take in carbon dioxide as a raw material for photosynthesis, and give out oxygen as a waste material of the process. Plants photosynthesize only during daylight, and this is when oxygen is released into the atmosphere. By night, plants take in some oxygen to power their respiration, but they use less than they produce.

CYCLES IN NATURE

The nitrogen cycle

Nitrogen is an essential component in amino acids, the basic units of protein, which all living creatures need. Therefore, all life needs a supply of nitrogen compounds. Animals cannot manufacture most amino acids themselves, so they obtain them from plant foods. Plants make amino acids from nitrates (a combination of nitrogen and oxygen) absorbed from the soil. The nitrates are added to the soil by bacteria that fix nitrogen from the air.

REAL WORLD
Carnivorous plant

The Venus flytrap grows in soils that lack nitrates, so the plant collects it from prey instead. It traps insects in its pressure-sensitive, pincer-shaped leaves. The leaves shut to form a stomachlike space, where enzymes digest the insect to release its nutrients.

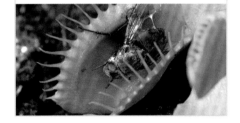

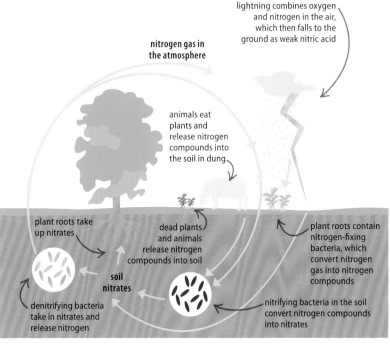

△ **Nitrates**
Nitrogen is not a very reactive element, mostly staying unchanged in the atmosphere. However, the enzymes in certain bacteria and the high energy of lightning can convert nitrogen into nitrates, a form that can be used by all life.

The water cycle

Earth's water is always on the move, collecting in vast quantities in the ocean, but rarely finding its way to deserts. Life cannot exist without water. It is one of the ingredients in the production of glucose in photosynthesis, and water is also the medium in which the metabolic process takes place inside cells. Most living bodies are mainly water—about 60 percent in the case of humans—and, where water is rare, so is life.

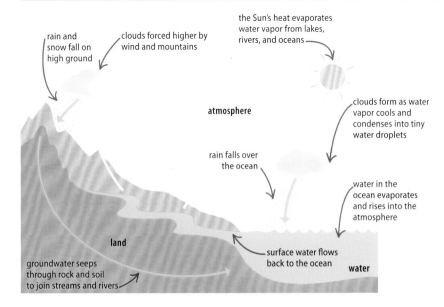

◁ **Movement of water**
Most of Earth's water is in the oceans, but it also moves constantly into the atmosphere, falling as rain to form freshwater running over and into the ground or freezing as ice on high mountains and in the polar regions.

Evolution

THE ORGANISMS MOST SUITED TO SURVIVE IN AN ENVIRONMENT ARE MOST LIKELY TO PASS ON THEIR GENES.

SEE ALSO	
‹ 20–21 Variety of life	
‹ 42–43 Reproduction I	
Adaptations	82–83 ›
Genetics I	84–85 ›

Set out by English naturalist Charles Darwin in 1859, the theory of evolution by natural selection was one of the most controversial scientific theories ever. It has become accepted since, and has been updated to include the role of genes.

The drive to breed

Everything an organism does is meant to increase the chance of it producing as many surviving offspring as possible. These offspring compete with each other and other species for limited resources, such as food, water, and a place to live. Those best able to survive are the ones that pass on their genes to the next generation. The individuals that cannot compete die without producing young, so their genes are not passed on.

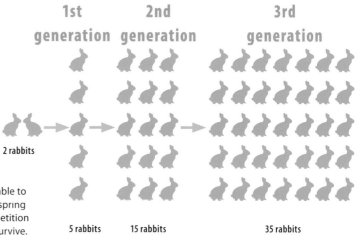

▷ **Increasing genes**
Rabbits have a very high reproduction rate, with one female able to produce 70 young in just one year. The following year, her offspring could potentially produce almost 5,000 more. In reality, competition between all these rabbits is so fierce that far fewer than this survive.

Natural selection

The most successful, or "fit," offspring are the ones with genes that allow them to out-compete their rivals. When they mate, their fit genes are passed on to the next generation. This is called natural selection. Eventually every animal in the species has the fit genes—meaning the species gradually evolves over time.

peppered moth gives rise to both dark and light colored offspring

△ **Adding variety**
Most variation between animals is the result of sexual reproduction. Every offspring inherits a slightly different mixture of genes from both parents. The variation in color of these moths ensures that at least some of the offspring will survive if the habitat begins to change.

pale peppered moth is harder for a predator to see

△ **Pale moths hidden**
Before the Industrial Revolution, most peppered moths were pale and could hide in the lichens growing on tree trunks, while the darker moths stood out.

pale peppered moths are easier to see for predators, so experience a decline in numbers

△ **Pale moths stand out**
Then soot from factories killed the lichens, making tree trunks darker. The pale moths then became more preyed upon, which made the dark moths more common.

EVOLUTION

A mass extinction known as the **Great Dying** wiped out 90 percent of all species on Earth about **252 million years ago**.

How new species evolve

A species is a group of organisms that look the same and survive in the same way, and can breed together to produce viable young in the wild. Some species of bat look very similar to one another and live in the same areas, but attract mates using different calls and cannot breed with each other. Speciation is the formation of a new species. Species can evolve sympatrically (from one ancestor) or allopatrically (when populations are isolated).

REAL WORLD
Extinction

Most of the knowledge of evolution comes from fossils of extinct species. An extinct species is one that has no members left alive. Fossils, such as this primitive bird, form when body parts are replaced with rocky minerals over a long period of time. Fossils show us what the ancestors of today's species looked like. If the lost species died out after it evolved into another species, experts call this pseudoextinction.

sympatric speciation

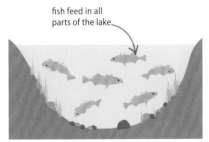

△ **1. One species of fish**
One species of fish lives in the lake. The fish feed mainly on small animals in the water and on the lakebed.

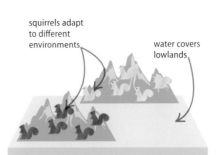

△ **2. Specialist feeders**
Gradually, the fish split into two groups as they specialize on catching certain animals. The groups evolve in different ways to exploit the different food sources.

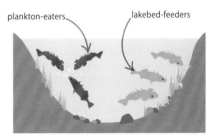

△ **3. Two species**
The groups rarely mix, and eventually they evolve into two distinct species that cannot breed with each other any more.

allopatric speciation

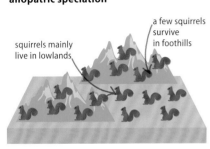

△ **1. One species of squirrel**
A species of squirrel has spread across a wide range. Although they do not meet, squirrels from either end of the range could breed with one another.

△ **2. Geographic isolation**
Rising sea levels turns the range into isolated islands. Squirrels on both islands adapt to life in their own mountain habitat, forming two new species.

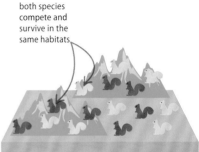

△ **3. Sharing habitat**
The sea level falls again, creating a new lowland habitat for the squirrels to exploit. Both species mix throughout the original range, but are no longer able to breed.

Adaptations

ORGANISMS CHANGE OVER TIME IN ORDER TO SURVIVE.

Adaptations are the visible results of evolution. Natural selection alters the anatomy and behavior of organisms so they become adapted to new ways of living.

SEE ALSO	
‹ 20–21 Variety of life	
‹ 44–45 Reproduction II	
‹ 80–81 Evolution	
Genetics I	84–85 ›

Adaptive radiation

When several different adaptations evolve from a single ancestor, it is known as adaptive radiation. The result is a group of species that share many features, but differ in ways that adapt them to a specific way of life. For example, rodents all have long, sharp incisors inherited from their common ancestor. However, in gophers these teeth are adapted to digging burrows, in beavers they fell trees, while squirrels use them to nibble through hard seed casings.

▷ **Darwin's finches**
Adaptive radiation can be seen in Darwin's finches—named after the discoverer of evolution. Most finches are seed-eaters, but the songbirds that live on the Galápagos Islands, Ecuador, have adapted to tackle other foods too.

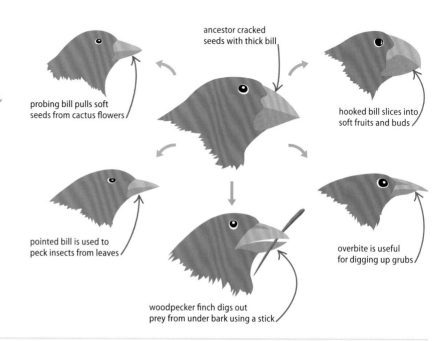

ancestor cracked seeds with thick bill

probing bill pulls soft seeds from cactus flowers

hooked bill slices into soft fruits and buds

pointed bill is used to peck insects from leaves

overbite is useful for digging up grubs

woodpecker finch digs out prey from under bark using a stick

Convergent evolution

A lot of evolution is divergent, with groups of related animals becoming less alike as they adapt to different environments. However, evolution can also be convergent, where unrelated species adapt to the same environment in the same way. For example, both birds and bats have evolved wings to enable them to fly. The shape, structure, and function of both kinds of wings are very similar, but birds and bats are only distantly related to each other, and their common ancestor did not have wings.

◁ **Marine hunters**
Sharks and toothed whales, such as dolphins and orcas, are all fast-swimming hunters. They look similar, but have very different body systems, because sharks are fish and whales are mammals.

dorsal fin keeps the animal from rolling as it powers through the water

whale breathes air at the surface through a blowhole

whale tail is made of two flukes

killer whale

dorsal fin stabilizes shark

shark breathes in water with gills

shark tail is made of two lobes

great white shark

ADAPTATIONS

Coevolution

Sometimes, two species evolve together, adapting to ways of life by relying on each other for survival. Each organism affects the other in small ways, so the two become better adapted to each other and surviving together. Many animals and flowering plants have undergone this coevolution.

Corals have coevolved with **microscopic algae**—the algae live inside them, and provide food in return.

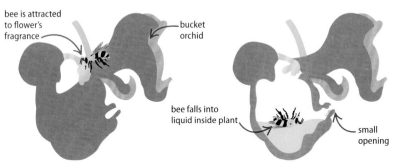

△ **Bucket orchid and bee**
This tropical flower attracts orchid bees with its fragrant oil. On landing, the bee slips on the oil and falls into a bucket, or pool, inside the petals.

△ **Escape route**
The bee cannot climb up the smooth walls of the bucket, but it can use a ladder of hairs that leads to a small opening on the side to escape.

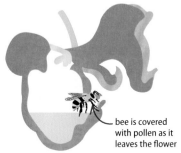

△ **Collecting pollen**
When the bee wriggles through the exit, the flower glues sticky pollen to its back. When the bee falls into the next flower it visits, this pollen will pollinate it.

Sexual selection

Not all adaptations increase an ability to survive in competition with others. Sexual selection can produce traits that can be a hindrance, such as unwieldy antlers or long, ornate tail feathers that make flying difficult. This type of selection happens because the female chooses a particular trait in the male. The female will select the mate with the best features, and, because of this, males with that trait pass on their genes, increasing the size of the trait in the next generation.

▽ **Bird tail tale**
To attract a mate, a male pheasant displays its tail feathers. The females prefer long, clean feathers because they show the male is a strong specimen. Sexual selection results in larger, more ornate tail feathers. The process stops only when the tail size hinders the male and so weakens it.

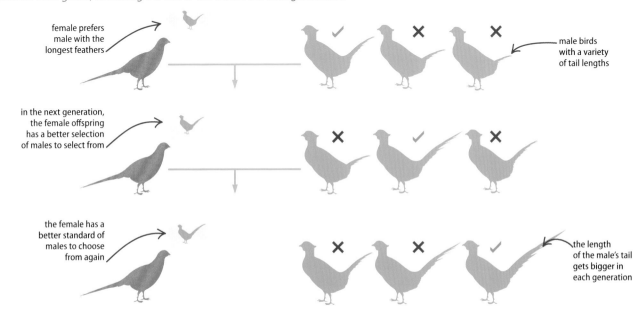

Genetics I

THE FIELD OF BIOLOGY THAT INVESTIGATES INHERITANCE OF CHARACTERISTICS FROM PARENTS IS CALLED GENETICS.

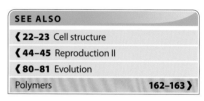

SEE ALSO
‹ 22–23 Cell structure
‹ 44–45 Reproduction II
‹ 80–81 Evolution
Polymers 162–163 ›

The instructions for making a living body are called genes. Each gene relates to a specific characteristic, such as eye color or height. A full set of genes is inherited from both parents, so a child shares many of his or her parents' characteristics.

Chromosomes

Genes are carried on long chemical chains of deoxyribonucleic acid (DNA). DNA is stored inside a cell's nucleus on chromosomes, which are the vehicles that carry the genes as they pass from one generation to the next. The number of chromosomes in a cell is called the diploid number. Sperm and eggs contain a half-set, or haploid number, of chromosomes.

Genes and alleles

Each gene has a specific position on its chromosome. Everyone has two versions of each chromosome, one from each parent. That means they have two versions, known as alleles, of each gene. The two alleles form a person's genotype. One allele is often dominant over the other, which is recessive, so just one characteristic (known as a person's phenotype) is expressed.

▽ **Genetic probability**
In this example, we see two parents and their possible offspring. Both parents give one allele to their children. The allele for brown eyes (B) is dominant, and the allele for blue eyes (b) is recessive. The mother has a recessive allele, so it is equally likely that they have a brown or a blue eyed child.

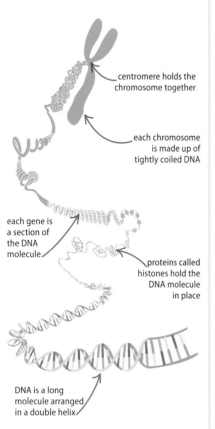

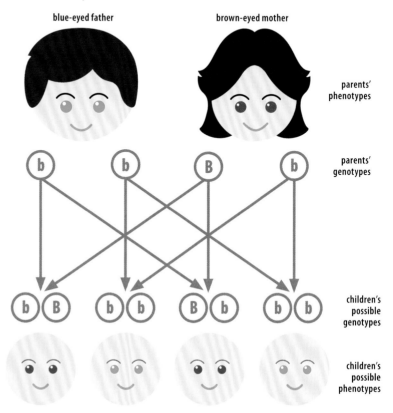

GENETICS I

Codominance

Not all alleles are dominant or recessive. Sometimes, both alleles are expressed at once in a system called codominance, or incomplete dominance. In the example below, the red parent flower has two red alleles (R), while the white parent flower has two white alleles (r). When the pair breed, all the offspring have the genotype Rr and codominance makes all the flowers pink. However, breeding two pink flowers produces red and white, as well as pink, blooms.

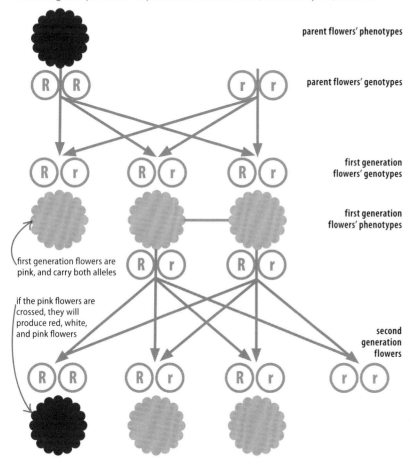

first generation flowers are pink, and carry both alleles

if the pink flowers are crossed, they will produce red, white, and pink flowers

Sex chromosomes

A person's sex is determined by inheriting particular chromosomes from the mother and father. Females have two X chromosomes, while males have an X and a Y chromosome—the Y is much smaller, and has fewer genes, than the X. A mother's gametes always contain an X, while a sperm can have an X or Y.

▽ **Determining gender**
Because the mother always gives an X chromosome, it is the father's gamete that determines the sex of the baby. If an X sperm fertilizes the egg, the baby will be female, and male if a Y sperm achieves it.

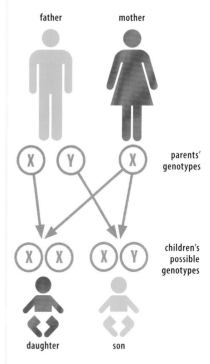

REAL WORLD
X-linked diseases

Males are more likely to be color blind, because they have a defective gene on their X chromosome and their shorter Y has no alternative allele for the problem. Females can carry the same defective gene, but have normal vision thanks to a healthy allele from their other X chromosome.

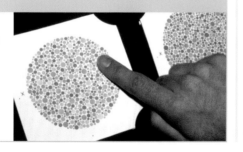

Humans have **46 chromosomes**, which is less than some rats, at **92**, but more than kangaroos, which have only **16**.

Genetics II

GENETIC CODES ARE USED TO MAKE
PROTEINS NECESSARY FOR THE BODY.

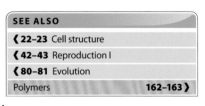

SEE ALSO	
‹ 22–23	Cell structure
‹ 42–43	Reproduction I
‹ 80–81	Evolution
Polymers	162–163 ›

Genetic information is held as a code stored on DNA molecules. This code is translated into the many proteins that do the work in a cell. When errors occur in this process, genetic illnesses are possible as a result.

Double helix

A DNA (deoxyribonucleic acid) molecule is a double helix, a ladder-shaped spiral. The "sides" are chiefly ribose sugars, while the "rungs" are made up of four chemical compounds called nucleotides, or bases. The bases are called thymine (T), adenine (A), cytosine (C), and guanine (G). The sequence of these bases is a code that adds up to the instructions for a particular gene.

▷ **Nucleotide bases**
Each rung has a pair of bases. Thymine always pairs with adenine, and cytosine with guanine. Most of the bases are not "read" by the cell, as they do not contain instructions for a gene.

Transcription

The first step in turning a gene into a protein involves making a copy of the gene's DNA stored in the nucleus. This involves transcribing the DNA's code onto ribonucleic acid (RNA). The DNA double helix is unzipped into two unwound strands, and an RNA strand forms next to one of them. The RNA has bases too, but instead of thymine it has a base called uracil (U). The RNA copies the DNA strand and then travels to a ribosome.

▷ **Matching up**
The bases in the RNA are ordered to match their partners in the DNA, so a cytosine in the DNA is matched by a guanine in the RNA, and uracil matches with adenine.

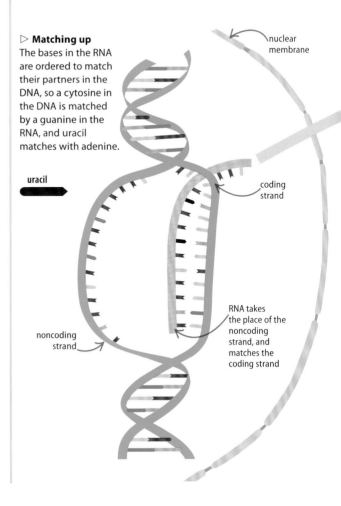

Translation

The genetic code is translated into a protein in the cell's ribosome. This tiny organelle pulls the RNA through itself three bases at a time. Every three bases form a triple-character sequence called a codon, which is specific to a certain amino acid. Proteins are composed of chains of these acids, and the codons on the RNA tell the ribosome in which order to arrange them.

▽ **Making proteins**
Anticodons carry specific amino acids to the ribosome to add to the chain. When the anticodon matches the codon on the RNA, the anticodon adds its amino acid to the chain, and the next codon is pulled into the ribosome.

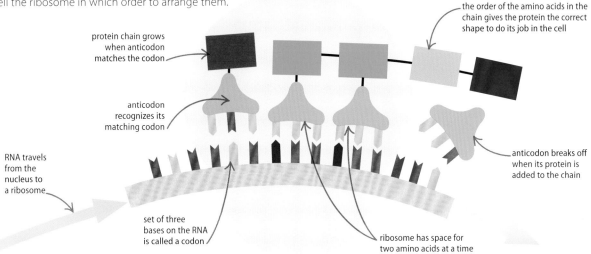

Mutations

When DNA is copied, mistakes can occur. These are called mutations. A mutation may be made in the unread part of DNA, and so have no effect. If it happens in the read section, the result can make the cell die. However, occasionally a mutation improves the way the cell and the body works. These useful mistakes are spread by natural selection and drive evolution.

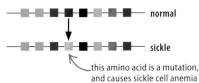

△ **Genetic disease**
Some mutations are not deadly, but cause diseases. For example, sickle cell anemia is caused by one different amino acid in the structure of hemoglobin, the chemical that carries oxygen in the blood. The mutant hemoglobin forms long chains, which makes a sufferer's blood cells sickle-shaped.

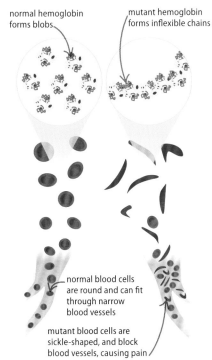

REAL WORLD

Human genome project

A genome is the complete collection of a species' genes. In 2003, scientists finished a complete record of the human genome. They identified about 25,000 genes and sequenced three billion base pairs. Below is a section of the genome, with a color for each base. However, geneticists have still to figure out what most of the genes do and record their many different versions, or alleles.

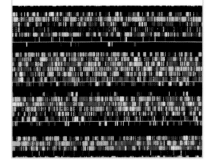

Pollution

CHEMICALS FROM HUMAN ACTIVITIES AFFECT
THE ECOSYSTEMS AND FUTURE OF THE EARTH.

SEE ALSO	
‹ 74–75 Ecosystems	
Human impact	90–91 ›
Acids and bases	144–145 ›
Electromagnetic waves	194–195 ›

Pollution is anything that is added to the environment in amounts large enough to have a harmful effect. Sound, light, and heat can be pollution, but the most damaging pollutants are chemicals in Earth's soil, water, and air.

Ozone hole

Ozone is a type of oxygen in the atmosphere that blocks dangerous ultraviolet light (UV) coming from the Sun. Large amounts of chlorofluorocarbon (CFC) gases, used in aerosols and refrigerators and thought to be inactive, were released in the 1980s. The CFCs reacted with ozone, and, over the years, have depleted the ozone layer in places, especially above the North and South Poles. CFCs are now banned and the ozone holes are shrinking.

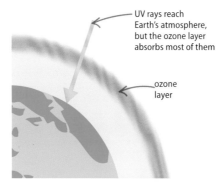

△ **Safe levels**
While some does hit the Earth's surface, the ozone layer, 25 km (15.5 miles) above Earth, deflects much of the harmful UV light back into space.

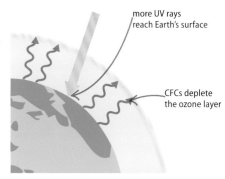

△ **High layer**
A chemical reaction between the CFCs and the ozone layer turns the latter into oxygen, which does not shield Earth from UV light, meaning more of it reaches the surface.

REAL WORLD
Global dimming

Burning fossil fuels releases carbon dioxide, which contributes to global warming. However, the soot released may also keep temperatures down in a process called global dimming. The tiny dark particles in the air reflect the Sun's light, reducing the amount that heats Earth's surface.

Greenhouse effect

The "greenhouse gases" of water vapor, carbon dioxide, and methane in the atmosphere stop heat being lost to space. Without this process, Earth's average surface temperature would be below freezing. However, human activities, such as burning fossil fuels and intensive farming, are increasing the amount of greenhouse gas. This greenhouse effect is gradually increasing Earth's surface temperature, resulting in more extreme weather, such as flooding and drought.

Venus, warm enough to melt lead, is the hottest planet, due to an **extreme** greenhouse effect.

▽ **Trapped heat**
Sunlight absorbed by the Earth's surface warms it up, and the surface sends out heat in the form of infrared radiation. Some infrared is absorbed in turn by the atmospheric greenhouse gases.

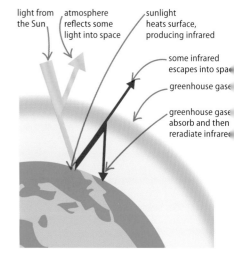

POLLUTION

Acid rain

All rainwater is slightly acidic. This is because carbon dioxide in the air dissolves in it, making weak carbonic acid (as found in carbonated drinks). However, sometimes oxides of sulfur and nitrogen are released into the atmosphere as industrial waste. When these dissolve in water, they form much more potent acids, which have a damaging effect on wildlife when they fall as rain.

▷ **Gases released**
Coal-burning power plants and engines fueled by oil or gasoline release gases that can form acid rain. The rain often falls far from its source. It has many effects, including killing animal and plant life and damaging buildings.

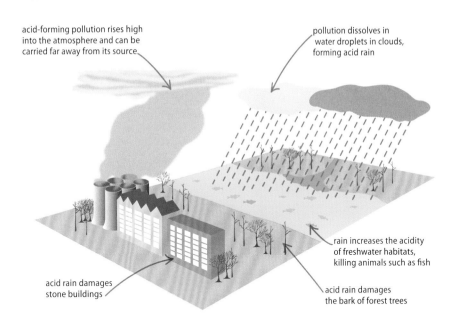

acid-forming pollution rises high into the atmosphere and can be carried far away from its source

pollution dissolves in water droplets in clouds, forming acid rain

rain increases the acidity of freshwater habitats, killing animals such as fish

acid rain damages stone buildings

acid rain damages the bark of forest trees

Eutrophication

Fertilizers provide crops with nutrients such as nitrates and phosphates. These compounds boost the growth of any plant, and cause thick blooms of algae if they are washed by heavy rains into lakes and rivers. This leads to a process of eutrophication, where these blooms choke out life in the water.

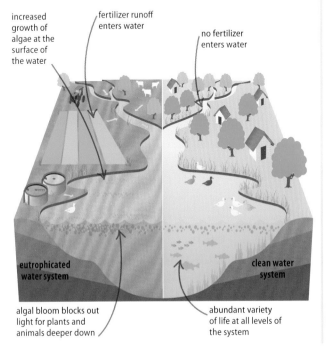

increased growth of algae at the surface of the water

fertilizer runoff enters water

no fertilizer enters water

eutrophicated water system

clean water system

algal bloom blocks out light for plants and animals deeper down

abundant variety of life at all levels of the system

Biomagnification

Even when present in tiny amounts, some pollutants can have an impact through a process called biomagnification. When an animal cannot break down a chemical, it is stored in its body, and is passed on to any predator that eats it. The concentration of this pollutant in animal tissues increases at each stage of the food chain, reaching damaging levels in top predators.

▷ **DDT disaster**
The biomagnification of an insecticide called DDT nearly wiped out many birds of prey in the USA in the 1940s and 1950s. DDT was thought harmless to vertebrates, but it built up in the bodies of fish and other animals in their environments. DDT poisoning resulted in birds, such as ospreys and bald eagles, laying eggs with very thin shells, so many eggs smashed in the nest.

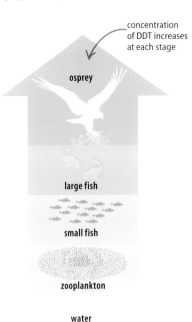

concentration of DDT increases at each stage

osprey

large fish

small fish

zooplankton

water

Human impact

ACTIVITIES BY HUMANS CAN CHANGE ECOSYSTEMS
AND THE PLANTS AND ANIMALS WITHIN THEM.

SEE ALSO
❰ 74–75 Ecosystems
❰ 82–83 Adaptations
❰ 84–85 Genetics I
❰ 88–89 Pollution

Scientists know there have been five mass extinctions in Earth's history, all with natural causes. Many of today's species are becoming extinct due to human activities. Some experts think we are living through a sixth mass extinction right now.

Habitat loss

Humans have the ability to alter a habitat to suit their needs, turning natural landscapes into artificial ones, such as farmland or urban developments. The wildlife from the original habitat has been evolving for millions of years, and its species are specialized to a life within that community. They cannot survive in other habitats, and sometimes face extinction as a result.

▽ **Climax habitat**
Climax habitats carry the maximum number of life forms possible. This patch of tropical forest has a unique community of species.

▽ **Slash and burn**
Humans need places to grow crops, so they cut down the forest and burn the logs. The ash makes a nutrient-rich soil for the first crops.

▽ **Fertile soil**
For a few years the ashy soil makes good farmland. However, the orginal jungle soil beneath does not hold nutrients for long, so eventually the crop yields fall.

▽ **Secondary forest**
The farmers abandon this plot, and move on, leaving a new forest habitat to develop. It will never recover to its original climax state.

  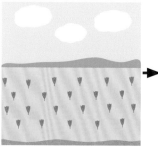 

Fragmentation

Many forest animals never leave their habitat. For example, the gibbons of Southeast Asia can walk only short distances on the ground—they move about by swinging from branch to branch. Even a narrow gap in the forest, such as a road, is enough to divide forest communities permanently. Fragmentation breaks forest animals into small groups, making it harder for them to survive.

▷ **Living with relatives**
The biggest problems caused by fragmentation are loss of diversity and inbreeding. In a small group, every member is closely related to each other. Relatives share the same genes and any offspring tend to be weak.

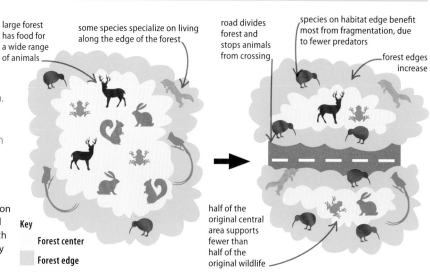

HUMAN IMPACT

Controlling pests

Pests are animals that impede human activities. They tend to be able to live in a wide variety of habitats, and can damage crops, spread disease, or infest homes. Pest control usually involves the use of chemicals, but this can cause pollution. By contrast, biological control makes use of natural predators and parasites to control pests.

▽ **Fly pests**
Flies that lay their eggs in animal waste and rotting food are a serious pest in stables, farms, and sewage treatment plants. Their maggot larvae eat the waste before pupating into adults that can spread diseases.

▽ **Parasitic wasp**
The spalangia wasp is native to Australia, but humans use it to kill flies naturally around the world. The wasp lays its eggs inside a fly pupa. The wasp larva hatches and eats the fly pupa from the inside out.

▽ **Becoming an adult**
The wasp then pupates itself inside the empty fly case. When fully grown, the adult wasp bites a hole in the case and flies away. After mating, the female wasps will lay more eggs on fly pupae, until all the flies are dead.

Introduced species

As humans move around the world, they take animals and plants with them. Introducing species to new habitats can upset the balance of an ecosystem. There have been several disastrous introductions, such as the introduction of the cane toad to Australia (below), or the 60 starlings that were released in New York City, in 1890. There are now 200 million starlings in North America, which have pushed many native birds close to extinction.

Key
■ Spread of cane toads today

△ **Beetle pest**
The grubs of a native beetle were damaging valuable plantations of sugar cane across tropical parts of eastern Australia. Farmers looked for a small predator to control the beetle numbers and protect the crops.

△ **Marine toad**
A large toad from South America was introduced in 1936 to tackle the beetles. It was known as the marine toad because it was tough enough to survive almost anywhere, even along the seashore.

△ **Spread across Australia**
The toads ate almost everything except the cane beetle, upsetting delicate ecosystems. They spread and became a major pest, renamed the cane toad. There are more than 200 million living in Australia today.

REAL WORLD
Genetic modification

Humans have been altering the genetic makeup of animals and plants for thousands of years by selectively breeding animals with desired characteristics. However, in recent years, genetic engineers have been adding completely new genes to animals in the laboratory. These fish glow in the dark because of a gene added from a bioluminescent (light-emitting) deep sea jellyfish.

Humans are the only species to live on all **seven continents**, including a permanent settlement in the Antarctic since 1956.

Chemistry

What is chemistry?

THE SCIENCE THAT DEALS WITH THE PROPERTIES OF SUBSTANCES AND LOOKS AT HOW THEY CAN CHANGE FROM ONE TYPE TO ANOTHER.

Chemistry is sometimes called the central science, because it forms the link between physics and biology. Chemistry builds on the knowledge of physics and then, in turn, is used to provide the basis for much of biology.

Understanding substances

Chemists seek to understand how the characteristics and structure of a substance, natural or artificial, can be described. What is it about water that makes it a flowing liquid, while the plastic bucket used to carry it is a rigid solid? A chemist finds the answer at the very smallest of scales. Every substance contains atoms, and the way they are arranged dictates how a substance behaves.

▽ **Describing materials**
Chemists have many ways of describing substances. They include the substance's state—solid, liquid, or gas—or whether it is metallic like the screw, or nonmetallic like the seashell.

water—liquid, nonmetallic

helium in balloon—gas, nonmetallic

seashell—solid, nonmetallic

screw—solid, metallic

Elements

Everything in the Universe is made out of raw materials called elements. There are about 91 naturally occurring elements. Most, such as gold or mercury, are pretty rare, while others, such as carbon, chlorine, and iron, are found in great quantities. Few elements are found pure in nature; they are usually combined with other elements to form entirely different materials called compounds. (Water is a compound of hydrogen and oxygen, for example.) Compounds can be separated into their elements, but an element cannot be broken down into anything simpler.

14
6   **12.011**
C
CARBON

carbon element

18
2   **4.0026**
He
HELIUM

helium element

◁ **Defining elements**
Chemists arrange the elements in the periodic table (see pages 116–117) according to the structure of their atoms. For example, the number of electrons (one of the parts of an atom) at a certain part of the atom means carbon is in group 14 whereas helium is in group 18.

WHAT IS CHEMISTRY?

Atoms

Atoms are the building blocks of all material on Earth and out in space (as far as we know). They are not all the same. In fact, every element is made up of its own type of atom. All atoms have positively charged protons in the central nucleus. These are surrounded by negatively charged electrons. The number of electrons and protons varies from element to element and this is what gives each element its properties.

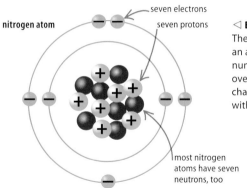

nitrogen atom — seven electrons, seven protons

most nitrogen atoms have seven neutrons, too

◁ **Balanced charge**
The number of protons in an atom always equals the number of electrons, so overall the atom has no charge. Neutrons are particles with no, or a neutral, charge.

Reactions

Chemists investigate how elements and compounds behave in reactions. During a chemical reaction, substances known as reactants are transformed into new substances called products. The reaction rearranges the atoms, breaking up the reactants and combining them in new ways to make the products. Most products are different compounds, but some may be pure elements.

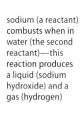

sodium (a reactant) combusts when in water (the second reactant)—this reaction produces a liquid (sodium hydroxide) and a gas (hydrogen)

◁ **Chemical energy**
Reactions take in and release energy, and can be very violent events. Explosions and combustion (burning) are among the most energetic reactions.

Analysis

One role of a chemist is to use knowledge of the physical and chemical properties of different elements and compounds to figure out the content of an unknown substance. This process is called analysis. It involves using a number of tests, such as burning substance (the flame's color gives clues to its contents) or reacting it with a known compound, to see the products created.

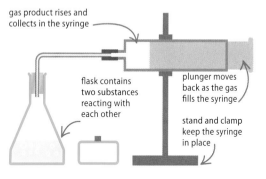

gas product rises and collects in the syringe

flask contains two substances reacting with each other

plunger moves back as the gas fills the syringe

stand and clamp keep the syringe in place

◁ **Laboratory apparatus**
Chemical reactions are carried out in laboratories. These science workshops contain a range of apparatus for containing and heating reactants, and collecting and measuring products.

Chemical industry

Chemistry is also used to manufacture useful substances. Manufacturing chemicals on an industrial scale is very different to making them in a laboratory. Scientists use their knowledge of what controls the speed of a reaction to come up with the best possible manufacturing process—making the most product for the least expenditure on heat and raw materials.

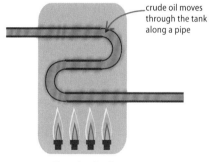

crude oil moves through the tank along a pipe

Heated crude oil

◁ **Petrochemicals**
The many hundreds of chemicals in crude oil are used as raw materials for making fuels, plastics, waxes, and medicines. The oil is heated to separate it into different materials (see page 157).

Properties of materials

SUBSTANCES CAN BE UNDERSTOOD BY OBSERVING THEIR PROPERTIES.

SEE ALSO	
Periodic table	116–117 ⟩
Corrosion	133 ⟩
What is mass?	172 ⟩
Stretching and deforming	174–175 ⟩

Every substance has its own unique set of properties—color, density, smell, and flammability. Chemists try to understand why the substances in nature have such varied properties.

Mass and density

All objects have a mass: a measure of how much matter they contain. Mass is not an indicator of size. A piece of lead has more mass than an identically sized piece of polystyrene, for example. The difference in mass is due to a property known as density: a measure of how tightly packed matter is inside a substance. Density is calculated as mass divided by volume, and expressed with the units kg/m^3—or often g/cm^3. Lead is one of the most dense elements of all, which is why it is used in weights—a small, manageable lead object contains a lot of matter and so weighs a large amount.

REAL WORLD
Physical versus chemical

The spokes of this bike are bent. The bending is due to the physical properties of the metal. Physical properties do not change the substance (in this case, metal). Some parts of the bike have rusted. The rusting is due to the chemical properties of the metal. Chemical properties relate to how the substance changes into other materials (rust) when it reacts with other substances (air and water).

Buoyancy

The density of a substance can be tested by putting it in water. If an object has a density higher than water, it will sink; if it is less dense than water, it will float.

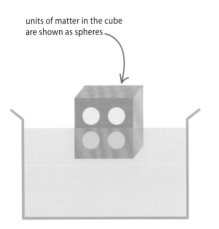

△ **Low-density object**
This cube is less dense than water. The matter in the cube is spread out more than the matter in water, so it weighs less than an equal volume of water.

units of matter in the cube are shown as spheres

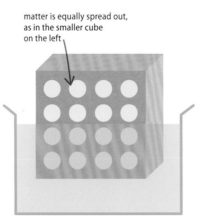

△ **Larger object**
This cube is made of the same material as the first, only it has four times the volume—and weighs four times as much. So it has the same density as the first and floats.

matter is equally spread out, as in the smaller cube on the left

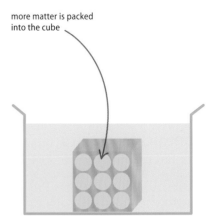

△ **High-density object**
This cube is the same size as the first cube, but has a higher density. In this case, the cube weighs more than the same volume of water, so it sinks.

more matter is packed into the cube

PROPERTIES OF MATERIALS

Comparing properties

Substances can be described and identified in terms of their properties. Chemists compare the properties of materials to find similarities and differences between them. Then they can start to investigate why these similarities and differences exist.

Substance	Floats in water?	Color	Transparency	Luster	Solubility	Conductivity	Texture
copper	no	red	opaque	shiny	in acid	conductor	smooth
natural chalk	no	white	opaque	dull	in acid	insulator	powdery
pencil lead (graphite)	no	black	opaque	shiny	no	conductor	slippery
pine wood	yes	brown	opaque	dull	only in special solvents	insulator	fibrous
salt crystals	no	white	translucent	shiny	in water	insulator when solid	gritty
glass	no	various	varies	shiny	only in special solvents	insulator	smooth
talc	no	various	opaque	waxy	in acid	insulator	greasy
diamond	no	various	transparent	sparkling when cut	no	insulator	smooth

Hardness

The hardness of a substance is normally measured on the Mohs scale, named after its inventor Friedrich Mohs. The scale is based on ten "guide" minerals, which all occur naturally in rocks. The hardness of a substance is measured in comparison with these guides. A material is harder than another when it can leave a scratch on it. For example, a piece of ordinary glass can scratch apatite but not orthoclase, and so its hardness is somewhere between 5 and 6.

▷ **Mohs scale**
The Mohs scale is only a comparative measure of hardness. In reality, a diamond is not ten times harder than talc. However, the Mohs scale is the preferred measure because it gives meaningful results using a quick and simple method.

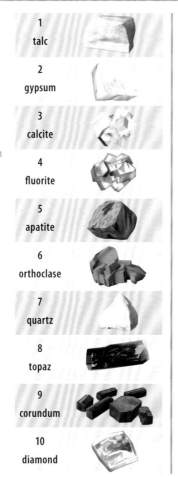

1 talc
2 gypsum
3 calcite
4 fluorite
5 apatite
6 orthoclase
7 quartz
8 topaz
9 corundum
10 diamond

Chemical properties

A substance can be described in terms of its chemical properties. It could be an element (a pure substance that cannot be reduced into simpler constituents), a compound (a combination of two or more elements), or be described as a metal, nonmetal, or semimetal. Chemists also look at a substance's chemical behavior, cataloguing its reactions and analyzing the products. A full set of properties—chemical and physical—can belong only to one substance.

▷ **Reactivity series**
Every element has a certain reactivity, which is part of its chemical behavior. Common metals are often ordered by how reactive they are. This is called the reactivity series. Metals at the top are most reactive. Potassium is so reactive that it is rarely found on its own. If two metals are competing to bond with another element, the one higher up the scale would win.

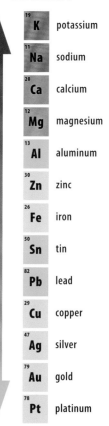

most reactive

- K potassium
- Na sodium
- Ca calcium
- Mg magnesium
- Al aluminum
- Zn zinc
- Fe iron
- Sn tin
- Pb lead
- Cu copper
- Ag silver
- Au gold
- Pt platinum

least reactive

States of matter

THERE ARE THREE MAIN STATES OF MATTER: SOLID, LIQUID, AND GAS.

SEE ALSO	
Changing states	100–101 ❯
Gas Laws	102–103 ❯
Intermolecular forces	115 ❯
Water	142–143 ❯
Stretching and deforming	174–175 ❯
Heat transfer	188–189 ❯

What sets each state apart is how the atoms and molecules (groups of atoms) are bonded together. This bonding is determined by factors such as temperature and pressure.

Physical difference

A solid that is melting into a liquid or boiling into a gas is changing physically. However, all three states share the same chemical formula.

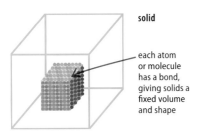

solid — each atom or molecule has a bond, giving solids a fixed volume and shape

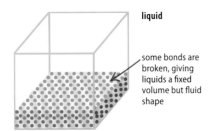

liquid — some bonds are broken, giving liquids a fixed volume but fluid shape

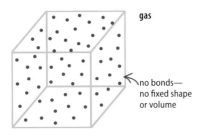

gas — no bonds—no fixed shape or volume

△ **Solid, liquid, gas**
As a substance gets warmer, its molecules break bonds. The substance's structure becomes more chaotic, and changes state, from a solid to a liquid to a gas.

Solids

A solid is the most ordered state of matter, with every atom or molecule connected to its neighbors, forming a fixed shape with a fixed volume. Solids are either crystalline, with their units built up in repeating units, or amorphous, with the units grouped together randomly.

△ **Crystalline halite**
Large crystals of common salt are called halite. The crystal is made up of sodium and chlorine atoms arranged in a cube.

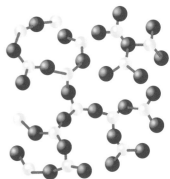

△ **Amorphous silica**
Glass is silica, the same material found in sand. It has an amorphous structure, with the units arranged randomly.

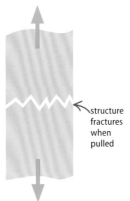

structure fractures when pulled

△ **Brittle solid**
In a brittle solid, the particles are held in a crystalline structure. Small forces do not alter the solid, but a force stronger than the bonds between the molecules can break it.

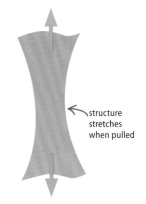

structure stretches when pulled

△ **Ductile solid**
Metals and some other solids can be pulled into a wire without breaking. This is because their molecules are held in an amorphous structure and can slide past each other.

Liquids

In a liquid, most of the atoms and molecules are still bonded together, but about one in ten of the links between them is broken. As a result, a liquid still has a more or less fixed volume and density—squeezing it does not really reduce its volume much. However, the constituents of the liquid are freer to move around than in a solid. Liquid can flow down slopes under the force of gravity, and take on the shape of any container it is poured into.

◁ **Liquid metal**
Mercury is the only metal that is liquid at room temperature. This is because its atoms form only weak bonds with each other.

◁ **Viscosity**
How a liquid flows is called its viscosity. When molecules are often blocked from moving past each other, the liquid is viscous (thick) and flows slowly. In low-viscosity liquids, molecules move around with little resistance.

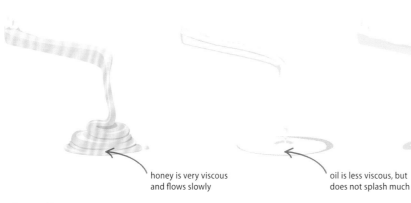

honey is very viscous and flows slowly

oil is less viscous, but does not splash much

water has low viscosity, and drips and splashes easily

REAL WORLD
Plasma

The aurora, or Northern Lights and Southern Lights, are an example of a fourth state of matter: plasma. Plasma is a mixture of high-energy charged atoms and smaller subatomic particles. The aurora is formed by plasma streaming from the Sun being trapped in the Earth's magnetic field. It crashes into the atmosphere over the polar regions, creating the amazing light show.

Gases

In a gas, there are no bonds at all between the atoms or molecules. The units are free to move independently of each other in any direction. As a result, a gas has no fixed shape or volume and can be squeezed into a small space or spread out to fill a container of any shape. Like a liquid, it can also be made to flow from one place to another.

▷ **Helium**
Helium is made up of just single atoms. As they move around, the atoms bounce off each other and the sides of the container.

Changing states

MATTER CHANGES FROM ONE STATE TO ANOTHER ACCORDING TO TEMPERATURE AND PRESSURE.

SEE ALSO	
‹ 96–97 Properties of materials	
‹ 98–99 States of matter	
Convection currents	189 ›

Every substance has a standard state. This is its state (solid, liquid, or gas) at 25°C (77°F)—just above room temperature. Increasing or decreasing that temperature eventually leads to a change in state.

States and energy

Changes in state are the result of energy being added to or removed from a substance. Taking energy from a gas results in it becoming a liquid and then a solid. Adding energy has the reverse effect. The energy within a substance makes its basic units—atoms or molecules—vibrate (wobble). This vibration, called internal energy, is measured when temperatures are recorded.

SEAgel is a spongelike solid made from seaweed. It is so light that it floats in thin air!

▷ **Melting and boiling point**
The temperatures at which a solid changes into a liquid or gas are called, respectively, the melting and boiling points. The temperatures are specific to each substance. They are always measured at standard atmospheric pressure. Changes in pressure affect the temperatures at which substances change state.

Sublimation
Sometimes a solid does not melt, but turns straight into a gas in a process called sublimation. Carbon dioxide sublimates almost all the time, while water ice changes straight into vapour if the air is very dry.

Deposition
The opposite process to sublimation, deposition, occurs when a gas turns into a solid without first becoming a liquid. Ice can be deposited from the vapor in air in very cold conditions.

solid

Freezing
In a liquid, the vibration or internal energy is just enough to break a few bonds—in fact, they are constantly breaking and reforming. A liquid freezes into a solid when its atoms or molecules no longer have enough energy to keep breaking bonds.

REAL WORLD
Salting ice

Adding salt to ice lowers the melting point of water by a couple of degrees. Salting roads in winter stops dangerous sheets of ice from forming—although if the conditions are well below 0°C (32°F) the water will still freeze. The salt dissolved in the water gets in the way of the water molecules, making it harder for them to form all the bonds they need to become ice.

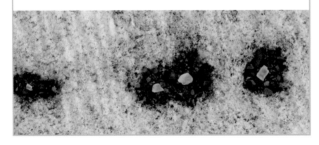

CHANGING STATES 101

Latent heat

Energy cannot be created from nothing, nor can it be made to disappear. So when a substance is condensing or freezing, rearranging its units into a lower-energy state, the unneeded energy is given out, warming the surroundings as latent heat. The same amount of heat moves the other way, from the surroundings to the substance, when it is boiling or melting and moving to a more energetic state.

▷ **Constant temperature**
This graph shows that the temperature stays constant at the melting and boiling points (when the change of state is taking place). The increase or decrease of energy at these points is the latent heat.

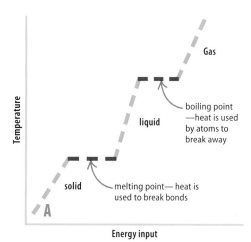

Condensation
The reverse of boiling, condensation, occurs when gas molecules are unable to escape and form bonds with other molecules that pass close by. Gradually the molecules gather together into larger droplets of liquid.

Boiling
A liquid boils into a gas when it has enough energy to break all of its bonds. Instead of vibrating around a fixed point, the molecules of gas are free to move in any direction.

Melting
The vibrations in solids are too weak to break the bonds connecting them. The solid melts only when its units have enough energy to break a few of the bonds and become a liquid. Substances with high melting points have strong bonds connecting their units, and so need a lot of heat energy to break them.

Changing states in mixtures

Mixtures contain ingredients that have different melting and boiling points. When a solid is dissolved in a liquid, such as the salt in seawater, the mixture looks and behaves like a liquid. However, when it is heated to boiling point, the mixture separates—the water evaporates, leaving behind the solid salt (which melts at a much higher temperature).

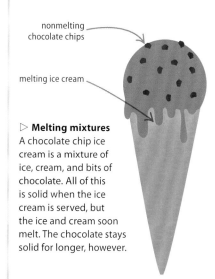

▷ **Melting mixtures**
A chocolate chip ice cream is a mixture of ice, cream, and bits of chocolate. All of this is solid when the ice cream is served, but the ice and cream soon melt. The chocolate stays solid for longer, however.

Gas laws

THE GAS LAWS STATE HOW GASES RESPOND TO CHANGE.

SEE ALSO	
‹ 28–29 Respiration	
‹ 99 Gases	
Pressure	141 ›
Pressure	184–185 ›

The three laws relate the movements of molecules in a gas to its volume, pressure, and temperature, and state how each measure responds when the others change. Each gas law is named after its discoverer.

Boyle's law

This law is named after Robert Boyle, who lived in Britain and Ireland in the 17th century and was one of the world's first chemists. His law states that if the temperature of a gas stays the same, then its volume is inversely proportional to its pressure. In other words, forcing a gas into a smaller volume results in it exerting a higher pressure.

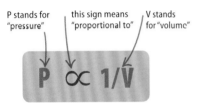

△ **Equation for Boyle's law**
This equation shows the relationship between a gas's pressure and its volume. Increasing the pressure decreases the volume.

P stands for "pressure"; this sign means "proportional to"; V stands for "volume"

$$P \propto 1/V$$

one weight produces pressure (P) in beaker

molecules spread evenly

△ **Diffusion**
The molecules in the gas spread out evenly to fill any container. This is called diffusion and means that molecules tend to move away from places where they are highly concentrated.

two weights produce double the pressure (2P) in beaker

high pressure squeezes molecules into half the original volume

△ **Pressure**
The force exerted on an area (its pressure) is caused by molecules in the gas hitting the inside of the container. Reducing the volume gives the molecules less room to move. They hit the sides more frequently, increasing the pressure.

REAL WORLD
Avogadro's law

There is a fourth gas law, which, although unrelated to the other three, was set out by the Italian Amedeo Avogadro (right) in 1811. It states that equal volumes of all gases at the same temperature and pressure contain the same number of molecules. Therefore a flask of hydrogen can contain the same number of molecules as an identical flask of oxygen, despite weighing a lot (16 times) less.

Robert Boyle was an alchemist and discovered his law while he was searching for a way to turn lead into gold.

Charles's law

This gas law, which is attributed to the French scientist Jacques Charles, states that the temperature of a gas is proportional to its volume. So if the gas is held in a container with an adjustable volume—a gas syringe, for example—increasing the temperature of the gas results in an increase in its volume.

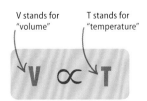

△ **Equation for Charles's law**
This equation shows the relationship between a gas's volume and its temperature. Increasing the temperature increases the volume.

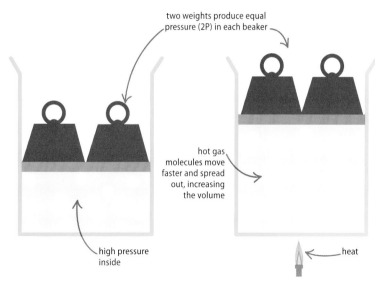

△ **Temperature**
Temperature is a measure of heat energy: the motion of a gas's molecules. Increasing the temperature of the gas increases the rate at which its molecules move.

△ **More motion**
Faster molecules hit each other and the container walls more often. If one wall is moveable, these impacts will push it outward, increasing the volume of the container.

Gay-Lussac's law

Named after French scientist Joseph Louis Gay-Lussac in 1808, this was the last of the three main gas laws to be formulated. It states that for a fixed volume of gas, the pressure is proportional to its temperature. In other words, when the temperature of a gas is increased, it also exerts a higher pressure. Similarly, squeezing a gas into a smaller volume increases its pressure (as per Boyle's law) and also raises the gas's temperature.

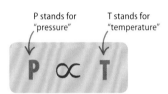

△ **Equation for Gay-Lussac's law**
This equation shows the relationship between the pressure of a gas and its temperature. Increasing the temperature increases the pressure.

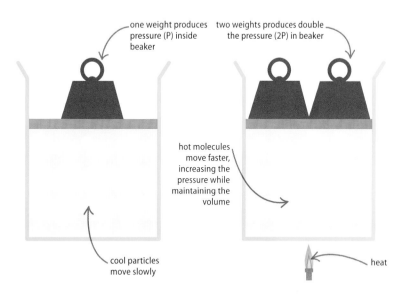

△ **Fewer collisions**
The molecules in the cool gas move slowly and they hit the sides of the container infrequently. These few, weak collisions combine to create a low gas pressure, overall.

△ **More collisions**
As the gas is heated, the molecules move around faster and hit the sides of the container more often and with greater force. Thus the pressure goes up.

Mixtures

A MIXTURE IS A COMBINATION OF SUBSTANCES THAT CAN BE SEPARATED BY PHYSICAL MEANS.

SEE ALSO	
Separating mixtures	106–107 ⟩
Compounds and molecules	110–111 ⟩
Water	142–143 ⟩

Mixtures are classified as solutions, suspensions, or colloids based on particle size. The substances in a mixture are not chemically linked.

Uneven and even

Every mixture has at least two ingredients. The first ingredient is known as the continuous medium. Into this, the second ingredient, known as the dispersed phase, is mixed. In an even or homogeneous mixture, the particles of the dispersed phase are evenly distributed among the molecules of the continuous medium, so the concentrations of each ingredient are constant. In an uneven or heterogeneous mixture, the dispersed phase is concentrated in some places and not in others. Some substances, normally liquids, cannot be mixed together because their molecules repel each other—they are described as immiscible.

REAL WORLD
Lava lamp

A lava lamp makes use of two immiscible liquids. The clear liquid is a mineral oil, while the colored "lava" is a wax. When the lamp is turned on, light heats the wax, reducing its density so it begins to rise up into the oil. The wax does not mix, however, and the colored bubbles rise and fall.

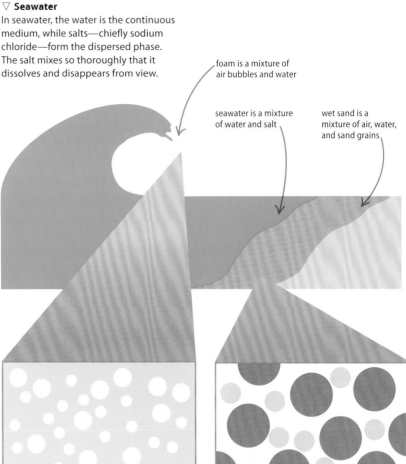

▽ **Seawater**
In seawater, the water is the continuous medium, while salts—chiefly sodium chloride—form the dispersed phase. The salt mixes so thoroughly that it dissolves and disappears from view.

foam is a mixture of air bubbles and water

seawater is a mixture of water and salt

wet sand is a mixture of air, water, and sand grains

△ **Foam**
The foam of a breaking wave is a heterogeneous mixture of air bubbles and water. The white appearance of the mixture is different from those of both the constituents.

△ **Wet sand**
The sand grains are much larger than the water molecules around them so they remain distinct and are visible when viewed close up. As the mixture dries, the water is replaced by air.

MIXTURES

Solutions

A homogeneous mixture is often referred to as a solution. The continuous medium is the solvent, and the dispersed phase is the solute. The solute disappears after it dissolves, although the color of the solvent may change.

SOLUTIONS			
Solvent	**Solute**	**Solution**	**Description**
helium	oxygen	deep-sea breathing gas	helium replaces other gases in the air
air	water	humid air	occurs on warm but damp days
air	smoke	smog	air pollution
water	carbon dioxide	soda water	fizzy water used in sodas
water	ethanoic acid	vinegar	sharp-tasting cooking ingredient
water	salt	seawater	salty water
palladium	hydrogen	palladium hydride	high-tech alloy used in industry
silver	mercury	amalgam	soft alloy used in dental fillings
iron	carbon	steel	high-strength alloy used in construction

Key
 Solid Liquid ▨ Gas

Suspensions

A common type of heterogeneous mixture is a suspension. In contrast to solutions, where the solute breaks up into tiny particles, the particles of the dispersed phase are considerably larger than those of the continuous medium—at least one micrometer across. Everyday examples include the dust carried in wind, tiny droplets in the gas of an aerosol spray, or silt in river water.

▽ **Hanging around**
The particles of the dispersed phase are suspended—they are too small to sink quickly. There are three ways that the mixture can separate.

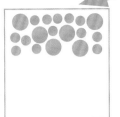

△ **Creaming**
If the suspended particles are less dense than the continuous phase, they will float. The particles will sit at the surface like cream floating on top of a cup of coffee.

△ **Sedimentation**
If the particles are denser than the continuous phase, they will sink. The particles will form a sediment, or layer, at the bottom of the mixture.

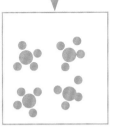

△ **Flocculation**
Sometimes the particles will clump to form larger particles, or floccs. Flocculation happens when the conditions change, or another substance is added to the mixture.

Colloids

A colloid is a mixture that is halfway between a solution and a suspension. The dispersed phase appears to be evenly distributed to the naked eye, but at a microscopic level the two constituents remain heterogeneously mixed. Ice cream, fog, and milk are examples of colloids.

▷ **Cloud**
A cloud is a colloid of liquid water droplets mixed into air. If the droplets grow beyond a certain size, they fall as rain.

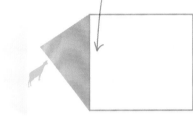

fat and water are immiscible (they won't mix), so the fat forms tiny blobs

△ **Milk**
Milk is a colloid of fat in water. Colloids are often white, because the larger size of the dispersed phase causes light to scatter when it passes through the mixture.

Separating mixtures

MIXTURES ARE MADE UP OF SEPARATE SUBSTANCES.

The constituents of mixtures are not chemically joined. Since they remain distinct substances, they can be separated using only physical means. The precise method depends on the type of mixture.

SEE ALSO
❮ 34–35 Waste materials
❮ 104–105 Mixtures
Refining metals 152–153 ❯
Crude oil distillation 157 ❯

Liquid mixtures

Dissolved solids can be separated by evaporating away the liquid solvent, leaving crystals of solid behind. This is how salt is separated from seawater. Collecting a pure sample of the solvent is more complicated. The vapor passes through a condenser, where it is cooled back into a liquid. A condenser is also used in distillation, which separates a mixture of two or more liquids.

Filtration

Silt in river water is an example of an uneven mixture—large, heavy solids are mixed into a continuous medium of much smaller particles. This kind of mixture can be separated using filters. A filter is a material that allows the smaller particles through but blocks the progress of the larger ones. Most laboratory filters are made from paper, but wire meshes can be used too.

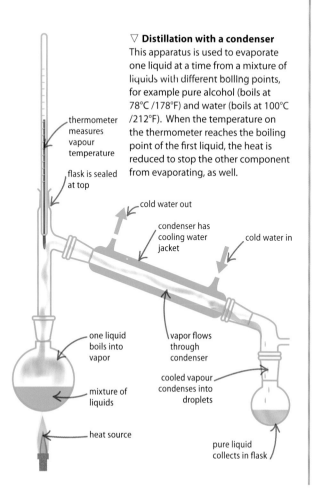

▽ **Distillation with a condenser**
This apparatus is used to evaporate one liquid at a time from a mixture of liquids with different boiling points, for example pure alcohol (boils at 78°C /178°F) and water (boils at 100°C /212°F). When the temperature on the thermometer reaches the boiling point of the first liquid, the heat is reduced to stop the other component from evaporating, as well.

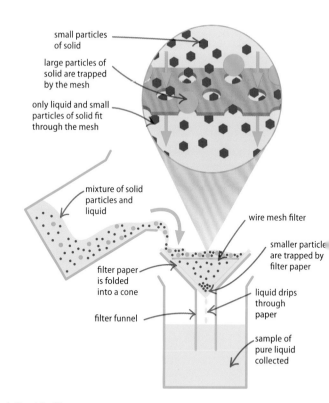

△ **Double filter**
The experiment above uses two different filters to separate out two different-sized consituents. Water and small particles pass through the first filter, made of wire mesh, but larger particles are trapped. The smaller particles are trapped in the second filter, made of paper, leaving just the pure liquid to drip into the beaker.

SEPARATING MIXTURES **107**

Centrifugal force

Another way to separate an uneven mixture is by using a centrifuge. In a suspension, the solid particles are often still too small to sink to the bottom under the pull of gravity alone. So the mixture is spun around at high speed, creating a centrifugal force that pushes the solid material down to the bottom of the test tube.

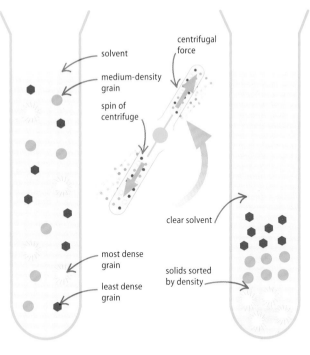

△ **Sorting mixtures**
The centrifugal force has the strongest effect on the densest particles in the mixture, so these move to the bottom fastest. This phenomenon can be used to sort suspended particles or grains—the densest ones form the lower layer, with successively less dense particles layered on top.

REAL WORLD
Butter churn

Butter is made by separating the solid fats from the liquid component in milk. This is done by mechanical disruption. The mixture is churned (spun) and this makes the blobs of fat stick together. The fat blobs get bigger and bigger until they separate from the water. The products from the churning are butter and buttermilk— a thinner, lower-fat liquid.

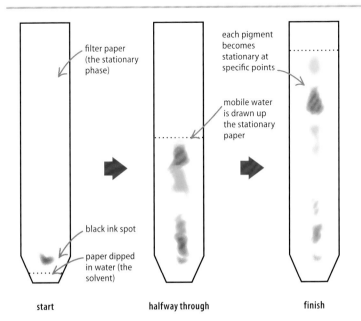

start · halfway through · finish

Chromatography

When the components of a mixture have the same particle sizes or similar boiling points, they are separated by chromatography. The mixture is dissolved in a solvent. The solvent, known as the mobile phase, is then drawn through a substance known as the stationary phase, often filter paper. The mobile phase moves forward, but each component in the mixture moves through the stationary phase at a different speed. As a result, each component becomes fixed in the stationary medium at a different point, forming separated samples of each substance.

◁ **Separating black ink**
Black ink is a mixture of colored pigments in water. These can be separated using chromatography. The word means "writing with color," and the drop of ink forms bands of its individual color components.

Elements and atoms

EVERYTHING IS BUILT FROM ELEMENTS AND ATOMS.

In ancient times, people believed that our world was made from just a few elemental substances: earth, air, fire, and water. Chemists now know that it is made from 90 naturally occurring elements.

SEE ALSO	
⟨ 78–79 Cycles in nature	
Octet rule	112 ⟩
Periodic table	116–117 ⟩
Size of atoms	118 ⟩
Inner and outer electrons	124 ⟩
Inside atoms	168–169 ⟩

What is an element?

An element is a substance that cannot be broken down into simpler constituents. Therefore a pure sample of an element is made entirely from one type of atom. The structure of that atom defines the element's physical and chemical properties.

REAL WORLD

Hennig Brand

The German Hennig Brand is the first historical figure known to have discovered a new element. In 1669, he found phosphorus after investigating the substances in his urine. The phosphorus glowed in the dark, making Brand think he had found a magic material.

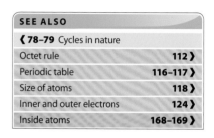

Atomic number
Every element has a unique atomic number, which is the total number of protons in the atom.

Atomic mass
Atomic mass is the mass of protons, neutrons, and electrons in the atom. The number is shown as an average of all isotopes (see pages 111 and 169).

1 1.0079	26 55.845	3 6.941	17 35.453
H	**Fe**	**Li**	**Cl**
HYDROGEN	IRON	LITHIUM	CHLORINE

Chemical symbol
Every element is abbreviated using a unique symbol of one or two letters. Mostly these relate to the English names, so H is for hydrogen and Cl is for chlorine. A few are based on other languages, for example iron is Fe, from the Latin word "ferrum."

Name
Many element names are very old. Newer ones are agreed by an international committee. Chlorine is named after khloros, the Greek word for "greenish yellow" (the gas's color).

Atomic structure

An atom is made up of positively charged protons and negatively charged electrons. The atoms of every element have a specific number of protons. Protons have a positive charge, but atoms are always neutral because the protons are balanced by an equal number of negatively charged electrons.

Proton
A proton is a positively charged particle that sits in the nucleus.

Nucleus
All atoms, except hydrogen atoms, have neutrons as well as protons in their nucleus.

Neutrons
Neutrons are neutral particles that have no charge.

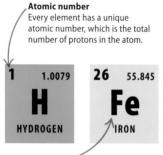

Electron shell
The electrons are arranged in shells, or energy levels, around the nucleus.

Electrons
An electron is a negatively charged particle that sits in the electron shell.

△ **Hydrogen**
With one proton and one electron, hydrogen atoms are the smallest, lightest, and simplest of any element.

△ **Nitrogen**
Nitrogen atoms have seven protons and seven electrons. Most nitrogen atoms also have seven neutrons.

Electron configurations

As the atomic number increases, atoms get heavier and larger, because the electrons are arranged in shells positioned farther and farther out from the nucleus. The first shell can hold two electrons and the second can hold eight. Once the third shell has eight, the fourth shell starts to fill up, although in some cases these shells can hold many more than eight electrons (see page 124).

Shell shape
In reality the electron shells are not round. Scientists draw them like this so they are easy to see and compare.

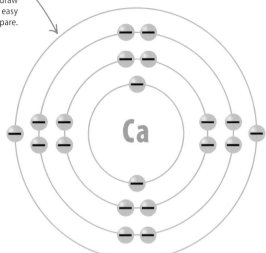

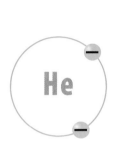

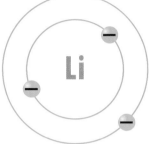

△ **Helium**
With an atomic number of 2, helium has two protons and therefore two electrons in a single shell.

△ **Lithium**
Lithium has an atomic number of 3. The first electron shell is full, so the third electron sits in another shell.

△ **Calcium**
With an atomic number of 20, the electrons in a calcium atom are arranged over four shells.

Outer shell

The electrons in an atom's outer shell are the ones that form bonds with other atoms and become involved in chemical reactions. So the number of outer electrons in an atom is a strong indicator of an element's physical and chemical properties. Atoms react with each other to achieve a full outer shell and therefore become more stable. The diagrams below show only the outer shell of each atom.

▽ **Octet rule**
Atoms need to have eight electrons in their outer shell to become stable. This is called the octet rule. They must either gain electrons to reach eight, or lose electrons so that the next shell down—which will be full—becomes their outer shell.

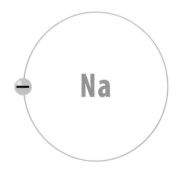

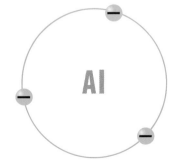

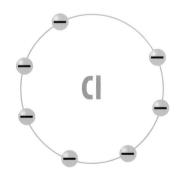

△ **Sodium**
A sodium atom has just one outer electron. To get a full outer shell, it must give that electron away.

△ **Aluminum**
An aluminum atom has three outer electrons. It has to lose all of these to become stable.

△ **Chlorine**
A chlorine atom has seven outer electrons. It has space for one more, which would fill its outer shell.

Compounds and molecules

ATOMS JOIN TOGETHER TO FORM COMPOUNDS AND MOLECULES.

Few elements exist naturally in their pure form. Gold is one example. Most other elements form compounds, when their atoms bond with those of other elements.

SEE ALSO
(104–105 Mixtures
(108–109 Elements and atoms
Ionic bonding 112–113)
Covalent bonding 114–115)

What is a compound?
Almost all everyday items are made up of chemical compounds, from the water coming out of the tap to the minerals in bricks and stones to the substances in the human body. A compound is a single substance made up of the atoms of two or more elements, which are chemically connected or bonded. This differentiates a compound from a mixture, which is made up of two or more separate substances.

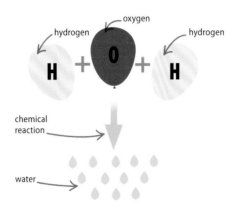

◁ **Fixed ratio**
A compound's constituent elements have a fixed ratio. Water (H_2O) has two parts of hydrogen (H) for every part of oxygen (O).

◁ **Chemical reactions**
A compound can only be formed when elements, or other compounds, react with each other.

◁ **Different properties**
A compound's properties are different to those of its constituent elements. Water is a liquid, for example, that is made up of two gases.

Molecules
A molecule is the smallest unit of a compound. Breaking the molecule down into simpler constituents would result in the compound ceasing to exist. The atoms in a molecule are connected by chemical bonds. The arrangement and strength of the bonds gives the molecule a certain shape.

At **very high pressures,** oxygen molecules transform into an eight-atom version that is bright red.

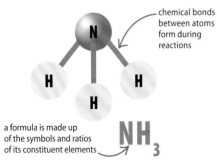

△ **Ammonia**
The molecules of this compound have a single nitrogen atom (N) bonded to three hydrogen atoms (H). Together they form a tetrahedron.

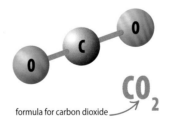

△ **Carbon dioxide**
As its name suggests, this compound has one carbon atom (C) bonded to two oxygen atoms (O). The three atoms form a straight molecule.

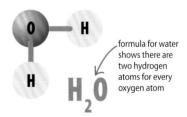

△ **Water**
Common compounds such as water have nonscientific names. Others, such as carbon dioxide, are named according to the elements they contain.

COMPOUNDS AND MOLECULES

Molecular elements

Atoms get involved in reactions and form molecules to become more stable. So even when they are pure, most elements do not exist as single unbonded atoms. However, the molecules they form consist of only one type of atom.

▷ **Increased stability**
The oxygen in the air exists as a molecule of two oxygen atoms (O_2). When bonded together, the oxygen atoms are in a more stable state.

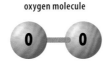
oxygen molecule

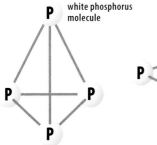
white phosphorus molecule

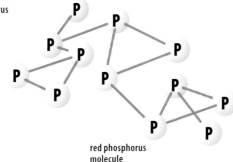
red phosphorus molecule

△ **Allotropes**
Some elements can form more than one shape of molecule and each form is called an allotrope. Phosphorus (P) has red and white allotropes. The red allotrope has stronger bonds and is more stable than the white one, which reacts very easily—even burning on contact with air.

Crystals

A crystal forms when the large numbers of molecules of an element or a compound are all joined together in a repeating pattern. For example, a diamond is a form of carbon made up of repeating tetrahedral units.

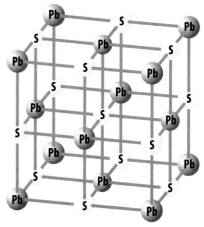

△ **Galena**
Galena is a compound of lead (Pb) and sulfur (S). Its formula is simply PbS and the lead and sulfur atoms form a cube of atoms. A galena crystal is made up of these cubic units.

Metallic bonds

Metal atoms lose their outer electrons easily, forming positively charged ions (see page 112) surrounded by a sea of shared electrons. The attraction between the negatively charged electrons and positively charged ions creates metallic bonds that "glue" the structure together.

▽ **Strong material**
The free electrons are shared by all neighboring ions and can slide past each other. This means that metal objects can be deformed, or bent, without breaking.

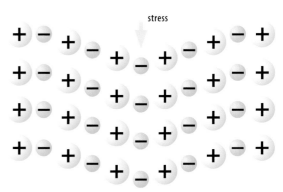
metal ion
electrons are not linked to any particular ion
stress

Ionic bonding

IONIC BONDING IS WHEN DIFFERENT ATOMS FORM BONDS BY GAINING OR LOSING ELECTRONS.

Atoms bond with each other so that they can fill the spaces in their outer electron shells. This makes them more stable.

SEE ALSO	
⟨ 110–111 Compounds and molecules	
Covalent bonding	114–115 ⟩
Ionization energy	119 ⟩
Redox reactions	132–133 ⟩
Electrochemistry	148–149 ⟩
Inside atoms	168–169 ⟩
Electricity	202–203 ⟩

What is an ion?

An atom has an equal number of protons and electrons so it has no overall charge. If the atom loses or gains an electron, it becomes a charged particle called an ion. Losing one electron produces a positive ion with a charge of 1+; losing two results in a charge of 2+. Ions formed by gaining electrons have negative charges, so gaining one electron results in a charge of 1−.

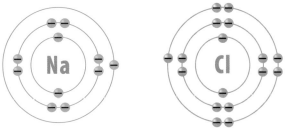

△ **A sodium atom** has one outer electron, while chlorine has seven electrons in the outer shell, with room for one more.

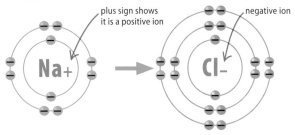

plus sign shows it is a positive ion

negative ion

△ **Sodium loses its outer electron**, passing it to chlorine. Both ions now have full outer shells.

sodium's second shell is now its outer shell, which is full and stable

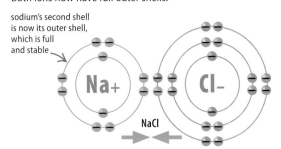

△ **The positive charge of the sodium** ion attracts the equal but negative charge of the chloride ion to form an ionic bond between the two. The resulting compound is sodium chloride (NaCl).

Octet rule

Atoms with low atomic numbers become full and stable when their outer shells contain eight electrons—the so-called octet rule (see page 109). Cations, or positive ions, are formed when atoms lose electrons, while anions, or negative ions, are formed when atoms gain electrons.

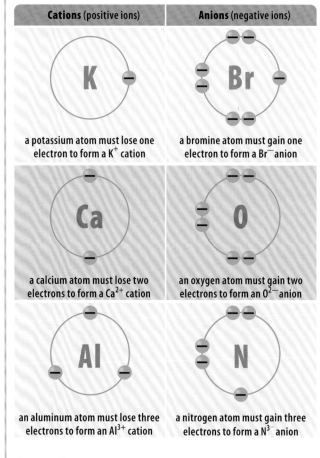

Cations (positive ions)	Anions (negative ions)
a potassium atom must lose one electron to form a K^+ cation	a bromine atom must gain one electron to form a Br^- anion
a calcium atom must lose two electrons to form a Ca^{2+} cation	an oxygen atom must gain two electrons to form an O^{2-} anion
an aluminum atom must lose three electrons to form an Al^{3+} cation	a nitrogen atom must gain three electrons to form a N^{3-} anion

△ **Outer electrons**
Atoms with between one and three outer electrons will lose them, whereas atoms with five to seven electrons will gain more. An atom with a complete outer shell is stable, so does not lose or gain electrons.

IONIC BONDING

Balancing charges

For a bond to form between ions, the positive and negative charges need to balance so that the overall molecule is neutral. As a result compounds are not always derived from one anion and one cation, but form with different proportions of ions.

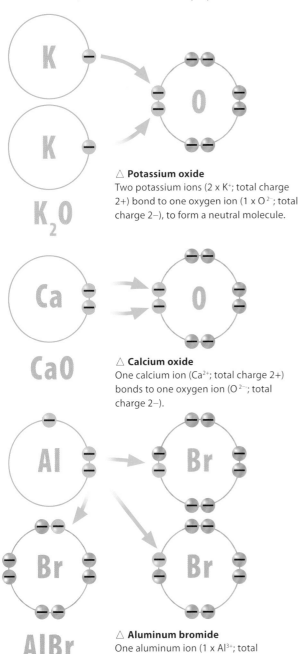

△ **Potassium oxide**
Two potassium ions (2 x K⁺; total charge 2+) bond to one oxygen ion (1 x O^{2-}; total charge 2–), to form a neutral molecule.

△ **Calcium oxide**
One calcium ion (Ca^{2+}; total charge 2+) bonds to one oxygen ion (O^{2-}; total charge 2–).

△ **Aluminum bromide**
One aluminum ion (1 x Al^{3+}; total charge 3+) bonds to three bromine ions (3 x Br⁻; total charge 3–).

Reactivity

Metal atoms give away electrons so they are electropositive. Nonmetals gain electrons so they are electronegative. Different atoms give away or gain electrons more easily than others.

▽ **Metal ions**
Magnesium (Mg) and sodium (Na) have three electron shells. However, magnesium has two outer electrons while sodium has one. It takes less energy to lose one electron than two, so sodium is more electropositive than magnesium. Potassium (K) also has one outer electron but it is in a fourth shell, farther away from the attractive pull of the nucleus. So potassium loses its outer electron more easily than sodium.

▽ **Nonmetal ions**
Oxygen (O) needs two electrons to complete the octet but nitrogen (N) needs three. It takes less energy to gain two electrons than three, so oxygen is more electronegative than nitrogen. Phosphorus (P) also needs three electrons but it has one more shell. The pull from the nucleus in this third shell is weaker than in a second shell, so it is harder for phosphorus to gain electrons than nitrogen.

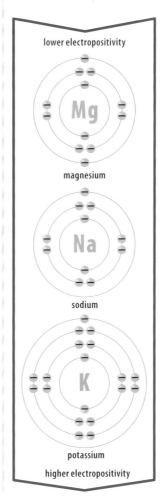

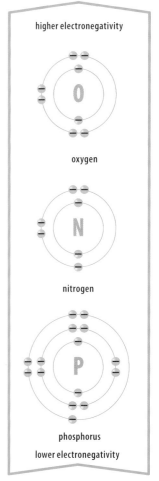

Covalent bonding

COVALENT BONDING IS WHEN ATOMS FORM BONDS BY SHARING ELECTRONS.

Rather than giving away or accepting electrons, some atoms share their outer electrons to achieve full outer shells.

SEE ALSO	
❮ 110–111 Compounds and molecules	
❮ 112–113 Ionic bonding	
Hydrogen bonds	142 ❯
Hydrocarbon chains	158 ❯
Inside atoms	168–169 ❯

Sharing electrons

Covalent bonds are formed of pairs of electrons, one from each atom. The pair is included in the outer electron shell of both atoms at once. This allows the atoms to have a full set of eight electrons in their outer shell and become stable. No electrons leave their original atoms—so the atoms always remain neutral.

▽ **Double bond**
Oxygen gas is made up of O_2 molecules. They form when oxygen atoms share not one but two pairs of electrons in what is known as a double bond.

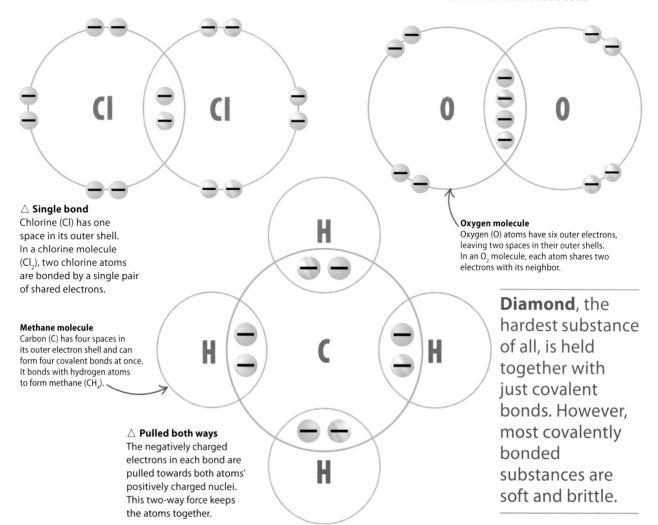

△ **Single bond**
Chlorine (Cl) has one space in its outer shell. In a chlorine molecule (Cl_2), two chlorine atoms are bonded by a single pair of shared electrons.

Methane molecule
Carbon (C) has four spaces in its outer electron shell and can form four covalent bonds at once. It bonds with hydrogen atoms to form methane (CH_4).

△ **Pulled both ways**
The negatively charged electrons in each bond are pulled towards both atoms' positively charged nuclei. This two-way force keeps the atoms together.

Oxygen molecule
Oxygen (O) atoms have six outer electrons, leaving two spaces in their outer shells. In an O_2 molecule, each atom shares two electrons with its neighbor.

Diamond, the hardest substance of all, is held together with just covalent bonds. However, most covalently bonded substances are soft and brittle.

Shapes and bonds

In a methane molecule (see page 114), every electron in the carbon atom's outer shell is shared with a hydrogen atom. However, in other molecules not all the electrons are involved in a bond. The ones that are not are called lone pairs. These lone pairs create a zone of electric charge that repels the bonded pairs and pushes them closer together. So the arrangement of bonded and lone pairs gives a molecule its shape.

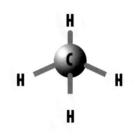

◁ **Methane**
In a methane molecule there is no lone pair, so the four bonds are repelled equally. This means that the hydrogen atoms are positioned equally around the carbon atom to create a regular shape called a tetrahedron.

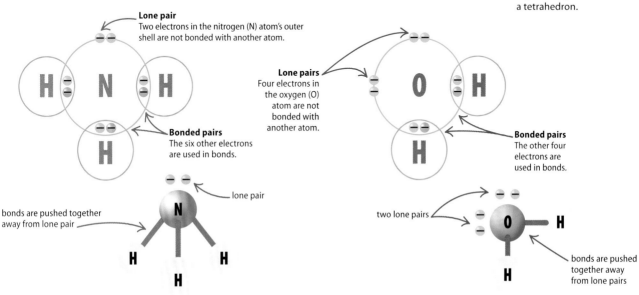

△ **Ammonia**
The lone pair on nitrogen repels the three bonds so they are pushed closer together.

△ **Water**
In a water molecule, two lone pairs of electrons push the molecule into a V shape.

Intermolecular forces

Most simple covalent compounds are gases, because their molecules stay separate from each other in normal conditions. However, in a liquid or solid, weak intermolecular forces act between the molecules to hold them together. A common type is the dipole-dipole interaction, which occurs between dipoles (molecules that have one negatively charged side and one positively charged side). A negative end of a dipole on one molecule will then attract a positive end of dipole on a neighbouring molecule, holding the two molecules together.

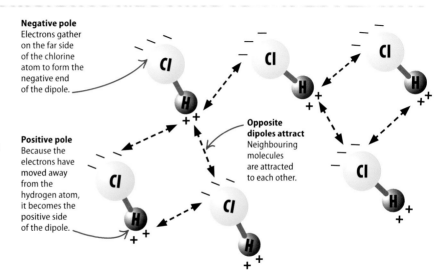

Periodic table

CHEMISTS ORGANIZE THE ELEMENTS USING THE PERIODIC TABLE.

The elements are arranged according to their atomic structure. Those with similar properties are grouped together.

SEE ALSO	
‹ 108–109	Elements and atoms
Understanding the periodic table	118–119 ›
Alkali metals and alkali earth metals	120–121 ›
The halogens and noble gases	122–123 ›
Transition metals	124–125 ›
Inside atoms	168–169 ›

Building the table

The periodic table we use today was formulated by Dmitri Mendeleev in 1869. The elements are arranged in rows in order of their atomic number. The atomic number is the number of protons each atom has in its nucleus (see page 108). By arranging the elements in this way, those with similar properties are grouped together. This means chemists can predict the likely characteristics of an element from its position in the table.

atoms of the elements in Group 1 have one electron in their outer shells

▷ **Individual entry**
Every element is most easily identified by its symbol. The atomic number is the number of protons in the nucleus.

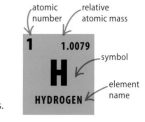

atomic number — relative atomic mass — symbol — element name

Groups
The table has 18 columns called groups.

Periods
The table has seven horizontal rows called periods.

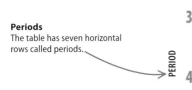

REAL WORLD
Precious metal

Gold was one of the first known elements. This was because gold is one of the few elements that occurs pure in nature, so it was easily discovered.

gold

Periods 6 and 7
These periods are too long to fit on the table, so the middle sections in Group 3 are shown at the bottom.

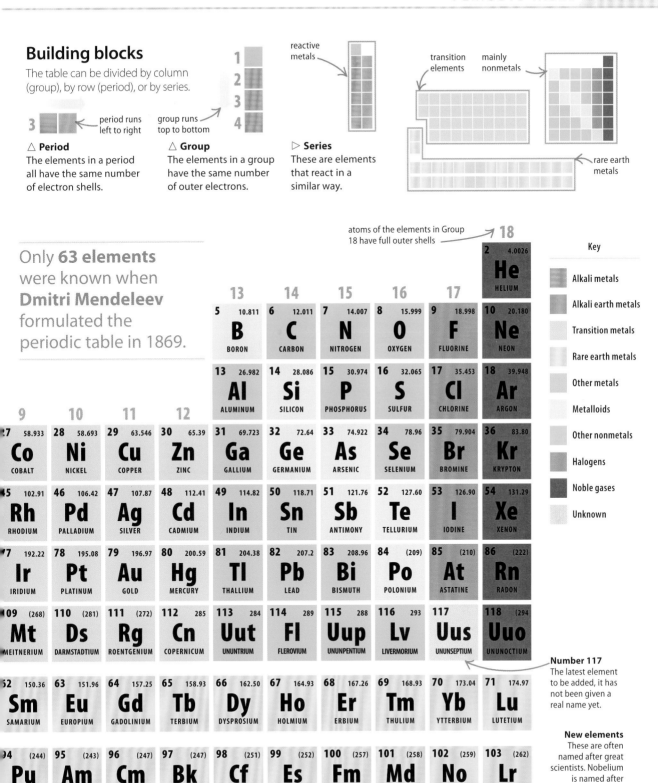

Understanding the periodic table

THERE ARE TRENDS IN THE PERIODIC TABLE.

SEE ALSO
‹ 113 Reactivity
‹ 116–117 Periodic table
Inside atoms 168–169 ›

The periodic table arranges the elements according to the arrangment of their atoms' electrons. This means that similar elements are grouped together.

Size of atoms

Atoms get bigger as you move down the table because each period, or row, begins when a new shell is added to the atom. However, they get smaller from left to right as the number of outer electrons increases. This is because atoms with more outer electrons are held together with greater force, pulling them into smaller volumes.

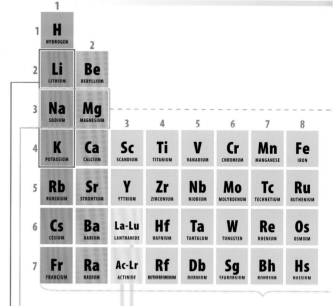

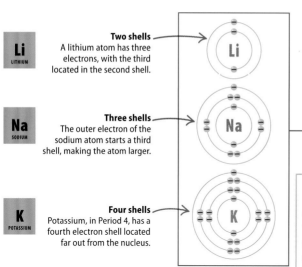

Two shells
A lithium atom has three electrons, with the third located in the second shell.

Three shells
The outer electron of the sodium atom starts a third shell, making the atom larger.

Four shells
Potassium, in Period 4, has a fourth electron shell located far out from the nucleus.

Metals and nonmetals

The left side of the periodic table is made up of metallic elements; the right side, nonmetallic. A metallic element has atoms that give up their outer electrons easily. The nonmetals hold firmly to their outer electrons and have very different properties from metals. Seven elements are semimetals, which have characteristics of both metals and nonmetals.

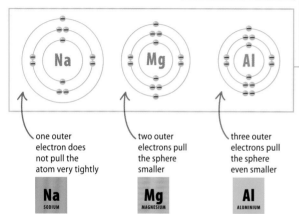

one outer electron does not pull the atom very tightly

two outer electrons pull the sphere smaller

three outer electrons pull the sphere even smaller

METALLIC AND NONMETALLIC	
Metallic	**Nonmetallic**
conducts heat	good insulator
conducts electricity	resists current
malleable and tough	brittle and crumbly
shiny and opaque	dull and translucent
high density	low density
low ionization energy	high ionization energy

◁ **Metallic vs nonmetallic**
Metal atoms have a certain set of characteristics due to their atomic structure. Nonmetals have an almost opposite set of characteristics.

UNDERSTANDING THE PERIODIC TABLE

decreasing atomic radius
increasing ionization energy
decreasing metallic character

semi-metals, called metalloids, form a diagonal boundary between metals and nonmetals—elements to the left of these are metals; those to the right are nonmetals

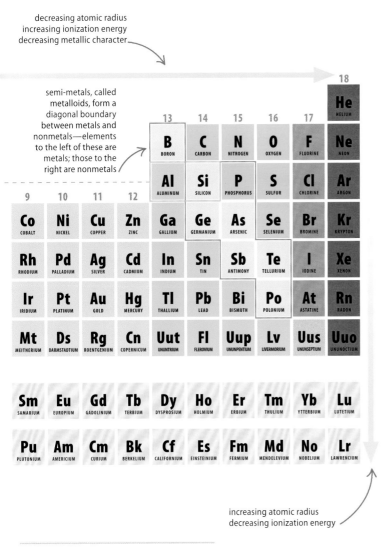

increasing atomic radius
decreasing ionization energy

Trends in the table are not always followed: the atoms of **zirconium** and **hafnium** are almost identical in size, even though hafnium has 32 more electrons!

Ionization energy

Ionization energy is the energy needed to take an electron out of an atom, making the atom a positively charged ion. The trend in the ionization energy of elements is the reverse of that of atomic size. In the periodic table, the required energy increases left to right and decreases top to bottom. Atoms with large numbers of outer electrons require more energy to ionize by losing an electron because their shells are held more tightly, closer to the nucleus. Large atoms, with outer electrons located far from the nucleus, lose them more easily.

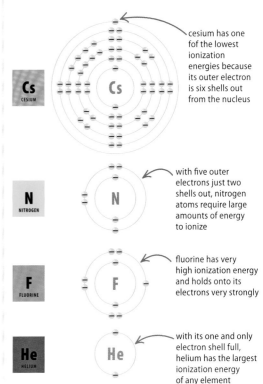

cesium has one of the lowest ionization energies because its outer electron is six shells out from the nucleus

with five outer electrons just two shells out, nitrogen atoms require large amounts of energy to ionize

fluorine has very high ionization energy and holds onto its electrons very strongly

with its one and only electron shell full, helium has the largest ionization energy of any element

REAL WORLD
Ekasilicon

After developing the periodic table, Dmitri Mendeleev used it to predict the properties of elements that had yet to be discovered—left as gaps in the table. He described element 32 as ekasilicon, predicting its melting point, color, density, and chemical characteristics. In 1886, ekasilicon—eventually named germanium—was isolated, and matched Mendeleev's predictions.

Alkali metals and alkali earth metals

SIX ELEMENTS IN GROUP 1 OF THE PERIODIC TABLE ARE CALLED ALKALI METALS. THE SIX IN GROUP 2 ARE ALKALI EARTH METALS.

SEE ALSO	
‹ 112–113 Ionic bonding	
‹ 116–117 Periodic table	
‹ 118–119 Understanding the periodic table	
The halogens and noble gases	122–123 ›
Transition metals	124–125 ›
What is a base?	144 ›

These elements get involved in chemical reactions with other elements easily because they have very few outer electrons.

Reactive metals

Elements in Group 1 have a single outer electron in their atoms, while those of Group 2 have two outer electrons. They form ions easily by losing these electrons, so they readily get involved in reactions, which makes them highly reactive. With just one electron to lose, a member of Group 1, such as potassium (K), will ionize more easily than a member of Group 2, which must lose two electrons.

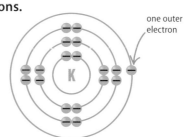

△ **Potassium (Group 1)**
As the third alkali metal, potassium has one electron in its fourth and outermost shell.

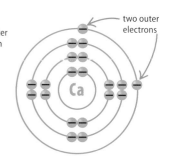

△ **Calcium (Group 2)**
Calcium also has four electron shells, but there are two electrons in its outer shell.

Releasing hydrogen

These metals all react strongly with water, producing brightly colored flames. The metal ion swaps places with (displaces) a hydrogen ion in the water, forming a substance called a hydroxide. The displaced hydrogen is released as bubbles of gas. For example, when potassium is added to water, the products are potassium hydroxide (KOH) and hydrogen gas: $2K + 2H_2O \rightarrow 2KOH + H_2$.

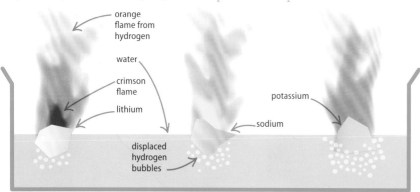

△ **Lithium**
When reacting with water, lithium burns with a crimson flame. The hydrogen released turns the flame orange.

△ **Sodium**
This metal produces an orange flame. It is the same color produced by sodium lamps used in street lights.

△ **Potassium**
Potassium burns with a lilac flame. It is more reactive than sodium and lithium and often explodes as it reacts.

REAL WORLD
In bodies

The alkali metals and alkali earth metals are common ingredients in living bodies. Sodium and potassium ions are used to create the electric pulses that fire through muscles and nerves, while calcium compounds are in bones, teeth, and the shells of snails.

Hydrogen and helium

Hydrogen is in Group 1 and has a single outer electron. However, it is not included in the alkali metals. This is because it has a distinct set of chemical properties compared to the other group members. Similarly, helium has two outer electrons, yet it is not included in Group 2. Instead it is in Group 18 with the noble gases, with which it shares most chemical properties.

△ **Hydrogen**
Hydrogen has just one electron, which it loses less easily than other elements in its group.

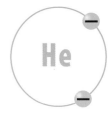

△ **Helium**
Helium has one electron shell, and with two electrons it is full. It does not form ions in chemical reactions.

Group trends

Members of Groups 1 and 2 become more reactive down the group as the atoms get bigger. This is because the atoms' negatively charged outer electrons are located farther away from the positively charged nucleus—and are held less strongly in the atom.

▽ **Alkali earth metals**
Earth metals are so called because they are found in compounds in the Earth's crust. Beryllium, for example, is found in gemstones such as emeralds. Although Group 2 metals react with water, they do so less strongly than those in Group 1.

◁ **Lithium**
With the lowest density of any metal, lithium even floats in water.

◁ **Sodium**
The most abundant alkali metal, sodium compounds are found in many rocks.

◁ **Potassium**
Potassium is named after potash—potassium—containing compounds in the ash of burned wood.

◁ **Rubidium**
This metal would melt on a hot day and is so reactive that it catches fire in air.

◁ **Cesium**
Cesium melts at 28°C (82°F), which is only just above room temperature.

◁ **Francium**
This radioactive metal is extremely rare and little is known about it.

high reactivity

◁ **Beryllium**
This metal has a very low density so it is used to make high-speed aircraft and satellites.

◁ **Magnesium**
This metal is named after the region Magnesia in Greece, which has lots of magnesium compounds.

◁ **Calcium**
Calcium is common in Earth's rocks. Natural calcium compounds are often known as limes.

◁ **Strontium**
While most strontium is relatively stable, some forms are radioactive and dangerous.

◁ **Barium**
Barium compounds are added to fireworks to produce green explosions.

◁ **Radium**
This metal is highly radioactive and gives off a faint blue glow.

high reactivity

The halogens and noble gases

THESE ARE GROUPS 17 AND 18 OF THE PERIODIC TABLE.

> **SEE ALSO**
> ‹ 113 Reactivity
> ‹ 118–119 Understanding the periodic table
> ‹ 120–121 Alkali metals and alkali earth metals
> Radioactivity 126–127 ›
> Types of reaction 129 ›

While the left side of the periodic table is dominated by metals, the right side—made up of Groups 17 and 18—are all nonmetals. The chemical characteristics of these two groups could not be more different.

The halogen group

There are five naturally occurring halogens. The reactivity decreases down the group as the atoms grow larger. The outer shell of a smaller atom is closer to the nucleus, so the electrons in it are held more strongly than in larger ones—and this includes the electron added during reactions to make an ion.

◁ **Fluorine**
This pale yellow gas is the most reactive nonmetal element of all, and so forms compounds easily. Sodium fluoride is found in toothpaste.

◁ **Chlorine**
This is a green gas that is used in many disinfectants and cleaning products, such as bleach. Chlorides are added to many swimming pools.

◁ **Bromine**
This is the only nonmetal element found in liquid form in standard conditions. Its compounds are used in fireproofing.

◁ **Iodine**
This purple-gray solid does not melt into a liquid at atmospheric pressure; it changes from a solid state straight into a purple gas.

◁ **Astatine**
The heaviest halogen is highly radioactive and is very rare. Its atoms break up into other elements quickly.

low reactivity

The salt formers

The members of Group 17 are also known as the halogens, meaning "salt formers." The atoms of halogens have outer shells with seven electrons—out of a maximum of eight. As a result, all the halogens are very electronegative, meaning that they form negatively charged ions easily by attracting an electron each to fill their outer shells. They do this by reacting with metals (which form positively charged ions) to form stable ionic compounds. These substances are called salts.

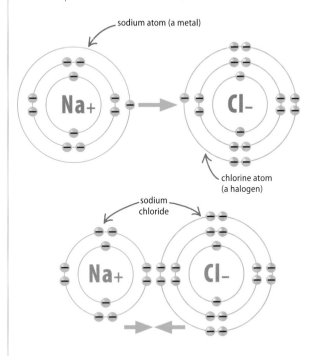

△ **Common salt**
It is perhaps no surprise that the most common salt is called common salt or table salt. This is a compound formed when the halogen chlorine (Cl) reacts with the metal sodium (Na), producing sodium chloride (NaCl).

Displacement

Halogens all react in the same way and form similar families of compounds. Therefore, a more highly reactive halogen will displace a less reactive one from its compounds. This can involve the two halogens swapping places in two compounds. When a pure halogen is used, the displaced element is also released in its pure form.

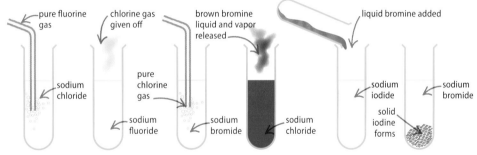

△ **Fluorine displaces chlorine**
Fluorine displaces chlorine from sodium chloride (NaCl). It will also displace bromine and iodine.

△ **Chlorine displaces bromine**
Chlorine displaces bromine from sodium bromide (NaBr). It will also displace iodine but not fluorine.

△ **Bromine displaces iodine**
Bromine displaces iodine from sodium iodide (NaI). It will not displace chlorine or fluorine.

Inert gases

The noble gases form Group 18 of the periodic table. Apart from helium, they all have atoms with eight electrons in their outer shells—a full set. This makes them chemically inactive or inert. In other words, they are noble and do not mix with the other elements, and hardly ever take part in chemical reactions. Their atoms do not form molecules, even with themselves, and all Group 18 elements exist as gases made up of single atoms.

◁ **Helium**
Helium has just two outer electrons, filling a single shell around the nucleus.

◁ **Neon**
Discovered in 1898, this gas's name means "the new one."

◁ **Argon**
The most common noble gas on Earth, it forms one percent of the atmosphere.

◁ **Krypton**
Much rarer than neon, this gas's name means "the hidden one."

◁ **Xenon**
Xenon—"the strange one"—is a dense gas; a balloon of it falls straight down.

◁ **Radon**
All radon atoms are radioactive. The gas is formed naturally when uranium in rocks breaks down.

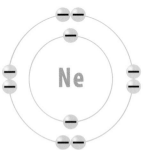

△ **Neon atom's shell**
Like all noble gases, neon does not bond ionically—it has no spaces to fill in its outer shell. Neon atoms do not share electrons in covalent bonds for the same reason.

Neon lights

When heated, noble gases glow a specific color. Helium was discovered by its characteristic colors coming from the Sun—and it was named after the Greek word helios for Sun. Electrifying noble gases has the same effect, and these are used in gas-discharge lamps—or neon lighting.

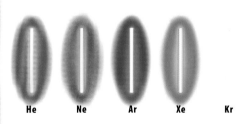

△ **Glowing gases**
In a neon light, electrical current runs through a tube of noble gas. As electrons are ripped off the atoms, they release a certain color of light.

REAL WORLD
Helium balloons

Helium is the second lightest gas in the Universe after hydrogen. Helium balloons float upward in the denser air gases. While hydrogen balloons and airships explode easily, helium balloons cannot burn, so they are safe to use in any size.

Transition metals

THE TRANSITION METALS ARE GROUPED IN A BLOCK THAT FORMS THE CENTER OF THE PERIODIC TABLE.

The transition metals make up a block from Groups 3 to 12 in the periodic table. They have distinct chemical properties because of the unique way that their electrons are arranged inside the atoms.

SEE ALSO	
⟨ 109 Electron configurations	
⟨ 112–113 Ionic bonding	
⟨ 118–119 Understanding the periodic table	
⟨ 120–121 Alkali metals and alkali earth metals	
Redox reactions	132–133 ⟩

Inner and outer electrons

The transition elements only have one or two outer electrons. This is because they can put more than eight electrons in the shell below the outermost shell. So as the atomic number of the elements increases along each period in this block, the extra electrons are not held in the atoms' outer shells, but are put in the next shell down, which can hold up to 18 electrons. This is known as back-filling.

▽ **Adding electrons**
Calcium is not a transition element. It has two outer electrons and eight in the next shell down (the third). However, next along in the periodic table is scandium—the first transition element. It has one more electron than calcium, but it sits in the third shell, so a scandium atom still has two outer electrons. Similarly, titanium has two outer electrons but ten in the third shell.

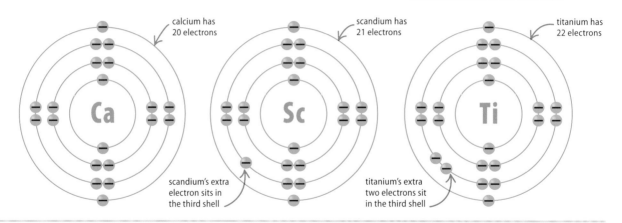

Different charges

Like other metals, transition elements lose their outer electrons easily to form positive ions. However, transition metals can then continue to lose electrons from the next shell down and so can form ions with a number of different charges, or oxidation states. An ion's oxidation state indicates how many electrons have been lost or gained: every electron lost increases the oxidation state by one; +2 means two electrons have been lost (see page 132). For example, manganese (Mn) forms ions with five common charges.

Oxidation state	Electrons lost by manganese
+2	two outer electrons
+3	two outer electrons and one inner electron
+4	two outer electrons and two inner elecrons
+6	two outer electrons and four inner electrons
+7	two outer electrons and five inner electrons

REAL WORLD
Most useful metals

Transition metals are less reactive than the alkali and alkali earth metals in Groups 1 and 2. Because of this, they have been used in technology for thousands of years. Iron is the most common transition metal. It is a very strong construction material. Nickel, another transition metal, is used in many coins.

Complex colors

A complex ion has a metal ion at its center with a number of other molecules or ions surrounding it. Transition elements form huge complex ions with molecules such as water, ammonia, and chlorine. The structures of these ions are very complicated and vary enormously. The wavelengths of light that these ions absorb and emit also varies enormously, so the compounds that they form come in a rainbow of different colors.

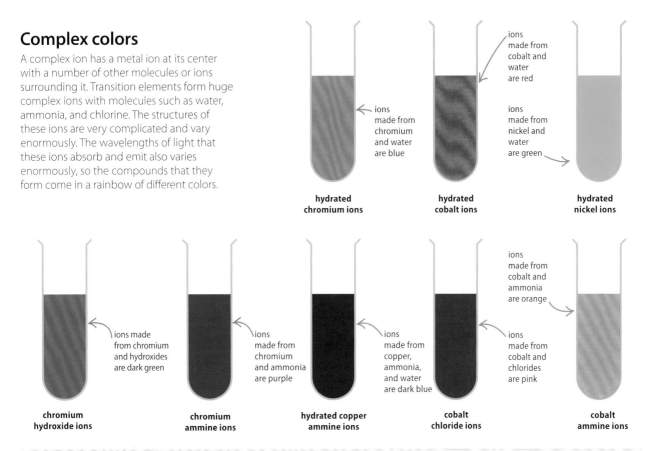

ions made from chromium and water are blue
hydrated chromium ions

ions made from cobalt and water are red
hydrated cobalt ions

ions made from nickel and water are green
hydrated nickel ions

ions made from chromium and hydroxides are dark green
chromium hydroxide ions

ions made from chromium and ammonia are purple
chromium ammine ions

ions made from copper, ammonia, and water are dark blue
hydrated copper ammine ions

ions made from cobalt and chlorides are pink
cobalt chloride ions

ions made from cobalt and ammonia are orange
cobalt ammine ions

Rare earth metals

The 30 rare earth metals are normally shown at the bottom of the periodic table, as there is no room to place them between Groups 2 and 3. They form in a similar way to the transition metals. Large atoms, from the sixth period on, grow by back-filling electrons, although this time the electrons are added two shells down, not one. The fourth and fifth atomic shells have room for 32 electrons.

▽ **Huge atoms**
Lanthanides are used to make high-tech alloys, while all of the actinides are radioactive. Uranium and thorium are used as nuclear fuels.

the rare earth metals are also referred to as the lanthanides and actinides, accordng to the first element in each period

many of the radioactive actinides only exist for a few seconds in laboratories

Radioactivity

WHEN AN ATOM HAS AN UNSTABLE NUCLEUS, IT CAN BREAK APART, EMITTING HIGH-ENERGY PARTICLES AND RADIATION.

SEE ALSO	
‹ 116–117 Periodic table	
Inside atoms	168–169 ›
Electromagnetic waves	194–195 ›
Energy from atoms	219 ›
The Sun	232–233 ›

A radioactive atom is generally very large, and its nucleus has a different number of neutrons from a stable atom. It is called a radioactive isotope of the element.

Radioactive decay

When an unstable nucleus breaks apart, or decays, it produces radiation. Gamma rays are one type of radiation. They are the highest energy waves in the electromagnetic spectrum. Sometimes a nucleus will emit fast-moving particles. Losing these alters the structure of the nucleus and produces a new element. Alpha particles are made up of two protons and two neutrons—the same as the nucleus of a helium atom. Beta particles are generally single electrons.

▽ **Alpha decay**
An alpha particle is formed when the parent atom's nucleus loses two protons and two neutrons. This decreases its atomic number (the number of protons in an atom) by two. So radioactive uranium (atomic number: 92) decays into thorium (90). The mass number (the number of protons and neutrons) decreases by four.

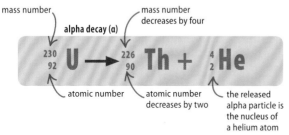

▽ **Beta decay**
A beta particle is formed when a neutron in the unstable nucleus splits into a proton and electron. The proton stays in the nucleus, raising the atomic number by 1, while the electron is pushed out. Therefore radioactive carbon atoms (atomic number: 6) form nitrogen (7). The nucleus has one less neutron but one more proton, so the mass number stays the same.

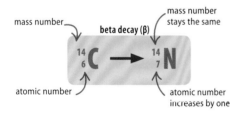

Dangerous radiation

Radioactive radiation is dangerous because it contains so much energy that it can ionize—knock electrons off—the atoms in living tissues. This damages the way cells work, causing them to die in large numbers, and can trigger cancers. Large alpha particles can only get into the body through food or drink, but can then cause a lot of damage. Gamma rays shine right through, but are less likely to hit a molecule and cause damage.

▽ **Penetrating power**
Alpha particles are blocked by the skin, although they can cause radiation burns. Beta particles bounce off thin sheets of metal, while it takes a thick layer of lead to shield against gamma rays.

REAL WORLD
Smoke detectors

Household smoke alarms contain tiny—and safe— amounts of americium, a radioactive element made in laboratories. The americium ionizes the air inside. A battery runs a current through it. When smoke gets in, the air is deionized and the current is blocked, triggering the alarm.

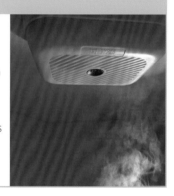

Half-life

Radioactive isotopes decay at a fixed rate that is measured as a half-life. This is the amount of time it takes for a sample to reduce its mass by half as it decays into other elements. Every radioactive isotope has a specific half-life. The more radioactive an isotope is, the shorter its half-life.

▷ **Fixed decay rate**
The half-life of a radioactive substance is the same whether there is a lot of it or a little. Here, the half-life is eight days. After eight days, 50 percent of the original sample is left, after another eight days only 25 percent of the sample is left, and so on.

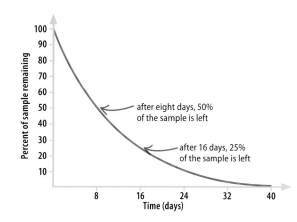

after eight days, 50% of the sample is left

after 16 days, 25% of the sample is left

Decay series

Radioactive isotopes often decay into daughter atoms that are also radioactive. The decay continues through a series of radioactive isotopes until finally stable atoms are formed. Members of a decay series may exist for just a fraction of a second, while others are around for years, only gradually breaking down into the next element in line.

▷ **Uranium 238 series**
This is the most common isotope of uranium. It decays in a series of alpha and beta emissions producing a series of radioactive isotopes before reaching a stable form of lead (Pb, mass number: 206). Each isotope decays at a different rate so each has a different half-life.

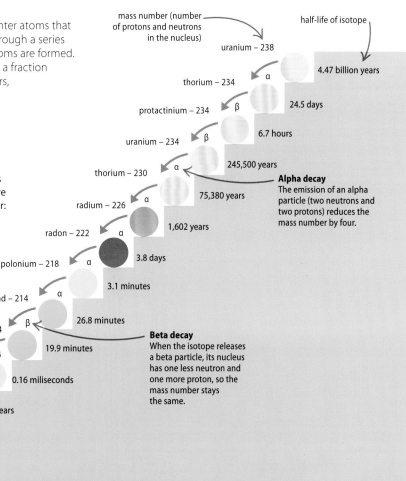

Alpha decay
The emission of an alpha particle (two neutrons and two protons) reduces the mass number by four.

Beta decay
When the isotope releases a beta particle, its nucleus has one less neutron and one more proton, so the mass number stays the same.

Chemical reactions

CHEMICAL REACTIONS ARE PROCESSES THAT CHANGE ONE SET OF SUBSTANCES INTO ANOTHER.

New bonds are made and existing ones are broken in a chemical reaction, which rearranges the atoms to form new substances.

SEE ALSO	
Combustion	130–131 ⟩
Redox reactions	132–133 ⟩
Energy and reactions	134–135 ⟩
Rates of reaction	136–137 ⟩
Catalysts	138–139 ⟩
Reversible reactions	140–141 ⟩

Start and end points

At the starting point of a chemical reaction are substances called reactants. Most reactions involve at least two reactants, although some involve only one reactant. The reactants can be compounds or pure elements. When they come into contact with each other, their ions and atoms are reorganized, resulting in the formation of a new set of substances, known as the products.

Self-rising flour produces gas bubbles by a chemical reaction to make cakes light.

▷ **Activating reaction**
During the reaction, the bonds between atoms in the reactants rearrange, which results in the formation of the products. In this case two reactants have combined to form one product.

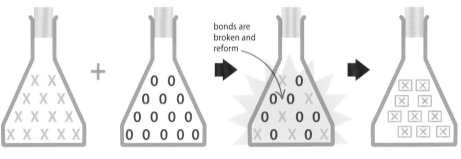

Conservation of matter

Atoms (or any other forms of matter) are neither created nor destroyed during chemical reactions. Every atom that was part of the reactants is present in the products, even if heat and flames are being released during the reaction. This principle is known as the conservation of matter.

▷ **Reactants**
Sodium reacts with water to produce the compound sodium hydroxide and bubbles of hydrogen gas.

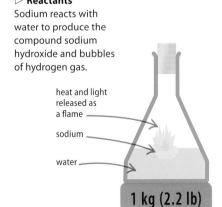

▷ **Products**
The weight of the products—sodium hydroxide and hydrogen—is the same as the weight of the reactants.

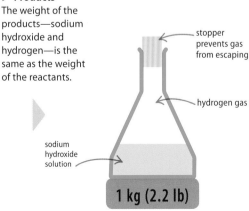

REAL WORLD
Sodas

The fizz of bubbles released when a sparkling drink is opened is produced by a decomposition reaction. Carbonic acid (H_2CO_3) dissolves in the water and breaks apart into carbon dioxide gas—which makes the refreshing bubbles—and more water.

CHEMICAL REACTIONS

Equations

Chemists use equations to represent what is happening during chemical reactions. The formula of each reactant is written on the left-hand side, and those of the products are shown on the right. An arrow indicates the direction in which the reaction occurs.

▽ Chemical symbols
Instead of using the elements' names, their chemical symbols are shown.

one iron atom · one sulfur atom · one iron sulfide molecule

$$Fe + S \rightarrow FeS$$

▽ Balanced equations
The number of atoms in the reactants is the same as the number of atoms in the products.

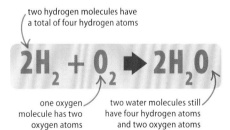

two hydrogen molecules have a total of four hydrogen atoms

$$2H_2 + O_2 \rightarrow 2H_2O$$

one oxygen molecule has two oxygen atoms · two water molecules still have four hydrogen atoms and two oxygen atoms

▽ Reaction conditions
The equation can also contain other information about the reaction, such as the state of the reactants and products.

two hydrogen chloride molecules · stands for "aqueous," or dissolved in water · two sodium atoms · stands for "solid" · two sodium chloride molecules · one hydrogen molecule has two hydrogen atoms · stands for "gas"

$$2HCl(aq) + 2Na(s) \rightarrow 2NaCl(aq) + H_2(g)$$

Types of reaction

There are three main types of chemical reactions. In a decomposition reaction, one complex product breaks apart into two (or perhaps more) simple products. In a synthesis reaction, two or more simple reactants join together to form a single, more complicated product. In displacement reactions, atoms or ions of one type swap places with those of another, forming new compounds.

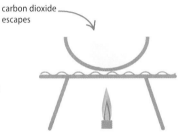

carbon dioxide escapes

◁ Decomposition reaction
Calcium carbonate ($CaCO_3$) decomposes into calcium oxide (CaO) and carbon dioxide (CO_2) when heated.

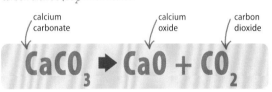

calcium carbonate · calcium oxide · carbon dioxide

$$CaCO_3 \rightarrow CaO + CO_2$$

◁ Synthesis reaction
Calcium oxide (CaO) powder and water (H_2O) combine in a synthesis reaction to form calcium hydroxide $Ca(OH)_2$), which dissolves in the remaining water.

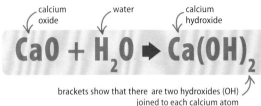

calcium oxide · water · calcium hydroxide

$$CaO + H_2O \rightarrow Ca(OH)_2$$

brackets show that there are two hydroxides (OH) joined to each calcium atom

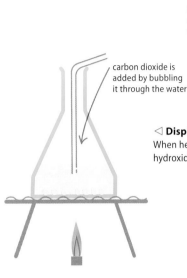

heat released makes the water boil

carbon dioxide is added by bubbling it through the water

◁ Displacement reaction
When heated gently, carbon dioxide (CO_2) displaces the hydroxide in calcium hydroxide ($Ca(OH)_2$) to make calcium carbonate ($CaCO_3$) and water (H_2O).

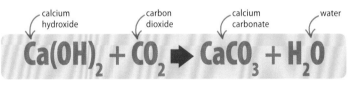

calcium hydroxide · carbon dioxide · calcium carbonate · water

$$Ca(OH)_2 + CO_2 \rightarrow CaCO_3 + H_2O$$

Combustion

COMBUSTION IS A REACTION THAT PRODUCES HEAT AND LIGHT IN THE FORM OF FLAMES AND EXPLOSIONS.

SEE ALSO	
Carbon and fossil fuels	156–157 ⟩
Hydrocarbons	158–159 ⟩
Heat transfer	188–189 ⟩
Using heat	190–191 ⟩

Most combustion reactions involve oxygen, heat, and fuel. All of these components are needed for the reaction to continue.

Heat and light

A flame is an area of hot glowing gases that have been released by a combustion reaction. For example, a candle wick is soaked with hot liquid wax that is a fuel and burns (undergoes a combustion reaction with oxygen in the air). The products of the reaction are carbon dioxide gas and water vapor. These glow briefly as they are released, contributing to the flame.

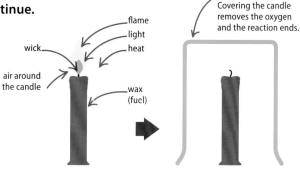

Gas tests

The gases commonly produced in chemistry experiments often look exactly the same. It may be dangerous to smell them—even if they have a characteristic odor. Chemists use combustion tests to identify the three most easily confused gases—hydrogen, oxygen, and carbon—in a safe way. A sample of each gas is exposed to a burning splint—a strip of dried wood used in a lab—and the gas can be identified by the characteristic way it combusts.

Combustion—and its fire—was the first chemical reaction that humans learned to control.

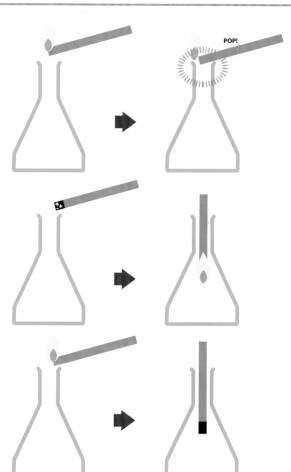

◁ **Hydrogen**
Hydrogen is very flammable and burns very quickly. A burning splint will pop before it even enters the flask as the hydrogen rushes out to the flame.

◁ **Oxygen**
Oxygen is the gas that fuels combustion. If a smouldering splint is exposed to a flask filled with oxygen, the wood will reignite and burst into flames.

◁ **Carbon dioxide**
Carbon dioxide is a common product of combustion reactions but it does not burn itself. A burning splint will go out when it is exposed to carbon dioxide.

COMBUSTION

Fuels

A fuel is a substance that burns readily and releases useful energy in the form of heat. Most fuels are carbon compounds. All fuels need to be handled with care so they do not burn too fast. Uncontrollably fast combustions create explosions in which large amounts of energy are released in a very short time.

△ **Wood**
Probably the first fuel used by humans, wood is largely cellulose, made from carbon molecules. Most dried wood burns at about 300°C (572°F), although some types get a lot hotter than this. Other materials are released as smoke when wood burns.

△ **Coal**
Coal is a flammable rock made from the remains of ancient trees exposed to pressure and heat over time. Its main constituent is pure carbon, although there are many other impurities, including sulfur. Most coals can burn at about 700°C (1,292°F).

△ **Methane**
Methane, or natural gas, is a simple gas made from hydrocarbons (see page 158). It is found in underground gas fields. It is also produced by natural processes in marshy areas and in the stomachs of herbivores. Its abundance makes it a very popular fuel.

△ **Gasoline**
Gasoline is a flammable liquid made from hydrocarbons, chiefly octane (C_8H_{18}). It is refined from crude oil (see page 157). The liquid is easy to store in tanks and pump around. It also ignites more easily than other fuels, even from its fumes.

△ **Paraffin wax**
Paraffin wax is a solid and is also made from refined crude oil. The solid does not burn easily, but when melted the liquid wax will ignite. Once lit, the process is self-sustaining—the heat of the combustion melts more of the solid into flammable liquid.

Fire control

Firefighters tackle fires using an understanding of combustion reactions. The fire triangle is a simple way of expressing the three things needed for combustion to continue: oxygen, heat, and fuel. Taking one of these components away will make the reaction end—and the fire go out.

▽ **Fire extinguishers**
Different fire extinguishers are designed to tackle fires fueled by different types of substances. For example, water is not used on burning liquid because the hot fuel bubbles up through it, making the water boil and spray the burning fuel into the air.

▷ **Oxygen**
This gas is one of the reactants in the combustion reaction. Firefighters smother a fire with foam, sand, or a blanket to cut off the oxygen supply.

◁ **Heat**
The heat released by the reaction is used to power the combustion of more fuel and oxygen. Adding water will cool the reaction and reduce its energy.

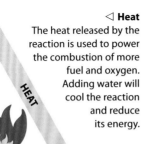

△ **Fuel**
Fire needs fuel. Firefighters have to consider what is burning before deciding how best to extinguish the fire safely and effectively.

Type of fire	Fire extinguishers			
	Water	Foam	CO_2	Powder
paper, wood, textiles, and plastics	✓	✓		✓
flammable liquids		✓	✓	✓
flammable gases				✓
electrical equipment			✓	✓

Redox reactions

IN A REDUCTION-OXIDATION (REDOX) REACTION, ELECTRONS ARE TRANSFERRED FROM ONE ATOM TO ANOTHER.

SEE ALSO	
⟨ 112–113 Ionic bonding	
Electrochemistry	148–149 ⟩
Refining metals	152–153 ⟩
Electric currents	203 ⟩

A redox reaction is one in which the oxidation state of one reactant rises as the oxidation state of the other falls to balance it. The oxidation state is the number of electrons added to or taken from an atom.

Oxidation states

Chemical reactions occur because most atoms have an incomplete outer shell of electrons, which makes them electrically unstable. To fill their outer shell they form bonds with other atoms in which they accept or donate electrons. The number of electrons that an atom needs to lose or gain to make itself stable is called its oxidation state. Any uncombined element has an oxidation state of zero.

△ **Positive or negative?**
The oxidation state, or number, shows the number of electrons that are gained or lost when an atom changes to an ion (see pages 112–113). The oxidation state of all uncombined elements is zero, as is the sum of the oxidation numbers in a neutral compound. For simple ions, the oxidation state is the same as the electrical charge of the ion.

Changing oxidation state

When atoms or ions undergo a reaction, their oxidation state changes. For example, the oxidation state of sodium changes from 0 to +1 because it has one electron in its outer shell to give away. It is easier for it to donate the electron than to try to fill up its shell with seven more electrons. On the other hand, chlorine has an oxidation state of -1 because it is lacking one electron to complete its outer shell.

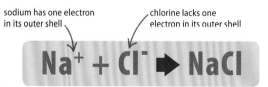

△ **Sodium chloride**
Sodium and chlorine make an ideal pair to form a compound because sodium has an electron to donate to chlorine.

Oxidation and reduction

When an atom (or ion) loses electrons during a chemical reaction it is said to have been "oxidized." The term "oxidation" originally applied to reactions where oxygen had combined with another substance, but now it is used in any reaction where electrons are donated. The atom or ion that gains electrons is said to have been "reduced." All redox reactions happen in pairs—for every reduction reaction there is a corresponding oxidation reaction.

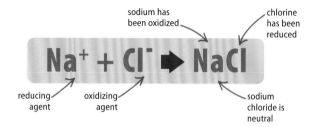

△ **Oxidizers and reducers**
The atom or ion that accepts the electrons is called the oxidizing agent, oxidant, or oxidizer. The atom or ion that donates the electrons is called the reducing agent.

REDOX REACTIONS

Electrochemistry

The exchange of electrons that occurs in redox reactions can be used to create an electric current in an apparatus called an electrochemical cell. The current forms when electrons are released from the oxidation reaction and made to travel to the reduction reaction, which will absorb the electrons. In this experiment, a piece of zinc metal is dipped in zinc sulfate and a piece of copper is put in copper sulfate. These two metals are connected by a conducting wire. The sulfate solutions have free ions, which can carry an electric current (see page 148).

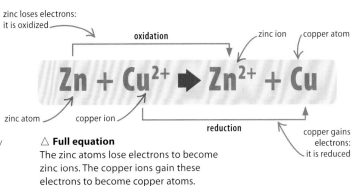

△ **Full equation**
The zinc atoms lose electrons to become zinc ions. The copper ions gain these electrons to become copper atoms.

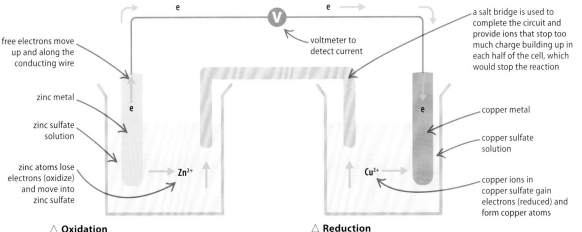

△ **Oxidation**
In the left half of the cell, oxidation occurs. The zinc metal atoms lose electrons to form zinc ions. The free electrons travel up and along the conducting wire to the reduction cell. The zinc ions (Zn^{2+}) move into the zinc sulfate solution.

△ **Reduction**
In the right half of the cell, reduction happens. Copper ions (Cu^{2+}) in the copper sulfate solution move to the piece of copper and accept two electrons each that have arrived from the oxidation cell. The copper ions thus become copper atoms.

Corrosion

A familiar phenomenon involving redox reactions is corrosion, in which metals and other materials are oxidized. Corrosion takes place in damp conditions, involving a reaction with oxygen or carbon dioxide and occasionally with pollutants such as hydrogen sulfide.

▷ **Types of corrosion**
The products of the reaction, such as rust, cause discolouration and weaken the original object.

Metal	Corrosion	Chemical name	Description
iron	rust	hydrated iron oxide	flaky rust expands and cracks the metal
copper	verdigris	copper carbonate	turns objects gray-green
aluminum	alumina	aluminum oxide	forms a dull layer on metal
silver	tarnish	silver sulfide	makes silver dark and dull
gold	no corrosion	none	gold always stays shiny

Energy and reactions

A LOOK AT THE WAY ENERGY IS INVOLVED IN CHEMICAL REACTIONS.

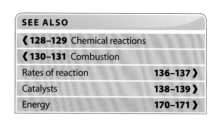

SEE ALSO
‹ 128–129 Chemical reactions
‹ 130–131 Combustion
Rates of reaction 136–137 ›
Catalysts 138–139 ›
Energy 170–171 ›

All chemical reactions require energy. Energy is needed to begin breaking and reforming atomic bonds. Most reactants need energy added to them before they will react.

Activation energy

The activation energy is the amount of energy that a reaction needs to begin. It is like a hill that the reactants have to get over. A reaction between a strong acid and alkali has low activation energy. It occurs as soon as the reactants are mixed because the molecules have enough energy already. The combustion of coal has a higher activation energy, so coal must be heated (adding energy) before it will burst into flames.

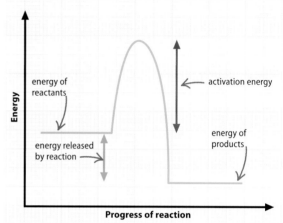

▷ **Energy graph**
When the energy involved in a reaction is shown as a graph, the activation energy forms a hump, over which the reactants must pass to form products.

Exothermic reaction

Chemical reactions need energy to begin, but they also release energy as the reactants reorganize into products. When the amount of energy released is greater than the activation energy, the reaction is exothermic. Exothermic reactions, such as the combustion of fuels, heat the surroundings with this release of energy.

▽ **Energy released**
In an exothermic reaction the energy in the products is lower than that in the reactants. This is because energy is lost as heat during the reaction.

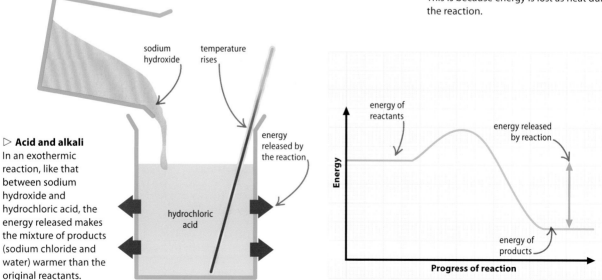

▷ **Acid and alkali**
In an exothermic reaction, like that between sodium hydroxide and hydrochloric acid, the energy released makes the mixture of products (sodium chloride and water) warmer than the original reactants.

Endothermic reaction

When the amount of energy released during a reaction is less than the activation energy, the process is decribed as endothermic. Because more energy is going into the reaction than is coming out, the reaction mixture and its surroundings become colder as their energy is taken in by the reaction.

▽ **Energy taken in**
In an endothermic reaction the products have more energy than the reactants. This is because energy is taken in from the surroundings during the reaction.

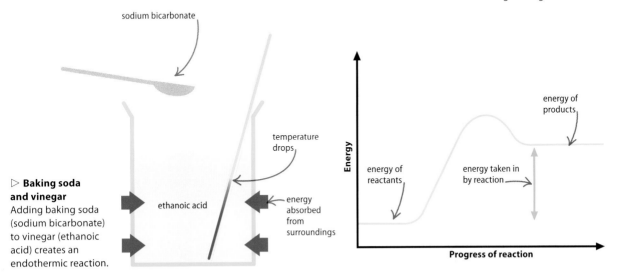

▷ **Baking soda and vinegar**
Adding baking soda (sodium bicarbonate) to vinegar (ethanoic acid) creates an endothermic reaction.

Calorimeter

All the energy used during a chemical reaction can be measured using a calorimeter. A reaction takes place in a central chamber, which is surrounded by water. The calorimeter is completely cut off from the outside, so any changes (rises and falls) in the water temperature can only be a result of the reaction taking place.

▷ **Bomb calorimeter**
This device is used to measure the energy in substances, including different foods. The sample is burned in pure oxygen and the amount of energy released is proportional to the rise in water temperature.

REAL WORLD

Hand warmers

Exothermic reactions are a convenient way of producing heat. Hand-warming packets and self-cooking cans contain two reactants in separate containers. When the hand warmer is bent in half, the containers rupture, mixing the reactants. Their reaction produces harmless products and enough heat to keep hands warm on cold days.

Rates of reaction

REACTANTS TURN INTO PRODUCTS AT DIFFERENT RATES.

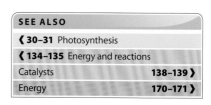

SEE ALSO	
‹ 30–31 Photosynthesis	
‹ 134–135 Energy and reactions	
Catalysts	138–139 ›
Energy	170–171 ›

Reaction rates depend on the substances involved. Dynamite burns so rapidly that it explodes in a fraction of a second, while an iron nail takes years to turn to rust.

Measuring rates

To understand what controls the speed of a reaction, a chemist first needs to be able to measure its rate—how quickly the reactants are converting into products. Only one product needs to be measured, since any others are produced at the same rate.

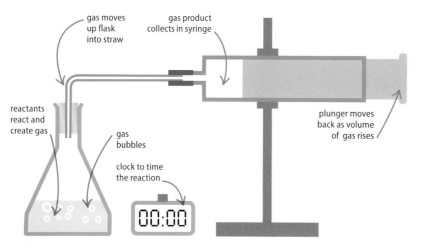

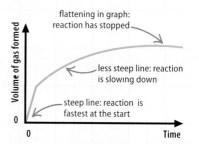

△ **Using a syringe to measure gas**
Measuring the increase in the volume of a gas product is relatively simple using a syringe. The measurements can be taken at regular intervals, timed by the clock. The volume will increase at a rate that is proportional to the reaction.

△ **Rate of reaction graph**
The volume measurements can be plotted against time on a graph. The steep line at the beginning shows that the rate of reaction starts very fast but then tails off.

Reactivity and temperature

Every reaction has an activation energy, which is the amount of energy the reactants need in order to break and reform atomic bonds. When a reaction has low activation energy, more of the reactants have the amount of energy needed and so the reaction occurs more quickly than a reaction with a higher activation energy. Heating the reactants—and increasing the pressure—adds energy and increases the rate of reaction.

▷ **Magnesium in water**
In cold water, magnesium reacts very slowly, forming magnesium oxide and bubbles of hydrogen. Heating the water to near its boiling point makes the same reaction run more quickly, making the water fizz with hydrogen bubbles.

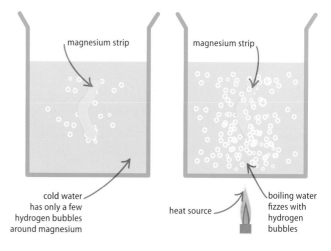

Concentration

Concentration is a measure of how much of a substance is present in a certain volume of a mixture. The rate of reaction is proportional to the concentrations of the reactants. Even if one reactant is present in large amounts, the reaction will only speed up as more of the other is added.

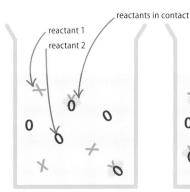

△ **Low concentration**
Reactants must make contact with each other to react. When reactants are mixed in low concentrations, they are widely dispersed and come into contact with each other infrequently.

△ **High concentration**
When reactants are mixed in higher concentrations, their molecules are less spread out and come into contact with each other more frequently. As a result, the rate of reaction is higher.

Particle size

When a solid reactant is added to a liquid or dissolved reactant, the reaction will proceed faster if the solid is crushed into powder rather than added as a single lump. The liquid reactant reacts with the surface of the solid, and the powdered reactant has a larger combined surface area than the single mass.

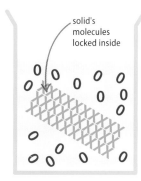

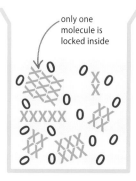

△ **Large solid, small area**
When the solid reactant is added as a big lump, the liquid reactant has fewer opportunities to react it. This is because many of the solid's molecules are locked away inside, out of reach of the liquid reactant.

△ **Small solids, large area**
The same amount of solid reacts much more quickly when broken up into smaller sizes. This is because more of its molecules are made available to take part in the reaction.

Light

Some reactions speed up when exposed to bright light or other higher energy forms of radiation, such as ultraviolet (UV) light. The reactants absorb the energy from certain wavelengths and this is enough to give them the activation energy to begin reacting. These reactions are called photochemical reactions. Photosynthesis, used in plants to turn carbon dioxide and water into glucose, needs light. Without it, the rate of reaction is negligible.

▷ **Ozone layer**
The reaction that creates ozone, a form of oxygen with three atoms per molecule happens mostly where high-energy light hits the high atmosphere. The ozone forms a layer in the high atmosphere and helps to absorb the dangerous UV rays in sunlight.

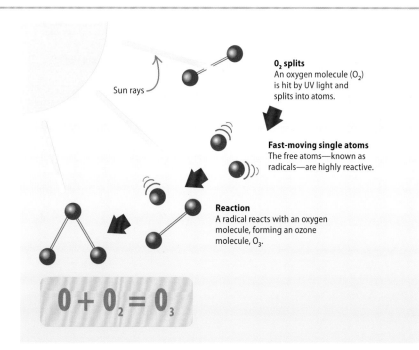

$O + O_2 = O_3$

Catalysts

CATALYSTS SPEED UP REACTIONS BY LOWERING THE ACTIVATION ENERGY REQUIRED.

SEE ALSO	
‹ 67 Digestive chemicals	
‹ 134 Activation energy	
‹ 136 Reactivity and temperature	
Energy	170–171 ›

Various catalysts used in laboratories and industry make chemical reactions run faster and allow unreactive materials to get involved in reactions. The enzymes that control reactions in cells are also catalysts.

Less energy needed

Many reactions have activation energies that are so high that the reactions never happen on their own—or happen so slowly that they are hardly noticeable. Catalysts make such reactions possible by reducing the activation energy needed.

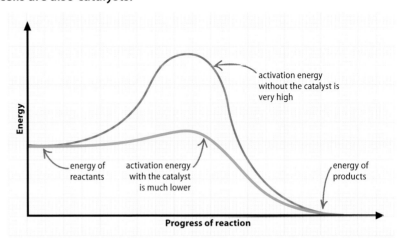

▷ **Energy graph**
Catalysts reduce the energy barrier between reactants and products. In industry, a catalyst can make reactions more economical.

How catalysts work

Catalysts are a highly varied group of materials. Many are porous substances with tiny spaces inside where the reactants are brought together in such a way that they react without the need for a lot of energy. The precise mechanisms vary but usually a catalyst facilitates a reaction by providing an intermediary phase between the reactants and the products. The catalyst is involved in the reaction but not consumed by it.

▷ **Reactant 1 bonds with catalyst**
One reactant bonds temporarily with the catalyst, forming a complex molecule.

▷ **Reactant 2 joins in**
The molecule bonds with the other reactant, bringing the reactants close together.

▷ **Product forms**
While held in this way, the reactants need much less energy to react. The product can form easily.

The word **"catalyst"** comes from the Greek word meaning "to untie."

▷ **Catalyst breaks away**
The product breaks from the catalyst, which is unchanged by the reaction and available to repeat its role.

Enzymes

Most of the chemical reactions that take place inside living bodies would not happen without the catalytic effect of enzymes. Enzymes are protein molecules that are highly folded into shapes specific to their roles. These shapes create an area known as the enzyme's active site. The reactants—known as substrates in biochemistry—are also molecules with complex shapes. They fit onto the enzyme's active site, where the reaction takes place. Enzymes are used in the digestive system to break down large molecules of food into smaller ones.

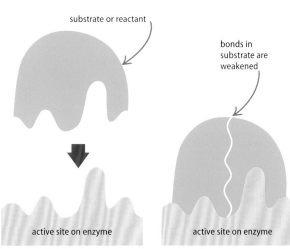

△ **Active site**
Only a specific substrate can bond to a specific enzyme's active site, like a key fitting into a lock.

△ **Catalyzed reaction**
When joined to the enzyme, the chemical reaction can take place. Bonds within the substrate are weakened.

△ **Products produced**
The substrate divides into two products. These break off the active site, leaving it free to collect a new substrate.

Catalytic converter

Every new car is fitted with a catalytic converter, or "cat." The engine exhaust passes through this device before it enters the air. Inside is a honeycomb-shaped ceramic coated with a thin layer of a platinum and rhodium alloy, which is the catalyst. The catalyst changes dangerous gases, such as carbon monoxide (CO), nitrogen oxides (NO), and unburned hydrocarbons, into comparatively harmless ones—carbon dioxide (CO_2), nitrogen (N_2), and water (H_2O).

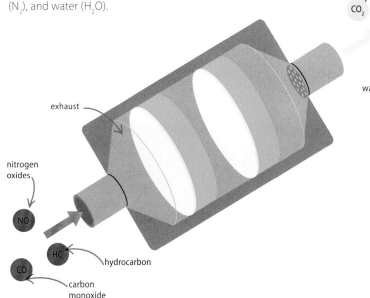

REAL WORLD
Margarine

Margarine is made using a catalyst. The starting materials are vegetable oils: long chain molecules made from carbon and hydrogen. The oils are unsaturated—their molecules have room for more hydrogen atoms. Hydrogen is bubbled through the oil over a nickel catalyst, which saturates the oil molecules, turning them into a butterlike solid.

Reversible reactions

SOME REACTIONS CAN BE REVERSED.

SEE ALSO
⟨ 100–101 Changing states
⟨ 102–103 Gas laws
⟨ 128–129 Chemical reactions
⟨ 134–135 Energy and reactions
Pressure 184–185 ⟩

In general, chemical reactions run in just one direction. The energy that is required to turn the products back into reactants is just too great for it to happen. However, some reactions are easily reversible.

Two-way reactions

A reversible reaction is one that can go backward as well as forward—products that form can easily be turned back into the original reactants. The amounts of energy needed to make the reaction run in either direction are rarely equal, but there is not a large difference between the two. A common reversible reaction is to use heat to drive water from a solid. This is reversed by simply adding water.

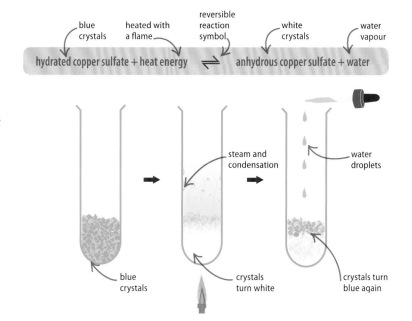

▷ **Hydrating crystals**
Copper sulfate crystals are blue due to water molecules locked inside them. Heating the crystals drives out water and they turn into the white anhydrous (without water) form. However, adding water easily reverses the process.

Dynamic equilibrium

Reversible reactions do not normally run one way and then the other. They run in both directions simultaneously. However, it is the rate of reaction in each direction that dictates the yield (the proportions of reactants and products). When the rate of reaction in both directions is the same, the reaction is in equilibrium.

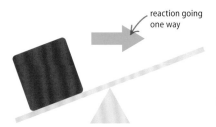

△ **One way**
At the start of the reaction, few products have formed so the reaction runs in one direction. The high concentration of reactants makes the rate of reaction high.

△ **Mostly one direction**
Although there is still a high concentration of reactants, the reaction is starting to go backward. However, the concentration of products is increasing.

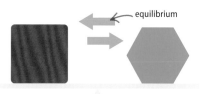

△ **Dynamic equilibrium**
Products are being made at the same speed as they turn back into reactants but the reactions continue. This stage in the reaction is called dynamic equilibrium.

Temperature

If a change such as temperature is made to a reaction in equilibrium, the speed of the forward or backward reaction will adjust to counter the effects of that change. Every reversible reaction has an exothermic direction (giving out energy) and an endothermic one (taking in energy). If heated, the reaction that takes in heat (the endothermic direction) will speed up to balance the effect of the heating.

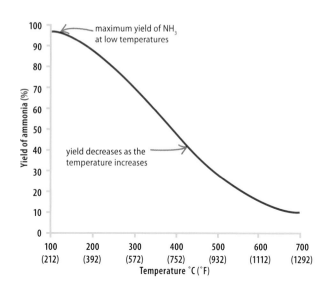

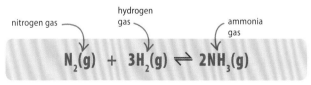

▷ **Making ammonia**
Nitrogen and hydrogen give out heat when they react to form ammonia. Adding heat reduces the yield of ammonia because more of the compound decomposes back into hydrogen and nitrogen.

Pressure

Pressure also affects the equilibrium in reactions involving gases. Pressure is caused by gas molecules hitting the sides of the container. The more molecules there are, the higher the pressure in the container. Increasing the pressure during a reversible reaction shifts the equilibrium toward the side with fewer molecules. In the equation for making ammonia there are four molecules of reactants (one molecule of nitrogen and three molecules of hydrogen) and two molecules of product (ammonia). An increase in pressure favors the forward direction of the reaction, which produces ammonia, rather than the reverse.

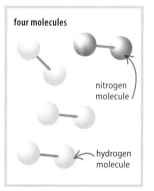

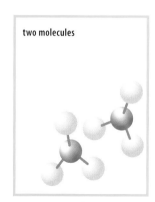

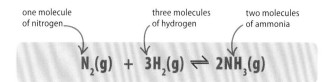

△ **Reactants**
Increasing the pressure pushes the hydrogen and nitrogen molecules together and drives the reaction to produce ammonia.

△ **Products**
Only two ammonia molecules are produced, which take up less space than the reactants. This makes the pressure fall.

Photosynthesis is a reversible reaction. If there is too much sugar and oxygen in a plant cell, **photorespiration** occurs, turning them back into carbon dioxide and water.

REAL WORLD
Quicklime

Quicklime is a chemical made by heating calcium carbonate. The heat makes the carbonate decompose into quicklime and carbon dioxide. However, these two products can then react back into calcium carbonate. To stop this, the kiln draws carbon dioxide away from the quicklime.

Water

ONE OXYGEN ATOM AND TWO HYDROGEN ATOMS BOND TO FORM THE COMPOUND WATER.

SEE ALSO
‹ 78–79 Cycles in nature
‹ 104–105 Mixtures
‹ 115 Intermolecular forces
The Earth 226–227 ›

Water is one of the very few natural substances that are liquid in everyday conditions. Its unusual properties stem from the oxygen atom in its molecules.

Hydrogen bonds

In addition to the covalent bonds that join the hydrogen and oxygen atoms in a water molecule, there are bonds between the molecules themselves. The electrons in the covalent bond are pulled closer to the oxygen atom than to the hydrogen atoms. This makes the oxygen atom negatively charged and the hydrogen atoms positive. These opposite charges on different molecules attract each other in what is known as a hydrogen bond.

▷ **Dipole** The areas of charge in the water molecule are called poles. A hydrogen bond is formed between the negative end of one molecule and the positive end of another.

— the oxygen atom forms the negative end of the dipole
— positive and negative ends attract each other and form a hydrogen bond between the molecules
— each hydrogen atom forms the positive end of the dipole

States of water

On Earth, water is mainly liquid—it covers 70 percent of the planet's surface. However, the other states of water are just as familiar—polar regions are covered in ice, while the atmosphere is filled with water vapor. Like all gases, water vapor has a lower density than water. However, almost uniquely among natural substances, when water freezes into ice (solid) it expands and has a lower density. As a result, ice floats on water. With other substances, their solid states have higher densities and sink under their liquid states.

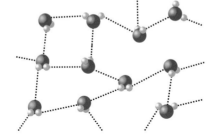

◁ **Ice**
An ice crystal is held together with hydrogen bonds. As the crystal forms, the molecules spread out so each molecule can bond with three others. This makes the molecules take up a larger volume.

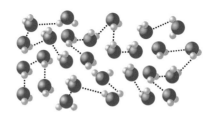

◁ **Liquid water**
In liquid water there are fewer hydrogen bonds. The molecules can get closer to each other, taking up less volume. The bonds break and reform, allowing the molecules to move around.

◁ **Water vapor**
In the gaseous form, the water molecules of water are independent of each other and can move around freely. Water vapor forms below the boiling point of water, while steam is technically vapor above 100°C (212°F).

Water is **densest at 4°C (39°F)**, which is the temperature at the bottom of the deepest ocean floors.

Universal solvent

Water is sometimes known as the universal solvent because so many substances dissolve in it. The property is another result of water molecules' polarity. Ionic substances are made up of charged particles bonded together. When they are added to water, the ions split from their opposite partners and form bonds with the positive and negative ends of the water molecules.

REAL WORLD
The Dead Sea
When things dissolve in water they make it more dense. Seawater is more dense than freshwater because it has salt dissolved in it. The water in the Dead Sea is so salty that it is much denser than the human body. That is why bathers can float so easily.

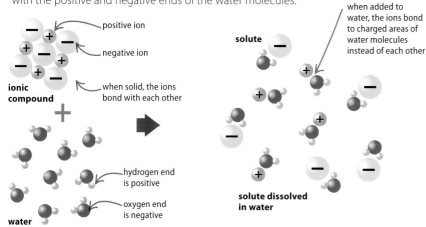

Water hardness

Hardness is the term used to describe how many minerals are dissolved in water. Temporary hardness is largely due to dissolved calcium hydrogen carbonate. When the water is heated it decomposes into carbon dioxide, water, and solid calcium carbonate. This solid is called limescale and builds up on heating equipment like kettles. Other calcium (and magnesium) compounds form permanent hardness. They can affect the taste of drinking water and the action of soaps. A water softener replaces minerals that cause hardness with sodium ions, which do not cause as many problems.

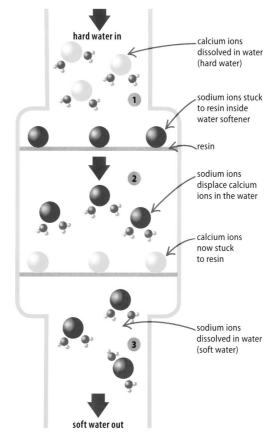

1. Hard water in
Dissolved calcium ions make the water hard. This hard water is fed into the softener before it reaches the tap.

2. Inside the softener
The softener contains a porous resin filled with sodium ions. As the hard water flows though, the sodium ions displace (swap places with) the less reactive calcium ions in the water.

3. Soft water out
The water flowing out of the softener contains sodium ions, while the calcium ions are left behind in the resin. The resin needs to be replaced regularly or washed with a sodium solution to restock the sodium ions.

Acids and bases

ACIDS AND BASES ARE CHEMICAL OPPOSITES, BUT THESE TWO TYPES OF COMPOUNDS ARE CLOSELY RELATED.

SEE ALSO	
‹ 89	Acid rain
‹ 112–113	Ionic bonding
‹ 114–115	Covalent bonding
‹ 120	Why alkali?
‹ 136–137	Rates of reaction

The chemistry of acids and bases is driven by hydrogen ions. Acids are substances that produce hydrogen ions; bases are substances that react with acids by accepting these hydrogen ions.

What is an acid?

Acids are compounds that release positively charged particles of hydrogen, called hydrogen ions (H^+), when dissolved in water. These ions are highly reactive and can bond to other substances and have a corrosive effect on them. The strength of an acid depends on the number of hydrogen ions that it can release.

DNA, the chemical that carries genetic code, is a type of acid.

▽ Strong acids
The most powerful acids are ionically bonded compounds (see page 112). They split into hydrogen and other ions completely when dissolved in water, thus releasing large quantities of free hydrogen ions.

Name	Formula	Where it is found
hydrochloric acid	HCl	the stomach
sulfuric acid	H_2SO_4	car batteries
nitric acid	HNO_3	process to make fertilizers

▽ Weak acids
Acids which have a covalent structure (see page 114) do not break up into ions so easily. They have complex molecules, but sometimes the bond holding a certain hydrogen ion weakens, allowing it to break off.

Name	Formula	Where it is found
citric acid	$C_6H_8O_7$	lemon juice
ethanoic acid	CH_3COOH	vinegar
formic acid	HCOOH	ant stings

What is a base?

A base is a compound that reacts with an acid by accepting its hydrogen ions. The most reactive bases are soluble compounds called alkalis. As it dissolves, an alkali releases hydroxide ions (OH^-). The hydrogen and hydroxide ions combine very readily to form water, so the reaction between an acid and an alkali is often vigorous.

▽ Common alkalis
Any compound with a hydroxide ion is known as an alkali. Alkalis are used in industry to make soaps and are added to waste to help it decay more rapidly.

Name	Formula	Where it is found
sodium hydroxide	NaOH	oven cleaner
magnesium hydroxide	$Mg(OH)_2$	indigestion tablets
potassium hydroxide	KOH	soap

Neutralization

The reaction between an acid and an alkali (or other base, such as an oxide) is called neutralization, because it results in products that are neither acid nor alkali. One of the products is always water. The other, known as the salt, is a compound formed from the left-over ions.

▽ General equation
An acid and base always react to produce a salt and water. The salt produced when hydrochloric acid (HCl) reacts with sodium hydroxide (NaOH) is sodium chloride (NaCl)— better known as common salt.

$$\text{acid} + \text{base} \rightarrow \text{salt} + \text{water}$$
$$HCl(aq) + NaOH(aq) \rightarrow NaCl(aq) + H_2O(l)$$

Measuring acidity

Acidity is measured in pH, which stands for "power of hydrogen." Neutral substances such as water have a pH of 7. A substance with a pH lower than this is acidic; one with a pH higher than this (up to 14) is alkaline. The pH measures the concentration of hydrogen ions. Each whole pH number on the scale is ten times more acidic or basic than the previous number. For example, a substance with a pH of 6 has ten times more hydrogen ions in it than water, which has a pH of 7.

▷ **Indicators**
Chemicals used to test whether a substance is acid or alkaline are called indicators. Litmus was the first indicator used to show pH. It produces a red color for acid and blue for alkali. However its range of colors is limited, making it hard to judge the precise pH. A dye called universal indicator is more practical and produces a wide range of colors indicating where the solution fits into the pH scale.

REAL WORLD
Indigestion tablets

The discomfort of indigestion is caused by digestive acids leaking out of the stomach into the esophagus. This causes a burning sensation as it attacks the soft lining of the throat. Antacid tablets contain alkalis—often magnesium hydroxide—that neutralize these acids into harmless salts.

Rainwater is slightly acidic because carbon dioxide dissolves in it, making carbonic acid.

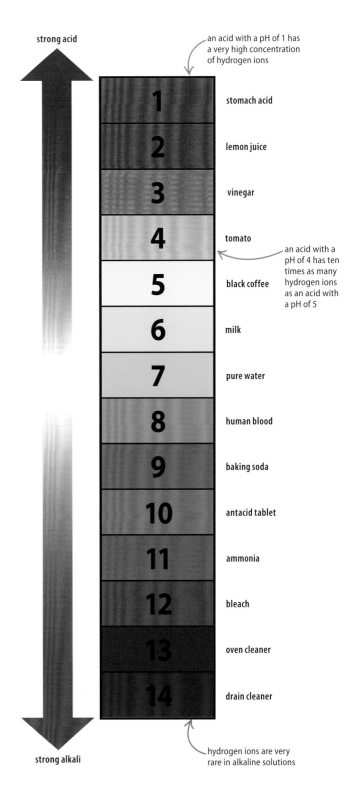

strong acid

1 stomach acid — an acid with a pH of 1 has a very high concentration of hydrogen ions
2 lemon juice
3 vinegar
4 tomato — an acid with a pH of 4 has ten times as many hydrogen ions as an acid with a pH of 5
5 black coffee
6 milk
7 pure water
8 human blood
9 baking soda
10 antacid tablet
11 ammonia
12 bleach
13 oven cleaner
14 drain cleaner — hydrogen ions are very rare in alkaline solutions

strong alkali

Acid reactions

ACIDS REACT WITH A RANGE OF OTHER SUBSTANCES IN PREDICTABLE WAYS.

SEE ALSO	
‹ 28–29 Respiration	
‹ 89 Acid rain	
‹ 128–129 Chemical reactions	
‹ 144–145 Acids and bases	
Alcohols	160–161 ›

Although acids come in many forms, they all react in the same way. When any acid is added to metals, oxides, or other compounds, the reaction generates the same set of products.

Acids and metals

If a metal is more reactive than the hydrogen in an acid, they will react to form a salt and hydrogen gas. The most reactive metals, such as potassium, even do this with water—which contains hydrogen but is, by definition, neutral. Metals such as copper and gold are less reactive than hydrogen, so they do not react with most acids.

▽ **General equation**
Iron displaces the hydrogen in the sulfuric acid (H_2SO_4), forming a salt, iron sulfate ($FeSO_4$), which is an ionically bonded compound. The hydrogen has nothing else to react with, so it is released as a gas.

acid + metal = salt + hydrogen
$H_2SO_4(aq) + Fe(s) \rightarrow FeSO_4(aq) + H_2(g)$

▽ **Iron plus sulfuric acid**
When solid iron is added to the acid, the mixture begins to fizz with hydrogen bubbles. The iron sulfate salt dissolves forming a green solution.

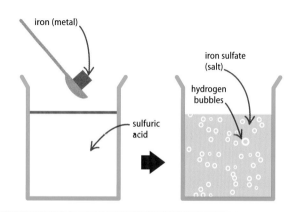

REACTION OF METALS			
Name	Reacts with water	Reacts with most acids	Level of reaction
potassium	yes	yes	high
sodium	yes	yes	
lithium	yes	yes	
calcium	yes	yes	
magnesium	no	yes	
aluminum	no	yes	
zinc	no	yes	
iron	no	yes	
tin	no	yes	
lead	no	yes	
copper	no	no	
mercury	no	no	
silver	no	no	
gold	no	no	no reaction

REAL WORLD
Acid rain

Rainwater is naturally slightly acidic because carbon dioxide gas in the air dissolves in it, making weak carbonic acid. When this acidic rain falls on certain stones it reacts with the chemicals in the stones, gradually eating away at them in a process called weathering.

ACID REACTIONS

Acids and oxides

When an acid reacts with an oxide (a compound with oxygen), it forms a salt and water. The hydrogen ions from the acid and the oxide ions form the water molecules. The cation (the positively charged portion of the oxide)—generally a metal ion—then forms a salt with the anion (the negative part of the acid).

▽ **General equation**
The acid–oxide reaction has the same products as an acid-base reaction (see page 144).

acid + oxide = salt + water
$H_2SO_4(aq) + CuO(s) \rightarrow CuSO_4(aq) + H_2O(l)$

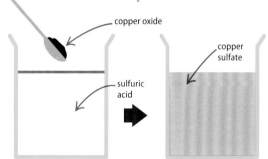

▽ **Sulfuric acid (H_2SO_4) plus copper oxide (CuO)**
The black copper oxide powder added to colorless sulfuric acid produces copper sulfate salt ($CuSO_4$) dissolved in the water (H_2O), a blue solution.

Acids and carbonates

When an acid reacts with a carbonate, the products are a salt, water, and carbon dioxide. A carbonate is an ionic compound in which the anion is CO_3^{2-}. The carbonate ion is displaced in the reaction by the anion from the acid. The carbonate ion then reacts with the free hydrogen ion to form water and carbon dioxide.

▽ **General equation**
The acid-carbonate reaction produces a salt, water, and also carbon dioxide gas.

acid + carbonate = salt + carbon dioxide + water
$H_2SO_4(aq) + CaCO_3(s) \rightarrow CaSO_4(aq) + CO_2(g) + H_2O(l)$

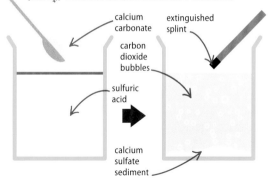

▽ **Sulfuric acid (H_2SO_4) + calcium carbonate ($CaCO_3$)**
White calcium carbonate powder added to sulfuric acid produces carbon dioxide (CO_2) and calcium sulfate ($CaSO_4$), which is insoluble and forms a sediment.

Acids and sulfites

A sulfite is a compound made up of at least one cation, often a metal, and a sulfite SO_3^{2-} ion. When a sulfite reacts with an acid, the products are a salt, water, and sulfur dioxide. The sulfite ion is displaced in the reaction by the anion from the acid. The sulfite ion then reacts with the free hydrogen to form water and sulfur dioxide gas.

▽ **General equation**
This reaction is very similar to that of the acid-carbonate reaction, except sulfur dioxide gas is formed instead of carbon dioxide.

acid + sulfite = salt + sulfur dioxide + water
$2HCl(aq) + CuSO_3(s) \rightarrow CuCl_2(aq) + SO_2(g) + H_2O(g)$

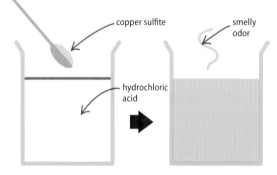

▽ **Hydrochloric acid (HCl) plus copper sulfite ($CuSO_3$)**
Blue copper sulfite crystals added to clear hydrochloric acid produces the green salt copper chloride ($CuCl_2$), dissolved in water, and smelly sulfur dioxide (SO_2).

Electrochemistry

ELECTRICITY IS USED IN CHEMISTRY TO ALTER COMPOUNDS OR TRANSFER MATERIALS.

SEE ALSO	
‹ 112–113 Ionic bonding	
‹ 133 Electrochemistry	
Refining metals	152–153 ›
Electricity	202–203 ›

The energy carried by electric currents can be used in chemistry. Currents are frequently used to force compounds apart, by converting ions back into atoms to produce pure elements.

Electrolytes

An electrolyte is a liquid that conducts electricity. It is an ionic compound and has to be liquid (molten or in a solution) so that its component ions are free to move. A power source is connected to two electrodes that are placed in the electrolyte. This creates a positive charge at one electrode (the anode) and a negative charge at the other (the cathode). The positive and negative ions in the electrolyte then move toward the electrode with the opposite charge, where they receive or donate electrons. This flow of ions carries electricity through the liquid.

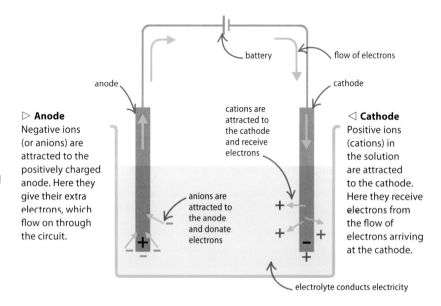

▷ **Anode**
Negative ions (or anions) are attracted to the positively charged anode. Here they give their extra electrons, which flow on through the circuit.

◁ **Cathode**
Positive ions (cations) in the solution are attracted to the cathode. Here they receive electrons from the flow of electrons arriving at the cathode.

Electrolysis

Passing an electric current through an ionic compound will split it into its component elements. This is called electrolysis and was the process used to isolate many new elements for the first time. When the power source is turned on, the positive and negative ions in the compound are attracted to their oppositely charged electrodes. At the cathode, positive ions receive electrons and, at the anode, negative ions lose electrons, so the ions become neutral atoms again. The pure elements build up at each electrode and can be collected. Water is an ionic compound (H_2O) that can be split into hydrogen (H) and oxygen (O) in this way.

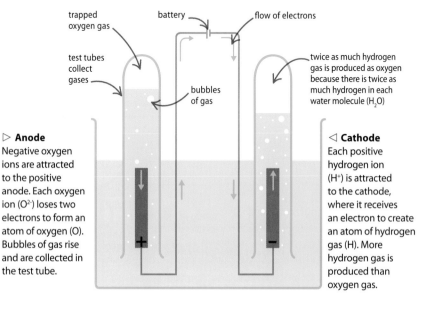

▷ **Anode**
Negative oxygen ions are attracted to the positive anode. Each oxygen ion (O^{2-}) loses two electrons to form an atom of oxygen (O). Bubbles of gas rise and are collected in the test tube.

◁ **Cathode**
Each positive hydrogen ion (H^+) is attracted to the cathode, where it receives an electron to create an atom of hydrogen gas (H). More hydrogen gas is produced than oxygen gas.

Purifying metals

Electrochemistry can be used to remove impurities from a metal and make an extremely pure sample. The piece of impure metal is used as the anode. A pure sliver of the same metal is the cathode. When the current is switched on, the metal ions in the impure metal leave the anode and dissolve in the electrolyte, a copper sulfate solution. Here they are free to move to the cathode, where they receive electrons and turn back into metal atoms.

Electrolysis hair removal uses electricity to turn salts in the hair into alkalis that kill the roots.

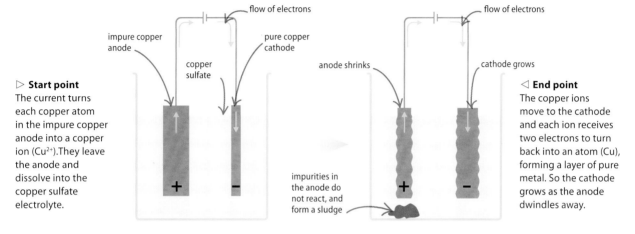

▷ **Start point**
The current turns each copper atom in the impure copper anode into a copper ion (Cu^{2+}). They leave the anode and dissolve into the copper sulfate electrolyte.

◁ **End point**
The copper ions move to the cathode and each ion receives two electrons to turn back into an atom (Cu), forming a layer of pure metal. So the cathode grows as the anode dwindles away.

Electroplating

A thin layer of precious metal can be added to a less expensive metal object using a process called electroplating. A piece of precious metal, such as gold or silver, is used as the anode. The item to be plated forms the cathode. The electrolyte also contains ions of the precious metal. The current makes the anode gradually dissolve and the precious metal ions transfer to the cathode, where they coat the object.

REAL WORLD
Galvanization

Electroplating can be used to coat and protect steel with a layer of zinc to make galvanized steel. This zinc-plated steel is more resistant to corrosion than iron (the main constituent of steel).

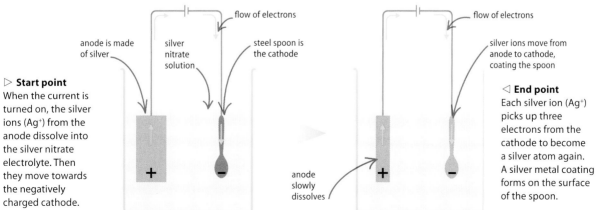

▷ **Start point**
When the current is turned on, the silver ions (Ag^+) from the anode dissolve into the silver nitrate electrolyte. Then they move towards the negatively charged cathode.

◁ **End point**
Each silver ion (Ag^+) picks up three electrons from the cathode to become a silver atom again. A silver metal coating forms on the surface of the spoon.

Lab equipment and techniques

A GUIDE TO THE BASIC APPARATUS IN A CHEMISTRY LAB AND HOW IT IS USED.

SEE ALSO
⟨ 98–99 States of matter
⟨ 106–107 Separating mixtures
⟨ 128–129 Chemical reactions
⟨ 130–131 Combustion

Every chemistry lab has some basic apparatus that can be used for heating substances, observing reactions, and finding out more about materials.

Bunsen burner

This simple gas burner was designed in the late 19th century by German chemist Robert Bunsen. It is used as the primary source of heat in chemistry experiments. The burner has two main settings that can be adjusted by opening and closing an air hole on its base. When the air hole is closed, the burner has a luminous flame. When the hole is opened, it lets in more air, which creates a very hot and roaring blue flame.

▷ **Different flames**
The roaring blue flame is used to heat reactants and boil liquids during experiments. The luminous flame, which is taller and not so hot, is used to ignite splints and burn powders in flame tests (see page 130).

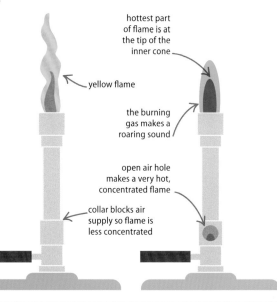

Measuring liquids

Chemists must be careful when measuring the volume of liquids. The surfaces of liquids are not flat, but have a curved edge called the meniscus. Water, like most liquids, has a concave meniscus. Other liquids, such as mercury, have a convex surface.

▷ **Measure at eye level**
To measure a volume, the eye should be level with the meniscus.

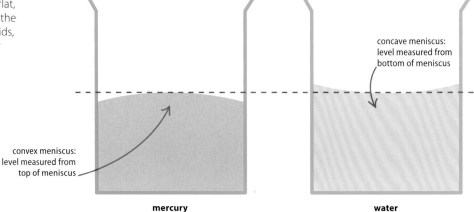

LAB EQUIPMENT AND TECHNIQUES

Moles

Chemists measure quantities of reactants and products in moles. A mole is a standard unit of atoms. It is defined as the number of atoms in 12 g (0.5 oz) of carbon. This mass is known as the relative atomic mass (RAM) of carbon. A mole of anything else contains this same number of atoms (roughly 6.02×10^{23}), but because atoms have different masses, a mole of one element will have a different mass from a mole of another. Compounds have relative formula masses (RFM), which are calculated by adding up the RAM of their constituents.

Element	RAM
hydrogen	1
carbon	12
oxygen	16
sodium	23
sulfur	32
iron	56
gold	197

△ **Relative atomic mass**
Atoms of different elements have different masses, so moles of different substances have different masses too. For example, one mole of carbon weighs twelve times more than one mole of hydrogen.

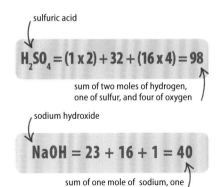

sulfuric acid
$$H_2SO_4 = (1 \times 2) + 32 + (16 \times 4) = 98$$
sum of two moles of hydrogen, one of sulfur, and four of oxygen

sodium hydroxide
$$NaOH = 23 + 16 + 1 = 40$$
sum of one mole of sodium, one of oxygen, and one of hydrogen

△ **Relative formula mass**
The RFM of a compound is the sum of the RAM of each of its constituent atoms.

Apparatus diagram

Chemists often draw the apparatus they use in experiments so that other scientists can replicate the equipment. The apparatus is drawn in a simple, two-dimensional style that makes each item easy to recognize. Test tubes, beakers, conical flasks, and other items of glassware are used to hold reactants during heating. They are frequently positioned on a steel tripod that holds them above the Bunsen burner.

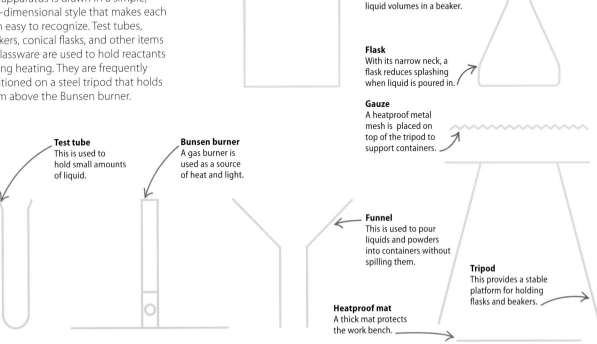

Test tube
This is used to hold small amounts of liquid.

Bunsen burner
A gas burner is used as a source of heat and light.

Beaker
The flat sides of a beaker make it easier to measure liquid volumes in a beaker.

Flask
With its narrow neck, a flask reduces splashing when liquid is poured in.

Gauze
A heatproof metal mesh is placed on top of the tripod to support containers.

Funnel
This is used to pour liquids and powders into containers without spilling them.

Heatproof mat
A thick mat protects the work bench.

Tripod
This provides a stable platform for holding flasks and beakers.

Refining metals

THE CHEMICAL PROCESSES THAT EXTRACT PURE METALS FROM ORES.

SEE ALSO
⟨ 124–125 Transition metals
⟨ 129 Types of reaction
⟨ 132–133 Redox reactions
⟨ 148–149 Electrochemistry

Few metals are found pure in nature. Most exist in ores, compounds rich in metals that have to be chemically altered to remove the pure metal.

Iron smelting

The most common iron ores are oxides (in which iron is bonded to oxygen), such as hematite (Fe_2O_3). The ores have their oxygen removed in a process called smelting, which takes place in a blast furnace. The reducing agent (the substance that removes the oxygen) is carbon monoxide, a gas that is sformed by burning coke, a form of coal. The heat from the combustion of coke also powers the various reactions taking place. Impurities such as silicon dioxide are also removed in the process.

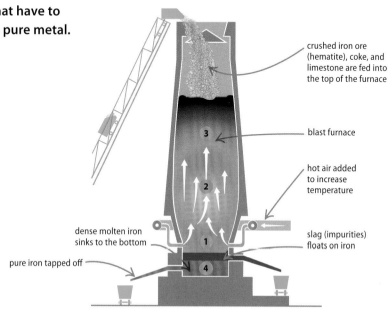

- crushed iron ore (hematite), coke, and limestone are fed into the top of the furnace
- blast furnace
- hot air added to increase temperature
- slag (impurities) floats on iron
- dense molten iron sinks to the bottom
- pure iron tapped off

1. $2C + O_2 \rightarrow CO_2 + C \rightarrow 2CO$
The coke is more or less pure carbon. It burns near the bottom of the furnace with oxygen, forming carbon dioxide. The carbon dioxide then reacts with more carbon to form carbon monoxide (CO).

2. $3CO + Fe_2O_3 \rightarrow 3CO_2 + 2Fe$
The carbon monoxide rises and reacts with the hot ore in the middle of the furnace. Because the carbon in the gas is more reactive than iron, it takes the oxygen ions from the ore, forming pure iron and carbon dioxide gas.

3. $CaCO_3 \rightarrow CaO + CO2$
Calcium carbonate (limestone) is also added to the furnace. The heat from the combustion at the bottom makes the calcium carbonate decompose into calcium oxide (quicklime) and carbon dioxide.

4. $CaO + SiO_2 \rightarrow CaSiO_3$
The quicklime moves to the bottom, where molten iron is being formed. Quicklime is very reactive and reacts with impurities in the iron, such as silicon dioxide, removing them to form a waste product called slag.

Thermite process

Another way to extract pure iron from its ores is to burn it with pure aluminum, a more reactive metal. This very rapid reaction is called the thermite process and it is exothermic (see page 134). Aluminum is more reactive than iron so it snatches the oxygen from the iron ore, leaving free elemental iron and aluminum oxide.

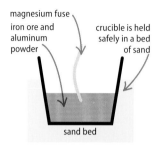

△ **Before**
Powdered iron ore and aluminum are mixed in a heat-resistant crucible. The reaction is ignited with a strip of magnesium that burns white hot.

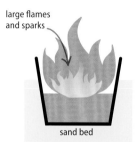

△ **Reaction**
The aluminum snatches the oxygen from the iron, forming aluminum oxide. The reaction releases a large amount of heat with sparks and flames.

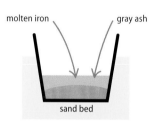

△ **After**
The heat melts the iron and it sinks to the bottom of the crucible. The molten iron is surrounded by the gray crystals of aluminum oxide.

Aluminum production

Aluminum cannot be reduced easily like iron. It is too reactive so there are no suitable reducing agents. Therefore this extremely useful metal is extracted from its ore—generally bauxite (Al_2O_3)—by electrolysis (see page 148). The ore is dissolved in molten cryolite (a mineral compound of sodium, aluminum, and fluorine). This electrolyte (liquid that can conduct electricity) is more than 1,000°C (1,832°F) and is held in a tank or cell, lined with graphite carbon. This lining acts as the negatively charged cathode, while more graphite blocks are used as the positively charged anodes.

> Before the invention of electrolysis in the 1880s, pure **aluminum was more expensive than gold.**

▷ **The Hall-Héroult process**
This process is named after Martin Hall and Paul Héroult, who invented it independently of each other in the late 1880s. When an electric current is passed through the electrolyte, it is broken down into positively charged aluminum ions and negatively charged oxygen ions, which are free to move.

1. Al^{3+} (l) + 3e⁻ ➡ Al (l)
Positive aluminum cations are attracted to the negative cathode. Here, each ion (Al3+) receives three electrons from the cathode lining, changing it into an atom of aluminum. The liquid aluminum pools on the cathode at the bottom of the cell and is drained off regularly.

2. $2O^{2-}$ (l) + C (s) ➡ CO_2 (g) + 4e⁻
Negative oxygen ions are attracted to the positive anodes, where each ion loses two electrons to form an oxygen atom. The oxygen reacts with the carbon in the anode to produce carbon dioxide gas, which bubbles out of the liquid. As the carbon is used up, the anodes gradually corrode and need to be replaced.

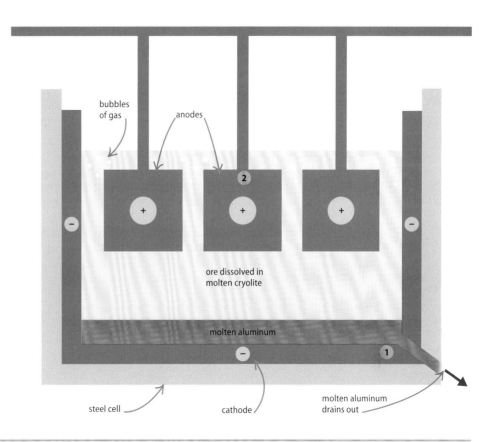

Alloys

Two or more metals—and sometimes other elements—are mixed together to form an alloy. Alloys exhibit some of the properties of all their individual constituents, so they can be adapted to suit many applications. The first metal implements created by humans were made of bronze, a mixture of copper and tin, two metals that were easy to extract from ores.

COMMON ALLOYS				
Name	Main metal	Other metal	Properties	Uses
carbon steel	iron	carbon	high strength	construction
stainless steel	iron	chromium	resistant to corrosion	eating utensils
bronze	copper	tin	easily worked	bells
brass	copper	zinc	does not corrode	zippers, keys
solder	tin	lead	low melting point	soldering
invar	iron	nickel	does not expand when hot	precision
amalgam	mercury	silver	starts soft, then hardens	dental fillings

Chemical industry

SOME CHEMICAL REACTIONS ARE PERFORMED ON A HUGE SCALE TO PRODUCE VALUABLE SUBSTANCES.

SEE ALSO	
‹ 78–79	Cycles in nature
‹ 128–129	Chemical reactions
‹ 144–145	Acids and bases
‹ 148–149	Electrochemistry

Many of the raw materials that humans need exist in nature. They are refined from ores or separated from mixtures such as seawater. Some compounds, however, are made in factories using chemical reactions.

The Haber process

Also known by its full name, the Haber-Bosch, this process turns nitrogen and hydrogen gas into ammonia (NH_3). Ammonia is used to make crop fertilizers and explosives, such as TNT and dynamite. Nitrogen is the most common gas on Earth—it makes up 78 percent of the air—but it is very unreactive. The Haber process uses a catalyst (see page 138) to make the reaction occur.

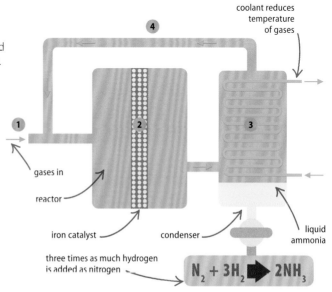

1. Gases mixed
A mixture of hydrogen (H_2) and nitrogen (N_2) gases is pumped into the reactor. Three times as much hydrogen is added as nitrogen to create the correct ratio for ammonia (3:1).

2. In the reactor The gases are passed over an iron catalyst, which brings them together so they react to form ammonia. The reaction takes place at 450°C (842°F) and at 200 times the atmospheric pressure.

3. Product separated
The ammonia gas leaving the reactor moves into the condenser, where it is cooled so that it turns into liquid ammonia that can then be tapped off.

4. Reactants recycled Not all of the reactants turn into ammonia. The unused nitrogen and hydrogen gases rise out of the condenser and are recycled back into the reactor.

Nitric acid production

One of the chemicals that is made from ammonia is nitric acid (HNO_3). This acid reacts with bases to form nitrate salts, which plants need to make proteins. Nitric acid is mainly used to make fertilizers, but it is also used as a rocket fuel and is one of the few solvents that can dissolve gold.

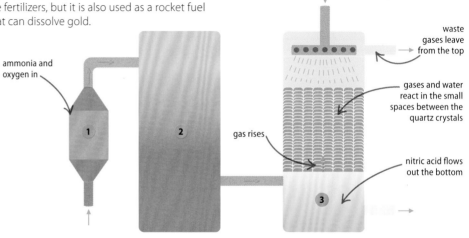

1. Converter
In the converter, ammonia (NH_3) and oxygen (O_2) react at 800°C (1,472°F) using a platinum catalyst to make nitric oxide (NO) and water.

2. Oxidation chamber
The gases from the converter are cooled to 100°C (212°F). More oxygen is added, some of which will react with the nitric oxide to make nitrogen dioxide (NO_2).

3. Absorption tower
Water trickles down through the quartz crystals while the gases rise. The nitrogen dioxide and left-over oxygen react with the water to form nitric acid.

CHEMICAL INDUSTRY

Contact process

This is the industrial process for making sulfuric acid. Sulfur dioxide gas reacts with water using a catalyst to produce the acid in a multistage process. Sulfuric acid is one of the most powerful acids. It is used in car batteries and its salts (the sulfates) are used in fertilizers. It is also used in papermaking.

1. Furnace
In the furnace, sulfur (S) is burned with oxygen (O) from the air to form sulfur dioxide (SO_2).

2. Cleaning the gas
In the next three chambers, the gas is filtered, washed, and dried to remove any impurities that could interfere with the catalyst.

3. Reactor
The vanadium oxide catalyst makes the sulfur dioxide react with more oxygen to form sulfur trioxide (SO_3).

4. Absorption tower
The sulfur trioxide is dissolved in a little sulfuric acid. This makes it safe to dilute with water to make a lot more sulfuric acid—the end product.

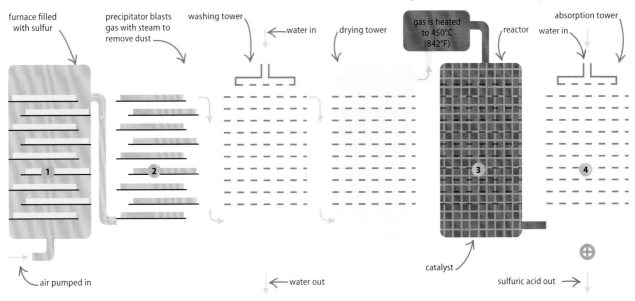

Downs cells

Pure chlorine gas (Cl_2) and sodium metal (Na) are made by the electrolysis of sodium chloride (common salt: NaCl). This takes place on an industrial scale in a large tank called a Downs cell. The tank contains liquid salt—it is heated to more than 600°C (1,112°F) so that the salt melts. When an electric current is run through the liquid, the molten salt breaks up into sodium and chloride ions, which move to the electrodes and turn into atoms. The pure elements can then be collected.

1. At the iron cathode ($2Na^+ + 2e^- \rightarrow 2Na$)
Positive sodium ions (Na^+) move to the cathode, where they gain an electron each to form sodium atoms (Na). This metal is less dense than the sodium chloride electrolyte so it floats to the surface where it can be collected.

2. At the carbon anode ($2Cl^- \rightarrow Cl_2 + 2e^-$)
Negative chlorine ions (Cl^-) are attracted to the positively charged anode, where they lose an electron each to form chlorine atoms (Cl). The element bubbles out of the liquid electrolyte as chlorine gas (Cl_2).

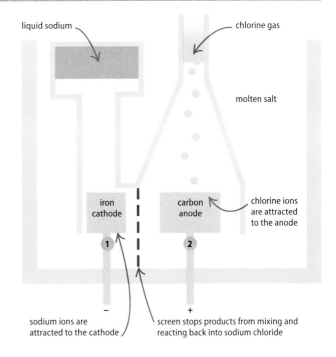

Carbon and fossil fuels

CARBON AND ITS COMPOUNDS FORM THE BASIS FOR ALL FOSSIL FUELS.

SEE ALSO	
‹ 78 The carbon cycle	
‹ 131 Fuels	
Hydrocarbons	158–159 ›

After hydrogen, carbon is the most common element in living things. When organisms die, their remains are preserved underground. Over millions of years are transformed into useful, carbon-rich compounds called fossil fuels.

Forms of carbon

Pure carbon exists in different forms, or allotropes (see page 111). The carbon atoms in each allotrope link up in different ways, which gives the allotropes very different properties. Diamond is an extremely hard and sparkling gem. The arrangement of the atoms in graphite, however, make it a slippery gray solid, often used as pencil lead.

△ **Diamond**
The carbon atoms are arranged in a very rigid crystal network based on repeating tetrahedra of four atoms.

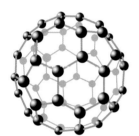

△ **Fullerene**
The atoms link together to form a ball-shaped cage. Fullerenes may contain 100, 80, or 60 carbon atoms.

△ **Graphite**
The atoms are arranged in sheets of hexagons. The sheets are only loosely bonded, so they slip over each other.

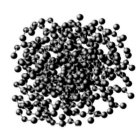

△ **Soot**
The atoms in this allotrope are arranged randomly. Soot forms from the uncombusted carbon released when fossil fuels burn.

Coal

Coal is a carbon-rich sedimentary rock made from the remains of trees. Most of the coal mined today formed from forests that grew around 300 million years ago. The plant material was buried in the absence of oxygen, so huge amounts were preserved as sediments, gradually forming coal.

▷ **Coal formation**
The process begins when plant remains sink in waterlogged, boggy soil. The lack of oxygen prevents the wood from decaying. These remains form a dense soil called peat, which can itself be used as a fuel when dried. Over time the peat is buried, and the increased pressure drives out the water to form lignite (soft, brown rock). Deeper down, heat hardens the lignite into coal.

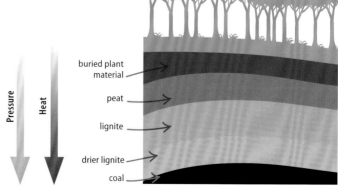

Petroleum

Petroleum—meaning "rock oil"—is a mixture of natural compounds known as hydrocarbons, which are made from carbon and hydrogen. Petroleum forms from a thick ooze of dead microorganisms that covered the beds of ancient seas. After being buried by other sediments, the biological material broke down into hydrocarbons over millions of years.

▷ **Oil and gas fields**
Petroleum oil or gas is a natural product that percolates up through porous rocks to the surface. When the petroleum's passage is blocked by nonpermeable rock, it accumulates as an oil (or gas) field.

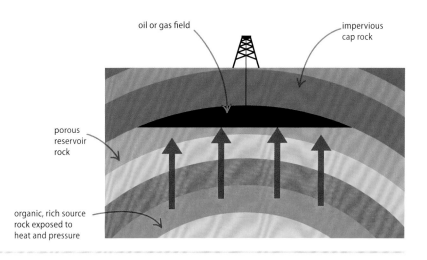

Crude oil distillation

The mixture of hydrocarbons collected from underground reservoirs of petroleum is known as crude oil. It contains thousands of mostly liquid compounds—the gas given off is known as natural gas. Crude oil is separated into useful fractions: groups of compounds that have similar boiling points, indicating that their molecules have a similar size.

▷ **Fractional distillation**
Oil is separated in a fractionating tower. The oil is heated and most of it boils and rises upward as vapor. It cools as it rises, and each fraction condenses at a certain height up the tower.

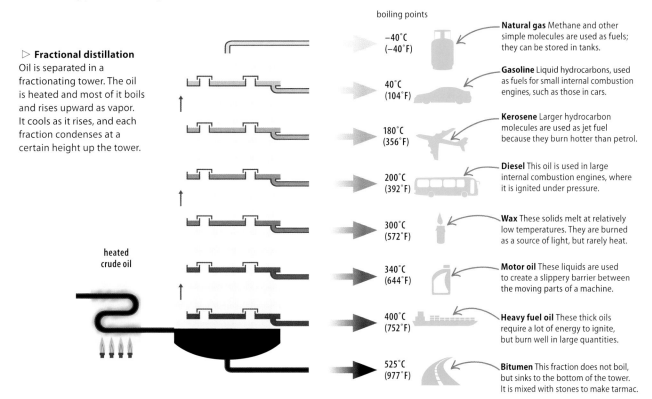

Natural gas Methane and other simple molecules are used as fuels; they can be stored in tanks.

Gasoline Liquid hydrocarbons, used as fuels for small internal combustion engines, such as those in cars.

Kerosene Larger hydrocarbon molecules are used as jet fuel because they burn hotter than petrol.

Diesel This oil is used in large internal combustion engines, where it is ignited under pressure.

Wax These solids melt at relatively low temperatures. They are burned as a source of light, but rarely heat.

Motor oil These liquids are used to create a slippery barrier between the moving parts of a machine.

Heavy fuel oil These thick oils require a lot of energy to ignite, but burn well in large quantities.

Bitumen This fraction does not boil, but sinks to the bottom of the tower. It is mixed with stones to make tarmac.

Hydrocarbons

THE DIFFERENT FAMILIES OF COMPOUNDS MADE PURELY FROM CARBON AND HYDROGEN.

SEE ALSO
‹ 110–111 Compounds and molecules
‹ 114–115 Covalent bonding
‹ 156–157 Carbon and fossil fuels

Hydrocarbons are the simplest compounds in living things. The study of chemicals found in living things is called organic chemistry.

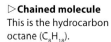

Hydrocarbon chains

Carbon atoms can form up to four covalent bonds. This allows carbon to form intricate hydrocarbon molecules. The carbon atoms are chained together, with hydrogen atoms bonded to the spare electrons. When hydrogen atoms are not available, two carbon atoms may form double, and even triple, bonds.

▷ **Chained molecule**
This is the hydrocarbon octane (C_8H_{18}).

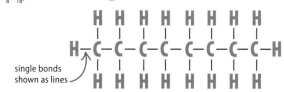

◁ **Letter diagram**
This is octane shown simply with the chemical symbols for carbon (C) and hydrogen (H).

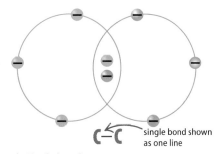

△ **Single bond**
The normal carbon-to-carbon covalent bond involves sharing a single pair of electrons.

△ **Double bond**
This bond has two pairs of electrons shared between the atoms. It is less stable than a single bond.

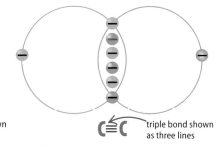

△ **Triple bond**
This very unstable bond contains three shared pairs of electrons to form a triple bond.

Naming system

Hydrocarbons with chained and branched molecules are known as aliphatics. They are named with a prefix that is specific to the number of carbon atoms in their longest chain. Side branches on the main chain are also named using the same prefixes. These branches are known as alkyl groups, and so the prefix is followed by the suffix "–yl" to show they relate to a branch other than the main chain. For example a methyl chain is a side branch with one carbon atom.

Prefix	Number of carbon atoms
meth	1
eth	2
prop	3
but	4
pent	5
hex	6

△ **Prefixes**
The first four prefixes are specific to hydrocarbons, while from five onward the prefixes are based on Latin and Greek numbers.

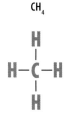

△ **Methane**
The simplest hydrocarbon is also known as natural gas and is burned as a fuel.

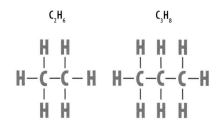

△ **Ethane**
Ethane has two carbon atoms, and is the compound used to make polythene plastic.

△ **Propane**
With three carbon atoms, propane gas is the fuel supplied in the tanks used in camping stoves.

HYDROCARBONS

Alkanes, alkenes, and alkynes

Chained hydrocarbons form families according to how their carbon atoms are bonded. Hydrocarbons with single bonds are called alkanes. Chains with at least one double bond are alkenes. A triple-bonded compound is an alkyne.

Suffix	Contains
ane	carbon–carbon single bonds
ene	carbon–carbon double bonds
yne	carbon–carbon triple bonds

◁ **Suffix**
Compounds are given a suffix to show which family they belong to.

◁ **Ethane**
The single bond in ethane makes this hydrocarbon relatively stable and unreactive.

◁ **Ethene**
The double bond makes ethene more flammable than ethane.

◁ **Ethyne**
The triple bond is very unstable. Ethyne and all alkynes are highly flammable and reactive.

reactivity increasing →

Isomers

Aliphatic compounds can have the same formula—the number of carbon and hydrogen atoms—but be arranged in different ways. These similar compounds are known as isomers. Side branches change the way isomers behave, making them react differently and have different melting and boiling points.

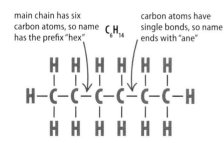

△ **Hexane**
This liquid alkane has six carbon atoms in a single chain. It has a total of four isomers and its main use is in petrol.

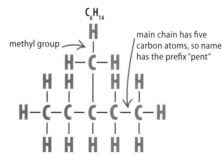

△ **Methylpentane**
The longest chain in this compound is a pentane. A methyl group (side chain with one carbon) adds the sixth carbon atom.

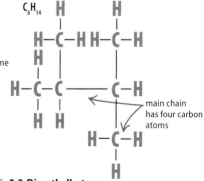

△ **2,3-Dimethylbutane**
The longest chain in this isomer is a butane. Two methyl groups are attached to second and third carbon atoms in the butane.

Aromatics

Hydrocarbons can also form ringed molecules called aromatics. The simplest of these is benzene (C_6H_6), which has six carbon atoms linked with alternating single and double bonds. The electron pairs forming the three double bonds are free and shared between all six carbon atoms, forming a ring-shaped "delocalized" bond.

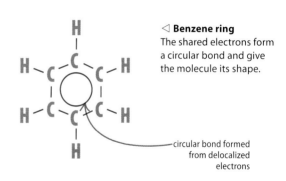

◁ **Benzene ring**
The shared electrons form a circular bond and give the molecule its shape.

circular bond formed from delocalized electrons

Functional groups

HYDROCARBONS CAN REACT WITH OTHER ELEMENTS.

> **SEE ALSO**
> ◀ 28–29 Respiration
> ◀ 78–79 Cycles in nature
> ◀ 144–145 Acids and bases

These "functional groups" of additional elements dominate the compound's chemical behavior.

Alcohols

These are organic molecules in which an oxygen and hydrogen (–OH) is added to the carbon chain, in the place of a hydrogen atom. Ethanol—the alcohol with two carbon atoms—is the compound in alcoholic drinks. It is produced by natural fermentation processes and can be metabolized by the body. However, all other alcohols are much more poisonous.

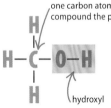

△ **Methanol**
This simplest alcohol is used as an antifreeze and solvent.

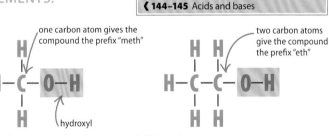

△ **Ethanol**
This alcohol is found in beer and wine and is purified into liquors.

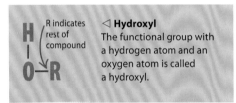

◁ **Hydroxyl**
The functional group with a hydrogen atom and an oxygen atom is called a hydroxyl.

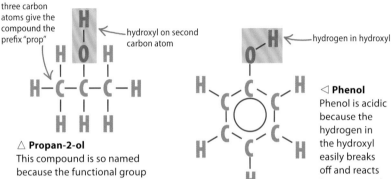

△ **Propan-2-ol**
This compound is so named because the functional group is on the second carbon atom.

◁ **Phenol**
Phenol is acidic because the hydrogen in the hydroxyl easily breaks off and reacts (see page 144).

Carboxylic acids

Organic acids have a carboxyl group (COOH). The hydrogen breaks off and reacts with alkali compounds and metals. The rest of the molecule forms a carboxylate ion with a charge of –1. The salts produced when the acid reacts are called carboxylates. Most carboxylic acids are weak and have a maximum pH of around 3 or 4.

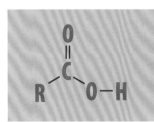

◁ **Carboxyl**
The carboxyl group is formed from the carbon at the end of a chain joined to one oxygen atom with a double bond and to a hydroxyl group with a single bond.

CFCs or chlorofluorocarbons, the chemicals that damage the ozone layer, are organic halide compounds.

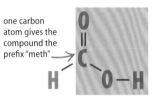

△ **Methanoic acid**
Also known as formic acid, this is the simplest carboxylic acid. It is used to soften animal hides into leather.

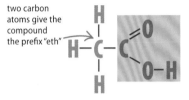

△ **Ethanoic acid**
Also known as acetic acid, this is the sour-tasting ingredient in vinegar. It forms naturally from ethanol due to the action of bacteria.

FUNCTIONAL GROUPS

Esters

When a carboxylic acid reacts with an alcohol, they form an ester. The functional group of the ester links the two original molecules together. The fats and oils in living things—including the lipids that form cell membranes—are esters. Soaps, oils, and fats are also all types of ester.

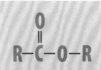

△ **Functional group**
The oxygen from alcohol bonds to the carboxyl (carbon and oxygen group) from the acid.

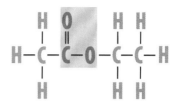

△ **Ethyl ethanoate**
This ester has a strong pear drop smell and is used as nail varnish remover.

△ **Thiol smells**
The odor in garlic as well as the noxious smell sprayed by skunks is due to a thiol. Its functional group is called a sulfydryl.

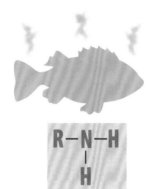

△ **Amine smells**
The smell of fish is due to the presence of a compound called trimethylamine. Its functional group includes nitrogen.

Thiols and amines

Thiols are similar to alcohols, except the functional group has a sulfur instead of an oxygen atom. The word "thiol" is a mixture of the Latin words for sulfur and alcohol. These compounds have strong smells. Amines are another smelly group of organic compounds. They have a functional group with one nitrogen and two hydrogen atoms. When an amine group attaches to a carboxylic acid, it forms an amino acid, one of the building blocks of proteins.

REAL WORLD
Ant stings

Some insect venoms, especially the stings of fire ants, have methanoic acid as their active ingredient. A fire ant squirts the acid onto attackers, causing small but painful burns. The original name, formic acid, is derived from the Latin word for "ant."

Organic halides

Members of the halogen group (see page 122) form only one bond in chemical reactions, just like hydrogen, but they are much more reactive. Halogens replace hydrogen atoms in hydrocarbon molecules, forming organic halides.

◁ **Chloromethane**
With just a single chlorine atom, this is the most reactive of this family of compounds. One of its uses is to make silicone rubbers.

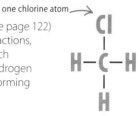

△ **Dichloromethane**
This sweet-smelling liquid is used in paint strippers, aerosol sprays, and to decaffeinate coffee.

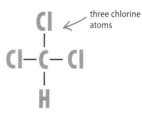

△ **Trichloromethane**
Better known as chloroform, this compound was one of the first anesthetics.

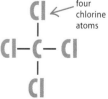

△ **Tetrachloromethane**
Also known as carbon tetrachloride, this toxic liquid is banned in some countries.

Polymers and plastics

COMPOUNDS FORMED FROM LONG CHAINS OF SMALLER MOLECULES ARE CALLED POLYMERS.

SEE ALSO	
‹ 84–85 Genetics	
‹ 96–97 Properties of materials	
‹ 158–159 Hydrocarbons	
Stretching and deforming	174–175 ›

Plastics and other artificial fibers, such as nylon, are familiar types of polymers. However, these long-chained molecules are also widespread in nature. Many of the chemicals in food are polymers too.

Monomers

The repeating units in a polymer are called monomers. A polymer may contain a single type of monomer or have two or more types of repeating units—known as copolymers. Monomers are held together by covalent bonds (see page 114). Many artificial polymers are derived from alkene monomers, which have double bonds that can be broken and reformed to make the chains.

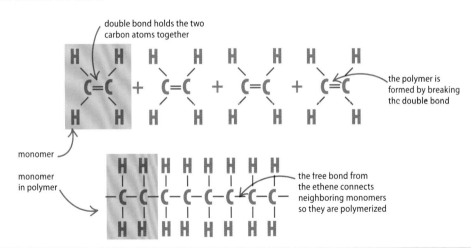

▷ **Ethene monomer**
One of the most common plastics is made from chains of ethene monomers. Ethene is the simplest alkene molecule. Its polymer is called polythene.

▷ **Polythene polymer**
While ethene is a gas, polythene (also known as polyethylene) is a transparent solid. It can be formed from an unlimited number of ethene monomers.

Natural polymers

The natural world contains many polymers. Living things frequently digest these large compounds, breaking them into their monomers, which are absorbed and then rebuilt into different polymers.

△ **Protein**
Muscles and many other features in a living body are made from proteins, which are polymers of amino acid monomers.

△ **DNA**
DNA is a complex copolymer. The sides are formed from chains of sugar, while the crosslinks are pairs of four monomers called nucleic acids.

△ **Cellulose**
The wall around a plant cell is made from a polymer of glucose called cellulose. Cellulose forms tough fiber and is a major component of wood and paper.

△ **Starch**
Found in potatoes and bread, starch is also made from glucose monomers. However, they are chained together differently to form globules rather than fibers.

Plastics

Many artificial polymers are plastics. A plastic is an incredibly useful material that can be molded into any shape while hot, becoming solid when cool. It can also be pulled into thin films and used as a protective coating. Plastic is made from monomers derived from crude oil.

▽ **Common plastics**
Several plastics have become very familiar over the last few decades, because they have a huge range of applications.

Polymer	Monomer	Properties of polymer
polythene (polyethylene)	ethene	makes flexible plastics; is used in packaging and to insulate electrical wires
polystyrene	styrene	used to make Styrofoam; is also added to other polymers to make them waterproof
PVC (polyvinyl chloride)	chloroethene (vinyl chloride)	makes very tough plastics; is not damaged by strong chemicals; is a good insulator
teflon (polytetrafluoroethylene)	tetrafluoroethylene	a very slippery substance that is used on nonstick pans

Properties of plastics

It is easier to shape plastic polymers while they are warm or melted into a liquid. There are two main types of plastic. Thermoplastics can be molded, melted, and reshaped repeatedly. Thermosets can only be molded once; after they have set, they will burn without melting if reheated.

▷ **Polymer properties**
The properties of a polymer result from the shape of the monomers. Thermosets form crosslinks when solid, which make the polymer into a rigid lattice.

REAL WORLD
Rubber

The bark of rubber trees produces an oily liquid called latex that contains the compound isoprene. Adding an acid makes the isoprene in the liquid polymerize into solid rubber, which can be made into sheets or molded before it dries out.

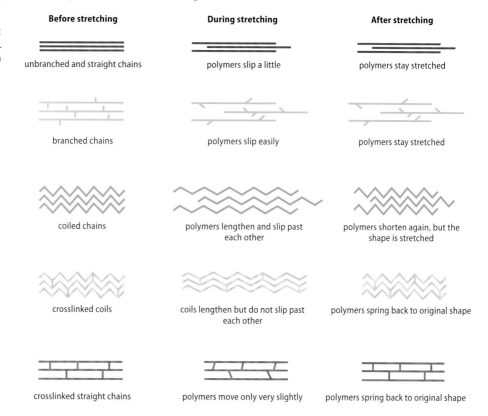

Physics

What is physics?

THIS FIELD OF SCIENCE SEEKS TO REVEAL THE WORKINGS OF THE UNIVERSE ON THE LARGEST AND SMALLEST SCALES

The word "physics" means "nature" in ancient Greek, and physicists tackle the most fundamental subjects in the Universe, such as the nature of energy, space, and even time.

Foundation of knowledge

Physics is the foundation of all scientific knowledge. Chemistry, biology, and other sciences are built on an understanding of physics. For example, physicists have revealed the structure of the atom, which chemists use to understand how chemicals react with each other. Meanwhile, physics has also explained how energy behaves, which is crucial knowledge for biologists figuring out how organisms stay alive. A few physicists, such as Albert Einstein and Isaac Newton, have become famous because their discoveries have had such a far-reaching effect.

▷ **Falling objects**
Physics explains many everyday phenomena. For example, Newton's theory of gravitation (see pages 178–179) explains why an apple—or any object—falls to the ground.

an apple falls due to gravity (a force of attraction)

Energy, mass, space, and time

Physics can express everything in the Universe in terms of mass, energy, and force, from the workings of a giant star to a raindrop falling from a cloud. A mass is an object that is affected by forces. What a force does is transfer energy from one mass to another, which changes the way the masses move or are shaped. For example, throwing a ball or stretching a rubber band requires force—even light shining on an object exerts a tiny force on it!

by throwing the ball, a basketball player applies a force that propels the ball at speed in a certain direction (hopefully into a basket)

◁ **In motion**
They may not know it, but basketball players use physics. They push the ball in just the right direction and with just the right force to score a basket.

WHAT IS PHYSICS? 167

Machines

Physics allows us to build machines that harness forces and the energy they transfer to do useful work. A machine is a device that carries out a task by changing forces in some way. Machines need not be complex; in fact, a piece of high-tech machinery, such as a robot or an engine, is really a series of much simpler machines working together. Simple machines include levers, wheels, screws, ramps, and pulleys. Machines make work easier by converting small forces into big ones.

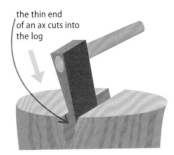

the thin end of an ax cuts into the log

◁ **Focusing force**
Even the blade of an ax is a machine. The force pressing on the wide end of the wedge-shaped blade is focused into the sharp edge so it slices through solid objects.

Radiation

People are often confused by the term "radiation," thinking it refers to the dangerous particles blasted out by nuclear reactions. However, in physics the word "radiation" normally refers to waves of light, heat, and other invisible rays that travel across the Universe. Together they form the electromagnetic spectrum, which is made up of mostly familiar types of radiation. As well as light, the spectrum includes radio waves, gamma rays, ultraviolet light, infrared (or heat), and X-rays. These are all examples of electromagnetic waves.

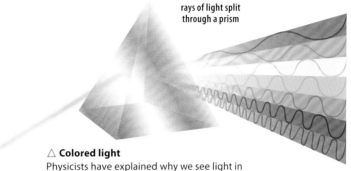

rays of light split through a prism

△ **Colored light**
Physicists have explained why we see light in different colors. Waves of red light are longer (and have less energy) than waves of violet light. All the other colors are in between.

Electricity

Thanks to physicists researching sparks and magnetic forces, most machines are powered by electric currents. This process began in ancient times, when early scientists examined magnetic, iron-rich stones that stuck to each other. Over the centuries, it was discovered that magnetism and electricity are linked—an area of physics called electromagnetism. This field also involves atomic structure and where radiation comes from.

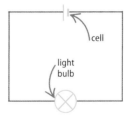

cell
light bulb

◁ **Electric circuits**
Electricity can be put to work using a circuit of different components. For example, a light bulb turns electric current into light when a cell is connected.

Astronomy

In many ways, astronomy was the first science of all, because ancient people saw patterns in the movement of the planets, Moon, and Sun. Modern astronomy still involves stargazing, but high-tech telescopes are used to gather light and other radiation from farther out in space than ever before. The laws of physics discovered on Earth work in just the same way on the other side of the Universe. Therefore, astronomers can use their knowledge to understand the many different objects they see out in space—and even figure out how the Universe came into existence.

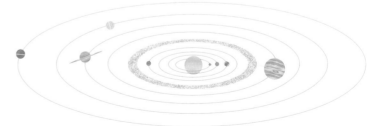

our Solar System

△ **Meet the neighbors**
Observations of the eight planets in our Solar System have taught us much about our own world. Astronomers are now searching for Earth-like planets around more distant stars.

Inside atoms

ATOMS ARE TOO SMALL TO SEE, EVEN WITH SOME OF THE MOST POWERFUL MICROSCOPES.

SEE ALSO	
‹ 98–99 States of matter	
‹ 108–109 Elements and atoms	
‹ 116–117 The periodic table	
‹ 126–127 Radioactivity	
Forces and mass	172–173 ›
Electricity	202–203 ›

Everything we can see in the Universe, from the stars to our own bodies, is made up of atoms.

What is an atom?

Atoms are not all the same. There are 92 different types that occur naturally—and a few more that are made by scientists in laboratories. Each atom belongs to a specific element, a substance that cannot be purified further into simpler ingredients. Familiar elements include hydrogen, carbon, and lead.

▽ **Different atoms**
The atoms of every element have a unique size and mass. The mass varies with the number of protons and neutrons in the nucleus.

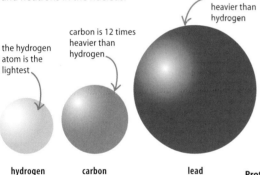

the hydrogen atom is the lightest

carbon is 12 times heavier than hydrogen

lead is 207 times heavier than hydrogen

hydrogen   carbon   lead

Nucleus
The protons and neutrons form the nucleus, a tiny core where most of the matter is packed.

Proton
Protons have positive charges that attract the negatively charged electrons, holding them in place around the nucleus.

Neutron
These particles have no charge. They make up the rest of the mass of the atom, each weighing slightly more than a proton.

Subatomic structure

Atoms are made up of even smaller particles called protons, neutrons, and electrons. The atoms of a certain element have a unique number and arrangement of particles, which is what gives the element its distinct properties—making it a gas or metal, for example. An atom always has the same number of protons as electrons. Each proton has a positive charge, which is matched by the negative charge of an electron, making the whole atom neutral.

△ **Carbon atom**
All carbon atoms have six protons in the nucleus and an equal number of electrons moving around it. Most carbon atoms also have six neutrons.

INSIDE ATOMS

Electron shell
The electrons move around the nucleus, arranged in shells. Shells have a fixed number of spaces for electrons. In most cases, when one shell becomes full, another begins farther away from the nucleus.

Isotopes

Atoms occur in different forms. While an element's atomic nucleus always has a certain number of protons, many contain different numbers of neutrons. These alternative versions of the atom are called isotopes. Atoms of different isotopes have varying weights.

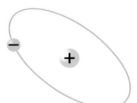

△ **Hydrogen**
The main isotope of hydrogen has no neutrons in its nucleus.

△ **Deuterium**
With one extra neutron, this atom weighs twice as much as the main hydrogen isotope.

△ **Tritium**
This hydrogen isotope is three times heavier than the main hydrogen isotope.

REAL WORLD
Radiocarbon dating

Scientists use the carbon-14 isotope to measure the age of ancient artifacts that are made from organic materials, such as wood or cotton. When new, the cotton wrapping of this mummy had a certain amount of carbon-14 in it. The isotope breaks down at a slow but fixed rate, and the amount left in the wrapping can tell scientists how old it is.

Atomic forces

There are three forces at work inside atoms. The first type is a strong force that pulls the particles in the nucleus together. The second types occurs when the electrons are bonded to the atom by an electromagnetic force, which also acts over a much larger distance outside of the atom. The third type is a weak force that is involved in radioactivity, pushing particles out of the nucleus.

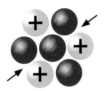

△ **Strong force**
This is the strongest force in nature, but it acts only over tiny distances.

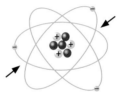

△ **Electromagnetic force**
This force is involved in light and electricity, and holds atoms together.

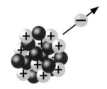

△ **Weak force**
This force causes radioactive decay in atoms.

Electron
The electron has a negative charge that is equal and opposite to that of the proton. However, the mass of an electron is just a tiny fraction of a proton's mass.

Energy

WE RELY ON ENERGY TO MAKE OUR WORLD FUNCTION.

Energy is what makes things happen. It is everywhere and in everything, giving objects the ability to move or glow with heat.

SEE ALSO	
‹ 28–29 Respiration	
‹ 70–71 Human health	
‹ 131 Fuels	
‹ 136 Reactivity and temperature	
Forces and mass	172–173 ›
Kinetic energy	182 ›
Electromagnetic waves	194–195 ›
Renewable energy	224–225 ›

Measuring energy

Energy can be put to work. To a physicist, the word "work" means the amount of energy involved in moving an object. Work is calculated as the amount of force multiplied by the distance. Since force is measured in newtons (N) and distance in meters (m), such a calculation results in a unit of work called a newton meter (Nm).

▽ **One joule of energy**
One joule (J) is the amount of energy transferred to an object by a force of 1 N over a distance of 1 m (3¼ ft). This is roughly equivalent to lifting an apple up 1 m (3¼ ft).

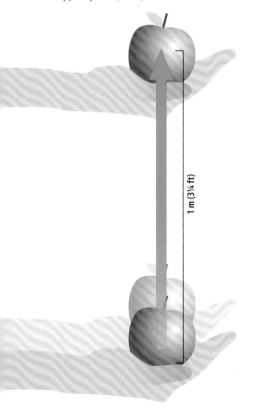

Types of energy

Energy can be seen working in many ways. Although they are given different names and appear in a wide range of contexts—from the energy released by an exploding star to the energy in a bouncing ball—all types of energy are closely related, and each one can change into other types (see the opposite page for examples).

◁ **Kinetic energy**
This is the energy of motion. As an object speeds up, it contains more kinetic energy.

◁ **Thermal energy**
The air blowing out from a hairdryer is hot because electrical energy is converted into thermal energy.

◁ **Electrical energy**
This type of energy is carried by an electric current that supplies all kinds of appliances.

◁ **Chemical energy**
This is the form of energy released when chemical reactions take place, such as burning fuel.

◁ **Radiant energy**
This is the form of energy carried by light and other types of electromagnetic radiation.

◁ **Nuclear energy**
This form of energy is released when atoms split apart (fission) or join together (fusion).

◁ **Sound energy**
This is a type of energy that objects produce when they vibrate in a medium, such as air.

◁ **Potential energy**
The diver has potential energy due to her or his height above the water, which changes to kinetic energy as the diver falls.

ENERGY 171

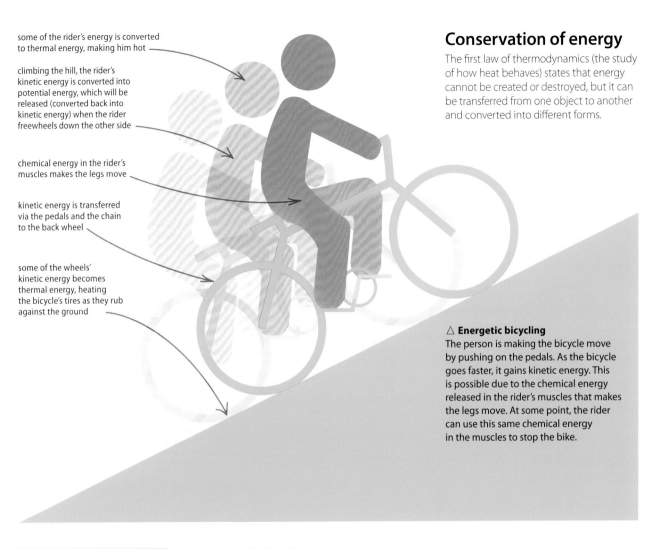

some of the rider's energy is converted to thermal energy, making him hot

climbing the hill, the rider's kinetic energy is converted into potential energy, which will be released (converted back into kinetic energy) when the rider freewheels down the other side

chemical energy in the rider's muscles makes the legs move

kinetic energy is transferred via the pedals and the chain to the back wheel

some of the wheels' kinetic energy becomes thermal energy, heating the bicycle's tires as they rub against the ground

Conservation of energy

The first law of thermodynamics (the study of how heat behaves) states that energy cannot be created or destroyed, but it can be transferred from one object to another and converted into different forms.

△ **Energetic bicycling**
The person is making the bicycle move by pushing on the pedals. As the bicycle goes faster, it gains kinetic energy. This is possible due to the chemical energy released in the rider's muscles that makes the legs move. At some point, the rider can use this same chemical energy in the muscles to stop the bike.

All machines will gradually lose energy, which, unfortunately, makes **perpetual motion impossible**.

REAL WORLD
Perpetual motion

For many years inventors have tried to develop a machine that could run forever. This machine shown right, designed by the German Ulrich von Cranach in 1664, was driven by cannonballs falling into the large wheel at the right. These would drop onto a curved track that fed them into an Archimedes screw. Powered by the wheel, the screw lifted the balls to the starting position. However, like all perpetual motion machines before and since, this clever design could not overcome the slowing effect of friction (see page 173).

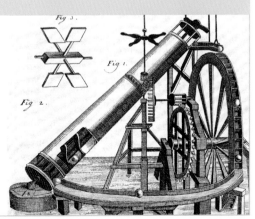

Forces and mass

ALL MOTION IS CAUSED BY FORCES ACTING ON MASSES.

SEE ALSO	
‹ 38–39 Movement	
‹ 170–171 Energy	
Gravity	178–179 ›
Electricity	202–203 ›

The effect of a force depends on the mass of the object. The greater the object's mass, the lower its resultant acceleration.

What is a force?

A force can affect an object in different ways. First, it may change the object's speed, so it moves faster or slower; second, a force can change the direction in which the object moves; third, the force may deform the shape of the object. Forces are measured in newtons (N). A force of 1 N results in a mass of 1 kilogram (kg) or 2.2 pounds (lb) reaching a speed of 1 meter (m) per second in one second.

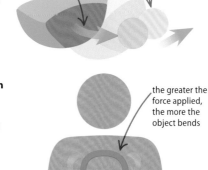

◁ **Changing speed**
The force of the golf club increases the speed of the ball from zero to a high speed, sending it down the golf course.

- ball reacts to the force of the golf club
- golf club connects with the ball

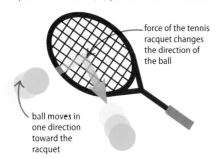

- force of the tennis racquet changes the direction of the ball
- ball moves in one direction toward the racquet

◁ **Changing direction**
The force of the tennis racquet on the ball makes it stop traveling in one direction, and moves the ball in a new direction.

- the greater the force applied, the more the object bends

◁ **Changing shape**
Depending on the toughness of the object, and strength of the person or machine used, the force exerted on an object may be able to change its shape.

What is mass?

Mass is a measure of how much an object resists a force. An object with a large mass contains more matter than one with a smaller mass. A force applied to a large mass results in a smaller acceleration than if it were applied to a small mass.

The precise kilogram unit is based on a single cylinder of the elements **platinum** and **iridium** kept in a safe in Paris, France.

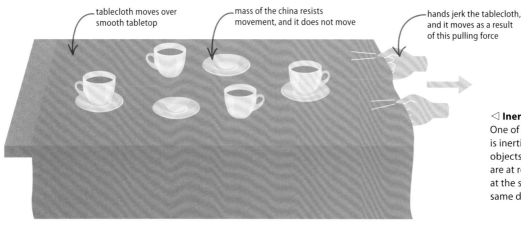

- tablecloth moves over smooth tabletop
- mass of the china resists movement, and it does not move
- hands jerk the tablecloth, and it moves as a result of this pulling force

◁ **Inertia**
One of the properties of mass is inertia. This is a tendency for objects to remain where they are at rest—or keep traveling at the same speed and in the same direction if on the move.

FORCES AND MASS

Friction and drag

Nothing in nature is perfectly smooth, so when objects slide past one another, their uneven surfaces push back against the direction of motion. This resistance force is known as friction. Drag is a similar phenomenon that occurs when an object pushes its way through air or water. The air or water pushes back, resisting the motion.

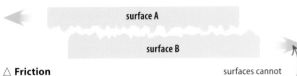

△ **Friction**
Even microscopic dips and bumps on a solid surface are enough to catch the uneven surface of another object moving over it, creating friction.

surfaces cannot move easily, due to friction

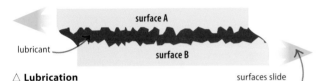

△ **Lubrication**
Adding a lubricant—generally a slippery liquid—reduces the friction. It provides a barrier that stops the solid surfaces touching as much.

surfaces slide past more easily

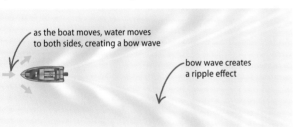

as the boat moves, water moves to both sides, creating a bow wave

bow wave creates a ripple effect

△ **Water resistance**
The boat is moving through the water, and must push the water in front out of the way. The water resists and rises up as a bow wave.

REAL WORLD
Tire tread

Travel would be impossible without friction. For example, a tire has a rough tread to increase the friction force between the wheel and the road, preventing the car from sliding. Running shoes have rough soles for the same reason.

Resultant forces

Several different forces may act on one object at the same time, but sometimes the object cannot respond to each one individually. In these cases, the forces are combined to produce a single effect, so it appears that the object is being moved by a single force in one direction—this is the resultant force.

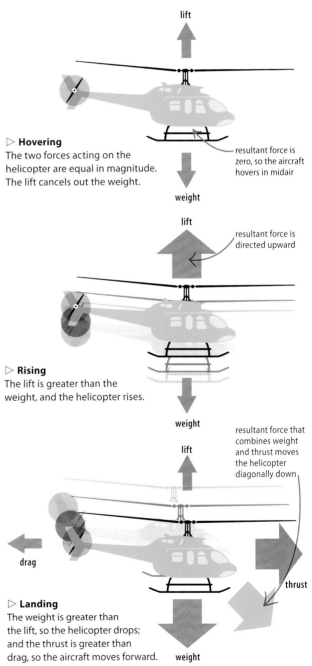

▷ **Hovering**
The two forces acting on the helicopter are equal in magnitude. The lift cancels out the weight.

resultant force is zero, so the aircraft hovers in midair

▷ **Rising**
The lift is greater than the weight, and the helicopter rises.

resultant force is directed upward

▷ **Landing**
The weight is greater than the lift, so the helicopter drops; and the thrust is greater than drag, so the aircraft moves forward.

resultant force that combines weight and thrust moves the helicopter diagonally down

Stretching and deforming

AS WELL AS MOVING OBJECTS FROM PLACE TO PLACE, FORCES CAN ALSO MAKE OBJECTS CHANGE SHAPE.

SEE ALSO
❰ 96–97 Properties of materials
❰ 98–99 States of matter
❰ 163 Plastics
❰ 172–173 Forces and mass

When a force acts on an object that cannot move, or when a number of different forces act in different directions, they make the object's molecules (or other small parts of it) move closer together or further apart, so the whole object changes shape.

Types of distortion
The type of distortion an object undergoes depends on the number, directions, and strengths of forces acting on it, and also on its structure and composition. Many objects simply snap or shatter when strong forces act on them. Those that do not are referred to as deformable, such as modeling clay.

Graphene is one of the **strongest** and **most elastic** materials. It is made of sheets of carbon atoms that are connected together in hexagons.

△ **Compression**
When two or more forces act in opposite directions and meet at the same point inside an object, the object will compress and bulge out on all sides.

△ **Tension**
When two or more forces act in opposite directions and pull away from a object, they apply tension, and elastic objects will stretch in response.

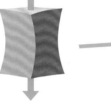
△ **Bending**
When several forces act on an object in different places, the object will either snap (if it is brittle) or bend (if it is malleable). Many materials, like wood, bend a little, and then snap.

△ **Torsion**
Turning forces, or torques, that act in opposite directions, but affect different parts of an object, result in the object being twisted.

△ **Shearing**
When forces act in opposite directions at the ends of an object that is not free to spin, its ends will move in two different directions.

Deformation
Forces that change the shape of an object are known as stresses. The change in shape of the object in response is called a strain. When an object is stressed, three things may happen: it may break; it may change shape permanently (in which case it is said to be "plastic"); or it may change shape until the stress is removed—and then return to its original shape (elastic).

▷ **Stress–strain curve**
Many materials behave elastically for small distortions, and then will start to behave plastically. Finally, they will break. The forces required vary a lot, depending on the material.

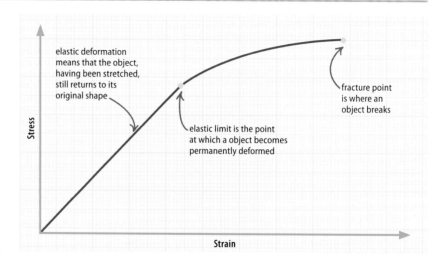
elastic deformation means that the object, having been stretched, still returns to its original shape

elastic limit is the point at which a object becomes permanently deformed

fracture point is where an object breaks

Hooke's Law

The English scientist Robert Hooke (1635–1703) discovered the law of elasticity. Hooke's Law states that the amount of stretch of a spring, or other stretchy object, is directly proportional to the force acting on it. The law is only true if the elastic limit of the spring has not been reached. If the elastic limit has been reached, the spring will not return to its original shape and may eventually break.

REAL WORLD
Bungee jump
If you fell a long distance while attached to a rope, you would stop suddenly, with a dangerous jerk. Elastic cords, such as those used by bungee jumpers, slow you down more gradually because the energy of the fall is slowly transferred to the cord as it stretches.

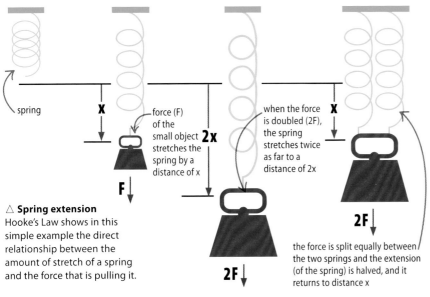

△ **Spring extension**
Hooke's Law shows in this simple example the direct relationship between the amount of stretch of a spring and the force that is pulling it.

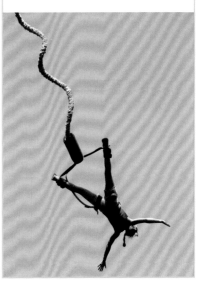

Young's modulus

The elasticity of an object depends on its shape, size, and structure. The English polymath Thomas Young (1773–1829) devised a way of measuring the elasticity of solids—known as Young's modulus—to compare different materials.

Stiffness of select materials	
rubber	0.01–0.1
nylon	3
oak	11
gold	78
glass	80
stainless steel	215.3

△ **Measuring stiffness**
Young's modulus is measured in gigapascals (GPa). The higher the number, the stiffer (less elastic) the material.

Material properties

Many properties of materials are related to the way they deform under stress. They depend partly on the molecules from which materials are made, but also on the shapes and sizes of larger structures inside the material, such as crystals or fibers.

Description of materials under stress	
hard	difficult to scratch or dent
tough	difficult to break or deform
plastic	changes shape permanently when stressed
elastic	returns to original size and shape when stress is removed
brittle	breaks suddenly under stress, with little deformation
ductile	can be drawn out into a wire
malleable	can be hammered into shape

△ **Describing materials**
These terms are used to describe the behavior of materials under stress. Many materials change their behaviors with temperature. For example, warm rubber is very elastic, but very cold rubber is brittle.

Velocity and acceleration

THESE QUANTITIES TELL US HOW QUICKLY SOMETHING IS MOVING.

SEE ALSO	
‹ 172–173 Forces and mass	
Gravity	178–179 ›
Newton's laws of motion	180–181 ›
Understanding motion	182–183 ›

When motion of an object changes in rate or direction, the motion is described in terms of velocity and acceleration.

Speed and velocity

Speed is a measure of the rate at which a distance is covered. It is commonly measured in kilometers per hour. Velocity is also measured in these units, however, this measure also takes direction into account. Thermodynamicists and nuclear physicists use speed more often than velocity.

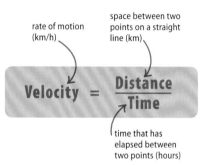

◁ **Increasing velocity**
An increase in the car's velocity is known as acceleration. A constant force gives a constant increase in velocity.

◁ **Changing direction**
The car continues at 60 km/h (37 mph), but then changes lanes. The car's speed is constant, but its velocity is changing.

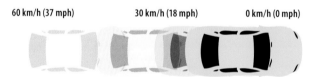

◁ **Decreasing velocity**
When a car slows, the change in velocity is known as a deceleration.

Relative velocity

The relative velocity compares how fast an object is traveling in comparison to another. If two objects are traveling in the same direction, the relative velocity can be calculated by subtracting the velocity of the slower object from the velocity of the quicker one. Two objects moving in the opposite direction along the same path would be heading for a collision. The relative velocity of these objects would be greater than either of their individual speeds.

▷ **Relative speed zero**
Runner A is moving at the same velocity as B, so their relative velocity is 0 km/h (0 mph).

▷ **Catching up**
Runner A is gaining on B because his velocity is 1 km/h (0.6 mph) faster.

▷ **Heading for collision**
Runner A and B are moving in opposite directions. Their relative velocity is the sum of their two speeds, which is 14 km/h (8.7 mph).

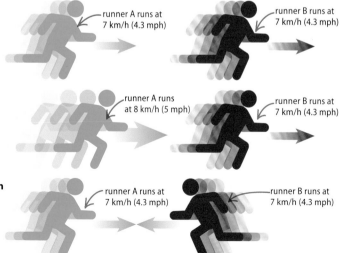

VELOCITY AND ACCELERATION

Changing velocity

Acceleration is a measure of the rate of change in velocity—how long it takes for an object to increase (or decrease) from one velocity to another. Acceleration is calculated by subtracting the starting velocity (V_1) from the final velocity (V_2) to obtain the change in velocity. This figure is then divided by the time that has passed.

rate of change of velocity (meters per second per second)

total change in velocity (meters per second)

time in which this change happened (seconds)

$$\text{Acceleration} = \frac{V_2 - V_1}{\text{Time}}$$

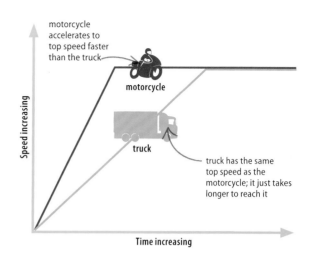

motorcycle accelerates to top speed faster than the truck

motorcycle

truck

truck has the same top speed as the motorcycle; it just takes longer to reach it

Speed increasing

Time increasing

▷ **Motorcycle versus truck**
This graph shows the greater acceleration of the motorcycle compared to the truck, before they both reach the same cruising speed.

Oscillation

An oscillation is a regular movement about a central point. Whether it is a pendulum swinging from side to side, a weight bouncing on the end of a spring, or the molecules vibrating inside a solid, the motion results from regular accelerations and decelerations. In turn, these produce an average velocity of zero because the object ends up coming back to the same central point. This phenomenon is caused by two opposing forces that accelerate the object to the center, but the resulting velocity moves the same distance in the opposite direction.

REAL WORLD
Timekeeping

Oscillations repeat at a constant rate. The time it takes for the oscillator to complete a full cycle is called the period. A pendulum oscillates with a fixed period, and the long pendulums in grandfather clocks have a period of two seconds. Each swing turns the cogs just enough to keep the hands moving at the right rate.

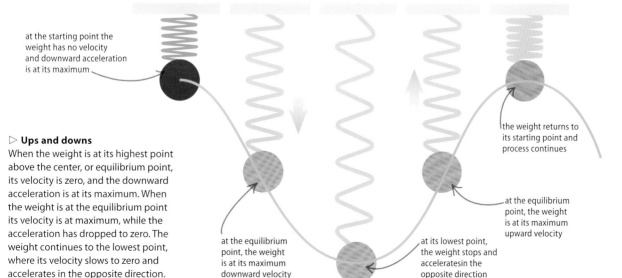

at the starting point the weight has no velocity and downward acceleration is at its maximum

at the equilibrium point, the weight is at its maximum downward velocity

at its lowest point, the weight stops and accelerates in the opposite direction

at the equilibrium point, the weight is at its maximum upward velocity

the weight returns to its starting point and process continues

▷ **Ups and downs**
When the weight is at its highest point above the center, or equilibrium point, its velocity is zero, and the downward acceleration is at its maximum. When the weight is at the equilibrium point its velocity is at maximum, while the acceleration has dropped to zero. The weight continues to the lowest point, where its velocity slows to zero and accelerates in the opposite direction.

Gravity

THE FORCE OF GRAVITY AFFECTS EVERY OBJECT IN THE UNIVERSE.

SEE ALSO	
‹ 172–173 Forces and mass	
Newton's laws of motion	180–181 ›
Rotational motion	183 ›
The Solar System I	234–235 ›

Gravity is the force that holds planets together and keeps them orbiting stars, as well as holding us to the Earth.

Attraction

Gravity is a force of attraction. Although all objects attract all others, gravity between objects on Earth is usually too small to notice. This is why it took a genius like Isaac Newton to understand that gravity does affect all objects, whatever their size.

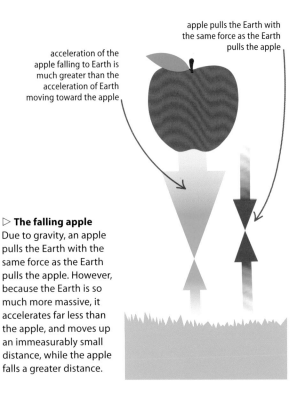

▷ **The falling apple**
Due to gravity, an apple pulls the Earth with the same force as the Earth pulls the apple. However, because the Earth is so much more massive, it accelerates far less than the apple, and moves up an immeasurably small distance, while the apple falls a greater distance.

Physicists think that the force of gravity is carried by **tiny particles called gravitons**—but they have yet to find any.

Universal law

Isaac Newton discovered that gravity affects everything in the Universe. He explained that the gravitational force between two objects, such as planets, depends on their masses and the distance between them. Newton also showed that spherical objects, such as the Earth, act as if all their mass is concentrated at their centers.

△ **Attraction**
All objects are attracted to each other by the force of gravity. Above, two objects of the same mass are attracted by the pull of this gravitational force.

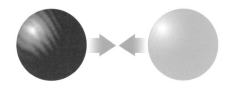

△ **Double the mass**
Changing the masses of the two objects so that they are twice as heavy will make the gravitational force between them four times as strong.

△ **Increase the distance**
Changing the distance between the two objects so that they are twice as far away from each other will make the gravitational force four times less.

Weight and mass

Weight is not the same thing as mass. Mass is the amount of matter an object contains, while weight is the force with which the Earth or another body pulls on the object. An object can have the same mass but weigh differently, depending on the gravitational force acting on the object.

Someone who weighs **40 kg (88 lb) on Earth** would weigh **more than one tonne on the Sun**—if it were possible to stand on its surface.

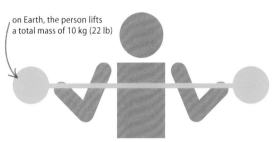

△ **On Earth**
Lifting a barbell requires this person to exert a greater force than the barbell's weight. Here, a weightlifter is lifting a barbell with weights whose total mass is 10 kg (22 lb).

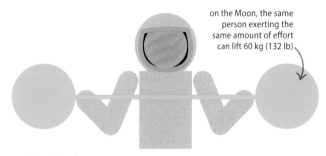

△ **On the Moon**
On the Moon, the force of gravity is about one sixth that on Earth. So the same effort is required to lift 60 kg (132 lb) on the Moon as it is to lift 10 kg (22 lb) on Earth.

Ballistics

A thrown object is pulled back down to Earth by the force of gravity. At the same time, its sideways motion is decelerated by the drag force applied by the air. If there were no atmosphere, the object would travel a much greater distance.

Orbit

The harder an object is thrown, the faster and farther it travels before its path takes it back to the Earth's surface. If the object is propelled hard enough, it will gain enough speed to counteract the pull of gravity so it will never land and will orbit the Earth.

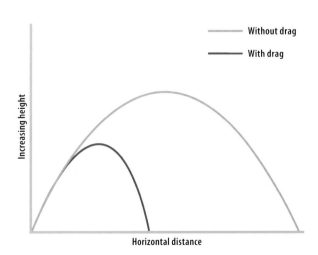

△ **Air resistance and motion**
On Earth, air resistance applies a drag force, slowing the object's motion (red line). Where there is no air resistance, such as on the Moon, a thrown object moves in a parabola (green line)—a steady speed in a horizontal direction, while moving up and then down.

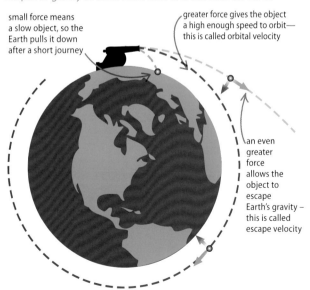

△ **Newton's satellite**
This diagram is based on an illustration by Isaac Newton. He showed that if a cannonball is fired with enough force, its speed will allow it to orbit or escape Earth completely.

Newton's laws of motion

NEWTON'S LAWS EXPLAIN HOW FORCES ACT ON OBJECTS.

When a force acts on an object that is free to move, the object will move in accordance with Newton's three laws of motion.

SEE ALSO	
❮ 38–39	Movement
❮ 172–173	Forces and mass
❮ 176–177	Velocity and acceleration
Understanding motion	182–183 ❯

A new direction for physics

Isaac Newton (1642–1727) published his laws of motion in 1687, setting the direction for physics over the next two centuries. He explained that when the forces acting on an object are balanced, there is no change in the way it moves. When the forces are unbalanced, there is an overall force in one direction, which alters the object's speed or the direction in which it is moving. Newton also emphasized the complicated relationship between objects and forces, which is due mainly to the effects of friction and air resistance. Without these effects, he concluded, the motions of objects are much simpler. So, his laws apply most obviously to bodies in space, such as planets and spacecraft.

REAL WORLD
Blast off!

Newton's laws of motion can be used to explain how a rocket blasts into space. At the start, there is no force acting on the rocket, so it does not move. Then, when the rocket's engines fire, the force they produce lifts the rocket up and off the launchpad. As the hot gases shoot down, an equal force pushes the rocket up.

First law of motion

The first law of motion states that any object will continue to remain stationary, or move in a straight line at a constant speed, unless an external force acts on it. So, a soccer ball is stationary until it is kicked, and then it moves until other forces bring it to a halt.

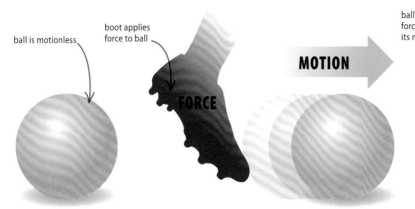
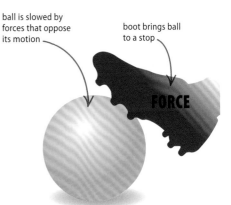

△ **At rest**
Although the force of gravity is acting on the soccer ball, the ground below it stops the ball from moving, so it remains in a state of rest.

△ **Force applied**
The impact of a boot applies a force to the ball. For as long as the boot is in contact with the ball, the ball will be accelerated by it.

△ **Motion is arrested**
The ball immediately begins to slow due to the resistance of the air and friction with the ground. It is brought to a stop when it encounters a stationary object (the boot).

Second law of motion

The second law of motion states that when a force acts on an object, it will tend to move in the direction of the force. The larger the force on an object, the greater its acceleration will be. The more massive an object is, the greater the force needed to accelerate it.

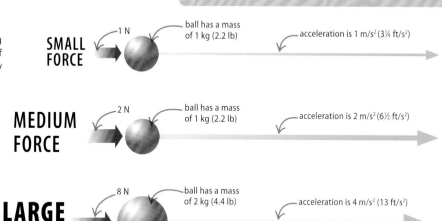

product of mass and acceleration (newtons (N))

amount of matter an object contains (kilograms)

increase in velocity over time (meters per second per second (m/s²))

Force = Mass x Acceleration

▷ **Small mass, small force**
A force of 1 N acting on a mass of 1 kg (2.2 lb) will produce an acceleration of 1 m/s² (3¼ ft/s²)—velocity increases by 1 m (3¼ ft) per second every second.

▷ **Small mass, medium force**
A force of 2 N acting on a mass of 1 kg (2.2 lb) will produce an acceleration of 2 m/s² (6½ ft/s²).

▷ **Double mass, large force**
A force of 8 N acting on a mass of 2 kg (4.4 lb) will produce an acceleration of 4 m/s² (13 ft/s²).

Third law of motion

The third law of motion states that any object will react to a force applied to it. The force of reaction is equal and acts in an opposite direction to the original force that produces it. In the diagram, two people of the same mass are each standing on a skateboard, which reduces friction. When they push together (action), the result (reaction) will be that they move in the opposite direction from each other.

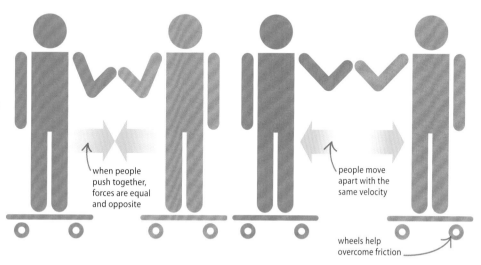

△ **Action**
The third law works when a force acts between two objects. Even if the second person does not make any effort to push back, her or his body will always react to the force in the same way.

△ **Reaction**
The forces between the two people are equal and opposite as they push away from each other on their skateboards. The masses are equal, so they move away from each other at the same velocity.

Understanding motion

FORCES ARE ABLE TO TRANSFER ENERGY TO MAKE OBJECTS MOVE.

Forces are rarely applied to an object one at a time and in straight lines. To understand how objects move, some principles are applied.

SEE ALSO	
❮ 170–171	Energy
❮ 172–173	Forces and mass
❮ 176–177	Velocity and acceleration
❮ 178–179	Gravity
❮ 180–181	Newton's laws of motion
The Solar System I	234–235 ❯

Momentum

A moving object carries on moving because it has momentum. It will keep moving until a force stops it. For example, when you catch a ball, you must exert a force on it to remove its momentum and stop it moving. However, when your hand and the ball collide, the ball will exert a force on your hand so that the momentum of your hand will change. The momentum gained by your hand is equal to the momentum lost by the ball. Momentum is calculated by multiplying the mass of an object by its velocity—the heavier an object and the faster it moves, the greater its momentum. This conservation of momentum, as shown in the illustration, is evidence that energy is never created or destroyed, but transferred between objects.

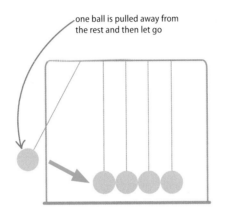

△ **Collision action**
As the left ball hits the line of other balls, its velocity decreases and its momentum drops to zero.

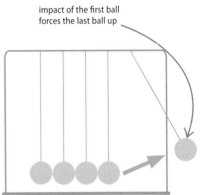

△ **Motion reaction**
The momentum of the first ball passes through its neighbors until it reaches the right ball, which is forced to move.

Kinetic energy

The energy of a moving object is described as kinetic energy. The more kinetic energy an object has, the faster it moves. Some objects can have a relatively small mass but great kinetic energy. For example, the asteroid that is thought to have killed the dinosaurs 65 million years ago had a huge impact despite having a relatively small mass. This is because it hit the ground at around 30 km (19 miles) per second, giving it as much energy as one million express trains.

The **purpose of an engine** is to convert the energy in fuel—or perhaps a battery—into kinetic energy.

▷ **Roller coaster**
At point A, a stationary train on a roller coaster has zero kinetic energy. However, when the train accelerates (in this case, by the pull of gravity) to a high speed, its kinetic energy increases. At point B, the train's kinetic energy will be reduced again by the decelerating effect of gravity as it starts to roll up the smaller slope.

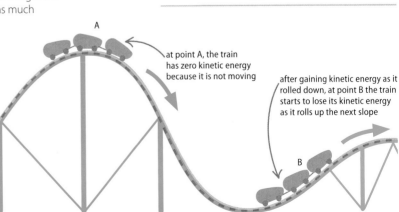

at point A, the train has zero kinetic energy because it is not moving

after gaining kinetic energy as it rolled down, at point B the train starts to lose its kinetic energy as it rolls up the next slope

UNDERSTANDING MOTION 183

Torque

This term refers to the turning effect of a force—its ability to create rotation rather than linear (straight-line) motion. Torque is dependent on the size of a force and its distance from the turning point, or pivot. Forces applied farther from the pivot result in a larger torque. The torque (or moment) of a force is calculated by multiplying force and distance.

> The great Greek mathematician **Archimedes of Syracuse** (c.287 BCE–c.212 BCE) reasoned that if he had a lever long enough, he could generate enough force to **lift up Earth**.

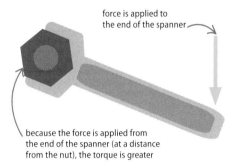

△ **Large torque**
Applying a force to the end of a spanner handle maximizes its torque, making it easier to undo a stiff nut.

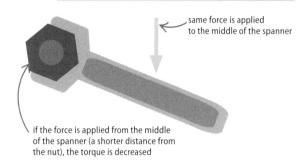

△ **Small torque**
Applying the same force to halfway along the handle results in half the torque, so turning the nut requires more effort.

Rotational motion

When an object moves in a circle, it is acted on by two forces. The centripetal force pulls it toward the center, such as gravity on a space satellite or the strength of a string attached to a ball. A second centrifugal force counteracts the centripetal force by pulling the object away from the center.

▷ **In a spin**
The object accelerates toward the center of the circle. This is balanced by a virtual force—called centrifugal force—which reacts to the centripetal force and keeps the object from moving to the center. The result is a continuous curving motion around the center.

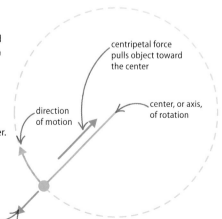

REAL WORLD
Angular momentum

Any spinning object has what is called angular momentum, which is proportional to the mass of the object, its rotational speed, and the average distance of the mass from the center of the spin. The ice skater uses this phenomenon to control the speed of her spins. When she stretches out her arms, she spreads her mass over a wider area, which creates a relatively slow rate of spin. When she draws them back in, all her mass is centered over the axis of rotation, and she spins faster.

Pressure

PRESSURE IS THE RESULT OF ONE THING PRESSING ON THE SURFACE OF ANOTHER.

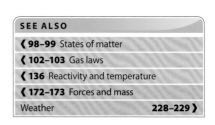

SEE ALSO	
‹ 98–99 States of matter	
‹ 102–103 Gas laws	
‹ 136 Reactivity and temperature	
‹ 172–173 Forces and mass	
Weather	228–229 ›

Pressure can be applied to or by any medium, including air and water.

What is pressure?

Pressure is defined as force per unit area, and is measured in pascals (Pa), which is equal to one newton per square meter. To calculate the pressure, divide the force pressing on the object by the area it is spread across.

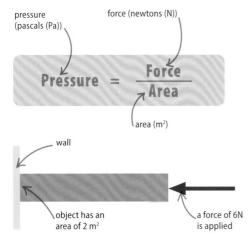

pressure (pascals (Pa))
force (newtons (N))
area (m²)

$$\text{Pressure} = \frac{\text{Force}}{\text{Area}}$$

wall
object has an area of 2 m²
a force of 6N is applied

△ **Larger area, lower pressure**
If a force of 6 N is spread over an area of 2 m², the applied pressure is 6 divided by 2, which equals 3 Pa.

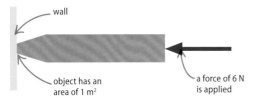

wall
object has an area of 1 m²
a force of 6 N is applied

△ **Smaller area, higher pressure**
If a force of 6 N is spread over an area of 1 m², the applied pressure is 6 divided by 1, which equals 6 Pa. This is why drawing pins and nails are pointed: their small-area tips apply very high pressures, so they penetrate materials easily.

Atmospheric pressure

At the Earth's surface, the atmosphere applies a pressure of about about 101,000 pascals to all objects. We cannot feel this pressure because it is balanced by an equal and opposite pressure inside our bodies. In different weather conditions and at different heights, the local atmospheric pressure changes. This can be measured using a barometer.

▽ **Height and pressure**
Gas molecules are constantly on the move and bumping into each other. When they hit another molecule or the wall of a container, they exert pressure on it. The air molecules close to the Earth are at the bottom of the atmosphere with all the other air molecules on top of them. Therefore, the pressure is higher and the air is denser. Air grows thinner higher from the Earth's surface.

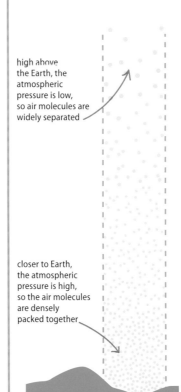

high above the Earth, the atmospheric pressure is low, so air molecules are widely separated

closer to Earth, the atmospheric pressure is high, so the air molecules are densely packed together

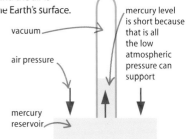

vacuum
mercury level is short because that is all the low atmospheric pressure can support
air pressure
mercury reservoir

△ **Low atmospheric pressure**
If the air pressure above the reservoir is low, it will not produce enough force to make the mercury rise up the tube.

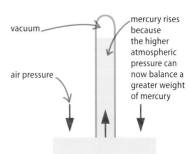

vacuum
mercury rises because the higher atmospheric pressure can now balance a greater weight of mercury
air pressure

△ **High atmospheric pressure**
If the air pressure above the reservoir is high, it will push the mercury up the tube.

PRESSURE

Water pressure

Water is far denser than air. This means that as one goes deeper under water the pressure increases rapidly. On Earth, the water pressure at 10 m (33 ft) depth is about one "atmosphere," which is roughly the air pressure at sea level. At a depth of 20 m (66 ft), the water pressure is about two atmospheres, and at 30 m (99 ft) it is about three atmospheres, and so on.

▷ **Under pressure**
In this milk carton, the pressure increases toward the base, so water will squirt out under greater pressure from the bottom hole than from the top one.

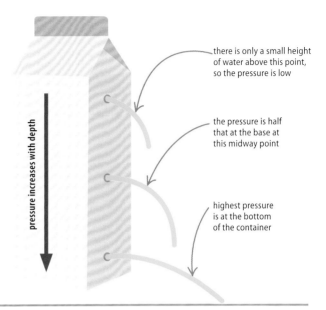

Bernoulli effect

Pressure varies according to the motion of a medium—this is called the Bernoulli effect. In an airplane wing, the top surface of the wing has more camber (longer curve) than the bottom surface, so the air flows faster over the top of the wing than it does underneath.

▷ **Taking flight**
There is less air pressure above the wing than there is beneath the wing. The difference in the air pressure above and below the wing causes lift.

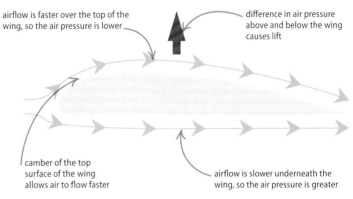

Hydraulics

In an hydraulic system, a liquid (often oil) is used to transfer force from one place to another. Usually, hydraulic systems also convert a low force at one place to a higher one at another. Hydraulic systems rely on the fact that liquids (unlike gases) are almost incompressible—if they are pressed, rather than reducing in volume they force objects like pistons to move away.

◁ **Hydraulic multiplication**
The increase in force created by an hydraulic system can be calculated from the areas of the two sides (shown here in cross-section): if one side has twice the area of the other, the force will be doubled.

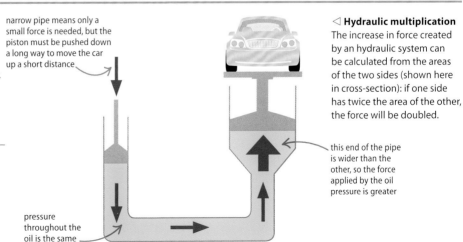

Machines

MACHINES MAKE WORK EASIER TO DO.

A simple machine is a device that increases the size, or changes the direction, of a force. Machines can use this energy to lift, cut, or move masses.

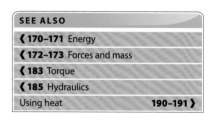

SEE ALSO	
‹ 170–171 Energy	
‹ 172–173 Forces and mass	
‹ 183 Torque	
‹ 185 Hydraulics	
Using heat	190–191 ›

Simple machines

Even the most complex devices can be broken down into half a dozen simple machines working together. All of these machines have been in use since ancient times, and at first glance some may not seem to be machines at all. However, the way they all multiply the force applied to them, or multiply the distance over which that force acts, makes them machines.

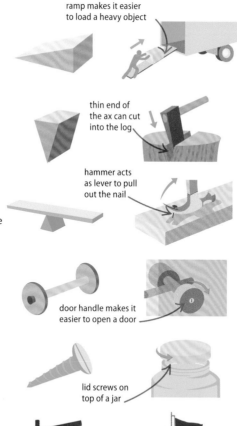

▷ **Ramp**
A heavy load can be pushed up a ramp in a continuous motion that requires a smaller force than lifting it straight up.

ramp makes it easier to load a heavy object

▷ **Wedge**
Any force applied to the thick end of a wedge is focused into the thin end, applying enough pressure to cut into materials.

thin end of the ax can cut into the log

▷ **Lever**
When a force is applied, the lever moves around a turning point (fulcrum), creating an opposite force at a different point along the lever.

hammer acts as lever to pull out the nail

▷ **Wheel and axle**
A wheel moves around an axle in the same way as a lever around a fulcrum, multiplying the distance over which a force acts.

door handle makes it easier to open a door

▷ **Screw**
A screw wraps around an axle, so the load moves up the screw as it turns. The tip of a screw is often pointed, so it also acts as a wedge.

lid screws on top of a jar

▷ **Pulley**
A pulley is a rope looped around one or more wheels. The pulley's wheel changes the direction of the force on the rope—so pulling down makes the weight go up.

person uses a pulley to raise a flag

Levers

Levers magnify a small force into a large force. They work by moving a load around a turning point. There are three types of levers; the difference between them depends on where the effort, load, and fulcrum are positioned.

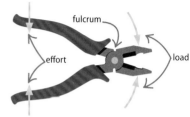

△ **First-class lever**
When you use pliers, the effort is applied on the opposite side of the fulcrum to the load.

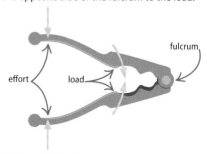

△ **Second-class lever**
When you use a nutcracker, the load is positioned between the effort and the fulcrum.

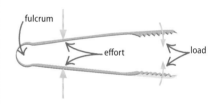

△ **Third-class lever**
When you use tongs, the effort is applied between the load and the fulcrum.

MACHINES   **187**

Pulleys

Compound pulleys are good examples of the way machines create a mechanical advantage—amplifying a small effort into a large force capable of lifting big loads. The double pulley is the simplest type. Single pulleys do not create a mechanical advantage, but they allow a force to be applied in a different direction.

The **first machine** ever created was the wedge-shaped handax from the Stone Age.

▷ **Single pulley**
A simple pulley is used to change the direction of a force. The effort and load are equal, so the force needed to lift this object is the same as that required to lift it by hand.

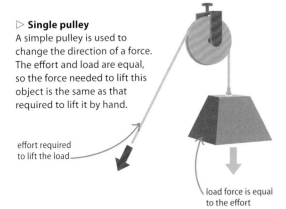

effort required to lift the load

load force is equal to the effort

▷ **Double pulley**
The rope runs around two pulleys, doubling the mechanical advantage. This allows a person to lift the same load with half the effort of a single pulley.

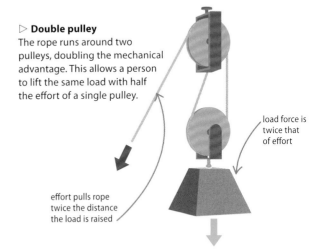

load force is twice that of effort

effort pulls rope twice the distance the load is raised

Gears

When wheels are given interlocking teeth they become cogs or gears, which are used to transmit a turning force, or torque. The magnitude of the transmission depends on the gear ratio, a comparison of the number of teeth on each gear. For example, when the driver gear (moved by the effort force) has twice the number of teeth of the driven gear, this second gear rotates twice as fast and with half the torque.

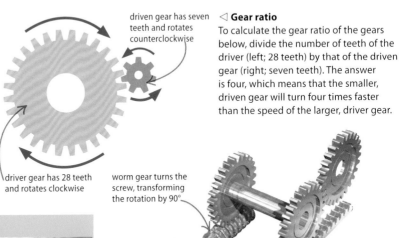

driven gear has seven teeth and rotates counterclockwise

◁ **Gear ratio**
To calculate the gear ratio of the gears below, divide the number of teeth of the driver (left; 28 teeth) by that of the driven gear (right; seven teeth). The answer is four, which means that the smaller, driven gear will turn four times faster than the speed of the larger, driver gear.

driver gear has 28 teeth and rotates clockwise

worm gear turns the screw, transforming the rotation by 90°

rack and pinion gear converts linear motion of toothed rail into rotation

△ **Transmission**
Several gears together are often called gear trains, or transmissions. They are used in machines to redirect force from one moving part to another.

bevel gears interlock at right angles to each other

REAL WORLD
Excavator

Construction machines, such as this excavator, show how simple machines are combined. The digger moves on tracks, which are driven by wheels acting as pulleys at each end. The shovel uses a wedge to cut into the ground, and moves using hydraulic levers.

Heat transfer

THERMODYNAMICS IS THE STUDY OF THE WAY HEAT MOVES FROM ONE SUBSTANCE TO ANOTHER.

SEE ALSO	
‹ 49 Thermoregulation	
‹ 100–101 Changing states	
‹ 103 Charles's law	
‹ 136 Reactivity and temperature	
Using heat	190–191 ›
The Earth	226–227 ›
Weather	228–229 ›

Heat is the name used for the type of energy that makes the atoms and molecules move inside a substance. Adding energy makes these particles move more quickly—and results in the substance heating up.

Measuring heat

Temperature is a measure of the heat in a substance. It is an average figure for the energy contained by every particle. Temperature and energy are not interchangeable. A spark from a fire can have a very high temperature, but it does not cause much of a burn because it contains only a small amount of energy. Temperature is measured using a scale. The difference between the upper and lower points is divided into a fixed number of units, or degrees, and any temperature can be expressed in multiples of degrees.

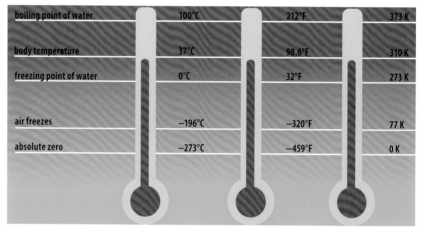

△ **What happens?**
This scale shows what happens at some significant temperatures.

△ **Celsius**
Water freezes at 0°C and boils at 100°C. Celsius was previously known as centigrade.

△ **Fahrenheit**
The Fahrenheit scale starts from the freezing point of saturated saltwater (0°F).

△ **Kelvin**
Absolute zero (0 K) is the temperature at which all particles cease to move completely.

Conduction

Heat always moves from areas with high thermal energy to areas with less. In other words, hot things always cool down, while cold things warm up to match their surroundings. Heat moves through a solid by conduction. This is a phenomenon in which the motion of particles in the hot part of the solid gradually transfers to neighboring ones, making them move faster and sending heat energy through the solid. Metals conduct heat better than nonmetals because their electrons are more free to move and pass their energy on.

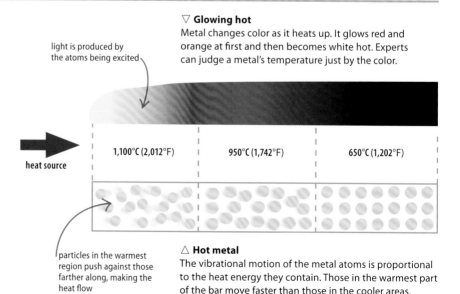

▽ **Glowing hot**
Metal changes color as it heats up. It glows red and orange at first and then becomes white hot. Experts can judge a metal's temperature just by the color.

△ **Hot metal**
The vibrational motion of the metal atoms is proportional to the heat energy they contain. Those in the warmest part of the bar move faster than those in the cooler areas.

Convection currents

Heat moves through liquids or gases by a process called convection. This works on the basis that hot fluids rise upward while cooler ones sink. As a fluid receives energy its particles move faster and spread out. That results in it becoming less dense and rising upward through the cooler, denser fluid. The cooler fluid sinks, and fills the space left by the warmer fluid. This cool fluid is then exposed to the same heat source, and it is heated and rises up. As a result, heat is transferred around the fluid in a continuous convection current of rising and falling fluids.

Convection currents are responsible for the movement of **tectonic plates** on the Earth's crust.

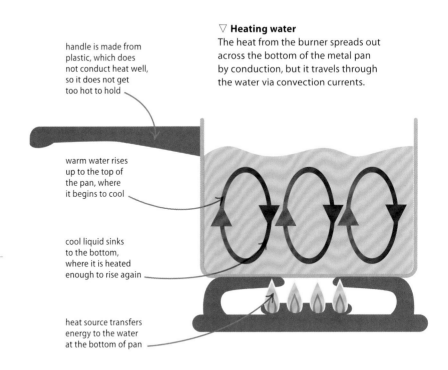

▽ **Heating water**
The heat from the burner spreads out across the bottom of the metal pan by conduction, but it travels through the water via convection currents.

handle is made from plastic, which does not conduct heat well, so it does not get too hot to hold

warm water rises up to the top of the pan, where it begins to cool

cool liquid sinks to the bottom, where it is heated enough to rise again

heat source transfers energy to the water at the bottom of pan

Radiating heat

Heat can travel in the form of electromagnetic radiation—mainly infrared and microwaves. In general, smaller objects radiate away their heat more quickly than larger ones. This is because small objects have large surface areas compared to their volumes: a cube with a surface area of 24 unit^2 (such as the example below, left) has a volume of 8 unit^3 and a cube with a surface area of 6 unit^2 has a volume of only 1 unit^3.

▷ **Comparing surface areas**
This cube has the same volume (8 unit^3) as the tower to the right, but has a smaller surface area (24 unit^2). Therefore, less of its heat energy has access to the surface, so it radiates heat more slowly. The tower has a larger surface area (28 unit^2) than the cube, so more of its heat energy has access to the surface, where it can radiate into space, making the object cool more quickly than the cube.

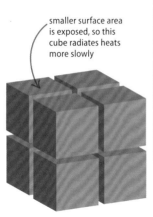

smaller surface area is exposed, so this cube radiates heats more slowly

greater surface area is exposed, so this tower radiates heat more quickly

REAL WORLD
Saving heat

Animals that live in cold parts of the world are larger than their relatives that live in warmer places. For example, polar bears are much larger than the sun bears of southern Asia. The big polar animal loses precious heat more slowly than its tropical cousins because its large body gives it a small surface area to volume ratio.

Using heat

SOME MACHINES HARNESS THE ENERGY IN HEAT TO CREATE MOTION, WHILE OTHERS TRANSFER HEAT TO WARM FOOD.

SEE ALSO	
‹ 130–131 Combustion	
‹ 157 Crude oil distillation	
‹ 186–187 Machines	
‹ 188–189 Heat transfer	
Power generation	218–219 ›

Many vehicles are powered by harnessing the heat energy released from fuels. By contrast, a fridge releases heat to keep the contents inside cool so they can last longer.

Internal combustion engine

Most road vehicles are powered by internal combustion engines. In external combustion engines, such as steam locomotives, the burning fuel is kept separate from the high-pressure steam that drives the engine. In internal combustion engines the power comes from burning fuel (gasoline or diesel) inside a cylinder, creating motion in a four-stroke cycle.

The first internal combustion engine design was fueled by **gunpowder**.

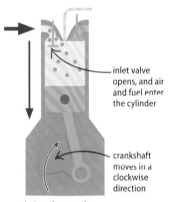

△ **Intake stroke**
The piston falls, drawing a mixture of fuel and air into the cylinder.

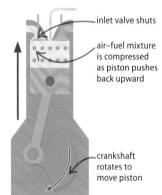

△ **Compression stroke**
The piston rises, compressing the fuel mixture and making it warm up.

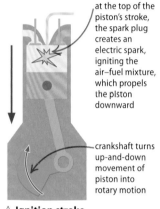

△ **Ignition stroke**
Spark explodes the fuel and the gases produced expand, pushing the piston down.

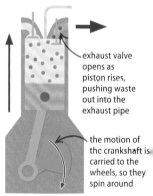

△ **Exhaust stroke**
The piston rises again, pushing the exhaust gases out of the engine.

Jet engine

Jet engines on aircraft and inside the fastest ships convert heat energy into motion using a turbine. This is a series of propeller-like blades that spin when fast-moving gases flow over them. The gases used are air and the exhaust produced by burning fuel. The spinning turbine drives a compressor, which draws air into the engine and squeezes it so it gets hot. The hot air makes the fuel burn more quickly, driving the turbine around faster. The aircraft is thrust forward by the jet of gas sent backward by the turbine.

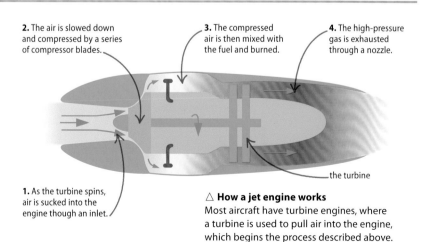

△ **How a jet engine works**
Most aircraft have turbine engines, where a turbine is used to pull air into the engine, which begins the process described above.

Rocket engine

Rocket engines do not burn their fuels in air. Instead, the fuel is mixed with another chemical, called an oxidizer, which creates a very hot and vigorous reaction. The hot expanding gases produced by the reaction are forced out of a small nozzle. The action of the gas leaving the engines results in a reaction force that drives the rocket forward.

▽ **How a liquid-fueled rocket engine works**
Unlike a jet engine, a rocket engine carries both the fuel and oxidizer on board. Smaller rockets, such as fireworks, use solid fuels, while the largest rockets have liquid fuels.

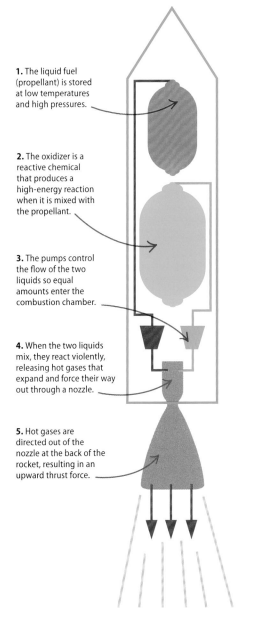

1. The liquid fuel (propellant) is stored at low temperatures and high pressures.

2. The oxidizer is a reactive chemical that produces a high-energy reaction when it is mixed with the propellant.

3. The pumps control the flow of the two liquids so equal amounts enter the combustion chamber.

4. When the two liquids mix, they react violently, releasing hot gases that expand and force their way out through a nozzle.

5. Hot gases are directed out of the nozzle at the back of the rocket, resulting in an upward thrust force.

Refrigeration

Cold is the absence of heat, and a refrigerator chills food by removing heat from the internal storage space. Heat energy always moves from hot places to cold ones. A refrigerator works by passing a cold gas behind the storage space, so heat from the air inside moves to that gas, making the air colder. The cold gas is produced by expanding a liquid very rapidly. The temperature drops as the molecules spread out, thus preserving food and drinks.

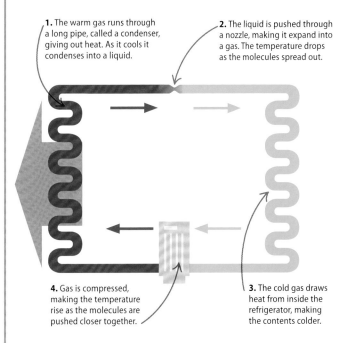

1. The warm gas runs through a long pipe, called a condenser, giving out heat. As it cools it condenses into a liquid.

2. The liquid is pushed through a nozzle, making it expand into a gas. The temperature drops as the molecules spread out.

3. The cold gas draws heat from inside the refrigerator, making the contents colder.

4. Gas is compressed, making the temperature rise as the molecules are pushed closer together.

△ **Refrigeration cycle**
In a refrigerator, a refrigerant (a substance used for cooling) travels around a system of pipes. First, heat radiates from the warm refrigerant. Second, the refrigerant begins to expand and cool. Third, the cold refrigerant cools the refrigerator because thermal energy moves from the refrigerator to the refrigerant. Finally, the compressor squeezes the refrigerant so it gets warmer as it begins to release its thermal energy.

REAL WORLD
Microwave oven

A microwave heats food using high-energy microwaves, which are absorbed by the bonds in water and fat molecules. These vibrate, which causes the food to heat up.

Waves

WAVES ARE VIBRATIONS THAT TRANSFER ENERGY.

Many different types of energy travel in waves. Sound waves carry noises through air, while seismic waves travel inside the Earth and cause earthquakes.

SEE ALSO	
‹ 64 Hearing	
Electromagnetic waves	194–195 ›
Optics	198–199 ›
Sound	200–201 ›

What is a wave?

Waves are vibrations that transfer energy as they travel. Some energy waves—sound waves, for example—need to travel through a medium, such as water or air. The medium does not travel with the wave, but moves back and forth as energy is passed through it, similar to the way a "wave" travels around a sports stadium as people move up and down in their seats. There are two main types of wave: transverse and longitudinal.

REAL WORLD
Seismic waves

Seismic waves are caused by the movement of rocks underground. As the vibrations travel up to the Earth's surface, they can produce earthquakes. The huge amounts of energy in seismic waves can be detected many thousands of kilometers away by sensitive instruments called seismometers.

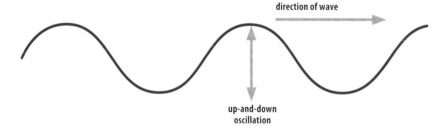

◁ **Transverse wave**
Light and other electromagnetic waves are transverse waves. This type of wave oscillates (vibrates) up and down at right angles (transversely) to the direction of travel of the wave, following an S-shaped path.

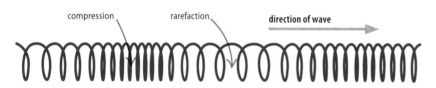

◁ **Longitudinal wave**
Sound energy travels in longitudinal waves. The effect is like releasing a stretched spring and watching the energy travel along the coils, squeezing them together (sections called compressions) and stretching them apart (sections called rarefactions). Sound moves through air by pushing and pulling air molecules in a similar pattern of compressions and rarefactions.

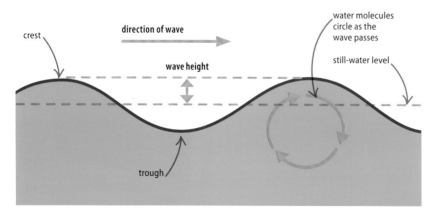

◁ **Ocean wave**
Ocean waves are formed by the action of the wind pushing against the surface of the water, and have qualities of both of the wave types above. At the surface, water rises and falls between its highest point (crest) and lowest point (trough), equidistant to the still-water level. As the wave passes, the water molecules below the surface do not move forward but loop in circles.

Measuring waves

Waves have three important measurements. These are wavelength, frequency, and amplitude.

▽ Wavelength
The wavelength is the length of one complete wave cycle. It is the distance measured between any point on a wave and the equivalent point on the next wave.

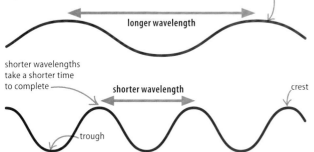

longer wavelengths take a longer time to complete

shorter wavelengths take a shorter time to complete

▽ Frequency
This is the number of waves passing any point in one second. The unit of frequency is the hertz (Hz).

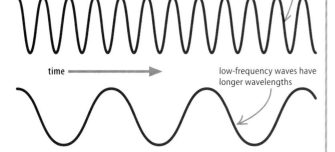

waves with a short wavelength have a higher frequency than those with longer wavelengths

low-frequency waves have longer wavelengths

▽ Amplitude
The amplitude is the height of a crest or trough as the wave travels, measured from the central rest position.

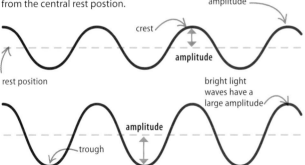

dim light waves have a small amplitude

bright light waves have a large amplitude

Wave speed
The speed of a wave is related to its frequency and wavelength. They are linked by this equation:

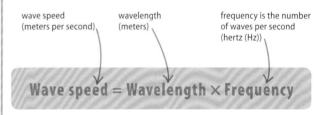

Wave speed = Wavelength × Frequency

- wave speed (meters per second)
- wavelength (meters)
- frequency is the number of waves per second (hertz (Hz))

Calculating wave speed
The waves below are traveling across water. To find the wave speed, multiply the wavelength by the frequency.

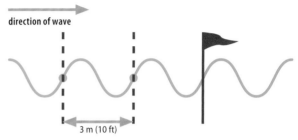

△ **The wavelength** has been worked out—each wave is 3 m (10 ft) long. A marker is used to help count the number of waves in one second.

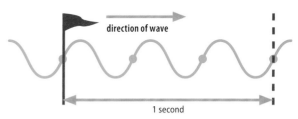

△ **One second later** Three waves have passed the marker, so the frequency is 3 Hz.

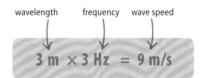

3 m × 3 Hz = 9 m/s

wavelength frequency wave speed

Electromagnetic waves

THESE ARE WAVES THAT CARRY ENERGY THROUGH SPACE.

Electromagnetic (EM) waves transfer energy from one place to another. There are different types but they all travel through a vacuum, such as space, at the speed of light.

SEE ALSO
❮ 30–31 Photosynthesis
❮ 168–169 Inside atoms
❮ 170–171 Energy
Light 196–197 ❯
Astronomy 230–231 ❯

Along the spectrum
Visible light is just one type of EM wave; other types are invisible. The full range of waves, called the electromagnetic spectrum, is made up of waves of different frequencies and wavelengths. At one end are radio waves, which have the longest wavelengths and lowest frequencies. At the other end are gamma rays, with the shortest wavelengths and highest frequencies.

▽ **Properties and uses**
The different types of electromagnetic radiation have different properties and uses, depending on their wavelength. Waves with shorter wavelengths, such as gamma rays and X rays, can carry large amounts of energy, while longer radio waves do not.

REAL WORLD
Snake sense

Some animals can sense infrared radiation well enough to find warm objects in the dark. Some snakes have pits —see the hollow depression on the snout of this viper—that contain heat receptor cells. At night, or when their prey is hiding, these sensors can detect the body heat of warm-blooded prey, such as mice.

Gamma rays | **X-rays** | **Ultraviolet** | **Visible light**

Increasing energy

Gamma rays
These are produced by radioactivity and can carry a lot of energy. They cannot be seen or felt but are very harmful. While they can cause cancer, they also kill cancer cells. Other uses include sterilizing food and surgical instruments.

X-rays
X-rays are used to make images of inside the body because they pass through skin and soft tissue, but are absorbed by harder materials such as bone. In high doses they can be harmful, so X-rays must be used with caution.

Ultraviolet (UV)
UV radiation is found naturally in sunlight. You cannot see it or feel it, although you can experience the effects of too much UV as sunburn. Sunblock and sunglasses should be worn to protect skin and eyes from UV damage.

Visible light
This set of wavelengths is the only one that our eyes can see. The color seen depends on the wavelength of light, with violet and blue having shorter wavelengths than green and yellow. Red has the longest wavelength of all.

ELECTROMAGNETIC WAVES

The source of EM radiation

EM radiation is associated with the force that holds electrons in place around atoms (see pages 168–169). However, the electrons can move around, jumping between higher and lower energy levels, or shells. These changes result in the atom absorbing or emitting energy in the form of EM radiation.

▽ Energy in
For an electron to jump from one shell to the next one up, it needs a specific amount of energy. It cannot make the move in small jumps, nor can it jump beyond the shell and fall back. It will only move if it receives radiation with exactly the right amount of energy.

▽ Energy out
When an electron jumps back to its original position nearer to the nucleus, it releases energy in the form of a specific wavelength of radiation. This process is what makes objects glow with visible light, give off heat, or emit other forms of radiation.

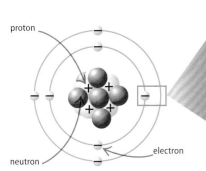

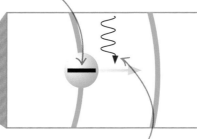

1. The electron is in a low-energy position near the center of the atom.

2. If the electron receives radiation of the correct wavelength, it will jump to the next level.

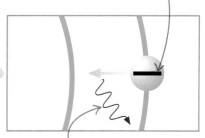

3. The electron is at a high-energy level, farther away from the nucleus than normal.

4. As it drops down to the lower level, the electron gives out radiation of a specific wavelength.

Infrared | Microwaves | Radio waves

Increasing wavelength

Infrared
Infrared means "below red," and has a lower frequency and longer wavelength than visible red light. We experience infrared waves as heat, and can see infrared at work in heaters, grills, and toasters. It is also used in television remote controls and in fiber optics.

Microwaves
This band of wavelengths is used in many types of personal communications, including mobile phones, wi-fi, and Bluetooth, as well as in microwave ovens. It is also used in radar technology, as a way of locating airplanes and ships.

Radio waves
Radio waves are the longest in the spectrum. They are used to transmit radio and TV signals around Earth. Television uses higher frequencies than radio. Radio waves from space can be picked up using radio telescopes and used to study the Universe.

Light

LIGHT ENABLES US TO SEE A BRIGHT AND COLORFUL WORLD.

Light is the only type of electromagnetic radiation we can see. We are able to perceive it as a wide range of colors.

SEE ALSO	
‹ 30–31 Photosynthesis	
‹ 137 Light	
‹ 194–195 Electromagnetic waves	
Optics	198–199 ›
Astronomy	230–231 ›

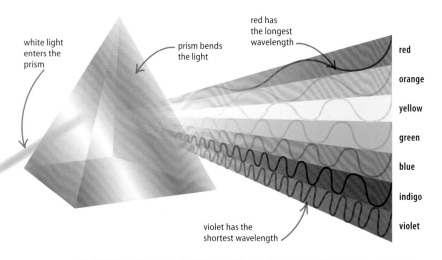

Color spectrum
If white light is shined into a triangular block of glass, called a prism, the glass refracts (bends) the light. In an effect called dispersion, the light is split into different wavelengths, the band of visible colors known as the spectrum. The spectrum begins with the longest wavelength (red), and ends with the shortest wavelength (violet). Most people see seven distinct colors, but the spectrum is really continuous changing color.

◁ **Splitting light**
A prism bends light by different amounts, according to its wavelength.

Making color
We see color based on information sent to the brain from millions of light-sensitive cells in the eye, called cones. There are three types of cone which respond to either red, green, or blue light. You see all colors as a mix of these three colors, known as primary colors.

▷ **Reflective colors**
Objects either reflect or absorb the different colors in white light. The reflected colors are the ones we see.

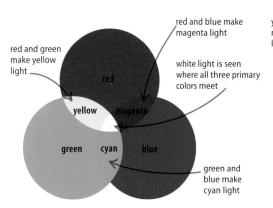

△ **Making colors with light**
If you shine three flashlights, one of each of the primary colors, at a white surface, where they overlap they will create white light. Different combinations will create magenta, yellow, and cyan, known as secondary colors. This effect is used in televisions to create a full-color picture.

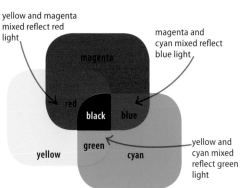

△ **Mixing pigments**
Making colors with pigments (inks and paints) is done in a very different way from colored light. The primary pigments are magenta, yellow, and cyan. Each reflects light of a different color. When the pigments are mixed the number of colors they reflect is reduced, and all three together make black.

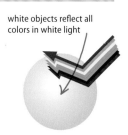
white objects reflect all colors in white light

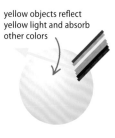
yellow objects reflect yellow light and absorb other colors

black objects absorb all colors and reflect none

Reflection

When rays hit a smooth, shiny, flat surface, such as a flat mirror, they are reflected perfectly to give a clear but reversed image. Rough surfaces cause light to bounce off in different directions, so there is no reflected image.

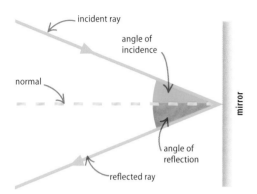

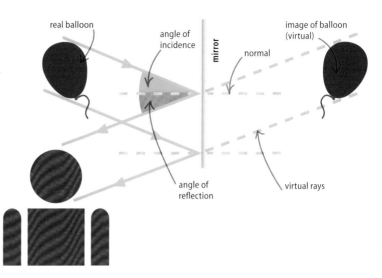

△ **Angles of incidence and reflection**
A reflection is made up of an incoming ray, called the incident ray, and an outgoing ray, called the reflected ray. The angle of incidence is equal to the angle of reflection, measured from a imaginary line at 90° to the mirror, called the normal.

△ **Virtual image**
The image in a mirror appears to be behind it—light rays appear to be focused there, but they do not actually meet at that point. This is called a virtual image. The image on a movie screen is called a real image because rays from the projector focus directly on the screen.

Refraction

Light rays usually travel in straight lines, but pass through different media (materials)—such as air, water, or glass—at different speeds. When light moves from one medium to another, the change in speed makes the beam change direction. This effect is known as refraction.

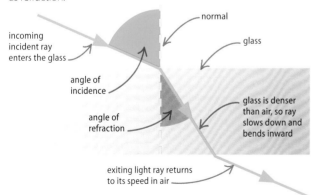

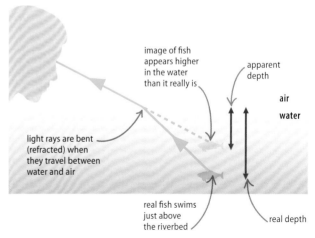

△ **Changing direction**
If light travels through air and then enters at an angle a more dense medium, such as glass, the rays slow down and refract inward. They travel in a straight line through the glass but at an angle to their original direction. As the rays pass out from the glass to the air, they return to their original path and speed up again.

△ **Real and apparent depth**
Light rays refract when they pass from water to the lighter medium of air. This means that when you look from an angle at an object in water, it is not in fact where you see it. A fish swimming in the water is actually deeper than it appears to be.

Optics

THE SCIENCE OF OPTICS EXPLAINS AND EXPLORES THE PROPERTIES AND BEHAVIOR OF LIGHT.

> **SEE ALSO**
> ‹ 64 Vision
> ‹ 196–197 Light
> Telescopes 230 ›
> The Sun 232–233 ›

Light is a type of electromagnetic radiation. It is carried by a stream of particles that can also behave like a wave.

Light sources

The Sun, lights, and TV screens all emit (send out) light—they are luminous. But most objects reflect and/or absorb light that bounces off them. Transparent materials, such as glass and water, let light pass right through them. They transmit light.

Features of light	
form of radiation	Light is a form of electromagnetic radiation (see pages 194–195). It radiates (spreads out) from its source.
light rays travel in straight lines	You can see this in the beams from lighthouses, flashlights, and lasers. Because light rays are straight, if an object blocks them you get a dark region of shadow.
transfers energy	Energy is needed to produce light. All materials gain energy when they absorb light—solar cells use the energy in sunlight to produce electricity.
stream of particles that can behave like a wave	Light is carried by a stream of particles, called photons, but in some situations this stream can also behave like a wave.
can travel through empty space	Electromagnetic waves do not need to travel through a medium (a material such as water or air). The light from the Sun and stars, for example, reaches us through empty space.
travels fast	Light is the fastest thing in the Universe. In a vacuum, such as space, its speed is exactly 299,792 km per second (roughly 186,282 miles per second).

△ **Understanding light**
The most important source of light on Earth is the Sun. Sunlight is produced by the energy generated deep in its core (see pages 232–233). In contrast, the Moon simply reflects the light of the Sun and shines much less brightly. The table above gives the main features of light.

Lenses

A lens is a piece of transparent glass or plastic that uses refraction (see page 197) to change the directions of light rays. Lenses are used to focus light in glasses, cameras, and telescopes. There are two main types—convex and concave.

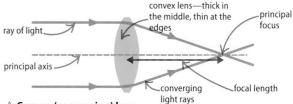

△ **Convex (converging) lens**
When rays pass through a convex lens they converge (bend inward) and meet at a point behind the lens, called the principal focus. The distance from the center of the lens to the principal focus is called the focal length.

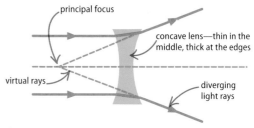

△ **Concave (diverging) lens**
A concave lens makes light diverge (spread out). When parallel rays pass through a concave lens they spread out as if they came from a focal point in front of the lens, called the principal focus.

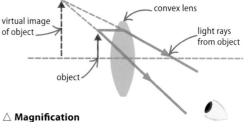

△ **Magnification**
If an object is placed between the center of a convex lens and the principal focus, the rays never converge. Instead they appear to come from a position behind the lens as a magnified image. It is a virtual image (see page 197).

Interference

Where two rays of light meet, they affect each other, a phenomemon known as interference. If the waves are in phase (in step), they reinforce each other. This is called constructive interference. If they are out of phase (out of step), they cancel each other out. This is called destructive interference. Astronomers use the interference between light beams from different parts of stars to image them.

> **REAL WORLD**
> ## Bubble colors
> When light is reflected from a soap bubble, some is reflected from the inner surface of the bubble, and some from the outer surface. The light rays from the two surfaces interfere to produce new wavelengths, seen as different colors.

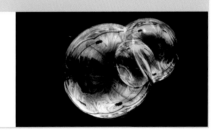

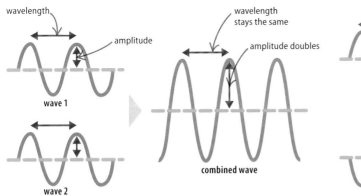

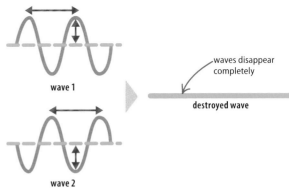

△ **In phase**
When two waves that are in phase meet, their amplitudes add together to make a single wave with double the amplitude. This is called constructive interference.

△ **Out of phase**
If the waves are out of phase, the interference is destructive. As the two waves come together, their amplitudes cancel each other out and the wave is destroyed.

Diffraction

Experiments with light have helped scientists to understand its properties. We know that light can travel as waves, because it behaves like other types of waves, such as sound. For example, both light and sound waves are reflected and refracted (see page 197). Another feature of waves is that, when they pass through a gap, or around an obstacle, they spread out. This effect is called diffraction.

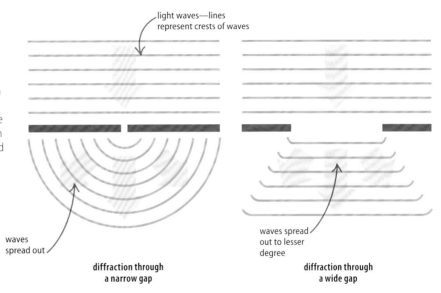

▷ **Spreading out**
Waves spread out like ripples as they pass through a narrow gap. Wider gaps cause less diffraction.

Sound

SOUNDS ARE VIBRATIONS, CARRIED EITHER BY SOLIDS, LIQUIDS, OR GASES.

SEE ALSO
‹ 64 Hearing
‹ 184 Atmospheric pressure
‹ 192–193 Waves

Sounds are of great benefit for communication and can also be harnessed for medical or industrial use. However, unwanted sound is a serious pollutant that damages health and well-being.

Pitch and loudness

The characteristics of sound that we experience as pitch and loudness are closely related to the physical properties of sound waves. Generally, the higher the frequency of a wave—the number of peaks and troughs that pass a point each second—the higher its pitch; the larger the amplitude of the wave, the louder it sounds.

We can hear sounds so quiet that they make our eardrums move **less than the width of an atom**.

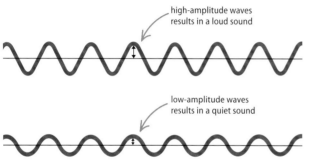

△ **Loudness**
These sound waves have the same frequency but different amplitudes. A higher amplitude indicates there is a larger variation in air pressure, and greater volume.

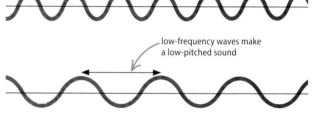

△ **Pitch**
These sound waves have the same amplitude but different frequencies. A higher frequency creates a more rapid variation in air pressure and results in a higher pitch.

Echoes

Sound waves reflect from surfaces, especially hard, smooth ones. If the surface is far enough from the sound source for an adequate time to pass before the reflection returns, it can be heard or detected as an echo. Underwater echoes are used by ships to scan the sea floor. The return time depends on the depth of the bed, so maps of the seafloor can be made in this way.

▷ **Mapping the seabed**
This diagram illustrates how a ship uses echoes to map the sea floor.

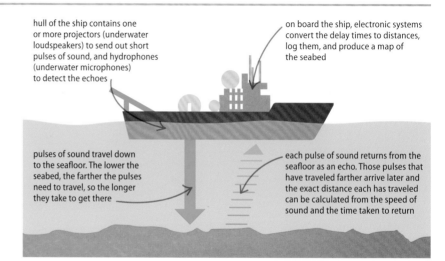

Doppler effect

If a sound source is moving toward a listener, the pulses of pressure that make up the sound waves get closer together because the source is moving a little closer to each one before sending out the next. This means that the sound's frequency is higher than if the source were stationary. If the source is receding, the pulses become farther apart and the frequency lowers. This is called the Doppler effect.

▽ **Police siren**
The Doppler effect explains why a siren on a police car changes in pitch as the vehicle drives by.

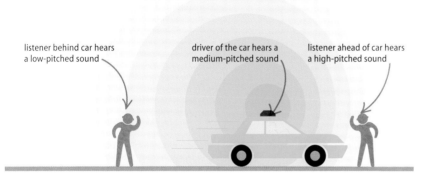

- sound waves emanating from the police car's siren
- listener behind car hears a low-pitched sound
- driver of the car hears a medium-pitched sound
- listener ahead of car hears a high-pitched sound

REAL WORLD
Sound underwater

Sound travels better in water than in air. Marine animals use sound for a wide range of tasks. Some use it to communicate over huge distances, others to probe their surroundings, while some even use it to stun their prey. Dolphins and some whale species are especially dependent on sound for communication, which makes them particularly vulnerable to underwater noise pollution.

Supersonic motion

Sound travels at a speed of around 343 m (1,340 ft) per second through air. However, when an object travels faster than sound, it overtakes the sound waves ahead of it. An example of this is the supersonic jet, which flies faster than the speed of sound, so a person cannot hear it coming toward him or her—the jet passes before the sound arrives. However, when the sound catches up, it arrives suddenly as a shock wave, which is heard on the ground as a sonic boom.

High-power, high-frequency sound can be used to **smash kidney stones apart**, avoiding the need for surgery.

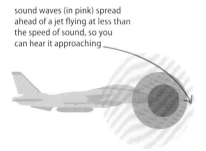

sound waves (in pink) spread ahead of a jet flying at less than the speed of sound, so you can hear it approaching

△ **Subsonic flight**
The sound waves ahead of an aircraft flying slower than the speed of sound have higher frequencies than those behind them.

sound waves pile up in front of a jet traveling at the speed of sound, forming a large shock wave

△ **The shock front**
When the speed of sound is reached, the sound waves can no longer spread ahead of the plane, creating a shock front.

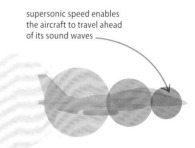

supersonic speed enables the aircraft to travel ahead of its sound waves

△ **Supersonic flight**
The shock front of a supersonic plane is heard as a sonic boom by anyone it passes over.

Electricity

ELECTRICITY IS THE PHENOMENON ASSOCIATED WITH EITHER MOVING OR STATIC ELECTRIC CHARGE.

SEE ALSO	
❰ 113 Reactivity	
❰ 148–149 Electrochemistry	
❰ 168–169 Inside atoms	
Circuits	206–207 ❱

Atoms contain tiny particles called electrons that carry negative electrical charge. These orbit the positively charged atomic nucleus, but can become detached.

Static electricity

When an object contains an excess of electrons, it is said to be negatively charged. It will repel other negatively charged objects. Objects containing many atoms that have lost electrons are positively charged. Such objects attract negatively charged objects, and repel other positively charged objects. Since the electrons are not flowing to or from such objects, this type of electricity is called static. Objects with static charge also attract neutral objects, by repelling electrons within them to leave an area of positive charge.

Static discharge

In stormy weather, electrons gradually move from the Earth to low clouds. Charges also separate within clouds. The ground and the upper parts of clouds become strongly positively charged, while the lower parts of clouds become strongly negative. Eventually, the clouds discharge as the charges neutralize each other. Discharges within clouds are seen as sheet lightning, while forked lightning is a cloud-to-ground discharge. The lightning can travel at a staggering 209,200 km/h (130,000 mph) with an electric current of around 300,000 amperes.

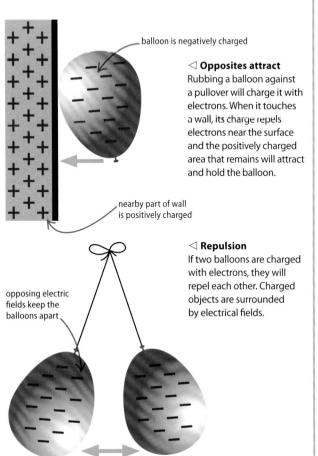

◁ **Opposites attract**
Rubbing a balloon against a pullover will charge it with electrons. When it touches a wall, its charge repels electrons near the surface and the positively charged area that remains will attract and hold the balloon.

◁ **Repulsion**
If two balloons are charged with electrons, they will repel each other. Charged objects are surrounded by electrical fields.

△ **Dangerous places**
When lightning strikes, it takes the shortest route to the ground. A lone tree is likely to be struck in a thunderstorm. High buildings are often struck, too, so they are fitted with lightning rods to conduct any lightning safely down to the ground.

Lightning can heat the air surrounding it to a temperature that is **more than five times hotter than the Sun's surface!**

ELECTRICITY 203

Electric currents

When electric charge flows through a material, it is called an electric current. It is caused by a drift of electrons through a material called a conductor (see below). In an electrical circuit (see page 206), a power source, such as a battery, gives the electrons energy so that the charge flows from the negative terminal (connection) of the power source around the circuit to the positive terminal. Current only flows when an electric circuit is complete, with no gaps. In a circuit, individual electrons actually travel extremely slowly (less than 1 mm (0.04 in) per second), but because they are closely situated to one another they are able to pass electrical energy around the circuit at more than 100 million m (328 million ft) per second.

Copper is a very good conductor of electricity, and is used to make a variety of cooking utensils and pipes for carrying hot water, both in homes and industry.

▷ **Disconnected conductor**
If a wire is not connected to a battery, the free electrons within it move randomly in all directions.

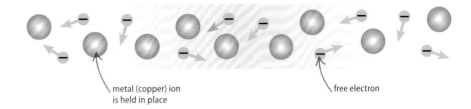

metal (copper) ion is held in place

free electron

▷ **Current-carrying conductor**
When the conductor forms part of a powered electrical circuit, the electrons drift toward the positive pole of the power supply.

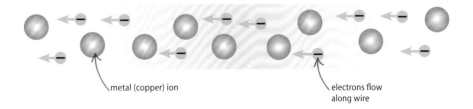

metal (copper) ion

electrons flow along wire

Controlling electricity

Some materials are better at carrying an electrical current than others and are called conductors. Many metals make good conductors, as their atoms easily release electrons to carry the current. Materials such as glass, rubber, and most plastics are made of atoms that do not easily release their electrons. As a result, these conduct electricity poorly, cannot carry a current, and are called insulators.

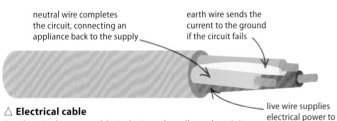

neutral wire completes the circuit, connecting an appliance back to the supply

earth wire sends the current to the ground if the circuit fails

live wire supplies electrical power to electrical appliances

△ **Electrical cable**
An electrical power cable is designed to allow electricity to flow easily along its copper wires. Each wire is separated by a plastic sleeve—a good insulator. The colors of the sleeves vary between countries.

REAL WORLD
Amber

Amber is the dried resin of certain trees, and it quickly collects a static charge when it is rubbed. A piece of charged amber will attract light objects, such as feathers. The ancient Greeks were aware of these effects, and the words "electron" and "electricity" come from the Greek word for amber.

Current, voltage, and resistance

THESE ARE THE FACTORS THAT DETERMINE HOW ELECTRICITY FLOWS THROUGH A CIRCUIT.

There are two variables that control the amount of current that flows around a circuit: voltage and electrical resistance.

What is voltage?

Voltage is a measure in volts (V) of potential difference—the difference in electrical energy between two points, such as the difference in potential energy at two different points of a circuit. A voltage is required to make electrons move and an electric current to flow. Batteries are labeled in terms of their voltage. A typical car battery is 12 volts, while a flashlight battery may be 1.5 volts.

SEE ALSO	
⟨ 112 What is an ion?	
⟨ 148–149 Electrochemistry	
⟨ 168–169 Inside atoms	
⟨ 203 Electric currents	
Circuits	206–207 ⟩

Volts, amperes, and ohms are named after three scientists who helped develop **the science of electricity**: Alessandro Volta, André-Marie Ampère, and Georg Simon Ohm.

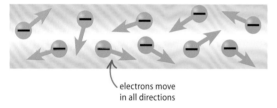

electrons move in all directions

△ **No voltage**
If a conductor's ends are not connected to a battery or other power source, the free electrons within it drift randomly in all directions.

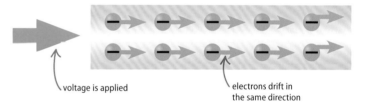

voltage is applied

electrons drift in the same direction

△ **Voltage**
If the ends of a conductor are connected to a battery, the battery's voltage makes electrons drift along, creating electrical current.

Resistance

Any piece of wire and any component in a circuit holds back the flow of electricity through it to some extent. This is usually because electrons moving around the circuit are scattered ("bounced") by the ions (charged atoms) of the material, which slows the electrons down and makes them lose energy. This "holding back" is called electrical resistance. The lost energy appears in the form of heat, sound, or light. The resistance of a wire depends on factors such as its length and diameter.

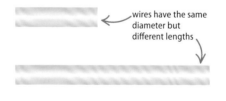

wires have the same diameter but different lengths

◁ **Length**
A shorter wire has less resistance than a longer wire of the same diameter. This is because electrons have less distance to travel and suffer fewer collisions and energy loss. In a longer wire, they have farther to go, so they encounter more collisions, greater resistance, and greater energy loss.

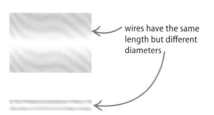

wires have the same length but different diameters

◁ **Diameter**
A thinner wire has a greater resistance than a thicker wire of the same length, because it has less room for electrons to move through. In the thicker wire, more electrons can travel side by side (like a crowd in a wide corridor), so the electron flow is greater.

Ohm's Law

Ohm's Law is a formula that shows the relationship between voltage, current, and resistance. Changing the value of one of these three variables will affect the other two. The resistance in a circuit, for example, can be increased by adding an extra component, such as a lamp or a resistor—a device designed to resist the current.

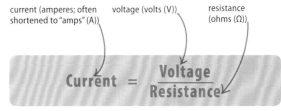

$$\text{Current} = \frac{\text{Voltage}}{\text{Resistance}}$$

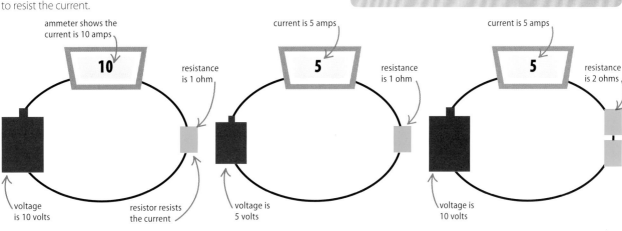

△ **Circuit 1**
In this circuit, the battery provides 10 volts and there is a resistance of just 1 ohm, so the current is 10 amps.

△ **Circuit 2**
In this second circuit, there is still 1 ohm of resistance, but the voltage has been halved, which reduces the current to 5 amps.

△ **Circuit 3**
Here, the voltage is again 10 volts, but another 1 ohm resistor has been added, which reduces the current to 5 amps.

Electric heat and light

When electricity flows along a conductor, the resistance that occurs converts some of the electrical energy into heat and sometimes light. The amount of resistance and heat produced can be increased by using a high-resistance wire.

△ **Electric heater**
An electric heater uses long lengths of high-resistance wire coiled tightly, so that more wire can be fitted into the heater, generating more heat.

REAL WORLD
Superconductors

Certain materials lose practically all of their electrical resistance at very low temperatures. This phenomenon, called superconductivity, can be used to create very efficient electromagnets. These powerful superconducting electromagnets are used in Magnetic Resonance Imaging (MRI) scanners in medicine, in large particle colliders, and in some magnetic levitation (Maglev) rail vehicles, including this Japanese train.

Circuits

ALL ELECTRONIC AND ELECTRICAL SYSTEMS AND EQUIPMENT ARE BUILT FROM CIRCUITS.

SEE ALSO
‹ 168–169 Inside atoms
‹ 172–173 Forces and mass
‹ 203 Electric currents
‹ 204 Resistance
‹ 205 Ohm's law
Electricity supplies 220–221 ›

Circuits are composed of power sources, conductors, and electronic or electrical components that carry out specific tasks.

Circuit basics

In any circuit, a power source—such as a cell—pushes electrical current along one or more conductors, often wires. When the current passes through a component, such as a light bulb, the component changes the electricity and also changes itself in response. For example, a resistor controls the flow of current to protect the device from overload. Similarly, a light bulb opposes the current and lights up. If the circuit is broken—by means of a switch, for example—the current ceases to flow.

△ **Switch**
This allows or halts the flow of current.

△ **Cell**
This causes current to flow around the circuit.

△ **Capacitor**
This device stores electrical charge.

△ **Light bulb**
This will light up when current flows through it.

△ **Voltmeter**
This device measures the voltage, in volts.

△ **Ammeter**
This component measures the current, in amps.

△ **Resistor**
The purpose of this is to resist the flow of current.

△ **Variable resistor**
This device controls the amount of current.

△ **Motor**
A motor moves when current flows through it.

In series

When components are connected in series, they share the voltage of the power source, such as a cell. If there are two identical components, then each will receive half the voltage. The current will stop flowing around the circuit if there is a break at any point.

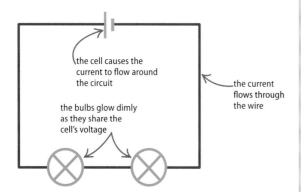
△ **Series circuit**
These two bulbs are arranged in series so they have to share the voltage. They glow dimly as a result.

In parallel

When components are connected in parallel, they are each subject to the whole voltage from the power source. The current will continue to flow through one bulb if the wire leading to the other is broken.

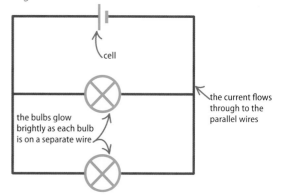
△ **Parallel circuit**
These two bulbs are arranged in parallel so they both receive the full voltage from the cell and glow brightly.

Capacitor

A capacitor is a component used in many circuits to store and release electric charge. There are many different types and sizes of capacitor, many of which are used in circuits to smooth out a varying electric current. At its simplest, a capacitor may consist of two plates of electrically conductive material separated by an insulator called a dielectric. In a direct current (DC) circuit (see page 216), the capacitor stops the flow of current once it has been fully charged.

Supercapacitors that store and release large electrical charges are being developed to replace electric vehicle batteries, since they can be **recharged far more quickly** and more often.

REAL WORLD
Camera flash

Some capacitors are used because they can release their entire charge in just a fraction of a second. Most digital cameras use capacitors, which are charged up by the camera's battery, to power their flash function. The capacitor releases all of its charge almost instantly to enable the flash to fire brightly so that it lights up a dim scene as a photo is taken.

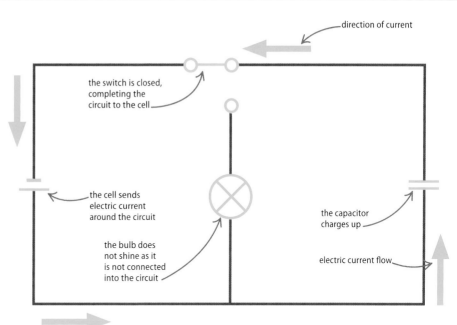

△ **Capacitor stores charge**
In this direct current (DC) circuit, charge flows from the cell to the capacitor. The electric charge builds up on the capacitor's plate while some current continues to flow across the capacitor and around the circuit. As its charge builds, the capacitor resists the flow of current. Once fully charged, it completely stops the flow of current through it.

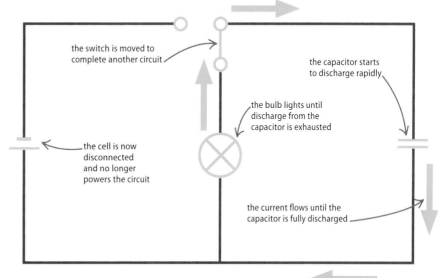

△ **Capacitor releases charge**
Moving the switch disconnects the cell from the circuit but closes and completes another circuit that still contains the capacitor. The capacitor discharges (releases its electrical charge) and the bulb lights up. The bulb will only shine for a short while and will stop once the capacitor is fully discharged.

Electronics

IN ELECTRONIC SYSTEMS, INFORMATION FLOWS IN THE FORM OF PRECISELY CONTROLLED ELECTRICAL SIGNALS THROUGH CIRCUITS.

Almost all modern machines, from computers and phones to washing machines and cars, contain electronic devices of many kinds.

SEE ALSO
‹ 202–203 Electricity
‹ 206–207 Circuits
Electromagnet 211 ›
Electric motors 212–213 ›
Electricity generators 214–215 ›
Transformers 216–217 ›

Electronic components

These are components designed to handle, control, and change the amount of electric current flowing through circuits in a device. The current acts like an electrical signal, instructing the circuit and device to perform specific tasks, from adding up numbers on a calculator to displaying a word on screen. When first invented, these devices were large and bulky, and individually built and wired together. Now they have been miniaturized so that thousands can exist together on a tiny silicon microchip. When electronic circuits are designed, each component is represented by a special symbol, including the ones on the right.

△ **Diode**
This makes current flow in one direction.

△ **Connected wires**
The symbol for wires that are connected.

△ **Overlapping wires**
These wires cross but are not connected.

△ **Light-emitting diode**
This converts electrical energy to light.

△ **Amplifier**
This device increases electrical power.

△ **Transistor**
This device controls the size of current.

△ **Piezo transducer**
Converts electrical energy to sound.

△ **Fuse**
This component burns out if the circuit shorts.

△ **Thermistor**
This device converts heat to electricity.

△ **Generator**
This generates electrical voltage.

△ **AC power supply**
This supplies energy as an alternating current.

△ **DC power supply**
This supplies energy as a direct current.

△ **Inductor**
This is a type of electromagnet.

△ **Transformer**
This varies the current and voltage.

△ **Microphone**
This changes sound into electrical energy.

△ **Aerial**
This device sends or receives radio waves.

Integrated circuits

Modern electronic circuits are built onto tiny rectangles of silicon to make microchips. They are called integrated circuits because the components are all constructed together. An integrated circuit is built up from layers of different materials. Some of these layers are insulators, some are conductors, and some are semiconductors, which allow electricity to flow, but only in certain conditions. Patterns etched in the layers produce the components and their interconnections.

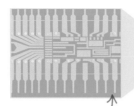
components and connections are etched onto layers of semi-conductor material

microchip is encased in a body with pins to connect to a circuit board

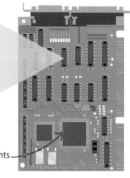
circuit board is fitted with microchips and other components

△ **Integrated circuit**
Electronic components are so small they are only visible under a microscope.

△ **Microchip**
This is constructed from a tiny wafer of silicon, and contains many integrated circuits.

△ **Circuit board**
Containing many microchips and other components, this forms a key part of many devices.

ELECTRONICS

Using codes

We use numbers made up of ten numerals (0, 1, 2, 3, 4, 5, 6, 7, 8, and 9), but computers use only two numerals: 0 and 1. This is because computer circuits store data in the form of switches. Each switch holds a single "bit" of information. If the switch is on, this information is a 1; if the switch is off, it is a 0. This means that all information must be coded for the computer as 1s and 0s. This leads to very long numbers, so, to make it easier for humans to handle, binary is often converted into hexadecimal (base 16) numbers.

Decimal	Binary	Hexadecimal
0	0000	0
1	0001	1
2	0010	2
3	0011	3
4	0100	4
5	0101	5
6	0110	6
7	0111	7
8	1000	8
9	1001	9
10	1010	A
11	1011	B
12	1100	C
13	1101	D
14	1110	E
15	1111	F

△ **Conversion table**
This table shows the decimal (base 10) number system we use converted to binary (base 2) numbers and hexadecimal (base 16) numbers.

The first electronic component was the **diode**, invented in 1904 by English scientist Ambrose Fleming.

Logic gates

A logic gate is used to make a simple decision. It accepts an electrical signal from its inputs (it can have one or two) and then outputs either an "on," high-voltage signal (representing 1) or an "off," low-voltage signal (representing 0). In computers and many other electronic devices, large numbers of logic gates are linked together to form complex circuits. The image below shows three commonly found logic gates and their possible inputs and outputs.

▷ **AND gate**
There will only be an output from the gate if both inputs are on.

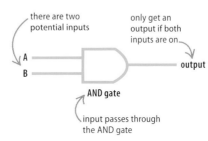

there are two potential inputs

only get an output if both inputs are on

input passes through the AND gate

AND gate		
Input A	Input B	Output
1	0	0
0	1	0
0	0	0
1	1	1

▷ **OR gate**
There will be an ouput if one or both inputs are on.

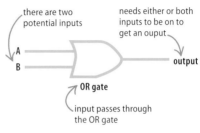

there are two potential inputs

needs either or both inputs to be on to get an ouput

input passes through the OR gate

OR gate		
Input A	Input B	Output
0	0	0
0	1	1
1	0	1
1	1	1

▷ **NOT gate**
The output is on only if the input is off. If the input is on, the output is off.

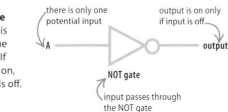

there is only one potential input

output is on only if input is off

input passes through the NOT gate

NOT gate	
Input	Output
0	1
1	0

REAL WORLD
Retinal implant

Modern electronic devices can be so small, reliable, and sensitive that they can be implanted in the human retina to help some partially sighted people see. Light falling onto the implant is converted into electrical signals that stimulate the optic nerve. The brain interprets these signals as patterns of dark and light, and allows the patient to see objects.

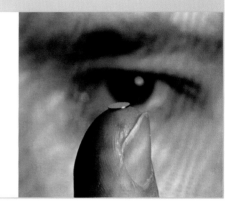

Magnets

MAGNETS PRODUCE A MAGNETIC FIELD, WHICH ATTRACTS SOME MATERIALS AND CAN ATTRACT OR REPEL OTHER MAGNETS.

SEE ALSO	
‹ 124–125 Transition metals	
‹ 172–173 Forces and mass	
‹ 203 Electric currents	
Electric motors	212–213 ›
Electricity generators	214–215 ›

Some magnets occur naturally, while some materials can be made magnetic by passing an electric current through them. Some materials can be permanently magnetized.

Magnetic force

In magnetic materials, areas called domains behave like tiny magnets. When not magnetized, these are all jumbled up and point in different directions, but when placed in a magnetic field or stroked repeatedly by a magnet, the domains all line up so that all their north poles point in one direction and the south poles in the opposite direction, making the material magnetic.

▷ **Single bar magnet**
The area around the magnet where its magnetism can affect other materials is called its magnetic field. A bar magnet has a north pole at one end and a south pole at the other. Cutting a bar magnet in two creates two magnets, each with their own north and south poles.

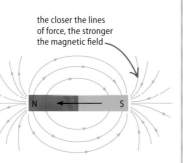

the closer the lines of force, the stronger the magnetic field

▷ **Horseshoe magnet**
Magnets come in all kinds of shapes, such as the horseshoe magnet. This type of magnet also has a north and south pole, but it is curved, so the poles are close together.

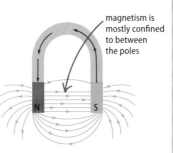

magnetism is mostly confined to between the poles

▽ **Attract or repel**
Two magnets will be attracted to each other if unlike poles (one north and one south) face each other. However, like poles repel, pushing each other away.

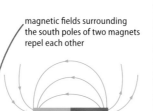

magnetic fields surrounding the south poles of two magnets repel each other

Permanent magnets

Some materials, including iron, nickel, cobalt, and their alloys (metals combined with metals or nonmetals), are ferromagnetic. These can be magnetized by an electric current or by stroking another magnet. Once magnetized, these materials stay magnetic unless demagnetized by a shock, excess heat, or a variable magnetic field.

▽ **Magnetic objects**
Steel is an alloy of iron, and is used to make cans and paper clips. "Copper" coins actually contain nickel.

▽ **Nonmagnetic objects**
Common plastics are not magnetic, nor are aluminum beer and soda cans, or brass musical instruments.

REAL WORLD
Lodestone compass

Lodestone is a naturally occurring magnetic mineral that was used thousands of years ago to make the first compasses. If a piece of lodestone is allowed to spin freely, it will align itself with the Earth's magnetic field, pointing in a north–south direction. The word "magnet" comes from "Magnesia," the area in Greece where lodestones and magnesium were found.

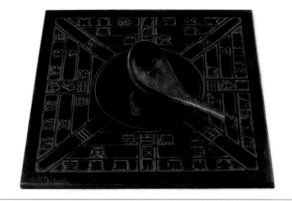

Earth's magnetic field

The Earth can be thought of as one big powerful magnet whose magnetic field, called the magnetosphere, stretches tens of thousands of kilometers out into space. The planet's magnetism is caused by the motion of liquid metals in its outer core. For an unknown reason, the direction of the Earth's field reverses suddenly, about once every million years.

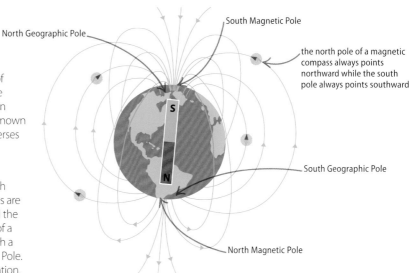

▷ **Magnetic Earth**
The magnetic pole at Earth's north is a south pole, because the north poles of compasses are attracted by it. Confusingly, it is often called the South Magnetic Pole. There is a difference of a few degrees between the direction in which a compass points and the North Geographic Pole. This difference is called the angle of declination.

Electromagnet

Magnets are not the only source of magnetic fields. An electric current flowing through a conductor produces a circular magnetic field at right angles to the conductor. The current creates an electromagnet—a device that is extremely useful since its magnetism can be controlled and switched on and off. The poles of an electromagnet will be reversed if the direction of the current is reversed.

▽ **Solenoid**
A solenoid is a common form of electromagnet. It consists of a coil of wire through which an electric current is passed to produce a magnetic field. The soft iron core in the middle of this solenoid helps produce a stronger magnetic field and does not retain its magnetism after the current is switched off.

▽ **Field direction**
The direction of the magnetic field can be remembered by making a loose fist with your fingers of your right hand as if grasping the conductor. Sticking your thumb up in the direction of the current, your fingers follow a curving path in the direction of the magnetic field.

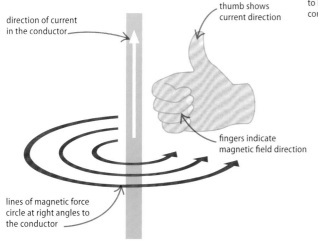

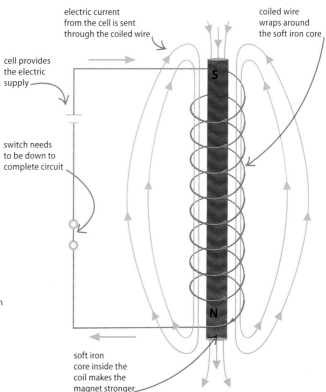

Electric motors

AN ELECTRIC CURRENT AND THE FORCES IN A MAGNETIC FIELD CAN COMBINE TO CREATE MOTION.

SEE ALSO
‹ 170–171 Energy
‹ 203 Electric currents
‹ 210–211 Magnets
Electricity generators 214–215 ›

An electric motor turns because of the forces of attraction and repulsion between a permanent magnet and an electromagnet.

Inside a motor
A wire coil sits between the opposite poles of one or more permanent magnets. When an electric current is passed through the wire coil, it generates a magnetic field, which interacts with the magnetic field of the surrounding permanent magnets, repelling like poles and attracting unlike poles, which make the wire coil rotate half a turn. The electric current is then reversed to switch the wire coil's magnetic poles, so that it moves another half-turn. Repeating this process results in the coil spinning around.

▽ **Left-hand rule**
This rule can be used to work out the direction an electric motor turns.

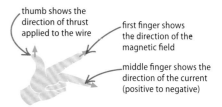

thumb shows the direction of thrust applied to the wire
first finger shows the direction of the magnetic field
middle finger shows the direction of the current (positive to negative)

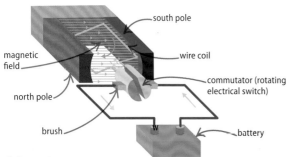

△ **Stage 1**
In this simple DC electric motor, current flows from the battery through the commutator and into the wire coil. This turns it into an electromagnet and generates a magnetic field, which interacts with the field of the permanent magnet.

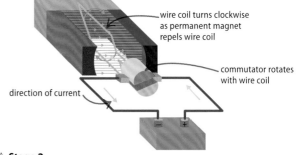

△ **Stage 2**
Repelled by the permanent magnet's like poles, the wire coil starts turning. After a quarter-turn, the permanent magnets also begin attracting the opposite pole of the wire coil, helping to complete the half-turn.

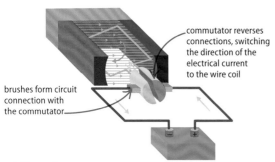

△ **Stage 3**
With the poles of the wire coil and permanent magnet now lining up, the commutator reverses the direction of the current in the wire coil. This switches the polarity of the wire coil's magnetic field.

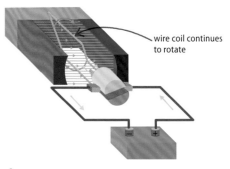

△ **Stage 4**
With the coil's current reversed, the like poles of the coil and permanent magnet repel again. The coil continues to rotate. When it completes another half-turn, the commutator will reverse the current again to keep the coil spinning.

Loudspeaker

A loudspeaker uses the motion generated by the forces between a permanent magnet and an electromagnet to reproduce sound. Fluctuating electric current enters the coil, producing a fluctuating magnetic field. The forces between this field and that of the permanent magnet move the coil rapidly in and out. The coil moves the cone and these movements generate sound waves.

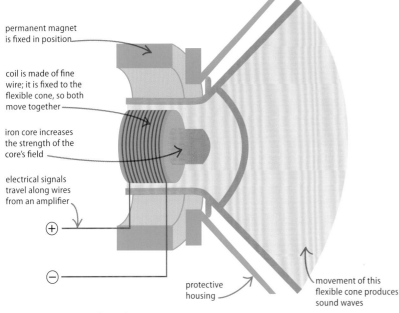

△ **Electromagnetism in action**
The forces acting on the moving parts of a loudspeaker are electromagnetic, produced by the interaction of the permanent magnet and the coil electromagnet.

REAL WORLD
Robotic arm

The joints and parts of an industrial robot arm, such as this car welding robot, are powered by electric stepper motors. A central rotor can be turned in steps by the magnets, making the motor capable of very precise movements.

The **world's smallest electric motor** is just 1nm (1 nanometer) across.

Linear motor

This type of electric motor creates a force in a straight line rather than the turning force of a traditional rotary motor. It achieves this by a continuous sequence of magnetic attraction and repulsion between electromagnets along a track and magnets attached to a sled, train, or some other object running along the track. The electromagnets repeatedly switch their polarity to move the object down the track without the need for wheels.

▷ **Magnetic motion**
Maglev (magnetic levitation) trains use powerful magnets to float above a track and are propelled forward at great speed by a linear motor.

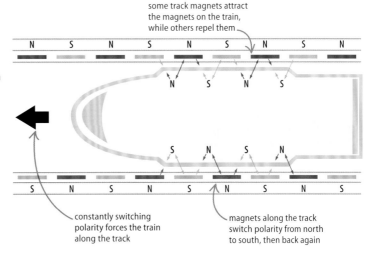

Electricity generators

GENERATORS USE INDUCTION TO CHANGE MOTION INTO ELECTRICAL POWER.

SEE ALSO	
❰ 170–171	Energy
❰ 186–187	Machines
❰ 210–211	Magnets
❰ 212–213	Electric motors
Power generation	218–219 ❱

Generators, also called dynamos, are vital in many areas of technology. For example, turbines use them to change the kinetic energy of moving wind, water, or steam into electrical energy.

Electromagnetic induction

In 1831, English scientist Michael Faraday (1797–1867) discovered that when a magnet was moved in or out of a coil of wire, an electric current was produced. A voltage and current is produced in a conductor (the coil of wire) when it cuts across a magnetic field because the magnetic field lines of force act on the free electrons in the conductor, causing them to move. This principle, known as induction, is the basis on which all generators work.

Built in 1871, the **Gramme dynamo** was the first electricity generator to generate power commercially.

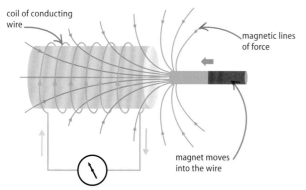

△ **Magnet moves in**
A generator works when the magnet moves into the wire. The induction effect is stronger if the conductor is coiled.

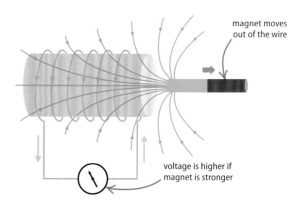

△ **Magnet moves out**
When the magnet moves out of the conductor, current is induced in the opposite direction.

Bicycle dynamo

A bicycle dynamo contains a permanent magnet fitted to a shaft. As the bicycle wheel turns, the dynamo shaft turns, rotating the permanent magnet inside a coil of wire wrapped around a soft iron core. The changing magnetic field of the turning permanent magnet induces a current in the coil, which flows from the dynamo to power the bicycle's front and rear lights.

▷ **Electromagnetic induction in action**
In this bicycle dynamo, the wire coil is fixed in place and the permanent magnet rotates inside it. Friction between the grooved dynamo wheel and the tire wall causes the shaft holding the magnet to rotate when the bicycle wheel turns.

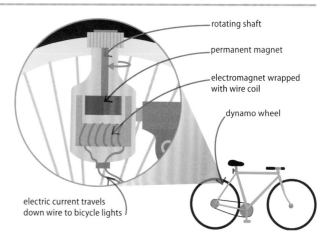

ELECTRICITY GENERATORS

Direct current generator

Generators can be built to produce either direct current (DC) or alternating current (AC) (see page 216). A DC generator has the same parts as a DC electric motor but works in reverse (see page 212). The wire coil of the conducting wire is turned inside a magnetic field that is generated by a large permanent magnet. As the wire in the coil cuts across the magnetic field lines, a voltage and current are created in the coil.

▷ **Right-hand rule**
This rule shows the direction in which a current will flow in a wire when the wire moves in a magnetic field.

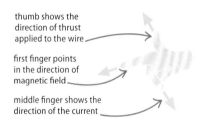

thumb shows the direction of thrust applied to the wire

first finger points in the direction of magnetic field

middle finger shows the direction of the current

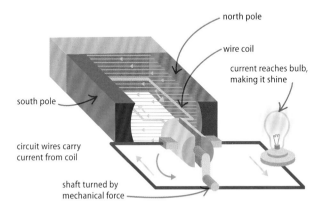

△ **Stage 1**
An experimental direct current generator sees the wire coil turned by a hand crank. As it passes through the magnetic field of the permanent magnet, a current is induced in the wire coil.

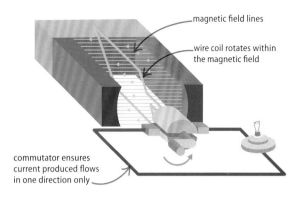

△ **Stage 2**
An electric current is only generated when the wire coil is cutting the horizontal magnetic field lines. When the wire coil is vertical, no current is produced and the bulb does not light up.

Alternating current generator

An alternating current (AC) generator, known as an alternator, does not use a commutator. As a result, the current produced changes direction twice for every complete 360° turn of the coil. Individual slip rings are fitted to each of the two ends of the coil to provide a path for the current to leave. Brushes contact the slip rings and complete the path for the current into the circuit to which the generator is attached.

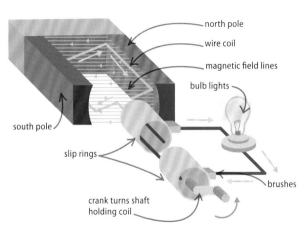

◁ **Alternator in action**
This simple alternator has a single loop of wire acting as the coil. Turning a hand crank rotates the coil between the poles of a permanent magnet. An alternating current is induced in the coil, which flows through the slip rings and brushes to light the bulb.

REAL WORLD
Wind-up electrics

In parts of the world where electricity is unreliable or absent, and batteries are expensive, radios (as below), laptops, and other electronic devices can be powered by hand. A small generator inside the device is turned by a hand crank to charge up the rechargeable batteries inside.

Transformers

TRANSFORMERS CHANGE THE VOLTAGE OF AC POWER.

Alternating current can be changed to a higher or lower voltage by a device called a transformer. For example, high voltage from a power station needs to be transformed to a lower voltage for use in homes.

SEE ALSO	
⟨ 186–187 Machines	
⟨ 200 Pitch and loudness	
⟨ 203 Electric currents	
⟨ 208–209 Electronics	
⟨ 214 Electromagnetic induction	
Power grid	220 ⟩

Direct and alternating current

There are two kinds of current: direct and alternating. Direct current (DC) is usually produced by batteries and it flows one way around a circuit. Electricity—as used in homes—has an alternating current (AC), in which the direction of the flow of electricity reverses dozens of times a second. Transformers are devices that can be used to change the voltages and currents of AC (see pages 204–205). They make it easy to change AC to a high-voltage form for transmission over long distances, and to a low-voltage form for domestic use.

▷ **AC and DC voltage**
In this graph, the green line represents DC voltage and the green area is the energy transferred by this voltage. To transfer the same energy in the same time (as shown by the blue areas), the AC voltage must rise higher than the DC voltage at some parts of its cycle, as the orange line shows.

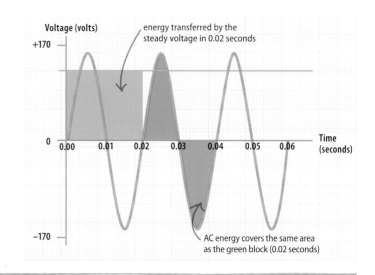

Transformers

An inductor is a coil of wire that stores energy in a magnetic field. A transformer is two inductors in one: two coils share the same core. When an alternating current passes through one coil, the core sets up currents in the other coil. If this second coil has more turns than the first, then the voltage across it is higher.

▷ **Voltage and coils**
The ratio of the number of volts that pass through the primary and secondary transformers is equal to the ratio of the number of turns in the primary and secondary coils.

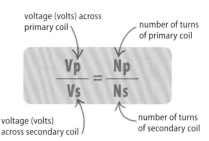

$$\frac{V_p}{V_s} = \frac{N_p}{N_s}$$

voltage (volts) across primary coil
number of turns of primary coil
voltage (volts) across secondary coil
number of turns of secondary coil

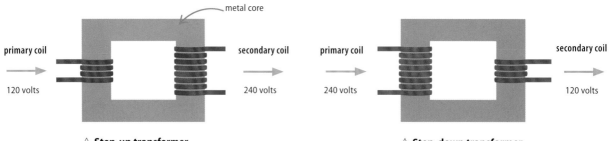

△ **Step-up transformer**
The second inductor has twice as many turns as the first, so its voltage is twice that in the first.

△ **Step-down transformer**
The second inductor has half as many turns as the first, so the voltage is halved as a result.

TRANSFORMERS 217

Induction in action

Induction is the production of an electrical current by a changing magnetic field. Many devices, from microphones (see below) to microcomputer parts, rely on it. Computer hard disks, for instance, store data magnetically on a stack of disklike platters. The surface of each platter contains billions of individual areas, each of which can be magnetized. The patterns of magnetism store data as binary digits (1s for magnetized areas and 0s for demagnetized areas) and are produced by induction caused by a tiny moving electromagnet.

▷ **Hard disk**
A hard disk drive consists of a set of disks called platters. Data is written, read, or deleted by an electromagnet on a moving arm.

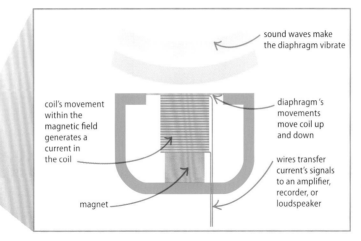

- magnet moves the arm from side to side
- arm is very light so that it can flick quickly to the correct position
- read–write head at the tip of the arm contains a tiny electromagnet
- disk spins at a high speed, and the head reads and writes as the surface passes beneath

- a metal mesh protects the delicate diaphragm. Outdoors, special shields are used to reduce the noise of the wind blowing across it
- sound waves make the diaphragm vibrate
- coil's movement within the magnetic field generates a current in the coil
- diaphragm's movements move coil up and down
- wires transfer current's signals to an amplifier, recorder, or loudspeaker
- magnet

◁ **Take a look inside**
In a microphone, sound waves vibrate a diaphragm, which is attached to a wire coil. As the coil moves, it induces currents, which form a changing electrical signal.

◁ **Microphone**
A microphone is carefully designed so that it mimics the sounds it receives, and does not overemphasize particular frequencies.

> Electromagnets are used to **lift heavy loads** of steel. The most powerful can lift single loads **weighing more than 250 tons**.

REAL WORLD
Induction cooking

The electromagnet in an induction stovetop generates a magnetic field. Some of its energy transfers to the metal pan via the process of induction, as circulating electric currents. The electrical resistance of the metal means that some of this electrical energy is converted to heat, warming the pan but not the surface.

Power generation

ELECTRICITY IS PRODUCED IN DIFFERENT WAYS.

Electricity is generated on a large scale in power stations. They work in different ways, but they all harness a source of energy and use it to power giant electricity generators.

SEE ALSO	
❰ 28 Respiration	
❰ 126–127 Radioactivity	
❰ 156–157 Carbon and fossil fuels	
❰ 214–215 Electricity generators	
Renewable energy	224–225 ❱

Thermal power station

This is the most common type of power station. Its source of energy is a fossil fuel, generally natural gas, coal, or oil. The heat released by burning the fuel boils water into steam. The steam is forced under high pressure through the turbine, making it spin. This rotation is transmitted to the generator.

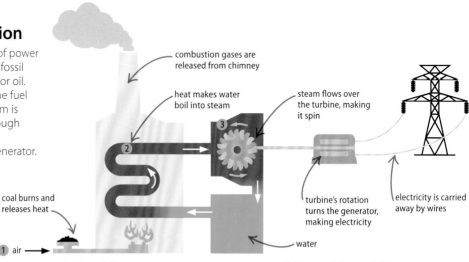

1. Heat from fuel
Solid fuels, like coal, are crushed into small particles, increasing its surface area so that it burns faster and hotter. The gases released by the combustion are released from a chimney.

2. Water into steam
The water boils in the furnace, turns into steam, and passes over the propeller-like blades. The steam then condenses back into water to begin the process again.

3. Motion into electricity
The rotational motion of the turbine is passed to the generator, where a conductor is spun around in a magnetic field, inducing an electric current.

Hydroelectricity

In a hydroelectric power station, the energy of falling water is used to generate electricity. A dam built across a river builds up a large reservoir of water behind it. The water is released through a pipe, or penstock, to form a high-pressure flow that spins a turbine at the bottom. A water-driven turbine has cup-shaped blades, unlike the wing shapes on a gas or steam turbine.

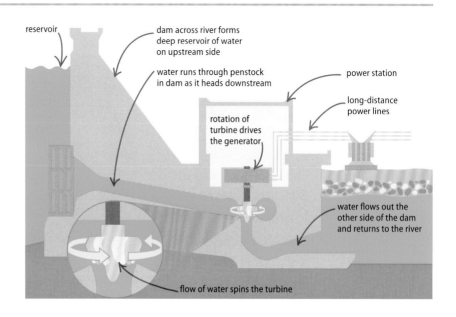

▷ **Power station**
The turbine inside the dam is connected to a generator in a power station on the downstream side of the dam.

POWER GENERATION | 219

Energy from atoms

Nuclear power stations use radioactive materials, such as uranium or thorium, as a source of heat. Radioactive elements produce heat as they decay, but a great deal more heat is produced by a process called nuclear fission. The fuel is refined to contain large amounts of a particular radioactive isotope (see pages 126–127) that can be split into two smaller atoms. Uncontrolled fission causes the explosion of a nuclear bomb, but the process is slowed down in nuclear reactors.

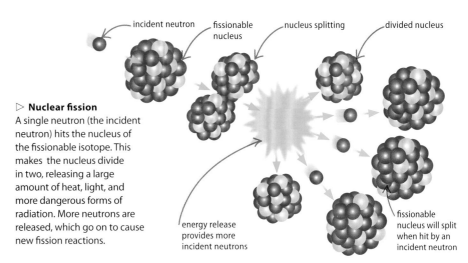

▷ **Nuclear fission**
A single neutron (the incident neutron) hits the nucleus of the fissionable isotope. This makes the nucleus divide in two, releasing a large amount of heat, light, and more dangerous forms of radiation. More neutrons are released, which go on to cause new fission reactions.

Nuclear reactor

The fission reaction takes place inside a reactor filled with water or gas. The reactor has a core containing fuel rods made of radioactive material. The reaction heats the water, which is pumped through a heat exchanger, where the superheated water makes steam that drives the turbines. There are also control rods, made largely of boron, which soak up some of the free neutrons, limiting the number of fissions that occur and so controlling the process.

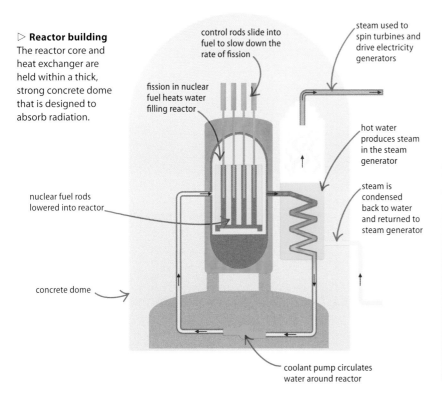

▷ **Reactor building**
The reactor core and heat exchanger are held within a thick, strong concrete dome that is designed to absorb radiation.

REAL WORLD
Cherenkov radiation

The water surrounding a nuclear reactor has an eerie blue color, which is caused by Cherenkov radiation, named after the Russian scientist Pavel Cherenkov (1904–1990). This happens because charged particles move through the water at an extremely high velocity.

Electricity supplies

ELECTRICITY IS SENT FROM POWER STATIONS FOR USE IN HOMES AND WORKPLACES VIA A HUGE NETWORK OF CABLES.

SEE ALSO	
‹ 202–203	Electricity
‹ 204	What is voltage?
‹ 206–207	Circuits
‹ 218–219	Power generation

Almost all the electricity used in homes, offices, and factories is generated at large power stations far from where people live. It is sent across country in a power grid, before being transformed into a usable current suitable for domestic use.

Power grid

Electricity is generated as an alternating current (AC). This is boosted to several hundred thousand volts by a transformer before it enters the power grid. The high voltage reduces the amount of energy lost as heat as currents travel along wires hundreds of kilometers long. Burying high-voltage lines is very expensive, so most of the power grid is made up of lightweight aluminum cables suspended from pylons, high in the air for safety.

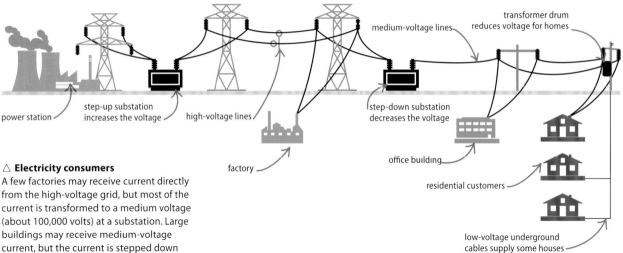

△ **Electricity consumers**
A few factories may receive current directly from the high-voltage grid, but most of the current is transformed to a medium voltage (about 100,000 volts) at a substation. Large buildings may receive medium-voltage current, but the current is stepped down again by transformers to between 110 and 250 volts before reaching homes.

Future power grids may use superconductors to carry **ten times as much current** as today's cables.

REAL WORLD
Power cuts

When the power grid fails, it results in a power cut. No current arrives at homes and offices, and the lights—and everything else—go off. A power cut can be caused by a simple failure of a transformer or a cable being damaged by a storm. However, huge power cuts have also been caused by solar storms, where a surge of charged particles from the Sun overloads the grid, causing it to shut down.

ELECTRICITY SUPPLIES

Domestic circuits

A domestic electricity supply connects to the grid at the consumer unit, or fuse box. Powerful electrical appliances, such as an oven, have a direct connection to the fuse box. Others are connected by ring or radial circuits. Ring circuits can use thinner wires to supply the same power as a radial circuit, but radial circuits can be extended easily and can carry smaller amounts of current. So, radial circuits are often used for lighting and ring circuits are used for power sockets.

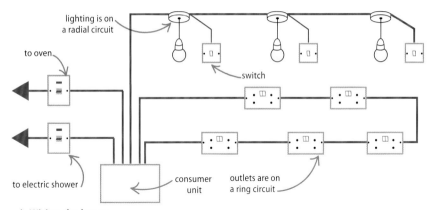

△ **Wiring the house**
This simplified diagram shows the wiring in a house. Normally each floor of a house has two circuits: one for the lighting, another for the electrical outlets.

Protecting circuits

If too much current runs through domestic circuits, the wiring or appliances connected to it may get very hot and cause a fire. The consumer unit contains automatic switches called circuit breakers that cut off the supply if dangerous electrical surges occur. The circuit breaker also responds to short circuits, where faulty wiring or a damaged appliance results in the circuit drawing much more current than is normal. Fuses in plugs will also cut dangerous currents.

▽ **Electrical plug**
Most appliances connect to the electrical supply via a plug that fits into an outlet in the wall. Every plug has a live wire that delivers the current to it. The neutral wire carries the current back to the main circuit.

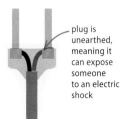

plug is unearthed, meaning it can expose someone to an electric shock

▽ **Earth wire**
A third wire is sometimes used in plugs. The earth wire connects the appliance to the ground via the domestic circuit. If a fault damages the insulation in the plug, any leaking current will flow safely to the ground via the earth wire.

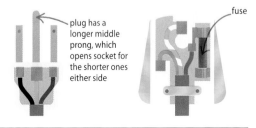

plug has a longer middle prong, which opens socket for the shorter ones either side

▽ **Fused plugs**
The plugs in many countries are fitted with fuses—thin wires through which the current passes. If too much current passes through, the fuse wire gets hot and melts, breaking the circuit before other components get too hot.

fuse

Adaptor

Many devices come equipped with an oversized plug, known as an adaptor. The current flowing through domestic circuits is AC, which is fine for simple devices such as light bulbs and heaters. However, the back-and-forth surges of an AC supply would damage sensitive electronics, such as microchips, so an adaptor is used to filter the AC into a direct current (DC), which only travels in one direction.

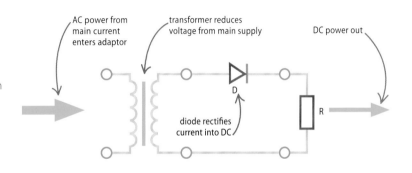

▷ **Rectifier**
The main component in an adaptor is the rectifier. This is a type of diode (D) that only lets current pass in one direction.

Energy efficiency

ENERGY IS LOST AS HEAT BY ALL MACHINES AND PROCESSES.

When a machine or activity is designed or planned, it should be as efficient as possible. This means that as much as possible of the energy output should be used for work.

SEE ALSO
‹ 170–171 Energy
‹ 188–189 Heat transfer
‹ 216–217 Transformers

Lost energy

At a subatomic scale, some processes occur with 100 percent transfer of energy from one form to another, but on a larger scale, this never happens. Some energy is always turned into heat, which is usually unwanted. Other types of unwanted energy may also be produced: many machines make a lot of noise, which is a wasteful and unpleasant form of acoustic energy.

▽ **Energy loss**
Only a third of the energy consumed by thermal power plants reaches customers as electricity.

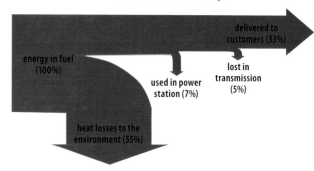

energy in fuel (100%)
used in power station (7%)
lost in transmission (5%)
delivered to customers (33%)
heat losses to the environment (55%)

▽ **Energy conversion**
Every type of energy conversion has a maximum possible efficiency. Some processes are wasteful, while others convert a very high proportion of one form of energy into another.

CONVERSION EFFICIENCIES		
Energy process	**Conversion taking place**	**Maximum possible efficiency**
photosynthesis	radiant energy from the Sun to chemical energy in the plant	6%
solar cell	radiant energy from the Sun to electrical energy, often produced by silicon crystals	28%
muscle	chemical energy from chemicals in the blood to kinetic energy as the muscle contracts	30%
coal-fired power station	chemical energy from coal to electrical energy from turbines	40%
internal combustion	chemical energy from gasoline or diesel to kinetic energy used to make vehicle move	50%
wind turbine	kinetic energy of the wind to electrical energy from a generator	60%
electric heater	electrical energy to thermal energy, produced by electrical resistance of the element	100%

REAL WORLD
Fiberoptic cable

Until a few decades ago, telephone and computer signals were usually sent in the form of electric currents that traveled down copper wires. Although copper conducts electricity very well, some of the electrical energy is lost in the form of heat. Now, optical fibers have replaced many copper wires. In an optical fiber, signals travel in the form of light, and only a tiny amount of the light energy is changed to heat, making it a far more efficient system.

Many **household appliances** are not energy efficent—the only 100 percent efficient device is the **electric heater**. However, they can be very expensive to use.

ENERGY EFFICIENCY

Heat loss and insulation

Sometimes we wish to produce as much heat as we can, rather than as little as possible. When we do, it is important to prevent the heat escaping. The main ways to reduce heat loss from buildings are to keep doors and windows closed and to install heat insulation.

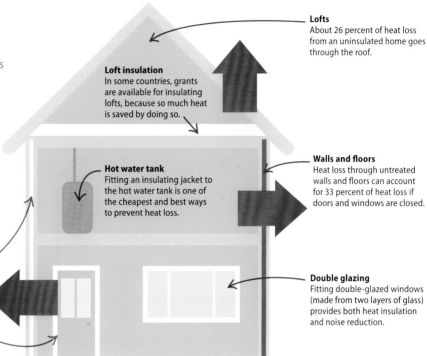

Lofts
About 26 percent of heat loss from an uninsulated home goes through the roof.

Loft insulation
In some countries, grants are available for insulating lofts, because so much heat is saved by doing so.

Hot water tank
Fitting an insulating jacket to the hot water tank is one of the cheapest and best ways to prevent heat loss.

Walls and floors
Heat loss through untreated walls and floors can account for 33 percent of heat loss if doors and windows are closed.

Double glazing
Fitting double-glazed windows (made from two layers of glass) provides both heat insulation and noise reduction.

▷ **Keeping warm for less**
Heating a well-insulated home costs only a small fraction of the amount required to heat an uninsulated one. Here are some ideas to help keep a house warm and save money.

Cavity wall insulation
Most houses are built with hollow outer walls. The gaps can be filled with foam, which sets hard and provides effective insulation.

Doors and windows
In an uninsulated house, gaps around doors and windows can account for 11 percent of heat loss.

Fluorescent bulbs

One of the easiest ways to save energy is to replace incandescent (filament) bulbs, with energy-efficient fluorescent versions. An incandescent bulb glows because the current passes through a high-resistance bare wire (the filament). The resistance means that enough electrical energy is converted to heat to make it glow with light.

▷ **Compact fluorescent lamps (CFL)**
Compact fluorescent lamps (CFLs) are gradually replacing domestic, incandescent bulbs because they are more energy efficient and last longer. CFLs feature a spiraling glass tube full of gases, which emit ultraviolet light when an electric current passes through them. This triggers a phosphor coating on the tube to shine brightly.

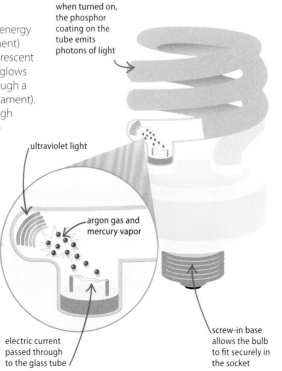

when turned on, the phosphor coating on the tube emits photons of light

ultraviolet light

argon gas and mercury vapor

electric current passed through to the glass tube

screw-in base allows the bulb to fit securely in the socket

▽ **Compact fluorescent lamp**
If 100 J (joules) of energy is passed through a CFL, most of the energy appears as light (75 J), so less electricity is required and less unnecessary heat (25 J) is produced.

electrical energy 100 J → light energy 75 J
heat energy 25 J

▽ **Domestic incandescent bulb**
From 100 J of electrical energy, most of the energy supplied to a domestic incandescent bulb is converted to heat (90 J), while only a small portion (10 J) is converted to light.

light energy 10 J
electrical energy 100 J
heat energy 90 J

Renewable energy

RENEWABLE ENERGY SOURCES ARE AN ACTIVE AREA OF RESEARCH WORLDWIDE.

SEE ALSO	
‹ 192–193 Waves	
‹ 218 Hydroelectricity	
Wind	228 ›
The Sun	232–233 ›

Fossil fuels (coal, oil, and natural gas) will not last forever, and they cause serious pollution. Nuclear energy produces waste that remains dangerous for many centuries. So, alternative sources of energy are being developed.

Solar energy

There are two main ways to convert sunlight into usable energy. The first way is in a solar thermal collector, where a liquid is heated by being pumped through sunlit pipes, and then used to heat a boiler. The second way is to turn it into electrical power by means of photovoltaic cells. These contain material such as the element selenium, which produces an electrical voltage when light falls on it.

▷ **Heat from the Sun**
Solar thermal collectors can be used to heat water for warming a house, as shown in this illustration.

1. The solar thermal collectors contain water-filled pipes, which are heated by the Sun.

2. Heated water is pushed from the top of the collectors down the pipe by the cooler water entering the collectors at the base.

3. The electronic controller controls the pump and checks water temperature in solar thermal collectors and tank.

4. The water passes through pipes in the tank, warming the water in the tank. This cools the water in the pipes.

5. The pipe takes the hot water to the hot faucets in the house.

6. The gas or electric boiler provides extra heat to the water tank if solar-heated water is too cold.

7. Cold water from main supply replaces hot water used in the house, so the water tank is always full.

8. A pump keeps the water moving through the pipes.

9. The water has lost heat to the water in the tank. The pump pushes it up the pipe to the solar thermal collectors, to be heated again.

Wind turbines

A wind turbine converts the motion of the wind into electrical power. Many wind turbines are grouped into arrays and these are often offshore, where conditions are windier. As winds do not always blow, the amount of energy from wind farms is variable. Wind farms can be unpopular because of their appearance and the noise they make, so careful siting is essential.

▷ **Inside a wind turbine**
When the wind turbine blades rotate, a generator (dynamo) produces electricity. A system of gears converts the relatively slow spin of the blades into a more rapid rotation in the dynamo, producing more electrical power.

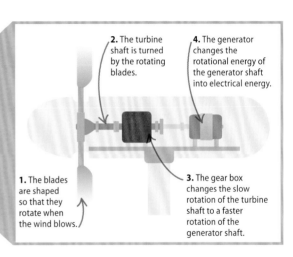

1. The blades are shaped so that they rotate when the wind blows.

2. The turbine shaft is turned by the rotating blades.

3. The gear box changes the slow rotation of the turbine shaft to a faster rotation of the generator shaft.

4. The generator changes the rotational energy of the generator shaft into electrical energy.

RENEWABLE ENERGY

Tidal power

The movements of the sea can be converted into usable power in a number of ways. In one type of tidal power system, both the incoming and outgoing tides produce electricity by turning turbines.

▽ **Inward tide**
The incoming tide passes through a gap in a sea wall and turns a turbine mounted in the gap.

▽ **Outward tide**
When the tide goes out, the water flows back through the gap, turning the turbines again, generating more electricity.

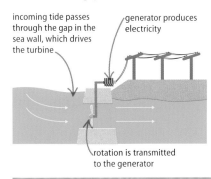

incoming tide passes through the gap in the sea wall, which drives the turbine

generator produces electricity

rotation is transmitted to the generator

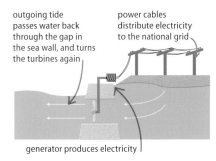

outgoing tide passes water back through the gap in the sea wall, and turns the turbines again

power cables distribute electricity to the national grid

generator produces electricity

REAL WORLD
Energy from the waves

The Pelamis wave energy converter draws power from sea waves. The converter is made of floating sections that are hinged together. As they bend with the waves, the "hinges" force fluid along pipes, and the pressure of the fluid is used to rotate turbines and generate electricity.

Geothermal energy

The interior of Earth is hotter than the surface—on average, the temperature increases by an interval of around 30°C (50°F) for every kilometer (0.6 miles) of depth. The difference between the surface and underground temperatures can be exploited to generate electricity, or simply to heat water for domestic use.

▷ **Electricity from underground**
In this geothermal system, water is pumped underground and pushes groundwater up to the surface. This water contains mineral salts and is referred to as geothermal brine. The brine is hot enough to boil and the high-pressure steam produced is used to turn turbines in a power station, generating electricity. The power station then distributes this electricity to the power grid, so it can be used in homes and buildings.

6. An array of turbines and electrical generators converts kinetic energy into electrical energy.

the power station adjusts voltage and distributes electricity to the power grid

5. The boiling brine produces high-pressure steam to rotate the turbine blades.

7. The cooler steam passes to the condenser, where the steam turns to water. The process then begins again.

4. The brine is so hot that it boils as soon as it leaves the pipe.

waste brine goes back into the injection well

1. The water is forced down the injection well.

very hot undergound area

3. The hot brine is forced up the production well.

2. The water from the injection well heats up, and, when chemicals dissolve in it, it turns into brine.

The Earth

OUR PLANET IS THE THIRD FROM THE SUN AND ONE OF FOUR IN THE SOLAR SYSTEM MADE MAINLY OF ROCK AND METAL.

Earth is the only planet where liquid water is known to exist. It is also the only place in the Universe known to support life.

SEE ALSO	
⟨ 20–21 Variety of life	
⟨ 100–101 Changing states	
⟨ 142 States of water	
⟨ 192–193 Waves	
⟨ 211 Earth's magnetic field	
The Solar System I	234–235 ⟩

Inside the Earth

Earth is a mixture of rock and metal. The solid inner core is made of iron and nickel, and the outer core is a mix of molten iron and nickel. The surrounding mantle is a thick layer of solid and semimolten rock. A thin, rocky outer shell consists of thick continental crust (land) and thinner oceanic crust (seafloor).

▷ **Inner heat**
Inside, the Earth is very hot. The temperature at the inner core reaches 4,700°C (8,500°F). The heat causes the semimolten rock in the mantle to circulate slowly.

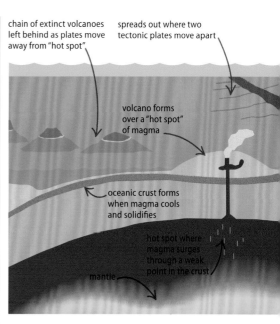

The seasons

Earth experiences seasons because it rotates on a tilted axis as it travels around the Sun, an orbit that takes one year. As different areas of the planet face toward or away from the Sun, the length of the day and temperature change, which affect plant growth and animal behavior.

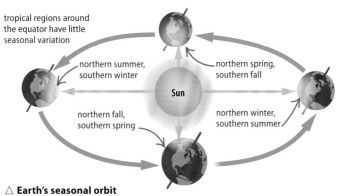

△ **Earth's seasonal orbit**
When the North Pole turns to face the Sun it is summer in the Northern Hemisphere and winter in the south. Six months later, when the South Pole tilts toward the Sun, it is summer in the south and winter in the north.

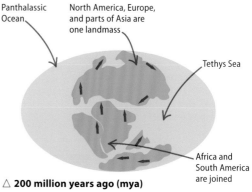

△ **200 million years ago (mya)**
From a single landmass called Pangaea, the continents begin breaking apart. The northern continents become separated from those in the south by the Tethys Sea.

Plate tectonics

Earth's crust is broken up into sections called tectonic plates. The plates drift on the mantle as it is slowly churned by currents caused by heat from the core. Where two plates move together, at a convergent boundary, one plate dives under another to form a mountain range. At a divergent boundary the plates move apart and molten material from the mantle, known as magma, erupts at the surface as a volcano. Where plates grind alongside each other, earthquakes occur as the rocks catch and then jerk free.

▽ **Violent Earth**
As plates constantly move, oceans are pulled apart, and continents may either crash into each other or break away.

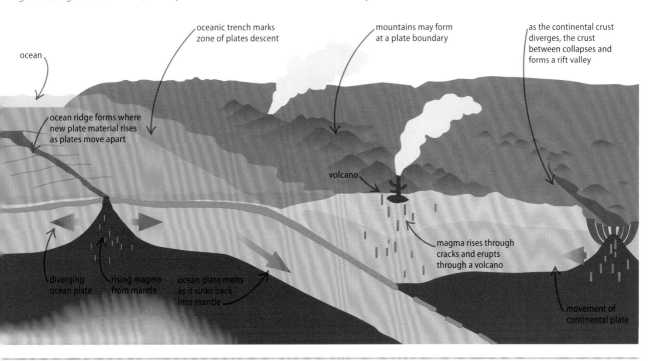

Continental drift

Over millions of years, the motion of Earth's plates has caused the continents to drift apart. If you could put them together, they would all fit, like a jigsaw puzzle. This idea is supported by matching patterns of rocks and fossils on lands now separated, and may explain why similar animals are found on opposite sides of the world.

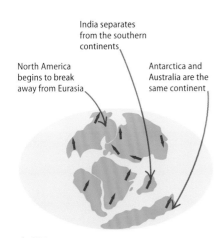

△ **130 mya**
At this point, North America begins to break up from Eurasia (the landmass comprising Europe and Asia). Australia and Antarctica are joined together.

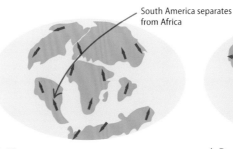

△ **70 mya**
Divergent plates continue to open up the Atlantic Ocean. South America drifts west, Antarctica heads for the South Pole, and India creeps towards Asia.

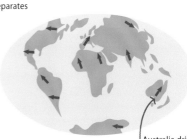

△ **Present day**
India is in place after colliding with the Eurasian mainland. Greenland separates from North America.

Weather

CHANGES IN CONDITIONS IN THE ATMOSPHERE PRODUCE DIFFERENT WEATHER EVENTS.

SEE ALSO	
‹ 74–75	Ecosystems
‹ 100–101	Changing states
‹ 102–103	Gas laws
‹ 184	Atmospheric pressure
‹ 202	Static discharge
‹ 226–227	The Earth

Weather changes occur when sections of atmosphere with different temperatures, pressures, and humidities (water content) come into contact.

Precipitation

Rain is an example of precipitation, where water vapor in the atmosphere condenses to a liquid and falls to the ground. Warm air can hold more water vapor than cool air. Precipitation occurs when air saturated with water vapor is forced to cool and the excess falls as raindrops. Hail and snow are also forms of precipitation. Hailstones are formed when rain is repeatedly blown upward into colder areas of the atmosphere, while snowflakes form when water vapor condenses in already freezing air. Precipitation occurs at weather fronts, where air masses of different temperatures meet. There are three types, shown below.

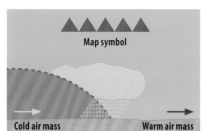

◁ **Cold front**
Cold air moves under warmer, wetter air. As the warm air rises, its pressure falls and it cools, dropping its water as rain.

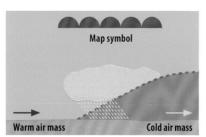

◁ **Warm front**
A mass of warm air flows over a block of cold air, forming rain and clouds. Warm fronts move more slowly than cold fronts, resulting in sustained rain.

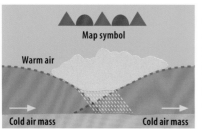

◁ **Occluded front**
This occurs when the warm air mass is pushed off the ground completely by cooler air. Occluded fronts also produce rain.

Wind

Wind forms when air rushes from an area of high pressure to an area of low pressure. The bigger the difference between the two pressures, the stronger the wind.

▽ **Beaufort wind scale**
This scale describes the strength of wind by its effects, so people can judge wind speeds without a measuring device.

Scale	Wind speed km/h (mph)	Strength	Observation
0	0–2 (0–1)	calm	smoke rises vertically
1	3–6 (2–3)	light air	smoke drifts slowly
2	7–11 (4–7)	light breeze	leaves rustle
3	12–19 (8–12)	gentle breeze	small flags fly
4	20–29 (13–18)	moderate breeze	trees toss, dust flies
5	30–39 (19–24)	fresh breeze	small branches sway
6	40–50 (25–31)	strong breeze	large branches sway
7	51–61 (32–38)	near gale	trees in motion
8	62–74 (39–46)	gale	twigs break
9	75–87 (47–54)	strong gale	branches break
10	88–101 (55–63)	storm	trees snap
11	102–119 (64–74)	violent storm	widespread damage
12	120+ (75+)	hurricane	extreme damage

REAL WORLD
Tornado

The fastest winds on Earth are inside tornadoes. They form when a column of spinning air inside a thunderstorm cloud makes contact with the ground. An average tornado is about 80 m (260 ft) across and the air in it moves at 170 km/h (110 mph), sucking objects off the ground, high into the air.

WEATHER

Clouds

Clouds are made of minute water droplets or ice condensed around tiny specks of dust that are blown in the air. Clouds are mostly white because their water droplets scatter a lot of light. When the cloud is filled with water and close to raining, it looks dark gray because it absorbs a lot of light.

▽ **Cloud types**
Below are types of cloud that are defined by their height and appearance.

1. Cirrostratus
These flat and wispy clouds form at high altitudes from ice crystals.

2. Cirrus
Cirrus are high, wispy clouds, and indicate that stormy weather is likely.

3. Cirrocumulus
These high, fluffy clouds means rain is on its way.

4. Altostratus
Sheets of cloud at medium altitudes suggest gray skies and light rain are likely.

5. Cumulonimbus
The largest cloud of all produces thunderstorms.

6. Altocumulus
These fluffy clouds form at a medium height, and indicate a cold front is coming.

7. Stratocumulus
The wide, fluffy clouds are closer to the ground than altocumulus.

8. Stratus
This cloud is characterized by its horizontal shape.

9. Nimbostratus
This is a stratus cloud with rain.

10. Cumulus
These low-level fluffy clouds form in mild weather.

11. Fog
This stratus cloud can touch the ground.

Weather maps

Meteorologists (people who study weather) show the current atmospheric conditions on weather maps. This is a useful tool for forecasting the weather. The map shows the weather fronts and areas of low and high pressure. An expert meteorologist can predict how the front will move, and so figure out what the weather will be like over a particular region.

▷ **Pressure gradients**
Isobars (the black lines on the map) link places where the atmospheric pressure is the same. The isobars form rings around centers of low and high pressure. The closer the rings are to each other, the stronger the wind.

Key: Warm front, Cold front, Occluded front

low-pressure zones, where there are usually strong winds and rainfall, are marked by rings of isobars with the lowest pressure near the center

high-pressure zones, where it is usually cloudless and sunny, are marked by rings of isobars with the highest pressure near the center

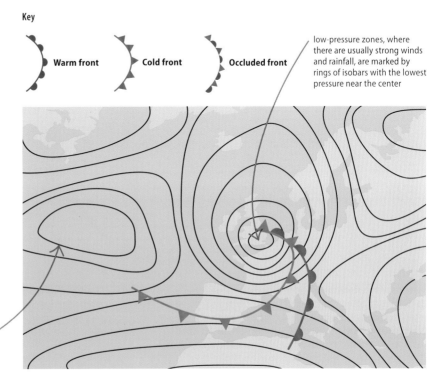

Astronomy

ASTRONOMY IS THE SCIENTIFIC STUDY OF STARS AND OTHER OBJECTS IN SPACE.

People have been mapping the stars and tracking the movements of planets for thousands of years.

SEE ALSO	
‹ 194–195 Electromagnetic waves	
‹ 198–199 Optics	
The Sun	232–233 ›
The Solar System I	234–235 ›
The Solar System II	236–237 ›
Origins of the Universe	240–241 ›

Telescopes

The first telescopes, developed in the early 17th century, gathered light from a distant source and magnified the image using either lenses (in refracting telescopes) or mirrors (in reflecting telescopes). These are called optical telescopes, because they focus light. Today, there also telescopes that reveal other types of radiation invisible to the human eye, such as gamma rays and radio waves. These have led to many important discoveries in astronomy, such as active galaxies and the Big Bang.

△ **Refracting telescope**
The large objective lens focuses the rays of light into a small image inside the device. Then an eyepiece lens magnifies the image.

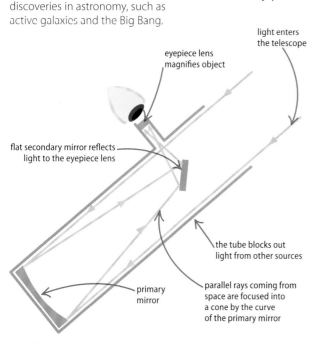

△ **Reflecting telescope**
This telescope collects light using a curved primary mirror, which reflects and focuses the light onto a flat secondary mirror. This shines the light toward the eyepiece lens, which magnifies the object. The world's most powerful astronomical telescopes are reflecting telescopes, some with mirrors up to 10 m (33 ft) across.

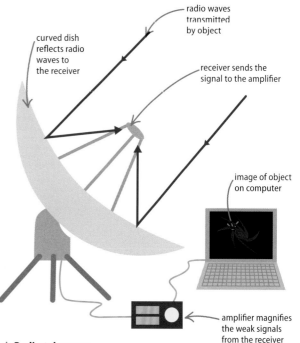

△ **Radio telescope**
A radio telescope is a huge antenna that picks up the longer wavelengths of radiation coming from space. The radio signals from stars are weak, so a large dish is used to reflect them onto the central receiver. The signals are amplified electronically, and a computer processes them to produce pictures, called radio images.

ASTRONOMY

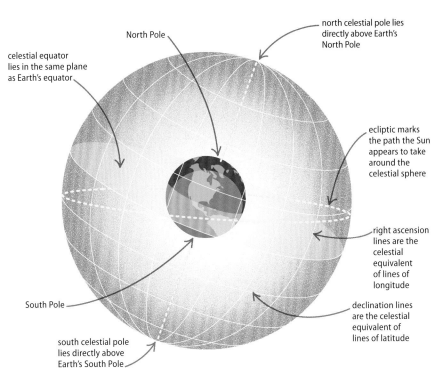

Celestial sphere

The objects seen in the night's sky are not all the same distance from Earth. The Moon is obviously much closer than Jupiter, but astronomers plot their movements and the positions of all the stars on an imaginary sphere that surrounds Earth. The view of the celestial sphere, as it is called, changes as Earth rotates within it, so stars appear to rise in the east and set in the west, just like the Sun. An observer on Earth can see a maximum of half of the sphere at one time.

◁ **Plotting the stars**
The Earth's poles and equator are projected onto the celestial sphere. A system of grid lines through the poles, called lines of right ascension, and lines parallel to the equator, called declination lines, means stars can be located by their coordinates.

Spectroscopy

In the laboratory, scientists investigate the chemical elements in hot gases using a technique called spectroscopy. Observing the gases through a spectroscope reveals the different wavelengths of light (see page 196). White light produces a continuous band of colors, but if atoms are present they affect the light and lines of color appear. The atoms of each element have their own unique pattern of lines, called an emission spectrum. Astronomers use spectroscopy to find out what materials are present many light-years away.

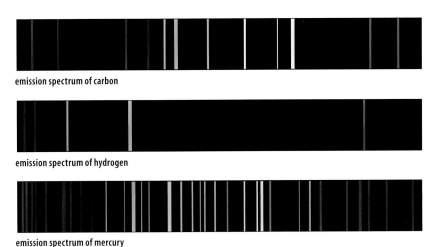

emission spectrum of carbon

emission spectrum of hydrogen

emission spectrum of mercury

REAL WORLD
Light-years

Distances in space are so immense that they are measured in light-years, or the distance light travels in a year—slightly more than 9 trillion km (6 trillion miles). The Sun is eight light-minutes away. Voyager 1 (right), the most distant space probe, is 16 light-hours away, while our next nearest star is four light-years out.

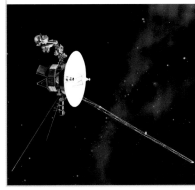

The Sun

THE SUN IS OUR NEAREST STAR. ITS HEAT AND LIGHT MAKE ALL LIFE ON EARTH POSSIBLE.

Although 100 times wider than Earth, the Sun is an average star in terms of its size and age. Studying the Sun has helped us understand how other stars in the Universe work.

SEE ALSO	
❮ 30–31 Photosynthesis	
❮ 126–127 Radioactivity	
❮ 194–195 Electromagnetic waves	
❮ 224 Solar panels	
❮ 226 The seasons	
The Solar System I	234–235 ❯
Stars and galaxies	238–239 ❯

Inside the Sun

The Sun is an immense ball of gas 1.4 million km (870,000 miles) wide. It is made up of almost three-quarters hydrogen, about a quarter helium, and small amounts of 65 or so other elements, all held together by gravity. The temperature, density, and pressure of the gas increase toward the center. At the core, nuclear reactions that convert hydrogen to helium are the source of the Sun's energy. The energy radiates out, taking many thousands of years to reach the surface, where it is released into space as light and heat.

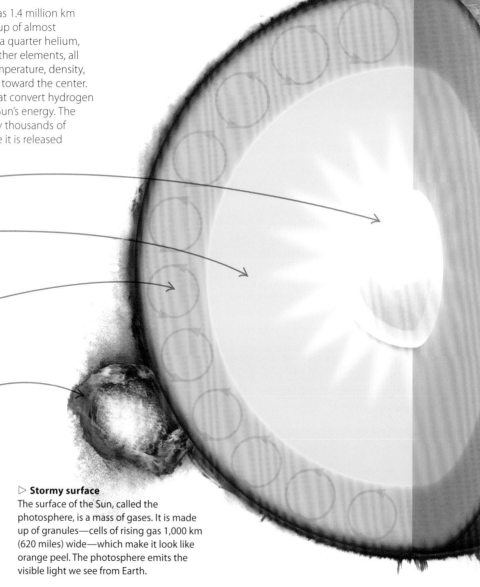

Core
The temperature at the center of the Sun is 15.7 million°C (28 million°F).

Radiative zone
In this region, energy slowly radiates from the core towards the convective zone.

Convective zone
Swirling currents of gas carry heat from the top of the radiative zone toward the surface, where they cool and then sink back.

Prominence
These looping clouds of gas can shoot out more than 100,000 km (62,000 miles).

The Sun's mass is about **750 times greater** than all the other objects in the Solar System put together.

▷ **Stormy surface**
The surface of the Sun, called the photosphere, is a mass of gases. It is made up of granules—cells of rising gas 1,000 km (620 miles) wide—which make it look like orange peel. The photosphere emits the visible light we see from Earth.

THE SUN

Chromosphere
The Sun is surrounded by layers of gas, forming an atmosphere. The inner layer is called the chromosphere. The outer layer is called the corona, and extends into space for millions of kilometers.

Spicules
Jets of gas called spicules shoot up to 10,000 km (6,200 miles) from the photosphere for bursts of up to 10 minutes.

Nuclear fusion

Nuclear fusion occurs when the nuclei of two atoms fuse (join) together to make a large nucleus and energy is released. Every element is made up of atoms with a different number of protons (positive particles) in the nucleus and neutrons (no charge). Hydrogen, the most common element in the Sun, has one proton and usually no neutrons. However, the heat and pressure in the Sun's core increases the chance for hydrogen isotopes to form, with one or two neutrons. They fuse to form helium.

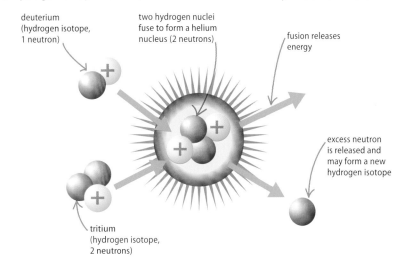

deuterium (hydrogen isotope, 1 neutron)

two hydrogen nuclei fuse to form a helium nucleus (2 neutrons)

fusion releases energy

excess neutron is released and may form a new hydrogen isotope

tritium (hydrogen isotope, 2 neutrons)

The **sunspots** on the Sun's surface may last from a few hours to **several weeks**.

△ **Activity in the Sun's core**
At the Sun's core hydrogen nuclei collide at great speed. The fusion process is complex, but one of the reactions that takes place is shown above. Here, two different hydrogen isotopes (see page 169) fuse to form helium, releasing energy and an excess neutron.

REAL WORLD
Little Ice Age

The number of sunspots rises and falls over an 11-year cycle. It is believed that sunspot activity may affect the climate on Earth. In the late 1600s, there was a long period when few sunspots were recorded, which coincided with a series of very cold winters in Europe that became known as the Little Ice Age. For about 100 years the Thames River, in London, England, froze almost every winter, and frost fairs were held on the thick ice.

Sunspots
These dark areas are around 1,500°C (2,700°F) cooler than the rest of the surface. They occur where magnetism prevents hot gas from reaching the surface.

The Solar System I

THE SUN AND THE OBJECTS THAT ORBIT IT, INCLUDING THE PLANETS AND SMALLER BODIES, MAKE UP OUR SOLAR SYSTEM.

SEE ALSO	
‹ 178–179 Gravity	
‹ 226–227 The Earth	
‹ 232–233 The Sun	
The Solar System II	236–237 ›

At the center of the Solar System, the powerful gravitational force of the Sun holds the eight planets in orbit around it.

The word "planet" comes from the Greek word "**planetos,**" which means "**wanderer.**"

Scale of the Solar System

Distances in space are so vast that they are hard to imagine. Earth is about 150 million km (93 million miles) from the Sun. To simplify things, astronomers call this distance an astronomical unit (AU)—so Earth is 1 AU from the Sun. Using this scale, Neptune, the furthest planet, is 30 AU from the Sun.

3. Earth
Diameter: 12,756 km (7,926 miles)
Distance from Sun: 1 AU
Year: 365 days
Day: 24 hours
Number of moons: 1
Average surface temperature: 15°C (59°F)

4. Mars
Diameter: 6,786 km (4,217 miles)
Distance from Sun: 1.5 AU
Year: 687 days
Day: 24.5 hours
Number of moons: 2
Average surface temperature: –63°C (–81°F)

▷ **The planets**
Each planet in the Solar System has its own features, such as distance from the Sun and number of moons. Every planet also has a different year (the time it takes to orbit the Sun), and length of day (the time it takes to rotate once about its axis).

2. Venus
Diameter: 12,104 km (7,521 miles)
Distance from Sun: 0.7 AU
Year: 225 days
Day: 243 days
Number of moons: 0
Average surface temperature: 464°C (867°F)

1. Mercury
Diameter: 4,879 km (3,031 miles)
Distance from Sun: 0.4 AU
Year: 88 days
Day: 58 days
Number of moons: 0
Average surface temperature: 167°C (333°F)

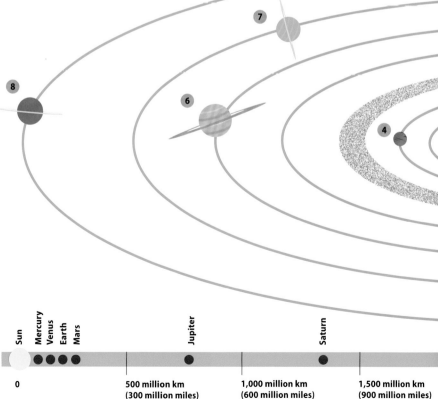

▷ **Inner and outer Solar System**
The first four planets—all small and rocky—form the inner Solar System. Beyond the Main Belt, in the outer Solar System, lie the four planets known as the gas giants.

THE SOLAR SYSTEM I

Beyond Neptune

Surrounding the planets is the Kuiper Belt, a region of mainly icy-rocky bodies and a small number of dwarf planets, such as Pluto. Beyond this lies the Oort Cloud, a sphere of yet more ice bodies left over from the formation of the Solar System.

▷ **The Oort Cloud**
More than one trillion comets make up the Oort Cloud. Its outer edge marks the end of the Solar System.

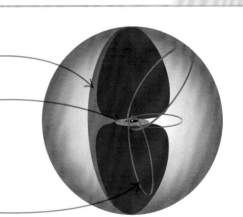

The outer limit
The Oort Cloud reaches 50,000 AU from the Sun.

Kuiper Belt
The Kuiper Belt merges with the Oort Cloud.

Comet orbits
Many comets are ice bodies from the Oort Cloud that have been pushed into closer orbits around the Sun. They travel in all directions, as shown by the orbits in pink.

---

5. Jupiter
Diameter: 142,984 km (88,846 miles)
Distance from Sun: 5.2 AU
Year: 11.9 years
Day: 10 hours
Number of moons: 63
Cloud-top temperature: −108°C (−162°F)

6. Saturn
Diameter: 120,536 km (74,897 miles)
Distance from Sun: 9.6 AU
Year: 29.5 years
Day: 10.5 hours
Number of moons: 62
Cloud-top temperature: −139°C (−218°F)

7. Uranus
Diameter: 51,118 km (31,763 miles)
Distance from Sun: 19.2 AU
Year: 84 years
Day: 17 hours
Number of moons: 27
Cloud-top temperature: −197°C (−323°F)

8. Neptune
Diameter: 49,528 km (30,775 miles)
Distance from Sun: 30 AU
Year: 165 years
Day: 16 hours
Number of moons: 14
Cloud-top temperature: −201°C (−330°F)

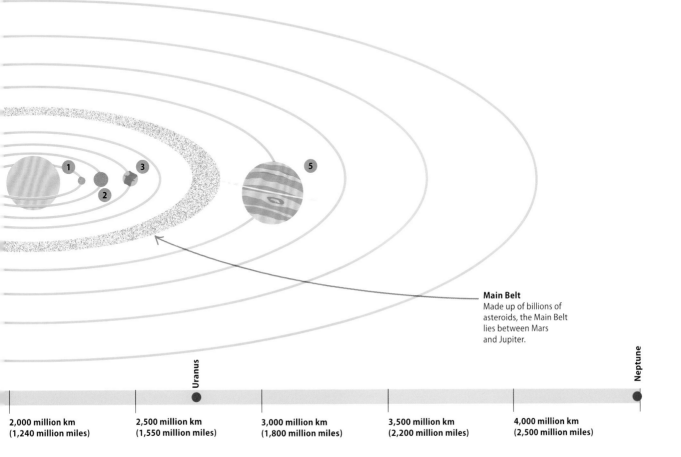

Main Belt
Made up of billions of asteroids, the Main Belt lies between Mars and Jupiter.

The Solar System II

AS WELL AS THE PLANETS, THE GRAVITY OF THE SUN ATTRACTS A HUGE NUMBER OF SMALLER OBJECTS.

SEE ALSO
‹ 232–233 The Sun
‹ 234–235 The Solar System I
Stars and galaxies 238–239 ›

Moons orbit most of the planets, including Earth, while smaller bodies, such as comets, follow independent paths.

The Moon
A moon is a body that orbits a planet and there are more than 160 in our Solar System. Earth has just one moon, a cratered ball of rock, which spins as it orbits. The Moon formed when a large asteroid collided with Earth during its formation and some of the debris went into orbit around the Earth, becoming the Moon.

Orbit of the Moon ▷
When we look at the Moon, only the sunlit part is visible. The Moon takes the same amount of time to orbit our planet as to spin once on its axis, so we only ever see one side from Earth. The side we don't see is called the far side of the Moon.

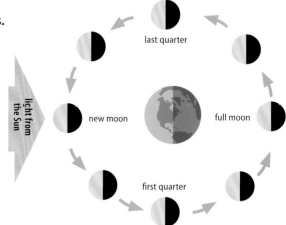

The lunar cycle ▷
Every month the face of the Moon appears to change from a dark shadow, called a new moon, to become a thin, shining crescent, to a full moon, and then back again. This is because, as the Moon orbits Earth, we see more or less of the half of the Moon that is lit by the Sun.

1. **new moon** (day 0)
2. **waxing crescent** — side facing the Earth is in darkness
3. **first quarter** (day 7)
4. **waxing gibbous**
5. **full moon** (day 14) — we see the whole sunlit surface
6. **waning gibbous**
7. **last quarter** (day 21)
8. **waning crescent**

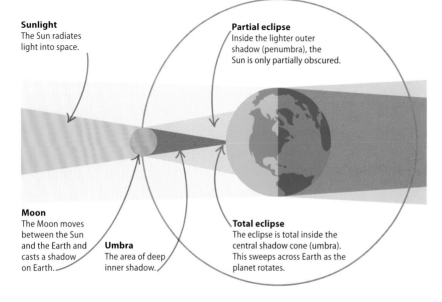

Sunlight
The Sun radiates light into space.

Partial eclipse
Inside the lighter outer shadow (penumbra), the Sun is only partially obscured.

Moon
The Moon moves between the Sun and the Earth and casts a shadow on Earth.

Umbra
The area of deep inner shadow.

Total eclipse
The eclipse is total inside the central shadow cone (umbra). This sweeps across Earth as the planet rotates.

Eclipses
Sometimes, as the Moon orbits Earth, it passes directly in front of the Sun and blocks out the light. This is called a solar eclipse. Sometimes the Moon's path takes it into Earth's shadow, causing a lunar eclipse. When this happens the Moon dims and appears red because the light is bent as it passes through Earth's atmosphere.

◁ **Solar eclipse**
There are only about three total solar eclipses each year, and each one is only seen from the narrow band of deep shadow, called the umbra, on the Earth's surface. More frequent is a partial solar eclipse, when the Moon's shadow covers just part of the Sun.

Dwarf planets

In 1930, a new planet was found beyond the orbit of Neptune. The new body was named Pluto, and it was found to be by far the smallest planet, even smaller than Earth's Moon. By 2005, improved survey techniques had found several bodies similar in size to Pluto in the same area of the Solar System, and one (Ceres) in the Main Belt of asteroids. It was then decided to name objects of this size range dwarf planets, and Pluto became one of them.

▷ **Independent bodies**
Dwarf planets are independent bodies large enough to have become almost spherical because of their internal gravity, but are too small to be called planets.

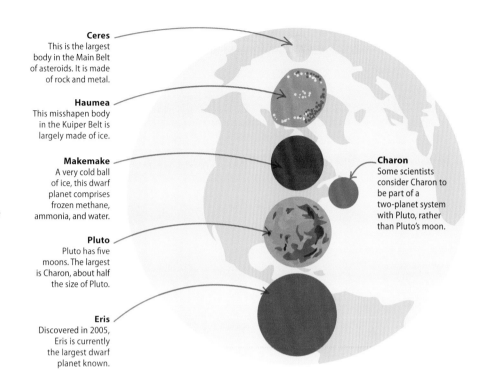

Ceres
This is the largest body in the Main Belt of asteroids. It is made of rock and metal.

Haumea
This misshapen body in the Kuiper Belt is largely made of ice.

Makemake
A very cold ball of ice, this dwarf planet comprises frozen methane, ammonia, and water.

Pluto
Pluto has five moons. The largest is Charon, about half the size of Pluto.

Eris
Discovered in 2005, Eris is currently the largest dwarf planet known.

Charon
Some scientists consider Charon to be part of a two-planet system with Pluto, rather than Pluto's moon.

Comets

Comets are "dirty snowballs" of dust and ice formed at the birth of the Solar System. They have highly elliptical (oval-shaped) orbits. Some travel far beyond Neptune, taking thousands of years to circle the Sun, while others have short paths of just a few years. As a comet nears the Sun it heats up and dust and gas stream out, forming tails millions of kilometers long.

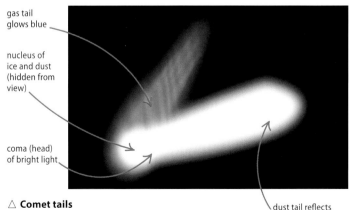

- gas tail glows blue
- nucleus of ice and dust (hidden from view)
- coma (head) of bright light
- dust tail reflects white sunlight

△ **Comet tails**
When a comet gets closer to the Sun, beyond the orbit of Mars, it becomes active, developing a coma and tails. When the comet travels out of the inner Solar System these disappear again.

REAL WORLD
Meteoroids and meteorites

Meteoroids are chunks of space rock that produce streaks of light, called meteors, as they burn up in Earth's atmosphere. Most are small and around 3,000 tons of space rock hits Earth every year as dust. A meteoroid that survives the atmosphere to land on Earth's surface is called a meteorite and these can form large impact craters. Roter Kamm in Namibia, for example, is more than five million years old, 2.5 km (1.5 miles) wide, and 130 m (425 ft) deep.

Stars and galaxies

GALAXIES ARE HUGE STAR SYSTEMS, MADE UP OF STARS AND LARGE AMOUNTS OF GAS AND DUST.

SEE ALSO	
‹ 178–179	Gravity
‹ 194–195	Electromagnetic waves
‹ 230–231	Astronomy
‹ 232–233	The Sun

Our Solar System is just one of billions in our local area, or galaxy. Our galaxy, the Milky Way, is one of hundreds of billions in the Universe.

Astronomical objects

Astronomers estimate that about 6,000 objects can be seen from Earth with the naked eye. Most appear as points of light, but a closer look through a powerful telescope reveals that there is a lot more than just stars and planets out there.

The Sun
Our local star is the source of almost all light and heat reaching Earth. However, it is a very average star, in terms of size and temperature. The next nearest star to Earth is Proxima Centauri, which is 4.2 light-years away.

Constellation
Ancient astronomers organized the visible stars into patterns called constellations, most based on images from Greek mythology, such as Ursa Major. Although the stars in a constellation look close together, they are at vastly differing distances from Earth.

Star cluster
Stars are seldom found alone; most travel either with one or more companions. Pairs are called binary stars. Small groups of stars are called clusters and are made up of stars that formed at the same time, held together in groups by gravity.

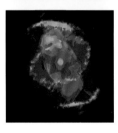

Planetary nebula
As some stars grow older they eject their outer layers to become planetary nebulae. The glowing, colored rings of hot gas and dust make stars such as the Cat's Eye Nebula some of the most stunning objects in space. The faint star at the center is known as a white dwarf.

Pulsar
Some dying stars blow apart in a massive explosion called a supernova. The core of the star may collapse to form a small, dense neutron star that emits beams of energy and rotates at amazing speeds. If the beams are detected on Earth, the star is known as a pulsar.

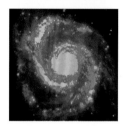

Galaxy
Galaxies are vast star systems that exist in a range of shapes and sizes. The smallest have a few million stars, and the largest, several trillion. Around half of galaxies are spiral-shaped disks, with a central bulge and arms spiraling away from it.

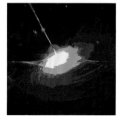

Quasar
Among the most distant of all objects are quasars—young galaxies seething with energy as billions of stars form. Light from distant objects takes many billions of years to reach Earth, so we see quasars as they were when the light left them all that time ago.

REAL WORLD
The Milky Way

Our galaxy is called the Milky Way. It is a spiral galaxy, but from Earth we see it as a pale strip across the night sky. The ancient Greeks called this the *galaktikos*, which means "milky path." The Solar System lies in an outer arm.

Star types

Stars have a life cycle and, as they age, their characteristics—size, color, luminosity (energy output)—change. Astronomers group stars according to the light they emit. The color of a star's light identifies how hot it is, with blue as the hottest. However, hot stars are not always the brightest. Arranging stars by luminosity and temperature shows they fall into certain groups.

▷ **Star groups**
When a star first produces energy by nuclear fusion—like our Sun— it is called a main sequence star.

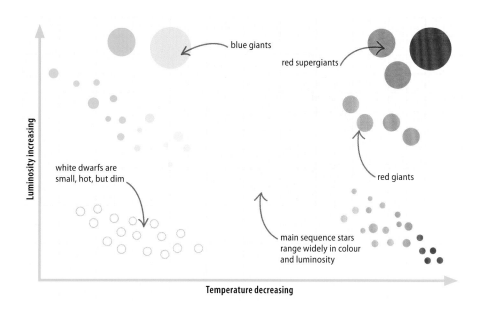

Star life cycle

Stars are born inside great clouds of gas and dust called nebulae. As the clouds collapse, the temperature and pressure rise, and eventually nuclear fusion begins in the star's core. The star then stabilizes on the main sequence of its life. When the fuel runs out, the star dies.

▽ **Birth, life, and death**
Stars spend around 90 percent of their lives in the main sequence phase. The mass of a star is crucial and will determine what happens to it and when it dies.

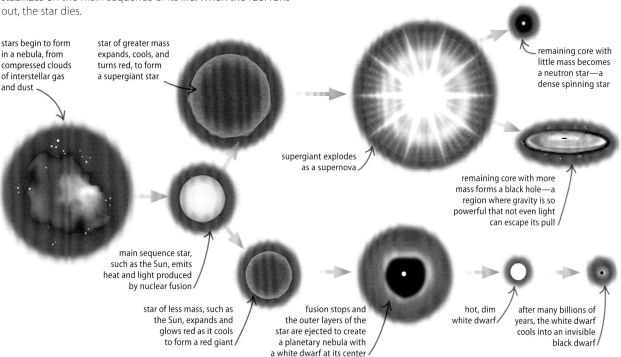

Origins of the Universe

THE BIG BANG THEORY EXPLAINS HOW THE UNIVERSE DEVELOPED.

Although nobody knows how the Universe began, evidence suggests that it started with an ancient burst of energy and is still expanding.

SEE ALSO
❮ 168–169 Inside atoms
❮ 170–171 Energy
❮ 178–179 Gravity
❮ 194–195 Electromagnetic waves
❮ 230 Telescopes
❮ 231 Spectroscopy
❮ 238–239 Stars and galaxies

The Big Bang theory

In the 1920s, it was discovered that our galaxy and the millions of galaxies that surround it are all moving away from each other because the Universe is expanding. This implies that the galaxies all began close together, billions of years ago. The idea that the Universe started as a hot burst of energy in the distant past was widely accepted once the remains of that energy were observed in the 1960s. In the 13.7 billion years that have passed since the Universe began, that energy has cooled to −270°C (−454°F), and is now known as cosmic microwave background radiation.

There are two theories that predict the way in which the Universe may end: it might be **torn to pieces** in a "**Big Rip**," or become cold and black in a "**Big Chill**."

▽ **The history of everything**
This diagram shows the story of the Universe. Moving from left to right, the intervals of time become longer: the halfway mark on the picture is 500,000 years, which is only 0.04 percent of the age of the Universe.

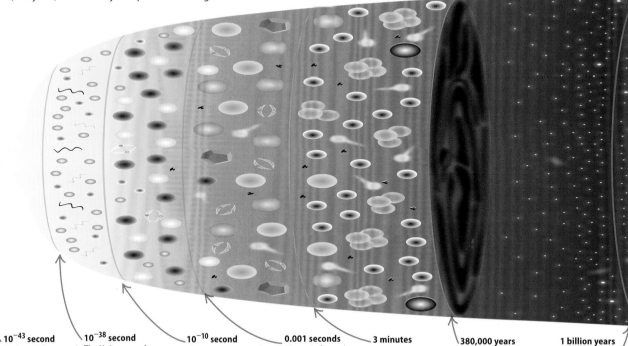

10^{-43} second
Nothing is known of the events that led to the Big Bang and the start of our Universe.

10^{-38} second
The Universe undergoes an enormous increase in its rate of expansion, called inflation, and emits a huge amount of heat and radiation.

10^{-10} second
Electromagnetic and weak forces become distinct. The Universe is cooling rapidly and forming a soup of primitive particles.

0.001 seconds
Matter is formed, as subatomic particles, and most of these destroy each other.

3 minutes
As the Universe continues to cool, the remaining particles are mostly protons, neutrons, electrons, and neutrinos.

380,000 years
The Universe is cool enough for atoms to form. Space becomes transparent, because there are fewer particles to obstruct photons of light.

1 billion years
Stars and galaxies form.

ORIGINS OF THE UNIVERSE   241

REAL WORLD
Cosmic microwave

Microwave radiation from the Big Bang was discovered by accident by radio astronomers who thought the radiation was background noise. Today, satellites have made very detailed maps of the radiation, which show slight temperature variations (shown as different colors below), revealing slight variations in the density of the young Universe.

Red shift

Galaxies exist in clusters, and the key piece of evidence for the Big Bang is that these clusters are all moving apart—in other words, the Universe is expanding. Astronomers know this because they can split the light from the galaxies into spectra, which are like rainbows containing lines of light or dark that show the substances present in them. In spectra from distant galaxies, the positions of the lines are all shifted to longer wavelengths—that is, toward the red end of the spectrum.

▷ **Red shift**
The light from a star, galaxy, or other bright object is reddened very slightly if it is moving away from the observer.

▷ **Blue shift**
When an object approaches the observer, its light shifts the other way, toward the blue end of the spectrum.

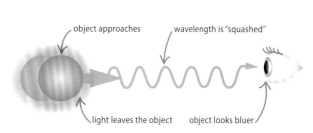

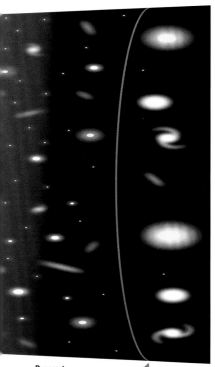

Present
The Universe as it is today, 13.7 billion years old.

What is out there?

Stars and galaxies are just a tiny part of the total mass of the Universe. Most is made up of forms of matter and energy that cannot be seen. Galaxies contain invisible dark matter, which scientists know is there by observing galaxy behavior. There is also an unknown force accelerating the expansion of the Universe, known as dark energy.

▽ **Universal matter**
These pie charts show the make-up of the Universe. The atoms that make the stars and galaxies are mainly hydrogen and helium. The additional heavier elements are made within stars. Those beyond iron (see pages 116–117) form when massive stars explode.

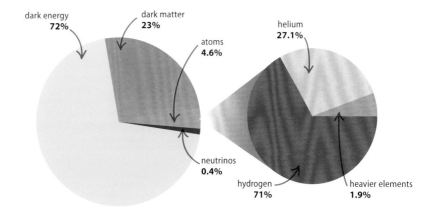

Biology reference

The plant kingdom

With the scientific name Plantae, this kingdom contains around 300,000 species, ranging from simple mosses to immense trees. The great majority of plants are photosynthetic and manufacture their own supply of sugars using the energy in sunlight.

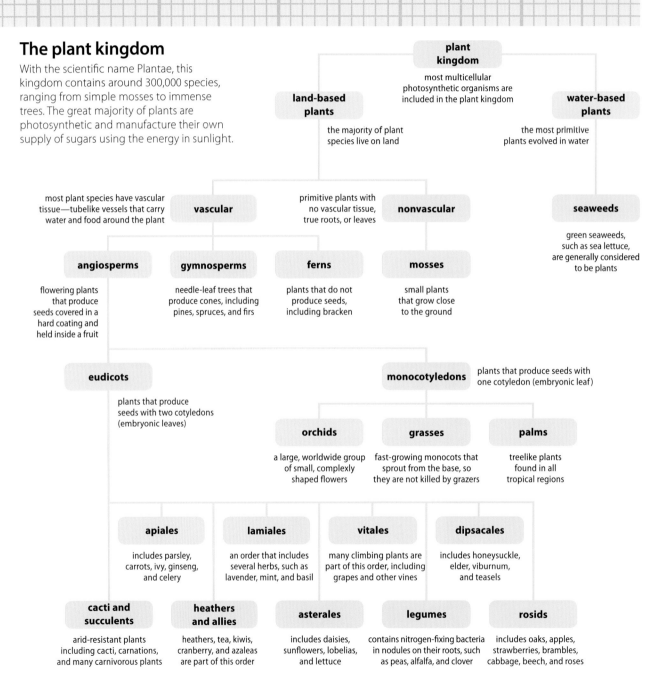

BIOLOGY REFERENCE

The animal kingdom

With the scientific name of Animalia, this kingdom contains more than a million species—the precise number is unclear. All animals are heterotrophs—they survive by feeding on other living things, using this food for fuel or as a source of raw materials.

animal kingdom — includes multicellular heterotrophic organisms that generally have an internal digestive system and head

invertebrates — all animals that do not have backbones (which are called vertebrates)

roundworms — also known as nematodes, found in soils and living as parasites

segmented worms — including marine worms, earthworms, and leeches

sponges — primitive, mainly aquatic animals that absorb food through their outer surface

mollusks — the second-largest phylum, including snails, squid, and clams

small phyla — includes microscopic creatures, such as worms and aquatic life

flatworms — mostly parasitic worms, including flukes and tapeworms

cnidarians — jellyfish, anemones, and corals

echinoderms — a widespread group of marine creatures, including starfish and sea urchins

bryozoans — small filter-feeding animals that frequently grow in colonies

arthropods — the largest phylum of invertebrates, which all have jointed limbs

millipedes — plant-eating arthropods with two pairs of legs on each body segment

centipedes — predatory arthropods with many body segments, each with a single pair of eggs

crustaceans — mainly aquatic arthropods including crabs, lobsters, but also woodlice

arachnids — eight-legged arthropods including spiders, scorpions, mites, and ticks

insects — largest class of arthropods, have six legs and are the only flying invertebrates

chordates (backbone) — contains all the vertebrates, and other animals that have a flexible supporting rod called a notochord

jawless fish — primitive fish that have a spiral of teeth, used to scrape mouthfuls of food

cartilaginous fish — sharks and rays that have skeletons made of cartilage and not bone

bony fish — the largest group of fish, mostly with fins supported by thin rays of bone

amphibians — the first land vertebrates, including frogs, toads, newts, and salamanders

reptiles — a large group of land animals that includes snakes, turtles, and crocodiles

birds — egg-laying animals with feathers; most are able to fly

mammals — hair-covered animals that produce milk to feed their young

monotremes — primitive egg-laying mammals from Australia and New Guinea, including the echidna and platypus

marsupials — pouched mammals from Australia and the Americas, including opossums, kangaroos, and wombats

placentals — carry developing young in an internal chamber, nourishing them with an organ called a placenta

Chemistry reference

Melting and boiling points

Every element has a specific melting and boiling point. This is the temperature at which a solid changes into a liquid or a gas respectively. All temperatures are measured at atmospheric pressure. Metals tend to have high melting points, while simple gases have boiling points below room temperature. However, carbon is a nonmetal, but has the highest melting point of all.

LIST OF ELEMENTS

Atomic number	Name/Symbol	Melting point °C	Melting point °F	Boiling point °C	Boiling point °F
1	hydrogen (H)	−259	−434	−253	−423
2	helium (He)	−272	−458	−269	−452
3	lithium (Li)	179	354	1,340	2,440
4	beryllium (Be)	1,283	2,341	2,990	5,400
5	boron (B)	2,300	4,170	3,660	6,620
6	carbon (C)	3,500	6,332	4,827	8,721
7	nitrogen (N)	−210	−346	−196	−321
8	oxygen (O)	−219	−362	−183	−297
9	fluorine (F)	−220	−364	−188	−306
10	neon (Ne)	−249	−416	−246	−410
11	sodium (Na)	98	208	890	1,634
12	magnesium (Mg)	650	1,202	1,105	2,021
13	aluminum (Al)	660	1,220	2,467	4,473
14	silicon (Si)	1,420	2,588	2,355	4,271
15	phosphorus (P)	44	111	280	536
16	sulfur (S)	113	235	445	832
17	chlorine (Cl)	−101	−150	−34	−29
18	argon (Ar)	−189	−308	−186	−303
19	potassium (K)	64	147	754	1,389
20	calcium (Ca)	848	1,558	1,487	2,709
21	scandium (Sc)	1,541	2,806	2,831	5,128
22	titanium (Ti)	1,677	3,051	3,277	5,931
23	vanadium (V)	1,917	3,483	3,377	6,111
24	chromium (Cr)	1,903	3,457	2,642	4,788
25	manganese (Mn)	1,244	2,271	2,041	3,706
26	iron (Fe)	1,539	2,802	2,750	4,980
27	cobalt (Co)	1,495	2,723	2,877	5,211
28	nickel (Ni)	1,455	2,641	2,730	4,950

LIST OF ELEMENTS

Atomic number	Name/Symbol	Melting point °C	Melting point °F	Boiling point °C	Boiling point °F
29	copper (Cu)	1,083	1,981	2,582	4,680
30	zinc (Zn)	420	788	907	1,665
31	gallium (Ga)	30	86	2,403	4,357
32	germanium (Ge)	937	1,719	2,355	4,271
33	arsenic (As)	817	1,503	613	1,135
34	selenium (Se)	217	423	685	1,265
35	bromine (Br)	−7	19	59	138
36	krypton (Kr)	−157	−251	−152	−242
37	rubidium (Rb)	39	102	688	1,270
38	strontium (Sr)	769	1,416	1,384	2,523
39	yttrium (Y)	1,522	2,772	3,338	6,040
40	zirconium (Zr)	1,852	3,366	4,377	7,911
41	niobium (Nb)	2,467	4,473	4,742	8,568
42	molybdenum (Mo)	2,610	4,730	5,560	10,040
43	technetium (Tc)	2,172	3,942	4,877	8,811
44	ruthenium (Ru)	2,310	4,190	3,900	7,052
45	rhodium (Rh)	1,966	3,571	3,727	6,741
46	palladium (Pd)	1,554	2,829	2,970	5,378
47	silver (Ag)	962	1,764	2,212	4,014
48	cadmium (Cd)	321	610	767	1,413
49	indium (In)	156	313	2,028	3,680
50	tin (Sn)	232	450	2,270	4,118
51	antimony (Sb)	631	1,168	1,635	2,975
52	tellurium (Te)	450	842	990	1,814
53	iodine (I)	114	237	184	363
54	xenon (Xe)	−112	−170	−107	−161
55	cesium (Cs)	29	84	671	1,240
56	barium (Ba)	725	1,337	1,640	2,984

CHEMISTRY REFERENCE

LIST OF ELEMENTS

Atomic number	Name/Symbol	Melting point °C	Melting point °F	Boiling point °C	Boiling point °F
57	lanthanum (La)	921	1,690	3,457	6,255
58	cerium (Ce)	799	1,470	3,426	6,199
59	praseodymium (Pr)	931	1,708	3,512	6,354
60	neodymium (Nd)	1,021	1,870	3,068	5,554
61	promethiium (Pm)	1,168	2,134	2,700	4,892
62	samarium (Sm)	1,077	1,971	1,791	3,256
63	europium (Eu)	822	1,512	1,597	2,907
64	gadolinium (Gd)	1,313	2,395	3,266	5,911
65	terbium (Tb)	1,356	2,473	3,123	5,653
66	dysprosium (Dy)	1,412	2,574	2,562	4,644
67	holmium (Ho)	1,474	2,685	2,695	4,883
68	erbium (Er)	1,529	2,784	2,863	5,185
69	thulium (Tm)	1,545	2,813	1,947	3,537
70	ytterbium (Yb)	819	1,506	1,194	2,181
71	lutetium (Lu)	1,663	3,025	3,395	6,143
72	hafnium (Hf)	2,227	4,041	4,602	8,316
73	tantalum (Ta)	2,996	5,425	5,427	9,801
74	tungsten (W)	3,410	6,170	5,660	10,220
75	rhenium (Re)	3,180	5,756	5,627	10,161
76	osmium (Os)	3,045	5,510	5,090	9,190
77	iridium (Ir)	2,410	4,370	4,130	7,466
78	platinum (Pt)	1,772	3,222	3,827	6,921
79	gold (Au)	1,064	1,947	2,807	5,080
80	mercury (Hg)	−39	−38	357	675
81	thallium (Tl)	303	577	1,457	2,655
82	lead (Pb)	328	622	1,744	3,171
83	bismuth (Bi)	271	520	1,560	2,840
84	polonium (Po)	254	489	962	1,764

LIST OF ELEMENTS

Atomic number	Name/Symbol	Melting point °C	Melting point °F	Boiling point °C	Boiling point °F
85	astatine (At)	300	572	370	698
86	radon (Rn)	−71	−96	−62	−80
87	francium (Fr)	27	81	677	1,251
88	radium (Ra)	700	1,292	1,200	2,190
89	actinium (Ac)	1,050	1,922	3,200	5,792
90	thorium (Th)	1,750	3,182	4,787	8,649
91	protactinium (Pa)	1,597	2,907	4,027	7,281
92	uranium (U)	1,132	2,070	3,818	6,904
93	neptunium (Np)	637	1,179	4,090	7,394
94	plutonium (Pu)	640	1,184	3,230	5,850
95	americium (Am)	994	1,821	2,607	4,724
96	curium (Cm)	1,340	2,444	3,190	5,774
97	berkelium (Bk)	1,050	1,922	710	1,310
98	californium (Cf)	900	1,652	1,470	2,678
99	einsteinium (Es)	860	1,580	996	1,825
100	fermium (Fm)	unknown		unknown	
101	mendelevium (Md)	unknown		unknown	
102	nobelium (No)	unknown		unknown	
103	lawrencium (Lr)	unknown		unknown	
104	rutherfordium (Rf)	unknown		unknown	
105	dubnium (Db)	unknown		unknown	
106	seaborgium (Sg)	unknown		unknown	
107	bohrium (Bh)	unknown		unknown	
108	hassium (Hs)	unknown		unknown	
109	meitnerium (Mt)	unknown		unknown	
110	darmstadtium (Ds)	unknown		unknown	
111	roentgenium (Rg)	unknown		unknown	
112	copernicum (Cn)	unknown		unknown	

Human elements

The human body contains 25 different chemical elements. Most are found in just tiny amounts. About two-thirds of the body is made of water (H_2O), and almost all of the rest is made up of carbon, nitrogen, calcium, and phosphorus atoms.

▷ **Human elements**
This chart shows the proportion of elements in the body by their mass—so 65 percent of body weight is made up of oxygen atoms, and so on.

Key
- Oxygen 65%
- Carbon 18%
- Hydrogen 10%
- Nitrogen 3%
- Calcium 1.5%
- Phosphorus 1%
- Potassium 0.25%
- Sulfur 0.25%
- Sodium 0.15%
- Chlorine 0.15%
- Others 0.7%

Physics reference

SI units

All scientists use seven basic units of measurement, known as the SI base units, listed below. "SI" stands for "Système International." The units are maintained by experts in the headquarters, located in Paris, France.

SI UNITS

Unit	Symbol	Quantity measured
meter	m	unit of length, defined as the distance light travels through a vacuum in 1/299,792,458th of a second
kilogram	kg	unit of mass, defined by the International Standard Kilogram made of a platinum-iridium alloy in Paris, France
second	s	unit of time, defined in terms of the frequency of a type of light radiated by a cesium atom
ampere	A	unit of electrical current, defined by the attraction force between two parallel conductors that are conducting one ampere
kelvin	K	unit on a scale of temperature that begins at absolute zero: 0 Kelvin or 459.67°F (-273.15°C)
candela	cd	a measure of luminous intensity (how powerful a light source is); one candle has a luminous intensity of one candela
mole	mol	a unit of quantity of a substance (generally very small particles such as atoms and molecules); one mole is made up of 6.02 x 10^{23} objects (atoms or molecules)

Derived SI units

This table contains just a few units that are derived from combinations of the seven base SI units. Nevertheless these units are very widely used and have been given their own names.

SI UNITS

Unit	Symbol	Quantity measured
becquerel	Bq	unit of radioactive decay; the quantity of material in which one nucleus decays per second
Celsius	°C	unit of temperature, with the same magnitude as a Kelvin, but zero is at water's freezing point
coulomb	C	closely related to an ampere, this is the quantity of charge carried each second by a current of one ampere
farad	F	unit of capacitance, which is a capacitor's ability to store charge
hertz	Hz	unit of frequency; the number of cycles or repeating events per second
joule	J	amount of energy transferred when a force of one newton is applied over one meter
newton	N	unit of force required to increase the velocity of a mass by 1 kg by 1 m per second every second
ohm	Ω	unit of resistance; a one ohm resistor allows a current of one ampere to flow when one volt is applied across it
pascal	Pa	unit of pressure; a pascal is a force of one newton applied across an area of one square meter
volt	V	unit of potential difference and the force that pushes electric current
watt	W	unit of power (the rate at which energy is expended); calculated as joules per second

PHYSICS REFERENCE

Formulas
Physicists calculate unknown quantities using formulas, in which known quantities are combined in specific ways. Formulas can be rearranged according to which quantity needs to be calculated. Here are some of the main formulas.

PHYSICS FORMULAS

Quantity	Description	Formula
Current	voltage / resistance	$I = \dfrac{V}{R}$
Voltage	current x resistance	$V = IR$
Resistance	voltage / current	$R = \dfrac{V}{I}$
Power	work / time	$P = \dfrac{W}{t}$
Time	distance / velocity	$t = \dfrac{d}{v}$
Distance	velocity x time	$d = vt$
Velocity	displacement (distance in a given direction) / time	$v = \dfrac{d}{t}$
Acceleration	final velocity − initial velocity / time	$a = \dfrac{v_2 - v_1}{t}$
Force	mass x acceleration	$F = ma$
Momentum	mass x velocity	$p = mv$
Pressure	force / area	$P = \dfrac{F}{A}$
Density	mass / volume	$\rho = \dfrac{m}{V}$
Volume	mass / density	$V = \dfrac{m}{\rho}$
Mass	volume x density	$m = V\rho$
Area	length x width	$A = lw$
Kinetic energy	½ mass x square of velocity	$E_k = \tfrac{1}{2}mv^2$
Weight	mass x acceleration due to gravity	$W = mg$
Work done	force x distance moved in direction of force	$W = Fs$

The planets
This table gives some basic information on the planets of the Solar System plus the number of observed moons that orbit them. The inner planets have rocky surfaces, while the larger outer planets are mainly made of gases and ice.

PLANETS AND MOONS

Planet	Description	Number of known moons
Mercury	rock, metal	0
Venus	rock, metal	0
Earth	rock, metal	1
Mars	rock, metal	2
Jupiter	gas, ice, rock	63
Saturn	gas, ice, rock	62
Uranus	gas, ice, rock	27
Neptune	gas, ice, rock	14

Earth's vital statistics
Our planet is the largest rocky planet in the Solar System. Many of the units scientists use to measure the Universe are based on the size and motion of the planet.

Average diameter	12,756 km (7,928 miles)
Average distance from Sun: km (miles)	149.6 million (93 million)
Average orbital speed around Sun: km (miles)	29.8 km/s (18.5 mps)
Sunrise to sunrise (at the Equator)	24 hours
Mass	5.98×10^{24} kg
Volume	1.08321×10^{12} km^3
Average density (water = 1)	5.52 g/cm^3
Surface gravity	9.81 m/s^2
Average surface temperature	15°C (59°F)
Ratio of water to land	70:30

Glossary

AC (alternating current)
AC is an electrical current that repeatedly changes in direction.

acceleration
An increase or decrease in an object's velocity (speed) due to a force being applied to it.

acid
A compound that breaks up into a negative ion and one or more positive hydrogen ions, which react easily with other substances.

activation energy
The energy needed to start a chemical reaction.

air resistance
A force that pushes against an object that is moving through the air, slowing it down; also called drag.

algae
Plantlike organisms that live in water or damp habitats; in general, they are single-celled.

alkali
A compound that dissociates into negative hydroxide (OH) ions and a positive ion; alkalis react easily with acids.

allotrope
A variant form of an element; for example, carbon can occur as graphite or diamond; while allotropes look different and have various physical properties, they all have identical chemical properties.

alloy
A mixture of two or more metals, or a metal and a nonmetal.

amplitude
The height of a wave.

anatomy
The science that studies the structure of living bodies to discover how they work.

anion
A negatively charged ion formed when an atom or group of atoms gains one or more electrons.

arthropod
A member of the largest animal phylum, which includes spiders, insects, and crustaceans.

atmosphere
A blanket of gases that surrounds a planet, moon, or star.

atom
The smallest unit of an element.

atomic number
The number of protons located in the nucleus of an atom; every element has atoms with a unique atomic number.

attraction
A force that pulls things together; opposite of repulsion.

bacteria (singular: bacterium)
Single-celled organisms that form a distinct kingdom of life; compared to other cells, bacterial cells are small and lack organelles.

base
An ionic compound that reacts with an acid.

biomass
A way of measuring the total mass of living things in a certain region; a useful way of comparing different types of organism in an ecosystem.

boiling point
The temperature at which a heated substance changes from a liquid into a gas; when the gas is cooled, it will condense into a liquid at this same temperature.

buoyancy
The tendency of a solid to float or sink in liquids.

capillary
A small blood vessel that delivers oxygen to body cells.

catalyst
A substance that lowers the activation energy of a chemical reaction, making the reaction occur much more rapidly.

cations
Positively charged ions, which form from atoms (or molecules) that lose one or more electrons.

cell
The smallest unit of a living body.

cellulose
A complex carbohydrate that makes up the wall that surrounds all plant cells.

chemical
A pure substance that has distinct properties.

chlorophyll
The green-colored compound that collects the energy in sunlight so it can be used to react with carbon dioxide and water to make sugar during photosynthesis.

chromosome
A structure in the nucleus of cells that is used to store coils of DNA.

circuit
A series of components (such as light bulbs) connected between the poles of a battery or other power source so an electric current runs through them.

combustion
A chemical process in which a substance reacts with oxygen, releasing heat and flames.

compound
A chemical that is made up of the atoms of two or more elements bonded together.

compression
Squeezing or pushing a substance into a smaller space.

concave
Having a curved surface that resembles the inside of a circle or sphere.

concentration
The amount of one substance mixed into a known volume of another.

condense
To turn from a gas to a liquid; for example, steam condenses into water.

conduction
The process by which energy is transferred through a substance. The energy being transferred is thermal (heat), acoustic, or electrical.

convection
A process that transfers heat through a liquid or gas, with warm areas rising and cooler ones sinking, thus creating a circulating current.

convex
Having a curved surface that resembles the outside of a circle or sphere.

current
A flow of a substance; electrical currents are a flow of electrons or other charged particles.

GLOSSARY 249

DC
Short for "direct current," an electric current that flows in one direction continuously.

deceleration
A decrease in velocity that occurs when a force pushes against a moving object in the opposite direction to its direction of motion.

decomposition
To break up into two or more simpler ingredients.

deformation
To be changed in shape by a force, such as being stretched, bent, or squeezed.

density
A quantity of how much matter is held within a known volume of a material.

diffraction
A behavior of waves, in which a wave spreads out in a number of directions after it passes through a small gap, with a width similar to its wavelength.

dipole
A molecule with two poles: one negative and one positive.

displacement
The moving aside of part of a medium by an object placed in that medium. Or the distance between one point and another.

distillation
A process that separates liquid mixtures by boiling away each component in turn, then cooling them back into pure liquids.

DNA
Short for "deoxyribonucleic acid," a complex chained molecule that carries genetic code, the instructions that a cell—and entire body—uses to make copies of itself.

drag
The resistance force formed when an object pushes through a fluid, such as air or water.

dynamic equilibrium
When a reversible reaction takes place at the same rate in both directions so, even though it is continuing in both directions, the overall quantities of the materials involved stay constant.

eclipse
An eclipse occurs when the Earth, Sun, and Moon line up, blocking out the view of one of the objects. In a solar eclipse, the Moon covers up the Sun as seen from Earth. In a lunar eclipse, the Earth sits between the Sun and the Moon.

ecosystem
A collection of living organisms that share a habitat and are reliant on each other for survival.

elasticity
The property of an object that allows it to change shape when forced to but return to its original form when the force is removed.

electrolysis
Dividing compounds into simpler substances using the energy in electricity.

electrolyte
A liquid that conducts electricity.

electromagnet
A magnet that can be turned on by running an electric current through it.

electron
A negatively charged particle that is located around the outside of an atom.

electronics
A field of science and technology that involves using semiconductors to make components for circuits.

element
A natural substance that cannot be divided or simplified into raw ingredients. There are around 90 natural elements on Earth.

endothermy
The ability of an animal to maintain a constant body temperature using energy burned from its food to heat or cool the body.

energy
Energy is what allows things to happen. For example, chemical energy in food allows us to live and move.

enzyme
A protein that is used to control a chemical reaction or other process taking place inside a living body.

evaporate
To turn from a liquid to a gas, such as a puddle drying out.

evolve
A change in the characteristics of a species due to its environment; evolution is driven by a process called natural selection.

exoskeleton
Hard tissue that forms the outer surface of a body, giving shape and structure to it.

exothermic
Describing an animal that does not maintain a constant body temperature but allows it to fluctuate with that of the surroundings.

fat
A solid lipid—a biological material that is used to store energy, insulate nerves, and form membranes. Liquid lipids are called oils.

filtration
The process of passing a substance through a filter to remove solid particles.

fission
Breaking apart; nuclear fission involves radioactive atoms splitting in two, releasing a huge amount of energy.

force
The means that causes a mass to change its momentum.

fossil fuel
A substance that burns easily, releasing heat formed from the remains of ancient plants and other organisms; fossil fuels include coal, natural gas, and oil.

friction
A force that occurs between moving objects, where the surfaces rub against each other, opposing their movement.

fusion
Joining together; nuclear fusion involves two small atoms fusing into a single larger one, releasing huge amounts of energy.

gene
A coded instruction for making a certain body feature that is passed from parent to offspring; the code is stored as a DNA molecule and is translated into proteins, each of which performs a specific job.

generator
A device for converting rotational motion into electric current.

gills
A breathing organ that takes oxygen from the water and releases carbon dioxide. Gills are used by fish and many underwater creatures.

gland
An organ in the body that secretes chemicals in large quantities; endocrine glands release chemicals into the blood stream, exocrine glands secrete onto the surface of the body.

glucose
A simple carbohydrate, or sugar, made by the process of photosynthesis and then used by cells as a source of energy.

gravity
A force that acts between all masses and which tends to pull them together.

habitat
The place where organisms live; every habitat has specific conditions, such as supply of water, range of temperatures, and amount of light.

half-life
The period of time that it takes for a sample of a radioactive element to halve in mass by decaying into other elements.

hormone
A chemical messenger that travels through the bloodstream to control certain life processes; hormones include epinephrine, insulin, and estrogen.

hydrocarbon
A compound composed largely, if not entirely, from hydrogen and carbon.

immiscible
A property where two liquids will not mix with each other because their molecules push away from each other.

indicator
A substance that changes color with pH, the measure of acidity.

induction
The process by which the energy of a moving conductor is converted into an electrical current when it passes through a magnetic field.

inertia
A mass's resistance to changing its state of motion.

insulation
A material with the function of stopping heat moving from a warm object to a colder one; animal insulation, such as hair or blubber, is used to save energy.

interference
The mixing of two or more light waves to produce new, different ones.

invertebrate
An animal with no backbone. Most animals are invertebrates, but are nevertheless not all closely related.

ion
An atom or a molecule that has lost or gained an electron and thus carries a positive or negative charge.

isotope
One of two or more forms of atom all with the same number of protons—and so belonging to the same element—but with varying numbers of neutrons.

keratin
A protein used by vertebrates to cover their bodies; feathers, hair, nails, claws, horns, and reptile scales are all made of keratin.

longitudinal
A wave that is made up of compressions and expansions of a medium.

main sequence star
An average star, like our Sun.

mass
A property of an object that allows it to have weight and be acted on by forces.

matter
Anything that has mass and occupies space.

membrane
A thin layer that surrounds a cell or other body structure; the layer is semipermeable, so only certain substances can cross it.

metabolism
The name used for all processes that support life that take place in a living body; catabolism is all the processes that break things into simpler substances; anabolic processes build simple substances into complex ones.

metal
An element that is likely to react by losing electrons, forming a cation; metals are generally shiny, heavy solids.

micrometer (μm)
A millionth of a meter.

microtubule
A fine fiber of protein that runs through the cytoplasm of a cell and is used to haul larger items around.

mixture
A collection of two or more substances mixed together but which are not chemically connected.

mole
A unit of quantity used to count huge numbers of objects, such as atoms and molecules; for example, one mole of hydrogen atoms is 6.0221415×10^{23} atoms.

molecule
Two or more atoms that are bonded together; the molecule is the smallest unit of a compound; breaking it up into simpler units would destroy the compound.

momentum
The product of the speed of an object and its mass.

nanometer (nm)
A billionth of a meter.

neutron
A neutral particle located in the nuclei of most atoms.

nucleus (plural: nuclei)
The central core of something. An atomic nucleus contains protons and neutrons, while a cell's nucleus contains DNA.

nutrient
A substance that is useful for life as a source of energy or as raw material.

octet
A collection of eight things.

orbit
The path of one mass around another mass under the influence of gravity.

organelle
A structure inside a cell that performs a certain task in the cell's metabolism.

organism
A living thing.

oscillation
A regular vibration around a fixed point.

oxidation
The loss of electrons by an atom, ion, or molecule.

phloem
The vascular tissue that carries sugar fuel around a plant.

pigment
A chemical substance that colors an object.

plasma
A high-energy state of matter where the atoms of a gas have been ripped into their constituent parts.

polarity
Relating to an object, such as a magnet, that has two opposite ends or poles.

polymer
A long chainlike molecule made up of smaller molecules connected together.

precipitation
A solid or liquid that falls from a cloud. Rain, snow, sleet, and hail

GLOSSARY

are examples of precipitation.

pressure
The amount of force that is applied to a surface per unit of area.

protein
A type of complex chemical found in all living things, used as enzymes and in muscles. A protein is a chain of simple units called amino acids. There are about 20 natural amino acids, and a protein has hundreds of these units connected in a specific order.

protist
A single-celled organism with a complex cell structure, including organelles and a nucleus.

proton
A positively charged particle that is located in the nuclei of all atoms.

pupate
To prepare to change from a larva to an adult form (imago); for example, a caterpillar pupates as a chrysalis before emerging as a butterfly.

radiation
Waves of energy that travel through space. Radiation includes visible light, heat, X-rays, and radio waves; nuclear radiation includes subatomic particles and fragments of atoms.

radicals
Atoms, molecules, or ions with unpaired electrons that cause them to react easily.

radioactive
Relating to atoms that are unstable and break apart, releasing high-energy particles.

rarefaction
A decrease in the pressure and density of molecules along a longitudinal wave.

reactivity
A description of how likely a substance is to become involved in a chemical reaction.

reduction
When a substance gains electrons during a chemical reaction and so its oxidation number is reduced.

reflection
When a wave bounces off a surface.

refraction
When a wave changes direction as it passes from one medium to another.

repulsion
A force that pushes things apart; the opposite of attraction.

respiration
The process occuring in all living cells that releases energy from glucose to power life.

rubisco
Short for "ribulose bisphosphate carboxylase oxidase," an enzyme that is responsible for taking carbon dioxide from the atmosphere and reacting it with water to make glucose as part of photosynthesis.

salt
An ionic compound formed by a reaction between an acid and base (including an alkali).

sedimentary rock
A rock that forms from sediments, which are layers of substances that have settled on the seabed or ground before becoming buried and compressed for millions of years.

solute
A substance that becomes dissolved in another.

solvent
A substance that can have other substances dissolved in it.

speed
The rate of how fast an object is moving.

states of matter
The three main forms of matter that a substance can take are: solid, liquid, or gas. Plasma is a fourth state of matter.

strain
The change of the shape of an object in response to stress.

stress
A force that alters the shape of an object, by stretching, bending, and sometimes breaking it.

subatomic particle
A particle that is smaller than an atom, such as a proton, neutron, and electron.

superconductor
A material that conducts electricity without warming up and so wastes none of the energy it is carrying.

suspension
A mixture in which small solids, blobs of liquid, or gas bubbles are spread throughout a liquid.

temperature
An average measure of the thermal energy or heat of an object.

torque
The turning effect of a force.

torsion
A twist caused by torque.

transformer
A device for altering the voltage of an electrical current.

transverse
A wave that moves by rising and falling perpendicular to the direction of its motion.

vapor
Another word for a gas.

vascular
Concerning vessels, tubes that transport substances around a body.

velocity
A speed of something in a particular direction.

vertebrate
An animal that has a vertebral column, a flexible spine made from a chain of smaller bones called vertebrae; the largest animals are vertebrates, and include fish, amphibians, reptiles, mammals, and birds.

vesicle
A membranous sac that contains a material being processed by a cell; a vesicle may be used to release substances from a cell.

voltage
A measure of the force that pushes electrons around an electric current.

xylem
The vascular tissue that transports water and minerals around a plant.

wavelength
The distance measured between any point on a wave and the equivalent point on the next wave.

weight
The force applied to a mass by gravity.

work
The amount of energy transferred when a force is being applied to a mass over a certain distance.

Index

A

acceleration 176, 177, 178, 181
acids 134, 144–147, 160, 161
actinides 125
activation energy 134, 136, 137, 138
adaptive radiation 82
adaptors 221
air resistance 179, 180
aircraft 185, 190, 201
alcohols 71, 160
algae 83, 89
aliphatics 158, 159
alkalis 134, 144, 145
alkanes, alkenes, and alkynes 159
alleles 84–85
allotropes 111
alloys 153
alpha particles and decay 126, 127
alternator 215
aluminum 109, 112, 118, 152, 153
amber 203
amines 161
amino acids 79, 87, 161
ammonia 34, 110, 115, 141, 154
amoebas 27, 32
amphibians 59
amplitude 193, 200
angiosperms 21, 55
animals 22, 29, 33, 34–35, 36
   classification 20–21, 56–61, 243
   human impact on 90–91
   movement 38–39, 57
   relationships 52–53
   reproduction 42–44, 47, 80
   senses 40–41
anions 112–113, 147
anodes 148, 149, 153
antigens and antibodies 50, 51
ants 52, 53, 161
aphids 42, 53
appliances, household 221, 222
applied science 11, 15
arachnids 56
Archaea 20, 26
Arctic Ocean 77
aromatics 159
arteries 36, 63, 69
arthropods 32, 39, 40, 56
astronomy 15, 167, 230–241
atomic mass 108, 151
atomic number 108, 116
atoms 95, 98–99, 108–109, 168–169, 195, 231
   bonding 109, 111, 112–115, 142
   nuclear power from 219, 233
   octet rule 109, 112
   periodic table 11, 94, 116–125
   radioactivity 126–127
   see also chemical reactions
ATP 28, 31
aurora 99
Avogadro's law 102

B

bacteria 20, 24, 26, 50, 51, 78, 79
ball games 172, 180, 182
ballistics 179
balloons 123, 202
bases 86–87, 144
batteries 204, 206, 215
bees 53, 83
Bernoulli effect 185
beta particles and decay 126, 127
bicycles 171, 214
Big Bang theory 240–241
binary digits 209, 217
biology 18–91, 242–243
   fields of 14, 18–19
biomagnification 89
biomass 76
biomes 75
birds 33, 38, 53, 60, 61, 83, 89
bivalves 57
bladder 35
blood 36, 50, 51, 63, 69, 71
blubber 60
body mass index 71
boiling points 100, 101, 244–245
bonding 109, 111, 112–115, 142, 143, 144, 158, 162
bones 62, 63, 120
botany 14, 54
Boyle's law 102
braille 65

brain, human 19, 68
Brand, Hennig 108
bromine 112, 122, 123
bubbles 199
bungee jumping 175
bunsen burner 150
buoyancy 96
butter churn 107
butterflies 47

C

cesium 119, 121
calcium 109, 112, 120, 121, 124
calorimeter 135
cameras 207
candle wax 130, 131, 157
capacitors 207
carbohydrates 70
carbon 30, 94, 126, 156–161, 168–169, 231
carbon cycle 78
carbon dioxide
   chemistry 100, 110, 130, 141
   in fizzy drinks 128
   life and 30, 31, 34, 78
   and pollution 88, 89
carbonates 147
carboxylic acids 160
carnivores 21, 33, 79
catalysts 138–139
catalytic converter 139
caterpillars 47
cathodes 148, 149, 153
cations 112–113, 147
cats 21, 40
celestial sphere 231
cell division 25
cells 18, 22–25, 27, 41, 64
   membrane 22–23, 24, 26, 161
   plant 18, 23, 30
   reproductive 43, 63, 72, 73
   respiration by 28
   single-celled life 26, 27, 32, 38, 42
   white blood cells 50, 51
cellulose 162
central nervous system 63, 68
centrifugal force 107, 183
cephalopods 57
CFCs (chlorofluorocarbons) 88, 160

Charles's law 103
chemical energy 170, 171
chemical industry 95, 154–155
chemical reactions 95, 109, 110, 128–131
   in the body 67, 139
   catalysts 138–139
   energy and 134–135, 136, 137, 138, 140
   rates of 136–137
   redox reactions 132, 133
   reversible 140–141
chemical symbols 108
chemistry 14, 92–163, 244–245
   basic explanation 94–95
   equipment/techniques 150–151
chlorine 108, 109, 114, 115, 122, 123, 132, 155, 161
chlorophyll 30, 31, 55
chloroplast 31
chordates 21, 58
chromatography 107
chromosomes 25, 43, 72, 84, 85
cicadas 47
cilia 27, 38
circuits 206–207, 208–209, 221
circulatory system 36, 63, 69, 71
clouds 105, 202, 229
Cnidaria 56
coal 131, 134, 156
cold 49, 65, 100, 189, 191
colloids 105
color blindness 85
colors 31, 125, 167, 194, 196, 199
combustion 130–131, 190
comets 235, 237
compounds 94, 97, 110–115, 123
computers 15, 209, 217
concentration (chemical) 137
condensation 101
conduction 188
conductors 203, 204, 205, 208, 214
conservation of matter 128
contact process 155
continental drift 227
convection 189
copper 133, 149, 203, 222
corrosion 133

INDEX

covalent bonding 114–115, 142, 144, 158, 162
creaming 105
crocodiles 32, 34, 59
crustaceans 56
crystals 98, 111
currents, electric 203, 204–205, 220–221
   direct and alternating 215, 216
cycles in nature 78–79
cytoplasm 22, 26

D

dark matter and dark energy 241
DDT 89
Dead Sea 143
deformation 174
density 96
deposition 100
detritivores 76
diamonds 114, 156
diatoms 27
diffraction 199
digestion 33, 63, 66–67, 145
diodes 208, 209
dipoles 115, 142
disease 50–51, 87
distillation 106
distortion 174
DNA 26, 50, 73, 84, 86, 87, 162
dolphins 20, 33, 201
Doppler effect 201
double helix 86
Downs cells 155
drag 173, 179
drug use 71
dynamo 214

E

ears 64, 200
Earth 225, 226–227, 231, 234, 247
   magnetic field 211
echoes 200
eclipses 236
ecology 14, 19
ecosystems 19, 74–75, 77, 90–91
ectothermy 59
eggs (ova) 43, 45, 49, 72–73, 84

elasticity 175
electricity 167, 170, 202–207
   generating 214–221, 224–225
   motors 212–213
electrochemistry 14, 133, 148–149
electrolysis 148, 149, 153, 155
electrolytes 148, 153
electromagnetic induction 214
electromagnetic radiation and spectrum 167, 194–199
electromagnetism 15, 167, 213
electromagnets 205, 211, 213, 217
electronics 208–209
electrons 95, 108, 109, 132, 168, 169, 195, 202, 203, 204
   back-filling 124, 125
   bonding 109, 111, 112–115, 142
electroplating 149
elements 94, 97, 108–109, 111, 168, 231, 244–245
   periodic table 11, 94, 116–125
embryo 73
endocrine system 48, 63, 68
endocytosis and exocytosis 24
endothermic reaction 135, 141
endothermy 60
energy 170–171, 182, 188, 195, 198
   cellular 28
   and changing states 100, 101
   in chemical reactions 134–135, 136, 137, 138, 140
   ionization 119, 120
energy efficiency 222–225
energy pyramid 76
engines 182, 190–191
enzymes 67, 139
epinephrine 48
equations, chemical 129
equilibrium 140–141, 177
esters 161
esophagus 66, 145
estrogen 49, 72
ethane 158, 159
ethene 159, 162
Eukaryota 20–21, 27
eutrophication 89
evolution 19, 80–83
excretion 34–35

exercise 71
exothermic reaction 134, 135, 141
extinctions 19, 81, 90
eyes 40, 64, 196
   aids to impaired sight 65, 209

F

fats 70, 161
feathers 60, 61
ferns 54
fertilization 43, 73
fertilizers 89, 154, 155
fetus 73
fiberoptics 222
filter feeding 32, 57
filtration 106
finches, Darwin's 19, 82
fire extinguishing 131
fish 34, 38, 40, 44, 47, 52, 58, 59, 77, 81, 91, 161
   gills 29, 58
flagella 26, 27, 38
fleas 53
flies 91
flocculation 105
flowers 21, 24, 45, 53, 55, 83
fluorine 119, 122, 123
food
   digestion 33, 63, 66–67, 145
   feeding habits 32–33, 57, 74, 75
   food chains 19, 76–77, 89
   food webs 77
   healthy eating 70–71
force 166, 167, 169, 172–175, 180–183
forensic science 14
formulas (physics) 247
fossil fuels 78, 88, 89, 156–157, 218, 224
fossils 33, 81
freezing 100, 191
frequencies 193, 200, 201
friction 173, 180
frogs 59
fruit 45, 55
fuels 131, 191
   see also fossil fuels
fungi 20–21, 26–27, 32, 42, 74
fur 60

G

galaxies 238, 240, 241
galvinization 149
gametes 43, 63, 72
gamma rays 126, 194
gas exchange 29
gases 98, 99, 100–101, 115
   halogens 122–123, 161
   laws of 102–103
   measuring 136
   natural gas 157
   noble (inert) 123
   pressure and 102–103, 141
   spectroscopy and 231
   testing for 130
   water vapor 142
gastropods 57
Gay-Lussac's law 103
gears 187
generators, electricity 214–215
genes 80, 84, 86
genetic modification 91
genetics 14, 84–87
genome, human 87
geothermal energy 225
germination 46
glands 48, 63
global dimming 88
glucose 28, 30, 31, 78, 79, 162
gold 116, 133, 154
gonads 44, 72
graphene 174
graphite 156
grasses 46
grasshoppers 32, 40
gravity 166, 178–179, 184
greenhouse effect 88
gymnosperms 54

H

Haber-Bosch process 154
half-life 127
Hall-Héroult process 153
halogens 122–123, 161
hardness 97
health 50–51, 70–71
heart 69
heat 130, 131, 135, 170, 188–191
   body and 49, 60, 65
   electrical 205, 222

helicopters 173
helium 94, 99, 109, 119, 121, 123, 232, 233
hemoglobin 36, 87
hemophilia 51
herbivores 33, 76
hermaphrodites 44
heterotrophs 32, 76
Hooke, Robert 23, 175
hormones 35, 48–49, 72
human beings 33, 35, 39, 41, 48–51, 62–73, 245
  brain 19, 68
  genome 87
  impact on ecosystems 90–91
hydra 42
hydraulics 185
hydrocarbons 157, 158–161
hydroelectricity 218
hydrogen 108, 121, 130, 168, 169, 231, 232, 233
hydrogen bonds 142
hydrogen ions 144, 145, 147
hyphae 27
hypothesis 12–13

I

ice 100, 142
Ice Age, Little 233
immune system 50–51
indicators 145
induction 216–217
inertia 172
infrared radiation 88, 194, 195
insects 32, 40, 45, 47, 56, 91
insulation 223
insulin 49
interference 199
intestines 66–67
invertebrates 56–57
ionic bonding 111, 112–113, 143, 144
ionization energy 119, 120
ions 112–113, 120, 143, 148
  complex 125
  hydrogen 144, 145, 147
  oxidation states 124, 132, 133
iron 108, 124, 133, 146, 152
isomers 159
isotopes 127, 169, 219

J

jellyfish 56
jet aircraft 190, 201
joints 62

K

kangaroos 44, 60
keratin 59, 60, 61
kidneys 35, 63, 201
kinetic energy 170, 171, 182
knowledge, development of 11
Kuiper Belt 235

L

laboratories 95, 150–151
lamps 104, 223
lancelets 58
lanthanides 125
lead 96, 168
leaves 30, 31, 37, 55
lenses 198
levers 186
life
  alkali metals in 120
  classification of 20–21
  cycles of 46–47
  seven requirements for 18
light 137, 192, 194, 196–199, 230
  electrical 205, 206, 207
  red and blue shift 241
  spectroscopy and 231
light bulbs 223
light-years 231
lightning 79, 202
limescale 143
lions 21, 33, 47, 52
liquids 98, 99, 100–101, 106, 150, 185, 189
lithium 108, 109, 118, 120, 121
liverworts 54
lizards 59
lodestone compass 210
logic gates 209
loudspeakers 213
lubrication 173
lungs 29, 63, 69
lymphatic system 63

M

machines 167, 171, 186–187
Maglev trains 205, 213
magnesium 113, 118, 121, 136
Magnetic Resonance Imaging (MRI) 68, 205
magnets 210–211, 217
  and electricity 212, 213, 214, 215
magnification 198, 230
mammals 21, 34, 60–61
margarine 139
marsupials 44, 60
mass 96, 166, 172, 178, 179, 181, 189
materials 94, 96–97, 175
matter 98–101, 128, 142, 241
measurements 10
medusae 56
melatonin 48
melting points 100, 101, 244–245
Mendeleev, Dmitri 11, 116, 117, 119
mercury 99, 150, 184, 231
metallic bonds 111
metalloids 119
metals 97, 118, 146
  alkali and alkali earth 120–121
  conduction 188, 203
  purifying and electroplating 149
  rare earth 125
  refining 152–153
  transition 124–125
metamorphosis 47, 59
meteorites 237
methane 114, 115, 131, 158
microbiology 14, 18
microchips 208
microphones 217
microscopes 18, 23
microwaves 191, 195, 241
Milky Way 238
minerals 97
  in food 70
mitochondria 22, 23, 28
mitosis 25
mixtures 101, 104–107
Mohs scale 97
molecules 98–99, 100, 110–111
  of gases 102–103, 115
  intermolecular forces 115
  in mixtures 104
moles (chemistry) 151
mollusks 57
momentum 182, 183
monomers 162, 163
monotremes 60
Moon 179, 198, 236
mosses 54
moths 47, 80
motion 180–183
motor vehicles 139, 173, 190, 207
motors, electric 212–213
mouth 65, 66, 67
movement (body) 38–39, 57
mucus 25, 66
muscles 39, 62, 66, 71, 120
mutations 87

N

natural selection 80
nebulae 238, 239
neon 123
nephrons 35
nerve cells (neurons) 41, 68
nerves 41, 63, 65, 120
neuroscience 68
neutralization 144
neutrons 95, 108, 168, 219
Newton, Isaac 178, 179, 180–181
nickel 124, 125
nitrates 79, 89
nitric acid 154
nitrogen 34, 108, 112, 113, 119, 126, 154
nitrogen cycle 79
nose 25, 65, 66
nuclear fission 219
nuclear fusion 233
nuclear power 170, 219, 224

O

oceans see seas
octopus 57
Ohm's Law 205
oil 95, 157
omnivores 33, 76

INDEX

Oort Cloud 235
optics 15, 198–199
orbits 179, 226
organelles 18, 22, 23, 24, 27, 28, 31
oscillation 177
osmoregulation 35
osmosis 24, 31, 37
ovulation 72
oxidation states 124, 132–133
oxides 147, 152
oxygen 110, 111, 112, 113, 114, 130, 131
    life and 29, 30–31, 34, 69
oxygen cycle 78
ozone layer 88, 137

P

pain 41, 65
pancreas 49, 66, 67
panda, giant 19
paraffin wax 131
parasites 53, 57, 91
parthenogenesis 42
Pascal's Principle 185
pathogens 50, 51
pendulums 177
periodic table 11, 94, 116–125
peristalsis 66
perpetual motion 171
pests 91
petrochemicals 95
petroleum/gasoline 131, 157
pH 145
phloem 37, 54
phosphates 89
phosphorus 108, 111, 113
photochemical reactions 137
photorespiration 141
photosynthesis 23, 27, 30–31, 34, 37, 54, 74, 78, 79, 137, 141
phototropism 40
physics 15, 164–241, 246–247
    basic explanation 166–167
physiology 19
placenta 44, 60, 73
planets 234–235, 247
    dwarf 237
plankton 38, 77
plants 32, 46, 76
    carnivorous 79
    cells 18, 23, 30

classification 20–21, 54–55, 242
reproduction 42, 45, 54, 55, 83
tropism 40
vascular system 37
see also photosynthesis
plasma (state of matter) 99
plasma, blood 36
plastics 163, 210
plate tectonics 189, 226–227
platelets 36, 51
plugs, electric 221
Pluto 237
polar bears 77, 189
poles 210, 211, 231
pollination 45, 53, 55, 83
pollution 88–89
polymers 162–163
polyps 56
polythene 162, 163
potassium 112, 113, 118, 120, 121
power grid 220
power stations 218–219, 220, 225
precipitation 228
    see also rain
predators and prey 75, 76
pressure 102–103, 141, 184–185
    atmospheric 184, 228, 229
prism 196
products 95, 128–129, 140, 141
proteins 70, 87, 162
protists 20–21, 22, 27
protons 95, 108, 112, 168, 233
pulleys 11, 187
pulsars 238

Q

quasars 238
quicklime 141

R

rabbits 80
Radiata 56
radiation 167, 189, 194–195,198
    Cherenkov 219
    cosmic microwave 241
radio waves 195, 230
radioactivity 126–127, 194, 219

radiocarbon dating 169
rain 79, 89, 145, 146, 228
reactants 95, 128–129, 134–138, 140, 141
reactivity 97, 113, 120, 121, 122, 136, 146
reflection 197, 230
reflex action 41
refraction 197, 198, 230
refrigeration 191
reproduction 42–45, 47, 80
    human 49, 63, 72–73
    plant 42, 45, 54, 55, 83
reptiles 59
resistance, electrical 204–205
respiration 28–29, 34, 63, 78
RNA 86–87
robots 213
rockets 180, 191
rubber 163
ruminants 33

S

salamanders 59
saliva 66, 67
salmon 47, 58
salt (sodium chloride) 34, 98, 100, 122, 132, 144, 155
saltwater 13, 26, 104, 106, 143
science
    definitions of 10
    fields of 14–15
scientific method 10, 12–13
scientists 11, 15
seas 77, 104, 143, 200, 201
    tidal power 225
    waves 192, 225
seasons 226
sedimentation 105
seeds 45, 46, 54, 55
seismic waves 192
senses 40–41, 64–65
sexual reproduction 43, 49, 63, 72
sexual selection 83
sharks 40, 53, 58, 82
SI units 10, 246
sickle-cell anemia 87
silver 133, 149
single-celled organisms 26, 27, 32, 38, 42

skeletal systems 39, 61, 62
skin 51, 65
smell 65, 161
smelting 152
smoke detectors 126
snails 57, 120
snakes 38, 40, 59, 194
social sciences 15
sodas 128
sodium 95, 109, 112, 113, 118, 120, 121, 128, 132, 155
sodium chloride *see* salt
solar panels 224
solar system 167, 234–237
solenoid 211
solids 98, 100–101
solutions 105
solvents 105, 106, 107, 143
sound 64, 170, 192, 200–201
    magnifying 213, 217
species 21, 81, 91
spectroscopy 231
spectrum 167, 196, 241
speed 176–177, 193
sperm 43, 72–73, 84
spinal cord 41, 58
spores 27, 42, 54
squamates 59
starch 162
stars 238–239
static electricity 202, 203
steel 149, 210, 217
stomach 66, 67
stresses 174
sublimation 100
sugars 28, 37, 49, 70, 162
sulfites 147
sulfuric acid 155
Sun 198, 232–235, 237, 238, 239
    eclipses 236
    and ecosystems 74
    energy from 224
    plants and 30, 31, 37, 40, 74
    solar storms 220
    ultraviolet light 88, 137, 194
sunspots 233
superconductors 205, 220
supersonic motion 201
suspensions 105
sweat 49, 65
symbiosis 53
synapses 41

T

tapeworm 53
taste 65, 66
taxonomy 18, 20–21
teeth 32, 33, 120
telescopes 230
temperature 10, 100, 101, 103, 141, 188
tension 174
testosterone 49
theory 10
thermite process 152
thermodynamics 15, 171, 188–189
thermometer 10
thermoregulation 49
thiols 161
tires 173
tissue 25
toads 59, 91
tobacco 71
tongue 65, 66
tornadoes 228
torque 183, 187
torsion 174
touch 65
transformers 216–217, 220
trees 31, 37, 46, 54, 55, 74
tropism 40
turtles and tortoises 59

U

ultraviolet light 88, 137, 194
universe, origins of 240–241
uranium 125, 126, 127
urinary system 35, 63

V

vaccination 51
veins 36, 63, 69
velocity 176–177
venom 59, 161
Venus 88, 234
vertebrates 21, 29, 32, 36, 58–59
villi 67
virtual image 197, 198
viruses 50
viscosity 99
vitamins 70
voltage 204, 205, 206, 216

W

waste removal 34–35, 66
water
  buoyancy 96
  chemistry 99, 110, 115, 120, 136, 142–143, 148, 150
  cold 49
  filtration 106
  hardness 143
  hydroelectricity 218
  physics 173, 189, 185, 197, 201
  plants and 37
  salt and 13, 26, 104, 106, 143
  states of 142
water cycle 79
waves 15, 192–193, 199, 200
  electromagnetic 194–196, 198
weather 79, 228–229, 233
weight 71, 179
whales 77, 82, 201
wind 45, 228
wind turbines 224
wings 38, 61, 82, 185
wood 131
worms 39, 57, 76

X, Y, Z

X-rays 194
xylem 37, 54, 55
Young's modulus 175
zinc 133, 149

Acknowledgments

DORLING KINDERSLEY would like to thank: Smiljka Surlja for her design assistance; Fran Baines, Clive Gifford, Clare Hibbert, Wendy Horobin, James Mitchem, Carole Stott, and Victoria Wiggins for their editorial assistance; Nikky Twyman for proofreading; and Jackie Brind for the index.

DORLING KINDERSLEY INDIA would like to thank Sudakshina Basu and Vandna Sonkariya for their design assistance.

The publisher would like to thank the following for their kind permission to reproduce their photographs:

(Key: a-above; b-below/bottom; c-center; f-far; l-left; r-right; t-top)

23 Science Photo Library: Dr. E. Walker (br). **24** Getty Images: Photographer's Choice / Tony Hutchings (br). **34** Corbis: Anup Shah (cr). **37** SuperStock: Stock Connection (bl). **47** Ardea: Alan Weaving (tr). **65** Corbis: Tetra Images (br). **68** Corbis: Owen Franken (cl). **73** Science Photo Library: Mehau Kulyk (br). **79** FLPA: Nigel Cattlin (cl). **81** Corbis: Louie Psihoyos (tr). **85** Science Photo Library: Andrew McClenaghan (bc). **87** Science Photo Library: James King-Holmes (br). **88** Dreamstime.com: Peter Wollinga (bl). **91** Corbis: Richard Chung / Reuters (bc). **99** Corbis: Radius Images (bl). **100** Corbis: Mark Schneider / Visuals Unlimited (bl). **102** Corbis: Bettmann (bc). **107** Corbis: FoodPhotography Eising / the food passionates (c). **108** Science Photo Library: Sheila Terry (cr). **119** Science Photo Library: Charles D. Winters (br). **123** Corbis: Louie Psihoyos / Science Faction (br). **124** Corbis: Thom Lang (br). **126** Alamy Images: Robert Cousins (br). **128** Corbis: Taro Yamada (br). **135** Science Photo Library: Martyn F. Chillmaid (br). **139** Alamy Images: Carol and Mike Werner / PHOTOTAKE Inc. (br). **141** Science Photo Library: Dirk Wiersma (br). **143** SuperStock: imagebroker.net (cra). **145** Dreamstime.com: Cammeraydave (br). **146** Science Photo Library: Cristina Pedrazzini (br). **149** Getty Images: Photolibrary / Wallace Garrison (crb). **161** Corbis: Alex Wild / Visuals Unlimited (bl). **163** Corbis: moodboard (bl). **169** Corbis: Roland Holschneider / DPA (c). **171** Science Photo Library: Middle Temple Library (br). **173** Corbis: Ken Welsh / Design Pics (bl). **175** Corbis: Mike Powell (cr). **180** Corbis: Gene Blevins / LA DailyNews (cra). **183** Corbis: Duomo (br). **187** Alamy Images: Chuck Franklin (bl). **189** Corbis: Barritt, Peter / SuperStock (br). **191** Alamy Images: Ange (br). **192** Corbis: Grantpix / Index Stock (cra). **194** Corbis: Joe McDonald (cra). **199** Science Photo Library: Sinclair Stammers (tr). **201** Corbis: Denis Scott (cra). **205** Science Photo Library: Andy Crump (br). **207** Corbis: Marcus Mok / Asia Images (bl). **209** Science Photo Library: Volker Steger / Peter Arnold Inc. (br). **210** Corbis: Liu Liqun (br). **213** Science Photo Library: David Parker (cra). **215** Alamy Images: Mark Boulton (br). **217** Alamy Images: MShieldsPhotos (br). **219** Science Photo Library: Patrick Landmann (br). **220** Corbis: Chip East / Reuters (br). **222** Corbis: Seth Resnick / Science Faction (bc). **225** Alamy Images: Mark Ferguson (cra). **228** Getty Images: Alan R Moller (cra). **231** Science Photo Library: NASA / JPL (br). **233** Corbis: Heritage Images / Museum of London (br). **237** Corbis: George Steinmetz (br). **238** NASA: ESA and The Hubble Heritage Team (STScI / AURA) (br). **241** Science Photo Library: NASA (cla)

All other images © Dorling Kindersley
For further information see: **www.dkimages.com**

HELP YOUR KIDS WITH math

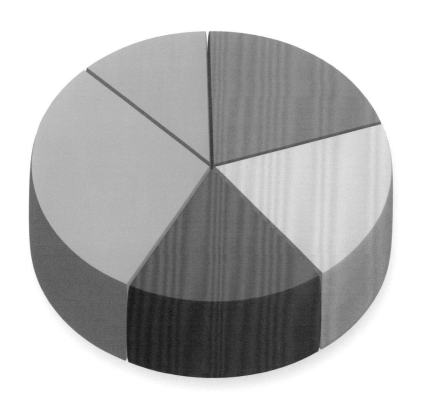

HELP YOUR KIDS WITH
m^a√th

A UNIQUE STEP-BY-STEP VISUAL GUIDE

Project Art Editor
Mark Lloyd

Project Editor
Nathan Joyce

Designers
Nicola Erdpresser, Riccie Janus,
Maxine Pedliham, Silke Spingies,
Rebecca Tennant

Editors
Nicola Deschamps, Martha Evatt,
Lizzie Munsey, Martyn Page, Laura Palosuo,
Peter Preston, Miezan van Zyl

Design Assistants
Thomas Howey, Fiona Macdonald

US Editor
Jill Hamilton

Production Editor
Luca Frassinetti

US Consultant
Alison Tribley

Production
Erika Pepe

Indexer
Jane Parker

Jacket Designer
Duncan Turner

Managing Editor
Sarah Larter

Managing Art Editor
Michelle Baxter

Publishing Manager
Liz Wheeler

Art Director
Phil Ormerod

Reference Publisher
Jonathan Metcalf

This American Edition, 2014
First American Edition, 2010
Published in the United States by DK Publishing
345 Hudson Street, New York, New York 10014

Copyright © 2010, 2014, 2019 Dorling Kindersley Limited
DK, a Division of Penguin Random House, LLC
11 12 13 14 10 9 8 7 6 5 4 3 2 1
001–313518 –Jan/2019

All rights reserved.
Without limiting the rights under the copyright reserved above,
no part of this publication may be reproduced, stored in or introduced into a retrieval system,
or transmitted, in any form, or by any means (electronic, mechanical, photocopying, recording,
or otherwise), without the prior written permission of the copyright owner.
Published in Great Britain by Dorling Kindersley Limited.

A catalog record for this book
is available from the Library of Congress.
ISBN 978-1-4654-2166-1

DK books are available at special discounts when purchased in bulk for sales promotions, premiums,
fund-raising, or educational use. For details contact: DK Publishing Special Markets,
345 Hudson Street, New York, New York 10014
SpecialSales@dk.com.

Printed in China

A WORLD OF IDEAS:
SEE ALL THERE IS TO KNOW

www.dk.com

CAROL VORDERMAN M.A.(Cantab), MBE is one of Britain's best-loved TV personalities and is renowned for her excellent math skills. She has hosted numerous shows, from light entertainment with **Carol Vorderman's Better Homes** and **The Pride of Britain Awards**, to scientific programs such as **Tomorrow's World**, on the BBC, ITV, and Channel 4. Whether co-hosting Channel 4's **Countdown** for 26 years, becoming the second-best-selling female nonfiction author of the 2000s in the UK, or advising Parliament on the future of math education in the UK, Carol has a passion for and devotion to explaining math in an exciting and easily understandable way.

BARRY LEWIS (Consultant Editor, Numbers, Geometry, Trigonometry, Algebra) studied math in college and graduated with honors. He spent many years in publishing, as an author and as an editor, where he developed a passion for mathematical books that presented this often difficult subject in accessible, appealing, and visual ways. He is the author of **Diversions in Modern Mathematics**, which subsequently appeared in Spanish as **Matemáticas modernas. Aspectos recreativos**.

He was invited by the British government to run the major initiative **Maths Year 2000,** a celebration of mathematical achievement with the aim of making the subject more popular and less feared. In 2001 Barry became the president of the UK's Mathematical Association, and was elected as a fellow of the Institute of Mathematics and its Applications, for his achievements in popularizing mathematics. He is currently the Chair of Council of the Mathematical Association and regularly publishes articles and books dealing with both research topics and ways of engaging people in this critical subject.

ANDREW JEFFREY (Author, Probability) is a math consultant, well known for his passion and enthusiasm for the teaching and learning of math. A teacher for over 20 years, Andrew now spends his time training, coaching, and supporting teachers and delivering lectures for various organizations throughout Europe. He has written many books on the subject of math and is better known to many schools as the "Mathemagician."

MARCUS WEEKS (Author, Statistics) is the author of many books and has contributed to several reference books, including DK's **Science: The Definitive Visual Guide** and **Children's Illustrated Encyclopedia**.

SEAN MCARDLE (Consultant) was head of math in two primary schools and has a Master of Philosophy degree in Educational Assessment. He has written or co-written more than 100 mathematical textbooks for children and assessment books for teachers.

Contents

FOREWORD by Carol Vorderman 8
INTRODUCTION by Barry Lewis 10

1 NUMBERS

Introducing numbers	14
Addition	16
Subtraction	17
Multiplication	18
Division	22
Prime numbers	26
Units of measurement	28
Telling the time	30
Roman numerals	33
Positive and negative numbers	34
Powers and roots	36
Surds	40
Standard form	42
Decimals	44
Binary numbers	46
Fractions	48
Ratio and proportion	56
Percentages	60
Converting fractions, decimals, and percentages	64
Mental math	66
Rounding off	70
Using a calculator	72
Personal finance	74
Business finance	76

2 GEOMETRY

What is geometry?	80
Tools in geometry	82
Angles	84
Straight lines	86
Symmetry	88
Coordinates	90
Vectors	94
Translations	98
Rotations	100
Reflections	102
Enlargements	104
Scale drawings	106
Bearings	108
Constructions	110
Loci	114
Triangles	116
Constructing triangles	118
Congruent triangles	120
Area of a triangle	122
Similar triangles	125
Pythagorean Theorem	128
Quadrilaterals	130
Polygons	134
Circles	138
Circumference and diameter	140

Area of a circle	142
Angles in a circle	144
Chords and cyclic quadrilaterals	146
Tangents	148
Arcs	150
Sectors	151
Solids	152
Volumes	154
Surface area of solids	156

3 TRIGONOMETRY

What is trigonometry?	160
Using formulas in trigonometry	161
Finding missing sides	162
Finding missing angles	164

4 ALGEBRA

What is algebra?	168
Sequences	170
Working with expressions	172
Expanding and factorizing expressions	174
Quadratic expressions	176
Formulas	177
Solving equations	180
Linear graphs	182
Simultaneous equations	186
Factorizing quadratic equations	190

The quadratic formula	192
Quadratic graphs	194
Inequalities	198

5 STATISTICS

What is statistics?	202
Collecting and organizing data	204
Bar graphs	206
Pie charts	210
Line graphs	212
Averages	214
Moving averages	218
Measuring spread	220
Histograms	224
Scatter diagrams	226

6 PROBABILITY

What is probability?	230
Expectation and reality	232
Combined probabilities	234
Dependent events	236
Tree diagrams	238

Reference section	240
Glossary	252
Index	258
Acknowledgments	264

Foreword

Hello

Welcome to the wonderful world of math. Research has shown just how important it is for parents to be able to help children with their education. Being able to work through homework together and enjoy a subject, particularly math, is a vital part of a child's progress.

However, math homework can be the cause of upset in many households. The introduction of new methods of arithmetic hasn't helped, as many parents are now simply unable to assist.

We wanted this book to guide parents through some of the methods in early arithmetic and then for them to go on to enjoy some deeper mathematics.

As a parent, I know just how important it is to be aware of it when your child is struggling and equally, when they are shining. By having a greater understanding of math, we can appreciate this even more.

Over nearly 30 years, and for nearly every single day, I have had the privilege of hearing people's very personal views about math and arithmetic.
Many weren't taught math particularly well or in an interesting way. If you were one of those people, then we hope that this book can go some way to changing your situation and that math, once understood, can begin to excite you as much as it does me.

CAROL VORDERMAN

π = **3.14**15926535897932384626433832
7950288419716939937510582097494
4592307816406286208998628034853
4211706798214808651328230664709
3844609550582231725359408128481
1174502841027019385211055964462
2948954930381964428810975665933
4461284756482337867831652712019
0914564856692346034861045432664
8213393607260249141273724587006
6063155881748815209209628292540
9171536436789259036001133053054 8
2046652138414695194511609433057
2703657595919530921861173819326
1179310511854807446237996274956 7
3518857527248912279381830119491

Introduction

This book concentrates on the math tackled in schools between the ages of 9 and 16. But it does so in a gripping, engaging, and visual way. Its purpose is to teach math by stealth. It presents mathematical ideas, techniques, and procedures so that they are immediately absorbed and understood. Every spread in the book is written and presented so that the reader will exclaim, "Ah ha—now I understand!" Students can use it on their own; equally, it helps parents understand and remember the subject and thus help their children. If parents too gain something in the process, then so much the better.

At the start of the new millennium I had the privilege of being the director of the United Kingdom's **Maths Year 2000**, a celebration of math and an international effort to highlight and boost awareness of the subject. It was supported by the British government and Carol Vorderman was also involved. Carol championed math across the British media, and is well known for her astonishingly agile ways of manipulating and working with numbers—almost as if they were her personal friends. My working, domestic, and sleeping hours are devoted to math—finding out how various subtle patterns based on counting items in sophisticated structures work and how they hang together. What united us was a shared passion for math and the contribution it makes to all our lives—economic, cultural, and practical.

How is it that in a world ever more dominated by numbers, math—the subtle art that teases out the patterns, the harmonies, and the textures that make up the relationships between the numbers—is in danger? I sometimes think that we are drowning in numbers.

As employees, our contribution is measured by targets, statistics, workforce percentages, and adherence to budget. As consumers, we are counted and aggregated according to every act of consumption. And in a nice subtlety, most of the products that we do consume come complete with their own personal statistics—the energy in a can of beans and its "low" salt content; the story in a newspaper and its swath of statistics controlling and interpreting the world, developing each truth, simplifying each problem. Each minute of every hour, each hour of every day, we record and publish ever more readings from our collective life-support machine. That is how we seek to understand the world, but the problem is, the more figures we get, the more truth seems to slip through our fingers.

The danger is, despite all the numbers and our increasingly numerate world, math gets left behind. I'm sure that many think the ability to do the numbers is enough. Not so. Neither as individuals, nor collectively. Numbers are pinpricks in the fabric of math, blazing within. Without them we would be condemned to total darkness. With them we gain glimpses of the sparkling treasures otherwise hidden.

This book sets out to address and solve this problem. Everyone can do math.

BARRY LEWIS

Former President, **The Mathematical Association**;
Director **Maths Year 2000.**

Numbers

Introducing numbers

COUNTING AND NUMBERS FORM THE FOUNDATION OF MATHEMATICS.

Numbers are symbols that developed as a way to record amounts or quantities, but over centuries mathematicians have discovered ways to use and interpret numbers in order to work out new information.

What are numbers?

Numbers are basically a set of standard symbols that represent quantities—the familiar 0 to 9. In addition to these whole numbers (also called integers) there are also fractions (see pp.48–55) and decimals (see pp.44–45). Numbers can also be negative, or less than zero (see pp.34–35).

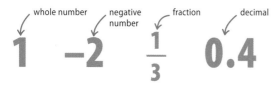

△ **Types of numbers**
Here 1 is a positive whole number and -2 is a negative number. The symbol ⅓ represents a fraction, which is one part of a whole that has been divided into three parts. A decimal is another way to express a fraction.

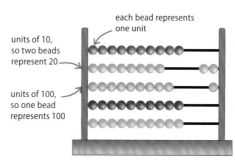

◁ **Abacus**
The abacus is a traditional calculating and counting device with beads that represent numbers. The number shown here is 120.

LOOKING CLOSER

Zero

The use of the symbol for zero is considered an important advance in the way numbers are written. Before the symbol for zero was adopted, a blank space was used in calculations. This could lead to ambiguity and made numbers easier to confuse. For example, it was difficult to distinguish between 400, 40, and 4, since they were all represented by only the number 4. The symbol zero developed from a dot first used by Indian mathematicians to act as placeholder.

◁ **Easy to read**
The zero acts as a placeholder for the "tens," which makes it easy to distinguish the single minutes.

zero is important for 24-hour timekeeping

▽ **First number**
One is not a prime number. It is called the "multiplicative identity," because any number multiplied by 1 gives that number as the answer.

▽ **Even prime number**
The number 2 is the only even-numbered prime number—a number that is only divisible by itself and 1 (see pp.26–27).

△ **Perfect number**
This is the smallest perfect number, which is a number that is the sum of its positive divisors (except itself). So, 1 + 2 + 3 = 6.

△ **Not the sum of squares**
The number 7 is the lowest number that cannot be represented as the sum of the squares of three whole numbers (integers).

INTRODUCING NUMBERS 15

REAL WORLD
Number symbols

Many civilizations developed their own symbols for numbers, some of which are shown below, together with our modern Hindu–Arabic number system. One of the main advantages of our modern number system is that arithmetical operations, such as multiplication and division, are much easier to do than with the more complicated older number systems.

Modern Hindu–Arabic	1	2	3	4	5	6	7	8	9	10
Mayan	•	••	•••	••••	—	•̇	••̇	•••̇	••••̇	=
Ancient Chinese	一	二	三	四	五	六	七	八	九	十
Ancient Roman	I	II	III	IV	V	VI	VII	VIII	IX	X
Ancient Egyptian	|	||	|||	||	|||	|||	||||	||||	||||	∩
Babylonian	𒐕	𒐖	𒐗	𒐘	𒐙	𒐚	𒐛	𒐜	𒐝	𒌋

▽ **Triangular number**
This is the smallest triangular number, which is a positive whole number that is the sum of consecutive whole numbers. So, 1 + 2 = 3.

▽ **Composite number**
The number 4 is the smallest composite number —a number that is the product of other numbers. The factors of 4 are two 2s.

▽ **Prime number**
This is the only prime number to end with a 5. A 5-sided polygon is the only shape for which the number of sides and diagonals are equal.

△ **Fibonacci number**
The number 8 is a cube number ($2^3 = 8$) and it is the only positive Fibonacci number (see p.171), other than 1, that is a cube.

△ **Highest decimal**
The number 9 is the highest single-digit whole number and the highest single-digit number in the decimal system.

△ **Base number**
The Western number system is based on the number 10. It is speculated that this is because humans used their fingers and toes for counting.

Addition

NUMBERS ARE ADDED TOGETHER TO FIND THEIR TOTAL. THIS RESULT IS CALLED THE SUM.

SEE ALSO	
Subtraction	17 ⟩
Positive and negative numbers	34–35 ⟩

Adding up

An easy way to work out the sum of two numbers is a number line. It is a group of numbers arranged in a straight line that makes it possible to count up or down. In this number line, 3 is added to 1.

◁ **Use a number line**
To add 3 to 1, start at 1 and move along the line three times—first to 2, then to 3, then to 4, which is the answer.

▷ **What it means**
The result of adding 3 to the start number of 1 is 4. This means that the sum of 1 and 3 is 4.

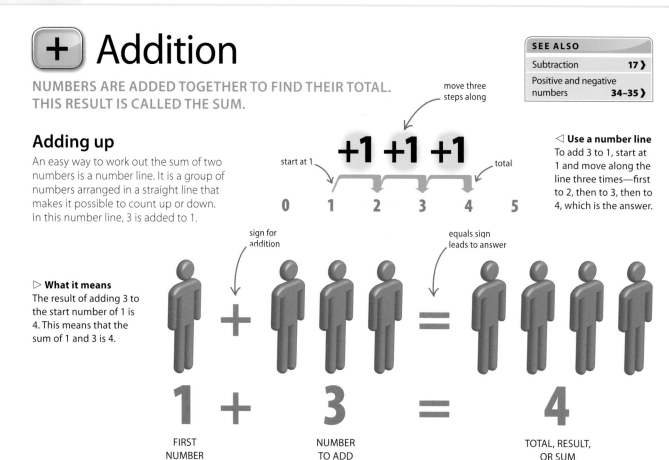

Adding large numbers

Numbers that have two or more digits are added in vertical columns. First, add the ones, then the tens, the hundreds, and so on. The sum of each column is written beneath it. If the sum has two digits, the first is carried to the next column.

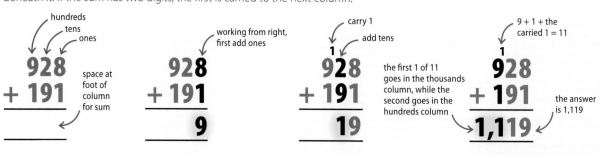

▷ **First, the numbers** are written with their ones, tens, and hundreds directly above each other.

▷ **Next, add** the ones 1 and 8 and write their sum of 9 in the space underneath the ones column.

▷ **The sum** of the tens has two digits, so write the second underneath and carry the first to the next column.

▷ **Then add the hundreds** and the carried digit. This sum has two digits, so the first goes in the thousands column.

ADDITION AND SUBTRACTION

Subtraction

SEE ALSO
◀ 16 Addition
Positive and negative numbers 34–35 ▶

A NUMBER IS SUBTRACTED FROM ANOTHER NUMBER TO FIND WHAT IS LEFT. THIS IS KNOWN AS THE DIFFERENCE.

Taking away

A number line can also be used to show how to subtract numbers. From the first number, move back along the line the number of places shown by the second number. Here 3 is taken from 4.

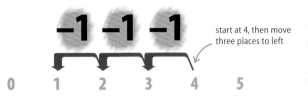

◁ **Use a number line**
To subtract 3 from 4, start at 4 and move three places along the number line, first to 3, then 2, and then to 1.

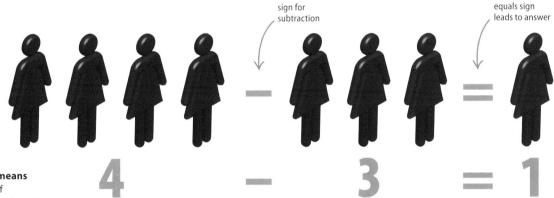

▷ **What it means**
The result of subtracting 3 from 4 is 1, so the difference between 3 and 4 is 1.

4 — FIRST NUMBER

3 — NUMBER TO SUBTRACT

1 — RESULT OR DIFFERENCE

Subtracting large numbers

Subtracting numbers of two or more digits is done in vertical columns. First subtract the ones, then the tens, the hundreds, and so on. Sometimes a digit is borrowed from the next column along.

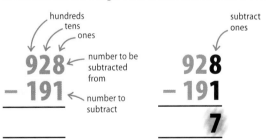

First, the numbers are written with their ones, tens, and hundreds directly above each other.

Next, subtract the unit 1 from 8, and write their difference of 7 in the space underneath them.

In the tens, 9 cannot be subtracted from 2, so 1 is borrowed from the hundreds, turning 9 into 8 and 2 into 12.

In the hundreds column, 1 is subtracted from the new, now lower number of 8.

18 NUMBERS

 # Multiplication

MULTIPLICATION INVOLVES ADDING A NUMBER TO ITSELF A NUMBER OF TIMES. THE RESULT OF MULTIPLYING NUMBERS IS CALLED THE PRODUCT.

SEE ALSO	
‹ 16–17 Addition and Subtraction	
Division	22–25 ›
Decimals	44–45 ›

What is multiplication?

The second number in a multiplication sum is the number to be added to itself and the first is the number of times to add it. Here the number of rows of people is added together a number of times determined by the number of people in each row. This multiplication sum gives the total number of people in the group.

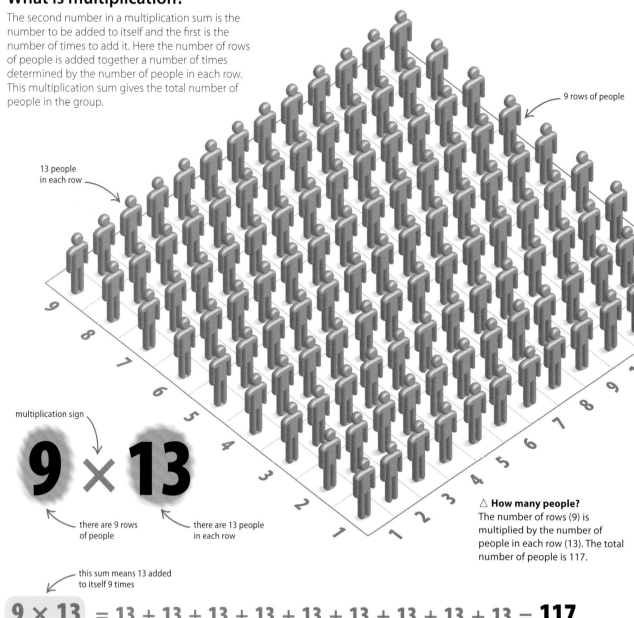

9 rows of people

13 people in each row

multiplication sign

9 × 13

there are 9 rows of people

there are 13 people in each row

△ **How many people?**
The number of rows (9) is multiplied by the number of people in each row (13). The total number of people is 117.

this sum means 13 added to itself 9 times

9 × 13 = 13 + 13 + 13 + 13 + 13 + 13 + 13 + 13 + 13 = **117**

product of 9 and 13 is 117

MULTIPLICATION

Works both ways
It does not matter which order numbers appear in a multiplication sum because the answer will be the same either way. Two methods of the same multiplication are shown here.

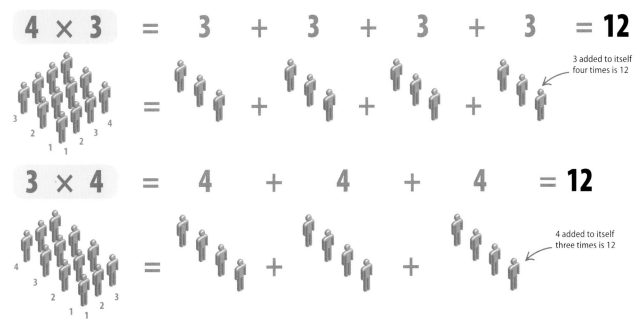

$4 \times 3 = 3 + 3 + 3 + 3 = \mathbf{12}$

3 added to itself four times is 12

$3 \times 4 = 4 + 4 + 4 = \mathbf{12}$

4 added to itself three times is 12

Multiplying by 10, 100, 1,000
Multiplying whole numbers by 10, 100, 1,000, and so on involves adding one zero (0), two zeroes (00), three zeroes (000), and so on to the right of the number being multiplied.

add 0 to end of number
$34 \times 10 = \mathbf{340}$

add 00 to end of number
$72 \times 100 = \mathbf{7,200}$

add 000 to end of number
$18 \times 1,000 = \mathbf{18,000}$

Patterns of multiplication
There are quick ways to multiply two numbers, and these patterns of multiplication are easy to remember. The table shows patterns involved in multiplying numbers by 2, 5, 6, 9, 12, and 20.

PATTERNS OF MULTIPLICATION		
To multiply	**How to do it**	**Example to multiply**
2	add the number to itself	$2 \times 11 = 11 + 11 = \mathbf{22}$
5	the last digit of the number follows the pattern 5, 0, 5, 0	5, 10, 15, 20
6	multiplying 6 by any even number gives an answer that ends in the same last digit as the even number	$6 \times 12 = \mathbf{72}$ $6 \times 8 = \mathbf{48}$
9	multiply the number by 10, then subtract the number	$9 \times 7 = 10 \times 7 - 7 = \mathbf{63}$
12	multiply the original number first by 10, then multiply the original number by 2, and then add the two answers	$12 \times 10 = 120$ $12 \times 2 = 24$ $120 + 24 = \mathbf{144}$
20	multiply the number by 10 then multiply the answer by 2	$14 \times 20 =$ $14 \times 10 = 140$ $140 \times 2 = \mathbf{280}$

MULTIPLES

When a number is multiplied by any whole number the result (product) is called a multiple. For example, the first six multiples of the number 2 are 2, 4, 6, 8, 10, and 12. This is because 2 × 1 = 2, 2 × 2 = 4, 2 × 3 = 6, 2 × 4 = 8, 2 × 5 = 10, and 2 × 6 = 12.

MULTIPLES OF 3

3 × 1 = **3**
3 × 2 = **6**
3 × 3 = **9**
3 × 4 = **12**
3 × 5 = **15**

first five multiples of 3

MULTIPLES OF 8

8 × 1 = **8**
8 × 2 = **16**
8 × 3 = **24**
8 × 4 = **32**
8 × 5 = **40**

first five multiples of 8

MULTIPLES OF 12

12 × 1 = **12**
12 × 2 = **24**
12 × 3 = **36**
12 × 4 = **48**
12 × 5 = **60**

first five multiples of 12

Common multiples

Two or more numbers can have multiples in common. Drawing a grid, such as the one on the right, can help find the common multiples of different numbers. The smallest of these common numbers is called the lowest common multiple.

Lowest common multiple
The lowest common multiple of 3 and 8 is 24 because it is the smallest number that both multiply into.

 multiples of 3

 multiples of 8

 multiples of 3 and 8

▷ **Finding common multiples**
Multiples of 3 and multiples of 8 are highlighted on this grid. Some multiples are common to both numbers.

MULTIPLICATION

Short multiplication
Multiplying a large number by a single-digit number is called short multiplication. The larger number is placed above the smaller one in columns arranged according to their value.

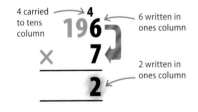

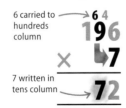

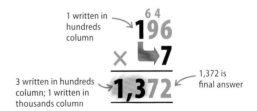

To multiply 196 and 7, first multiply the ones 7 and 6. The product is 42, the 4 of which is carried.

Next, multiply 7 and 9, the product of which is 63. The carried 4 is added to 63 to get 67.

Finally, multiply 7 and 1. Add its product (7) to the carried 6 to get 13, giving a final product of 1,372.

Long multiplication
Multiplying two numbers that both contain at least two digits is called long multiplication. The numbers are placed one above the other, in columns arranged according to their value (ones, tens, hundreds, and so on).

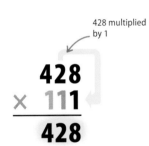

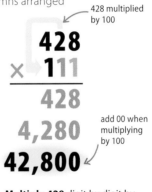

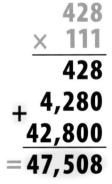

First, multiply 428 by 1 in the ones column. Work digit by digit from right to left so 8×1, 2×1, and then 4×1.

Multiply 428 digit by digit by 1 in the tens column. Remember to add 0 when multiplying by a number in the tens place.

Multiply 428 digit by digit by 1 in the hundreds column. Add 00 when multiplying by a digit in the hundreds place.

Add together the products of the three multiplications. The answer is 47,508.

LOOKING CLOSER
Box method of multiplication

The long multiplication of 428 and 111 can be broken down further into simple multiplications with the help of a table or box. Each number is reduced to its hundreds, tens, and ones, and multiplied by the other.

▷ **The final step**
Add together the nine multiplications to find the final answer.

		428 WRITTEN IN 100S, 10S, AND ONES		
		400	20	8
111 WRITTEN IN 100S, 10S, AND ONES	100	400×100 = 40,000	20×100 = 2,000	8×100 = 800
	10	400×10 = 4,000	20×10 = 200	8×10 = 80
	1	400×1 = 400	20×1 = 20	8×1 = 8

```
  40,000
   2,000
     800
   4,000
     200
      80
     400
      20
+      8
= 47,508
```
this is the final answer

Division

DIVISION INVOLVES FINDING OUT HOW MANY TIMES ONE NUMBER GOES INTO ANOTHER NUMBER.

SEE ALSO
‹ 16–17 Addition and subtraction
‹ 18–21 Multiplication
Ratio and proportion 56–59 ›

There are two ways to think about division. The first is sharing a number out equally (10 coins to 2 people is 5 each). The other is dividing a number into equal groups (10 coins into piles containing 2 coins each is 5 piles).

How division works

Dividing one number by another finds out how many times the second number (the divisor) fits into the first (the dividend). For example, dividing 10 by 2 finds out how many times 2 fits into 10. The result of the division is known as the quotient.

◁ **Division symbols**
There are three main symbols for division that all mean the same thing. For example, "6 divided by 3" can be expressed as $6 \div 3$, $6/3$, or $\frac{6}{3}$.

▽ **Division as sharing**
Sharing equally is one type of division. Dividing 4 candies equally between 2 people means that each person gets the same number of candies: 2 each.

4 CANDIES ÷ **2** PEOPLE = **2** CANDIES PER PERSON

DIVIDEND The number that is being divided or shared by another number

DIVISOR The number that is being used to divide the dividend

LOOKING CLOSER
How division is linked to multiplication

Division is the direct opposite or "inverse" of multiplication, and the two are always connected. If you know the answer to a particular division, you can form a multiplication from it and vice versa.

◁ **Back to the beginning**
If 10 (the dividend) is divided by 2 (the divisor), the answer (the quotient) is 5. Multiplying the quotient (5) by the divisor of the original division problem (2) results in the original dividend (10).

$10 \div 2 = 5 \quad 5 \times 2 = 10$

DIVISION

▽ Introducing remainders
In this example, 10 candies are being divided among 3 girls. However, 3 does not divide exactly into 10—it fits 3 times with 1 left over. The amount left over from a division sum is called the remainder.

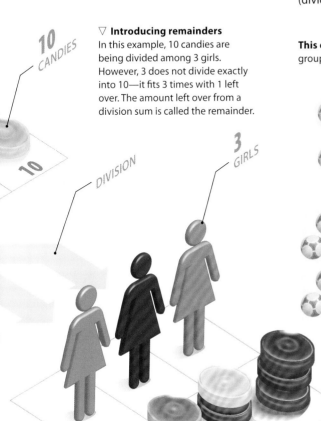

Another approach to division
Division can also be viewed as finding out how many groups of the second number (divisor) are contained in the first number (dividend). The operation remains the same in both cases.

This example shows 30 soccer balls, which are to be divided into groups of 3:

There are exactly 10 groups of 3 soccer balls, with no remainder, so 30 ÷ 3 = **10**.

DIVISION TIPS		
A number is divisible by	**If...**	**Examples**
2	the last digit is an even number	12, 134, 5,000
3	the sum of all digits when added together is divisible by 3	18 1+8 = 9
4	the number formed by the last two digits is divisible by 4	732 32÷4 = 8
5	the last digit is 5 or 0	25, 90, 835
6	the last digit is even and the sum of its digits when added together is divisible by 3	3,426 3+4+2+6 = 15
7	no simple divisibility test	
8	the number formed by the last three digits is divisible by 8	7,536 536 ÷ 8 = 67
9	the sum of all of its digits is divisible by 9	6,831 6+8+3+1 = 18
10	the number ends in 0	30, 150, 4,270

Short division

Short division is used to divide one number (the dividend) by another whole number (the divisor) that is less than 10.

start on the left with the first 3 (divisor)

dividing line

$$\begin{array}{r} 1 \\ 3\overline{)396} \end{array}$$

396 is the dividend

Divide the first 3 into 3. It fits once exactly, so put a 1 above the dividing line, directly above the 3 of the dividend.

result is 132

$$\begin{array}{r} 13 \\ 3\overline{)396} \end{array}$$

Move to the next column and divide 3 into 9. It fits three times exactly, so put a 3 directly above the 9 of the dividend.

$$\begin{array}{r} 132 \\ 3\overline{)396} \end{array}$$

Divide 3 into 6, the last digit of the dividend. It goes twice exactly, so put a 2 directly above the 6 of the dividend.

Carrying numbers

When the result of a division gives a whole number and a remainder, the remainder can be carried over to the next digit of the dividend.

start on the left — divisor

$$5\overline{)2{,}765}$$

2,765 is the dividend

Start with number 5. It does not divide into 2 because it is larger than 2. Instead, 5 will need to be divided into the first two digits of the dividend.

divide 5 into first 2 digits of dividend

$$5\overline{)2{,}^{2}7^{2}65}$$

Divide 5 into 27. The result is 5 with a remainder of 2. Put 5 directly above the 7 and carry the remainder.

carry remainder 2 to next digit of dividend

$$\begin{array}{r} 5 \\ 5\overline{)2{,}^{2}7^{2}65} \end{array}$$

carry remainder 1 to next digit of dividend

$$\begin{array}{r} 55 \\ 5\overline{)2{,}^{2}7^{2}6^{1}5} \end{array}$$

Divide 5 into 26. The result is 5 with a remainder of 1. Put 5 directly above the 6 and carry the remainder 1 to the next digit of the dividend.

the result is 553

$$\begin{array}{r} 553 \\ 5\overline{)2{,}^{2}7^{2}6^{1}5} \end{array}$$

Divide 5 into 15. It fits three times exactly, so put 3 above the dividing line, directly above the final 5 of the dividend.

LOOKING CLOSER

Converting remainders

When one number will not divide exactly into another, the answer has a remainder. Remainders can be converted into decimals, as shown below.

remainder

$$4\overline{)9^{1}0}\;\;\text{r}\,2$$

$$\begin{array}{r} 22. \\ 4\overline{)9^{1}0.0} \end{array}$$

Remove the remainder, 2 in this case, leaving 22. Add a decimal point above and below the dividing line. Next, add a zero to the dividend after the decimal point.

$$\begin{array}{r} 22. \\ 4\overline{)9^{1}0.^{2}0} \end{array}$$

Carry the remainder (2) from above the dividing line to below the line and put it in front of the new zero.

$$\begin{array}{r} 22.5 \\ 4\overline{)9^{1}0.^{2}0} \end{array}$$

Divide 4 into 20. It goes 5 times exactly, so put a 5 directly above the zero of the dividend and after the decimal point.

LOOKING CLOSER

Making division simpler

To make a division easier, sometimes the divisor can be split into factors. This means that a number of simpler divisions can be done.

$$816 \div 6$$

divisor is 6, which is 2 × 3. Splitting 6 into 2 and 3 simplifies the sum

result is 136

$$816 \div 2 = 408 \quad \Rightarrow \quad 408 \div 3 = 136$$

divide by first factor of divisor   divide by second factor of divisor

This method of splitting the divisor into factors can also be used for more difficult divisions.

$$405 \div 15$$

splitting 15 into 5 and 3, which multiply to make 15, simplifies the problem

result is 27

$$405 \div 5 = 81 \quad \Rightarrow \quad 81 \div 3 = 27$$

divide by first factor of divisor   divide result by second factor of divisor

Long division

Long division is usually used when the divisor is at least two digits long and the dividend is at least 3 digits long. Unlike short division, all the workings out are written out in full below the dividing line. Multiplication is used for finding remainders. A long division sum is presented in the example on the right.

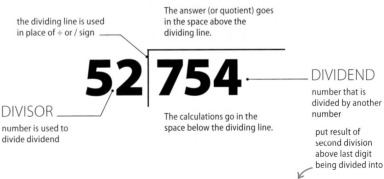

the dividing line is used in place of ÷ or / sign

The answer (or quotient) goes in the space above the dividing line.

DIVISOR number is used to divide dividend

The calculations go in the space below the dividing line.

DIVIDEND number that is divided by another number

put result of second division above last digit being divided into

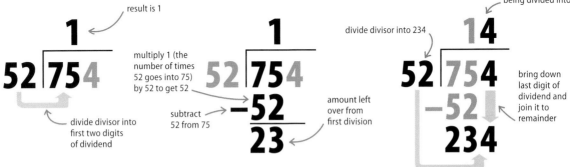

result is 1

divide divisor into first two digits of dividend

multiply 1 (the number of times 52 goes into 75) by 52 to get 52

subtract 52 from 75

amount left over from first division

divide divisor into 234

bring down last digit of dividend and join it to remainder

▸ **Begin by dividing** the divisor into the first two digits of the dividend. 52 fits into 75 once, so put a 1 above the dividing line, aligning it with the last digit of the number being divided.

▸ **Work out the first remainder.** The divisor 52 does not divide into 75 exactly. To work out the amount left over (the remainder), subtract 52 from 75. The result is 23.

▸ **Now, bring down the last digit** of the dividend and place it next to the remainder to form 234. Next, divide 234 by 52. It goes four times, so put a 4 next to the 1.

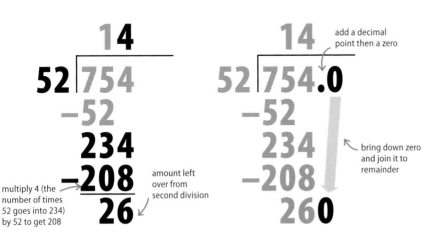

multiply 4 (the number of times 52 goes into 234) by 52 to get 208

amount left over from second division

add a decimal point then a zero

bring down zero and join it to remainder

add decimal point above other one

put result of last sum after decimal point

▸ **Work out the second remainder.** The divisor, 52, does not divide into 234 exactly. To find the remainder, multiply 4 by 52 to make 208. Subtract 208 from 234, leaving 26.

▸ **There are no more** whole numbers to bring down, so add a decimal point after the dividend and a zero after it. Bring down the zero and join it to the remainder 26 to form 260.

▸ **Put a decimal point** after the 14. Next, divide 260 by 52, which goes five times exactly. Put a 5 above the dividing line, aligned with the new zero in the dividend.

Prime numbers

ANY WHOLE NUMBER LARGER THAN 1 THAT CANNOT BE DIVIDED BY ANY OTHER NUMBER EXCEPT FOR ITSELF AND 1.

SEE ALSO
‹ 18–21 Multiplication
‹ 22–25 Division

Introducing prime numbers

Over 2,000 years ago, the Ancient Greek mathematician Euclid noted that some numbers are only divisible by 1 or the number itself. These numbers are known as prime numbers. A number that is not a prime is called a composite—it can be arrived at, or composed, by multiplying together smaller prime numbers, which are known as its prime factors.

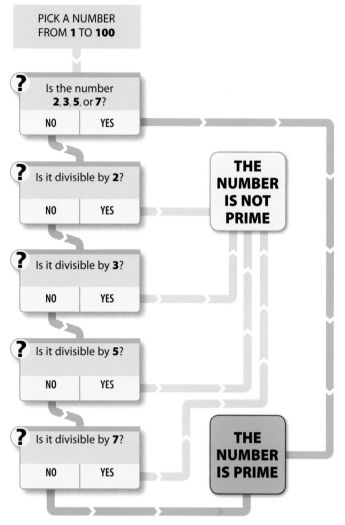

△ **Is a number prime?**
This flowchart can be used to determine whether a number between 1 and 100 is prime by checking if it is divisible by any of the primes 2, 3, 5, and 7.

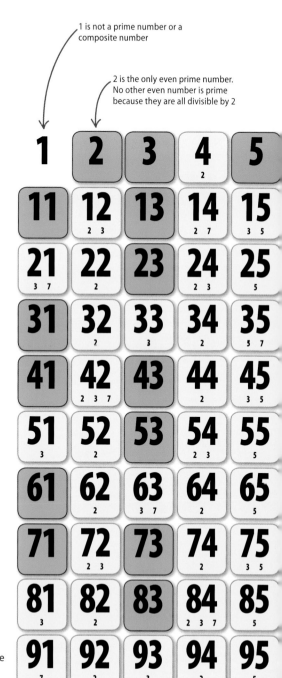

▷ **First 100 numbers**
This table shows the prime numbers among the first 100 whole numbers.

PRIME NUMBERS **27**

KEY

17 — **Prime number**
A blue box indicates that the number is prime. It has no factors other than 1 and itself.

42 2 3 7 — **Composite number**
A yellow box denotes a composite number, which means that it is divisible by more than 1 and itself.

smaller numbers show whether the number is divisible by 2, 3, 5, or 7, or a combination of them

6 (2 3)	7	8 (2)	9 (3)	10 (2 5)
16 (2)	17	18 (2 3)	19	20 (2 5)
26 (2)	27 (3)	28 (2 7)	29	30 (2 3 5)
36 (2 3)	37	38 (2)	39 (3)	40 (2 5)
46 (2)	47	48 (2 3)	49 (7)	50 (2 5)
56 (2 7)	57 (3)	58 (2)	59	60 (2 3 5)
66 (2 3)	67	68 (2)	69 (3)	70 (2 5 7)
76 (2)	77 (7)	78 (2 3)	79	80 (2 5)
86 (2)	87 (3)	88 (2)	89	90 (2 3 5)
96 (2 3)	97	98 (2 7)	99 (3)	100 (2 5)

Prime factors

Every number is either a prime or the result of multiplying together prime numbers. Prime factorization is the process of breaking down a composite number into the prime numbers that it is made up of. These are known as its prime factors.

prime factor — remaining factor

$30 = 5 \times 6$

To find the prime factors of 30, find the largest prime number that divides into 30, which is 5. The remaining factor is 6 (5 × 6 = 30), which needs to be broken down into prime numbers.

largest prime factor

$6 = 3 \times 2$

Next, take the remaining factor and find the largest prime number that divides into it, and any smaller prime numbers. In this case, the prime numbers that divide into 6 are 3 and 2.

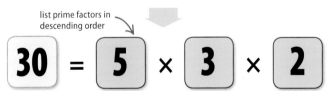

list prime factors in descending order

$30 = 5 \times 3 \times 2$

It is now possible to see that 30 is the product of multiplying together the prime numbers 5, 3, and 2. Therefore, the prime factors of 30 are 5, 3, and, 2.

REAL WORLD
Encryption

Many transactions in banks and stores rely on the Internet and other communications systems. To protect the information, it is coded using a number that is the product of just two huge primes. The security relies on the fact that no "eavesdropper" can factorize the number because its factors are so large.

▷ **Data protection**
To provide constant security, mathematicians relentlessly hunt for ever bigger primes.

Units of measurement

UNITS OF MEASUREMENT ARE STANDARD SIZES USED TO MEASURE TIME, MASS, AND LENGTH.

SEE ALSO	
Volumes	154–155 ⟩
Formulas	177–179 ⟩
Reference	242–245 ⟩

Basic units

A unit is any agreed or standardized measurement of size. This allows quantities to be accurately measured. There are three basic units: time, weight (including mass), and length.

△ **Time**
Time is measured in milliseconds, seconds, minutes, hours, days, weeks, months, and years. Different countries and cultures may have calendars that start a new year at a different time.

△ **Weight and mass**
Weight is how heavy something is in relation to the force of gravity acting upon it. Mass is the amount of matter that makes up the object. Both are measured in the same units, such as grams and kilograms, or ounces and pounds.

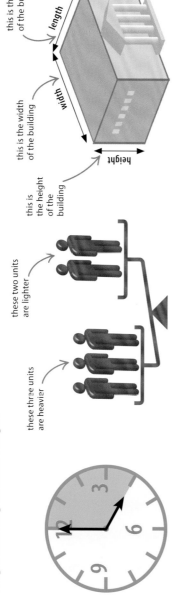

△ **Length**
Length is how long something is. It is measured in centimeters, meters, and kilometers in the metric system, or in inches, feet, yards, and miles in the imperial system (see pp.242–245).

LOOKING CLOSER

Distance

Distance is the amount of space between two points. It expresses length, but is also used to describe a journey, which is not always the most direct route between two points.

- plane flies set distance between two cities
- distance between cities A and B

Compound measures

A compound unit is made up of more than one of the basic units, including using the same unit repeatedly. Examples include area, volume, speed, and density.

▽ **Area**
Area is measured in squared units. The area of a rectangle is the product of its length and width; if they were both measured in meters (m) its area would be m × m, which is written as m².

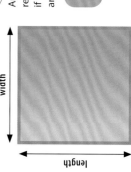

$$area = length \times width$$

← area is made up of two of the same units, because width is also a length

▽ **Volume**
Volume is measured in cubed units. The volume of a cuboid is the product of its height, width, and length; if they were all measured in meters (m), its area would be m × m × m, or m³.

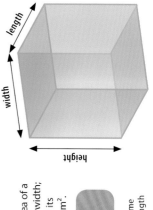

$$volume = length \times width \times height$$

← volume is a compound of three of the same units, because width and height are technically lengths

Speed

Speed measures the distance (length) traveled in a given time. This means that the formula for measuring speed is length ÷ time. If this is measured in kilometers and hours, the unit for speed will be km/h.

$$\text{Speed} = \frac{\text{distance}}{\text{time}}$$

△ Speed formula triangle

The relationships between speed, distance, and time can be shown in a triangle. The position of each unit in the triangle indicates how to use the other two measurements to calculate that unit.

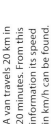

$$S = \frac{D}{T}$$

← speed = distance ÷ time

this line acts as a division sign

$$D = S \times T$$

→ distance = speed × time

this line acts as a multiplication sign

$$T = \frac{D}{S}$$

→ time = distance ÷ speed

▷ Finding speed

A van travels 20 km in 20 minutes. From this information its speed in km/h can be found.

20 km

divide 20 by 60 to find its value in hours

$$20 \text{ minutes} = \frac{20}{60} = \frac{1}{3} \text{ hour}$$

First, convert the minutes into hours. To convert minutes into hours, divide them by 60, then cancel the fraction—divide the top and bottom numbers by 20. This gives an answer of ⅓ hour.

distance is 20 km

$$S = \frac{D}{T} = 60 \text{ km/h}$$

time is ⅓ hour

Then, substitute the values for distance and time into the formula for speed. Divide the distance (20 km) by the time (⅓ hour) to find the speed, in this case 60 km/h.

Density

Density measures how much matter is packed into a given volume of a substance. It involves two units—mass and volume. The formula for measuring density is mass ÷ volume. If this is measured in grams and centimeters, the unit for density will be g/cm³.

$$\text{Density} = \frac{\text{mass}}{\text{volume}}$$

△ Density formula triangle

The relationships between density, mass, and volume can be shown in a triangle. The position of each unit of measurement in the triangle shows how to calculate that unit using the other two measurements.

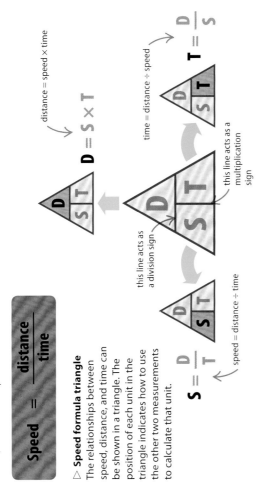

$$D = \frac{M}{V}$$

← density = mass ÷ volume

this line acts as a division sign

$$M = D \times V$$

→ mass = density × volume

this line acts as a multiplication sign

$$V = \frac{M}{D}$$

→ volume = mass ÷ density

▷ Finding volume

Lead has a density of 0.0113 kg/cm³. With this measurement, the volume of a lead weight that has a mass of 0.5 kg can be found.

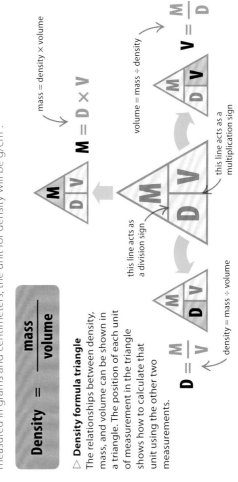

0.5 kg

density of lead is constant, regardless of mass

mass is 0.5 kg

$$V = \frac{M}{D} = 44.25 \text{ cm}^3$$

density is 0.0113 kg/cm³

△ Using the formula

Substitute the values for mass and density into the formula for volume. Divide the mass (0.5 kg) by the density (0.0113 kg/cm³) to find the volume, in this case 44.25 cm³.

NUMBERS

 # Telling the time

TIME IS MEASURED IN THE SAME WAY AROUND THE WORLD. THE MAIN UNITS ARE SECONDS, MINUTES, AND HOURS.

> **SEE ALSO**
> ⟨ 14–15 Introducing numbers
> ⟨ 28–29 Units of measurement

Telling the time is an important skill and one that is used in many ways: What time is breakfast? How long until my birthday? Which is the quickest route?

Measuring time

Units of time measure how long events take and the gaps between the events. Sometimes it is important to measure time exactly, in a science experiment for example. At other times, accuracy of measurement is not so important, such as when we go to a friend's house to play. For thousands of years time was measured simply by observing the movement of the sun, moon, or stars, but now our watches and clocks are extremely accurate.

◁ **Units of time**
The units we use around the world are based on 1 second as measured by International Atomic Time. There are 86,400 seconds in one day.

There are 60 seconds in each minute.

There are 60 minutes in each hour.

There are 24 hours in each day.

Bigger units of time

This is a list of the most commonly used bigger units of time. Other units include the Olympiad, which is a period of 4 years and starts on January 1st of a year in which the summer Olympics take place.

7 days is 1 week

▼

Fortnight is short for 14 nights and is the same as 2 weeks

▼

Between 28 and 31 days is 1 month

▼

365 days is 1 year (366 in a leap year)

▼

10 years is a decade

▼

100 years is a century

▼

1000 years is a millennium

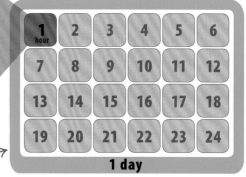

TELLING THE TIME

Reading the time

The time can be told by looking carefully at where the hands point on a clock or watch. The hour hand is shorter and moves around slowly. The minute hand is longer than the hour hand and points at minutes "past" the hour or "to" the next one. Most clock faces show the minutes in groups of five and the in-between minutes are shown by a short line or mark. The second hand is usually long and thin, and sweeps quickly around the face every minute, marking 60 seconds.

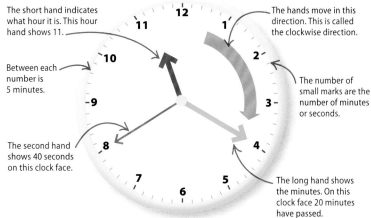

△ **A clock face**
A clock face is a visual way to show the time easily and clearly. There are many types of clock and watch faces.

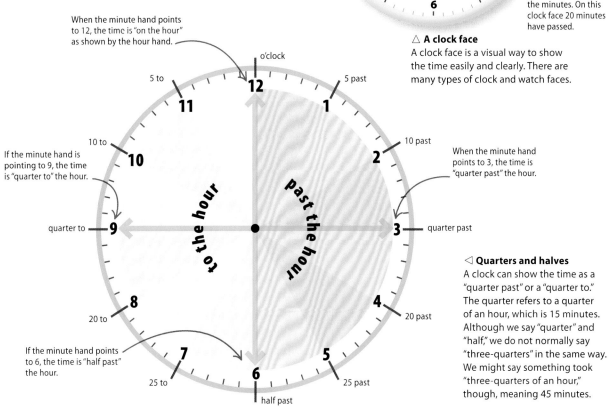

◁ **Quarters and halves**
A clock can show the time as a "quarter past" or a "quarter to." The quarter refers to a quarter of an hour, which is 15 minutes. Although we say "quarter" and "half," we do not normally say "three-quarters" in the same way. We might say something took "three-quarters of an hour," though, meaning 45 minutes.

10 o'clock

Quarter past 1

Half past 3

Quarter to 7

Analogue time

Most clocks and watches only go up to 12 hours, but there are 24 hours in one day. To show the difference between morning and night, we use AM or PM. The middle of the day (12 o'clock) is called midday or noon.

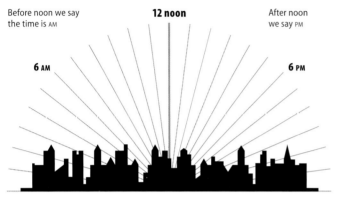

Before noon we say the time is AM — 12 noon — After noon we say PM

6 AM — 6 PM

△ **AM or PM**
The initials AM and PM stand for the Latin words **a**nte **m**eridiem (meaning "before noon") and **p**ost **m**eridiem (meaning "after noon"). The first 12 hours of the day are called AM and the second 12 hours of the day are called PM.

Digital time

Traditional clock faces show time in an analogue format but digital formats are also common, especially on electrical devices such as computers, televisions, and mobile phones. Some digital displays show time in the 24-hour system; others use the analogue system and also show AM or PM.

△ **Hours and minutes**
On a digital clock, the hours are shown first followed by a colon and the minutes. Some displays may also show seconds.

△ **24-hour digital display**
If the hours or minutes are single digit numbers, a zero (called a leading zero) is placed to the left of the digit.

△ **Midnight**
When it is midnight, the clock resets to 00:00. Midnight is an abbreviated form of "middle of the night."

△ **12-hour digital display**
This type of display will have AM and PM with the relevant part of the day highlighted.

24-hour clock

The 24-hour system was devised to stop confusion between morning and afternoon times, and runs continuously from midnight to midnight. It is often used in computers, by the military, and on timetables. To convert from the 12-hour system to the 24-hour system, you add 12 to the hour for times after noon. For example, 11 PM becomes 23:00 (11 + 12) and 8:45 PM becomes 20:45 (8:45 + 12).

12-hour clock	24-hour clock
12:00 midnight	00:00
1:00 AM	01:00
2:00 AM	02:00
3:00 AM	03:00
4:00 AM	04:00
5:00 AM	05:00
6:00 AM	06:00
7:00 AM	07:00
8:00 AM	08:00
9:00 AM	09:00
10:00 AM	10:00
11:00 AM	11:00
12:00 noon	12:00
1:00 PM	13:00
2:00 PM	14:00
3:00 PM	15:00
4:00 PM	16:00
5:00 PM	17:00
6:00 PM	18:00
7:00 PM	19:00
8:00 PM	20:00
9:00 PM	21:00
10:00 PM	22:00
11:00 PM	23:00

XVII Roman numerals

DEVELOPED BY THE ANCIENT ROMANS, THIS SYSTEM USES LETTERS FROM THE LATIN ALPHABET TO REPRESENT NUMBERS.

SEE ALSO
◁ 14–15 Introducing numbers

Understanding Roman numerals

The Roman numeral system does not use zero. To make a number, seven letters are combined. These are the letters and their values:

I	V	X	L	C	D	M
1	5	10	50	100	500	1000

Forming numbers

Some key principles were observed by the ancient Romans to "create" numbers from the seven letters.

First principle When a smaller number appears after a larger number, the smaller number is added to the larger number to find the total value.

$$XI = X + I = 11 \qquad XVII = X + V + I + I = 17$$

Second principle When a smaller number appears before a larger number, the smaller number is subtracted from the larger number to find the total value.

$$IX = X - I = 9 \qquad CM = M - C = 900$$

Third principle Each letter can be repeated up to three times.

$$XX = X + X = 20 \qquad XXX = X + X + X = 30$$

Using Roman numerals

Although Roman numerals are not widely used today, they still appear on some clock faces, with the names of monarchs and popes, and for important dates.

Time

Names

Henry VIII
Henry the eighth

Dates

MMXIV
2014

Number	Roman numeral
1	I
2	II
3	III
4	IV
5	V
6	VI
7	VII
8	VIII
9	IX
10	X
11	XI
12	XII
13	XIII
14	XIV
15	XV
16	XVI
17	XVII
18	XVIII
19	XIX
20	XX
30	XXX
40	XL
50	L
60	LX
70	LXX
80	LXXX
90	XC
100	C
500	D
1000	M

Positive and negative numbers

A POSITIVE NUMBER IS A NUMBER THAT IS MORE THAN ZERO, WHILE A NEGATIVE NUMBER IS LESS THAN ZERO.

A positive number is shown by a plus sign (+), or has no sign in front of it. If a number is negative, it has a minus sign (−) in front of it.

SEE ALSO
‹ 14–15 Introducing numbers
‹ 16–17 Addition and subtraction

Why use positives and negatives?

Positive numbers are used when an amount is counted up from zero, and negative numbers when it is counted down from zero. For example, if a bank account has money in it, it is a positive amount of money, but if the account is overdrawn, the amount of money in the account is negative.

negative numbers

number line continues forever

Adding and subtracting positives and negatives

Use a number line to add and subtract positive and negative numbers. Find the first number on the line and then move the number of steps shown by the second number. Move right for addition and left for subtraction.

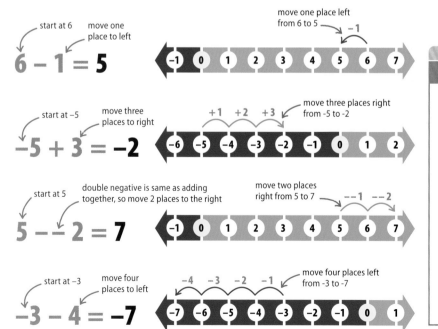

start at 6, move one place to left
$6 - 1 = 5$
move one place left from 6 to 5

start at −5, move three places to right
$-5 + 3 = -2$
move three places right from -5 to -2

start at 5, double negative is same as adding together, so move 2 places to the right
$5 - -2 = 7$
move two places right from 5 to 7

start at −3, move four places to left
$-3 - 4 = -7$
move four places left from -3 to -7

LOOKING CLOSER
Double negatives

If a negative or minus number is subtracted from a positive number, it creates a double negative. The first negative is cancelled out by the second negative, so the result is always a positive, for example 5 minus −2 is the same as adding 2 to 5.

 =

△ **Like signs equal a positive**
If any two like signs appear together, the result is always positive. The result is negative with two unlike signs together.

POSITIVE AND NEGATIVE NUMBERS   35

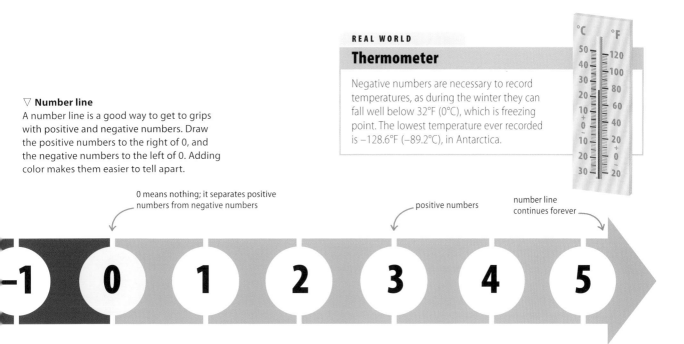

REAL WORLD
Thermometer
Negative numbers are necessary to record temperatures, as during the winter they can fall well below 32°F (0°C), which is freezing point. The lowest temperature ever recorded is −128.6°F (−89.2°C), in Antarctica.

▽ **Number line**
A number line is a good way to get to grips with positive and negative numbers. Draw the positive numbers to the right of 0, and the negative numbers to the left of 0. Adding color makes them easier to tell apart.

- 0 means nothing; it separates positive numbers from negative numbers
- positive numbers
- number line continues forever

Multiplying and dividing
To multiply or divide any two numbers, first ignore whether they are positive or negative, then work out if the answer is positive or negative using the diagram on the right.

$2 \times 4 = 8$ — 8 is positive because $+ \times + = +$

$-1 \times 6 = -6$ — −6 is negative because $- \times + = -$

$-4 \div 2 = -2$ — −2 is negative because $- \div + = -$

$-2 \times 4 = -8$ — −8 is negative because $- \times + = -$

$-2 \times -4 = 8$ — 8 is positive because $- \times - = +$

$-10 \div -2 = 5$ — 5 is positive because $- \div - = +$

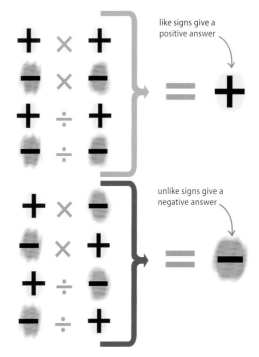

△ **Positive or negative answer**
The sign in the answer depends on whether the signs of the values are alike or not.

Powers and roots

A POWER IS THE NUMBER OF TIMES A NUMBER IS MULTIPLIED BY ITSELF. THE ROOT OF A NUMBER IS A NUMBER THAT, MULTIPLIED BY ITSELF, EQUALS THE ORIGINAL NUMBER.

SEE ALSO	
⟨ 18–21 Multiplication	
⟨ 22–25 Division	
Standard form	42–43 ⟩
Using a calculator	72–73 ⟩

Introducing powers

A power is the number of times a number is multiplied by itself. This is indicated as a smaller number positioned to the right above the number. Multiplying a number by itself once is described as "squaring" the number; multiplying a number by itself twice is described as "cubing" the number.

5^4 ← this is the power, which shows how many times to multiply the number (5^4 means $5 \times 5 \times 5 \times 5$)

← this is the number that the power relates to

$5 \times 5 = 5^2$
$= 25$

this is the power; 5^2 is called "5 squared"

△ **The square of a number**
Multiplying a number by itself gives the square of the number. The power for a square number is ^{2}, for example 5^2 means that 2 number 5's are being multiplied.

▷ **Squared number**
This image shows how many units make up 5^2. There are 5 rows, each with 5 units—so $5 \times 5 = 25$.

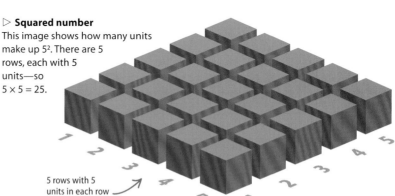

5 rows with 5 units in each row

$5 \times 5 \times 5 = 5^3$
$= 125$

this is the power; 5^3 is called "5 cubed"

△ **The cube of a number**
Multiplying a number by itself twice gives its cube. The power for a cube number is ^{3}, for example 5^3, which means there are 3 number 5's being multiplied: $5 \times 5 \times 5$.

5 vertical rows

▷ **Cubed number**
This image shows how many units make up 5^3. There are 5 horizontal rows and 5 vertical rows, each with 5 units in each one, so $5 \times 5 \times 5 = 125$.

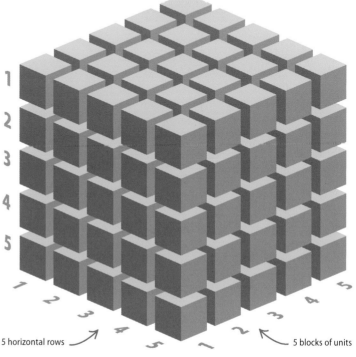

5 horizontal rows

5 blocks of units

POWERS AND ROOTS

Square roots and cube roots

A square root is a number that, multiplied by itself once, equals a given number. For example, one square root of 4 is 2, because 2 × 2 = 4. Another square root is –2, as (–2) × (–2) = 4; the square roots of numbers can be either positive or negative. A cube root is a number that, multiplied by itself twice, equals a given number. For example, the cube root of 27 is 3, because 3 × 3 × 3 = 27.

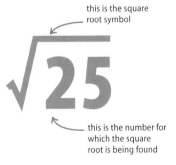

this is the square root symbol

this is the number for which the square root is being found

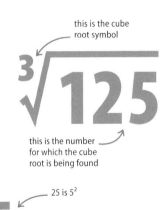

this is the cube root symbol

this is the number for which the cube root is being found

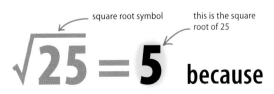

square root symbol

this is the square root of 25

$5 \times 5 = 25$ — 25 is 5^2

△ **The square root of a number**
The square root of a number is the number which, when squared (multiplied by itself), equals the number under the square root sign.

cube root symbol

this is the cube root of 125

125 is 5^3

$5 \times 5 \times 5 = 125$

△ **The cube root of a number**
The cube root of a number is the number that, when cubed (multiplied by itself twice), equals the number under the cube root sign.

COMMON SQUARE ROOTS		
Square root	Answer	Why?
1	1	Because 1 × 1 = 1
4	2	Because 2 × 2 = 4
9	3	Because 3 × 3 = 9
16	4	Because 4 × 4 = 16
25	5	Because 5 × 5 = 25
36	6	Because 6 × 6 = 36
49	7	Because 7 × 7 = 49
64	8	Because 8 × 8 = 64
81	9	Because 9 × 9 = 81
100	10	Because 10 × 10 = 100
121	11	Because 11 × 11 = 121
144	12	Because 12 × 12 = 144
169	13	Because 13 × 13 = 169

LOOKING CLOSER
Using a calculator

Calculators can be used to find powers and square roots. Most calculators have buttons to square and cube numbers, buttons to find square roots and cube roots, and an exponent button, which allows them to raise numbers to any power.

△ **Exponent**
This button allows any number to be raised to any power.

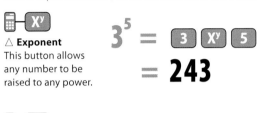

◁ **Using exponents**
First enter the number to be raised to a power, then press the exponent button, then enter the power required.

△ **Square root**
This button allows the square root of any number to be found.

$\sqrt{25} = \boxed{\sqrt{}}\ \boxed{25}$
$= 5$

◁ **Using square roots**
On most calculators, find the square root of a number by pressing the square root button first and then entering the number.

Multiplying powers of the same number

To multiply powers that have the same base number, simply add the powers. The power of the answer is the sum of the powers that are being multiplied.

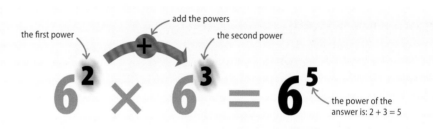

▷ **Writing it out**
Writing out what each of these powers represents shows why powers are added together to multiply them.

Dividing powers of the same number

To divide powers of the same base number, subtract the second power from the first. The power of the answer is the difference between the first and second powers.

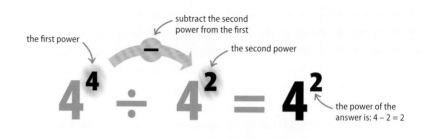

▷ **Writing it out**
Writing out the division of the powers as a fraction and then canceling the fraction shows why powers to be divided can simply be subtracted.

LOOKING CLOSER
Zero power

Any number raised to the power 0 is equal to 1. Dividing two equal powers of the same base number gives a power of 0, and therefore the answer 1. These rules only apply when dealing with powers of the same base number.

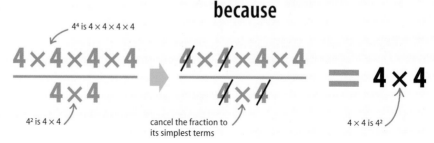

▷ **Writing it out**
Writing out the division of two equal powers makes it clear why any number to the power 0 is always equal to 1.

POWERS AND ROOTS **39**

Finding a square root by estimation
It is possible to find a square root through estimation, by choosing a number to multiply by itself, working out the answer, and then altering the number depending on whether the answer needs to be higher or lower.

$\sqrt{25} = 5$ and $\sqrt{36} = 6$, so the answer must be somewhere between 5 and 6. Start with the midpoint between the two, 5.5:

$5.5 \times 5.5 = 30.25$ — Too low
$5.75 \times 5.75 = 33.0625$ — Too high
$5.65 \times 5.65 = 31.9225$ — Too low
$5.66 \times 5.66 = \mathbf{32.0356}$

↙ the square root of 32 is approximately 5.66   ↙ this would round down to 32

$\sqrt{1{,}600} = 40$ and $\sqrt{900} = 30$, so the answer must be between 40 and 30. 1,000 is closer to 900 than 1,600, so start with a number closer to 30, such as 32:

$32 \times 32 = 1{,}024$ — Too high
$31 \times 31 = 961$ — Too low
$31.5 \times 31.5 = 992.25$ — Too low
$31.6 \times 31.6 = 998.56$ — Too low
$31.65 \times 31.65 = 1{,}001.72$ — Too high
$31.62 \times 31.62 = \mathbf{999.8244}$

↙ the square root of 1,000 is approximately 31.62   ↙ this would round up to 1,000 as the nearest whole number

Finding a cube root by estimation
Cube roots of numbers can also be estimated without a calculator. Use round numbers to start with, then use these answers to get closer to the final answer.

$3 \times 3 \times 3 = 27$ and $4 \times 4 \times 4 = 64$, so the answer is somewhere between 3 and 4. Start with the midpoint between the two, 3.5:

$3.5 \times 3.5 \times 3.5 = 42.875$ — Too high
$3.3 \times 3.3 \times 3.3 = 35.937$ — Too high
$3.1 \times 3.1 \times 3.1 = 29.791$ — Too low
$3.2 \times 3.2 \times 3.2 = 32.768$ — Too high
$3.18 \times 3.18 \times 3.18 = \mathbf{32.157432}$

↙ the cube root of 32 is approximately 3.18   ↙ this would be 32.2 rounded to the tenths place, which would round to 32

$9 \times 9 \times 9 = 729$ and $10 \times 10 \times 10 = 1{,}000$, so the answer is somewhere between 9 and 10. 800 is closer to 729 than 1000, so start with a number closer to 9, such as 9.1:

$9.1 \times 9.1 \times 9.1 = 753.571$ — Too low
$9.3 \times 9.3 \times 9.3 = 804.357$ — Too high
$9.27 \times 9.27 \times 9.27 = 796.5979$ — Too low
$9.28 \times 9.28 \times 9.28 = 799.1787$ — Very close
$9.284 \times 9.284 \times 9.284 = \mathbf{800.2126}$

↙ the cube root of 800 is approximately 9.284   ↙ this would round down to 800

Surds

A SURD IS A SQUARE ROOT THAT CANNOT BE WRITTEN AS A WHOLE NUMBER. IT HAS AN INFINITE NUMBER OF DIGITS AFTER THE DECIMAL POINT.

SEE ALSO
‹ 36–39 Powers and roots
Fractions 48–55 ›

Introducing surds

Some square roots are whole numbers and are easy to write. But some are irrational numbers—numbers that go on forever after the decimal point. These numbers cannot be written out in full, so the most accurate way to express them is as square roots.

$\sqrt{5} = 2.2360679774...$ ← irrational number

$\sqrt{4} = 2$ ← rational number

△ **Surd**
The square root of 5 is an irrational number—it goes on forever. It cannot accurately be written out in full, so it is most simply expressed as the surd √5.

△ **Not a surd**
The square root of 4 is not a surd. It is the number 2, a whole, or rational, number.

Simplifying surds

Some surds can be made simpler by taking out factors that can be written as whole numbers. A few simple rules can help with this.

▷ **Square roots**
A square root is the number that, when multiplied by itself, equals the number inside the root.

$$\sqrt{a} \times \sqrt{a} = a$$

$$\sqrt{3} \times \sqrt{3} = 3$$

← multiply the surd by itself to get the number inside the square root

▷ **Multiplying roots**
Multiplying two numbers together and taking the square root of the result equals the same answer as taking the square roots of the two numbers and multiplying them together.

$$\sqrt{ab} = \sqrt{a} \times \sqrt{b}$$

$\sqrt{16} = 4$, so this can be written as $4 \times \sqrt{3}$

$$\sqrt{48} = \sqrt{16 \times 3} = \sqrt{16} \times \sqrt{3} = 4 \times \sqrt{3}$$

look for factors that are square numbers

48 can be written as 16 × 3

the square root of 16 is a whole number

the square root of 3 is an irrational number, so it stays in surd form

SURDS **41**

▷ Dividing roots
Dividing one number by another and taking the square root of the result is the same as dividing the square root of the first number by the square root of the second.

$$\sqrt{\frac{a}{b}} = \frac{\sqrt{a}}{\sqrt{b}}$$

$$\sqrt{\frac{7}{16}} = \frac{\sqrt{7}}{\sqrt{16}} = \frac{\sqrt{7}}{4}$$

√7 is irrational (2.6457...), so leave as a surd

16 is 4 squared

▷ Simplifying further
When dividing square roots, look out for ways to simplify the top as well as the bottom of the fraction.

$$\sqrt{\frac{8}{9}} = \frac{\sqrt{8}}{\sqrt{9}} = \frac{\sqrt{8}}{3} = \frac{2 \times \sqrt{2}}{3}$$

√9 = 3 (3 × 3 = 9)

final, simplified form

$$\sqrt{8} = \sqrt{4} \times \sqrt{2} = 2 \times \sqrt{2}$$

8 is 4 × 2

4 is 2 squared

Surds in fractions
When a surd appears in a fraction, it is helpful to make sure it appears in the numerator (top of the fraction) not the denominator (bottom of the fraction). This is called rationalizing, and is done by multiplying the whole fraction by the surd on the bottom.

▷ Rationalizing
The fraction stays the same if the top and bottom are multiplied by the same number.

$$\frac{1}{\sqrt{2}} = \frac{1 \times \sqrt{2}}{\sqrt{2} \times \sqrt{2}} = \frac{\sqrt{2}}{2}$$

the surd √2 is now on top of the fraction

multiply top and bottom by the surd √2

▷ Simplifying further
Sometimes rationalizing a fraction gives us another surd that can be simplified further.

12 and 15 can both be divided by 3 to simplify further

$$\frac{12}{\sqrt{15}} = \frac{12 \times \sqrt{15}}{\sqrt{15} \times \sqrt{15}} = \frac{12 \times \sqrt{15}}{15} = \frac{4 \times \sqrt{15}}{5}$$

multiply both top and bottom by √15

multiplying √15 by √15 gives 15

NUMBERS

 # Standard Form

STANDARD FORM IS A CONVENIENT WAY OF WRITING VERY LARGE AND VERY SMALL NUMBERS.

> **SEE ALSO**
> ‹ 18–21 Multiplication
> ‹ 22–25 Division
> ‹ 36–39 Powers and roots

Introducing standard form

Standard form makes very large or very small numbers easier to understand by showing them as a number multiplied by a power of 10. This is useful because the size of the power of 10 makes it possible to get an instant impression of how big the number really is.

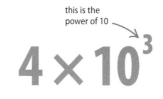

this is the power of 10

4×10^3

◁ **Using standard form**
This is how 4,000 is written as standard form—it shows that the decimal place for the number represented, 4,000, is 3 places to the right of 4.

How to write a number in standard form

To write a number in standard form, work out how many places the decimal point must move to form a number between 1 and 10. If the number does not have a decimal point, add one after its final digit.

▷ **Take a number**
Standard form is usually used for very large or very small numbers.

very large number
1,230,000

very small number
0.0006

▷ **Add the decimal point**
Identify the position of the decimal point if there is one. Add a decimal point at the end of the number, if it does not already have one.

add decimal point
1,230,000.

decimal point is already here
0.0006

▷ **Move the decimal point**
Move along the number and count how many places the decimal point must move to form a number between 1 and 10.

6 5 4 3 2 1
1,230,000.
the decimal point moves 6 places to the left

1 2 3 4
0.0006
the decimal point moves 4 places to the right

▷ **Write as standard form**
The number between 1 and 10 is multiplied by 10, and the small number, the "power" of 10, is found by counting how many places the decimal point moved to create the first number.

the power is 6 because the decimal point moved six places; the power is positive because the decimal point moved to the left

1.23×10^6

the first number must always be between 1 and 10

the power is negative because the decimal point moved to the right

6×10^{-4}

the power is 4 because the decimal point moved four places

STANDARD FORM **43**

Standard form in action

Sometimes it is difficult to compare extremely large or small numbers because of the number of digits they contain. Standard form makes this easier.

The mass of Earth is 5,974,200,000,000,000,000,000,000 kg

The decimal point moves **24 places** to the left.

The mass of the planet Mars is

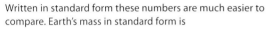

The decimal point moves **23 places** to the left.

Written in standard form these numbers are much easier to compare. Earth's mass in standard form is

$$5.9742 \times 10^{24} \text{ kg}$$

The mass of Mars in standard form is

$$6.4191 \times 10^{23} \text{ kg}$$

▷ **Comparing planet mass**
It is immediately evident that the mass of the Earth is bigger than the mass of Mars because 10^{24} is 10 times larger than 10^{23}.

EXAMPLES OF STANDARD FORM

Example	Decimal form	Standard form
Weight of the Moon	73,600,000,000,000,000,000,000 kg	7.36×10^{22} kg
Humans on Earth	6,800,000,000	6.8×10^{9}
Speed of light	300,000,000 m/sec	3×10^{8} m/sec
Distance of the Moon from the Earth	384,000 km	3.8×10^{5} km
Weight of the Empire State building	365,000 tons	3.65×10^{5} tons
Distance around the Equator	40,075 km	4×10^{4} km
Height of Mount Everest	8,850 m	8.850×10^{3} m
Speed of a bullet	710 m/sec	7.1×10^{2} m/sec
Speed of a snail	0.001 m/sec	1×10^{-3} m/sec
Width of a red blood cell	0.00067 cm	6.7×10^{-4} cm
Length of a virus	0.000 000 009 cm	9×10^{-9} cm
Weight of a dust particle	0.000 000 000 753 kg	7.53×10^{-10} kg

LOOKING CLOSER

Standard form and calculators

The exponent button on a calculator allows a number to be raised to any power. Calculators give very large answers in standard form.

△ **Exponent button**
This calculator button allows any number to be raised to any power.

Using the exponent button:

4×10^{2} is entered by pressing

On some calculators, answers appear in standard form:

$$1234567 \times 89101112 =$$
$$1.100012925 \times 10^{14}$$

so the answer is approximately 110,001,292,500,000

Decimals

NUMBERS WRITTEN IN DECIMAL FORM ARE CALLED DECIMAL NUMBERS OR, MORE SIMPLY, DECIMALS.

SEE ALSO	
‹ 18–21 Multiplication	
‹ 22–25 Division	
Using a calculator	72–73 ›

Decimal numbers

In a decimal number, the digits to the left of the decimal point are whole numbers. The digits to the right of the decimal point are not whole numbers. The first digit to the right of the decimal point represents tenths, the second hundredths, and so on. These are called fractional parts.

whole number part is 1,234

fractional part is 56

1,234.56

decimal point separates the whole numbers (on the left) from the fractional numbers (on the right)

△ **Whole and fractional parts**
The whole numbers represent – moving left from the decimal point – ones, tens, hundreds, and thousands. The fractional numbers – moving right from the decimal place – are tenths then hundredths.

Multiplication

To multiply decimals, first remove the decimal point. Then perform a long multiplication of the two numbers, before adding the decimal point back in to the answer. Here 1.9 (a decimal) is multiplied by 7 (a whole number).

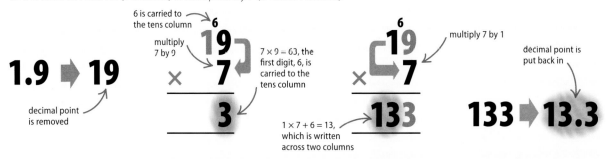

▶ **First, remove any** decimal points, so that both numbers can be treated as whole numbers.

▶ **Then multiply** the two numbers, starting in the ones column. Carry ones to the tens if necessary.

▶ **Next multiply the tens.** The product is 7, which, added to the carried 6, makes 13. Write this across two columns.

▶ **Finally, count** the decimal digits in the original numbers – there is 1. The answer will also have 1 decimal digit.

DECIMALS

DIVISION
Dividing one number by another often gives a decimal answer. Sometimes it is easier to turn decimals into whole numbers before dividing them.

Short division with decimals
Many numbers do not divide into each other exactly. If this is the case, a decimal point is added to the number being divided, and zeros are added after the point until the division is solved. Here 6 is divided by 8.

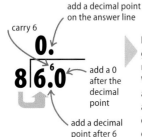

Both numbers are whole. As 8 will not divide into 6, put in a decimal point with a 0 after it and carry the 6.

carry 6
add a decimal point after 6
add a 0 after the decimal point

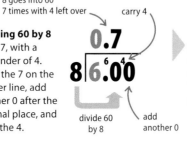

Dividing 60 by 8 gives 7, with a remainder of 4. Write the 7 on the answer line, add another 0 after the decimal place, and carry the 4.

add a decimal point on the answer line
8 goes into 60 7 times with 4 left over
carry 4
divide 60 by 8

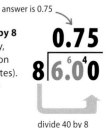

Dividing 40 by 8 gives 5 exactly, and the division ends (terminates). The answer to 6 ÷ 8 is 0.75.

answer is 0.75
divide 40 by 8

Dividing decimals
Above, short division was used to find the decimal answer for the sum 8 ÷ 6. Long division can be used to achieve the same result.

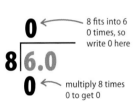

8 fits into 6 0 times, so write 0 here
multiply 8 times 0 to get 0

First, divide 8 into 6. It goes 0 times, so put a 0 above the 6. Multiply 8 × 0, and write the result (0) under the 6.

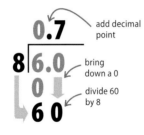

add decimal point
bring down a 0
divide 60 by 8

Subtract 0 from 6 to get 6, and bring down a 0. Divide 8 into 60 and put the answer, 7, after a decimal point.

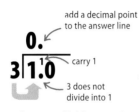

multiply 8 times 7 to get 56
first remainder is 4

Work out the first remainder by multiplying 8 by 7 and subtracting this from 60. The answer is 4.

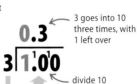

8 goes into 40 exactly 5 times
bring down a 0
divide 40 by 8

Bring down a zero to join the 4 and divide the number by 8. It goes exactly 5 times, so put a 5 above the line.

LOOKING CLOSER

Decimals that do not end

Sometimes the answer to a division can be a decimal number that repeats without ending. This is called a "repeating" decimal. For example, here 1 is divided by 3. Both the calculations and the answers in the division become identical after the second stage, and the answer repeats endlessly.

add a decimal point to the answer line
carry 1
3 does not divide into 1

3 does not divide into 1, so enter 0 on the answer line. Add a decimal point after 0, and carry 1.

3 goes into 10 three times, with 1 left over
divide 10 by 3

10 divided by 3 gives 3, with a remainder of 1. Write the 3 on the answer line and carry the 1 to the next 0.

3 goes into 10 three times, with 1 left over
symbol for a repeating decimal

Dividing 10 by 3 again gives exactly the same answer as the last step. This is repeated infinitely. This type of repeating decimal is written with a line over the repeating digit.

Binary numbers

NUMBERS ARE COMMONLY WRITTEN USING THE DECIMAL SYSTEM, BUT NUMBERS CAN BE WRITTEN IN ANY NUMBER BASE.

SEE ALSO
◁ 14–15 Introducing numbers
◁ 33 Roman numerals

What is a binary number?

The decimal system uses the digits 0 through to 9, while the binary system, also known as base 2, uses only two digits—0 and 1. Binary numbers should not be thought of in the same way as decimal numbers. For example, 10 is said as "ten" in the decimal system but must be said as "one zero" in the binary system. This is because the value of each "place" is different in decimal and binary.

Decimal numbers

Binary numbers
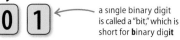

a single binary digit is called a "bit," which is short for **b**inary dig**it**

Counting in the decimal system

When using the decimal system for column sums, numbers are written from right to left (from lowest to highest). Each column is worth ten times more than the column to the right of it. The decimal number system is also known as base 10.

Counting in binary

Each column in the binary system is worth two times more than the column to the right of it and, as in the decimal system, 0 represents zero value. A similar system of headings may be used with binary numbers but only two symbols are used (0 and 1).

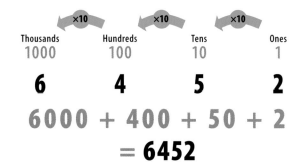

← written in the decimal system

Decimal	Binary	
0	0	0
1	1	1 one
2	1 0	1 two
3	1 1	1 two + 1 one
4	1 0 0	1 four
5	1 0 1	1 four + 1 one
6	1 1 0	1 four + 1 two
7	1 1 1	1 four + 1 two + 1 one
8	1 0 0 0	1 eight
9	1 0 0 1	1 eight + 1 one
10	1 0 1 0	1 eight + 1 two
11	1 0 1 1	1 eight + 1 two + 1 one
12	1 1 0 0	1 eight + 1 four
13	1 1 0 1	1 eight + 1 four + 1 one
14	1 1 1 0	1 eight + 1 four + 1 two
15	1 1 1 1	1 eight + 1 four + 1 two + 1 one
16	1 0 0 0 0	1 sixteen
17	1 0 0 0 1	1 sixteen + 1 one
18	1 0 0 1 0	1 sixteen + 1 two
19	1 0 0 1 1	1 sixteen + 1 two + 1 one
20	1 0 1 0 0	1 sixteen + 1 four
50	1 1 0 0 1 0	1 thirty-two + 1 sixteen + 1 two
100	1 1 0 0 1 0 0	1 sixty-four + 1 thirty-two + 1 four

Adding in binary

Numbers written in binary form can be added together in a similar way to the decimal system, and column addition may be done like this:

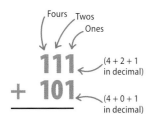

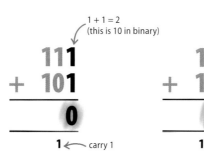

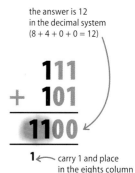

Align the numbers under their correct place-value columns as in the decimal system. It may be helpful to write in the column headings when first learning this system.

Add the ones column. The answer is 2, which is 10 in binary. The twos are shown in the next column so carry a 1 to the next column and leave 0 in the ones column.

Now the digits in the twos column are added together with the 1 carried over from the ones column. The total is 2 again (10 in binary) so a 1 needs to be carried and a 0 left in the twos column.

Finally, add the 1s in the fours column, which gives us 3, (11 in binary). This is the end of the equation so the final 1 is placed in the eights column.

Subtracting in binary

Subtraction works in a similar way to the decimal system but "borrows" in different units to the decimal system—borrowing by twos instead of tens.

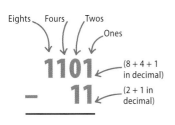

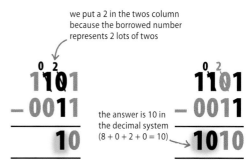

The numbers are written in their correct place-value columns as in the decimal system.

Add zeros so that there are the same number of digits in each column. Then begin by subtracting the ones column: 1 minus 1 is 0, so place a 0 in the answer space. Now move on to the twos column on the left.

The lower 1 cannot be subtracted from the 0 above it so borrow from the fours column and replace it with a 0. Then put a 2 above the twos column. Subtract the lower 1 from the upper 2. This leaves 1 as the answer.

Now subtract the digits in the fours column, which gives us 0. Finally, in the eights column we have nothing to subtract from the upper 1, so 1 is written in the answer space.

NUMBERS

 # Fractions

A FRACTION REPRESENTS A PART OF A WHOLE NUMBER.
THEY ARE WRITTEN AS ONE NUMBER OVER ANOTHER NUMBER.

SEE ALSO
⟨ 22–25 Division
⟨ 44–45 Decimals
Ratio and proportion 56–59 ⟩
Percentages 60–61 ⟩
Converting fractions, decimals, and percentages 64–65 ⟩

Writing fractions

The number on the top of a fraction shows how many equal parts of the whole are being dealt with, while the number on the bottom shows the total number of equal parts that the whole has been divided into.

$\frac{1}{2}$

- **Numerator** The number of equal parts examined.
- **Dividing line** This is also written as /.
- **Denominator** Total number of equal parts in the whole.

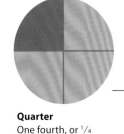

Quarter
One fourth, or $^1/_4$ (a quarter), shows 1 part out of 4 equal parts in a whole.

$\frac{1}{4}$

$\frac{1}{8}$

$\frac{1}{16}$

$\frac{1}{32}$ $\frac{1}{64}$ $\frac{1}{64}$

Eighth
$^1/_8$ (one eighth) is 1 part out of 8 equal parts in a whole.

Sixteenth
$^1/_{16}$ (one sixteenth) is 1 part out of 16 equal parts in a whole.

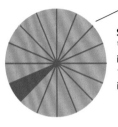

One thirty-second
$^1/_{32}$ (one thirty-second) is 1 part out of 32 equal parts in a whole.

One sixty-fourth
$^1/_{64}$ (one sixty-fourth) is 1 part out of 64 equal parts in a whole.

▷ **Equal parts of a whole**
The circle on the right shows how parts of a whole can be divided in different ways to form different fractions.

FRACTIONS

Types of fractions

A proper fraction—where the numerator is smaller than the denominator—is just one type of fraction. When the number of parts is greater than the whole, the result is a fraction that can be written in two ways—either as an improper fraction (also known as a top-heavy fraction) or a mixed fraction.

$\frac{1}{4}$ — numerator has lower value than denominator

◁ **Proper fraction**
In this fraction the number of parts examined, shown on top, is less than the whole.

$\frac{35}{4}$ — numerator has higher value than denominator

◁ **Improper fraction**
The larger numerator indicates that the parts come from more than one whole.

$10\frac{1}{3}$ — whole number / fraction

◁ **Mixed fraction**
A whole number is combined with a proper fraction.

Depicting fractions

Fractions can be illustrated in many ways, using any shape that can be divided into an equal number of parts.

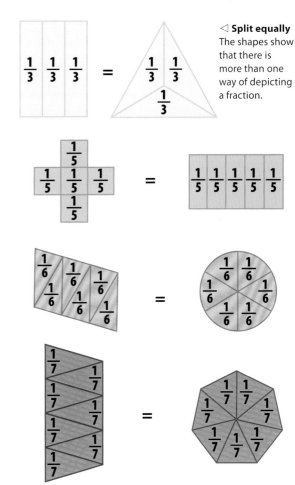

◁ **Split equally**
The shapes show that there is more than one way of depicting a fraction.

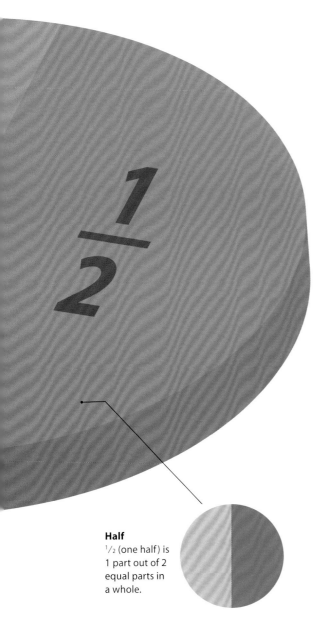

Half
$\frac{1}{2}$ (one half) is 1 part out of 2 equal parts in a whole.

Turning top-heavy fractions into mixed fractions

A top-heavy fraction can be turned into a mixed fraction by dividing the numerator by the denominator.

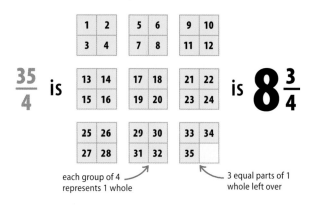

Draw groups of four numbers—each group represents a whole number. The fraction is eight whole numbers with ³/₄ (three quarters) left over.

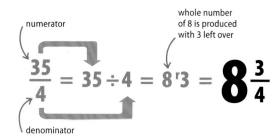

Divide the numerator by the denominator, in this case, 35 by 4.

The result is the mixed fraction 8³/₄ made up of the whole number 8 and 3 parts—or ³/₄ (three quarters)—left over.

Turning mixed fractions into top-heavy fractions

A mixed fraction can be changed into a top-heavy fraction by multiplying the whole number by the denominator and adding the result to the numerator.

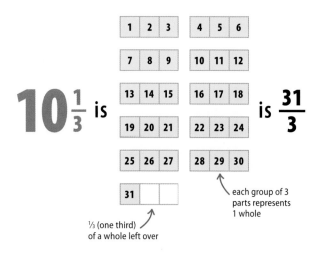

Draw the fraction as ten groups of three parts with one part left over. In this way it is possible to count 31 parts in the fraction.

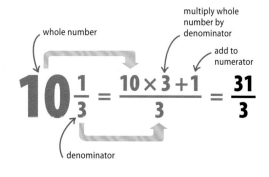

Multiply the whole number by the denominator—in this case, 10 × 3 = 30. Then add the numerator.

The result is the top-heavy fraction ³¹/₃, with a numerator (31) greater than the denominator (3).

FRACTIONS

Equivalent fractions

The same fraction can be written in different ways. These are known as equivalent (meaning "equal") fractions, even though they look different.

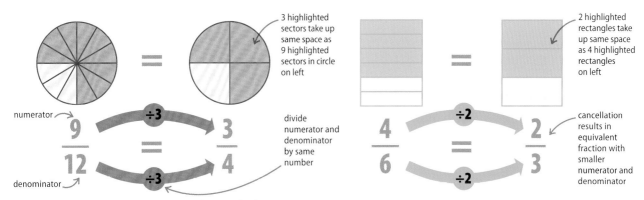

△ **Cancellation**
Cancellation is a method used to find an equivalent fraction that is simpler than the original. To cancel a fraction divide the numerator and denominator by the same number.

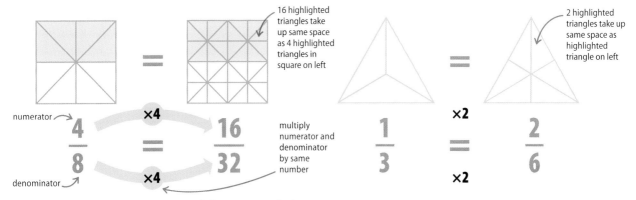

△ **Reverse cancellation**
Multiplying the numerator and denominator by the same number is called reverse cancellation. This results in an equivalent fraction with a larger numerator and denominator.

Table of equivalent fractions									
$1/1 =$	$2/2$	$3/3$	$4/4$	$5/5$	$6/6$	$7/7$	$8/8$	$9/9$	$10/10$
$1/2 =$	$2/4$	$3/6$	$4/8$	$5/10$	$6/12$	$7/14$	$8/16$	$9/18$	$10/20$
$1/3 =$	$2/6$	$3/9$	$4/12$	$5/15$	$6/18$	$7/21$	$8/24$	$9/27$	$10/30$
$1/4 =$	$2/8$	$3/12$	$4/16$	$5/20$	$6/24$	$7/28$	$8/32$	$9/36$	$10/40$
$1/5 =$	$2/10$	$3/15$	$4/20$	$5/25$	$6/30$	$7/35$	$8/40$	$9/45$	$10/50$
$1/6 =$	$2/12$	$3/18$	$4/24$	$5/30$	$6/36$	$7/42$	$8/48$	$9/54$	$10/60$
$1/7 =$	$2/14$	$3/21$	$4/28$	$5/35$	$6/42$	$7/49$	$8/56$	$9/63$	$10/70$
$1/8 =$	$2/16$	$3/24$	$4/32$	$5/40$	$6/48$	$7/56$	$8/64$	$9/72$	$10/80$

Finding a common denominator

When finding the relative sizes of two or more fractions, finding a common denominator makes it much easier. A common denominator is a number that can be divided exactly by the denominators of all of the fractions. Once this has been found, comparing fractions is just a matter of comparing their numerators.

▷ **Comparing fractions**
To work out the relative sizes of fractions, it is necessary to convert them so that they all have the same denominator. To do so, first look at the denominators of all the fractions being compared.

▷ **Make a list**
List the multiples – all the whole number products of each denominator – for all of the denominators. Pick a sensible stopping point for the list, such as 100.

multiples of 3: 3, 6, 9, 12, 15, 18, 21, 24, 27, 30…
multiples of 8: 8, 16, 24, 32, 40, 48, 56, 64, 72…
multiples of 12: 12, 24, 36, 48, 60, 72, 84, 96…

▷ **Find the lowest common denominator**
List only the multiples that are common to all three sets. These numbers are called common denominators. Identify the lowest one.

lowest common denominator of 3, 8, and 12

common denominators

24, 48, 72, 96…

▷ **Convert the fractions**
Find out how many times the original denominator goes into the common denominator. Multiply the numerator by the same number. It is now possible to compare the fractions.

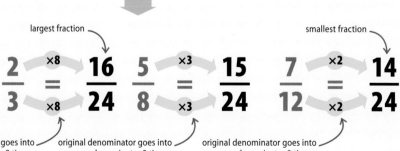

largest fraction — $\frac{2}{3} \times 8 = \frac{16}{24}$

$\frac{5}{8} \times 3 = \frac{15}{24}$

smallest fraction — $\frac{7}{12} \times 2 = \frac{14}{24}$

original denominator goes into common denominator 8 times, so multiply both numerator and denominator by 8

original denominator goes into common denominator 3 times, so multiply both numerator and denominator by 3

original denominator goes into common denominator 2 times, so multiply both numerator and denominator by 2

FRACTIONS

ADDING AND SUBTRACTING FRACTIONS
Just like whole numbers, it is possible to add and subtract fractions. How it is done depends on whether the denominators are the same or different.

Adding and subtracting fractions with the same denominator
To add or subtract fractions that have the same denominator, simply add or subtract their numerators to get the answer. The denominators stay the same.

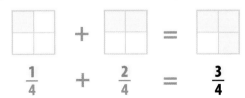

To add fractions, add together only the numerators. The denominator in the result remains unchanged.

To subtract fractions, subtract the smaller numerator from the larger. The denominator in the result stays the same.

Adding fractions with different denominators
To add fractions that have different denominators, it is necessary to change one or both of the fractions so they have the same denominator. This involves finding a common denominator (see opposite).

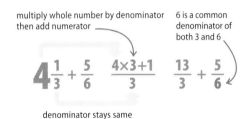

First, turn any mixed fractions that are being added into improper fractions.

The two fractions have different denominators, so a common denominator is needed.

Convert the fractions into fractions with common denominators by multiplying.

If necessary, divide the numerator by the denominator to turn the improper fraction back into a mixed fraction.

Subtracting fractions with different denominators
To subtract fractions with different denominators, a common denominator must be found.

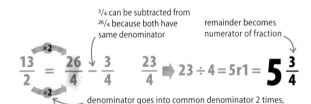

First, turn any mixed fractions in the equation into improper fractions by multiplying.

The two fractions have different denominators, so a common denominator is needed.

Convert the fractions into fractions with common denominators by multiplying.

If necessary, divide the numerator by the denominator to turn the improper fraction back into a mixed fraction.

MULTIPLYING FRACTIONS

Fractions can be multiplied by other fractions. To multiply fractions by mixed fractions or whole numbers, they first need to be converted into improper (top-heavy) fractions.

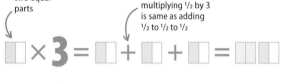

- two equal parts
- multiplying $\frac{1}{2}$ by 3 is same as adding $\frac{1}{2}$ to $\frac{1}{2}$ to $\frac{1}{2}$

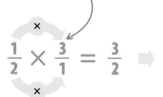

- whole number an improper fraction with whole number as numerator and 1 as denominator
- remainder becomes numerator of fraction
- denominator stays the same

Imagine multiplying a fraction by a whole number as adding the fraction to itself that many times. Alternatively, imagine multiplying a whole number by a fraction as taking that portion of the whole number, here $\frac{1}{2}$ of 3.

Convert the whole number to a fraction. Next, multiply both numerators together and then both denominators.

Divide the numerator of the resulting fraction by the denominator. The answer is given as a mixed fraction.

Multiplying two proper fractions

Proper fractions can be multiplied by each other. It is useful to imagine that the multiplication sign means "of"—the problem below can be expressed as "what is $\frac{1}{2}$ of $\frac{3}{4}$?" and "what is $\frac{3}{4}$ of $\frac{1}{2}$?".

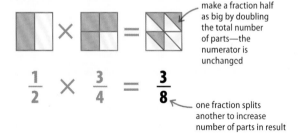

- make a fraction half as big by doubling the total number of parts—the numerator is unchanged
- one fraction splits another to increase number of parts in result

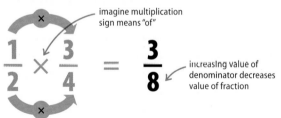

- imagine multiplication sign means "of"
- increasing value of denominator decreases value of fraction

Visually, the result of multiplying two proper fractions is that the space taken by both together is reduced.

Multiply the numerators and the denominators. The resulting fraction answers both questions: "what is $\frac{1}{2}$ of $\frac{3}{4}$?" and "what is $\frac{3}{4}$ of $\frac{1}{2}$?".

Multiplying mixed fractions

To multiply a proper fraction by a mixed fraction, it is necessary to first convert the mixed fraction into an improper fraction.

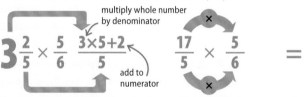

- multiply whole number by denominator
- add to numerator

$$\frac{17}{5} \times \frac{5}{6} = \frac{85}{30} \Rightarrow 85 \div 30 = 2r25 = 2\frac{25}{30}$$

- remainder becomes numerator of fraction
- to show in its lowest form divide both numbers by 5 to get $\frac{5}{6}$
- denominator stays the same

First, turn the mixed fraction into an improper fraction.

Next, multiply the numerators and denominators of both fractions to get a new fraction.

Divide the numerator of the new improper fraction by its denominator. The answer is shown as a mixed fraction.

DIVIDING FRACTIONS

Fractions can be divided by whole numbers. Turn the whole number into a fraction and find the reciprocal of this fraction by turning it upside down, then multiply it by the first fraction.

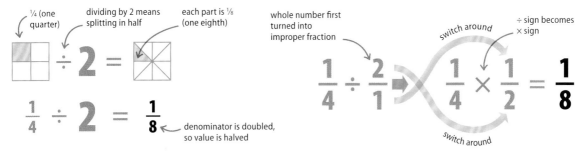

Picture dividing a fraction by a whole number as splitting it into that many parts. In this example, ¼ is split in half, resulting in twice as many equal parts.

To divide a fraction by a whole number, convert the whole number into a fraction, turn that fraction upside down, and multiply both the numerators and the denominators.

Dividing two proper fractions

Proper fractions can be divided by other proper fractions by using an inverse operation. Multiplication and division are inverse operations—they are the opposite of each other.

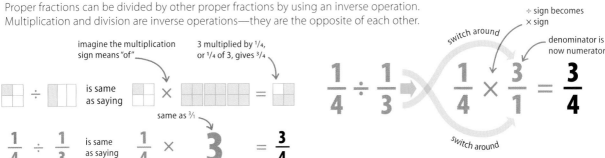

Dividing one fraction by another is the same as turning the second fraction upside down and then multiplying the two.

To divide two fractions use the inverse operation—turn the last fraction upside down, then multiply the numerators and the denominators.

Dividing mixed fractions

To divide mixed fractions, first convert them into improper fractions, then turn the second fraction upside down and multiply it by the first.

$$1\tfrac{1}{3} \div 2\tfrac{1}{4} \;\Rightarrow\; \frac{1\times 3+1}{3} \;\; \frac{2\times 4+1}{4} \;\Rightarrow\; \frac{4}{3} \div \frac{9}{4} \;\Rightarrow\; \frac{4}{3} \times \frac{4}{9} = \frac{16}{27}$$

- whole number
- denominator
- multiply whole number by denominator
- add to numerator
- switch around
- ÷ sign becomes × sign
- denominator is now numerator
- switch around

First, turn each of the mixed fractions into improper fractions by multiplying the whole number by the denominator and adding the numerator.

Divide the two fractions by turning the second fraction upside down, then multiplying the numerators and the denominators.

Ratio and proportion

RATIO COMPARES THE SIZE OF QUANTITIES. PROPORTION COMPARES THE RELATIONSHIP BETWEEN TWO SETS OF QUANTITIES.

SEE ALSO
‹ 18–21 Multiplication
‹ 22–25 Division
‹ 48–55 Fractions

Ratios show how much bigger one thing is than another. Two things are in proportion when a change in one causes a related change in the other.

Writing ratios

Ratios are written as two or more numbers with a colon between each. For example, a fruit bowl in which the ratio of apples to pears is 2 : 1 means that there are 2 apples for every 1 pear in the bowl.

▷ **Supporters**
This group represents fans of two football clubs, the "greens" and the "blues."

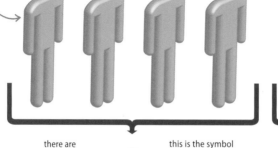

▷ **Forming a ratio**
To compare the numbers of people who support the two different clubs, write them as a ratio. This makes it clear that for every 4 green fans there are 3 blue fans.

these are the fans of the "greens"

there are 4 green supporters

this is the symbol for the ratio between the fans

there are 3 blue supporters

▽ **More ratios**
The same process applies to any set of data that needs to be compared. Here are more groups of fans, and the ratios they represent.

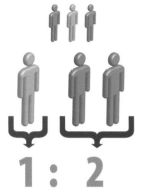
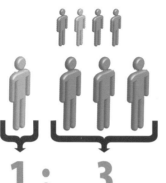
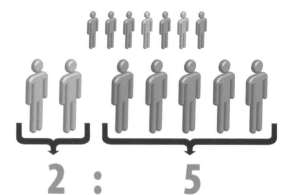

△ **1 : 2**
One fan of the greens and 2 fans of the blues can be compared as the ratio 1 : 2. This means that in this case there are twice as many fans of the blues as of the greens.

△ **1 : 3**
One fan of the greens and 3 fans of the blues can be shown as the ratio 1 : 3, which means that, in this case, there are three times more blue fans than green fans.

△ **2 : 5**
Two fans of the greens and 5 fans of the blues can be compared as the ratio 2 : 5. There are more than twice as many fans of the blues as of the greens.

RATIO AND PROPORTION

Finding a ratio

Large numbers can also be written as ratios. For example, to find the ratio between 1 hour and 20 minutes, convert them into the same unit, then cancel these numbers by finding the highest number that divides into both.

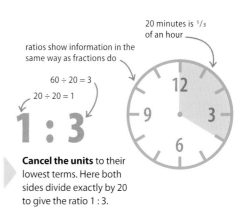

20 minutes is $1/3$ of an hour

ratios show information in the same way as fractions do

minutes are the smaller unit

20 mins, 60 mins

Convert one of the quantities so that both have the same units. In this example use minutes.

1 hour is the same as 60 minutes, so convert

this is the symbol for ratio

20 : 60

Write as a ratio by inserting a colon between the two quantities.

$60 \div 20 = 3$
$20 \div 20 = 1$

1 : 3

Cancel the units to their lowest terms. Here both sides divide exactly by 20 to give the ratio 1 : 3.

Working with ratios

Ratios can represent real values. In a scale, the small number of the ratio is the value on the scale model, and the larger is the real value it represents.

▷ **Scaling down**
1 : 50,000 cm is used as the scale on a map. Find out what a distance of 1.5 cm represents on this map.

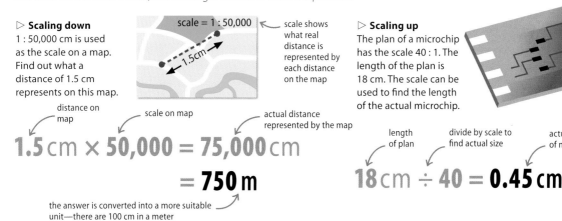

▷ **Scaling up**
The plan of a microchip has the scale 40 : 1. The length of the plan is 18 cm. The scale can be used to find the length of the actual microchip.

distance on map · scale on map · actual distance represented by the map

1.5 cm × 50,000 = 75,000 cm
= 750 m

the answer is converted into a more suitable unit—there are 100 cm in a meter

length of plan · divide by scale to find actual size · actual length of microchip

18 cm ÷ 40 = 0.45 cm

Comparing ratios

Converting ratios into fractions allows their size to be compared. To compare the ratios 4 : 5 and 1 : 2, write them as fractions with the same denominator.

$1 : 2 = \dfrac{1}{2}$ ← fraction that represents ratio 1 : 2

and

$4 : 5 = \dfrac{4}{5}$ ← fraction that represents ratio 4 : 5

First write each ratio as a fraction, placing the smaller quantity in each above the larger quantity.

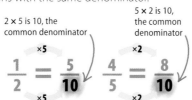

2×5 is 10, the common denominator

5×2 is 10, the common denominator

$\dfrac{1}{2} \xrightarrow{\times 5} \dfrac{5}{10}$ $\dfrac{4}{5} \xrightarrow{\times 2} \dfrac{8}{10}$

Convert the fractions so that they both have the same denominator, by multiplying the first fraction by 5 and the second by 2.

compare the numerators

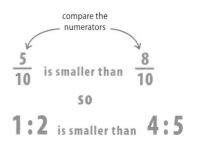

$\dfrac{5}{10}$ **is smaller than** $\dfrac{8}{10}$

so

1 : 2 is smaller than **4 : 5**

Because the fractions now share a denominator, their sizes can be compared, making it clear which ratio is bigger.

PROPORTION

Two quantities are in proportion when a change in one causes a change in the other by a related number. Two examples of this are direct and indirect (also called inverse) proportion.

Direct proportion

Two quantities are in direct proportion if the ratio between them is always the same. This means, for example, that if one quantity doubles then so does the other.

▷ **Direct proportion**
This table and graph show the directly proportional relationship between the number of gardeners and the number of trees planted.

Gardeners	Trees
1	2
2	4
3	6

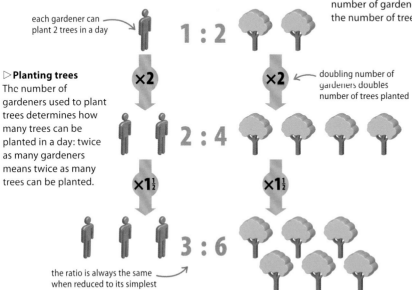

▷ **Planting trees**
The number of gardeners used to plant trees determines how many trees can be planted in a day: twice as many gardeners means twice as many trees can be planted.

the ratio is always the same when reduced to its simplest terms, in this case 1 : 2

each gardener can plant 2 trees in a day

doubling number of gardeners doubles number of trees planted

2 gardeners can plant 4 trees in a day

line showing direct proportion is always straight

Indirect proportion

Two quantities are in indirect proportion if their product (the answer when they are multiplied by each other) is always the same. So if one quantity doubles, the other quantity halves.

▷ **Indirect proportion**
This table and graph show the indirectly proportional relationship between the vans used and the time taken to deliver the parcels.

Vans	Days
1	8
2	4
4	2

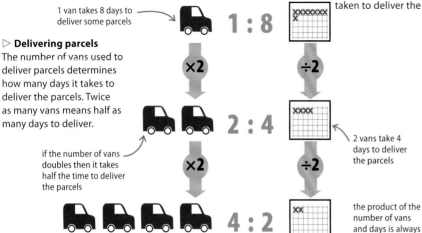
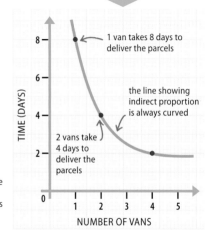

▷ **Delivering parcels**
The number of vans used to deliver parcels determines how many days it takes to deliver the parcels. Twice as many vans means half as many days to deliver.

1 van takes 8 days to deliver some parcels

if the number of vans doubles then it takes half the time to deliver the parcels

2 vans take 4 days to deliver the parcels

the product of the number of vans and days is always the same: 8

1 van takes 8 days to deliver the parcels

2 vans take 4 days to deliver the parcels

the line showing indirect proportion is always curved

RATIO AND PROPORTION

Dividing in a given ratio

A quantity can be divided into two, three, or more parts, according to a given ratio. This example shows how to divide 20 people into the ratios 2 : 3 and 6 : 3 : 1.

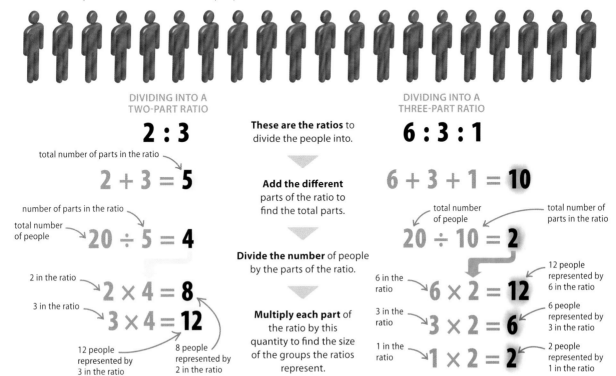

Proportional quantities

Proportion can be used to solve problems involving unknown quantities. For example, if 3 bags contain 18 apples, how many apples do 5 bags contain?

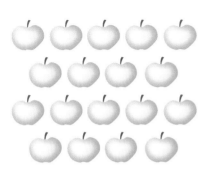
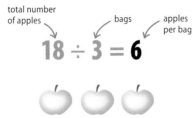
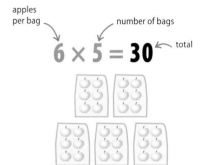

There is a total of 18 apples in 3 bags. Each bag contains the same number of apples.

To find out how many apples there are in 1 bag, divide the total number of apples by the number of bags.

To find the number of apples in 5 bags, multiply the number of apples in 1 bag by 5.

Percentages

A PERCENTAGE SHOWS AN AMOUNT AS A PART OF 100.

Any number can be written as a part of 100 or a percentage. Percent means "per hundred," and it is a useful way of comparing two or more quantities. The symbol "%" is used to indicate a percentage.

SEE ALSO	
‹ 44–45 Decimals	
‹ 48–55 Fractions	
Ratio and proportion	56–59 ›
Rounding off	70–71 ›

Parts of 100

The simplest way to start looking at percentages is by dealing with a block of 100 units, as shown in the main image. These 100 units represent the total number of people in a school. This total can be divided into different groups according to the proportion of the total 100 they represent.

100%

▷ **This is simply** another way of saying "everybody" or "everything." Here, all 100 figures —100%—are blue.

50%

▷ **This group** is equally divided between 50 blue and 50 purple figures. Each represents 50 out of 100 or 50% of the total. This is the same as half.

1%

▷ **In this group** there is only 1 blue figure out of 100, or 1%.

FEMALE TEACHERS 10% or 10 out of 100

MALE STUDENTS 19% or 19 out of 100

MALE TEACHERS 5% or 5 out of 100

△ **Adding up to 100**
Percentages are an effective way to show the component parts of a total. For example, male teachers (blue) account for 5% (5 out of 100) of the total.

PERCENTAGES

FEMALE STUDENTS
66% or 66 out of 100

▽ **Examples of percentages**
Percentages are a simple and accessible way to present information, which is why they are often used by the media.

Percentage	Facts
97%	of the world's animals are invertebrates
92.5%	of an Olympic gold medal is composed of silver
70%	of the world's surface is covered in water
66%	of the human body is water
61%	of the world's oil is in the Middle East
50%	of the world's population live in cities
21%	of the air is oxygen
6%	of the world's land surface is covered in rain forest

WORKING WITH PERCENTAGES

A percentage is simply a part of a whole, expressed as a part of 100. There are two main ways of working with percentages: the first is finding a percentage of a given amount, and the second is finding what percentage one number is of another number.

Calculating percentages

This example shows how to find the percentage of a quantity, in this case 25% of a group of 24 people.

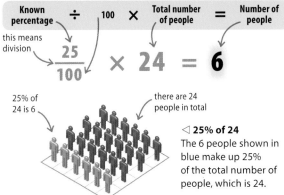

Known percentage ÷ 100 × Total number of people = Number of people

this means division

$$\frac{25}{100} \times 24 = 6$$

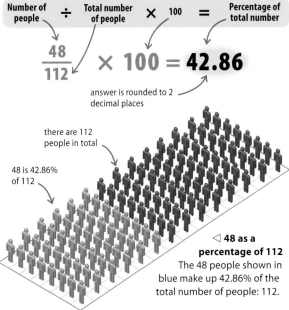

25% of 24 is 6

there are 24 people in total

◁ **25% of 24**
The 6 people shown in blue make up 25% of the total number of people, which is 24.

This example shows how to find what percentage one number is of another number, in this case 48 people out of a group of 112 people.

Number of people ÷ Total number of people × 100 = Percentage of total number

$$\frac{48}{112} \times 100 = 42.86$$

answer is rounded to 2 decimal places

there are 112 people in total

48 is 42.86% of 112

◁ **48 as a percentage of 112**
The 48 people shown in blue make up 42.86% of the total number of people: 112.

PERCENTAGES AND QUANTITIES

Percentages are a useful way of expressing a value as a proportion of the total number. If two out of three of a percentage, value, and total number are known, it is possible to find out the missing quantity using arithmetic.

Finding an amount as a % of another amount

Out of 12 pupils in a class, 9 play a musical instrument. To find the known value (9) as a percentage of the total (12), divide the known value by the total number and multiply by 100.

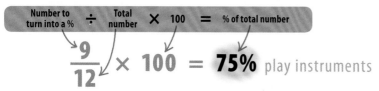

Divide the known number by the total number (9 ÷ 12 = 0.75).

Multiply the result by 100 to get the percentage (0.75 × 100 = 75).

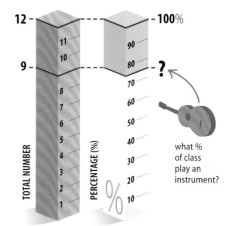

what % of class play an instrument?

Finding the total number from a %

In a class, 7 children make up 35% of the total. To find the total number of students in the class, divide the known value (7) by the known percentage (35) and multiply by 100.

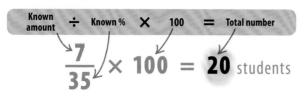

Divide the known amount by the known percentage (7 ÷ 35 = 0.2).

Multiply the result by 100 to get the total number (0.2 × 100 = 20).

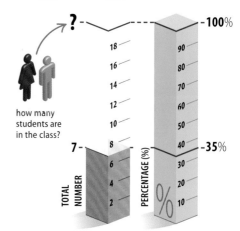

how many students are in the class?

REAL WORLD
Percentages

Percentages are all around us—in stores, in newspapers, on TV—everywhere. Many things in everyday life are measured and compared in percentages—how much an item is reduced in a sale; what the interest rate is on a mortgage or a bank loan; or how efficient a light bulb is by the percentage of electricity it converts to light. Percentages are even used to show how much of the recommended daily intake of vitamins and other nutrients is in food products.

PERCENTAGES 63

PERCENTAGE CHANGE

If a value changes by a certain percentage, it is possible to calculate the new value. Conversely, when a value changes by a known amount, it is possible to work out the percent increase or decrease compared to the original.

Finding a new value from a % increase or decrease

To find how a 55% increase or decrease affects the value of 40, first work out 55% of 40. Then add to or subtract from the original to get the new value.

Known % ÷ 100 × Original value = % of total value   THEN   Original value + or − % of total value = New value

$$\frac{55}{100} \times 40 = 22$$

$$40 \underset{\text{or} -}{+} 22 = \begin{array}{c} 62 \\ \text{or } 18 \end{array}$$

Divide the known % by 100 (55 ÷ 100 = 0.55).

Multiply the result by the original value (0.55 × 40 = 22).

Add the original value to 22 to find the % increase, or **subtract** 22 to find the % decrease.

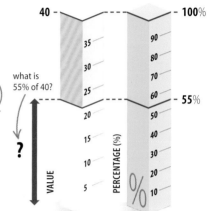
what is 55% of 40?

Finding an increase in a value as a %

The price of a donut in the school cafeteria has risen 30 cents—from 99 cents last year to $1.29 this year. To find the increase as a percent, divide the increase in value (30) by the original value (99) and multiply by 100.

Increase in value ÷ Original value × 100 = Increase in value as %

$$\frac{30}{99} \times 100 = 30.3\% \text{ increase}$$

Divide the increase in value by the original value (30 ÷ 99 = 0.303).

Multiply the result by 100 to find the percentage (0.303 × 100 = 30.3), and round to 3 significant figures.

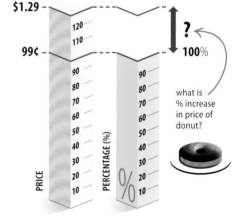
what is % increase in price of donut?

Finding a decrease in a value as a %

There was an audience of 245 at the school play last year, but this year only 209 attended—a decrease of 36. To find the decrease as a percent, divide the decrease in value (36) by the original value (245) and multiply by 100.

Decrease in value ÷ Original value × 100 = Decrease in value as %

$$\frac{36}{245} \times 100 = 14.7\% \text{ decrease}$$

Divide the decrease in value by the original value (36 ÷ 245 = 0.147).

Multiply the result by 100 to find the percentage (0.147 × 100 = 14.7), and round to 3 significant figures.

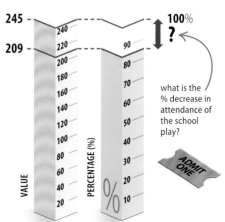
what is the % decrease in attendance of the school play?

Converting fractions, decimals, and percentages

SEE ALSO
◀ 44–45 Decimals
◀ 48–55 Fractions
◀ 60–63 Percentages

DECIMALS, FRACTIONS, AND PERCENTAGES ARE DIFFERENT WAYS OF WRITING THE SAME NUMBER.

The same but different
Sometimes a number shown one way can be shown more clearly in another way. For example, if 20% is the grade required to pass an exam, this is the same as saying that 1/5 of the answers in an exam need to be answered correctly to achieve a pass mark or that the minimum score for a pass is 0.2 of the total.

Changing a **decimal** into a **percentage**
To change a decimal into a percentage, multiply by 100.

$$0.75 \rightarrow 75\%$$

$$0.75 \times 100 = 75\%$$

Decimal — Multiply by 100 — Percentage

decimal point in 0.75 moved two places to right to make 75

75%
PERCENTAGE
A percentage shows a number as a proportion of 100.

▷ **All change**
The three ways of writing the same number are shown here: decimal (0.75), fraction (¾), and percentage (75%). They look different, but they all represent the same proportion of an amount.

Changing a **percentage** into a **decimal**
To change a percentage into a decimal, divide it by 100.

$$75\% \rightarrow 0.75$$

decimal point added two places to left of last digit

$$75\% \div 100 = 0.75$$

Percentage — Divide by 100 — Decimal

Changing a **percentage** into a **fraction**
To change a percentage into a fraction, write it as a fraction of 100 and then cancel it down to simplify it, if possible.

$$75\% \rightarrow \frac{3}{4}$$

divide by highest number that goes into 75 and 100

$$75\% \rightarrow \frac{75}{100} \xrightarrow[\div 25]{\div 25} \frac{3}{4}$$

Percentage — Turn the percentage into the numerator of a fraction with 100 as the denominator. — Fraction canceled down into its lowest terms.

CONVERTING FRACTIONS, DECIMALS, AND PERCENTAGES

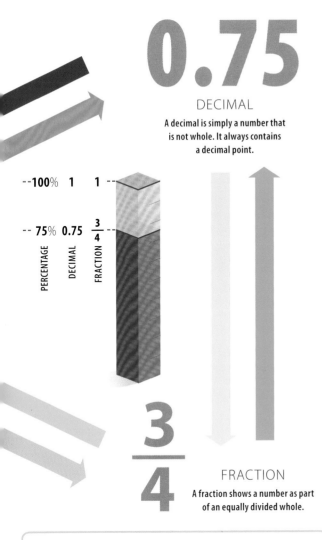

0.75
DECIMAL
A decimal is simply a number that is not whole. It always contains a decimal point.

FRACTION
A fraction shows a number as part of an equally divided whole.

Everyday numbers to remember
Many decimals, fractions, and percentages are used in everyday life—some of the more common ones are shown here.

Decimal	Fraction	%	Decimal	Fraction	%
0.1	1/10	10%	0.625	5/8	62.5%
0.125	1/8	12.5%	0.666	2/3	66.7%
0.25	1/4	25%	0.7	7/10	70%
0.333	1/3	33.3%	0.75	3/4	75%
0.4	2/5	40%	0.8	4/5	80%
0.5	1/2	50%	1	1/1	100%

Changing a **decimal** into a **fraction**
First, make the fraction's denominator (its bottom part) 10, 100, 1,000, and so on for every digit after the decimal point.

$0.75 \Rightarrow \dfrac{3}{4}$ divide by highest number that goes into 75 and 100

$0.75 \Rightarrow \dfrac{75}{100} \xrightarrow{\div 25 / \div 25} \dfrac{3}{4}$

Decimal number with two digits after the decimal point.

Count the decimal places—if there is 1 digit, the denominator is 10; if there are 2, it is 100. The numerator is the number after the decimal point.

Cancel the fraction down to its lowest possible terms.

Changing a **fraction** into a **percentage**
To change a fraction into a percentage, change it to a decimal and then multiply it by 100.

$\dfrac{3}{4} \Rightarrow 75\%$

divide the denominator (4) into the numerator (3)

$\dfrac{3}{4} \Rightarrow 3 \div 4 = 0.75 \Rightarrow 0.75 \times 100 = 75\%$

Fraction   **For decimal, divide the numerator by the denominator.**   **Multiply by 100**

Changing a **fraction** into a **decimal**
Divide the fraction's denominator (its bottom part) into the fraction's numerator (its top part).

$\dfrac{3}{4} \Rightarrow 0.75$

numerator   denominator

$\dfrac{3}{4} = 3 \div 4 = 0.75$

Fraction   **Divide the numerator by the denominator.**   **Decimal**

Mental math

EVERYDAY PROBLEMS CAN BE SIMPLIFIED SO THAT THEY CAN BE EASILY DONE WITHOUT USING A CALCULATOR.

> **SEE ALSO**
> ‹ 18–21 Multiplication
> ‹ 22–25 Division
> Using a calculator 72–73 ›

MULTIPLICATION

Multiplying by some numbers can be easy. For example, to multiply by 10 either add a 0 or move the decimal point one place to the right. To multiply by 20, multiply by 10 and then double the answer.

▷ **Multiplying by 10**
A sports club hired 2 people last year, but this year it needs to hire 10 times that number. How many staff members will it recruit this year?

◁ **Finding the answer**
To multiply 2 by 10 add a 0 to the 2. Multiplying 2 people by 10 results in an answer of 20.

number of staff members recruited last year
2 staff members recruited last year
×10
2 × 10
20 new members of staff
zero added to give 20, which is new number of staff members

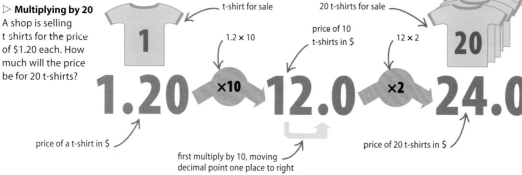

▷ **Multiplying by 20**
A shop is selling t-shirts for the price of $1.20 each. How much will the price be for 20 t-shirts?

◁ **Finding the answer**
First multiply the price by 10, here by moving the decimal point one place to the right, and then double that to give the final price of $24.

price of a t-shirt in $
t-shirt for sale
1.2 × 10
×10
first multiply by 10, moving decimal point one place to right
20 t-shirts for sale
price of 10 t-shirts in $
12 × 2
×2
price of 20 t-shirts in $

▷ **Multiplying by 25**
An athlete runs 16 miles a day. If the athlete runs the same distance every day for 25 days, how far will he run in total?

◁ **Finding the answer**
First multiply the 16 miles for one day by 100, to give 1,600 miles for 100 days, then divide by 4 to give the answer over 25 days.

athlete runs every day
16 × 100
×100
16 miles run in a day
athlete runs every day for 25 days
1,600 miles run in 100 days
1,600 ÷ 4
÷4
400 miles run in 25 days

MENTAL MATH

▽ Multiplication using decimals
Decimals appear to complicate the problem, but they can be ignored until the final stage. Here the amount of carpet required to cover a floor needs to be calculated.

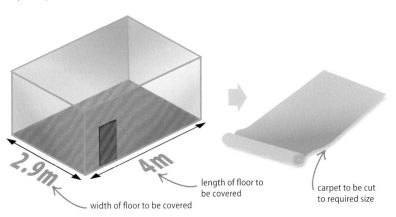

length of floor to be covered
carpet to be cut to required size
width of floor to be covered

LOOKING CLOSER
Checking the answer
Because 2.9 is almost 3, multiplying 3×4 is a good way to check that the calculation to 2.9×4 is correct.

$$2.9 \approx 3 \text{ and}$$
symbol for approximately equal to

$$3 \times 4 = 12$$

close to real answer of 11.6

$$\text{so } 2.9 \times 4 \approx 12$$

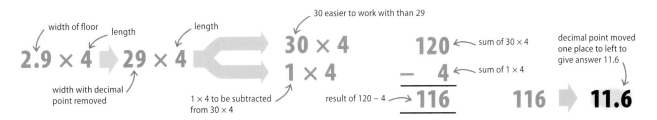

width of floor
length
2.9×4
width with decimal point removed

length
29×4

30 easier to work with than 29
30×4
1×4
1×4 to be subtracted from 30×4

120 — sum of 30×4
$- 4$ — sum of 1×4
116
result of $120 - 4$

decimal point moved one place to left to give answer 11.6
116 ▶ 11.6

First, take away the decimal point from the 2.9 to make the calculation 29×4.

▶ **Change 29×4** to 30×4 since it is easier to work out. Write 1×4 below (the difference between 29×4 and 30×4).

▶ **Subtract 4** (product of 1×4) from 120 (product of 30×4) to give the answer of 116 (product of 29×4).

▶ **Move the decimal point** one place to the left (it was moved one place to the right in the first step).

Top tricks
The multiplication tables of several numbers reveal patterns of multiplications. Here are two good mental tricks to remember when multiplying the 9 and 11 times tables.

multipliers 1 to 10

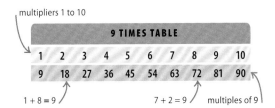

$1 + 8 = 9$
$7 + 2 = 9$
multiples of 9

△ **Two digits are added together**
The two digits that make up the first 10 multiples of 9 each add up to 9. The first digit of the multiple (such as 1, in 18) is always 1 less than the multiplier (2).

multipliers 1 to 9

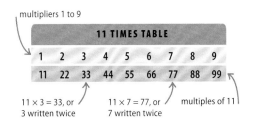

$11 \times 3 = 33$, or 3 written twice
$11 \times 7 = 77$, or 7 written twice
multiples of 11

△ **Digit is written twice**
To multiply by 11, merely repeat the two multipliers together. For example, 4×11 is two 4s or 44. It works all the way up to $9 \times 11 = 99$, which is 9 written twice.

DIVISION

Dividing by 10 or 5 is straightforward. To divide by 10, either delete a 0 or move the decimal point one place to the left. To divide by 5, again divide by 10 and then double the answer. Using these rules, work out the divisions in the following two examples.

▷ **Dividing by 10**
In this example, 160 travel vouchers are needed to rent a 10-seat mini bus. How many travel vouchers are needed for each of the 10 children to travel on the bus?

◁ **How many each?**
To find the number of travel vouchers for each child, divide the total of 160 by 10 by deleting a 0 from the 160. It gives the answer of 16 travel vouchers each.

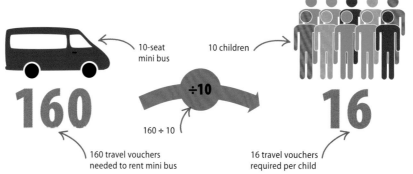

▷ **Dividing by 5**
The cost of admission to a zoo for a group of five children is 75 tokens. How many tokens are needed for 1 of the 5 children to enter the zoo?

◁ **How many each?**
To find the admission for 1 child, divide the total of 75 by 10 (by moving a decimal point in 75 one place to the left) to give 7.5, and then double that for the answer of 15.

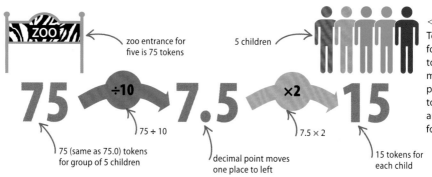

LOOKING CLOSER

Top tips

There are various mental tricks to help with dividing larger or more complicated numbers. In the three examples below, there are tips on how to check whether very large numbers can be divided by 3, 4, and 9.

▷ **Divisible by 3**
Add together all of the digits in the number. If the total is divisible by 3, the original number is too.

original number → 1665233198172 ➡ digits add up to 54 → 1+6+6+5+2+3+3+1+9+8+1+7+2 = 54

54 ÷ 3 = 18, so the original number is divisible by 3

▷ **Divisible by 4**
If the last two digits are taken as one single number, and it is divisible by 4, the original number is too.

original number → 123456123456123456 ➡ 5 and 6 seen as one number: 56 → 56 ÷ 4 = 14

56 ÷ 4 = 14, so the original number is divisible by 4

▷ **Divisible by 9**
Add together all of the digits in the number. If the total is divisible by 9, the original number is too.

original number → 1643951142 ➡ add together all digits of number, their sum is 36 → 1+6+4+3+9+5+1+1+4+2 = 36

36 ÷ 9 = 4, so the original number is divisible by 9

PERCENTAGES

A useful method of simplifying calculations involving percentages is to reduce one difficult percentage into smaller and easier-to-calculate parts. In the example below, the smaller percentages include 10% and 5%, which are easy to work out.

▷ **Adding 17.5 percent**
Here a shop wants to charge $480 for a new bike. However, the owner of the shop has to add a sales tax of 17.5 percent to the price. How much will it then cost?

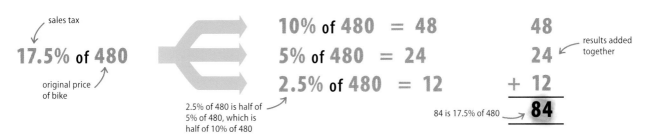

▷ **First, write down** the percentage price increase required and the original price of the bike.

▷ **Next,** reduce 17.5% into the easier stages of 10%, 5%, and 2.5% of $480, and calculate their values.

▷ **The sum** of 48, 24, and 12 is 84, so $84 is added to $480 for a price of $564.

Switching

A percentage and an amount can both be "switched," to produce the same result with each switch. For example, 50% of 10, which is 5, is exactly the same as 10% of 50, which is 5 again.

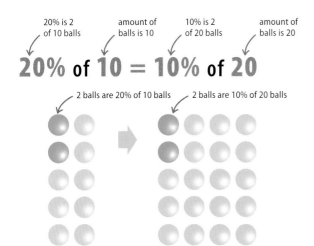

Progression

A progression involves dividing the percentage by a number and then multiplying the result by the same number. For example, 40% of 10 is 4. Dividing this 40% by 2 and multiplying 10 by 2 results in 20% of 20, which is also 4.

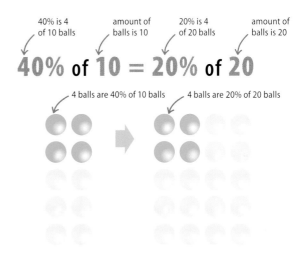

NUMBERS

Rounding off

THE PROCESS OF ROUNDING OFF INVOLVES REPLACING ONE NUMBER WITH ANOTHER TO MAKE IT MORE PRACTICAL TO USE.

SEE ALSO
‹ 44–45 Decimals
‹ 66–67 Mental math

Estimation and approximation
In many practical situations, an exact answer is not needed, and it is easier to find an estimate based on rounding off (approximation). The general principle of rounding off is that a number at or above the midpoint of a group of numbers, such as the numbers 15–19 in the group 10–20, rounds up, while a number below the midpoint rounds down.

▽ **Rounding to the nearest 10**
The midpoint between any two 10s is 5. If the last digit of each number is 5 or over it rounds up, otherwise it rounds down.

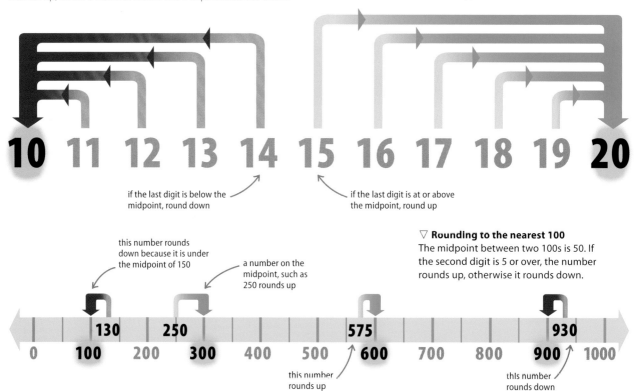

if the last digit is below the midpoint, round down

if the last digit is at or above the midpoint, round up

▽ **Rounding to the nearest 100**
The midpoint between two 100s is 50. If the second digit is 5 or over, the number rounds up, otherwise it rounds down.

this number rounds down because it is under the midpoint of 150

a number on the midpoint, such as 250 rounds up

this number rounds up

this number rounds down

LOOKING CLOSER

Approximately equal

Many measurements are given as approximations, and numbers are sometimes rounded to make them easier to use. An "approximately equals" sign is used to show when numbers have been rounded up or down. It looks similar to a normal equals sign (=) but with curved instead of straight lines.

wavy lines mean "approximately"

$31 \approx 30$ and $187 \approx 200$

△ **Approximately equal to**
The "approximately equals" sign shows that the two sides of the sign are approximately equal instead of equal. So 31 is approximately equal to 30, and 187 is approximately equal to 200.

ROUNDING OFF

Decimal places

Any number can be rounded to the appropriate number of decimal places. The choice of how many decimal places depends on what the number is used for and how exact an end result is required.

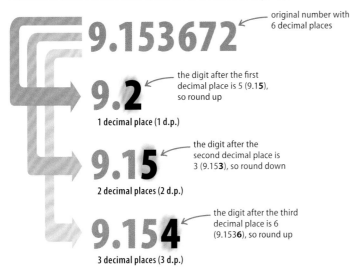

LOOKING CLOSER

How many decimal places?

The more decimal places, the more accurate the number. This table shows the accuracy that is represented by different numbers of decimal places. For example, a distance in miles to 3 decimal places would be accurate to a thousandth of a mile, which is equal to 5 feet.

Decimal places	Rounded to	Example
1	1/10	1.1 mi
2	1/100	1.14 mi
3	1/1,000	1.135 mi

Significant figures

A significant figure in a number is a digit that counts. The digits 1 to 9 are always significant, but 0 is not. However, 0 becomes significant when it occurs between two significant figures, or if an exact answer is needed.

200 — 1 significant figure
Real value anywhere between 150–249

200 — 2 significant figures
Real value anywhere between 195–204

200 — 3 significant figures
Real value anywhere between 199.5–200.4

◁ **Significant zeros**
The answer 200 could be the result of rounding to 1, 2, or 3 significant figures (s.f.). Below each example is the range in which its true value lies.

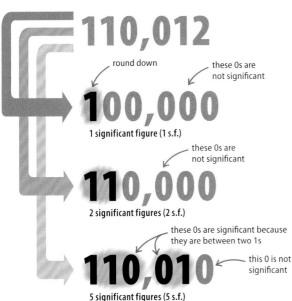

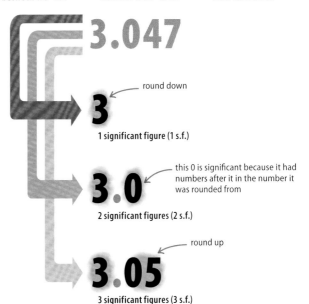

72 NUMBERS

 # Using a calculator

CALCULATORS ARE MACHINES THAT WORK OUT THE ANSWERS TO SOME MATHEMATICAL PROBLEMS.

SEE ALSO	
Tools in geometry	82–83 ⟩
Collecting and organizing data	204–205 ⟩

Calculators are designed to make math easier, but there are a few things to be aware of when using them.

Introducing the calculator
A modern calculator is a handheld electronic device that is used to find the answers to mathematical problems. Most calculators are operated in a similar way (as described here), but it may be necessary to read the instructions for a particular model.

Using a calculator
Be careful that functions are entered in the correct order, or the answers the calculator gives will be wrong.

For example, to find the answer to the calculation:

$(7 + 2) \times 9 =$

Enter these keys, making sure to include all parts of the calculation, including the parentheses.

(7 + 2) × 9 = 81

Not

7 + 2 × 9 = 25 ← calculator does product 2 × 9 = 18, then sum 18 + 7 = 25

Estimating answers
Calculators can only give answers according to the keys that have been pressed. It is useful to have an idea of what answer to expect since a small mistake can give a very wrong answer.

For example

2 0 0 6 × 1 9 8

must be close to ← this would give the answer 400,000

2 0 0 0 × 2 0 0

So if the calculator gives the answer **40,788** it is clear that the numbers have not been entered correctly—one "0" is missing from what was intended:

2 0 6 × 1 9 8

FREQUENTLY USED KEYS

ON
This button turns the calculator on—most calculators turn themselves off automatically if they are left unused for a certain period of time.

Number pad
This contains the basic numbers that are needed for math. These buttons can be used individually or in groups to create larger numbers.

Standard arithmetic keys
These cover all the basic mathematical functions: multiplication, division, addition, and subtraction, as well as the essential equals sign.

Decimal point
This key works in the same way as a written decimal point—it separates whole numbers from decimals. It is entered in the same way as any of the number keys.

Cancel
The cancel key clears all recent entries from the memory. This is useful when starting a new calculation because it makes sure no unwanted values are retained.

Delete
This clears the last value that was entered into the calculator, rather than wiping everything from the memory. It is sometimes labeled "CE" (clear entry).

Recall button
This recalls a value from the calculator's memory—it is useful for calculations with many parts that use numbers or stages from earlier in the problem.

USING A CALCULATOR 73

△ **Scientific calculator**
A scientific calculator has many functions—a standard calculator usually only has the number pad, standard arithmetic keys, and one or two other, simpler functions, such as percentages. The buttons shown here allow for more advanced math.

FUNCTION KEYS

Cube
This is a short cut to cubing a number, without having to key in a number multiplied by itself, and then multiplied by itself again. Key in the number to be cubed, then press this button.

ANS
Pressing this key gives the answer to the last sum that was entered. It is useful for sums with many steps.

Square root
This finds the positive square root of a positive number. Press the square root button first, then the number, and then the equals button.

Square
A short cut to squaring a number, without having to key in the number multiplied by itself. Just key in the number then this button.

Exponent
Allows a number to be raised to a power. Enter the number, then the exponent button, then the power.

Negative
Use this to make a number negative. It is usually used when the first number in a calculation is negative.

sin, cos, tan
These are mainly used in trigonometry, to find the sine, cosine, or tangent values of angles in right triangles.

Parentheses
These work the same way as enclosing part of a calculation in parentheses, to make sure the order of operations is correct.

Personal finance

KNOWING HOW MONEY WORKS IS IMPORTANT FOR MANAGING YOUR PERSONAL FINANCES.

Personal finance includes paying tax on income, gaining interest on savings, or paying interest on loans.

SEE ALSO
‹ 34–35 Positive and negative numbers
Business finance 76–77 ›
Formulas 177–179 ›

Tax
Tax is a fee charged by a government on a product, income, or activity. Governments collect the money they need to provide services, such as schools and defense, by taxing individuals and companies. Individuals are taxed on what they earn—income tax—and also on some things they buy—sales tax.

GOVERNMENT
Part of the cost of government spending is collected in the form of income tax

◁ **Income tax**
Each person is taxed on what they earn; "take home" is the amount of money they have left after paying their income tax and other deductions.

TAXPAYER
Everybody pays tax—through their wages and through the money that they spend

WAGE
This is the amount of money that is earned by a person who is employed

FINANCIAL TERMS

Financial words often seem complicated, but they are easy to understand. Knowing what the important ones mean will enable you to manage your finances by helping you understand what you have to pay and the money you will receive.

Bank account	This is the record of whatever a person borrows from or saves with the bank. Each account holder has a numeric password called a personal identification number (PIN), which should never be revealed to anyone.
Credit	Credit is money that is borrowed—for example, on a 4-year pay-back agreement or as an overdraft from the bank. It always costs to borrow money. The money paid to borrow from a bank is called interest.
Income	This is the money that comes to an individual or family. This can be provided by the wages that are paid for employment. Sometimes it comes from the government in the form of an allowance or direct payment.
Interest	This is the cost of borrowing money or the income received when saving with a bank. It costs more to borrow money from a bank than the interest a person would receive from the bank by saving the same amount.
Mortgage	A mortgage is an agreement to borrow money to buy a home. A bank lends the money for the purchase and this is paid back, usually over a long period of time, together with interest on the loan and other charges.
Savings	There are many forms of savings. Money can be saved in a bank to earn interest. Saving through a pension plan involves making regular payments to ensure an income after retirement.
Break-even	Break-even is the point where the cost, or what a company has spent, is equal to revenue, which is what the company has earned—at break-even the company makes neither a profit nor a loss.
Loss	Companies make a loss if they spend more than they earn—if it costs them more to produce their product than they earn by selling it.
Profit	Profit is the part of a company's income that is left once their costs have been paid—it is the money "made" by a company.

PERSONAL FINANCE

INTEREST

Banks pay interest on the money that savers invest with them (capital), and charge interest on money that is borrowed from them. Interest is given as a percentage, and there are two types, simple and compound.

Simple interest

This is interest paid only on the sum of money that is first saved with the bank. If $10,000 is put in a bank account with an interest rate of 0.03, the amount will increase by the same figure each year.

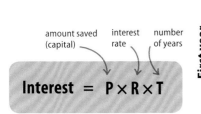

△ **Simple interest formula**
To find the simple interest made in a given year, substitute real values into this formula.

First year

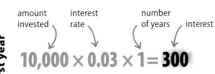

Substitute the values in the formula to work out the value of the interest for the year.

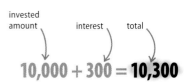

After one year, this is the total amount of money in the saver's bank account.

Second year

Substitute the values in the formula to work out the value of the interest for the year.

After two years the interest is the same as the first year, as it is only paid on the initial investment.

Compound interest

This is where interest is paid on the money invested and any interest that is earned on that money. If $10,000 is paid into a bank account with an interest rate of 0.03, then the amount will increase as follows.

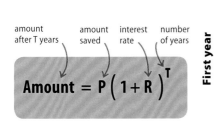

△ **Compound interest formula**
To find the compound interest made in a given year, substitute values into this formula.

First year

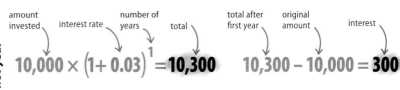

Substitute the values in the formula to work out the total for the first year.

After one year the total interest earned is the same as that earned with simple interest (see above).

Second year

Substitute the values in the formula to work out the total for the second year.

After two years there is a greater increase because interest is also earned on previous interest.

Business Finance

BUSINESSES AIM TO MAKE MONEY, AND MATH PLAYS AN IMPORTANT PART IN ACHIEVING THIS AIM.

The aim of a business is to turn an idea or a product into a profit, so that the business earns more money than it spends.

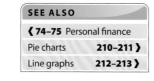

SEE ALSO	
⟨ 74–75 Personal finance	
Pie charts	210–211 ⟩
Line graphs	212–213 ⟩

What a business does

Businesses take raw materials, process them, and sell the end product. To make a profit, the business must sell its end product at a price higher than the total cost of the materials and the manufacturing or production. This example shows the basic stages of this process using a cake-making business.

▷ **Making cakes**
This diagram shows how a cake-making business processes inputs to produce an output.

◁ **Small business**
A business can consist of just one person or a whole team of employees.

1 INPUTS
Inputs are raw materials that are used in making a product. For cake making, the inputs would include the ingredients such as flour, eggs, butter, and sugar.

△ **Costs**
Costs are incurred at the input stage, when the raw materials have to be paid for. The same costs occur every time a new batch of cakes is made.

Revenue and profit

There is an important difference between revenue and profit. Revenue is the money a business makes when it sells its product. Profit is the difference between revenue and cost—it is the money that the business has "made."

profit is money a business "makes"
revenue is earned by selling final product

Profit = Revenue − Costs

costs are incurred in production, for example, wages and rent

some costs are fixed, and the money is spent however much of the product is sold—so costs do not start at 0

▷ **Cost graph**
This graph shows where a business begins to make a profit: where its revenue is greater than its costs.

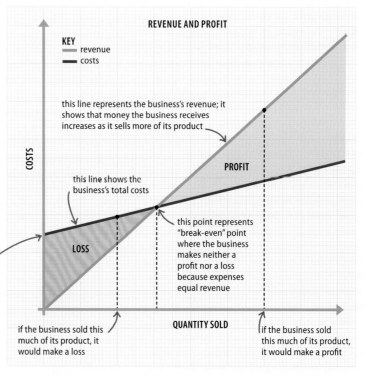

REVENUE AND PROFIT

KEY
— revenue
— costs

this line represents the business's revenue; it shows that money the business receives increases as it sells more of its product

this line shows the business's total costs

PROFIT

this point represents "break-even" point where the business makes neither a profit nor a loss because expenses equal revenue

LOSS

if the business sold this much of its product, it would make a loss

QUANTITY SOLD

if the business sold this much of its product, it would make a profit

BUSINESS FINANCE

2 PROCESSING
Processing occurs when a business takes raw materials and turns them into something else that it can sell at a higher value.

△ **Costs**
Processing costs include rent, wages paid to staff, and the costs of utilities and equipment used for processing. These costs are often ongoing, long-term expenses.

3 OUTPUT
Output is what a business produces at the end of processing, in a form that is sold to customers; for example, the finished cake.

△ **Revenue**
Revenue is the money that is received by the business when it sells its output. It is used to pay off the costs. Once these are paid, the money that is left is profit.

Where the money goes
A business's revenue is not pure profit because it must pay its costs. This pie chart shows an example of where a business's revenue might be spent, and the amount left as profit.

▷ **Costs and profit pie chart**
This pie chart shows some costs that a business might have. Businesses that make different products have different expenses, which reflect the makeup of their products and the efficiency of the business. When all the costs have been paid, the money left is profit.

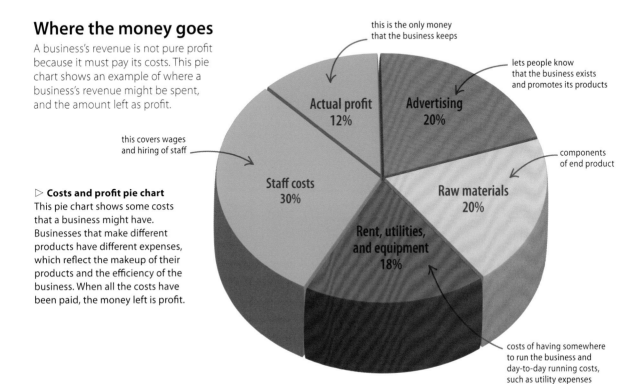

- this is the only money that the business keeps
- lets people know that the business exists and promotes its products
- components of end product
- this covers wages and hiring of staff
- costs of having somewhere to run the business and day-to-day running costs, such as utility expenses

Actual profit 12%
Advertising 20%
Raw materials 20%
Rent, utilities, and equipment 18%
Staff costs 30%

Geometry

What is geometry?

GEOMETRY IS THE BRANCH OF MATHEMATICS CONCERNED WITH LINES, ANGLES, SHAPES, AND SPACE.

Geometry has been important for thousands of years, its practical uses include working out land areas, architecture, navigation, and astronomy. It is also an area of mathematical study in its own right.

Lines, angles, shapes, and space

Geometry includes topics such as lines, angles, shapes (in both two and three dimensions), areas, and volumes, but also subjects like movements in space, such as rotations and reflections, and coordinates.

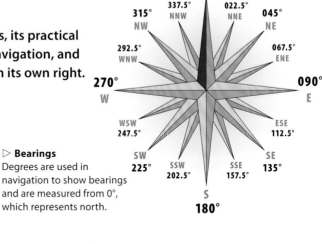

▷ **Bearings**
Degrees are used in navigation to show bearings and are measured from 0°, which represents north.

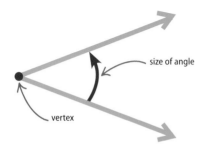

△ **Angles**
An angle is formed when two lines meet at a point. The size of an angle is the amount of turn between the two lines, measured in degrees.

△ **Parallel lines**
Lines that are parallel are the same distance apart along their entire length, and never meet, even if they are extended.

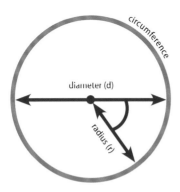

△ **Circle**
A circle is a continuous line that is always the same distance from a central point. The length of the line is the circumference. The diameter runs from one side to the other through the center. The radius runs from the center to the circumference.

REAL WORLD

Geometry in nature

Although many people think of geometry as a purely mathematical subject, geometric shapes and patterns are widespread in the natural world. Perhaps the best-known examples are the hexagonal shapes of honeycomb cells in a beehive and of snowflakes, but there are many other examples of natural geometry. For instance, water droplets, bubbles, and planets are all roughly spherical. Crystals naturally form various polyhedral shapes—common table salt has cubic crystals, and quartz often forms crystals in the shape of a six-sided prism with pyramid shaped ends.

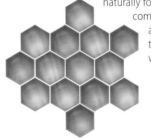

◁ **Honeycomb cells**
Cells of honeycomb are naturally hexagons, which can fit together (tessellate) without leaving any space between them.

WHAT IS GEOMETRY? 81

LOOKING CLOSER
Graphs and geometry

Graphs link geometry with other areas of mathematics. Plotting lines and shapes in graphs with coordinates makes it possible to convert them into algebraic expressions, which can then be manipulated mathematically. The reverse is also true: algebraic expressions can be shown on a graph, enabling them to be manipulated using the rules of geometry. Graphical representations of objects enables positions to be given to them, which makes it possible to apply vectors and calculate the results of movements, such as rotations and translations.

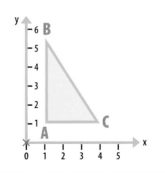

◁ **Graph**
The graph here shows a right triangle, ABC, plotted on a graph. The vertices (corners) have the coordinates A = (1, 1), B = (1, 5.5), and C = (4, 1).

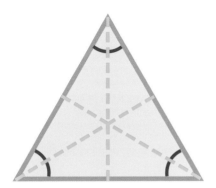

△ **Triangle**
A triangle is a three-sided, two-dimensional polygon. All triangles have three internal angles that add up to 180°.

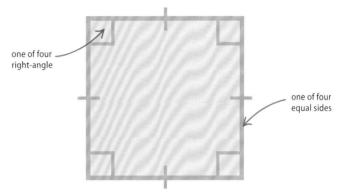

△ **Square**
A square is a four-sided polygon, or quadrilateral, in which all four sides are the same length and all four internal angles are right angles (90°).

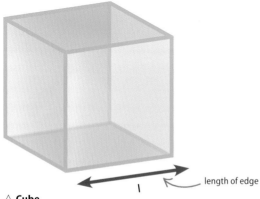

△ **Cube**
A cube is a three-dimensional polygon in which all its edges are the same length. Like other rectangular solids, a cube has 6 faces, 12 edges, and 8 vertices (corners).

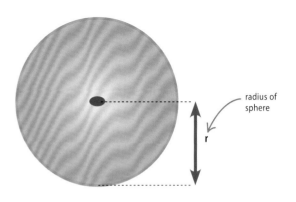

△ **Sphere**
A sphere is a perfectly round three-dimensional shape in which every point on its surface is the same distance from the center; this distance is the radius.

Tools in geometry

MATHEMATICAL INSTRUMENTS ARE NEEDED FOR MEASURING AND DRAWING IN GEOMETRY.

SEE ALSO	
Angles	84–85 ⟩
Constructions	110–113 ⟩
Circles	138–139 ⟩

Tools used in geometry

Tools are vital to measure and construct geometric shapes accurately. The essential tools are a ruler, a compass, and a protractor. A ruler is used for measuring and to draw straight lines. A compass is used to draw a whole circle or a part of a circle (called an arc). A protractor is used to measure and draw angles.

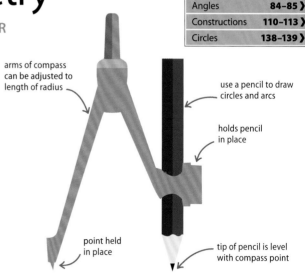

Using a compass

A tool for drawing circles and arcs, a compass is made up of two arms attached at one end. To use a compass, hold the arm that ends in a point still, while pivoting the other arm, which holds a pencil, around it. The point becomes the center of the circle.

▽ Drawing a circle when given the radius
Set the distance between the arms of a compass to the given radius, then draw the circle.

Use a ruler to set the arms of the compass to the given radius.

With the compass set to the radius, hold the point down and drag the pencil around.

▽ Drawing a circle when given its center and one point on the circumference
Put the point of the compass where the center is marked and extend the other arm so that the tip of the pencil touches the point on the circumference. Then, draw the circle.

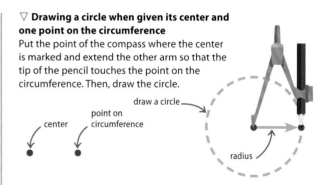

Set the compass to the distance between the two points.

Hold the point of the compass down and draw a circle through the point.

▽ Drawing arcs
Sometimes only a part of a circle—an arc—is required. Arcs are often used as guides to construct other shapes.

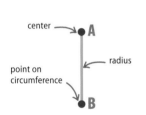

Draw a line and mark the ends with a point—one will be the center of the arc, the other a point on its circumference.

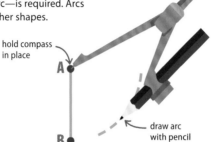

Set the compass to the length of the line—the radius of the arc—and hold it on one of the points to draw the first arc.

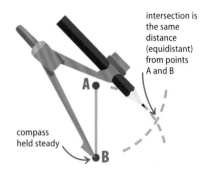

Draw a second arc by holding the point of the compass on the other point. The intersection is equidistant from A and B.

TOOLS IN GEOMETRY

Using a ruler
A ruler can be used to measure straight lines and the distances between any two points. A ruler is also necessary for setting the arms of a compass to a given distance.

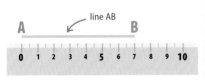

◁ **Measuring lines**
Use a ruler to measure straight lines or the distance between any two given points.

▷ **Drawing lines**
A ruler is also used as a straight edge when drawing lines between two points.

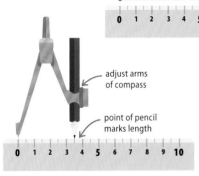

◁ **Setting a compass**
Use a ruler to measure and set the width of a compass to a given radius.

Other tools
Other tools may prove useful when creating drawings and diagrams in geometry.

△ **Set square**
A set square looks like a right triangle and is used for drawing parallel lines. There are two types of set square, one has interior angles 90°, 40° and 45°, the other 90°, 60°, and 30°.

△ **Calculator**
A calculator provides a number of key options for geometry calculations. For example, functions such as Sine can be used to work out the unknown angles of a triangle.

Using a protractor
A protractor is used to measure and draw angles. It is usually made of transparent plastic, which makes it easier to place the center of the protractor over the point of the angle. When measuring an angle, always use the scale starting with zero.

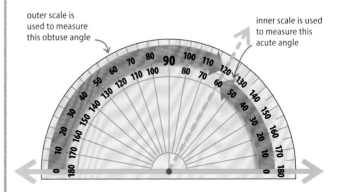

▽ **Measuring angles**
Use a protractor to measure any angle formed by two lines that meet at a point.

Extend the lines if necessary to make reading easier.

Place the protractor over the angle and read the angle measurement, making sure to read up from zero.

The other scale measures the external angle.

▽ **Drawing angles**
When given the size of an angle, use a protractor to measure and draw the angle accurately.

Draw a line and mark a point on it.

Place the protractor on the line with its center over the point. Read the degrees up from zero to mark the point.

Draw a line through the two points, and mark the angle.

 Angles

AN ANGLE IS A FIGURE FORMED BY TWO RAYS THAT SHARE A COMMON ENDPOINT CALLED THE VERTEX.

SEE ALSO	
❰ 82–83 Tools in geometry	
Straight lines	86–87 ❱
Bearings	108–109 ❱

Angles show the amount two lines "turn" as they extend in different directions away from the vertex. This turn is measured in degrees, represented by the symbol °.

Measuring angles

The size of an angle depends on the amount of turn. A whole turn, making one rotation around a circle, is 360°. All other angles are less than 360°.

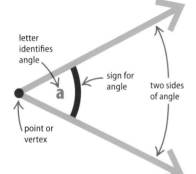

△ **Parts of an angle**
The space between these two rays is the angle. An angle can be named with a letter, its value in degrees, or the symbol ∠.

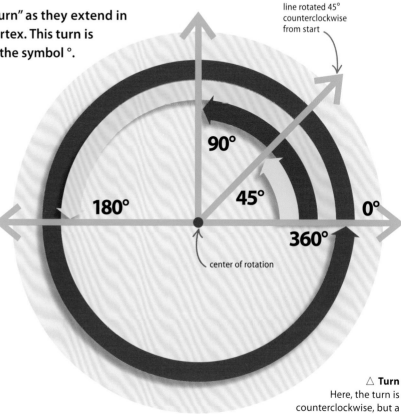

△ **Turn**
Here, the turn is counterclockwise, but a turn can also be clockwise.

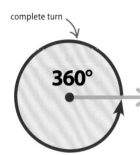

△ **Whole turn**
An angle that is a whole turn is 360°. Such a rotation brings both sides of the angle back to the starting point.

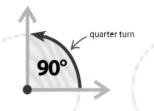

△ **Half turn**
An angle that is a half turn is 180°. Its two sides form a straight line. The angle is also known as a straight angle.

△ **Quarter turn**
An angle that is a quarter turn is 90°. Its two sides are perpendicular (L-shaped). It is also known as a right angle.

△ **Eighth turn**
An angle that is one eighth of a whole turn is 45°. It is half of a right angle, and eight of these angles are a whole turn.

ANGLES **85**

Types of angle
There are four important types of angle, which are shown below. They are named according to their size.

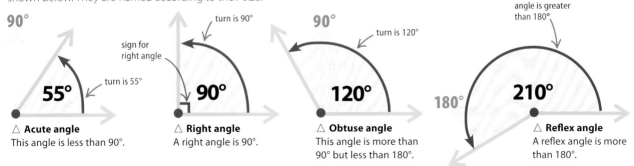

△ **Acute angle**
This angle is less than 90°.

△ **Right angle**
A right angle is 90°.

△ **Obtuse angle**
This angle is more than 90° but less than 180°.

△ **Reflex angle**
A reflex angle is more than 180°.

Naming angles
Angles can have individual names and names that reflect a shared relationship.

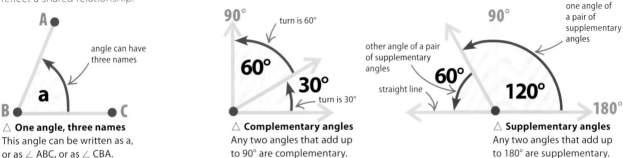

△ **One angle, three names**
This angle can be written as a, or as ∠ ABC, or as ∠ CBA.

△ **Complementary angles**
Any two angles that add up to 90° are complementary.

△ **Supplementary angles**
Any two angles that add up to 180° are supplementary.

Angles on a straight line
The angles on a straight line make up a half turn, so they add up to 180°. In this example, four adjacent angles add up to the 180° of a straight line.

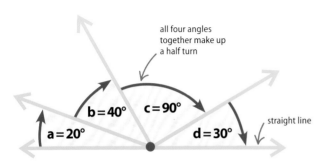

$a + b + c + d = 180°$
$20° + 40° + 90° + 30° = 180°$

Angles at a point
The angles surrounding a point, or vertex, make up a whole turn, so they add up to 360°. In this example, five adjacent angles at the same point add up to the 360° of a complete circle.

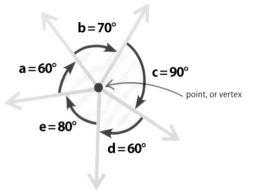

$a + b + c + d + e = 360°$
$60° + 70° + 90° + 60° + 80° = 360°$

Straight lines

A STRAIGHT LINE IS USUALLY JUST CALLED A LINE. IT IS THE SHORTEST DISTANCE BETWEEN TWO POINTS ON A SURFACE OR IN SPACE.

SEE ALSO	
‹ 82–83 Tools in geometry	
‹ 84–85 Angles	
Constructions	110–113 ›

Points, lines, and planes

The most fundamental objects in geometry are points, lines, and planes. A point represents a specific position and has no width, height, or length. A line is one dimensional—it has infinite length extending in two opposite directions. A plane is a two-dimensional flat surface extending in all directions.

△ **Points**
A point is used to represent a precise location. It is represented by a dot and named with a capital letter.

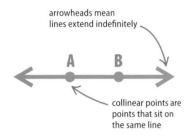

△ **Lines**
A line is represented by a straight line and arrowheads signify that it extends indefinitely in both directions. It can be named by any two points that it passes through—this line is AB.

△ **Line segments**
A line segment has fixed length, so it will have endpoints rather than arrowheads. A line segment is named by its endpoints—this is line segment CD.

△ **Planes**
A plane is usually represented by a two-dimensional figure and labeled with a capital letter. Edges can be drawn, although a plane actually extends indefinitely in all directions.

Sets of lines

Two lines on the same surface, or plane, can either intersect—meaning they share a point—or they can be parallel. If two lines are the same distance apart along their lengths and never intersect, they are parallel.

△ **Nonparallel lines**
Nonparallel lines are not the same distance apart all the way along; if they are extended they will eventually meet in a point.

LOOKING CLOSER
Parallelograms

A parallelogram is a four-sided shape with two pairs of opposite sides, both parallel and of equal length.

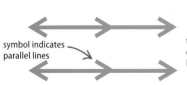

△ **Parallel lines**
Parallel lines are two or more lines that never meet, even if extended. Identical arrows are used to indicate lines that are parallel.

△ **Transversal**
Any line that intersects two or more other lines, each at a different point, is called a transversal.

△ **Parallel sides**
The sides AB and DC are parallel, as are sides BC and AD. The sides AB and BC, and AD and CD are not parallel—shown by the different arrows on these lines.

STRAIGHT LINES

Angles and parallel lines

Angles can be grouped and named according to their relationships with straight lines. When parallel lines are crossed by a transversal, it creates pairs of equal angles—each pair has a different name.

▽ **Labeling angles**
Lines AB and CD are parallel. The angles created by the intersecting transversal line are labeled with lower-case letters.

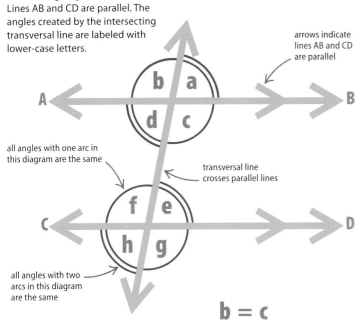

arrows indicate lines AB and CD are parallel

all angles with one arc in this diagram are the same

transversal line crosses parallel lines

all angles with two arcs in this diagram are the same

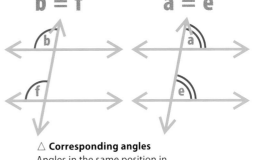

△ **Corresponding angles**
Angles in the same position in relation to the transversal line and one of a pair of parallel lines, are called corresponding angles. These angles are equal.

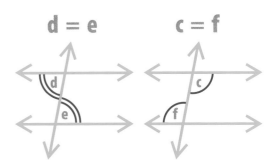

△ **Alternate angles**
Alternate angles are formed on either side of a transversal between parallel lines. These angles are equal.

▷ **Vertical angles**
When two lines cross, equal angles are formed on opposite sides of the point. These angles are known as vertical angles.

b = c

Drawing a parallel line

Drawing a line that is parallel to an existing line requires a pencil, a ruler, and a protractor.

mark position of second line

Draw a straight line with a ruler. Mark a point—this will be the distance of the new, parallel line from the original line.

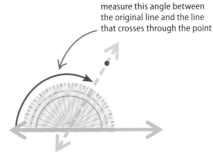

measure this angle between the original line and the line that crosses through the point

Draw a line through the mark, intersecting the original line. This is the transversal. Measure the angle it makes with the original line.

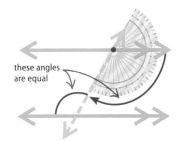

these angles are equal

Measure the same angle from the transversal. Draw the new line through the mark with a ruler; this line is parallel to the original line.

GEOMETRY

Symmetry

THERE ARE TWO TYPES OF SYMMETRY—
REFLECTIVE AND ROTATIONAL.

SEE ALSO
❮ 86–87 Straight lines	
Rotations	100–101 ❯
Reflections	102–103 ❯

▽ **Lines of symmetry**
These are the lines of symmetry for some flat or two-dimensional shapes. Circles have an unlimited number of lines of symmetry.

A shape has symmetry when a line can be drawn that splits the shape exactly into two, or when it can fit into its outline in more than one way.

Reflective symmetry

A flat (two-dimensional) shape has reflective symmetry when each half of the shape on either side of a bisecting line (mirror line) is the mirror image of the other half. This mirror line is called a line of symmetry.

▷ **Isosceles triangle**
This shape is symmetrical across a center line—the sides and angles on either side of the line are equal, and the line cuts the base in half at right angles.

equilateral triangles have three lines of symmetry

an isosceles triangle has a single line of symmetry through its center

◁ **Equilateral triangle**
An equilateral triangle has a line of symmetry through the middle of each side—not just the base.

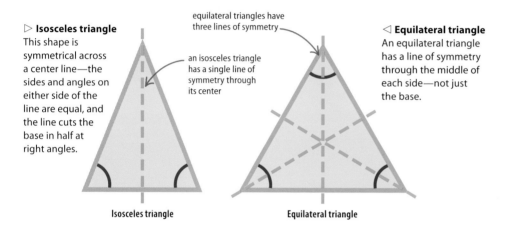

Isosceles triangle   Equilateral triangle

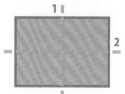
Lines of symmetry of a rectangle

Lines of symmetry of a square

Lines of symmetry of a regular pentagon

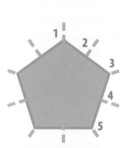

Planes of symmetry

Solid (three-dimensional) shapes can be divided using "walls" known as planes. Solid shapes have reflective symmetry when the two sides of the shape split by a plane are mirror images.

◁ **Rectangle-based pyramid**
A pyramid with a rectangular base and triangles as sides can be divided into mirror images in two ways.

a rectangle-based pyramid has two planes of symmetry

▽ **Cuboid**
Formed by three pairs of rectangles, a cuboid can be divided into two symmetrical shapes in three ways.

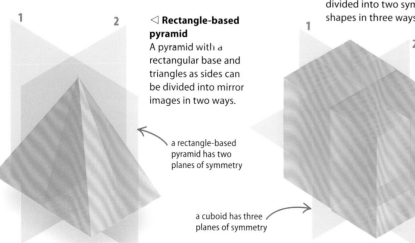

a cuboid has three planes of symmetry

Every line through the middle of a circle is a line of symmetry

Rotational symmetry

A two-dimensional shape has rotational symmetry if it can be rotated about a point, called the center of rotation, and still exactly fit its original outline. The number of ways it fits its outline when rotated is known as its "order" of rotational symmetry.

▷ **Equilateral triangle**
An equilateral triangle has rotational symmetry of order 3—when rotated, it fits its original outline in three different ways.

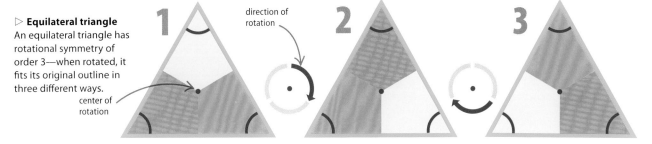

▽ **Square**
A square has rotational symmetry of order 4—when rotated around its center of rotation, it fits its original outline in four different ways.

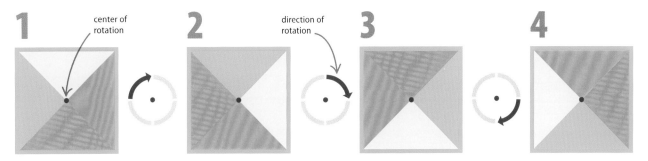

Axes of symmetry

Instead of a single point as the center of rotation, a three-dimensional shape is rotated around a line known as its axis of symmetry. It has rotational symmetry if, when rotated, it fits into its original outline.

▽ **Rectangle-based pyramid**
A rectangle-based pyramid can rotate into two different positions around its axis.

▽ **Cylinder**
A cylinder can rotate into an unlimited number of positions around its vertical axis.

▽ **Cuboid**
A cuboid can rotate into two different positions around each of its three axes.

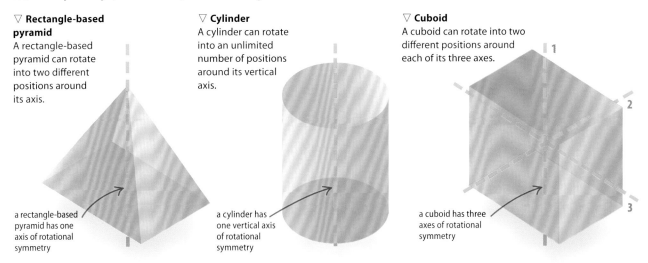

GEOMETRY

 # Coordinates

COORDINATES GIVE THE POSITION OF A PLACE OR POINT ON A MAP OR GRAPH.

SEE ALSO	
Vectors	94–97 ⟩
Linear graphs	182–185 ⟩

Introducing coordinates

Coordinates come in pairs of numbers or letters, or both. They are always written in parentheses separated by a comma. The order in which coordinates are read and written is important. In this example, (E, 1), means five units, or squares on this map, to the right (along the horizontal row) and one square down, or up in some cases (the vertical column).

▽ **City Map**
A grid provides a framework for locating places on a map. Every square is identified by two coordinates. A place is found when the horizontal coordinate meets the vertical coordinate. On this city map, the horizontal coordinates are letters and the vertical coordinates are numbers. On other maps only numbers may be used.

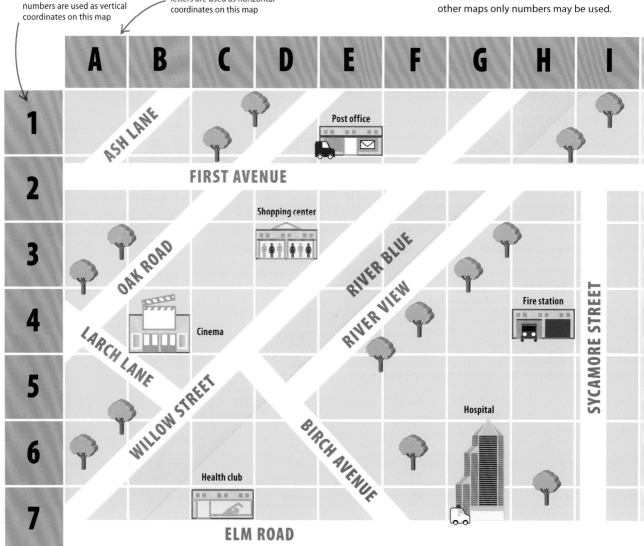

numbers are used as vertical coordinates on this map

letters are used as horizontal coordinates on this map

COORDINATES

Map reading
The horizontal coordinate is always given first and the vertical coordinate second. On the map below, a letter and a number are paired together to form a coordinate.

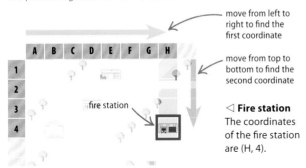

move from left to right to find the first coordinate

move from top to bottom to find the second coordinate

◁ **Fire station**
The coordinates of the fire station are (H, 4).

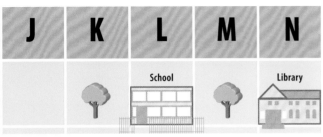

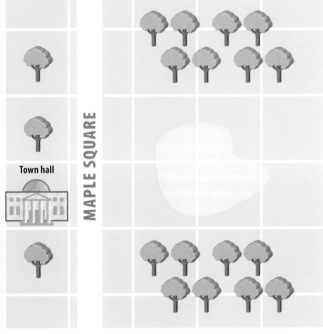

Using coordinates
Each place of interest on this map can be found using the given coordinates. Remember when reading this map to first read across (horizontal) and then down (vertical).

◁ **Cinema**
Find the cinema using coordinates (B, 4). Starting at the second square on the right, move 4 squares down.

◁ **Post office**
The coordinates of the post office are (E, 1). Find the horizontal coordinate E then move down 1 square.

◁ **Town hall**
Find the town hall using coordinates (J, 5). Move 10 squares to the right, then move 5 squares down.

◁ **Health club**
Using the coordinates (C, 7), find the location of the health club. First, find C. Next, find 7 on the vertical column.

◁ **Library**
The coordinates of the library are (N, 1). Find N first then move down 1 square to locate the library.

◁ **Hospital**
The hospital can be found using the coordinates (G, 7). To find the horizontal coordinate of G, move 7 squares to the right. Then go down 7 squares to find the vertical coordinate 7.

◁ **Fire station**
Find the fire station using coordinates (H, 4). Move 8 squares to the right to find H, then move 4 squares down.

◁ **School**
The coordinates of the school are (L, 1). First find L, then move down 1 square to find the school.

◁ **Shopping center**
Using the coordinates (D, 3), find the location of the shopping center. Find D. Next, find 3 on the vertical column.

Graph coordinates

Coordinates are used to identify the positions of points on graphs, in relation to two axes—the y axis is a vertical line, and the x axis is a horizontal line. The coordinates of a point are written as its position on the x axis, followed by its position on the y axis, (x, y).

▷ **Four quadrants**
Coordinates are measured on axes, which cross at a point called the "origin." These axes create four quadrants. There are positive values on the axes above and to the right of the origin, and negative values below and to its left.

the origin
quadrant

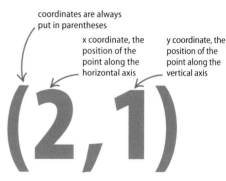

△ **Coordinates of a point**
Coordinates give the position of a point on each axis. The first number gives its position on the x axis, the second its position on the y axis.

Plotting coordinates

Coordinates are plotted on a set of axes. To plot a given point, first read along to its value on the x axis, then read up or down to its value on the y axis. The point is plotted where the two values cross each other.

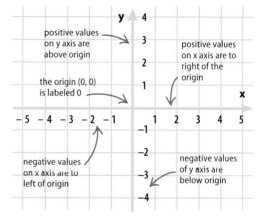

Using graph paper, draw a horizontal line to form the x axis, and a vertical line for the y axis. Number the axes, with the origin separating the positive and negative values.

$$A = (2, 2) \quad B = (-1, -3)$$
$$C = (1, -2) \quad D = (-2, 1)$$

These are four sets of coordinates. Each gives its x value first, followed by its y value. Plot the points on a set of axes.

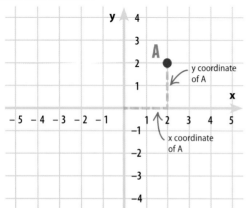

To plot each point, look at its x coordinate (the first number), and read along the x axis from 0 to this number. Then read up or down to its y coordinate (the second number).

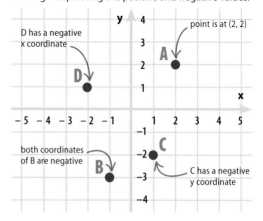

Plot each point in the same way. With negative coordinates, the process is the same, but read to the left instead of right for an x coordinate, and down instead of up for a y coordinate.

Equation of a line

Lines that pass through a set of coordinates on a pair of axes can be expressed as equations. For example, on the line of the equation y = x + 1, any point that lies on the line has a y coordinate that is 1 unit greater than its x coordinate.

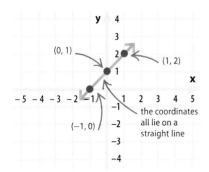

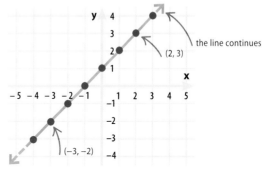

The equation of a line can be found using only a few coordinates. This line passes through the coordinates (−1, 0), (0, 1), and (1, 2), so it is already clear what pattern the points follow.

The graph of the equation is of all the points where the y coordinate is 1 greater than the x coordinate (y = x + 1). This means that the line can be used to find other coordinates that satisfy the equation.

World map

Coordinates are used to mark the position of places on the Earth's surface, using lines of latitude and longitude. These work in the same way as the x and y axes on a graph. The "origin" is the point where the Greenwich Meridian (0 for longitude) crosses the Equator (0 for latitude).

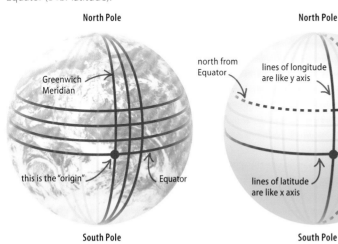

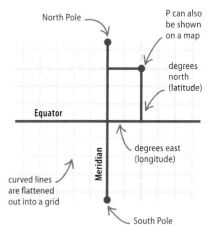

Lines of longitude run from the North Pole to the South Pole. Lines of latitude are at right-angles to lines of longitude. The origin is where the Equator (x axis) crosses the Greenwich Meridian (y axis).

The coordinates of a point such as P are found by finding how many degrees East it is from the Meridian and how many degrees North it is from the Equator.

This is how the surface of the Earth is shown on a map. The lines of latitude and longitude work as axes—the vertical lines show longitude and horizontal lines show latitude.

Vectors

A VECTOR IS A LINE THAT HAS SIZE (MAGNITUDE) AND DIRECTION.

A vector is a way to show a distance in a particular direction. It is often drawn as a line with an arrow on it. The length of the line shows the size of the vector and the arrow gives its direction.

SEE ALSO
⟨ 90–93 Coordinates
Translations 98–99 ⟩
Pythagorean Theorem 128–129 ⟩

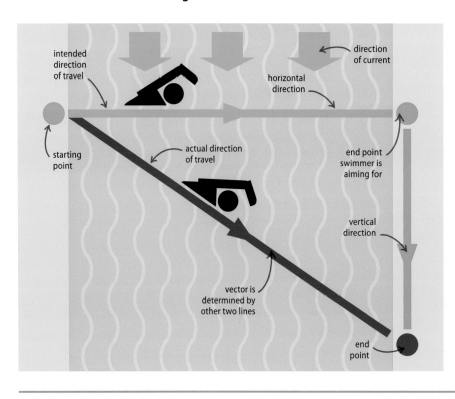

What is a vector?
A vector is a distance in a particular direction. Often, a vector is a diagonal distance, and in these cases it forms the diagonal side (hypotenuse) of a right-angled triangle (see pp.128–129). The other sides of the triangle determine the vector's length and direction. In the example on the left, a swimmer's path is a vector. The other two sides of the triangle are the distance across to the opposite shore from the starting point, and the distance down from the end point that the swimmer was aiming for to the actual end point where the swimmer reaches the shore.

◁ **Vector of a swimmer**
A man sets out to swim to the opposite shore of a river that is 30m wide. A current pushes him as he swims, and he ends up 20m downriver from where he intended. His path is a vector with dimensions 30 across and 20 down.

Expressing vectors
In diagrams, a vector is drawn as a line with an arrow on it, showing its size and direction. There are three different ways of writing vectors using letters and numbers.

v =   A "v" is a general label for a vector, used even when its size is known. It is often used as a label in a diagram.

$\vec{ab}$ **=**   Another way of representing a vector is by giving its start and end points, with an arrow above them to show direction.

$\binom{6}{4}$ **=**   The size and direction of the vector can be shown by giving the horizontal units over the vertical units.

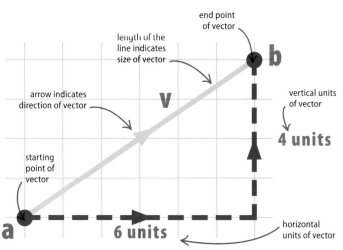

VECTORS

Direction of vectors

The direction of a vector is determined by whether its units are positive or negative. Positive horizontal units mean movement to the right, negative horizontal units mean left; positive vertical units mean movement up, and negative vertical units mean down.

▷ **Movement up and left**
This movement has a vector with negative horizontal units and positive vertical units.

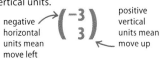

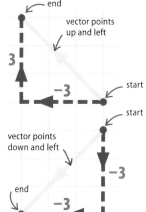
vector points up and left

▷ **Movement up and right**
This movement has a vector with both sets of units positive.

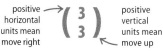

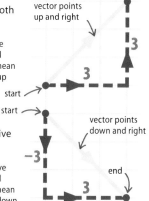
vector points up and right

▷ **Movement down and left**
This movement has a vector with both sets of units negative.

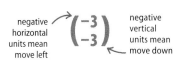

vector points down and left

▷ **Movement down and right**
This movement has a vector with positive horizontal units and negative vertical units.

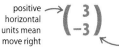

vector points down and right

Equal vectors

Vectors can be identified as equal even if they are in different positions on the same grid, as long as their horizontal and vertical units are equal.

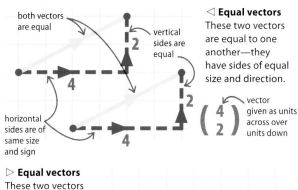

◁ **Equal vectors**
These two vectors are equal to one another—they have sides of equal size and direction.

▷ **Equal vectors**
These two vectors are equal to one another because their horizontal and vertical sides are each the same size and have the same direction.

numerical expression of both vectors

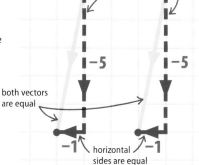

Magnitude of vectors

With diagonal vectors, the vector is the longest side (c) of a right triangle. Use the Pythagorean theorem to find the length of a vector from its vertical (a) and horizontal (b) units.

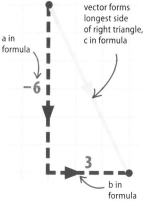

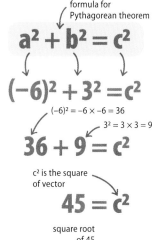

formula for Pythagorean theorem

$$a^2 + b^2 = c^2$$

$$(-6)^2 + 3^2 = c^2$$

$(-6)^2 = -6 \times -6 = 36$
$3^2 = 3 \times 3 = 9$

$$36 + 9 = c^2$$

c^2 is the square of vector

$$45 = c^2$$

square root of 45

c is equal to the square root of 45 → $c = \sqrt{45}$

length of vector → $c = 6.7$

Put the vertical and horizontal units of the vector into the formula.

Find the squares by multiplying each value by itself.

Add the two squares. This total equals c^2 (the square of the vector).

Find the square root of the total value (45) by using a calculator.

The answer is the magnitude (length) of the vector.

Adding and subtracting vectors

Vectors can be added and subtracted in two ways. The first is by using written numbers to add the horizontal and vertical values. The second is by drawing the vectors end to end, then seeing what new vector is created.

▷ **Addition**
Vectors can be added in two different ways. Both methods give the same answer.

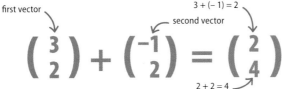

△ **Adding the parts**
To add vectors numerically, add the two top numbers (the horizontal values) and then the two bottom numbers (the vertical values).

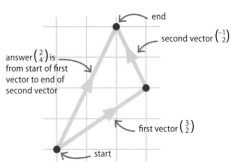

△ **Addition by drawing vectors**
Draw one vector, then draw the second starting from the end point of the first. The answer is the new vector that has been created, from the start of the first vector to the end of the second.

▷ **Subtraction**
Vectors can be subtracted in two different ways. Both methods give the same answer.

$$\begin{pmatrix}3\\2\end{pmatrix} - \begin{pmatrix}-1\\2\end{pmatrix} = \begin{pmatrix}4\\0\end{pmatrix}$$

△ **Subtracting the parts**
To subtract one vector from another, subtract its vertical value from the vertical value of the first vector, then do the same for the horizontal values.

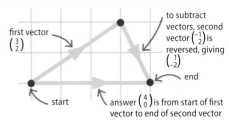

△ **Subtraction by drawing vectors**
Draw the first vector, then draw the second vector reversed, starting from the end point of the first vector. The answer to the subtraction is the vector from the start point to the end point.

Multiplying vectors

Vectors can be multiplied by numbers, but not by other vectors. The direction of a vector stays the same if it is multiplied by a positive number, but is reversed if it is multiplied by a negative number. Vectors can be multiplied by drawing or by using their numerical values.

▽ **Vector a**
Vector a has −4 horizontal units and +2 vertical units. It can be shown as a written vector or a drawn vector, as shown below.

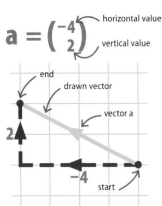

▽ **Vector a multiplied by 2**
To multiply vector a by 2 numerically, multiply both its horizontal and vertical parts by 2. To multiply it by 2 by drawing, simply extend the original vector by the same length again.

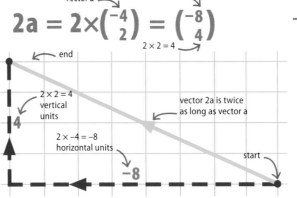

▽ **Vector a multiplied by −½**
To multiply vector a by −½ numerically, multiply each of its parts by −½. To multiply it by −½ by drawing, draw a vector half the length and in the opposite direction of a.

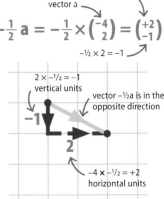

Working with vectors in geometry

Vectors can be used to prove results in geometry. In this example, vectors are used to prove that the line joining the midpoints of any two sides of a triangle is parallel to the third side of the triangle, as well as being half its length.

First, choose 2 sides of triangle ABC, in this example AB and AC. Mark these sides as the vectors a and b. To get from B to C, go along BA and then AC, rather than BC. BA is the vector −a because it is the opposite of AB, and AC is already known (b). This means vector BC is −a + b.

Second, find the midpoints of the two sides that have been chosen (AB and AC). Mark the midpoint of AB as P, and the midpoint of AC as Q. This creates three new vectors: AP, AQ, and PQ. AP is half the length of vector a, and AQ is half the length of vector b.

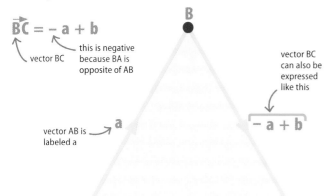

Third, use the vectors ½a and ½b to find the length of vector PQ. To get from P to Q go along PA then AQ. PA is the vector −½a because it is the opposite of AP, and AQ is already known to be ½b. This means vector PQ is −½a + ½b.

Fourth, make the proof. The vectors PQ and BC are in the same direction and are therefore parallel to each other, so the line PQ (which joins the midpoints of the sides AB and AC) must be parallel to the line BC. Also, vector PQ is half the length of vector BC, so the line PQ must be half the length of the line BC.

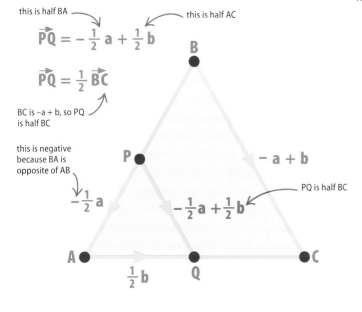

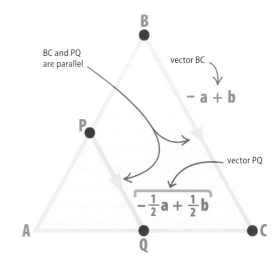

Translations

A TRANSLATION CHANGES THE POSITION OF A SHAPE.

A translation is a type of transformation. It moves an object to a new position. The translated object is called an image, and it is exactly the same size and shape as the original object. Translations are written as vectors.

SEE ALSO	
⟨ 90–93 Coordinates	
⟨ 94–97 Vectors	
Rotations	100–101 ⟩
Reflections	102–103 ⟩
Enlargements	104–105 ⟩

How translations work

A translation moves an object to a new position, without making any other changes—for example to size or shape. Here, the triangle named ABC is translated so that its image is the triangle $A_1B_1C_1$. This translation is named T_1. The triangle $A_1B_1C_1$ is then translated again and its image is the triangle $A_2B_2C_2$. This second translation is named T_2.

triangle ABC is original object before translation

▽ T_1
Translation T_1 moves triangle 6 units horizontally to the right.

▽ T_2
Translation T_2 moves triangle 6 units to right and 2 units upward.

each point on triangle $A_2B_2C_2$ is 6 units right and 2 units up from each point on triangle $A_1B_1C_1$

each point on triangle $A_1B_1C_1$ is 6 units to the right of each point on triangle ABC

T_1 moves triangle ABC 6 units right

T_2 moves triangle $A_1B_1C_1$ 6 units right and 2 units up

Writing translations

Translations are written as vectors. The top number shows the horizontal distance an object moves, while the bottom number shows the vertical distance moved. The two numbers are contained within a set of parentheses. Each translation can be numbered—for example, T_1, T_2, T_3—to make it clear which one is being referred to if more than one translation is shown.

△ **Translation T_1**
To move triangle ABC to position $A_1B_1C_1$, each point moves 6 units horizontally, but does not move vertically. The vector is written as above.

△ **Translation T_2**
To move triangle $A_1B_1C_1$ to position $A_2B_2C_2$ each point moves 6 units horizontally, then moves 2 units vertically. The vector is written as above.

Direction of translations

The numbers used to show a translation's vector are positive or negative, depending on which direction the object moved. If it moves to the right or up, it is positive; to the left or down, it is negative.

▽ **Negative translation**
The rectangle ABCD, moves down and left, so the values in its vector are negative.

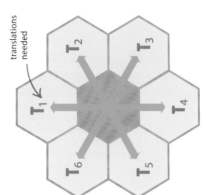

$$T_1 = \begin{pmatrix} -3 \\ -1 \end{pmatrix}$$

▽ **Translation T_1**
The translation T_1 moves rectangle ABCD to the new position $A_1B_1C_1D_1$. It is written as the vector shown—both its parts are negative.

LOOKING CLOSER

Tessellations in action

A tessellation is a pattern created by using shapes to cover a surface without leaving any gaps. Two shapes can be tessellated with themselves using only translation (and no rotation)—the square and the regular hexagon. To tessellate a hexagon using translation requires 6 different translations; to tessellate a square requires 8.

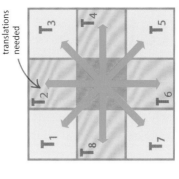

△ **Hexagons**
Each of the hexagons around the outside is a translated image of the central hexagon. The tessellation continues in the same way.

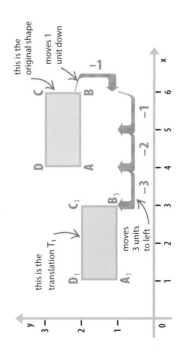

△ **Squares**
Each of the squares around the edge is a translated image of the central square. The tessellation continues in the same way.

Rotations

A ROTATION IS A TYPE OF TRANSFORMATION THAT MOVES AN OBJECT AROUND A GIVEN POINT.

SEE ALSO	
❮ 84–85 Angles	
❮ 90–93 Coordinates	
❮ 98–99 Translations	
Reflections	102–103 ❯
Enlargements	104–105 ❯
Constructions	110–113 ❯

The point around which a rotation occurs is called the center of rotation, and the distance a shape turns is called the angle of rotation.

Properties of a rotation

Rotations occur around a fixed point called the center of rotation, and are measured by angles. Any point on an original object and the corresponding point on its rotated image will be exactly the same distance from the center of rotation. The center of rotation can sit inside, outside, or on the outline of an object. A rotation can be drawn, or the center and angle of an existing rotation found, using a compass, ruler, and protractor.

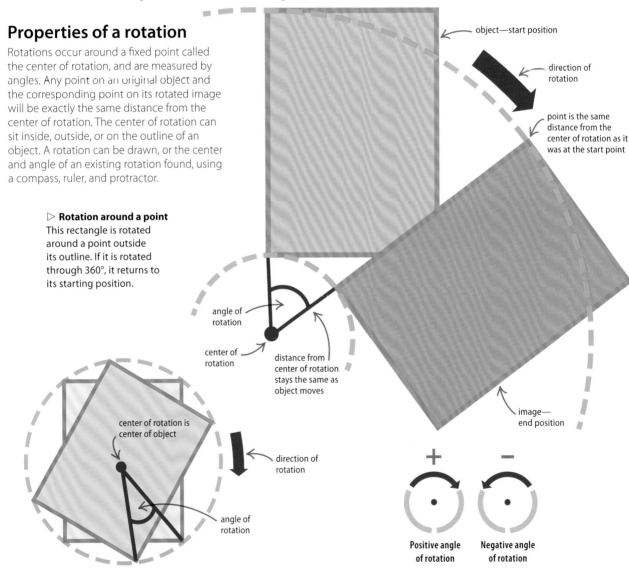

▷ **Rotation around a point**
This rectangle is rotated around a point outside its outline. If it is rotated through 360°, it returns to its starting position.

△ **Rotation around a point inside an object**
An object can be rotated around a point that is inside it rather than outside—this rectangle has been rotated around its center point. It will fit into its outline again if it rotates through 180°.

△ **Angle of rotation**
The angle of rotation is either positive or negative. If it is positive, the object rotates in a clockwise direction; if it is negative, it rotates counterclockwise.

Construction of a rotation

To construct a rotation, three elements of information are needed: the object to be rotated, the location of the center of rotation, and the size of the angle of rotation.

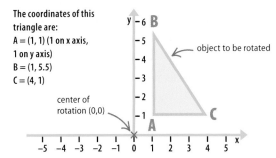

The coordinates of this triangle are:
A = (1, 1) (1 on x axis, 1 on y axis)
B = (1, 5.5)
C = (4, 1)

Given the position of the triangle ABC (see above) and the center of rotation, rotate the triangle −90°, which means 90° counterclockwise. The image of triangle ABC will be on the left-hand side of the y axis.

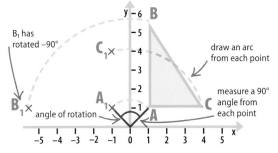

Place a compass point on the center of rotation and draw arcs counterclockwise from points A, B, and C (counterclockwise because the rotation is negative). Then, placing the center of a protractor over the center of rotation, measure an angle of 90° from each point. Mark the point where the angle meets the arc.

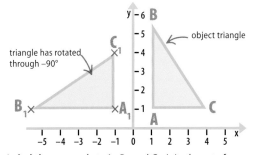

Label the new points A_1, B_1, and C_1. Join them to form the image. Each point on the new triangle $A_1B_1C_1$ has rotated 90° counterclockwise from each point on the original triangle ABC.

Finding the angle and center of a rotation

Given an object and its rotated image, the center and angle of rotation can be found.

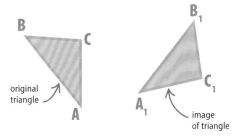

The triangle $A_1B_1C_1$ is the image of triangle ABC after a rotation. The center and angle of rotation can be found by drawing the perpendicular bisectors (lines that cut exactly through the middle—see pp.110–111) of the lines between two sets of points, here A and A_1 and B and B_1.

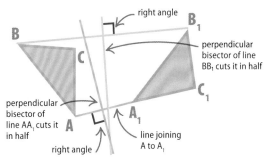

Using a compass and a ruler, construct the perpendicular bisector of the line joining A and A_1 and the perpendicular bisector of the line that joins B and B_1. These bisectors will cross each other.

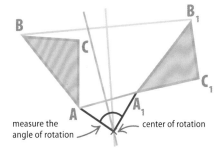

The center of rotation is the point where the two perpendicular bisectors cross. To find the angle of rotation, join A and A_1 to the center of rotation and measure the angle between these lines.

Reflections

A REFLECTION SHOWS AN OBJECT TRANSFORMED INTO ITS MIRROR IMAGE ACROSS AN AXIS OF REFLECTION.

SEE ALSO
‹ 88–89 Symmetry
‹ 90–93 Coordinates
‹ 98–99 Translations
‹ 100–101 Rotations
Enlargements 104–105 ›

Properties of a reflection

Any point on an object (for example, A) and the corresponding point on its reflected image (for example, A_1) are on opposite sides of, and equal distances from, the axis of reflection. The reflected image is effectively a mirror image whose base sits along the axis of reflection.

▽ **Reflected mountain**
The mountain on which the points A, B, C, D, and E are marked has a reflected image, which includes the points A_1, B_1, C_1, D_1, and E_1.

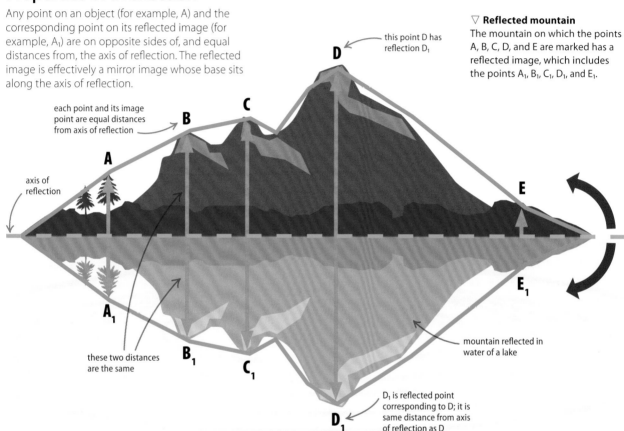

each point and its image point are equal distances from axis of reflection

this point D has reflection D_1

axis of reflection

these two distances are the same

mountain reflected in water of a lake

D_1 is reflected point corresponding to D; it is same distance from axis of reflection as D

LOOKING CLOSER

Kaleidoscopes

A kaleidoscope creates patterns using mirrors and colored beads. The patterns are the result of beads being reflected and then reflected again.

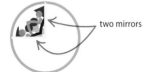

two mirrors

A simple kaleidoscope contains two mirrors at right angles (90°) to each other and some colored beads.

this is one reflection of the original beads

The beads are reflected in the two mirrors, producing two reflected images on either side.

the final reflection, which completes image

Each of the two reflections is reflected again, producing another image of the beads.

REFLECTIONS

Constructing a reflection

To construct the reflection of an object it is necessary to know the position of the axis of reflection and the position of the object. Each point on the reflection will be the same distance from the axis of reflection as its corresponding point on the original. Here, the reflection of triangle ABC is drawn for the axis of reflection $y = x$ (which means that each point on the axis has the same x and y coordinates).

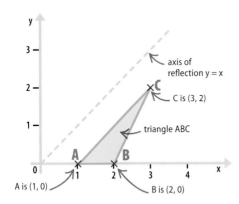

▷ **First, draw the axis of reflection.** As $y = x$, this axis line crosses through the points (0, 0), (1, 1), (2, 2), (3, 3), and so on. Then draw in the object that is to be reflected—the triangle ABC, which has the coordinates (1, 0), (2, 0), and (3, 2). In each set of coordinates, the first number is the x value, and the second number is the y value.

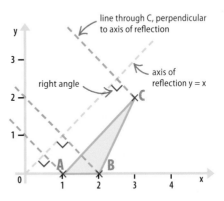

▷ **Second, draw lines** from each point of the triangle ABC that are at right-angles (90°) to the axis of reflection. These lines should cross the axis of reflection and continue onward, as the new coordinates for the reflected image will be measured along them.

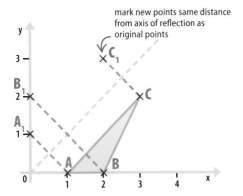

▷ **Third, measure the distance** from each of the original points to the axis of reflection, then measure the same distance on the other side of the axis to find the positions of the new points. Mark each of the new points with the letter it reflects, followed by a small 1, for example A_1.

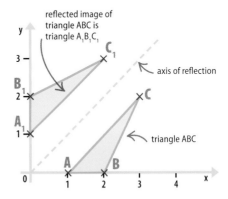

▷ **Finally, join the points** A_1, B_1, and C_1 to complete the image. Each of the points of the triangle has a mirror image across the axis of reflection. Each point on the original triangle is an equal distance from the axis of reflection as its reflected point.

Enlargements

AN ENLARGEMENT IS A TRANSFORMATION OF AN OBJECT THAT PRODUCES AN IMAGE OF THE SAME SHAPE BUT OF DIFFERENT SIZE.

SEE ALSO
⟨ 56–59 Ratio and proportion
⟨ 98–99 Translations
⟨ 100–101 Rotations
⟨ 102–103 Reflections

Enlargements are constructed through a fixed point known as the centre of enlargement. The image can be larger or smaller. The change in size is determined by a number called the scale factor.

Properties of an enlargement

When an object is transformed into a larger image, the relationship between the corresponding sides of that object and the image is the same as the scale factor. For example, if the scale factor is 5, the sides of the image are 5 times bigger than those of the original.

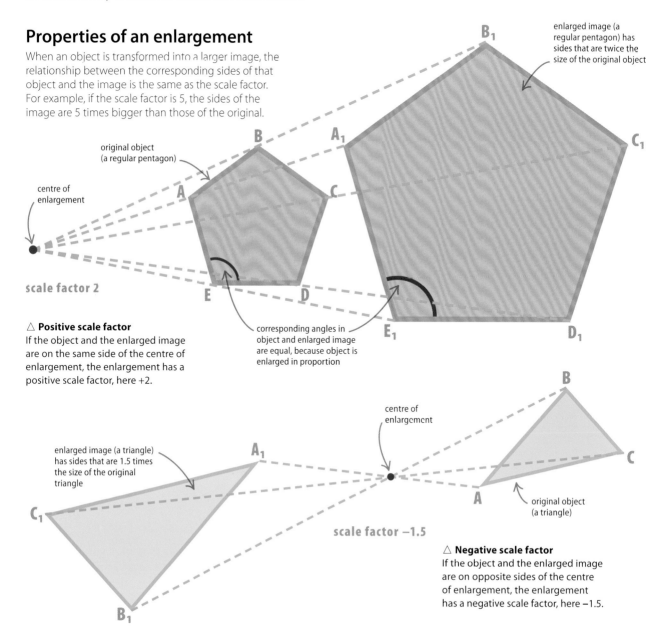

△ **Positive scale factor**
If the object and the enlarged image are on the same side of the centre of enlargement, the enlargement has a positive scale factor, here +2.

△ **Negative scale factor**
If the object and the enlarged image are on opposite sides of the centre of enlargement, the enlargement has a negative scale factor, here −1.5.

Constructing an enlargement

An enlargement is constructed by plotting the coordinates of the object on squared (or graph) paper. Here, the quadrilateral ABCD is measured through the centre of enlargement (0, 0) with a given scale factor of 2.5.

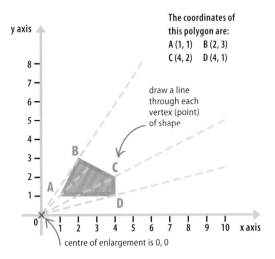

The coordinates of this polygon are:
A (1, 1)   B (2, 3)
C (4, 2)   D (4, 1)

▶ **Draw the polygon** ABCD using the given coordinates. Mark the centre of enlargement and draw lines from this point through each of the vertices of the shape (points where sides meet).

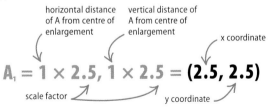

$$A_1 = 1 \times 2.5,\ 1 \times 2.5 = (2.5,\ 2.5)$$

(horizontal distance of A from centre of enlargement × scale factor, vertical distance of A from centre of enlargement × scale factor = x coordinate, y coordinate)

The same principle is then applied to the other points, to work out their x and y coordinates.

$$B_1 = 2 \times 2.5,\ 3 \times 2.5 = (5,\ 7.5)$$

$$C_1 = 4 \times 2.5,\ 2 \times 2.5 = (10,\ 5)$$

$$D_1 = 4 \times 2.5,\ 1 \times 2.5 = (10,\ 2.5)$$

▶ **Then, calculate the positions** of A_1, B_1, C_1, and D_1 by multiplying the horizontal and vertical distances of each point from the centre of enlargement (0, 0) by the scale factor 2.5.

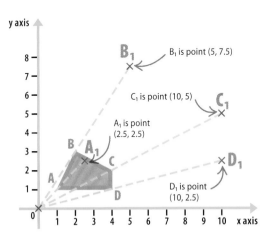

▶ **Read along the x axis and the y axis** to plot the vertices (points) of the enlarged image. For example, B_1 is point (5, 7.5) and C_1 is point (10, 5). Mark and label all the points A_1, B_1, C_1, and D_1.

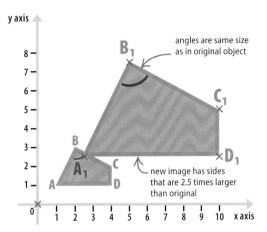

▶ **Join the new coordinates** to complete the enlargement. The enlarged image is a quadrilateral with sides that are 2.5 times larger than the original object, but with angles of exactly the same size.

Scale drawings

A SCALE DRAWING SHOWS AN OBJECT ACCURATELY AT A PRACTICAL SIZE BY REDUCING OR ENLARGING IT.

Scale drawings can be scaled down, such as a map, or scaled up, such as a diagram of a microchip.

SEE ALSO
‹ 56–59 Ratio and proportion
‹ 104–105 Enlargements
Circles 138–139 ›

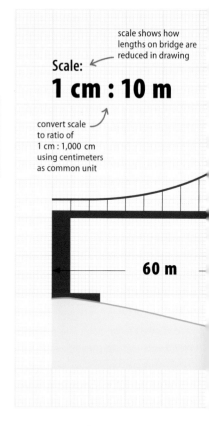

scale shows how lengths on bridge are reduced in drawing
Scale:
1 cm : 10 m
convert scale to ratio of 1 cm : 1,000 cm using centimeters as common unit
60 m

Choosing a scale
To make an accurate plan of a large object, such as a bridge, the object's measurements need to be scaled down. To do this, every measurement of the bridge is reduced by the same ratio. The first step in creating a scale drawing is to choose a scale—for example, 1 cm for each 10 m. The scale is then shown as a ratio, using the smallest common unit.

length (in cm) on scale drawing
length (in cm) of real length

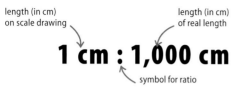

1 cm : 1,000 cm

symbol for ratio

◁ **Scale as a ratio**
A scale of 1 cm to 10 m can be shown as a ratio by using centimeters as a common unit. There are 100 cm in a meter, so 10 × 100 cm = 1,000 cm.

How to make a scale drawing
In this example, a basketball court needs to be drawn to scale. The court is 30 m long and 15 m wide. In its center is a circle with a radius of 1 m, and at either end a semicircle, each with a radius of 5 m. To make a scale drawing, first make a rough sketch, noting the real measurements. Next, work out a scale. Use the scale to convert the measurements, and create the final drawing using these.

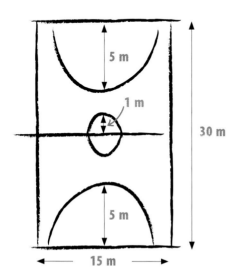

Draw a rough sketch to act as a guide, marking on it the real measurements. Make a note of the longest length (30 m). Based on this and the space available for your drawing, work out a suitable scale.

Since 30 m (the longest length in the drawing) needs to fit into a space of less than 10 cm, a convenient scale is chosen:

measurement on drawing **1 cm : 5 m** measurement on real court

By converting this to a ratio of 1 cm : 500 cm, it is now possible to work out the measurements that will be used in the drawing.

real measurements changed from meters to centimeters to make calculation easier
scale
length for drawing

length of court = 3,000 cm ÷ 500 = **6 cm**
width of court = 1,500 cm ÷ 500 = **3 cm**
radius of center circle = 100 cm ÷ 500 = **0.2 cm**
radius of semicircle = 500 cm ÷ 500 = **1 cm**

Choose a suitable scale and convert it into a ratio by using the lowest common unit, centimeters. Next, convert the real measurements into the same units. Divide each measurement by the scale to find the measurements for the drawing.

SCALE DRAWINGS 107

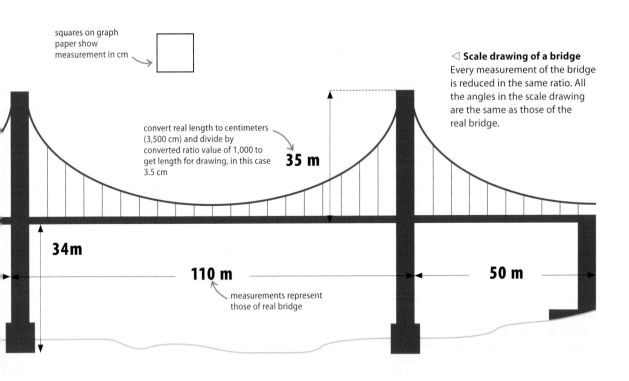

squares on graph paper show measurement in cm

◁ **Scale drawing of a bridge**
Every measurement of the bridge is reduced in the same ratio. All the angles in the scale drawing are the same as those of the real bridge.

convert real length to centimeters (3,500 cm) and divide by converted ratio value of 1,000 to get length for drawing, in this case 3.5 cm

35 m

34 m

110 m

50 m

measurements represent those of real bridge

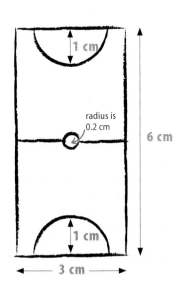

Make a second rough sketch, this time marking on the scaled measurements. This provides a guide for the final drawing.

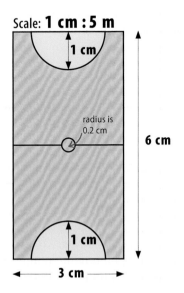

Scale: **1 cm : 5 m**

Construct a final, accurate scale drawing of the basketball court. Use a ruler to draw the lines, and a compass to draw the circle and semicircles.

REAL WORLD
Maps

The scale of a map varies according to the area it covers. To see a whole country such as France a scale of 1 cm : 150 km might be used. To see a town, a scale of 1 cm : 500 m is suitable.

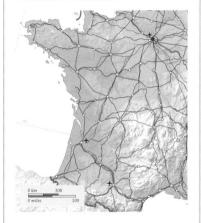

Bearings

A BEARING IS A WAY OF SHOWING A DIRECTION.

Bearings show accurate directions. They can be used to plot journeys through unfamiliar territory, where it is vital to be exact.

What are bearings?

Bearings are angles measured clockwise from the compass direction north. They are usually given as three-digit whole numbers of degrees, such as 270°, but they can also use decimal numbers, such as with 247.5°. Compass directions are given in terms such as "WSW," or "west-southwest."

SEE ALSO
< 82–83 Tools in geometry
< 84–85 Angles
< 106–107 Scale drawings

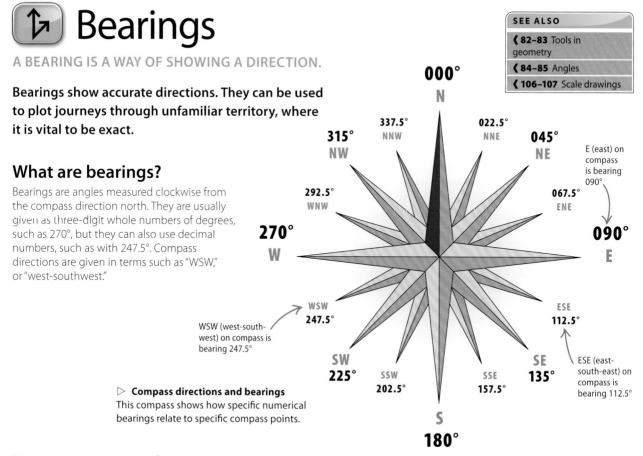

▷ **Compass directions and bearings**
This compass shows how specific numerical bearings relate to specific compass points.

How to measure a bearing

Begin by deciding on the starting point of the journey. Place a protractor at this start or center point. Use the protractor to draw the angle of the bearing clockwise from the compass direction north.

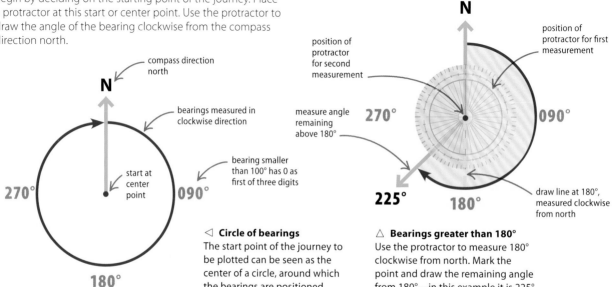

◁ **Circle of bearings**
The start point of the journey to be plotted can be seen as the center of a circle, around which the bearings are positioned.

△ **Bearings greater than 180°**
Use the protractor to measure 180° clockwise from north. Mark the point and draw the remaining angle from 180°—in this example it is 225°.

BEARINGS

Plotting a journey with bearings

Bearings are used to plot journeys of several direction changes. In this example, a plane flies on the bearing 290° for 300 mi, then turns to the bearing 045° for 200 mi. Plot its last leg back to the start, using a scale of 1 in for 100 mi.

SCALE
1 in : 100 mi

▷ **First, draw the bearing 290°.** Set the protractor at the center and draw 180°. Draw a further 110°, giving a total of 290°.

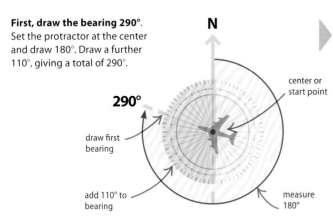

290°
draw first bearing
add 110° to bearing
center or start point
measure 180°

▷ **Second, work out** the distance traveled on the bearing 290°. Using the scale, the distance is 3 in, because 1 in equals 100 mi.

mark first part of flight
3 in
start point
actual distance
distance on scale drawing

300 ÷ 100 = 3 in

▷ **Set the protractor** at the end point of the 3 in and draw a new north line. The next bearing is 045° from this north.

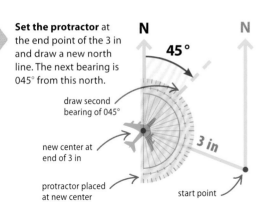

45°
draw second bearing of 045°
new center at end of 3 in
protractor placed at new center
3 in
start point

▷ **Work out the** distance traveled on the bearing 045°. Using the scale of 1 in for every 100 mi, the distance is 200 mi.

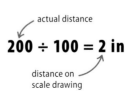

actual distance

200 ÷ 100 = 2 in

distance on scale drawing

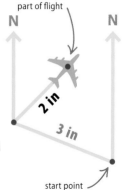

mark second part of flight
2 in
3 in
start point

▷ **Set the protractor** at the end point of the 2 in and draw a new north line. The next bearing is found to be 150° from this latest north. This direction takes the plane back to the start point.

x = 150°

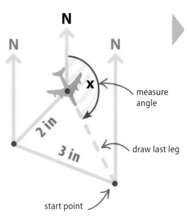

x
measure angle
2 in
3 in
draw last leg
start point

▷ **Finally, draw the** distance traveled on the bearing 150°. Using the scale, the distance is 2.8 in, meaning the final leg of the journey is 280 mi.

y = 2.8 in

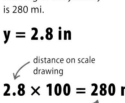

distance on scale drawing

2.8 × 100 = 280 mi

actual distance of last leg of journey

2 in
y
3 in
return to start point

Constructions

MAKING PERPENDICULAR LINES AND ANGLES USING A COMPASS AND A STRAIGHT EDGE.

SEE ALSO	
‹ 82–83 Tools in geometry	
‹ 84–85 Angles	
Triangles	116–117 ›
Congruent triangles	120–121 ›

An accurate geometric drawing is called a construction.
These drawings can include line segments, angles, and shapes.
The tools needed are a compass and a straight edge.

Constructing perpendicular lines

Two line segments are perpendicular when they intersect (or cross) at 90°, or right angles. There are two ways to construct a perpendicular line—the first is to draw through a point marked on a given line segment; the second is to use a point above or below the segment.

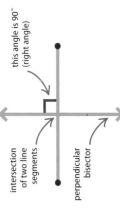

▷ **Perpendicular bisector**
A perpendicular bisector cuts another line segment exactly in half, crossing through its midpoint at right angles, or 90°.

Using a point on the line segment

A perpendicular line can be constructed using a point marked on a line segment. The point marked is where the two lines will intersect (cross) at right angles.

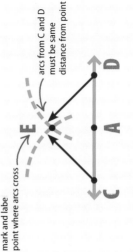

▲ **Draw a line segment** and mark a point or the segment with a letter, for example, A. Place the point of a compass on point A, and draw two arcs of the same distance from this point.

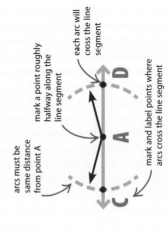

▲ **Place the point of a compass** on point C, and draw an arc above the line segment. Do the same from point D. The arcs intersect (cross) at a point, label this point E.

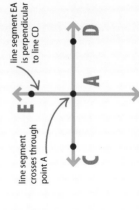

▲ **Now, draw a line segment** from E through A. This line segment is perpendicular (at right angles) to the original one.

Using a point above the line

Perpendicular lines can be constructed by marking a point above the first line segment, through which the second, perpendicular, one will pass.

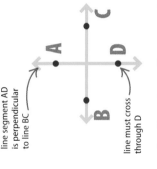

Draw a line segment and mark a point above it. Label this point with a letter, for example, A.

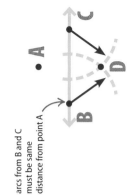

Place a compass on point A. Draw two arcs that intersect the line segment at two points. Label these points B and C.

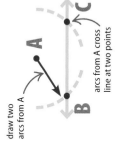

With the compass on points B and C, draw two arcs of the same length beneath the line segment. Label the intersection of the two arcs point D.

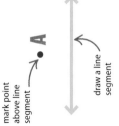

▶ **Now, draw a line segment** from points A to D. This is perpendicular (at right angles) to line segment BC.

Constructing a perpendicular bisector

A line that passes exactly through the midpoint of a line segment at right angles, or 90°, is called a perpendicular bisector. It can be constructed by marking points above and below the line segment.

First, draw a line segment, and label each end point, for example P and Q.

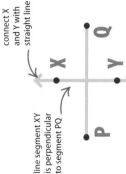

Place a compass on point P and draw an arc with a distance just over half the length of line segment PQ.

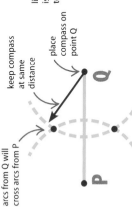

Draw another arc from point Q with the compass kept at the same length. This arc will intersect the first arc at two points.

▶ **Label the points** where the arcs intersect X and Y. Draw a line connecting X and Y; this is the perpendicular bisector of PQ.

Bisecting an angle

The bisector of an angle is a straight line that intersects the vertex (point) of the angle, splitting it into two equal parts. This line can be constructed by using a compass to mark points on the sides of the angle.

▷ **An angle bisector**
The interior bisector of an angle intersects the vertex and divides the angle into two equal parts.

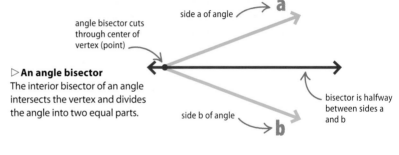

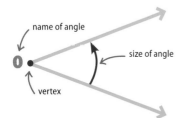

First, draw an angle of any size. Label the vertex of this angle with a letter, for example, o.

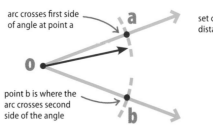

Draw an arc by placing the point of a compass on the vertex. Mark the points at which the arc intersects the angle's sides and label them a and b.

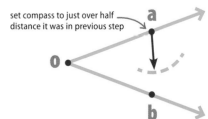

Place the compass on point a and draw an arc in the space between the angle's sides.

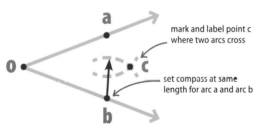

Keep the compass set at the same length and place it on point b, and draw another arc, and then on point a. The two arcs intersect at a point, c.

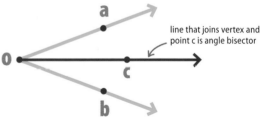

Draw a line from the vertex, o, through point c—this is the angle bisector. The angle is now split into two equal parts.

LOOKING CLOSER

Congruent triangles

Triangles are congruent if all their sides and interior angles are equal. The points that are marked when drawing an angle bisector create two congruent triangles —one above the bisector and one below.

▷ **Constructing triangles**
By connecting the points made after drawing a bisecting line through an angle, two congruent triangles are formed.

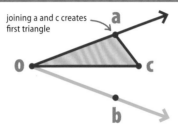

Draw a line from a to c, to make the first triangle, which is shaded red here.

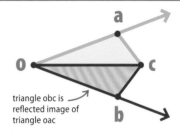

Now, draw a line from b to c to construct the second triangle—shaded red here.

Constructing 90° and 45° angles

Bisecting an angle can be used to construct some common angles without using a protractor, for example a right angle (90°) and a 45° angle.

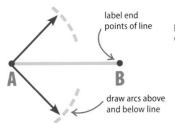

▶ **Draw a straight line** (AB). Place a compass on point A, set it to a distance just over half of the line's length, and draw an arc above and below the line.

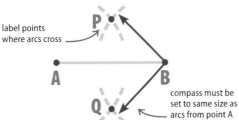

▶ **Then, draw two arcs** with the compass set to the same length and placed on point B. Label the points where the arcs cross each other P and Q.

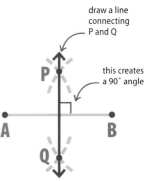

▶ **Draw a line** from point P to point Q. This is a perpendicular bisector of the original line and it creates four 90° angles.

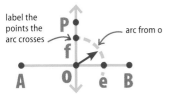

▶ **Draw an arc** from point o that crosses two lines on either side, this creates a 45° angle. Label the two points where the arc intersects the lines, f and e.

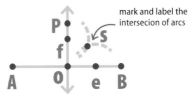

▶ **Keep the compass** at the same length as the last arc and draw arcs from points f and e. Label the intersection of these arcs with a letter (s).

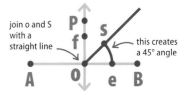

▶ **Draw a line** from point o through s. This line is the angle bisector. The 90° angle is now split into two 45° angles.

Constructing 60° angles

An equilateral triangle, which has three equal sides and three 60° angles, can be constructed without a protractor.

▶ **Draw a line,** which will form one arm of the first angle. Here the line is 2.5 cm long, but it can be any length. Mark each end of the line with a letter.

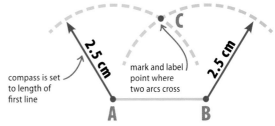

▶ **Now, set the compass** to the same length as the first line. Draw an arc from point A, then another from point B. Mark the point where the two arcs cross, C.

▶ **Now, draw a line** to connect points A and C. Line AC is the same length as line AB. A 60° angle has been created.

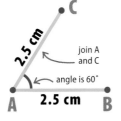

▶ **Construct an equilateral triangle** by drawing a third line from B to C. Each side of the triangle is equal and each internal angle of the triangle is 60°.

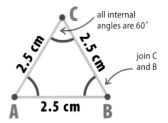

Loci

A LOCUS (PLURAL LOCI) IS THE PATH FOLLOWED BY A POINT THAT ADHERES TO A GIVEN RULE WHEN IT MOVES.

SEE ALSO
❰ 82–83 Tools in geometry
❰ 106–107 Scale drawings
❰ 110–113 Constructions

What is a locus?

Many familiar shapes, such as circles and straight lines, are examples of loci because they are paths of points that conform to specific conditions. Loci can also produce more complicated shapes. They are often used to solve practical problems, for example pinpointing an exact location.

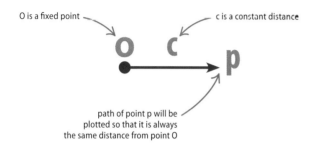

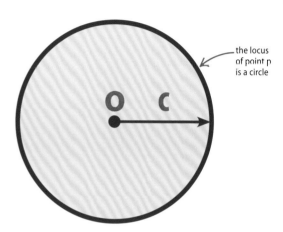

▷ **A compass and a pencil** are needed to construct this locus. The point of the compass is held in the fixed point, O. The arms of the compass are spread so that the distance between its arms is the constant distance, c.

▷ **The shape drawn** when turning the compass a full rotation reveals that the locus is a circle. The center of the circle is O, and the radius is the fixed distance between the compass point and the pencil (c).

Working with loci

To draw a locus it is necessary to find all the points that conform to the rule that has been specified. This will require a compass, a pencil, and a ruler. This example shows how to find the locus of a point that moves so that its distance from a fixed line AB is always the same.

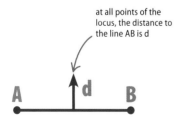

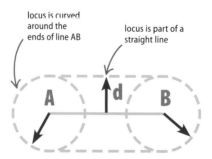

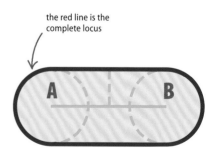

▷ **Draw the line segment AB.** A and B are fixed points. Now, plot the distance of d from the line AB.

▷ **Between points A and B**, the locus is a straight line. At the end of these lines, the locus is a semicircle. Use a compass to draw these.

▷ **This is the completed locus.** It has the shape of a typical athletics track.

LOOKING CLOSER
Spiral locus

Loci can follow more complex paths. The example below follows the path of a piece of string that is wound around a cylinder, creating a spiral locus.

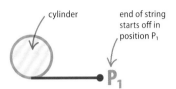

The string starts off lying flat, with point P_1 the position of the end of the string.

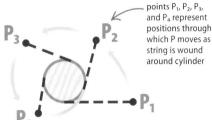

As the string is wound around the cylinder, the end of the string moves closer to the surface of the cylinder.

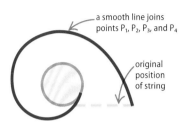

When the path of point P is plotted, it forms a spiral locus.

Using loci

Loci can be used to solve difficult problems. Suppose two radio stations, A and B, share the same frequency, but are 200 km apart. The range of their transmitters is 150 km. The area where the ranges of the two transmitters overlap, or interference, can be found by showing the locus of each transmitter and using a scale drawing (see pp.106–107).

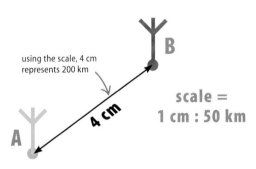

To find the area of interference, first choose a scale, then draw the reach of each transmitter. An appropriate scale for this example is 1 cm : 50 km.

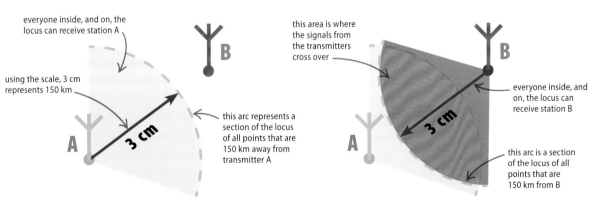

▶ **Construct the reception area** for radio station A. Draw the locus of a point that is always 150 km from station A. The scale gives 150 km = 3 cm, so draw an arc with a radius of 3cm, with A as the center.

▶ **Construct the reception area** for radio station B. This time draw an arc with the compass set to 3cm, with B as the center. The interference occurs in the area where the two paths overlap.

Triangles

A TRIANGLE IS A POLYGON WITH THREE ANGLES AND THREE SIDES.

A triangle has three sides and three interior angles. A vertex (plural vertices) is the point where two sides of a triangle meet. A triangle has three vertices.

SEE ALSO
❮ 84–85 Angles
❮ 86–87 Straight lines
Constructing triangles 118–119 ❯
Polygons 134–137 ❯

Introducing triangles

A triangle is a three-sided polygon. The base of a triangle can be any one of its three sides, but it is usually the bottom one. The longest side of a triangle is opposite the largest angle. The shortest side of a triangle is opposite the smallest angle. The three interior angles of a triangle add up to 180°.

△ **Labeling a triangle**
A capital letter is used to identify each vertex. A triangle with vertices A, B, and C is known as △ABC. The symbol "△" can be used to represent the word triangle.

vertex the point where two sides meet

perimeter the length of the outside frame

side one of three sides

angle the amount of turn between two straight lines about a fixed point

base side on which a triangle "rests"

Types of triangles

There are several types of triangles, each with specific features, or properties. A triangle is classified according to the length of its sides or the size of its angles.

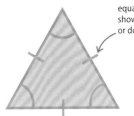

equal sides are shown by a dash or double dash

◁ **Equilateral triangle**
A triangle with three equal sides and three equal angles, each of which measures 60°.

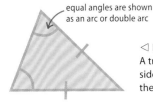

equal angles are shown as an arc or double arc

◁ **Isosceles triangle**
A triangle with two equal sides. The angles opposite these sides are also equal.

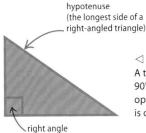

hypotenuse (the longest side of a right-angled triangle)

◁ **Right triangle**
A triangle with an angle of 90° (a right angle). The side opposite the right angle is called the hypotenuse.

right angle

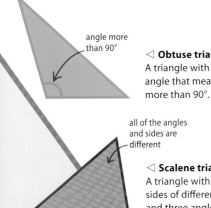

angle more than 90°

◁ **Obtuse triangle**
A triangle with one angle that measures more than 90°.

all of the angles and sides are different

◁ **Scalene triangle**
A triangle with three sides of different length, and three angles of different size.

Interior angles of a triangle

A triangle has three interior angles at the points where each side meets. These angles always add up to 180°. If rearranged and placed together on a straight line, the interior angles would still add up to 180°, because a straight angle always measures 180°.

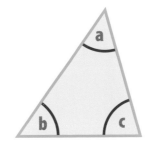

Proving that the angle sum of a triangle is 180°

Adding a parallel line produces two types of relationships between angles that help prove that the interior sum of a triangle is 180°.

Draw a triangle, then add a line parallel to one side of the triangle, starting at its base, to create two new angles.

▷ **Corresponding angles** are equal and alternate angles are equal; angles c, a, and b sit on a straight line so together add up to 180°.

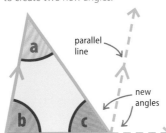

parallel line

new angles

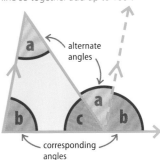

alternate angles

corresponding angles

Exterior angles of a triangle

In addition to having three interior angles a triangle also has three exterior angles. Exterior angles are found by extending each side of a triangle. The exterior angles of any triangle add up to 360°.

$$x + y + z = 360°$$

each exterior angle of a triangle is equal to the sum of the two opposite interior angles, so y = p + q

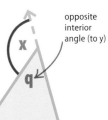

opposite interior angle (to y)

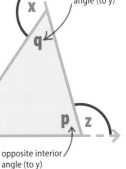

opposite interior angle (to y)

Constructing triangles

DRAWING (CONSTRUCTING) TRIANGLES REQUIRES A COMPASS, A RULER, AND A PROTRACTOR.

SEE ALSO
‹ 82–83 Tools in geometry
‹ 110–113 Constructions
‹ 114–115 Loci

To construct a triangle, not all the measurements for its sides and angles are required, as long as some of the measurements are known in the right combination.

What is needed?

A triangle can be constructed from just a few of its measurements, using a combination of the tools mentioned above, and its unknown measurements can be found from the result. A triangle can be constructed when the measurements of all three sides (SSS) are known, when two angles and the side in between are known (ASA), or when two sides and the angle between them are known (SAS). In addition, knowing either the SSS, the ASA, or the SAS measurements of two triangles will reveal whether they are the same size (congruent)—if the measurements are equal, the triangles are congruent.

REAL WORLD
Using triangles for 3-D graphics

3-D graphics are common in films, computer games, and the internet. What may be surprising is that they are created using triangles. An object is drawn as a series of basic shapes, which are then divided into triangles. When the shape of the triangles is changed, the object appears to move. Each triangle is colored to bring the object to life.

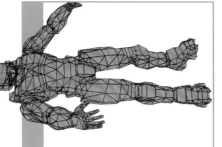

▷ **Computer animation**
To create movement, a computer calculates the new shape of millions of shapes.

Constructing a triangle when three sides are known (SSS)

If the measurements of the three sides are given, for example, **5 cm**, **4 cm**, and **3 cm**, it is possible to construct a triangle using a ruler and a compass, following the steps below.

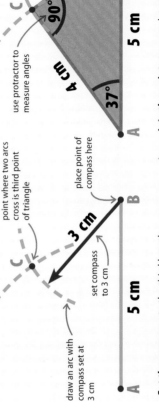

Draw the baseline, using the longest length. Label the ends A and B. Set the compass to the second length, 4 cm. Place the point of the compass on A and draw an arc.

Set the compass to the third length, 3 cm. Place the point of the compass on B and draw another arc. Mark the spot where the arcs intersect (cross) as point C.

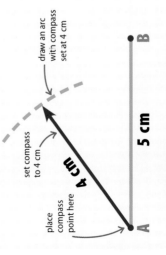

Join the points to complete the triangle. Now use a protractor to find out the measurements of the angles. These will add up to 180° (90° + 53° + 37° = 180°).

Constructing a triangle when two angles and one side are known (AAS)

A triangle can be constructed when the two angles, for example, **73°** and **38°**, are given, along with the length of the side that falls between them, for example, **5 cm**.

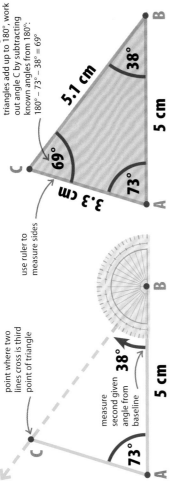

Draw the baseline of the triangle, here 5 cm. Label the ends A and B. Place the protractor over point A and measure the first angle, 73°. Draw a side of the triangle from A.

Place the protractor over point B and mark 38°. Draw another side of the triangle from B. Point C is where the two new lines meet.

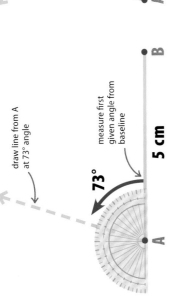

Join the points to complete the triangle. Calculate the unknown angle, and use a ruler to measure the two unknown sides.

Constructing a triangle when two sides and the angle in between are known (SAS)

Using the measurements for two of a triangle's sides, for example, **5 cm** and **4.5 cm**, and the angle between them, for example **50°**, it is possible to construct a triangle.

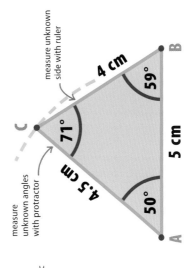

Draw the baseline, using the longest length. Label the ends A and B. Place the protractor over point A and mark 50°. Draw a line from A that runs through 50°. This line will be the next side of the triangle.

Set the compass to the second length, 4.5 cm. Place the compass on point A and draw an arc. Point C is found when the arc intersects the line through point A.

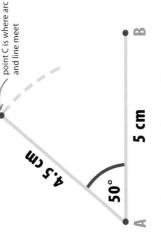
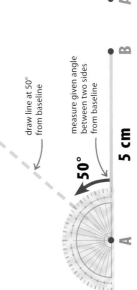

Join the points to complete the triangle. Use a protractor to measure the unknown angles and a ruler to measure the length of the unknown side.

Congruent triangles

TRIANGLES THAT ARE EXACTLY THE SAME SHAPE AND SIZE.

SEE ALSO
‹ 98–99 Translations
‹ 100–101 Rotations
‹ 102–103 Reflections

Identical triangles

Two or more triangles are congruent if their sides are the same length and their corresponding interior angles are the same size. In addition to sides and angles, all other properties of congruent triangles are the same, for example, area. Like other shapes, congruent triangles can be translated, rotated, and reflected, so they may appear different, even though they remain the same size and have identical angles.

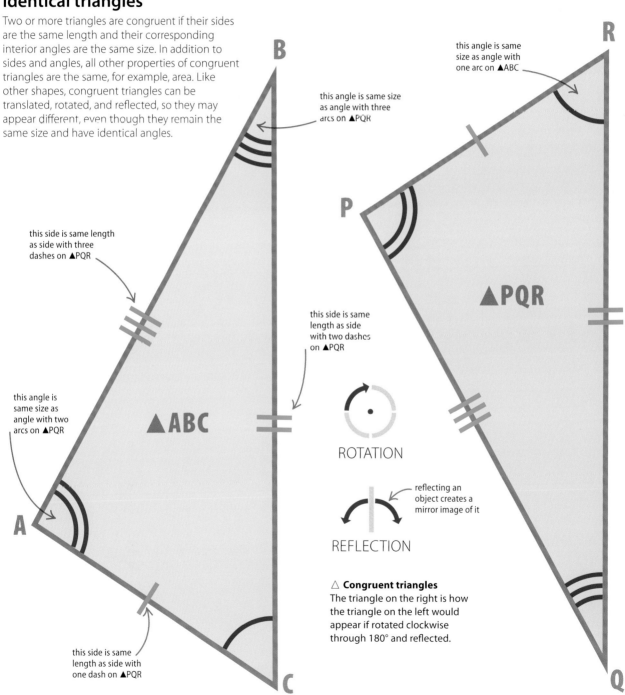

△ **Congruent triangles**
The triangle on the right is how the triangle on the left would appear if rotated clockwise through 180° and reflected.

CONGRUENT TRIANGLES

How to tell if triangles are congruent
It is possible to tell if two triangles are congruent without knowing the lengths of all of the sides or the sizes of all of the angles—knowing just three measurements will do. There are four groups of measurements.

▷ **Side, side, side (SSS)**
When all three sides of a triangle are the same as the corresponding three sides of another triangle, the two triangles are congruent.

▷ **Angle, angle, side (AAS)**
When two angles and any one side of a triangle are equal to two angles and the corresponding side of another triangle, the two triangles are congruent.

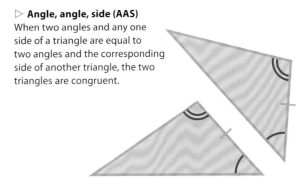

▷ **Side, angle, side (SAS)**
When two sides and the angle between them (called the included angle) of a triangle are equal to two sides and the included angle of another triangle, the two triangles are congruent.

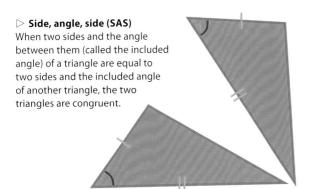

▷ **Right angle, hypotenuse, side (RHS)**
When the hypotenuse and one other side of a right triangle are equal to the hypotenuse and one side of another right triangle, the two triangles are congruent.

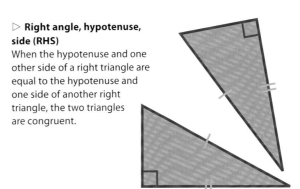

Proving an isosceles triangle has two equal angles
An isosceles triangle has two equal sides. Drawing a perpendicular line helps prove that it has two equal angles too.

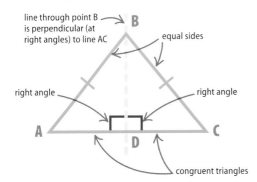

Draw a line perpendicular (at right angles) to the base of an isosceles triangle. This creates two new right triangles. They are congruent—identical in every way.

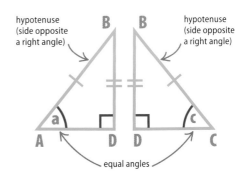

▶ **The perpendicular line** is common to both triangles. The two triangles have equal hypotenuses, another pair of equal sides, and right angles. The triangles are congruent (RHS) so angles "a" and "c" are equal.

Area of a triangle

AREA IS THE COMPLETE SPACE INSIDE A TRIANGLE.

What is area?

The area of a shape is the amount of space that fits inside its outline, or perimeter. It is measured in squared units, such as cm². If the length of the base and vertical height of a triangle are known, these values can be used to find the area of the triangle, using a simple formula, which is shown below.

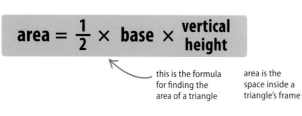

this is the formula for finding the area of a triangle

area is the space inside a triangle's frame

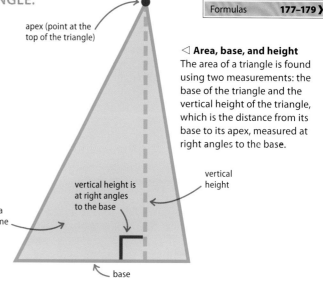

apex (point at the top of the triangle)

◁ **Area, base, and height**
The area of a triangle is found using two measurements: the base of the triangle and the vertical height of the triangle, which is the distance from its base to its apex, measured at right angles to the base.

vertical height is at right angles to the base

vertical height

base

Base and vertical height

Finding the area of a triangle requires two measurements, the base and the vertical height. The side on which a triangle "sits" is called the base. The vertical height is a line formed at right angles to the base from the apex. Any one of the three sides of a triangle can act as the base in the area formula.

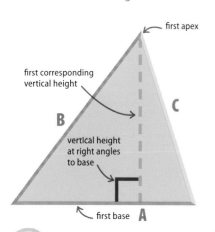

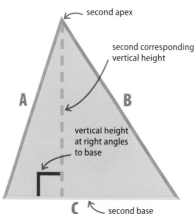

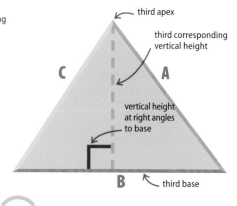

△ **First base**
The area of the triangle can be found using the orange side (A) as the "base" needed for the formula. The corresponding vertical height is the distance from the base of the triangle to its apex (highest point).

△ **Second base**
Any one of the triangle's three sides can act as its base. Here the triangle is rotated so that the green side (C) is its base. The corresponding vertical height is the distance from the base to the apex.

△ **Third base**
The triangle is rotated again, so that the purple side (B) is its base. The corresponding vertical height is the distance from the base to the apex. The area of the triangle is the same, whichever side is used as the base in the formula.

AREA OF A TRIANGLE 123

Finding the area of a triangle

To calculate the area of a triangle, substitute the given values for the base and vertical height into the formula. Then work through the multiplication shown by the formula (½ × base × vertical height).

▷ **An acute-angled triangle**
The base of this triangle is 6 cm and its vertical height is 3 cm. Find the area of the triangle using the formula.

First, write down the formula for the area of a triangle.

Then, substitute the lengths that are known into the formula.

Work through the multiplication in the formula to find the answer. In this example, ½ × 6 × 3 = 9. Add the units of area to the answer, here cm².

▷ **An obtuse triangle**
The base of this triangle is 3 cm and its vertical height is 4 cm. Find the area of the triangle using the formula. The formula and the steps are the same for all types of triangles.

First, write down the formula for the area of a triangle.

Then, substitute the lengths that are known into the formula.

Work through the multiplication to find the answer, and add the appropriate units of area.

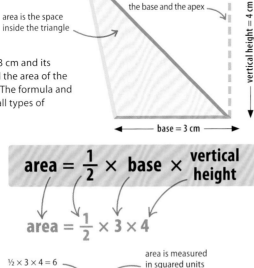

LOOKING CLOSER
Why the formula works

By adjusting the shape of a triangle, it can be converted into a rectangle. This process makes the formula for a triangle easier to understand.

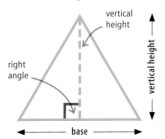

Draw any triangle and label its base and vertical height.

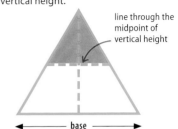

Draw a line through the midpoint of the vertical height that is parallel to the base.

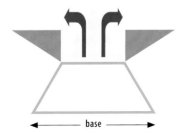

This creates two new triangles. These can be rotated around the triangle to form a rectangle. This has exactly the same area as the original triangle.

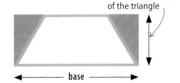

The original triangle's area is found using the formula for the area of a rectangle (b × h). Both shapes have the same base; the rectangle's height is ½ the height of the triangle. This gives the area of the triangle formula: ½ × base × vertical height.

Finding the base of a triangle using the area and height

The formula for the area of a triangle can also be used to find the length of the base, if the area and height are known. Given the area and height of the triangle, the formula needs to be rearranged to find the length of the triangle's base.

First, write down the formula for the area of a triangle. The formula states that the area of a triangle is equal to ½ multiplied by the length of the base, multiplied by the height.

Substitute the known values into the formula. Here the values of the area (12cm²) and the height (3cm) are known.

Simplify the formula as far as possible, by multiplying the ½ by the height. This answer is 1.5.

Make the base the subject of the formula by rearranging it. In this example both sides are divided by 1.5.

Work out the final answer by dividing 12 (area) by 1.5. In this example, the answer is 8cm.

Finding the vertical height of a triangle using the area and base

The formula for area of a triangle can also be used to find its height, if the area and base are known. Given the area and the length of the base of the triangle, the formula needs to be rearranged to find the height of the triangle.

First, write down the formula. This shows that the area of a triangle equals ½ multiplied by its base, multiplied by its height.

Substitute the known values into the formula. Here the values of the area (8cm²) and the base (4cm) are known.

Simplify the equation as far as possible, by multiplying the ½ by the base. In this example, the answer is 2.

Make the height the subject of the formula by rearranging it. In this example both sides are divided by 2.

Work out the final answer by dividing 8 (the area) by 2 (½ the base). In this example the answer is 4cm.

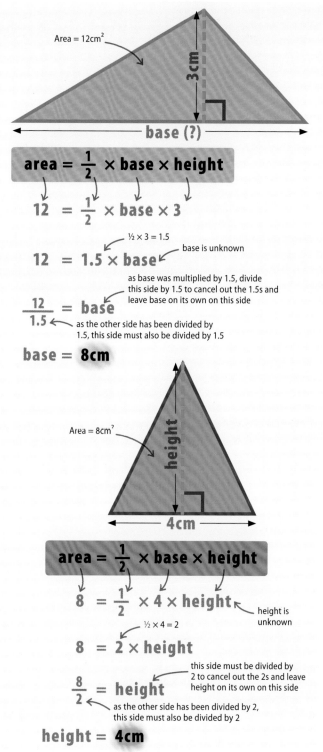

Similar triangles

SEE ALSO
◁ 56–59 Ratio and proportion
◁ 104–105 Enlargements
◁ 116–117 Triangles

TWO TRIANGLES THAT ARE EXACTLY THE SAME SHAPE BUT NOT THE SAME SIZE ARE CALLED SIMILAR TRIANGLES.

What are similar triangles?

Similar triangles are made by making bigger or smaller copies of a triangle—a transformation known as enlargement. Each of the triangles have equal corresponding angles, and corresponding sides that are in proportion to one another, for example each side of triangle ABC below is twice the length of each side on triangle $A_2B_2C_2$. There are four different ways to check if a pair of triangles are similar (see p.126), and if two triangles are known to be similar, their properties can be used to find the lengths of missing sides.

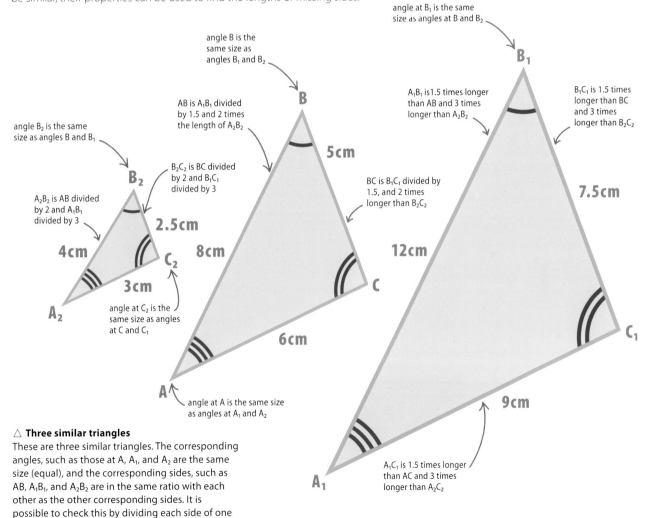

△ **Three similar triangles**
These are three similar triangles. The corresponding angles, such as those at A, A_1, and A_2 are the same size (equal), and the corresponding sides, such as AB, A_1B_1, and A_2B_2 are in the same ratio with each other as the other corresponding sides. It is possible to check this by dividing each side of one triangle by the corresponding side of another triangle – if the answers are all equal, the sides are in proportion to each other.

WHEN ARE TWO TRIANGLES SIMILAR?

It is possible to see if two triangles are similar without measuring every angle and every side. This can be done by looking at the following corresponding measurements for both triangles: two angles, all three sides, a pair of sides with an angle between them, or if the triangles are right triangles, the hypotenuse and another side.

Angle, angle AA

When two angles of one triangle are equal to two angles of another triangle then all the corresponding angles are equal in pairs, so the two triangles are similar.

$$U = U_1$$
$$V = V_1$$

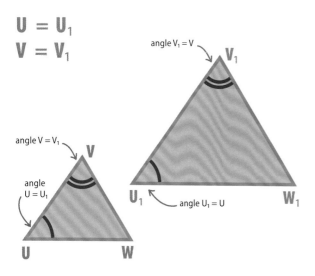

Side, angle, side (S) A (S)

When two triangles have two pairs of corresponding sides that are in the same ratio and the angles between these two sides are equal, the two triangles are similar.

$$\frac{PR}{P_1R_1} = \frac{PQ}{P_1Q_1} \text{ and } P = P_1$$

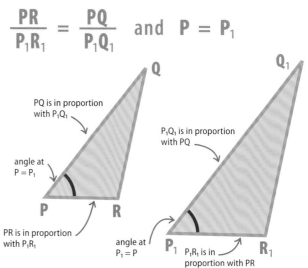

Side, side, side (S) (S) (S)

When two triangles have three pairs of corresponding sides that are in the same ratio, then the two triangles are similar.

$$\frac{AB}{A_1B_1} = \frac{AC}{A_1C_1} = \frac{BC}{B_1C_1}$$

Right-angle, hypotenuse, side R (H) (S)

If the ratio between the hypotenuses of two right triangles is the same as the ratio between another pair of corresponding sides, then the two triangles are similar.

$$\frac{LN}{L_1N_1} = \frac{ML}{M_1L_1} \left(\text{or } \frac{MN}{M_1N_1} \right)$$

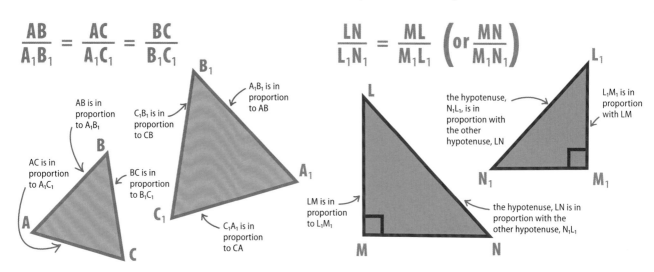

MISSING SIDES IN SIMILAR TRIANGLES

The proportional relationships between the sides of similar triangles can be used to find the value of sides that are missing, if the lengths of some of the sides are known.

▷ **Similar triangles**
Triangles ABC and ADE are similar (AA). The missing values of AD and BC can be found using the ratios between the known sides.

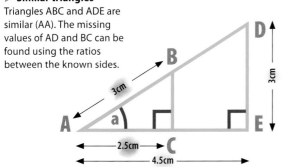

Finding the length of BC

To find the length of BC, use the ratio between BC and its corresponding side DE, and the ratio between a pair of sides where both the lengths are known – AE and AC.

Write out the ratios between the two pairs of sides, each with the longer side above the shorter side. These ratios are equal.

$$\frac{DE}{BC} = \frac{AE}{AC}$$

▽

Substitute the values that are known into the ratios. The numbers can now be rearranged to find the length of BC.

$$\frac{3}{BC} = \frac{4.5}{2.5}$$

▽

Rearrange the equation to isolate BC. This may take more than one step. First multiply both sides of the equation by BC.

multiply both sides by BC   multiply both sides by BC

$$3 = \frac{4.5}{2.5} \times BC$$

▽

Then rearrange the equation again. This time multipy both sides of the equation by 2.5.

multiply both sides by 2.5

$$3 \times 2.5 = 4.5 \times BC$$

multiply both sides by 2.5

▽

BC can now be isolated by rearranging the equation one more time – divide both sides of the equation by 4.5.

divide both sides by 4.5

$$BC = \frac{3 \times 2.5}{4.5}$$

divide both sides by 4.5

▽

Do the multiplication to find the answer, add the units, and round to a sensible number of decimal places.

1.6666.... is rounded to 2 decimal places

$$BC = 1.67\text{cm}$$

Finding the length of AD

To find the length of AD, use the ratio between AD and its corresponding side AB, and the ratio between a pair of sides where both the lengths are known – AE and AC.

Write out the ratios between the two pairs of sides, each with the longer side above the shorter side. These ratios are equal.

$$\frac{AD}{AB} = \frac{AE}{AC}$$

▽

Substitute the values that are known into the ratios. The numbers can now be rearranged to find the length of AD.

AD is the unknown

$$\frac{AD}{3} = \frac{4.5}{2.5}$$

▽

Rearrange the equation to isolate AD. In this example this is done by multiplying both sides of the equation by 3.

$$AD = 3 \times \frac{4.5}{2.5}$$

multiply by 3 to isolate AD

▽

Do the multiplication to find the answer, and add the units to the answer that has been found. This is the length of AD.

$$AD = 5.4\text{cm}$$

Pythagorean Theorem

SEE ALSO
⟨ 36–39 Powers and roots
⟨ 116–117 Triangles
⟨ 122–124 Area of a triangle
Formulas 177–179 ⟩

THE PYTHAGOREAN THEOREM IS USED TO FIND THE LENGTH OF MISSING SIDES IN RIGHT TRIANGLES.

If the lengths of two sides of a right triangle are known, the length of the third side can be worked out using Pythagorean Theorem.

What is the Pythagorean Theorem?

The basic principle of the Pythagorean Theorem is that squaring the two smaller sides of a right triangle (multiplying each side by itself) and adding the results will equal the square of the longest side. The idea of "squaring" each side can be shown literally. On the right, a square on each side shows how the biggest square has the same area as the other two squares put together.

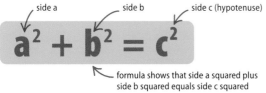

$$a^2 + b^2 = c^2$$

formula shows that side a squared plus side b squared equals side c squared

▷ **Squared sides**
The squares of the shorter sides are shown here with the square of the longest side (the hypotenuse).

$c^2 = c \times c$
c^2 is the area of the square formed from sides of length c

$a^2 = a \times a$
a^2 is the area of the square formed with sides of length a

$b^2 = b \times b$
b^2 is the area of the square formed from sides of length b

hypotenuse

If the formula is used with values substituted for the sides a, b, and c, the Pythagorean Theorem can be shown to be true. Here the length of c (the hypotenuse) is 5, while the lengths of a and b are 4 and 3.

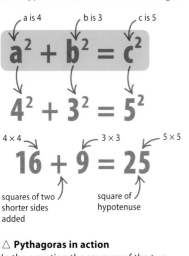

a is 4, b is 3, c is 5

$$a^2 + b^2 = c^2$$

$$4^2 + 3^2 = 5^2$$

4 × 4, 3 × 3, 5 × 5

$$16 + 9 = 25$$

squares of two shorter sides added

square of hypotenuse

△ **Pythagoras in action**
In the equation the squares of the two shorter sides (4 and 3) added together equal the square of the hypotenuse (5), proving that the Pythagorean Theorem works.

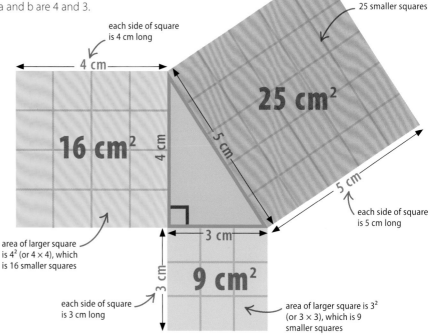

each side of square is 4 cm long

4 cm

16 cm²

area of larger square is 4² (or 4 × 4), which is 16 smaller squares

each side of square is 3 cm long

3 cm

9 cm²

25 cm²

4 cm

5 cm

5 cm

3 cm

each side of square is 5 cm long

area of larger square is 5² (or 5 × 5), which is 25 smaller squares

area of larger square is 3² (or 3 × 3), which is 9 smaller squares

PYTHAGOREAN THEOREM

Find the value of the hypotenuse

The Pythagorean Theorem can be used to find the value of the length of the longest side (the hypotenuse) in a right triangle when the lengths of the two shorter sides are known. This example shows how this works, if the two known sides are 3.5 cm and 7.2 cm in length.

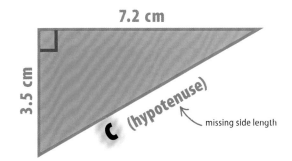

First, take the formula for the Pythagorean Theorem.

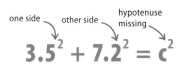

Substitute the values given into the formula, in this example, 3.5 and 7.2.

Calculate the squares of each of the triangle's known sides by multiplying them.

Add these answers together to find the square of the hypotenuse.

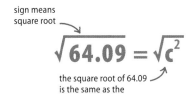

Use a calculator to find the square root of 64.09. This gives the length of side c.

The square root is the length of the hypotenuse.

Find the value of another side

The theorem can be rearranged to find the length of either of the two sides of a right triangle that are not the hypotenuse. The length of the hypotenuse and one other side must be known. This example shows how this works with a side of 5 cm and a hypotenuse of 13 cm.

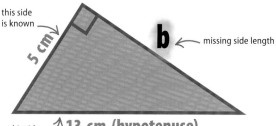

To calculate the length of side b, take the formula for the Pythagorean Theorem.

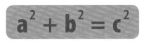

Substitute the values given into the formula. In this example, 5 and 13.

$$5^2 + b^2 = 13^2$$

Rearrange the equation by subtracting 5^2 from each side. This isolates b^2 on one side because $5^2 - 5^2$ cancels out.

$$13^2 - 5^2 = b^2$$

Calculate the squares of the two known sides of the triangle.

$$169 - 25 = b^2$$

Subtract these squares to find the square of the unknown side.

$$144 = b^2$$

Find the square root of 144 for the length of the unknown side.

$$\sqrt{144} = \sqrt{b^2}$$

The square root is the length of side b.

$$b = 12 \text{ cm}$$

130 GEOMETRY

 # Quadrilaterals

A QUADRILATERAL IS A FOUR-SIDED POLYGON.
"QUAD" MEANS FOUR AND "LATERAL" MEANS SIDE.

SEE ALSO	
‹ 84–85 Angles	
‹ 86–87 Straight lines	
Polygons	134–137 ›

Introducing quadrilaterals

A quadrilateral is a two-dimensional shape with four straight sides, four vertices (points where the sides meet), and four interior angles. The interior angles of a quadrilateral always add up to 360°. An exterior angle and its corresponding interior angle always add up to 180° because they form a straight line. There are several types of quadrilaterals, each with different properties.

△ **Interior angles**
If a single diagonal line is drawn from any one corner to the opposite corner, the quadrilateral is divided into two triangles. The sum of the interior angles of any triangle is 180°, so the sum of the interior angles of a quadrilateral is 2 × 180°.

▽ **Types of quadrilaterals**
Each type of quadrilateral is grouped and named according to its properties. There are regular and irregular quadrilaterals. A regular quadrilateral has equal sides and angles, whereas an irregular quadrilateral has sides and angles of different sizes.

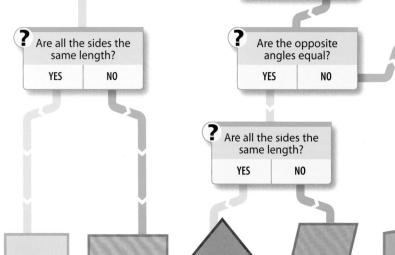

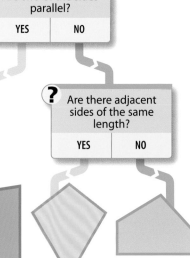

PROPERTIES OF QUADRILATERALS

Each type of quadrilateral has its own name and a number of unique properties. Knowing just some of the properties of a shape can help distinguish one type of quadrilateral from another. Six of the more common quadrilaterals are shown below with their respective properties.

Square

A square has four equal angles (right angles) and four sides of equal length. The opposite sides of a square are parallel. The diagonals bisect cut into two equal parts—each other at 90° (right angles).

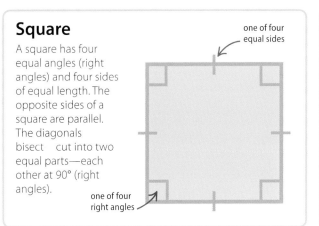

Rectangle

A rectangle has four right angles and two pairs of opposite sides of equal length. Adjacent sides are not of equal length. The opposite sides are parallel and the diagonals bisect each other.

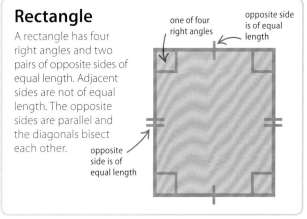

Rhombus

All sides of a rhombus are of equal length. The opposite angles are equal and the opposite sides are parallel. The diagonals bisect each other at right angles.

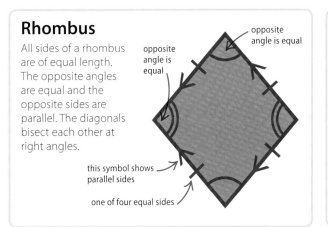

Parallelogram

The opposite sides of a parallelogram are parallel and are of equal length. Adjacent sides are not of equal length. The opposite angles are equal and the diagonals bisect each other in the center of the shape.

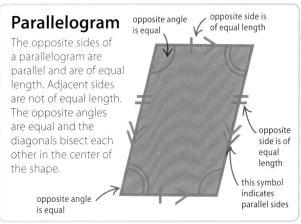

Trapezoid

A trapezoid, also known as a trapezium, has one pair of opposite sides that are parallel. These sides are not equal in length.

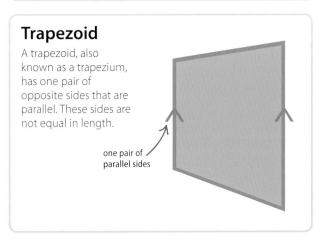

Kite

A kite has two pairs of adjacent sides that are equal in length. Opposite sides are not of equal length. It has one pair of opposite angles that are equal and another pair of angles of different values.

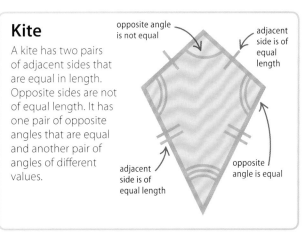

FINDING THE AREA OF QUADRILATERALS

Area is the space inside the frame of a two-dimensional shape. Area is measured in square units, for example, cm^2. Formulas are used to calculate the areas of many types of shapes. Each type of quadrilateral has a unique formula for calculating its area.

Finding the area of a square

The area of a square is found by multiplying its length by its width. Because its length and width are equal in size, the formula is the square of a side.

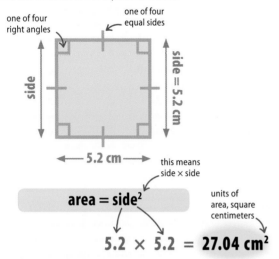

△ **Multiply sides**
In this example, each of the four sides measures 5.2 cm. To find the area of this square, multiply 5.2 by 5.2.

Finding the area of a rectangle

The area of a rectangle is found by multiplying its base by its height.

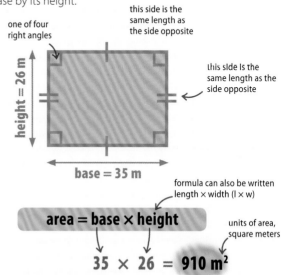

△ **Multiply base by height**
The height (or width) of this rectangle is 26 m, and its base (or length) measures 35 m. Multiply these two measurements together to find the area.

Finding the area of a rhombus

The area of a rhombus is found by multiplying the length of its base by its vertical height. The vertical height, also known as the perpendicular height, is the vertical distance from the top (vertex) of a shape to the base opposite. The vertical height is at right angles to the base.

▷ **Vertical height**
Finding the area of a rhombus depends on knowing its vertical height. In this example, the vertical height measures 8 cm and its base is 9 cm.

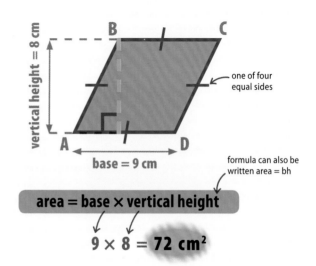

Finding the area of a parallelogram

Like the area of a rhombus, the area of a parallelogram is found by multiplying the length of its base by its vertical height.

▷ **Multiply base by vertical height**
It is important to remember that the slanted side, AB, is not the vertical height. This formula only works if the vertical height is used.

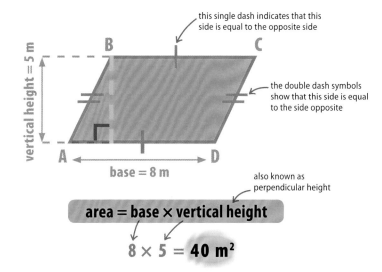

area = base × vertical height

8 × 5 = **40 m²**

Proving the opposite angles of a rhombus are equal

Creating two pairs of isosceles triangles by dividing a rhombus along two diagonals helps prove that the opposite angles of a rhombus are equal. An isosceles triangle has two equal sides and two equal angles.

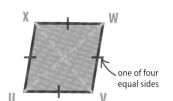 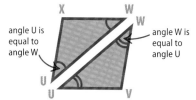 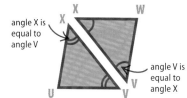

▷ **All the sides** of a rhombus are equal in length. To show this a dash is used on each side.

▷ **Divide the rhombus** along a diagonal to create two isosceles triangles. Each triangle has a pair of equal angles.

▷ **Dividing along the other diagonal** creates another pair of isosceles triangles.

Proving the opposite sides of a parallelogram are parallel

Creating a pair of congruent triangles by dividing a parallelogram along two diagonals helps prove that the opposite sides of a parallelogram are parallel. Congruent triangles are the same size and shape.

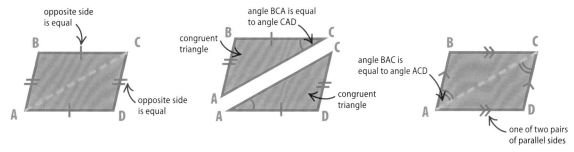

▷ **Opposites sides** of a parallelogram are equal in length. To show this a dash and a double dash are used.

▷ **The triangles ABC and ADC** are congruent. Angle BCA = CAD, and because these are alternate angles, BC is parallel to AD.

▷ **The triangles are congruent**, so angle BAC = ACD; because these are alternate angles, DC is parallel to AB.

Polygons

A CLOSED TWO-DIMENSIONAL SHAPE OF THREE OR MORE SIDES.

Polygons range from simple three-sided triangles and four-sided squares to more complicated shapes such as trapezoids and dodecagons. Polygons are named according to the number of sides and angles they have.

SEE ALSO
‹ 84–85 Angles
‹ 116–117 Triangles
‹ 120–121 Congruent triangles
‹ 130–133 Quadrilaterals

What is a polygon?

A polygon is a closed two-dimensional shape formed by straight lines that connect end to end at a point called a vertex. The interior angles of a polygon are usually smaller than the exterior angles, although the reverse is possible. Polygons with an interior angle of more than 180° are called concave.

▷ **Parts of a polygon**
Regardless of shape, all polygons are made up of the same parts—sides, vertices (connecting points), and interior and exterior angles.

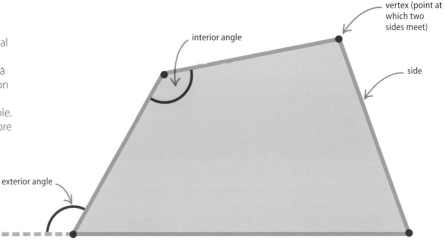

Describing polygons

There are several ways to describe polygons. One is by the regularity or irregularity of their sides and angles. A polygon is regular when all of its sides and angles are equal. An irregular polygon has at least two sides or two angles that are different.

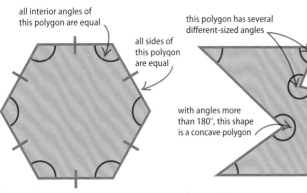

△ **Regular**
All the sides and all the angles of regular polygons are equal. This hexagon has six equal sides and six equal angles, making it regular.

△ **Irregular**
In an irregular polygon, all the sides and angles are not the same. This heptagon has many different-sized angles, making it irregular.

LOOKING CLOSER

Equal angles or equal sides?

All the angles and all the sides of a regular polygon are equal—in other words, the polygon is both equiangular and equilateral. In certain polygons, only the angles (equiangular) or only the sides (equilateral) are equal.

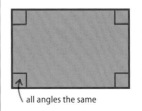

◁ **Equiangular**
A rectangle is an equiangular quadrilateral. Its angles are all equal, but not all its sides are equal.

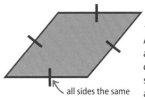

◁ **Equilateral**
A rhombus is an equilateral quadrilateral. All its sides are equal, but all its angles are not.

Naming polygons

Regardless of whether a polygon is regular or irregular, the number of sides it has always equals the number of its angles. This number is used in naming both kinds of polygons. For example, a polygon with six sides and angles is called a hexagon because "hex" is the prefix used to mean six. If all of its sides and angles are equal, it is known as a regular hexagon; if not, it is called an irregular hexagon.

Triangle
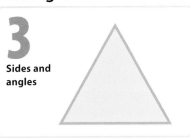
3 Sides and angles

Quadrilateral

4 Sides and angles

Pentagon
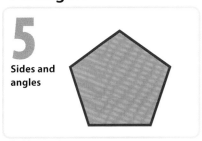
5 Sides and angles

Hexagon
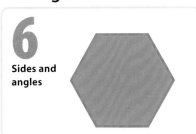
6 Sides and angles

Heptagon

7 Sides and angles

Octagon
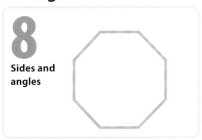
8 Sides and angles

Nonagon
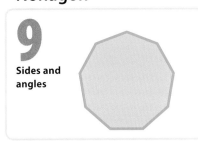
9 Sides and angles

Decagon
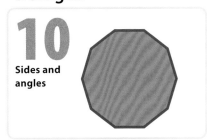
10 Sides and angles

Hendecagon

11 Sides and angles

Dodecagon
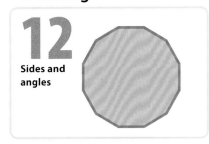
12 Sides and angles

Pentadecagon
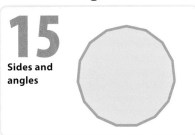
15 Sides and angles

Icosagon
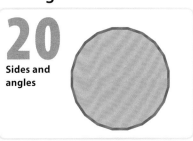
20 Sides and angles

PROPERTIES OF A POLYGON

There are an unlimited number of different polygons that can be drawn using straight lines. However, they all share some important properties.

Convex or concave

Regardless of how many angles a polygon has, it can be classified as either concave or convex. This difference is based on whether a polygon's interior angles are over 180° or not. A concave polygon can be easily identified because at least of one its angles is over 180°.

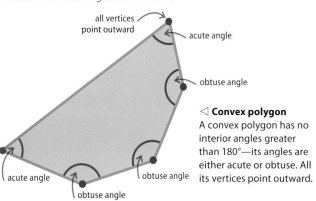

◁ **Convex polygon**
A convex polygon has no interior angles greater than 180°—its angles are either acute or obtuse. All its vertices point outward.

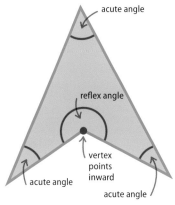

◁ **Concave polygon**
At least one angle of a concave polygon is over 180°. This type of angle is known as a reflex angle. The vertex of the reflex angle points inward, toward the center of the shape.

Interior angle sum of polygons

The sum of the interior angles of both regular and irregular convex polygon depends on the number of sides the polygon has. The sum of the angles can be worked out by dividing the polygon into triangles.

This quadrilateral is convex—all of its angles are smaller than 180°. The sum of its interior angles can be found easily, by breaking the shape down into triangles. This can be done by drawing in a diagonal line that connects two vertices that are not next to one another.

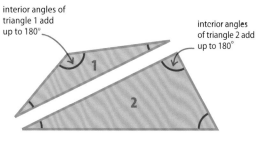

▷ **A quadrilateral can be split** into two triangles. The sum of the angles of each triangle is 180°, so the sum of the angles of the quadrilateral is the sum of the angles of the two triangles added together: 2 × 180° = 360°.

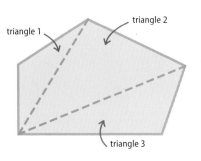

◁ **Irregular pentagon**
This pentagon can be split up into three triangles. The sum of its interior angles is the sum of the angles of the three triangles: 3 × 180° = 540°.

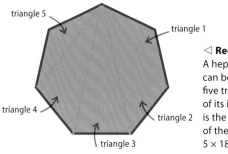

◁ **Regular heptagon**
A heptagon (7 sides) can be split up into five triangles. The sum of its interior angles is the sum of the angles of the five triangles: 5 × 180° = 900°.

A formula for the interior angle sum

The number of triangles a convex polygon can be split up into is always 2 fewer than the number of its sides. This means that a formula can be used to find the sum of the interior angles of any convex polygon.

Sum of interior angles = (n − 2) × 180°

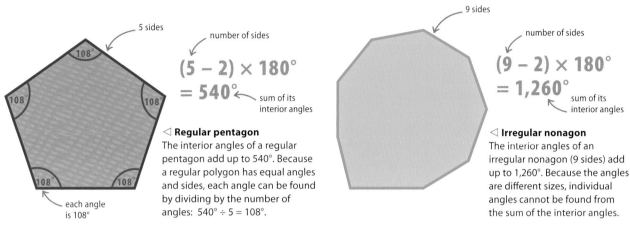

◁ **Regular pentagon**
The interior angles of a regular pentagon add up to 540°. Because a regular polygon has equal angles and sides, each angle can be found by dividing by the number of angles: 540° ÷ 5 = 108°.

◁ **Irregular nonagon**
The interior angles of an irregular nonagon (9 sides) add up to 1,260°. Because the angles are different sizes, individual angles cannot be found from the sum of the interior angles.

Sum of exterior angles of a polygon

Imagine walking along the exterior of a polygon. Start at one vertex, and facing the next, walk toward it. At the next vertex, turn the number of degrees of the exterior angle until facing the following vertex, and repeat until you have been around all the vertices. In walking around the polygon, you will have turned a complete circle, or 360°. The exterior angles of any polygon always add up to 360°.

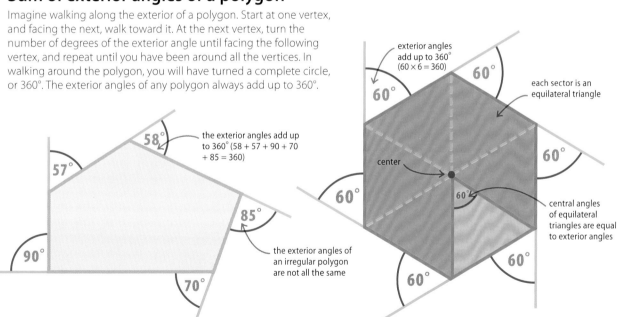

△ **Irregular pentagon**
The exterior angles of a polygon, regardless of whether it is regular or irregular add up to 360°. Another way to think about this is that, added together, the exterior angles of a polygon would form a complete circle.

△ **Regular hexagon**
The size of the exterior angles of a regular polygon can be found by dividing 360° by the number of sides the polygon has. A regular hexagon's central angles (formed by splitting the shape into 6 equilateral triangles) are the same as the exterior angles.

Circles

A CIRCLE IS A CLOSED CURVED LINE SURROUNDING A CENTER POINT. EVERY POINT OF THIS CURVED LINE IS OF EQUAL DISTANCE FROM THE CENTER POINT.

SEE ALSO	
‹ 82–83 Tools in geometry	
Circumference and diameter	140–141 ›
Area of a circle	142–143 ›

Properties of a circle

A circle can be folded into two identical halves, which means that it possesses "reflective symmetry" (see p.88). The line of this fold is one of the most important parts of a circle—its diameter. A circle may also be rotated about its center and still fit into its own outline, giving it a "rotational symmetry" about its center point.

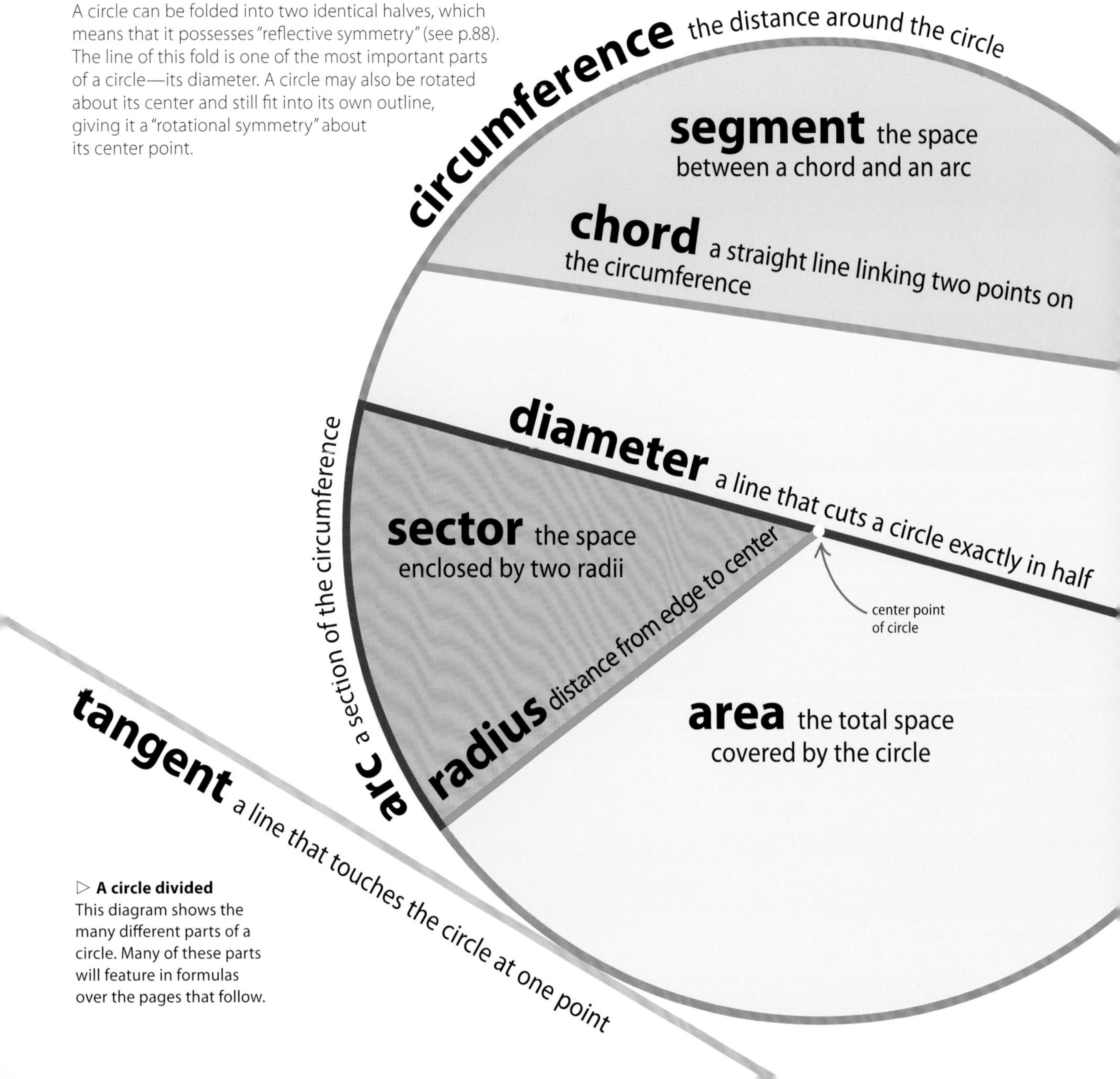

circumference the distance around the circle

segment the space between a chord and an arc

chord a straight line linking two points on the circumference

diameter a line that cuts a circle exactly in half

sector the space enclosed by two radii

center point of circle

radius distance from edge to center

area the total space covered by the circle

arc a section of the circumference

tangent a line that touches the circle at one point

▷ **A circle divided**
This diagram shows the many different parts of a circle. Many of these parts will feature in formulas over the pages that follow.

CIRCLES

Parts of a circle

A circle can be measured and divided in various ways. Each of these has a specific name and character, and they are all shown below.

Radius
Any straight line from the center of a circle to its circumference. The plural of radius is radii.

Diameter
Any straight line that passes through the center from one side of a circle to the other.

Chord
Any straight line linking two points on a circle's circumference, but not passing through its center.

Segment
The smaller of the two parts of a circle created when divided by a chord.

Circumference
The total length of the outside edge (perimeter) of a circle.

Arc
Any section of the circumference of a circle.

Sector
A "slice" of a circle, similar to the slice of a pie. It is enclosed by two radii and an arc.

Area
The amount of space inside a circle's circumference.

Tangent
A straight line that touches the circle at a single point.

How to draw a circle

Two instruments are needed to draw a circle—a compass and a pencil. The point of the compass marks the center of the circle and the distance between the point and the pencil attached to the compass forms the circle's radius. A ruler is needed to measure the radius of the circle correctly.

Set the compass. First, decide what the radius of the circle is, and then use a ruler to set the compass at this distance.

"x" stands for distance in inches between compass point and pencil or length of radius

use ruler to set length of radius

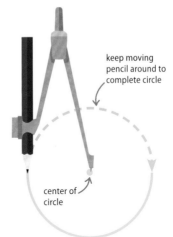

Decide where the center of the circle is and then hold the point of the compass firmly in this place. Then put the pencil on the paper and move the pencil around to draw the circumference of the circle.

keep moving pencil around to complete circle

center of circle

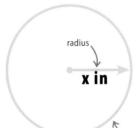

The completed circle has a radius that is the same length as the distance that the compass was originally set to.

radius

circumference

Circumference and diameter

> **SEE ALSO**
> ‹ 56–59 Ratio and proportion
> ‹ 104–105 Enlargements
> ‹ 138–139 Circles
> Area of a circle 142–143 ›

THE DISTANCE AROUND THE EDGE OF A CIRCLE IS CALLED THE CIRCUMFERENCE; THE DISTANCE ACROSS THE MIDDLE IS THE DIAMETER.

All circles are similar because they have exactly the same shape. This means that all their measurements, including the circumference and the diameter, are in proportion to each other.

The number pi

The ratio between the circumference and diameter of a circle is a number called pi, which is written π. This number is used in many of the formulas associated with circles, including the formulas for the circumference and diameter.

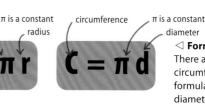

symbol for pi

$$\pi \approx 3.14$$

value to 2 decimal places

◁ **The value of pi**
The numbers after the decimal point in pi go on for ever and in an unpredictable way. It starts 3.1415926 but is usually given to two decimal places.

Circumference (C)

The circumference is the distance around the edge of a circle. A circle's circumference can be found using the diameter or radius and the number pi. The diameter is always twice the length of the radius.

circumference — π is a constant — radius

$$C = 2\pi r$$

circumference — π is a constant — diameter

$$C = \pi d$$

◁ **Formulas**
There are two circumference formulas. One uses diameter and the other uses radius.

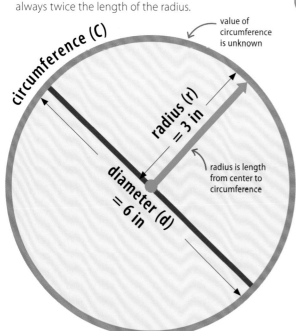

value of circumference is unknown

radius is length from center to circumference

The formula for circumference shows that the circumference is equal to pi multiplied by the diameter of the circle.

$$C = \pi d$$

d is the same as 2 × r, the formula can also be written C=2πr

Substitute known values into the formula for circumference. Here, the radius of the circle is known to be 3 in.

$$C = 3.14 \times 6$$

pi is 3.14 to two decimal places

Multiply the numbers to find the length of the circumference. Round the answer to a suitable number of decimal places.

$$C = 18.8 \text{ in}$$

18.84 is rounded to one decimal place

△ **Finding the circumference**
The length of a circle's circumference can be found if the length of the diameter is known, in this example the diameter is 6 in long.

Diameter (d)

The diameter is the distance across the middle of a circle. It is twice the length of the radius. A circle's diameter can be found by doubling the length of its radius, or by using its circumference and the number pi in the formula shown below. The formula is a rearranged version of the formula for the circumference of a circle.

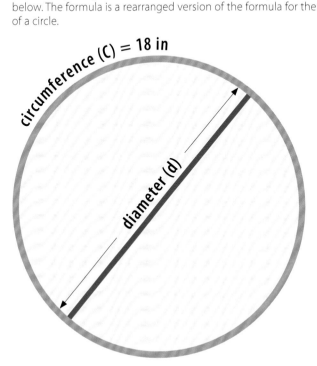

△ **Finding the diameter**
This circle has a circumference of 18 in. Its diameter can be found using the formula given above.

The formula for diameter shows that the length of the diameter is equal to the length of the circumference divided by the number pi.

$$d = \frac{C}{\pi}$$

π is a constant

Substitute known values into the formula for diameter. In the example shown here, the circumference of the circle is 18 in.

$$d = \frac{18}{\pi}$$

Divide the circumference by the value of pi, 3.14, to find the length of the diameter.

$$d = \frac{18}{3.14}$$

more accurate to use π button on a calculator

Round the answer to a suitable number of decimal places. In this example, the answer is given to two decimal places.

$$d = 5.73 \text{ in}$$

the answer is given to two decimal places

LOOKING CLOSER

Why π?

All circles are similar to one another. This means that corresponding lengths in circles, such as their diameters and circumferences, are always in proportion to each other. The number π is found by dividing the circumference of a circle by its diameter—any circle's circumference divided by its diameter always equals π—it is a constant value.

▷ **Similar circles**
As all circles are enlargements of each other, their diameters (d1, d2) and circumferences (C1, C2) are always in proportion to one another.

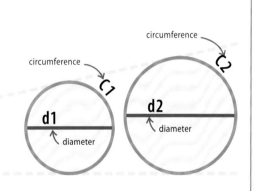

Area of a circle

THE AREA OF A CIRCLE IS THE AMOUNT OF SPACE ENCLOSED INSIDE ITS PERIMETER (CIRCUMFERENCE).

SEE ALSO
‹ 138–139 Circles
‹ 140–141 Circumference and diameter
Formulas 177–179 ›

The area of a circle can be found by using the measurements of either the radius or the diameter of the circle.

Finding the area of a circle

The area of a circle is measured in square units. It can be found using the radius of a circle (r) and the formula shown below. If the diameter is known but the radius is not, the radius can be found by dividing the diameter by 2.

In the formula for the area of a circle, πr² means π (pi) × radius × radius.

$$\text{area} = \pi r^2$$

- area of a circle
- π is a fixed value
- radius

Substitute the known values into the formula; in this example, the radius is 4 in.

$$\text{area} = 3.14 \times 4^2$$

π is 3.14 to 3 significant figures; a more accurate value can be found on a calculator

this means 4 × 4

Multiply the radius by itself as shown—this makes the last multiplication simpler.

$$\text{area} = 3.14 \times 16$$

4 × 4 = 16

Make sure the answer is in the right units (in² here) and round it to a suitable number.

$$\text{area} = 50.24 \text{ in}^2$$

answer is 50.24 exactly

- edge of circle is circumference
- radius (r) = 4 in
- the value of the radius is given
- area is the total space inside the circle, shown in yellow

LOOKING CLOSER
Why does the formula for the area of a circle work?

The formula for the area of a circle can be proved by dividing a circle into sectors, and rearranging the sectors into a rectangular shape. The formula for the area of a rectangle is simpler than that of the area for a circle—it is just height × width. The rectangular shape's height is simply the length of a circle sector, which is the same as the radius of the circle. The width of the rectangular shape is half of the total sectors, equivalent to half the circumference of the circle.

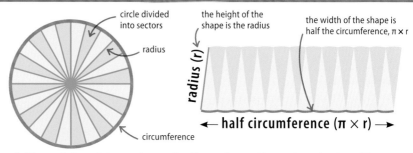

- circle divided into sectors
- radius
- circumference
- the height of the shape is the radius
- the width of the shape is half the circumference, π × r
- radius (r)
- ← half circumference (π × r) →

Split any circle up into equal sectors, making them as small as possible.

Lay the sectors out in a rectangular shape. The area of a rectangle is height × width, which in this case is radius × half circumference, or r × πr, which is πr².

AREA OF A CIRCLE

Finding area using the diameter

The formula for the area of a circle usually uses the radius, but the area can also be found if the diameter is given.

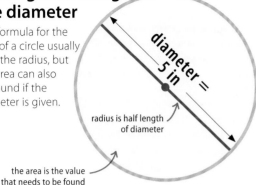

radius is half length of diameter

the area is the value that needs to be found

The formula for the area of a circle is always the same, whatever values are known.

$$\text{area} = \pi\, r^2$$

Substitute the known values into the formula—the radius is half the diameter—2.5 in this example.

Multiply the radius by itself (square it) as shown by the formula—this makes the last multiplication simpler.

Make sure the answer is in the right units, in² here, and round it to a suitable number.

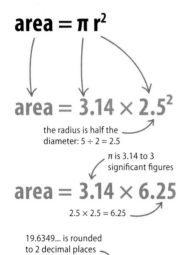

the radius is half the diameter: $5 \div 2 = 2.5$

π is 3.14 to 3 significant figures

$2.5 \times 2.5 = 6.25$

19.6349... is rounded to 2 decimal places

$$\text{area} = 19.63 \text{ in}^2$$

Finding the radius from the area

The formula for area of a circle can also be used to find the radius of a circle if its area is given.

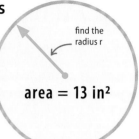

find the radius r

area = 13 in²

The formula for the area of a circle can be used to find the radius if the area is known.

$$\text{area} = \pi\, r^2$$

Substitute the known values into the formula—here the area is 13 in².

$$13 = 3.14 \times r^2$$

Rearrange the formula so r² is on its own on one side: divide both sides by 3.14.

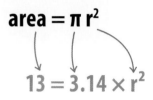

divide this side by 3.14

r² was multiplied by 3.14, so divide by 3.14 to isolate r²

$$\frac{13}{3.14} = r^2$$

Round the answer, and switch the sides so that the unknown, r², is shown first.

r² is shown first

$$r^2 = 4.14$$

4.1380... is rounded to 2 decimal places

Find the square root of the last answer in order to find the value of the radius.

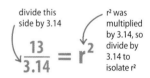

$$\sqrt{r^2} = \sqrt{4.14}$$

2.0342... is rounded to 2 decimal places

Make sure the answer is in the right units (in here) and round it to a suitable number.

$$r = 2.03 \text{ in}$$

LOOKING CLOSER
Areas of compound shapes

When two or more different shapes are put together, the result is called a compound shape. The area of a compound shape can be found by adding the areas of the parts of the shape. In this example, the two different parts are a semicircle, and a rectangle. The total area is 1,414 in² (area of the semicircle, which is ½ × πr², half the area of a circle) + 5,400 in² (the area of the rectangle) = 6,814 in².

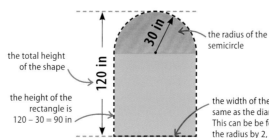

the total height of the shape

the height of the rectangle is $120 - 30 = 90$ in

120 in

30 in

the radius of the semicircle

◁ **Compound shapes**
This compound shape consists of a semicircle and a rectangle. Its area can be found using only the two measurements given here.

the width of the rectangle is the same as the diameter of the circle. This can be be found by multiplying the radius by 2, $30 \times 2 = 60$ in.

144 GEOMETRY

 # Angles in a circle

THE ANGLES IN A CIRCLE HAVE A NUMBER OF SPECIAL PROPERTIES.

SEE ALSO
‹ 84–85 Angles
‹ 116–117 Triangles
‹ 138–139 Circles

If angles are drawn to the center and the circumference from the same two points on the circumference, the angle at the center is twice the angle at the circumference.

Subtended angles

Any angle within a circle is "subtended" from two points on its circumference—it "stands" on the two points. In both of these examples, the angle at point R is the angle subtended, or standing on, points P and Q. Subtended angles can sit anywhere within the circle.

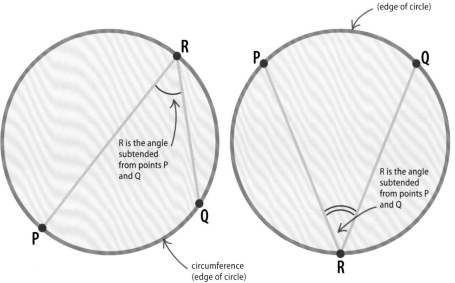

▷ **Subtended angles**
These circles show how a point is subtended from two other points on the circle's circumference to form an angle. The angle at point R is subtended from points P and Q.

Angles at the center and at the circumference

When angles are subtended from the same two points to both the center of the circle and to its circumference, the angle at the center is always twice the size of the angle formed at the circumference. In this example, both angles R at the circumference and O at the center are subtended from the same points, P and Q.

$$\text{angle at center} = 2 \times \text{angle at circumference}$$

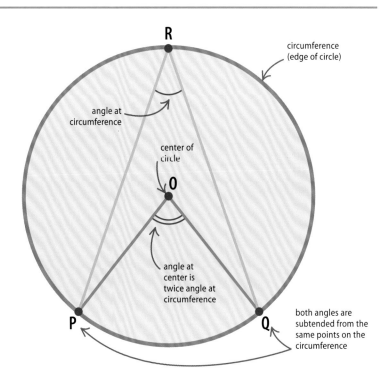

▷ **Angle property**
The angles at O and R are both subtended by the points P and Q at the circumference. This means that the angle at O is twice the size of the angle at R.

ANGLES IN A CIRCLE   **145**

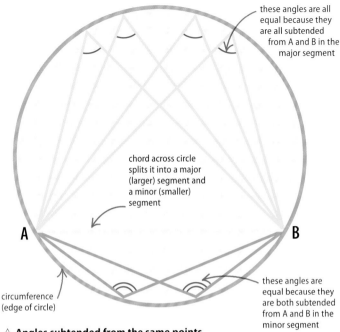

△ **Angles subtended from the same points**
Angles at the circumference subtended from the same two points in the same segment are equal. Here the angles marked with one red line are equal, as are the angles marked with two red lines.

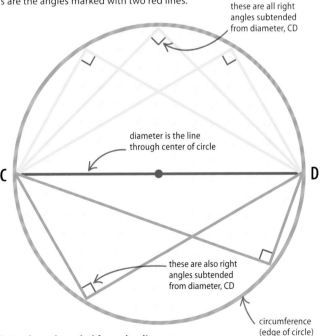

△ **Angles subtended from the diameter**
Any angle at the circumference that is subtended from two points either side of the diameter is equal to 90°, which is a right angle.

Proving angle rules in circles
Mathematical rules can be used to prove that the angle at the center of a circle is twice the size of the angle at the circumference when both the angles are subtended from the same points.

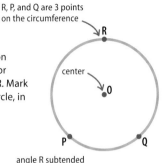

Draw a circle and mark any 3 points on its circumference, for example, P, Q, and R. Mark the center of the circle, in this example it is O.

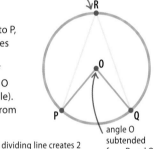

Draw straight lines from R to P, R to Q, O to P, and O to Q. This creates two angles, one at R (the circumference of the circle) and one at O (the center of the circle). Both are subtended from points P and Q.

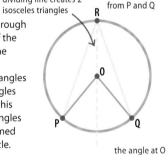

Draw a line from R through O, to the other side of the circle. This dividing line creates two isosceles triangles. Isosceles triangles have 2 sides and 2 angles that are the same. In this case, two sides of triangles POR and QOR are formed from 2 radii of the circle.

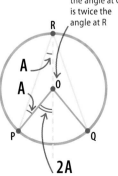

For one triangle the two angles on its base are equal, and labeled A. The exterior angle of this triangle is the sum of the opposite interior angles (A and A), or 2A. Looking at both triangles, it is clear that the angle at O (the center) is twice the angle at R (the circumference).

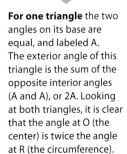

Chords and cyclic quadrilaterals

A CHORD IS A STRAIGHT LINE JOINING ANY TWO POINTS ON THE CIRCUMFERENCE OF A CIRCLE. A CYCLIC QUADRILATERAL HAS FOUR CHORDS AS ITS SIDES.

Chords vary in length—the diameter of a circle is also its longest chord. Chords of the same length are always equal distances from the center of the circle. The corners of a cyclic quadrilateral (four-sided shape) touch the circumference of a circle.

SEE ALSO
‹ 130–133 Quadrilaterals
‹ 138–139 Circles

Chords

A chord is a straight line across a circle. The longest chord of any circle is its diameter because the diameter crosses a circle at its widest point. The perpendicular bisector of a chord is a line that passes through its center at right angles (90°) to it. The perpendicular bisector of any chord passes through the center of the circle. The distance of a chord to the center of a circle is found by measuring its perpendicular bisector. If two chords are equal lengths they will always be the same distance from the center of the circle.

▷ **Chord properties**
This circle shows four chords. Two of these chords are equal in length. The longest chord is the diameter, and one is shown on the right with its perpendicular bisector (a line that cuts it in half at right angles).

LOOKING CLOSER

Intersecting chords

When two chords cross, or "intersect," they gain an interesting property: the two parts of one chord, either side of where it is split, multiply to give the same value as the answer found by multiplying the two parts of the other chord.

▷ **Crossing chords**
This circle shows two chords, which cross one another (intersect). One chord is split into parts A and B, the other into parts C and D.

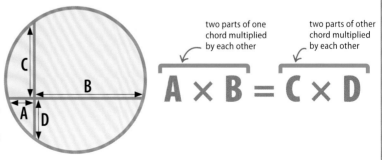

$$A \times B = C \times D$$

CHORDS AND CYCLIC QUADRILATERALS

Finding the center of a circle

Chords can be used to find the center of a circle. To do this, draw any two chords across the circle. Then find the midpoint of each chord, and draw a line through it that is at right angles to that chord (this is a perpendicular bisector). The center of the circle is where these two lines cross.

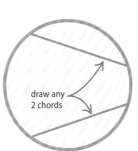

First, draw any two chords across the circle of which the center needs to be found.

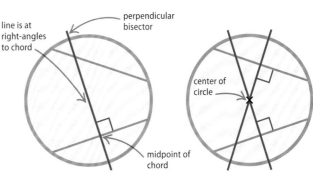

Then measure the midpoint of one of the chords, and draw a line through the midpoint at right-angles (90°) to the chord.

Do the same for the other chord. The center of the circle is the point where the two perpendicular lines cross.

Cyclic quadrilaterals

Cyclic quadrilaterals are four-sided shapes made from chords. Each corner of the shape sits on the circumference of a circle. The interior angles of a cyclic quadrilateral add up to 360°, as they do for all quadrilaterals. The opposite interior angles of a cyclic quadrilateral add up to 180°, and their exterior angles are equal to the opposite interior angles.

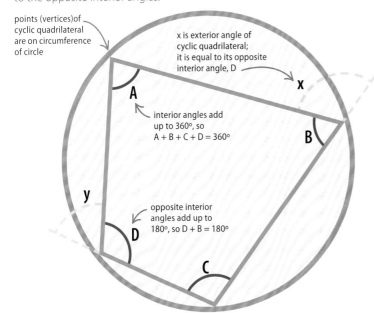

$$A + B + C + D = 360°$$

△ **Interior angle sum**
The interior angles of a cyclic quadrilateral always add up to 360°. Therefore, in this example $A + B + C + D = 360°$.

$$A + C = 180°$$
$$B + D = 180°$$

△ **Opposite angles**
Opposite angles in a cyclic quadrilateral always add up to 180°. In this example, $A + C = 180°$ and $B + D = 180°$.

$$y = B$$
$$x = D$$

△ **Exterior angles**
Exterior angles in cyclic quadrilaterals are equal to the opposite interior angles. Therefore, in this example, $y = B$ and $x = D$.

△ **Angles in a cyclic quadrilateral**
The four interior angles of this cyclic quadrilateral are A, B, C, and D. Two of the four exterior angles are x and y.

Tangents

A TANGENT IS A STRAIGHT LINE THAT TOUCHES THE CIRCUMFERENCE (EDGE) OF A CIRCLE AT A SINGLE POINT.

SEE ALSO
❮ 110–113 Constructions
❮ 128–129 Pythagorean Theorem
❮ 138–139 Circles

What are tangents?

A tangent is a line that extends from a point outside a circle and touches the edge of the circle in one place, the point of contact. The line joining the centre of the circle to the point of contact is a radius, at right-angles (90°) to the tangent. From a point outside the circle there are two tangents to the circle.

▷ **Tangent properties**
The lengths of the two tangents from a point outside a circle to their points of contact are equal.

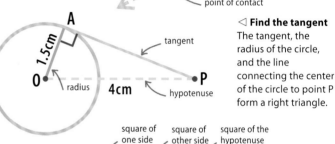

Finding the length of a tangent

A tangent is at right-angles to the radius at the point of contact, so a right triangle can be created using the radius, the tangent, and a line between them, which is the hypotenuse of the triangle. Pythagorean theorem can be used to find the length of any one of the three sides of the right triangle, if two sides are known.

◁ **Find the tangent**
The tangent, the radius of the circle, and the line connecting the center of the circle to point P form a right triangle.

Pythagorean theorem shows that the square of the hypotenuse (side facing the right-angle) of a right triangle is equal to the the sum of the two squares of the other sides of the triangle.

$$a^2 + b^2 = c^2$$

square of one side, square of other side, square of the hypotenuse

Substitute the known numbers into the formula. The hypotenuse is side OP, which is 4cm, and the other known length is the radius, which is 1.5cm. The side not known is the tangent, AP.

$$1.5^2 + AP^2 = 4^2$$

the value of the tangent is unknown

Find the squares of the two known sides by multiplying the value of each by itself. The square of 1.5 is 2.25, and the square of 4 is 16. Leave the value of the unknown side, AP^2 as it is.

$1.5 \times 1.5 = 2.25$
$4 \times 4 = 16$

$$2.25 + AP^2 = 16$$

Rearrange the equation to isolate the unknown variable. In this example the unknown is AP^2, the tangent. It is isolated by subtracting 2.25 from both sides of the equation.

subtract 2.25 from both sides to isolate the unknown term — 2.25 must be subtracted from both sides to isolate the unknown

$$AP^2 = 16 - 2.25$$

Carry out the subtraction on the right-hand side of the equation. The value this creates, 13.75, is the squared value of AP, which is the length of the missing side.

this means AP × AP
$16 - 2.25 = 13.75$

$$AP^2 = 13.75$$

Find the square root of both sides of the equation to find the value of AP. The square root of AP^2 is just AP. Use a calculator to find the square root of 13.75.

the square root of AP^2 is just AP
this is the sign for a square root

$$AP = \sqrt{13.75}$$

Find the square root of the value on the right, and round the answer to a suitable number of decimal places. This is the length of the missing side.

3.708... is rounded to 2 decimal places

$$AP = 3.71\text{cm}$$

TANGENTS

Constructing tangents

To construct a tangent accurately requires a compass and a straight edge. This example shows how to construct two tangents between a circle with center O and a given point outside the circle, in this case, P.

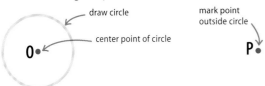

Draw a circle using a compass, and mark the center O. Also, mark another point outside the circle and label it (in this case P). Construct two tangents to the circle from the point.

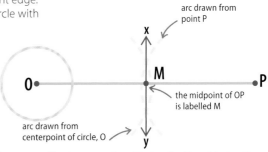

Draw a line between O and P, then find its midpoint. Set a compass to just over half OP, and draw two arcs, one from O and one from P. Join the two points where the arcs cross with a straight line (xy). The midpoint is where xy crosses OP.

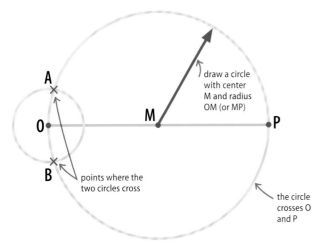

Set the compass to distance OM (or MP which is the same length), and draw a circle with M as its center. Mark the two points where this new circle intersects (crosses) the circumference of the original circle as A and B.

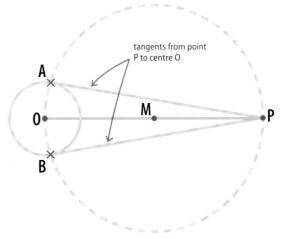

Finally, join each point where the circles intersect (cross), A and B, with point P. These two lines are the tangents from point P to the circle with center O. The two tangents are equal lengths.

Tangents and angles

Tangents to circles have some special angle properties. If a tangent touches a circle at B, and a chord, BC, is drawn across the circle from B, an angle is formed between the tangent and the chord at B. If lines (BD and CD) are drawn to the circumference from the ends of the chord, they create an angle at D that is equal to angle B.

▷ **Tangents and chords**
The angle formed between the tangent and the chord is equal to the angle formed at the circumference if two lines are drawn from either end of the chord to meet at a point on the circumference.

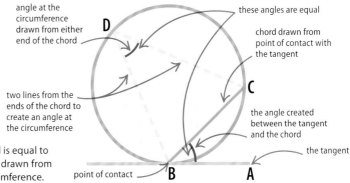

Arcs

AN ARC IS A SECTION OF A CIRCLE'S CIRCUMFERENCE. ITS LENGTH CAN BE FOUND USING ITS RELATED ANGLE AT THE CENTER OF THE CIRCLE.

> **SEE ALSO**
> ⟨ **56–59** Ratio and proportion
> ⟨ **138–139** Circles
> ⟨ **140–141** Circumference and diameter

What is an arc?

An arc is a part of the circumference of a circle. The length of an arc is in proportion with the size of the angle made at the center of the circle when lines are drawn from each end of the arc. If the length of an arc is unknown, it can be found using the circumference and this angle. When a circle is split into two arcs, the bigger is called the "major" arc, and the smaller the "minor" arc.

formula for finding the length of an arc

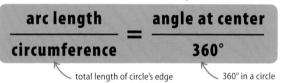

total length of circle's edge — 360° in a circle

▷ **Arcs and angles**
This diagram shows two arcs: one major, one minor, and their angles at the center of the circle.

angle created at the center when two lines are drawn from the ends of the major arc

minor arc

major arc

angle created at the center when two lines are drawn from the ends of the minor arc

Finding the length of an arc

The length of an arc is a proportion of the whole circumference of the circle. The exact proportion is the ratio between the angle formed from each end of the arc at the center of the circle, and 360°, which is the total number of degrees around the central point. This ratio is part of the formula for the length of an arc.

◁ **Find the arc length**
This circle has a circumference of 10 cm. Find the length of the arc that forms an angle of 120° at the center of the circle.

circumference is 10cm

Take the formula for finding the length of an arc. The formula uses the ratios between arc length and circumference, and between the angle at the center of the circle and 360° (total number of degrees).

$$\frac{\text{arc length}}{\text{circumference}} = \frac{\text{angle at center}}{360°}$$

Substitute the numbers that are known into the formula. In this example, the circumference is known to be 10 cm, and the angle at the center of the circle is 120°; 360° stays as it is.

$$\frac{\text{arc length}}{10} = \frac{120}{360}$$

this side has been multiplied by 10 to leave arc length on its own (÷10 × 10 cancels out)

this side has also been multiplied by 10 because what is done to one side must be done to the other

Rearrange the equation to isolate the unknown value—the arc length—on one side of the equals sign. In this example the arc length is isolated by multiplying both sides by 10.

$$\text{arc length} = \frac{10 \times 120}{360}$$

Multiply 10 by 120 and divide the answer by 360 to get the value of the arc length. Then round the answer to a suitable number of decimal places.

3.333... is rounded to 2 decimal places

$$C = 3.33\text{cm}$$

 Sectors

A SECTOR IS A SLICE OF A CIRCLE'S AREA. ITS AREA CAN BE FOUND USING THE ANGLE IT CREATES AT THE CENTER OF THE CIRCLE.

SEE ALSO
⟨ 56–59 Ratio and proportion
⟨ 138–139 Circles
⟨ 140–141 Circumference and diameter

What is a sector?

A sector of a circle is the space between two radii and one arc. The area of a sector depends on the size of the angle between the two radii at the center of the circle. If the area of a sector is unknown, it can be found using this angle and the area of the circle. When a circle is split into two sectors, the bigger is called the "major" sector, and the smaller the "minor" sector.

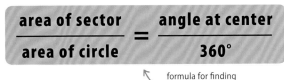

formula for finding the area of a sector

▷ **Sectors and angles**
This diagram shows two sectors: one major, one minor, and their angles at the center of the circle.

Finding the area of a sector

The area of a sector is a proportion, or part, of the area of the whole circle. The exact proportion is the ratio of the angle formed between the two radii that are the edges of the sector and 360°. This ratio is part of the formula for the area of a sector.

◁ **Find the sector area**
This circle has an area of 7 cm². Find the area of the sector that forms a 45° angle at the center of the circle.

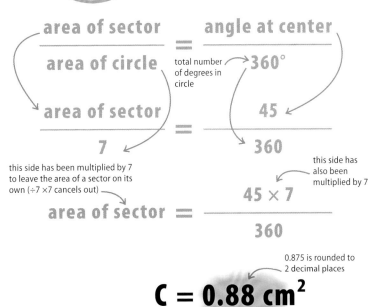

Take the formula for finding the area of a sector. The formula uses the ratios between the area of a sector and the area of the circle, and between the angle at the center of the circle and 360°.

Substitute the numbers that are known into the formula. In this example, the area is known to be 7 cm², and the angle at the center of the circle is 45°. The total number of degrees in a circle is 360°.

Rearrange the equation to isolate the unknown value—the area of the sector—on one side of the equals sign. In this example, this is done by multiplying both sides by 7.

Multiply 45 by 7 and divide the answer by 360 to get the area of the sector. Round the answer to a suitable number of decimal places.

152 GEOMETRY

 # Solids

A SOLID IS A THREE-DIMENSIONAL SHAPE.

SEE ALSO	
‹ 134–137 Polygons	
Volumes	154–155 ›
Surface area of solids	156–157 ›

Solids are objects with three dimensions: width, length, and height. They also have surface areas and volumes.

Prisms

Many common solids are polyhedrons—three-dimensional shapes with flat surfaces and straight edges. Prisms are a type of polyhedron made up of two parallel shapes of exactly the same shape and size, which are connected by faces. In the example to the right, the parallel shapes are pentagons, joined by rectangular faces. Usually a prism is named after the shape of its ends (or bases), so a prism whose parallel shapes are rectangles is known as a rectangular prism. If all its edges are equal sizes, it is called a cube.

▷ **A prism**
The cross section of this prism is a pentagon (a shape with five sides), so it is called a pentagonal prism.

◁ **Volume**
The amount of space that a solid occupies is called its volume.

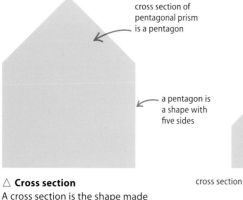

cross section of pentagonal prism is a pentagon

a pentagon is a shape with five sides

△ **Cross section**
A cross section is the shape made when an object is sliced from top to bottom.

cross section

cut out net and fold along edges to construct

this net forms a shape with seven faces

◁ **Surface area**
The surface area of a solid is the total area of its net—a two-dimensional shape, or plan, that forms the solid if it is folded up.

SOLIDS

vertex — a point where edges meet

face — a surface of the solid bordered by edges

length — distance of longest side

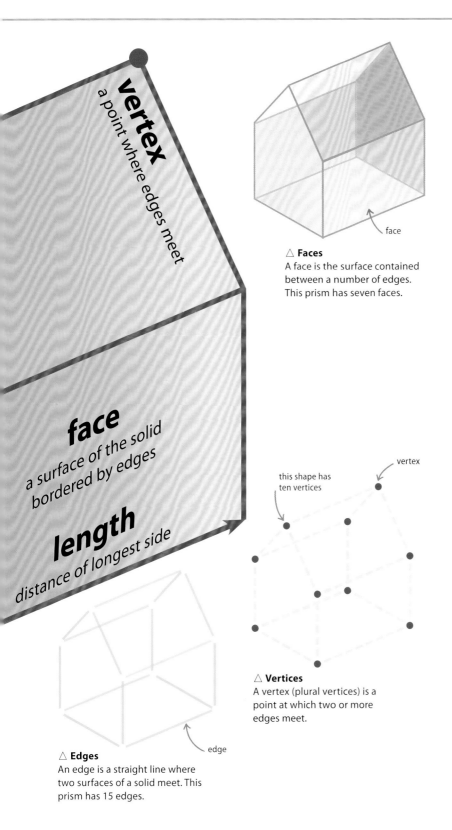

△ **Faces**
A face is the surface contained between a number of edges. This prism has seven faces.

△ **Vertices**
A vertex (plural vertices) is a point at which two or more edges meet.

△ **Edges**
An edge is a straight line where two surfaces of a solid meet. This prism has 15 edges.

Other solids

A solid with only flat surfaces is called a polyhedron and a solid with a curved surface is called a nonpolyhedron. Each common solid also has a name of its own.

▷ **Cylinder**
A cylinder is a prism with two circular ends joined by a curved surface.

▷ **Rectangular prism**
A rectangular prism is a prism whose opposite faces are equal. If all its edges are equal in length, it is a cube.

▷ **Sphere**
A sphere is a round solid in which the surface is always the same distance from its center.

▷ **Pyramid**
A pyramid has a polygon as its base and triangular faces that meet at a vertex (point).

▷ **Cone**
A cone is a solid with a circular base that is connected by a curved surface to its apex (highest point).

154 GEOMETRY

Volumes

THE AMOUNT OF SPACE WITHIN A THREE-DIMENSIONAL SHAPE.

SEE ALSO	
‹ 28–29 Units of measurement	
‹ 152–153 Solids	
Surface area of solids	156–157 ›

Solid space

When measuring volume, unit cubes, also called cubic units, are used, for example, cm^3 and m^3. An exact number of unit cubes fits neatly into some types of three-dimensional shapes, also known as solids, such as a cube, but for most solids, for example, a cylinder, this is not the case. Formulas are used to find the volumes of solids. Finding the area of the base, or the cross section, of a solid is the key to finding its volume. Each solid has a different cross-section.

▷ **Unit cubes**
A unit cube has sides that are of equal size. A 1 cm cube has a volume of $1 \times 1 \times 1$ cm, or $1\ cm^3$. The space within a solid can be measured by the number of unit cubes that can fit inside. This cuboid has a volume of $3 \times 2 \times 2$ cm, or $12\ cm^3$.

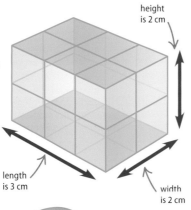

height is 2 cm
length is 3 cm
width is 2 cm

Finding the volume of a cylinder

A cylinder is made up from a rectangle and two circles. Its volume is found by multiplying the area of a circle with the length, or height, of the cylinder.

$$\text{volume} = \pi \times r^2 \times l$$

← formula for finding volume of a cylinder

The formula for the volume of a cylinder uses the formula for the area of a circle multiplied by the length of the cylinder.

equals 3.14   or r × r

$$\text{area} = \pi \times r^2$$

← formula for finding area of a circle

$$3.14 \times 3.8 \times 3.8 = \mathbf{45\ cm^2}$$

← area of cross section, given to 2 significant figures

First, find the area of the cylinder's cross-section using the formula for finding the area of a circle. Insert the values given on the illustration of the cylinder below.

$$\text{volume} = \text{area} \times \text{length}$$

$$45 \times 12 = \mathbf{544\ cm^3}$$

Next, multiply the area by the length of the cylinder to find its volume.

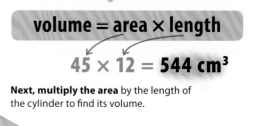

▷ **Circular cross-section**
The base of a cylinder is a circle. When a cylinder is sliced widthwise, the circles created are identical, so a cylinder is said to have a circular cross-section.

LENGTH = 12 cm
RADIUS = 3.8 cm
area of a cross section

VOLUMES

Volume of a rectangular prism

A rectangular prism has six flat sides and all of its faces are rectangles. Multiply the length by the width by the height to find the volume of a rectangular prism.

formula also written
v = l × w × h, or v = lwh

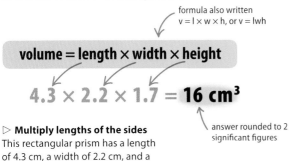

volume = length × width × height

$4.3 \times 2.2 \times 1.7 =$ **16 cm³**

answer rounded to 2 significant figures

▷ **Multiply lengths of the sides**
This rectangular prism has a length of 4.3 cm, a width of 2.2 cm, and a height of 1.7 cm. Multiply these measurements to find its volume.

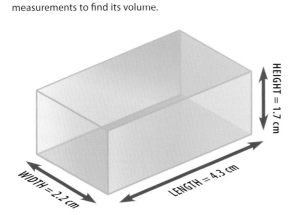

Finding the volume of a cone

Multiply the distance from the tip of the cone to the center of its base (the vertical height) with the area of its base (the area of a circle), then multiply by ⅓.

also called the perpendicular height

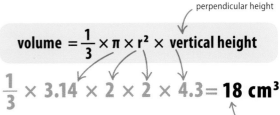

volume = $\frac{1}{3}$ × π × r² × vertical height

$\frac{1}{3} \times 3.14 \times 2 \times 2 \times 4.3 =$ **18 cm³**

answer rounded to 2 significant figures

▷ **Using the formula**
To find the volume of this cone, multiply together ⅓, π, the radius squared, and the vertical height.

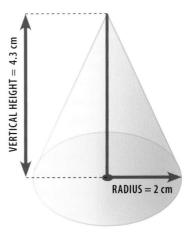

Finding the volume of a sphere

The radius is the only measurement needed to find the volume of a sphere. This sphere has a radius of 2.5 cm.

multiply radius by itself twice

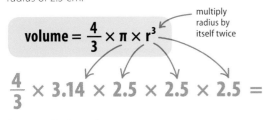

volume = $\frac{4}{3}$ × π × r³

$\frac{4}{3} \times 3.14 \times 2.5 \times 2.5 \times 2.5 =$ **65 cm³**

answer rounded to 2 significant figures

▷ **Using the formula**
To find the volume of this sphere, multiply together ⁴/₃, π, and the radius cubed (the radius multiplied by itself twice).

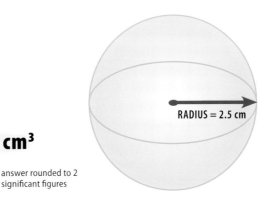

Surface area of solids

SURFACE AREA IS THE SPACE OCCUPIED BY A SHAPE'S OUTER SURFACES.

SEE ALSO
‹ 28–29 Units of measurement
‹ 152–153 Solids
‹ 154–155 Volumes

For most solids, surface area can be found by adding together the areas of its faces. The sphere is the exception, but there is an easy formula to use.

Surfaces of shapes

For all solids with straight edges, surface area can be found by adding together the areas of all the solid's faces. One way to do this is to imagine taking apart and flattening out the solid into two-dimensional shapes. It is then straightforward to work out and add together the areas of these shapes. A diagram of a flattened and opened out shape is known as its net.

▷ **Cylinder**
A cylinder has two flat faces and a curved surface. To create its net, the flat surfaces are separated and the curved surface opened up.

radius is the length from center of circle to its perimeter

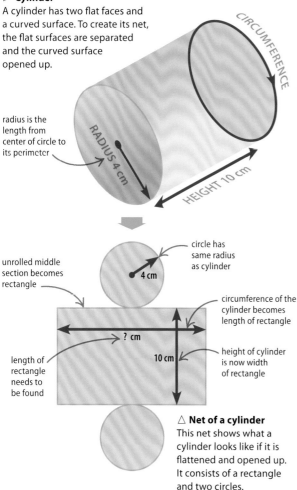

unrolled middle section becomes rectangle

circle has same radius as cylinder

circumference of the cylinder becomes length of rectangle

length of rectangle needs to be found

height of cylinder is now width of rectangle

△ **Net of a cylinder**
This net shows what a cylinder looks like if it is flattened and opened up. It consists of a rectangle and two circles.

Finding the surface area of a cylinder

Breaking the cylinder down into its component parts creates a rectangle and two circles. To find the total surface area, work out the area of each of these and add them together.

formula for area of circle

$$\text{Area} = \pi \times r^2$$

area of circle

$$3.14 \times 4 \times 4 = 50.24 \text{ cm}^2$$

The area of the circles can be worked out using the known radius and the formula for the area of a circle. π (pi) is usually shortened to 3.14, and area is always expressed in square units.

formula for circumference

$$\text{Circumference} = 2 \times \pi \times r$$

circumference of cylinder

$$2 \times 3.14 \times 4 = 25.12 \text{ cm}$$

Before the area of the rectangle can be found, it is necessary to work out its width—the circumference of the cylinder. This is done using the known radius and the formula for circumference.

length of rectangle = circumference of cylinder

width of rectangle = height of cylinder

area of rectangle

$$25.12 \times 10 = 251.2 \text{ cm}^2$$

The area of the rectangle can now be found by using the formula for the area of a rectangle (length × width).

surface area of cylinder

$$50.24 + 50.24 + 251.2 = 351.68 \text{ cm}^2$$

The surface area of the cylinder is found by adding together the areas of the three shapes that make up its net—two circles and a rectangle.

SURFACE AREA OF SOLIDS

Finding the surface area of a rectangular prism

A rectangular prism is made up of three different pairs of rectangles, here labeled A, B, and C. The surface area is the sum of the areas of all its faces.

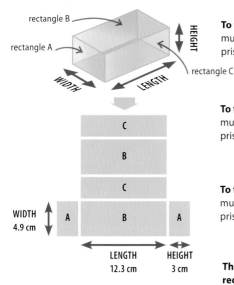

△ **Net of a rectangular prism**
The net is made up of three different pairs of rectangles.

To find the area of **rectangle A**, multiply together the rectangular prism's height and width.

To find the area of **rectangle B**, multiply together the rectangular prism's length and width.

To find the area of **rectangle C**, multiply together the rectangular prism's height and length.

The surface area of the **rectangular prism** is the total of the areas of its sides—twice area A, added to twice area B, added to twice area C.

Area of A = height × width

$3 \times 4.9 = $ **14.7 cm²**

Area of B = length × width

$12.3 \times 4.9 = $ **60.27 cm²**

Area of C = height × length

$3 \times 12.3 = $ **36.9 cm²**

parentheses used to separate operations

$(2 \times A) + (2 \times B) + (2 \times C)$

$(2 \times 14.7) + (2 \times 60.27) + (2 \times 36.9)$

$= $ **223.74 cm²**

Finding the surface area of a cone

A cone is made up of two parts—a circular base and a cone shape. Formulas are used to find the areas of the two parts, which are then added together to give the surface area.

Area = π × r × h ← slant height
surface area of cone without base

$3.14 \times 3.9 \times 9 = $ **110.21 cm²**

$\pi \times r^2$ ← formula for area of a circle
surface area of base

$3.14 \times 3.9 \times 3.9 = $ **47.76 cm²**

total surface area of cone

$110.21 + 47.76 = $ **157.97 cm²**

▷ **Cone**
Find the surface area of a cone by using formulas to find the area of the cone shape and the area of the base, and adding the two.

To find the area of the cone, multiply π by the radius and slant length.

To find the area of the base, use the formula for the area of a circle, $\pi \times r^2$.

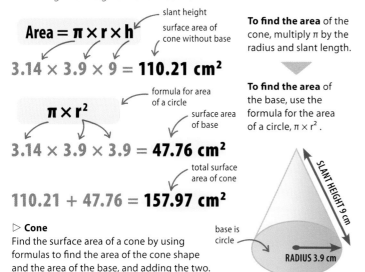

Finding the surface area of a sphere

Unlike many other solid shapes, a sphere cannot be unrolled or unfolded. Instead, a formula is used to find its surface area.

Area = 4 × π × r² ← formula for the surface area of a sphere

$4 \times 3.14 \times 17 \times 17$

$= $ **3,629.84 cm²**

▷ **Sphere**
The formula for the surface area of a sphere is the same as 4 times the formula for the area of a circle (πr^2). This means that the surface area of a sphere is equal to the surface area of 4 circles with the same radius.

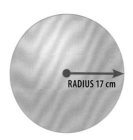

Trigonometry

What is trigonometry?

TRIGONOMETRY DEALS WITH THE RELATIONSHIPS BETWEEN THE SIZES OF ANGLES AND LENGTHS OF SIDES IN TRIANGLES.

SEE ALSO
⟨ 56–59 Ratio and proportion
⟨ 125–127 Similar triangles

Corresponding triangles

Trigonometry uses comparisons of the lengths of the sides of similar right triangles (which have the same shape but different sizes) to find the sizes of unknown angles and sides. This diagram shows the Sun creating shadows of a person and a building, which form two similar triangles. By measuring the shadows, the height of the person, which is known, can be used to find the height of the building, which is unknown.

▽ **Similar triangles**
The shadows the sun makes of the person and the building create two corresponding triangles.

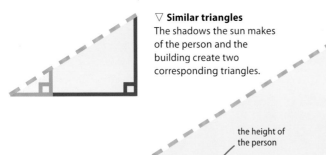

▷ **The ratio between** corresponding sides of similar triangles is equal, so the building's height divided by the person's height equals the length of the building's shadow divided by the length of the person's shadow.

▷ **Substitute the values** from the diagram into this equation. This leaves only one unknown—the height of the building (h)—which is found by rearranging the equation.

▷ **Rearrange the equation** to leave h (the height of the building) on its own. This is done by multiplying both sides of the equation by 6, then canceling out the two 6s on the left side, leaving just h.

▷ **Work out the right side** of the equation to find the value of h, which is the height of the building.

$$\frac{\text{height of building}}{\text{height of person}} = \frac{\text{length of building's shadow}}{\text{length of person's shadow}}$$

the value of h is unknown → $\frac{h}{6} = \frac{250}{9}$

whatever is done to one side of the equation must be done to the other, so this side must also be multiplied by 6

this side has been multiplied by 6 to cancel out the ÷ 6 and isolate h → $h = \frac{250}{9} \times 6$

the answer is rounded to 2 decimal places

$$h = 166.67 \text{ ft}$$

Using formulas in trigonometry

TRIGONOMETRY FORMULAS CAN BE USED TO WORK OUT THE LENGTHS OF SIDES AND SIZES OF ANGLES IN TRIANGLES.

SEE ALSO
⟨ 56–59 Ratio and proportion
⟨ 125–127 Similar triangles
Finding missing sides 162–163 ⟩
Finding missing angles 164–165 ⟩

Right triangles
The sides of these triangles are called the hypotenuse, opposite, and adjacent. The hypotenuse is always the side opposite the right angle. The names of the other two sides depend on where they are in relation to the particular angle specified.

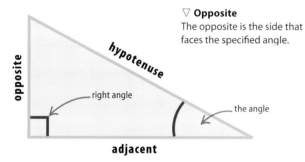

▽ **Opposite**
The opposite is the side that faces the specified angle.

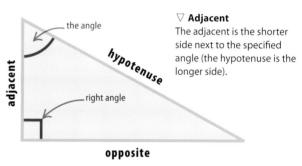

▽ **Adjacent**
The adjacent is the shorter side next to the specified angle (the hypotenuse is the longer side).

Trigonometry formulas
There are three basic formulas used in trigonometry. "A" stands in for the angle that is being found (this may also sometimes be written as θ). The formula to use depends on the sides of the triangle that are known.

$$\sin A = \frac{\text{opposite}}{\text{hypotenuse}}$$

△ **The sine formula**
The sine formula is used when the lengths of the opposite and hypotenuse are known.

$$\cos A = \frac{\text{adjacent}}{\text{hypotenuse}}$$

△ **The cosine formula**
The cosine formula is used when the lengths of the adjacent and hypotenuse are known.

$$\tan A = \frac{\text{opposite}}{\text{adjacent}}$$

△ **The tangent formula**
The tangent formula is used when the lengths of the opposite and adjacent are known.

Using a calculator
The values of sine, cosine, and tangent are set for each angle. Calculators have buttons that retrieve these values. Use them to find the sine, cosine, or tangent of a particular angle.

△ **Sine, cosine, and tangent**
Press the sine, cosine, or tangent button then enter the value of the angle to find its sine, cosine, or tangent.

 then

△ **Inverse sine, cosine, and tangent**
Press the shift button, then the sin, cosine, or tangent button, then enter the value of the sine, cosine, or tangent to find the inverse (the angle in degrees).

Finding missing sides

GIVEN AN ANGLE AND THE LENGTH OF ONE SIDE OF A RIGHT TRIANGLE, THE OTHER SIDES CAN BE FOUND.

The trigonometry formulas can be used to find a length in a right triangle if one angle (other than the right angle) and one other side are known. Use a calculator to find the sine, cosine, or tangent of an angle.

SEE ALSO
‹ 160 What is trigonometry?
Finding missing angles 164–165 ›
Formulas 177–179 ›

▽ **Calculator buttons**
These calculator buttons recall the value of sine, cosine, and tangent for any value entered.

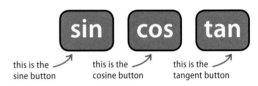

this is the sine button • this is the cosine button • this is the tangent button

Which formula?
The formula to use depends on what information is known. Choose the formula that contains the known side as well as the side that needs to be found. For example, use the sine formula if the length of the hypotenuse is known, one angle other than the right angle is known, and the length of the side opposite the given angle needs to be found.

$$\sin A = \frac{\text{opposite}}{\text{hypotenuse}}$$

△ **The sine formula**
This formula is used if one angle, and either the side opposite it or the hypotenuse are given.

$$\cos A = \frac{\text{adjacent}}{\text{hypotenuse}}$$

△ **The cosine formula**
Use this formula if one angle and either the side adjacent to it or the hypotenuse are known.

$$\tan A = \frac{\text{opposite}}{\text{adjacent}}$$

△ **The tangent formula**
This formula is used if one angle and either the side opposite it or adjacent to it are given.

Using the sine formula
In this right triangle, one angle other than the right angle is known, as is the length of the hypotenuse. The length of the side opposite the angle is missing and needs to be found.

Choose the right formula—because the hypotenuse is known and the value for the opposite side is what needs to be found, use the sine formula.

Substitute the known values into the sine formula.

Rearrange the formula to make the unknown (x) the subject by multiplying both sides by 7.

Use a calculator to find the value of sin 37°—press the sin button then enter 37.

Round the answer to a suitable size.

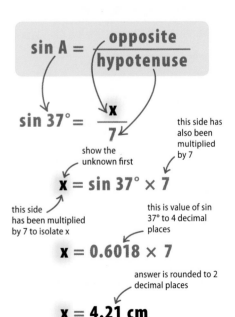

$$\sin A = \frac{\text{opposite}}{\text{hypotenuse}}$$

$$\sin 37° = \frac{x}{7}$$

this side has also been multiplied by 7

show the unknown first

$$x = \sin 37° \times 7$$

this side has been multiplied by 7 to isolate x

this is value of sin 37° to 4 decimal places

$$x = 0.6018 \times 7$$

answer is rounded to 2 decimal places

$$x = 4.21 \text{ cm}$$

hypotenuse is side opposite right angle

7 cm (hypotenuse)

x (opposite)

missing length

37°

use this angle in calculation

FINDING MISSING SIDES 163

Using the cosine formula

In this right triangle, one angle other than the right angle is known, as is the length of the side adjacent to it. The hypotenuse is the missing side that needs to be found.

Choose the right formula—because the side adjacent to the angle is known and the value of the hypotenuse is missing, use the cosine formula.

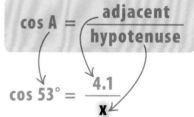

$$\cos A = \frac{\text{adjacent}}{\text{hypotenuse}}$$

Substitute the known values into the formula.

$$\cos 53° = \frac{4.1}{x}$$

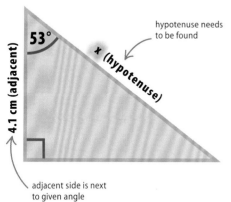

hypotenuse needs to be found

Rearrange to make x the subject of the equation—first multiply both sides by x.

$$\cos 53° \times x = 4.1$$

this side has been multiplied by x

this side has also been multiplied by x, leaving 4.1 on its own

Divide both sides by cos 53° to make x the subject of the equation.

$$x = \frac{4.1}{\cos 53°}$$

ths side has been divided by cos 53° to isolate x

this side has also been divided by cos 53°

Use a calculator to find the value of cos 53°—press the cos button then enter 53.

$$x = \frac{4.1}{0.6018}$$

value of cos 53° is rounded to 4 decimal places

adjacent side is next to given angle

Round the answer to a suitable size.

$$x = 6.81 \text{ cm}$$

answer is rounded to 2 decimal places

Using the tangent formula

In this right triangle, one angle other than the right angle is known, as is the length of the side adjacent to it. Find the length of the side opposite the angle.

Choose the right formula—since the side adjacent to the angle given are known and the opposite side is sought, use the tangent formula.

$$\tan A = \frac{\text{opposite}}{\text{adjacent}}$$

Substitute the known values into the tangent formula.

$$\tan 53° = \frac{x}{3.7}$$

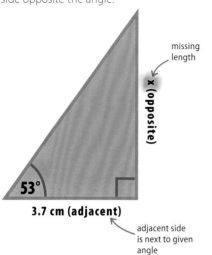

missing length

show the unknown first

Rearrange to make x the subject by multiplying both sides by 3.7.

$$x = \tan 53° \times 3.7$$

this side has been multiplied by 3.7 to isolate x

this side has also been multiplied by 3.7

value of tan 53° is rounded to 4 decimal places

Use a calculator to find the value of tan 53° – press the tan button then enter 53.

$$x = 1.3270 \times 3.7$$

adjacent side is next to given angle

Round the answer to a suitable size.

$$x = 4.91 \text{ cm}$$

the answer is rounded to 2 decimal places

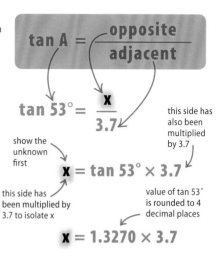

164 TRIGONOMETRY

 # Finding missing angles

IF THE LENGTHS OF TWO SIDES OF A RIGHT TRIANGLE ARE KNOWN, ITS MISSING ANGLES CAN BE FOUND.

SEE ALSO
‹ 72–73 Using a calculator
‹ 160 What is trigonometry?
‹ 162–163 Finding missing sides
Formulas 177–179 ›

To find the missing angles in a right triangle, the inverse sine, cosine, and tangent are used. Use a calculator to find these values.

Which formula?
Choose the formula that contains the pair of sides that are given in an example. For instance, use the sine formula if the lengths of the hypotenuse and the side opposite the unknown angle are known, and the cosine formula if the lengths of the hypotenuse and the side next to the angle are given.

▽ **Calculator functions**
To find the inverse values of sine, cosine, and tangent, press shift before sine, cosine, or tangent.

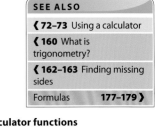

$$\sin A = \frac{\text{opposite}}{\text{hypotenuse}}$$

△ **The sine formula**
Use the sine formula if the lengths of the hypotenuse and the side opposite the missing angle are known.

$$\cos A = \frac{\text{adjacent}}{\text{hypotenuse}}$$

△ **The cosine formula**
Use the cosine formula if the lengths of the hypotenuse and the side adjacent (next to) to the missing angle are known.

$$\tan A = \frac{\text{opposite}}{\text{adjacent}}$$

△ **The tangent formula**
Use the tangent formula if the lengths of the sides opposite and adjacent to the missing angle are known.

Using the sine formula
In this right triangle the hypotenuse and the side opposite angle A are known. Use the sine formula to find the size of angle A.

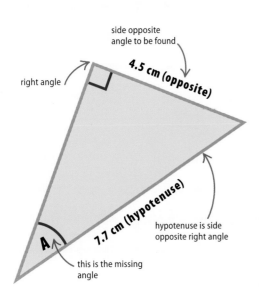

Choose the right formula—in this example the hypotenuse and the side opposite the missing angle, A, are known, so use the sine formula.

$$\sin A = \frac{\text{opposite}}{\text{hypotenuse}}$$

Substitute the known values into the sine formula.

$$\sin A = \frac{4.5}{7.7}$$

Work out the value of sin A by dividing the opposite side by the hypotenuse.

$$\sin A = 0.5844$$

answer is rounded to 4 decimal places

Find the value of the angle by using the inverse sine function on a calculator.

press shift then the sine button to get inverse sine

$$A = \sin^{-1}(0.5844)$$

Round the answer to a suitable size. This is the value of the missing angle.

this is rounded to 2 decimal places

$$A = 35.76°$$

FINDING MISSING ANGLES   **165**

Using the cosine formula

In this right triangle the hypotenuse and the side adjacent to angle A are known. Use the cosine formula to find the size of angle A.

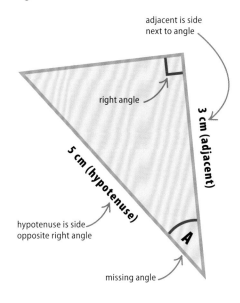

Choose the right formula. In this example the hypotenuse and the side adjacent to the mssing angle, A, are known, so use the cosine formula.

$$\cos A = \frac{\text{adjacent}}{\text{hypotenuse}}$$

Substitute the known values into the formula.

$$\cos A = \frac{3}{5}$$

Work out the value of cos A by dividing the adjacent side by the length of the hypotenuse.

$$\cos A = 0.6$$

Find the value of the angle by using the inverse cosine function on a calculator.

$$A = \cos^{-1}(0.6)$$

press shift then cosine button to get inverse cosine

Round the answer to a suitable size. This is the value of the missing angle.

$$A = 53.13°$$

answer is rounded to 2 decimal places

Using the tangent formula

In this right triangle the sides opposite and adjacent to angle A are known. Use the tangent formula to find the size of angle A.

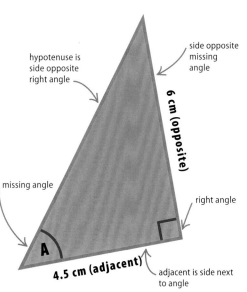

Choose the right formula—here the sides opposite and adjacent to the missing angle, A, are known, so use the tangent formula.

$$\tan A = \frac{\text{opposite}}{\text{adjacent}}$$

Substitute the known values into the tangent formula.

$$\tan A = \frac{6}{4.5}$$

answer rounded to 1 decimal place

Work out the value of tan A by dividing the opposite by the adjacent.

$$\tan A = 1.3$$

press shift then tangent button to get inverse tangent

Find the value of the angle by using the inverse tangent function on a calculator.

$$A = \tan^{-1}(1.3)$$

answer is rounded to 2 decimal places

Round the answer to a suitable size. This is the value of the missing angle.

$$A = 52.43°$$

Algebra

What is algebra?

ALGEBRA IS A BRANCH OF MATHEMATICS IN WHICH LETTERS AND SYMBOLS ARE USED TO REPRESENT NUMBERS AND THE RELATIONSHIPS BETWEEN NUMBERS.

Algebra is widely used in maths, in sciences such as physics, as well as in other areas, such as economics. Formulas for solving a wide range of problems are often given in algebraic form.

Using letters and symbols

Algebra uses letters and symbols. Letters usually represent numbers, and symbols represent operations, such as addition and subtraction. This allows relationships between quantities to be written in a short, generalized way, eliminating the need to give individual specific examples containing actual values. For instance, the volume of a rectangular solid can be written as lwh (which means length × width × height), enabling the volume of any cuboid to be found once its dimensions are known.

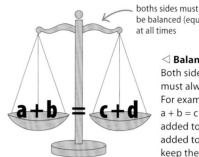

◁ **Balancing**
Both sides of an equation must always be balanced. For example, in the equation $a + b = c + d$, if a number is added to one side, it must be added to the other side to keep the equation balanced.

TERM
The parts of an algebraic expression that are separated by symbols for operations, such as + and −. A term can be a number, a variable, or a combination of both

OPERATION
A procedure carried out on the terms of an algebraic expression, such as addition, subtraction, multiplication, and division

VARIABLE
An unknown number or quantity represented by a letter

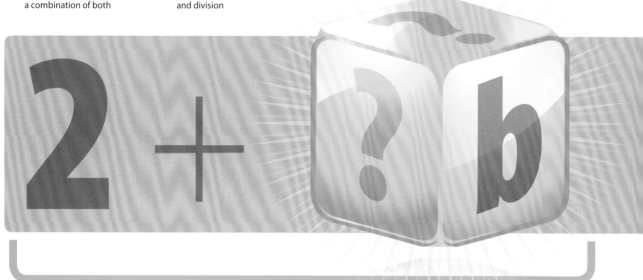

EXPRESSION
An expression is a statement written in algebraic form, 2 + b in the example above. An expression can contain any combination of numbers, letters, and symbols (such as + for addition)

△ **Algebraic equation**
An equation is a mathematical statement that two things are equal. In this example, the left side (2 + b) is equal to the right side (8).

WHAT IS ALGEBRA? 169

REAL WORLD
Algebra in everyday life

Although algebra may seem abstract, with equations consisting of strings of symbols and letters, it has many applications in everyday life. For example, an equation can be used to find out the area of something, such as a tennis court.

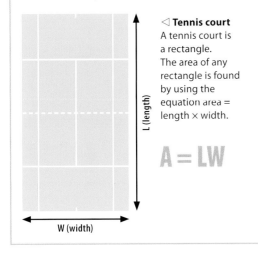

◁ **Tennis court**
A tennis court is a rectangle. The area of any rectangle is found by using the equation area = length × width.

$A = LW$

BASIC RULES OF ALGEBRA
Like other areas of maths, algebra has rules that must be followed to get the correct answer. For example, one rule is about the order in which operations must be done.

Addition and subtraction
Terms can be added together in any order in algebra. However, when subtracting, the order of the terms must be kept as it was given.

$$a + b = b + a$$

△ **Two terms**
When adding together two terms, it is possible to start with either term.

$$(a + b) + c = a + (b + c)$$

△ **Three terms**
As with adding two terms, three terms can be added together in any order.

Multiplication and division
Multiplying terms in algebra can be done in any order, but when dividing the terms must be kept in the order they were given.

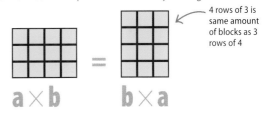

4 rows of 3 is same amount of blocks as 3 rows of 4

$$a \times b = b \times a$$

△ **Two terms**
When multiplying together two terms, the terms can be in any order.

EQUALS	CONSTANT
The equals sign means that the two sides of the equation balance each other	A number with a value that is always the same

THE ANSWER IS:
b = 6

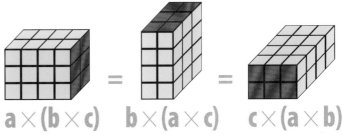

$$a \times (b \times c) = b \times (a \times c) = c \times (a \times b)$$

△ **Three terms**
Multiplication of three terms can be done in any order.

Sequences

A SEQUENCE IS A SERIES OF NUMBERS WRITTEN AS A LIST THAT FOLLOWS A PARTICULAR PATTERN, OR "RULE."

SEE ALSO	
‹ 36–39 Powers and roots	
‹ 168–169 What is algebra?	
Working with expressions	172–173 ›
Formulas	177–179 ›

Each number in a sequence is called a "term." The value of any term in a sequence can be worked out by using the rule for that sequence.

The terms of a sequence

The first number in a sequence is the first term, the second number in a sequence is the second term, and so on.

▷ **A basic sequence**
For this sequence, the rule is that each term is the previous term with 2 added to it.

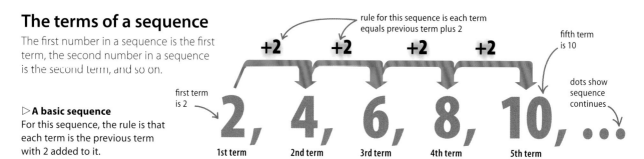

Finding the "nth" value

The value of a particular term can be found without writing out the entire sequence up until that point by writing the rule as an expression and then using this expression to work out the term.

▷ **The rule as an expression**
Knowing the expression, which is $2n$ in this example, helps find the value of any term.

expression used to find value of term— 1 is substituted for n in 1st term, 2 in 2nd term, and so on

$2n = 2 \times 1 = 2$
1st term
To find the first term, substitute 1 for n.

$2n = 2 \times 2 = 4$
2nd term
To find the second term, substitute 2 for n.

$2n = 2 \times 41 = 82$
41st term
To find the 41st term, substitute 41 for n.

$2n = 2 \times 1,000 = 2,000$
1,000th term
For the 1,000th term, substitute 1,000 for n. The term here is 2,000.

In the example below, the expression is $4n - 2$. Knowing this, the rule can be shown to be: each term is equal to the previous term plus 4.

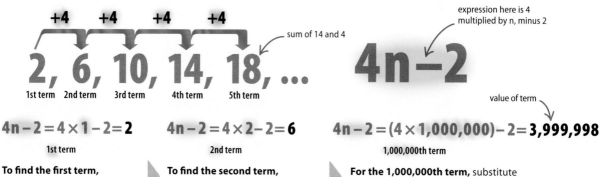

$4n - 2 = 4 \times 1 - 2 = 2$
1st term
To find the first term, substitute 1 for n.

$4n - 2 = 4 \times 2 - 2 = 6$
2nd term
To find the second term, substitute 2 for n.

$4n - 2 = (4 \times 1,000,000) - 2 = 3,999,998$
1,000,000th term
For the 1,000,000th term, substitute 1,000,000 for n. The term here is 3,999,998.

SEQUENCES 171

IMPORTANT SEQUENCES
Some sequences have rules that are slightly more complicated; however, they can be very significant. Two examples of these are square numbers and the Fibonacci sequence.

Square numbers
A square number is found by multiplying a whole number by itself. These numbers can be drawn as squares. Each side is the length of a whole number, which is multiplied by itself to make the square number.

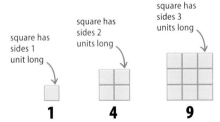

Fibonacci sequence
The Fibonacci sequence is a widely recognized sequence, appearing frequently in nature and architecture. The first two terms of the sequence are both 1, then after this each term is the sum of the two terms that came before it.

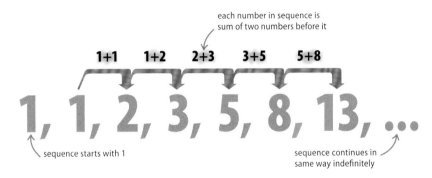

REAL WORLD
Fibonacci and nature
Evidence of the Fibonacci sequence is found everywhere, including in nature. The sequence forms a spiral (see below) and it can be seen in the spiral of a shell (as shown here) or in the arrangement of the seeds in a sunflower. It is named after Leonardo Fibonacci, an Italian mathematician.

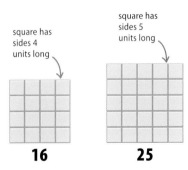

How to draw a Fibonacci spiral
A spiral can be drawn using the numbers in the Fibonacci sequence, by drawing squares with sides as long as each term in the sequence, then drawing a curve to touch the opposite corners of these squares.

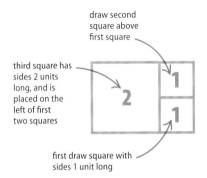

First, draw a square that is 1 unit long by 1 unit wide. Draw an identical one above it, then a square with sides 2 units long next to the 1 unit squares. Each square represents a term of the sequence.

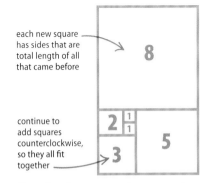

Keep drawing squares that represent the terms of the Fibonacci sequence, adding them in a counterclockwise direction. This diagram shows the first six terms of the sequence.

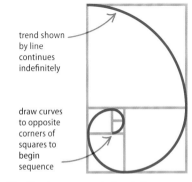

Finally, draw curves to touch the opposite corners of each square, starting at the center and working outward counterclockwise. This curve is a Fibonacci spiral.

Working with expressions

AN EXPRESSION IS A COLLECTION OF SYMBOLS, SUCH AS X AND Y, AND OPERATIONS, SUCH AS + AND –. IT CAN ALSO CONTAIN NUMBERS.

SEE ALSO
‹ 168–169 What is algebra?
Formulas 177–179 ›

Expressions are important and occur everywhere in mathematics. They can be simplified to as few parts as possible, making them easier to understand.

Like terms in an expression
Each part of an expression is called a "term." A term can be a number, a symbol, or a number with a symbol. Terms with the same symbols are "like terms" and it is possible to combine them.

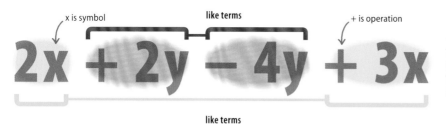

◁ **Identifying like terms**
The terms 2x and 3x are like terms because they both contain the symbol x. Terms 2y and –4y are also like terms because each contains the symbol y.

Simplifying expressions involving addition and subtraction
When an expression is made up of a number of terms that are to be added or subtracted, there are a number of important steps that need to be followed in order to simplify it.

▷ **Write down the expression**
Before simplifying the expression, write it out in a line from left to right.

$$3a - 5b + 6b - 2a + 3b - 7b$$

▷ **Group the like terms**
Then group the like terms together, keeping the operations as they are.

$$3a - 2a - 5b + 6b + 3b - 7b$$
like terms   like terms

▷ **Work out the result**
The next step is to work out the result of each like term.

$3a - 2a = 1a$ → $1a - 3b$ ← $-5b + 6b + 3b - 7b = -3b$

▷ **Simplify the result**
Further simplify the result by removing any 1s in front of symbols.

term 1a always written as a → $a - 3b$

WORKING WITH EXPRESSIONS

Simplifying expressions involving multiplication

To simplify an expression that involves terms linked by multiplication signs, the individual numbers and symbols first need to be separated from each other.

$6a \times 2b$

The term **6a** means $6 \times a$. Similarly, the term **2b** means $2 \times b$.

➡

$6 \times a \times 2 \times b$

Separate the expression into the individual numbers and symbols involved.

➡

$12 \times ab =$ 12ab

simplified expression written without multiplication signs

The product of multiplying 6 and 2 is 12, and that of multiplying a and b is ab. The simplified expression is 12ab.

Simplifying expressions involving division

To simplify an expression involving division, look for any possible cancellation. This means looking to divide all terms of the expression by the same number or letter.

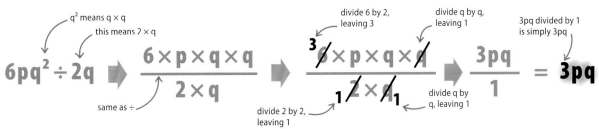

q^2 means $q \times q$ this means $2 \times q$

$6pq^2 \div 2q$ same as ÷

➡ $\dfrac{6 \times p \times q \times q}{2 \times q}$

divide 6 by 2, leaving 3; divide q by q, leaving 1

➡ $\dfrac{\overset{3}{\cancel{6}} \times p \times q \times \cancel{q}}{\underset{1}{\cancel{2}} \times \cancel{q}_1}$

divide 2 by 2, leaving 1; divide q by q, leaving 1

➡ $\dfrac{3pq}{1} =$ **3pq**

3pq divided by 1 is simply 3pq

Any chance to cancel the expression down makes it smaller and easier to understand.

Both terms (top and bottom) are canceled down by dividing them by 2 and q.

Canceling down by dividing each term equally makes the expression smaller.

Substitution

Once the value of each symbol in an expression is known, for example that y = 2, the overall value of the expression can be found. This is called "substituting" the values in the expression or "evaluating" the expression.

Substitute the values in the expression $2x - 2y - 4y + 3x$ if **x = 1** and **y = 2**

W = WIDTH

◁ **Substituting values**
The formula for the area of a rectangle is length × width. Substituting 5 in for the length and 8 in for the width, gives an area of 5 in × 8 in = 40 in².

like terms
$2x - 2y - 4y + 3x$
like terms

grouped terms are easier to substitute

➡ $5x - 6y$

substitute 1 for x

➡ $5x = 5 \times 1 = 5$
$-6y = -6 \times 2 = -12$

substitute 2 for y

answer is −7

➡ $5 - 12 =$ **−7**

Group like terms together to simplify the expression.

The expression has now been simplified.

Now substitute the given values for x and y.

The final answer is shown to be −7.

2(a + 2) Expanding and factorizing expressions

> **SEE ALSO**
> ‹ 172–173 Working with expressions
> Quadratic expressions 176 ›

THE SAME EXPRESSION CAN BE WRITTEN IN DIFFERENT WAYS—MULTIPLIED OUT (EXPANDED) OR GROUPED INTO ITS COMMON FACTORS (FACTORIZED).

How to expand an expression

The same expression can be written in a variety of ways, depending on how it will be used. Expanding an expression involves multiplying all the parts it contains (terms) and writing it out in full.

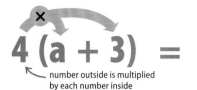

number outside is multiplied by each number inside

first term is multiplied by number
second term is multiplied by number

$4 \times a = 4a$ $4 \times 3 = 12$

$= 4a + 12$

sign between terms remains the same

▸ **To expand an expression** with a number outside a parenthesis, multiply all the terms inside the parenthesis by that number.

▸ **Multiply each term** inside the parenthesis by the number outside. The sign between the two terms (letters and numbers) remains the same.

▸ **Simplify the resulting terms** to show the expanded expression in its final form. Here, $4 \times a$ is simplified to $4a$ and 4×3 to 12.

Expanding multiple parentheses

To expand an expression that contains two parentheses, each part of the first one is multiplied by each part of the second parenthesis. To do this, split up the first (blue) parenthesis into its parts. Multiply the second (yellow) parenthesis by the first part and then by the second part of the first parenthesis.

second parenthesis multiplied by first part of first parenthesis

$3x \times 2y = 6xy$ $3x \times 3 = 9x$ $1 \times 2y = 2y$ $1 \times 3 = 3$

$(3x + 1)(2y + 3) = 3x(2y + 3) + 1(2y + 3) = 6xy + 9x + 2y + 3$

first parenthesis   second parenthesis

second parenthesis multiplied by second term of first parenthesis

these signs remain

▸ **To expand an expression** of two parentheses, multiply all the terms of the second by all the terms of the first.

▸ **Break down the first parenthesis** into its terms. Multiply the second parenthesis by each term from the first in turn.

▸ **Simplify the resulting terms** by carrying out each multiplication. The signs remain the same.

Squaring a parenthesis

Squaring a parenthesis simply means multiplying a parenthesis by itself. Write it out as two parentheses next to each other, and then multiply it to expand as shown above.

parenthesis means multiply

$x \times x = x^2$ $x \times -3 = -3x$ $-3 \times x = -3x$ $-3 \times -3 = 9$

$(x - 3)^2 = (x - 3)(x - 3) = x(x - 3) - 3(x - 3) = x^2 - 3x - 3x + 9 = x^2 - 6x + 9$

multiply second parenthesis by first part of first one

sign remains the same

multiply second parenthesis by second part of first parenthesis

▸ **To expand a squared parenthesis**, first write the expression out as two parentheses next to each other.

▸ **Split the first parenthesis** into its terms and multiply the second parenthesis by each term in turn.

▸ **Simplify the resulting terms,** making sure to multiply their signs correctly. Finally, add or subtract like terms (see pp.172–173) together.

EXPANDING AND FACTORIZING EXPRESSIONS

How to factorize an expression

Factorizing an expression is the opposite of expanding an expression. To do this, look for a factor (number or letter) that all the terms (parts) of the expression have in common. The common factor can then be placed outside a parenthesis enclosing what is left of the other terms.

4 is common to both 4b and 12 (because they can both be divided by 4)

$$4b + 12$$

↖ this means $4 \times b$

To factorize an expression, look for any letter or number (factor) that all its parts have in common.

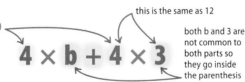

this is the same as 12

both b and 3 are not common to both parts so they go inside the parenthesis

In this case, 4 is a common factor of both 4b and 12, because both can be divided by 4. Divide each by 4 to find the remaining factors of each part. These go inside the parenthesis.

place 4 outside parenthesis

remaining factors go inside parenthesis

$$4(b + 3)$$

parenthesis means multiply

Simplify the expression by placing the common factor (4) outside a parenthesis. The other two factors are placed inside the parenthesis.

Factorizing more complex expressions

Factorizing can make it simpler to understand and write complex expressions with many terms. Find the factors that all parts of the expression have in common.

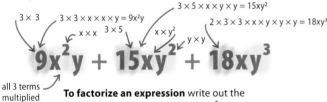

3×3 $3 \times 3 \times x \times x \times x \times y = 9x^2y$ $3 \times 5 \times x \times x \times y \times y = 15xy^2$

$x \times x$ 3×5 $x \times y^2$ $2 \times 3 \times 3 \times x \times y \times y \times y = 18xy^3$ $y \times y$

$$9x^2y + 15xy^2 + 18xy^3$$

all 3 terms multiplied

To factorize an expression write out the factors of each part, for example, y^2 is $y \times y$. Look for the numbers and letters that are common to all the factors.

common factor of numbers

common factor of x variables

common factor of y variables

All the parts of the expressions contain the letters x and y, and can be factorized by the number 3. These factors are combined to produce one common factor.

3xy is common factor of all parts of the expression

$9x^2y \div 3xy = 3x$ $15xy^2 \div 3xy = 5y$

$18xy^3 \div 3xy = 6y^2$

$$3xy(3x + 5y + 6y^2)$$

Set the common factor (3xy) outside a set of parentheses. Inside, write what remains of each part when divided by it.

LOOKING CLOSER

Factorizing a formula

The formula for finding the surface area (see pp.156–157) of a shape can be worked out using known formulas for the areas of its parts. The formula can look daunting, but it can be made much easier to use by factorizing it.

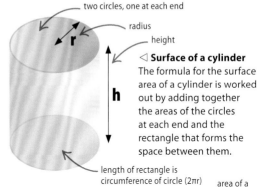

two circles, one at each end

radius

height

◁ **Surface of a cylinder**
The formula for the surface area of a cylinder is worked out by adding together the areas of the circles at each end and the rectangle that forms the space between them.

length of rectangle is circumference of circle ($2\pi r$)

area of rectangle is length ($2\pi r$) height (h)

area of a circle is πr^2, for 2 circles it is $2\pi r^2$

$$2\pi rh + 2\pi r^2$$

To find the formula for the surface area of a cylinder, add together the formulas for the areas of its parts.

$2\pi r$ is common to both expressions

means multiply by

h and r are not common to both terms so they sit inside the parenthesis

$$2\pi r(h + r)$$

To make the formula easier to use, simplify it by identifying the common factor, in this case $2\pi r$, and setting it outside the parentheses.

Quadratic expressions

A QUADRATIC EXPRESSION CONTAINS AN UNKNOWN TERM (VARIABLE) SQUARED, SUCH AS X^2.

SEE ALSO	
‹ 174–175 Expanding and factorizing expressions	
Factorizing quadratic equations	190–191 ›

An expression is a collection of mathematical symbols, such as x and y, and operations, such as + and –. A quadratic expression typically contains a squared variable (x^2), a number multiplied by the same variable (x), and a number.

What is a quadratic expression?

A quadratic expression is usually given in the form $ax^2 + bx + c$, where a is the multiple of the squared term x^2, b is the multiple of x, and c is the number. The letters a, b, and c all stand for different positive or negative numbers.

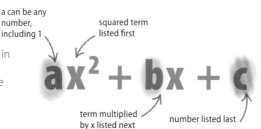

- a can be any number, including 1
- squared term listed first
- term multiplied by x listed next
- number listed last

◁ **Quadratic expression**
The standard form of a quadratic expression is one with squared term (x^2) listed first, terms multiplied by x listed second, and the number listed last.

From two parentheses to a quadratic expression

Some quadratic expressions can be factorized to form two expressions within parentheses, each containing a variable (x) and an unknown number. Conversely, multiplying out these expressions gives a quadratic expression.

Multiplying two expressions in parentheses means multiplying every term of one parenthesis with every term of the other. The final answer will be a quadratic equation.

To multiply the two parentheses, split one of the parentheses into its terms. Multiply all the terms of the second parenthesis first by the x term and then by the numerical term of the first parenthesis.

Multiplying both terms of the second parenthesis by each term of the first in turn results in a squared term, two terms multiplied by x, and two numerical terms multiplied together.

Simplify the expression by adding the x terms. This means adding the numbers together inside parentheses and multiplying the result by an x outside.

Looking back at the original quadratic expression, it is possible to see that the numerical terms are added to give b, and multiplied to give c.

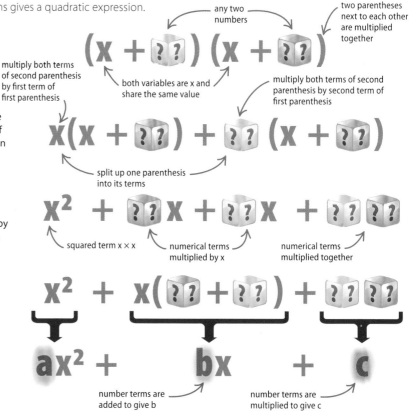

Formulas

IN MATHS, A FORMULA IS BASICALLY A "RECIPE" FOR FINDING THE VALUE OF ONE THING (THE SUBJECT) WHEN OTHERS ARE KNOWN.

SEE ALSO	
‹ 74–75 Personal finance	
‹ 172–173 Working with expressions	
Solving equations	180–181 ›

A formula usually has a single subject and an equals sign, together with an expression written in symbols that indicates how to find the subject.

Introducing formulas

The recipe that makes up a formula can be simple or complicated. However, formulas usually have three basic parts: a single letter at the beginning (the subject); an equals sign that links the subject to the recipe; and the recipe itself, which when used, works out the value of the subject.

This is the formula to find the area of a rectangle when its length (L) and width (W) are known:

$$A = LW$$

- subject of the formula
- equals sign
- the recipe—to find A we must multiply the length (L) and the width (W). LW means the same as L × W

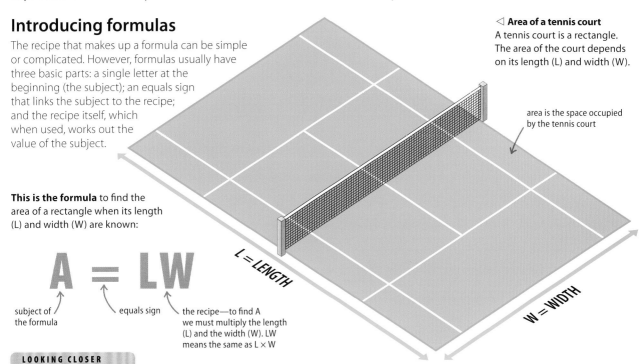

◁ **Area of a tennis court**
A tennis court is a rectangle. The area of the court depends on its length (L) and width (W).

area is the space occupied by the tennis court

L = LENGTH

W = WIDTH

LOOKING CLOSER
Formula triangles

Formulas can be rearranged to make different parts the subject of the formula. This is useful if the unknown value to be found is not the subject of the original formula—the formula can be rearranged so that the unknown becomes the subject, making solving the formula easier.

◁ **Simple rearrangement**
This triangle shows the different ways the formula for finding a rectangle can be rearranged.

- area (A) is the subject of the formula
- $A = L \times W$
- area (A) = length (L) multiplied by width (W)
- A stands for area
- L stands for length
- W stands for width

length (L) = area (A) divided by width (W)

$$L = \frac{A}{W}$$

length (L) is the subject of the formula

width (W) = area (A) divided by length (L)

$$W = \frac{A}{L}$$

width (W) is the subject of the formula

CHANGING THE SUBJECT OF A FORMULA

Changing the subject of a formula involves moving letters or numbers (terms) from one side of the formula to the other, leaving a new term on its own. The way to do this depends on whether the term being moved is positive (+c), negative (-c), or whether it is part of a multiplication (bc) or division (b/c). When moving terms, whatever is done to one side of the formula needs to be done to the other.

Moving a positive term

To make b the subject, +c needs to be moved to the other side of the equals sign.

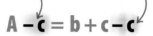

−c is brought in to the left of the equals sign. −c is brought in to the right of the equals sign.

Add −c to both sides. To move +c, its opposite (−c) must first be added to both sides of the formula to keep it balanced.

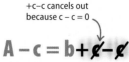

+c−c cancels out because c − c = 0.

Simplify the formula by canceling out −c and +c on the right, leaving b by itself as the subject of the formula.

a formula must have a single symbol on one side of the equals sign.

The formula can now be rearranged so that it reads $b = A − c$.

Moving a negative term

$A = b − c$

To make b the subject, −c needs to be moved to the other side of the equals sign.

+c is brought in to the left of the equals sign. +c is brought in to the right of the equals sign.

Add +c to both sides. To move −c, its opposite (+c) must first be added to both sides of the formula to keep it balanced.

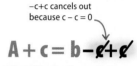

−c+c cancels out because c − c = 0.

Simplify the formula by canceling out −c and +c on the right, leaving b by itself as the subject of the formula.

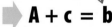

a formula must have a single symbol on one side of the equals sign.

The formula can now be rearranged so that it reads $b = A + c$.

Moving a term in a multiplication problem

bc means b × c

In this example, b is multiplied by c. To make b the subject, c needs to move to the other side.

÷c (or /c) is brought in to the left of the equals sign. ÷c (or /c) is brought in to the right of the equals sign.

Divide both sides by c. To move the c to the other side, you must do the opposite of multiplying, which is dividing.

$$\frac{A}{c} = \frac{bc}{c}$$

c/c cancels out because c/c equals 1.

Simplify the formula by canceling out c/c on the right, leaving b by itself as the subject of the formula.

a formula must have a single symbol on one side of the equals sign.

The formula can now be rearranged so that it reads $b = A/c$.

Moving a term in a division problem

b/c means b ÷ c

In this example, b is divided by c. To make b the subject, c needs to move to the other side.

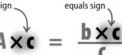

×c is brought in to the left of the equals sign. ×c is brought in to the right of the equals sign.

Multiply both sides by c. To move the c to the other side, you must do the opposite of dividing, which is multiplying.

c/c cancels out because c/c equals 1.

Simplify the formula by canceling out c/c on the right, leaving b by itself as the subject of the formula.

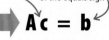

remember that A × c is written as Ac.

a formula must have a single symbol on one side of the equals sign.

The formula can now be rearranged so that it reads $b = Ac$.

FORMULAS IN ACTION

A formula can be used to calculate how much interest (the amount a bank pays someone in exchange for being able to borrow their money) is paid into a bank account over a particular period of time. The formula for this is principal (or amount of money) × rate of interest × time. This formula is shown here.

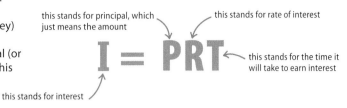

$$I = PRT$$

- this stands for interest
- this stands for principal, which just means the amount
- this stands for rate of interest
- this stands for the time it will take to earn interest

There is a bank account with $500 in it, earning simple interest (see pp.74–75) at 2% a year. To find out how much time (T) it will take to earn interest of $50, the formula above is used. First, the formula must be rearranged to make T the subject. Then the real values can be put in to work out T.

▷ **Move P**
The first step is to divide each side of the formula by P to move it to the left of the equals sign.

$$I = PRT \quad \Rightarrow \quad \frac{I}{P} = RT$$

to remove P from the right side, divide each side of the formula by P

remember that dividing the right side by **P** gives **P**RT/P, but the **P**s cancel out, leaving **RT**

▷ **Move R**
The next step is to divide each side of the formula by R to move it to the left of the equals sign.

$$\frac{I}{P} = RT \quad \Rightarrow \quad \frac{I}{PR} = T$$

to remove R from the right side, divide each side of the formula by R

remember that dividing the right side by **R** gives **R**T/R, but the **R**s cancel out, leaving **T**.

▷ **Put in real values**
Put in the real values for I ($50), P ($500), and R (2%) to find the value of T (the time it will take to earn interest of $50).

$$T = \frac{I}{PR} \quad \Rightarrow \quad \frac{50}{500 \times 0.02} = 5 \text{ years}$$

- interest (I) is $50
- principal (P) is $500
- rate of interest (R) is 2%, written as a decimal as 0.02
- length of time (T) to earn interest of $50 is 5 years

Solving equations

AN EQUATION IS A MATHEMATICAL STATEMENT THAT CONTAINS AN EQUALS SIGN.

SEE ALSO
‹ 168–169 What is algebra?
‹ 172–173 Working with expressions
‹ 177–179 Formulas
Linear graphs 182–185 ›

Equations can be rearranged to find the value of an unknown variable, such as x or y.

Simple equations

Equations can be rearranged to find the value of an unknown number, or variable. A variable is represented by a letter, such as x or y. Whatever action is taken on one side of an equation must also be made on the other side, so that both sides remain equal.

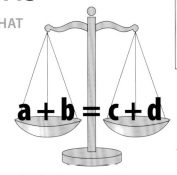

◁ **Balancing**
The expressions on either side of the equals sign in an equation are always equal.

To find the value of x the equation must be rearranged so that x is by itself on one side of the equation.

to get rid of this 2, 2 must also be taken from the other side

variable

$2 + x = 8$

this expression has the same value as the expression on the other side of the equals sign

Changes made to one side of the equation must also be made to the other side. Subtract 2 from both sides to isolate x.

subtract 2 on this side

$2 + x - 2 = 8 - 2$

2 was subtracted from the other side, so it must also be subtracted from this side

Simplify the equation by canceling out the +2 and −2 on the left side. This leaves x on its own on the left.

cancel out +2 and −2, which gives 0

$\cancel{2} + x \cancel{-2} = 8 - 2$

Once x is the subject of the equation, working out the right side of the equation gives the value of x.

x is now the subject of the equation

$x = 6$

working out the right side of the equation (8 − 2) gives the value of (6)

LOOKING CLOSER

Creating an equation

Equations can be created to explain day-to-day situations. For example, a taxi firm charges $3 to pick up a customer, and $2 per mile traveled. This can be written as an equation.

If a customer pays $18 for a trip, the equation can be used to work out how far the customer traveled.

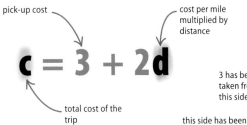

pick-up cost

cost per mile multiplied by distance

$c = 3 + 2d$

total cost of the trip

total cost of trip

cost per mile multiplied by distance

$18 = 3 + 2d$

pick-up cost

Substitute the cost of the trip into the equation.

$15 = 2d$

3 has been taken from this side

3 has been taken from this side

Rearrange the equation – subtract 3 from both sides.

this side has been divided by 2

$7\frac{1}{2} \text{ mi} = d$

to get rid of 2 in 2d, divide both sides by 2

Find the distance traveled by dividing both sides by 2.

MORE COMPLICATED EQUATIONS

More complicated equations are rearranged in the same way as simple equations—anything done to simplify one side of the equation must also be done to the other side so that both sides of the equation remain equal. The equation will give the same answer no matter where the rearranging is started.

Example 1

This equation has numerical and unknown terms on both sides, so it needs several rearrangements to solve.

First, rearrange the numerical terms. To remove the −9 from the right-hand side, add 9 to both sides of the equation.

Next, rearrange so that the a's are on the opposite side to the number. This is done by subtracting 2a from both sides.

Then rearrange again to make a the only subject of the equation. Since the equation contains 3a, divide the whole equation by 3.

The subject of the equation, a, is now on its own on the right side of the equation, and there is only a number on the other side.

Reverse the equation to show the unknown variable (a) first. This does not affect the meaning of the equation, because both sides are equal.

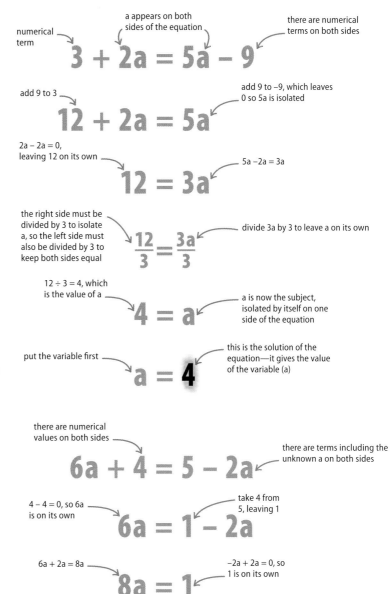

Example 2

This equation has unknown and numerical terms on both sides, so it will take several rearrangements to solve.

First rearrange the numerical terms. Subtract 4 from both sides of the equation so that there are numbers on only one side.

Then rearrange the equation so that the unknown variable is on the opposite side to the number, by adding 2a to both sides.

Finally, divide each side by 8 to make a the subject of the equation, and to find the solution of the equation.

182 ALGEBRA

Linear graphs

GRAPHS ARE A WAY OF PICTURING AN EQUATION. A LINEAR EQUATION ALWAYS HAS A STRAIGHT LINE.

SEE ALSO
⟨ 90–93 Coordinates
⟨ 180–181 Solving equations
Quadratic graphs 194–197 ⟩

Graphs of linear equations

A linear equation is an equation that does not contain a squared variable such as x^2, or a variable of a higher power, such as x^3. Linear equations can be represented by straight line graphs, where the line passes through coordinates that satisfy the equation. For example, one of the sets of coordinates for $y = x + 5$ is (1, 6), because $6 = 1 + 5$.

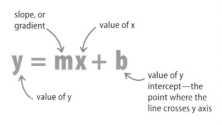

△ **The equation of a straight line**
All straight lines have an equation. The value of m is the slope (or slope) of the line and b is where it cuts the y axis.

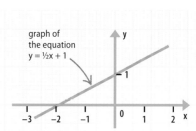

△ **A linear graph**
The graph of an equation is a set of points with coordinates that satisfy the equation.

Finding the equation of a line

To find the equation of a given line, use the graph to find its slope and y intercept. Then substitute them into the equation for a line, $y = mx + b$.

To find the slope of the line (m), draw lines out from a section of the line as shown. Then divide the vertical distance by horizontal distance—the result is the slope.

To find the y intercept, look at the graph and find where the line crosses the y axis. This is the y intercept, and is b in the equation.

$$y \text{ intercept} = (0, 4)$$

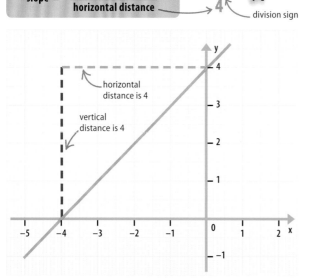

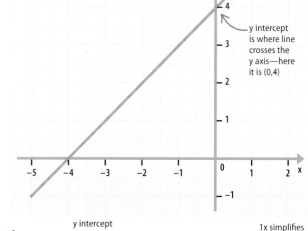

Finally, substitute the values that have been found from the graph into the equation for a line. This gives the equation for the line shown above.

slope is +1   y intercept is 4   1x simplifies to x

$$y = mx + b \implies y = x + 4$$

LINEAR GRAPHS

Positive slopes

Lines that slope upward from left to right have positive slopes. The equation of a line with a positive slope can be worked out from its graph, as described below.

Find the slope of the line by choosing a section of it and drawing horizontal (green) and vertical (red) lines out from it so they meet. Count the units each new line covers, then divide the vertical by the horizontal distance.

$$\text{slope} = \frac{\text{vertical distance}}{\text{horizontal distance}} = \frac{6}{3} = +2$$

\+ sign means line slopes upward from left to right

The y intercept can be easily read off the graph —it is the point where the line crosses the y axis.

$$y \text{ intercept} = (0,1)$$

Substitute the values for the slope and y intercept into the equation of a line to find the equation for this given line.

slope is +2, y intercept is 1

$$y = mx + b \quad \Rightarrow \quad y = 2x + 1$$

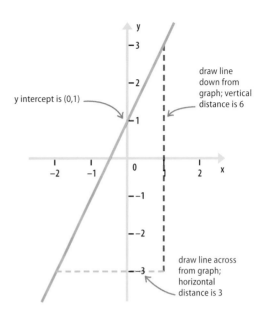

y intercept is (0,1)

draw line down from graph; vertical distance is 6

draw line across from graph; horizontal distance is 3

Negative slopes

Lines that slope downward from left to right have negative slopes. The equation of these lines can be worked out in the same way as for a line with a positive slope.

Find the slope of the line by choosing a section of it and drawing horizontal (green) and vertical (red) lines out from it so they meet. Count the units each new line covers, then divide the vertical by the horizontal distance.

$$\text{slope} = \frac{\text{vertical distance}}{\text{horizontal distance}} = \frac{4}{1} = 4 \rightarrow -4$$

insert minus sign to show line slopes downward from left to right

The y intercept can be easily read off the graph —it is the point where the line crosses the y axis.

$$y \text{ intercept} = (0,-4)$$

Substitute the values for the slope and y intercept into the equation of a line to find the equation for this given line.

y intercept is (0,−4), slope is −4

$$y = mx + b \quad \Rightarrow \quad y = -4x - 4$$

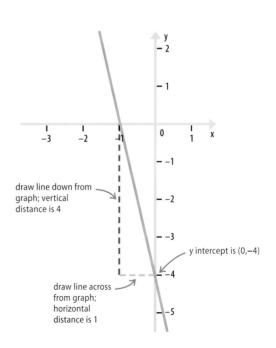

draw line down from graph; vertical distance is 4

draw line across from graph; horizontal distance is 1

y intercept is (0,−4)

How to plot a linear graph

The graph of a linear equation can be drawn by working out several different sets of values for x and y and then plotting these values on a pair of axes. The x values are measured along the x axis, and the y values along the y axis.

▷ **The equation**
This shows that each of the y values for this equation will be double the size of each of the x values.

this means 2 multiplied by x

$y = 2x$

first, choose some possible values of x

x	y = 2x
1	2
2	4
3	6
4	8

then find corresponding values of y by doubling each x value

First, choose some possible values of x—numbers below 10 are easiest to work with. Find the corresponding values of y using a table. Put the x values in the first column, then multiply each number by 2 to find the corresponding values for y.

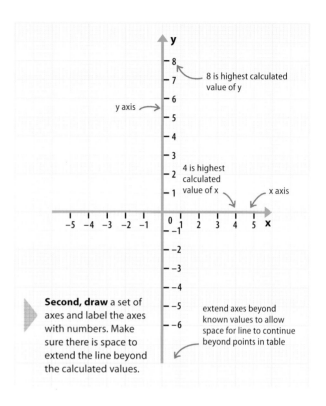

8 is highest calculated value of y

4 is highest calculated value of x

▷ **Second, draw** a set of axes and label the axes with numbers. Make sure there is space to extend the line beyond the calculated values.

extend axes beyond known values to allow space for line to continue beyond points in table

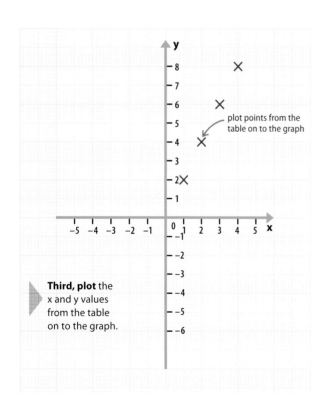

plot points from the table on to the graph

▷ **Third, plot** the x and y values from the table on to the graph.

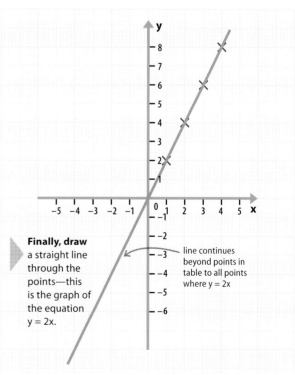

▷ **Finally, draw** a straight line through the points—this is the graph of the equation $y = 2x$.

line continues beyond points in table to all points where $y = 2x$

LINEAR GRAPHS

Downward-sloping graph

Graphs of linear equations are read from left to right and slope down or up. Downward-sloping graphs have a negative gradient; upward-sloping ones have a positive gradient.

The equation here contains the term −2x. Because x is multiplied by a negative number (−2), the graph will slope downward.

this means x multiplied by −2

$$y = -2x + 1$$

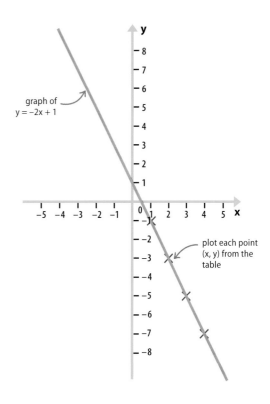

graph of $y = -2x + 1$

plot each point (x, y) from the table

Use a table to find some values for x and y. This equation is more complex than the last, so add more rows to the table: −2x and 1. Calculate each of these values, then add them to find y. It is important to keep track of negative signs in front of numbers.

x	−2x	+1	y=−2x+1
1	−2	+1	−1
2	−4	+1	−3
3	−6	+1	−5
4	−8	+1	−7

write down some possible values of x

values of x multiplied by −2

+1 is constant

work out corresponding values for y by adding together the parts of the equation

REAL WORLD
Temperature conversion graph

A linear graph can be used to show the conversion between the two main methods of measuring temperature—Fahrenheit and Celsius. To convert any temperature from Fahrenheit into Celsius, start at the position of the Fahrenheit temperature on the y axis, read horizontally across to the line, and then vertically down to the x axis to find the Celsius value.

°F	°C
32.0	0
50.0	10

△ **Temperature conversion**
Two sets of values for Fahrenheit (F) and Celsius (C) give all the information that is needed to plot the conversion graph.

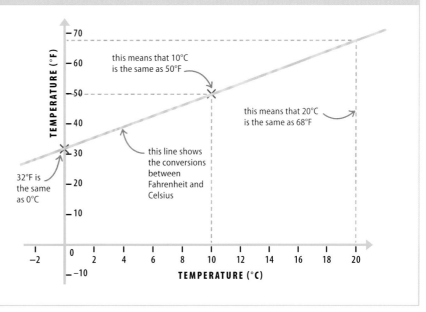

this means that 10°C is the same as 50°F

this means that 20°C is the same as 68°F

this line shows the conversions between Fahrenheit and Celsius

32°F is the same as 0°C

Simultaneous equations

SEE ALSO

‹ 172–173 Working with expressions
‹ 177–179 Formulas

SIMULTANEOUS EQUATIONS ARE PAIRS OF EQUATIONS WITH THE SAME UNKNOWN VARIABLES, THAT ARE SOLVED TOGETHER.

Solving simultaneous equations

Simultaneous equations are pairs of equations that contain the same variables and are solved together. There are three ways to solve a pair of simultaneous equations: elimination, substitution, and by graph; they all give the same answer.

both equations contain the variable x
both equations contain the variable y

$$3x - 5y = 4$$
$$4x + 5y = 17$$

◁ **A pair of equations**
These simultaneous equations both contain the unknown variables x and y.

Solving by elimination

Make the x or y terms the same for both equations, then add or subtract them to eliminate that variable. The resulting equation finds the value of one variable, which is then used to find the other.

▷ **Equation pair**
Solve this pair of simultaneous equations using the elimination method.

$$10x + 3y = 2$$
$$2x + 2y = 6$$

Multiply or divide one of the equations to make one variable the same as in the other equation. Here, the second equation is multiplied by 5 to make the x terms the same.

the second equation is multiplied by 5

$$2x + 2y = 6 \xrightarrow{\times 5} 10x + 10y = 30$$

$$10x + 3y = 2 \quad \text{← first equation stays as it is}$$

the second equation is multiplied by 5, so both equations now have the same value of x (10x)

this is the second equation
the x term is now the same as in the first equation

Then add or subtract each set of terms in the second equation from or to each set in the first, to remove the matching terms. The new equation can then be solved. Here, the second equation is subtracted from the first, and the remaining variables are rearranged to isolate y.

this will cancel out the x terms

$$10x - 10x + 3y - 10y = 2 - 30$$

subtract the numerical terms from each other as well as the unknown terms

the x terms have been eliminated as 10x − 10x = 0

$$-7y = -28$$

this side is divided by −7 to isolate y

$$y = \frac{-28}{-7}$$

this side must also be divided by −7

$$y = 4 \quad \text{← this gives the value of y}$$

Choose one of the two original equations—it does not matter which—and put in the value for y that has just been found. This eliminates the y variable from the equation, leaving only the x variable. Rearranging the equation means that it can be solved, and the value of the x can be found.

$$2x + 2y = 6 \quad \text{← the second equation has been chosen}$$

$$2x + (2 \times 4) = 6 \quad \text{← it is already known that y = 4 so 2y = 8}$$

$$2x + 8 = 6 \quad \text{← } 2 \times 4 = 8$$

subtracting 8 from this side to isolate 2x

$$2x = -2 \quad \text{← subtract 8 from this side: } 6 - 8 = -2$$

divide this side by 2 to isolate x

$$x = \frac{-2}{2} \quad \text{← this side must also be divided by 2}$$

$$x = -1 \quad \text{← this is the value of x}$$

Both unknown variables have now been found—these are the solutions to the original pair of equations.

$$x = -1 \qquad y = 4$$

SIMULTANEOUS EQUATIONS

Solving by substitution

To use this method, rearrange one of the two equations so that the two unknown values (variables) are on different sides of the equation, then substitute this rearranged equation into the other equation. The new, combined equation contains only one unknown value and can be solved. Substituting the new value into one of the equations means that the other variable can also be found. Equations that cannot be solved by elimination can usually be solved by substitution.

▷ **Equation pair**
Solve this pair of simultaneous equations using the substitution method.

$$x + 2y = 7$$
$$4x - 3y = 6$$

Choose one of the equations, and rearrange it so that one of the two unknown values is the subject. Here x is made the subject by subtracting 2y from both sides of the equation.

choose one of the equations; this is the first equation

$$x + 2y = 7$$

make x the subject by subtracting 2y from both sides of the equation

$$x = 7 - 2y$$

2y must be subtracted from both sides of the equation

Then substitute the expression that has been found for that variable ($x = 7 - 2y$) into the other equation. This gives only one unknown value in the newly compiled equation. Rearrange this new equation to isolate y and find its value.

substitute the expression for x which has been found in the previous step

$$4x - 3y = 6$$ ← take the other equation

$$4(7 - 2y) - 3y = 6$$ ← this equation now has only one unknown value so it can be solved

multiply out the parentheses above: $4 \times 7 = 28$ and $4 \times -2y = -8y$

$$28 - 8y - 3y = 6$$

$$28 - 11y = 6$$ ← simplify the two y terms: $-8y - 3y = -11y$

isolate the y term by subtracting 28 from this side

$$-11y = -22$$ ← 28 must also be subtracted from this side: $6 - 28 = -22$

divide this side by −11 to isolate y ($-11y \div -11 = y$)

$$\frac{-11y}{-11} = \frac{-22}{-11}$$ ← this side must also be divided by −11

$$y = 2$$ ← this is the value of y

Substitute the value of y that has just been found into either of the original pair of equations. Rearrange this equation to isolate x and find its value.

choose one of the equations; this is the first one

$$x + 2y = 7$$

$$x + (2 \times 2) = 7$$ ← because $y = 2$, 2y is $2 \times 2 = 4$

$$x + 4 = 7$$

work out the terms in the parentheses: $2 \times 2 = 4$

subtract 4 from this side to isolate x

$$x = 3$$ ← 4 has been subtracted from the other side of the equation, so it must also be subtracted from this side: $7 - 4 = 3$

Both unknown variables have now been found—these are the solutions to the original pair of equations.

$$x = 3 \qquad y = 2$$

Solving simultaneous equations with graphs

Simultaneous equations can be solved by rearranging each equation so that it is expressed in terms of y, using a table to find sets of x and y coordinates for each equation, then plotting the graphs. The solution is the coordinates of the point where the graphs intersect.

▷ **A pair of equations**
This pair of simultaneous equations can be solved using a graph. Each equation will be represented by a line on the graph.

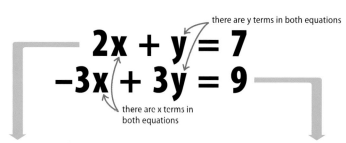

there are y terms in both equations

$$2x + y = 7$$
$$-3x + 3y = 9$$

there are x terms in both equations

To isolate y in the first equation, rearrange the equation so that y is left on its own on one side of the equals sign. Here, this is done by subtracting 2x from both sides of the equation.

$2x + y = 7$ is the first equation

$$2x + y = 7$$

−2x has been added to this side to cancel out the 2x and isolate y

−2x has also been added to this side

$$y = 7 - 2x$$

To isolate y in the second equation, rearrange so that y is left on its own on one side of the equals sign. Here, this is done by first adding 3x to both sides, then dividing both sides by 3.

$-3x + 3y = 9$ is the second equation

$$-3x + 3y = 9$$

3x must also be added to this side

3x has been added to this side to cancel out −3x; this isolates 3y

$$3y = 9 + 3x$$

divide both sides of equation by 3 to isolate y

$$y = 3 + x$$

$3y \div 3 = y$ $9 \div 3 = 3$ $3x \div 3 = x$

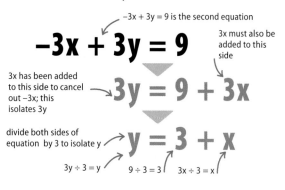

Find the corresponding x and y values for the rearranged first equation using a table. Choose a set of x values that are close to zero, then work out the y values using a table.

Find the corresponding x and y values for the rearranged second equation using a table. Choose the same set of x values as for the other table, then use the table to work out the y values.

the 7 does not depend on x

choose a set of values for x that are close to 0

x	1	2	3	4
7	7	7	7	7
−2x	−2	−4	−6	−8
y (7 − 2x)	5	3	1	−1

work out the value of −2x for each value of x

the y value is the sum of 7 and −2x   7 − 6 = 1

the 3 does not depend on the value of x

the value of +x is the same as x

choose the same values of x as in the other table

x	1	2	3	4
3	3	3	3	3
+x	1	2	3	4
y (3 + x)	4	5	6	7

the y value is the sum of 3 and x   3 + 3 = 6

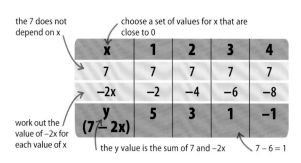
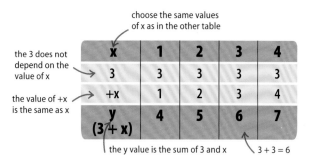

SIMULTANEOUS EQUATIONS 189

Draw a set of axes, then plot the two sets of x and y values. Join each set of points with a straight line, continuing the line past where the points lie. If the pair of simultaneous equations has a solution, then the two lines will cross.

> **LOOKING CLOSER**
> ## Unsolvable simultaneous equations
> Sometimes a pair of simultaneous equations does not have a solution. For example, the graphs of the two equations $x + y = 1$ and $x + y = 2$ are always equidistant from each other (parallel) and, because they do not intersect, there is no solution to this pair of equations.

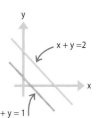

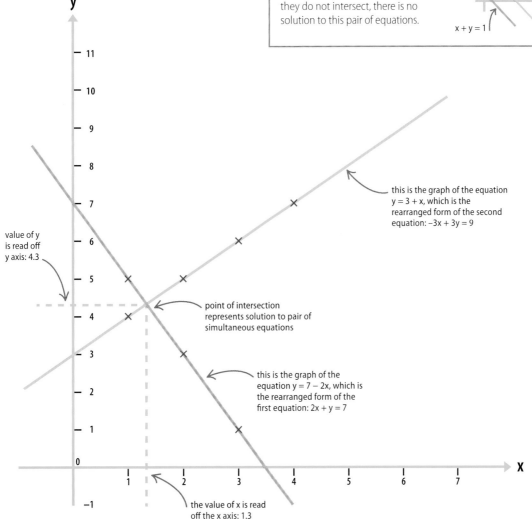

value of y is read off y axis: 4.3

this is the graph of the equation $y = 3 + x$, which is the rearranged form of the second equation: $-3x + 3y = 9$

point of intersection represents solution to pair of simultaneous equations

this is the graph of the equation $y = 7 - 2x$, which is the rearranged form of the first equation: $2x + y = 7$

the value of x is read off the x axis: 1.3

The solution to the pair of simultaneous equations is the coordinates of the point where the two lines cross. Read from this point down to the x axis and across to the y axis to find the values of the solution.

$x = 1.3 \quad y = 4.3$

Factorizing quadratic equations

SOME QUADRATIC EQUATIONS (EQUATIONS IN THE FORM $AX^2 + BX + C = 0$) CAN BE SOLVED BY FACTORIZING.

SEE ALSO	
‹ 176 Quadratic expressions	
The quadratic formula	192–193 ›

Quadratic factorization
Factorization is the process of finding the terms that multiply together to form another term. A quadratic equation is factorized by rearranging it into two bracketed parts, each containing a variable and a number. To find the values in the parentheses, use the rules from multiplying parentheses (see p.176)—that the numbers add together to give b and multiply together to give c of the original quadratic equation.

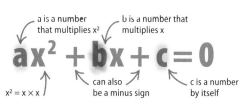

- a is a number that multiplies x^2
- $x^2 = x \times x$
- b is a number that multiplies x
- can also be a minus sign
- c is a number by itself

△ **A quadratic equation**
All quadratic equations have a squared term (x^2), a term that is multiplied by x, and a numerical term. The letters a, b, and c all stand for different numbers.

parentheses set next to each other are multiplied together

△ **Two parentheses**
A quadratic equation can be factorized as two parentheses, each with an x and a number. Multiplied out, they result in the equation.

these two unknown numbers add together to give b and multiply together to give c of the original equation

Solving simple quadratic equations
To solve quadratic equations by factorization, first find the missing numerical terms in the parentheses. Then solve each one separately to find the answers to the original equation.

To solve a quadratic equation, first look at its b and c terms. The terms in the two parentheses will need to add together to give b (6 in this case) and multiply together to give c (8 in this case).

- x^2 means $1x^2$
- c term is 8
- b term is 6
- answer is always 0

these two numbers add together to give 6 and multiply together to give 8

To find the unknown terms, draw a table. In the first column, list the possible combinations of numbers that multiply together to give the value of c = 8. In the second column, add these terms together to see if they add up to b = 6.

list possible factors of c=8

Two numbers that multiply to give c=8	The sum of the two numbers
8 and 1	8 + 1 = 9
4 and 2	4 + 2 = 6

all sets of numbers in this column multiply to give c=8

add factors to find their sum

✗ not all the factors add up to produce the needed sum (b), which is 6

✓ 4 and 2 are the factors needed, as 4 + 2 = 6, which is b

Insert the factors into the parentheses after the x terms. Because the two parentheses multiplied together equal the original quadratic expression, they can also be set to equal 0.

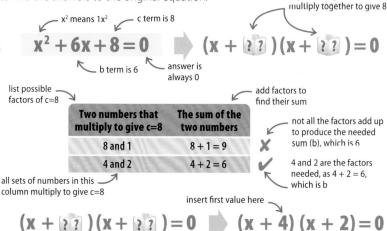

insert first value here
insert second value here
solve for first value
subtract 4 from both sides to isolate x
one possible solution is −4

For the two parentheses to multiply to equal 0, the value of either one needs to be 0. Set each one equal to 0 and solve. The resulting values are the two solutions of the original equation.

solve for second value
subtract 2 from both sides to isolate x
another possible solution is −2

Solving more complex quadratic equations

Quadratic equations do not always appear in the standard form of $ax^2 + bx + c = 0$. Instead, several x^2 terms, x terms, and numbers may appear on both sides of the equals sign. However, if all terms appear at least once, the equation can be rearranged in the standard form, and solved using the same methods as for simple equations.

This equation is not written in standard quadratic form, but contains an x^2 term and a term multiplied by x so it is known to be one. In order to solve it needs to be rearranged to equal 0.

$$x^2 + 11x + 13 = 2x - 7$$

these terms need to be moved to other side of equation for it to equal 0

Start by moving the numerical term from the right-hand side of the equals sign to the left by adding its opposite to both sides of the equation. In this case, −7 is moved by adding 7 to both sides.

7 has been added to this side (13 + 7 = 20)

$$x^2 + 11x + 20 = 2x$$

7 has been added to this side, which cancels out −7, leaving 2x on its own

Next, move the term multiplied by x to the left of the equals sign by adding its opposite to both sides of the equation. In this case, 2x is moved by subtracting 2x from both sides.

adding −2x to 11x gives 9x

$$x^2 + 9x + 20 = 0$$

subtracting 2x from this side cancels out 2x

It is now possible to solve the equation by factorizing. Draw a table for the possible numerical values of x. In one column, list all values that multiply together to give the c term, 20; in the other, add them together to see if they give the b term (9).

list possible factors of c = 20

add the factors to find their sum

Factors of +20	Sum of factors	
20, 1	21	✗
2, 10	12	✗
5, 4	9	✓

stop when the factors add to the b term, 9

all sets of numbers in this column multiply to give 20

Write the correct pair of factors into parentheses and set them equal to 0. The two factors of the quadratic (x + 5) and (x + 4) multiply together to give 0, therefore one of the factors must be equal to 0.

parentheses set next to each other are multiplied together

$$(x + 5)(x + 4) = 0$$

entire equation equals 0

Solve the quadratic equation by solving each of the bracketed expressions separately. Make each bracketed expression equal to 0, then find its solution. The two resulting values are the two solutions to the quadratic equation: −5 and −4.

solve for first value

$$x + 5 = 0 \quad \Rightarrow \quad x = -5$$

subtract 5 from both sides to isolate x

one possible solution is −5

solve for second value

$$x + 4 = 0 \quad \Rightarrow \quad x = -4$$

subtract 4 from both sides to isolate x

another possible solution is −4

LOOKING CLOSER

Not all quadratic equations can be factorized

Some quadratic equations cannot be factorized, as the sum of the factors of the purely numerical component (c term) does not equal the term multiplied by x (b term). These equations must be solved by formula (see pp.192–193).

b term (3) — c term (1)

$$x^2 + 3x + 1 = 0$$

both sets of numbers multiply together to give c (1)

Factors of +1	Sum of factors	
1, 1	2	✗
−1, −1	−2	✗

a sum of +3 is needed as the b term is 3

The equation above is a typical quadratic equation, but cannot be solved by factorizing.

Listing all the possible factors and their sums in a table shows that there is no set of factors that add to b (3), and multiply to give c (1).

The quadratic formula

QUADRATIC EQUATIONS CAN BE SOLVED USING A FORMULA.

The quadratic formula

The quadratic formula can be used to solve any quadratic equation. Quadratic equations take the form $ax^2 + bx + c = 0$, where a, b, and c are numbers and x is the unknown.

▷ **A quadratic equation**
Quadratic equations include a number multiplied by x^2, a number multiplied by x, and a number by itself.

▷ **The quadratic formula**
The quadratic formula allows any quadratic equation to be solved. Substitute the different values in the equation into the quadratic formula to solve the equation.

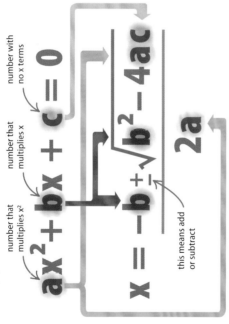

LOOK CLOSER
Quadratic variations

Quadratic equations are not always the same. They can include negative terms or terms with no numbers in front of them ("x" is the same as "1x"), and do not always equal 0.

$$-4x^2 + x - 3 = 8$$

- the values in the equation can be negative as well as positive
- quadratic equations are not always equal to 0
- when an x appears without a number in front of it, x=1

Using the quadratic formula

To use the quadratic formula, substitute the values for a, b, and c in a given equation into the formula, then work through the formula to find the answers. Take great care with the signs (+, –) of a, b, and c.

Given a quadratic equation, work out the values of a, b, and c. Once these values are known, substitute them into the quadratic formula, making sure that their positive and negative signs do not change. In this example, a is 1, b is 3, and c is –2.

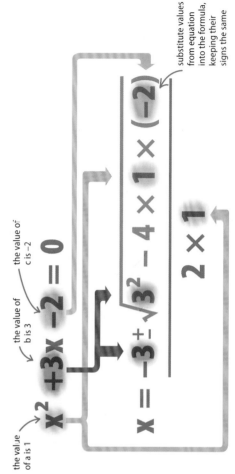

▷

Work through the formula step-by-step to find the answer to the equation. First simplify the values under the square root sign. Work out the square of 3 (which equals 9), then work out the value of $4 \times 1 \times -2$ (which equals -8).

$$x = \frac{-3 \pm \sqrt{9 - (-8)}}{2}$$

$3 \times 3 = 9$

$4 \times 1 \times (-2) = -8$

two minus signs cancel out, so $9 - (-8) = 9 + 8$

Work out the numbers under the square root sign: $9 - (-8)$ equals 17. Then, use a calculator to find the square root of 17.

$$x = \frac{-3 \pm \sqrt{17}}{2}$$

$9 + 8 = 17$

Once the sum is simplified, it must be split to find the two answers—one when the second value is subtracted from the first, and the other where they are added.

$$x = \frac{-3 \pm 4.12}{2}$$

4.12 is the square root of 17 rounded to 2 decimal places.

+

−

Add the two values on the top part of the fraction; here the values are -3 and 4.12.

$$x = \frac{-3 + 4.12}{2}$$

Subtract the second value on the top part of the fraction from the first value; here the values are -3 and -4.12.

$$x = \frac{-3 - 4.12}{2}$$

$-3 - 4.12 = -7.12$

Divide the top part of the fraction by the bottom part to find an answer.

$$x = \frac{1.12}{2}$$

$-3 + 4.12 = 1.12$

Divide the top part of the fraction by the bottom part to find an answer.

$$x = \frac{-7.12}{2}$$

Give both answers, because quadratic equations always have two solutions.

$$x = 0.56$$

quadratic equations always have two solutions

$$x = -3.56$$

Quadratic graphs

THE GRAPH OF A QUADRATIC EQUATION IS A SMOOTH CURVE.

SEE ALSO
‹ 34–35 Positive and negative numbers
‹ 176 Quadratic expressions
‹ 182–185 Linear graphs
‹ 190–191 Factorizing quadratic equations
‹ 192–193 The quadratic formula

The exact shape of the curve of a quadratic graph varies, depending on the values of the numbers a, b, and c in the quadratic equation $y = ax^2 + bx + c$.

Quadratic equations all have the same general form: $y = ax^2 + bx + c$. With a particular quadratic equation, the values of a, b, and c are known, and corresponding sets of values for x and y can be worked out and put in a table. These values of x and y are then plotted as points (x,y) on a graph. The points are then joined by a smooth line to create the graph of the equation.

A quadratic equation can be shown as a graph. Pairs of x and y values are needed to plot the graph. In quadratic equations, the y values are given in terms of x—in this example each y value is equal to the value of x squared (x multiplied by itself), added to 3 times x, added to 2.

$$y = x^2 + 3x + 2$$

this group of terms is used to find the y value for each value of x

y value gives position of each point on y axis of the graph

Find sets of values for x and y in order to plot the graph. First, choose a set of x values. Then, for each x value, work out the different values (x^2, 3x, 2) for each value at each stage of the equation. Finally, add the stages to find the corresponding y value for each x value.

choose some values of x around 0

x	y
−3	
−2	
−1	
0	
1	
2	
3	

$y = x^2 + 3x + 2$, so it is difficult to work out the y values right away

work out x^2 in this column — work out 3x in this column — +2 is the same for each x value

x	x^2	3x	+2	y
−3	9	−9	2	
−2	4	−6	2	
−1	1	−3	2	
0	0	0	2	
1	1	3	2	
2	4	6	2	
3	9	9	2	

add values in each purple row to find y values

x	x^2	3x	+2	y
−3	9	−9	2	2
−2	4	−6	2	0
−1	1	−3	2	0
0	0	0	2	2
1	1	3	2	6
2	4	6	2	12
3	9	9	2	20

y is the sum of numbers in each purple row

△ **Values of x**
The value of y depends on the value of x, so choose a set of x values and then find the corresponding values of y. Choose x values either side of 0 as they are easiest to work with.

△ **Different parts of the equation**
Each quadratic equation has 3 different parts—a squared x value, a multiplied x value, and an ordinary number. Work out the different values of each part of the equation for each value of x, being careful to pay attention to when the numbers are positive or negative.

△ **Corresponding values of y**
Add the three parts of the equation together to find the corresponding values of y for each x value, making sure to pay attention to when the different parts of the equation are positive or negative.

QUADRATIC GRAPHS 195

▷ **Draw the graph of the equation.** Use the values of x and y that have been found in the table as the coordinates of points on the graph. For example, x = 1 has the corresponding value y = 6. This becomes the point on the graph with the coordinates (1, 6).

▷ **Draw the axes and plot the points**
Draw the axes of the graph so that they cover the values found in the tables. It is often useful to make the axes a bit longer than needed, in case extra values are added later. Then plot the corresponding values of x and y as points on the graph.

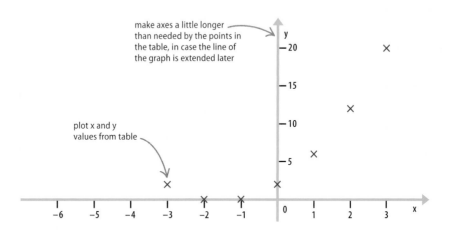

make axes a little longer than needed by the points in the table, in case the line of the graph is extended later

plot x and y values from table

▷ **Join the points**
Draw a smooth line to join the points plotted on the graph. This line is the graph of the equation y = x² + 3x + 2. Bigger and smaller values of x could have been chosen, so the line continues past the values that have been plotted.

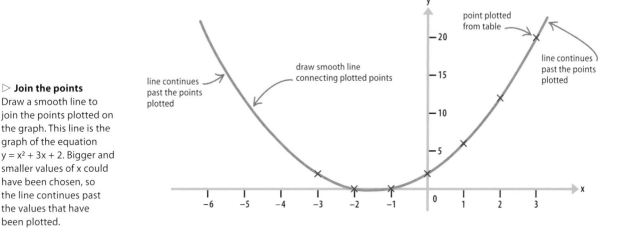

point plotted from table

line continues past the points plotted

draw smooth line connecting plotted points

line continues past the points plotted

LOOKING CLOSER
The shape of a quadratic graph

The shape of a quadratic graph depends on whether the number that multiplies x² is positive or negative. If it is positive, the graph is a smile; if it is negative, the graph is a frown.

◁ **y = ax² + bx + c**
If the value of the a term is positive, then the graph of the equation is shaped like this.

◁ **y = −ax² + bx + c**
If the value of the a term is negative, then the graph of the equation is shaped like this.

Using graphs to solve quadratic equations

A quadratic equation can be solved by drawing a graph. If a quadratic equation has a y value that is not 0, it can be solved by drawing both a quadratic and a linear graph (the linear graph is of the y value that is not 0) and finding where the two graphs cross. The solutions to the equation are the x values where the two graphs cross.

This equation has two parts: a quadratic equation on the left and a linear equation on the right. To find the solutions to this equation, draw the quadratic and linear graphs on the same axes. To draw the graphs, it is necessary to find sets of x and y values for both sides of the equation.

$$-x^2 - 2x + 3 = -5$$

- linear part of equation
- quadratic part of equation
- y values for quadratic part of equation are dependent on value of x
- y values for linear part of equation are all −5

$$y = -x^2 - 2x + 3$$

$$y = -5$$

◁ **y = −5**
This graph is very simple: whatever value x takes, y is always −5. This means that the graph is a straight horizontal line that passes through the y axis at −5.

Find values of x and y for the quadratic part of the equation using a table. Choose x values either side of 0 and split the equation into parts ($-x^2$, $-2x$, and $+3$). Work out the value of each part for each value of x, then add the values of all three parts to find the y value for each x value.

choose some values of x around 0

$y = -x^2 - 2x + 3$, so it is difficult to work out the y values right away

work out x^2 first then put a minus sign in front to give values

work out $-2x$ in this column

$+3$ is the same for each x value

add values in each purple row to find y values

x	y
−4	
−3	
−2	
−1	
0	
1	
2	

x	$-x^2$	$-2x$	3	y
−4	−16	+8	+3	
−3	−9	+6	+3	
−2	−4	+4	+3	
−1	−1	+2	+3	
0	0	0	+3	
1	−1	−2	+3	
2	−4	−4	+3	

x	$-x^2$	$-2x$	3	y
−4	−16	+8	+3	−5
−3	−9	+6	+3	0
−2	−4	+4	+3	3
−1	−1	+2	+3	4
0	0	0	+3	3
1	−1	−2	+3	0
2	−4	−4	+3	−5

y is the sum of numbers in each purple row

△ **Values of x**
Each value of y depends on the value of x. Choose a number of values for x, and work out the corresponding values of y. It is easiest to include 0 and values of x that are on either side of 0.

△ **Different parts of the equation**
The equation has 3 different parts: $-x^2$, $-2x$, and $+3$. Work out the values of each part of the equation for each value of x, being careful to pay attention to whether the values are positive or negative. The last part of the equation, $+3$, is the same for each x value.

△ **Corresponding values of y**
Finally, add the three parts of the equation together to find the corresponding values of y for each x value. Make sure to pay attention to whether the different parts of the equation are positive or negative.

QUADRATIC GRAPHS 197

Plot the quadratic graph. First draw a set of axes, then plot the points of the graph, using the values of x and y from the table as the coordinates of each point. For example, when x = −4, y has the value y = −5. This gives the coordinates of the point (−4, −5) on the graph. After plotting the points, draw a smooth line to join them.

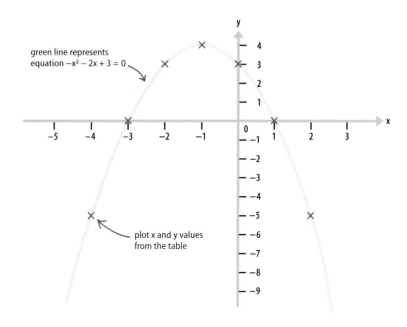

green line represents equation $-x^2 - 2x + 3 = 0$

plot x and y values from the table

Then plot the linear graph. The linear graph (y = −5) is a horizontal straight line that passes through the y axis at −5. The points at which the two lines cross are the solutions to the equation $-x^2 - 2x + 3 = -5$.

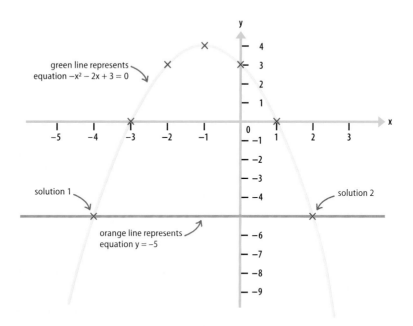

green line represents equation $-x^2 - 2x + 3 = 0$

solution 1

solution 2

orange line represents equation y = −5

The solutions are read off the graph—they are the two x values of the points where the lines cross: −4 and 2.

coordinates of first solution

coordinates of second solution

first solution to the equation

second solution to the equation

$(-4, -5)$ and $(2, -5)$ ▶ $x = -4$ $x = 2$

≠ Inequalities

AN INEQUALITY IS USED TO SHOW THAT ONE QUANTITY IS NOT EQUAL TO ANOTHER.

SEE ALSO
❰ 34–35 Positive and negative numbers
❰ 172–173 Working with expressions
❰ 180–181 Solving equations

Inequality symbols

An inequality symbol shows that the numbers on either side of it are different in size and how they are different. There are five main inequality symbols. One simply shows that two numbers are not equal, the others show in what way they are not equal.

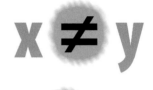

◁ **Not equal to**
This sign shows that x is not equal to y; for example, 3 ≠ 4.

△ **Greater than**
This sign shows that x is greater than y; for example, 7 > 5.

△ **Greater than or equal to**
This sign shows that x is greater than or equal to y.

△ **Less than**
This sign shows that x is less than y. For example, −2 < 1.

△ **Less than or equal to**
This sign shows that x is less than or equal to y.

▽ **Inequality number line**
Inequalities can be shown on a number line. The empty circles represent greater than (>) or less than (<), and the filled circles represent greater than or equal to (≥) or less than or equal to (≤).

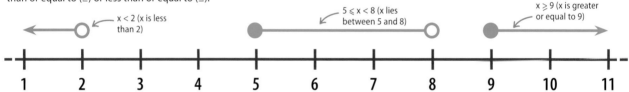

LOOKING CLOSER
Rules for inequalities

Inequalities can be rearranged, as long as any changes are made to both sides of the inequality. If an inequality is multiplied or divided by a negative number, then its sign is reversed.

▷ **Multiplying or dividing by a positive number**
When an inequality is multiplied or divided by a positive number, its sign does not change.

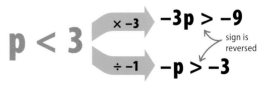

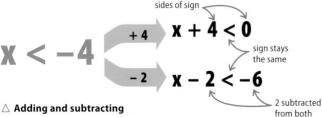

△ **Adding and subtracting**
When an inequality has a number added to or subtracted from it, its sign does not change.

△ **Multiplying or dividing by a negative number**
When an inequality is multiplied or divided by a negative number, its sign is reversed. In this example, a less than sign becomes a greater than sign.

INEQUALITIES

Solving inequalities

Inequalities can be solved by rearranging them, but anything that is done to one side of the inequality must also be done to the other. For example, any number added to cancel a numerical term from one side must be added to the numerical term on the other side.

To solve this inequality, add 2 to both sides then divide by 3.

$$3b - 2 \geqslant 10$$

To isolate 3b, −2 needs to be removed, which means adding +2 to both sides.

adding 2 to 3b − 2 leaves 3b on its own — 10 + 2 = 12

$$3b \geqslant 12$$

Solve the inequality by dividing both sides by 3 to isolate b.

3b divided by 3 leaves b on its own

$$b \geqslant 4 \quad 12 \div 3 = 4$$

To solve this inequality, subtract 3 from both sides then divide by 3.

$$3a + 3 < 12$$

subtracting 3 leaves 3a on its own — 12 − 3 = 9

Rearrange the inequality by subtracting 3 from each side to isolate the a term on the left.

$$3a < 9$$

3a divided by 3 leaves a on its own — 9 ÷ 3 = 3

Solve the inequality by dividing both sides by 3 to isolate a. This is the solution to the inequality.

$$a < 3$$

Solving double inequalities

To solve a double inequality, deal with each side separately to simplify it, then combine the two sides back together again in a single answer.

This is a double inequality that needs to be split into two smaller inequalities for the solution to be found.

$$-1 \leqslant 3x + 5 < 11$$

These are the two parts the double inequality is split into; each one needs to be solved separately.

$$-1 \leqslant 3x + 5$$

subtracting 5 from −1 gives −6

$$-6 \leqslant 3x$$

subtracting 5 from 3x + 5 leaves 3x on its own

Isolate the x terms by subtracting 5 from both sides of the smaller parts.

$$3x + 5 < 11$$

subtracting 5 from 3x + 5 leaves 3x on its own

subtracting 5 from 11 gives 6

$$3x < 6$$

−6 ÷ 3 = −2

$$-2 \leqslant x$$

3x ÷ 3 = x

Solve the part inequalities by dividing both of them by 3.

3x ÷ 3 = x

6 ÷ 3 = 2

$$x < 2$$

$$-2 \leqslant x < 2$$

Finally, combine the two small inequalities back into a single double inequality, with each in the same position as it was in the original double inequality.

Statistics

What is statistics?

STATISTICS IS THE COLLECTION, ORGANIZATION, AND PROCESSING OF DATA.

Organizing and analyzing data helps make large quantities of information easier to understand. Graphs and other visual charts present information in a way that is instantly understandable.

Working with data

Data is information, and it is everywhere, in enormous quantities. When data is collected, for example from a questionnaire, it often forms long lists that are hard to understand. It can be made easier to understand if the data is reorganized into tables, and even more accessible by taking the table and plotting its information as a graph or circle graph. Graphs show trends clearly, making the data much easier to analyze. Circle graphs present data in an instantly accessible way, allowing the relative sizes of groups to be seen immediately.

group	number
Female teachers	10
Male teachers	5
Female students	66
Male students	19
Total people	100

△ **Collecting data**
Once data has been collected, it must be organized into groups before it can be effectively analyzed. A table is the usual way to do this. This table shows the different groups of people in a school.

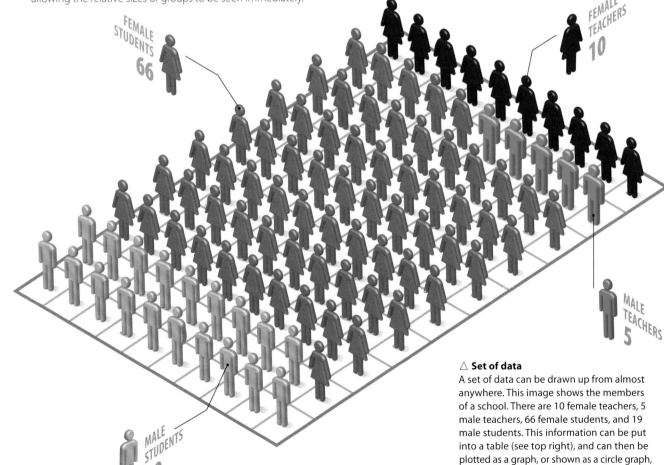

△ **Set of data**
A set of data can be drawn up from almost anywhere. This image shows the members of a school. There are 10 female teachers, 5 male teachers, 66 female students, and 19 male students. This information can be put into a table (see top right), and can then be plotted as a graph, or shown as a circle graph, allowing it to be analyzed more easily.

Presenting data

There are many ways of presenting statistical data. It can be presented simply as a table, or in visual form, as a graph or diagram. Bar graphs, pictograms, line graphs, circle graphs, and histograms are among the most common ways of showing data visually.

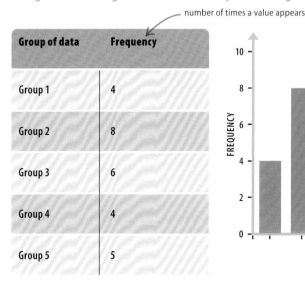

△ **Table of data**
Information is put into tables to organize it into categories, to give a better idea of what trends the data shows. The table can then be used to draw a graph or pictogram.

△ **Bar graph**
Bar graphs show groups of data on the x axis, and frequency on the y axis. The height of each "bar" shows what frequency of data there is in each group.

△ **Pictogram**
Pictograms are a very basic type of bar graph. Each image on a pictogram represents a number of pieces of information, for example, it could represent four musicians.

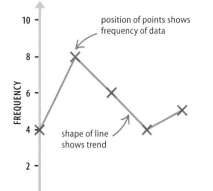

△ **Line graph**
Line graphs show data groups on the x axis, and frequency on the y axis. Points are plotted to show the frequency for each group, and lines between the points show trends.

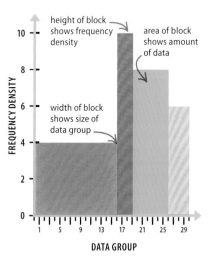

△ **Histogram**
Histograms use the area of rectangular blocks to show the different sizes of groups of data. They are useful for showing data from groups of different sizes.

△ **Circle graph**
Circle graphs show groups of information as sections of a circle. The bigger the section of the circle, the larger the amount of data it represents.

Collecting and organizing data

BEFORE INFORMATION CAN BE PRESENTED AND ANALYZED, THE DATA MUST BE CAREFULLY COLLECTED AND ORGANIZED.

SEE ALSO	
Bar graphs	206–209 ⟩
Pie charts	210–211 ⟩
Line graphs	212–213 ⟩

What is data?

In statistics, the information that is collected, usually in the form of lists of numbers, is known as data. To make sense of these lists, the data needs to be sorted into groups and presented in an easy-to-read form, for example as tables or diagrams. Before it is organized, it is sometimes called raw data.

choice of drinks

COLA, ORANGE JUICE,

PINEAPPLE JUICE, MILK,

APPLE JUICE, WATER

◁ **Questions**
Before designing a questionnaire, start with an idea of a question to collect data, for example, which drinks do children prefer?

Collecting data

A common way of collecting information is in a survey. A selection of people are asked about their preferences, habits, or opinions, often in the form of a questionnaire. The answers they give, which is the raw data, can then be organized into tables and diagrams.

information from these answers is collected as lists of data

Beverage questionnaire

This questionnaire is being used to find out what children's favorite soft drinks are. Put a cross in the box that relates to you.

1) Are you a boy or a girl?

[X] boy   [ ] girl

2) What is your favorite drink?

[ ] pineapple juice   [ ] orange juice   [X] apple juice

[ ] milk   [ ] cola   [ ] other

3) How often do you drink it?

[ ] once a week or less   [X] 2–3 times a week   [ ] 4–5 times a week

[ ] over 5 times a week

4) Where is you favorite drink usually bought from?

[ ] supermarket   [X] deli   [ ] other

▷ **Questionnaire**
Questionnaires often take the form of a series of multiple choice questions. The replies to each question are then easy to sort into groups of data. In this example, the data would be grouped by the drinks chosen.

Tallying

Results from a survey can be organized into a chart. The left-hand column shows the groups of data from the questionnaire. A simple way to record the results is by making a tally mark in the chart for each answer. To tally, mark a line for each unit and cross through the lines when 5 is reached.

making tally marks in groups of five makes chart easier to read; the line that goes across is the 5th

Soft drink	Tally
Cola	ЖII I
Orange juice	ЖII ЖII I
Apple juice	II
Pineapple juice	I
Milk	II
Other	I

△ **Tally chart**
This tally chart shows the results of the survey with tally marks.

Soft drink	Tally	Frequency
Cola	ЖII I	6
Orange juice	ЖII ЖII I	11
Apple juice	II	2
Pineapple juice	I	1
Milk	II	2
Other	I	1

△ **Frequency table**
Counting the tally marks for each group, the results (frequency) can be entered in a separate column to make a frequency table.

Tables

Tables showing the frequency of results for each group are a useful way of presenting data. Values from the frequency column can be analyzed and used to make charts or graphs of the data. Frequency tables can have more columns to show more detailed information.

Drink	Frequency
Cola	6
Orange juice	11
Apple juice	2
Pineapple juice	1
Milk	2
Other	1

△ **Frequency table**
Data can be presented in a table. In this example, the number of children that chose each type of drink is shown.

Drink	Boy	Girl	Total
Cola	4	2	6
Orange juice	5	6	11
Apple juice	0	2	2
Pineapple juice	1	0	1
Milk	1	1	2
Other	1	0	1

△ **Two-way table**
This table has extra columns that break down the information further. It also shows the numbers of boys and girls and their preferences.

Bias

In surveys it is important to question a wide selection of people, so that the answers provide an accurate picture. If the survey is too narrow, it may be unrepresentative and show a bias toward a particular answer.

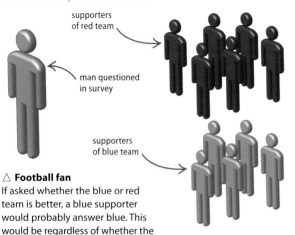

△ **Football fan**
If asked whether the blue or red team is better, a blue supporter would probably answer blue. This would be regardless of whether the reds had proved their superiority.

LOOKING CLOSER
Data logging

A lot of data is recorded by machines—information about the weather, traffic, or internet usage for instance. The data can then be organized and presented in charts, tables, and graphs that make it easier to understand and analyze.

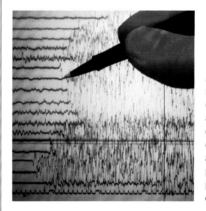

◁ **Seismometer**
A seismometer records movements of the ground that are associated with earthquakes. The collected data is analyzed to find patterns that may predict future earthquakes.

206 STATISTICS

Bar graphs

BAR GRAPHS ARE A WAY OF PRESENTING DATA AS A DIAGRAM.

A bar graph displays a set of data graphically. Bars of different lengths are drawn to show the size (frequency) of each group of data in the set.

SEE ALSO	
⟨ 204–205 Collecting and organizing data	
Pie charts	210–211 ⟩
Line graphs	212–213 ⟩
Histograms	224–225 ⟩

Using bar graphs

Presenting data in the form of a diagram makes it easier to read than a list or table. A bar graph shows a set of data as a series of bars, with each bar representing a group within the set. The height of each bar represents the size of each group—a value known as the group's "frequency." Information can be seen clearly and quickly from the height of the bars, and accurate values for the data can be read from the vertical axis of the chart. A bar graph can be drawn with a pencil, a ruler, and graph paper, using information from a frequency table.

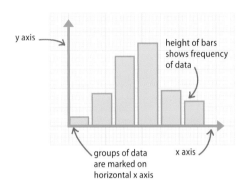

◁ **A bar graph**
In a bar graph, each bar represents a group of data from a particular data set. The size (frequency) of each data group is shown by the height of the corresponding bar.

This frequency table shows the groups of data and the size (frequency) of each group in a data set.

To draw a bar graph, first choose a suitable scale for your data. Then draw a vertical line for the y axis and a horizontal line for the x axis. Label each axis according to the columns of the table, and mark with the data from the table.

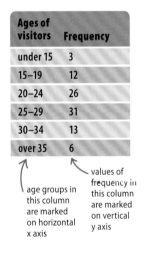

Ages of visitors	Frequency
under 15	3
15–19	12
20–24	26
25–29	31
30–34	13
over 35	6

age groups in this column are marked on horizontal x axis

values of frequency in this column are marked on vertical y axis

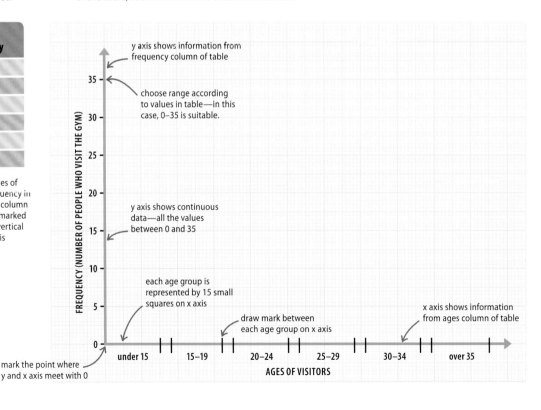

From the table, take the number (frequency) for the first group of data (3 in this case) and find this value on the vertical y axis. Draw a horizontal line between the value on the y axis and the end of the first age range, marked on the x axis. Next, draw a line for the second frequency (in this case, 12) above the second age group marked on the x axis, and similar lines for all the remaining data.

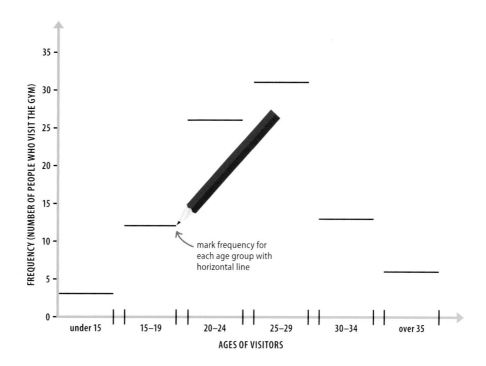

mark frequency for each age group with horizontal line

To complete the bar graph, draw vertical lines up from the dividing marks on the x axis. These will meet the ends of the lines you have drawn from the frequency table, making the bars. Coloring in the bars makes the graph easier to read.

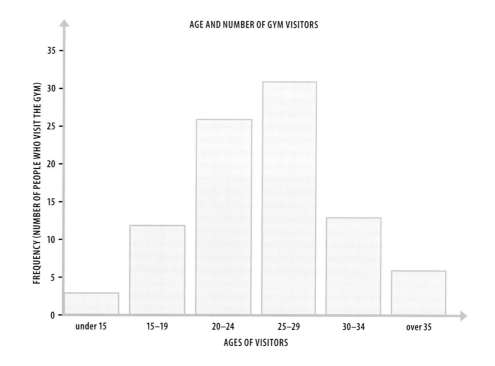

STATISTICS

Different types of bar graph

There are several different ways of presenting information in a bar graph. The bars may be drawn horizontally, as three-dimensional blocks, or in groups of two. In every type, the size of the bar shows the size (frequency) of each group of data.

Hobby	Frequency (number of children)
Reading	25
Sports	45
Computer games	30
Music	19
Collecting	15

◁ **Table of data**
This data table shows the results of a survey in which a number of children were asked about their hobbies.

▷ **Horizontal bar graph**
In a horizontal bar graph, the bars are drawn horizontally rather than vertically. Values for the number of children in each group, the frequency, can be read on the horizontal x axis.

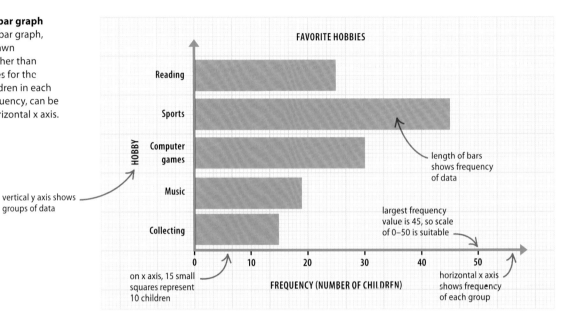

▷ **Three-dimensional bar graph**
The three-dimensional blocks in this type of bar graph give it more visual impact, but can make it misleading. Because of the perspective, the tops of the blocks appear to show two values for frequency—the true value is read from the front edge of the block.

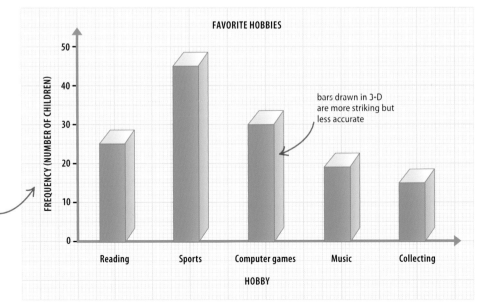

Compound and composite bar graphs

For data divided into sub-groups, compound or composite bar graphs can be used. In a compound bar graph, bars for each sub-group of data are drawn side by side. In a composite bar graph, two sub-groups are combined into one bar.

Hobby	Boys	Girls	Total frequency
Reading	10	15	25
Sports	25	20	45
Computer games	20	10	30
Music	10	9	19
Collecting	5	10	15

◁ **Table of data**
This data table shows the results of the survey on children's hobbies divided into separate figures for boys and girls.

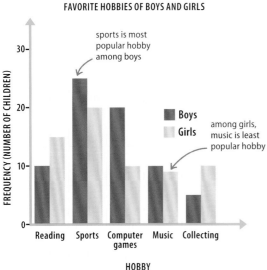

△ **Double bar graph**
In a double bar graph, each data group has two or more bars of different colors, each of which representing a subgroup of that data. A key shows which color represents which groups.

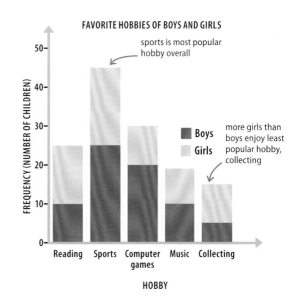

△ **Stacked bar graph**
In a stacked bar graph, two or more subgroups of data are shown as one bar, one subgroup on top of the other. This has the advantage of also showing the total value of the group of data.

Frequency polygons

Another way of presenting the same information as a bar graph is in a frequency polygon. Instead of bars, the data is shown as a line on the chart. The line connects the midpoints of each group of data.

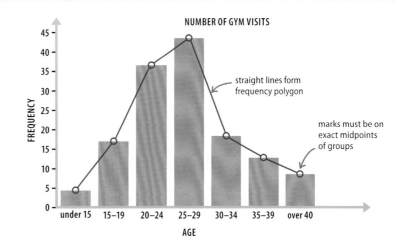

▷ **Drawing a frequency polygon**
Mark the frequency value at the midpoint of each group of data, in this case, the middle of each age range. Join the marks with straight lines.

Pie charts

PIE CHARTS ARE A USEFUL VISUAL WAY TO PRESENT DATA.

A pie chart shows data as a circle divided into segments, or slices, with each slice representing a different part of the data.

> SEE ALSO
> ‹ 84–85 Angles
> ‹ 150–151 Arcs and Sectors
> ‹ 204–205 Collecting and organizing data
> ‹ 206–209 Bar graphs

Why use a pie chart?
Pie charts are often used to present data because they have an immediate visual impact. The size of each slice of the pie clearly shows the relative sizes of different groups of data, which makes the comparison of data quick and easy.

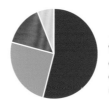

◁ **Reading a pie chart**
When a pie chart is divided into slices, it is easy to understand the information. It is clear in this example that the red section represents the largest group of data.

Identifying data
To get the information necessary to calculate the size, or angle, of each slice of a pie chart, a table of data known as a frequency table is created. This identifies the different groups of data, and shows both their size (frequency of data) and the size of all of the groups of data together (total frequency).

Country of origin	Frequency of data
United Kingdom	375
United States	250
Australia	125
Canada	50
China	50
Unknown	150
TOTAL FREQUENCY	1,000

◁ **Frequency table**
The table shows the number of hits on a website, split into the countries where they occurred.

"frequency of data" is broken down country by country

data from each country is used to calculate size of each slice

"total frequency" is total number of website hits from all countries

United Kingdom 135°

▽ **Calculating the angles**
To find the angle for each slice of the pie chart, take the information in the frequency table and use it in this formula.

$$\text{angle} = \frac{\text{frequency of data}}{\text{total frequency}} \times 360°$$

For example:

$$\text{angle for United Kingdom} = \frac{375}{1,000} \times 360° = 135°$$

number of website hits — divide both numbers — angle for pie chart — total number of website hits

The angles for the remaining slices are calculated in the same way, taking the data for each country from the frequency table and using the formula. The angles of all the slices of the pie should add up to 360°—the total number of degrees in a circle.

$$\text{United States} = \frac{250}{1,000} \times 360 = 90°$$

$$\text{Australia} = \frac{125}{1,000} \times 360 = 45°$$

$$\text{Canada} = \frac{50}{1,000} \times 360 = 18°$$

$$\text{China} = \frac{50}{1,000} \times 360 = 18°$$

$$\text{Unknown} = \frac{150}{1,000} \times 360 = 54°$$

PIE CHARTS   211

Drawing a pie chart
Drawing a pie chart requires a compass to draw the circle, a protractor to measure the angles accurately, and a ruler to draw the slices of the pie.

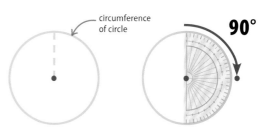

First, draw a circle using a compass (see pp.82–83).

Draw a straight line from the center point of the circle to the circumference (edge of the circle).

Measure the angle of a slice from the center and straight line. Mark it on the edge of the circle. Draw a line from the center to this mark.

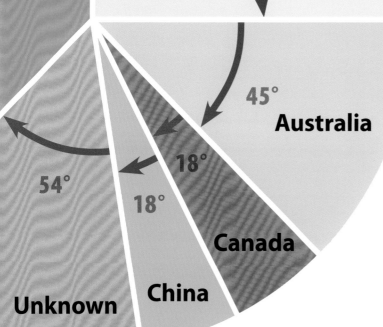

◁ **Finished pie chart**
After drawing each slice on the circle, the pie chart can be labeled and color coded, as necessary. The angles add up to 360°, so all of the slices fit into the circle exactly.

LOOKING CLOSER
Labeling pie charts
There are three different ways to label the different slices of a pie chart: with annotation (a,b), with labels (c,d), or with a key (e,f). Annotation and keys can be useful tools when slices are too small to label the required data.

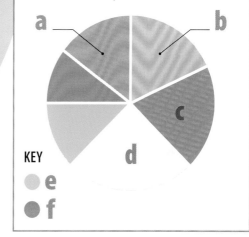

212 STATISTICS

Line graphs

LINE GRAPHS SHOW DATA AS LINES ON A SET OF AXES.

SEE ALSO
‹ 182–185 Linear graphs
‹ 204–205 Collecting and organizing data

Line graphs are a way of accurately presenting information in an easy-to-read form. They are particularly useful for showing data over a period of time.

Drawing a line graph
A pencil, a ruler, and graph paper are all that is needed to draw a line graph. Data from a table is plotted on the graph, and these points are joined to create a line.

Day	Sunshine (hours)
Monday	12
Tuesday	9
Wednesday	10
Thursday	4
Friday	5
Saturday	8
Sunday	11

The columns of the table provide the information for the horizontal and vertical lines—the x and y axes.

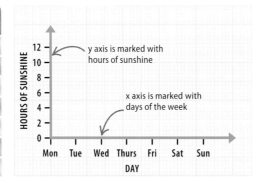

Draw a set of axes. Label the x axis with data from the first column of the table (days). Label the y axis with data from the second (hours of sunshine).

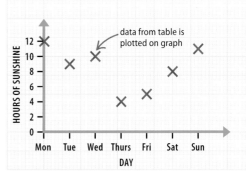

Read up the y axis from Monday on the x axis and mark the first value. Do this for each day, reading up from the x axis and across from the y axis.

Use a ruler and a pen or pencil to connect the points and complete the line graph once all the data has been marked (or plotted). The resulting line clearly shows the relationship between the two sets of data.

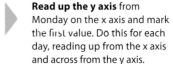

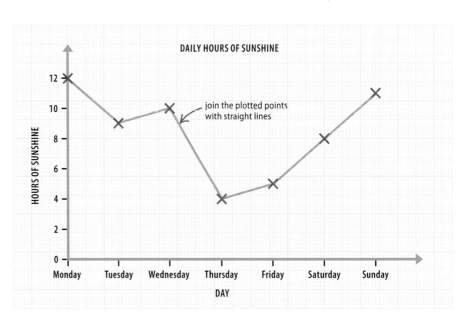

Interpreting line graphs

This graph shows temperature changes over a 24-hour period. The temperature at any time of the day can be found by locating that time on the x axis, reading up to the line, and then across to the y axis.

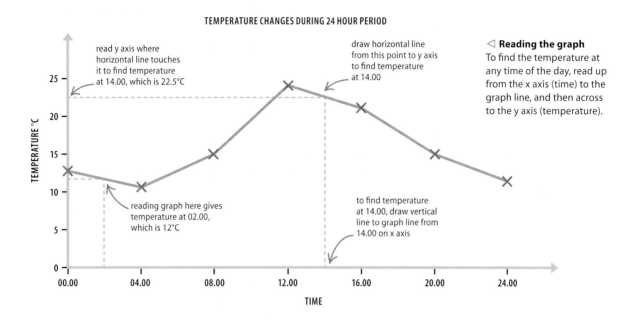

Cumulative frequency graphs

A cumulative frequency diagram is a type of line graph that shows how often each value occurs in a group of data. Joining the points of a cumulative frequency graph with straight lines usually creates an "S" shape, and the curve of the S shows which values occur most frequently within the set of data.

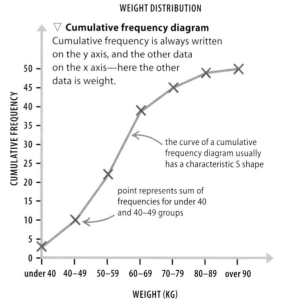

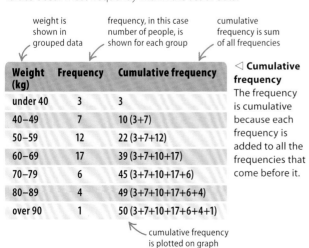

Weight (kg)	Frequency	Cumulative frequency
under 40	3	3
40–49	7	10 (3+7)
50–59	12	22 (3+7+12)
60–69	17	39 (3+7+10+17)
70–79	6	45 (3+7+10+17+6)
80–89	4	49 (3+7+10+17+6+4)
over 90	1	50 (3+7+10+17+6+4+1)

◁ **Cumulative frequency**
The frequency is cumulative because each frequency is added to all the frequencies that come before it.

Averages

AN AVERAGE IS A "MIDDLE" VALUE OF A SET OF DATA. IT IS A TYPICAL VALUE THAT REPRESENTS THE ENTIRE SET OF DATA.

SEE ALSO
◁ 204–205 Collecting and organizing data
Moving averages 218–219 ▷
Measuring spread 220–223 ▷

Different types of averages

There are several different types of average. The main ones are called the mean, the median, and the mode. Each one gives slightly different information about the data. In everyday life, the term "average" usually refers to the mean.

The mode

The mode is the value that appears most frequently in a set of data. It is easier to find the mode if you put the data list into an ascending order of values (from lowest to highest). If different values appear the same number of times, there may be more than one mode.

150, 160, 170, 180, 180

working out averages often requires listing a set of data arranged in ascending order

this color represents mode because it appears most often

◁ **The mode color**
The set of data in this example is a series of colored figures. The pink people appear the most often, so pink is the mode value.

150, 160, 170, 180, 180

180 occurs twice in this list, more often than any other value, so it is the mode, or most frequent, value

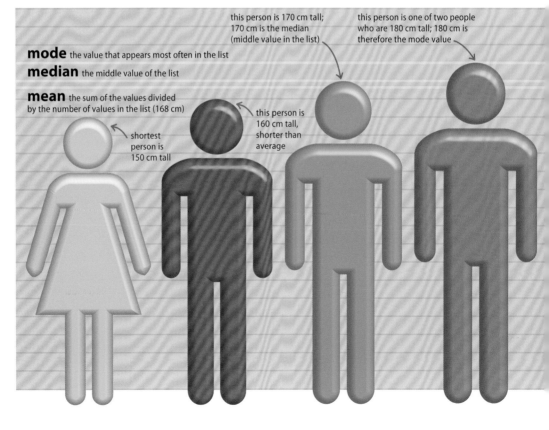

▷ **Average heights**
The heights of this group of people can be arranged as a list of data. From this list, the different types of average can be found—mean, median, and mode.

mode the value that appears most often in the list
median the middle value of the list
mean the sum of the values divided by the number of values in the list (168 cm)

shortest person is 150 cm tall

this person is 160 cm tall, shorter than average

this person is 170 cm tall; 170 cm is the median (middle value in the list)

this person is one of two people who are 180 cm tall; 180 cm is therefore the mode value

AVERAGES

The mean

The mean is the sum of all the values in a set of data divided by the number of values in the list. It is what most people understand by the word "average." To find the mean, a simple formula is used.

$$\text{Mean} = \frac{\text{Sum total of values}}{\text{Number of values}}$$

formula to find mean

First, take the list of data and put it in order. Count the number of values in the list. In this example, there are five values.

150, 160, 170, 180, 180

there are five numbers in list

Add all of the values in the list together to find the sum total of the values. In this example the sum total is 840.

$150 + 160 + 170 + 180 + 180 = 840$

add numbers together — sum total of values

Divide the sum total of the values, in this case 840, by the number of values, which is 5. The answer, 168, is the mean value of the list.

$$\frac{840}{5} = 168$$

sum total of values — number of values — 168 is the mean

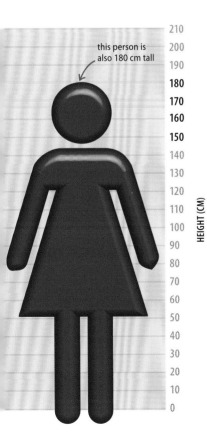

this person is also 180 cm tall

HEIGHT (CM)

The median

The median is the middle value in a set of data. In a list of five values, it is the third value. In a list of seven values, it would be the fourth value.

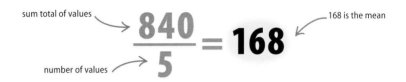

median is middle value, in this case the orange figure

Firstly, put the data in ascending order (from lowest to highest)

170, 180, 180, 160, 150

The median is the middle value in a list with an odd number of values.

150, 160, **170**, 180, 180

in this list of five values, third value is the median

LOOKING CLOSER

Median of an even number of values

In a list with an even number of values, the median is worked out using the two middle values. In a list of six values, these are the third and fourth values.

150, 160, **170**, **180**, 180, 190

3rd value — 4th value — middle values

▷ **Calculating the median**
Add the two middle values and divide by two to find the median.

$$\frac{170 + 180}{2} = \frac{350}{2} = 175$$

median value

STATISTICS

WORKING WITH FREQUENCY TABLES
Data that deals with averages is often presented in what is known as a frequency table. Frequency tables show the frequency with which certain values appear in a set of data.

Finding the median using a frequency table
The process for finding the median (middle) value from a frequency table depends on whether the total frequency is an odd or an even number.

The following marks were scored in a test and entered in a frequency table:

20, 20, 18, 20, 18, 19, 20, 20, 20

Mark	Frequency
18	2
19	1 (2 + 1 = 3)
20	6 (3 + 6 = 9)
	9

— number of times each mark appears
— median frequency (entry contains 5th value in list)
— total frequency
median mark

Because the total frequency of 9 is odd, to find the median first add 1 to it and then divide it by 2. This makes 5, meaning that the 5th value is the median. Count down the frequency column adding the values until reaching the row containing the 5th value. The median mark is 20.

The following marks were scored in a test and entered in a frequency table:

18, 17, 20 19, 19, 18, 19, 18

Mark	Frequency
17	1
18	3 (1 + 3 = 4)
19	3 (4 + 3 = 7)
20	1 (7 + 1 = 8)
	8

— frequency contains 4th value
— frequency contains 5th value
— total frequency

The total frequency of 8 is even (8), so there are two middle values (4th and 5th). Count down the frequency column adding values to find them.

▽ **An even total frequency**
If the total frequency is even, the median is calculated from the two middle values.

$$\text{Median} = \frac{\text{1st middle value} + \text{2nd middle value}}{2}$$

$$\frac{18 + 19}{2} = \mathbf{18.5}$$

— 1st middle value
— 2nd middle value
— median

The two middle values (4th and 5th) represent the marks 18 and 19 respectively. The median is the mean of these two marks, so add them together and divide by 2. The median mark is 18.5.

Finding the mean from a frequency table
To find the mean from a frequency table, calculate the total of all the data as well as the total frequency. Here, the following marks were scored in a test and entered into a table:

16, 18, 20, 19, 17, 19, 18, 17, 18, 19, 16, 19

Mark	Frequency
16	2
17	2
18	3
19	4
20	1

↑ range of values ↑ frequency shows number of times each mark was scored

Enter the given data into a frequency table.

Mark	Frequency	Total marks (mark × frequency)
16	2	16×2=32
17	2	17×2=34
18	3	18×3=54
19	4	19×4=76
20	1	20×1=20
	12	216

— add frequencies together to get total frequency
— total marks

Find the total marks scored by multiplying each mark by its frequency. The total sum of each part of the data is the sum of values.

$$\text{Mean} = \frac{\text{Sum of values}}{\text{Number of values}}$$

— total marks
— total frequency

$$216 \div 12 = \mathbf{18}$$

— total frequency   — mean mark

To find the mean, divide the sum of values, in this example, the total marks, by the number of values, which is the total frequency.

AVERAGES

Finding the mean of grouped data

Grouped data is data that has been collected into groups of values, rather than appearing as specific or individual values. If a frequency table shows grouped data, there is not enough information to calculate the sum of values, so only an estimated value for the mean can be found.

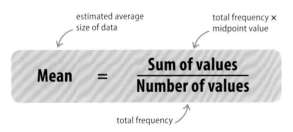

$$\text{Mean} = \frac{\text{Sum of values}}{\text{Number of values}}$$

- estimated average size of data
- total frequency × midpoint value
- total frequency

In grouped data the sum of the values can be calculated by finding the midpoint of each group and multiplying it by the frequency. Then add the results for each group together to find the total frequency × midpoint value. This is divided by the total number of values to find the mean. The example below shows a group of marks scored in a test.

LOOKING CLOSER
Weighted mean

If some individual values within grouped data contribute more to the mean than other individual values in the group, a "weighted" mean results.

Students in group	15	20	22
Mean exam mark	18	17	13

$$\frac{(15 \times 18) + (20 \times 17) + (22 \times 13)}{15 + 20 + 22} = 15.72$$

- students × mean
- sum of these three values is total number students
- weighted mean

△ **Finding the weighted mean**
Multiply the number of students in each group by the mean mark and add the results. Divide by the total students to give the weighted mean.

Mark	Frequency
under 50	2
50–59	1
60–69	8
70–79	5
80–89	3
90–99	1

Mark	Frequency	Midpoint	Frequency × midpoint
under 50	2	25	2 × 25 = 50
50–59	1	54.5	1 × 54.5 = 54.5
60–69	8	64.5	8 × 64.5 = 516
70–79	5	74.5	5 × 74.5 = 372.5
80–89	3	84.5	3 × 84.5 = 253.5
90–99	1	94.5	1 × 94.5 = 94.5
	20		1,341

$$\frac{1{,}341}{20} = 67.05$$

- total frequency × midpoint
- total frequency
- estimated mean mark

To find the midpoint of a set of data, add the upper and lower values and divide the answer by 2. For example, the midpoint in the 90–99 mark group is 94.5.

Multiply the midpoint by the frequency for each group and enter this in a new column. Add the results to find the total frequency multiplied by the midpoint.

Dividing the total frequency × midpoint by the total frequency gives the estimated mean mark. It is an estimated value as the exact marks scored are not known – only a range has been given in each group.

LOOKING CLOSER
The modal class

In a frequency table with grouped data, it is not possible to find the mode (the value that occurs most often in a group). But it is easy to see the group with the highest frequency in it. This group is known as the modal class.

▷ **More than one modal class**
When the highest frequency in the table is in more than one group, there is more than one modal class.

Mark	0–25	26–50	51–75	76–100
Frequency	2	6	8	8

modal class

STATISTICS

 # Moving averages

MOVING AVERAGES SHOW GENERAL TRENDS IN DATA OVER A CERTAIN PERIOD OF TIME.

What is a moving average?
When data is collected over a period of time, the values sometimes change, or fluctuate, noticeably. Moving averages, or averages over specific periods of time, smooth out the highs and lows of fluctuating data and instead show its general trend.

Showing moving averages on a line graph
Taking data from a table, a line graph of individual values over time can be plotted. The moving averages can also be calculated from the table data, and a line of moving averages plotted on the same graph.

The table below shows sales of ice cream over a two-year period, with each year divided into four quarters. The figures for each quarter show how many thousands of ice cream cones were sold.

	YEAR ONE				YEAR TWO			
Quarter	1st	2nd	3rd	4th	5th	6th	7th	8th
Sales (in thousands)	1.25	3.75	4.25	2.5	1.5	4.75	5.0	2.75

△ **Table of data**
These figures can be presented as a line graph, with sales shown on the y axis and time (measured in quarters of a year) shown on the x axis.

▷ **Sales graph**
The sales graph shows quarterly highs and lows (pink line), while a moving average (green line) shows the trend over the two-year period.

REAL WORLD
Seasonality
Seasonality is the name given to regular changes in a data series that follow a seasonal pattern. These seasonal fluctuations may be caused by the weather, or by annual holiday periods such as Christmas or Easter. For example, retail sales experience a predictable peak around the Christmas period and low during the summer vacation period.

▷ **Ice cream sales**
Sales of ice cream tend to follow a predictable seasonal pattern.

Calculating moving averages
From the figures in the table, an average for each period of four quarters can be calculated and a moving average on the graph plotted.

Average for quarters 1–4
Calculate the mean of the four figures for year one. Mark the answer on the graph at the midpoint of the quarters.

$$1.25 + 3.75 + 4.25 + 2.5 = 11.75$$

sum of sales figures for quarters 1–4

mean value (rounded to 2 decimal places)

$$\frac{11.75}{4} = 2.94$$

number of values

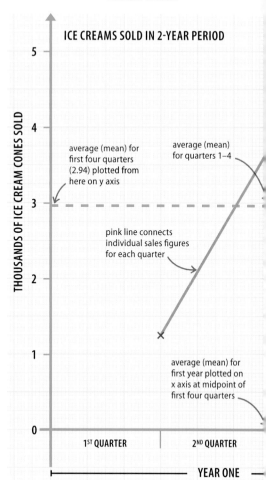

ICE CREAMS SOLD IN 2-YEAR PERIOD

average (mean) for first four quarters (2.94) plotted from here on y axis

average (mean) for quarters 1–4

pink line connects individual sales figures for each quarter

average (mean) for first year plotted on x axis at midpoint of first four quarters

1ST QUARTER   2ND QUARTER

YEAR ONE

MOVING AVERAGES

Average (mean) = **Sum total of values / Number of values**

◁ **Calculating the mean**
Use this formula to find the average (or mean) for each period of four quarters.

Average for quarters 2–5
Calculate the mean of the figures for quarters 2–5 and mark it at the quarters' midpoint.
$3.75 + 4.25 + 2.5 + 1.5 = 12$

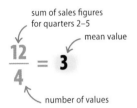

Average for quarters 3–6
Calculate the mean of the figures for quarters 3–6 and mark it at the quarters' midpoint.
$4.25 + 2.5 + 1.5 + 4.75 = 13$

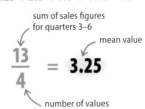

Average for quarters 4–7
Calculate the mean of the figures for quarters 4–7 and mark it at the quarters' midpoint.
$2.5 + 1.5 + 4.75 + 5 = 13.75$

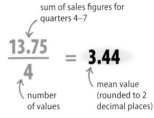

Average for quarters 5–8
Find the mean for quarters 5–8, mark it on the graph, and join all of the marks.
$1.5 + 4.75 + 5 + 2.75 = 14$

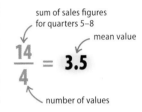

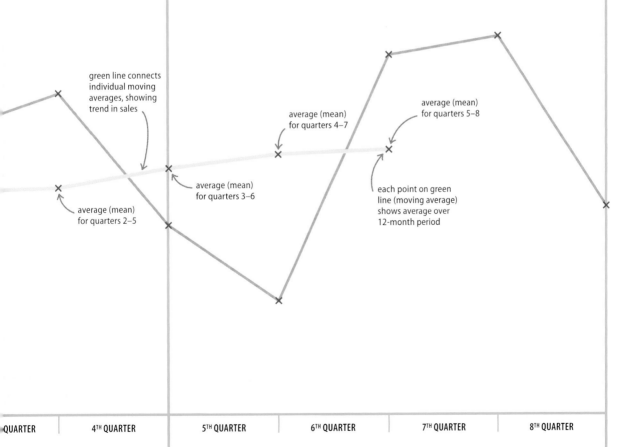

Measuring spread

MEASURES OF SPREAD SHOW THE RANGE OF DATA, AND ALSO GIVE MORE INFORMATION ABOUT THE DATA THAN AVERAGES ALONE.

SEE ALSO
‹ 204–205 Collecting and organizing data
Histograms 224–225 ›

Diagrams showing the measure of spread give the highest and lowest figures (the range) of the data and give information about how it is distributed.

Range and distribution

From tables or lists of data, diagrams can be created that show the ranges of different sets of data. This shows the distribution of the data, whether it is spread over a wide or narrow range.

Subject	Ed's results	Bella's results
Math	47	64
English	95	68
French	10	72
Geography	65	61
History	90	70
Physics	60	65
Chemistry	81	60
Biology	77	65

This table shows the marks of two students. Although their average (see pp.214–215) marks are the same (65.625), the ranges of their marks are very different.

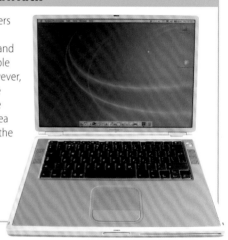

REAL WORLD
Broadband bandwidth
Internet service providers often give a maximum speed for their broadband connections, for example 20Mb per second. However, this information can be misleading. An average speed gives a better idea of what to expect, but the range and distribution of the data is the information really needed to get the full picture.

lowest mark ↘   highest mark ↙
Ed: **10**, 47, 60, 65, 77, 81, 90, **95**

Bella: **60**, 61, 64, 65, 65, 68, 70, **72**

◁ **Finding the range**
To calculate the range of each student's marks, subtract the lowest figure from the highest in each set. Ed's lowest mark is 10, and highest 95, so his range is 85. Bella's lowest mark is 60, and highest 72, giving a range of 12.

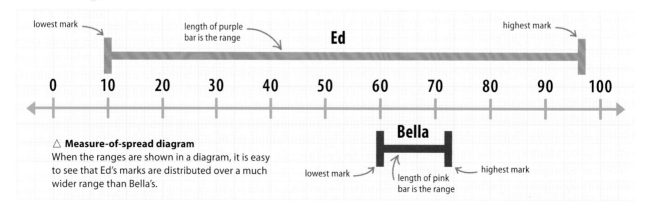

△ **Measure-of-spread diagram**
When the ranges are shown in a diagram, it is easy to see that Ed's marks are distributed over a much wider range than Bella's.

Stem-and-leaf diagrams

Another way of showing data is in stem-and-leaf diagrams. These give a clearer picture of the way the data is distributed within the range than a simple measure-of-spread diagram.

This is how the data appears before it has been organized.

34, 48, 7, 15, 27, 18, 21, 14, 24, 57, 25, 12, 30, 37, 42, 35, 3, 43, 22, 34, 5, 43, 45, 22, 49, 50, 34, 12, 33, 39, 55

Sort the list of data into numerical order, with the smallest number first. Add a zero in front of any number smaller than 10.

03, 05, 07, 12, 12, 14, 15, 18, 21, 22, 22, 24, 25, 27, 30, 33, 34, 34, 34, 35, 37, 39, 42, 43, 43, 45, 48, 49, 50, 55, 57

To draw a stem-and-leaf diagram, draw a cross with more space to the right of it than the left. Write the data into the cross, with the tens in the "stem" column to the left of the cross, and the ones for each number as the "leaves" on the right hand side. Once each value of tens has been entered into the stem, do not repeat it, but continue to repeat the values entered into the leaves.

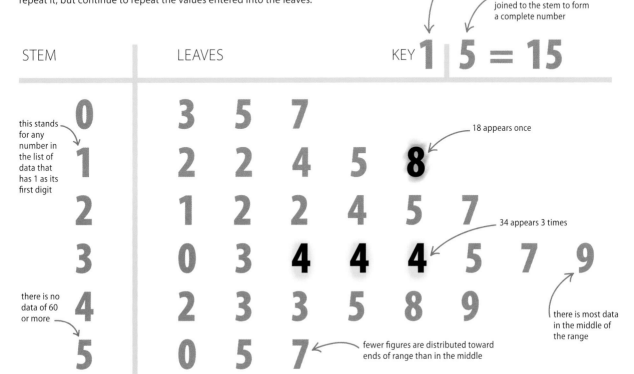

QUARTILES

Quartiles are dividing points in the range of a set of data that give a clear picture of distribution. The median marks the center point, the upper quartile marks the midpoint between the median and the top of the distribution, and the lower quartile the midpoint between the median and the bottom. Estimates of quartiles can be found from a graph, or calculated precisely using formulas.

Estimating quartiles

Quartiles can be estimated by reading values from a cumulative frequency graph (see p.213).

Make a table with the data given for range and frequency, and add up the cumulative frequency. Use this data to make a cumulative frequency graph, with cumulative frequency on the y axis, and range on the x axis.

Range	Frequency	Cumulative frequency
30–39	2	2
40–49	3	5 (= 2+3)
50–59	4	9 (= 2+3+4)
60–69	6	15 (= 2+3+4+6)
70–79	5	20 (= 2+3+4+6+5)
80–89	4	24 (= 2+3+4+6+5+4)
>90	3	27 (= 2+3+4+6+5+4+3)

this sign means greater than — add each number to those before it to find cumulative frequency

Divide the total cumulative frequency by 4 (this will be the cumulative frequency of the last entry in the table), and use the result to divide the y axis into 4 parts.

total cumulative frequency

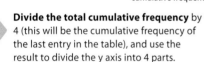

divide the y axis into sections of this length

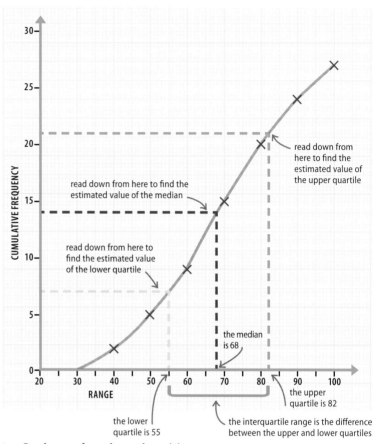

read down from here to find the estimated value of the upper quartile

read down from here to find the estimated value of the median

read down from here to find the estimated value of the lower quartile

the median is 68

the upper quartile is 82

the lower quartile is 55

the interquartile range is the difference between the upper and lower quartiles

Read across from the marks and down to the x axis to find estimated values for the quartiles. These are only approximate values.

Calculating quartiles

Exact values of quartiles can be found from a list of data. These formulas give the position of the quartiles and median in a list of data in ascending order, using the total number of data items in the list, n.

n is the total number of values in the list

$$\frac{(n+1)}{4}$$

△ **Lower quartile**
This shows the position of the lower quartile in a list of data.

$$\frac{(n+1)}{2}$$

△ **Median**
This shows the position of the median in a list of data.

$$\frac{3(n+1)}{4}$$

△ **Upper quartile**
This shows the position of the upper quartile in a list of data.

MEASURING SPREAD **223**

How to calculate quartiles

To find the values of the quartiles in a list of data, first arrange the list of numbers in ascending order from lowest to highest.

37, 38, 45, 47, 48, 51, 54, 54, 58, 60, 62, 63, 63, 65, 69, 71, 74, 75, 78, 78, 80, 84, 86, 89, 92, 94, 96

▷ **Using the formulas,** calculate where to find the quartiles and the median in this list. The answers give the position of each value in the list.

n is the total number of values in the list

position of lower quartile (7th value)

position of median (14th value)

position of upper quartile (21st value)

$$\frac{(n+1)}{4} = \frac{(27+1)}{4} = 7 \qquad \frac{(n+1)}{2} = \frac{(27+1)}{2} = 14 \qquad \frac{3(n+1)}{4} = \frac{3(27+1)}{4} = 21$$

formula to find lower quartile · formula to find median · formula to find upper quartile

△ **Lower quartile**
This calculation gives the answer 7, so the lower quartile is the 7th value in the list.

△ **Median**
The answer to this calculation is 14, so the median is the 14th value in the list.

△ **Upper quartile**
The answer to this calculation is 21, so the upper quartile is the 21st value in the list.

▷ **To find the values** of the quartiles and the median, count along the list to the positions that have just been calculated.

```
                    lower quartile              median                  upper quartile
 1  2  3  4  5  6   7   8  9 10 11 12 13  14  15 16 17 18 19 20  21  22 23 24 25 26 27
37,38,45,47,48,51, 54, 54,58,60,62,63,63, 65, 69,71,74,75,78,78, 80, 84,86,89,92,94,96
```

LOOKING CLOSER

Box-and-whisker diagram

Box-and-whisker diagrams are a way of showing the spread and distribution of a range of data in an graphic way. The range is plotted on a number line, with the interquartile range between the upper and lower quartiles shown as a box.

▽ **Using the diagram**
This box-and-whisker diagram shows a range with a lower limit of 1 and an upper limit of 9. The median is 4, the lower quartile 3, and the upper quartile 6.

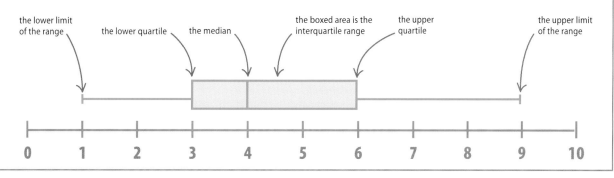

Histograms

A HISTOGRAM IS A TYPE OF BAR GRAPH. IN A HISTOGRAM, THE AREA OF THE BARS, NOT THEIR LENGTH, REPRESENTS THE SIZE OF THE DATA.

> **SEE ALSO**
> ‹ 204–205 Collecting and organizing data
> ‹ 206–209 Bar graphs
> ‹ 220–223 Measuring spread

What is a histogram?
A histogram is a diagram made up of blocks on a graph. Histograms are useful for showing data when it is grouped into groups of different sizes. This example looks at the number of downloads of a music file in a month (frequency) by different age groups. Each age group (class) is a different size because each covers a different age range. The width of each block represents the age range, known as class width. The height of each block represents frequency density, which is calculated by dividing the number of downloads (frequency) in each age group (class) by the class width (age range).

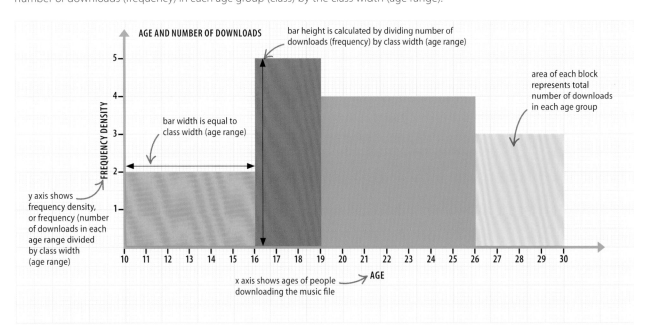

LOOKING CLOSER
Histograms and bar graphs

Bar graphs look like histograms, but show data in a different way. In a bar graph, the bars are all the same width. The height of each bar represents the total (frequency) for each group, while in a histogram, totals are represented by the area of the blocks.

▷ **Bar graph**
This bar graph shows the same data as shown above. Although class widths are different, the bar widths are the same.

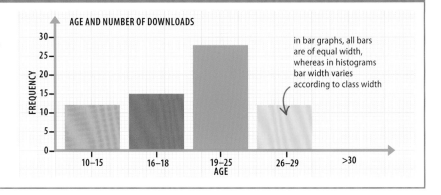

in bar graphs, all bars are of equal width, whereas in histograms bar width varies according to class width

HISTOGRAMS

How to draw a histogram

To draw a histogram, begin by making a frequency table for the data. Next, using the class boundaries, find the width of each class of data. Then calculate frequency density for each by dividing frequency by class width.

Age (year)	Frequency (downloads in a month)
10–15	12
16–18	15
19–25	28
26–29	12
>30	0

upper class boundary for any group is lower boundary of next group

class boundaries for this data are 10, 16, 19, 26, and 30

find class width by subtracting lower class boundary from the upper class boundary, for example 16 – 10 = 6

number of downloads per month

divide frequency by class width to find frequency density

Age	Class width	Frequency	Frequency density
10–15	6	12	2
16–18	3	15	5
19–25	7	28	4
26–29	4	12	3
>30	–	0	–

there is no data to enter for this group

The information needed to draw a histogram is the range of each class of data and frequency data. From this information, the class width and frequency density can be calculated.

To find class width, begin by finding the class boundaries of each group of data. These are the two numbers that all the values in a group fall in between—for example, for the 10–15 group they are 10 and 16. Next, find class width by subtracting the lower boundary from the upper for each group.

To find frequency density, divide the frequency by the class width of each group. Frequency density shows the frequency of each group in proportion to its class width.

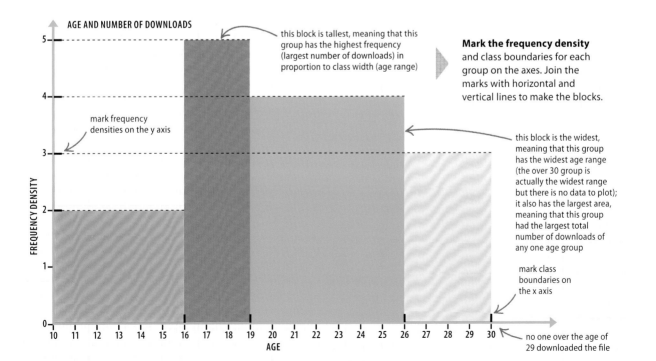

this block is tallest, meaning that this group has the highest frequency (largest number of downloads) in proportion to class width (age range)

Mark the frequency density and class boundaries for each group on the axes. Join the marks with horizontal and vertical lines to make the blocks.

mark frequency densities on the y axis

this block is the widest, meaning that this group has the widest age range (the over 30 group is actually the widest range but there is no data to plot); it also has the largest area, meaning that this group had the largest total number of downloads of any one age group

mark class boundaries on the x axis

no one over the age of 29 downloaded the file

Scatter diagrams

> **SEE ALSO**
> ‹ 204–205 Collecting and organizing data
> ‹ 212–213 Line graphs

SCATTER DIAGRAMS PRESENT INFORMATION FROM TWO SETS OF DATA AND REVEAL THE RELATIONSHIP BETWEEN THEM.

What is a scatter diagram?

A scatter diagram is a graph made from two sets of data. Each set of data is measured on an axis of the graph. The data always appears in pairs—one value will need to be read up from the x axis, the other read across from the y axis. A point is marked where each pair meet. The pattern made by the points shows whether there is any connection, or correlation, between the two sets of data.

▽ **Table of data**
This table shows two sets of data—the height and weight of 13 people. With each person's height the corresponding weight measurement is given.

Height (cm)	173	171	189	167	183	181	179	160	177	180	188	186	176
Weight (kg)	69	68	90	65	77	76	74	55	70	75	86	81	68

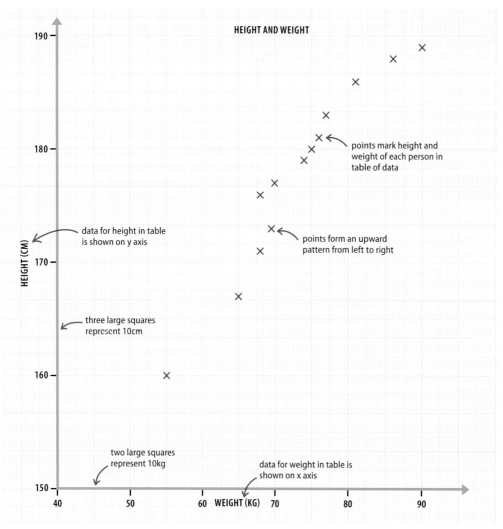

◁ **Plotting the points**
Draw a vertical axis (y) and a horizontal axis (x) on graph paper. Mark out measurements for each set of data in the table along the axes. Read each corresponding height and weight in from its axis and mark where they meet. Do not join the points marked.

◁ **Positive correlation**
The pattern of points marked between the two axes shows an upward trend from left to right. An upward trend is known as positive correlation. The correlation between the two sets of data in this example is that as height increases, so does weight.

Negative and zero correlations

The points in a scatter diagram can form many different patterns, which reveal different types of correlation between the sets of data. This can be positive, negative, or nonexistent. The pattern can also reveal how strong or how weak the correlation is between the two sets of data.

Energy used (kwh)	1,000	1,200	1,300	1,400	1,450	1,550	1,650	1,700
Temperature (°C)	55	50	45	40	35	30	25	20

IQ	141	127	117	150	143	111	106	135
Shoe size	8	10	11	6	11	10	9	7

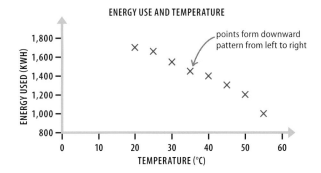

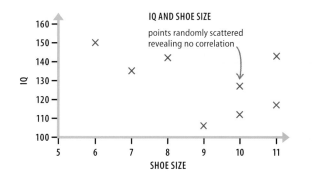

△ **Negative correlation**
In this graph, the points form a downward pattern from left to right. This reveals a connection between the two sets of data—as the temperature increases, energy consumption goes down. This relationship is called negative correlation.

△ **No correlation**
In this graph, the points form no pattern at all—they are widely spaced and do not reveal any trend. This shows there is no connection between a person's shoe size and their IQ, which means there is zero correlation between the two sets of data.

Line of best fit

To make a scatter diagram clearer and easier to read, a straight line can be drawn that follows the general pattern of the points, with an equal number of points on both sides of the line. This line is called the line of best fit.

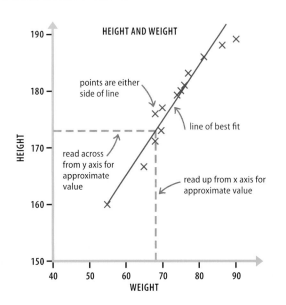

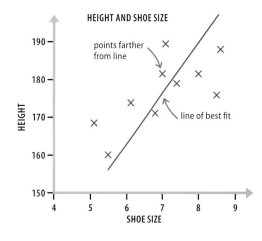

◁ **Finding approximate values**
When the line of best fit is drawn, approximate values of any weight and height can be found by reading across from the y axis, or up from the x axis.

△ **Weak correlation**
Here the points are farther away from the line of best fit. This shows that the correlation between height and shoe size is weak. The farther the points are from the line, the weaker the correlation.

Probability

230 PROBABILITY

 ## What is probability?

PROBABILITY IS THE LIKELIHOOD OF SOMETHING HAPPENING.

Math can be used to calculate the likelihood or chance that something will happen.

SEE ALSO	
‹ 48–55 Fractions	
‹ 64–65 Converting fractions, decimals, and percentages	
Expectation and reality	232–233 ›
Combined probabilities	234–235 ›

How is probability shown?

Probabilities are given a value between 0, which is impossible, and 1, which is certain. To calculate these values, fractions are used. Follow the steps to find out how to calculate the probability of an event happening and then how to show it as a fraction.

$$\frac{1}{8}$$

total of specific events that can happen

total of all possible events that can happen

◁ **Writing a probability**
The top number shows the chances of a specific event, while the bottom number shows the total chances of all of the possible events happening.

▷ **Total chances**
Decide what the total number of possibly outcomes is. In this example, with 5 candies to pick 1 candy from, the total is 5—any one of 5 candies may be picked.

 there are 5 candies, 4 are red and 1 is yellow

▷ **Chance of red candy**
Of the 5 candies, 4 are red. This means that there are 4 chances out of 5 that the candy chosen is red. This probability can be written as the fraction ⁴/₅.

$$\frac{4}{5}$$
total number of red candies that can be chosen
total of 5 candies to choose from

▷ **Chance of yellow candy**
Because 1 candy is yellow there is 1 chance in 5 of the candy picked being yellow. This probability can be written as the fraction ¹/₅.

$$\frac{1}{5}$$
1 yellow candy can be chosen
total of 5 candies to choose from

△ **Identical snowflakes**
Every snowflake is unique and the chance that there can be two identical snowflakes is 0 on the scale, or impossible.

▷ **A hole in one**
A hole in one during a game of golf is highly unlikely, so it has a probability close to 0 on the scale. However, it can still happen!

 0

IMPOSSIBLE

UNLIKELY

▷ **Probability scale**
All probabilities can be shown on a line known as a probability scale. The more likely something is to occur the further to the right, or towards 1, it is placed.

LESS LIKELY

WHAT IS PROBABILITY? **231**

Calculating probabilities

This example shows how to work out the probability of randomly picking a red candy from a group of 10 candies. The number of ways this event could happen is put at the top of the fraction and the total number of possible events is put at the bottom.

number of red candies that can be chosen

$$\frac{3 \text{ red}}{10 \text{ candies}}$$

total that can be chosen

chance of red candy being chosen, as fraction

$$\frac{3}{10} \text{ or } 0.3$$

chance of red candy being chosen, as decimal

△ **Pick a candy**
There are 10 candies to choose from. Of these, 3 are colored red. If one of the candies is picked, what is the chance of it being red?

△ **Red randomly chosen**
One candy is chosen at random from the 10 colored candies. The candy chosen is one of the 3 red candies available.

△ **Write as a fraction**
There are three reds that can be chosen, so 3 is put at the top of the fraction. As there are ten candies in total, 10 is at the bottom.

△ **What is the chance?**
The probability of a red candy being picked is 3 out of 10, written as the fraction ³⁄₁₀, the decimal 0.3, or the percentage 30%.

◁ **Heads or tails**
If a coin is tossed there is a 1 in 2, or even, chance of throwing either a head or a tail. This is shown as 0.5 on the scale, which is the same as half, or 50%.

▷ **Earth turning**
It is a certainty that each day the Earth will continue to turn on its axis, making it a 1 on the scale.

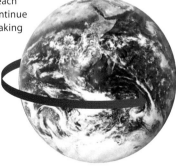

majority of people are right-handed

◁ **Being right-handed**
The chances of picking at random a right-handed person are very high—almost 1 on the scale. Most people are right-handed.

0.5
EVEN CHANCE

LIKELY

1
CERTAIN

MORE LIKELY

232 PROBABILITY

 # Expectation and reality

SEE ALSO
‹ 48–55 Fractions
‹ 230–231 What is probability?
Combined probabilities 234–235 ›

EXPECTATION IS AN OUTCOME THAT IS ANTICIPATED TO OCCUR; REALITY IS THE OUTCOME THAT ACTUALLY OCCURS.

The difference between what is expected to occur and what actually occurs can often be considerable.

What is expectation?

There is an equal chance of a 6-sided dice landing on any number. It is expected that each of the 6 numbers on it will be rolled once in every 6 throws ($\frac{1}{6}$ of the time). Similarly, if a coin is tossed twice, it is expected that it will land on heads once and tails once. However, this does not always happen in real life.

WHAT ARE THE CHANCES?	
Two random phone numbers ending in same digit	1 chance in 10
Randomly selected person being left-handed	1 chance in 12
Pregnant woman giving birth to twins	1 chance in 33
An adult living to 100	1 chance in 50
A random clover having four leaves	1 chance in 10,000
Being struck by lightning in a year	1 chance in 2.5 million
A specific house being hit by a meteor	1 chance in 182 trillion

chance of rolling each number is 1 in 6

△ **Roll a dice**
Roll a dice 6 times and it seems likely that each of the 6 numbers on the dice will be seen once.

Expectation versus reality

Mathematical probability expects that when a dice is rolled 6 times, the numbers 1, 2, 3, 4, 5, and 6 will appear once each, but it is unlikely this outcome would actually occur. However, over a longer series of events, for example, throwing a dice a thousand times, the total numbers of 1s, 2s, 3s, 4s, 5s, and 6s thrown would be more even.

reasonable to expect 4 in first 6 throws

▷ **Expectation**
Mathematical probability expects that, when a dice is rolled 6 times, a 4 will be thrown once.

unexpected third 5 in 6 throws

unexpected third 6 in 6 throws

▷ **Reality**
Throwing a dice 6 times may create any combination of the numbers on a dice.

EXPECTATION AND REALITY

Calculating expectation

Expectation can be calculated. This is done by expressing the likelihood of something happening as a fraction, and then multiplying the fraction by the number of times the occurrence has the chance to happen. This example shows how expectation can be calculated in a game where balls are pulled from a bucket, with numbers ending in 0 or 5 winning a prize.

◁ **Numbered balls**
There are 30 balls in the game and 5 are removed at random. The balls are then checked for winning numbers—numbers that end in 0 or 5.

6 winning balls

There are 6 winning balls that can be picked out of the total of 30 balls.

number of winning balls in game
6

30 numbered balls to pick from

The total number of balls that can be picked in the game is 30.

total number of balls in game
30

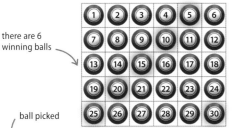
there are 6 winning balls

The probability of a winning ball being picked is 6 (balls) out of 30 (balls). This can be written as the fraction $6/30$, and is then reduced to $1/5$. The chance of picking a winning ball is 1 in 5, so the chance of winning a prize is 1 in 5.

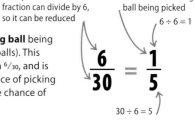
both parts of the fraction can divide by 6, so it can be reduced

chances of winning ball being picked
$6 \div 6 = 1$

$$\frac{6}{30} = \frac{1}{5}$$

$30 \div 6 = 5$

ball picked

It is expected that a prize will be won exactly 1 out of 5 times. The probability of winning a prize is therefore $1/5$ of 5, which is 1.

1 prize "probably" won

$$\frac{1}{5} \times 5 = 1$$

probability of picking a winning ball is 1 in 5

opportunities to pick a ball

"expect" 1 prize

winning ball

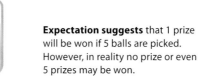

Expectation suggests that 1 prize will be won if 5 balls are picked. However, in reality no prize or even 5 prizes may be won.

1 prize won?

234 PROBABILITY

 # Combined probabilities

THE PROBABILITY OF ONE OUTCOME FROM TWO OR MORE EVENTS HAPPENING AT THE SAME TIME, OR ONE AFTER THE OTHER.

> SEE ALSO
> ‹ 230–231 What is probability?
> ‹ 232–233 Expectation and reality

Calculating the chance of one outcome from two things happening at the same time is not as complex as it might appear.

What are combined probabilities?

To find out the probability of one possible outcome happening from more than one event, all of the possible outcomes need to be worked out first. For example, if a coin is tossed and a dice is rolled at the same time, what is the probability of the coin landing on tails and the dice rolling a 4?

coin has 2 sides — dice has 6 sides

COIN   DICE

Coin and dice
A coin has 2 sides (heads and tails) while a dice has 6 sides—numbers 1 through to 6, represented by numbers of dots on each side.

▷ **Tossing a coin**
There are 2 sides to a coin, and each is equally likely to show if the coin is tossed. This means that the chance of the coin landing on tails is exactly 1 in 2, shown as the fraction ½.

chance of heads is 1 in 2

HEADS   TAILS

chance of tails is 1 in 2

$\dfrac{1}{2}$

— 1 represents chance of single event, for example chance of coin landing on tails
— 2 represents total possible outcomes if coin is tossed

▷ **Rolling a dice**
Because there are 6 sides to a dice, and each side is equally likely to show when the dice is rolled, the chance of rolling a 4 is exactly 1 in 6, shown as the fraction ⅙.

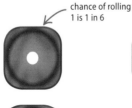
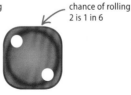
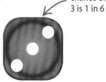

chance of rolling 1 is 1 in 6   chance of rolling 2 is 1 in 6   chance of rolling 3 is 1 in 6

chance of rolling 4 is 1 in 6   chance of rolling 5 is 1 in 6   chance of rolling 6 is 1 in 6

$\dfrac{1}{6}$

— 1 represents chance of single event, for example chance of rolling a 4
— 6 represents total possible outcomes if dice is thrown

▷ **Both events**
To find out the chances of both a coin landing on tails and a dice simultaneously rolling a 4, multiply the individual probabilities together. The answer shows that there is a 1/12 chance of this outcome.

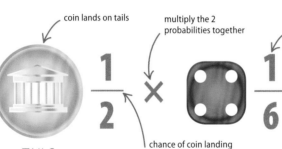
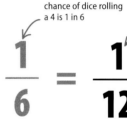

coin lands on tails   multiply the 2 probabilities together   chance of dice rolling a 4 is 1 in 6

$$\dfrac{1}{2} \times \dfrac{1}{6} = \dfrac{1}{12}$$

TAILS

chance of coin landing on tails is 1 in 2

— chance of specific outcome
— chance of coin landing on tails and rolling a 4 is 1 in 12
— total possible outcomes

COMBINED PROBABILITIES

Figuring out possible outcomes

A table can be used to work out all the possible outcomes of two combined events. For example, if two dice are rolled, their scores will have a combined total of between 2 and 12. There are 36 possible outcomes, which are shown in the table below. Read down from each red dice and across from each blue dice for each of their combined results.

red dice throws

blue dice throws

Blue \ Red	⚀	⚁	⚂	⚃	⚄	⚅
⚀	2	3	4	5	6	7
⚁	3	4	5	6	7	8
⚂	4	5	6	7	8	9
⚃	5	6	7	8	9	10
⚄	6	7	8	9	10	11
⚅	7	8	9	10	11	12

- 6 ways out of 36 to throw 7, for example blue dice rolling 1 and red dice rolling 6
- 5 ways out of 36 to throw 8, for example blue dice rolling 2 and red dice rolling 6
- 4 ways out of 36 to throw 9, for example blue dice rolling 3 and red dice rolling 6
- 3 ways out of 36 to throw 10, for example blue dice rolling 4 and red dice rolling 6
- 2 ways out of 36 to throw 11, for example blue dice rolling 5 and red dice rolling 6
- 1 way out of 36 to throw 12

KEY

 Least likely
The least likely outcome of throwing 2 dice is either 2 (each dice is 1) or 12 (each is 6). There is a $1/36$ chance of either result.

 Most likely
The most likely outcome of throwing 2 dice is a 7. With 6 ways to throw a 7, there is a $6/36$, or $1/6$, chance of this result.

Dependent events

SEE ALSO
‹ 232–233 Expectation and reality

THE CHANCES OF SOMETHING HAPPENING CAN CHANGE ACCORDING TO THE EVENTS THAT PRECEDED IT. THIS IS A DEPENDENT EVENT.

Dependent events
In this example, the probability of picking any one of four green cards from a pack of 40 is 4 out of 40 (4/40). It is an independent event. However, the probability of the second card picked being green depends on the color of the card picked first. This is known as a dependent event.

▷ **Color-coded**
This pack of cards contains 10 groups, each with its own color. There are 4 cards in each group.

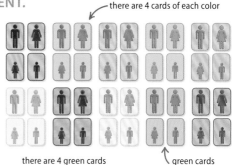

there are 4 cards of each color

there are 4 green cards — green cards

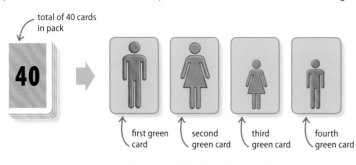

total of 40 cards in pack

first green card / second green card / third green card / fourth green card

◁ **What are the chances?**
The chances of the first card picked being green is 4 in 40 (4/40). This is independent of other events because it is the first event.

$$\frac{4}{40}$$

there are 40 cards in total

Dependent events and decreasing probability
If the first card chosen from a pack of 40 is one of the 4 green cards, then the chances that the next card is green are reduced to 3 in 39 (3/39). This example shows how the chances of a green card being picked next gradually shrink to zero.

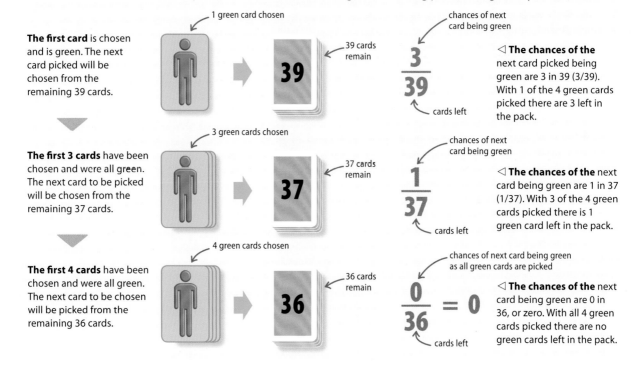

The first card is chosen and is green. The next card picked will be chosen from the remaining 39 cards.

1 green card chosen — 39 cards remain

chances of next card being green

$$\frac{3}{39}$$

cards left

◁ **The chances of the** next card picked being green are 3 in 39 (3/39). With 1 of the 4 green cards picked there are 3 left in the pack.

The first 3 cards have been chosen and were all green. The next card to be picked will be chosen from the remaining 37 cards.

3 green cards chosen — 37 cards remain

chances of next card being green

$$\frac{1}{37}$$

cards left

◁ **The chances of the** next card being green are 1 in 37 (1/37). With 3 of the 4 green cards picked there is 1 green card left in the pack.

The first 4 cards have been chosen and were all green. The next card to be chosen will be picked from the remaining 36 cards.

4 green cards chosen — 36 cards remain

chances of next card being green as all green cards are picked

$$\frac{0}{36} = 0$$

cards left

◁ **The chances of the** next card being green are 0 in 36, or zero. With all 4 green cards picked there are no green cards left in the pack.

Dependent events and increasing probability

If the first card chosen from a pack of 40 is not one of the 4 pink cards, then the probability of the next card being pink grow to 4 out of the remaining 39 cards (4/39). In this example, the probability of a pink card being the next to be picked grows to a certainty with each non-pink card picked.

The first card has been chosen and is not pink. The next card to be picked will be chosen from the remaining 39 cards.

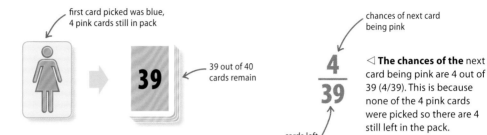

◁ **The chances of the** next card being pink are 4 out of 39 (4/39). This is because none of the 4 pink cards were picked so there are 4 still left in the pack.

The first 12 cards have been chosen, none of which were pink. The next card to be picked will be chosen from the remaining 28 cards.

◁ **The chances of the** next card being pink are 4 out of 28 (4/28). With none of the 4 pink cards picked there are still 4 left in the pack.

24 cards have been chosen and none of which were pink. The next card to be picked will be chosen from the remaining 16 cards.

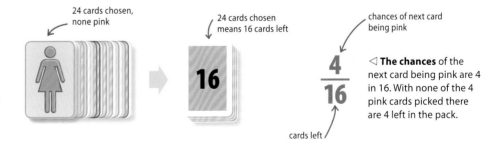

◁ **The chances** of the next card being pink are 4 in 16. With none of the 4 pink cards picked there are 4 left in the pack.

The first 36 cards have been chosen. None of them were pink. The next card to be picked will be chosen from the remaining 4 cards.

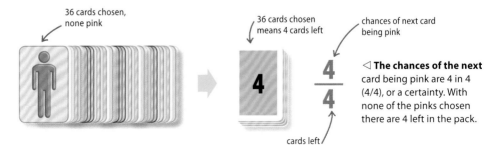

◁ **The chances of the next** card being pink are 4 in 4 (4/4), or a certainty. With none of the pinks chosen there are 4 left in the pack.

238 PROBABILITY

Tree diagrams

TREE DIAGRAMS CAN BE CONSTRUCTED TO HELP CALCULATE THE
PROBABILITY OF MULTIPLE EVENTS OCCURRING.

> **SEE ALSO**
> ‹ 230–231 What is probability?
> ‹ 234–235 Combined probabilities
> ‹ 236–237 Dependent events

A range of probable outcomes of future events can be shown using arrows, or the "branches" of a "tree," flowing from left to right.

Building a tree diagram

The first stage of building a tree diagram is to draw an arrow from the start position to each of the possible outcomes. Here, the start is a cell phone, and the outcomes are 5 messages sent to 2 other phones, with each of these other phones at the end of 1 of 2 arrows. Because no event came before, they are single events.

▷ **Single events**
Of 5 messages, 2 are sent to the first phone, shown by the fraction $2/5$, and 3 out of 5 are sent to the second phone, shown by the fraction $3/5$.

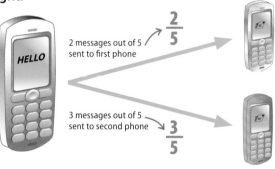

2 messages out of 5 sent to first phone — $\frac{2}{5}$

3 messages out of 5 sent to second phone — $\frac{3}{5}$

Tree diagrams showing multiple events

To draw a tree diagram that shows multiple events, begin with a start position, with arrows leading to the right to each of the possible outcomes. This is stage 1. Each of the outcomes of stage 1 then becomes a new start position, with further arrows each leading to a new stage of possible outcomes. This is stage 2. More stages can then follow on from the outcomes of previous stages. Because one stage of events comes before another, these are multiple events.

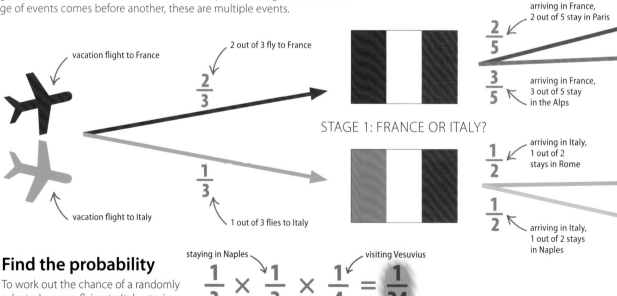

Find the probability

To work out the chance of a randomly selected person flying to Italy, staying in Naples, and visiting Vesuvius, multiply the chances of each stage of this trip together for the answer.

staying in Naples $\frac{1}{3}$ × $\frac{1}{2}$ × $\frac{1}{4}$ = $\frac{1}{24}$ visiting Vesuvius

1 out of 3 flies to Italy

chance of person visiting Italy, then Naples, then Vesuvius

△ **Multiple events in 3 stages**
The tree diagram above shows 3 stages of a vacation. In stage 1, people fly to France or Italy.

TREE DIAGRAMS **239**

When multiple events are dependent
Tree diagrams show how the chances of one event can depend on the previous event. In this example, each event is someone picking a fruit from a bag and not replacing it.

△ **Dependent events**
The first person picks from a bag of 10 fruits (3 oranges, 7 apples). The next picks from 9 fruits, when the chances of what is picked are out of 9.

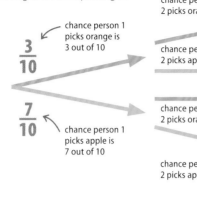

chance person 1 picks orange is 3 out of 10

$\frac{3}{10}$

chance person 1 picks apple is 7 out of 10

$\frac{7}{10}$

chance person 2 picks orange → $\frac{2}{9}$

chance person 2 picks apple → $\frac{7}{9}$

chance person 2 picks orange → $\frac{3}{9}$

chance person 2 picks apple → $\frac{6}{9}$

person 1 chooses from 10 fruits

person 2 chooses from 9 fruits

Find the probability
What are the chances that the first and second person will each choose an orange? Multiply the chances of both events together.

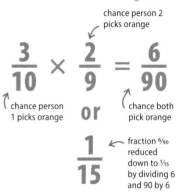

$$\frac{3}{10} \times \frac{2}{9} = \frac{6}{90}$$

chance person 1 picks orange

chance person 2 picks orange

or

chance both pick orange

$\frac{1}{15}$ ← fraction 6/90 reduced down to 1/15 by dividing 6 and 90 by 6

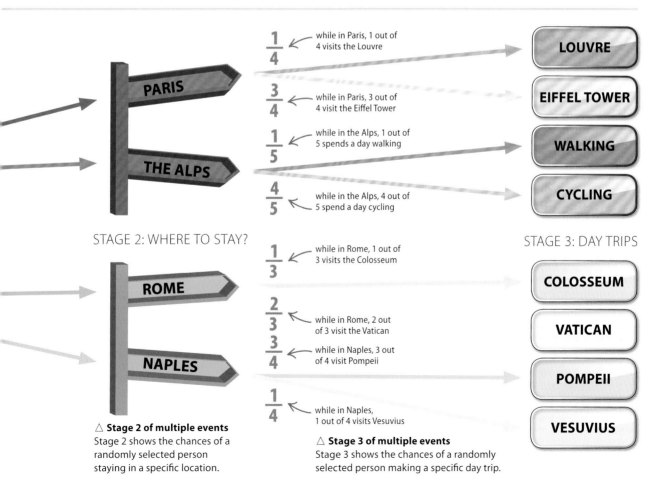

△ **Stage 2 of multiple events**
Stage 2 shows the chances of a randomly selected person staying in a specific location.

△ **Stage 3 of multiple events**
Stage 3 shows the chances of a randomly selected person making a specific day trip.

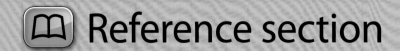
Reference section

Mathematical signs and symbols

This table shows a selection of signs and symbols commonly used in mathematics. Using signs and symbols, mathematicians can express complex equations and formulas in a standardized way that is universally understood.

Symbol	Definition
$+$	plus; positive
$-$	minus; negative
$\pm$	plus or minus; positive or negative; degree of accuracy
$\mp$	minus or plus; negative or positive
$\times$	multiplied by (6×4)
$\cdot$	multiplied by ($6 \cdot 4$); scalar product of two vectors ($A \cdot B$)
$\div$	divided by ($6 \div 4$)
$/$	divided by; ratio of ($6/4$)
$—$	divided by; ratio of ($\frac{6}{4}$)
$\bigcirc$	circle
$\blacktriangle$	triangle
$\square$	square
$\square$	rectangle
$\square$	parallelogram
$=$	equals
$\neq$	not equal to
$\equiv$	identical with; congruent to
$\not\equiv, \neq$	not identical with
$\triangleq$	corresponds to

Symbol	Definition
$:$	ratio of (6:4)
$::$	proportionately equal (1:2::2:4)
$\approx, \doteq, \stackrel{\frown}{=}$	approximately equal to; equivalent to; similar to
$\cong$	congruent to; identical with
$>$	greater than
$\gg$	much greater than
$\not>$	not greater than
$<$	less than
$\ll$	much less than
$\not<$	not less than
$\geqslant, \geq, \geqq$	greater than or equal to
$\leqslant, \leq, \leqq$	less than or equal to
$\propto$	directly proportional to
$()$	parentheses, can mean multiply
$—$	vinculum: division (a-b); chord of circle or length of line (AB);
$\overrightarrow{AB}$	vector
$\overline{AB}$	line segment
$\overleftrightarrow{AB}$	line

Symbol	Definition
∞	infinity
n^2	squared number
n^3	cubed number
n^4, n^5, etc	power, exponent
$\sqrt{}$	square root
$\sqrt[3]{}, \sqrt[4]{}$	cube root, fourth root, etc.
$\%$	percent
$°$	degrees (°F); degree of arc, for example 90°
$\angle, \angle^s$	angle(s)
$\stackrel{\angle}{=}$	equiangular
π	(pi) the ratio of the circumference to the diameter of a circle ≈ 3.14
α	alpha (unknown angle)
θ	theta (unknown angle)
$\perp$	perpendicular
$\llcorner$	right angle
$\parallel, \rightleftharpoons$	parallel
$\therefore$	therefore
$\because$	because
$\stackrel{m}{=}$	measured by

REFERENCE

Prime numbers

A prime number is any number that can only be exactly divided by 1 and itself without leaving a remainder. By definition, 1 is not a prime. There is no one formula for yielding every prime. Shown here are the first 250 prime numbers.

2	3	5	7	11	13	17	19	23	29
31	37	41	43	47	53	59	61	67	71
73	79	83	89	97	101	103	107	109	113
127	131	137	139	149	151	157	163	167	173
179	181	191	193	197	199	211	223	227	229
233	239	241	251	257	263	269	271	277	281
283	293	307	311	313	317	331	337	347	349
353	359	367	373	379	383	389	397	401	409
419	421	431	433	439	443	449	457	461	463
467	479	487	491	499	503	509	521	523	541
547	557	563	569	571	577	587	593	599	601
607	613	617	619	631	641	643	647	653	659
661	673	677	683	691	701	709	719	727	733
739	743	751	757	761	769	773	787	797	809
811	821	823	827	829	839	853	857	859	863
877	881	883	887	907	911	919	929	937	941
947	953	967	971	977	983	991	997	1,009	1,013
1,019	1,021	1,031	1,033	1,039	1,049	1,051	1,061	1,063	1,069
1,087	1,091	1,093	1,097	1,103	1,109	1,117	1,123	1,129	1,151
1,153	1,163	1,171	1,181	1,187	1,193	1,201	1,213	1,217	1,223
1,229	1,231	1,237	1,249	1,259	1,277	1,279	1,283	1,289	1,291
1,297	1,301	1,303	1,307	1,319	1,321	1,327	1,361	1,367	1,373
1,381	1,399	1,409	1,423	1,427	1,429	1,433	1,439	1,447	1,451
1,453	1,459	1,471	1,481	1,483	1,487	1,489	1,493	1,499	1,511
1,523	1,531	1,543	1,549	1,553	1,559	1,567	1,571	1,579	1,583

Squares, cubes, and roots

The table below shows the square, cube, square root, and cube root of whole numbers, to 3 decimal places.

No.	Square	Cube	Square root	Cube root
1	1	1	1.000	1.000
2	4	8	1.414	1.260
3	9	27	1.732	1.442
4	16	64	2.000	1.587
5	25	125	2.236	1.710
6	36	216	2.449	1.817
7	49	343	2.646	1.913
8	64	512	2.828	2.000
9	81	729	3.000	2.080
10	100	1,000	3.162	2.154
11	121	1,331	3.317	2.224
12	144	1,728	3.464	2.289
13	169	2,197	3.606	2.351
14	196	2,744	3.742	2.410
15	225	3,375	3.873	2.466
16	256	4,096	4.000	2.520
17	289	4,913	4.123	2.571
18	324	5,832	4.243	2.621
19	361	6,859	4.359	2.668
20	400	8,000	4.472	2.714
25	625	15,625	5.000	2.924
30	900	27,000	5.477	3.107
50	2,500	125,000	7.071	3.684

Multiplication table

This multiplication table shows the products of each whole number from 1 to 12, multiplied by each whole number from 1 to 12.

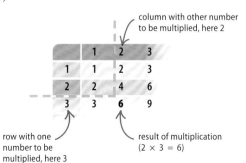

row with one number to be multiplied, here 3

column with other number to be multiplied, here 2

result of multiplication (2 × 3 = 6)

	1	2	3	4	5	6	7	8	9	10	11	12
1	1	2	3	4	5	6	7	8	9	10	11	12
2	2	4	6	8	10	12	14	16	18	20	22	24
3	3	6	9	12	15	18	21	24	27	30	33	36
4	4	8	12	16	20	24	28	32	36	40	44	48
5	5	10	15	20	25	30	35	40	45	50	55	60
6	6	12	18	24	30	36	42	48	54	60	66	72
7	7	14	21	28	35	42	49	56	63	70	77	84
8	8	16	24	32	40	48	56	64	72	80	88	96
9	9	18	27	36	45	54	63	72	81	90	99	108
10	10	20	30	40	50	60	70	80	90	100	110	120
11	11	22	33	44	55	66	77	88	99	110	121	132
12	12	24	36	48	60	72	84	96	108	120	132	144

Units of measurement

A unit of measurement is a quantity used as a standard, allowing values of things to be compared. These include seconds (time), meters (length), and kilograms (mass). Two widely used systems of measurement are the metric system and the imperial system.

AREA		
metric		
100 square millimeters (mm²)	=	1 square centimeter (cm²)
10,000 square centimeters (cm²)	=	1 square meter (m²)
10,000 square meters (m²)	=	1 hectare (ha)
100 hectares (ha)	=	1 square kilometer (km²)
1 square kilometer (km²)	=	1,000,000 square meters (m²)
imperial		
144 square inches (sq in)	=	1 square foot (sq ft)
9 square feet (sq ft)	=	1 square yard (sq yd)
1,296 square inches (sq in)	=	1 square yard (sq yd)
43,560 square feet (sq ft)	=	1 acre
640 acres	=	1 square mile (sq mile)

LIQUID VOLUME		
metric		
1,000 milliliters (ml)	=	1 liter (l)
100 liters (l)	=	1 hectoliter (hl)
10 hectoliters (hl)	=	1 kiloliter (kl)
1,000 liters (l)	=	1 kiloliter (kl)
imperial		
8 fluid ounces (fl oz)	=	1 cup
20 fluid ounces (fl oz)	=	1 pint (pt)
4 gills (gi)	=	1 pint (pt)
2 pints (pt)	=	1 quart (qt)
4 quarts (qt)	=	1 gallon (gal)
8 pints (pt)	=	1 gallon (gal)

MASS		
metric		
1,000 milligrams (mg)	=	1 gram (g)
1,000 grams (g)	=	1 kilogram (kg)
1,000 kilograms (kg)	=	1 tonne (t)
imperial		
16 ounces (oz)	=	1 pound (lb)
14 pounds (lb)	=	1 stone
112 pounds (lb)	=	1 hundredweight
20 hundredweight	=	1 ton

LENGTH		
metric		
10 millimeters (mm)	=	1 centimeter (cm)
100 centimeters (cm)	=	1 meter (m)
1,000 millimeters (mm)	=	1 meter (m)
1,000 meters (m)	=	1 kilometer (km)
imperial		
12 inches (in)	=	1 foot (ft)
3 feet (ft)	=	1 yard (yd)
1,760 yards (yd)	=	1 mile
5,280 feet (ft)	=	1 mile
8 furlongs	=	1 mile

TIME		
metric and imperial		
60 seconds	=	1 minute
60 minutes	=	1 hour
24 hours	=	1 day
7 days	=	1 week
52 weeks	=	1 year
1 year	=	12 months

TEMPERATURE				
		Fahrenheit	Celsius	Kelvin
Boiling point of water	=	212°	100°	373°
Freezing point of water	=	32°	0°	273°
Absolute zero	=	−459°	−273°	0°

Conversion tables

The tables below show metric and imperial equivalents for common measurements for length, area, mass, and volume. Conversions between Celcius, Fahrenheit, and Kelvin temperature require formulas, which are also given below.

LENGTH

metric		imperial
1 millimeter (mm)	=	0.03937 inch (in)
1 centimeter (cm)	=	0.3937 inch (in)
1 meter (m)	=	1.0936 yards (yd)
1 kilometer (km)	=	0.6214 mile
imperial		**metric**
1 inch (in)	=	2.54 centimeters (cm)
1 foot (ft)	=	0.3048 meter (m)
1 yard (yd)	=	0.9144 meter (m)
1 mile	=	1.6093 kilometers (km)
1 nautical mile	=	1.853 kilometers (km)

AREA

metric		imperial
1 square centimeter (cm^2)	=	0.155 square inch (sq in)
1 square meter (m^2)	=	1.196 square yard (sq yd)
1 hectare (ha)	=	2.4711 acres
1 square kilometer (km^2)	=	0.3861 square miles
imperial		**metric**
1 square inch (sq in)	=	6.4516 square centimeters (cm^2)
1 square foot (sq ft)	=	0.0929 square meter (m^2)
1 square yard (sq yd)	=	0.8361 square meter (m^2)
1 acre	=	0.4047 hectare (ha)
1 square mile	=	2.59 square kilometers (km^2)

MASS

metric		imperial
1 milligram (mg)	=	0.0154 grain
1 gram (g)	=	0.0353 ounce (oz)
1 kilogram (kg)	=	2.2046 pounds (lb)
1 tonne/metric ton (t)	=	0.9842 imperial ton
imperial		**metric**
1 ounce (oz)	=	28.35 grams (g)
1 pound (lb)	=	0.4536 kilogram (kg)
1 stone	=	6.3503 kilogram (kg)
1 hundredweight (cwt)	=	50.802 kilogram (kg)
1 imperial ton	=	1.016 tonnes/metric tons

VOLUME

metric		imperial
1 cubic centimeter (cm^3)	=	0.061 cubic inch (in^3)
1 cubic decimeter (dm^3)	=	0.0353 cubic foot (ft^3)
1 cubic meter (m^3)	=	1.308 cubic yard (yd^3)
1 liter (l)/1 dm^3	=	1.76 pints (pt)
1 hectoliter (hl)/100 l	=	21.997 gallons (gal)
imperial		**metric**
1 cubic inch (in^3)	=	16.387 cubic centimeters (cm^3)
1 cubic foot (ft^3)	=	0.0283 cubic meters (m^3)
1 fluid ounce (fl oz)	=	28.413 milliliters (ml)
1 pint (pt)/20 fl oz	=	0.5683 liter (l)
1 gallon/8 pt	=	4.5461 liters (l)

TEMPERATURE

To convert from Fahrenheit (°F) to Celsius (°C)	=	C = (F − 32) × 5 ÷ 9
To convert from Celsius (°C) Fahrenheit (°F)	=	F = (C × 9 ÷ 5) + 32
To convert from Celsius (°C) to Kelvin (K)	=	K = C + 273
To convert from Kelvin (K) to Celsius (°C)	=	C = K − 273

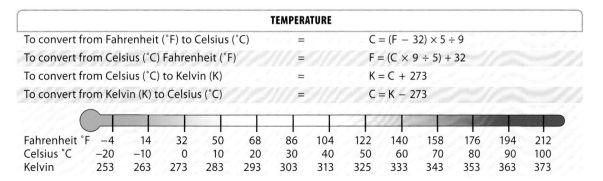

Fahrenheit °F	−4	14	32	50	68	86	104	122	140	158	176	194	212
Celsius °C	−20	−10	0	10	20	30	40	50	60	70	80	90	100
Kelvin	253	263	273	283	293	303	313	325	333	343	353	363	373

How to convert

The table below shows how to convert between metric and imperial units of measurement. The left table shows how to convert from one unit to its metric or imperial equivalent. The right table shows how to do the reverse conversion.

HOW TO CONVERT METRIC and IMPERIAL MEASURES			HOW TO CONVERT METRIC and IMPERIAL MEASURES		
to change	to	multiply by	to change	to	divide by
acres	hectares	0.4047	hectares	acres	0.4047
centimeters	feet	0.03281	feet	centimeters	0.03281
centimeters	inches	0.3937	inches	centimeters	0.3937
cubic centimeters	cubic inches	0.061	cubic inches	cubic centimeters	0.061
cubic feet	cubic meters	0.0283	cubic meters	cubic feet	0.0283
cubic inches	cubic centimeters	16.3871	cubic centimeters	cubic inches	16.3871
cubic meters	cubic feet	35.315	cubic feet	cubic meters	35.315
feet	centimeters	30.48	centimeters	feet	30.48
feet	meters	0.3048	meters	feet	0.3048
gallons	liters	4.546	liters	gallons	4.546
grams	ounces	0.0353	ounces	grams	0.0353
hectares	acres	2.471	acres	hectares	2.471
inches	centimeters	2.54	centimeters	inches	2.54
kilograms	pounds	2.2046	pounds	kilograms	2.2046
kilometers	miles	0.6214	miles	kilometers	0.6214
kilometers per hour	miles per hour	0.6214	miles per hour	kilometers per hour	0.6214
liters	gallons	0.2199	gallons	liters	0.2199
liters	pints	1.7598	pints	liters	1.7598
meters	feet	3.2808	feet	meters	3.2808
meters	yards	1.0936	yards	meters	1.0936
meters per minute	centimeters per second	1.6667	centimeters per second	meters per minute	1.6667
meters per minute	feet per second	0.0547	feet per second	meters per minute	0.0547
miles	kilometers	1.6093	kilometers	miles	1.6093
miles per hour	kilometers per hour	1.6093	kilometers per hour	miles per hour	1.6093
miles per hour	meters per second	0.447	meters per second	miles per hour	0.447
millimeters	inches	0.0394	inches	millimeters	0.0394
ounces	grams	28.3495	grams	ounces	28.3495
pints	liters	0.5682	liters	pints	0.5682
pounds	kilograms	0.4536	kilograms	pounds	0.4536
square centimeters	square inches	0.155	square inches	square centimeters	0.155
square inches	square centimeters	6.4516	square centimeters	square inches	6.4516
square feet	square meters	0.0929	square meters	square feet	0.0929
square kilometers	square miles	0.386	square miles	square kilometers	0.386
square meters	square feet	10.764	square feet	square meters	10.764
square meters	square yards	1.196	square yards	square meters	1.196
square miles	square kilometers	2.5899	square kilometers	square miles	2.5899
square yards	square meters	0.8361	square meters	square yards	0.8361
tonnes (metric)	tons (imperial)	0.9842	tons (imperial)	tonnes (metric)	0.9842
tons (imperial)	tonnes (metric)	1.0216	tonnes (metric)	tons (imperial)	1.0216
yards	meters	0.9144	meters	yards	0.9144

Numerical equivalents

Percentages, decimals, and fractions are different ways of presenting a numerical value as a proportion of a given amount. For example, 10 percent (10%) has the equivalent value of the decimal 0.1 and the fraction 1/10.

%	Decimal	Fraction	%	Decimal	Fraction	%	Decimal	Fraction	%	Decimal	Fraction	%	Decimal	Fraction
1	0.01	1/100	12.5	0.125	1/8	24	0.24	6/25	36	0.36	9/25	49	0.49	49/100
2	0.02	1/50	13	0.13	13/100	25	0.25	1/4	37	0.37	37/100	50	0.5	1/2
3	0.03	3/100	14	0.14	7/50	26	0.26	13/50	38	0.38	19/50	55	0.55	11/20
4	0.04	1/25	15	0.15	3/20	27	0.27	27/100	39	0.39	39/100	60	0.6	3/5
5	0.05	1/20	16	0.16	4/25	28	0.28	7/25	40	0.4	2/5	65	0.65	13/20
6	0.06	3/50	16.66	0.166	1/6	29	0.29	29/100	41	0.41	41/100	66.66	0.666	2/3
7	0.07	7/100	17	0.17	17/100	30	0.3	3/10	42	0.42	21/50	70	0.7	7/10
8	0.08	2/25	18	0.18	9/50	31	0.31	31/100	43	0.43	43/100	75	0.75	3/4
8.33	0.083	1/12	19	0.19	19/100	32	0.32	8/25	44	0.44	11/25	80	0.8	4/5
9	0.09	9/100	20	0.2	1/5	33	0.33	33/100	45	0.45	9/20	85	0.85	17/20
10	0.1	1/10	21	0.21	21/100	33.33	0.333	1/3	46	0.46	23/50	90	0.9	9/10
11	0.11	11/100	22	0.22	11/50	34	0.34	17/50	47	0.47	47/100	95	0.95	19/20
12	0.12	3/25	23	0.23	23/100	35	0.35	7/20	48	0.48	12/25	100	1.00	1

Angles

An angle shows the amount that a line "turns" as it extends in a direction away from a fixed point.

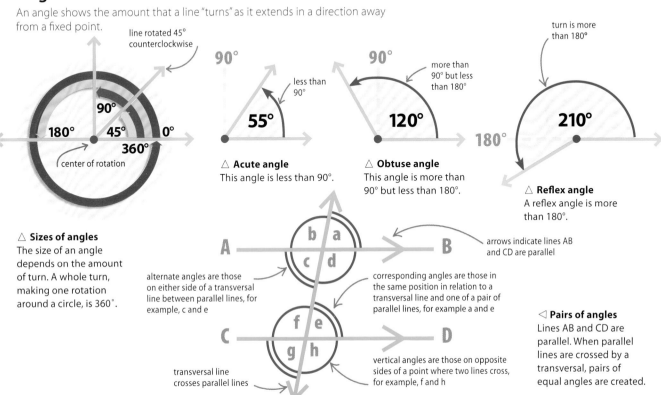

△ **Sizes of angles**
The size of an angle depends on the amount of turn. A whole turn, making one rotation around a circle, is 360°.

△ **Acute angle**
This angle is less than 90°.

△ **Obtuse angle**
This angle is more than 90° but less than 180°.

△ **Reflex angle**
A reflex angle is more than 180°.

alternate angles are those on either side of a transversal line between parallel lines, for example, c and e

corresponding angles are those in the same position in relation to a transversal line and one of a pair of parallel lines, for example a and e

vertical angles are those on opposite sides of a point where two lines cross, for example, f and h

arrows indicate lines AB and CD are parallel

◁ **Pairs of angles**
Lines AB and CD are parallel. When parallel lines are crossed by a transversal, pairs of equal angles are created.

transversal line crosses parallel lines

Shapes

Two-dimensional shapes with straight lines are called polygons. They are named according to the number of sides they have. The number of sides is also equal to the number of interior angles. A circle has no straight lines, so it is not a polygon although it is a two-dimensional shape.

△ **Circle**
A shape formed by a curved line that is always the same distance from a central point.

△ **Triangle**
A polygon with three sides and three interior angles.

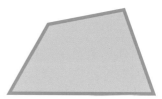

△ **Quadrilateral**
A polygon with four sides and four interior angles.

△ **Square**
A quadrilateral with four equal sides and four equal interior angles of 90° (right angles).

△ **Rectangle**
A quadrilateral with four equal interior angles and opposite sides of equal length.

△ **Parallelogram**
A quadrilateral with two pairs of parallel sides and opposite sides of equal length.

△ **Pentagon**
A polygon with five sides and five interior angles.

△ **Hexagon**
A polygon with six sides and six interior angles.

△ **Heptagon**
A polygon with seven sides and seven interior angles.

△ **Nonagon**
A polygon with nine sides and nine interior angles.

△ **Decagon**
A polygon with ten sides and ten interior angles.

△ **Hendecagon**
A polygon with eleven sides and eleven interior angles.

Sequences

A sequence is a series of numbers written as an ordered list where there is a particular pattern or "rule" that relates each number in the list to the numbers before and after it. Examples of important mathematical sequences are shown below.

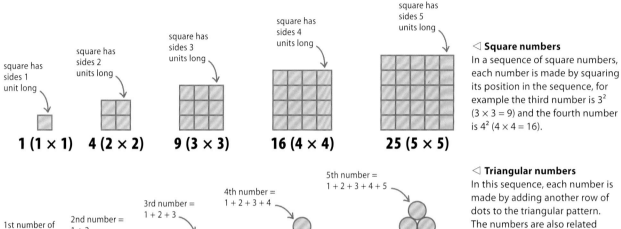

◁ **Square numbers**
In a sequence of square numbers, each number is made by squaring its position in the sequence, for example the third number is 3^2 ($3 \times 3 = 9$) and the fourth number is 4^2 ($4 \times 4 = 16$).

◁ **Triangular numbers**
In this sequence, each number is made by adding another row of dots to the triangular pattern. The numbers are also related mathematically, for example, the fifth number in the sequence is the sum of all numbers up to 5 ($1 + 2 + 3 + 4 + 5$).

Fibonacci sequence

Named after the Italian mathematician Leonardo Fibonacci (c.1175–c.1250), the Fibonacci sequence starts with 1. The second number is also 1. After that, each number in the sequence is the sum of the two numbers before it, for example, the sixth number, 8, is the sum of the fourth and fifth numbers, 3 and 5 ($3 + 5 = 8$).

Pascal's Triangle

Pascal's triangle is a triangular arrangement of numbers. The number at the top of the triangle is 1, and every number down each side is also 1. Each of the other numbers is the sum of the two numbers diagonally above it; for example, in the third row, the 2 is made by adding the two 1s in the row above.

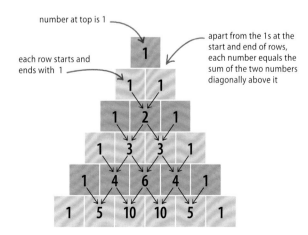

FORMULAS

Formulas are mathematical "recipes" that relate various quantities or terms, so that if the value of one is unknown, it can be worked out if the values of the other terms in the formula are known.

Interest

There are two types of interest – simple and compound. In simple interest, the interest is paid only on the capital. In compound interest, the interest itself earns interest.

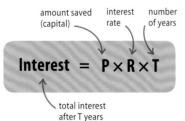

◁ **Simple interest formula**
To find the simple interest made after a given number of years, substitute real values into this formula.

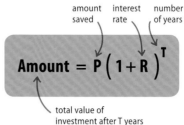

◁ **Compound interest formula**
To find the total value of an investment (capital + interest) after a given number of years, substitute values into this formula.

Formulas in algebra

Algebra is the branch of mathematics that uses symbols to represent numbers and the relationship between them. Useful formulas are the standard formula of a quadratic equation and the formula for solving it.

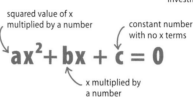

△ **Quadratic equation**
Quadratic equations take the form shown above. They can be solved by using the quadratic formula.

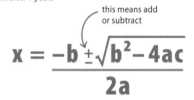

△ **The quadratic formula**
This formula can be used to solve any quadratic equation. There are always two solutions.

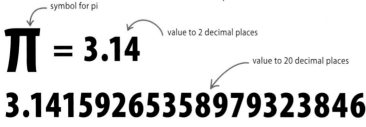

◁ **The value of pi**
Pi occurs in many formulas, such as the formula used for working out the area of a circle. The numbers after the decimal point in pi go on for ever and do not follow any pattern.

Formulas in trigonometry

Three of the most useful formulas in trigonometry are those to find out the unknown angles of a right triangle when two of its sides are known.

$$\sin A = \frac{\text{opposite}}{\text{hypotenuse}}$$

△ **The sine formula**
This formula is used to find the size of angle A when the side opposite the angle and the hypotenuse are known.

$$\cos A = \frac{\text{adjacent}}{\text{hypotenuse}}$$

△ **The cosine formula**
This formula is used to find the size of angle A when the side adjacent to the angle and the hypotenuse are known.

$$\tan A = \frac{\text{opposite}}{\text{adjacent}}$$

△ **The tangent formula**
This formula is used to find the size of angle A when the sides opposite and adjacent to the angle are known.

Area

The area of a shape is the amount of space inside it. Formulas for working out the areas of common shapes are given below.

area = πr^2

△ **Circle**
The area of a circle equals pi (π = 3.14) multiplied by the square of its radius.

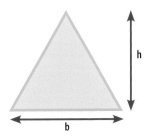

area = $\frac{1}{2}bh$

△ **Triangle**
The area of a triangle equals half multiplied by its base multiplied by its vertical height.

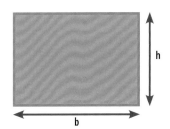

area = bh

△ **Rectangle**
The area of a rectangle equals its base multiplied by its height.

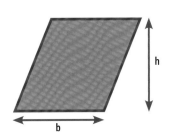

area = bh

△ **Parallelogram**
The area of a parallelogram equals its base multiplied by its vertical height.

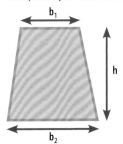

area = $\frac{1}{2}h(b_1+b_2)$

△ **Trapezoid**
The area of a trapezoid equals the sum of the two parallel sides, multiplied by the vertical height, then multiplied by $1/2$.

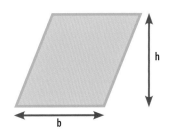

area = bh

△ **Rhombus**
The area of a rhombus equals its base multiplied by its vertical height.

Pythagorean Theorem

This theorem relates the lengths of all the sides of a right triangle, so that if any two sides are known, the length of the third side can be worked out.

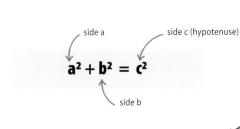

$a^2 + b^2 = c^2$

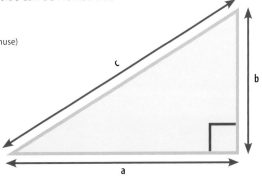

◁ **The theorem**
In a right triangle the square of the hypotenuse (the largest side, c) is the sum of the squares of the other two sides (a and b).

Surface and volume area

The illustrations below show three-dimensional shapes and the formulas for calculating their surface areas and their volumes. In the formulas, two letters together means that they are multiplied together, for example "2r" means "2" multiplied by "r". Pi (π) is 3.14 (to 2 decimal places).

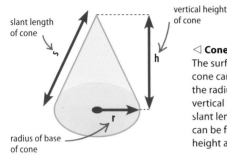

◁ **Cone**
The surface area of a cone can be found from the radius of its base, its vertical height, and its slant length. The volume can be found from the height and radius.

surface area = πrs + πr²
volume = $\frac{1}{3}$πr²h

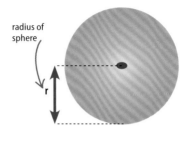

◁ **Sphere**
The surface area and volume of a sphere can be found when only its radius is known, because pi is a constant number (equal to 3.14, to 2 decimal places).

surface area = 4πr²
volume = $\frac{4}{3}$πr³

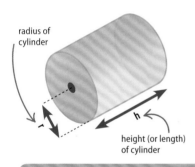

◁ **Cylinder**
The surface area and volume of a cylinder can be found from its radius and height (or length).

surface area = 2πr² + 2πrh
volume = πr²h

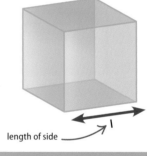

◁ **Cube**
The surface area and volume of a cube can be found when only the length of its sides is known.

surface area = 6l²
volume = l³

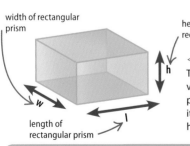

◁ **Rectangular prism**
The surface area and volume of a rectangular prism can be found from its length, width, and height.

surface area = 2(lh+lw+hw)
volume = lwh

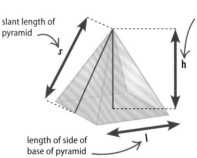

◁ **Square pyramid**
The surface area of a square pyramid can be found from the slant length and the side of its base. Its volume can be found from its height and the side of its base.

surface area = 2ls+l²
volume = $\frac{1}{3}$l²h

Parts of a circle

Various properties of a circle can be measured using certain characteristics, such as the radius, circumference, or length of an arc, with the formulas given below. Pi (π) is the ratio of the circumference to the diameter of a circle; pi is equal to 3.14 (to 2 decimal places).

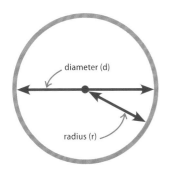

◁ **Diameter and radius**
The diameter of a circle is a straight line running right across the circle and through its center. It is twice the length of the radius (the line from the center to the circumference).

$$\text{diameter} = 2r$$

◁ **Diameter and circumference**
The diameter of a circle can be found when only its circumference (the distance around the edge) is known.

$$\text{diameter} = \frac{c}{\pi}$$

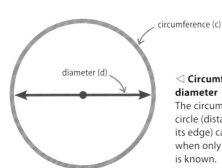

◁ **Circumference and diameter**
The circumference of a circle (distance around its edge) can be found when only its diameter is known.

$$\text{circumference} = \pi d$$

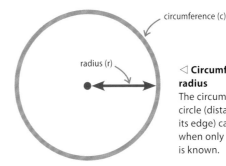

◁ **Circumference and radius**
The circumference of a circle (distance around its edge) can be found when only its radius is known.

$$\text{circumference} = 2\pi r$$

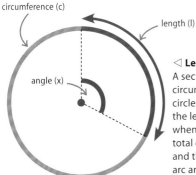

◁ **Length of an arc**
A section of the circumference of a circle is known as an arc, the length can be found when the circle's total circumference and the angle of the arc are known.

$$\text{length of an arc} = \frac{x}{360} \times c$$

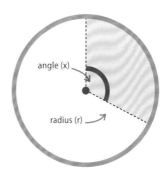

◁ **Area of a sector**
The area of a sector (or "slice") of a circle can be found when the circle's area and the angle of the sector are known.

$$\text{area of a sector} = \frac{x}{360} \times \pi r^2$$

Glossary

Acute
An acute angle is an angle that is smaller than 90°.

Addition
Working out the sum of a group of numbers. Addition is represented by the + symbol, e.g. 2 + 3 = 5. The order the numbers are added in does not affect the answer: 2 + 3 = 3 + 2.

Adjacent
A term meaning "next to". In two-dimensional shapes two sides are adjacent if they are next to each other and meet at the same point (vertex). Two angles are adjacent if they share a vertex and a side.

Algebra
The use of letters or symbols in place of unknown numbers to generalize the relationship between them.

Alternate angle
Alternate angles are formed when two parallel lines are crossed by another straight line. They are the angles on the opposite sides of each of the lines. Alternate angles are equal.

Angle
The amount of turn between two lines that meet at a common point (the vertex). Angles are measured in degrees, for example, 45°.

Apex
The tip of something e.g. the vertex of a cone.

Arc
A curve that is part of the circumference of a circle.

Area
The amount of space within a two-dimensional outline. Area is measured in units squared, e.g. cm².

Arithmetic
Calculations involving addition, subtraction, multiplication, division, or combinations of these.

Average
The typical value of a group of numbers. There are three types of average: median, mode, and mean.

Axis (plural: axes)
Reference lines used in graphs to define coordinates and measure distances. The horizontal axis is the x-axis, the vertical axis is the y-axis.

Balance
Equality on every side, so that there is no unequal weighting, e.g. in an equation, the left-hand side of the equals sign must balance with the right-hand side.

Bar graph
A graph where quantities are represented by rectangles (bars), which are the same width but varying heights. A greater height means a greater amount.

Base
The base of a shape is its bottom edge. The base of a three-dimensional object is its bottom face.

Bearing
A compass reading. The angle measured clockwise from the North direction to the target direction, and given as 3 figures.

Bisect
To divide into two equal halves, e.g. to bisect an angle or a line.

Box-and-whisker diagram
A way to represent statistical data. The box is constructed from lines indicating where the lower quartile, median, and upper quartile measurements fall on a graph, and the whiskers mark the upper and lower limits of the range.

Brackets
1. Brackets indicate the order in which calculations must be done—calculations in brackets must be done first e.g. 2 x (4 +1) = 10.
2. Brackets mark a pair of numbers that are coordinates, e.g. (1, 1).
3. When a number appears before a bracketed calculation it means that the result of that calculation must be multiplied by that number.

Break even
In order to break even a business must earn as much money as its spends. At this point revenue and costs are equal.

Calculator
An electronic tool used to solve arithmetic.

Chart
An easy-to-read visual representation of data, such as a graph, table, or map.

Chord
A line that connects two different points on a curve, often on the circumference of a circle.

Circle
A round shape with only one edge, which is a constant distance from the centre point.

Circle graph
A circular graph in which segments represent different quantities.

Circumference
The edge of a circle.

Clockwise
A direction the same as that of a clock's hand.

Coefficient
The number in front of a letter in algebra. In the equation $x^2 + 5x + 6 = 0$ the coefficient of 5x is 5.

Common factor
A common factor of two or more numbers divides exactly into each of those numbers, e.g. 3 is a common factor of 6 and 18.

Compass
1. A magnetic instrument that shows the position of North and allows bearings to be found.
2. A tool that holds a pencil in a fixed position, allowing circles and arcs to be drawn.

Composite number
A number with more than two factors. A number is composite if it is not a prime number e.g. 4 is a composite factor as it has 1, 2, and 4 as factors.

Concave
Something curving inwards. A polygon is concave if one of its interior angles is greater than 180°.

Cone
A three-dimensional object with a circular base and a single point at its top.

Congruent/congruence
Two shapes are congruent if they are both the same shape and size.

Constant
A quantity that does not change and so has a fixed value, e.g. in the equation y = x + 2, the number 2 is a constant.

Construction
The drawing of shapes in geometry accurately, often with the aid of a compass and ruler.

Conversion
The change from one set of units to another e.g. the conversion from miles into kilometers.

Convex
Something curving outwards. A polygon is convex if all its interior angles are less than 180°.

Coordinate
Coordinates show the position of points on a graph or map, and are written in the form (x,y), where x is the horizontal position and y is the vertical position.

Correlate/correlation
There is a correlation between two things if a change in one causes a change in the other.

Corresponding angles
Corresponding angles are formed when two parallel lines are crossed by another straight side. They are the angles in the same position i.e. on the same side of each of the lines. Corresponding angles are equal.

Cosine
In trigonometry, cosine is the ratio of the side adjacent to a given angle with the hypotenuse of a right triangle.

Counter clockwise
Movement in the opposite direction to that of a clock's hand.

Cross section
A two-dimensional slice of a three-dimensional object.

Cube
A three-dimensional object made up of 6 identical square faces, 8 vertices, and 12 edges.

Cube root
A number's cube root is the number which, multiplied by itself three times, equals the given number. A cube root is indicated by this sign $\sqrt[3]{}$.

Cubed number
Cubing a number means multiplying it by itself three times e.g. 8 is a cubed number because 2 x 2 x 2 = 8, or 2^3.

Currency
A system of money within a country e.g. the currency in the US is $.

Curve
A line that bends smoothly. A quadratic equation represented on a graph is also a curve.

Cyclic quadrilateral
A shape with 4 vertices and 4 edges, and where every vertex is on the circumference of a circle.

Cylinder
A three-dimensional object with two parallel, congruent circles at opposite ends.

Data
A set of information, e.g. a collection of numbers or measurements.

Debit
An amount of money spent and removed from an account.

Debt
An amount of money that has been borrowed, and is therefore owed.

Decimal
1. A number system based on 10 (using the digits 0, 1, 2, 3, 4, 5, 6, 7, 8, and 9).
2. A number containing a decimal place.

Decimal point
The dot between the whole part of a number and the fractional part e.g. 2.5.

Decimal place
The position of the digit after the decimal point.

Degrees
The unit of measurement of an angle, represented by the symbol °.

Denominator
The number on the bottom of a fraction e.g. 3 is the denominator of $^2/_3$.

Density
The amount of mass per unit of volume, i.e. density = mass ÷ volume.

Diagonal
A line that joins two vertices of a shape or object that are not adjacent to each other.

Diameter
A straight line touching two points on the edge of a circle and passing through the center.

Difference
The amount by which one quantity is bigger or smaller than another quantity.

Digit
A single number, e.g. 34 is made up of the digits 3 and 4.

Dimension
The directions in which measurements can be made e.g. a solid object has three dimensions: its length, height, and width.

Direct proportion
Two numbers are in direct proportion if they increase or decrease proportionately, e.g. doubling one of them means the other also doubles.

Distribution
In probability and statistics, the distribution gives the range of values unidentified random variables can take and their probabilities.

Division/divide
The splitting of a number into equal parts. Division is shown by the symbol ÷ e.g. 12 ÷ 3 = 4 or by / as used in fractions, e.g. $^2/_3$.

Double negative
Two negative signs together create a double negative, which then becomes equal to a positive e.g. 5 − (−2) = 5 + 2.

Enlargement
The process of making something bigger, such as a transformation, where everything is multiplied by the same amount.

Equal
Things of the same value are equal, shown by the equals sign, =.

Equation
A mathematical statement that things are equal.

Equiangular
A shape is equiangular if all its angles are equal.

Equidistant
A point is equidistant to two or more points if it is the same distance from them.

Equilateral triangle
A triangle that has three 60° angles and sides of equal length.

Equiprobable events
Two events are equiprobable if they are equally likely to happen.

Equivalent fractions
Fractions that are equal but have different numerators and denominators e.g. $^1/_2$, $^2/_4$, and $^5/_{10}$ are equivalent fractions.

Estimation
An approximated amount or an approximation the answer to a calculation, often made by rounding up or down.

Even number
A number that is divisible by 2 e.g. -18, -6, 0, 2.

254 GLOSSARY

Exchange rate
The exchange rate describes what an amount of one currency is valued at in another currency.

Exponent
See power

Expression
A combination of numbers, symbols, and unknown variables that does not contain an equal sign.

Exterior angle
1. An angle formed on the outside of a polygon, when one side is extended outwards.
2. The angles formed in the region outside two lines intersected by another line.

Faces
The flat surfaces of a three-dimensional object, bordered by edges.

Factor
A number that divides exactly into another, larger number, e.g. 2 and 5 are both factors of 10.

Factorisation/factorize
1. Rewriting a number as the multiplication of its factors, e.g. 12 = 2 x 2 x 3.
2. Rewriting an expression as the multiplication of smaller expressions e.g. $x^2 + 5x + 6 = (x + 2)(x + 3)$.

Fibonacci sequence
A sequence formed by adding the previous two numbers in the sequence together, which begins with 1, 1. The first ten numbers in the sequence are 1, 1, 2, 3, 5, 8, 13, 21, 34, and 55.

Formula
A rule that describes the relationship between variables, and is usually written as symbols, e.g. the formula for calculating the area of a circle is $A = 2\pi r$, in which A represents the area and r is the radius.

Fraction
A part of an amount, represented by one number (the numerator) on top of another number (the denominator) e.g. $^2/_3$.

Frequency
1. The number of times something occurs during a fixed period of time.
2. In statistics, the number of individuals in a class.

Geometry
The mathematics of shapes. Looks at the relationships between points, lines, and angles.

Gradient
The steepness of a line.

Graph
A diagram used to represent information, including the relationship between two sets of variables.

Greater than
An amount larger than another quantity. It is represented by the symbol >.

Greater than or equal to
An amount either larger or the same as another quantity. It is represented by the symbol ≥.

Greatest common factor
The largest number that divides exactly into a set of other numbers. It is often written as GCF, e.g. the GCF of 12 and 18 is 6.

Height
The upwards length, measuring between the lowest and highest points.

Hexagon
A two-dimensional shape with 6 sides.

Histogram
A bar graph that represents frequency distribution.

Horizontal
Parallel to the horizon. A horizontal line goes between left and right.

Hypotenuse
The side opposite the right-angle in a right triangle. It is the longest side of a right triangle.

Impossibility
Something that could never happen. The probability of an impossibility is written as 0.

Improper fraction
Fraction in which the numerator is greater than the denominator.

Included angle
An angle formed between two sides with a common vertex.

Income
An amount of money earned.

Independent events
Occurrences that have no influence on each other.

Indices (singular: index)
See power.

Indirect proportion
Two variables x and y are in indirect proportion if e.g. when one variable doubles, the other halves, or vice versa.

Inequalities
Inequalities show that two statements are not equal.

Infinite
Without a limit or end. Infinity is represented by the symbol ∞.

Integers
Whole numbers that can be positive, negative, or zero, e.g. -3, -1, 0, 2, 6.

Interest
An amount of money charged when money is borrowed, or the amount earned when it is invested. It is usually written as a percentage.

Interior angle
1. An included angle in a polygon.
2. An angle formed when two lines are intersected by another line.

Intercept
The point on a graph at which a line crosses an axis.

Interquartile range
A measure of the spread of a set of data. It is the difference between the lower and upper quartiles.

Intersection/intersect
A point where two or more lines or figures meet.

Inverse
The opposite of something, e.g. division is the inverse of multiplication and vice versa.

Investment/invest
An amount of money spent in an attempt to make a profit.

Isosceles triangle
A triangle with two equal sides and two equal angles.

Least common multiple
The smallest number that can be divided exactly into a set of values. It is often written LCM, e.g. the LCM of 4 and 6 is 12.

Length
The measurement of the distance between two points e.g. how long a line segment is between its two ends.

Less than
An amount smaller than another quantity. It is represented by the symbol <.

Less than or equal to
An amount smaller or the same as another quantity. It is represented by the symbol ≤.

Like terms
An expression in algebra that contains the same symbols, such as x or y, (the numbers in front of

GLOSSARY 255

the x or y may change). Like terms can be combined.

Line
A one-dimensional element that only has length (i.e. no width or height).

Line graph
A graph that uses points connected by lines to represent a set of data.

Line of best fit
A line on a scatter diagram that shows the correlation or trend between variables.

Line of symmetry
A line that acts like a mirror, splitting a figure into two mirror-image parts.

Loan
An amount of money borrowed that has to be paid back (usually over a period of time).

Locus (plural: loci)
The path of a point, following certain conditions or rules.

Loss
Spending more money than has been earned creates a loss.

Major
The larger of the two or more objects referred to. It can be applied to arcs, segments, sectors, or ellipses.

Mean
The middle value of a set of data, found by adding up all the values, then dividing by the total number of values.

Measurement
A quantity, length, or size, found by measuring something.

Median
The number that lies in the middle of a set of data, after the data has been put into increasing order. The median is a type of average.

Mental arithmetic
Basic calculations done without writing anything down.

Minor
The smaller of the two or more objects it referred to. It can be applied to arcs, segments, sectors, or ellipses.

Minus
The sign for subtraction, represented as −.

Mixed operations
A combination of different actions used in a calculation, such as addition, subtraction, multiplication, and division.

Mode
The number that appears most often in a set of data. The mode is a type of average.

Mortgage
An agreement to borrow money to pay for a house. It is paid back with interest over a long period of time.

Multiply/multiplication
The process of adding a value to itself a set number of times. The symbol for multiplication is ×.

Mutually exclusive events
Two mutally exclusive events are events that cannot both be true at the same time.

Negative
Less than zero. Negative is the opposite of positive.

Net
A flat shape that can be folded to make a three-dimensional object.

Not equal to
Not of the same value. Not equal to is represented by the symbol ≠, e.g. 1 ≠ 2.

Numerator
The number at the top of a fraction, e.g. 2 is the numerator of $^2/_3$.

Obtuse angle
An angle measuring between 90° and 180°.

Octagon
A two-dimensional shape with 8 sides and 8 angles.

Odd number
A whole number that cannot be divided by 2, e.g. -7, 1, and 65.

Operation
An action done to a number, e.g. adding, subtracting, dividing, and multiplying.

Operator
A symbol that represents an operation, e.g. +, −, ×, and ÷.

Opposite
Angles or sides are opposite if they face each other.

Parallel
Two lines are parallel if they are always the same distance apart.

Parallelogram
A quadrilateral which has opposite sides that are equal and parallel to each other.

Pascal's triangle
A number pattern formed in a triangle. Each number is the sum of the two numbers directly above it. The number at the top is 1.

Pentagon
A two-dimensional shape that has 5 sides and 5 angles.

Percentage/per cent
A number of parts out of a hundred. Percentage is represented by the symbol %.

Perimeter
The boundary all the way around a shape. The perimeter also refers to the length of this boundary.

Perpendicular bisector
A line that cuts another line in half at right-angles to it.

Pi
A number that is approximately 3.142 and is represented by the Greek letter pi, π.

Plane
A completely flat surface that can be horizontal, vertical, or sloping.

Plus
The sign for addition, represented as +.

Point of contact
The place where two or more lines intersect or touch.

Polygon
A two-dimensional shape with 3 or more straight sides.

Polyhedron
A three-dimensional object with faces that are flat polygons.

Positive
More than zero. Positive is the opposite of negative.

Power
The number that indicates how many times a number is multiplied by itself. Powers are shown by a small number at the top-right hand corner of another number, e.g. 4 is the power in $2^4 = 2 × 2 × 2 × 2$.

Prime number
A number which has exactly two factors: 1 and itself. The first 10 prime numbers are 2, 3, 5, 7, 11, 13, 17, 19, 23, and 29.

Prism
A three-dimensional object with ends that are identical polygons.

Probability
The likelihood that something will happen. This likelihood is given a value between 0 and 1. An impossible event has probability 0 and a certain event has probability 1.

Glossary

Product
A number calculated when two or more numbers are multiplied together.

Profit
The amount of money left once costs have been paid.

Proper fraction
A fraction in which the numerator is less than the denominator, e.g. $^2/_5$ is a proper fraction.

Proportion/proportionality
Proportionality is when two or more quantities are related by a constant ratio, e.g. a recipe may contain three parts of one ingredient to two parts of another.

Protractor
A tool used to measure angles.

Pyramid
A three-dimensional object with a polygon as its base and triangular sides that meet in a point at the top.

Pythagorean theorem
A rule that states that the squared length of the hypotenuse of a right-angled triangle will equal the sum of the squares of the other two sides as represented by the equation $a^2 + b^2 = c^2$.

Quadrant
A quarter of a circle, or a quarter of a graph divided by the x- and y-axis.

Quadratic equation
Equations that include a squared variable, e.g. $x^2 + 3x + 2 = 0$.

Quadratic formula
A formula that allows any quadratic equation to be solved, by substituting values into it.

Quadrilateral
A two-dimensional shape that has 4 sides and 4 angles.

Quartiles
In statistics, quartiles are points that split an ordered set of data into 4 equal parts. The number that is a quarter of the way through is the lower quartile, halfway is the median, and three-quarters of the way through is the upper quartile.

Quotient
The whole number of times a number can be divided into another e.g. if 11 ÷ 2 then the quotient is 5 (and the remainder is 1).

Radius (plural: radii)
The distance from the center of a circle to any point on its circumference.

Random
Something that has no special pattern in it, but has happened by chance.

Range
The span between the smallest and largest values in a set of data.

Ratio
A comparison of two numbers, written either side of the symbol : e.g. 2:3.

Rectangle
A quadrilateral with 2 pairs of opposite, parallel sides that are equal in length, and 4 right angles.

Rectangular prisms
A three-dimensional object made of 6 faces (2 squares at opposite ends with 4 rectangles between), 8 vertices, and 12 edges.

Recurring
Something that repeats over and over again, e.g. $^1/_9 = 0.11111...$ is a recurring decimal and is shown as $0.\dot{1}$.

Reflection
A type of transformation that produces a mirror-image of the original object.

Reflex angle
An angle between 180° and 360°.

Regular polygon
A two-dimensional shape with sides that are all the same length and angles that are all the same size.

Remainder
The number left over when a dividing a number into whole parts e.g. 11 ÷ 2 = 5 with remainder 1.

Revolution
A complete turn of 360°.

Rhombus
A quadrilateral with 2 pairs of parallel sides and all 4 sides of the same length.

Right angle
An angle measuring exactly 90°.

Root
The number which, when multiplied by itself a number of times, results in the given value, e.g. 2 is the fourth root of 16 as 2 x 2 x 2 x 2 = 16.

Rotation
A type of transformation in which an object is turned around a point.

Rounding
The process of approximating a number by writing it to the nearest whole number or to a given number of decimal places.

Salary
An amount of money paid regularly for the work that someone has done.

Sample
A part of a whole group from which data is collected to give information about the whole group.

Savings
An amount of money kept aside or invested and not spent.

Scale/scale drawing
Scale is the amount by which an object is made larger or smaller. It is represented as a ratio. A scale drawing is a drawing that is in direct proportion to the object it represents.

Scalene triangle
A triangle where every side is a different length and every angle is a different size.

Scatter plot
A graph in which plotted points or dots are used to show the correlation or relationship between two sets of data.

Sector
Part of a circle, with edges that are two radii and an arc.

Segment
Part of a circle, whose edges are a chord and an arc.

Semi-circle
Half of a full circle, whose edges are the diameter and an arc.

Sequence
A list of numbers ordered according to a rule.

Similar
Shapes are similar if they have the same shape but not the same size.

Simplification
In algebra, writing something in its most basic or simple form, e.g. by cancelling terms.

Simultaneous equation
Two or more equations that must be solved at the same time.

Sine
In trigonometry, sine is the ratio of the side opposite to a given angle with the hypotenuse of a right triangle.

Solid
A three-dimensional shape that has length, width, and height.

Sphere
A three-dimensional, ball-shaped, perfectly round object, where each point on its surface is the same distance from its center.

Spread
The spread of a set of data is how the data is distributed over a range.

Square
A quadrilateral in which all the angles are the same (90°) and every side is the same length.

Square root
A number that, multiplied by itself, produces a given number, shown as $\sqrt{\ }$, e.g. $\sqrt{4} = 2$.

Squared number
The result of multiplying a number by itself, e.g. $4^2 = 4 \times 4 = 16$.

Standard deviation
A measure of spread that shows the amount of deviation from the mean. If the standard deviation is low the data is close to the mean, if it is high, it is widely spread.

Standard form
A number (usually very large or very small) written as a positive or negative number between 1 and 9 multiplied by a power of 10, e.g. 0.02 is 2×10^{-2}.

Statistics
The collection, presentation, and interpretation of data.

Stem-and-leaf diagram
A graph showing the shape of ordered data. Numbers are split in two digits and separated by a line. The first digits form the stem (written once) and the second digits form leaves (written many times in rows).

Substitution
Putting something in place of something else, e.g. using a constant number in place of a variable.

Subtraction/subtract
Taking a number away from another number. It is represented by the symbol –.

Sum
The total, or the number calculated when two numbers are added together.

Supplementary angle
Two angles that add up to 180°.

Symmetry/symmetrical
A shape or object is symmetrical if it looks the same after a reflection or a rotation.

Table
Information displayed in rows and columns.

Take-home pay
Take-home pay is the amount of earnings left after tax has been paid.

Tangent
1. A straight line that touches a curve at one point.
2. In trigonometry, tangent is the ratio of the side opposite to a given angle with the side adjacent to the given angle, in a right-angled triangle.

Tax
Money that is paid to the government, either as part of what a person buys, or as a part of their income.

Terms
Individual numbers in a sequence or series, or individual parts of an expression, e.g. in $7a^2 + 4xy - 5$ the terms are $7a^2$, 4xy, and 5.

Tessellation
A pattern of shapes covering a surface without leaving any gaps.

Theoretical probability
The likelihood of an outcome based on mathematical ideas rather than experiments.

Three-dimensional
Objects that have length, width, and height. Three-dimensions is often written as 3D.

Transformation
A change of position, size, or orientation. Reflections, rotations, enlargements, and translations are all transformations.

Translation
Movement of an object without it being rotated.

Trapezoid
A quadrilateral with a pair of parallel sides that can be of different lengths.

Triangle
A two-dimensional shape with 3 sides and 3 angles.

Trigonometry
The study of triangles and the ratios of their sides and angles.

Two-dimensional
A flat figure that has length and width. Two-dimensions is often written as 2D.

Unit
1. The standard amount in measuring, e.g. cm, kg, and seconds.
2. Another name for one.

Unknown angle
An angle which is not specified, and for which the number of degrees need to be determined.

Variable
A quantity that can vary or change and is usually indicated by a letter.

Vector
A quantity that has both size and direction, e.g. velocity and force are vectors.

Velocity
The speed and direction in which something is moving, measured in metres per second m/s.

Vertex (plural: vertices)
The corner or point at which surfaces or lines meet.

Vertical
At right-angles to the horizon. A vertical line goes between up and down directions.

Volume
The amount of space within a three-dimensional object. Volume is measured in units cubed, e.g. cm^3.

Wage
The amount of money paid to a person in exchange for work.

Whole number
Counting numbers that do not have any fractional parts and are greater than or equal to 0, e.g. 1, 7, 46, 108.

Whole turn
A rotation of 360°, so that an object faces the same direction it started from.

Width
The sideways length, measuring between opposite sides. Width is the same as breadth.

X-axis
The horizontal axis of a graph, which determines the x-coordinate.

X-intercept
The value at which a line crosses the x-axis on a graph.

Y-axis
The vertical axis of a graph, which determines the y-coordinate.

Index

A

abacus 14
accuracy 71
acute-angled triangles, area 123
acute angles 85, 245
addition 16
    algebra 169
    binary numbers 47
    calculators 72
    expressions 172
    fractions 53
    inequalities 198
    multiplication 18
    negative numbers 34
    positive numbers 34
    vectors 96
algebra 166–99, 248
allowance, personal finance 74
alternate angles 87
AM (ante meridiem) 32
analoge time 32
angle of rotation 100, 101
angles 84–85, 245
    45° 113
    60° 113
    90° 113
    acute 85
    alternate 87
    arcs 150
    bearings 108
    bisecting 112, 113
    in a circle 144–45
    complementary 85
    congruent triangles 120, 121
    constructions 110
    corresponding 87
    cyclic quadrilaterals 147
    drawing triangles 118, 119
    geometry 80
    obtuse 85
    pairs of 245
    parallel lines 87
    pie charts 210
    polygons 134, 135, 136
    protractor 82, 83
    quadrilaterals 130, 131
    reflex 85
    rhombus 133
    right-angled 85, 113
    sectors 151
    size of 245
    supplementary 85
    tangents 149
    triangles 116, 117
    trigonometry formulas 161, 162, 163, 164–65
annotation, pie charts 211
answer, calculator 73
approximately equals sign 70
approximation 70
arcs 138, 139, 150
    compasses 82
    length of 251
    sectors 151
area
    circles 138, 139, 142–43, 151, 155, 249
    congruent triangles 120
    conversion tables 243
    cross-sections 154
    formulas 177, 249–50
    measurement 28, 242
    quadrilaterals 132–33
    rectangles 28, 249
    triangles 122–24, 249
arithmetic keys, calculators 72
arrowheads 86
averages 214–15
    frequency tables 216
    moving 218–19
axes
    bar graphs 206
    graphs 92, 184, 212, 213
axis of reflection 102, 103
axis of symmetry 89

B

balancing equations 180
banks, personal finance 74, 75
bar graphs 203, 206–209, 224
base numbers 15
bearings 80, 108–109
bias 205
binary numbers 46–47
bisectors 112, 113
    angles 112, 113
    perpendicular 110, 111, 146, 147
    rotation 101
borrowing, personal finance 74, 75
box-and-whisker diagrams 223
box method of multiplication 21
brackets
    calculators 72, 73
    expanding expressions 174
break-even, finance 74, 76
business finance 76–77

C

calculators 72–73, 83
    cosine (cos) 161, 164
    exponent button 37
    powers 37
    roots 37
    sine (sin) 161, 164
    standard form 43
    tangent (tan) 161, 164
calendars 28
cancel key, calculators 72
cancellation
    equations 180
    expressions 173
    formulas 178
    fractions 51, 64
    ratios 56
capital 75
carrying numbers 24
Celsius temperature scale 185, 242, 243
centimeters 28, 29
center of a circle 138, 139
    angles in a circle 144
    arcs 150
    chords 146, 147
    pie charts 211
    tangents 148, 149
center of enlargement 104, 105
center of rotation 89, 100, 101
centuries 30
chance 230, 231, 234, 236, 237
chances
    dependent events 236, 237
    expectation 232
change
    percentages 63
    proportion 58
charts 203, 205
chords 138, 139, 146–47
    tangents 149
circles 138–39, 246, 251
    angles in a 84, 85, 144–45
    arcs 150, 251
    area of 142–43, 151, 154, 155, 251
    chords 138, 139, 146–47
    circumference 140, 251
    compasses 82
    cyclic quadrilaterals 147
    diameter 140, 141, 251
    formulas 249
    geometry 80
    loci 114
    pie charts 210, 211
    sectors 151
    symmetry 88
    tangents 148, 149
circular prism 152
circumference 138, 139, 140, 251
    angles in a circle 144, 145
    arcs 150
    chords 146
    cyclic quadrilaterals 147
    pie charts 211
    tangents 148, 149
clocks 31–32, 33
codes 27
combined probabilities 234–35
common denominator 52–53
    ratio fractions 57
common factors 174, 175
common multiples 20
comparing ratios 56, 57
compass directions 108
compass points 108
compasses (for drawing circles) 139
    constructing tangents 149
    constructions 110
    drawing a pie chart 211
    drawing triangles 118, 119
    geometry tools 82
complementary angles 85
component bar graphs 209
composite bar graphs 209
composite numbers 15, 26, 27
compound bar graphs 209
compound interest 75
compound measurement units 28
compound shapes 143
computer animation 118
concave polygons 136
cones 153
    surface area 157, 250

INDEX 259

volumes 155, 250
congruent triangles 112, 120–21
   drawing 118
   parallelograms 133
constructing reflections 103
constructing tangents 149
constructions 110–11
conversion tables 243–44
convex polygons 136, 137
coordinates 90–91
   constructing reflections 103
   enlargements 105
   equations 93, 188, 189, 195, 197
   graphs 92, 182
   linear graphs 182
   maps 93
   quadratic equations 195, 197
   rotation 101
   simultaneous equations 188, 189
correlations, scatter diagrams 226, 227
corresponding angles 87
cosine (cos)
   calculators 73
   formula 161, 162, 163, 164, 165
costs 74, 76, 77
credit 74
cross-sections
   solids 152
   volumes 154
cube roots 37, 241
   estimating 39
   surds 40–41
cubed numbers 241
   calculator 73
   powers 36
   units 28
cubes 153, 250
   geometry 81
cubic units 154
cuboids 152, 153
   surface area 157, 250
   symmetry 88, 89
   volume 28, 155, 250
cumulative frequency graphs 213
   quartiles 222
curves, quadratic equation
   graphs 194

cyclic quadrilaterals 146, 147
cylinders 152, 153, 250
   nets 156
   surface area 156, 175
   symmetry 89
   volume 154

D

data 202–205
   averages 214, 215, 218–19
   bar graphs 203, 206, 207, 208, 209
   cumulative frequency graphs 213
   frequency tables 216
   grouped 217
   line graphs 212
   moving averages 218–19
   quartiles 222, 223
   ratios 56
   scatter diagrams 226, 227
   spread 220
   stem-and-leaf diagrams 221
data logging 205
data presentation
   histograms 224, 225
   pie charts 210
data protection 27
data table 208
dates, Roman numerals 33
days 28, 30
decades 30
decagons 135, 246
decimal numbers 15, 44–45, 245
   binary numbers 46–47
   converting 64–65
   division 24, 25
   mental mathematics 67
decimal places
   rounding off 71
   standard form 42
decimal points 44
   calculators 72
   standard form 42
decrease as percentages 63
degrees
   angles 84
   bearings 108
deletion, calculators 72
denominators
   adding fractions 53

common 52–53
   fractions 48, 49, 50, 51, 53, 64, 65
   ratio fractions 57
   subtracting fractions 53
density measurement 28, 29
dependent events 236–37
   tree diagrams 239
diagonals in quadrilaterals 130, 131
diameter 138, 139, 140, 141, 251
   angles in a circle 145
   area of a circle 142, 143
   chords 146
difference, subtraction 17
digital time 32
direct proportion 58
direction
   bearings 108
   vectors 94
distance
   bearings 109
   loci 114
   measurement 28, 29
distribution
   data 220, 239
   quartiles 222, 223
dividend 22, 23, 24, 25
division 22–23
   algebra 169
   calculators 72
   cancellation 51
   decimal numbers 45
   expressions 173
   formulas 178
   fractions 50, 55
   inequalities 198
   long 25
   negative numbers 35
   positive numbers 35
   powers 38
   proportional quantities 59
   quick methods 68
   ratios 57, 59
   short 24
   top-heavy fractions 50
divisor 22, 23, 24, 25
dodecagons 134, 135
double inequalities 199
double negatives 73
drawing constructions 110
drawing triangles 118–19

E

earnings 74
edges of solids 153
eighth fraction 48
elimination, simultaneous equations 186
employees, finance 76
employment, finance 74
encryption 27
endpoints 86
enlargements 104–105
equal vectors 95
equals sign 16, 17
   approximately 70
   calculators 72
   equations 180
   formulas 177
equations
   coordinates 93
   factorizing quadratic 190–91
   graphs 194, 195
   linear graphs 182, 183, 184, 185
   Pythagorean Theorem 128, 129
   quadratic 190–93, 194, 195
   simultaneous 186–89
   solving 180–81
equiangular polygons 134
equilateral polygons 134
equilateral triangles 113, 117
   symmetry 88, 89
equivalent fractions 51
estimating
   calculators 72
   cube roots 39
   quartiles 222
   rounding off 70
   square roots 39
Euclid 26
evaluating expressions 173
even chance 231
expanding expressions 174
expectation 232–33
exponent button, calculators 37, 43, 73
expressions 172–73
   equations 180
   expanding 174–75
   factorizing 174–75
   quadratic 176
   sequences 170

exterior angles
  cyclic quadrilaterals 147
  polygons 137
  triangles 117

F

faces of solids 153, 156
factorizing 27
  expressions 174, 175, 176
  quadratic equations 190–91
  quadratic expressions 176
factors 174, 175
  division 24
  prime 26, 27
Fahrenheit temperature scale 185, 242, 243
feet 28
Fibonacci sequence 15, 171, 247
finance
  business 76–77
  personal 74–75
flat shapes, symmetry 88
formulas 177, 248–49
  algebra 248
  area of quadrilaterals 132
  area of rectangles 173
  area of triangles 122, 123, 124
  factorizing 174
  interest 75
  moving terms 178–79
  Pythagorean Theorem 128, 129, 249
  quadratic equations 191, 192–93
  quartiles 222, 223
  speed 29
  trigonometry 161–65, 248
fortnights 30
fractional numbers 44
fractions 48–55, 245
  adding 53
  common denominators 52
  converting 64–65
  division 55
  mixed 50
  multiplication 54
  probability 230, 233, 234
  ratios 57
  subtracting 53
  top-heavy 50
frequency
  bar graphs 206, 207, 208
  cumulative 213
frequency density 224, 225
frequency graph 222
frequency polygons 209

frequency tables 216, 217
  bar graphs 206, 207
  data presentation 205
  histograms 225
  pie charts 210
function keys, scientific calculator 73
functions, calculators 72, 73

G

geometry 78–157
geometry tools 82–83
government, personal finance 74
gradients, linear graphs 182, 183
grams 28, 29
graphs
  coordinates 90, 92
  cumulative frequency 213
  data 205
  and geometry 81
  line 212–13
  linear 182–85
  moving averages 218–19
  proportion 58
  quadratic equations 194–97
  quartiles 222
  scatter diagrams 226, 227
  simultaneous equations 186, 188–89
  statistics 203
greater than symbol 198
grouped data 217

H

half fraction 49
hendecagons 135, 246
heptagons 135, 136, 246
hexagons 134, 135, 137, 246
  tessellations 99
histograms 203, 224–25
horizontal bar chart 208
horizontal coordinates 90, 91
hours 28, 29, 30
  kilometers per 29
hundreds
  addition 16
  decimal numbers 44
  multiplication 21
  subtraction 17
hypotenuse 117
  congruent triangles 121
  Pythagoream Theorem 128, 129
  tangents 148
  trigonometry formulas 161, 162, 163, 164, 165

I

icosagons 135
imperial measurements 28
  conversion tables 242–43
inches 28
included angle, congruent triangles 121
income 74
income tax 74
increase, percentages 63
independent events 236
inequalities 198–99
infinite symmetry 88
inputs, finance 76
interest 75
  formulas 179, 248
  personal finance 74
interior angles
  cyclic quadrilaterals 147
  polygons 136, 137
  triangles 117
International Atomic Time 30
interquartile range 223
intersecting chords 146
intersecting lines 86
inverse cosine 164
inverse multiplication 22
inverse proportion 58
inverse sine 164
inverse tangent 164
investment 74
  interest 75
irregular polygons 134, 135, 136, 137
irregular quadrilaterals 130
isosceles triangles 117, 121
  rhombus 133
  symmetry 88

K

kaleidoscopes 102
Kelvin temperature scale 242, 243
keys
  calculators 72
  pie charts 211
kilograms 28
kilometers 28
kilometers per hour 29
kite quadrilaterals 130, 131

L

labels on pie charts 211
latitude 93
leaf diagrams 221

leap years 30
length measurement 28, 242
  conversion tables 243
  speed 29
less than symbol 198
letters, algebra 168
like terms in expressions 172
line of best fit 227
line graphs 203, 212–13
line segments 86
  constructions 111
  vectors 94
line of symmetry 103
linear equations 182, 183, 184, 185
linear graphs 182–85
lines 86
  angles 84, 85
  constructions 110, 111
  geometry 80
  loci 114
  parallel 80
  rulers 82, 83
  straight 85, 86–87
  of symmetry 88
liquid volume, measurement 242
loans 74
location 114
locus (loci) 114–15
long division 25
long multiplication 21
  decimal numbers 44
longitude 93
loss
  business finance 76
  personal finance 74
lowest common denominator 52
lowest common multiple 20

M

magnitude, vectors 94, 95
major arcs 150
major sectors 151
map coordinates 90, 91, 93
mass measurement 28, 242
  conversion tables 243
  density 29
mean
  averages 214, 215, 218, 219
  frequency tables 216
  grouped data 217
  moving averages 218, 219
  weighted 217
measurement
  drawing triangles 118
  scale drawing 106, 107

INDEX

units of 28–29, 242
measuring spread 220–21
measuring time 30–32
median
    averages 214, 215
    quartiles 222, 223
memory, calculators 72
mental math 66–69
meters 28
metric measurement 28, 242–43
midnight 32
miles 28
millennium 30
milliseconds 28
minor arcs 150
minor sectors 151
minus sign 34
    calculator 73
minutes 28, 29, 30
mirror image
    reflections 102
    symmetry 88
mixed fractions 49, 50, 54
    division 55
    multiplication 54
modal class 217
mode 214
money 76
    business finance 77
    interest 75
    personal finance 74
months 28, 30
mortgage 74
multiple bar graphs 209
multiple choice questions 204
multiples 20
    division 24
multiplication 18–21
    algebra 169
    calculators 72
    decimal numbers 44
    expanding expressions 174
    expressions 173
    formulas 178
    fractions 50, 54
    indirect proportion 58
    inequalities 198
    long 21
    mental mathematics 66
    mixed fractions 50
    negative numbers 35
    positive numbers 35
    powers 36, 38
    proportional quantities 59
    reverse cancellation 51
    short 21
    tables 67, 241
    vectors 96

N

nature, geometry in 80
negative correlations 227
negative gradients 183
negative numbers 34–35
    addition 34
    calculators 73
    dividing 35
    inequalities 198
    multiplying 35
    quadratic graphs 195
    subtraction 34
negative scale factor 104
negative terms in formulas 178
negative translation 99
negative values on graphs 92
negative vectors 95
nets 152, 156, 157
non-parallel lines 86
non-polyhedrons 153
nonagons 135, 137, 246
nought 34
"nth" value 170
number line
    addition 16
    negative numbers 34–35
    positive numbers 34–35
    subtraction 17
numbers 14–15
    binary 46–47
    calculators 72
    composite 26
    decimal 15, 44–45, 245
    negative 34–35
    positive 34–35
    prime 26–27, 241
    Roman 33
    surds 40–41
    symbols 15
numerator 48, 49, 50, 51, 64, 65
    adding fractions 53
    comparing fractions 52
    ratio fractions 57
    subtracting fractions 53
numerical equivalents 245

O

obtuse-angled triangle 123
obtuse angles 85, 245
obtuse triangles 117
octagons 135
operations
    calculators 73
    expressions 172
order of rotational symmetry 89
origin 92
ounces 28
outputs, business finance 76, 77
overdraft 74

P

parallel lines 80, 86, 87
    angles 87
parallel sides of a parallelogram 133
parallelograms 86, 130, 131, 246
    area 133, 249
Pascal's triangle 247
patterns
    sequences 170
    tessellations 99
pension plan 74
pentadecagon 135
pentagonal prism 152
pentagons 135, 136, 137, 246
    symmetry 88
percentages 60–63, 245
    converting 64–65
    interest 75
    mental mathematics 69
perfect numbers 14
perimeters
    circles 139
    triangles 116
perpendicular bisectors 110, 111
    chords 146, 147
    rotation 101
perpendicular lines, constructions 110, 111
perpendicular (vertical) height
    area of quadrilaterals 132, 133
    area of triangles 122, 123
    volumes 155
personal finance 74–75
personal identification number (PIN) 74
pi (SYMBOL) 140, 141
    surface area of a cylinder 175
    surface area of a sphere 157
    volume of sphere 155
pictograms 203
pie charts 203, 210–11
    business finance 77
planes 86
    symmetry 88
    tessellations 99
plotting
    bearings 108, 109
    enlargements 105
    graphs 92
    line graphs 212
    linear graphs 184
    loci 115
    simultaneous equations 188, 189
plus sign 34
PM (post meridiem) 32
points
    angles 84, 85
    constructions 110, 111
    lines 86
    loci 114
    polygons 134
polygons 134–37
    enlargements 104, 105
    frequency 209
    irregular 134, 135
    quadrilaterals 130
    regular 134, 135
    triangles 116
polyhedrons 152, 153
positive correlation 226, 227
positive gradients 183
positive numbers 34–35
    addition 34
    dividing 35
    inequalities 198
    multiplying 35
    quadratic graphs 195
    subtraction 34
positive scale factor 104
positive terms in formulas 178
positive translation 99
positive values on graphs 92
positive vectors 95
pounds (mass) 28
power of ten 42, 43
power of zero 38
powers 36
    calculators 73
    dividing 38
    multiplying 38
prime factors 26, 27
prime numbers 14, 15, 26–27, 241
prisms 152, 153
probabilities, multiple 234–35
probability 228–39
    dependent events 236
    expectation 232, 233
    tree diagrams 238
probability fraction 233
probability scale 230

processing costs 77
product
    business finance 76
    indirect proportion 58
    multiples 20
    multiplication 18
profit
    business finance 76, 77
    personal finance 74
progression, mental mathematics 69
proper fractions 49
    division 55
    multiplication 54
properties of triangles 117
proportion 56, 58
    arcs 150
    enlargements 104
    percentages 62, 64
    sectors 151
    similar triangles 125, 127
proportional quantities 59
protractors
    drawing pie charts 211
    drawing triangles 118, 119
    geometry tools 82, 83
    measuring bearings 108, 109
pyramids 153, 250
    symmetry 88, 89
Pythagorean Theorem 128–129, 249
    tangents 148
    vectors 95

Q

quadrants, graphs 92
quadratic equations 192–93
    factorizing 190–91
    graphs 194–97
quadratic expressions 176
quadratic formulas 192–93
quadrilaterals 130–33, 136, 246
    area 132–33
    cyclic 146, 147
    polygons 135
quantities
    proportion 56, 58, 59
    ratio 56
quarter fraction 48
quarters, telling the time 31
quartiles 222–23
quotient 22, 23
    division 25

R

radius (radii) 138, 139, 140, 141, 251
area of a circle 142, 143
compasses 82
sectors 151
tangents 148
volumes 155
range
    data 220, 221
    histograms 225
    quartiles 222
rate, interest 75
ratio 56–57, 58
    arcs 150
    scale drawing 106
    similar triangles 126, 127
    triangles 59, 126, 127
raw data 204
re-entrant polygons 134
reality 232–33
recall button, calculators 72
rectangle-based pyramid 88, 89
rectangles 246
    area of 28, 132, 173, 249
    polygons 134
    quadrilaterals 130, 131
    symmetry 88
rectangular prism 152
recurring decimal numbers 45
reflections 102–103
    congruent triangles 120
reflective symmetry 88
    circles 138
reflex angles 85, 245
    polygons 136
regular pentagons 88
regular polygons 134, 135, 136, 137
regular quadrilaterals 130
relationships, proportion 58
remainders 23, 24, 25
revenue 74, 76, 77
reverse cancellation 51
rhombus
    angles 133
    area of 132, 249
    polygons 134
    quadrilaterals 130, 131, 132
right-angled triangles 117
    calculators 73
    Pythagorean Theorem 128, 129
    set squares 83
    tangents 148
    trigonometry formulas 161, 162, 163, 164, 165

vectors 95
right angles 85
    angles in a circle 145
    congruent triangles 121
    constructing 113
    hypotenuse 121
    perpendicular lines 110
    quadrilaterals 130, 131
Roman numerals 33
roots 36, 37, 241
rotational symmetry 88, 89
    circles 138
rotations 100–101
    congruent triangles 120
rounding off 70–71
rulers
    drawing circles 139
    drawing a pie chart 211
    drawing triangles 118, 119
    geometry tools 82, 83

S

sales tax 74
savings, personal finance 74, 75
scale
    bar graphs 206
    bearings 109
    drawing 106–107
    probability 230
    ratios 57
scale drawing 106–107
scale factor 104, 105
scalene triangles 117
scaling down 57, 106
scaling up 57, 106
scatter diagrams 226–27
scientific calculators 73
seasonality 218
seconds 28, 30
sectors 138, 139, 151
segments
    circles 138, 139
    pie charts 210
seismometer 205
sequences 170–71, 247
series 170
set squares 83
shapes 246
    compound 143
    constructions 110
    loci 114
    polygons 134
    quadrilaterals 130
    solids 152
    symmetry 88, 89
    tessellations 99

shares 74
sharing 22
short division 24
short multiplication 21
sides
    congruent triangles 120, 121
    drawing triangles 118, 119
    polygons 134, 135
    quadrilaterals 130, 131
    triangles 116, 117, 118, 119, 120, 121, 162–63, 164, 165
significant figures 71
signs 240
    addition 16
    approximately equals 70
    equals 16, 17, 72, 177
    minus 34, 73
    multiplication 18
    negative numbers 34, 35
    plus 34
    positive numbers 34, 35
    subtraction 17
    see also symbols
similar triangles 125–27
simple equations 180
simple interest 75
    formula 179
simplifying
    equations 180, 181
    expressions 172–73
simultaneous equations 186–89
sine
    calculators 73
    formula 161, 162, 164
size
    measurement 28
    ratio 56
    vectors 94
solids 152–53
    surface areas 152, 156–57, 250
    symmetry 88
    volumes 154, 250
solving equations 180–81
solving inequalities 199
speed measurement 28, 29
spheres
    geometry 81
    solids 153
    surface area 157, 250
    volume 155, 250
spirals
    Fibonacci sequence 171
    loci 115
spread 220–21
    quartiles 223
square numbers sequence 171
square roots 37, 241, 246

INDEX

calculators 73
estimating 39
Pythagorean Theorem 129
surds 40–41
square units 28, 132
squared numbers 241
powers 36
quadratic equations 192
squared variables
quadratic equations 190
quadratic expressions 176
squares
area of quadrilaterals 132
calculators 73
geometry 81
polygons 134
quadrilaterals 130, 131
symmetry 88, 89
tessellations 99
squaring
expanding expressions 174
Pythagorean Theorem 128
standard form 42–43
statistics 200–227
stem-and-leaf diagrams 221
straight lines 86–87
angles 85
subject of a formula 177
substitution
equations 180, 186, 187, 192
expressions 173
quadratic equations 192
simultaneous equations 186, 187
subtended angles 144, 145
subtraction 17
algebra 169
binary numbers 47
calculators 72
expressions 172
fractions 53
inequalities 198
negative numbers 34
positive numbers 34
vectors 96
sums 16
calculators 72, 73
multiplication 18, 19
supplementary angles 85
surds 40–41
surface area
cylinder 175
solids 152, 156–57, 250
surveys, data collection 204–205
switch, mental mathematics 69
symbols 240
algebra 168

cube roots 37
division 22
expressions 172, 173
greater than 198
inequality 198
less than 198
numbers 15
ratio 56, 106
square roots 37
triangles 116
see also signs
symmetry 88–89
circles 138

T

table of data 226
pie charts 210
tables
data collection 203, 204, 205, 208
frequency 206, 207, 216
proportion 58
taking away (subtraction) 17
tally charts 205
tangent formula 161, 162, 163, 164, 165
tangents 138, 139, 148–49
calculators 73
tax 74
temperature 35
conversion graph 185
conversion tables 243
measurement 242
tens
addition 16
decimal numbers 44
multiplication 21
subtraction 17
tenths 44
terms
expressions 172, 173
moving 178
sequences 170
tessellations 99
thermometers 35
thousands
addition 16
decimal numbers 44
three-dimensional bar chart 208
three-dimensional shapes 152
symmetry 88, 89
time measurement 28, 30–32, 242
speed 29
times tables 67, 241
tonnes 28

top-heavy fractions 49, 50, 54
transformations
enlargements 104
reflections 102
rotation 100
translation 98
translation 98–99
transversals 86, 87
trapezium (trapezoid) 130, 131, 134, 249
tree diagrams 238–39
triangles 116–17, 246
area of 122–24, 249
calculators 73
congruent 112, 133
constructing 118–19
equilateral 113
formulas 29, 177
geometry 81
parallelograms 133
Pascal's triangle 247
polygons 134, 135
Pythagorean Theorem 128, 129, 249
rhombus 133
right-angled 73, 83, 95, 117, 128, 129, 148, 161, 163, 164, 165
set squares 83
similar 125–27
symmetry 88, 89
tangents 148
trigonometry formulas 161, 163, 164, 165
vectors 95, 97
triangular numbers 15
trigonometry 158–65
calculators 73
formulas 161–65, 248
turns, angles 84
24-hour clock 32
two-dimensional shapes, symmetry 88, 89
two-way table 205

U

units of measurement 28–29, 242
cubed 154
ratios 57
squared 132
time 30
units (numbers)
addition 16
decimal numbers 44
multiplication 21
subtraction 17

unsolvable simultaneous, equations 189

V

variables
equations 180
simultaneous equations 186, 187
vectors 94–97
translation 98, 99
vertex (vertices) 116
angles 85
bisecting an angle 112
cyclic quadrilaterals 147
polygons 134
quadrilaterals 130, 147
solids 153
vertical coordinates 90, 91
vertical (perpendicular) height
area of quadrilaterals 132, 133
area of triangles 122, 123
volumes 155
vertically-opposite angles 87
volume 152, 154–55
conversion tables 243
density 29
measurement 28, 242, 250

W

wages 74
watches 32
weeks 30
weight measurement 28
weighted mean 217

X

x axis,
bar graphs 206, 207
graphs 92

Y

y axis
bar graphs 206, 207
graphs 92
yards 28
years 28, 30

Z

zero 14, 34
zero correlations 227
zero power 38

Acknowledgments

BARRY LEWIS would like to thank Toby, Lara, and Emily, for always asking why.

The publisher would like to thank David Summers, Cressida Tuson, and Ruth O'Rourke-Jones for additional editorial work; and Kenny Grant, Sunita Gahir, Peter Laws, Steve Woosnam-Savage, and Hugh Schermuly for additional design work. We would also like to thank Sarah Broadbent for her work on the glossary.

The publisher would like to thank the following for their kind permission to reproduce their photographs:

(Key: b-bottom; c-center; l-left; r-right; t-top)

Alamy Images: Bon Appetit 218bc (tub); K-PHOTOS 218bc (cone);
Corbis: Doug Landreth/Science Faction 171cr; Charles O'Rear 205br;
Dorling Kindersley: NASA 43tr, 93bl, 231br; Lindsey Stock 27br, 220cr; **Character from Halo 2 used with permission from Microsoft:** 118tr; **NASA:** JPL 43cr

All other images © Dorling Kindersley
For further information see: www.dkimages.com